JOHN JAMES AUDUBON

John James Audubon

WRITINGS AND DRAWINGS

THE LIBRARY OF AMERICA

CHRISTOPH IRMSCHER
SELECTED THE CONTENTS AND
WROTE THE NOTES FOR THIS VOLUME

Contents

Plates

MISSISSIPPI RIVER JOURNAL

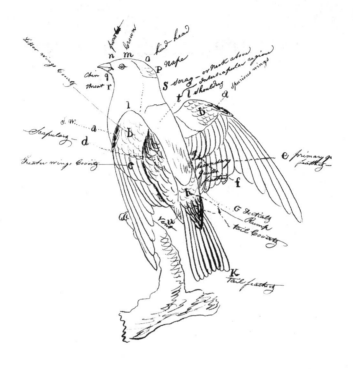

Audubon's copy of an illustration from William Turton's 1806 edition of Linnaeus's *Systema naturae*, in the manuscript of the Mississippi River Journal. (Houghton Library, Harvard University)

Mississippi River Journal

Thursday—Ohio River Oct—12th 1820

I left Cincinnati this afternoon at half Past 4 'oclock, on Board of M[r] Jacob Aumack's flat Boat—bound to New Orleans—the feelings of a Husband and a Father, were My Lot when I Kiss[d] My Beloved Wife & Children with an expectation of being absent for Seven Months—

I took with me Joseph Mason a Young Man of about 18 Years of age of good familly and naturally an Aimiable Youth, he is intended to be a Companion, & a Friend; and if God will grant us a safe return to our famillies Our Wishes will be congenial to our present feelings Leaving Home with a Determined Mind to fullfill our Object =

Without *any* Money My Talents are to be My Support and My anthusiasm My Guide in My Dificulties, the whole of which I am ready to exert to keep, and to surmount—

The Watter is Low, although a Litle fresh, raised the River a few days since, about 4½ feet, We only floated 14 Miles by the Break of the 13th of Oct[r]—the Day Was fine, I prayed for the health of My familly prepared Our Guns and Went on Shore in Kentucky—Cap[e] Sam[l] Cummings Who left Cincinnati with an Intention of Noting the Channels of this River and the Mississippi accompanied us—We Shot Thirty Partridges—1 Wood Cock—27 Grey Squirels—a Barn Owl—a Young Turkey Buzard and an Autumnal Warbler as M[r] A. Willson as being pleased to denominate the Young of the Yellow Rump Warbler—this Was a Young Male in beautifull plumage for the season and I Drew it—as I feel perfectly Convinced that M[r] Willson has Made an Error in presenting the Bird as a New Specie I shall Only recommand You to Examine attentively my Drawing of Each and his Description.— its Stomach was filled With the remains of Small Winged Insects and 3 Seeds of Some Berries, the Name of Which I Could not determine—

Early in the Morning the Wind rose and we Came to on the Ohio side by G[l] W[am] Harrison's Plantation and remained untill Nine o'clock *PM*—

I saw several Flocks of Ducks in the Morning before We had cleaned our Guns—hundreds of Meadow Lark Alauda Magna   few travelling Southwest—

———

the Wind Rose and brought us to Shore, it rain^d and blowed Violantly untill the Next Day—

Saturday Oct 14th 1820

After an early Breakfast We took to the Woods   I say *We* because Joseph Mason, Capt^e Cummings & Myself I believe Are allways together—

I Shot a *Fish Hawk Falco Aliætus* at the Mouth of the Big Miami River a handsome Male in good Plumage. he was wing^d only and in attempting to Seize Joseph's hand, he ran One of his Claws through the Lower Mandible of his Bill and exibited a very Ludicrous object—these Birds Walk with great dificulty and Like all of The Falco and Strix Genus throw themselves on their backs to defend themselves.—

We return^d to our Boat with a Wild Turkey 7 Partriges a Tall Tale Godwit and a *Hermit* Thrush which was too much torn to make a drawing of it   this Was the first time I had Met with this Bird and felt particularly Mortified at its Situation—

We pass^d the Small Town of Laurenceburgh—in Indianna, Petersburgh in K.^y, We Walked in the afternoon to *Bellevue* the former residence of a *Far Famed* Lady Your acquaintance Mrs Bruce; Saw Thomas Newell and Old Cap^e Green—if My Eyes did Not err I saw my Suspicions of her conduct that Evening *justified*   We killed 4 Small Grebes at one Shot from a Flock of about 30   We approached them with ease to within about 40 Yards, they were chassing each other and quite Mery   When the Destructive fire through the whole in consternation, the Many Wounded escaped by Diving, the rest flew off—this is the second time I have seen this kind, and they must be extremely rare, in this part of America—

about Three Miles above Bellevue in Kentucky We Walked through a Fissure of Rocks really romantic   the Passage in that form of a half Moon is about 6 feet wide, the rocks are composed of Large Round pebles cimented with Coarse sand about 100 feet High on one Side and Sixty on the other—I Made a Sketch of it for Your future Pleasure—We walked this day about 40 Miles saw one Deer Crossing the River

Sunday Oct. 15. 1820—

there Was this morning as heavy a white frost as I Ever Saw, the Wind blew Cold and heavy from the North   Shott 2 Tell *Tale Godwits*—and Chased a Deer in the River for some Considerable time, but a Canoe with Two Indianna Men had the advantage of us and Caught it as I rose to shoot it—the Wind being fair We floated tolerably Well, killed *5 Teal* and one Blue Wing^d Teal, 2 Doves 3 Partriges and fortunatly another Hermit Thrush Turdus Solitarius—We Met and Went on Board the Steam Boat *Velocipede*   Saw Co^l Oldham, Mr Bruce, Mr Talbut & Lady Passengers besides a Consider Number of Strangers, Open^d a Letter directed to Your Mother by Your Uncle W^am B—Mr Aumack killed a Young Malard Duck—the Contents of the Gizard of one of the 4 *Grebes* I open was Nothing else than a solid Mass of fine hair apparently belonging to some Very Small quadrupeds—

Saw a Chimney Swallow; the Number of Ducks Increasing —and an Appearance of a cold Night.—Killed a *Great Carolina Wren*   the Grebes were Cooked and eat but extremely Fishy rancid and fat—

at 10 'oclock We were roused from sound Sleep by the Boat's having ran on Rocks—the hands had to go in the Watter to take them off, it was cold and Windy—

Monday Oct 16th 1820

the frost much as yesterday; Turkeys being heard close by We took a Walk after them unsuccessfully, they answered to My Calls but kept off—

I did not feel well, took some Medicine and Drew the *Hermit Thrush Turdus Solitarius* that I killd Yesterday—this Bird Can easily be know from the Turdus auracapillus being about ⅓ Larger, and from the Tawny Thrush, by Looking at the inner parts of its Wings which exhibit a handsome Light band of Buff—its Stomack contained the remains of Insects and the

Seed of the Winter Grape—was very fat and delicate eating—
these Birds are Scarce and not generally known   there Note
a plaintive soft one—Seldom more than 2 are seen together
= some of the Country We saw is extremely high, hilly and
broken—saw a Wood Grouse—Many Ducks Several *Northern
Divers* or Loons—some Cormorants, Many Crows—several
flocks of Cow Buntings moving Southwest—Killed Two Partriges and One Turkey—

the Boats ran askue sand bar at Seven o'clock, with great
Exersions one was brought off   it was the one I was living
in   the other staid fast all night, the Hands suffered Much
from the Cold—

Tuesday Oct 17th 1820

The weather desagreably Cold, but Clear, the other Boat Still
fast   We went early on Shore,—in Kentucky—a Long Walk
through the woods was fruitless, I saw 4 Ravens—Many Winter Hawks—some Red breasted Thrushes or Robins = the
Woods full of Grey & Black Squirels   returned to the Boats
the *other* having Joined us with Two Turkeys & One Wood
Grouse or Pheasant—

The Turkeys, extremely plenty and Crossing the River
hourly from the North Side, great Number destroyed falling
in the Stream from want of Strength—the Partriges where
Crossing also, and in fact all the Game that Cannot properly
be Called Migratorius =

Saw a Great Number of Chimney Swallows going South-
west—these Birds travells much More advantageously than
Most all others being able to feed without halting—Killed a
fine *American Buzard Falco Levrianus*   he was feeding on a
Grey Squirel on a Stump tree, he fell to the ground and
Raised again loosing his praise—his Stomack Was filled with
that Last Prey—a Large Turkey Cock Was Stolen from us by
Some Travellers—killed to day 17. Partridges—One *Wood
Grouse* 4 Turkeys   I killed 2 at one Shot—One Hare—One
Robin & the American Buzzard—We put Some fish Lines
out having Landed for the Night all hands being very Much
fatigued—

Could My Wishes be fullfilled I would have You well fed on

Such game as the rich calls[d] richest—the Thermometer down at 36—

Wednesday Oct[r] 18th 1820

Jacob Aumack went hunting with us, saw some fine Turkeys, killed a Common Crow Corvus Americanus Which I drew; Many Robins in the woods and thousands of Snow Buntings Emberiza Nivalis—several Rose Breasted Gros Beaks—We killed 2 Pheasants, 15 Partridges—1 Teal, 1 T. T. Godwit—1 Small Grebe all of these I have Seen precisely alike in all parts—and one Bared Owl this is undoutedly the Most plentifull of his Genus—I felt poorly all day and Drawing in a Boat Were a Man cannot stand erect gave me a Violent headache—The Watter raising a litle gave Me some Hopes of reaching Louisville before sunday—anxious to know My Fate—I am comfortably Situated and would be sorry to be obliged to part with them—the Weather Milder & Cloudy— Caught No Fish Last night—

Tuesday Oct[r] 19th 1820

Cap[e] Cummings M[r] Aumack and Joseph after a Long Walk return to Dinner with only 7 Partridges and 1 Pheasant—M[r] Shaw Shot 1 Pheasant—I finished My Drawing of the *Common Crow* and after Dinner Went a Shore with the Company—saw many Cedar Birds killed a Young Blackburnian Warbler—a Young Carolina Cuckow so much reduce by the hard Weather that he could scarcely fly—Killed 5 pheasants 14 Partridges 1 Squirel and 3 Turkeys Shot *at once* by *Joseph* who was Not a litle proud when he heard 3 Chears given him from the Boats this was his first Essay on Turkeys—

While absent the boats having put to to Make Sweeps a flock of Turkeys came amongst them and in tring to Kill some with Aumacks' pistols One was bursted and the other Wounded Joseph's Scull pretty severely—saw an astonishing Number of Grey Squirels—the Country being extremely hilly opposite *Wells Point* the hunting Was Laborious and fatiguing—

The Stomack of the Cuckoo Contained 2 Entire Grass

Hopers One Large Green *Kid diddid* and the remainder of remains of Diferents Colopterous Insects—

Wednesday November 1ˢᵗ 1820—
Weather drizly and windy   Landed a few hundred yards below *Evansville* in Indianna on a/c of Mʳ Aumack Who had some Money to Collect—he brought on Board only a french Double Barrel Gun and a Gold Watch the Whole Made for Sale = I Wrote to My Beloved Wife & Mʳ H. W. Wheeler = saw Large flocks of Snow Geese but only one in perfect Plumage—

Not so Stupid as Mentionᵈ in Linné = Left Evansville at 2 o'clock PM—Capᶜ Cummings & Joseph started in the skiff for Henderson to Get *Dash* a slut I had Left in the Charge of Mʳ Brigs—about 3 Miles down we Saw 3 of these Birds that I have Considered as being the Brown Pelican   they Alighted on a Red Maple Tree—after many hard Trials:—they made a Noise somewhat Like a raven—We Landed below them and Went a Shore with great expectation of Procuring one—Mʳ Aumack drew Near them but Missed 2 that Were together and that I expected and Hopeᵈ to see fall   the Wind raising it Was Concluded We Should remain = rather sorry that the Capᶜ and Joseph were absent—as We had expected to go within 2 Miles of Henderson & Meet them on their return—

the People at Evansville very Sickly, could not see Mʳ Dᵈ Negley as it was My Will, he being at his House 4 Miles up Pigeon Creek—

Extremely tired of My Indolent Way of Living not having procured any thing to draw since Louisville—

Thursday Novembʳ 2ᵈ 1820
Capᶜ Cummings Joseph & *Dash* arrived at One o'clock this Morning—having a Severe rowing Match of it—We Started about 5 and floated down slowly within 2 Miles of Henderson when We experienced quite a *Gale* and Put to on the Indianna Shore Opposite Henderson—The Wind Blew so Violently that I could only Make a very rough Drawing of that

Place—I can scarcely conceive that I staid there 8 Years and Passed them Comfortably for it undoubtedly is one of the poorest Spots in the Western County according to My Present opinion =

Saw some Large Sea Gulls Larus argentatus*—Some Geese, Ducks, &ᶜ. So Warm to Night that Bats are flying Near the Boats = extremely Anxious to be doing something in the Drawing Way—

Friday Novembʳ 3ᵈ 1820

We left our harbour at day Break and passed Henderson about Sun raise, I Looked on the Mill perhaps for the Last Time, and with thoughts that Made My Blood almost Cold bid it an eternal farewell—

here One of the hands left us a Poor Sickly Devil who had been acting as Cook, called Luke a Shoe Maker Of Cincinnati—

the *Indian Summer* this extraordinary Phenomenon of North America, is now in All its Splendour, the Blood Red Raising Sun—and the Constant *Smokey* atmosphere, is undoubtedly Not easily to be accounted for = it has been often supposed that the Indians firing the Prairies of the West were the Cause, but since we have left C. the Eastwardly Winds have prevailed without diminishing in any degree the Smoke—it is extremely bad to Most Eyes and particularly so to Mine—

Capᶜ Cumming, Mʳ Shaw & Joseph took a Long Walk but saw Nothing, killed 4 Squirels—one Butcher Bird—and a Swamp Blackbird—Large flocks of them seen travelling Southwest = I shot a Turkey Buzard, *Vulture aura* about 120 yards off with a ball.

saw when We Landed at the foot of Diamond Island a Fine *snow Goose* a Young One—

saw several N. Divers, Some Geese. a few Sand Hill Cranes—& Some Ducks—

---

*they Are Pale blue above, Tail & Belly White—a few of the outer primaries Black and about the size of a Raven—

Saturday Novemb^r 4th 1820—

Landed Last evening Opposite the Midle of *Diamond* Island Lately the property of Walter Alves Deceased of Henderson— about 9 'oclock the Wind Rose & Blowed—tremendous Gales which continued all Night, fortunately We Were under the Lee of the Land—

this Morning the Wind had abated alitle, but we could Not go, the River making imediately below us a Turn south-west^d—5 of us took guns and Went to the Island, we walked almost all over it—Saw great Many Turkeys—and Many Dears—I killed a Large Buck that died in the Cane, and Lost it—We Brought Nothing on Board, if 2 of us only had been there, probably We Could have Made a good hunt =

I Shot a *Winter Wren* but cut it so much that It Could Not be drawn—

Returned to our Boats about 5 o'clock the Wind Still Blowing, but rounding to the Northeast and Weather very Cold— Watter falling—

I Remarked this Morning that the Turkey Buzzards that had roosted over a dead Hog last Night, Took a Long flight eastwardly this Morning as if to excite their appetite and re-turne^d to Consume their filthy Meal about 2 o'clock the Number considerably Increased = While sailing high several Hawks for the Sake of amusement Chased them and sailed Many of them almost to the ground—

My Slut Dash apparently good for Nothing for the Want of Employment—

Now & Then We see a Blue Crane—

Saw many *Wood Groos* on the Island—

Sunday November 5th 1820

the Weather fair this Morning, the Thermometer down at 30—the sun rose beautifull and reflected through the Trees, on the Placid Stream much like a Column of Lively fire = the frost was heavy on the decks and when the Sun Shun of it it Looked beautifull beyond expression—

We floated tolerably well the river being here contracted by Large Sand Barrs—

Early we were overtaken by a Skiff containing a Couple of

Gentill Young Men, Bound to New Orleans, they had Mattresses, Trunks, a Gun & Provisions—

Saw about the Same time a fine Brown Eagle—Shot at it without effect—

Many Dears where Merily Gamboling on the Sand Barrs and excited us

We passed *Mount Vernon* a Small Village in Indianna about one Mile above the upper end of Slim Island—Mr Shaw & Cap^c Cummings went to the Island but returned without any thing—this Part of the River rather Dificult—

We Landed about 3 Miles above the Mouth of *High Land Creek* in the *Mississippi* Bend—

Saw Many Geese, some Sand Hill Cranes—a few Loons— some *Red Breasted Thrushes*, many Sparrows & parokets—

Killed only one Winter Hawk, & Shot at one Wood Cock

as I promessed You a Picture of the Caracters We have on Board of Both Boats I will attempt to Copy them, Could My Pen Act as a Black Chalk by the help of my fingers you might rely on the Exibition of the figures—Yet I undertake it with pleasure, Knowing how Sweet this May be to you & Myself some Years hence, while sitting together by the fireside Looking at Your Dear Mother reading to us—

being on Board of Boats Much in the situation of Passengers I am of Course Bound to give the preference to those who are termed *Capitains* and Mr Aumack is the First that I will bring to Your attention—

You have seen him and of Course I have Not Much to say   the acquaintance of Man When unconnected by Interest is *plain* easily *understood* & Seldom Deviates—

he is a good Strong, Young Man, Generously Inclined rather Timorous on the River, Yet Brave, and accustomed to hardships—he Commands the Boat Where I am—

Mr Loveless is a good Natured, rough fellow, brought up to Work without pride, rather Anxious to Make Money— Playfull & found of Jokes & Woman—

Mr Shaw the owner of Most of the Cargo puts Me in Mind of some Jews, who are all Intent on their Interests & Wellfare; of a keen Visage & Manners; a Bostonian—Weak of Constitution but Strong of Stomack—Would Live Well if at any one else's Expense =

the Crew is Composed as follows

Ned Kelly a Wag of 21. Stout Well Made, handsome if Clean, possessed of Much Low Wit, produces Mirth to the Whole even in his Braggardism—Sings, dances and fiels allways happy—he is Baltimorian—

2 Men from Pennsilvania although Not brothers, are possessed of a great sameness of Caracters—these are *Anthony P. Bodley*—& *Henry Sesler*—they Work Well, talk but Litle and are Carpenter by Trade—

The Last is Much Like the Last of every thing, the Worst Part—Joseph Seeg, Lazy, found of Grog, says Nothing because it Cannot help himself, Sleeps Sound, for he burns all his Cloths, While in the Ashes—

Cap^{e} Cummings Joseph & Myself form the Rear at Times & at Times the Van—You have seen the Life and these Likeness could Not give you a better Impression than that You have formed,—We Agree Well, and are Likely to agree Still—

Monday Novemb^{r} 6th 1820

the Thermometer this morning was down at 28 and it felt very desagreable—Took to the Shore and walked 9 Miles to the Mouth of the Wabash, but saw Nothing to Shoot at—about One Mile below that the Wind springing ahead Brought us to on the Illinois Shore and 5 Guns went hunting, I shot 6 Dear!—

the people here have a dreadfull sickly Aspect and their Deportment not the Most Intissing—

the Game plenty—

Our Boats Started about One Hour before sun down, & Cap^{e} Cummings having extended his hunt up the Wabash had a Long Walk for nothing—

We Landed for the Night about 6 Miles above Shawaney Town on the Kentucky Shore—

Weather Appearance of rain, and blowing, Much Warmer—saw some Robins, a few Blue Jeays, a few Blue Birds, Geese, S. H. Cranes, Ducks,—Buzards & the Usual Number of W. Peckers common at this season—

Tuesday Novemb^r 7th 1820

Weather at 50 this morning, rainy & Desagreable; Landed at Shawaney Town where we staid six hours—I staid snugg on Board Mr Aumack having Nail^d up the only Accessible hole to Our Boat—

I Wrote to My Wife & Directed it to Mr Wheeler—We left Shawaney town at half 5 & went only to the Lower end of it, the Wind raising again with an Appearance of a very Boisterous Night—

Jacob Aumack killed a *Rusty Grakle* a beautifull Male and as these Birds are scarce I intend Drawing it tomorrow = it is but seldom that Many of these Birds are seen together, they walk^d with great Statliness and Elegance, are swifter of flight than the Swamp Blackbirds.

I felt very anxious during all the time of our stay to be off from this Place—

this Evening Ned Kelly & his Companion Joe seeg having Drank rather freely of Grog they had a Litle Scrape at the Expense of Mr Seeg's Eyes & Nose—

the People of Shawny Compleining of Sickness—the place improved but Litle—

Wednesday Novemb^r 8th 1820—

the Weather Calm & beautifull this Morning We Started with a good prospect and our Landing within Two Miles of the famous *Rock in Cave* to night prove it—

I Drew this Morning My *Rusty Grakle, Gracula Ferruginea*, and made a handsome piece of it—

Cap^e Cummings hunted all day but saw Nothing—since 3 Days we have been particularly unfortunate in our Hunts =

Near our Landing Place We Went on Shore to procure some Venaison Hams—Mr Shaw bought 4 p^{rs} for 2$ remarkly fine—the young man who sold them had killed 3 Dear to day and had hung one Large Buck for his Dogs to feed on—

Killed to day One Grey Squirel & 3 Tall Tale Godwits—these Birds Wade so deep that one Would Suppose they are swimming, fly a few Yards into Shallower Watter, holding their wings up untill perfectly satisfied of their being on the Bottom—then run about briskly & ketch small fishes with great dexterity—

Saw one Sea Gull a Large One—a few Gold Finchs, Many Cardinals—some Divers—but Neither Ducks or Geese—the Weather had become Cloudy & raining by Intervals   is Now beautifull with an appearance of Frost

about Two hours before sun sett a *Barred Owl* teazed by some Crows and Chased from the tree where he was Lit raised up in the Manner of a Hawk in the Air so high that we Lost Entire sight of him, he acted as if Lost—Now & then making very Short Cirkles and flapping his Wings quickly, then zig zag Lines—this was quite a New Sight and I expect take place but Seldom—I felt anxious to See his Descent to the Earth but Could Not—

The Trees here have Lost all their foliage, the Cane & a few Green Briars is all that animate the Woods—the Shore are thickly sett with Cotton Wood Trees—

Thursday Novemb^r 9th 1820

The Wind blowed nearly all day a head, the Weather Cold— Saw No Game although We Walked a great deal in the Woods   the Country extremely poor here—

We Landed at Sun set at the *Rock in Cave* having Come only about 2 Miles—

I began My Sketch of it immediatly, regretting that We had not reached this place Last Night—

We Purchased a Skiff from a flat Boat—

Ducks & Geese very numerous flying down the Stream— Shot 2 Ducks of the flocking Fowl Kind—& 3 Squirels

the Thermometer in the Watter at sun set was down to 27. appearance of a Very Cold Night—

a Man on the Shore told me that Last Winter he had Caught a Large Number of Malard Ducks with a Trap, set with a figure of 4 & shaped Like a Partridge trap—

the Tell Tales we eat to Day were very fat but very fishy— I eat the purple Grakle   it tasted well—

Friday Novemb[r] 10th 1820—

as soon as Day Light permitted me this Morning—I Took Joseph on Shore and Lighted a good fire—took also my Drawing Book &[c] with a Skiff—the Morning pleasant and the Thermometer raised to 50°—While I was taking My Sketch of the *Rockin Cave* Cap[c] Cummings took a Good Walk through the Woods—at 9 My Drawing was Compleat—this Cave is One of the Curiosities that attracts the attention of allmost every Traveller on the Ohio—and thousands of Names & Dates ornement the Sides & Cealing—there is a Small upper room dificult of Access imediatly above & through the Cealing of the Ground floord One, Large enough to Contain 4 or 5 persons when Sitted on their hams—this place is Said to have been for Many Years the *rendez Vous* of a Noted Robber of the Name of Mason   it is about 20 Miles below Shawaney town on the same side; had our Boats spent a Day there, I would have been pleased to take several Diferent Views of it = the Rocks are Blue Lime Stone containing in Many Parts Round Masses of a fine flinty Appearance Darker than the Main Body—

at Nine oclock it became Cloudy & Cold, We Left for our Boats, but before We reached them, it snowed & Hailed & Wetted us Compitly—Our Boats had parted to Cross & Run through the *Walker's Barr* and *Hurricane Island*—We Landed only about One Mile below the Latter, the rain Increasing and the Weather extremely Disagreable. Never have seen so Much snow at this season in this Latitude—

saw a fine Black Hawk Falco niger—& Black Gull,—Shott Two Ducks =

Saturday November 11th 1820

It rained hard during the whole of the Night and the day   floated only about 7 Miles—

saw a few Turkeys,—

a Flock of *Carrion Crows* made us go to the shore but they where so excidingly shy that they would fly several hundred Yards Off—while the Turkey Buzzards that accompanied them would suffer us to walk under the trees on which they alighted—the Carrion Crows are very scarce in this Part of the Country and Keep Generally Lower to the South—their flight is heavy and their Appearance while on the Wing Awkward

We Landed for the Night at Golconda a Small Town of the Illinois—Titles disputed of course the place not Improving—Court was sitting—

Sunday Novemb^r 12th 1820

The Wind Blowed this Morning and We did Not Leave the Shore untill 9 'oclock—Wind fair—weather, raw & Cloudy—Mr *Aumack* killed a Duck (Ruddy Duck) out of a Flock of 5 that proved to be a *Nondescript*—and also a *Imber Diver*—the Wind rendered our Cabin smoaky I Could Not begin to Draw untill after Dinner—I had the Pleasure of Seing Two of the Same Ducks Swimming Deep, with their Tail *erect*, and Diving for food = having never seen these Birds before, it was highly satisfactorily to Me = Tomorrow I will give a thorough Description of it =

The *Imber Diver* was Shot Dead and proved a beautifull specimen—of Course I will give You a Drawing of it—for Some time before I procured one of them; they Were Called *Northern Divers*, the Moment I saw this, the size and Coloring Made Me Sure of it being an *Imber Diver*—

saw a Large flock of Turkeys fly across from an Island to the Main, killed None—

We are Landed about half a Mile above the *Cumberland Island* the weather not So cold as it feels the Thermometer at 38—had some spits of Snow in the forenoon—

Vast flocks of Ducks & Geese flying Southwardly—

Monday November 13th—1820

a Beautifull Morning enable^d me to go on with my Drawing very early—a Light frost embelished the raising of the Sun =

We Landed at the Middle of Cumberland Island to dispatch a Skiff to take Soundings—

finished My Duck by Dinner Time and was Lucky enough to Kill another of the same kind, precisely a Like but rather

Less in Size, it is with apparent Dificulty or a Sluggish disposition that these Birds rise out of the Watter & yet Will Not dive at the flash of a Gun—while on the wing are very Swift—

this afternoon I Begun the Drawing of the Imber Diver had Two Long Chasses after a Couple of others, that out Managed our Skill—they would Dive as if Going down the Stream and raised from One to Two hundred Yards above us—they frequently Dipp their Bill in the Watter, and I think have the power of Judging in that Way if the place Contains Fish = One I shot at; dove & raised again Imediatly as if to see Where I was or What Was the Matter.

I saw severall of the *Fin Tail Ducks*, all acting the same Way i.e. Swimming Deep & the Tail Erect—No Doubt this appendage is very usefull to them when under the Watter =

Saw a Bear on a Sand Barr, had a great run after it—to no purpose =

saw 2 of these Birds I take for Black Pelicans—Many Loose flocks of Blackbirds Ducks & Geese—Mr *Aumack* saw an *Eagle* with a White head and *Brown Body & Tail*, this Corroborates with the Idea of Willson of its being the Same Bird with the Brown Eagle—

Landed about the Midle of *Tennessee Island* Weather Much Milder,—

Joseph Made a *Faux Pas* this day—the Whole of our Folks Not in the best humor—Killed 7 Partriges.

Tuesday Novemb^r 14th 1820
Drawing this Morning as soon as the Light would permit me—Started early—

Went out in the Skiff to try to Shoot the *Largest* White *Crane* with Black tips, but I walk^d off from the Shore and I return^d knowing that it would be vain to attempt to follow him on a Large naked Sand Barr—felt great anxiety to procure Such for he appeared Beautifull—

Saw several Eagles, *Brown* & White *headed*—

Although I drew nearly the Whole of this day I did finished my *Imber Diver*.

Cap^e Cummings Killed 26 Starlings, Sturnus Pradetorius, all

Young—eat them at our Supper, good & Delicate—1 Golden Plover & Two Squirels—

Mr Shaw Killed an Owl that unfortunatly he did not fetch; = We passed this Day *Fort Massacre* here the Ohio is Magnificent, the river about One & ¼ Mile Wide affords a view of 14 or 15 Miles, and this Afternoon being Calm with one of those *Whimsical* Sunsetts that only belong to America rendered the Scene extremely Interesting.

We Landed about One Mile below what is Called the Litle Chain a partial Obstruction to the Navigation of this queen of Rivers—

Saw several *Swans* flying very high—Geese are in Constant View but have so far outwited us, these Birds are Wilder on the Rivers than when in the Ponds or Small Lake that in Many places run Parralel with the Ohio at a Small distance in Land—

Cap^c C. Brought an Oppossum, Dash after having broke I thought all its bones Left it—it was thrown over Board as if dead, Yet the Moment he touchd the Watter he swam for the Boats—so tenacious of Life are these Animals that it tooked a heavy blow of the Axe to finish him—Tomorrow We Hope to Pass the Last Dificulty & Two Days More May take us to the Mississipi

Total Length of the Fin Tailed Duck 15½ Inches—¾ Hinds Shorter to Side of Tail   Bill Dark Blue   Broad for the size of the Bird—& Sharply hook^d at the point—Legs & feet L. Blue the palms Black, Tang Fleshy—upper Part of the Head Back Wings & Tail Dark Brown Zig Zags with transversal Bars of Light D^o—Irides Dark Chestnut Eye rather Small   Neck Breast & Belly Light Brown with transversal Black Drops—a Triangular White Spot forming the under Tail Coverts—

Tail Composed of 18 Feathers rounding   each feather narrow Sharp & Terminating in Spoon Like Shape points—this is White—the Head & Neck Short and Thick—

Swims Deep   White part of the Belly Silvery White—

Breadth 22 Inches—Wings Brown Not reaching the Tail by ½ Inch—No Wing Stripes—

When I saw these Birds the Weather was Boisterous   since fair have not Seen One—

Imber Diver Weighed	6 lb.	
Total Length	$2^{8}/_{12}$	feet—
to end of Tail	$2^{4½}/_{12}$	—"—
Width tip to tip	4	—"—
Length of the Gut	$5^{8}/_{12}$	—"—

Contents of Gutt & Gizard Small Fish, Bones & Scales and Large Gravel—Body extremely fat & rancid—Belly & Vest White but Not silvery as in the Grebes—

Wednesday 15th 1820 November—
at Work again this Morning as early as could be, a beautifull Day—finished My Drawing to my Liking having Sketch[d] Our Boats in the View of this Magnificent Part of the Ohio = saw More than a Dozen of Eagles and One I had a good View of had a White Tail & a Brown head, Again I remark[d] that the *Brown Eagles* i.e. S. Eagles Were at Least ¼ Larger than the White headed Ones =

Saw a Large flock of Large White Gulls With Black Wing Tips very Shy While on the Wing but not at all so when swimming   fired Two Guns Without effect.

Passed the famous Chain of Rocks, Much diversion to see M[r] Aumack's Movements =

having Seen Steam Boats allmost every day fast on Sand Barrs I have taken no particular Notice of any of their Names & Positions—have Passed this day 3 flat Boats belonging to

W^{am} Noble of Cincinnati that Left that Place early in August
—3 out of 6 are Lost—

Landed about 2 Miles above New America on the Illinois
Shore = Broken Land, fine Timber of Oak & Poplar =
Killed an Opposum—

Our People Much MELOWED =

saw Winter & Shore Larks Many Geese & Ducks 2 Swans =

Thursday November 16th 1820

We floated only about Two Miles & Landed at *America* to
sell some *Articles*; people very Sickly, a Miserable place altogether = took a Long Walk this Morning—this afternoon
Cap^e. C. Joseph & I took a Skiff and Spent the Afternoon
hunting, but killed Nothing—saw two Black Hawks =

at our Return at Night found Mr *Aumack* in Bad humor,
and after We had retired to our Cabin for the Night, Received
a *Humorous Lesson* that I Shall Never forget—

My Dear Children if Ever you read these trifling remarks
pay some attention to what follows—

Never be under what is Call^d Obligations to Men not
Aware of the Value or the Meaness of their Conduct

Never take a Passage in any Stage or Vessel without a well
understood agreement betwen You & the owners or Clerks &
of all things Never go for Nothing if You Wish to save Mental Troubles & Body Viscissitude—

Well aware that I shall Never forget this Night as Long as I
Live, I Close here—

the Old *Washington* Steam Boat came along side of us
Took 70 Barrels of Salt raised Steam and made herself fast
about 2 Miles Below—

Friday November 17th 1820

We left early—I took the Skiff and Went to the Mouth of the
Ohio, and round the point up the Mississipi—

Eleven Years ago on the 2^d of January I ascended that
Stream to St Genevieve Ferdinand Rozier of *Nantes* My Part-
ner in a Large Keel Boat Loaded with Sundries to a Large
Amount *our* property—

the 10th of May 1819 I passed this place in an Oppen Skiff Bound to New Orleans with Two of My Slaves—

Now I enter it *poor* in fact *Destitute* of all things and reliing only on that providential Hope the Comforter of this Wearied Mind—in a flat Boat a Passenger—

the Meeting of the Two Streams reminds me a Litle of the Gentle Youth who Comes in the World, Spotless he presents himself, he is gradually drawn in to Thousands of Dificulties that Makes him wish to keep Apart, but at Last he is over done Mixed and Lost in the Vortex—

the Beautifull & Transparent Watter of the Ohio when first entering the Mississipi is taken in Small Drafts and Looks the More agreable to the Eye as it goes down Surrounded by the Muddy Current, it keep off as much as possible by running down on the Kentucky side for Several Miles but reduces to a Narrow Strip & is Lost—I saw here Two Indians in a Canoe they spoke some French, had Beaver Traps, uncomonly Clean Kept, a few Venaison hams a Gun and Looked so Independant, free, & unconcerned with the World that I Gazed on them, admired their Spirits, & Wished for their Condition = here the Traveller enters a New World, the Current of the stream about 4 Miles p^r hour, puts the Steersman on the alert and Awakes him to troubles and Difficulties unknown on the Ohio, the Passenger feels a different Atmosphere, a very Diferent Prospect = the Curling Stream & its hue are the first objects—the Caving in of the Banks and the Thick Set Growth of the Young Cotton Wood is the Next = the Watter's dencity reduced the Thermometer from 62 to 20 Degrees = We Landed Very Early, Cap^e C. & I Walked Through the Woods, and remark^d the Great Diference of Temperature so suddenly felt—

I bid My farewell to the Ohio at 2 o'clock P. M. and felt a Tear gushing involuntarily, every Moment draws me from all that is Dear to Me My Beloved Wife & Children—

the Boats separated on Entering the Mississipi, as being safer to Navigate it singly—We fealt the better for this. and Hope good Cheer Will revive again—

although I hunted a good Deal this Day I saw but Litle and Nothing New, a few King Fishers, some Divers, Geese Ducks —some Gold Finches the Notes of Which reminded Me of the *Canary Birds*. a few Blue Geays, Now & then the Plaintive farewell note of the *Blue Bird*: rather sorry that the Strong Current We are in Will Not permit Me to go a Shore unless Landed by the force of Contrary Winds—

The Mississipi is a good Midle Stage at present—

Saturday November 18th 1820—

floated within about 2 Miles of the Iron Banks and Land in Kentucky at about ½ past 3 oclock—

I took a sketch of the River below us Comprehending on our Left the Iron Banks, the Chalk Bank on our Right in the Back Ground Wolff Island and Part of the Missoury Shore =

My Drawing, finished took a Walk in the Woods the Country full of Ponds of Stagnant Watters, Shot 2 Malards While Dash was bringing out the Last One a White headed Eagle *Dashed* at the Duck   the Bitch brought it—

Killed an Oppossum Many Blackbirds   the Thermometer at 64. Bats in the Evening and Butterflies seen to day in quantity as well as Many other Insects—

the Game Not so plenty as on the Ohio and Much Shier—

Sunday 19th November 1820

When We Left Cincinnati, we agreed to Shave & Clean completly every Sunday = and often have been anxious to See the day Come for Certainly a Shirt worn One week, hunting every day and Sleeping in Buffaloe Robes at night soon became soild and Desagreable—We passed this morning the famous Wolf Island—the History of which is amply given in the Ohio Navigator—here said Mr Lovelace "a Man Called *White* having become a Lunatic as I was going up the River, Jumped over Board in the Night Made the Shore although he could not swim and I was then at anchor in 7 feet of Watter and Never seen afterwards, I sent several *hands* to Look for him, his tracks only Led on the Top of the Bank—the Muskitoes being then remarkly Bad—he Must have Died in the Same Bend of the River found 2 dead Men Shot through the head Could Not burrie them their Stench was too Great—"

We floated to day about 30 Miles   killed Nothing—saw Mr *James Asley* who told Me that Mr *Thomas Litton* & himself Lived with a Mile of *Chalk Banks*—

Ivory Billed Wood Peckers are Now Plenty, Bears Wolf &^{c} but the Country extremely Difficult of Access, the *Canes* Extending in Many Places several Miles from the River—

On Sundays I Look at My Drawings and particularly at that of My Beloved Wife—& Like to spend about one hour in thoughts devoted to My familly—

Landed apposite the Head of N° 8. at the foot of N° 7—in Missoury—put out our Lines caught a Cat fish—Weather agreable,

saw Many Gulls unknown—

the Woods deserted almost by Small Birds—

heard some Partriges—

the Wild Geese here sits on the Banks Many feet above Watter and feed on the seeds of a Tall Grapes somewhat resembling *Fol Avoine*—but are extremly Shy—

Monday 20th November 1820

The Winds on this River are Contrary to our Wishes as those of an Old Rich *Maid* to the Wishes of a Lover of Wealth, We are anxious to Make progress on account of our Situation but it is disposed off Diferently by a *Superior Power*—

We Came but a few Miles and Landed about Noon in Such a Dreary place that Neither the Woods Nor the Stream Would afford it any benefit—

it rain^d in the evening—

Killed to day a *Red Tailed Awk* a great distance with a Ball—a Red Owl *Strix Asio*—One Goose—Nothing in the Woods that are rendered almost Impenitrabl by the Canes—being on a Very Loose Muddy Ground caught no Fish—

Tuesday November 21st 1820

the Wind High all Day   Landed at New Madrid at 3 o'clock P. M.—

this allmost deserted Village is one of the poorest that is seen on this River bearing a name; the Country Back was represented to us as being good, but the Looks of the Inhabitants contradicted strongly their assertions—

they are Clad in Bukskin pantaloons and a Sort of Shirt of the same, this is seldom put aside unless So ragged or so Blooded & Greased, that it will become desagreable even to the poor Wrecks that bear it on—

The Indian is More decent, better off, and a Thousand time More happy—here family dicensions are at their Zenith, and to Kill a Neighbour is but Litle More than a Kill Dear or a Racoon—

a Mrs *Maddis* formerly the Lawfull Wife of Mr *Reignier* of St *Geneviève* resides and keeps a Small Store in Company with a French Gentleman. We where told the Partnership was rendered agreable to both by a Mutual wish of Nature = went to this Lady's house Who knew me first and exibited Much of the french Manners

felt dull, this evening for every object that brings *forward* the *Background* of My Life's Picture shew too often with poignancy the diference of Situation—

Made some Inquiries about the regulations of the Post Office, none suficiently encouraging to enable my Writting a few Lines to My Beloved Wife & You—

saw some Geese   killed one, 2 Golden Plovers and Two Shore Larks—Caught No Fish—

a Black Hawk passed within a few Yards of me to day when I had a Rifle and could not kill it on the Wing, these Birds become more Aboundant as we descend; a few Swans are now & then seen very High.

All Our Hands Playing Cards untill bed Tim about 9. oclock = —the *Swamp Sparrow* and Snow Birds are Plenty in the High Dry Grass that Lines the Bends of this River, but the Woods have Nothing in More than the *Pait Pait Pait* of the Monogamous Wood Peckers—

Wednesday November 22^d 1820

We Left New Madrid at day Break, we had gone but a Very Short Distance when the Wind Rose, yet we made best day's run since in this River and Landed after Dark 3 Miles above the *Litle* Prairie on the Misoury Shore—

Joseph & Myself floated before the Boats almost all day in hunt of a White headed Eagle, in Vain, I Shot at & Missed a Beautifull *Black Hawk* and a *Brown Eagle*

having a very Long *Bend* to run through, we helped Mr Lovelace's; While We where rowing, a White headed Eagle Dashed off from the Top of a High Cypress Tree, after a Litle *Duck* the *Spirit* and Was on the point of being in Possession of it—When I sent him Two heavy Loads from My Gun that Wounded him badly—

I Called this Morning at *Belle Vue* Wood Yard to see Mr Dela Roderie, he was absent to a Cypress Swamp, I saw his Wife & Sister, and Left My Respects—

the Weather quite Pleasant, although We have Light White frosts every Night—

some Minutes after Landed, *Dash* Started an Oppossum that took Every Man to Shore thinking it Was a Bear, the Poor Oppossum came on Board with us—

fishing Lines all out   Lost One, and a Large *Cat Fish* in tringing to hawl him in—Geese, Sands Hill Cranes Plentifull on the Sand Barr opposite us, they regularly resort to these for roosts

Thursday November 23^d 1820

as soon as We had eat our *Common Breakfast*, fried Bacon and Soaked Biskuit—Joseph went to his station and I to Mine, i.e. he rowed the Skiff and I steering it—Went to the *Litle Prairie* shot at a Brown Eagle probably 250 Yards and Yet Cut one of its Legs—

at this Place We Saw a great Number of Birds, Mostly *Red Breasted Thrushes*—the Songs of Which revived our Spirits and Imparted Within us the Sweet sensation that Spring brings to Minds of *our Kind*.

the Rusty Grakles extremely Plenty—snow Birds—& Many Sparows—

I Shot a Beautifull *White headed Eagle Falco Leucocephalus*—probably 150 Yards off, My Ball Went through its body—

Returned to our Boats immediatly and began My Drawing—it is a Handsome Male—

Many Shots at Geese, but We find them so Shy that We Loose Much Ammunition in Contending With them—

floated 23 Miles   Landed Opposite Island N° 20 according to the Old Navigator, some Indians Camped on it, Made us Load all our pieces—

I saw Two Eagles Nest, One of them I remembered seing as I went to New Orleans 18 Months ago   it had being worked upon and No doubt Youngs Where raised in it, it is in a Large Cypress Tree, Not very high, Made of Very Large & Dead Sticks and about 8 feet in Diameter—

Since I killed the One before me I am Convinced that the *Bald Eagle* and the *Brown Eagle* are Two Diferent Species—

Friday November 24th 1820

high Winds, remained at our Last Night's harbour all day—at Day Break saw a Deer Crossing the River below us, ran him down and Brought him to the Boats; Cleaned, it Weighed 162^{lb} had 9 Points to its horns and so Much run down that its Neck Was swolen ½ the Size of its Body—

I Spent the greater Part of the day drawing; all hands hunting—Killed Two Geese, 1 Racoon & 1 Oppossum—

the Woods here are so Dreadfully tangled with *Bull rushes*, Green Briars and Canes that the Travelling through them is extremely Irksome =

saw some *Carrion Crows* and some *Turkey Buzards* that were attracted by the scent?? of the Deer we had hung in the Woods??—

immediatly below us is a familly of Three people in Two Skiffs a Woman & 2 Men; they are Too Lazy to Make themselves Comfortable, Lie on the Damp Earth, near the Edge of the Watter, have *Racoons* to Eat and Muddy Watter to help that food down, are from the Mouth of Cumberland and Moving to a Worst Part of the World Without Doubt—

saw some Ivory Billed Wood Peckers, these Birds allways go in Paires and When they Leave a Tree to fly to another they Sail and Look not unlike a *Raven*—I shot & killed a Turkey Buzzard a great Distance, Mistaking it for a Carrion Crow—

unfortunatly We are in bad part of the River for Fish—

Saturday November 25th 1820

I spent the whole of this day drawing the *White headed Eagle*, the Weather excidingly warm, the Thermometer rose to 70°, the Wind Blowing Strong a head We remained Still; in the Course of the Afternoon a Small Steam Boat, the *Independance* passed us, I saw with the Spy Glass Old Cap[c] Nelson of Louisville; *Butterflies Wasps,* & *Bees* plenty all day about us = the Skiff familly of Yesterday a few hundred Yards below us, the Woman Washed for us—

at sun set the Wind Shifted, A heavy Cloud Came over us and Made a great difference in the Atmosphere =

Killed 2 Geese and Two Racoons—

saw a few *Carrion Crows* attracted by the Guts of the Deer We Caught Yesterday—

Our Hands sailing all day—

Sunday November 26th 1820

Drawed all day, floated 18 Miles—the familly in the Skiffs came on Board this Morning Nearly frosen, the Thermometer down at 22—the ground very hard, and My being Without a Shirt—Made Me feel rather unpleasant—

the Woman of the Skiffs Mending My Good Brown Breeches—

to Look on those people, and consider Coolly their Condition, then; compare it to Mine, they certainly are More Miserable to Common Eyes—but, it is all a Mistaken Idea, for poverty & Independance are the only friend that Will travel together through this World =

Shot at an Eagle With a White head and Brown Tail =

Ducks, Geese, Swans, & Other Birds all going southwardly—

Monday November 27th 1820—

The weather raw and Cloudy, Finished my drawing of the White headed Eagle, having been 4 days at it—

that Noble Bird weighed 8½[lb], Measured 6 feet 7½/12 his Total Length 2[f]: 7½/12—it proved a Male, the heart extremely

Large, My Ball having passed through his Gizzard I could not see any of the Contents =

these Birds are becoming very Numerous, hunt in paires, and roost on the Tall trees above their Nests—One this Morning took up the head of a Wild Goose thrown over board, with as Much ease as a Man Could with the hand—they chase Ducks and if they force one from the Flock he is undoutedly taken, Carried on a Sand Bank and eat by Both Eagles—they are more Shy in the afternoon than in the morning—they seldom Sail High at this season, Watch from the Tops of trees and Dash at any thing that comes near them—to secure a Goose, the Male & femelle, Dive alternatively after it and give it so little time to breath that the poor fellow is forced in a few Minutes—

We are all unwell having eat too freely of the Buck Mr Shaw went off this Morning to Mr Lovelace's Boat—Made a good run—saw a Large Flock of White Gulls—but Not a Land Bird—Much to My Surprise I have Not Yet seen a Pelican, Nor a Swan on the Barrs or in the River = Malards are the only Ducks We now see—No Game, to be procured Not able to hunt on the Shores—We are Landed at the foot of Flour Island, opposite the first Chicasaw Bluff—the First High Ground since the Chalk banks—

While Looking at My Beloved Wife's Likeness this day I thought it was Altered and Looked sorowfull, it produced an Imediate sensation of Dread of her being in Want—

Yet I cannot hear from her for Weeks to Come—but Hope She and Our Children are Well—

The Eagles along the Banks of this River, retire in bad weather to the Inner parts of High Cypress woods and remain on Low Limbs for whole day, I had an opportunity of seeing several from our Landing place, with my Spy Glass—

Tuesday November 28th 1820—

as it is a rainy Morning, I Cannot, hunt, and will take this opportunity of relating to you such Incidents relative to my Life as I think you May at some future period be glad to know.=

My Father John Audubon, was born at *Sables D'Olonne* in France; the son of a Man who had a very Large familly, being

20 Males & one femelle, his Father started him at a very Early age *Cabin Boy* on Board a Whaleing Ship—of Course by education he Was Nothing; but he Naturally was, quick, Industrious and soberly Inclined; his Voyage was a hard one but he often asured me he never regretted it—it rendered him Robust, Active and fit to go through the World's rugged Paths. he soon became Able to Command a Fishing Smack, to purchase it, and so rapidly did he proceed on the road of Fortune, that when of Age, he commanded a Small Vessel belonging to him, trading to St Domingo—

a Man of Such Natural Talents and enterprise Could Not be confined to the common drudgery of the Money Making Animal, and entered an officer in the French Navy's Service under Louis the 16th was fortunate and Employed an Agent at St Domingo to Carry this trade—Every Movement was a Happy hit, he became Wealthy = the American Revolution brought him to this Country Commander of a Frigate under the Count Rochambeau, he had the honor of being presented to the Great Washington, and Major Croghan of Kentucky who has told me often that he then Looked Much Like me was particularly well acquainted with him, My Father was in several Engagement in the American service and at the taking of Lord Cornwallis—

before his Return to Europe he purchased a Beautifull Farm on the *Schuillkill* and *Perkioming* Creek in Pennsylvania; the Civil Wars of France and St Domingo, brought such heavy reverses of Fortune on his head, that it Was with the utmost Dificulty that his Life was Spared—

he along with thousands more saw his Wealth, Torn from him, and had Litle More left than was Necessary to Live and Educate Two Children Left out of five—having 3 Younger Brothers Killed in the Wars—

he remained in France reentered in the Service under Bonaparte; but the French Navy prospered not and he retired to a Small beautifull Country Seat, Three Leagues from *Nantes* in Sight of the Loire and ended his Life happy = Most Men have faults, he had One that never Left him untill sobered by a Long Life Common to Many Individual, but this was Counterbalanced by Many qualities—his Generosity was often too great—as a Father I never complained of him and the Many Durable Friends he had prove him to have been a *good* Man =

My Mother, who I have been told was an Extraordinary beautifull Woman, died Shortly after My Birth and My Father having Maried in France I was removed there when only Two Years Old and receive by that Best of Women, raised and Cherished to the utmost of her Means—My Father gave me and My Sister *Rosa* An education appropriate to his purse   I studied Mathematicks at an early Age, and had Many Teachers of Agreable Talents, I perhaps would have Much stored up, if The Continual Wars in Which France Was engaged had Not forced Me away when only Fourteen Years Old = I entered in the Navy and Was Rec^d a Midshipman at Rochefort Much against my Inclinations—the Short Peace of 1802 betwen England & France ended my Military Carreer, & the Conscription determined My Father on sending me to *America* and Live on the *Mill Grove* Farm I have Mentioned above—he sent me to the Care of *Miers Fisher* Es^{qr} a rich and honest Quaker of Philadelphia, who had been his agent for Many Years and who received Me so Polittely that I was sure he Estimed My Name—

a Young Man of *Seventeen* sent to America to *Make Money* (for Such was My Fathers Wish) brought up in France in easy Circumstance who had never thought on the Want of an article I had had at Discretion, was but ill fitted for it—I spent much Money and One Year of My Life as Happy as the Young Bird; that having Left the parents sight, carolls Merily, While Hawks of All Species are Watching him for an easy prey—

I had a Partner with whom I did Not agreed, he tried his opportunity   we parted for ever.

here it is well I should Mentioned, that I Landed in *New York*, took the Yellow Fever and did Not reach Philadelphia for Three Months—

Shortly after My Arrival on My Farm, Your Mother *Lucy Bakewell* came with her Father's Familly to a Farm Called *Fatland Ford* and divided from Mine only by the Philadelphia Road—

We soon became acquainted and attached to each other. I went to France to Obtain My Father's Consent to Marry her, and returned with a Partner, Ferdinand Rozier of Nantes entered in Business for the thoughts of Marriage brought Ideas so New to me that I began with pleasure in the way to secure My Future Wife and Familly the Comforts We had both been used to—I travelled through the Western Country and Made Louisville my Choice for a residence—on my return and being of Age I Married Your Beloved Mother on the 5th of April 1807 and removed to Kentucky—Louisville did Not Suit our Plans and We Left that Place with a View to Visit Sᵗ Louis on the Mississipi; but it is so seldom that our Wishes are favored that we did not reach that Place, for My Partner not being on good Terms with My Wife, I left her and You *Victor* at Henderson, you Where then a babe, having reached Sᵗ Genevieve through Many Dificulties, Ice, &ᶜ I parted from Mʳ Rozier and Walked to Henderson in Four Days 165 Miles—

Your present Uncle T. W. Bakewell Joined me in opening a House at New Orleans that the War with England Made us remove to Henderson,—

this Place saw My best days, My Happiness, My Wife having blessed Me with Your Brother Woodhouse and a sweet Daughter I calculated, to Live and Die in Comfort, Our Business Was good of course We agreed. but I was intended to Meet Many Events of a Desagreable Nature; a Third Partner was taken in and the Building of a Large Steam Mill, the Purchasing of Too Many goods sold on Credit of Course Lost reduced us—Divided us—

Your Uncle who had Maried a Short time previous, removed to Louisville—Men with whom I had Long been connected offered Me a Partnership, I acepted and a small ray of Light reappeared in My Business, but a *Revolution* occasioned by a Numberless quantities of Failures, put all to an end; the Loss of My Darling Daughter affected Me Much; My Wife apparently had Lost her spirits, I felt No wish to try the Mercantile Business, I paid all I could, and Left Henderson, Poor, & Miserable of thoughts,—

My Intention to go to France to See My Mother and Sister was frustrated, and at Last I resorted to My Poor Talents to Maintain, You and Your Dear Mother, Who fortunately apparently became easy at her Change of Condition, and gave

Me a spirit such as I really Needed, to Meet the surly Looks and Cold receptions of those who so Shortly before Where pleased to Call me Their Friend =

in Attempting the Likeness of James Berthoud Es^qr—a Particularly good Man and I believe the Only *Sincere* Friend of Myself and Wife We ever had—, to please his Son & Lady I discovered such Talents that I was engaged to proceed and succeeded in a Few Weeks beyond My Expectations

Your Mother who had remained at Henderson to come by Watter, was at Last obliged to come in a Carriage, and for the Second time You had a sweet sister born, How I have dwelt on her Lovely features, when Sucking the Nutritious food from her Dear Mother—Yet She was torn away from us when only 7 Months Old = having taken all the Likeness Louisville could afford I removed to Cincinnati, leaving You all behind untill satisfied of some Means of Making something for a Maintainance—Through Talents in Stuffing Fishes I entered in the service of the Western Museum at One hundred and Twenty five Dollars per Months, and raised a Drawing School of 25 Pupils, made some Likeness, and had You around Me Once More—but small towns do not afford a support for any time.

Ever since Boy I have had an astonishing desire to see much of the World, & particularly to Acquire a true knowledge of the Birds of North America, consequently, I hunted when Ever I had an Opportunity, and Drew every New Specimen as I Could or dared *steel time* from my Business and having a Tolerably Large Number of Drawings that have been generally admired, I Concluded that perhaps I Could Not do better than to Travel, and finish My Collection or so nearly that it would be a Valuable Acquisition = My Wife Hoped it might do Well, and I left her Once More with an intention of returning in Seven or Eight Months; I wrote to Henry Clay Es^qr with Whom I Was acquainted and he Enclosed Me in a Very Polite & Friendly Letter One of General Introduction = I receive Many from others—General Harrisson, &^c—

from the day I left Cincinnati untill the present My Journal gives you a rough Idea of My Way of Spending the tedious Passage in a Flat Boat to New Orleans =

We moved from our Landing of Last Night and only

crossed the River for the rain Lowered the *Smoake* so Much that it was impossible to see, beyond 20, or 30, Yards; played great deal on the flutes, Looked at My Drawings, read as Much as I Could and yet found the day very Long and heavy for Although I am Naturally of light spirits and have often tried to keep these good, When off from my Home, I have often dull moments of anguish = the rain abated for a few Minutes Cap^e C. Joseph & I took a walk to a Sand Barr Where Joseph Killed a Large bleu Crane, unfortunatly a Young one—saw few Geese, many *Cardinals*, Some *Carolina Wrens*—We are better to day = Luckily our Boat does not Leek—Saw a few Purple Finches =

Wednesday November 29th 1820—

the rain that begun Two days since, accompanied us the whole of this day, yet We Left our Harbour at about 7 this morning and runned 20 Miles—We passed the Second Chicasaw Bluff, raining so much that I could Not draw them; they are Much More Interesting than the Chalk Banks indeed they Look^d grand and Imposing. thcy arc from 150 to 200 feet High irregularly Caving down and Variegated in stratas of Red, Yellow, Black, and deep Lead Colors, the Whole of Such Soapy and Washing Nature as to give an interesting contrast to the Dashing of the Wash down to the edge of the Watter Which Here is very deep the upper Strata (the Whole run horizontali) is perferated with Thousands of holes, the Nests of the *Bank Swallow*—these Bluffs are about Two Miles ½ Long, the Country back, Barrens & Poor—

Confincd to the Inside of the Boat nearly the day, saw but a few Gulls, apparently all White, found White headed Eagle, & a few Cranes—a Large flock of Gold Finches—a few Bleu Jeays, & *Cardinals*, the Ivory Bill Wood Peckers heard from time to time,—

We are Landed at the foot of N° 35 a few Miles above What the Navigators call the Devil's Raceground—but the whole of the Mississipi being so much of the same Nature, it feels quite immaterial to follow the Devil's track any where along its Muddy Course—

Thursday Novemb[r] 30th 1820

We found the race path of the Devil well cleared and beaten, and went through it with great Ease, Many Places on this River are rendered more terrible in Idea by their Extraordinary Names than real dificulties—

We run a Race with M[r] Lovelace's Boat, of several miles that was well nigh terminating in a Dispute = it remembered me of Gamblers that although playing for Nothing are allways grieved at Loosing—

We came 25 Miles and Landed a litle below the Twelve Outlets, passed the third Chicasaw Bluffs, the view of these was intercepted by our Running on the Right of an Island— the Weather Cold, & very disagreable, Wind blowing all day Mostly ahead = some Men came on Board M[r] L. Boat who said had killed Three Bears a few days before—saw a few Indians at a Small Encampment—this morning I remarked Two Flocks of *American Teals* flying up the River; the Parokeets Numerous in the Woods—a Large flock of Sand Hill Cranes Sailed over us for some time, rounding & Elevating themselves to a Considerable Hight, took a southwardly Course— One swan Was seen on a Barr, been so Shy that he flew several times at shore as he Perceived the Boats. Wherever We Land a Number of *Swamp Sparrows* are seen Scullking through the High Grass that borders the Banks, the seeds of Which cover the hearth or more properly Mud; the Geese feed freely on these Whilst the Grass affords them an agreable place during the day—Saw a few Gulls, a Large flock of Sprig Tail Ducks going all southwardly =

the Cedar Birds, Ampellis Americana, fly Northeast.

We passed this afternoon 19 Flat Boats Lying at the Shore, some of Which had Left the Falls 10 days previous to our Departure—

I saw to day 2 Common Crows the only I have seen on the Mississipi—

Friday December 1st 1820—

This Morning was Cold and Cloudy, Flocks of Ducks Geese, &[c] sailing High, plentifully, all bound to the Southwest—I remarked Large Flocks of Merganzers, I Mean, The Large.

these Birds seldom Leave, the Clear Ohio—or its tributary streams untill Compell^d by the Ice Closing Most parts of them; their passing Southwardly so early Indicates a severe Winter above us*—their Flight is Direct, regularly forward in Acute Angles and so swift that One Might suppose the Noise over head as proceeded from a Violent storm of Wind = saw Early to day several Hundreds of Gull playing over a large Barr—when We attempted to Close on them, they rose high and off South—4 White headed Eagles where at the same time regalling themselves on the Carcass of a Deer—The swarms of Grakles that are passing us is astonishing—the Purple Finches also very Numerous saw several hundreds in one flock—when the Weather is Intensely Cold, scarcely a Fowl is to be seen along the Banks, the ponds offering themselves at that time food & Shelter—passed a Large Settlement of Wood Cutters = Mr Shaw killed 5 Geese 4 at one Shot

saw Two *Slate Colored Hawks, Falco Pennsylvanicus*, and a *Winter Hawk*, I went a Shore to a House about 5 Miles about *Wolf River*, in a sharp running Bend, saw 2 Beautifull Trees *The Pride of China* here the High Land is within 2 Miles of the River and the Spot on which the Plantation stands never overflows, these are remarkable *Spots* =

We are Landed immediatly at the foot of Old *Fort Pickering*, We Walked up to it through a very narrow crooked path, and found in a very decayed situation; the Position a Beautifull one and the Land Rich about it—and were told that when the Spaniards own it it was an agreable spot to Live at = about 2 Miles above this, the Mouth of Wolff river come in from the East, and is the Landing place of a Town called *Memphis* = have runned 24 Miles—Saw some *Towe* Buntings and Many Sparrows—at the Watter Edge (then about Milde Stage) there is a Bed of Coals running Orisontally about 2

---

*At New Orleans on the 25th of February same Year saw an a/c in a New York Paper saying that the Weather had been Intensely Severe that the Mercury had been so Low as 24 Degrees below o = that the Port of New York Was Completly Enclosed by Ice and that all the Streams in that State & Pensylvania where Closed—Much Pleased to See that particularly the Migrations of a Swift Moving Bird Such as the Merganser can So truly be considered as the herald of Weather in its Movements—when going Northward & Southwardly—.

feet Deep above the surface—this and the Eligeability of the Situation May become Valuable =

I saw this afternoon Two Eagles Coabiting—the femelle was on a Very high Limb of a Tree and Squated at the approach of the Male, who came Like a Torrent, alighted on her and quakled Shrill untill he sailed off, the femelle following him and Zig zaging herself through the air—this is a scarce proof I have had the pleasure of Witnessing of these Birds and all of the *Falco Genus* breeding Much Earlier than any other Land Birds—

We Lost one of our Fishing Lines, a Large Fish must have Carried it, its being very Strong and Well fastened to a Strong Willow Pole—

The Beard of the Turkeys Shews about one Inch Long the 1st Year and one of the Male in full growth and plumage Must be 3 Years old =

———

so well exercised are the Geese at extricating themselves from danger when a Flat Boat Come Near them that they will Walk off from the Edge of the Watter, Out, into the Young Willows & Cotton Wood several 100 yards—but when in a Bend Where the Shore is Steep they May be reached With more Ease—

Saturday December 2d 1820

Cloudy & Cold, took the Skiff and went ahead of the Boats, the only way I have now of hunting, and When any game is on Sight Lay down in the Bow and float untill distance—Shot at a Large W. H. Eagle and a *Black Hawk* Missed both, this Latter in going off *flapped* his Wings Like a Pigeon, they move swifter than any bird in their Common flight, I could Not Well account My Missing these Birds, they were Not More than 100 yds off—I shot 3 Turkeys at 2 Shots—their Crops compleatly filled With *winter Grapes* Gizzards of the Seeds of the Same and Large Gravel—they were extremely gentle I floated immediatly to them and Came within 25 yds; Cold days force the geese away from Shore—the Woods Literally filled with Parokeets great Many Squirels—and Many *Snow Birds*—begun raining at about one—Now & then a

Wood Cutter's Hut is seen in a Small Parcel of Char^d Land betwen Two Thick Cane Breaks—

The Lights or *Pulmons* of the Turkeys I Examined This Day, had Much the Appearance of *Waddles* Connected by a Thin Skin, the *Wadles* about 1½ Inch Long = the Thin Skin about ¼ of an Inch—

Many *Golden Wings* Woodpeckers — a few Sparrow Hawks—

We Landed on What is Named a *Tow head* a litle above the Island N° 51—a Tow head is a Small Willow Island overflowed in High Watter—

it was not Dark and We Walk Round it—saw Many Geese, and a Young *Bear*, but its being So Late dash was Called out, and gave it up,—

Raining & very Desagreable,—Many Gulls flew about us to day and Picked up the Lights & fat of the Turkeys & Geese that were thrown over Board—

Sunday December 3^d 1820

It rained Heavy all Night, this morning it was concluded the Boats would not Leave, yet, our *Captains* went hunting. the Wind Blowing at Intervals and their Ceasing, made some diference of the force of the rain, — saw several Crows Many *Brown Larks*, Many Geese, and Malards = Killed to day 3 Geese, 2 Malards and 2 *Mergansers*, both femelles—measuring 25 Inches—the Bill & Legs Not so bright a cealing Wax Color as usual—tongue Sharp Triangular and Toothed—think them young—One of them had Caught a Fish about 9 Inches of the *Sucker* Kind and had only partly down its Throat when Killed—there was 5 Together we drove them several times out of a Pond in the inner part of an Island, and at Last Shot these on the Wing =

the Geese very Shy—Three Keel Boats passed us about 2 o'clock P.M—they had left the Falls of Ohio 3 Weeks ago— Left our Harbour and floated about 4 Miles to the foot of Buck Island—here I saw with the setting Sun hundreds of Malards travelling *South* and the Finest rainbow I ever beheld, the Clouds were also beautifull Opposite it = Looked at my Beloved Wife's Likeness Shaved and Cleaned, One of the few enjoyments Flat Boats Can afford—the Goose we eat at Dinner extremely fishy—

Joseph who now is Obliged to officiate as Cook does not appear to relish the thing—the More I see Cap^c C. the More I like him = Wish that we could say the same of all the World—

The Tow head or Litle Island on which laid Last Night and to day had *Vast Many* dry Nests of Thrushes on the small Willows Trees—the Tall Grass with many Sparows—Saw 2 Flocks of Partridges Many Parokeets.

Saw a Blue Crane—

Monday December 4th 1820

We had a dreadfull night of Wind, the hands obliged to move the boats, I did not sleep, the knocking of the Boat against the sand barr very desagreable—this Morning the Wind still blowing hard, Went to a Small Lake to Shoot—there I saw a *Keeldeer plover*, a *King Fisher*, Many Geese & Ducks—but no *Swans* as we had been led to expect from reports of a Squater = Killed 3 Geese and 3 *American Teals*—saw a few Turkeys— this Lake about 2 Miles from the River, contains some of the Largest Muscles I ever saw, and Vast Many perewinkles that appeared to be of a Peculiar Species and I put some in my Pockets—I found these in round Parcels of about 20 to 30 close together = My Slut Dash brought out of the Watter very well = When returned to our Boats, 9 of the Boats We had passed some days previous went by, and we Pushed off immediatly = We floated Only about 4 Miles—and Landed on the Tennessee Shore—

Saw to day great Many *Autumnal Warblers*, the first I have seen since on the Mississipi; a few C. *Crows* some *Winter Wren*, some *Eagles W. H^d*—it is very Seldom that brown Eagles are seen; the others are Now *Courting* seeing them every day chassing off the Bachelors—

I doubt not that the Migrations of the *Autumnal Warblers* is the Latest of all of that Genus—

I was taken off Suddenly a few Minutes ago to take a Cat Fish of our Line, I had some trouble for a few Moments but having drowned him put my Left Hand in his Geels and hauled it in the Skiff—it Weighed 64½^{lb} and Looked fat—Killed It by Stabbing it about the center of its head, this was so Effectual that in a few Second it Was quite Motion-less—

I would be Inclined that, from *shape, Size, Color* & habits so diferent to those of the Cat Fish Caught in the River Ohio the present One is a diferent *Species*

Tuesday December 5th 1820—

Skinning the Cat Fish was the first Job this Morning—this was done *by cutting through the Skin* (which is very Tough) in Narrow Long Strips and tearing these off with a Strong paire of Pincers = While at this Saw Several hundred of these Black Birds Yet unknown to Me that I denominate *Black Pelicans* flying South forming a very Obtuse Angle, without uttering any Noise—have some Hopes therefore to see some of them on the Watters of Red River or Washita—Sand Hill Cranes now also flying and We saw More Geese than usual—Joseph Killed 4 American Teals—these fly up Stream—

saw 3 Swans—While Geese are flying in a Travelling order the Young or Smallest are about the Center of the *Lines* and the Larger Gander Leads the Van, the Oldest Goose Drives the Rear—the Weather beautifull but Cold, and No Doubt that the Frogs that Wistled so merily Yesterday are well buried in the Mud this Morning =

We made an Awkward Landing, Lodged on the Mud for about ½ an hour, and our Commander had a good opportu-nity of Exercising his Powers at Swearing—More particularly when Anthony broke his Sweep oar. this Took Place about 30 Miles from our Starting place of the Morning, opposite the heads of 57 & 58—"*fine Weather but No Fish*" says Cap^c Cummings—

Wednesday December 6th 1820—

Light frost, Rich Clouds of Purple & Light Green Indicates Wind—extremely anxious to overtake the fleet a head our Commanders have Yesterday and this Morning exerted them-selves more than usual and have Left our harbours as soon as

Day Light would permit—how beneficiary a fleet Constantly a head would be!—

saw 2 Large White Cranes with Black Tips—too shy to get in shooting distance;—Many A^n Teals and As Many Geese as Ever—

Passed the St *Francis River* the Mouth of Which at the time appeared Closed by a Mud Barr—but the people Who Lived on the Point formed by that Stream and the Mississipi told us that there was plenty, and that Keel Boats go up it 400 Miles, Many Setlements on its Banks the first about 15 Miles—the same People told us that they had seen Many *Pelicans* a few days previous our Passing—saw some *Old Blue Cranes* on the Trees but could not go within 150^{yds} of any of them—a Litle before we passed the Place Called the *Big Prairie* shot a Monstrous Turkey Cock, I think the Largest I ever saw; it appear considerably Larger than One I weighed that was over 31^{lb} = My anxiety to have it Made Me Miss = the *Big Prairie* is a Tolerable sized Plantation rather higher than the usual on this River, about ¼ of a Mile Back the Land rises in Gentle Hills, and where told is extremely Rich there, I first saw the *Mississipi Kite** ascending in the Steam Boat *Paragon* in June 1819—Bought some Delicious *sweet Potatoes* at ½ Dollar p^r Bushel the Squatter assured me that a few Weeks previous, the Pelicans were so numerous that Hundreds where often in sight on a Barr below this Place—people very sickly—Landed on the Tennessee Shore about 7 Miles from the *Setlement of the Hills.* the wonderfull fleet Still about 4 Miles a head, Our Comodores had a Meeting, the result was that We Should *Start* One hour before day and run down the D^d Rascals—

Thursday December 7th 1820—

Caught a Nice *Cat Fish* weighing 29^{lb} at 3 o'clock this Morning—$stab^d$ him as we had the former but it did Not die for One hour = at Day Break the Wind stiff a head, a Couple of

---

*the Mississipi Kite Were Busily Employed in Catching small Lizards Off the Bark of Dead Cypress Trees, this effected by Sliding beautifully by the Trees and suddenly Turning on their side and Graple the prey—having, At that time No Crayons or Paper, did not Draw One, and determined Never to Draw from a Stuffed Specimen, Carried No skins—

Light Showers Lulle^d it, and we put off—Mr Aumack Winged a *White headed Eagle*, brought it a live on board, the Noble Fellow Looked at his Ennemies with a Contemptible Eye. I tied a String on one of its Legs this made him Jump over Board, My Surprise at Seeing it Swim well Was very great, it used its Wing with great Effect and Would have Made the Shore distant then about 200^yds Dragging a Pole Weighing at Least 15^lb—Joseph went after it with a Skiff, the Eagle Defended itself = I was glad to find that its Eyes were Corresponding With My Drawing—this Specimen rather Less than the One I drew—the femelle overed over us and Shrieked for some time, exibiting the *true Sorow* of the *Constant Mate*. = Prepared a Bed for My Slut *Dash* expecting her to be delivered from her Burthen every Day =

Our Eagle Eat of Fish freely about one hour after we had him, by fixing a piece on a Stick and puting it to its Mouth—however while I was friendly Inclined toward it it Lanced one of its feet and caught hold of my right thum, Made it feel very sore—

Went to an Eagle's Nest; busily Employed Building Shot at the femelle, which is at all times distinguished by her size, the Male was Asisting—Kiled *One Goose*—as we reach^d the head of the Sand Barr close to Island N° 62 We passed the *Fleet* at Anchor but they all pushed off when they saw us go through this Place = One Boat suffered Much, by being runned down by another in Landing = Came 25 Miles—the Evening Looking Stormy, the Current strong at our Landing Could not put out our Lines—

Our Comodores Much Elated—

Friday December 8th 1820

not satisfied about our Landing in a strong Current I slept but litle, whenever I walk^d on the deck, the Eagle Hissed at Me, and rufled itself in the Manner that Owls do generally—the Weather Warm, Cloudy, & Windy—put off late and only run about 3½ Miles forced by the Storm to land at the foot of what I supposed the Island N° 63—leaving all the fleet behind us—

with Some Hopes of Shortly being at the Arkansas Fort I

feel Inclined to Copy a few of the Letters I had for that Place
Particularly those of Generals *Harrisson* & *Lytle.*

Cincinnati Sepr 7th 1820—

Dear General
     Mr Audubon who will have the honor to hand You
this, is upon a Tour through the extensive forests of
Western America for a Scientific Purpose—that of Completing a Collection of American Birds—I beg leave to
Introduce him to you & to request Your aid and Countenance in the Accomplishment of his highly laudable
project—
     Mrs Harrison is well & my daughter Lucy & Son
Symmes both maried since you were at my House, the
latter to a Daughter of Genl *Pikes*—

Your Friend
W. H. Harrison

Governor J. Miller
Arkansas T.^{y}—

————

Cincinati Ohio Octr 9th 1820

Dear Sir—
     Permit me to Introduce to your Acquaintance John J.
Audubon Es^{qr} who is on a Visit to the Territory of
Arkansaw and the Norwest as an Ornithologist—for the
taking drawings of Birds—Fowls &^{c} for a Work he has
on hand   Any facility You May have it in Your Power to
offer him towards promoting the Object in view Will be
thankfully received by him and duly Appreciated by

Your friend and Hble serv^t
W^{am} *Lytle*

————

Cincinnati Octr 10th 1820—

Rev^r Gentlemen—
     Permit me to Introduce to your kind regards John J.
Audubon Es^{qr} who proposes traversing Louisianna for
the purpose of Compleating a Collection of Drawings of
the Birds of the U. States which he proposes to publish

at some Future Period—he has been engaged in our Museum for 3 or 4 Months & his performances do honor to his Pencil—

I regreat to hear that you have been Visited by Sickness, I hope You May get safe to your Journey end, & be prospered in the great & glorious work on Which you have Entered—I should be Pleased to hear from you frequently

I remain Your Sincere Friend & Brother in the *Lord*
Elijah *Slack*—

Reverend Veil & Chapman

Elijah Slack was then President of the Cincinnati College

———

besides the above I received several Letters from Doc^r *Drake* Directed to the Reverend Mr *Chapman* Osage Mission = Col^l *Brearly* Indian agent—& *Governor Miller*,—

I Will give You here the Copy of the Letters I Received from the Honorable Henry Clay to the one I Wrote from Cincinnati the Copy of Which is Annexed at the Begaining of the Part of My Journal

Sir—

I received your letter of the 12th inst—and now do Myself the pleasure to transmit to you inclosed such a letter as I presume you want—I suppose a general letter would answer all the purposes of special introduction, Which I should have been at a loss to give as I do not know the particular points which you may Visit—and even if I did, I might not have there any personal acquaintances—

Will it not be well for you before you commit Yourself to any great Expenses in the preparation and publication of your Contemplated Work to ascertain the Success which attended a Similar undertaking of Mr Wilson?

With Great Respect—
I am Yours
H. Clay

Lexington—25. Augt 1820—

I have had the satisfaction of a personal acquaintance with Mr John J. Audubon; and I have learn.^t from others, who have Known him longer and better, that his Character and Conduct have been uniformly good: being about to take a Journey, through the Southwestern portion of our Country with a laudable Object Connected with its Natural History, I take great Pleasure in recommanding him to the kind Offices of the Officers, and Agents of Government and other Citizens whom he may meet, as a Gentleman of Aimiable and Excellent qualities, Well qualified, as I believe, to execute the object which he has undertaken

H. Clay

H. Clay was then the Speaker of the House of Representatives, and I hope to rec.^e some benefits from this Letter—

Mr Aumack killed a Goose and Joseph an *Intrepid Hawk*, swans extremely Plenty   fired at them Many Times with Balls without Success—

Drifted at 3 o'clock P.M—about 4 Miles—and Landed at foot of N.º 64—

I began a letter to My Beloved Lucy with some Hopes of reaching the Fort of Arkansas Tomorow, but Hopes are Shy Birds fliing at a great Distance seldom reached by the best of Guns—

Saturday 9th December 1820—

I have nothing to say for this day, I drew a litle, seeing a Green Briar with seeds on—Wrote to My Lucy, and Lived on Sweet-Potatoes—how Surly the Looks of Ill fortune are to the poor

I Hope to see the fort of Arkansas tomorow and Hope to Leave the Boat I am now in if there is What the Kentuckians Term a "*half Chance*"   our Commanders Looks and Actions are so strange that I have become quite Sickened—

the Weather quite rough, all day, cleared at Night, the Flat

Boats passed us this evening—We have made a bad Landing according to my Ideas—

Sunday 10th December 1820

We floated down to the *Caladonian point* or *Petit* Landing about 4 Miles above the *real* Mouth of *White River*

here it was Concluded that Mr Aumack walk to the old *Post of Arkansas* of course I & Joseph prepared and having made Enquiries concerning the road we determined to go by Watter to the Mouth of the *Cut off* and thence Walk the remainder; Anthony, Joined us, and the Skiff doubled oared was taken; We left at 10 o'clock with Light hearts, Small Botle of Whiskey a few Biscuits, and the determination of Reaching the Post that Night—

at the Entrance of White River We discovered that that Stream was full and run^d Violently, the Watter a Dull Red Clay Color; We soon found ourselves forced to Land to make a Natural Cordel of several *Grape Vines* and pull up by it— the distance to the Cut off is Seven Miles that Appeared at Least 10 to us; here we Mett 2 Canoes of Indians from the *Osage Nation*, Landed our Skiff on the opposite side of White River Which We have found a *beautifull Clear Stream* and Backed by the Watters of Arkansas running through the Cut off; We Walked through a *Narow Path* often So thickly beset with green Briars that We Would be forced give back and go round—this followed through *Cipress Swamps* and round *Ponds* and Cane Breakes untill We reached the first Setlement Owned by a Frenchman Called Monsr Duval this Friendly Man about going to bed offered us his assistance put on Shoes & Clothing and Lead us 7 Miles Through the Mud & Watter to the Post; and at 9 o'clock P.M We Entered the Only Tavern in the Country—*Wearied*, Muddy, Wet, & hungry— the Supper was soon Call^d for, and soon served, and to see 4 Wolf tearing an Old Carcass would Not give you a bad Idea of our Manners While helping *Ourselves*, the *Bright Staring Eyes* of the Land Ladies Notwithstanding—

however I found Mrs Montgomery a handsome woman of good Manners and rather superior to those in her rank of Life—to Bed and to sleep sound was the next Wish for 32 Miles in such a Country May be Calculated a full dose for any *Pedestrian per day*—Led into a Large Building that formerly perhaps saw the great *Concils of Spanish Dons* We saw 3 Beds containing 5 Men, Yet, all was arranged in a Few Moments and as the Breaches were Camming off our Legs, Mr Aumack & Anthony Slided by into one and Joseph & Myself into Another; to force acquaintance with the Strangers being of Course Necessary a Conversation ensued that Lulld Me a Sleep, and Nothing but the Want of *Blankets* kept Me from Resting well, for I soon found a Place betwen the *Tugs* that Supported about 10^lb of Wild Turkey Feathers to Secure, My roundest Parts from the Sharp Edges of An Homespun Bedstead—

the Morning broke and with it, Mirth, *all about us*, the *Cardinals*, the Towe Buntings, the Meadow Larks and Many Species of Sparrows, chearing the approach of a Benevolent sun shining day—dressed and about to take a View of *all things* in this Place, Met a Mr *Thomas* known formerly when in the Paragon Steam Boat—he Introduced Me Generally to the Medley Circle around, and from thence took Me to a Keel Boat to receive the Information I Wanted about the Upper Countries through Which this Noble Stream Meanders— think of My Surprise at seeing here a Man Who 13 Years ago gave Me Letters of Introduction at Pittsburgh (Penn) for Men in Kentucky—this Was Mr *Barbour* the former Partner of Cromwell = he Met Me with great Cordiality, Told Me of the Absence of the *Governor*, the Indian adgent and also that the Osage Missionaries had proceeded about 150 Miles up to a Place called the *Rocky* Point.

The Cadron is beyond that. where a New town, the seat of Gover^t was expected to be situated—

disapointed to the utmost in Not Meeting those who I supposed would of Course give me the best Information I requested of Mr Thomas, to give the Governor My Letters and beg of him to Write Me a few Lines at New Orleans to the Care of Governor Robertson—Mr Barbour told Me that he had for Several Years past gone up to the Osage Nation about 960 Miles and that his Last Voyage he fell in with *Nutall* the *Botanist* and had him on board for 4 Months—that Many species of *Birds* were in that Country unknown in this and that the Navigation was an agreable One, at the same time that it was rendered profitable by the enormous profits derived from the Trade with the Indians, whom he represented as friendly and Honorouble in all there dealings—that he would be extremely Happy of My Company and that of My Companions and that if I did Not go with him at present that he Hoped I would Meet him when coming down the Arkansas Next Spring or summer for he is about 6 Months employd each Voyage = The Post of Arkansas is now a poor, Nearly deserted Village, it flourished in the time that the Spaniards & French kept it, and one 100 years passed it could have been called an agreable Small Town—at present, the decrepid Visages of the Wornout Indian Traders and a few American famillies are all that gives it Life, the Natural situation is a handsome One, on a high Bank formerly the Edge of *a Prairie*, but rendered Extremely sickly by the Back Neighbourhood of Many overflowing Lakes & Swamps—

I was assured that Only Two frosts had been felt here this Season and that the Ice in the River never Stopped the navigation—the Town now Prospering at *Point Rock* is high, healthy and in the Center of a Rich tract of Wood & Prairie Lands—and probably may flourish—the *Arkansas River* flows a Thick Current of red Clay & Sand, and if not for its Coloring would have Much of the Appearance of the Mississipi—

Cotton is raised here with some advantage—Corn grows Well, game & Fishes are plenty—

I here feel Inclined to tell you than an oportunit. of Good, Fresh Flour, Whiskey, Candles, Cheese, Apples, Porter, Cider, Butter Onions—, Tow Linen and Blankets would Meet with advantageous Sales during Winter, accompanied by *Powder Lead*, *Flint*, Butchers Knifes, Rifles, and *blue Shrouds* for the Indians—

After Breakfast We Left the Post of Arkansas with a Wish to see the Country above, and so *Strong* is my Anthusiast to Enlarge the Ornithological Knowledge of My Country that I felt as if I wish Myself *Rich again* and thereby able to Leave my familly for a Couple of Years = here I saw a French Gentleman who but a few Weeks passed had killed a *Hawk* of a Large size *perfectly White* except the Tail Which Was a *bright red*. unfortunatly, no remains of its skin Legs or Bill were to be found—

We travelled fast—reach[d] the Cutt off and Lannd our Skiff, having killed 5 *Crows* for their quills, Never before did I see these Birds so easily approach[d] and in fact all the Birds We saw, 2 Hawks I did not know hovered high over us—the Indians still at their Canoes, We Hailed, and gave them a Drachm of Whiskey, and as they Could Not Speak either french or English, I *Drew* a *Deer* with a stroke across its hind parts, *Snufled* and thereby Made them Know our Want of Venaison hams—

they brought 2 We gave them 50[cts] and a Couple Loads of Gun Powder to each, brought out smiles, and a Cordial Shaking of Hands = a Squaw with them a *Handsome Woman* Waded to us as Well as the Men and Drank freely—Whenever I meet *Indians* I feel the greatness of our Creator in all its splendor, for there I see the Man Naked from his Hand and Yet free from Acquired Sorrow =

in White River We saw a great Number of Geese Malards and some Blue Cranes—also Two Large Flocks of these *unknown Divers* or *Pelicans*—

reached our Boats about 6 in the afternoon fatigued but Contented   a good Supper, Merry Chat—and good Looks all round—Went to bed all Well—

before I leave the Trip to the *Arkansas Post*—I think I will give you More of it—We saw there a *Velocipede*   Judge how fast the Arts & Sciences Improved in this Southwestern Country—I wanted also to tell You that the *Squaw* on White River Wading out to us Craked a Large *Louse* taken from under her Arm—

———

The *Intrepid Hawks* are extremely plenty along the Banks of the Mississipi where they feed aboundantly on the *Swamp Sparows* as also on the *Sturnus depradatorius*, some of these are so strong and daring that they Will attack some Ducks on the Wings and often Carry them off several hundreds of yards to the Sand Bars—

———

The Brown Eagles that were so plenty on the Ohio have entirely disapeared and Nothing but White Headed Ones are to be seen—

———

The Lakes found in the Interior are stored with the finest of Fishes Such as Pikes, Salmons—Rock, Bass, Sun Perches &ᶜ and the bottom covered with thousands of Muskle Shells and Perrywinkles of many Species—these Latter of Course find their Way while the Spring floods are so general—the Bottom of Most of these Lakes is firm and Level—

Tuesday Decembᵣ 12ᵗʰ 1820

This day, Mᵣ *Shaw* and *Anthony* Walked off to the Post—and We floated down to the Mouth of that River—this We reached and Landed, I Was So fortunate as to Meet the *Steam Boat* the *Maid* of *Orleans* on board of Which I put a Letter for My Dearest Friend My Wife—with order to Put it in the Sᵣ *Louis* Post Office = saw to Day Many Crows Mergansers and Geese, some *Dun Divers*—and a Large flock of My unknown Divers—

the Blue Jeays are now & then seen—the great *Carolina Wrens* are Very aboundant—but the snow Birds have desapeared, the weather is so Warm that *Buterflies, Bats, Bees*, & Many Insects are flying about us and at the Arkansa I was assured that they had had but *Two* Light frosts—

Mᵣ Shaw is Expected Tomorow Night and perhaps Will Leave us here to Proceed up that River, for we are told the Orleans Market is Extremely dull—Killed a Gull precisely Such as I Shot at *New Port Kentucky*, rather Fatter

The Wild Geese we now Shoot have Eggs swollen to the size of Nᵒ 3 Blister Shots =

An Indian Chief at the Mouth of the arkansas killed *Three Swans* one of Which I was told Measured 9 feet from Tip to Tip—These Indians had Left when We arrived—a View of Such Noble Specimen would have been very agreable—

The *Prairie Hawk* that I see here is not the *Marsh Hawk* of Willson it is much Less—Lighter Colour, the Tip of the Wings Black and Only One Large Bend of Dark ending the Tail—they fly Much Like the *Night Hawk* and Catch Small Birds on the Grass Without Stopping their course—

Wednesday December 13th 1820—

a Beautifull day, Walked up the Arkansas in Search of a Lake but the Cane so thick that we give it up—Killed Two Geese, Mr Aumack Shot at a *Prairie Hawk* but did not Kill it—I wrote to Governor Miller the Copy of which is here annexed—

To his Excellency Govr Miller of the Arkansas—Sir— having had the Honor to receive several letters of rec- ommandation to your Excellency, from Genl *Harrison*, *Genl Lytle* and other Gentlemen, I felicite myself with the pleasure of an Interview with you—I Reached the Post of Arkansas but was foiled by your Absence; having only a few Moments to remain at that place I begged of Mr Thomas to present you the Letters I was the Bearer of—these I even was not able to seal—

My ardent Wish to Compleat a collection of drawings of the *Birds* of our Country, from *Nature* all of Natural *Size*, begun about 15 Years since, and to Acquire either by *occular*, or reliable observations of others the knowl- edge of their Habits, & residence; makes me wish to travel as far at Least as the Osage Nations on the Arkansas as also along the whole of our Frontiers—

Should your arduous avocations admit—I would Consider myself very Highly honored and under great obligations to receive from your Excellency a few lines of Information respecting the *Time*, the Manner of trav- elling and what might be necessary to render Such a Journey fruitfull to my Views—as well as your Personal Information of the discoveries you have made in Or- nithology, in that part of America—My Intention is to Visit the country around New Orleans as far East as the Florida Keys—then assend Red River, and to go to the Hot Springs—thence across to the Arkansas and Come down to its Mouth When on My return to Cincinnati at present my familly Residence—Yet My Plans are Alter- able as advised by Gentlemen of More Experience^d—

Should your Excellency contemplate any expedition upon Your River and I was sufered to Join it, I would be Anxious to Meet any Wishes my Humbler talents could afford at any time—

With Hopes that you will not be displeased at the liberty I have here taken

I remain with high respect
Your V. H. S^t
J. J. A.

P. S. if agreable please
Direct to Governor
Robertson

———

saw some Turkey Buzzard—
Some Mergansers and Sand Hill Cranes—Malards—Crows—Towe Buntings—Winter Wrens—Meadow Larks—Partridges Red Winged Starlings—and Vast Number of Swamp Sparows in the High Mississipi grass Parokeets—Golden Crowned Wrens—

———

Mr Shaw & Anthony returned at Eleven o'clock, but did not effect their Business, they returned in a Canoe, 30 Miles down the Arkansas to the *cut off* through that about 6 Miles down White River 7 and down the Mississipi 15 = this Makes 58 and the Distance from Arkansas Post to the Mouth of that River is 60—
about One Mile below the Mouth of Arkansas in a Thick patch of *Cane* are Two *Women* the remainder of a party of Wandering Vagabonds that about 2 years ago Left some part of the Eastern State to proceed to the *Promised Land*—these Two Wretches, Never Wash, Comb or Scarcely clad themselves, and subsist from the Scant generosity of the Neighbours—Now and then doing alitle sawing and washing—

Thursday Decemb^r 14th 1820

after Long considerations, our Gentlemen determined to do *Nothing*, and We *Cutt Loose* about 10 this Morning, the Weather quite Warm   Distant frequent Clapps, of Thunder announcing a Change—it soon begain to Rain, the Fog raised and We Landed again about 2 o'clock—saw here 5 Ivory Bill Wood Peckers feeding on the Berries of Some Creepers   they were gentle = keeping a Constant Cry of *Pet Pet Pet*—Killed a Crow on the Drift wood   it was not untill then that I discovered that a Crow killed by Mr Shaw while I was at the Arkansas—Was a *Fish Crow*—it rained all Night Watter raising fast—

Friday Decemb^r 15th 1820

rainy & Cold, floated about 6 Miles—at One o'clock the Steam Boat, *James Ross* passed us—in the afternoon I had the good fortune to kill a Beautifull *Marsh Hawk Falco Eulogi-nosus*—feeding on a Swamp Sparrow that I saw him Catch— When I approach him before I Shot he saw me first and flew a few yards where he sat tearing at his prey untill death reached him = the *Prairie Hawk* seen Yesterday is entirely diferent, in size, Color, & manner of flying and as it is a Non-descript I Hope I may Meet it again—Killed 4 Teals and 2 Geese—the Watter rose 20 Inches, this day—

I have seen the Marsh Hawks about September flying down the Ohio River, and several times about that season I have seen *flocks* of them travelling high and southwesterly—finding them Now plenty on these Shores where great deal of rich food is afforded them by the Numerous quantity of Swamp Sparows the Mildness of the Weather, no doubt assures them a good Winter Residence—

the one I killed Was a Male, in good order Weighing Only ¾^lb—Measured 18 Inches full Length, breadth 3½ feet—the Insides of the Mouth Black—

Saturday December 16th 1820—

the weather much the same, heard this Morning that the Ohio had raised Immensely—spent the day Drawing my Hawk but so dark and desagreable that I could not finish it— having Landed for 3 or 5 hours at the Head of the *Cypress Bend* We floated but a Short Distance,—

Vast Many Geese seen to day—Joseph killed a *Pewee fly catcher* Close by the Boat—the litle fellow Was very active and in very good Order—a femelle—

this Evening About *100 Pelicans* were in view on a sand Barr, and although I had no expectations of reaching them We put off in the Skiff, when about 200 yards off from them, they flew and I sent them my Ball, without effect = these are the first I have seen this Journey, I hope I Will have one to draw before I reach N. Orleans—

The generality of the geese We kill are very poor and Scarcely fit to eat = the Steam Boat *Govr Shelby* pass^d us heavily Laden—

When I was trying to approach the Pelicans, they rose from their slumber One at a time, and Shook their Wings as if to try if Able to fly in Case of need—the Nearer We Came the faster they gethered and walked off untill they all flew without uttering any Noise—

Sunday December 17th 1820

Raining all day, I finished my Drawing—Landed at *Pointe Chico*, a few Miles before this the *Spanish Beard* is seen,—Pointe Chico is a handsome spot on the river that never overflows—and answers well for the Growth of Cotton Corn &^c—Peach & Aple Trees flourish well here, but sugar will not grow—

a Man of good Manners assured me that the *Marsh Hawks* were very plenty here all winter, but not to be seen in Summer—and that the *Pelicans* desapear at this season for the South and return early in April with young—Many Red Winged Starlings—and Many *Bleu Birds* these were pleasing to me, the sweet Note of these is allways wellcome to Mine ears—

the Watter raising very fast—

Last Night Mr Aumack who was *rather Merry*—Went to shoot a Pelican about 10 o'clock P. M to Cool himself return^d—without a Shot—

saw Winter Wrens and a beautifull plant in full Bloom—*Ivory Billed Wood Peckers* becoming More plenty—

Monday Decr 18th 1820—

Raining all day, floated but a few Miles—Landed at a Place where Geese and Ducks abounded—Killed a Crow, *a Great Horned Owl*, and a Winter *Falcon*—

Tuesday Decemb^r. 19th 1820—

Rain and fog all day—Landed within 7 Miles of Last Night's = Killed a *Carrion Crow*, a *Winter Wren* and 16 *Parokeets*, I heard and saw once a *Thrush* unknown to Me but could Not get a Shot at it—Immense flocks of Parokeets and Swamp *Blackbirds*—the *Carrion Crow* I Shot at Would Not suffer us to go near than about 100 yards and forced Me to draw My Shot and Put in a Ball   this brought him down Lifeless =

This Morning I Shot at a Bird unknown to Me and no doubt a Non Descript—it was of the Sparow Genus—

saw several Thrushes, very Shy, they sung Sweetly and also Constantly, took for the Golden *Crown^d thrush Turdus Auracapillus*, Also a *French Mocking Bird Turdus Rufus*—the Trees in Many places in the Thick Canes full of Leaves—and during this Rainy *Spell* the Weather as felt Much Like the begaining of May—

Wednesday Decemb^r 20th 1820—

The Weather as desagreable as one could wish it—Raining and so foggy that We Could not see 50 yards—drawing all day—in the Morning the *Winter Wren Sylvia trogloditus*—and afterwards the *Carrion Crow, Vultur atratus*—at Twelve o'clock A Short Clearing taking place We floated about 4 Miles and Landed Opposite side of the River—Cap^e Cummings Shot at an *Ivory Billed Wood Pecker Picus Principallis* broke his Wing and When he Went to take it up it Jump up and Claimed a tree, as fast as Squirel to the Very Top, he gave it up having but a few Loads of Shot—Joseph Came and Saw it—Shot at it and brought him down =

We Boiled 10 Parokeet to night for Dash, Who has had 10 Welps—purposely to try the effect of the Poisonous effect of their hearts on Animals   Yesterday we Were told that 7 Cats had been Killed Last Summer by Eating as Many Parokeets—

Killed two Geese—

several Boats Landed along us to night—

Thursday Decemb^r 21st 1820—

We at last had fine weather, floated about 35 Miles   this brought us to the upper Part of *Stack Island* Now only a Barr the former having being sunk by the Earthquakes—Drawing nearly all day I finished the Carrion Crow, it stunk so intolerably, and Looked so disgusting that I was very glad when I through it over Board—

Saw in the Afternoon a *Black Hawk*, a flock of *Pelicans* at which I shot at about 200 yards as near as I could approach, without effect, the sand Barr where they were was Literally covered with excrements and their Feathers.

Vast Many Geese seen all day, these Birds Now *pairing*. Spanish Moss very aboundant on all the Cypress trees—Large flocks of *American Teals* and the constant Cry of Ivory Billed Wood Peckers about us—scarcely any other except a few *Peleated*, & Golden Wings—have not seen a red head Wood Pecker for some time—the *Carolina Wrens* and *Cardinals* exercising their Vocal Powers all day—

We received the Visits of 2 Men, Wood Cutters from the Shore—they assured me that *Pelicans* were here at all seasons but that when the Weather is bad they keep in the Lakes in Great Flocks along with the Geese, Swans, Ducks, Cranes—and there find an aboundance of food = they spoke of a *Black Hawk* that Lives on Fish but I could Not assertain Much about size or any thing else Concerning it –

they reported that a few Weeks passed a Youth of about 12 Years having Met a Large *Brown Tiger*, or *Cougar*, called here a *Painter* was so frightened that he died after reaching his Parents' house—these annimals are now scarce, but Dear, Bears and Wolfs are plenty—Anxious to know if Alligators were seen during this season, they answered in the Affirmative, they could be seen every few day—some keeping in Small ponds too Shallow to cover their back and there Catch, the *Garr Fishes*, root for frogs &c that one killed Lately had a Large quantity of Black Walnuts and Hickorys—they are killed here for the Skin, that when tannd gives a fine Leather preserving the Lozanges of the Scales. One of the Men, said he owed them a Grudge for killing an excellent hunting Dog—while following a wounded Dear across a Lake, and that he retaliates on the Whole species whenever an Opportunity offered—a Boy told us that one that had dugged a hole about 20 feet under the ground to resort to, in bad weather, Was taken a few days ago; the earth having falen on him during a heavy Dash of rain. they are easily killed with a Clubb—the usual way of destroying them = they Move slow on the ground—but swiftly in the Watter—this is all hear say and put it here to Compare it with My Own future Observations—

Friday December 22ᵈ 1820

Started at 5 o'clock this Morning, and certainly deserves Noting,—after breakfast Joseph & I push off as usual in the Skiff in which we remained untill near Sun Down—saw *Three Black Hawks*, Shot at this Twice, but these Birds are So Shy that I dared not advance nearer than Rifle Shot and Missed them = Went to a house, to Warm our fingers, the wind blowing rather Sharp this Morning—found a Handsome familly of Young Brats, who as well as their Mamma Looked Clean and healthy = here We saw the *Pameta* Plants along the Fences—

in the afternoon the sun Shown warm, the Geese where in Thousands on the Willow Bar, fighting and Mating—Malards, Teals and Wood Ducks aboundant = killed One Malard and Two Wood Ducks—saw One Swan—One Red tailed *Hawk*, several *Sparrow Hawks*—Many Crested titmouse—Autumnal Warblers all through the Shaggy *Beards*—The *Carrion Crow* plenty, and their relation the Buzzard

the *Pewee Fly Catchers* very busy diving at Insects and Singing Merily—saw several Bald Eagles that I Might have Shot at—

a litle before Sun down a Steam Boat Called the *Mars* passed us, a poor running Machine—Apparently an Old Barge—

Our Commander Spoke of *Cutting a Stick* at 12 o'clock, but the Axes were dull and We did not get up untill 3;—

Saturday Decembʳ 23ᵈ 1820

the Moon shining beautifully Clear, the Weather, calm a heavy White frost—started at 3 o'clock—

as soon as the fog desapeared, J. & I sett off for the Mouth of the *Yazoo River*, seing some Geese Made for them and killed one—in the Mouth of that River I perceived a Large flocks of My unknown *Blackbirds* that I suppose Brown Pelicans—Landed below them, and after crawling on My belly for about 300 yards I arrived within about 45 Yards I fired at 3 that were perched Close together on a dead Stick about 7 feet above the Watter, At My Shot they all fell as so many Stones, I expected them to be all dead but to My Surprise, those and about 20 swimming under them had dove, they Soon rose and took wing after running on the Watter about 50^{yds} at the exception of the One I had taken aim on—it could not raise, the Skiff brought up We rowed after it, diving below us up the Yazoo Nearly one Mile, Yet I could not give it up, it became Waried, & remained Less under Watter the Nearer We Approach when at Last Joseph Shot at its *head* & Neck (the Only part in view Looking much Like a Snake) and keeled it over—I took it up with great pleasure and anxiety—but I could Not ascertain its Genus—for I could not Make it an *Albatros* the only Bird I can discover any relation to—

We had to exert ourselves to reach our Boats—this done, I began Drawing—We passed to day the *Walnut Hills* a handsome situation on the Mississipi covered with Cotton plantations—We also passed the Small Village of *Warren* commonly Called Warington   Opposite this place (Not Improving) Met the St. *Elba S.-B.*

The *Yazoo River* flowed a Beautifull Stream of transparent Watter, Covered with 1000^{ds} of Geese & Ducks and filled With Fish—the Entrance Low Willows & Cotton Trees—We run^{d} to day 49 Miles—the Weather rather Too Warm=

Monday December 25th 1820 Chrismas day
We passed, the Petit Gulf = early this morning—the Steam Boat Comet passed by from Louisville 9 Days =

I had the pleasure of seeing Mr Aumack Killed a *Great Footed Hawk*, the Bird that Alexander Willson heard So Many wonderfull Tales of—these Birds are plenty on this River at this season every Year according to all the accounts I have Collected, but allways extremely Shy, and I Believe few Men Can Boast of having killed Many of them, for 15 Years, that I have hunted and seen probably one hundred I Never had the

Satisfaction of bringing one to the Ground—I often have seen
them after hearing their Canon Ball Like wistling Noise
through the Air seize their Prey on the Wing particularly at
Henderson Kentucky, where I watched for Weeks near a Pigeon House, that furnished one of these daring Robbers,
with food & Exercise—No doubt that the Clouds of Ducks of
Some many Species as are found on this River, renders it a
pleasant and fruitfull Winter Residence,—

We have seen about 50 Since a few Weeks—they fly fast,
with Quick Motions of their Wings, seldom Sailing except
when about alighting:—the Specimen before me is a very Old
Bird and a beautifull One, When on the Wing they appear
Black and are often Mistaken for the *Falco Niger*—Killed 3
Geese;—

saw a *Tell Tale Godwit*, the Only one seen Since I Left the
Ohio—but understanding that that River is now considerably
raised, I expect they are forced to abandon it—

Cap^c Cummings saw 4 Deer this Evening—We are Now
Landed about 15 Miles above Natchez, and if No head Wind
takes place Must reach that City Tomorow

I Hope that My Familly wishes me as good a Christmas as
I do them—Could I have spent it with my Beloved Wife &
Children, the exchange of Situation would have been Most
Agreable—I hope to have Some tidings of them Tomorow =
the shores are now Lined with Green Willows the Weather
Much Like May—at *Henderson*

The Thermometer is allmost every day from 60 to 65—

Tuesday Decemb^r 26th 1820
Beautifull Morning, Light frost—I began my drawing as soon
as I could see—drawing all day—

We saw to day probably *Millions* of those *Irish Geese* or
Cormorants, flying Southwest—they flew in Single Lines for
several Hours extremely high—

at half Past 11 o'clock The Boats Landed at the Natchez
Bluffs amongst about 100 More, several S. B.^s were also at
this place = the Carrion Crows first attracted my Attention,
hundreds of them flying constantly Low over the Shores and
alighting on the Houses—

I Rec^d Two Letters from my Beloved Wife, dated 7th & 14th of Novr the Last date contained one from My Brother *G. Loyen Dupuygaudeau* dated July 24, 1820.

so Busy I have been all day drawing, that I did not even go to the Shore—a litle before Dusk I Saw from our Boat Roof, the Magnolia & Pines that ornement the Hills above this Place—

I Wrote a Long Letter to My Lucy with Hopes that it would be in time for the Mail of Tomorow =

Our Commanders and Mr Shaw found every article of Produce Low, perhaps too Low to refound themselves.

———

I found the Stomack of the Great footed Hawk filled with Bones, feathers, and the Gizzard of a Teal, also the Eyes of a Fish and Many scales—it was a femelle—Egg numerous and 4 of them the size of Green Peas—

as We approach Natchez I remarked in several places—Saw Mills, placed over ditches cut from the River and running to the Swamps which in times of floods afford a Good Current—these ditches also serve to furnish these Mills with timbers floated through them from the Interior =

We have also seen very Large Rafts of Long Logs Intended for Mr Livingston's Warf at New Orleans—a Rafter assured us of having rec^d 6000$ for the Last Parcel he Stole from the Governments Land—

Wednesday Decemb^r 27th 1820

as soon as my drawing was finished, I Cleaned and Went to Natchez properly speaking—there to my utmost surprise I met Nicholas Berthoud, who accosted me kindly, and ask^d me to go down to New Orleans in his Boat—I accepted his Offer—

from the River opposite Natchez, that place presents a Most Romantick scenery, the Shore Lined by Steam Vessels Barges & flat Boats, seconded by the Lower town, consisting of Ware Houses, Grogg, Chops, Decayed Boats proper for the use of Washer Women and the sidling Road raising along the Caving Hills, on an oblique of a quarter of a Mile and about 200 feet High covered with Goats feeding peaceably on its declivities, while hundreds of Carts, Horses and foot travellers Are Constantly, meeting and Crossing each Others reduced to Miniatures by the distance, renders the whole really picturesk—; on the Top of this the Traveller comes in sight of the town as he enters Avenues of regularly plented Trees Leading to the diferent Streets running at right Angles towards the River; on the left the *Theater* a poor framed Building and a New and Elegant Mansion the property of Mr Postlewait attract the Anxious eye—on the right the rollings of the hearth thinly diversified by poor habitations soon close the prospect—advancing, he is Led into Main Street; this as well as the generality of the place too Narrow to be Handsome, is rendered Less Interesting by the poorness & Iregularity of the Houses, few of which are Bricks—and at this season very much encumbered by Bales of Cotton—the Jail, & Court Houses are new and tolerable in their form the Lower part of the former, a Boarding House of some Note. there are Two Miserable Looking Churches; I dare not say, unattended; but think so—

the Natchez's Hotel is a good House built on the spanish plan i.e. with Large Piazas and Many Doors and windows— Well Kept by Mr John Garnier and is the rendez vous of all Gentill Travellers and Boarders—several Large tavern which I did Not Visit furnish amply the Wants of the Strangers that at all times abound from diferent parts of the Union—this place now Contain about 2000 inhabitants and Houses, has a Bank in good Credit—a Post Office receiving the Diferent Mails Thrice per Week, a Public reading Room and 2 printing offices—

the Naturalist will imediatly remark, the General Mildness of the temperature on seeing at this season premature Growth of Lettuces, Radishes and other vegetables that in our Eastern Latitudes are Carefully nursed in April and sometimes in May—

the *Pewee* fly Catcher, the Notable Mocking Bird, constant residents Assure him that if frosts are seen they must be of Short duration, and the Numberless prostrated Carrion Crows in the less frequented Streets prove to him the unhalthiness of the Atmosphere—those Certainly may be considered as necessary Evils, for no Birds are more desagreable at the same time that few are More Valuable in Climates like this—

I saw here a Gentleman with whom I travelled some distance down the Mississippi My first Voyage but as he did Not or Would Not recognize my features I spoke not to him—

the Country back of Natchez was represented as Good and setled by rich Planters who once raised a Large quantity of Cotton the principal Article of Export—Opposite this the Lands are extremely Low and overflow to a great Extent and Depth the Mail in Times of flood goes by Watter through the Woods nearly 40 Miles Toward Natchitoches on Red River.

Indians are Daily seen here with diferent sorts of Game— for which they receive high Prices, I saw Small Wild Turkeys sold by them for One Dollar each, Malards at 50^{cts}

Although the Weather is Comparatively Mild, the Orange trees will not bear the Winters in open air = and sometimes the frosts for a day or Two are severely felt—the remains of an Ancient Spanish fort are perceivable, the Center is now Honored by the Gallows and the Ditch serves as buriing ground for Slaves = the Cemetiere Lies at the extremity of the Town—About 2 Years ago a Large part of the Hill gave Way, sunk probably 150 feet and Carried Many Houses into the River—this was Occasioned, by the quick sand Running Springs, that flows under the Strata of Clay and pebles of Which the Hills is Composed=

this sunken part is Now used as the depot of Dead Carcasses, and oftentimes during the Summer emits Such Exalaisons as attracts hundred, Nay I was told Thousands of Carrion Crows = an Engine is now Nearly in Operation Intended to raise the Watter of one of the Springs or *ecoulement* or drains to Suply the City—this indeed is much wanted, Watter hawled from the River is sold at 50^{cts} p^r Barrel taken out of the Eddy very Impure = I found few Men Interested towards Ornithology except those who had heard or pleased to Invent Wonderfull Stories respecting a few Species—

Mr Garnier on whom I can rely told me that he had given Liberty to a Mocking Bird after several Years confinement and that for several Years afterwards the Bird came daily in the House as if to thank him for his Generosity and Past kind attentions = Mr James Willkins to whom A. Willson had Letters of Introduction assured me that his Work was far from

Compleat, that through his Mere transient observations he had discovered several New Specimens but being *a Man of Business* he Never had Noted any—

A Bird Much resembling the femelle humming Bird is often seen (it is said) during Summer, feeding by Suctions amongst the Magnolias   He is about Twice the Size of a Wren—

The Carrion Crows Never breed in or Near the Town— having Not one Cent when I Landed here I imediatly Looked for something to do in the Likeness way for our Support (unfortunatly Naturalists are obliged to eat and have some sort of Garb)   I Rented the room of a Portrait Painter Naming himself *Cook* but I assure You he was Scarcely fit for a Scullion, Yet *the Gentleman* had some politeness and procured me the drawing of Two sketches for 5$ each, this was fine Sauce to our empty stomacks—

One was imediatly Paid for, the other a very excellent resemblance of Mr *Mathewson* probably never will be, for that Gentleman absented the same Evening and never Left orders to anybody to pay—I Merely put this down to give You the Best advice a Father Can present you with. Never to sell or Buy without imediatly paying for the same = a Constant adherence of this Maxim will keep your Mind and person at all times free, & Happy—Mr Cook much pleased with My Drawings and quickness of performance, desired to travel with us if Suitable Mutual Arrangements could be Made; I asked him to pay me Two Dollars per day Monthly in advance and furnish besides, One Third of the Whole Expenses, providing himself with Whatever Materials might be necessary—

he spoke of Joining us in a Couple of Weeks; I thought it very uncertain = the awkwardness I felt when I sat to Dinner at the Hotel was really surprising to me; having not used a fork and Scarcely even a Plate since I left Louisville, I involuntarily took Meat and Vegetables with my fingers several times; on Board the flat Boats, We seldom eat together and very often, the hungry Cooked; this I perform^d when in need by Plucking & Cleaning a Duck, or a Partridge and throwing it on the hot embers; few Men have eat a Teal with better appetite than I have, dressed in this manner =

Others prepairing Bacon would Cut a Slice from the *Side*

that hung by the Chimney and Chew that raw with a hard Biscuit = Such Life is well intended to drill Men Gradually to hardships, to go to Sleep with Wet Muddy Clothing on a Buffaloe Skin Stretch on a Board, to hunt through Woods filled with fallen trees, Entengled with Vines, Briars, Canes, high Rushes and at the same time giving under foot; produced heavy Swets, Strong Appetite, & keeps the Imagination free, from Worldly thoughts, I would advise Many *Citizens* particularly our Eastern *Dandys* to try the experiment—leaving their high heeled Boots, but Not their *Corsets*, for, this would no doubt be Serviceable, whenever food giving way, they might wish to depress their Stomacks for the Occasion—

Thursday December 28th 1820—
Weather sultry, saw some Mocking Birds and was assured that they remained during the Winters here—Nicholas having invited me to stay at his Lodgings I Breakfasted at the Hotel of M[r] Garnier a French Gentleman of Agreable Manners who kindly procured Me Willson's Ornithology from M[r] James Wilkins to whom I was introduced to by Nicholas—

Friday December 29th 1820
The weather this Morning had taken a remarquable Change the Thermometer had fallen from 72 to 36—it snowed and blew hard from the Northwest—Last Night the Musquitoes, were quite troublesome—

I made Two Sketches, to day for $5 each; after many Inquiries for the 9th Volume of Willson. I was disapointed in my wish of examining it none of the subscribers have rec[d] it—

Joseph and Cap[e] Cummings still remaining on Board of M[r] Aumack' Boat = I had the satisfaction of ransacking the *Fables* of *Lafontaine*, with Engravings = Wrote to D[r] Drake and Mr Rob[d] Best—

Saturday Decemb[r] 30th 1820—
the Weather very Cold, the Thermometer at 25 =
Spent all day Writting the Name and Such Descriptions of the Watter Birds in Willson as would Enable Me to Judge Whenever a New Specimen falls My Praise—

Mr Aumack Left this Morning in our Boat taking With him Cap^e Cummings—I felt Sorry at parting With that really agreable Compagnion   I Wrote to My Beloved Wife =

Sunday Decemb^r 31st 1820—

Early this Morning We prepared for our Departure, our things were Collected, and Carried to the Keel Boat—however it Was Not untill One o'clock that the Steam Boat Columbus hailed off the Landing—

We Made fast to her Stern with Two Ropes and went very Swiftly the Moment She was under full headway—

I drew this afternoon—and here I have to tell a sad Misfortune that took place this Morning—having Carried under My Arm My Smallest Port Folio and Some other Articles I Laid the Whole on the Ground and ordered Mr Berthouds Servant to take them on Board

I unfortunately Went off to Natchez again to breakfast   the Servant forgot My Folio on the Shore and Now I am Without, any Silver Paper, to preserve my Drawings, have Lost some very Valuable Drawings, and My Beloved Wife's Likeness = the greatest Exercions I now Must Make to try to find it again, but so dull do I feel about it that I am nearly Made Sick

I wrote to Mr John Garnier, requesting him to Advertise and procure someone to try to find My Port Folio but no Hopes can I have of ever seing it, when Lost amongst 150 or 160 flat Boats and Houses filled with the Lowest of Caracters—No doubt My Drawings will serve to ornement their Parlours or will be nailed on Some of the Steering Oars—

We passed to day A long Line of Bluffs exquisitively grand to the sight—

My Port Folio Contained 15 Drawings Three of Which Were Non Descripts—one a Duck extremely Curious and rare—that I had Named the *Fintail*: Should I not get it again, it may retard my return home very Considerably =

Monday January 1st 1821—

This day 21 Years since I was at *Rochefort* in France, I spent most of that day at Copying Letters of My Father to the Minister of the Navy—

What I have seen, and felt since, would fill a Large Volume—the Whole of Which Would end at *this Day January 1ˢᵗ 1821 I am on Board a Keel Boat going down to New Orleans the poorest Man on it*—½ What I have seen and felt has brought some very dearly purchased Experience, and Yet Yesterday I forgot that No servant could do for me what I might do Myself; had I acted accordingly; my Port Folio would now have been safe in my possession—

Not Willing to dwel on Ideal futurity, I do not at present attempt to forsee where My poor Body may be this day 12 Months

at 12 o'clock to day the *Columbus* Came too at Bayou *Sarah*—a Small Village at the Mouth of that Inlet—Many flat Boats, 3 Steam Boat and 2 Briggs waiting for Cotton = the steam Boat *Alabama* put off as we came to, and about half an hour after; the Columbus Left us to ourselves to try to reach Baton Rouge before her, to procure the freight there—promising to Wait 3 hours—

the Lands are flatening fast—the orange trees are Now and then seen Near the Rich Planter's habitation—and the Verdure Along all the Shore is very Luxuriant and agreable = the Thermometer at—68 at 12 o'clock in the Shade, the Day Beautifully fairr—Expected to see some Alligators = Many *Irish Geese* in the Eddys—Malards but few Geese = at half Past 6 o'clock P.M. We came opposite *Baton Rouge* but the Steam Boat had left and of Course we proceeded on our Way floating = this Last Place is a Thrifty Village in the New Orlean State—from some distance above *Levées* have made their appearance—I saw a Negro man fishing by deeping a Scoup Net every moment in the Watter immediatly at a point where the current ran swift forming an eddy below, he had taken several tolerably Large Cat fishes =

Tuesday January 2ᵈ 1821

We floated all night without accidents, the river since Natchez is much deeper, and free of Sawers and Snaggs—at day breake found ourselves about 50 Miles below Baton Rouge; the day Cloudy, raw, and some Wind ahead—

the Plantations increase in number, and the Shores have

Much the Appearance of those on Some of the Large river of France, their Lowness Excepted = the points are quite diferent to those on the River above, One May see the River below them by Looking across in Many places = and from the Boat we can only have a View of the upper windows, Roofs and Tops of the Trees about them. the Whole is backed by a dark Curtain of Thickly moss covered Cypresses—flat Boats are Landed at nearly every Plantation, this being a Sure method of disposing of their produce to a better profit—travellers on horse Back or Gigs go by us full Gallop as if their Life depended on the accelerity of their movements = I have Seen More Common Crows since Natchez than I ever saw in My Whole Life before, the Shores and Trees are Covered with them; but Yet very few fish Crows have been Seen—saw some Pelicans, Many Gulls, Buzzards & C. Crows—

our Situation in this Boat is quite Comfortable—We have, a good Servant to wait on us, are served with regular Meals, Clean and in Plates = Move much faster than With Messrs Aumack & Lovelace, having here 8 Roaers who dare not contradict orders =

it rained and blowed hard a head, about one Mile below *Bayou Lafourche*, We Came to—the weather did not stop Joseph and Myself from taking a Walk to the Swamp back of Plantation in front of which the Boat was moored = after Chasing the Note of what I supposed a New Bird for a considerable time, I found the deceiving Mocking Bird close by me and Exulting with the Towe Bunting's *Cheap*—Joseph was More fortunate   he killed Two Warblers, One the *Red Poll* (of this We saw about a dozen)—the other I have Not yet ascertained—although in Beautifull plumage; Both Male = how Sweet for me to find Myself the 1st of January in a Country where the woods are filled with Warblers, Thrushes, and at the same time see the Rivers and Lakes covered with all kinds of Watter Birds—

the Pewees, are quite gaily, I have seen this day 3 Cat Birds = if this is not the winter retreat of all our Summer Birds it is at all Events that of very many = how happy would I feel to see some future January Surrounded by the diferents species of Swallows Skeeping about, with the Whippoorwill & Night-Hawk =

—I drew the Likeness of Mr *Dickerson* the Master of the Boat—he paid me in Gold = —took the outlines of Both the Warblers by Candle Light to afford Me time to morow to finish both—

—3^d—

Raining & Blowing hard all Night   the weather cooled Considerably, much Like some of our April days at Henderson = took a Walk Early, while waiting for the Light to Increase and enable Me to work = passed through a Large Cotton Plantation yet unpluked Looked Like if a Heavy Snow had fell and frosen on every Bud—

the great regularity with which this is sowed and raised Attracts the Eye imediatly; it Lays in rows I believe allways running at right Angle to the River, about 6 feet distant from each other and the plants about 3 and so Straight that your Eye is Carried to the farthest extremety of the field without the Least Obstruction—even at this time that the Cotton has Ceased to be attended for Many weeks, it is quite free from Weeds of any Sort =

the Woods here have a new and very romantic Appearance—the Plant Called Pamitta raises promiscously through them the Moss on every trees darkens the under growth and affords to the melancholy Mind, a retreat—thooted by the Chirpings of hundreds of Beautifully Plumed inhabitants =

the flocks of *Blackbirds* taking the Species En Masse, feel the Air, they pass southwest constantly; forming a Line Like disbanded Soldiers all anxious to reach the point of destination each hurring to pass the Companion before him =

Doves are plenty, the Cardinal Gros Beaks very numerous and all Species of Sparrow inabiting the Interior are here—I remark great Many *Brown Larks* busy feeding on the Drift Wood that feels Many Eddys =

I drew both My Birds, the first on A plant in full bloom that I plucked Near the Boat = saw about 50 Mocking Birds Some of them extremely Gentle, and holding their tail Leaning back allmost over their Heads—We Were Visited by several *french Creoles* this is a Breed of Annimals, that

Neither speak french English nor Spanish corectly but have a Jargon composed of the Impure parts of these three—

they Stared at My Drawings, and when a litle Composed Gazed and Complimented Me very Highly—on asking them the names of about a dozen diferent Birds then lying on the Table they Made at once and without hesitating a Solid Mass of *Yellow Birds* of the Whole = One of them a young Man told Me that he Could procure 3 or 4 dozen of them every Night by hunting the Orange trees with a Lantern—I Can said he "see the Rascalls' White bellies and knok them down with a Stick very handy" = few of these good Natured fools could answer any valuable account of the Country =

some toads were hoping about this evening, and on turning a Dead Tree over, we found several Lizards, who moved with great Vigour = at Sunset the Wind Lulled, the Captain, Sailors and passengers all anxious to reach New Orleans, it was determined that after a good supper the Oars would be used untill day break tomorow, if so We May see the City early

———

I shot this Evening at a *Sparrow Hawk* that being badly Wounded sailed directly for a hole, (probably that of a Woodpecker) and no doubt died there—a few Moments previous he Was teazing an American Buzzard—

Joseph killed One Teal—with several Goldfinches and Warblers, some Sparrows, but Nothing New—

Thursday January 4th 1821—

at 4 o'clock this morning the wind was so high, that it forced us to Come to a litle above *Bonné Caré*'s Church = the weather was rather cold, as soon as day broke walk^d over to the Swamp,

saw, some Birds that I took for Large non described *Cukoos* as they flew high over us, they had a new Note to me = Many Warblers, Robins, blue Birds, Cardinals, Grakles, Sparows, Goldfinches, doves, Golden Wing Woodpeckers, One Redheaded one—Many, Carolina & Winter Wrens = Sparrow Hawks, and a Large one unknown = on our return to the boat we Started with Hopes that We could make *some* headway—but were forced to, about a Mile below the Church = I paid my Respects to the Pastor, to make some Inquiries respecting M*r* *Lecorgne, George Croghan,* and the country, but I found only a tall thin dirty Creole who could not say much besides the prayer for the prosperity of the Brick Church now erecting = from this pensionnary of Bigots I went to a School House; there I had the pleasure if meeting an Old, polite, and well Instructed French Gentleman in Charge of about a dozen of Pupils of Both sexes—he told me that *George Croghan* resided about 3 Miles from this Place across the Mississipi, that he was not acquainted with Lecorgne's Name—that this Country was a fine field for my Wishes; walked to the Boat, examined attentively My Drawings and told me that having Left Europe and the World of Talents for So many Years Such a Sight was very gratifying = We hunted again and Saw more of the *Cuckoos* these this time I saw on the Ground and knew them at Once for some of the same Birds I had Shot my preceeding Voyage and had taken for *Boat Tailed Grakles*—I killed 3, Two femelles and one Male and had the pleasure of examining their Manners very Closely—their Voice is Loud and Sweet and their Movements elegantly airy—a Beautifull male was very busily Engage*d* in carrying some Straws to a Large Live Oak, but loosing the Bird every time through the Spanish Moss, I Could Not see any appearance of Nest, and So early in the season could Not presume it was for the purpose of building one—I Shot him—and Joseph killed another femelle—these Birds are considerably More Shy than any other Grakle—fly very Loosely when in flocks, uttering constantly a Chuck diferent to that of the *purple Grakle—Gracula quiscala*. and their flight resembles that of our Cuckoos and that of the Cukoo of Europe = While on the ground their walk is Elegant and Stately carrying their Long concave tails rather high—feed Closer to each others than swamp Black Birds: Turton Speaks of their Shortish Bills and gives for total length 13 Inches—this was taken no doubt from a Young femelle—the Male now before me Measures 15¾ Inches—my drawing Shews you Male & femelle, and tomorow it being finished I will give you a description = the French here call them Starlings—but on all questions respecting them or any other birds their Answer is a Constant *Oh Oui* = the country is here richly adorned by handsome dwelling Houses, Many Sugar and Cotton Plantations running about One Mile and half to the Swamp, free from Old trees and Stumps = every house a *D'Espagnole*—orange trees, now hanging with their golden fruits forming avenues and Edges = the fields Well fenced in and dreaned by ditches running to the Swamps =

the Mocking Birds are so Gentle that I followed one along a fence this morning for nearly one Mile keeping only one pannel betwen us the whole of the distance = I have Not heard one sing yet; but imitating many Birds =

about 5 o'clock we again ventured off and again the Wind drove us in Shore and now we are Landed on a point Where our Boat rolls merily = raining hard—thermometer to day at 52—this morning the french Gentlemen Wrap^d up in their Cloaks kept their Handkerchiefs to their Noses = What would become of them on the Rocky Mountains at this season = our Captain Exchange some Apples for Oranges receiving 2 for 1—

Friday January 5th 1821

We had some Light Snow this morning, drawing nearly all day, the wind blowing violently—Shortly after Breakfast saw Some *Terns Winowing* in the Eddy below us, killed Two on the wing—on the Falling of the first, the Second approach^d as if to see What was the Matter, I Shot it dead, when the remaining Two that where coming fast wheeled and flew out of our Sight imediatly = those Birds flew Lightly with their Bills perpendicular over the Watter on which they appeared to keep a close attention, Now & then falling to it and taking up Small fragments of Buiscuit thrown from our Boat = I finished my *Gracula Barita* but not the drawing; the rocking of the Boat quite desagreable—took a Long Walk towards Evening, saw Many Warblers particularly the *Maryland Yellow throat,* Shot an *Hermit Thrush*; paid a Visit to a Cottager a French Creole, handsome Children who were all afraid of me—the Lady *remarkably handsome* their Litle Garden was adorned with a few orange Trees—Some fine Lettuces filled the Borders; Green Peas nearly in bloom, Artichaux, reminding one of the happy days Spent in France = bought some delightfull radishes, and Enquired of Birds of Course; one League distant is a fine Lake, now the rendez vous of Ducks, Geese, &ᶜ—but could not obtain Valuable remarks = the transient Cool Weather as rendered the Mocking Birds So gentle that they Scarcely would move out of the Way—

at Night I drew the Outlines of the Tern I had Shot and ransacked Turtons but all without effect, Yet I do not Consider this as a New Specie, untill I See Willson's 9ᵗʰ Volume = the Gracule Male I draw Measured in Breadth 22 Inches— Tongue bifid—and I found to day that their Carrying Straws up in the Trees was simply to pick the rice contained in the heads = I saw this day thousands of them—particularly found of Cattle pens, alighting close to them and hunting in the fresh Dung, in the Manner of the Uropean Starling

Saturday January 6ᵗʰ 1821

the Thermother fell by Sun rise to 30, We had some ice on the running Boards; after So much Warm weather experienced since the Latitude 33 this felt very uncomfortable, and our Litle Stove was good Company, the Wind blew hard ahead Yet—I drew slowly, the Tern I killed Yesterday; Joseph Made his first attempt from Nature on the femelle—I was very much pleased with his essay = the wind falling alot at 8 o'clock We pushᵈ off—and rowed 12 Miles with much Dificulty, I did not expect our Commander would Leave our Harbour with as dull a prospect—We even blown a Shore opposite *Monsieur Sʳ Amand*'s Sugar Plantation =

Out on Shore with Guns imediatly—the Swamps about 3 Miles back we gave up going to them fearing the departure of our boat while absent that far = here was the finest Plantation we have seen, Mʳ S. Aᵈ own 70 Negroes and Makes about 400 Hogsheads of Sugar—besides raising, Corn, Hay, Rice &ᶜ = this Gentleman, apparently Young was Shooting Red Winged Starlings on the Wing for his amusement, had a richly ornemented Double Barelled Gun of which he Made excellent use = the Slaves employed at Cutting the Sugar Cane = this they perform with Large heavy Knifes not unlike those used by Butchers to Chop—some cutting the Head of the Plants and Others the Cane itself—tying the Last in small fagots with the Tops, Carts with Entire Wooden Wheels drawn by 4 Oxen haul it to the House where it is, bruised, pressed Boiled & Made into Sugar = the Miserable Wretches at Work begged a Winter Falcon We had killed, saying *it Was a great treat for them*; the Overseer a Good Looking Black Man, told us of his being in the same Employ for 8 Years and had Now obtain so much of his Master's Confidence, as to have the Entire Care of the Plantation—he Spoke roughly to his under servants but had a good indulgent Eye, and No doubt does what he Can to Accomodate, Master and All =

these Immense Sugar Plantations Looked Like Prairies early in Summer for Scarce a Tree is to be seen, and particularly here, where the Horison was bounded by Cleared Land =

We saw Many Catle, Horses, and Sheep, but all poor and Slack, the Latters have but Litle Wool and that only on the back the Rams wear a Long kind of hairy beard Like Goats=

the Gardens were beautifull, Roses in full bloom revive the Eye of the Traveller who for Eighty Days has been confined to the Smoaky inside of a Dark flat Bottomed Boat = the Wind entirely lulled away at Sun Set—the Moon's Disk assured us of a fine Night and We Left our Station to drop within a few Miles of the City. Tomorow perhaps May take us there, yet so uncertain is this World, that I Should Not be Surprised if I never was to reach it = the further removed, the Stronger my Anxiety to see My familly again presses on my mind—and Nothing but the astonishing desire I have of Compleating my work keeps my Spirits at par—

saw a few Fish Crows; a Marsh Hawk—a Red Shouldered Hawk, one the Boatman killed a *Barred Owl*, this and the Winter falcon Much Lighter Colored than usual—

Several Steam Boats passed us going up & down

Length of the Tern 13 Inches—to the end of the tail— Wings extending 2 Inches beyond, tail 12 feathers—tongue Longer Slender and bifid, Mouth Orange Color—Breadth 2:7¼/12 = Eye dark brown = Legs & feet red Orange—

Sunday January 7th 1821

at *New Orleans* at Last—We arrived here about 8 o'clock this Morning; hundreds of Fish Crows hovering Near the

Shipping and dashing down to the Watter Like Gulls for food—uttering a cry very much like the young of the *Common Crow* when they first Leave the Nests = I saw Mr Prentice, who directed me to the House of Messrs *Gordon* & *Grant* where he told me N. Berthoud Was; I saw him and was Introduced to Mr Gordon of whom I shall have opportunity of Speaking probably frequently hereafter and the *British Consul* Mr Daviss   I heard that my familly Was Well, and saw a Note from My Wife to N. Berthoud, that accompanied a p^{re} of Gloves made by her for him—

We walked out, met Col^l George Croghan, our former acquaintance   saw Many of the Louisville Gentry too tedious to mention names—

Arrived at the House of Mr Arnauld an Old friend of N. B^{ds} father, we were invited to take dinner, and although We had engaged previously to Mr Gordon, we staid = We had a good dinner, and great deal of Mirth that I Call *french Gayety*, that really sickened me. I thought myself in Bedlam, every body talk^d Loud at once and the topics dry Jokes—Yet every one appeared good, well disposed, Gentlemen, and were very polite to us = a Monkey Amused the Company a good deal by his Gambols and pranks—formerly I Would have been able as well as anxious to go to the Theater but now I can only partake of the Last, and after having paid a Short Visit to Mr Gordon I retired to the Keel Boat; with a bad head Hake, occasioned by drinking some Wine—and very sorry that I probably Could not have Letters from the Post Office untill Tuesday, Tomorow being a grand French Fete the aniversary of the Memorable Batle of Orleans

Joseph had spent his time visiting the Town and was not prepossessed in its favor =

I saw at Mr Arnauld 2 American Doves who have been Caged for Two Years, they Laid Eggs Last Spring, and Incubated them for four days, but they were broke by accident =

Monday January 8th 1821

at Day breake, went to Market, having received information that Much and great variety of game was brought to it— We found Vast Many Malards, some teals, some American

Widgeons, Canada Geese Snow Geese, Mergansers, Robins; Blue Birds; Red wing Starlings—Tell Tale Godwits—every thing selling extremely high $1.25 for one p^{re} of Ducks, 1.50 for a Goose &^{c} Much surprised and diverted at finding a *Barred owl* Clean^d and Exposed for sale Value 25^{cts}—some fine Fish; Indiferent Meat—found Vegetables both of this Country and West Indies = these Latters are put up in Small parcels on the ground opposite the owner, who has fixed prices for each Lot = I went to the review and will remember it and the 8th of January for ever—My Pocket was rifled of my pocket Book taken in this morning with an intention of going to the Governor with the Letters I had received for him, and to Mr Wheelers brother in Law—when I mention^d my Loss to N. Berthoud he called me a *Green Horn*, I do not know the Color of my Horns but well, *those* of some Neighbours of Mine—

Not blaming fortune as is generally the Case I peaceably pack the whole to Myself and will try to grow Wiser if possible—I think the Knave who took it is now good deal disapointed and probably wishes I had it—the Parade was only tolerable I had a view of the Governor that is no dout all I May Expect, he Looked about 60—a french face of good Countenance—We Walked to Bayou St John absolutly to Kill the time, the whole City taken with the festivals of the day = Joseph rec^d a Letter from his Parents—this evening one of our Men Called *Smith* fell over board drunk and Would have drowned if Providence had not interfered a Woman heard the Noise and the Yawl of the S. B^t U. States Saw him =

—9th—

Breakfasted with J. B. Gilly, Rec^d a letter from My Wife—My Spirits very Low—Weather Cloudy & Sultry—begun raining paid a Visit to Jarvis the P. Painter—Saw W^{am} Croghan,— Wrote to My Wife—Wished I had remained at Natchez— having found No Work to do remained on Board the Keel Boat opposite the Market, the Dirtiest place in all the Cities of the United States—Wrote to John. Garnier about my Port Folio =

Wednesday Jany. 10th 1821

Raining hard all day   wrote my Brother G. L. Dupuygaudeau
and to My Mother = in the afternoon Cap^e Cummings arrived and dined with us—his appearance much worst—the
Weather so bad that I had No opportunity of doing any thing
toward procuring Work = Strong thoughts of returning to
Natchez   Saw Cap^e Penniston who rec^d me very Politely—

—11—

Spent the Day Walking about trying to find some work—
Shewed My Drawings to Mr Gordon & the British Consul M^r
Davison—spoke good of the Publication—the former raised
my Expectations of their value—

Remarked in Market, Blue Cranes, great Many Coots—
Caldwall Ducks, snow Geese, Keeldeers—1 White Crane or
Heron and one Sand Hill Crane—

Was sometimes with Mr Prentice, who gave me a letter to
Doctor Hunter, whom I wished to see, to procure the Infor-
mation I so much Need about the Red River, Whashita &^c—
Joseph Employed in Making Enquiries about the Lost Port
Folio from every Boat Landing from Natchez—

No Work yet—rain, Warm, the Frogs all piping—

—12th—

Early this Morning I Met an Italian, painter at the Theatre, I
took him to N. B^d Rooms and Shewed me the Drawing of the
White Headed Eagle—he was much pleased, took me to his
painting appartement at the Theatre, then to the Directors
who very roughly offered me 100$ per Month to paint with
Mons. L'Italian

I believe really now that my talents must be poor or the
Country—Dined with Mr Gordon, conversation Birds &
Drawings, Must exibit some again and again as New Guests
came in—

I Rec^d to day a Letter from My Beloved Wife Dated Nov^r
28th 1820—gave My Letter for Mr Garnier to the Columbus =
No work yet—

paid a Visit to Monsieur *Pamar* but Audubon was poor to
day and he knew it when I made my bow—Wrote this
Evening to Henry Clay Es^{qr} for another Letter of Recommandation—

Weather, Warm, rainy, foggy, and altogether Desagreable
= saw One Wood Cock in Market—

Saturday 13th January 1821

I rose early tormented by many desagreable thoughts, nearly
again without a cent, in a Busling City where no one cares a
fig for a Man in my Situation—I Walked to *Jarvis* the Painter
and Shewed him some of my Drawings—he overlooked them,
said nothing then Leaned down and examined them Minutly
but never said they Were good or bad—Merely that when he
drew an Eagle for Instance, he made it resemble a Lyon, and
coverted it with Yellow hair and not Feathers—some fools
who entered the room, were So pleased at seeing my Eagle
that they prised it, and Jarviss wistled = I called him a side,
while Joseph Rolled up our Papers and asked him if he
needed Assistance to finish his Portraits i.e. the Clothing and
Grounds—he Stared, I repeated my question and told him I
would not turn my Back to any one and for Such employment and that I had received good Lessons from good Masters—he then Asked me to Come the following Day and
Would think about it—

in following N. B. through the Street while nothing better
could be done, We entered the Warehouse of Mr *Pamar* and
at once Was Surprised to hear *him* ask what I Charged for my
Drawing of Faces; 25$—but said he I have 3 Children and You
may put them all on one piece; then I must have 100$—

N. B^d requested me to Make a Sketch of the Little Girl
then present; a Sheet of Paper was procured, My Pencil
Sharped and Sitting on a Crate was soon at Work and soon
finished; the Likeness was Striking; the Father Smiled, the
Clerks Stared me emased and the Servant was dispatched to
Shew my Success (as it Was Called) to Mistress = Monsieur
Pamar *Civilly* told me that I Must do my Best for him and
Left it to my self as to the Price = I have Liked to Earn, the
half of the Money that day, but the Heldest Daughter could

not be ready perhaps for Several Days—Yet here is some Hopes—how I Calculated on 100 Dollars; What relief to My Dear Wife and Children, for Said I if I get this, I may Send it her and No doubt I will Soon procure Some more Work—

I spent the remainder of this day in better Spirits took a Long Walk With Joseph towards the Lake—Saw an Aligator—

Wrote this Evening to Doct[r] D[l] Drake—and read Some Interesting tales, borrowed from M[r] Prentice—

Sunday 14th January 1821

I dispatch Joseph and *Simon* (N. B. Servant) across the river for some Live Oak to draw, brought Some not fit—Dressed I Went to Jarvis—he took me imediatly in his painting room, and asked me many questions, untill *I thought* that he *feared* My assistance; he very Simply told me he could not believe, that I might help him in the Least—I rose, bowed, and Walk[d] out without One Word, and No doubt he Looked on Me as I did on him as an Original, and as a Craked Man =

the Levée early was Crowded by people of all Sorts as well as Colors, the Market, very aboundant, the Church Bells ringing the Billiard Balls knocking, the Guns heard all around, What a Display this is for a Steady quaker of Philad[a] or Cincinnati—the day was beautifull and the crowd Increased considerably—I saw however no handsome Woman and the Citron hüe of allmost all is very disgusting to one who Likes the rosy Yankée or English Cheeks =

I took My Gun, rowed out to the edge of the Eddy and killed a Fish Crow, those Birds are plenty on the River every fair day—(when otherwise, the food is plenty in the swamps, the Crabs, Young Frogs, Watter Snakes, &[c] Shewing out in great numbers)—When the one I killed fell, hundreds flew to him, and appeared as if about to Carry him off, but they soon found it their Interest to let me have him, I drew Near and Loaded for another; they all rose in Circling Like Hawks extremely High and then flew down the Stream, out of sight calling aloud all the times. they Suffer their Legs & feet to hang down as if broken—

I brought it on Board and began to Work imediatly—at Dusk took a Walk to M[r] Gordon, from then on to M[r] *Laville*

where We saw some *White Ladies* and Good Looking ones—
returning on Board the quartroon Ball attracted My View—
but as it cost 1$ Entrance I Merely Listened a Short time to
the Noise and came Home as We are pleased to Call it—

Monday   15th January 1821—
Tuesday— 16   —″   —″
Wednesday 17th   —″   —″
Thursday   18th   —″   —″

This is a way of Cutting Matter Short, but indeed the time
has been so Long and dull during these days that I think it a
good ridence to use them thus—I spent them running about
to procure Work, being sadly disapointed by Mr Pamar who
said the Lady Wanted Oil Colors—

Yesterday I Made My Long acquaintance's Likeness John
B. Gilly purposely to expose it to the Public—it is consider^d
by every one who knows him to be perfect—and to Shew it
this Morning (for I made it in a few hours) to Pamar procured me the Making of that of his eldest Daughter; by the
time We receive the pay for it, We will be penny Less =

to day I rec^d a letter from My Beloved Wife who rufled My
Spirits Sadly it Was dated Cincinnati Decr 31. 1820—I answered it,

Saw in Market—2 White Herons—one New Species of
Snipe, but could not Draw any of them, being partly pluck^d
= Joseph who hunted all day Yesterday, killed Nothing New
—saw Many Warblers—

19th	Friday	British Consul's Likeness		$ 25.00
20	Saturday	Euphemie Pamar's Likeness		25.00
21	Sunday	another Sister	″	25.00
22	Monday	Mr Pamar		25.00
23	Tuesday	Litle Daughter of D^o		25.00
24	Wednesday	Mr Forestall	D^o	25.00
25	Thursday	Young Lucin	D^o	25.00
26	Friday	Mrs Lucin	D^o	20.00
27	Saturday	Mr Carabie	D^o	25.00
				220.00

28	Sunday	Drawing a Brown Pelican		

fatigued, Wearied of Body but in good Spirits having plenty to do at good Prices, and My Work much admired—only sorry that the Sun Sets—

Monday January 29th 1821—
Drawing all day the Brown Pelican, Collected My Earnings, purchased a Crate of queens Ware for My Beloved Wife, Wrote to her, W^{am} Bakewell and Charley Briggs forwarding her by Letter and Parcel care of Mr Buckanan of Louisville 270 Dollars—the Crate Cost 36:33$—

Tuesday 30th   Mr Duchamp's Likeness 25$
Wednesday 31   Nothing   disapointed by M. Laville—

Thursday February 1st 1821—
Began a Likeness of Mr Louallier—and Drew a Common Gull—

_____

Friday 2^d   Mr Smith began hunting for Me at 25$ per Month   Stopped Thursday Morning—and the Girl Began Cooking for us at 10$ per Month with washing

_____

Saturday 3^d   Wrote to My Beloved Wife—

_____

Sunday 4th   Disapointed again by M. Laville, returned to the Boat and Drew a *Grey Snipe*—Joseph & Mr Smith out hunting all day, brought a few Red Breasted Thrushes, some Pewee fly Catchers and Many Swamp Sparrows and Savanah Finches—Complaining very much of the Hardships of hunting in the Cypress Swamps = Remarked in the Markets many *Purple Galinules*: but all so Mangled that I could not see one fit to draw—Saw also several *Rails or soras*—

Monday February 5th 1821—
Running about pretty much all day trying to procure some More Work and also Enquiring about Willson's Ornithology,

but in Vain—the high value set on that Work more Particularly Lately as rendered it extremely rare and the few who possess it will not Lend it = the Weather extremely sultry and Damp heavy Rains and thunder—saw to day at Mr Pamar, where I often Breakfast and Dine Mr *Delaroderie*—

having been so extremely engaged the Two Days that I Drew the *Brown Pelican* I had not time to make such Memoranda as I wished—it was given me by Mr Aumack, the Bird was killed on a Lake in this Vicinity and are rare—it was a Male, in tolerable order—Mr Gordon who before he had seen my Drawing thought it a Pelican Common in some of the West Indies, was much pleased at finding it a diferent species = I was assured that these Birds were seen in Immense flocks in the Neighborhood of *Buenos-aires* by a Scotch Gentleman, of respectability = here the hunters Call them *Grand Gozier* and say that seldom more than Two are seen together—and only for Short Periods after heavy Gales from the Sea—

———

the Common Gulls pay us regular Visits With their usual Companions the Fish Crows every Morning about Sun Rise —Comming across the Land from the Lakes Barataria where I am told they resort to Roost—I was not a litle surprised at finding the stomacks of several We killed a few days since filled with *Beetles* of diferent Kinds; Joseph examined the River and found Vast Many of these Last floating dead on the surface, the Crows also feed freely on the same = the Gulls often Chase the Crows for some Considerable distance but Never successfully, the Crows being much swifter on the Wing = the quantity of Robins or Red breasted Thrushes killed here is astonishing, the Market abound with them and Yet they bring 6¼ cents each—they are at present the principal Game to be found, Birds of all description are destroyed and eat, our Men Cooked the Gulls and found them excellent food—

———

I saw 12 of the Grey Snipes Similar to the one I Made My Drawing from, all alike in size and Markings, but the Stupid Ass who sold me one knew Nothing; Not even where *he* had Killed them—

February 9th 1821—

In walking this morning about a mile below this city I had the pleasure of remarking thousands of purple martins travelling eastwardly they flew high and circling feeding on insects as they went they moved onwardly about ¼ miles an hour Thermometer at 68 weather Drisly—hundreds of Coots wher in the market this morning

February 15th 1821

Wrote to My Beloved Wife this Day per N. Berthoud

List of Drawings sent My Beloved Wife February 17th by Nicholas Berthoud of Shippingport Es^{qr}

1. Common Gallinule—Not Described by Willson
2. D° Gull—   D°   D°   D°
3. Marsh Hawk
4. Boat Tailed Grakles Male & femelle—Not Describ^d by Willson
5. Common Crow—
6. Fish Crow
7. Rail or Sora—
8. Marsh Tern—
9. Snipe Not Described by Willson—
10. Hermit Thrush
11. Yellow Red Pole Warbler—
12. Savannah Finch
13. Batle Ground Warbler Not Described by Willson—
14. Brown Pelican—   D°   D°   D°
15. Great footed Hawk
16. Turkey Hen Not Described by Willson—
17. Cormorant   D°   D°   D°
18. Carrion Crow or Black Vulture—
19. Imber Diver—
20. White Headed or Bald Eagle—

May I have the Satisfaction of Looking at these and Many More in good Order on My return the fruits of a Long Journey—

Monday 19th February 1821—

the Weather beautifull, Clear & Warm, the Wind having blown hard from the Southwest for 2 days & Nights—

saw this Morning Three Immense Flocks of *Bank Swallows* that past over Me with the rapidity of a Storm, going Northeast, their Cry was heard distinctly, and I knew them first by the Noise they made in the air coming from behind me; the falling of their Dung resembled a heavy but thinly falling Snow; No appearance of any feeding while in our Sight— Which Lasted but a few Minutes—

I was much pleased to see these arbingers of Spring but Where could they be moving So rapidly at this early Season I am quite at a Loss to think, & yet their Passage here was about as long after the Purple Martin that Went By on the 9th Instant as is their Arrival in Kentucky a Month hence—perhaps Were they forced by the east Winds and now Enticed to proceed by the Mildness of the Weather the Thermometer being at 68°—

how far More south must I go Next January & February to see these Millions of Swallows Spending their Winter as Thousands of Warblers, fly Catchers, Thrushes and Myriads of Ducks, Geese, Snipes &[c] Do here?—

the Market is regularly furnished with the *English Snipe* Which the french Call[d] *Cache cache*, Robins Blue Wing[d] Teals Common Teals, Spoon Bill Ducks, Malards, Snow Geese, Canada Geese, Many Cormorants, Coots, Watter Hens, Tell Tale Godwits, Call[d] here *Clou Clou* Yellow Shank Snipes, some Sand Hills Cranes, Strings of Blew Warblers, Cardinal Grosbeaks, Common Turtle Doves, Golden Wing[d] Wood Peckers &[c].

Wednesday 21st February 1821—

I met this morning with one of those discouraging Incidents connected with the life of the artists; I had a Likeness Spoken of in very rude terms by the fair Lady it was made for, and perhaps will Loos my time and the reward expected for my Labours,—Mrs *André* I here mention the Name as I May speak more of the Likeness as the occasion Will require =

Saw Many Green Baked White Belied Swallows to day and Also some *Martins* Hirundo Purpurea—All of them very Lively and not exibiting much of the Muddy Appearance that immersion in the Swamps about this City would undoubtedly give them had they remained buried in it since Last December at Which time late in that Month they were plenty and re-marked Passing by arriving from North & East moving South Westwardly = here they Must Make a Long Pause or Move Eastwardly very Slowly as Seldom do they arrive in Pennsyl-vania before the 25 of *March* and more frequently in the first days of *April*—they find now here an aboundance of Insects, and the Millions of Musquitoes that raise from the Swamps would Sufice to feed the Swallows of all the World =

saw Many Brown Larks,—

the Fish Crows are remarkably found of alighting in flocks on some Pacan trees about 12 Mile below this City about 9 o'clock in the Morning when they retire On these to rest from their Fishing excursions and remain Croaking untill the Midle of the day—

Thursday New Orleans February 22ᵈ 1821

We at Last have the Keel Boat off and have moved on the hearth again—Our present situation is quite a Curious one to Me, the room we are in and for which we pay 10$ per Month is situated in Barraks Street near the Corner of that & Royal Street—betwen Two Shops of Grocers and devided from them and our Yellow Landlady by Mere Board Partitions, re-ceiving at once all the new Matter that Issues from the Thun-dering Mouths of all these Groupes—the *Honest Woman* spoke much of honesty in Strangers and required one Month paid in Advance, this however I could not do, and satisfied her with one half Not taking a Receipt although She Ap-peared very urgent—

I walked a good deal about the City in search of Work & Willsons Ornithology but was not favoured with any suc-cess—extremely anxious to receive some news from My familly—and very much fatigued of New Orleans where I Cannot *shoot Two Birds with one Stone* I retired to our Lodg-ings at Dusk—

saw Capᶜ Barton's of Henderson who said he would Not have known me if I had not Spoke within his hearing

Saturday 24ᵗʰ February 1821

Idle, and the weather fair, took a *Wade* in the Woods the veg-etation, forwarded beyond my expectations, saw some handsome Plants in Bloom that made me regret of having sent My Drawings home—Birds extremely Shy and nothing new;— in the afternoon Paid a Visit to Mr John F. Miller from whom (I was told) I might expect an uncommon Share of Politeness, perhaps I walked in at a bad time but be this as it May, I was received and Dispatched as promptly as the case would permit; the subject of Course During the few Moments I Lost there rolled on Birds, I was asked if Many Ducks, such as the *Canvas Back* &^{c} (fine food) where residents of this Part of America, had I put these queries I might have expected a No from One that had resided 10 Years here, and yet this No I Was obliged to give—No doubt for want of True Knowledge for the Birds in question are said to be plenty here during Winter, = and are Most Likely the Sheldrakes Dun Divers and Mergansers having Many of these Latters offered for Sale—

This Morning the Market was well Stocked with Green Backed Swallows *Hirundo Veridis*, the Whole very fat and in beautifull plumage; if these Dear Litle Cherubs have preserved their coats and there flesh so fresh during the pretended Torpor Occasioned by Winter's frost how much more fortunate they are than the Pork Beef & Butter of Kentucky that sowers however well Salted.

I have been assured by Men on whom I can rely that some Winters are so Mild that Swallows are seen from time to time during every Months =

the Swallows in Markets were caught in the holes about houses their resorting places during the Nights—this Morning the Weather is quite Cold, and Yet the Swallows are flying about the Streets, over the River &^{c} twitering very Lively =

Sunday 25th February 1821—

Killed Some Green backed White bellied Swallows Hirundo Veridis—extremely fat, the Gizards completely filled with the remains of Winged Insects,—could not perceive any outward diference betwen the sexes,—the femelles however were well Stored with eggs and the Males strongly marked—the Brother of Mr Pamar killed a Beautifull White Robin, but his Dog Mangled it so much that I did not draw it—this extraordinary change of Color appeared as the Cause of Old Age, the Bill of the Bird much worn and the Legs were cicatrised in Several parts, the Bird however was very fat, as well as nearly all the others he killed this Day =

saw a few Partridges these Birds are here much Sought and hunted down without Mercy, not even do the Sportsmen permit a few Paires to remain untouch & thereby the race is nearly extinguished Near the City = We Waded to day through an extensive Swamp with hopes of Meeting Some new Species, but Saw Nothing of the Kind to my astounishment—

March Saturday 10th 1821

sent My Letter to My Lucy, Victor; Wm Bakewell & N. Berthoud by the Steam Boat Car of Commerce—

saw in Market this Morning some *Ampellis Americana.* Vast Number of *Common Snipes,* but the Robbins have nearly disapeared and are not even to be seen in the Woods—Was assured to Day that the *Baltimore Oriole* Wintered on the Island of *Cuba* and that the West Side of this Island was the resort of Millions of Swallows during November, December & January; So Strongly was this afirmed, that it has determined me to go there Next Winter and to the bay of hondurass, where it is said they also are plenty during these Months Only—

Recd this Morning a Letter from My Beloved Wife dated Shippingport written a few days previous to the one I red by the S. B. James Ross—

This Evening Capn Cummings saw a Night Hawk or a *Chuck Will's Widow* flying about the Street Near our Lodgings—I presume it was the Latter Bird having been assured that in the first days of April they are seen in numbers at the Bay of St Louis—

Sunday March 11th 1821

Walkd out this Morning with Joseph to try my *Souvenir* Gun and found it an excellent one, Shot Many Green Backed Swallows on the Wing—Some red Wing Starling, Savannah

Finches, one fish Crow, &ᶜ but Nothing New Yet in the Woods, which unfortunatly are now very deep with Watter, the River being about 4 or 5 feet higher than the ground behind the *Levée*—

During a Walk this afternoon a Beautifull Mississipi Kite sailed by me, unfortunatly I had no Gun—

Near our House a Mocking Bird regullarly resorts to the South Angle of a Chimney top and salutes us with Sweetest Notes from the rising of the Moon untill About Midnight, and every Morning from about 8 o'clock untill 11, when it flys to the Convent Garden to feed—I have remarked that Bird allways in the Same Spot and Same Position, and have been particularly pleased at hearing him Imitate the Watchman's Cry of *All's Well* that Issues from the fort about 3 Squares Distant, and So well, has he sometimes performed that I Could have been mistaken if he had not repeated too often in the Space of a 10 Minutes.

March 15ᵗʰ Thursday 1821

Wrote to My Beloved Wife and Mʳ Rob Best—

———

Last Night—saw Many *Chuck will's Widow* flying about the streets and some *Night Hawks*—

———

I Made a Likeness to day for a Lady's Sadle a thing I had not the Least use for, but the Man I had Made a portrait for, Wanted his wife's Very much and Could Not spare Money, and Not to disapoint him I Sufered Myself to be Sadled—

While at Dinner We Were all surprised at the astonishing Leaps that Some *Maggots* took about our Table,

they Issued out of a Very good piece of Cheese   To perform this I remarked them drawing up their heads towards the Tail untill Nearly runing both half of their Body Parallel and Then Suddenly Striking One of the ends Could not see which   they through themselves About 50 or 60 Times their Length some times One Way sometimes Another, apparently in Search of the Cheese—

March 16th Friday 1821

I had the pleasure of receiving a Letter this morning from M[r] A. P. Bodley dated Natchez 8th Inst[t] Informing me of My Port Folio having been found and Deposited at the office of the *Mississipi Republican* and that I could have it by writting—

I acknowledge with a very sensible pleasure the kindness of M[r] P, who worked his Passage down in M[r] Aumack Boats = and at the same time cannot Conceive how the Book had escaped the researches of M[r] Garnier—

M[r] Gordon had the goodness to write to a friend to have it forwarded imediatly and pay whatever Charges there might be, the Politeness of that Gentleman is remarkable to a Man who is no more than a Stranger to him, but No doubt it would be impossible for a Good heart to act otherwise—

I took a Walk with my Gun this afternoon to see the Passage of Millions of *Golden Plovers* Coming from the North Est and going Nearly Ouest—the destruction of these innocent fugitives from a Winter Storm above us was really astonishing—the Sportsmen are here more numerous and at the same time more expert at Shooting on the Wing than any where in the U. States   on the first sight of these birds Early this Morning assembled in Parties of from 20 to 100 at Diferent places where they Knew by experience they told me the Birds pass and Arranged themselves at Equal distances squaked on their hams, as a flock Came Near every Man Called in a Masterly astonishing Manner, the Birds Imediatly Lowered and Wheeled and Coming about 40 or 50 Yards run the Gantlet, every Gun goes off in Rotation, and so well aimed that I Saw Several times a flock of 100 or More Plovers destroyed at the exception of 5 or 6—the Dogs after each Voleys while the Shooters charged their Pieces brought the Same to each Individuals—this continued all day, when I left One of those Lines of Sharp Shooters then the Sun Setting, they appeared as Intent on Killing More As When I arrived at the Spot at 4 'o'clock—

a Man Near Where I Was seated had killed 63 dozens—from the firing below & behind us I would Suppose that 400 Gunners where out, Supposing each Man to have killed 30 Doz that day 144,000 must have been destroyed—On

Enquiring if these passages Where frequent I was told that Six Years ago there was about Such an Instance, imediatly after 2 or 3 days of very Warm Weather a blow from the Northeast brought them, Which Was Nearly the Same to day—some few Were fat but the Greatest Numbers Lean, and all that I opened Shewed No food—the femelles Eggs extremely small—

Saturday 17th March 1821

This Morning the Market was plentifully suplied with Golden Plovers and *Pures*—I also saw a White Crane, Spent the day Walking about at the exception of an hour Drawing at a Likeness—

Sunday March 18th 1821

This Morning I was Witness and in some measure contributed to the performing of a Farce of a new kind at Least to Me,—Walking along the Levee to Mr Pamar Where I had an appointment for a Likeness, I was Invited to breakfast by Mr A. Liautaud—I walked in and Met a Large Party, Well engaged round an old Gentleman at Pleasing him by the most extravagant rounds of praises—I understood the Caracter Was rather Moony, and very gay When well maneged, productive of Much Mirth to his hearers = During the Breakfast that Certainly Was a good One & On which Our *Prime Guest* touch^d heavily, We were several times struck^d by unexpected Voleys of Verses, composed for the Occasion and that could not Indeed have had a better Effect than that produced,— Every one enjoyed himself Very Much, particularly the Compositors who were highly Clapped, sometimes to be sure to put an end to his Loquacity.

Breakfast over I was told to remain and see the best part, Mr Liautaud said the Learned Guest Was about being rec^d a *Mason* and My being a Brother entitled me at Once to a seat—this was conducted in the most Ludicrous Manner Any one can conceive, and I really pitied the Newly Initiated— When all Ceremonies Were over—the Man, Was Burned in several parts, baptized in a Large Bucket of Watter, Tossed in a Blanket, and Make to Crawl Over about 50 Casks of Wine, on his belly and knees, and When at Last given up for want of Invention, the Poor Devils Who had been praying for Mercy during all this, was Left in the Necessary—

To this Man this Might be done perhaps again, but few Could bear such treatment and I expected several times that his Cries or a Change of sensation from Cowardice to Courage would Shew a very diferent scene—all however was Ended as Intended and the poor fellow took it for Granted that he really Was a Mason—

I left and Made Mrs Dourillier, Guesnon Likeness—

We purchased this Morning in Market a Beautifull *Blue Crane Ardea Cerulea*, the choice of 5 that Were nearly alike— these I was told Were come earlier than usual—And extremely dificult of Access—

I Drew it and its Coresponding so well with A. Willson Description Stop^d Me from writting it Myself—

Total Length	30½ Inches—
to end of Tail	23½ —"—
Breadth	39¼ —"—
Tail Feathers	12 —"—
Weight	11—onces—Midle Claw Serrate—in-wardly—

The Cotonny Substance on the Breast followed the Breast Bones only—and reapeared on each side of the rump—I was assured it a very beautifull Male—

Wednesday March 21st 1821

in reading the Papers this morning at Mr Pamar, I saw the Treaty betwen spain and our Country,

the 4th Article Speaking of an expedition to run the Line of Division formed by both Parties and to leave Natchitoches during the Course of this Year, I imediatly went to Mr Gordon to know from him what steps would be necessary to procure an Appointment as Draftsman for this So Long wished for Journey—he advised me to see Mr Hawkins Who would introduce me to Governor Robertson—

I saw Mr Hawkins who very politly promessed to See the

Governor and Mention to him my Wishes and to Call at his Office on the 23^d—

to Join in Such an enterprise and to leave all I am attach^d to, perhaps for ever, produced Many diferents sensations & thoughts, but all are Counterbalanced when persuaded as I am that My Labours Are all for their use & benefit—

I did not wait late on the 23^d but My Spirits were sadly dampened when Mr Hawkins told me that is was the Governor's opinion that Nothing more Would be done than to run the Line in question and that none but surveyors would be Necessary;

Disapointed but not less anxious to try further I Call^d on Mr Gordon, he Joined me in the Idea of My adressing the President Directly and that he could Not think that a Journey so Interesting would be perform^d only to say that Men had gone & Come back—in leaving this truly Kind Gentleman, I Met Mr Grasson of Louisville   spoke to him of my thoughts and Wishes,

"I Can render a Service I believe M^r A and I Will do it, I will give you some Letters to diferent Member of Congress With whom I am Well Acquaint^d and that will be glad to Meet Your Views, but Write to the President—"

This sounded better to my Ears—

full of My plans I went home & Wrote to N. Berthoud to request his Imediate assistance—Walk^d out in the afternoon seeing Nothing but hundreds of New Birds, in Imagination and supposed Myself often on the Journey—

on the 24th I called again on Mr Hawkins, Mr Gordon had spoke of me to him and the former again to the Governor, I spoke of adressing the President, he Acquiest^d and promess^d to give a Letter for the same and procure one from the Governor =

going through the Streets Not unlike (I dare Say) a Wild Man thinking too much to think at all My Eyes were attracted by a handsome faced Man, I knew it was My Old Acquaintance & Friend George Croghan, We Met freely and I was eased, he knew what I was going to say having dined the day previous at the Governor's with Mr Hawkins, he said he had spoke of me but Would do more and promised to send Some Letters to Mr Hawkins for my case, and Invited Me with such forcible Kindness to go and spend Some time at his Plantation that I Accepted his offer—see me again Walking fast and Looking Wild, but recollecting the high price of time I hunted Mr D^d Prentice, and asked him if he would form a letter for Me—he answered Yes but told Me that I would do better by writting Myself and that he would freely give his advice and help if Needed—I Was then reduced to My poor thoughts to Express My Wishes—

Anxious, and Determined to leave no power of Mine untried I set to the Paper & Wrote in as Great a Hurry as I am Now doing, a Letter, that Mr Prentice to My utmost astonishment pronounced, *all suficient* = he spoke much About the Journey and anticipated he said the pleasure of reading My Journal on My return—feeling a great Weight off My Shoulders I returned to My Room, took Gun Amunition & Joseph & to the Woods Went in Search of New Species =

My Life has been Strewed with Many thorns but Could I see Myself, & the fruits of my Labours safe, with My Beloved familly *all Well* after a return from Such an expedition, how grateful Would I feel to My Country and full of the Greatness of My Author—

In market this Morning I saw Three of What Willson *Calls Bartrams's* Snipes, they Where very fat—are Called here *Papabots*—saw a Beautifull White Crane but without legs—Vast Many Green Wing^d & blue winged Teals—hundreds of Snipes, *pures*, Solitary Snipes—Green back^d Swallows—but robbins have desapeared—

The Migration of Birds does Not go a pace with the végétable Kingdom in this Part of America—When, The Trees are as much in Leaves in Pensylvania, or Ohio, or Kentucky or even the upper Parts of Tennessee (and *this is about the Midle of May*) Birds back to the 25 of April have reach^d these Parts and are preparing to Answer the Calls of Nature—

to My Astonishment, the Many Species of Warblers, Thrushes &^{c} that Were numerous during the Winter have all Moved on Eastwardly, and None of the Species that resort this Part have yet reach^d at the exception of Swallows and a few Watter Birds—

this Would tempt me to believe that Most of Our Migratory Birds Leave their Winter resorts With such Certainty of knowledge about the Weather and Such Swiftness of Move- ment over the Country as does Not give us even the oppor- tunity of remarking their Passage and the greater number at once at the time appointed by the Strength of Passion—

Sunday 25th March 1821

Bought a beautifull Specimen of the *Great White Heron* in perfect order   it had been sent me by a hunter with Whom I had formed acquaintance a few days ago—Worked on it the Whole day and found it the most dificult to Imitate of any Bird I have Yet undertaken—Took a Walk in the Afternoon and heard the Voice of a Warbler new to Me, but could Not reach it—

Monday 26th   Walked early this Morning in search of Plants to form the back ground of my Drawing—Left Joseph Out who killed a beautifull, *Blue Yellow back Warbler Male Sylvia Pusilla*, I had seen some in the Swamp but the litle fel- lows were So Nimble and brisk that they had all escaped Me—Worked Nearly all Day Not having time to go and Pur- chase some articles I wanted to send My Lucy—

saw M[r] Gordon, who on reading My adress to the Presi- dent Twice told Me that he would Make some Alteration to its form—I left it with him—

Tuesday 27th March 1821—

Drawing at My Heron yet, it Smelt so dreadfully bad that When I opened it I could only take time to See *how plainly it proved a Male*—the Cottony Substance, Was round the breast bone, on each Side of the Vent and on each Side of the romp—the Midle Claws very pectinated—

I Drew to Day Male & femelle of the *Blue Yellow back Warbler Sylvia Pusilla*—and in a Short Walk taken this Evening saw perhaps thousands of the same Species   Killed several all alike in their sexes—

forwarded My Beloved Lucy per M[r] Prentice who left at 12 o'clock in the James Ross a piece of Linen, some Stockings, a piece of goods for our Boys and the Woman's Sadle I was almost forced to take some time since—

Gave Mʳ Forestale who also went in the same boat an order to get my Port Folio at Natchez and begged of him to forward it to Mʳ Gordon—

Saturday March 31ˢᵗ 1821

I spent my time these 3 Last Days More at thinking than any thing else and often indeed have I thought My Head very heavy—

This Morning I Waited on Mʳ Gordon with a Wish to receive from him an amendment to my Letter to the President, for all in my head is the Pacific Expedition   he Wrote, I read it, but was not altogether Satisfied—I Called on Mʳ *Vanderlyn* the Historical Painter With my Port Folio—to Shew him some of my Birds with a View to ask him for a few Lines of recommandation—he examined them attentively and *Called* them *handsomely done*; but being *far* from possessing any Knowledge of Ornithology or Natural History, I was quite Satisfied *he* Was No Judge but of their being better or Worse *Shaded* Yet he spoke of the beautifull Coloring and Good Positions and told me that he would With pleasure give me a Certificate of his having *Inspected* them—Are all Men of Talents fools and Rude purposely or Naturally? I cannot assert, but have often thought that *they* were one or the other—

When I arrived at Mʳ V.'s Room, he spoke to me as if I had been an abject slave, and told Me in Walking away to Lay my Drawings down *there the Dirty Entry* that he would return *presently* and Look them over,—I felt so vexed that My first Intention Was to *Pack* off, but the Expedition Was in View, I thought how Long Kempbell the Actor Waitted Once at the Theatre in England, and stood patiently *although* not Laying My Drawings *Down there*—

About 30 Minutes Elapsed, he returned with an Officer and with an air More becoming a Man Who *Once Was Much* in My situation ask me in his private room, Yet I could plainly see in his Eye that selfish Confidence that allways destroy in some degree the Greatest Man's Worth, the swet ran down My face as I hastily openᵈ My Drawings and Laid them on the floor; I Lookᵈ up to him, he Was looking at them, the Officer's *By God* that's handsome, struck my eyars, Vanderlyn

took up a Bird Look[d] at it closely put it down and said they
Were *handsomely done*

I breathed—Not because I thought him a Man of the Most
superior Talents, for to come to such a Pitch one Must have no
faults, and I With My Eyes *half Closed* (as you know the pretended Juges of our Day Look at Painting) saw a great Deffect
in One of his figures of Women, (the deffect that had being
Corrected by the Lady I drew Lately.) but because this Gentleman had *some Talents*, that he Was Look[d] on as a Very Excellent Judge and that I had been Told that a few Words from
him Might be serviceable—of my Likenesses he spoke very
diferently, the one I had Was, he said, hard, and without Effect,
although he aknowledged it Must have been a Strong one =

he sat, he Wrote, and I, thinking More of Journeying to the
Pacific Ocean, than of Likenesses; Cared Not a *Pecayon* about
these Later Observations—

as I was Walking away from his house corner of S[t] Louis
and Royal Streets—the *Corner of Events* the officer who had
followed me, ask[d] Me, the price of My *Black Chalk Likenesses*
and Where I resided—all answered; I thought how Strange it
was that a poor Devil Like me Could Steal the Custom of the
Great *Vanderlin* but fortune if not *bland* certainly Must have
her Lunatic Moments—the officer said he would Call on Me
Liking My Style Very Much=

M[r] Hawkings saw this afternoon some of my Drawings and
I gave him *My* Letter to the President, he was Apparently
Much pleased With both—and told me he Would do all in his
Power for me—

I Put My Letters to My Beloved Wife—N. Berthoud &
Judge Towles in the Mail, that Leaves every Sunday at 8
o'clock, and return[d] to our Lodging with a Compound of Ideas
Not Easily to be described—

I had Shot during a Short Walk I took yesterday afternoon
a *White Eyed fly Catcher* that the Rats having eat Last Night
I could Not of course draw to day—Joseph to day Shot a
Tyrant Fly *Catcher* and a *Yellow belied Wood Pecker*

The Politeness of M[r] Vanderlyn Will be remembered a long
time by me; and when ever I Look over these Scrawls, it will
do me good to have a litle of the same feelings—the following is the Copy of the Lines he handed me—

Mr John. J. Audubon has Shewn me several Specimens of his Drawings in Natural history—Such as Birds, with their Natural Colors, & other Drawings in plain Black & White Which appear to be done with great truth & accuracy of representation as much so, as any I have seen in any Country—The Above Gentleman Wishes me to give this as my opinion in Writting believing it may Serve as a recommendation to his being employed as a Draftsman in any Expedition to the interiors of our Country.

J. Vanderlyn

New Orleans, 30th March 1821.

April 5th 1821

I have Just now recovered My Lost Port Folio   Mr Garnier sent it me a fortnight ago to the Care of his son   the trouble this gave me I will mention hereafter—I have to thank Mr Garnier but More *he* that found it on the River Bank and took Such very remarkable good Care of it—for on opening it I found the Contents in as good order as the day it was Lost and *Only* One Plate missing =

Blue Yellow-Back Warblers—

Orchard Orioles—

Cardinal Grosbeaks—

Yellow Eyed Cuckoos—

Large Crested Fly Catchers

White Eyed —" — "—

Night Hawks at Dawn of Day Plenty—

Turkey Buzards

Carrion Crows

Common Gulls—

Carolina Wrens by Vast Number—

Partridges a few Very Shy—

to see these in hunt of others I Walked since half past 2 o'clock this Morning untill 4 this afternoon Wading often to our Midles through the Swamps and then Walking through the Thickest Woods I believe I have Yet seen—

Cap^e Cummings Left us on the 10th for Philadelphia   the Poor Man had Not *One Cent* with him—saw Mr Hoytema who arrived in the Columbus—Rec^d by that Vessel Letters from Lucy. William Bakewell, Charles, Briggs, N. Berthoud—Carr of Commerce brought another from My Wife and One from Mr *Matabon* the great flute Player—answered—

Painted Bunting—
Although these Birds are taken now and quite tamed in a few days, so much so as to sing as if at Large, when Caught Next Month they Die in a few hours, and Shew dejection from the Instant they are caged—they are found of Nestling in Live Oaks, Wild plum-tree Briars, Orange Groves—when domesticated Are fed on Rice—*Breed Twice*—femelles opened on the 15 April had Eggs the size of N° 5 Shots—

I had from reliable Source that One Made his Escape from a Cage and returned Thirty odd Days after to the house, Went to the Cage, and remained Many Years—a femelle Was seen in Cage to carry and Arrange the Materials given her to form a Nest and Compleated it—but Never Laid—

Saw Some Young Mocking Birds in Market this Morning able to fly—these Birds are said by People here to breed as often as 4 Times during one season—I also was told that Young Ones sufered to be approach^d by the Parents after a separation of Several days are Often *Poisonned* by them, this *unatural* conduct demands *Self* Confirmation—

Monday April 16th 1821
having received a Visit from D^r heermann and Lady While hunting Last Saturday, I Called on him at his House, he wished I would give a few Lessons of Drawing to M^rs H—I acquiessd and am to begain tomorow;—Joseph Hunting nearly all day killed a Red Headed Wood Pecker, a Red bellied one—Orchard Orioles, Black headed Titmouse—*Green* Painted Buntings—drew one With a blue head = Joseph saw a *Yellow Breasted Chat* and Some Baltimore Orioles—

spent part of the Day with Mr Hoytema & *Young Towns* of Henderson on Board =

Was sorry as well as Surprised Not to have a word by the S. B^t Manattan—from My Beloved Lucy—

Thursday 19th—April 1821

Low in funds again—Left home with my *Port Folio* My *Best friend* as to Introduction and travelled as far as Dr *Hunter* the renowned *Man* of Jefferson—We came on him rather *unaware* the good Man Was Pxxxxxg. We Waited and I gave him My Letter of *D^d Prentice*—

This *Phisician* May have been a Great *Doctor formerly* but Now deprived of all that I Call Mind I found it *Necessary* to leave to his Mill's Drudgery =

Called on a New Phenomenon in Painting Mr *Earl* I believe & there Saw Mr *Earls Jackson*—*Great God* forgive Me if My Jugment is Erroneous—I Never saw a Worst painted Sign *in the Street of Paris* =

April Sunday 22^d—1821

Rec^d Yesterday a letter from My Beloved Lucy, answered it Last Night and this Morning Wrote to N. Berthoud & W^{am} Bakewell—sent Home One Box & 1 one Bag the Whole by the Steam Boat Car of *Commerce* that Left at 9 'o'clock P. M.

Dinned at Mr Pamar as I usually do on Sundays, My Pupils all religiously enclined did not give them Lessons = the great Ease and of Course Comfort that I find in the Company of Mrs Pamar's familly renders my visits at that house quite what I wish and often need for a relief of Exersions = Finished to day a Drawing of a *Snowy Heron Ardea Candidissima* a beautifull Male—Joseph Drawing Flowers all day—

Monday 23^d

found in Market a Gallinule that differs much from What I call the *Purple* one—the Yellow Legs & feet, their Stoutness—the Blue band Tops—& All Coloring—the hunters assured me they Never saw *one* with red Legs—but I cannot depend on their Memory = We also found another Male of Blue Grosbeak Loxia Purpurea =

Saw My Old Acquaintance John Gwathmey of Louisville, he was *a la guettée* on the Levée the appearance of My Clothes, did Not please him we talk but Litle together,

Tuesday April 24th 1821

Much in want of Cash Walked to the Columbus Steam Boat and Made *Baxter Towns* Portrait for 25$—gave my Lessons and Drew the *Black Poll* Warbler Male—*Sylvia Striata*, pleased with my days Work, rec[d] a letter from My Son Victor,—Much pleased also at his emproved hand write—

Wednesday 25—

Went again on Board Columbus rec[d] my Pay from Towns— Made M[r] *Hall*'s *Portrait* one of the best I believe I ever have taken = Met Gwathmey & Thompson from Louisville— Dined at M[r] Pamar   had a great Wish to See General Jackson but no time to Spare yet—Paid our Board rent & Washing to day—15$ the 2 first Items and 5 for the Latter—raining hard— Mr Hoytema Still in the Columbus—his THOUGHTS—

I am forced here to Complain of the bad figure that my friend Willson has given of the Warbler I drew Yesterday, in the Bill only the length exceed that of Nature ⅛ of an Inch— an enormous diférence—and he has runed a broad White line round over the Eye that does not exist =

April Friday 27th 1821

Walked on Board of the Columbus at 6 o'clock this morning, Made John De Hart's Portrait—Mr Hoytema came alitle before breakfast, had been absent all Night, Much Irked by the other passengers

General Jackson Left the City about Twelve—I saw him *thrice*   found Vanderlyn's Likeness the Only good one I have seen, *Sully*'s Plate *Miserable*—John De Harts Likeness being Intended for M[rs] Hall, took it there, spent a few Hours with her extremely agreably—Wrote to Charles Briggs—

Saturday 28th 1821

Rose early and went on Board the Hecla to take M[r] *Bossier* Portrait, made it good   Young *Guesnon* and *Hetchberger* the Painter Spent the Evening with Me, Joseph Sick, Wrote to My Beloved Lucy—

Sunday 29th 1821

Rose purposely to go and Collect some Money to forward home, received 105$ sent 100 in a U. S. Note N° 152. Mark A dated Philad^a april 5th 1817 payable at N. O. to B. Morgan's order—I gave it to John De Hart in an open Letter to remit to My Wife—Columbus left at 12 'o'clock—Dined at Hetchberger   Made his Lady's Likeness—coming home Walked in *Painter of Feather*'s room, very Civil, asked for My Card—Hoytema p^d me a Short Visit—Joseph better.

Monday April 30th 1821

Steam Boat Paragon Arrived   No Letter for me—Mr Gordon had one from Mr Berthoud—sadly disapointed almost sicken, could not do any thing—

May 1st Tuesday 1821

Walked some, Wrote to My Wife but the boat I Intended for, not going– extremely uneasy about My Wife's health or her Children—done Nothing—

May 2 Wednesday—

Wrote again to Lucy   give the letter to Baxter Towns—drew a Long Legged Plover—Contents Shrimpes & Insects and at the Diference of Size only found it nearly coresponding to Bewicks description—it was a Male I received it from Mr Duval the Miniature Painter who assured me that he had Killed 6 or 7 since he leaves here, all alike no diference whatever in the size or Coloring—there they are often seen on Lake *Borgne* during the Summer Months—was pleased with the Position in my drawing—

Thursday—3^d

Bought 15 Y^{ds} Nankeen for Summer Clothes   found Mrs H. More aimiable if Possible than usual, talked freely to Me—became acquainted With an other Sister—Work^d at Mrs Hechbergers Portrait—Weather since Monday Morning very

Desagreably Hot—Thermometer, at 88–89—and to day at 3
'oclock in the Shade at 90—
    Cases of Yellow fever in the City I was told—

May Sunday 1821

Rec[d] a Letter by the Cincinnati from My Wife, Not Very agreable to My feelings, surprised at having Nothing from N.
Berthoud—appraised *Joseph* of his Father's Death, Bore it
well—saw M[r] Jesse Embrie of the Cincinnati Museum =
spent all day very Dull   dined at *Hetchberger*—

    Monday—Counfounded Hot—Young *Guesnon* afronted
and Ceased Speaking to me—
    Tuesday 7th   Wrote to My Wife but did not Close my
Letter—M[r] Hoytema paid us a Short Visit—Much exasperated against M[r] Gordon—M[r] Gordon sent to England for Me
for 10[lb] *Italian Chalk*, 6 doz Black Lead Pencils, 2 Grosses
Pastels—but did Not advance the Money =

Wednesday 8th—

finished My Letter to My Lucy and Wrote a Short one to N.
Berthoud—put them on Board the Fayette, the Ross, the one
I expected to Leave first not being ready = —*thought* to day
that a Certain Gentleman to Whom I go to dayly felt *uncomfortable* While I was present, seldom before My coming to
New Orleans did *I* think that I was Looked on so favourably
by the *fair* sex as I Have *Discovered* Lately—
    saw Hoytema at M[r] Hawkins in an High state of Spirits I
dare not Call it Intoxication—he Sailed this Evening for Liverpool = —paid a Visit to the Aimiable Vanderlyn, this Gentleman Like all substantial Men gained on acquaintance   saw
his Portrait of My Fair Pupil M[rs] H—the Likeness good but
roughly painted—he complimented me on My Drawings I
thought too Much to be true = saw Gilly about setling for
Our Passage to Shippingport Should I determine on going
there—

Wrote to My Wife, N. Berthoud, Henry Clay, D^l Drake, on the 16th forwarded all by S. B.^{t} Paragon =
Dined at Governor Robertson, Polite reception, promessed Me a recommendatory letter to Mr Monroe—
No news from Mr Berthoud yet,—

7th May 1821—

begun lessons with Young Mr Bollin @ 1.50 per Lessons
"—   "—   "— Miss Perry   2.00—" —"—
"—   "—   "— Miss Dimitry   2.00—" —"—

New Orleans May 20th 1821

Sent a few Lines to My Wife by the S. B.^{t} Tamerlane—Last Week I Rec^d a Letter from Mr J. Hawkins and one from Mr Robertson the Governor for the President of the U. States—favors from Men of High Stations are favors indeed—
The Governor a Man of Strong Information—extremely Polite—
Since So Long, without any news from my familly, My Spirits have failed me, and it is With Dificulty that I set to Write at all—My Journal Suffers through the same Cause that Affects me—attention—

June 16th New Orleans—1821—

Left the City at about ½ past 12 o'clock—in the Steam Boat Columbus Cap^e John de Hart—bound to Shippingport Kentucky—
pressed by much work on hand within some weeks passed, during every day and too much incommodated by Musquitoes at evenings My poor Journal as been put a side—but events and a wish not to discontinue to put down incidents that are of some Note and agreable to My Mind I come again to it—
a personnage who had some weeks ago boasted of his Interest towards me, and who on One occasion carried his ostentation quite too far and awkwardly must first take my

attention—and here I will give you a Lesson, Should you ever be Employed as a Teacher to any ostentatious oppolent person—*flatter*, keep flattering and end in flattery or else expect No pay—

My Misfortunes often occur through a want of Attention to that Maxim in similar Cases   after having with assiduity attended on a Gentleman's Lady (Whose Name I will not at present Mention) for forty Days, I received the rudest of dismisal—and My pride would not admit me to the House to ever ask any compensation—how agreable the first Lessons were I shall allways remember, *She thought* herself endowed with superior talents, and her Looking glass pleasing her vanity I dare say made her believe She Was a Star dropped from the heavens to Ornement this Hearth—but dificulties augmented and of Course drawing seassed to please, I could not well find time to finish every piece that I had began for her, and Constancy the Lady Said was never to be found the Companion of Genius—towards the Last She would be unwell when I walk^d in, Yawn^d and postpon^d to the Morow—I believe the Husband saw her Weakness, but the good Man, Like *one* or *Two* More of My Acquaintance Was Weaker still—

I knew well that My conduct had been correct and I felt a great pleasure in Leaving them, and, the one hundred Dollars I had earned *with them*—

The *Dimitry* familly, on Whose's Daughters I had the pleasure of *attending* as a Drawing Master had become peculiarly agreable and I left them with anxiety for their wellfare and the pleasure that Anticipation produces, having some Hopes of Seing them Next Winter,—Young Dimitry I never will forget. a Youth of More genuine Natural Ability I never have Met—his sarcastism had much the Turn of Dr Walcot's—I Rec^d from the Young Ladies Miss *Aimée* & *Euphrosine* Two handsome Plants for My Beloved Lucy that I forward^d under the Care of Cap^e De Hart—

My True Friend R. Pamar and his most Aimiable and kind Wife I have to thank for all that I can Call the pleasures I felt Wilst at New Orleans—I Eat there whenever I could find time, and I Was so Loved by the Children that I felt as if I parted from Mine when I left them—I had form^d a very slight acquaintance With Mr P. some Years, ago as he descended the

Ohio on his way home—I had been Polite to him When he called at My Poor Log House at Henderson and he said often that kindnesses had not been profuted to him; that he was Well able to remember the Instances and that if I did Not please to Make free with his house *he* Would be sorry for it—

I Rec^d Many Attentions from Mr Laville and Lady—Mr Hollander the Partner of My old but too rich Acquaintance Vincent Nolte I had the pleasure of Seing—

he I believe saw that I had No wish to disgrace the Handsome Rich Furniture of the Wealthy with My Intrusions when reduced to My Grey Breeches, and taking Me by both Hands One day as I was trying to Make Way from him; he said My Dear Mr Audubon Come and see me, I promise you I Shall Not have any one at table and I will try to Raise your Spirits, I have some fine Paintings, and please bring Your Birds that I am Anxious to see—then You see that although I lived extremely retired and generally Shon^d those that I thought I Would Incomodate I Now & then Stumble on an Less Indiferent Member of this Life towards his fellows Who like Me have been rich and poor alternatly—

I had attended on Miss Pirrie to Enhance her Natural taste for Drawing, for some days When her Mother Whom I intend Noticing in due time, asked Me to think about My spending the summer and fall at their farm Near Bayou Sarah; I Was glad of such an overture, but would have greatly prefared her living in the Floridas—We Concluded the Bargain promessing Me 60 Dollars per Month for One half of My time to teach Miss Eliza all I could in Drawing Music Dancing &^c &^c—furnishing us with a Room &^c for Joseph & Myself—so that after the One hundred Diferent Plans I had form^d as Opposite as Could be to this, I found Myself bound for several Months on a Farm in Louisianna.

We Left our abode in Quartier Street and Old Miss Louise without the Least regret, the filthiness of her Manners, did not agree with our feeling; and by this time We had fully discovered that a Clean sweet Housekeeper is quite necessary to Naturalists—

Our Good Spanish Neighbour Mr Jack We Loved, his Nieces sung Well, and his own Jokes now and then amused us—

We Came to our Landing at the Mouth of Bayou Sarah of a hot sultry day without any Accidents; bid farewell to M[r] Gordon and after Mounting the Hill at S[t] francis Ville Rested ourselves some Moments at a M[r] Semple   dinner Was set, but Not my Heart for it, I wished Myself on Board the Columbus, I Wished for My Beloved Lucy, My Dear Boys—I felt that I would be Awkward at table and a good opportunity having offered to go to M[r] Pirrie place, We Walked slowly on guided by some of their servants dispatch[d] with the News of our Coming and some Light Baggage—

the Aspect of the Country entirely New to us distracted My Mind from those objects that are the occupation of My Life— the Rich Magnolia covered with its Odoriferous Blossoms, the Holy, the Beech, the Tall Yellow Poplar, the Hilly ground, even the Red Clay I Looked at with amasement,—such entire Change in so Short a time, appears, often supernatural, and surrounded Once More by thousands of Warblers & thrushes, I enjoy[d] Nature

My Eyes soon Met hovering over us the Long Wished for, Mississipi Kite and Swallow tailed Hawk, but our Guns were pack[d] and We could only then anticipate the pleasure of procuring them Shortly—the 5 Miles We Walked appear[d] Short   We arived and Met M[r] Pirrie at his House, Anxious to Know him I Inspected his features by Lavaters directions,— *We Were received Kindly*—

July 4th 1821—

during the diferent excursions We have made through the Woods here, and from Report of Such persons as are thought proper to Lessen to on the subject, I have made the following remarks—Viz—

The Blue Jeay Corvus Cristatus is scarc in Lower Louisianna during the summer, not having met With More than a dozen Individuals in All on our rambles—Last April Immense Numbers of these Birds, so annoyed the Corn rows in this Neighborhood as to force the planters to Poison them with Corn boiled with Arsenic which had a great Effect— Killed the Thiefs often instantly—

Yellow Bird   frigilla Tristis
saw a very few during Last Winter Near N. Orleans   None at present—these do not breed here—

Baltimore Oriole, Oriolus Baltimore—
Not an Individual to be met With at any season—

Wood Thrush   Turdus Melodus—
Extremely plenty, in its usual haunts, i.e. deep Shady Woods—the first bird that Sings at the dawn of day—Never killed one Coresponding with Willson's figure—

Robin—Turdus Migratorius—
Resorts here during Winter in vast Numbers and become very fat—the sport to all the Gunners—leaves early in March—

White Breasted Black Cap[d] Nuthatch
Sitta Carolinensis—
Scarce, have killed a few, Nestle here—Young quite Grown Midle of June, first brood—

Sitta Varia   Red bellied Nutatch—
Not found—

Gold Wing[d] Wood Pecker—Picus auratus—
Plentifull—

Black-throated Bunting, Emberiza Americana
Not an Individual Met With—

Blue Bird, Sylvia Sialis—
Scarce, about one paire to each Plantation—Yet Nesting in holes of Peach & Apple Trees—

Orchard Oriole, Oriolus Mutatus—
Very Aboundant, this Country appears to be Chosen by them   I found seventeen Nests on M[r] Pirrie's Plantations With Eggs or Young, during Two days Looking for them—the Young of Many already flying about Midle June—first brood—Was deceived one day by one imitating the Cry of the Loggerhead Shrieke and followed it a great distance before I found My Mistake; it kept on the tops of high trees in the forest, a very unusual circumstance, the figure of Willson has the bill Much too Large & Long, the figure of the Egg is also too large—

Great American Shrieke   Lanius exubitor
a few seen during winter—

Ruby Crowned Wren—sylvia Calendula
a few during Winter seen Near N. Orleans—

Shore Lark   Alauda Alpestris—
None at any season—

Pine Gros Beak, Loxia Enucleator
None—

Maryland Yellow throat. Sylvia Marilandica.
Great Numbers during the Winter, Leaves early in March

Yellow Breasted Chat. Pipra Poliglotta
as Many here as I have met in any other state—that is, One
about each Plantation, Never have seen a femelle—

Summer Red Bird, Tanagra Aestiva
Tolerably plenty—

Indigo Bunting, Fringilla Cyanea
Tolerably plenty   Not so much as in Kentucky or Pensylvania, but More so than in Ohio—

American Red Start, Muscicapa Ruticilla
Very plenty, Young quite grown Midle of June—

Cedar Bird   Ampellis Americana—
Was remarked this Spring feeding on the Holy berries and remained to reap the fruit of the Wild Cherries—in Immense
flocks, extremely fat—disappeared at once—

Red Bellied Wood Pecker, Picus Carolinus
plentifull as any where else—

Yellow throated fly Catcher   Muscicapa Sylvicola—
Never Met With—

Purple finch—Fringilla purpurea
a few during Winter seen Near N. Orleans—allways in litle
flocks of 4 to 6—

Brown Creeper—Certhia familiaris—
Not seen—

House Wren—
Not seen—

Black Cap[d] Titmouse, Parus atricapillus
Very plenty—Young quite grown Midle of June—

Crested Titmouse—Parus bicolor
the same—

Winter Wren—Sylvia trogloditus—
during Winter, numerous in the Cypress Swamps—

Red headed Wood Pecker, Picus Erythrocephalus
plenty—Young quite Grown 15. June—

Yellow Bellied Wood Pecker—
a few during Winter—

Hairy Wood Pecker—
Not seen—

Downy Wood Pecker, P. Pubescens
scarce,—

Mocking Bird—Turdus polyglottus
Extremely plenty—Nestles in all sorts of Situations having
found Nests in the higher parts of Tall trees in, Small Bushes
and even betwen fence rails garded only by the rail imediatly
over the Nest—the Egg represented by Willson very Litle
Like any of the great Number I examined = these Birds
Mock indiscriminatly every Note of Birds—are very Gentle
with every thing but the Bird of Prey, these they give chase to
and follow a great distance with much apparent Courage—
here during Winter—

Humming Bird. Trochilus Colubris—
Plentifull—Was assured of the existence of Two Species by
Many—represented as Much Larger—have Not Met with any
individual yet and fear it to be a Mistake—these Birds are
easily Caught by pouring Sweeten[d] Wine in the Calices of
flowers—they fall antoxicated Willson erroneously says that
this sweet Bird does not sing—I have many times lessened to
its Low toned Melody with great pleasure and can assure
you that if its Voice was as sonorous as it is varied and Musical
it would be considered as surpassed by few other Species—

Towee Bunting—Emberiza Erythropthalma
Saw a very few Near New Orleans during Winter Not one
found at present—

Cardinal Gross Beak. Loxia Cardinalis
Extremely plenty—during the Whole Season increasing still

by vast Numbers that come from the Eastward to spend their
Winter here, very depradatory to Corn Crebs—Young very
Large 15 June, Second brood Hatching—

Scarlet Tanager, Tanagra Rubra—
Plentifull—but do not find them by any Means confined to
the Interior of the forests, but to the contrary found on the
bordering Tall trees of Plantations—

Rice Bunting—Emberiza Oryzivora
passes early in spring from further Southern parts going eastwardly, remarked Some Last february and March—

Red Eyed Fly Catcher.
Sylvia Olivacea—
plentifull—Young quite grown early in June—

Marsh Wren—Certhia Palustris
Never saw one Like Willson's drawing—but have killed Many
Individual of the Marking & Shape of My Drawings—some
of them a few Miles Above New Orleans in April—but never
imediatly Near Rivers—

Great Carolina Wren—
Certhia Caroliniana—
almost constantly in sight or hearing—about the field or the
forest—young full grown now. found of damp places—

Yellow Throat Warbler—
Sylvia Flavicollis
Never Met With—

Tyrant Fly Catcher, Lanius Tirannus
plentifull—young full grown now—

Great Crested fly Catcher—
Muscicapa Crinita—
Very Common—young full grown, very Timorous & Shy—

Small green Crested fly Catcher.
Muscicapa querula—
Extremely plenty—found of the road Sides from where it
dashes at flies from Low Bushes—

Pewit Fly Catcher—
Muscicapa Nonciala—
Plentifull during winter Near N. Orleans, a few remains in the
Hilly parts of Louisianna during summer—

Wood Pewée—Muscicapa Rapax—
Plentifull in the Woods—this Bird hunts latter than any of its
Genus, I have heard it uttering its Note Long after Dark—

Ferruginous Thrush. Turdus Rufus—
have a very few Individuals, that had more the appearance of
Lost Strangers, than of happy residents, rarely seeing more
than one at a time—

Golden Crown Thrush.
Turdus Aurocapilla—
Not Met at all during summer   many seen during the Winter
Months—

Cat Bird, Turdus Lividus
Not One seen Since Last March When one Evening I saw
Many on the Canal row of Willows, the public Walk Near N.
Orleans—

Bay Breasted Warbler
Sylvia Castanea—
None Seen—

Chestnut Sided Warbler. Sylvia Pensylva.[a]
None seen—

Mourning Warbler. sylvia Philadelphia—
Never Met with—

Red Cockaded W. Pecker P. querulus.
have seen and killed one Only, but it Lodged and I Lost it—
Not seen Near plantations, unless the weather be very Cold—
Mostly in Pine Woods—

Brown Headed Nuthatch—
Sitta Pusilla—
Never seen—

Pigeon Hawk falco Columbarius—
Never Met with—

Blue Wing[d] Yellow Warbler
Sylvia Solitaria—
Not Met with here—

Blue Eyed Yellow Warbler
Sylvia Citrinella—
So many of these about New Orleans early in March Nimbly

hunting for insects amongst the willows—but could not find
one in the month of May, having past I Suppose Eastwardly
where it is so common in all our orchards—

Golden winged Warbler
Sylvia Chrysoptera—

Not seen here, a plenteous bird in the Lower parts of Kentucky—

Black Throated Blue Warbler—
Sylvia Canadensis—

Never have seen these Birds since I left Pensylvania   Very
Numerous in the Lower parts of that state in April and May—

American Sparrow Hawk
Falco sparverius—

very Common, Nestle allways in hole, mostly that of the
Wood Peckers—Young quite grown, Midle of June here—

Field Sparrow—
Fringilla Pussilla

Not here—
Not a single Species of Sparrow to be met with at this season =

Yellow Rump Warbler
Sylvia Coronata—

remains here during the whole winter, in aboundance—saw
them every day every where   there was a Few even in the
City of N. Orleans—in May Not one to be found—

Maryland Yellow throat—
Sylvia Marilandica

plenty during Winter, and very Gentle—

Blue small grey fly Catcher
Muscicapa Cœrulea—

plenty during summer, Nestles in Willows, Keeps in small parties of 6 or 7—has much the manners of the Long tailed Titmouse of Europe—

White Eyed fly Catcher—
Muscicapa Cantatrix—

the Commonest of all the Birds in our Woods—the young of
which Two brood Are raised in the season   full grown Midle
of July—

saw 3 Red Ibises pass over the plantation Yesterday—

Chuck-Will's-Widow
Caprimulgus Carolinensis femelle
Yesterday 21st of July 1821 an Indian of the Chactaw Nation, who habitually hunts for Mr Pirrie—brought me a femelle of the Chuck Will's Widow in full and handsome plumage, it measured One foot in length, 25 Inches in breadth, the tail composed of Ten Feathers is rounded, but has not the white in any degree that Willson mentions in the inner vanes of the 2 exterior feathers = the Craw of this was filled with the heads of many of that kind of bugs commonly called *pinching* Bugs, one of them a very Curious Large One Armed with *Two equal* paires of Pincers—

these Birds generally Aboundant in this part of Louisianna, are at present very scarce, Not having been able to Meet one in any of our Excursions that often are of Twenty Miles—a few Weeks previous to our Arrival they where heard from all parts of the adjacent Woods Loud during the day—a few have been seen and a few heard since, all of which have eluded My pursuits—they remain here untill Late in September, I suppose them at this time so occupied in search of food for their young that it has put an end to their Crying = Many of the Planter thinks that this bird has the Power and Judgment of removing its eggs when discovered sometimes several hundred yards—these are usually laid on the bare earth under a small bush or by the side of a Log—

Saw 3 of these birds on the 20th of August one Evening while I was Watching the arrival of Some Wood Ibisses—they flew Lightly in the manner of the Night Hawk but Close to the Cotton plant Tops, passing and repassing by me untill I could see No more,—Not one of these Birds have I heard since Early in June—

On the 22^d a beautifull femelle of this Bird was brought me by Mr Perrie's Overseer who had Shot it the preceding evening on a small dead Tree, where the Chuck will's Widow had taken a Stand to watch Beetles & Seized on them as they passed by, he saw it raise several times and Catch them in the Manner that Mocking Birds often do Whilt enchanting the Observer of his Melodies—this Man's Wife had seen it for several evenings precious at the

July 26th 1821

Rec[d] yesterday from New Orleans a Packet of Letters, 4 from My Wife, One from Benj. Bakewell & one from M[r] N. Berthoud. much afraid that My Wife has not rec[d] My Packet for the President forwarded her by the Cap[e] of the Steam boat Car of Commerce =

Remarked to day that a Male of the *Orchard* Oriole, that I had wounded in the Tip of the wing and Caged had Violent fits of Convultions, that lasted for as much as ten Minutes each, this I atributed to the uncommon exertions he made to escape through the Wire of the upper part of the Cage—

Yet he eat freely of Fruits and also rice—

saw Yesterday an unknown Awk of a Large Size, that at first appearance I took for an *Ash Colored Awk.* but at a dash he Made at some Pigeons I was able to see him Well and could not recognize it for any of the 22 Species I am acquainted with—our pices not being Loaded, I Lost him—

The Martins have for about Two Weeks Every day followed a Course of Conduct quite New to me & very remarkable, they are seen Every Morning about 50 in number, the Whole of Which were inhabitants of the Boxes put up for them, assembled on the top of a Dead tree Close by the House, from 8 o'clock untill dinner time about 2 P. M. they amuse themselves over the Yard, after this the Whole disapear and Spend the Night, I know not where—going every time they Leave due West—and returning from that point about sun rise—every Morning—do they spend their Nights in Large trees at a great distance? or do they fly to & fro that While to try their power is uncertain; however I Suppose the first Case the true one—

Same spot and sport—These Birds differ Much in plumage, particularly in being darker or Lighter as they are Older or younger, this had Many Minute eggs, very fat—finding Birds of Migratory habits generally in good order during this season it May be concluded that it is a preparatory necessary Incident to them to make them to bear the fatigues and probably the unavoidable wants of food during their travels—the Stomack of this had entire Locusts, Green Wood Lice, Ground Crikets and 2 of these Long Beetles Called usually by the french *Scarabées*—as Most Birds are at present, Many of the Tail & wing feathers were tender from the Moult—

Carrion Crows are extremely attached to their roosting Dead Trees and will Spend the Whole of the Summer nights on the Same,—Leaving it very late every morning When flying on a long Course they much resemble the True Turkey—flapping their wings 8 or 10 times, then sailing about 50 Yards, & again flap—

Almost every Genus of Migratory Birds, begain to depart as soon as the Young are fully able—saw to day Large flocks of the Tyrant fly Catchers going due south—

July 29th 1821

I had the pleasure of Meeting with Several Red Cockaded Wood Peckers yesterday during a Walk We took to the Pine Woods and procure^d Two beautifull Males, both alive, being slightly wounded each in the Wing—the particular & very remarkable cry of this Bird can be heard at a very considerable distance of a Still day, in articulation it resembles that of the Hairy Wood Pecker, but is much more Shrill & *Loud*. the Tall pine trees are its Chosen haunts and seldom does it alight on any other kind of Timber—its Motions are quick, gracefull and easy, it Moves in all directions cither on the Trunk or Limbs, Looking often very cunningly under the Loose pieces of bark for Insects: is more Shy than any of its Genus, Watching attentively all our Movements below, they kept allways on the opposite side, peeping carefully at us—The second one Shot did not Loose a Moment to think of its Misfortune, the moment it fell to the ground it Hoped briskly to the Nearest tree, and Would soon have reach its top had I not secured it—it defended itself with courage and so powerfully did it pcck at my fingers that I was forced to let him go =

Confined in my Hat on my head, they remained Still and Stubborn, I looked at them several times, when I found them trying to hide their Heads as if ashamed to have lost their Liberty—the report of my Gun alarmed them every time I Shot when they both uttered a Plaintive Cry—

through the pain of the wound or the heat felt in my hat one died before We reach^d Mr Pirries's house—the Other I put in a Cage,—he imediatly review^d the Premises hoping about and hunting for a place to Work through, and used his

Chisel bill with great adroitness sending the small Chips he cut to the right & left and having made his way to the floor, run to the Wall and Climb^d up it as easily as if the bark of his favorite Pine had been his foot hold, picking betwen the Bricks and Swallowing every Insect he found = remarking often his looking under Craks and the litle Shelves in the rough wall, I drew him in that Position = Sorry I am to have to say that Mr Willson's Drawing could not have been Made from the Bird *fresh killed* or if so it was in very bad order about the head, he having put the Small striek of red feathers of the head imediatly over the Eye, where there is a White Line, the red being placed far back of the ear—and the whole of the wing not at all Marked Like that of the Bird—the sides of the breast is also badly represented, the Lines in Nature are Longitudinal only, and Show more of a body—the appearance of this Bird when on the pine trees Would Make one suppose it to be Black all over and the Red Line is often covered by the Crown feathers in the living Bird = I first Met with this Species a few Miles from Nashville, when on My Way to Philadelphia in 1806, seing them from time to time untill I left the first range of Mountains, Called the Cumberland—of the Nest, or time of Incubation I Cannot speak, I am told that during severe winter they will leave the pine Woods and Approach Plantations—

the Length of Both those I attentively examined Was 8½ Inches, Breadth 14½—the Gizzard filled with heads of Small Ants and a few Minute Insects—the bird smells Strongly of Pine; as I Hope to be soon able to procure the femelle, I May probably with her portrait give More information—

Shot also a Young of the Great White Heron, entirely destitute of the Pendant silky feathers of the Shoulders, but so well grown that it Might easily in that stage be taken for another Species = Killed Two Young of the Snowy Heron, that

This afternoon having finished My Drawing of the Red Cockaded Woodpecker and satisfied of its Correctness by a Close comparison to the living original I gave it its Liberty, and was glad to think that it most Likely would do well as it flew 40 to 50 Yards at times and seemed Much refreshed by its return to Liberty—

Where with an old One, Neither of these had the recumbent feathers of the back and their Legs & feet were all of a Yellowish Green instead of the former Black and feet highly Yellow—saw some Killdeer plovers. King fisher, Green Heron, and a ferruginous Thrush—Low Lands bordering Watter courses are usually preferred by these—

—————

The Martins Hirundo Purpurea that leave this place daily, Congregate with a parcel raised Near Thompson's Creek, about 5 Miles from this—and I have no doubt will take their flight from thence, for their Winter resort =

Wednesday August 1ˢᵗ 1821

We were awakened Last night by a Servant desiring that I Should rise & Dress to accompany Mʳˢ P. to a Dying Neighbour's house, about one Mile,—We Went, but arrived *rather late* for Mʳ James O'conner Was dead, I had the displeasure of keeping his body's Company the remainder of the night, On Such Occasions time flys very slow indeed, so much so that it lookedt as if it Stood Still like the Hawk that Poises in the Air over its prey = the Poor Man had drink himself Literally to an everlasting Sleep; peace to his Soul   I Made a good Sketch of his head and Left the House and the Ladies engaged at preparing the ceremonial Dinner—the weather Sultry Thermometer at 93—it had Not raised yet this Season here above 96—

Our Sparrow Hawk Was killed to day by a Hen engaged in guarding her Brood—Nero had become extremely Temeraire, Would Fall on a Grown duck as if thinking all must answer his Wishes when hungry—he flew at liberty about the Place, caught, Grasshopers with great ease and Would Catch in the air any of the unfortunate Small birds killed in our dayly walks when thrown towards him for food—he regularly refuse all putrid flesh, Never would touch Woodpeckers, but dearly received Bats & Mice,—he had grown handsome from an apparent parcel of Moving Cotton—sailed with the Wild Birds of his Species, retiring every Night to the Inner upper part of a Sash in Mʳ P.'s Room—he seldom made use of the Note of the Old Birds but allmost constantly uttered his Cree, Cree, Cree,—

Our Orchard Oriole I gave Liberty to seeing that the Departure of every number of his tribe, had rendered him melancholy to excess; I have No doubt that that Specie could be Kept in cages Without much trouble, and its Sprightly songs certainly would well repay for the care employed to furnish them with food & Drink—

August—4th 1821 Saturday—

Louisianna Warbler. Sylvia Ludovicianna

I Shot this morning the same Bird or one of the same kind that I pursued yesterday So eagerly and then without success—and Was Much pleased to discover in it a New Species = during my Chase of yesterday it flew briskly from one tree or small bush to another, Not as if afraid of me, but as if Anxious for food, hanging its Wings very much like the Hooded fly Catcher and constantly keeping its tail Much spread like the American Red Start the Only Note it repeated every time it left a place for another Was a simple soft single *Tweet*, All its Movements extremely quick gave Me much trouble to shoot it—this Bird I Never have Met before, and of Course I Consider it as a Very Scarce One, its Note attracted me as that of all New Species do; More of its habits I would Like to know—Total Length 5. Inches Breadth 8—Whole upper part of a rich Olive Yellow—deeper on the Shoulders & back, Wing feathers Black edged with bright Olive—tail Much rounded, composed of 12 Feathers the 3 first exterior on each side Outwarding edged with brownish black and Yellow inwardly these edges broadening more as they goes to the Midle feathers that are of a dark brown nearly black edged

August 29th saw Two of those Birds, to day a Male & femelle that I approach^d and Examined very attentively for some Minutes they were in a Low damp & Shady part of the wood, I killed the femelle & have Joined it to my drawing of a Male—I was anxious to procure her mate but the discharge of my Gun so alarmed it that it flew off and I could not see it more—these Birds resemble the young of the Blue eyed Warbler of Willson in much of their plumage but not in Manners and are a scarc species—

with Olive—Under wing Coverts rich yellow—under tail Coverts the same, very long—

Eyes full, Irids deep brown, bill the true Warbler horn col^d above and Clay below, very Sharp with a few black bristle, tongue forked & slender—Legs feet & Claws, Yellowish Clay. it proved on dissection a Male, extremely fat—Gizzard containing, remains of Caterpillars, Small beetles and diferent kinds of Small flies with a few fine Clear Sands—

Sunday August 12th 1821

We left this Morning after an early breakfast to go and explore a Famous Lake about 5½ Miles from this where we were to find (as told) great many Very fine Birds = the walk to it was pleasant being mostly through rich Magnolia Woods, We killed Two Wood Ducks in a Small pond that we had to leave on a/c of the depth of the Hole, but that were excellently wellcome to Two *Red Shouldered Hawks* that Carried them off in our Sight—these Last are the only Birds of this kind I have seen at this season in this part of Louisianna—We saw a Singularly rich col^d Spider that finding a Horse fly Just entangled in her Net move to it and covers it in a Moment with the silk of her bag, Shooting it out in a Stream and at the same time rolling the fly untill the whole Assumed the appearance of a Small oblong ball of White Silk, the Spider then return^d to the center of its Nest—No doubt this is a Way of preserving the flies when the Spider is not hungry;—When we left the ridges We at once saw a diferent Country in Aspect, the Tall White & Red Cypress being the principal Trees in Sight with their thousand Knees raising Like so Many Loafs of Sugar—Our eagerness to see the Lake engage us to force our Way through Deep stiff Mud & Watter—We came to it and saw several Large Alligator Sluggishly moving on the surface; Not in the least disturb^d by our approach—

saw a White Ibis on a Log where it sat a Long time arranging its feathers using its scythe Shape^d bill very dexterously; Could have killed it but having No boat and afraid of Sending a Dog in the Lake Left it setting peaceably—

saw a great Number of Prothonotary Warblers on the Low

Bushes of the Swamp—Many *Yellow throated Warblers* these
have all the habits of a Creeper, Moving quickly round, up
and down the Limbs and trunks of the Cypress trees, fly
swiftly in the Manner of the brown Creeper alighting generally low on the trunk assending it searching nimbly for small
Insects; these birds have so much the appearance of the *White
& Black Creeper* that had I Not seen one fly directly toward
me and discovering then the beautifull & rich Yellow Throat
I would Not have shot one. This however I effected and
found Myself in possession of a Beautifull Male that Measured
5½ Inches in Length & 8¼ in extend answering Willson Descriptions, on Dissection the Bird was very fat as all the Warblers We Shoot Now Are, and had its gizard filled with Shells
of Minute Insects—so found of the Cypress trees is this beautiful spirited litle bird that I Was Tempted to Call it the Cypress swamp Warbler, when it is only to be Met in this part of
the Country—

I Was also fortunate in Shooting a Male of the *Green blue*
Warbler—One Week ago I had shot one but Never could find
it, there was at that time five in Company, and within only
a few feet of Me Mr Willson Shot a femelle on the Cumberland
River, and Never any more; about Two Months since I Discovered One in a small swamp Nearer Mr Pirrie—these birds
sing sweetly, and No doubt breed here; Look Much like the
blue Yellow Backs Warblers and hang downwards by the feet
like these and the Titmouse. saw only the one I shot to day
and having as much as I Know I could Well draw before they
would be Spoiled by the heat of the Wheather *returned* to the
House.

This Male Measured 5 Inches in Length and 7¾ in
breadth—all the Colors brighter & Stronger than Willson's
femelle, every Tail feathers having White on their inner Vane
except the Two Midle ones—so fat was this bird and of so
solid a Nature was that fat that it Cut like Mutton fat; its
gizard Was filled entirely with some Small brown Shelly Insects and the remains of the same Kind that are extremely
plenty on the Cipresses of these Swamps—

Shot a Watter Thrush, have found many here,

Went to the Lake that We Visited Last sunday and in Going there, I Was much pleased to observe that the *sound* that

We heard on sunday and had taken for the Plaintive Note of
the *Wood Pewee* was in fact that of a Young Mississipi Kite,
whilt waitting for the return of the Parent with food—this
Young it seems had Actually remained on the same tree
Where we had heard it before but could not then discover
it—this morning perceiving that a long Vine reach[d] near to
the Top of the Tree and hearing the Noise without knowing
it nor where it actually issued from, I walked toward it still
looking up to the Topmost branches When I perceived something Like a dead stick Lodged Cross ways on a limb—I Eyed
it particularly and saw it Moved, I Shot at it and the Noise
stop[d] but the Young M. Kite Closed her wings and destroyed
the Dead Stik like appearance it had before my fire—I Waited
for it to fall, it cried again shortly and I then saw the Old Bird
bringing food and Alight Close to the young with one of
these Large Grass hopers that abound in the Mississipy flats—
but the young was too far gone to relish food   the Mother
exibited much distress and after several trials to Make the
young Bird take it it dropt it and taking old of her Offspring
by the feathers of the back carried it off with ease for about 25
yards to another tree where I follow[d] and killed both at One
Shot—the Young instead of having the head of a Light blue
Ash color like its Mother had it of a handsome buff   the remainder of the body Was nearly black   I intended drawing
Both and I purposely hided them under a Log, but on my return some quadrupedes had discovered them and eat both—
I regret much the Loss   the young Bird was nearly full
grown   saw several paires of Ivory Bill *Wood Peckers* Killed a
handsome Male,—Louisianna affords all the *Picus Genus* of
the U. States—

Arrived at the Swamp and then saw a great Number of
Small Birds; Shot a beautifull *new* species of Fly Catcher,
Muscicapa, which I Will give you Tomorrow when my Drawing of it Will be finished, I had the pleasure of seing Two that
appeared Much alike, they were quarelling when I Shot at
them but fell only One—cannot say Any More of this truly
handsome bird having never seen any thing of them before to
Day—

saw within a few feet a beautifull *Mourning Warbler* but
Was so situated Knee deep in the Mud that I could Not ret-

rograde without Alarming it   I preferred gazing at it as it in-
nocently gazed at me hoping it would fly at a Short distance,
but it Moved with a *Tweet* and out of sight in an instant.
Much disapointed at My having lost the only opp.[y] I Ever
have had of procuring this rare Bird—

Shot several of the *Yellow Throated* Warbler all alike and all
Males   the woods were full of them and yet Not a femelle
could I Shoot—they move sideways on the small limbs of the
Cypress in a Hoping Manner extremely quickly   hangs often
to the ends of Limbs like the titmouse and runs up or down
the Large Trunks much like the Nuthatches—Killed Many
Blue Yellow Back Warblers, saw Many *Prothonotarys*, several
Watter Thrushes, that I Consider More Like Warblers the
Habits of which genus they exibit to a very great degree and
the Bill of Which they have—Alligators as numerous as before
basking in the Sun that this day was more than ordinarily uncomfortable = saw several Ibiss at respectfull Distances in
their common dull postures—

My Litle fly Catcher had only One wing touch[d] When I
presented Myself to pick it up, it spread its Tail & open its
Wings and Snap its bill about 20 times in the same Manner
that Many of this Genus do when they seize a fly, particularly
those that are Nearest the Standard of the Genus—I seldom
have seen a bird of Such Small size With so Large & beautifull an Eye, I took it home to James Pirrie's Es[qr] and had the
pleasure of drawing it While a live and full of Spirit, it often
Made off from My fingers by Starting suddenly and unexpectedly, and then would hop round the room as quick as a
Carolina or Winter Wren would have done, uttering its *tweet*
tweet Tweet all the while, and Snapping every time I took it
up, I put it in a Cage for a few Moments but it obstinately
forced the forepart of its head through the Lower part of the
Wires and I relieved it, but Confining it in My hat for the
Night anxious to see More of its Movements—

Joseph unwell With a sick head Hacke—

Length of the *Cypress Swamp Fly Catcher Muscicapa Rara.*
5¼ Inches—breadth 7¾ Inches   Whole upper parts handsome ash Color appearing blue at a distance, the front of the
Head mixed with Yellow, a Yellow Line Surround the Eye

Length of the Cypress Swamp Fly Catcher
Muscicapa Rara. 5¼ Inches — breadth 9¾ Dm

Facsimile of a page from the manuscript of Audubon's Mississippi River Journal. (Houghton Library, Harvard University)

that is very Large   Irids deep brown, pupil Black, betwen the
eye & Bill & under the eye Shaded with darker ash   Tail
Coverts lighter than the back, tail Slightly forked of 12 Feathers all plain brownish ash shafts deep brown as well as those
of the wings   under tail Coverts Long & White—the Throat,
breast belly & Vent Rich citron Yellow without intermission
of Shade in any of these parts, Breast Spotted With black
forming Small Chains falling to the begaining of the Spurious
wings—Bill, hooked at the Tip & broad at the base, Legs feet
& Claws horn Colors the last Long & Sharp   Nostrils very
prominent, Tongue much Jagged, Mouth flesh color^d & furnish outwardly With many Long black bristles—it proved a
male, Gizzard fleshy filled with wings of Different Insects,—
Cheeks also ash col^d—My Drawing a very excellent one—
finding this Bird very Weak in the Morning killed it and put
it in Whiskey—

Monday 20th August 1821

I spent the Night Nearly in pursuit of the Wood Ibiss and although I Killed One I could never find it this Morning, some
Fox or Racoon had no doubt a good Repast of it—I saw 4
Coming, sailing & flapping alternatly; their Necks & Legs
Strached out a little over the tops of the Trees afew Moments
after sun Setting, No Note, they alighted on the Largest Top
Branches of the dead trees in A Large Cotton Plantation,
drew their Necks & Heads on their shoulders, Standing perpendicularly, Now & then arranging the feathers of their
breast as if to put their Immense bill at Rest on it—I ap-
proach^d them untill they Were immediatly over My head, but
they never minded Me, it growing Dusky I shot at the
Largest—it open its Wings and sailed to the hearth without a
groan, the others raised and Sailed on Some other trees, the
Darkness of the Night then prevented My Seing them any
More and Also forced Me to Look for the One I had undoubtedly Killed. After a Long Search this Morning begun with the
dawn of Day I had to return, fatigued & Much Disapointed—
the Planter and Negroes Assured Me that for Many Years
these Birds some time as Many as 60 & 70 in Numbers, and
at other times only a few had resorted to these Dead Trees to

roost Nearly Said they the round Year, Missing a few Weeks only early in Spring and in Winter, Could Not ascertain the Months—About 2 Weeks since 3 had been killed the Negroes pronounced their flesh Excellent food—

While sitting waiting for the Arrival of these curious Birds saw Several flocks of the White Ibiss and blew Herons, Moving from the Lake to their rendezvouzing place of Rest—to a Large Sand Barr at the Mouth of Thomson's Creek that empty a few Miles below Bayou Sarah—the first flew in single waving Lines silently—the blew Herons in Acute Angles passing the Word of March from the first to the Last in a Simple *qua*, these are easily known by their drawn in Necks and Notes, the others, allways Keeping their Necks at its full Length—

these passages take place every Evening from about One hour before Sunset untill Dark when the Noises of the One and the Pure Whiteness of the others, are the only evidence of Straglers still being going over—

—August 25—

Finished drawing a very fine Specimen of a Rattle Snake—that measured 5$\frac{7}{12}$ feet Weighed 6$\frac{1}{4}$^{lb} had 10 Rattles—

Anxious to give it such a Position as I thought would rendered it most interesting to Naturalists, I put it in that which that Reptile generally takes when on point to Inflict a Most severe wound—I had examined the Fangs of Many before and their position along the Superior Jaw Bones, but had never seen one Shewing the Whole exposed at the same time having before this thought that the probability was that those Laying Inclosed below the Upper one in Most Specimen Were to Replace these upper ones, Which I thought might drop periodically as the Annimal Changes its Skin and Rattles = however on Dissection of these from the Ligament by Which they are fixed to the Jaw bones I found them strongly and I think permanently attached & as follows—Two Superior or Next the upper Lips (I Speak of one side of the Jaw only) connected Well together at their bases & running parrallel their whole Length. They had appertures on the upper & Lower sides of their bases to receive the Venom connect-

edly and the discharging one a short distance from the Sharp
points on the Inner part of the fangs—the Two next Fangs
about one quarter of an Inch below connected and running
in the same Manner, but with only one base apperture on the
Lower Side of each and the one at the point that issues the
venom to the Wound—the 5th rather smaller is also about a
quarter of an Inch below, Lonely. Appertures as in the Secondaries—the scales of the belly to the Under part of the Mouth
where they finished Numbered 170. and 22 from the vent to
the tail = My Drawing I Hope Will give you a good Idea of
a Rattle Snake although the Heat of the weather Would not
permit me to Spend more than 16 hours at it = My Aimiable
Pupil Miss Eliza Pirrie also drew the Same Snake; it is With
Much pleasure that I Now Mention her Name Expecting to
remember often her sweet disposition and the Happy Days
spent near her—

Octr 10th sent 100$ to M^{rs} A—

Octr 20th 1821

This Morning about 6 o'clock We Left Mr *Pirrie's* Plantation
for New Orleans, Which Place we Reach^d on Monday the 21st
at 2 'oclock but before I alight in that City I Must Poise Myself and give you a Short a/c of the Most Remarkable Incidents that have taken Place With us During our Stay at
Oakley the name of James P. Plantation—

three Months out of the 4 we Lived there Were Spent in
peaceable tranquility; giving regular Daily Lessons to Miss P.
of Drawing, Music, Dancing, Arithmetick, and Some trifling
acquirements such as Working Hair &^{c} Hunting and Drawing
My Cherished Birds of America, Seldom troublesome of Disposition, and not Caring for or Scarcely ever partaking or
Mixing with the constant Transient Visitors at the House, *We*
were Called *good Men* and Now & then received a Chearing
Look from the Mistress of the House and *sometimes* also one
Glance of approbation of the more Circumspect Miss Eliza =
Governor Robertson Visited us and then I formed a Still

stronger oppinion of that mans agreableness and Strength of Mind than I had before, & Consider him as a really true Philosopher of the Age = amongst our other Visitors the Brother of Henry *Clay* Mr John Clay of this City I found a good agreable Man to all appearance—a Rather Singular Caracter, *Rich* W^{am} Brand also spent some days at this House and Married in the Neighborhood = all Kindly Polite to us;

Miss P— had No Particular admirers of her beauties but several very anxious for her fortunes amongst Which a Certain Mr Colt a Young Lawer Who appeared quite Pressing although Very uncivilly Received at Times =

Mr P. a Man of Strong Mind but extremely Weak of Habit and degenerating sometimes into a State of Intoxication, remarkable in its Kind, Never associating With any body on such occasions and Exibiting all the Madman's action wilst under its Paroxism = When Sober; truly a good Man a *Free Mason*, generous and Intertaining—his Wife Raised to opulence by Dint of Industry an Extraordinary Woman—Generous I believed but giving Way for want of understanding at times to the Whole force of her Violent Passions = found of quizing her husband and Idolatring her Daughter Eliza=

This Daughter Eliza of age 15 Years, of a good form of *body*, not Handsome of face, proud of her Wealth and of herself, cannot well be too Much fed on Praise—and God Knows how hard I tryed to Please her in Vain—and God Knows also that I have vowed Never to try as much again for any Pupil of mine—as usual *I* had to do ⅔ of all *her* Work of Course her progresses Were Rapid to the Eyes of every body and truly astonishing to the eyes of Some good Observers =

a Sister Mrs Smith I Cannot say that I Knew or rather I never did Wish to Know; of Temper Much like her Mother, of Heart Not so good. Yet God forgive her the Injuries She did me—

her Husband a good, Honest Man and Citisen Viewed all the faults of her he Wedded With Patient Kindness and felt his reward through his own Correctness of Conduct—I admire him Much—

I saw there a Mrs Harwood of London England a *good* Little Woman Very kind to us in Mending our Linen &^{c}—her

Little Daughter a sweet Child about 5 Years Old, Hated by Mrs P.—a Certain Miss *Throgmorton* Was also good deal Disliked, the poor Girl was nearly drove off as We Were by the Ladies—although She had been Invited there to spend the Summer—

about a Month before We left Miss P. was taken seriously Ill, and as She was the only remaining Child unmaried and the 2^d of 7, 5 of which had died in the Course of a very few years, much fear were entertained of the Survival of this One, and No doubt much too much Care Was taken of her; kept in bed Long after She was convalescent and Not permitted to leave her room for a Long time She became, Low of flesh and Crabed of Speech, every thing must have gone on the Smoothest way to hurt her feelings—her Phisician the *Man She Loved*, Would not permit her reassuming her Avocations near Me and told the Mother that it would be highly Improper Miss Eliza Should Draw, Write &^{c} untill some Months; but that She Might Eat any thing Pleasing to her fancy—this fancy Was not Confined into small bounds, She Eat so plentifully of everything that could be procured that She had several Relapses of fevers—I saw her during this Illness at appointed hours as if I was an Extraordinary ambassador to some Distant Court—had to keep the utmost Decorum of Manners and I believe Never Laughed once with her the Whole 4 Months I was there

Mrs P. on the 10th of Octr Dismissed me—Not anxious to revisit New Orleans So soon, I begged of her that We Should remain 8 or 10 Days Longer if the familly Would please to Consider us as Visitors, this agreed on, I Continued My Close application to My Ornithology Writting every day from Morning untill Night, Correcting, arranging from My Scattered Notes all My Ideas and posted up partially all My Land Birds = the great Many Errors I found in the Work of Willson astonished Me   I tried to speak of them With Care and as seldom as Possible; Knowing the good Wish of that Man the Hurry he was in and the Vast Many hear say he depended on—

We perceived however during all this While a remarkable Coolness had taken place from the Ladies toward us, seldom seing any of them except at table and then With Looks far from Chearing My Spirits that Were during the Whole of My Stay there unfortunately very Low—Mrs Smith took an utter dislike to Me and one day Whilst I was engaged in finishing a Portrait of Mrs P. begun by her Daughter Eliza, Mrs S. addressed the Work and Me in the grossest Words of Insult, and afterward Never Looked Directly at Me—

She Bursted at another time in a ridiculous Laugh at table, when her good Husband Interfere^{d} and told her She ought to Make Me some amends for her Conduct—I left the table unwilling to hear any More of this—

Saturday Came and a Settlement of Money Matter Was Necessary—I Charged for 15 days of Miss E. Ill time   My Bill Was 204$ and Mrs P. in a perfect Rage fit told Me that I Cheated her out of 20$—My Coolness sufered all her Vociferations to flow, I simply told her our former mutual Engagements on that score—I figurd the Bill and sent it to Mr P. Who Was then Labouring under one of his unfortunate fits of Antoxication—

he Came to see Me, apologized in the kindest Manner for his Lady's Conduct; ordered his Son in Law Mr Smith to pay Me, and shewed me all the politeness he his possessed of—Mr Smith Congratulate My firmness of Acting—and all Went on pretty Well that Day—

the Ladies early that Morning Left for St Francisville Without bidding us any adieu, and expected that on their Return at night We could be gone; this however was a disapointment; for Mr *Pirrie* requested we Should Stay, representing how easily We would reach the Steam Boat the next Morning before her time of departure—in the Course of this Afternoon Mrs P. sent for Joseph and presented him with a full suit of fine Clothes of her Deceased son—to the acceptation of Which I positively refused to acquiesce, knowing too Well how far Some gifts are talked of—and Not willing that My Companion Should diminish the Self Respect I think Necessary for every Man to keep towards himself however poor, when able by *Talents*, Health and Industry to Procure his own Necessities =

unfortunatly there was Much Company in the evening sometimes after Supper We Left our Room Were Mr Pirrie and Mr Smith had Joined us on leaving the Table to go and bid our farewell to the female Part of the familly = My Entry before the Circle possessed none of that Life and Spirit I formerly Enjoyed on Such occasions, I would gladly have wished to be excused from the fatiguing Ceremonie, yet I Walk^d in followed by Joseph and Approaching to M^{rs} P— bid her good bye as simply as Ever any Honest quaker Did, touch^d Slightly Mrs Smith's Hand as I boughed to her—My Pupil Raised from the Sopha and Expected a kiss from Me—but None Were to be disposed off, I pressed her Hand and With a general Salute to the Whole Made My Retreat No doubt Much to the great Surprise of Every One Present Who had heard those very Women Speak Constantly before of Me in Highest Tones of Respects, scarcely Deigning to Look at me Now—as Joseph Was following me he received a Voley of farewells from the 3 Ladies of the House, sent after him Ridiculously to Affect Me, but the Effect Was lost and it Raised a Smile on My Lips—We Joined again the Two good Husbands in our Lodging Chamber = they remained with us untill bed time; Cordially parted With us, retired to repose Without Joining the Company—

Day Light of Sunday Saw us Loading our Trunks and Drawing Table, Vaulted our Sadles and Left this abode of unfortunate Opulence without a single Sigh of regret =

Not so with the sweet Woods around us, to leave them was painfull, for in them We allways enjoyd Peace and the sweetest pleasures of admiring the greatn. of the Creator in all his unrivalled Works, I often felt as if anxious to retain the fill of My lungs with the purer air that Circulate through them, Looked With pleasure and Sorrow on the few Virgin blooming Magnolias—the 3 Colored Vines and as We descended the Hills of St Francisville bid that farewell to the Country, that under diferent Circumstances, We Would have Willingly divided With the Ladies of Oakley =

We Left the Mouth of Bayou Sarah at 10 o'clock in the Morning in the Steam Boat Ramapo with a Midley of Passengers and with a few Stoppages to Land and take occasional Travellers Reached the City on Monday =

the Weather Cool and Rainy, I left the Boat and Walked to My good acquaintance R. Pamar = I had perceived that My Long flowing buckled hair was Looked on with astonishment by the Passengers on board and saw that the effect Was stronger in town—My Large Loose Dress of Whitened Yellow Nankeen and the unfortunate *Cut* of my features Made me decide to be Dressed as soon as Possible Like other folks and I had My Chevelure parted from My head   the Reception of Mr Pamar's familly was very gratefull to My Spirits, I Was Looked upon as if a Son returned from a Long Painfull voyage, the Children, the Parents the servants, all hung about Me; What Pleasures for the Whole of us—

I dined there, Afterwards Visiting the famous hunter Lewis adam—and the Dimitry familly Who also Received me very kindly—

Rented an Chambre garnie in Rue St Anne N° 29 for 16$ per Month and removed our baggage thereto from the boat—

We Spent Tuesday Wednesday & Thursday, Looking over the City for a Suitable House for My Little familly—this appeared a very dificult task and I nearly Concluded to take one we visited in Dauphine Street =

My Clothes being extremely Shabby and forced against My Will to provide some New ones, I bought some cloth and Now Wait very impatiently on the Gentleman Taylor for them that I May go and Procure some Pupils with a better grace—

having renewed our early Morning Visits to the Market to Look at All there—We found it almost as Well suplied of Vegetables fruits, fish, Meats flowers &^{c} as in the Spring—delightfull radishes, Letuce &^{c} plenty—Wrote to My Wife Yesterday—per Mail it is Now 15 days since I forwarded her a Draft on Mr Gordon Which May probably have reach today—

I found at Messrs Gordon Grant & Co a Box of Oil Colors and a Letter from Mr Briggs, I was sorry to See both, the first did not Contain What I Wish, and I Cannot say that I felt any pleasure in Reading the Latter—

I answered Mr Briggs's Letter this Evening—the 25th of Oct^r—

Octr 25th 1821—

Raining hard the Whole of the day spent the greater part of it at R. Pamar and his Relation *Louis adam the hunter*, Rented a House in *Dauphine* Street for 17$ per Month—

Joseph found the time rather Long to himself Not a Thing to be found to Draw =

26th   Wrote a few Lines to James Pirrie Es^{qr} to Inform him that Messrs D. & G. Flower had not Paid the House of Gordon & C° One hundred Dollars according to Promess = Wrote a few Words to My Lucy and forwarded it by Mail Covering Briggs's Letter;

Walked a good Deal, Visited the familly Dimitry, Spend Much of the Day at Pamar's—in the evening Went some distance down the Levee, the Sky beautifull & serene = Miss Pamar Much Improved in Music and Manners—Many Men formerly *My Friends* passed ME without uttering a Word to me and *I as Willing* to Shun those Rascals—

fatigued of being *Idle* so powerfull are habits of all kinds that to spend a Month they would render me sick of Life—

Hetchberger Visited us Much Pleased at my addition of Drawings since I Left Cincinnati Octr 12th 1820   I have finished 62 Drawings of *Birds & Plants,* 3 quadrupeds, 2 Snakes, 50 Portraits of all sorts and My Father *Don Antonio*— have Made out to Live in humble Comfort with only My Talents and Industry, Without *One Cent* to begin on at my Departure—

I have now 42 Dollars, health, and as much Anxiety to pursue My Plans of accomplishing My Collection as Ever I had and Hope God Will Grant Me the same Powers to Proceed—

My Present Prospects to Procure Birds this Winter are More Ample than ever being now Well Known by the Principal Hunters on Lake Borgne, Barataria—Ponchartrain, and the Country of Terre a Bœuf—

Octr 27th Sunday—

Dressed all new, Hair Cut, my appearance altered beyond My expectations, fully as much as a handsome Bird is when robbed of all its feathering, the Poor thing Looks, Bashfull dejected and is either entirely Neglected or Look^d upon With Contempt; such was my situation Last Week = but When the Bird is Well fed, taken care of, sufered to Enjoy Life and dress himself; he is cherished again, Nai admired—Such my Situation this day—Good God that 40 Dollars Should thus be *enough* to Make a *Gentleman*—ah my Beloved Country When will thy Sons value more Intrinsectly each Brother's worth? never!!

Exibited My Drawings at My good acquaintance Pamars—received much valuable Intelligence coroborating With My own observations on them, (things that trully pleases My feelings)—Dined there—

Payd a Visit to Mrs Clay and the young Ladies there, with My Portfolio—unknown, Passed for a *German* untill the Latter part of My Stay—the Company Much Pleased with my Work—but no Pupil as I expected to have—

took a Long Walk to the Canal, talked much with My Hunter *Gilbert* Who Leaves for Barataria Tomorow—Weather Beautifull and Very Warm, good Deal of Game in Market this Morning—

Green Back Swallows, Gamboling over the City and the River the Whole day have great Hopes of assertaining their Winter quarters Not far from this

Octr 29th 1821.

Spent this infructuously in search of Employment; Visited several Public Institutions where I cannot say that I Was very politely received; in one or Two Notable ones (Not Willing to Mention Names) I was invitd to Walk in and then out in very quick order =

Dined at Pamar; Was Visited by John Gwathmey of Louisville K^y = Wrote to F^d Rozier to Procure my Drawing of the *Male Grous* or Prairie Hen—Determined on Exibiting some of My Drawings at Public Places for I well recollect the effect of *Lafontaine* Fable, that says that "*a l'œuvre on connoit L'Artizan*"—unknown by most people here, I am like Many others who appear as advanturors look^d on with Care, and Suspicion—but so Moves the World, and no doubt it is *Wright* it Should be So—

Visited Rich Mrs *Brand* was there very Politely received, "must Call again"—Mrs Brand Maried a Large fortune, the Honey Moon is not yet *Set* and She Looks well even on her Decline, promissing full fullness—for the Next quarter—

Rec^d a Letter from My Beloved Friend My Lucy, unfortu-

natly of old Date, and the one also sent by Mr Ecard dated
Nearly 2 Months—

Octr 30th 1821 New Orleans—
Returned to W^{am} Brand and Procured his Son for a Pupil at
2$ per Leçon of one hour, and have Some Hopes of Having
Mrs B. a Pupil of *French* and Painting—

Visited another College, Politly Received by the Ladies
Who examined My Port Folio with apparent satisfaction, No
Pupils however, a Certain Mr *Torain* having antecedented Me
every Where—

Dined at Pamar and Drew My American Hare—to Exibit
to the Public—Joseph at Work Preparing Father Antonio
Coat—

the Market Well Suplied With game & Vegetables—have
resumed our Habit of taking a Walk there as soon as the Day
Downs—

the Day Warm, Swallows Plenty and quite as gay in their
flight as in June—

to find here these Bird in aboundance 3 Months after they
have left the Midle States, and to know that they Winter
Within 40 Miles in Multitudes is one of the gratifications the
Most Exquisite I ever Wish^d to feel in Ornithological Subjects
and that puts a compleat *Dash* over *all* the Nonsense Wrote
about their Torpidity during Cold Weather; No Man could
ever have Enjoyed the Study of Nature in her all Inclusive Bo-
somy Wilds and err^d so Wide—

Octr 31st 1821 New Orleans—
Begun giving Lessons of Drawing to Mrs Brand and Young
Master W^{am} Brand this Day at 3 Dollars per Lesson =

Spent some time at Work on Father Antoine and My Drawings of My American Hare—

Received a Visit of Mr Pamar, Mr Dimitry and Dumatras =

Weather Warm in the Morning, Much fish Condemned in
the Market—also some game—Excellent regulations—the
Wind Shifted to the Northward and I premeditated Cold
Weather by the Swallows flying South about Noon   at Night

quite Cool—What Knowledge these Litle Creature Possess and how true they are in their Movements

November 1ˢᵗ 1821.

Weather beautifull—gave Lessons at Wᵃᵐ Brand's—Dined at My good Pamar's House—

Very unwell at Night with Violent Cholicks and was forced to My bed by seven o'clock a thing I have not done for Very Many Years = Visited M. Basterop, Painter—

at 12 o'clock Disturbd by the Cries of Fire—but as it Was Not in our imediate Neighbourhood did not Suffer *Joseph* to go—

November 2ᵈ Friday—

felt Well at day light and Went to see the Market   Much Game, but nothing for Me—gave My Lessons at Wᵃᵐ Brand's—Much pleased to find his Lady possessed of a *Natural* talent for Painting—Wᵃᵐ Brand extremely kind and Polite, very anxious to give his Son a good Education—

Recᵈ the Visit of *Bruster* the Painter, the good Man Very sory to see My *Father* Antonio—fearing an Engraving after it =

I determind to have My Drawing framed although it Cost Me about 30$ having some Hopes that it Would procure Me some Pupils of Note—

Saturday 3ᵈ November.

give My Lesson = John Gwathmey announced me the Death of my *Constant* Ennemy Mʳˢ Bakewell My Wife's Mother's in Law = God forgive her faults—Etchberger the Painter Spent the evening with us—Mʳ Hails borowd My Shot Bag at 10 o'clock P.M. = sufered some Mortifications this Morning in a House Were I shewed My Birds—Weather Cloudy & Raw—

1821. Sunday 4ᵗʰ November N. Orleans

Breakfasted at Pamar's   saw a School Mistress there who requested that I should Call at her House to Shew My

Drawings = Did so at 11 o'clock tolerable reception there, the Lady Drawing Well herself anxious to acquire My Style but Complaining Much of the extraordinary price I asked her—expect there several Pupils but Nothing very Certain—

Dined at Pamar's, Steam Boat Ramapo arrived Without James Pirrie Es^{qr} Much Disapointed on a/c of the 100$ that he was to Pay Messrs Gordon Grant & C° on the 20th ultimo—

took a Long Walk Down the River Shore and out to the Swamps—Swallows More Plenty than yesterday, generally Moving Eastwardly to the Lakes—Weather Delightfull, Much such that is felt in May in Kentucky—Many of the trees having a beautifull set of New foliage, Vast Many Plants in Bloom—Particularly the *Elder*—

No Lessons at W^{am} Brand to day—

—Monday. 5th—

give My Leçons at W. Brand—

Drawing at My F. Antoine—Paid Mr Forestal 100$—

—Tuesday 6th—

gave My Lecons at W^{am} Brand—

Swallows plenty—Appearance of *Indian Summer* Took a Long Walk and Much Work Done at My Drawing

—Wednesday 7th—

Gave My Lecon to Mrs Brand & Son—Procured Two Pupils to begain Next Monday—Drew an American Avoset—Weather Beautifull—

———

Brown Pelican—

Length 4 feet 2½ Inches from the Tip of the Bill to the end of the Toes which extend about 1½ Inches beyond the Tail—The Bill Measured 12½ Inches the upper Mandible armed with a strong Hooked Point projecting beyond the blade of the upper Mandible ½ Inch—and fitting the Lower one in its Whole Length to the Nail Which runs to the forehead in Two furrows and Contains the Nostrils that are Extremely small, Linear, within ½ an Inch of the forehead and scarce perceivable—the outer edges of this Mandible as Well as those of the Lower and Sharp Cutting edges—3 Process edges are contained in the inner part of the upper Mandible also Sharp edged—the whole of this upper Part bony stiff & Strong Substance—of a Greyish Blue edging in Yellow—the edges of the Lower Mandible are the same Color avaraging in Width about ½ an Inch truncated at the end and Capable of distention from their Natural depth of 1⅜ of an Inch to 6 Inches and furnished with a bag or pouch of a Bluish Distending skin begaining at the under point of the Lower Mandible and Loosing itself along the Neck about 9½ Inches below the Junction of the Mandible from Which part to its utmost stratch point with the hand it Measured a foot—the Tongue is a Mere Knot about 12 Inches from the Tip of the Lower Mandible fast to this Bag—the Eye is Brown pretty Large and situated in the Skin that covers the Cheeks and Jaws of the Bill—the upper of the Head and side of the Neck running along the Pouch of a Mole Cole Color, the hind head ornemented with a Crest of slender feathers of 1½ Inch in Length —the upper Plumage of the Neck, assuming a Silky appearance and Much Worn by resting on the back and Shoulders of the Bird—Shoulders & Back Covered With pointed, Small feathers the formers Light ash in their Centers edge With Rufous & Some with brown—the Latter silvery in the Center edge With deep black to the Rump Where the Plumage is Larger yet Pointed ash & Rufous—the Tail Rounded Composed of 18 feathers quills Black blades Silvery Ash—

the Wings Extended Measured 7½ feet—the second Joint 9 Inches Closing on the Body reaching to the beginning of the Neck—and When closed the Tips reach the end of the Tail— the first 9 Primiry quills White to their points below and about ½ above, the feathering brownish black cast. secondaries much the same—Tertials Broad falling over the back part of the body to the root of the Tail, feathers of the Shoulders of a Light ash some edged With brown, others With Black, quills Very slender and Black—Whole under part White and in some Specimen Silvery—Legs Strong and Muscular, far behind = 4 Toes Webbed in Connection, the Whole of a Bluish, greenish, Yellow Claws blunt, Much Hooked the Longest Pectinated Inwardly = the Bird immitting a Strong desagreable fishy smell Weighed 6½^{lb} femorals Much as the shoulders = On dissection it was a Male—the Stomack Very Long and slender, fleshy—Containing only about 50 slender Blue Worm all alive about 2½ Inches Long—the Gut Measured 10 feet about the size of a Moderate Swans quill—the Bird Was killed on Lake Barataria by My Hunter Gilbert = the rump and the root of the Tail was Covered With a Thin Coating of Oily Yellow fat extremely rancid, and Much air Was Contained betwen the Whole of the Skin and flesh of the body; the Bones of the Wings & Legs although Extremely hard and dificult to Breake, were very thin Light and perfectly empty—

—Thursday 8th—

gave My Lecons at Mrs Brand's = Weather extremely sultry— Anxious to hear from My Wife—

New Orleans November, Friday 9.th 1821.

Weather quite Cool a diference in the atmosphere of 22 Degrees from that of yesterday and the Swallows that Were Numerous Last Evening are all gone for the Present—gave my Lecons at Mrs Brand's =

Carried My Port follio to Mrs Dimitry this Morning to Show Miss Euphrosine the Progress of Joseph—Dinned and Breakfasted at Good *Pamar's*—

Visited this afternoon Miss *Bornet*'s academy of Young Ladies and Shew^{d} some Drawings—but all to No purpose the Ladies there entirely in favor of Mr Torain's Talents—

Mr Hawkins during My absence brought an Engraving of Vanderling's head of Adriane for Me to Copy and requested Joseph to tell Me Not to Spare My Time on it = Mr Basterop also Called Whilst I was out—

My feelings Much harassed about My Beloved Wife from Whom I have Not heard for 2 Weaks—

—Saturday 10th—

Gave My Lecons at Mrs Brand = Called on Mr Hawkins who visited me to see father Antoines Drawing = Concluded to

have the Engraving he Wished Me to Copy for not exceeding
50$ wishing it could be done as Soon as possible = Saw M^r
John Clay—very Polite to Me =

Weather Very beautiful but Cold Drew a female of the
Gadwall Duck a remarkably fine Specimen—sent Me by My
Hunter Gilbert =

Mr Basterop at My Lodgings = Wished that I Should Join
him in a Painting of a Panorama of this City—but My Birds
My Beloved Birds of America feel all my time and nearly My
thoughts I do not Wish to See any other *Perspective* than
the Last Specimen of them Drawn—No News from My
Beloved Lucy nor Children, Very uneasy on their Silence—
Mississipi falling fast—

New Orleans Sunday November 11th 1821

Saw John Gwathmey early this Morning, who told me that
My Wife Intended Leaving Louisville about the first Instant
in a Small Steam Boat for this Place—and this News kept me
nearly Wild all day, Yet No Boat arrived No Wife No Friend
yet near—

The Weather Beautifull & Warm Dined at Pamars—Drew
a good Deal, Visited Basterop—Joseph hunting all day with
Young Dimitry, killed Nothing—Swallows Very plenty and as
gay as could be—Saw Some Common Gull, but Not a *Fish
Crow* come yet = Mr Bermudas Visited Me a Short time this
Evening—The Nearer the Moment that I Expect to see My
Beloved Lucy Approaches the greater My Impatience, my dis-
apointment Dayly When evening draws on—

Monday 12th 1821

Began Given Lesson to Miss Delafosse and Miss   at 2 Dollars per hour for both—

Gave My Lecon also at Mrs Brand—

Saw Eliza Throgmorton there—

Weather Beautifull but *No Ducks*—Drew a good Deal—
Dined at Pamar—had a Conversation Mr John Clay Respecting M^r P = Mr Bermudas brought Me a *Green Winged* Teal
as a great Rarity—No News from My Wife yet—

—Tuesday 13th—

Gave Leçons at Mrs Brand but Miss Lafosse Wishes only to receive them 3 times per Week—Drew a Wild Goose Not represented by Willson—Weather quite Cool—Very Busy all day—(The white fronted)

Wednesday New Orleans November 14th 1821

Wednesday—gave my Lecons at Mrs Brand's and Miss Delafosse's =

Work Constantly the whole day—Drew a female of the *White Nun or Smew* Merganser—

Weather Rainy & Raw—

Dined on Bread & Cheese—

Rec[d] a Letter from M[rs] A. the purport of Which Lower My Spirits very Considerably—alas were does Comfort keep herself now; retired certainly on a Desolate Rock unwilling to Cast even a Look on our Wretched Species—

M[r] E. Fiske formerly our Agent in this City presented Me this Morning with a Bill of Fellows & Rugles—I Spoke to him on that Subject in Terms that astonished him, but My determination is bent and I Shall Philosophise Now on all things—

Little Expectations of Seing My family before the Latter Part of Winter—

—Thursday 15th—

gave Lesson at M[rs] Brand's—

Drew Closely all day finishing 3 Drawings of Birds and Continued after sun Set by Candle light untill 10 at Vanderlyn's Head—

Weather fair but Cool—Very Low of Spirits

Wished myself off this Miserable Stage—

—16th—

Friday—

Gave Lesson to M[rs] Brand—but Miss Delafosse Was unwell and Postponed taking untill tomorow—Sent a Bill to D[r]

Heermann—it was accepted and Promised Joseph Payment for Next Week—

—17th—
Saturday—
Gave Lessons, at Mrs Brands & Miss Delafosse also—her Mother Knew My father—Drew Much to day and Late this Evening—

November Sunday 18th 1821.
Drawing all day; Dined at Mr Pamar—Rec^d a Visit of Philip Guesnon—also one from the famous Hunter Louis Adams Who however had No Knowledge of the Small Merganzer I had drawn.

—19th—
Monday   Gave Lessons at Mrs Brands and Miss Dellfosse—these Latters have Concluded to have one every day Much to My satisfaction—Needing this acumulation of Income very Much—
   Draw a Black Bellied Darter Male a Superb Specimen—
   Was Visited by Mr Hawkins, an agreable Man Possessing Taste, Information & Judgment—

—20th—
Tuesday =
Gave Lessons at Mrs Brand & Miss Dellfosse
   Drew Much and finished both My Black Bellied Darter and the Vanderlyn's Head—
   Shabbyly used by Dr Heermann—Who refused Paying My Well earned Bill—Visited by My good acquaintance Pamar—
   Basterop the Painter = Much Talk With My good Hunter Gilbert Who Procured Me a Superb Specimen of the *Great Sand Hill Crane*—
   Sufering Much from Sore Eyes and Violent Headache the Whole Day—

—Wednesday 21ˢᵗ—
Gave Lessons at Mʳˢ Brand, & Miss Delfose—Drawing all Day
at My Whooping Crane—
    Weather Extremely Sultry—

November Thursday 22ᵈ 1821
Gave Lessons at Mʳˢ Brand =
    My fair Pupill Miss Delfosse engaged otherwise =
    Recᵈ 40$ on a/c from Mʳ Hawkins who appeared to be
Much Pleased with the Drawing I give him of *Arianne* =
Weather Summer Heat—Swallows Plenty = Recᵈ a Letter
from My Wife, my Spirits yet very Low—Drew Much to
day—received 100$ from Mʳ Forestal as Mʳ Gordon had Not
paid any Money to My Wife at Louisville =

—23ᵈ—
Friday—Gave my Lessons to Mʳˢ Brand and Miss Dellfosse—
Rainy and Warm—drawing all day—bought a Portfollio from
Vigny—for 8$.

—24ᵗʰ—
Gave my Lessons at Mʳˢ Brand and Miss Dellfosse and also at
Pamar to his Daughter who exibited the brightest Genius I
believe I ever Met With.—Miss Dellfosse beautifull and extremely agreable =
    Wrote to My Wife and Wᵃᵐ Bakewell and forwarded to
each a Check on the U. S. Bank of Philadelphia Procured by
Mʳ Bermudas for me and for Which I Paid one per Cent—of
100$—Weather extremely Changed Cold and Windy—

—25ᵗʰ—
Sunday—
Weather Very Cold and raw—Gave Two lessons of Drawing
to Euphemie Pamar =

—26—

Gave My lessons to Mrs Brand. Miss Dellfosse and Euphemie Pamar—Weather rather Milder   Swallows plenty—Ship Fulton arrived   120 Passenger on Board—

November Tuesday 27th 1821.

Gave My lessons at Both Places—

Visited the Maire's Lady Mrs Rofignac Who had evinced a desire to see some of My Pencils Productions—Expect her Daughter for a Pupil   Weather Charming—Drew 2 Ducks. Called by Willson the *Tufted Ducks* Male & female, the Clerk of the Steam Boat Ramapo Called on us   Mr *Laurent* an agreable Man—

—28th—

Wednesday   Gave My lessons at Both Houses   Weather fine Rec^d a Visit from Mr Brand & his Lady = Basterop Not Much Pleased at this; Drew a good deal

—29th—

Thursday—Gave Lessons to Mrs Brand's only   Rec^d a Letter from My Wife of an older date than the former one—Weather beautifull—Painted Joseph Likeness—

—30th—

Friday   Gave My Lessons to Mrs Brand's and at Miss Dellfosse =

New Orleans Decr 1st 1821

Saturday   Gave My Lessons to both houses and Miss Pamar—
Rec^d a Letter from My Beloved Wife—
Expect her in a few Days—
U. S. Steam Boat arrived—
weather uncommonly pleasant
Rec^d this Evening a Non Descript Hawk—

Sunday 2^{d}

Gave 2 Lessons to Euphemie Pamar and one to Miss Dellfosse *only*—Weather beautifull finished My Drawing of the *Crested Hawk* Which proved a female with Many Minute Eggs   how Rare this bird is I need Not Say being the only Specimen I Ever have Met with—although I once before found some Tail feathers of another killed by a Squatter on the Ohio—Which Tail feathers having kept—Corespond exactly With those of the present bird—

Regret Much that I Cannot Save the Skin but the Weather being Warm and My Drawing having taken Nearly Two Days it was not possible to Skin it—

—Monday 3^{d}—

Gave Lesson to E. Pamar. at Mrs Brand and Miss Delfosse = saw Mr Wheeler who arrived this day—how Little I Expected to have Ever Met with him—Weather quite Warm—

—Tuesday 4—

Gave Lessons to Mrs Brand and Miss Delfosse also   Rec^{d} 40$ from the former and paid the rent of the house in Dauphine Street   Weather very Warm   drew an American Bitern—

New Orleans Decemb^{r} 5th 1821.

½ quire of Paper to Miss Josephine =

Wednesday—Gave Lessons at Mrs Brands and Miss Delfosse Weather Cool and Rainy—

Visited Basterop and Was Introduced to Mr Sell another of the Trade = another day of Disapointment My Lucy Not arrived—

—6—

Thursday   Begun taking & Giving Lesson to Mr Lombar Gave my lessons at Mrs Brand and today Miss Delfosse—Mrs Pirrie Arrived to Day

—7th—

Friday Gave Lessons at Mrs Brand's & Miss Delfosse—Mr Lombar Give Me Lesson on the Violin & I to his Son of Drawing in Exchange—
Rainy & Cold all day—

—8th—

Saturday—Gave Lessons at Mrs Brand's and gave her 1 doz^e Black Chalks Making 1½ 6 Pencil handles—at Miss Delfosse and Miss Pamar—at night Music & Drawing With young Lombard—had the Pleasure of Seing Mrs *Harwood* from London and Rec^d by her My Bitch *Belle*—Weather Rain & Cloudy—

—9th—

Sunday Weather Extremely Desagreable the Steam Boat Hero arrived from Louisville but No Regular Information about My familly by it = Gave 2 Lessons at Mrs Pamar where I Spent the greater part of the Day =
Young Lombar Drawing at my House the whole Day—

—10th—

Gave Lessons 2 to Miss Pamar, Mrs Brand's house and Miss Delfosse—Received a Visit from Mr Selle & Mr Jany Painters—

New Orleans Decr 11th Tuesday 1821.

I have but little time to spare at present to write the Many Incidents connected with the Life I am forced to follow for My Maintainance and of Course hundreds of them are passed and forgotten although I am well assured that a Rearsal would at future periods amuse My thoughts. *One* however so curious appeared Me this day that I Cannot let it escape—May you My Dear Sons reap some benefit from the details
I am a Teacher of Drawing and have some Pupils My Style of giving Lessons and the high rate I charge for My

Tuition have procured Me the Ill will of Every other Artist in the City who Knows me or has heard of my Maxims—I Called on a *Bastard of Apollon* this Day to see *his Labours* I was unknown, tolerably well received and had the Pleasure of Seing the *Annimal in* Action—I also heard *his Barkings* and saw his Eyes gladening at the Sight produced on the canvass before them—a Third unfortunate Dauber came in, who it appeared Was an old acquaintance that Criticised at once with ease on all that Was around us—as Every day arrivals by Sea and Land bring New hands to the bellows the Names of Many Were Called forth and Mine amongst them—I kept Myself Waited & the following Picture was given Me Without any Varnishings I assure You—"That Man Came No one Knows from Whence—he goes throu the Streets Like the Devil I am told that he has as Many Pupils as he Wishes for and Makes a Wonderfull quantity of What he Calls Portraits and Assures the good folks who employ him that in a few Months by his Method any One May become able Painter— and Yet from What I am told the Man Never Drew has bought a set of handsome Drawings of Beasts Birds Flowers &ᶜ Which he Shews and Says are his own—all this a Lye and take in While I Who Was Naturally Intended to Paint Teach &ᶜ am Without a Pupil or Portrait!"—

here I took My Hat told the Gentleman where I resided and that I Would be happy to See him giving him the Initials of My Name only for a Guide = from this Eloquent Member of the *Sans Culottes of the Trade*, I moved pretty briskly to Mʳ Basterop's Room were in few Minutes I had the Satisfaction of Seing Messʳˢ. selle & Janin—all artists and agreable Men, Not Well setled about the a/c of Myself I had so Lately heard but thinking how Strangely the good Man Will feel When *he* Calls on Me—if ever he does =

I Gave My lessons first to Miss Pamar—Mʳˢ Brands at Miss Dellfosse and then according to Promess Went to a *Pension-nat* (were My Young Friend Miss Pamar receives the *Larger* portion of her Education) to give her regular Lessons of Drawing = When I Entered the Room, I saw a Degree of Coolness in the Appearance of the *Lady* of the Institution that along with My unfortunate or foolish Natural awkwardness in similar Cases rendered My stay extremely desagreable; My Pupil who is generally Lively and full of Confidence in her actions Was at this time so astonishingly astray from Her Work that not a line was properly Copied—I perceived the sarcastic Looks of the Diferent Teachers who Were present going the round and Was highly relieved When the Clock struck My Departure—

a few Expressions uttered on my Entering, Joined to a few that reach[d] My Ears (that burnt all this while) as I was Making My Escape Made Me take the resolution Never again to trespass on that Threshold or any other Without first knowing Well how it May agree with the Will of the first Caracters attached to them—

My Lovely Miss Pirrie of oackley Passed by Me this Morning, but did not remember how beautifull I had rendered her face once by Painting it at her Request with Pastelles; She knew not the Man who with the utmost patience and in fact attention *waitted* on her Motions to please her—but thanks to My humble talents I can run the gantlet throu this world without her help—

—Wednesday 12th—

Gave Lessons at M[rs] Brands—Miss Delfosse absent to day— gave Lesson also to E. Pamar   having taken all in Consideration I put aside the Shadow and hang to the bone—and with a *White Lye* arranged the Matter quite Well with M[rs] Pamar to Whom I had said that I Should Not return there any More =

December Thursday 13th 1821.

Gave Lessons at M[rs] Brand's and E. Pamar Miss Dellfosse finding the Weather Too Cold—So anxious am I during the Whole of My present days to see My familly that My head is scarce at right With My Movements and yet I Must feel My sad Disapointments and retire to rest without the comfort of her so much Wanted Company—

I saw to day a Work on Natural History with Colord Plates rather better than usual

—14—

Friday   Gave Lessons to all this afternoon—but Miss Delfosse appeared dejected and Work but Indiferently—

It is Now 26 days since the Last Letter I have from my Wife
is dated, Three Steam Boats have arrived since from Louisville
and No News of her departure have reached Me—My anxiety
renders every Moment painfull and Irksome—

I Met quite unexpectedly My Pupil Miss Pirrie at M^{rs}
Brand, the interview was Short more friendly than I expected
and We parted as if We Might see each others again With
some Pleasure at some future Period—

—15th—

Saturday   Gave My Lessons to All this afternoon   Weather
Cool & Clear; feeling much relieved from My Anxiety about
My familly having heard that the Steam Boat the Rocket by
Which they are to Come, had not Left on the 28th ultimo and
that Probably they would Not Arrive for 4 or 5 Days yet—M^r
Jany Visited us this Evening and Stayd Very Late—

December 16th 1821

Sunday—Gave 2 Lessons to E. Pamar & 2 to Miss Dellfosse
only—Weather fine but Cool   begun Drawing a Young
Swan Sent me by My Hunter Gilbert from Barataria—

Young Lombar at Work all Day in My Room Drawing—

—17—

Monday   Gave My Lessons all round—I Drew at My *Swan*
Mr Jarviss paid me a Visit and I returned it imediatly—Gave
him 3 pieces of Canvas—Weather very Dark & Rainy

—18th—

Tuesday—Gave a Lesson to Miss Pamar and One to M^{rs}
Brand—My Wife & My Two sons arived at 12 'o'clock all in
good health—I took them to Mr Pamar Where We all dined
and then Moved to our Lodgings in Dauphine Street   after

14 Months absence the Meeting of all that renders Life agre-able to Me, was gratefully Wellcome and I thanked My Maker for this Mark of Mercy—

—19th—

Wednesday   I only gave Lesson to Mrs Brand having Much to do arranging My familly—Examined My Drawings & found them not so good as I Expected them to be; When Compared with those Drawn since Last Winter = Bona-parte's Service Was performed this Day here—

—20th—

Thursday—Gave My Lessons all round—Weather Extremely Warm—Rec^d a *Nondescript Rail*

—21st—

Friday   Gave Lessons at Mrs Brand's & Miss Delfosse but so Wet and Damp that I Declined going to see E. Pamar—Drew a Streaked Rail—

New Orleans December 22^d 1821.

Saturday—Gave my Lessons all round—Weather very De-sagreable—Rec^d 20$ on a/c from R. Pamar = Young Lom-bar Resumed his Lessons this Evening having Missed Coming Whilst I was arranging My familly at home—

—23^d—

Sunday   Gave 2 Lessons to E. Pamar and 1 to Miss Delfosse—Weather Extremely Cold, having some Ice this Morning, Nearly one Inch Thick—

—24—

Monday   Gave a Lessons to E. Pamar Young Brand and 2 to Miss Delfosse =

Weather very Cold—Mr Rozier Came to Pay us a Visit—it is Eleven Years since he, I, and My familly, Were all together =

—25—

Tuesday—Gave 2 Lessons to Miss Delfosse but not any were else—

Snowed from Day Light untill Twelve o'clock and afterwards frose hard—

—26—

Wednesday—Gave 2 Lessons to Miss Delfosse and 1 to Miss Pamar—

Mr Gordon Visited us this Morning and Mr Colas the Miniature Painter this Evening to see My Birds—

—27th—

Thursday—Gave 2 Lessons to E. Pamar 2 to Miss Delfosse and One at Mrs Brands—Weather beautiful   Paid our Rent this morning—

—28th—

Friday   Gave My Lessons all round 2 to Miss D.

—29th—

Saturday   Gave My Lessons all round—

Decr Sunday—30th 1821

Gave 1 Lesson to E. Pamar and 1 to Miss Delfosse—Mr Pamar Dined with us—I Drew this Day a Ferruginous Thrush and am to Draw 99 Birds in that Number of Days for Which I am to Pay One Dollar for each to *Robert* the Hunter—Who is to furnish Me With one hundred Specimen of Diferent kinds Should he Not fulfill the Contracts, he is to have only 50^{cts} for each furnished.

—31—

Monday—Gave 2 Lesson to Miss Pamar 1 At Mrs Brand and 1 at Miss Delfosse & Drew an *Ampellis Americana*

Descriptions of the Water Birds of the United States, with their Generic characters—according to the arrangement of Latham—as Described by Alexander Willson—the Species discovered by Myself are Marked with My Initials—

Spoon Bill

Bill Long, thin, the tip dilated, Orbicular, flat, Nostrils Small, placed near the base of the Bill, tongue Short, pointed; feet four toed, Semipalmate.

Roseate Spoonbill, Platalea Ajaja. 7. 123—

La Spatule couleur de Rose de Brisson—1 sent Willson from Natchez, Measured 2 feet $^6/_{12}$ and 4 feet in extent, Bill 6½ Inches Long from the Corner of the Mouth 7 from its upper base, 2 Inches its greatest Width ¾ Inch Narowest place— ½. Black covered with Scaly protuberances like the edge of Oister Shells—waitish Stained with red—Nostrils oblong in the Midle of the upper Mandible—a deep groove runs along the Mandible about ¼ Inch from the edge—Crown & Chin bare covered with a greenish Skin; that below the Lower Mandible dilatable as in Pelicans—orange round the eye, Irides blood red; cheeks & hind head bare black Skin; Neck Long covered with Short White fathers, tipt on the Neck with Crimson; breast White its Sides burnt brown Color, a Long tuft of hair Like plumage proceeds from the breast pale rose Color   back White Slightly tinged with brownish, Wings pale rose Color, Shafts of Same Lake; Shoulders of the Wings covered with Long hairy plumage deep & Splendid Carmine; upper & Lower tail Coverts Same; belly rosy; rump paler; tail equal at the end   12   bright brownish orange feathers, Skalp redish; Legs and Naked part of the thigh dark dirty red; feet ½ Webbed—toes Very Long particularly hind one, inside of the Wing richer than Outside—

List of the Water Birds of North America taken from Turton's Linne—

American Avoset, head, Neck & Breast rufous—Bill Black, Legs pale blue—

———

Blue Crane, Head, & Neck dark purple—3 Long, narrow pendant feathers 6 Inches beyond Eye—Length—23 Inches extent 3 feet—

———

Snowy Heron—2½₂ feet—extent 3⅔₂—orange Yellow round the Eye—Irids vivid Orange—Whole plumage White—(Head Largely Crested—4 Inches) breast D° upper back feathers recumbent and Loose—

———

Night Heron, Bill Blk 4¼ Inch, Skin about eye Blue, Irids red, Cap^d deep Blue—3 White feathers Issuing—Back deep blue—Vent & belly White, Legs & feet Light Buff—Length, ? 2⁴⁄₁₂—extent 4 feet—

———

Great White Heron Bill yellow, Legs & feet claws Blk—Whole body White, Back feathers falling far over tail—Length 3 feet 6 to end of tail, 7 or 8 Inches Long to extremities of back feathers—

———

Stormy Petrel—

———

Great Tern, Bill & feet red, Black Cap^d, tail very forked, upper parts, Light Bluish ash—Belly White—

———

Lesser Tern, Bill & Legs Yellow, Blk Cap^d tail very forked—

———

Short tail Tern, Bill & Legs Black, Cap & Cheek Blk, Tail Shorter than Wings—

———

Black Skimmer—

———

Spotted Sand piper; Bartram, Sand Snipe, ring plover, Sanderling plover, Golden P. Kildeer P—

———

Red Breasted Snipe—Long Legged Avoset   Bill Blk Red purpleish red, Eye red, whole upper part, Deep Olive
Solitary Sandpiper, Yellow Shank Snipe—Tell tail D°—

Turn Stone, Bill Black   Leg deep Orange—Breast Side of Neck and Spot under the Eye Black, Much of Brick Color on Wings—belly White—4 Toes—

Ash Colored Sandpiper   Legs dull Yellow   4 Toes

Pure—Bill Black, Legs & feet D°   4 Toes

Black Bellied Plover—4 Toes the Hind one Small and very high

Red Breasted Sandpiper   Bill Short   Vent White, Bill breast and under Neck Deep Rufous—

Esquimaux Corlew—Legs Greenish Blue—4 Toes—

Red Backed Snipe—, Bill Much Curved Blk behind Bend

Semi Palmated Snipe—*have this

Marbled Godwit—Bill Long   rather inclined upwards

Lousianna Heron, Legs Yellow Bill blue—upper head Purpled, Crest White, Back Feathers very Long Light Buff—Tail, Wing & Back Deep Blue—

Picd Oister Catcher—

Hooping Crane—Black Tips—Bill Yellow

Long Bill Curlew, Legs Blewish—

Yellow Crowned Heron   Bill dark Blue, Legs Yellow White Crested Very Long, throat and Head black with an Ovale White Spot—

Great Heron, thighs Deep Rufous, under Crest Long Blk, upper White—Breast, & Back fathers Long & Loose

———

American Bittern, Dirty Yellow Ockre, Zig Zagged with dark Brown—a Black Triangular Line runs from the Mouth to the Back of Neck—

———

Least Bittern—

———

Wood Ibis   Gros becs

———

Scarlet Ibis—

———

Flamingo

———

White Ibis

———

Black Surf Duck Singular Bill—3 White Marks about the head—Legs Red—

———

Buffel Headed Duck—the Spirit—

———

Canada Goose

———

Tufted Duck   Bill Blue—Head neck and breast Blk   a Rufous bend over the Lower part of Neck—

———

Golden Eye Duck

———

Shoveller Duck

———

Goosander, Head Changeable Green

———

Pin Tail Duck   Sprigg Tail

———

Blue Wing^d Teal

———

Snow Goose

———

Pied Duck   Legs & feet Light Ockre, Ring round the Neck

Connected with Back, Back Tail Belly and Line over the Eye Black, primaries also Black, the Remainder White

Red Breasted Merganser—have this

American Widgeon, Bald Pate

Blue Bill—head Neck & Breast Dark Brown—Back Canvassed—Rump Tail & Tail Coverts Blk

Hooded or Crested Merganser—

Long Tail Duck—Old Wife—

Summer Duck

Green Winged Teal

Canvas Back Duck

Red Headed Duck—Head and neck half Way—Bright Rufous —Lower part of Neck & breast Blk Back Canvassed—

Malard

Cadwall Duck

Eider Duck   Male & femelle—

the Smew, the Black Spectacled Goosander

Ruddy Duck, Blue Bill, Legs Rosy—upper head Black, Neck & whole upper part Brick Color—Cheeks, chin, & Side of Head White—
    femelle Dark Olive all upper Part—sides of Head Dusty Yellow—Breast transversally Barred with Brick Colored Lines—Belly & Vent dirty Yellow =

Brant

Scotter Duck   Wholy Black, upper Mandible Yellow, Lower
& Nails Blk—Protuberances Red—Legs Red—

Velvet Duck—have it   Large Blk Sea Duck

Harlequin Duck   a Narrow regular White ring around the
Lower part of Neck—

Black Duck   Dusky Duck

Marsh Tern   Black Cap^d Wings, Back & Tail Light Ash or
Blue—the first Very Long the Latter Slightly forked—Legs &
palmate feet Lead—

Sooty Tern—Bill Black, front and whole under part White,
upper Blk tail Much forked, the Tips White edged inwardly
with Blk—

the 9th Volume I believe Contains—the Loon = Purple
Gallinule = Coot = Darter = Black Headed Gull = Great
Footed hawk &^{c} =

Copy of a Letter Written to the Honorable Henry Clay
Speaker of the House of Representatives Lexington Kentucky—

Sir

After having spent the greater part of Fifteen Years in
procuring and Drawing the Birds of the United States
with a view of Publishing them I find Myself possessed
of a Large Number of Such Specimen as usually resort
to the Midle States only. having a desire to complete the
Collection before I present it to My Country in perfect
order, I intend to Explore the Territories Southwest of
the Mississipi.

I shall leave this place about the Midle of Sepr for the
purpose of Visiting the Red River, Arkansas and the
Countries adjacent, and Well aware of the good Recep-

tion that a few lines from one on whom our Country looks up with respectfull Admiration, would procure me, I have taken the liberty of requesting Such Introductory Aid, as you, May deem Necessary to a Naturalist, While at the Frontier forts and Agencies of the United States

I Remain
Respectfully
Your Ob' Servt
J. J. A.

Cincinnati *Ohio. Augt 12th 1820*

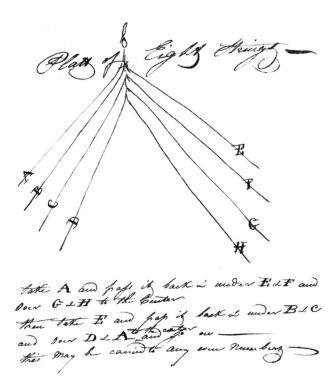

Plait of Eight Strings—

take A and pass it back & under E & F and
over G & H to the Center
then take E and pass it back under B & C
and over D & A to the center and so on—
this may be carried to any even Numbers—
(Houghton Library, Harvard University)

FROM

1826 JOURNAL

1826 Journal

July 9th 1826. at Sea—
My leaving the U. S. had for some time the Appearance and feelings of a Dream—I could scarce make up My Mind fixedly on the Subject—I thought continually that I still saw My Beloved Friend, and My Dear Children. I still believed when every Morning I awak^d that the land of America Was beneath me, that I would in a Moment throw myself in her Shady Woods, and watch for, and lessen, to the Voice of her many Lovely Warblers. but now that I have positively been at Sea since *51 days* Tossing to and fro, without the sight nor the touch of those objects so Dear to me, I feel fully convinced, and Look forward with an Anxiety that I do not believe ever rufled my Mind before; when I calculate that Not Less than 4 Months, (the third of a Year) must elapse, before My Friend & Children can receive any tidings of my Arrival on the Distant Shores that now soon will divide us = When I think that Many more Months must run from the Life's Sand Glass alotted to my existence, and that the time of my returning to my Country, & Friends is yet an unfolded and unknown event; My body & face feels a Sudden Glow of aprehension that I neither can describe or represent = I know only the acuteness of the feelings that act through My whole frame Like an Ellectric Shock, I Imediately feel chilled and sullenly throw my body on My Matrass and Cast My Eyes towards the asure Canopy of Heaven scarce able to hold the Tears from flowing—

Our 4th of July was passed Near the Grand Banks; how diferently from My Last, and how diferently from any that I can recollect ever having spent—The weather was Thick foggy and as Dull as myself, Not a sound of rejoicing did reach my ear, Not once did I hear the sublime "Hail Columbia happy Land" No Nothing, perhaps nothing could have so forcibly awakened me from My Dozing situation than this Like of a Pleasure so powerfully felt by me when at Home—it was then that I suddenly arose from my Lethargy and remarked the reality of My absence and present situation.

The day passed as I conceive One spent by a General who has Lost a Great advantage over an Ennemy, I complained of my-self, I attributed all my disapointment to my want of fore-sight, but I complained to No one Else   I felt Sorrowful in the extreme as if america had Lost much this day—My Compagnon passengers, Lay strewed about the Deck and on the Cotton Bales, basking like Crocodiles during all the Intervals granted to the Sun to peep at them through the Smoacky heaziness that accompanied us—yet the Breeze was strong, the Waves moved Majestically and Thousands of Large Petrells displayed their elegant aerial Movements to Me—how much I envied their power of Flight to enable me to be here, there, and all over the Globe comparatively Speaking in a Moment—throwing themselves Edgeways against the Brese as if a well sharpen^d arrow sent with the Strength and grace of One Issuing from the Bow of an Appollo—

I had remarked a singular Increase in the number of these Petrels ever since the capes of Florida, but here they were so numerous & for part of a Day flew in Such succession to-wards the West & South west that I Concluded they were Migrating to some well Known Shore to deposit their Eggs or perhaps Leading their Young—these very seldom alighted, they were full the size of a common Gull and, as they flew they shewed in quick Alternativeness The whole upper or un-der parts of their body—sometimes skimming Low, at other forming Imense curves, then Dashing along the deep troughs of the Sea, going round our Vessel (allways out of Gun Shot reach) as if She had been at Anchor—their Lower parts are White, a broad white patch on the rump; the head Apparently all White, & the upper parts of the Body, & Wings above, sooty Brown—I would conceive that one of these petrels fly over as Much Distance in one hour as the little black petrels in our Wake do in 12—

since we have left the Neighbourhood of the Banks these birds have gradually disapeared, and Now in Latitude 44.53— I see none—Our sailors and Captain speak of them as Companions in storms as much as the little relations the Mother Carey's Chickens—

as sudenly as if We had Just Turned the summit of a

Mountain Deviding a Country south of the Equator from Iceland, the Weather Altered in the present Latitude & Longitude My Light Summer Clothing, Was Not suficient, Indeed a Cloth Coat felt Light & Scanty, and the Dews that fell during the Night rendered the Deck were I allways slept too damp now to be comfortable = This however of Two evils I prefer^d for I could not withstand the More desagreable Odor of the Cabin, Where Now, the captain, officers & Mr Swift eat their Meals Daily =

setting during the day as I am Now, with my poor Book in My Lap on a Parcel of Coiled Cables Near the helm's Man, (who bye the Bye Gazes at Me as much as he Looks at his Compass) I Spend Nearly all My Time, part of it reading; thoughtlessly leaning over the railing, Looking on the noisy braking waves that urge us on, and again thinking of America as the sun to our eyes towards her reposing place declines I am forced To make a better choice of Situation and perhaps Will go and Lie on the Starboard Side of the Long Boat, where Our Cook, ready at trying to Please Will talk to me untill wearied of this from the Spot I remove again = Night gradually brings on the *Wish to repose in Sleep* when after a few Stories told, each gradually leaves the Spot and goes and lays down, either in his Hamock, his Birth or the Harder Chicken Coop, that Line both Sides of our Compagnon Way—

here the days have Increased astonishingly at Nine o'clock I Can easily read Large print the day opens at 2, and 25 Minutes after 4 Phoebus enlivens the Globe and promises a fair, prosperous sixteen hours.—

Our unconcerned, Happy mariners, set to their daily Labor at 6 of the Morn and chearly spend the day, Improving the appearance of all about our Ship, rendering her the more secure all this while—their Joviality, their Industry, their Witticisms, would enable probably any other than a Friend away from his Friend to pass the Time away—

I have told you that I sat frequently on a parcel of Coiled Cables, but you are still Ignorant, that since I Left New Orleans I have sheared My Beard but once—that It now profusedly expands from each ear out, and from out My Chin and neck around like a Crowd of Stifen^d Bristles which, along with the Tawny acquired hue of My Skin since On Board of this floating Prison renders Me as unlike the Daughter of Titian as Satan is to God—

We had for several days a stiff propitious Breese that Wafted us over the Briny deep at full Nine Miles per hour, this was congenial to My Wishes, but not to my feelings; the vessel felt the motion before me and Chifted My Body too soon or unwarily; Caused me Violent head aches far more distresfull than any sea sick feeling ever experienced—during this Period I found food Highly season^d and spirituous Liquors of great benefit—

here, for the 3^d or 4th time I read of Thomson's the 4 seasons and I believe enjoyed them better than ever when I came to his Castle of Indolence, I felt the all powerfull extent of his Genius operating on Me as a Cathartic swallowed when well aware that My Body was not in a fit condition (through situation) to be benefited by it—

as we drew Nearer the Shores of the far-famed Spot, even the Clouds seem^d to prefer a diference of consistancy and Shapes; No Longer did the Vivifying Orb, settle with her globular shape all fiery beyond the deep, it Shewed dull, pale, sickly, and as if sorry that *through diferences that for ever must exist* the light refulgent was not to be extended over the Globe untill the Omnipotent God had granted to each of all its portions that real sense of freedom that now better felt in the Western Hemisphere = here foggs succeeded foggs; the Englishmen on Board pronounced it, *Clear weather of England*, but I Named it the Blasting atmosphere of Comfort—

I would continue now but the dampness is So powerfull although the Sun Still Straks through the haze, that My Paper is Damp and receives the Ink quite too finely. Dear Friend Adieu.

    *   *   *

At Sea July 1826.

Our Captain is again Turning; we have a Brigg in sight and not very far—but we have not the Land in sight: no! and God knows when we will have it

My time is really dull not a Book on Board that I have not read Twice since here (I mean on Board this Ship) and I believe Twice before—thought as I said yesterday of Every thing

I can well remember throw the Mist of Times and feel as Dull as ever = I move from the Deck here; from here to the deck; lay there a little, and down here longer: it is all a Like; dull, uncomfortable: nay: was it uncomfortable only, I do not believe I would Complain, but it is all Iddle time I spend here; all dreary, Iddle time: the most misirable. pitifull. sinfull way of Spending even One moment—

I have this very Instant Cut the quill afresh; Now Much could be said about this goose quill; but I will not pretend to Philosophize on a goose quill—I would rather weigh the Pros & Cons of the all Genus Anas—yet who Knows but that single quill, Now cut and Sharpen^d, to a very acutte Angle, did; or did not, belong to The offspring of an Egg laid as Near the North Poles, as Geese Dare go—I can safely say that John Hotchkiss (a handsome youth) of the Firm of Hotchkiss & Co of New Orleans, and I believe of New York, and I believe by birth of New England: sold me this very quill for 4 cents Lawfull money of the U. States—more or Less &^{c}, &^{c}: Now do not think all at once, that I am Merry because we are Nearing Land—No by Heavens!! Never in my life would I feel Less concerned about Land than I do Now, did not My Knees ache so dreadfully—and did I Not Long as much as I do for a Large Bowl of Milk and a full pound of fresh bread = ah yes, even such Loaf as our Franklin devoured in our Philadelphia Market, When somewhat in My Situation—for if I have not ran off from My Mother & friends: I am sure, I have from the Country that has nourished Me and brought me up with all these feelings I now possess = What was I writing about when this soliloquy was begun—Let me think—I began about a quill and—this very quill reminded me that I saw a few Minutes since when I ran on Deck for the purpose of disposing of a certain portion of —— a Bird that allways resides Near soundings; it looked Like a small Merganser Birds that you well know are used to diving—the 1st Mate Call^d it a Mure!!! Lineus never described this Bird. neither have I; nor any of my Precedents: Not Even the very highly, Celebrated and most Conspicuous Mr Ord of the City of Philadelphia state of Pennsylvania: Member of all the societies of &^{c} &^{c} &^{c}—he perfect *Academician*, that Laughed *because* a Turkey could Swim!—

Now where the devil are you running To, Audubon?—running—why—Towards the shores of that England that Gave
Birth to a Milton!! to a Shakespeare!!—To a Driden—that
raised West: that Enabled Thomson to prove his Merits =
that Called Goldsmith by a well deserved Name—where
Johnson flourish^d—that gazed on the penciled productions of
Hogarth!—with admiration laughed with Smollet—Might
have cried with Young—was delighted of LATE with Scott and
shed Tears for her Byron—

Oh England! renowned Isle! how Shall I Enter thee? Good
God? what have I pronounced—I am fit to enter her dominions at all? My Heart swells. The Bird seazed when sitting on
her Nest could not be more terrified—I Look up: Yes, for
Mercy—I Look up; and Yet, how much I dread! how far I
would thus have gone, When Captn Hatch call^d out and said
the Brigg Homer was Close to us—The preliminary greet-
tings of "Brig oh! and Ship I!" were returned—Where
from, whence came you? &^c &^c had being all Interchanged
with a few hundred of &^c besides. I reach the rail way and saw
the brig *Homer*, which was 26 days less from New Orleans,
than we are a—(a mere Moment in the Life of Man and
scarce an Atom in eternal Calculations) *She Looked well* although her sails were packed with Russia Duck to save Duty
on Importation   ah England? is it possible that thou shouldst
be untroubled by thy own sons? I can scarce believe it—thy
hoary head used and *connected* with all Kinds of Tricks, ought
not to suffer this.—Now again, what strange itching will prevail and Lead a poor Devil to Think on matters entirely unconnected with him—It is almost Dark. I will drink The
residue of my Glass and Write Perhaps again Tomorrow.—

The Word *perhaps* brings *a thousand and one* recollections
to Mind = I recollect Just now that when I first I knew thee,
Dearest Friend: Frequently I was asked if this *Passion* of mine
would be of Lasting Duration—help, I am now Entering on
a Sacred Subject = husband, Shut thy Book, pray =

Liverpool July 25th 1826

Burst My Brains: Burst My coarse scull, and give the whole of
Your slender powers to enable me to describe My feelings this

day?—I must begin slow gradually Warm my powers, and—
oh poor head; never can I Express threw thee the extent of all
I saw in the Beautifull Picture surveyed during an—"Stop,—
take time—consider and proceed gradually. No rashness—recollect thou art now going to attempt a very dificult Task—I
advise thee waite".—

My Beloved Friend I will follow thee. yes, threw Worlds of
Futurity, as well and receive thy affectionate advises with
Loyal pleasure!!!—

I waited full dressed nearly 15 minutes before the sweet lark
(My reveille Matin) had turn^d his head from its soft pillow towards the Orb of Appolo.—I waitd anxiously.—I felt gay
and—no. not Happy, but the sweet Jingling Melody of the
Lark help^d my Spirits much = Mr Swift raised and dress^d in a
moment and the Black Chalk once more Touched the paper
to Animate it.—ah yes, I have drawn in England! Ah, how
much I have drawn in My America!!—

I finished early so much so indeed, that when seven Struck
my ear from the clock, we where on the pavement bound toward the West to Near thee a Step—Naked streets look dull—
we soon returned and eat a beneficial repast—Isued again
and—My Dear Lucy I bought a beautifull Watch for thee
from Mr Roschel's & Son Church street and One Also for Me
from the same polite Gentleman—Ten of the morning was
positively past and I positively felt much ashamed when after
reaching Dale Street where are our Lodgings, that a Note
from Mr Rathbone had been there sometime waiting for me.
A hackney coach was produced in a Moment I entered it
with my Port Folio N° 2, and ordered quickly for Duke
Street. They were gone to Mrs Rathbone's Mother—I enquired the way but before My sentence Was finished; I saw
Their carriage Turning back making for me—and I had Once
More the pleasure of being near These Kind persons—their
Youngest sweet little son Basil look^d at me and I wished
him—well—Mr James Pyke was Introduced to me—we proceeded slowly and I thought of My situation—in England, in
the carriage of a man Generous, and Noble of heart. dressed
(although perhaps Queerly to him) very diferently to my
Indian Guarb—Gun cocked dashing threw the deep swamps
of Lower Louisiana after the Wood Ibises in company of my

good Friend Bourgeat.—The country open^d to our View gradually, and after having passed under a cool Harbour of English Trees, I entered the habitation of—Philemon & Baucis!!! yes a Venerable Happy paire received their Children with Kisses all Kindness, and bid me well come and with natural ease that I thought had deserted this hearth with the Golden age =

I felt painfully awkward (as I allways do in new company) for a while. but so much truth was about me that I became calmer and—the good Venerable Couple walked me round a Garden transplanted from abroad, and—my Port Folio was Opened in the presence of several females and a younger Rathbone—now I am allways in too great a Haste—I saw as I entered this happy dwelling a Beautifull Collection of the Birds of England well prepared. Yes well prepared.—what sensations I had whilst I help^d to untie the fastening of My Folio Book. I knew by all around me that All was full of best Taste and strong Judgment, but I did not know if I would at all please—a Small book was open^d I was panting like the wing^d pheasant he dreads the well taught Friend of Man, that may perhaps prove him too weak, to proceed in full sight of his learned Eye—

Ah Lucy these kind *Friends* praised *my Birds*, and I felt the praise—yes breathed as if some Celestial being fanned me in Elysium—

Praises are of many Kinds, but Kindly praises are true and these *good friends* praised me Kindly!!!—

Farewell, venerable double one. ah yes you will, must farewell in the Heavenly Gardens above.—

Tender embraces were again Interchanged—I again was held by those sacred hands again in the seat next R^d Rathbone and moved threw the avenue by the same way to Liverpool again—

I am now Leaping out of the Carriage I have bid farewell to all My Friends and—Lucy. R^d Rathbone Steped towards me and in a low tone said Mr Audubon the coachman has been satisfied. —my blood ran high then cold—I felt and— Too much abashed then My self in the Vehicle that brought me to Dale Street again—could such incidents ever be forgotten?—

No. give my Life the lasting solidity of the adamante, and the Deep Touches of the Keenest Graver will be effaced sooner from the Rock than from my Heart.—

The good American Consul had Called on Me—I must thank him tomorrow—

The reverend W. Goddard with the Rector of Liverpool and several Ladies called on me and saw some Drawings—all praised them—

oh what can I Hope?—

Beloved Wife Good night—

An Orange Woman.

Shall I describe her—

She sells sweets during day and Poisons at night—

My Cards—

Call^d on Mr Maury—

Liverpool England July 31st 1826.

This day, Lucy was one of Trial to me, believe thy Friend.—This Was Monday, and it was appointed to exhibit partially my Collection to the Public and my kind Liverpool Friends—

at 9 this morning I was quite Busy—Arranging and disposing in sets my Drawings to be fairly inspected by the Public—the Connaisseurs—the Critics = this last word has something very savage in its nature as well as in its orthography or its pronunciation—I know not why—yet I know that I dread the very cast, askance, of a Single eye of those dangerous personnages of whom I have so much heard of, but whom fortunately thus far, I have only met in scanty forms—and of Little value.—

I drew my New Watch and by its regular movements in 5 Minutes it proved to be at the Meridian—The Door of the Royal Institution were thrown open and the Ladies flocked in, I however saw but one Mrs R. There I was—all in view of the World—how many glances to meet—questions to Answer and repeat = *"ha, that's Beautifull"*. again and again repeated made me wish to be in the Forests of america to be able myself to say at meeting a New Specimen = ah! how beautifull!!—the time past however—My drawings were on

the Floor and a Gentleman walking up directly toward me
said "Sir did you Ever reside in New York"—I answered "yes
Sir."—"pray Sir did you Mary a Miss Bakewell?"—now to
this, Answer thy own Self?—This proved to be a M[r] Jackson
who lived at Bloomingdale near M[r] Thomas Kinder and who
knew thee well for he said—*"Your lady was very handsome"*—
yes he might say that but he said Imediately—"Your
Drawings are Charming."—I could have slapped the Man for
bringing My paltry pictures with thy face all of a breath =
but it is past 2—the Doors are Closed—and I run to My
Chamber to Dress a little, and wait for M[r] Adam Hodgsons
= four a Clock. half past four. I am Looking from my window for his gig   is it here? Let me see?—aye that it is! = My
Port Folio is under my arm and 3 by 3 I Leap down the
Stairs—Shake the friendly hand and am seated on his Left,
moving toward his Cottage = I am sorry I cannot paint portraits—I would represent to thee, the Meekness of his Blue
Eyes—his sweetness of Language—his comely movements.
but My Dear Lucy, thou knowest that in all my attempts I
never yet reach[d] the original.—We are going, talking about
me, thee, and Ours; and—the little pony has Stop[d] I am out
of the Little Chair—and conducted into a Neat *English*
Setting Room—wert thou not an English Lady Born Thyself,
I would Describe this one, as being considered by Myself a
fair Specimen, really scientifically—but—I will merely say—It
was beautifully Snug and had Ghothic Windows, threw which
the Eye was freely permitted to extend its desires over an uncommon extent of Picturesque Scenery.—"M[rs] Hodgson. M[r]
Audubon My Dear"—a fairly, Tall, Young female, with the
Freshness of Spring, entered the room and wish[d] me welcome with an air of plain contentedness—that not *even my
Eye* could deny to Mean, Letter after Letter, all that was
spoken.—

We Dined!—Lucy like at Home.—These good people gave
me in perfect friendship Lessons of English Politeness = I
spoke plainly about My Past diferences of Conditions to M[r]
H.—and moved from the Dining, into the setting room,
rather after the setting of the Sun =

We had four visitors a Cap[e] Somebody his Lady and Son—
and a pert young Woman the name of which I do not care

half so much about as I do for those of the others but I must Let them all go bye, as my poor head will not remember Names (unless they may chance to be Friends names).

The Calmness existing in the Country soon reach[d] my heart and soon did I contemplate such Scenery in Imagination in America = I thought of Such an Evening Walking Gently arm in arm together towards the Watters of the Bayou Sara to Watch thee Bathe thy gentle form in its current. I thought of the Happiness I have enjoyed, whilt gazing on the Happy Couple before me. I thought!—ah my Dearest Friend M[r] Hodgson asks me if I will retire to rest or lessen to his usual habit of reading prayers to his Little Flock and servants—I prefer[d] the Latter, and silently mute each bent on Devotion prayed With this good Man.—

Liverpool August 6th, Sunday, 1826

When I arrived in this City I felt dejected, yes miserably So— The uncertainty of being kindly received, of having My works approved off where all acting on Both my Phisical and Mental Powers—I felt as if nutritive food was within my Sight was not to be touched—Now how diferently my sensations—I am well received where ever I am Known—every Object Known to me smiles as I meet it—and my poor heart is at Last relieved from the great anxiety that has for So many years agitated it by thinking now that I have not work[d] altogether in Vain—that I may no Longer be positively ashamed of the Productions of my Pencil (whatever may become of those of my pen are yet very far in the distant ground of the future, and I dread will never produce an Effect unless indeed it be a bad one and then I doubt if Speaking like an Artist it would be effect at all)—well my Dear LaForest these thoughts of thine have been known to Me these 11 Years at Least "give me pray thy day's Expenditure" ah Expenditure—Let us see—Bed Last Night 1 shilling. Breakfast 2—Dinner 3.—Boots 6 pence —Maids—6 pence Waiter, Nothing this day—wine Extra 3 Shillings and 6 pence at the Blind asilum's church—that makes 10/6—within 6 pence sterling of Two Dollars. I will Manage diferently when I reach *Town* speaking as Lord Stanley and as I dare venture to say many more lords do

without ennumerating the Gentlemen that do so also—it is
rather a High way of Living for *a Naturalist*; nay Let me fully
Write *an author!* however it is about the rate We pay at the
Mansion house in Philadelphia—and the City Hotel in New
York—it is indeed less than in Washington City—but to return to the true meaning of thy question (for which I would
give half my authorship to have it Natura *personnalis*) I will
say: up early as usual and will not Mention it again—Indeed I
must beg thy Pardon for thus Miserably tormenting thy kind
Patience—well I went to Church as thou seest per *Bill annexed* Now there's Mercantile stuff for thee—Bill annexed
yet Many could I bring forward as Living Specimens I assure
thee—but Let go to Church—it was filled to a Crany—I had
drop^d my Six pence in the Silver plate and had walk^d with that
Natural awkwardness that I possess so Iminently smack into
the Midle of the centerial aisle, when so many female
Constellations flashed on my staring Eyes that I stop^d—drop^d
My head and waited patiently for events.—Now do not believe that I was thoughtless no Indeed—I really then thought
of thee Dearest Wife and wish^d thee at my Elbow to urge Me
and To ——. The Conductor walks up—takes old of My
Soiled Glove with his snow White hand, and Leads me politely in the Pew Next to the Priest—the Music was exquisitely
fine—I am rather a Judge, thou knowest that by my Ears.—
but the sermon was not so—It was delevered by a *Closet
Priest* I Mean by One who had not studied *Nature herself*
Beautifull Nature devoid of Art however I understood that he
was a young Man of great promess: I Called on sister Ann
and Chatted some there. I understood that she was writing to
sister Eliza Berthoud and it gave me a desire to write also—
She had evinced a wish to see thy Watch and I gratified her in
that:—the more I see of Miss Donathan the more I like her
She is very aimiable and not ugly, believe me—Mr Gordon
had my Bonaparte's Birds carried to Dr Trail to whom I had
promised a view of it—I dined as thou hast already been informed by bill of Fare at 2 o'clock in Company with the
American gentleman of Charleston = I remained Too long at
table—I dress^d afterwards, pack^d up Harlan's Fauna neatly for
Mrs E. Rathbone and having taken my cane push^d for the
Institution where Mr Munro was to be to escort me to M^r

W^{am} Roscoe s^r where I was to take tea. No Mr Munro but I found his Wife and some Little Children Clean and pretty enough to be Kiss^d, so I kiss them. fatigued of waiting I am under Way. have delivered the packet for Mrs Rathbone to a servant at her Door—and passed the Botanic Garden—entered *Lodge Lane* and Mr Roscoe's Habitation.—It was full of Ladies and Gentlemen all of his *own familly*, and as I knew almost the whole I was soon at my ease—great deal said about Lord Stanley, his Birds and my Birds. I was ask^d to Imitate the Wild Turkey call, and I did to the surprise of the all circle. hooted like the Barred Owl. and cooed like the dove—I am glad really that I was not desired to Bray!—"Why"? why! because an ass is an ass and it would have been rude even in an ass, to Bray in such Company.—Lucy remark my position. I sat rather reclining, my legs extended before me at the upper end of the room between Mr W^{am} Roscoe and his son Edward fronting the whole of the aimiable circle before me—and have to answer to questions after questions as fast as I dare answer—Mrs Ed^d Roscoe has raised from her seat Twenty times to come and ask me questions about my style of Drawing—

The Good old gentleman and myself retire from the Groupe into the Dining room to talk about my *Plans* = he strongly advises me not to Exibit my Work without remuneration—he repeats his wish that I may succeed and desires that I should Take Tea on Tuesday evening with him when he will give me Letters for London = Tea his presented and I take one Cup of *Coffee!* A Beautifull young lady called *here a Miss* is at my side and asks with the volubility of Interesting youth and anthusiasms Many Many questions about America—but they all Appear very much surprised that I have no Wonderful Talcs to relate—that for Instance *I* so much in the Woods have not been devoured at least 6 times by Tigers, Bears, Wolfs, Foxes or—a rat.—no I never was troubled in the woods by any larger Annimals than Ticks and Musquitoes and that is quite enough—is it not Dearest Lucy?

I must acknowledge however that I would like to have rode a few hundred miles on a Wild Elk or a Unicorn—or an Alligator. "Alligator!!!! Who in the known world ever heard of Such things?" heard Lucy I do not know; but I am sure hundreds of Persons have *Read* of the like having been

performed by a Man Just about the size of Common Men.
"come, come." but indeed it is a fact the ride was taken by an
Englishman—now I am sure thy wonder has vanished, for
thou Knowest as well as myself and much better to how
Many Many Wonders and Wonderful things *they* have performed—

Well it is late; Son after Son with each a sweet wife under
his care bids me and their Venerable Father *Good Night*
Lucy the well bred society of England is sublimity of
Manners. Such tone of voices I never heard in America except
when with—thee My Wife!—and the Gentlemen are—no it is
impossible to be more truly polite.—a gentleman at Church
this Morning who knew me for a Stranger handed me Book
after books   The book that contained the Hyms then with
the page open and with a gentle bow pointed the Verse with
a finger covered by a beautifully White Glove—have I not reasons to like England thus far—Indeed I have.

I bid good Night myself and accompanied by a young Man
came all the way to Norton Street where I stop^d to rest and
talk to Mr Gordon about my views of the Exibition of my
Drawings for *Nothing*—he is of my way of thinking. We talk^d
also about thy relations in England &^c &^c &^c and being now
6 Minutes Past 12 I will bid thee Good Night, My Love!!!!—

Liverpool 9th August 1826.
So poor Audubon thy Birds will be seen by the Shilling's
worth. and Criticized no doubt by the Pound. the Fruits of
thy Life's Labour ought now to rippe fast or thy Winter may
be yet spent without the ambers thou art been used to, during thy Happy Youthful Days—1 am almost sorry for it,
Indeed I have more than once felt vexation at heart on the
occasion and yet perhaps with all, it may prove Best. as to me,
rest for ever assured that it will never in the least diminish the
affectionate regards and Estime that has been felt by me ever
since I found thee for the first time reclining at the foot of a
Magnolia thy Eyes humid with the watters of admiration
casted on the Beauties of thy resplendissant Friend Nature! no
Audubon! what ever may become of thee (speaking in a
Phisical way) will never ender me from speaking of thee, and

thinking of thee, as I conceived thee to be then, ever since then, and Now!!—then for ever thy Thine. xxxxxxxx

My Beloved Wife the above note, (the handwriting of which as well as the Composition thou knowest well) Acquaints thee as quickly as all the Liverpool papers that My Birds of America (about one half by the bye for the Port folio Nº 1 is yet sacred) will be seen Next Monday at the Royal Institution not *Probono Publico* but for the benefit of E Pluribus Unum.

    *   *   *

Manchester Monday 25ᵗʰ Septʳ 1826.

who would Come this Morning in my room about 7 whilt I was busily finishing the grounds of my Male Pheasant? a Handsome quaker perhaps 30 years of Age and very neatly dressed "My friends are going out of Manchester before *thee* opens thy exhibition rooms—can we see thy Collection at 9 o'clock?"—I ask the Stranger to set— answer Yes to all he asks, and Shew him my Drawing: Now were all the people in this good Land of England quakers I might perhaps have some encouragement but really My Lucy My times are dull, heavy, long, painfull and Harrass My Mind allmost too much = 5 Minutes before nine I was Standing waitting for the quaker and his Friends in the Loby of the Exchange where 2 persons Standing also held the following discourse = "pray have you seen Mʳ Audubon's Collection of Birds   I am told it is Well worth a Shilling   suppose we go now—"   "puh— it is all a Hoax   save your Shilling for better use, I have seen them, Why the fellow ought to be Drummed out of Town" = did I Blush Lucy? no I turned pale and dared not raise my eyes least I Might be Known, but depend upon it I wished Myself in America again =

the quakers however made all up again, for they praised My Drawings so much that I *blushed then* in Spite of my old age = Now Lucy comes in 2 Cards of Invitation for the Concert One from Dʳ Holme the second from Mʳ Loyd the Banker = I also received a short Letter from Mʳ Edᵈ Roscoe all about drawing = but I am rather, Indeed I will say good deal surprised that I have not a word from either Miss Hanah

Rathbone or Mr Gordon—and that I have not heard a Word
about my Album =

I took my Drawing of the Pheasant to Mr Tanetti's Chop
and had it put in a good light, to prove to the good people
of Manchester that I really did wish to see more of them =
then Lucy I purchased 25 yards of good Linen for £ 4.3.4. being 3 & 4 pence per yard and I will have in 10 days a fresh
supply of Comfortables = the old dog that attends the rooms
of the Exchange, gave me due Notice that my time was out
and that I Must Clear My Birds because an Exibition of Deaf
and Dumbs must take place = I have no Objection, far from
this—I have already made Arrangements for my new place in
King Street and Hope to do better there next week—at 5 I
took down 240 drawings and packed them ready for removal
in Less than one hour = I am quite sure that a Stranger
might have thought I was about escaping to save being really
drummed out of Manchester—Now for the Concert = It was
6 o'clock and raining very agreably when I left My room for
Fountain Street where already Carriages and foot people had
accumulated to a great Number, I by elbowing arrive at the
entrance and present My Ticket—am asked if a Stranger and
requested to Write My Name & Residence = no objections
again and J. J. Audubon Louisiana, America is wrote Just as
handsomely as Napoleon himself would have done it when
pressed by time = the Room is full of Red, White, Blue &
Green Turbans well fitted to the handsome heads of the
Ladies that already are seated all attention = I Glide modestly
on one side and settle my Self were I conceive that my
Heart, My Eye and My Intellect may be well satisfied and suplied in Course without being myself observed = but no it
would not do, My Long hairs are seen and the bearer pointed
at in such ridiculous Manner that I needed to recollect that I
was an Honest plain Man and ranked as high as any other in
the eye of God   therefore stood the brunt and Lessened to
the Music = It was fine but it sank my Spirits and Could I
have left the Assembly I would certainly have done so =
Many ladies were richly Beautifull = several Old dames
twiged at me with their Lorgnettes and I wish them Younger
in unison with themselves on that score but a remarkably
Elegant woman who set on the bench before me turned so

frequently round to examine (I suppose) the shape of my
Nose, that I took several times within my fingers to torment
this fair one   I have passed many uncomfortable evenings in
Company and this may be added = at last "God save the
King" came and I went squeezing myself side ways, pocket
Hafs in side Pocket, Coat buttoned, One hand on My Watch
and the other ready to seize Any rascal who might dare to attempt to steal from me   I soon reach[d] home with the Head
ache, and have wrote this = tomorow this time I intend being at Liverpool again = So My Sweet Wife good Night.—

Carlisle England Tuesday 24th 1826.

At 5 I had Left Manchester, the morning was Clear & beautifull but as no dependence can be placed on the weather in
this Country I thought but little of it—I was rather amused at
the Observations made about my Folio at the Stage Office =
a Clerk there Laughed allmost as much as the Reverend J.
Clowes but the poor Fellow Lived in Manchester and consequently had not heard of either the owner or his Works = I
was alone in the Inside of the Carriage (for truly Coaches in
England are very good) and had been there for some time
lamenting myself and feeling much dissatisfied at having no
Company when a very Tall Gentleman came in from the Top
and said that he wished to Sleep, he turned on his Side, I
look[d] at him and envied his condition, could I have Slept also,
I would certainly have prefered this to being the companion
of a Drowsy Man = We rolled on however and Arrived at the
village of Preston, were breakfast was swallowed as quickly
and with as Much avidity as our Kentuckians usually do =
Coaches were exchanged, passage transferred &[c] and I entered the Carriage to Meet 2 New Gentlemen; their appearance was goodly and to break on the silence, I offered both
of them a pinch of N[o] 37   it was taken by one and smelled at
by the other—the Chat begun and in less than 10 Minutes we
all had travelled thro America, part of India, Crossed the
Ocean in New York Packets discussed the Emancipation of
Slavery and reach[d] the point of Political Starvation of the poor
of England & Ireland, the Corn Law—tranquilly going I peeping frequently thro each window—I saw Little Girls running

along the side of the Coach with Nosegays Loosely fastened
to a Long Stick and Offered to passengers for a Penny. I took
One for a 6 pence and again resumed the chat = At a little
Village where the Horses were changed it was discovered that
a Chocking smell existed on the Top of the Coach   The man
is called the Guard spoke of it and told us that he could not
keep his seat   I felt Anxious to view the Country, when Still
and got out to Mount up and behind but the Smell was so
Insuferable and the Appearance of the Man near whom I
must have seated myself so far from being pleasant that I
Imediatly Jump^d down to take my Inside seat = Judge of My
Dismay Lucy when I was asked if *My Trunk belonged to me*
and if it did not contain a Dead Body intended for dissection
at Edinburgh = I answered no thou may be sure = The
Guard smiled as if quite sure my trunk contained such a thing
and told My Companions that he would inform against me at
Lancaster, I bore all this very well, I was Innocent! I offered
to Open my Trunk and would have certainly done so at
Lancaster but whilst we were proceeding the Guard came to
the door and Made an Apology, said the smell had been removed, and that it was positively *attached to the Inside parts
of the Man's Breeches* who was on the seat by him = this
caused much Laughter and many Course Jockes; *my* Subject
was a source of Conversation when every thing else failed =
I became quite pleased with all my Companions, my being a
Stranger was suficient to be well treated by them, and Indeed
what better mark of Superior Politeness is it not over all other
countrymen = the English gentlemen are gentlemen at all
points and in all Circumstances. The approach of Lancaster is
beautifull, the view of the well planted Castle is commanding,
the Sea seen from this also was agriable as it is bounded by
Picturesque Shores = We dined at Kendal, having passed
thro Bolton & Burton but before we dined at a Stage before
which the Horses were Changing, My Companions were left
behind and had to run for nearly one Mile to overtake the
Coach; This caused many altercations betwen the Gentlemen
and the Driver & Guard and one of the Proprietors a M^r
Saunders who Interfered and who was unfortunately *rather*
Drunk made matters much Worse, a Complaint was lodged
against the Driver, and he received No More Shillings from

My Companions = I saw & heard all very peaceably, Mr Walton the Tall Gentleman who had Slept so well during the Morning was extremely attentive to me = but The Messrs Patisson from *Cornwall* were Still more so. The Father Kindly gave me his Card and begged that I would call on him if ever I travelled in the South of England = We now entered a most Dreary Country poor beyond Conception, Immense Hills rolling one by the other in constant succession, Spotted here & there with miserable Cotts the residence of poor Shepperds —No game was seen, the weather was bleak & rainy and I Cannot say that I enjoyed the ride at all beyond the conversation of my Companions, we passed thro Penrith and arrived at Carlisle at ½ past 9, having rode 122 Miles = I was told that in hard winters the road becomes at times Impassable, choaked with snow and that when not entirely obstructed it was necessary to see some Posts placed every 100 yards and painted black at the top to be guided Surely = we had a Miserable Supper but good beds and I enjoyed mine for I felt very wearied, my Cold & cough having very much Increased by my having rode some 20 Miles outside to view the Country = I was praying and wishing thee Well when Two female voices Struck my ears and I discovered that the noise was close by my door = a conversation was Kept low and undistinguishable for some minutes when one of the persons began weeping and continued Increasing untill it became most piteously Hideous = I felt a Strong Inclination to raise, to open my Door and to inquire into the cause when I recollected that it could not be about me and that consequently it was not my Business to Interfer, a part of conduct in man that I allways strongly will recommend to our Beloved Sons = the females at last retired into a room next me and the noise subsided, I felt fatigued and bid thee Good Night full of thought of apprehension for the future =

Thursday Octr 26th George Street

*   *   *

I walk^d a good Deal and admired this City very much, the great breadth of the streets, their good pavement and foot ways, the beautifull uniformity of the Buildings, their Natural

Grey Coloring and wonderfull Cleanliness of the all perhaps was felt more powerfully coming direct from Dirty
Manchester = But the Picturesque tout Ensemble here is
wonderfull, a High Castle, here, another there, on to a Bridge
Looking at a Second City below, here a Rugged Mountain
and there beautifull Public Grounds, Monuments, the Sea,
the Landscape Around, all wonderfully managed indeed. it
would require 50 diferent good Views at least of it or of its
parts to give thee a true Idea, but I will try day after day In
my humble way of writing to describe more particularly all
that I may see either in the Old or new part of this Town =
I could not Spend the day without having a peep at my own
handy work. I disengaged my Birds and look^d at them with
pleasure and yet with a considerable degree of fear that they
never would be published—I felt very much alone again and
longed for some one to dispose to of my Ideas. whilt at my
dinner, how much I thought of the country that I have left
behind, and of thee particularly, some dark thoughts came
across my mind, feared thee sick, perhaps Lost for ever to me
and felt deadly sick—My Dinner was there cooling fast whilt
each part I Swallowed went down slowly as if Choaking, I felt
frequently tears about my eyes and I forced myself out of the
Room to destroy this painfull Gloom that I dread at all times
and that sometime I fear may do more =

   After a good walk I returned rather more at ease and
looked at the paire of Stuffed Pheasants on the large Buffet
that ornements my present seating room; at the Sweetly
scented Geraniums opposite them, at the Black Haired Sopha,
the Armed Chairs; the studying little Cherubs on the Mantle
piece, the Painted landscape on my right, the Print exibiting
Charity well appropriated by Free Masonry and my own face
at last in the Mirror in my front = I saw in it not only my
own face but such powerful resemblance of that of my
Venerable Father that I almost Imagined it was him that I saw
= The thought of my Mother flew about me, my sister was
also present my young days, those I have enjoyed with thee
and those I have spent miserable from thee All were alterna-
tivly at hand, and yet how far away—ah how far is even the
Last moment that is never to return again = but my Lucy,
such reflexions will not do, I must close my Book, think of

Tomorow yes of the future that allways as we reach it evapo-
rates and becomes a mere yesterday, not thought of but with
regret, if passed either right or wrong. My Sweet Beloved
Lucy God forever bless thee. Good night.

Edinburgh Scotland Oct[r] 27th 1826. Friday.
I visited the Market this morning but to go to it I first
Crossed from the New Town into the begaining of the Old
over the North bridge; went down many flights of winding
steps, and at Last reached the desired Spot = I was then positively under the Bridge that no doubt was built to save the
trouble of descending & mounting from one side to another
of Edinburgh Which is Mostly built on the Slopes of Two
long ranges of High broken Hills = the Vegetable Markets
are well arranged and Looked well as well as the Fruits &
Meats but the Low Situation and narrow Kind of Booths in
which the whole is exibited was not agreable and Compared
with the Famous New Market of Liverpool, Nothing = I ascended the Stairs Leading to the New Town and seeing before me, after turning a Little to the right the Monument in
Honor of Nelson, I walk[d] towards it and reach[d] it—its elevated Situation, the Broken Rocks along which I went made
it very Picturesque, but a tremendous Shower of rain accompanied by a Heavy Gust of Cold wind made me hurry from
the Spot without being quite Satisfied—and I returned *home*
to Breakfast = I was Struck with the relative Appearance of
the Woman of the Lower Class with that of our Indian
Squaws of the West, their Walk is precisely the same and their
Mode of Carrying Burthens also—they have a leather Strap
passed over and poised on the forehead attached to Large
Baskets without covers, and waddle thro the streets with Toes
Inward Just as the Shawanées for Instance = their complex-
ion if Fair is beyond rosy partaking indeed of Purple, i e cold
and Desagreable—if Dark they are dark Indeed—Many of the
men wear Long Whiskers & beards are extremely uncouth
of Manners & Still more so of Language = I had eat my
breakfast when Messrs Patisson came to see my Drawings and
brought with them a Miss *Ewart* whom M[r] P. senior said
drew *uncomonly beautifully* I thought that according to

Johnson this, if well applied, must mean a great deal and I open^d my Book with a certain portion of reluctance—I thought I could soon discover if she *thought So herself*—several drawings were looked at—She remained mute, Mr P. pronounced them Surpassing all he had ever seen—I watched the Ladie's eyes and the Coloring of her fair cheeks, she look^d closer and said with a smile that it seemed America would certainly surpass all other Countries in point of Arts & Sciences in Less than another Century = Now I Shall not be a live then, neither My name recollected and I Still longed for an acquiescence from the Mouth of the fair Stranger—I thought that perhaps a Picture of lovers would bring my wish to bear—I turned untill I found My Doves and held them in a good light "how beautifull, Exquisitely beautifull! how delighted Sir Walter Scot will be to see Your Magnificent Collection!" Now that I found the Steam was High, that perhaps some explosion might be produced, I exibited the Rattlesnake attack^d by the Mocking Birds—this had the desired Effect—the Lady was pleased & I was satisfied that She drew well = Mr P. said that Mr Selby never would publish another Bird was he to see mine = We parted all friends; I having begged of each of them to bring or send any of their Friends to View my Work any morning from 10 untill 12 =

    *   *   *

Edinburgh Octr 30th 1826. Monday

I waitted most Impatiently to day until one o'clock, getting up from my chair and looking down in the street thro my window to see some one coming to view My Work; but all my anxiety, & my Ill humour availed not, and to vent it I took my umbrella and Marched direct, rather stiffened, to Fish Market Close, and passed the files of printers in Mr Neill's office as if the World was about being convulsed. I reach^d the owner of the establishment & all my pomposity evaporated and dispersed like a morning's Mist before the Sun. I became at once as quiet as a Lamb and merely told him that I regretted very much my not deserving the attentions of those for whom I had Letters, and that if So I must off to London = he gave me good words and in Such calculated cool manner, that none but an Ass could have resisted his reasonement; he accompanied me Instantly to one of the most Scientific Men, who after looking at me as I Look at the Eye of a Bird as it looses its brilliancy & I fear to Lose its caracter. he noted down, name & residence, and promissed to send Amateurs. Mr Neill not satisfied any more than myself took me to a Mr Lizars in St James Square the engraver of Mr Selby's Birds, who at once followed me to see my Work = he talk^d of nothing else (as he walk^d along under the same umbrella) besides the astonishing talent of his Employer, how quick he drew, and how well, had I seen the work &^{c} &^{c} untill having ascended the stairs of my lodgings and entered my room, his Eye fell on my Port folio and gave him some other thoughts I am quite Sure = It is a doubt with me if I open^d my Lips at all during all this; I slowly unbuckled the Straps, and putting a chair for him to set without uttering a Word, I turned up a Drawing!—Now Lucy poor Mr Selby was the suferer by that movement—Mr Lizars quite surprised exclaimed "My God I never saw any thing like that before" now Lucy Lawson the *Philadelphia Brute* never gave an Inch, and to this day swears that I Know nothing about Drawing. that Willson did more with one Bird than I ever will with thousands! = Mr Lizars was so astonished that he said Sir somebody must see them that he would write Imediately, and so he did = that Mr Selby must see them and to him also he wrote and going as it grew dark, he called it seems on a Mr W. Heath, a great Artist from London, who came Imediatly to see me = I had however made my Exit in search of a handsome peble for thee, and missed him then = I called at the Post office but it was not open—Shocking arrangement for a Traveller, that if in town for a few hours only cannot be told if, or not, there are letters for him; I found it the same case in England =

I returned and found 2 Lines from Mr Heath and not knowing who he was I parted to go and see who he might be = N° 4 St James Street—up 3 paires of Stairs (a L'artisan) met a very dark Brunette who acknowledged herself to be the better half of her husband, who in a moment after, Shewed me two Enormous Mustachios on his upper lip, and great many various Drawings & Etchings—I will not say that they were without faults, as thou knowest there are faults in every thing—I thought some of them very good = he will come tomorow = I Met accidentally this day My 3ᵈ Companion from Manchester Mʳ Walton, I was glad to see him and he reciprocated my feeling very amicably—tomorow he also comes =

Edinburgh November 1ˢᵗ 1826 Wednesday

Well my Good Lovely Wife, I breakfasted with *Professor Jameson!* Most splendid House, splendid every thing, a good breakfast to boot! the professor wears his hair three distinct diferent courses; when he sets fronting the South for Instance, those on the upper forehead are bent westwardly; towards the East those that cover both Ears are Inclined; and the very Short Sheared portion behind mounts directly upwards perhaps Somewhat alike the Stiffer quills of the "fretfull Porcupine." but Dearest Lucy notwithstanding all this curious economy of the outward ornemental appendages of his Scull; the Sense within is Great, and If I mistake not, it feels of the Suavity of a Kind Generous Heart = Professor Jameson to day is no more the Man I took him to be, he accosted me most friendly, chatted with an uncommon degree of cordiality and promessed me his Powerfull assistance so forcibly convincingly that I am quite Sure I can depend upon him = I Left him and his Sister at 10 as we both have a good deal to do besides drinking hot, well creamed Coffee.—the separation however was Short, for when the Clock Struck 12, he entered my room (then filled with fair females) accompanying a Notable Baronet and perhaps a couple more Gentlemen = *he* Lucy made them Praise My Work—Said he would call again and I saw him pull my Door after him quite Sorry. for as I said Just Now Professor Jameson is quite the Man for me now = ah and Mʳ Neill also, and Mʳ Lizars and Dʳ Hibbert and Dʳ Henry, and Dʳ Knox, and for all I Know a full Score double twice—at 4 o'clock I was still turning very patiently drawings one after the other, holding at full arms Length, the Larger ones—and pushing quite under the delicate beauties noses the Small ones to give their fair Eyes all Kinds of opp.ᵗⁱᵉˢ (and yet God knows how all this will end)   I

felt very fatigued my Left arm once I thought had some
Idea of revolutionizing I thought once that my Left fist was
about to assailling my own so well formed Nose—I took the
hint and saved both—I Walk^d out and was Look^d at by many
= as I passed one I could here—"that's a German Phisician I
Know"—I answered *Low* Fudge!—another "that's a French
Nobleman" I answered *Low* bah!—took plenty of needed
exercise, Enquired in Vain after Chalks, called in vain at the
Post office = thought often of My Good Friends of Green
Bank, and of thee. and at Last peep^d in at Mr Lizars Just As
he was about supping several Cups of Tea into his supping in
place—well I could not remain quite a blank the while. M^r
Lizars uncorked a bottle of warm^d London Porter, Lady N° 1
handed it me with a Smile and I handed it to my mouth with
thanks!— Whilt down in his counting room I Expressed the
wish to purchase a set of views of *Superb Edinburgh*, the book
was brought upstairs for me to look at—he ask^d me to Draw
a Vignette for him and wrote on the first Sheet of his book
the exact following transfer of Properties in fee simply thus:

> To John J. Audubon as a very imperfect expression of
> the regard entertained for his Abilities as an Artist, and
> for his worth as a Friend
> by
> Will. H. Lizars
> Engraver of the
> Views of Edin^g

Any Kentucky lawyer who would pretend to acknowledge the
whole *un bona fide* I would knock down; But as our advocates
are all of the *Good Clay kind*, I neither fear the contestation
nor that of being conquered by Phisical Power in such an encounter—now we walked and purchased Chalks. Yes: for 3
pounds and one Shilling and 8 pence I took home 3 Boxes of
Crayons, 2 brushes of Sable hair, and 2 handles of God Knows
the genera or the Specie of the Wood = I had seen some
Artists of Mr Lizars coloring by Gass light, printing on copper
&^{c} &^{c} for the 1st time of my life! = how little I Yet Know. My
God how Ignorant I am!—Well, I went to bed after reading
untill I was so pleased with the book that I put it under My
head to dream about it Like Children are wont to do at

Christmas Eve I believe   however My senses all operated another way   I Dreamed of the Beech Woods, of a House
there! of a female there; Of a—

God bless thee, sweetest Friend Good night.

Edinburgh Novr 30th 1826.

*   *   *

My invitation to dine with the Antiquarians of this city was
not forgotten—I was at at 5 at Mr Lizars when having already
found Mr Moule we proceeded to the Watterloo hotel—The
Setting room was soon filled   I met many that I knew and a
few Minutes after the Earl of Elgin had made his entry I was
presented to him by Mr Innes of Stow—he Shook hands with
me and Spoke in very Kind terms complimenting me at the
same time about my Pencil's Production—at 6 I suppose we
walked in couples to the Dinning room—I had the arm of My
Good friend P. Neill—Mr Lizars Sat on one side of me, and
Mr N. on the other and then I was helped from a Sumptuous
dinner Indeed = It at first consisted Entirely of Scotch
messes of old Fashion—Such as Marrow Bones—Cod fishes
heads stuffed with Oat Meal and Garlick—Black Puddings—
Sheeps Heads—Trachea of the same and I do not know what
all—then a Second Dinner was served quite a L'Anglaise   I
finished with a nice bit of Grouse—then my Lucy Came on
the Toasts—Lord Elgin being President and provided with an
Auctioneering Mallet brought all the company to order by
rapping Smartly on the Table with this Instrument, he rose
and Simply Said, "The King, 4 times 4"   every one rose,
Drink to the Monarch's health and the President saying "ip
ip ip" Sixteen Sheers were loudly called out—the Duke of
York, of Clarence, and Many others had their health, then Sir
Walter Scot (who was not present to my great discomfiture)
Then one and then an other untill My Lucy thy Husband's
Health was proposed by Mr Skin the first Secretary to the
Royal Institution of the Antiquarian Society &^c &^c—Whilt he
was engaged in a handsome Panageric the Swet ran down me
I thought I would faint and I was seated in that Situation
when Every body Rose and Earl President called Out "M^r
Audubon"   I had seen each Toasted Individual rise and de-
liver a Speech. that being the case could I remain Speechless

like a fool—No I Summoned Resolution and for the first time in My Life addressed A Large assembly thus "Gentlemen My Powers of Voice are as Humble as those of the Birds now hanging on the Walls of the Institution, I am truly obliged for your favor   permit me to Say May God bless You all and may this Society Prosper"—I felt my hands and they were positively covered with Perspiration   I felt It runing down along my Legs and Mr Lizars Seeing how I was, poured out a Glass of Wine and said "Bravo take this"—the Company went Toasting—a Delightful old Scotch song was granted us by Mr Innes   the refrain was "put on Thy Cloak about thee"   then Mr Donald gave us another, W^{am} Allan, Es^{qr} the famous Painter told a beautifull Story—then rose and Imitated the busing of a Bumble bee confined in a room and followed it as if flying off from him beating it down with his Hafs &^{c} most admirably—at 10 the Earl Rose and bid us Well.—at ½ past 10 I proposed to Mr Lizars to go and We did.—I was now much pleased of My having been there particularly as Lord Elgin expressed a Wish to see me again—I went to Mr Lizars where I took Some Scotch Grog and return^d home well = The Lad that Copied My Letter to Mrs Rathbone was yet at Work   he took the Letter to the office and I took Myself to bed—It is again One o'clock Sweet Wife and another day has Elapsed without a word from thee—God Bless thee Good Night—I forgot to say that I visited Mr Allan the Artist in the Morning and saw there a most superb Picture of his own Pencil—

Edinburgh Tuesday 12th Decr 1826.

I Took one of my Manuscripts Imediatly after breakfast, i.e. 10 o'clock—to Dr Brewster—I found him writting in a Large room where several fine Pictures hung around = he received me very politely and in a few minutes, having blown my Nose, and put my neck in a good attitude to suffer my lungs to operate freely I began reading my Letter on the manners of the Carrion Crow—Vultur attratus—when about midway my respiration becoming encumbered, I rested a moment to breath when the doctor took this opportunity to say "that it was very Interesting"—I soon resumed and went thro thank

God!—he who has all his Life being an Auctioneer or brought up in the Green Room of Covent Garden Theater for Instance, with all his Knowledge of Business and of Man knows nothing about the feelings that agitate me on such an Occasion. thou art probably the only one sweet Wife that ever analized them as I felt them = a Man who never Look^d into an English grammar, and very seldom, unfortunatly in a French or a Spanish One—a Man who has allways felt awkward and very Shy in the presence of a Stranger—One habituated to ramble alone with his thoughts allways bent on the beauties of *Nature herself*—This *man me* in Edinburgh to be seated opposite Dr Brewster reading one of my puny efforts at describing habits of birds that None but an Almighty Creator can ever know = Was so ridiculously Absurd in my estimation during all this while, and whilst I felt the riveting looks of Observation of the Learned Personnage before me, that to say that a Cold sweat ran over my body much Worse than when I dined with the Antiquarians and that to say this to thee is only giving thee one of the ten thousand tormenting thoughts that crossed my mind whilt my Eyes & mouth were reading = however a Large Black Dog not altogether of the Newfound Land Breed came in, caressed his Master and Chassed my most dismall agitations = I was afterwards Introduced through a sliding partition into a Large Drawing Room and presented to the Doct^{rs} Lady = again I repeat it the well bred people of this Country are uncommonly kind to Strangers, and I must add My Lucy that thy sex possesses here the most astonishing power of rendering *me* for Instance, in an Instant quite at My Ease!—I Left = A proof Sheet was to be sent me tomorrow. I was told that I would be Introduced to Sir Walter Scot on Monday Next at the Royal Academy = Poor me—far from Walter Scot I could talk to him. hundreds of times have I said quite Loud in the Woods, as I Looked on a silvery Streamlet, or the Sickly Swamp, or the Noble Ohio, or on Mountain tops loosing their picks in Grey mist—Oh Walter Scot where art thou? wilt thou not come to my Country? Wrestle with Mankind and Stop their Increasing ravages on Nature & describe her Now for the Sake of Future Ages—neither this Little Stream—this Swamp, this Grand Sheet of Flowing Watter nor these Mountains will be seen in

a Century hence, as I see them now.—Nature will have been
rob^d of her brilliant Charms—the currents will be tormented
and turned astray from their primitive courses—the Hills will
be levelled with the Swamp and probably this very swamp
have become a Mound covered with a Fortress of a thousand
Guns—Scarce a Magnolia will Louisiana possess—the Timid
Deer will exist nomore—Fishes will no longer bask on this
surface. the Eagle scarce ever alight, and these Millions of
Songsters will be drove away by Man—Oh Walter Scot come,
Come to America! set thee here, look upon Her and See her
Grandeur now, Nature Still Nurses her, Cherishes her, but a
Tear flows in her eye, her Cheek has Already changed from
the Peach Blossom, to sallow hue—her frame Enclines to
Emaciation, her Step is Arrested. Without thee Walter Scot,
unknown to the World She must Die—Such things I often
have repeated but the Echos only have answered me—Walter
Scot did not, does not, Never will know this, nor my feelings
towards him—but if he did—what have I to say more than a
World of others who all admire him perhaps more than I do
because more enlightened they and better judges of his
Worth—ah, Walter Scot when I am presented to thee—my
head will droop, my heart will swell, my Limbs will tremble,
my lips quiver, my tongue congeal I shall be mute and
perhaps not even my Eyes will dare turn towards thee—Great
Man nevertheless will I feel Elevated that I was permitted to
touch thy hand and I Shall Bless thee within in Spite of all the
deadness of my Phisical faculties = Lucy Walter Scot resides
the next door from Dr Brewster in Coats Crescent N° 11.

My Exhibition Appeared to have been abandoned and I ordered the News Papers to say that it would Close saturday
next—Mr Skene had advised me to do so—and he also told
me this morning that he Would present me as a Member to
the Antiquarian Society at the Next Meeting—

I expected to have seen Mr Selby and Sir W^{am} Jardine but
neither came to town—

I went to Mrs Welbank N° 41 Albany Street to Dine with
W^{am} Gregg—Dr Gardner was there—Mrs Wellbank has a Red
Nose Lucy—now when I say red, I do not mean to say that it
is covered with that soft downy, velvety Light substance that
I often have seen and felt on thine, composed in its Coloring

of pure White, with a thought of vermillion—Not I—I Infer that the strongest decoction of the little Insect called Cochenille would only be a very poor color compared with the Truly red colored Nose of the Lady here mention[d]   This redeness extended from the Center of the ridge, off and over the Cheeks, the forehead, & the Chin in rich profusion, and along with the Cap, the Ribbands and the dress I thought that Nothing so very red had ever met my Eye before = She is aimiable however, and so are her Daughters, and so Lucy never mind the Color!—

*   *   *

Monday 18th Decemb[r] 1826

My Painting of the Cats fighting like Two Devils for a Dead Squirrel I finished at 3 o'clock having been 10 hours at it = this is Turning out Work of the hands as a Journeyman Carpenter would do =

I received a delightfull Letter from My Friend Thomas Sully Dated 9th of Last Month Inclosing one to Sir Thomas Lawrence to Introduce me = how Strange that D[r] Mease Should now advise me not to cut my Locks when he was So Strenuously desirous to have me do so when in Philad[a]   I dressed and took my painting to M[rs] Lizars to shew it her as it rained all day and had been prevented from coming to see me—I was at 5 at George Combe where I dined—the conversation positively Phrenology—George Combe extremely Agreable Companion and witte—I Left them all at seven, called for M[r] Lizars and went to the Royal Academy Meeting = Two of my Plates were laid on the Table = Doc[r] Brewster and M[r] Allan wished the Society to Subscribe for My Work and the comittee retired to act on it and other Business no doubt =

the Meeting was very Numerous and no doubt very Learned one. thou knowest I cannot well say but according to M[r] Ord *who is Learned and an Academician* I Suppose each member here quite as much so at Least as M[r] *George Ord* =

Sir W[am] Jardine and M[r] Selby arrived and came in a little before the Seating of the whole = the door of the Hall was oppen and We all marched in and seated Ourselves on well dressed hair clothed Seats = the Room is rich and beautifull—it is a large Oblong lined with brilliant Scarlet paper imitation of Morocco = the ceiling is divided in Large Oblong Compartments raised from the ground of it painted imitation oak = the Windows are Imensely Large decorated with borders resembling those of the Ceiling and had thin Green Jalousies = Two sets of lamps each composed of six Large globular ground Glass prisims hung from above and lighted with gas gave a light in every part of the Room suficient to Read by—the President sat in an Immense arm chair Lined with Red Morocco—and after the results of the last meeting were read—Professor   gave us a long, tedious, laboured Lecture on the origin of Languages, their formation, &^{c}—It was a very poor Mess I assure thee although I ought to say so who am not an Academician—Now My Friend Ord would have swallowed it Whole with delight no doubt but I could not make either head or Tail of it = a few fossil Bones of a Mammoth were offered to View, and thank God We raised the Siege = Sir Walter Scot sent Dr Brewster an Apology, for not coming this Evening I saw the hand writting but not the contents =

Sir W. J. and Mr Selby had brought Birds with them from Jardine Hall and wish to see my Style tomorow and Tomorow they Shall—

Mr Witham Subscribed to my Work but I went Away with Mr Lizars at 10 without Knowing the result from the Comittee who sat much latter—I had to go to Supper at Doc^r & Professor Russel in Abercromby Place = I entered a Set of two Large Rooms upstairs well furnished and exibiting much Wealth in the Owner Some Pictures were about the Walls (this is of course in this country it seems)—but Lucy I Entered with as much ease as if I had been going to work at Home = I walked about and Chated with several of the Academiccians that had also come and was rather Surprised to find that Many Although Great Men in that Way Knew Nothing of America beyond her Laws or the Situation of her Principal Cities = We went down to Supper at about 11 every thing Magnificently rich I Look^d on each a Tart and wished myself by thy side. I felt quite Worn out—at work since 6 o'clock either writting or Painting or Thinking hard—dining here—going to the Academy—Supping at this house I felt quite sick of the Whole and when the Company rose at ½ past 12 I was glad to leave and run here—in 3 minutes I will be in bed and May God Bless thee Good Night—

Edinburgh Decr 19th 1826 Tuesday.

My Writing generally takes me full two hours every morning and as Soon as I finished this day dressed Smart to go to breakfast with Sir W. Jardine and Mr Selby at Barry's Hotel Princes Street where I believe they allways take their abode when they visit Edinburgh it was just 9. the morning was pure and beautifull—the Sun was about raising Higher than the line of the old Town—the Orizon was all like burnished Gold—the walls of the castle white in the light and allmost black in their Shade along with many of the detached buildings in the distance had a Surprising effect on my feelings = I thought of the Grandeur of the scene = of the Power of the great Creator that formed it all with a thought. of the Power of Imitative man and was launched in deepest reflections when a Child, bear-footed, ragged and apparently on the eve of Starvation Shook my Views and altered my whole devotion. I gave him a Shilling the poor Child complained so of want that I dared I would have taken It to Sir William and made it breakfast at the Hotel = but thinking how Novel such an act might appear, how little I yet knew Sir W. and how Strange the world is, I told him to come with me—I returned home = took all my clothes from my Trunk and having made an Honest parcel of all the linen I had that I resolved at the moment Never to wear again—I gave it the Child. I gave it 5 more Shillings—I gave it my blessings, and I felt—oh my Lucy I felt such pleasure—I felt as if God Smiled on me!—

Now I soon reached the hotel and was in a Moment with My New Friends = they had brought—Ducks, Hawks and other Birds to draw after my Fashion—I breakfasted well, the thoughts of the little mendicant gave me an Appetite not felt for some days past—we then came to my Lodgings. I Shewed the Ornithologists how I put My Specimens Squared My paper &^{c} and had them both Intently Occupied drawing a little Squirrel—they call^d this a Lesson—Is it the first my Beloved

Wife? It was to me like a Dream that I should have come from America to Teach Men so much my superiors—they work very well Indeed although I perceived at once that Mr Selby was more Anthusiastic and work^d therefore faster than Sir W. but this one finished Closely as he went, so that on the whole it was difficult to give to either the Supremacy = they were delighted—Of course Mr Selby particularly so—he already cut out much Work to himself for Said he "I will paint all our own Quadrupeds in Oil for my own house" = they remained with me untill we could see no more =

I read them my Letter of the Carrion Crow but Dr Brewster had altered it so much that I was quite Chock^d at it—it made me quite Sick—he had Improved the Style and destroyed the Matter—

I dined at Major Dods 19 Pitt Street with a compleat set of Military Gentry—Colonels & Cap^c & Majors and G^{ls} I found there to my great astonishment Young Pattison My companion in the coach from Manchester here—he was cousin to Mrs Dods—Major Dods is the Uncle of John Crawford who was the clerk of N. Berthoud—I retired early I did not like the Blustery talk of all those Warriors—I went Direct to Mrs Lizars and having found the Ladies by themselves I felt as if enjoying a pleasant bath after a day's march of 50 miles—Miss hannah offered to play on the Piano for me—I felt delighted at this mark of kind attention and I compar^d her at once to my Sweet good Friend of Green Bank—from whom I fear I never will have an Answer to any of my Letters to her =

Mr Lizars came in with Sir W^{am} and Mr Selby and Announced that I was Ellected by acclamation a Member of the Society of Arts of this City. thus I possess one Tittle in Foreign Lands!—We talk^d agreat Deal about Ornithology—My Work, their Work &^{c} and at ½ past 10 we all three came away Linked closely together untill we reach^d their Hotel—I am again at My Lodgings and find a Kind Note from Cap^c Basil Hall of thanks &^{c} and Inclosing one to Cap^c Campbell of the R. N. at Glasgow—Now My Beloved Wife I feel extremely Anxious to set up all Night and write a dozen long letters but then If I do I fear that I will suffer tomorow and so May God Bless thee for ever! = Good night My Love.

Edinburgh Dec. 1826

Sunday Night 12 o'clock—

and Now My Dear book, must I part with thee? Back America, and fed in England and Scotland, and at sea—go to My best Friend. To My Wife, to my Beloved Lucy—yes, go back, return to thy own native soil and give her pleasure a while. *She* will be glad to hold conference with thee now—for she will look on thy sheets as the reflectors of my daily Life. Simple, either in times of Nothing or of wondrous events, and whilst she reads them, she will observe my very gradual advancement into a World yet unknown, and dangerous to be known. A World wherein I may prosper but wherein it is the easiest thing to sink into compleat oblivion. When I open thy sheets again where will *we* be? God only knows, and how happy or miserable shall I be—I will not pretend, at present, to investigate—or torment my brain about—for this simple reason, that God being my Supreme commander I am, and for ever will be, contented to act, to enjoy, to suffer or feel whatever in his Wisdom he may think best fit for me—and so well aware do I think him right in all he does, that happy or miserable, I will enjoy or suffer, perfectly satisfied that it is all for the best at last. Go, that My Wife read this, let my children read it. Let the world know these my heartfelt sentiments, and believe me, my Dear Book, for ever thy most obliged, yes truly obliged Friend.

John J. AUDUBON
—Citizen of the United States of North America

FROM

ORNITHOLOGICAL BIOGRAPHY

OR AN ACCOUNT OF THE HABITS OF THE

BIRDS OF THE UNITED STATES OF AMERICA

The Wild Turkey

Meleagris Gallopavo, LINN.

(PLATE I)

THE GREAT size and beauty of the Wild Turkey, its value as a delicate and highly prized article of food, and the circumstances of its being the origin of the domestic race now generally dispersed over both continents, render it one of the most interesting of the birds indigenous to the United States of America.

The unsettled parts of the States of Ohio, Kentucky, Illinois, and Indiana, an immense extent of country to the north-west of these districts, upon the Mississippi and Missouri, and the vast regions drained by these rivers from their confluence to Louisiana, including the wooded parts of Arkansas, Tennessee, and Alabama, are the most abundantly supplied with this magnificent bird. It is less plentiful in Georgia and the Carolinas, becomes still scarcer in Virginia and Pennsylvania, and is now very rarely seen to the eastward of the last mentioned States. In the course of my rambles through Long Island, the State of New York, and the country around the Lakes, I did not meet with a single individual, although I was informed that some exist in those parts. Turkeys are still to be found along the whole line of the Alleghany Mountains, where they have become so wary as to be approached only with extreme difficulty. While, in the Great Pine Forest, in 1829, I found a single feather that had been dropped from the tail of a female, but saw no bird of the kind. Farther eastward, I do not think they are now to be found. I shall describe the manners of this bird as observed in the countries where it is most abundant, and having resided for many years in Kentucky and Louisiana, may be understood as referring chiefly to them.

The Turkey is irregularly migratory, as well as irregularly gregarious. With reference to the first of these circumstances, I have to state, that whenever the *mast** of one portion of the

---

*In America, the term *mast* is not confined to the fruit of the beech, but is used as a general name for all kinds of forest fruits, including even grapes and berries.

country happens greatly to exceed that of another, the Turkeys are insensibly led toward that spot, by gradually meeting in their haunts with more fruit the nearer they advance towards the place where it is most plentiful. In this manner flock follows after flock, until one district is entirely deserted, while another is, as it were, overflowed by them. But as these migrations are irregular, and extend over a vast expanse of country, it is necessary that I should describe the manner in which they take place.

About the beginning of October, when scarcely any of the seeds and fruits have yet fallen from the trees, these birds assemble in flocks, and gradually move towards the rich bottom lands of Ohio and Mississippi. The males, or, as they are more commonly called, the *gobblers*, associate in parties of from ten to a hundred, and search for food apart from the females; while the latter are seen either advancing singly, each with its brood of young, then about two-thirds grown, or in connexion with other families, forming parties often amounting to seventy or eighty individuals, all intent on shunning the old cocks, which, even when the young birds have attained this size, will fight with, and often destroy them by repeated blows on the head. Old and young, however, all move in the same course, and on foot, unless their progress be interrupted by a river, or the hunter's dog force them to take wing. When they come upon a river, they betake themselves to the highest eminences, and there often remain a whole day, or sometimes two, as if for the purpose of consultation. During this time, the males are heard *gobbling*, calling, and making much ado, and are seen strutting about, as if to raise their courage to a pitch befitting the emergency. Even the females and young assume something of the same pompous demeanour, spread out their tails, and run round each other, *purring* loudly, and performing extravagant leaps. At length, when the weather appears settled, and all around is quiet, the whole party mounts to the tops of the highest trees, whence, at a signal, consisting of a single *cluck*, given by a leader, the flock takes flight for the opposite shore. The old and fat birds easily get over, even should the river be a mile in breadth; but the younger and less robust frequently fall into the water,—not to be drowned, however, as might be imagined. They bring their wings close to their body, spread out their tail as a support, stretch forward their neck, and, striking out their legs with great vigour, proceed rapidly towards the shore; on approaching which, should they find it too steep for landing, they cease their exertions for a few moments, float down the stream until they come to an accessible part, and by a violent effort generally extricate themselves from the water. It is remarkable, that immediately after thus crossing a large stream, they ramble about for some time, as if bewildered. In this state, they fall an easy prey to the hunter.

When the Turkeys arrive in parts where the mast is abundant, they separate into smaller flocks, composed of birds of all ages and both sexes, promiscuously mingled, and devour all before them. This happens about the middle of November. So gentle do they sometimes become after these long journeys, that they have been seen to approach the farm-houses, associate with the domestic fowls, and enter the stables and corncribs in quest of food. In this way, roaming about the forests, and feeding chiefly on mast, they pass the autumn and part of the winter.

As early as the middle of February, they begin to experience the impulse of propagation. The females separate, and fly from the males. The latter strenuously pursue, and begin to gobble or to utter the notes of exultation. The sexes roost apart, but at no great distance from each other. When a female utters a call-note, all the gobblers within hearing return the sound, rolling note after note with as much rapidity as if they intended to emit the last and the first together, not with spread tail, as when fluttering round the females on the ground, or practising on the branches of the trees on which they have roosted for the night, but much in the manner of the domestic turkey, when an unusual or unexpected noise elicits its singular hubbub. If the call of the female comes from the ground, all the males immediately fly towards the spot, and the moment they reach it, whether the hen be in sight or not, spread out and erect their tail, draw the head back on the shoulders, depress their wings with a quivering motion, and strut pompously about, emitting at the same time a succession of puffs from the lungs, and stopping now and then to listen and look. But whether they spy the female or not, they continue to puff and strut, moving with as much celerity as their ideas of ceremony seem to admit. While thus occupied, the males often encounter each other, in which case desperate battles take place, ending in bloodshed, and often in the loss of many lives, the weaker falling under the repeated blows inflicted upon their head by the stronger.

I have often been much diverted, while watching two males in fierce conflict, by seeing them move alternately backwards and forwards, as either had obtained a better hold, their wings drooping, their tails partly raised, their body-feathers ruffled, and their heads covered with blood. If, as they thus struggle, and gasp for breath, one of them should lose his hold, his chance is over, for the other, still holding fast, hits him violently with spurs and wings, and in a few minutes brings him to the ground. The moment he is dead, the conqueror treads him under foot, but, what is strange, not with hatred, but with all the motions which he employs in caressing the female.

When the male has discovered and made up to the female (whether such a combat has previously taken place or not), if she be more than one year old, she also struts and gobbles, turns round him as he continues strutting, suddenly opens her wings, throws herself towards him, as if to put a stop to his idle delay, lays herself down, and receives his dilatory caresses. If the cock meet a young hen, he alters his mode of procedure. He struts in a different manner, less pompously and more energetically, moves with rapidity, sometimes rises from the ground, taking a short flight around the hen, as is the manner of some Pigeons, the Red-breasted Thrush, and many other birds, and on alighting, runs with all his might, at the same time rubbing his tail and wings along the ground, for the space of perhaps ten yards. He then draws near the timorous female, allays her fears by purring, and when she at length assents, caresses her.

When a male and a female have thus come together, I believe the connexion continues for that season, although the former by no means confines his attentions to one female, as I have seen a cock caress several hens, when he happened to fall in with them in the same place, for the first time. After this the hens follow their favourite cock, roosting in his immediate neighbourhood, if not on the same tree, until they begin to lay, when they separate themselves, in order to save their eggs from the male, who would break them all, for the purpose of protracting his sexual enjoyments. The females then carefully avoid him, excepting during a short period each day. After this the males become clumsy and slovenly, if one may say so, cease to fight with each other, give up gobbling or calling so frequently, and assume so careless a habit, that the hens are obliged to make all the advances themselves. They *yelp* loudly and almost continually for the cocks, run up to them, caress them, and employ various means to rekindle their expiring ardour.

Turkey-cocks when at roost sometimes strut and gobble, but I have more generally seen them spread out and raise their tail, and emit the pulmonic puff, lowering their tail and other feathers immediately after. During clear nights, or when there is moonshine, they perform this action at intervals of a few minutes, for hours together, without moving from the same spot, and indeed sometimes without rising on their legs, especially towards the end of the love-season. The males now become greatly emaciated, and cease to gobble, their *breast-sponge* becoming flat. They then separate from the hens, and one might suppose that they had entirely deserted their neighbourhood. At such seasons I have found them lying by the side of a log, in some retired part of the dense woods and cane thickets, and often permitting one to approach within a few feet. They are then unable to fly, but run swiftly, and to a great distance. A slow turkey-hound has led me miles before I could flush the same bird. Chases of this kind I did not undertake for the purpose of killing the bird, it being then unfit for eating, and covered with ticks, but with the view of rendering myself acquainted with its habits. They thus retire to recover flesh and strength, by purging with particular species of grass, and using less exercise. As soon as their condition is improved, the cocks come together again, and recommence their rambles. Let us now return to the females.

About the middle of April, when the season is dry, the hens begin to look out for a place in which to deposit their eggs. This place requires to be as much as possible concealed from the eye of the Crow, as that bird often watches the Turkey when going to her nest, and, waiting in the neighbourhood until she has left it, removes and eats the eggs. The nest, which consists of a few withered leaves, is placed on the ground, in a hollow scooped out, by the side of a log, or in the fallen top of a dry leafy tree, under a thicket of sumach or briars, or a few feet within the edge of a cane-brake, but always in a dry place. The eggs, which are of a dull cream colour, sprinkled with red dots, sometimes amount to twenty, although the more usual number is from ten to fifteen. When depositing her eggs, the female always approaches the nest with extreme caution, scarcely ever taking the same course twice; and when about to leave them, covers them carefully with leaves, so that it is very difficult for a person who may have seen the bird to discover the nest. Indeed, few Turkeys' nests are found, unless the female has been suddenly started from them, or a cunning Lynx, Fox, or Crow has sucked the eggs and left their shells scattered about.

Turkey hens not unfrequently prefer islands for depositing their eggs and rearing their young, probably because such places are less frequented by hunters, and because the great masses of drifted timber which usually accumulate at their heads, may protect and save them in cases of great emergency. When I have found these birds in such situations, and with young, I have always observed that a single discharge of a gun made them run immediately to the pile of drifted wood, and conceal themselves in it. I have often walked over these masses, which are frequently from ten to twenty feet in height, in search of the game which I knew to be concealed in them.

When an enemy passes within sight of a female, while laying or sitting, she never moves, unless she knows that she has been discovered, but crouches lower until he has passed. I have frequently approached within five or six paces of a nest, of which I was previously aware, on assuming an air of carelessness, and whistling or talking to myself, the female remaining undisturbed; whereas if I went cautiously towards it, she would never suffer me to approach within twenty paces, but would run off, with her tail spread on one side, to a distance of twenty or thirty yards, when assuming a stately gait, she would walk about deliberately, uttering every now and then a cluck. They seldom abandon their nest, when it has been discovered by men; but, I believe, never go near it again, when a snake or other animal has sucked any of the eggs. If the eggs have been destroyed or carried off, the female soon yelps again for a male; but, in general, she rears only a single brood each season. Several hens sometimes associate together, I believe for their mutual safety, deposit their eggs in the same nest, and rear their broods together. I once found three sitting on forty-two eggs. In such cases, the common nest is always watched by one of the females, so that no Crow, Raven, or perhaps even Pole-cat, dares approach it.

The mother will not leave her eggs, when near hatching, under any circumstances, while life remains. She will even allow an enclosure to be made around her, and thus suffer imprisonment, rather than abandon them. I once witnessed the hatching of a brood of Turkeys, which I watched for the purpose of securing them together with the parent. I concealed myself on the ground within a very few feet, and saw her raise herself half the length of her legs, look anxiously upon the eggs, cluck with a sound peculiar to the mother on such occasions, carefully remove each half-empty shell, and with her bill caress and dry the young birds, that already stood tottering and attempting to make their way out of the nest. Yes, I have seen this, and have left mother and young to better care than mine could have proved,—to the care of their Creator and mine. I have seen them all emerge from the shell, and, in a few moments after, tumble, roll, and push each other forward, with astonishing and inscrutable instinct.

Before leaving the nest with her young brood, the mother shakes herself in a violent manner, picks and adjusts the feathers about her belly, and assumes quite a different aspect. She alternately inclines her eyes obliquely upwards and sideways, stretching out her neck, to discover hawks or other enemies, spreads her wings a little as she walks, and softly clucks to keep her innocent offspring close to her. They move slowly along, and as the hatching generally takes place in the afternoon, they frequently return to the nest to spend the first night there. After this, they remove to some distance, keeping on the highest undulated grounds, the mother dreading rainy weather, which is extremely dangerous to the young, in this tender state, when they are only covered by a kind of soft hairy down, of surprising delicacy. In very rainy seasons, Turkeys are scarce, for if once completely wetted, the young seldom recover. To prevent the disastrous effects of rainy weather, the mother, like a skilful physician, plucks the buds of the spice-wood bush, and gives them to her young.

In about a fortnight, the young birds, which had previously rested on the ground, leave it and fly, at night, to some very large low branch, where they place themselves under the deeply curved wings of their kind and careful parent, dividing themselves for that purpose into two nearly equal parties. After this, they leave the woods during the day, and approach the natural glades or prairies, in search of strawberries, and subsequently of dewberries, blackberries and grasshoppers, thus obtaining abundant food, and enjoying the beneficial influence of the sun's rays. They roll themselves in deserted ants' nests, to clear their growing feathers of the loose scales, and prevent ticks and other vermin from attacking them, these insects being unable to bear the odour of the earth in which ants have been.

The young Turkeys now advance rapidly in growth, and in the month of August are able to secure themselves from unexpected attacks of Wolves, Foxes, Lynxes, and even Cougars, by rising quickly from the ground, by the help of their powerful legs, and reaching with ease the highest branches of the tallest trees. The young cocks shew the tuft on the breast about this time, and begin to gobble and strut, while the young hens pur and leap, in the manner which I have already described.

The old cocks have also assembled by this time, and it is probable that all the Turkeys now leave the extreme northwestern districts, to remove to the Wabash, Illinois, Black River, and the neighbourhood of Lake Erie.

Of the numerous enemies of the Wild Turkey, the most formidable, excepting man, are the Lynx, the Snowy Owl, and the Virginian Owl. The Lynx sucks their eggs, and is extremely expert at seizing both young and old, which he effects in the following manner. When he has discovered a flock of Turkeys, he follows them at a distance for some time, until he ascertains the direction in which they are proceeding. He then makes a rapid circular movement, gets in advance of the flock, and lays himself down in ambush, until the birds come up, when he springs upon one of them by a single bound, and secures it. While once sitting in the woods, on the banks of the Wabash, I observed two large Turkey-cocks on a log, by the river, pluming and picking themselves. I watched their movements for a while, when of a sudden one of them flew across the river, while I perceived the other struggling under the grasp of a lynx. When attacked by the two large species of Owl above mentioned, they often effect their escape in a way which is somewhat remarkable. As Turkeys usually roost in flocks, on naked branches of trees, they are easily discovered by their enemies, the owls, which, on silent wing, approach and hover around them, for the purpose of reconnoitring. This, however, is rarely done without being discovered, and a single *cluck* from one of the Turkeys announces to the whole party the approach of the murderer. They instantly start upon their legs, and watch the motions of the Owl, which, selecting one as its victim, comes down upon it like an arrow, and would inevitably secure the Turkey, did not the latter at that moment lower its head, stoop, and spread its tail in an inverted manner over its back, by which action the aggressor is met by a smooth inclined plane, along which it glances without hurting the Turkey; immediately after which the latter drops to the ground, and thus escapes, merely with the loss of a few feathers.

The Wild Turkeys cannot be said to confine themselves to any particular kind of food, although they seem to prefer the pecan-nut and winter-grape to any other, and, where these fruits abound, are found in the greatest numbers. They eat grass and herbs of various kinds, corn, berries, and fruit of all descriptions. I have even found beetles, tadpoles, and small lizards in their crops.

Turkeys are now generally extremely shy, and the moment they observe a man, whether of the red or white race, instinctively move from him. Their usual mode of progression is what is termed walking, during which they frequently open each wing partially and successively, replacing them again by folding them over each other, as if their weight were too great. Then, as if to amuse themselves, they will run a few steps, open both wings and fan their sides, in the manner of the common fowl, and often take two or three leaps in the air and shake themselves. Whilst searching for food among the leaves or loose soil, they keep their head up, and are unremittingly on the lookout; but as the legs and feet finish the operation, they are immediately seen to pick up the food, the presence of which, I suspect, is frequently indicated to them through the sense of touch in their feet, during the act of scratching. This habit of scratching and removing the dried leaves in the woods, is pernicious to their safety, as the spots which they thus clear, being about two feet in diameter, are seen at a distance, and, if fresh, shew that the birds are in the vicinity. During the summer months they resort to the paths or roads, as well as the ploughed fields, for the purpose of rolling themselves in the dust, by which means they clear their bodies of the ticks which at that season infest them, as well as free themselves of the moschettoes, which greatly annoy them, by biting their heads.

When, after a heavy fall of snow, the weather becomes frosty, so as to form a hard crust on the surface, the Turkeys remain on their roosts for three or four days, sometimes much longer, which proves their capability of continued abstinence. When near farms, however, they leave the roosts, and go into the very stables and about the stacks of corn, to procure food. During melting snow-falls, they will travel to an extraordinary distance, and are then followed in vain, it being impossible for hunters of any description to keep up with them. They have then a dangling and straggling way of running, which, awkward as it may seem, enables them to outstrip any other animal. I have often, when on a good horse, been obliged to abandon the attempt to put them up, after following them for several hours. This habit of continued running, in rainy or very damp weather of any kind, is not peculiar to the Wild Turkey, but is common to all gallinaceous birds. In America, the different species of Grouse exhibit the same tendency.

In spring, when the males are much emaciated, in consequence of their attentions to the females, it sometimes happens that, on plain and open ground, they may be overtaken by a swift dog, in which case they squat, and allow themselves to be seized, either by the dog, or the hunter who has followed on a good horse. I have heard of such occurrences, but never had the pleasure of seeing an instance of them.

Good dogs scent the Turkeys, when in large flocks, at extraordinary distances,—I think I may venture to say half a mile. Should the dog be well trained to this sport, he sets off at full speed, and in silence, until he sees the birds, when he instantly barks, and pushing as much as possible into the centre of the flock, forces the whole to take wing in different directions. This is of great advantage to the hunter, for should the Turkeys all go one way, they would soon leave their perches and run again. But when they separate in this manner, and the weather happens to be calm and lowering, a person accustomed to this kind of sport finds the birds with ease, and shoots them at pleasure.

When Turkeys alight on a tree, it is sometimes very difficult to see them, which is owing to their standing perfectly motionless. Should you discover one, when it is down on its legs upon the branch, you may approach it with less care. But if it is standing erect, the greatest precaution is necessary, for should it discover you, it instantly flies off, frequently to such a distance that it would be vain to follow.

When a Turkey is merely winged by a shot, it falls quickly to the ground in a slanting direction. Then, instead of losing time by tumbling and rolling over, as other birds often do when wounded, it runs off at such a rate, that unless the hunter be provided with a swift dog, he may bid farewell to it. I recollect coming on one shot in this manner, more than a mile from the tree where it had been perched, my dog having traced it to this distance, through one of those thick canebrakes that cover many portions of our rich alluvial lands near the banks of our western rivers. Turkeys are easily killed if shot in the head, the neck, or the upper part of the breast; but if hit in the hind parts only, they often fly so far as to be lost to the hunter. During winter many of our *real* hunters shoot them by moonlight, on the roosts, where these birds will frequently stand a repetition of the reports of a rifle, although they would fly from the attack of an owl, or even perhaps from his presence. Thus sometimes nearly a whole flock is secured by men capable of using these guns in such circumstances.

They are often destroyed in great numbers when most worth-less, that is, early in the fall or autumn, when many are killed in their attempt to cross the rivers, or immediately after they reach the shore.

Whilst speaking of the shooting of Turkeys, I feel no hesitation in relating the following occurrence, which happened to myself. While in search of game, one afternoon late in autumn, when the males go together, and the females are by themselves also, I heard the clucking of one of the latter, and immediately finding her perched on a fence, made towards her. Advancing slowly and cautiously, I heard the yelping notes of some gobblers, when I stopped and listened in order to ascertain the direction in which they came. I then ran to meet the birds, hid myself by the side of a large fallen tree, cocked my gun, and waited with impatience for a good opportunity. The gobblers continued yelping in answer to the female, which all this while remained on the fence. I looked over the log and saw about thirty fine cocks advancing rather cautiously towards the very spot where I lay concealed. They came so near that the light in their eyes could easily be perceived, when I fired one barrel, and killed three. The rest, instead of flying off, fell a-strutting around their dead companions, and had I not looked on shooting again as murder without necessity, I might have secured at least another. So I shewed myself, and marching to the place where the dead birds were, drove away the survivors. I may also mention, that a friend of mine shot a fine hen, from his horse, with a pistol, as the poor thing was probably returning to her nest to lay.

Should you, good-natured reader, be a sportsman, and now and then have been fortunate in the exercise of your craft, the following incident, which I shall relate to you as I had it from the mouth of an honest farmer, may prove interesting. Turkeys were very abundant in his neighbourhood, and, resorting to his corn fields, at the period when the maize had just shot up from the ground, destroyed great quantities of it. This induced him to swear vengeance against the species. He cut a long trench in a favourable situation, put a great quantity of corn in it, and having heavily loaded a famous duck gun of his, placed it so as that he could pull the trigger by means of a string, when quite concealed from the birds. The Turkeys soon discovered the corn in the trench, and quickly disposed of it, at the same time continuing their ravages in the fields. He filled the trench again, and one day seeing it quite black with the Turkeys, whistled loudly, on which all the birds raised their heads, when he pulled the trigger by the long string fastened to it. The explosion followed of course, and the Turkeys were seen scampering off in all directions, in utter discomfiture and dismay. On running to the trench, he found nine of them extended in it. The rest did not consider it expedient to visit his corn again for that season.

During spring, Turkeys are *called*, as it is termed, by drawing the air in a particular way through one of the second joint bones of a wing of that bird, which produces a sound resembling the voice of the female, on hearing which the male comes up, and is shot. In managing this, however, no fault must be committed, for Turkeys are quick in distinguishing counterfeit sounds, and when *half civilized* are very wary and cunning. I have known many to answer to this kind of call, without moving a step, and thus entirely defeat the scheme of the hunter, who dared not move from his hiding-place, lest a single glance of the gobbler's eye should frustrate all further attempts to decoy him. Many are shot when at roost, in this season, by answering with a rolling gobble to a sound in imitation of the cry of the Barred Owl.

But the most common method of procuring Wild Turkeys, is by means of *pens*. These are placed in parts of the woods where Turkeys have been frequently observed to roost, and are constructed in the following manner. Young trees of four or five inches diameter are cut down, and divided into pieces of the length of twelve or fourteen feet. Two of these are laid on the ground parallel to each other, at a distance of ten or twelve feet. Two other pieces are laid across the ends of these, at right angles to them; and in this manner successive layers are added, until the fabric is raised to the height of about four feet. It is then covered with similar pieces of wood, placed three or four inches apart, and loaded with one or two heavy logs to render the whole firm. This done, a trench about eighteen inches in depth and width is cut under one side of the cage, into which it opens slantingly and rather abruptly. It is continued on its outside to some distance, so as gradually to attain the level of the surrounding ground. Over the part of this trench within the pen, and close to the wall, some sticks are placed so as to form a kind of bridge about a foot in breadth. The trap being now finished, the owner places a quantity of Indian corn in its centre, as well as in the trench, and as he walks off drops here and there a few grains in the woods, sometimes to the distance of a mile. This is repeated at every visit to the trap, after the Turkeys have found it. Sometimes two trenches are cut, in which case the trenches enter on opposite sides of the trap, and are both strewn with corn. No sooner has a Turkey discovered the train of corn, than it communicates the circumstance to the flock by a cluck, when all of them come up, and searching for the grains scattered about, at length come upon the trench, which they follow, squeezing themselves one after another through the passage under the bridge. In this manner the whole flock sometimes enters, but more commonly six or seven only, as they are alarmed by the least noise, even the cracking of a tree in frosty weather. Those within, having gorged themselves, raise their heads, and try to force their way through the top or sides of the pen, passing and repassing on the bridge, but never for a moment looking down, or attempting to escape through the passage by which they entered. Thus they remain until the owner of the trap arriving, closes the trench, and se-cures his captives. I have heard of eighteen Turkeys having been caught in this manner at a single visit to the trap. I have had many of these pens myself, but never found more than seven in them at a time. One winter I kept an account of the produce of a pen which I visited daily, and found that sev-enty-six had been caught in it, in about two months. When these birds are abundant, the owners of the pens sometimes become satiated with their flesh, and neglect to visit the pens for several days, in some cases for weeks. The poor captives thus perish for want of food; for, strange as it may seem, they scarcely ever regain their liberty, by descending into the trench, and retracing their steps. I have, more than once, found four or five, and even ten, dead in a pen, through inat-tention. Where Wolves or Lynxes are numerous, they are apt to secure the prize before the owner of the trap arrives. One morning, I had the pleasure of securing in one of my pens, a fine Black Wolf, which, on seeing me, squatted, supposing me to be passing in another direction.

Wild Turkeys often approach and associate with tame ones, or fight with them, and drive them off from their food. The cocks sometimes pay their addresses to the domesticated females, and are generally received by them with great pleasure, as well as by their owners, who are well aware of the advantages resulting from such intrusions, the half-breed being much more hardy than the tame, and, consequently, more easily reared.

While at Henderson, on the Ohio, I had, among many other wild birds, a fine male Turkey, which had been reared from its earliest youth under my care, it having been caught by me when probably not more than two or three days old. It became so tame that it would follow any person who called it, and was the favourite of the little village. Yet it would never roost with the tame Turkeys, but regularly betook itself at night to the roof of the house, where it remained until dawn. When two years old, it began to fly to the woods, where it remained for a considerable part of the day, to return to the enclosure as night approached. It continued this practice until the following spring, when I saw it several times fly from its roosting place to the top of a high cotton-tree, on the bank of the Ohio, from which, after resting a little, it would sail to the opposite shore, the river being there nearly half a mile wide, and return towards night. One morning I saw it fly off, at a very early hour, to the woods, in another direction, and took no particular notice of the circumstance. Several days elapsed, but the bird did not return. I was going towards some lakes near Green River to shoot, when, having walked about five miles, I saw a fine large gobbler cross the path before me, moving leisurely along. Turkeys being then in prime condition for the table, I ordered my dog to chase it, and put it up. The animal went off with great rapidity, and as it approached the Turkey, I saw, with great surprise, that the latter paid little attention. Juno was on the point of seizing it, when she suddenly stopped, and turned her head towards me. I hastened to them, but you may easily conceive my surprise when I saw my own favourite bird, and discovered that it had recognised the dog, and would not fly from it; although the sight of a strange dog would have caused it to run off at once. A friend of mine happening to be in search of a wounded deer, took the bird on his saddle before him, and carried it home for me. The following spring it was accidentally shot, having been taken for a wild bird, and brought to me on being recognised by the red ribbon which it had around its neck. Pray, reader, by what word will you designate the recognition made by my favourite Turkey of a dog which had been long associated with it in the yard and grounds? Was it the result of instinct, or of reason,—an unconsciously revived impression, or the act of an intelligent mind?

At the time when I removed to Kentucky, rather more than a fourth of a century ago, Turkeys were so abundant, that the price of one in the market was not equal to that of a common barn-fowl now. I have seen them offered for the sum of three pence each, the birds weighing from ten to twelve pounds. A first-rate Turkey, weighing from twenty-five to thirty pounds avoirdupois, was considered well sold when it brought a quarter of a dollar.

The weight of Turkey hens generally averages about nine pounds avoirdupois. I have, however, shot barren hens in strawberry season, that weighed thirteen pounds, and have seen a few so fat as to burst open on falling from a tree when shot. Male Turkeys differ more in their bulk and weight. From fifteen to eighteen pounds may be a fair estimate of their ordinary weight. I saw one offered for sale in the Louisville market, that weighed thirty-six pounds. Its pectoral appendage measured upwards of a foot.

Some closet naturalists suppose the hen Turkey to be destitute of the appendage on the breast, but this is not the case in the full-grown bird. The young males, as I have said, at the approach of the first winter, have merely a kind of protuberance in the flesh at this part, while the young females of the same age have no such appearance. The second year, the males are to be distinguished by the hairy tuft, which is about four inches long, whereas in the females that are not barren, it is yet hardly apparent. The third year, the male Turkey may be said to be adult, although it certainly increases in weight and size for several years more. The females at the age of four are in full beauty, and have the pectoral appendage four or five inches long, but thinner than in the male. The barren hens do not acquire it until they are very old. The experienced hunter knows them at once in the flock, and shoots them by preference. The great number of young hens destitute of the appendage in question, has doubtless given rise to the idea that it is wanting in the female Turkey.

The long downy *double* feathers* about the thighs and on the lower parts of the sides of the Wild Turkey, are often used for making tippets, by the wives of our squatters and farmers. These tippets, when properly made, are extremely beautiful as well as comfortable.

A long account of the habits of this remarkable bird has already been given in Bonaparte's American Ornithology, vol. i. As that account was in a great measure derived from notes furnished by myself, you need not be surprised, good reader, to find it often in accordance with the above.

Having now said all that I have thought it might be agreeable to you to know of the history and habits of the Wild Turkey, I proceed to the technical description of that interesting bird.

Purple Grakle or Common Crow-Blackbird

Quiscalus versicolor, VIEILL.

(PLATE 2)

I COULD not think of any better mode of representing these birds than that which I have adopted, as it exhibits them in the exercise of their nefarious propensities. Look at them: The male, as if full of delight at the sight of the havoc which he has already committed on the tender, juicy, unripe corn on which he stands, has swelled his throat, and is calling in

---

*The peculiarities in the structure of the plumage of different species of birds might, if duly attended to, prove of essential service to the systematic ornithologist, as conducing, along with other circumstances, to the elucidation of the natural affinities of birds. On this subject, I would refer the system-makers to the valuable observations of Mr. MACGILLIVRAY in the Edinburgh New Philosophical Journal for 1828.

exultation to his companions to come and assist him in demolishing it. The female has fed herself, and is about to fly off with a well-loaded bill to her hungry and expectant brood, that, from the nest, look on their plundering parents, joyously anticipating the pleasures of which they shall ere long be allowed to participate. See how torn the husk is from the ear, and how nearly devoured the grains of corn already are! This is the tithe our Blackbirds take from our planters and farmers; but it was so appointed, and such is the will of the beneficent Creator.

These birds are constant residents in Louisiana. I say they are so, because a certain number of them, which in some countries would be called immense, is found there at all seasons of the year. No sooner has the cotton or corn planter begun to turn his land into brown furrows, than the Crow-Blackbirds are seen sailing down from the skirts of the woods, alighting in the fields, and following his track along the ridges of newly-turned earth, with an elegant and elevated step, which shews them to be as fearless and free as the air through which they wing their way. The genial rays of the sun shine on their silky plumage, and offer to the ploughman's eye such rich and varying tints, that no painter, however gifted, could ever imitate them. The coppery bronze, which in one light shews its rich gloss, is, by the least motion of the bird, changed in a moment to brilliant and deep azure, and again, in the next light, becomes refulgent sapphire or emerald-green.

The bird stops, spreads its tail, lowers its wings, and, with swelled throat and open bill, sounds a call to those which may chance to be passing near. The stately step is resumed. Its keen eye, busily engaged on either side, is immediately attracted by a grub, hastening to hide itself from the sudden exposure made by the plough. In vain does it hurry, for the Grakle has seen and marked it for its own, and it is snatched up and swallowed in a moment.

Thus does the Grakle follow the husbandman as he turns one furrow after another, destroying a far worse enemy to the corn than itself, for every worm which it devours would else shortly cut the slender blade, and thereby destroy the plant when it would perhaps be too late to renew it by fresh seed.

Every reflecting farmer knows this well, and refrains from disturbing the Grakle at this season. Were he as merciful at another time, it would prove his grateful recollection of the services thus rendered him. But man is too often forgetful of the benefit which he has received; he permits his too commonly weak and selfish feelings to prevail over his reason; and no sooner does the corn become fit for his own use, than he vows and executes vengeance on all intruders. But to return to our Blackbird.

The season of love has arrived. Each male having, by assiduity, valour, or good fortune, received the affectionate regards of a faithful mate, unites with her in seeking a safe and agreeable retreat. The lofty dead trees left standing in our newly cultivated fields, have many holes and cavities, some of which have been bored by woodpeckers, and others caused by insects or decay. These are visited and examined in succession, until a choice being made, and a few dry weeds and feathers collected, the female deposits her eggs, which are from four to six in number, of a bluish tint, blotched and streaked with brown and black. She sits upon them while her valiant mate and guardian mounts to the summit of a broken branch, pours forth his rude notes, and cheers and watches her with the kindest and most unremitting care. I think I see him plunging through the air and overtaking the Red-headed or the Golden-winged Woodpecker, which, in search of their last year's nest, have imprudently alighted at the entrance of the already chosen and occupied hole. The conflict is but momentary; the creeping bird is forced to yield, and after whirling round in the air as it defends itself, and very nearly comes to the ground, makes the best of its way off, well knowing that there its opponent is more formidable than even in the air.

This over, the Grakle roams in quest of food. Little heaps of grubs, with a few grains of corn, afford delicious repasts to himself and his mate. They thus share the labours of incubation, and see the time pass in eager and pleasant expectation. And now the emerging brood shake off the shell that so long enclosed them; their tottering heads are already raised toward their mother, while she, with intense anxiety, dries and cherishes them. They grow up day after day. The hole becomes nearly filled with their increased bulk. The vigilance and industry of the parents also augment apace. I wish, good-natured reader, you would seek out such a sight: it would gladden your heart, for the rearing of such a family is worthy of your contemplation.

It is with regret that I must turn from this picture. I have already told you that the Grakles are at least as fond of corn as the lords of the land are. Hark to the sound of rattles, and the hallooing of the farmer's sons and servants, as they spread over the field! Now and then the report of a gun comes on the ear. The Grakles have scarcely a single moment of quiet; they are chased, stolen upon, and killed in great numbers, all the country round; but the hungry birds heed not the slaughter of their brethren. They fly in flocks from place to place, and, in spite of all that the farmer has done or threatens to do, continue their depredations. Food must be had. Grubs and worms have already retired to their winter quarters within the earth; no beech-nuts or acorns have yet fallen from the trees; corn is now their only resource, and the quantity of it which they devour is immense.

Now gloomy November brings up its cold blasts from the north, and drives before it the Grakles from the Eastern States. They reach Louisiana and all the Southern States when autumn has not yet retired, when the weather is still mild and serene, and the yellow foliage of the wide woods gives shelter to myriads of birds. The Grakles, congregated in prodigious flocks, alight on the trees that border the vast forests, covering every twig and bough in such astonishing masses, that the most unskilful or most avaricious gunner finds no difficulty in satisfying his wish for sport or game. This is the time to listen to their choruses. They seem to congratulate each other on their escape, and vociferate at such a rate as to make one imagine their number double what it is.

Beech-nuts and acorns are now abundant in the woods, having by this time fallen from the trees, and the Grakles roam in quest of them in immense bodies, rising on wing when disturbed, uttering at the same time a tremendous noise, then making a few rounds, and alighting again. They thus gradually clear away the mast, in the same manner as the wild pigeons are wont to do. As the weather becomes colder, they frequent the farms, and even resort to the cattle pens, where, from among the litter and refuse straw, they pick the scattered grains that have fallen from the stores with which the farmer has supplied his stock. They remain about the farms until the commencement of spring. They are easily caught in traps, and shew little fear when seized, biting so severely as often to draw blood, and laying hold with their claws in a very energetic manner.

During the winter of 1821, I caught a number of them, as well as many other birds, for the purpose of sending them alive to Europe. The whole of my captives were confined together in a large cage, where they were well fed and watered, and received all necessary attention. Things went on favourably for several days, and I with pleasure saw them becoming daily more gentle. An unexpected change, however, soon took place, for as the Grakles became reconciled to confinement, they began to attack the other birds, beating and killing one after another so fast that I was obliged to remove them from the cage. Even this did not prevent further breach of the peace, for the strong attacked and killed the weak of their own race, so that only a few remained in the end. The Grakles thus mangled, killed and partially devoured several Cardinal Grosbeaks, Doves, Pigeons, and Blue Jays. I look upon this remarkable instance of ferocity in the Grakle with the more amazement, as I never observed it killing any bird when in a state of freedom.

What I have said respecting the Purple Grakle (which by some is improperly named the Boat-tailed Grakle) refers particularly to the habits of those in the south, where some of them are found at all seasons. I shall now speak of those of the Western and Middle States. Most of these birds leave the south about the middle of February, setting out in small detached flocks. They reach the State of New York in this straggling manner about the middle of May. Their migratory flight is performed in short undulating lines, resembling small segments of very large circles. It may be explained in this manner. Supposing the bird poised in the air and intent on moving forwards, it propels itself by a strenuous flap of the wings, which carries it forward in a curve, along which it ascends until it attains the level of its original point of departure, when it flaps its wings again, and performs another curve. In this form of flight they pursue their long journey, during which they keep up a continual low chattering, as if they were discussing some important question. When they reach Pennsylvania, they commence the avocations which I have already described, and are seen following the plough, while their kindred that have been left in Louisiana are probably by this time feeding their young, as the difference of climate between these latitudes leaves the northern states a month later in their seasons than the southern.

In the Northern States these birds construct their nests in a much more perfect, and therefore more natural manner. A pine tree, whenever it occurs in a convenient place, is selected by preference, its dense foliage and horizontal branches being well adapted for nidification. There the Grakle forms a nest, which from the ground might easily be mistaken for that of our Robin, the *Turdus migratorius*, were it less bulky. But it is much larger, and instead of being placed by itself, is associated with others, often to the number of a dozen or more, on the horizontal arms of the pine, forming tier above tier, from the lowest to the highest branches. The centre of the nest is what I would call *saddled* on the bough, the materials being laid so that the nest is thinner in its middle part and thicker at the two opposite sides, so as to have a firm hold. It is about six inches in diameter outside, and four inches within, the depth being the same, and is composed of grass, slender roots and mud, lined with hair and finer grasses. I had a white pine-tree in one of my fields on Mill Grove Farm, on which many of these birds bred every spring, when some mischievous lads frequently amused themselves with beating down the nests with long fishing-rods, to my great annoyance. Some of the Pennsylvanian farmers, from a very laudable motive, have given out that Grakles are fond of pulling up the garlic plant, so injurious to the pastures of the Middle States; but I am sorry to say this assertion is by no means correct, and were these good people to look to the Grakles for the clearing of their fields from that evil, they might wait long enough.

The flesh of the Purple Grakle is little better than that of the Crow, being dry and ill-flavoured, notwithstanding which it is frequently used, with the addition of one or two Golden-winged Woodpeckers or Redwings, to make what is here called *pot pie*, even amidst a profusion of so many better things. The eggs, on the contrary, are very delicate, and I am astonished that those who are so anxious for the destruction of these birds do not gratify their wishes by eating them while yet in embryo in the egg. In some parts of Louisiana, the farmers, or, as they are styled, the planters, steep the seed corn for a few hours in a solution of Glauber's salt, to deter the Grakles and other birds from eating the grains when just *planted*, as we term it in America, the word *sow* being seldom employed there to denote the act of depositing in the earth even the smallest seed.

The Purple Grakle travels very far north. I have found it everywhere during my peregrinations, and in one or two instances have seen it form its nest in the fissures of rocks.

The Bird of Washington
Falco Washingtonii
(PLATE 3)

IT WAS in the month of February 1814, that I obtained the first sight of this noble bird, and never shall I forget the delight which it gave me. Not even HERSCHEL, when he discovered the planet which bears his name, could have experienced more rapturous feelings. We were on a trading voyage, ascending the Upper Mississippi. The keen wintry blasts whistled around us, and the cold from which I suffered had, in a great degree, extinguished the deep interest which, at other seasons, this magnificent river has been wont to awake in me. I lay stretched beside our patroon. The safety of the cargo was forgotten, and the only thing that called my attention was the multitude of ducks, of different species, accompanied by vast flocks of swans, which from time to time passed us. My patroon, a Canadian, had been engaged many years in the fur trade. He was a man of much intelligence, and, perceiving that these birds had engaged my curiosity, seemed anxious to find some new object to divert me. An eagle flew over us. "How fortunate!" he exclaimed; "this is what I could have wished. Look, sir! the Great Eagle, and the only one I have seen since I left the lakes." I was instantly on my feet, and having observed it attentively, concluded, as I lost it in the distance, that it was a species quite new to me. My patroon assured me that such birds were indeed rare; that they sometimes followed the hunters, to feed on the entrails of animals which they had killed, when the lakes were frozen over, but that when the lakes were open, they would dive in the daytime after fish, and snatch them up in the manner of the Fishing Hawk; and that they roosted generally on the shelves of the rocks, where they built their nests, of which he had discovered several by the quantity of white dung scattered below.

Convinced that the bird was unknown to naturalists, I felt particularly anxious to learn its habits, and to discover in what particulars it differed from the rest of its genus. My next meeting with this bird was a few years afterwards, whilst engaged in collecting crayfish on one of those flats which border and divide Green River, in Kentucky, near its junction with the Ohio. The river is there bordered by a range of high cliffs, which, for some distance, follow its windings. I observed on the rocks, which, at that place, are nearly perpendicular, a quantity of white ordure, which I attributed to owls that might have resorted thither. I mentioned the circumstance to my companions, when one of them, who lived within a mile and a half of the place, told me it was from the nest of the Brown Eagle, meaning the White-headed Eagle (*Falco leucocephalus*) in its immature state. I assured him this could not be, and remarked that neither the old nor the young birds of that species ever build in such places, but always in trees. Although he could not answer my objection, he stoutly maintained that a brown eagle of some kind, above the usual size, had built there; and added that he had espied the nest some days before, and had seen one of the old birds dive and catch a fish. This he thought strange, having, till then, always observed that both Brown Eagles and Bald Eagles procured this kind of food by robbing the fish-hawks. He said that if I felt particularly anxious to know what nest it was, I might soon satisfy myself, as the old birds would come and feed their young with fish, for he had seen them do so before.

In high expectation, I seated myself about a hundred yards from the foot of the rock. Never did time pass more slowly. I could not help betraying the most impatient curiosity, for my hopes whispered it was a Sea Eagle's nest. Two long hours had elapsed before the old bird made his appearance, which was announced to us by the loud hissings of the two young ones, which crawled to the extremity of the hole to receive a fine fish. I had a perfect view of this noble bird as he held himself to the edging rock, hanging like the Barn, Bank, or Social Swallow, his tail spread, and his wings partly so. I trembled lest a word should escape from my companions. The slightest murmur had been treason from them. They entered into my feelings, and, although little interested, gazed with me. In a few minutes the other parent joined her mate, and from the difference in size (the female of rapacious birds being much larger), we knew this to be the mother bird. She also had brought a fish; but, more cautious than her mate, she glanced her quick and piercing eye around, and instantly perceived that her abode had been discovered. She dropped her prey, with a loud shriek communicated the alarm to the male, and, hovering with him over our heads, kept up a growling cry, to intimidate us from our suspected design. This watchful solicitude I have ever found peculiar to the female:—must I be understood to speak only of birds?

The young having concealed themselves, we went and picked up the fish which the mother had let fall. It was a white perch, weighing about 5½ lb. The upper part of the head was broken in, and the back torn by the talons of the eagle. We had plainly seen her bearing it in the manner of the Fish-Hawk.

This day's sport being at an end, as we journeyed homewards, we agreed to return the next morning, with the view of obtaining both the old and young birds; but rainy and tempestuous weather setting in, it became necessary to defer the expedition till the third day following, when, with guns and men all in readiness, we reached the rock. Some posted themselves at the foot, others upon it, but in vain. We passed the entire day, without either seeing or hearing an eagle, the sagacious birds, no doubt, having anticipated an invasion, and removed their young to new quarters.

I come at last to the day which I had so often and so ardently desired. Two years had gone by since the discovery of the nest, in fruitless excursions; but my wishes were no longer to remain ungratified. In returning from the little village of Henderson, to the house of Doctor RANKIN, about a mile distant, I saw an eagle rise from a small enclosure not a hundred yards before me, where the Doctor had a few days before slaughtered some hogs, and alight upon a low tree branching over the road. I prepared my double-barrelled piece, which I constantly carry, and went slowly and cautiously towards him. Quite fearlessly he awaited my approach, looking upon me with undaunted eye. I fired and he fell. Before I reached him he was dead. With what delight did I survey the magnificent bird! Had the finest salmon ever pleased him as he did me?—Never. I ran and presented him to my friend, with a pride which they alone can feel, who, like me, have devoted themselves from their earliest childhood to such pursuits, and who have derived from them their first pleasures. To others I must seem to "prattle out of fashion." The Doctor, who was an experienced hunter, examined the bird with much satisfaction, and frankly acknowledged he had never before seen or heard of it.

The name which I have chosen for this new species of Eagle, "The Bird of Washington," may, by some, be considered as preposterous and unfit; but as it is indisputably the noblest bird of its genus that has yet been discovered in the United States, I trust I shall be allowed to honour it with the name of one yet nobler, who was the saviour of his country, and whose name will ever be dear to it. To those who may be curious to know my reasons, I can only say, that, as the new world gave me birth and liberty, the great man who ensured its independence is next to my heart. He had a nobility of mind, and a generosity of soul, such as are seldom possessed. He was brave, so is the eagle; like it, too, he was the terror of his foes; and his fame, extending from pole to pole, resembles the majestic soarings of the mightiest of the feathered tribe. If America has reason to be proud of her Washington, so has she to be proud of her Great Eagle.

In the month of January following, I saw a pair of these eagles flying over the Falls of the Ohio, one in pursuit of the other. The next day I saw them again. The female had relaxed her severity, had laid aside her coyness, and to a favourite tree they continually resorted. I pursued them unsuccessfully for several days, when they forsook the place.

The flight of this bird is very different from that of the White-headed Eagle. The former encircles a greater space, whilst sailing keeps nearer to the land and the surface of the water, and when about to dive for fish falls in a spiral manner, as if with the intention of checking any retreating movement which its prey might attempt, darting upon it only when a few yards distant. The Fish-hawk often does the same. When rising with a fish, the Bird of Washington flies to a considerable distance, forming, in its line of course, a very acute angle with the surface line of the water. My last opportunity of seeing this bird, was on the 15th of November 1821, a few miles above the mouth of the Ohio, when two passed over our boat, moving down the river with a gentle motion. In a letter from a kind relative, Mr W. BAKEWELL, dated, "Falls of the Ohio, July 1819," and containing particulars relative to the Swallow-tailed Hawk (*Falco furcatus*), that gentleman says:—"Yesterday, for the first time, I had an opportunity of viewing one of those magnificent birds, which you call the Sea Eagle, as it passed low over me, whilst fishing. I shall be really glad when I can again have the pleasure of seeing your drawing of it."

Whilst in Philadelphia, about twelve months ago, I had the gratification of seeing a fine specimen of this Eagle at Mr BRANO's museum. It was a male in fine plumage, and beautifully preserved. I wished to purchase it with a view to carry it to Europe, but the price put upon it was above my means.

My excellent friend RICHARD HARLAN, M. D. of that city, speaking of this bird in a letter dated "Philadelphia, August 19, 1830," says, "That fine specimen of *Washington Eagle*, which you noticed in BRANO's museum, is at present in my possession. I have deposited it in the Academy, where it will most likely remain." I saw the specimen alluded to, which, in as far as I could observe, agreed in size and markings exactly with my drawing, to which, however, I could not at the time refer, as it was, with the whole of my collection, deposited in the British Museum, under the care of my ever kind and esteemed friend J. G. CHILDREN, Esq. of that Institution.

The glands containing the oil used for the purpose of anointing the surface of the plumage were, in the specimen represented in the plate, extremely large. Their contents had the appearance of hog's lard, which had been melted and become rancid. This bird makes more copious use of that substance than the White-headed Eagle, or any of the tribe to which it belongs, excepting the Fish-hawk, the whole plumage looking, upon close examination, as if it had received a general coating of a thin clear dilution of gum-arabic, and presenting less of the downy gloss exhibited in the upper part of the White-headed Eagle's plumage. The male bird weighs 14½ lb. avoirdupois, and measures 3 feet 7 inches in length, and 10 feet 2 inches in extent.

The Great-footed Hawk

Falco peregrinus, GMEL.

(PLATE 8)

THE French and Spaniards of Louisiana have designated all the species of the genus Falco by the name of "*Mangeurs de Poulets*;" and the farmers in other portions of the Union have bestowed upon them, according to their size, the appellations of "Hen Hawk," "Chicken Hawk," "Pigeon Hawk," &c. This mode of naming these rapacious birds is doubtless natural enough, but it displays little knowledge of the characteristic manners of the species. No bird can better illustrate the frequent inaccuracy of the names bestowed by ignorant persons than the present, of which on referring to the plate, you will see a pair enjoying themselves over a brace of ducks of different species. Very likely, were tame ducks as plentiful on the plantations in our States, as wild ducks are on our rivers, lakes and estuaries, these hawks might have been named by some of our settlers "*Mangeurs de Canards.*"

Look at these two pirates eating their *dejeuné à la fourchette*, as it were, congratulating each other on the savouriness of the food in their grasp. One might think them real epicures, but they are in fact true gluttons. The male has obtained possession of a Green-winged Teal, while his mate has procured a Gadwal Duck. Their appetites are equal to their reckless daring, and they well deserve the name of "Pirates," which I have above bestowed upon them.

The Great-footed Hawk, or Peregrine Falcon, is now frequently to be met with in the United States, but within my remembrance it was a very scarce species in America. I can well recollect the time when, if I shot one or two individuals of the species in the course of a whole winter, I thought myself a fortunate mortal; whereas of late years I have shot two in one day, and perhaps a dozen in the course of a winter. It is quite impossible for me to account for this increase in their number, the more so that our plantations have equally increased, and we have now three gunners for every one that existed twenty years ago, and all of them ready to destroy a hawk of any kind whenever an occasion presents itself.

The flight of this bird is of astonishing rapidity. It is scarcely ever seen sailing, unless after being disappointed in its attempt to secure the prey which it has been pursuing, and even at such times it merely rises with a broad spiral circuit, to attain a sufficient elevation to enable it to reconnoitre a certain space below. It then emits a cry much resembling that of the Sparrow Hawk, but greatly louder, like that of the European Kestrel, and flies off swiftly in quest of plunder. The search is often performed with a flight resembling that of the tame pigeon, until perceiving an object, it redoubles its flappings, and pursues the fugitive with a rapidity scarcely to be conceived. Its turnings, windings and cuttings through the air are now surprising. It follows and nears the timorous quarry at every turn and back-cutting which the latter attempts. Arrived within a few feet of the prey, the Falcon is seen protruding his powerful legs and talons to their full stretch. His wings are for a moment almost closed; the next instant he grapples the prize, which, if too weighty to be carried off directly, he forces obliquely toward the ground, sometimes a hundred yards from where it was seized, to kill it, and devour it on the spot. Should this happen over a large extent of water, the Falcon drops his prey, and sets off in quest of another. On the contrary, should it not prove too heavy, the exulting bird carries it off to a sequestered and secure place. He pursues the smaller Ducks, Water-hens, and other swimming birds, and if they are not quick in diving, seizes them, and rises with them from the water. I have seen this Hawk come at the report of a gun, and carry off a Teal not thirty steps distant from the sportsman who had killed it, with a daring assurance as surprising as unexpected. This conduct has been observed by many individuals, and is a characteristic trait of the species. The largest duck that I have seen this bird attack and grapple with on the wing is the Mallard.

The Great-footed Hawk does not however content himself with water-fowl. He is generally seen following the flocks of Pigeons and even Blackbirds, causing great terror in their ranks, and forcing them to perform various aerial evolutions to escape the grasp of his dreaded talons. For several days I watched one of them that had taken a particular fancy to some tame pigeons, to secure which it went so far as to enter their house at one of the holes, seize a bird, and issue by another hole in an instant, causing such terror among the rest as to render me fearful that they would abandon the place. However, I fortunately shot the depredator.

They occasionally feed on dead fish that have floated to the shores or sand bars. I saw several of them thus occupied while descending the Mississippi on a journey undertaken expressly for the purpose of observing and procuring different specimens of birds, and which lasted four months, as I followed the windings of that great river, floating down it only a few miles daily. During that period, I and my companion counted upwards of fifty of these Hawks, and killed several, among which was the female represented in the plate now before you, and which was found to contain in its stomach bones of birds, a few downy feathers, the gizzard of a Teal, and the eyes and many scales of a fish. It was shot on the 26th December 1820. The ovary contained numerous eggs, two of which were as large as pease.

Whilst in quest of food, the Great-footed Hawk will frequently alight on the highest dead branch of a tree in the immediate neighbourhood of such wet or marshy grounds as the Common Snipe resorts to by preference. His head is seen moving in short starts, as if he were counting every little space below; and while so engaged, the moment he spies a Snipe, down he darts like an arrow, making a rustling noise with his wings that may be heard several hundred yards off, seizes the Snipe, and flies away to some near wood to devour it.

It is a cleanly bird, in respect to feeding. No sooner is the prey dead than the Falcon turns its belly upward, and begins to pluck it with his bill, which he does very expertly, holding it meantime quite fast in his talons; and as soon as a portion is cleared of feathers, tears the flesh in large pieces, and swallows it with great avidity. If it is a large bird, he leaves the refuse parts, but, if small, swallows the whole in pieces. Should he be approached by an enemy, he rises with it and flies off into the interior of the woods, or if he happens to be in a meadow, to some considerable distance, he being more wary at such times than when he has alighted on a tree.

The Great-footed Hawk is a heavy, compact, and firmly built bird for its size, and when arrived at maturity, extremely muscular, with very tough flesh. The plumage differs greatly according to age. I have seen it vary in different individuals, from the deepest chocolate-brown to light grey. Their grasp is so firm, that should one be hit while perched, and not shot quite dead, it will cling to the branch until life has departed.

Like most other Hawks, this is a solitary bird, excepting during the breeding season, at the beginning of which it is seen in pairs. Their season of breeding is so very early, that it might be said to be in winter. I have seen the male caressing the female as early as the first days of December.

This species visits Louisiana during the winter months only; for although I have observed it mating then, it generally disappears a few days after, and in a fortnight later none can be seen. It is scarce in the Middle States, where, as well as in the Southern Districts, it lives along water-courses, and in the neighbourhood of the shores of the sea and inland lakes. I should think that they breed in the United States, having shot a pair in the month of August near the Falls of Niagara. It is extremely tenacious of life, and if not wounded in the wings, though mortally so in the body, it flies to the last gasp, and does not fall until life is extinct. I never saw one of them attack a quadruped, although I have frequently seen them perched within sight of squirrels, which I thought they might easily have secured, had they been so inclined.

Once when nearing the coast of England, being then about a hundred and fifty miles distant from it, in the month of July, I obtained a pair of these birds, which had come on board our vessel, and had been shot there. I examined them with care, and found no difference between them and those which I had shot in America. They are at present scarce in England, where I have seen only a few. In London, some individuals of the species resort to the cupola of St Paul's Cathedral, and the towers of Westminster Abbey, to roost, and probably to breed. I have seen them depart from these places at day dawn, and return in the evening.

The achievements of this species are well known in Europe, where it is even at the present day trained for the chase. Whilst on a visit at Dalmahoy, the seat of the Earl of Morton, near Edinburgh, I had the pleasure of seeing a pair of these birds hooded, and with small brass bells on their legs, in excellent training. They were the property of that nobleman.

These birds sometimes roost in the hollows of trees. I saw one resorting for weeks every night to a hole in a dead sycamore, near Louisville in Kentucky. It generally came to the place a little before sunset, alighted on the dead branches, and in a short time after flew into the hollow, where it spent the night, and from whence I saw it issuing at dawn. I have known them also retire for the same purpose to the crevices of high cliffs, on the banks of Green River in the same state. One winter, when I had occasion to cross the Homochitta River, in the State of Mississippi, I observed these Hawks in greater numbers than I had ever before seen.

Many persons believe that this Hawk, and some others, never drink any other fluid than the blood of their victims; but this is an error. I have seen them alight on sand bars, walk to the edge of them, immerse their bills nearly up to the eyes in the water, and drink in a continued manner, as Pigeons are known to do.

The Mocking Bird

Turdus polyglottus, LINN.

(PLATE 4)

IT IS where the Great Magnolia shoots up its majestic trunk, crowned with evergreen leaves, and decorated with a thousand beautiful flowers, that perfume the air around; where the forests and fields are adorned with blossoms of every hue; where the golden Orange ornaments the gardens and groves; where Bignonias of various kinds interlace their climbing stems around the White-flowered Stuartia, and mounting still higher, cover the summits of the lofty trees around, accompanied with innumerable Vines, that here and there festoon the dense foliage of the magnificent woods, lending to the vernal breeze a slight portion of the perfume of their clustered flowers; where a genial warmth seldom forsakes the atmosphere; where berries and fruits of all descriptions are met with at every step;—in a word, kind reader, it is where Nature seems to have paused, as she passed over the Earth, and opening her stores, to have strewed with unsparing hand the diversified seeds from which have sprung all the beautiful and splendid forms which I should in vain attempt to describe, that the Mocking Bird should have fixed its abode, there only that its wondrous song should be heard.

But where is that favoured land?—It is in that great continent to whose distant shores Europe has sent forth her adventurous sons, to wrest for themselves a habitation from the wild inhabitants of the forest, and to convert the neglected soil into fields of exuberant fertility. It is, reader, in Louisiana that these bounties of nature are in the greatest perfection. It is there that you should listen to the love-song of the Mocking Bird, as I at this moment do. See how he flies round his mate, with motions as light as those of the butterfly! His tail is widely expanded, he mounts in the air to a small distance, describes a circle, and, again alighting, approaches his beloved one, his eyes gleaming with delight, for she has already promised to be his and his only. His beautiful wings are gently raised, he bows to his love, and again bouncing upwards, opens his bill, and pours forth his melody, full of exultation at the conquest which he has made.

They are not the soft sounds of the flute or of the hautboy that I hear, but the sweeter notes of Nature's own music. The mellowness of the song, the varied modulations and gradations, the extent of its compass, the great brilliancy of execution, are unrivalled. There is probably no bird in the world that possesses all the musical qualifications of this king of song, who has derived all from Nature's self. Yes, reader, all!

No sooner has he again alighted, and the conjugal contract has been sealed, than, as if his breast was about to be rent with delight, he again pours forth his notes with more softness and richness than before. He now soars higher, glancing around with a vigilant eye, to assure himself that none has witnessed his bliss. When these love-scenes, visible only to the ardent lover of nature, are over, he dances through the air, full of animation and delight, and, as if to convince his lovely mate that to enrich her hopes he has much more love in store, he that moment begins anew, and imitates all the notes which nature has imparted to the other songsters of the grove.

For a while, each long day and pleasant night are thus spent; but at a peculiar note of the female he ceases his song, and attends to her wishes. A nest is to be prepared, and the choice of a place in which to lay it is to become a matter of mutual consideration. The Orange, the Fig, the Pear-tree of the gardens are inspected; the thick briar patches are also visited. They appear all so well suited for the purpose in view, and so well does the bird know that man is not his most dangerous enemy, that instead of retiring from him, they at length fix their abode in his vicinity, perhaps in the nearest tree to his window. Dried twigs, leaves, grasses, cotton, flax, and other substances, are picked up, carried to a forked branch, and there arranged. The female has laid an egg, and the male redoubles his caresses. Five eggs are deposited in due time, when the male having little more to do than to sing his mate to repose, attunes his pipe anew. Every now and then he spies an insect on the ground, the taste of which he is sure will please his beloved one. He drops upon it, takes it in his bill, beats it against the earth, and flies to the nest to feed and receive the warm thanks of his devoted female.

When a fortnight has elapsed, the young brood demand all their care and attention. No cat, no vile snake, no dreaded hawk, is likely to visit their habitation. Indeed the inmates of the next house have by this time become quite attached to the lovely pair of Mocking Birds, and take pleasure in contributing to their safety. The dew-berries from the fields, and many kinds of fruit from the gardens, mixed with insects, supply the young as well as the parents with food. The brood is soon seen emerging from the nest, and in another fortnight, being now able to fly with vigour, and to provide for themselves, they leave the parent birds, as many other species do.

The above account does not contain all that I wish you to know of the habits of this remarkable songster; so, I shall shift the scene to the woods and wilds, where we shall examine it more particularly.

The Mocking Bird remains in Louisiana the whole year. I have observed with astonishment, that towards the end of October, when those which had gone to the Eastern States, some as far as Boston, have returned, they are instantly known by the "southrons," who attack them on all occasions. I have ascertained this by observing the greater shyness exhibited by the strangers for weeks after their arrival. This shyness, however, is shortly over, as well as the animosity displayed by the resident birds, and during the winter there exists a great appearance of sociality among the united tribes.

In the beginning of April, sometimes a fortnight earlier, the Mocking Birds pair, and construct their nests. In some instances they are so careless as to place the nest between the rails of a fence directly by the road. I have frequently found it in such places, or in the fields, as well as in briars, but always so easily discoverable that any person desirous of procuring one, might do so in a very short time. It is coarsely constructed on the outside, being there composed of dried sticks of briars, withered leaves of trees, and grasses, mixed with wool. Internally it is finished with fibrous roots disposed in a circular form, but carelessly arranged. The female lays from four to six eggs the first time, four or five the next, and when there is a third brood, which is sometimes the case, seldom more than three, of which I have rarely found more than two hatched. The eggs are of a short oval form, light green, blotched and spotted with umber. The young of the last brood not being able to support themselves until late in the season, when many of the berries and insects have become scarce, are stunted in growth;—a circumstance which has induced some persons to imagine the existence in the United States of two species of Mocking Bird, a larger and a smaller. This, however, in as far as my observation goes, is not correct. The first brood is frequently brought to the bird-market in New Orleans as early as the middle of April. A little farther up the country, they are out by the fifteenth of May. The second brood is hatched in July, and the third in the latter part of September.

The nearer you approach to the sea-shores, the more plentiful do you find these birds. They are naturally fond of loose sands, and of districts scantily furnished with small trees, or patches of briars, and low bushes.

During incubation, the female pays such precise attention to the position in which she leaves her eggs, when she goes to a short distance for exercise and refreshment, to pick up gravel, or roll herself in the dust, that, on her return, should she find that any of them has been displaced, or touched by the hand of man, she utters a low mournful note, at the sound of which the male immediately joins her, and they are both seen to condole together. Some people imagine that, on such occasions, the female abandons the nest; but this idea is incorrect. On the contrary, she redoubles her assiduity and care, and scarcely leaves the nest for a moment; nor is it until she has been repeatedly forced from the dear spot, and has been much alarmed by frequent intrusions, that she finally and reluctantly leaves it. Nay, if the eggs are on the eve of being hatched, she will almost suffer a person to lay hold of her.

Different species of snakes ascend to their nests, and generally suck the eggs or swallow the young; but on all such occasions, not only the pair to which the nest belongs, but many other Mocking Birds from the vicinity, fly to the spot, attack the reptiles, and, in some cases, are so fortunate as either to force them to retreat, or deprive them of life. Cats that have abandoned the houses to prowl about the fields, in a half wild state, are also dangerous enemies, as they frequently approach the nest unnoticed, and at a pounce secure the mother, or at least destroy the eggs or young, and overturn the nest. Children seldom destroy the nests of these birds, and the planters generally protect them. So much does this feeling prevail throughout Louisiana, that they will not willingly permit a Mocking Bird to be shot at any time.

In winter, nearly all the Mocking Birds approach the farm-houses and plantations, living about the gardens or out-houses. They are then frequently seen on the roofs, and perched on the chimney-tops; yet they always appear full of animation. Whilst searching for food on the ground, their motions are light and elegant, and they frequently open their wings as butterflies do when basking in the sun, moving a step or two, and again throwing out their wings. When the weather is mild, the old males are heard singing with as much spirit as during the spring or summer, while the younger birds are busily engaged in practising, preparatory to the love sea-son. They seldom resort to the interior of the forest either during the day or by night, but usually roost among the fo-liage of evergreens, in the immediate vicinity of houses in Louisiana, although in the Eastern States they prefer low fir trees.

The flight of the Mocking Bird is performed by short jerks of the body and wings, at every one of which a strong twitch-ing motion of the tail is perceived. This motion is still more apparent while the bird is walking, when it opens its tail like a fan and instantly closes it again. The common *cry* or *call* of this bird is a very mournful note, resembling that uttered on similar occasions by its first cousin the *Turdus rufus*, or, as it is commonly called, the "*French Mocking Bird*." When travel-ling, this flight is only a little prolonged, as the bird goes from tree to tree, or at most across a field, scarcely, if ever, rising higher than the top of the forest. During this migration, it generally resorts to the highest parts of the woods near water-courses, utters its usual mournful note, and roosts in these places. It travels mostly by day.

Few hawks attack the Mocking Birds, as on their approach, however sudden it may be, they are always ready not only to defend themselves vigorously and with undaunted courage, but to meet the aggressor half way, and force him to abandon his intention. The only hawk that occasionally surprises it is the *Falco Stanleii*, which flies low with great swiftness, and carries the bird off without any apparent stoppage. Should it happen that the ruffian misses his prey, the Mocking Bird in turn becomes the assailant, and pursues the Hawk with great courage, calling in the mean time all the birds of its species to its assistance; and although it cannot overtake the marauder, the alarm created by their cries, which are propagated in succession among all the birds in the vicinity, like the watchwords of sentinels on duty, prevents him from succeeding in his attempts.

The musical powers of this bird have often been taken notice of by European naturalists, and persons who find pleasure in listening to the song of different birds whilst in confinement or at large. Some of these persons have described the notes of the Nightingale as occasionally fully equal to those of our bird. I have frequently heard both species in confinement, and in the wild state, and without prejudice, have no hesitation in pronouncing the notes of the European Philomel equal to those of a *soubrette* of taste, which, could she study under a MOZART, might perhaps in time become very interesting in her way. But to compare her essays to the finished talent of the Mocking Bird, is, in my opinion, quite absurd.

The Mocking Bird is easily reared by hand from the nest, from which it ought to be removed when eight or ten days old. It becomes so very familiar and affectionate, that it will often follow its owner about the house. I have known one raised from the nest kept by a gentleman at Natchez, that frequently flew out of the house, poured forth its melodies, and returned at sight of its keeper. But notwithstanding all the care and management bestowed upon the improvement of the vocal powers of this bird in confinement, I never heard one in that state produce any thing at all approaching in melody to its own natural song.

The male bird is easily distinguished in the nest, as soon as the brood is a little fledged, it being larger than the female, and shewing more pure white. It does not shrink so deep in the nest as the female does, at the sight of the hand which is about to lift it. Good singing birds of this species often bring a high price. They are long-lived, and very agreeable companions. Their imitative powers are amazing, and they mimic with ease all their brethren of the forests or of the waters, as well as many quadrupeds. I have heard it asserted that they possess the power of imitating the human voice, but have never met with an instance of the display of this alleged faculty.

The Carolina Parrot

Psittaccus carolinensis, LINN.

(PLATES 5, 6, 7)

DOUBTLESS, kind reader, you will say, while looking at the seven figures of Parakeets represented in the plate, that I spared not my labour. I never do, so anxious am I to promote your pleasure.

These birds are represented feeding on the plant commonly named the *Cockle-bur.* It is found much too plentifully in every State west of the Alleghanies, and in still greater profusion as you advance towards the Southern Districts. It grows in every field where the soil is good. The low alluvial lands along the Ohio and Mississippi are all supplied with it. Its growth is so measured that it ripens after the crops of grain are usually secured, and in some rich old fields it grows so exceedingly close, that to make one's way through the patches of it, at this late period, is no pleasant task. The burs stick so thickly to the clothes, as to prevent a person from walking with any kind of ease. The wool of sheep is also much injured by them; the tails and manes of horses are converted into such tangled masses, that the hair has to be cut close off, by which the natural beauty of these valuable animals is impaired. To this day, no useful property has been discovered in the Cockle-bur, although in time it may prove as valuable either in medicine or chemistry*as many other plants that had long been considered of no importance.

Well, reader, you have before you one of these plants, on the seeds of which the parrot feeds. It alights upon it, plucks the bur from the stem with its bill, takes it from the latter with one foot, in which it turns it over until the joint is properly placed to meet the attacks of the bill, when it bursts it open, takes out the fruit, and allows the shell to drop. In this manner, a flock of these birds, having discovered a field ever so well filled with these plants, will eat or pluck off all their seeds, returning to the place day after day until hardly any are left. The plant might thus be extirpated, but it so happens that it is reproduced from the ground, being perennial, and our farmers have too much to do in securing their crops, to attend to the pulling up the cockle-burs by the roots, the only effectual way of getting rid of them.

The Parrot does not satisfy himself with Cockle-burs, but eats or destroys almost every kind of fruit indiscriminately, and on this account is always an unwelcome visitor to the planter, the farmer, or the gardener. The stacks of grain put up in the field are resorted to by flocks of these birds, which frequently cover them so entirely, that they present to the eye the same effect as if a brilliantly coloured carpet had been thrown over them. They cling around the whole stack, pull out the straws, and destroy twice as much of the grain as would suffice to satisfy their hunger. They assail the Pear and Apple-trees, when the fruit is yet very small and far from being ripe, and this merely for the sake of the seeds. As on the stalks of Corn, they alight on the Apple-trees of our orchards, or the Pear-trees in the gardens, in great numbers; and, as if through mere mischief, pluck off the fruits, open them up to the core, and, disappointed at the sight of the seeds, which are yet soft and of a milky consistence, drop the apple or pear, and pluck another, passing from branch to branch, until the trees which were before so promising, are left completely stripped, like the ship water-logged and abandoned by its crew, floating on the yet agitated waves, after the tempest has ceased. They visit the Mulberries, Pecan-nuts, Grapes, and even the seeds of the Dog-wood, before they are ripe, and on all commit similar depredations. The Maize alone never attracts their notice.

Do not imagine, reader, that all these outrages are borne without severe retaliation on the part of the planters. So far from this, the Parakeets are destroyed in great numbers, for whilst busily engaged in plucking off the fruits or tearing the grain from the stacks, the husbandman approaches them with perfect ease, and commits great slaughter among them. All the survivors rise, shriek, fly round about for a few minutes, and again alight on the very place of most imminent danger. The gun is kept at work; eight or ten, or even twenty, are killed at every discharge. The living birds, as if conscious of the death of their companions, sweep over their bodies, screaming as loud as ever, but still return to the stack to be shot at, until so few remain alive, that the farmer does not consider it worth his while to spend more of his ammunition. I have seen several hundreds destroyed in this manner in the course of a few hours, and have procured a basketful of these birds at a few shots, in order to make choice of good specimens for drawing the figures by which this species is represented in the plate now under your consideration.

The flight of the Parakeet is rapid, straight, and continued through the forests, or over fields and rivers, and is accompanied by inclinations of the body which enable the observer to see alternately their upper and under parts. They deviate from a direct course only when impediments occur, such as the trunks of trees or houses, in which case they glance aside in a very graceful manner, merely as much as may be necessary. A general cry is kept up by the party, and it is seldom that one of these birds is on wing for ever so short a space without uttering its cry. On reaching a spot which affords a supply of food, instead of alighting at once, as many other birds do, the Parakeets take a good survey of the neighbourhood, passing over it in circles of great extent, first above the trees, and then gradually lowering until they almost touch the ground, when suddenly re-ascending they all settle on the tree that bears the fruit of which they are in quest, or on one close to the field in which they expect to regale themselves.

They are quite at ease on trees or any kind of plant, moving side-wise, climbing or hanging in every imaginable posture, assisting themselves very dexterously in all their motions with their bills. They usually alight extremely close together. I have seen branches of trees as completely covered by them as they could possibly be. If approached before they begin their plundering, they appear shy and distrustful, and often at a single cry from one of them, the whole take wing, and probably may not return to the same place that day. Should a person shoot at them, as they go, and wound an individual, its cries are sufficient to bring back the whole flock, when the sportsman may kill as many as he pleases. If the bird falls dead, they make a short round, and then fly off.

On the ground these birds walk slowly and awkwardly, as if their tail incommoded them. They do not even attempt to run off when approached by the sportsman, should he come upon them unawares; but when he is seen at a distance, they lose no time in trying to hide, or in scrambling up the trunk of the nearest tree, in doing which they are greatly aided by their bill.

Their roosting-place is in hollow trees, and the holes excavated by the larger species of Woodpeckers, as far as these can be filled by them. At dusk, a flock of Parakeets may be seen alighting against the trunk of a large Sycamore or any other tree, when a considerable excavation exists within it. Immediately below the entrance the birds all cling to the bark, and crawl into the hole to pass the night. When such a hole does not prove sufficient to hold the whole flock, those around the entrance hook themselves on by their claws, and the tip of the upper mandible, and look as if hanging by the bill. I have frequently seen them in such positions by means of a glass, and am satisfied that the bill is not the only support used in such cases.

When wounded and laid hold of, the Parakeet opens its bill, turns its head to seize and bite, and, if it succeed, is capable of inflicting a severe wound. It is easily tamed by being frequently immersed in water, and eats as soon as it is placed in confinement. Nature seems to have implanted in these birds a propensity to destroy, in consequence of which they cut to atoms pieces of wood, books, and, in short, every thing that comes in their way. They are incapable of articulating words, however much care and attention may be bestowed upon their education; and their screams are so disagreeable as to render them at best very indifferent companions. The woods are the habitation best fitted for them, and there the richness of their plumage, their beautiful mode of flight, and even their screams, afford welcome intimation that our darkest forests and most sequestered swamps are not destitute of charms.

They are fond of sand in a surprising degree, and on that

account are frequently seen to alight in flocks along the gravelly banks about the creeks and rivers, or in the ravines of old fields in the plantations, when they scratch with bill and claws, flutter and roll themselves in the sand, and pick up and swallow a certain quantity of it. For the same purpose, they also enter the holes dug by our Kingsfisher. They are fond of saline earth, for which they visit the different Licks interspersed in our woods.

Our Parakeets are very rapidly diminishing in number; and in some districts, where twenty-five years ago they were plentiful, scarcely any are now to be seen. At that period, they could be procured as far up the tributary waters of the Ohio as the Great Kenhawa, the Scioto, the heads of the Miami, the mouth of the Manimee at its junction with Lake Erie, on the Illinois River, and sometimes as far north-east as Lake Ontario, and along the eastern districts as far as the boundary line between Virginia and Maryland. At the present day, very few are to be found higher than Cincinnati, nor is it until you reach the mouth of the Ohio that Parakeets are met with in considerable numbers. I should think that along the Mississippi there is not now half the number that existed fifteen years ago.

Their flesh is tolerable food, when they are young, on which account many of them are shot. The skin of their body is usually much covered with the mealy substances detached from the roots of the feathers. The head especially is infested by numerous minute insects, all of which shift from the skin to the surface of the plumage, immediately after the bird's death. Their nest, or the place in which they deposit their eggs, is simply the bottom of such cavities in trees as those to which they usually retire at night. Many females deposit their eggs together. I am of opinion that the number of eggs which each individual lays is two, although I have not been able absolutely to assure myself of this. They are nearly round, and of a light greenish white. The young are at first covered with soft down, such as is seen on young Owls. During the first season, the whole plumage is green; but towards autumn a frontlet of carmine appears. Two years, however, are passed before the male or female are in full plumage. The only material differences which the sexes present externally are, that the male is rather larger, with more brilliant plumage. I have represented a female with two supernumerary feathers in the tail. This, however, is merely an accidental variety.

The White-headed Eagle

Falco leucocephalus, LINN.

(PLATES 10, 11)

THE FIGURE of this noble bird is well known throughout the civilized world, emblazoned as it is on our national standard, which waves in the breeze of every clime, bearing to distant lands the remembrance of a great people living in a state of peaceful freedom. May that peaceful freedom last for ever!

The great strength, daring, and cool courage of the White-headed Eagle, joined to his unequalled power of flight, render him highly conspicuous among his brethren. To these qualities did he add a generous disposition towards others, he might be looked up to as a model of nobility. The ferocious, overbearing, and tyrannical temper which is ever and anon displaying itself in his actions, is, nevertheless, best adapted to his state, and was wisely given him by the Creator to enable him to perform the office assigned to him.

To give you, kind reader, some idea of the nature of this bird, permit me to place you on the Mississippi, on which you may float gently along, while approaching winter brings millions of water-fowl on whistling wings, from the countries of the north, to seek a milder climate in which to sojourn for a season. The Eagle is seen perched, in an erect attitude, on the highest summit of the tallest tree by the margin of the broad stream. His glistening but stern eye looks over the vast expanse. He listens attentively to every sound that comes to his quick ear from afar, glancing now and then on the earth beneath, lest even the light tread of the fawn may pass unheard. His mate is perched on the opposite side, and should all be tranquil and silent, warns him by a cry to continue patient. At this well known call, the male partly opens his broad wings, inclines his body a little downwards, and answers to her voice in tones not unlike the laugh of a maniac. The next moment, he resumes his erect attitude, and again all around is silent. Ducks of many species, the Teal, the Wigeon, the Mallard and others, are seen passing with great rapidity, and following the course of the current; but the Eagle heeds them not: they are at that time beneath his attention. The next moment, however, the wild trumpet-like sound of a yet distant but approaching Swan is heard. A shriek from the female Eagle comes across the stream,—for, kind reader, she is fully as alert as her mate. The latter suddenly shakes the whole of his body, and with a few touches of his bill, aided by the action of his cuticular muscles, arranges his plumage in an instant. The snow-white bird is now in sight: her long neck is stretched forward, her eye is on the watch, vigilant as that of her enemy; her large wings seem with difficulty to support the weight of her body, although they flap incessantly. So irksome do her exertions seem, that her very legs are spread beneath her tail, to aid her in her flight. She approaches, however. The Eagle has marked her for his prey. As the Swan is passing the dreaded pair, starts from his perch, in full preparation for the chase, the male bird, with an awful scream, that to the Swan's ear brings more terror than the report of the large duck-gun.

Now is the moment to witness the display of the Eagle's powers. He glides through the air like a falling star, and, like a flash of lightning, comes upon the timorous quarry, which now, in agony and despair, seeks, by various manœuvres, to elude the grasp of his cruel talons. It mounts, doubles, and willingly would plunge into the stream, were it not prevented by the Eagle, which, long possessed of the knowledge that by such a stratagem the Swan might escape him, forces it to remain in the air by attempting to strike it with his talons from beneath. The hope of escape is soon given up by the Swan. It has already become much weakened, and its strength fails at the sight of the courage and swiftness of its antagonist. Its last gasp is about to escape, when the ferocious Eagle strikes with his talons the under side of its wing, and with unresisted power forces the bird to fall in a slanting direction upon the nearest shore.

It is then, reader, that you may see the cruel spirit of this dreaded enemy of the feathered race, whilst, exulting over his prey, he for the first time breathes at ease. He presses down his powerful feet, and drives his sharp claws deeper than ever into the heart of the dying Swan. He shrieks with delight, as he feels the last convulsions of his prey, which has now sunk under his unceasing efforts to render death as painfully felt as it can possibly be. The female has watched every movement of her mate; and if she did not assist him in capturing the Swan, it was not from want of will, but merely that she felt full assurance that the power and courage of her lord were quite sufficient for the deed. She now sails to the spot where he eagerly awaits her, and when she has arrived, they together turn the breast of the luckless Swan upwards, and gorge themselves with gore.

At other times, when these Eagles, sailing in search of prey, discover a Goose, a Duck, or a Swan, that has alighted on the water, they accomplish its destruction in a manner that is worthy of your attention. The Eagles, well aware that water-fowl have it in their power to dive at their approach, and thereby elude their attempts upon them, ascend in the air in opposite directions over the lake or river, on which they have observed the object which they are desirous of possessing. Both Eagles reach a certain height, immediately after which one of them glides with great swiftness towards the prey; the latter, meantime, aware of the Eagle's intention, dives the moment before he reaches the spot. The pursuer then rises in the air, and is met by its mate, which glides toward the water-bird, that has just emerged to breathe, and forces it to plunge again beneath the surface, to escape the talons of this second assailant. The first Eagle is now poising itself in the place where its mate formerly was, and rushes anew to force the quarry to make another plunge. By thus alternately gliding, in rapid and often repeated rushes, over the ill-fated bird, they soon fatigue it, when it stretches out its neck, swims deeply, and makes for the shore, in the hope of concealing itself among the rank weeds. But this is of no avail, for the Eagles follow it in all its motions, and the moment it approaches the margin, one of them darts upon it, and kills it in an instant, after which they divide the spoil.

During spring and summer, the White-headed Eagle, to procure sustenance, follows a different course, and one much less suited to a bird apparently so well able to supply itself without interfering with other plunderers. No sooner does the Fish-Hawk make its appearance along our Atlantic shores, or ascend our numerous and large rivers, than the Eagle follows it, and, like a selfish oppressor, robs it of the hard-earned fruits of its labour. Perched on some tall summit, in view of the ocean, or of some water-course, he watches every motion of the Osprey while on wing. When the latter rises from the water, with a fish in its grasp, forth rushes the Eagle in pursuit. He mounts above the Fish-Hawk, and threatens it by actions well understood, when the latter, fearing perhaps that its life is in danger, drops its prey. In an instant, the Eagle, accurately estimating the rapid descent of the fish, closes his wings, follows it with the swiftness of thought, and the next moment grasps it. The prize is carried off in silence to the woods, and assists in feeding the ever-hungry brood of the Eagle.

This bird now and then procures fish himself, by pursuing them in the shallows of small creeks. I have witnessed several instances of this in the Perkioming Creek in Pennsylvania, where, in this manner, I saw one of them secure a number of *Red-fins*, by wading briskly through the water, and striking at them with his bill. I have also observed a pair scrambling over the ice of a frozen pond, to get at some fish below, but without success.

It does not confine itself to these kinds of food, but greedily devours young pigs, lambs, fawns, poultry, and the putrid flesh of carcasses of every description, driving off the vultures and carrion-crows, or the dogs, and keeping a whole party at defiance until it is satiated. It frequently gives chase to the vultures, and forces them to disgorge the contents of their stomachs, when it alights and devours the filthy mass. A ludicrous instance of this took place near the city of Natchez, on the Mississippi. Many Vultures were engaged in devouring the body and entrails of a dead horse, when a White-headed Eagle accidentally passing by, the vultures all took to wing, one among the rest with a portion of the entrails partly swallowed, and the remaining part, about a yard in length, dangling in the air. The Eagle instantly marked him, and gave chase. The poor vulture tried in vain to disgorge, when the Eagle, coming up, seized the loose end of the gut, and dragged the bird along for twenty or thirty yards, much against its will, until both fell to the ground, when the Eagle struck the vulture, and in a few moments killed it, after which he swallowed the delicious morsel.

I have heard of several attempts made by this bird to destroy children, but have never witnessed any myself, although I have little doubt of its having sufficient daring to do so.

The flight of the White-headed Eagle is strong, generally uniform, and protracted to any distance, at pleasure. Whilst travelling, it is entirely supported by equal easy flappings, without any intermission, in as far as I have observed it, by following it with the eye or the assistance of a glass. When looking for prey, it sails with extended wings, at right angles to its body, now and then allowing its legs to hang at their full length. Whilst sailing, it has the power of ascending in circular sweeps, without a single flap of the wings, or any apparent motion either of them or of the tail; and in this manner it often rises until it disappears from the view, the white tail remaining longer visible than the rest of the body. At other times, it rises only a few hundred feet in the air, and sails off in a direct line, and with rapidity. Again, when thus elevated, it partially closes its wings, and glides downwards for a considerable space, when, as if disappointed, it suddenly checks its career, and reassumes its former steady flight. When at an immense height, and as if observing an object on the ground, it closes its wings, and glides through the air with such rapidity as to cause a loud rustling sound, not unlike that produced by a violent gust of wind passing amongst the branches of trees. Its fall towards the earth can scarcely be followed by the eye on such occasions, the more particularly that these falls or glidings through the air usually take place when they are least expected.

This bird has the power of raising from the surface of the water any floating object not heavier than itself. In this manner it often robs the sportsman of ducks which have been killed by him. Its audacity is quite remarkable. While descending the Upper Mississippi, I observed one of these Eagles in pursuit of a Green-winged Teal. It came so near our boat, although several persons were looking on, that I could perceive the glancings of its eye. The Teal, on the point of being caught, when not more than fifteen or twenty yards from us, was saved from the grasp of its enemy, one of our party having brought the latter down by a shot, which broke one of its wings. When taken on board, it was fastened to the deck of our boat by means of a string, and was fed with pieces of cat-fish, some of which it began to eat on the third day of its confinement. But, as it became a very disagreeable and dangerous associate, trying on all occasions to strike at some one with its talons, it was killed and thrown overboard.

When these birds are suddenly and unexpectedly approached or surprised, they exhibit a great degree of cowardice. They rise at once and fly off very low, in zig-zag lines, to some distance, uttering a hissing noise, not at all like their usual disagreeable imitation of a laugh. When not carrying a gun, one may easily approach them; but the use of that instrument being to appearance well known to them, they are very cautious in allowing a person having one to get near them. Notwithstanding all their caution, however, many are shot by approaching them under cover of a tree, on horseback, or in a boat. They do not possess the power of smelling gunpowder, as the crow and the raven are absurdly supposed to do; nor are they aware of the effects of spring-traps, as I have seen some of them caught by these instruments. Their sight, although probably as perfect as that of any bird, is much affected during a fall of snow, at which time they may be approached without difficulty.

The White-headed Eagle seldom appears in very mountainous districts, but prefers the low lands of the sea-shores, those of our large lakes, and the borders of rivers. It is a constant resident in the United States, in every part of which it is to be seen. The roosts and breeding places of pigeons are resorted to by it, for the purpose of picking up the young birds that happen to fall, or the old ones when wounded. It seldom, however, follows the flocks of these birds when on their migrations.

When shot at and wounded, it tries to escape by long and quickly repeated leaps, and, if not closely pursued, soon conceals itself. Should it happen to fall on the water, it strikes powerfully with expanded wings, and in this manner often reaches the shore, when it is not more than twenty or thirty yards distant. It is capable of supporting life without food for a long period. I have heard of some, which, in a state of confinement, had lived without much apparent distress for twenty days, although I cannot vouch for the truth of such statements, which, however, may be quite correct. They defend themselves in the manner usually followed by other Eagles and Hawks, throwing themselves backwards, and furiously striking with their talons at any object within reach, keeping their bill open, and turning their head with quickness to watch the movements of the enemy, their eyes being apparently more protruded than when unmolested.

It is supposed that Eagles live to a very great age,—some persons have ventured to say even a hundred years. On this subject, I can only observe, that I once found one of these birds, which, on being killed, proved to be a female, and which, judging by its appearance, must have been very old. Its tail and wing-feathers were so worn out, and of such a rusty colour, that I imagined the bird had lost the power of moulting. The legs and feet were covered with large warts, the claws and bill were much blunted, it could scarcely fly more than a hundred yards at a time, and this it did with a heaviness and unsteadiness of motion such as I never witnessed in any other bird of the species. The body was poor and very tough. The eye was the only part which appeared to have sustained no injury. It remained sparkling and full of animation, and even after death seemed to have lost little of its lustre. No wounds were perceivable on its body.

The White-headed Eagle is seldom seen alone, the mutual attachment which two individuals form when they first pair seeming to continue until one of them dies or is destroyed. They hunt for the support of each other, and seldom feed apart, but usually drive off other birds of the same species. They commence their amatory intercourse at an earlier period than any other *land bird* with which I am acquainted, generally in the month of December. At this time, along the Mississippi, or by the margin of some lake not far in the interior of the forest, the male and female birds are observed making a great bustle, flying about and circling in various ways, uttering a loud cackling noise, alighting on the dead branches of the tree on which their nest is already preparing, or in the act of being repaired, and caressing each other. In the beginning of January incubation commences. I shot a female, on the 17th of that month, as she sat on her eggs, in which the chicks had made considerable progress.

The nest, which in some instances is of great size, is usually placed on a very tall tree, destitute of branches to a considerable height, but by no means always a dead one. It is never seen on rocks. It is composed of sticks, from three to five feet in length, large pieces of turf, rank weeds, and Spanish moss in abundance, whenever that substance happens to be near. When finished, it measures from five to six feet in diameter, and so great is the accumulation of materials, that it sometimes measures the same in depth, it being occupied for a great number of years in succession, and receiving some augmentation each season. When placed in a naked tree, between the forks of the branches, it is conspicuously seen at a great distance. The eggs, which are from two to four, more commonly two or three, are of a dull white colour, and equally rounded at both ends, some of them being occasionally granulated. Incubation lasts for more than three weeks, but I have not been able to ascertain its precise duration, as I have observed the female on different occasions sit for a few days in the nest, before laying the first egg. Of this I assured myself by climbing to the nest every day in succession, during her temporary absence,—a rather perilous undertaking when the bird is sitting.

I have seen the young birds when not larger than middle-sized pullets. At this time, they are covered with a soft cottony kind of down, their bill and legs appearing disproportionately large. Their first plumage is of a greyish colour, mixed with brown of different depths of tint, and before the parents drive them off from the nest, they are fully fledged. As a figure of the Young White-headed Eagle will appear in the course of the publication of my Illustrations, I shall not here trouble you with a description of its appearance. I once caught three young Eagles of this species, when fully fledged, by having the tree on which their nest was, cut down. It caused great trouble to secure them, as they could fly and scramble much faster than any of our party could run. They, however, gradually became fatigued, and at length were so exhausted as to offer no resistance, when we were securing them with cords. This happened on the border of Lake Pontchartrain, in the month of April. The parents did not think fit to come within gun-shot of the tree while the axe was at work.

The attachment of the parents to the young is very great, when the latter are yet of a small size; and to ascend to the nest at this time would be dangerous. But as the young advance, and, after being able to take wing and provide for themselves, are not disposed to fly off, the old birds turn them out, and beat them away from them. They return to the nest, however, to roost, or sleep on the branches immediately near it, for several weeks after. They are fed most abundantly while under the care of the parents, which procure for them ample supplies of fish, either accidentally cast ashore, or taken from the Fish-Hawk, together with rabbits, squirrels, young lambs, pigs, oppossums, or raccoons. Every thing that comes in the way is relished by the young family, as by the old birds.

The young birds begin to breed the following spring, not always in pairs of the same age, as I have several times observed one of these birds in brown plumage mated with a full-coloured bird, which had the head and tail pure white. I once shot a pair of this kind, when the brown bird (the young one) proved to be the female.

This species requires at least four years before it attains the full beauty of its plumage when kept in confinement. I have known two instances in which the white of the head did not make its appearance until the sixth spring. It is impossible for me to say how much sooner this state of perfection is attained, when the bird is at full liberty, although I should suppose it to be at least one year, as the bird is capable of breeding the first spring after birth.

The weight of Eagles of this species varies considerably. In the males, it is from six to eight pounds, and in the females from eight to twelve. These birds are so attached to particular districts, where they have first made their nest, that they seldom spend a night at any distance from the latter, and often resort to its immediate neighbourhood. Whilst asleep, they emit a loud hissing sort of snore, which is heard at the distance of a hundred yards, when the weather is perfectly calm. Yet, so light is their sleep, that the cracking of a stick under the foot of a person immediately wakens them. When it is attempted to smoke them while thus roosted and asleep, they start up and sail off without uttering any sound, but return next evening to the same spot.

Before steam-navigation commenced on our western rivers, these Eagles were extremely abundant there, particularly in the lower parts of the Ohio, the Mississippi, and the adjoining streams. I have seen hundreds going down from the mouth of the Ohio to New Orleans, when it was not at all difficult to shoot them. Now, however, their number is considerably diminished, the game on which they were in the habit of feeding, having been forced to seek refuge from the persecution of man farther in the wilderness. Many, however, are still observed on these rivers, particularly along the shores of the Mississippi.

In concluding this account of the White-headed Eagle, suffer me, kind reader, to say how much I grieve that it should have been selected as the Emblem of my Country. The opinion of our great Franklin on this subject, as it perfectly coincides with my own, I shall here present to you. "For my part," says he, in one of his letters, "I wish the Bald Eagle had not been chosen as the representative of our country. He is a bird of bad moral character; he does not get his living honestly; you may have seen him perched on some dead tree, where, too lazy to fish for himself, he watches the labour of the Fishing-Hawk; and when that diligent bird has at length taken a fish, and is bearing it to his nest for the support of his mate and young ones, the Bald Eagle pursues him, and takes it from him. With all this injustice, he is never in good case, but, like those among men who live by sharping and robbing, he is generally poor, and often very lousy. Besides, he is a rank coward: the little King Bird, not bigger than a Sparrow, attacks him boldly, and drives him out of the district. He is, therefore, by no means a proper emblem for the brave and honest Cincinnati of America, who have driven all the *King Birds* from our country; though exactly fit for that order of knights which the French call *Chevaliers d'Industrie*."

It is only necessary for me to add, that the name by which this bird is universally known in America is that of *Bald Eagle*, an erroneous denomination, as its head is as densely feathered as that of any other species, although its whiteness may have suggested the idea of its being bare.

The Ruby-throated Humming Bird

Trochilus Colubris, LINN.

(PLATE 9)

WHERE is the person who, on seeing this lovely little creature moving on humming winglets through the air, suspended as if by magic in it, flitting from one flower to another, with motions as graceful as they are light and airy, pursuing its course over our extensive continent, and yielding new delights wherever it is seen;—where is the person, I ask of you, kind reader, who, on observing this glittering fragment of the rainbow, would not pause, admire, and instantly turn his mind with reverence toward the Almighty Creator, the wonders of whose hand we at every step discover, and of whose sublime conceptions we everywhere observe the manifestations in his admirable system of creation?—There breathes not such a person; so kindly have we all been blessed with that intuitive and noble feeling—admiration!

No sooner has the returning sun again introduced the vernal season, and caused millions of plants to expand their leaves and blossoms to his genial beams, than the little Humming Bird is seen advancing on fairy wings, carefully visiting every opening flower-cup, and, like a curious florist, removing from each the injurious insects that otherwise would ere long cause their beauteous petals to droop and decay. Poised in the air, it is observed peeping cautiously, and with sparkling eye, into their innermost recesses, whilst the etherial motions of its pinions, so rapid and so light, appear to fan and cool the flower, without injuring its fragile texture, and produce a delightful murmuring sound, well adapted for lulling the insects to repose. Then is the moment for the Humming Bird to secure them. Its long delicate bill enters the cup of the flower, and the protruded double-tubed tongue, delicately sensible, and imbued with a glutinous saliva, touches each insect in succession, and draws it from its lurking place, to be instantly swallowed. All this is done in a moment, and the bird, as it leaves the flower, sips so small a portion of its liquid honey, that the theft, we may suppose, is looked upon with a grateful feeling by the flower, which is thus kindly relieved from the attacks of her destroyers.

The prairies, the fields, the orchards and gardens, nay, the deepest shades of the forests, are all visited in their turn, and everywhere the little bird meets with pleasure and with food. Its gorgeous throat in beauty and brilliancy baffles all competition. Now it glows with a fiery hue, and again it is changed to the deepest velvety black. The upper parts of its delicate body are of resplendent changing green; and it throws itself through the air with a swiftness and vivacity hardly conceivable. It moves from one flower to another like a gleam of light, upwards, downwards, to the right, and to the left. In this manner, it searches the extreme northern portions of our country, following with great precaution the advances of the season, and retreats with equal care at the approach of autumn.

I wish it were in my power at this moment to impart to you, kind reader, the pleasures which I have felt whilst watching the movements, and viewing the manifestation of feelings displayed by a single pair of these most favourite little creatures, when engaged in the demonstration of their love to each other:—how the male swells his plumage and throat, and, dancing on the wing, whirls around the delicate female; how quickly he dives towards a flower, and returns with a loaded bill, which he offers to her to whom alone he feels desirous of being united; how full of ecstacy he seems to be when his caresses are kindly received; how his little wings fan her, as they fan the flowers, and he transfers to her bill the insect and the honey which he has procured with a view to please her; how these attentions are received with apparent satisfaction; how, soon after, the blissful compact is sealed; how, then, the courage and care of the male are redoubled; how he even dares to give chase to the Tyrant Fly-catcher, hurries the Blue-bird and the Martin to their boxes; and how, on sounding pinions, he joyously returns to the side of his lovely mate. Reader, all these proofs of the sincerity, fidelity, and courage, with which the male assures his mate of the care he will take of her while sitting on her nest, may be seen, and have been seen, but cannot be portrayed or described.

Could you, kind reader, cast a momentary glance on the nest of the Humming Bird, and see, as I have seen, the newly-hatched pair of young, little larger than humble-bees, naked, blind, and so feeble as scarcely to be able to raise their little bill to receive food from the parents; and could you see those parents, full of anxiety and fear, passing and repassing within a few inches of your face, alighting on a twig not more than a yard from your body, waiting the result of your unwelcome visit in a state of the utmost despair,—you could not fail to be impressed with the deepest pangs which parental affection feels on the unexpected death of a cherished child. Then how pleasing is it, on your leaving the spot, to see the returning hope of the parents, when, after examining the nest, they find their nurslings untouched! You might then judge how pleasing it is to a mother of another kind, to hear the physician who has attended her sick child assure her that the crisis is over, and that her babe is saved. These are the scenes best fitted to enable us to partake of sorrow and joy, and to determine every one who views them to make it his study to contribute to the happiness of others, and to refrain from wantonly or maliciously giving them pain.

I have seen Humming Birds in Louisiana as early as the 10th of March. Their appearance in that State varies, however, as much as in any other, it being sometimes a fortnight later, or, although rarely, a few days earlier. In the Middle Districts, they seldom arrive before the 15th of April, more usually the beginning of May. I have not been able to assure myself whether they migrate during the day or by night, but am inclined to think the latter the case, as they seem to be busily feeding at all times of the day, which would not be the case had they long flights to perform at that period. They pass through the air in long undulations, raising themselves for some distance at an angle of about 40 degrees, and then falling in a curve; but the smallness of their size precludes the possibility of following them farther then fifty or sixty yards without great difficulty, even with a good glass. A person standing in a garden by the side of a Common Althæa in bloom, will be as surprised to hear the humming of their wings, and then see the birds themselves within a few feet of him, as he will be astonished at the rapidity with which the little creatures rise into the air, and are out of sight and hearing the next moment. They do not alight on the ground, but easily settle on twigs and branches, where they move sidewise in prettily measured steps, frequently opening and closing their wings, pluming, shaking and arranging the whole of their apparel with neatness and activity. They are particularly fond of spreading one wing at a time, and passing each of the quill-feathers through their bill in its whole length, when, if the sun is shining, the wing thus plumed is rendered extremely transparent and light. They leave the twig without the least difficulty in an instant, and appear to be possessed of superior powers of vision, making directly towards a Martin or a Blue-bird when fifty or sixty yards from them, and reaching them before they are aware of their approach. No bird seems to resist their attacks, but they are sometimes chased by the larger kinds of humble-bees, of which they seldom take the least notice, as their superiority of flight is sufficient to enable them to leave these slow moving insects far behind in the short space of a minute.

The nest of this Humming Bird is of the most delicate nature, the external parts being formed of a light grey lichen found on the branches of trees, or on decayed fence-rails, and so neatly arranged round the whole nest, as well as to some distance from the spot where it is attached, as to seem part of the branch or stem itself. These little pieces of lichen are glued together with the saliva of the bird. The next coating consists of cottony substance, and the innermost of silky fibres obtained from various plants, all extremely delicate and soft. On this comfortable bed, as in contradiction to the axiom that the smaller the species the greater the number of eggs, the female lays only two, which are pure white and almost oval. Ten days are required for their hatching, and the birds raise two broods in a season. In one week the young are ready to fly, but are fed by the parents for nearly another week. They receive their food directly from the bill of their parents, which disgorge it in the manner of Canaries or Pigeons. It is my belief that no sooner are the young able to provide for themselves than they associate with other broods, and perform their migration apart from the old birds, as I have observed twenty or thirty young Humming Birds resort to a group of Trumpet-flowers, when not a single old male was to be seen. They do not receive the full brilliancy of their colours until the succeeding spring, although the throat of the male bird is strongly imbued with the ruby tints before they leave us in autumn.

The Ruby-throated Humming Bird has a particular liking for such flowers as are greatly tubular in their form. The Common Jimpson-weed or Thorn-apple (*Datura Stramonium*) and the Trumpet-flower (*Bignonia radicans*) are among the most favoured by their visits, and after these, Honeysuckle, the Balsam of the gardens, and the wild species which grows on the borders of ponds, rivulets, and deep ravines; but every flower, down to the wild violet, affords them a certain portion of sustenance. Their food consists principally of insects, generally of the coleopterous order, these, together with some equally diminutive flies, being commonly found in their stomach. The first are procured within the flowers, but many of the latter on wing. The Humming Bird might therefore be looked upon as an expert fly-catcher. The nectar or honey which they sip from the different flowers, being of itself insufficient to support them, is used more as if to allay their thirst. I have seen many of these birds kept in partial confinement, when they were supplied with artificial flowers made for the purpose, in the corollas of which water with honey or sugar dissolved in it was placed. The birds were fed on these substances exclusively, but seldom lived many months, and on being examined after death, were found to be extremely emaciated. Others, on the contrary, which were supplied twice a-day with fresh flowers from the woods or garden, placed in a room with windows merely closed with moschetto gauze-netting, through which minute insects were able to enter, lived twelve months, at the expiration of which time their liberty was granted them, the person who kept them having had a long voyage to perform. The room was kept artificially warm during the winter months, and these, in Lower Louisiana, are seldom so cold as to produce ice. On examining an orange-tree which had been placed in the room where these Humming Birds were kept, no appearance of a nest was to be seen, although the birds had frequently been observed caressing each other. Some have been occasionally kept confined in our Middle Districts, but I have not ascertained that any one survived a winter.

The Humming Bird does not shun mankind so much as birds generally do. It frequently approaches flowers in the windows, or even in rooms when the windows are kept open, during the extreme heat of the day, and returns, when not interrupted, as long as the flowers are unfaded. They are extremely abundant in Louisiana during spring and summer, and wherever a fine plant of the trumpet-flower is met with in the woods, one or more Humming Birds are generally seen about it, and now and then so many as ten or twelve at a time. They are quarrelsome, and have frequent battles in the air, especially the male birds. Should one be feeding on a flower, and another approach it, they are both immediately seen to rise in the air, twittering and twirling in a spiral manner until out of sight. The conflict over, the victor immediately returns to the flower.

If comparison might enable you, kind reader, to form some tolerably accurate idea of their peculiar mode of flight, and their appearance when on wing, I would say, that were both objects of the same colour, a large sphinx or moth, when moving from one flower to another, and in a direct line, comes nearer the Humming Bird in aspect than any other object with which I am acquainted.

Having heard several persons remark that these little creatures had been procured with less injury to their plumage, by shooting them with water, I was tempted to make the experiment, having been in the habit of killing them either with remarkably small shot, or with sand. However, finding that even when within a few paces, I seldom brought one to the ground when I used water instead of shot, and was moreover obliged to clean my gun after every discharge, I abandoned the scheme, and feel confident that it can never have been used with material advantage. I have frequently secured some by employing an insect-net, and were this machine used with dexterity, it would afford the best means of procuring Humming Birds.

I have represented ten of these pretty and most interesting birds, in various positions, flitting, feeding, caressing each other, or sitting on the slender stalks of the trumpet-flower and pluming themselves. The diversity of action and attitude thus exhibited, may, I trust, prove sufficient to present a faithful idea of their appearance and manners. A figure of the nest you will find elsewhere. The nest is generally placed low, on the horizontal branch of any kind of tree, seldom more than twenty feet from the ground. They are far from being particular in this matter, as I have often found a nest attached by one side only to a twig of a rose-bush, currant, or the strong stalk of a rank weed, sometimes in the middle of the forest, at other times on the branch of an oak, immediately over the road, and again in the garden close to the walk.

The Red-tailed Hawk

Falco Borealis, GMEL.

(PLATE 12)

THE Red-tailed Hawk is a constant resident in the United States, in every part of which it is found. It performs partial migrations, during severe winters, from the Northern Districts towards the Southern. In the latter, however, it is at all times more abundant, and I shall endeavour to present you with a full account of its habits, as observed there.

Its flight is firm, protracted, and at times performed at a great height. It sails across the whole of a large plantation, on a level with the tops of the forest-trees which surround it, without a single flap of its wings, and is then seen moving its head sidewise to inspect the objects below. This flight is generally accompanied by a prolonged mournful cry, which may be heard at a considerable distance, and consists of a single sound resembling the monosyllable *Kae*, uttered in such a manner as to continue for three or four minutes, without any apparent inflection or difference of intensity. It would seem as if uttered for the purpose of giving notice to the living objects below that he is passing, and of thus inducing them to bestir themselves and retreat to a hiding-place, before they attain which he may have an opportunity of pouncing upon some of them. When he spies an animal, while he is thus sailing over a field, I have observed him give a slight check to his flight, as if to mark a certain spot with accuracy, and immediately afterwards alight on the nearest tree. He would then instantly face about, look intensely on the object that had attracted his attention, soon after descend towards it with wings almost close to his body, and dart upon it with such accuracy and rapidity as seldom to fail in securing it.

When passing over a meadow, a cotton-field, or one planted with sugar-canes, he performs his flight close over the grass or plants, uttering no cry, but marking the prey in the manner above described, and on perceiving it, ascending in a beautiful curved line to the top of the nearest tree, after which he watches and dives as in the former case. Should he not observe any object worthy of his attention, while passing over a meadow or a field, he alights, shakes his feathers, particularly those of the tail, and after spending a few minutes in pluming himself, leaves the perch, uttering his usual cry, and ascending in the air, performs large and repeated circular flights, carefully inspecting the field, to assure himself that there is in reality nothing in it that may be of use to him. He then proceeds to another plantation. At other times, as if not assured that his observations have been duly made, he rises in circles over the same field to an immense height, where he looks like a white dot in the heavens. Yet from this height he must be able to distinguish the objects on the ground, even when these do not exceed our little partridge or a young hare in size, and although their colour may be almost the same as that of surrounding bodies; for of a sudden his circlings are checked, his wings drawn close to his body, his tail contracted to its smallest breadth, and he is seen to plunge headlong towards the earth, with a rapidity which produces a loud rustling sound nearly equal to that of an Eagle on a similar occasion.

Should he not succeed in discovering the desired object in the fields, he enters the forest and perches on some detached tree, tall enough to enable him to see to a great distance around. His posture is now erect, he remains still and silent, moving only his head, as on all other occasions, to enable his keen eye to note the occurrences which may take place in his vicinity. The lively Squirrel is seen gaily leaping from one branch to another, or busily employed in searching for the fallen nuts on the ground. It has found one. Its bushy tail is beautifully curved along its back, the end of it falling off with a semicircular bend; its nimble feet are seen turning the nut quickly round, and its teeth are already engaged in perforating the hard shell; when, quick as thought, the Red-tailed Hawk, which has been watching it in all its motions, falls upon it, seizes it near the head, transfixes and strangles it, devours it on the spot, or ascends exultingly to a branch with the yet palpitating victim in his talons, and there feasts at leisure.

As soon as the little King-bird has raised its brood, and when its courage is no longer put in requisition for the defence of its young or its mate, the Red-tailed Hawk visits the farm-houses, to pay his regards to the poultry. This is done without much precaution, for, while sailing over the yard where the chickens, the ducklings, and the young turkeys are, the Hawk plunges upon any one of them, and sweeps it off to the nearest wood. When impelled by continued hunger, he now and then manages to elude the vigilance of the Martins, Swallows and King-birds, and watching for a good opportunity, falls upon and seizes an old fowl, the dying screams of which are heard by the farmer at the plough, who swears vengeance against the robber. He remembers that he has observed the Hawk's nest in the woods, and full of anger at the recollection of the depredations which the plunderer has already committed, and at the anticipation of its many visits during the winter, leaves his work and his horses, strides to his house, and with an axe and a rifle in his hands proceeds towards the tree, where the hopes of the Red-tailed Hawk are snugly nestled among the tall branches. The farmer arrives, eyes the gigantic tree, thinks for a moment of the labour which will be required for felling it, but resolves that he shall not be overreached by a Hawk. He throws aside his hat, rolls up his sleeves, and applies himself to the work. His brawny arms give such an impulse to the axe, that at every stroke large chips are seen to fall off on all sides. The poor mother-bird, well aware of the result, sails sorrowfully over and around. She would fain beg for mercy towards her young. She alights on the edge of the nest, and would urge her off-spring to take flight. But the farmer has watched her motions. The axe is left sticking in the core of the tree, his rifle is raised to his shoulder in an instant, and the next moment the whizzing ball has pierced the heart of the Red-tailed Hawk, which falls unheeded to the earth. The farmer renews his work, and now changes sides. A whole hour has been spent in the application of ceaseless blows. He begins to look upwards, to judge which way the giant of the forest will fall, and hav-ing ascertained this, he redoubles his blows. The huge oak be-gins to tremble. Were it permitted to speak, it might ask why it should suffer for the deeds of another; but it is now seen slowly to incline, and soon after with an awful rustling pro-duced by all its broad arms, its branches, twigs and leaves, passing like lightning through the air, the noble tree falls to the earth, and almost causes it to shake. The work of revenge is now accomplished: the farmer seizes the younglings, and carries them home, to be tormented by his children, until death terminates their brief career.

Notwithstanding the very common occurrence of such acts of retribution between man and the Hawk, it would be diffi-cult to visit a plantation in the State of Louisiana, without ob-serving at least a pair of this species hovering about, more especially during the winter months. Early in February, they begin to build their nest, which is usually placed within the forest, and on the tallest and largest tree in the neighbour-hood. The male and female are busily engaged in carrying up dried sticks, and other materials, for eight or ten days, during which time their cry is seldom heard. The nest is large, and is fixed in the centre of a triply forked branch. It is of a flattish form, constructed of sticks, and finished with slender twigs and coarse grasses or Spanish moss. The female lays four or five eggs, of a dull white colour, splatched with brown and black, with a very hard, smooth shell. The male assists the fe-male in incubating, but it is seldom that the one brings food to the other while thus employed.

I have seen one or two of these nests built in a large tree which had been left standing in the middle of a field; but oc-currences of this kind are rare, on account of the great enmity shewn to this species by the farmers. The young are abundantly supplied with food of various kinds, particularly grey squirrels, which the parents procure while hunting in pairs, when nothing can save the squirrel from their attacks excepting its retreat into the hole of a tree; for should the animal be observed ascending the trunk or branch of a tree by either of the Hawks, this one immediately plunges toward it, while the other watches it from the air. The little animal, if placed against the trunk, when it sees the Hawk coming towards it, makes swiftly for the opposite side of the trunk, but is there immediately dived at by the other Hawk, and now the murderous pair chase it so closely, that unless it immediately finds a hole into which to retreat, it is caught in a few minutes, killed, carried to the nest, torn in pieces, and distributed among the young Hawks. Small hares, or, as we usually call them, *rabbits*, are also frequently caught, and the depredations of the Red-tailed Hawks at this period are astonishing, for they seem to kill every thing, fit for food, that comes in their way. They are great destroyers of tame Pigeons, and woe to the Cock or Hen that strays far from home, for so powerful is this Hawk, that it is able not only to kill them, but to carry them off in its claws to a considerable distance.

The continued attachment that exists between Eagles once paired, is not exhibited by these birds, which, after rearing their young, become as shy towards each other as if they had never met. This is carried to such a singular length, that they are seen to chase and rob each other of their prey, on all occasions. I have seen a couple thus engaged, when one of them had just seized a young rabbit or a squirrel, and was on the eve of rising in the air with it, for the purpose of carrying it off to a place of greater security. The one would attack the other with merciless fury, and either force it to abandon the prize, or fight with the same courage as its antagonist, to prevent the latter from becoming the sole possessor. They are sometimes observed flying either one after the other with great rapidity, emitting their continued cry of *kae*, or performing beautiful evolutions through the air, until one or other of them becomes fatigued, and giving way, makes for the earth, where the battle continues until one is overpowered and obliged to make off. It was after witnessing such an encounter between two of these powerful marauders, fighting hard for a young hare, that I made the drawing now before you, kind reader, in which you perceive the male to have greatly the advantage over the female, although she still holds the hare firmly in one of her talons, even while she is driven towards the earth, with her breast upwards.

I have observed that this species will even condescend to pounce on wood-rats and meadow-mice; but I never saw one of these birds seize even those without first alighting on a tree before committing the act.

During the winter months, the Red-tailed Hawk remains perched for hours together, when the sun is shining and the weather calm. Its breast is opposed to the sun, and it then is seen at a great distance, the pure white of that portion of its plumage glittering as if possessed of a silky gloss. They return to their roosting-places so late in the evening, that I have frequently heard their cry after sun-set, mingling with the jovial notes of Chuck-will's-widow, and the ludicrous laugh of the Barred Owl. In the State of Louisiana, the Red-tailed Hawk roosts amongst the tallest branches of the *Magnolia grandiflora*, a tree which there often attains a height of a hundred feet, and a diameter of from three to four feet at the base. It is also fond of roosting on the tall Cypress-trees of our swamps, where it spends the night in security, amidst the mosses attached to the branches.

The Red-tailed Hawk is extremely wary, and difficult to be approached by any one bearing a gun, the use of which it seems to understand perfectly; for no sooner does it perceive a man thus armed than it spreads its wings, utters a loud shriek, and sails off in an opposite direction. On the other hand, a person on horseback, or walking unarmed, may pass immediately under the branch on which it is perched, when it merely watches his motions as he proceeds. It seldom alights on fences, or the low branches of trees, but prefers the highest and most prominent parts of the tallest trees. It alights on the borders of clear streams to drink. I have observed it in such situations, immersing its bill up to the eyes, and swallowing as much as was necessary to quench its thirst at a single draught.

I have seen this species pounce on soft-shelled tortoises,

and amusing enough it was to see the latter scramble towards the water, enter it, and save themselves from the claws of the Hawk by immediately diving. I am not aware that this Hawk is ever successful in these attacks, as I have not on any occasion found any portion of the skin, head, or feet of tortoises in the stomachs of the many Hawks of this species which I have killed and examined. Several times, however, I have found portions of bull-frogs in their stomach.

All our Falcons are pestered with parasitic flying ticks. Those found amongst the plumage of the Red-tailed Hawk, like all others, move swiftly sidewise between the feathers, issue from the skin, and shift from one portion of the body to another on wing, and do not abandon the bird for a day or two after the latter is dead. These ticks are large, and of an auburn colour.

The body of the Red-tailed Hawk is large, compact, and muscular. These birds protrude their talons beyond their head in seizing their prey, as well as while fighting in the air, in the manner shown in the Plate. I have caught several birds of this species by baiting a steel-trap with a live chicken.

The animal represented as held in one of the feet of the female, is usually called a *rabbit* in all parts of the United States, but is evidently a true hare. It never burrows, but has a *form* to rest in, and to which it returns in the manner of the common hare of Europe. I may hereafter present you, kind reader, with a full account of this American species, which occurs in great abundance in the United States.

I have only here to add, that amongst the American farmers the common name of our present bird is the *Hen-hawk*, while it receives that of *Grand mangeur de poules* from the Creoles of Louisiana.

The Passenger Pigeon

Columba migratoria, LINN.

(PLATES 14, 15)

THE Passenger Pigeon, or, as it is usually named in America, the Wild Pigeon, moves with extreme rapidity, propelling itself by quickly repeated flaps of the wings, which it brings more or less near to the body, according to the degree of velocity which is required. Like the Domestic Pigeon, it often flies, during the love season, in a circling manner, supporting itself with both wings angularly elevated, in which position it keeps them until it is about to alight. Now and then, during these circular flights, the tips of the primary quills of each wing are made to strike against each other, producing a smart rap, which may be heard at a distance of thirty or forty yards. Before alighting, the Wild Pigeon, like the Carolina Parrot and a few other species of birds, breaks the force of its flight by repeated flappings, as if apprehensive of receiving injury from coming too suddenly into contact with the branch or the spot of ground on which it intends to settle.

I have commenced my description of this species with the above account of its flight, because the most important facts connected with its habits relate to its migrations. These are entirely owing to the necessity of procuring food, and are not performed with the view of escaping the severity of a northern latitude, or of seeking a southern one for the purpose of breeding. They consequently do not take place at any fixed period or season of the year. Indeed, it sometimes happens that a continuance of a sufficient supply of food in one district will keep these birds absent from another for years. I know, at least, to a certainty, that in Kentucky they remained for several years constantly, and were nowhere else to be found. They all suddenly disappeared one season when the mast was exhausted, and did not return for a long period. Similar facts have been observed in other States.

Their great power of flight enables them to survey and pass over an astonishing extent of country in a very short time. This is proved by facts well known in America. Thus, Pigeons have been killed in the neighbourhood of New York, with their crops full of rice, which they must have collected in the fields of Georgia and Carolina, these districts being the nearest in which they could possibly have procured a supply of that kind of food. As their power of digestion is so great that they will decompose food entirely in twelve hours, they must in this case have travelled between three hundred and four hundred miles in six hours, which shews their speed to be at an average about one mile in a minute. A velocity such as this would enable one of these birds, were it so inclined, to visit the European continent in less than three days.

This great power of flight is seconded by as great a power of vision, which enables them, as they travel at that swift rate, to inspect the country below, discover their food with facility, and thus attain the object for which their journey has been undertaken. This I have also proved to be the case, by having observed them, when passing over a sterile part of the country, or one scantily furnished with food suited to them, keep high in the air, flying with an extended front, so as to enable them to survey hundreds of acres at once. On the contrary, when the land is richly covered with food, or the trees abundantly hung with mast, they fly low, in order to discover the part most plentifully supplied.

Their body is of an elongated oval form, steered by a long well-plumed tail, and propelled by well-set wings, the muscles of which are very large and powerful for the size of the bird. When an individual is seen gliding through the woods and close to the observer, it passes like a thought, and on trying to see it again, the eye searches in vain; the bird is gone.

The multitudes of Wild Pigeons in our woods are astonishing. Indeed, after having viewed them so often, and under so many circumstances, I even now feel inclined to pause, and assure myself that what I am going to relate is fact. Yet I have seen it all, and that too in the company of persons who, like myself, were struck with amazement.

In the autumn of 1813, I left my house at Henderson, on the banks of the Ohio, on my way to Louisville. In passing over the Barrens a few miles beyond Hardensburgh, I observed the pigeons flying from north-east to south-west, in greater numbers than I thought I had ever seen them before, and feeling an inclination to count the flocks that might pass within the reach of my eye in one hour, I dismounted, seated myself on an eminence, and began to mark with my pencil, making a dot for every flock that passed. In a short time finding the task which I had undertaken impracticable, as the birds poured in in countless multitudes, I rose, and counting the dots then put down, found that 163 had been made in twenty-one minutes. I travelled on, and still met more the farther I proceeded. The air was literally filled with Pigeons; the light of noon-day was obscured as by an eclipse; the dung fell in spots, not unlike melting flakes of snow; and the continued buzz of wings had a tendency to lull my senses to repose.

Whilst waiting for dinner at YOUNG's inn, at the confluence of Salt-River with the Ohio, I saw, at my leisure, immense legions still going by, with a front reaching far beyond the Ohio on the west, and the beech-wood forests directly on the east of me. Not a single bird alighted; for not a nut or acorn was that year to be seen in the neighbourhood. They consequently flew so high, that different trials to reach them with a capital rifle proved ineffectual; nor did the reports disturb them in the least. I cannot describe to you the extreme beauty of their aerial evolutions, when a Hawk chanced to press upon the rear of a flock. At once, like a torrent, and with a noise like thunder, they rushed into a compact mass, pressing upon each other towards the centre. In these almost solid masses, they darted forward in undulating and angular lines, descended and swept close over the earth with inconceivable velocity, mounted perpendicularly so as to resemble a vast column, and, when high, were seen wheeling and twisting within their continued lines, which then resembled the coils of a gigantic serpent.

Before sunset I reached Louisville, distant from Hardensburgh fifty-five miles. The Pigeons were still passing in undiminished numbers, and continued to do so for three days in succession. The people were all in arms. The banks of the Ohio were crowded with men and boys, incessantly shooting at the pilgrims, which there flew lower as they passed the river. Multitudes were thus destroyed. For a week or more, the population fed on no other flesh than that of Pigeons, and talked of nothing but Pigeons. The atmosphere, during this time, was strongly impregnated with the peculiar odour which emanates from the species.

It is extremely interesting to see flock after flock performing exactly the same evolutions which had been traced as it were in the air by a preceding flock. Thus, should a Hawk have charged on a group at a certain spot, the angles, curves, and undulations that have been described by the birds, in their efforts to escape from the dreaded talons of the plunderer, are undeviatingly followed by the next group that comes up. Should the bystander happen to witness one of these affrays, and, struck with the rapidity and elegance of the motions exhibited, feel desirous of seeing them repeated, his wishes will be gratified if he only remain in the place until the next group comes up.

It may not, perhaps, be out of place to attempt an estimate of the number of Pigeons contained in one of those mighty flocks, and of the quantity of food daily consumed by its members. The inquiry will tend to shew the astonishing bounty of the great Author of Nature in providing for the wants of his creatures. Let us take a column of one mile in breadth, which is far below the average size, and suppose it passing over us without interruption for three hours, at the rate mentioned above of one mile in the minute. This will give us a parallelogram of 180 miles by 1, covering 180 square miles. Allowing two pigeons to the square yard, we have One billion, one hundred and fifteen millions, one hundred and thirty-six thousand pigeons in one flock. As every pigeon daily consumes fully half a pint of food, the quantity necessary for supplying this vast multitude must be eight millions seven hundred and twelve thousand bushels per day.

As soon as the Pigeons discover a sufficiency of food to entice them to alight, they fly round in circles, reviewing the country below. During their evolutions, on such occasions, the dense mass which they form exhibits a beautiful appearance, as it changes its direction, now displaying a glistening sheet of azure, when the backs of the birds come simultaneously into view, and anon, suddenly presenting a mass of rich deep purple. They then pass lower, over the woods, and for a moment are lost among the foliage, but again emerge, and are seen gliding aloft. They now alight, but the next moment, as if suddenly alarmed, they take to wing, producing by the flappings of their wings a noise like the roar of distant thunder, and sweep through the forests to see if danger is near. Hunger, however, soon brings them to the ground. When alighted, they are seen industriously throwing up the withered leaves in quest of the fallen mast. The rear ranks are continually rising, passing over the main-body, and alighting in front, in such rapid succession, that the whole flock seems still on wing. The quantity of ground thus swept is astonishing, and so completely has it been cleared, that the gleaner who might follow in their rear would find his labour completely lost. Whilst feeding, their avidity is at times so great that in attempting to swallow a large acorn or nut, they are seen gasping for a long while, as if in the agonies of suffocation.

On such occasions, when the woods are filled with these Pigeons, they are killed in immense numbers, although no apparent diminution ensues. About the middle of the day, after their repast is finished, they settle on the trees, to enjoy rest, and digest their food. On the ground they walk with ease, as well as on the branches, frequently jerking their beautiful tail, and moving the neck backwards and forwards in the most graceful manner. As the sun begins to sink beneath the horizon, they depart *en masse* for the roosting-place, which not unfrequently is hundreds of miles distant, as has been ascertained by persons who have kept an account of their arrivals and departures.

Let us now, kind reader, inspect their place of nightly rendezvous. One of these curious roosting-places, on the banks of the Green River in Kentucky, I repeatedly visited. It was, as is always the case, in a portion of the forest where the trees were of great magnitude, and where there was little underwood. I rode through it upwards of forty miles, and, crossing it in different parts, found its average breadth to be rather more than three miles. My first view of it was about a fortnight subsequent to the period when they had made choice of it, and I arrived there nearly two hours before sunset. Few Pigeons were then to be seen, but a great number of persons, with horses and waggons, guns and ammunition, had already established encampments on the borders. Two farmers from the vicinity of Russelsville, distant more than a hundred miles, had driven upwards of three hundred hogs to be fattened on the pigeons which were to be slaughtered. Here and there, the people employed in plucking and salting what had already been procured, were seen sitting in the midst of large piles of these birds. The dung lay several inches deep, covering the whole extent of the roosting-place, like a bed of snow. Many trees two feet in diameter, I observed, were broken off at no great distance from the ground; and the branches of many of the largest and tallest had given way, as if the forest had been swept by a tornado. Every thing proved to me that the number of birds resorting to this part of the forest must be immense beyond conception. As the period of their arrival approached, their foes anxiously prepared to receive them. Some were furnished with iron-pots containing sulphur, others with torches of pine-knots, many with poles, and the rest with guns. The sun was lost to our view, yet not a Pigeon had arrived. Every thing was ready, and all eyes were gazing on the clear sky, which appeared in glimpses amidst the tall trees. Suddenly there burst forth a general cry of "Here they come!" The noise which they made, though yet distant, reminded me of a hard gale at sea, passing through the rigging of a close-reefed vessel. As the birds arrived and passed over me, I felt a current of air that surprised me. Thousands were soon knocked down by the pole-men. The birds continued to pour in. The fires were lighted, and a magnificent, as well as wonderful and almost terrifying, sight presented itself. The Pigeons, arriving by thousands, alighted everywhere, one above another, until solid masses as large as hogsheads were formed on the branches all round. Here and there the perches gave way under the weight with a crash, and, falling to the ground, destroyed hundreds of the birds beneath, forcing down the dense groups with which every stick was loaded. It was a scene of uproar and confusion. I found it quite useless to speak, or even to shout to those persons who were nearest to me. Even the reports of the guns were seldom heard, and I was made aware of the firing only by seeing the shooters reloading.

No one dared venture within the line of devastation. The hogs had been penned up in due time, the picking up of the dead and wounded being left for the next morning's employment. The Pigeons were constantly coming, and it was past midnight before I perceived a decrease in the number of those that arrived. The uproar continued the whole night; and as I was anxious to know to what distance the sound reached, I sent off a man, accustomed to perambulate the forest, who, returning two hours afterwards, informed me he had heard it distinctly when three miles distant from the spot. Towards the approach of day, the noise in some measure subsided, long before objects were distinguishable, the Pigeons began to move off in a direction quite different from that in which they had arrived the evening before, and at sunrise all that were able to fly had disappeared. The howlings of the wolves now reached our ears, and the foxes, lynxes, cougars, bears, raccoons, oppossums and pole-cats were seen sneaking off, whilst eagles and hawks of different species, accompanied by a crowd of vultures, came to supplant them, and enjoy their share of the spoil.

It was then that the authors of all this devastation began their entry amongst the dead, the dying, and the mangled. The pigeons were picked up and piled in heaps, until each had as many as he could possibly dispose of, when the hogs were let loose to feed on the remainder.

Persons unacquainted with these birds might naturally conclude that such dreadful havock would soon put an end to the species. But I have satisfied myself, by long observation, that nothing but the gradual diminution of our forests can accomplish their decrease, as they not unfrequently quadruple their numbers yearly, and always at least double it. In 1805 I saw schooners loaded in bulk with Pigeons caught up the Hudson River, coming in to the wharf at New York, when the birds sold for a cent a piece. I knew a man in Pennsylvania, who caught and killed upwards of 500 dozens in a clap-net in one day, sweeping sometimes twenty dozens or more at a single haul. In the month of March 1830, they were so abundant in the markets of New York, that piles of them met the eye in every direction. I have seen the Negroes at the United States' Salines or Saltworks of Shawanee Town, wearied with killing Pigeons, as they alighted to drink the water issuing from the leading pipes, for weeks at a time; and yet in 1826, in Louisiana, I saw congregated flocks of these birds as numerous as ever I had seen them before, during a residence of nearly thirty years in the United States.

The breeding of the Wild Pigeons, and the places chosen for that purpose, are points of great interest. The time is not much influenced by season, and the place selected is where food is most plentiful and most attainable, and always at a convenient distance from water. Forest-trees of great height are those in which the Pigeons form their nests. Thither the countless myriads resort, and prepare to fulfil one of the great laws of nature. At this period the note of the Pigeon is a soft *coo-coo-coo-coo*, much shorter than that of the domestic species. The common notes resemble the monosyllables *kee-kee-kee-kee*, the first being the loudest, the others gradually diminishing in power. The male assumes a pompous demeanour, and follows the female whether on the ground or on the branches, with spread tail and drooping wings, which it rubs against the part over which it is moving. The body is elevated, the throat swells, the eyes sparkle. He continues his notes, and now and then rises on the wing, and flies a few yards to approach the fugitive and timorous female. Like the domestic Pigeon and other species, they caress each other by billing, in which action, the bill of the one is introduced transversely into that of the other, and both parties alternately disgorge the contents of their crop by repeated efforts. These preliminary affairs are soon settled, and the Pigeons commence their nests in general peace and harmony. They are composed of a few dry twigs, crossing each other, and are supported by forks of the branches. On the same tree from fifty to a hundred nests may frequently be seen:—I might say a much greater number, were I not anxious, kind reader, that however wonderful my account of the Wild Pigeon is, you may not feel disposed to refer it to the marvellous. The eggs are two in number, of a broadly elliptical form, and pure white. During incubation, the male supplies the female with food. Indeed, the tenderness and affection displayed by these birds towards their mates, are in the highest degree striking. It is a remarkable fact, that each brood generally consists of a male and a female.

Here again, the tyrant of the creation, man, interferes, disturbing the harmony of this peaceful scene. As the young birds grow up, their enemies, armed with axes, reach the spot, to seize and destroy all they can. The trees are felled, and made to fall in such a way that the cutting of one causes the overthrow of another, or shakes the neighbouring trees so much, that the young Pigeons, or *squabs*, as they are named, are violently hurried to the ground. In this manner also, immense quantities are destroyed.

The young are fed by the parents in the manner described

above; in other words, the old bird introduces its bill into the mouth of the young one in a transverse manner, or with the back of each mandible opposite the separations of the mandibles of the young bird, and disgorges the contents of its crop. As soon as the young birds are able to shift for themselves, they leave their parents, and continue separate until they attain maturity. By the end of six months they are capable of reproducing their species.

The flesh of the Wild Pigeon is of a dark colour, but affords tolerable eating. That of young birds from the nest is much esteemed. The skin is covered with small white filmy scales. The feathers fall off at the least touch, as has been remarked to be the case in the Carolina Turtle. I have only to add, that this species, like others of the same genus, immerses its head up to the eyes while drinking.

In March 1830, I bought about 350 of these birds in the market of New York, at four cents a piece. Most of these I carried alive to England, and distributed amongst several noblemen, presenting some at the same time to the Zoological Society.

The Ivory-billed Woodpecker

Picus principalis, LINN.

(PLATES 16, 17)

I HAVE always imagined, that in the plumage of the beautiful Ivory-billed Woodpecker, there is something very closely allied to the style of colouring of the great VANDYKE. The broad extent of its dark glossy body and tail, the large and well-defined white markings of its wings, neck, and bill, relieved by the rich carmine of the pendent crest of the male, and the brilliant yellow of its eye, have never failed to remind me of some of the boldest and noblest productions of that inimitable artist's pencil. So strongly indeed have these thoughts become ingrafted in my mind, as I gradually obtained a more intimate acquaintance with the Ivory-billed Woodpecker, that whenever I have observed one of these birds flying from one tree to another, I have mentally exclaimed, "There goes a Vandyke!"

This notion may seem strange, perhaps ludicrous, to you, good reader, but I relate it as a fact, and whether or not it may be found in accordance with your own ideas, after you have inspected the plate in which is represented this great chieftain of the Woodpecker tribe, is perhaps of little consequence.

The Ivory-billed Woodpecker confines its rambles to a comparatively very small portion of the United States, it never having been observed in the Middle States within the memory of any person now living there. In fact, in no portion of these districts does the nature of the woods appear suitable to its remarkable habits.

Descending the Ohio, we meet with this splendid bird for the first time near the confluence of that beautiful river and the Mississippi; after which, following the windings of the latter, either downwards toward the sea, or upwards in the direction of the Missouri, we frequently observe it. On the Atlantic coast, North Carolina may be taken as the limit of its distribution, although now and then an individual of the species may be accidentally seen in Maryland. To the westward of the Mississippi, it is found in all the dense forests bordering the streams which empty their waters into that majestic river, from the very declivities of the Rocky Mountains. The lower parts of the Carolinas, Georgia, Alabama, Louisiana, and Mississippi, are, however, the most favourite resorts of this bird, and in those States it constantly resides, breeds, and passes a life of peaceful enjoyment, finding a profusion of food in all the deep, dark, and gloomy swamps dispersed throughout them.

I wish, kind reader, it were in my power to present to your mind's eye the favourite resort of the Ivory-billed Woodpecker. Would that I could describe the extent of those deep morasses, overshadowed by millions of gigantic dark cypresses, spreading their sturdy moss-covered branches, as if to admonish intruding man to pause and reflect on the many difficulties which he must encounter, should he persist in venturing farther into their almost inaccessible recesses, extending for miles before him, where he should be interrupted by huge projecting branches, here and there the massy trunk of a fallen and decaying tree, and thousands of creeping and twining plants of numberless species! Would that I could represent to you the dangerous nature of the ground, its oozing, spongy, and miry disposition, although covered with a beautiful but treacherous carpeting, composed of the richest mosses, flags, and water-lilies, no sooner receiving the pressure of the foot than it yields and endangers the very life of the adventurer, whilst here and there, as he approaches an opening, that proves merely a lake of black muddy water, his ear is assailed by the dismal croaking of innumerable frogs, the hissing of serpents, or the bellowing of alligators! Would that I could give you an idea of the sultry pestiferous atmosphere that nearly suffocates the intruder during the meridian heat of our dogdays, in those gloomy and horrible swamps! But the attempt to picture these scenes would be vain. Nothing short of ocular demonstration can impress any adequate idea of them.

How often, kind reader, have I thought of the difference of the tasks imposed on different minds, when, travelling in countries far distant from those where birds of this species and others as difficult to be procured are now and then offered for sale in the form of dried skins, I have heard the amateur or closet-naturalist express his astonishment that half-a-crown was asked by the person who had perhaps followed the bird when alive over miles of such swamps, and after procuring it, had prepared its skin in the best manner, and carried it to a market thousands of miles distant from the spot where he had obtained it. I must say, that it has at least grieved me as much as when I have heard some idle fop complain of the poverty of the Gallery of the Louvre, where he had paid nothing, or when I have listened to the same infatuated idler lamenting the loss of his shilling, as he sauntered through the Exhibition Rooms of the Royal Academy of London, or any equally valuable repository of art. But, let us return to the biography of the famed Ivory-billed Woodpecker.

The flight of this bird is graceful in the extreme, although seldom prolonged to more than a few hundred yards at a time, unless when it has to cross a large river, which it does in deep undulations, opening its wings at first to their full extent, and nearly closing them to renew the propelling impulse. The transit from one tree to another, even should the distance be as much as a hundred yards, is performed by a single sweep, and the bird appears as if merely swinging itself from the top of the one tree to that of the other, forming an elegantly curved line. At this moment all the beauty of the plumage is exhibited, and strikes the beholder with pleasure. It never utters any sound whilst on wing, unless during the love season; but at all other times, no sooner has this bird alighted than its remarkable voice is heard, at almost every leap which it makes, whilst ascending against the upper parts of the trunk of a tree, or its highest branches. Its notes are clear, loud, and yet rather plaintive. They are heard at a considerable distance, perhaps half a mile, and resemble the false high note of a clarionet. They are usually repeated three times in succession, and may be represented by the monosyllable *pait, pait, pait.* These are heard so frequently as to induce me to say that the bird spends few minutes of the day without uttering them, and this circumstance leads to its destruction, which is aimed at, not because (as is supposed by some) this species is a destroyer of trees, but more because it is a beautiful bird, and its rich scalp attached to the upper mandible forms an ornament for the war-dress of most of our Indians, or for the shot-pouch of our squatters and hunters, by all of whom the bird is shot merely for that purpose.

Travellers of all nations are also fond of possessing the upper part of the head and the bill of the male, and I have frequently remarked, that on a steam-boat's reaching what we call a *wooding-place*, the *strangers* were very apt to pay a quarter of a dollar for two or three heads of this Woodpecker. I have seen entire belts of Indian chiefs closely ornamented with the tufts and bills of this species, and have observed that a great value is frequently put upon them.

The Ivory-billed Woodpecker nestles earlier in spring than any other species of its tribe. I have observed it boring a hole for that purpose in the beginning of March. The hole is, I believe, always made in the trunk of a live tree, generally an ash or a hagberry, and is at a great height. The birds pay great regard to the particular situation of the tree, and the inclination of its trunk; first, because they prefer retirement, and again, because they are anxious to secure the aperture against the access of water during beating rains. To prevent such a calamity, the hole is generally dug immediately under the junction of a large branch with the trunk. It is first bored horizontally for a few inches, then directly downwards, and not in a spiral manner, as some people have imagined. According to circumstances, this cavity is more or less deep, being sometimes not more than ten inches, whilst at other times it reaches nearly three feet downwards into the core of the tree. I have been led to think that these differences result from the more or less immediate necessity under which the female may be of depositing her eggs, and again have thought that the older the Woodpecker is, the deeper does it make its hole. The average diameter of the different nests which I have examined was about seven inches within, although the entrance, which is perfectly round, is only just large enough to admit the bird.

Both birds work most assiduously at this excavation, one waiting outside to encourage the other, whilst it is engaged in digging, and when the latter is fatigued, taking its place. I have approached trees whilst these Woodpeckers were thus busily employed in forming their nest, and by resting my head against the bark, could easily distinguish every blow given by the bird. I observed that in two instances, when the Woodpeckers saw me thus at the foot of the tree in which they were digging their nest, they abandoned it for ever. For the first brood there are generally six eggs. They are deposited on a few chips at the bottom of the hole, and are of a pure white colour. The young are seen creeping out of the hole about a fortnight before they venture to fly to any other tree. The second brood makes its appearance about the 15th of August.

In Kentucky and Indiana, the Ivory-bills seldom raise more than one brood in the season. The young are at first of the colour of the female, only that they want the crest, which, however, grows rapidly, and towards autumn, particularly in birds of the first breed, is nearly equal to that of the mother. The males have then a slight line of red on the head, and do not attain their richness of plumage until spring, or their full size until the second year. Indeed, even then, a difference is easily observed between them and individuals which are much older.

The food of this species consists principally of beetles, larvæ, and large grubs. No sooner, however, are the grapes of our forests ripe than they are eaten by the Ivory-billed

Woodpecker with great avidity. I have seen this bird hang by its claws to the vines, in the position so often assumed by a Titmouse, and, reaching downwards, help itself to a bunch of grapes with much apparent pleasure. Persimons are also sought for by them, as soon as the fruit becomes quite mellow, as are hagberries.

The Ivory-bill is never seen attacking the corn, or the fruit of the orchards, although it is sometimes observed working upon and chipping off the bark from the belted trees of the newly-cleared plantations. It seldom comes near the ground, but prefers at all times the tops of the tallest trees. Should it, however, discover the half-standing broken shaft of a large dead and rotten tree, it attacks it in such a manner as nearly to demolish it in the course of a few days. I have seen the remains of some of these ancient monarchs of our forests so excavated, and that so singularly, that the tottering fragments of the trunk appeared to be merely supported by the great pile of chips by which its base was surrounded. The strength of this Woodpecker is such, that I have seen it detach pieces of bark seven or eight inches in length at a single blow of its powerful bill, and by beginning at the top branch of a dead tree, tear off the bark, to an extent of twenty or thirty feet, in the course of a few hours, leaping downwards with its body in an upward position, tossing its head to the right and left, or leaning it against the bark to ascertain the precise spot where the grubs were concealed, and immediately after renewing its blows with fresh vigour, all the while sounding its loud notes, as if highly delighted.

This species generally moves in pairs, after the young have left their parents. The female is always the most clamorous and the least shy. Their mutual attachment is, I believe, continued through life. Excepting when digging a hole for the reception of their eggs, these birds seldom, if ever, attack living trees, for any other purpose than that of procuring food, in doing which they destroy the insects that would otherwise prove injurious to the trees.

I have frequently observed the male and female retire to rest for the night, into the same hole in which they had long before reared their young. This generally happens a short time after sunset.

When wounded and brought to the ground, the Ivory-bill immediately makes for the nearest tree, and ascends it with great rapidity and perseverance, until it reaches the top branches, when it squats and hides, generally with great effect. Whilst ascending, it moves spirally round the tree, utters its loud *pait, pait, pait,* at almost every hop, but becomes silent the moment it reaches a place where it conceives itself secure. They sometimes cling to the bark with their claws so firmly, as to remain cramped to the spot for several hours after death. When taken by the hand, which is rather a hazardous undertaking, they strike with great violence, and inflict very severe wounds with their bill as well as claws, which are extremely sharp and strong. On such occasions, this bird utters a mournful and very piteous cry.

The Wood Thrush

Turdus mustelinus, GMEL.

(PLATES 18, 19)

KIND READER, you now see before you my greatest favourite of the feathered tribes of our woods. To it I owe much. How often has it revived my drooping spirits, when I have listened to its wild notes in the forest, after passing a restless night in my slender shed, so feebly secured against the violence of the storm, as to shew me the futility of my best efforts to rekindle my little fire, whose uncertain and vacillating light had gradually died away under the destructive weight of the dense torrents of rain that seemed to involve the heavens and the earth in one mass of fearful murkiness, save when the red streaks of the flashing thunderbolt burst on the dazzled eye, and, glancing along the huge trunk of the stateliest and noblest tree in my immediate neighbourhood, were instantly followed by an uproar of crackling, crashing, and deafening sounds, rolling their volumes in tumultuous eddies far and near, as if to silence the very breathings of the unformed thought! How often, after such a night, when far from my dear home, and deprived of the presence of those nearest to my heart, wearied, hungry, drenched, and so lonely and desolate as almost to question myself why I was thus situated, when I have seen the fruits of my labours on the eve of being destroyed, as the water, collected into a stream, rushed through my little camp, and forced me to stand erect, shivering in a cold fit like that of a severe ague, when I have been obliged to wait with the patience of a martyr for the return of day, trying in vain to destroy the tormenting moschettoes, silently counting over the years of my youth, doubting perhaps if ever again I should return to my home, and embrace my family!—how often, as the first glimpses of morning gleamed doubtfully amongst the dusky masses of the forest-trees, has there come upon my ear, thrilling along the sensitive cords which connect that organ with the heart, the delightful music of this harbinger of day!—and how fervently, on such occasions, have I blessed the Being who formed the Wood Thrush, and placed it in those solitary forests, as if to console me amidst my privations, to cheer my depressed mind, and to make me feel, as I did, that never ought man to despair, whatever may be his situation, as he can never be certain that aid and deliverance are not at hand.

The Wood Thrush seldom commits a mistake after such a storm as I have attempted to describe; for no sooner are its sweet notes heard than the heavens gradually clear, the bright refracted light rises in gladdening rays from beneath the distant horizon, the effulgent beams increase in their intensity, and the great orb of day at length bursts on the sight. The grey vapour that floats along the ground is quickly dissipated, the world smiles at the happy change, and the woods are soon heard to echo the joyous thanks of their many songsters. At that moment, all fears vanish, giving place to an inspiriting hope. The hunter prepares to leave his camp. He listens to the Wood Thrush, while he thinks of the course which he ought to pursue, and as the bird approaches to peep at him, and learn somewhat of his intentions, he raises his mind towards the Supreme Disposer of events. Seldom, indeed, have I heard the song of this Thrush, without feeling all that tranquillity of mind, to which the secluded situation in which it delights is so favourable. The thickest and darkest woods always appear to please it best. The borders of murmuring streamlets, over-shadowed by the dense foliage of the lofty trees growing on the gentle declivities, amidst which the sunbeams seldom penetrate, are its favourite resorts. There it is, kind reader, that the musical powers of this hermit of the woods must be heard, to be fully appreciated and enjoyed.

The song of the Wood Thrush, although composed of but few notes, is so powerful, distinct, clear, and mellow, that it is impossible for any person to hear it without being struck by the effect which it produces on the mind. I do not know to what instrumental sounds I can compare these notes, for I really know none so melodious and harmonical. They gradually rise in strength, and then fall in gentle cadences, becoming at length so low as to be scarcely audible; like the emotions of the lover, who at one moment exults in the hope of possessing the object of his affections, and the next pauses in suspense, doubtful of the result of all his efforts to please.

Several of these birds seem to challenge each other from different portions of the forest, particularly towards evening, and at that time nearly all the other songsters being about to retire to rest, the notes of the Wood Thrush are doubly pleasing. One would think that each individual is anxious to excel his distant rival, and I have frequently thought that on such occasions their music is more than ordinarily effective, as it then exhibits a degree of skilful modulation quite beyond my power to describe. These concerts are continued for some time after sunset, and take place in the month of June, when the females are sitting.

This species glides swiftly through the woods, whilst on wing, and performs its migrations without appearing in the open country. It is a constant resident in the State of Louisiana, to which the dispersed individuals resort, as to winter quarters, from the different parts of the United States, to which they had gone to breed. They reach Pennsylvania about the beginning or middle of April, and gradually proceed farther north.

Their food consists of different kinds of berries and small fruits, which they procure in the woods, without ever interfering with the farmer. They also occasionally feed on insects and various lichens.

The nest is usually placed in a low horizontal branch of the Dogwood Tree, occasionally on smaller shrubs. It is large, well saddled on the branch, and composed externally of dry leaves of various kinds, with a second bed of grasses and mud, and an internal layer of fine fibrous roots. The eggs are four or five, of a beautiful uniform light blue. The nest is generally found in deep swampy hollows, on the sides of hills.

On alighting on a branch, this Thrush gives its tail a few jets, uttering at each motion a low chuckling note peculiar to itself, and very different from those of the Hermit or Tawny Thrush. It then stands still for a while, with the feathers of the hind part a little raised. It walks and hops along the branches with much ease, and often bends down its head to peep at the objects around. It frequently alights on the ground, and scratches up the dried leaves in search of worms and beetles, but suddenly flies back to the trees, on the least alarm.

The sight of a fox or raccoon causes them much anxiety, and they generally follow these animals at a respectful distance, uttering a mournful *cluck*, well known to hunters. Although, during winter, these birds are numerous in Louisiana, they never form themselves into flocks, but go singly at this period, and only in pairs in the breeding season. They are easily reared from the nest, and sing nearly as well in confinement as while free. Their song is occasionally heard during the whole winter, particularly when the sun reappears after a shower. Their flesh is extremely delicate and juicy, and many of them are killed with the blow-gun.

Having given you a description of the Dogwood before, when I presented that tree in bloom, I have only to say here, that you now see it in its autumnal colouring, adorned with its berries, of which the Wood Thrush is fond.

The Fish Hawk, or Osprey

(PLATE 13)

COMPARING the great size of this bird, its formidable character, its powerful and protracted flight, and the dexterity with which, although a land bird, it procures its prey from the waters of the ocean, with the very inferior powers of the bird named the Kingsfisher, I should be tempted to search for a more appropriate appellation than that of Fish-Hawk, and, were I not a member of a republic, might fancy that of *Imperial Fisher* more applicable to it.

The habits of this famed bird differ so materially from those of almost all others of its genus, that an accurate description of them cannot fail to be highly interesting to the student of nature.

The Fish Hawk may be looked upon as having more of a social disposition than most other Hawks. Indeed, with the exception of the Swallow-tailed Hawk (*Falco furcatus*), I know none so gregarious in its habits. It migrates in numbers, both during spring, when it shews itself along our Atlantic shores, lakes, and rivers, and during autumn, when it retires to warmer climes. At these seasons, it appears in flocks of eight or ten individuals, following the windings of our shores in loose bodies, advancing in easy sailings or flappings, crossing each other in their gyrations. During the period of their stay in the United States, many pairs are seen nestling, rearing their young, and seeking their food, within so short a distance of each other, that while following the margins of our eastern shores, a Fish Hawk or a nest belonging to the species, may be met with at every short interval.

The Fish Hawk may be said to be of a mild disposition. Not only do these birds live in perfect harmony together, but they even allow other birds of very different character to approach so near to them as to build their nests of the very materials of which the outer parts of their own are constructed. I have never observed a Fish Hawk chasing any other bird whatever. So pacific and timorous is it, that, rather than encounter a foe but little more powerful than itself, it abandons its prey to the White-headed Eagle, which, next to man, is its greatest enemy. It never forces its young from the nest, as some other Hawks do, but, on the contrary, is seen to feed them even when they have begun to procure food for themselves.

Notwithstanding all these facts, a most erroneous idea prevails among our fishermen, and the farmers along our coasts, that the Fish Hawk's nest is the best *scare-crow* they can have in the vicinity of their houses or grounds. As these good people affirm, no Hawk will attempt to commit depredations on their poultry, so long as the Fish Hawk remains in the country. But the absence of most birds of prey from those parts at the time when the Fish Hawk is on our coast, arises simply from the necessity of retiring to the more sequestered parts of the interior for the purpose of rearing their young in security, and the circumstance of their visiting the coasts chiefly at the period when myriads of water-fowl resort to our estuaries at the approach of winter, leaving the shores and salt-marshes at the return of spring, when the Fish Hawk arrives. However, as this notion has a tendency to protect the latter bird, it may be so far useful, the fisherman always interposing when he sees a person bent upon the destruction of his favourite bird.

The Fish Hawk differs from all birds of prey in another important particular, which is, that it never attempts to secure its prey in the air, although its rapidity of flight might induce an observer to suppose it perfectly able to do so. I have spent weeks on the Gulf of Mexico, where these birds are numerous, and have observed them sailing and plunging into the water, at a time when numerous shoals of flying-fish were emerging from the sea to evade the pursuit of the dolphins. Yet the Fish Hawk never attempted to pursue any of them while above the surface, but would plunge after one of them or a bonita-fish, after they had resumed their usual mode of swimming near the surface.

The motions of the Fish Hawk in the air are graceful, and as majestic as those of the Eagle. It rises with ease to a great height by extensive circlings, performed apparently by mere inclinations of the wings and tail. It dives at times to some distance with the wings partially closed, and resumes its sailing, as if these plunges were made for amusement only. Its wings are extended at right angles to the body, and when thus flying it is easily distinguishable from all other Hawks by the eye of an observer accustomed to note the flight of birds. Whilst in search of food, it flies with easy flappings at a moderate height above the water, and with an apparent listlessness, although in reality it is keenly observing the objects beneath. No sooner does it spy a fish suited to its taste, than it checks its course with a sudden shake of its wings and tail, which gives it the appearance of being poised in the air for a moment, after which it plunges headlong with great rapidity into the water, to secure its prey, or continue its flight, if disappointed by having observed the fish sink deeper.

When it plunges into the water in pursuit of a fish, it sometimes proceeds deep enough to disappear for an instant. The surge caused by its descent is so great as to make the spot around it present the appearance of a mass of foam. On rising with its prey, it is seen holding it in the manner represented in the Plate. It mounts a few yards into the air, shakes the water from its plumage, squeezes the fish with its talons, and immediately proceeds towards its nest, to feed its young, or to a tree, to devour the fruit of its industry in peace. When it has satisfied its hunger, it does not, like other Hawks, stay perched until hunger again urges it forth, but usually sails about at a great height over the neighbouring waters.

The Fish Hawk has a great attachment to the tree to which it carries its prey, and will not abandon it, unless frequently disturbed, or shot at whilst feeding there. It shews the same attachment to the tree on which it has built its first nest, and returns to it year after year.

This species arrives on the southern coasts of the United States early in the month of February, and proceeds eastward as the season advances. In the Middle Districts, the fishermen hail its appearance with joy, as it is the harbinger of various species of fish which resort to the Atlantic coasts, or ascend the numerous rivers. It arrives in the Middle States about the beginning of April, and returns southward at the first appearance of frost. I have occasionally seen a few of these birds on the muddy lakes of Louisiana, in the neighbourhood of New Orleans, during the winter months; but they appeared emaciated, and were probably unable to follow their natural inclinations, and proceed farther south.

As soon as the females make their appearance, which happens eight or ten days after the arrival of the males, the love-season commences, and soon after, incubation takes place. The loves of these birds are conducted in a different way from those of the other Falcons. The males are seen playing through the air amongst themselves, chasing each other in sport, or sailing by the side or after the female which they have selected, uttering cries of joy and exultation, alighting on the branches of the tree on which their last year's nest is yet seen remaining, and doubtless congratulating each other on finding their home again. Their caresses are mutual. They begin to augment their habitation, or to repair the injuries which it may have sustained during the winter, and are seen sailing together towards the shores, to collect the drifted sea-weeds with which they line the nest anew. They alight on the beach, search for the driest and largest weeds, collect a mass of them, clench them in their talons, and fly towards their nest with the materials dangling beneath. They both alight and labour together. In a fortnight the nest is complete, and the female deposits her eggs, which are three or four in number, of a broadly oval form, yellowish-white, densely covered with large irregular spots of reddish-brown.

The nest is generally placed in a large tree in the immediate vicinity of the water, whether along the seashore, on the margins of the inland lakes, or by some large river. It is, however, sometimes to be seen in the interior of a wood, a mile or more from the water. I have concluded that, in the latter case, it was on account of frequent disturbance, or attempts at destruction, that the birds had removed from their usual haunt. The nest is very large, sometimes measuring fully four feet across, and is composed of a quantity of materials sufficient to render its depth equal to its diameter. Large sticks, mixed with sea-weeds, tufts of strong grass, and other materials, form its exterior, while the interior is composed of sea-weeds and finer grasses. I have not observed that any particular species of tree is preferred by the Fish Hawk. It places its nest in the forks of an oak or a pine with equal pleasure. But I have observed that the tree chosen is usually of considerable size, and not unfrequently a decayed one. I dare not, however, affirm that the juices of the plants which compose the nest, ever become so detrimental to the growth of a tree as ultimately to kill it. In a few instances, I have seen the Fish Crow and the Purple Grakle raising their families in nests built by them among the outer sticks of the Fish Hawk's nest.

The male assists in incubation, during the continuance of which the one bird supplies the other with food, although each in turn goes in quest of some for itself. At such times the male bird is now and then observed rising to an immense height in the air, over the spot where his mate is seated. This he does by ascending almost in a direct line, by means of continued flappings, meeting the breeze with his white breast, and occasionally uttering a cackling kind of note, by which the bystander is enabled to follow him in his progress. When the Fish Hawk has attained its utmost elevation, which is sometimes such that the eye can no longer perceive him, he utters a loud shriek, and dives smoothly on half-extended wings towards his nest. But before he reaches it, he is seen to expand his wings and tail, and in this manner he glides towards his beloved female, in a beautifully curved line. The female partially raises herself from her eggs, emits a low cry, resumes her former posture, and her delighted partner flies off to the sea, to seek a favourite fish for her whom he loves.

The young are at length hatched. The parents become more and more attached to them, as they grow up. Abundance of food is procured to favour their development. So truly parental becomes the attachment of the old birds, that an attempt to rob them of those dear fruits of their love, generally proves more dangerous than profitable. Should it be made, the old birds defend their brood with great courage and perseverance, and even sometimes, with extended claws and bill, come in contact with the assailant, who is glad to make his escape with a sound skin.

The young are fed until fully fledged, and often after they have left the nest, which they do apparently with great reluctance. I have seen some as large as the parents, filling the nest, and easily distinguished by the white margins of their upper plumage, which may be seen with a good glass at a considerable distance. So much fish is at times carried to the nest, that a quantity of it falls to the ground, and is left there to putrify around the foot of the tree. Only one brood is raised each season.

The Fish Hawk seldom alights on the ground, and when it does so, walks with difficulty, and in an extremely awkward manner. The only occasions on which it is necessary for them to alight, are when they collect materials for the purpose of repairing their nest at the approach of autumn, or for building a new one, or repairing the old, in spring.

I have found this bird in various parts of the interior of the United States, but always in the immediate neighbourhood of rivers or lakes. When I first removed to Louisville in Kentucky, several pairs were in the habit of raising their brood annually on a piece of ground immediately opposite the foot of the Falls of the Ohio in the State of Indiana. The ground belonged to the venerable General CLARK, and I was several times invited by him to visit the spot. Increasing population, however, has driven off the birds, and few are now seen on the Ohio, unless during their migrations to and from Lake Erie, where I have met with them.

I have observed many of these birds at the approach of winter, sailing over the lakes near the Mississippi, where they feed on the fish which the Wood Ibis kills, the Hawks themselves being unable to discover them whilst alive in the muddy water with which these lakes are filled. There the Ibises wade among the water in immense flocks, and so trample the bottom as to convert the lakes into filthy puddles, in which the fishes are unable to respire with ease. They rise to the surface, and are instantly killed by the Ibises. The whole surface is sometimes covered in this manner with dead fish, so that not only are the Ibises plentifully supplied, but Vultures, Eagles and Fish Hawks, come to participate in the spoil. Except in such places, and on such occasions, I have not observed the Fish Hawk to eat of any other prey than that which it had procured by plunging headlong into the water after it.

I have frequently heard it asserted that the Fish Hawk is sometimes drawn under the water and drowned, when it has attempted to seize a fish which is too strong for it, and that some of these birds have been found sticking by their talons to the back of Sturgeons and other large fishes. But, as nothing of this kind ever came under my observation, I am unable to corroborate these reports. The roosting place of this bird is generally on the top-branches of the tree on which its nest is placed, or of one close to it.

Fish Hawks are very plentiful on the coast of New Jersey, near Great Egg Harbour, where I have seen upwards of fifty of their nests in the course of a day's walk, and where I have shot several in the course of a morning. When wounded, they defend themselves in the manner usually exhibited by Hawks, erecting the feathers of the head, and trying to strike with their powerful talons and bill, whilst they remain prostrate on their back.

The largest fish which I have seen this bird take out of the water, was a Weak-Fish, such as is represented in the plate, but sufficiently large to weigh more than five pounds. The bird carried it into the air with difficulty, and dropped it, on hearing the report of a shot fired at it.

The Broad-winged Hawk

Falco pennsylvanicus, WILS.

(PLATE 20)

ONE FINE May morning, when nature seemed to be enchanted at the sight of her own great works, when the pearly dew-drops were yet hanging at the point of each leaf, or lay nursed in the blossoms, gently rocked, as it were, by the soft breeze of early summer, I took my gun, and, accompanied by my excellent brother-in-law, WILLIAM G. BAKEWELL, Esq. at that time a youth, walked towards some lovely groves, where many songsters attracted our attention by their joyous melodies. The woods were all alive with the richest variety, and, divided in choice, we kept going on without shooting at any thing, so great was our admiration of every bird that presented itself to our view. As we crossed a narrow skirt of wood, my young companion spied a nest on a tree of moderate height, and, as my eye reached it, we both perceived that the parent bird was sitting in it. Some little consultation took place, as neither of us could determine whether it was a Crow's or a Hawk's nest, and it was resolved that my young friend should climb the tree, and bring down one of the eggs. On reaching the nest, he said the bird, which still remained quiet, was a Hawk and unable to fly. I desired him to cover it with his handkerchief, try to secure it, and bring it down, together with the eggs. All this was accomplished without the least difficulty. I looked at it with indescribable pleasure, as I saw it was new to me, and then felt vexed that it was not of a more spirited nature, as it had neither defended its eggs nor itself. It lay quietly in the handkerchief, and I carried it home to my father-in-law's, shewed it to the family, and went to my room, where I instantly began drawing it. The drawing which I then made is at this moment before me, and is dated "Fatland Ford, Pennsylvania, May 27, 1812."

I put the bird on a stick made fast to my table. It merely moved its feet to grasp the stick, and stood erect, but raised its feathers, and drew in its neck on its shoulders. I passed my hand over it, to smooth the feathers by gentle pressure. It moved not. The plumage remained as I wished it. Its eye, directed towards mine, appeared truly sorrowful, with a degree of pensiveness, which rendered me at that moment quite uneasy. I measured the length of its bill with the compass, began my outlines, continued measuring part after part as I went on, and finished the drawing, without the bird ever moving once. My wife sat at my side, reading to me at intervals, but our conversation had frequent reference to the singularity of the incident. The drawing being finished, I raised the window, laid hold of the poor bird, and launched it into the air, where it sailed off until out of my sight, without uttering a single cry, or deviating from its course. The drawing from which the plate is taken, was subsequently made, as I had to wait until I should procure a male, to render it complete.

The above incident you will doubtless consider as extraordinary as I myself did, and perhaps some may feel disposed to look upon it as a specimen of travellers' tales; but as I have resolved to present you with the incidents as they occurred, I have felt no hesitation in relating this.

The Broad-winged Hawk is seldom seen in Louisiana, and I believe never except during the severe winters that occasionally occur in our Middle and Eastern Districts. I have observed that its usual range seldom extends far west of the Alleghany Mountains; but in Virginia, Maryland, and all the States to the eastward of these, it is by no means a rare species. I have shot several in the Jerseys, the State of New York, near the Falls of Niagara, and also in the Great Pine Forest.

Its flight, which is easy and light, is performed in circles. When elevated in the air, it is fond of partially closing its wings for a moment, and thus gliding to a short distance, as if for amusement. It seldom chases other birds of prey, but is itself frequently teased by the Little Sparrow-hawk, the King-bird, or the Martin. It generally attacks birds of weak nature, particularly very young chickens and ducklings, and during winter feeds on insects and other small animals. It flies singly, unless during the breeding season, and after feeding retires to the top of some small tree, within the woods, where it rests for hours together. It is easily approached. When wounded by a shot so as to be unable to fly, it, like most birds of its tribe, throws itself on its back, opens its bill, protrudes its tongue, utters a hissing sound, erects the top-feathers of its head, and defends itself by reiterated attempts to lay hold with its talons. If a stick is presented to it in this state, it will clench it at once, and allow itself to be carried hanging to it for some distance, indeed until the muscles become paralyzed, when it drops, and again employs the same means of defence.

When feeding, it generally holds its prey with both feet, and tears and swallows the parts without much plucking. I must here remark, that birds of prey never cover their victims by extending the wings over them, unless when about to be attacked by other birds or animals, that evince a desire to share with them or carry off the fruit of their exertions. In the stomach of this bird I have found wood-frogs, portions of small snakes, together with feathers, and the hair of several small species of quadrupeds. I do not think it ever secures birds on the wing, at least I never saw it do so.

The nest, which is about the size of that of the Common Crow, is usually placed on pretty large branches, and near the stem or trunk of the tree. It is composed externally of dry sticks and briars, internally of numerous small roots, and is lined with the large feathers of the Common Fowl and other birds. The eggs are four or five, of a dull greyish-white, blotched with dark brown. They are deposited as early as the beginning of March, in low places, but not until a fortnight later in the mountainous parts of the districts in which the bird more frequently breeds.

The tree on which I have placed a pair of these birds is known nearly throughout the Union by the name of *Pig-nut Hickory*. I have represented it along with them, not because the birds themselves feed on the nuts, as some people have supposed on seeing the drawing, but because it occurs abundantly in those States where the Broad-winged Hawk resides, and, again, because I have found the nest of that bird more frequently placed on its branches than on those of any other tree. The nuts have an excessively hard shell. The kernel is sweet, but as it is of small size, the nuts are seldom gathered for any other purpose than that of feeding tame squirrels. The hogs which run at large in our woods feed on them, as do all our different species of squirrels, and sometimes the raccoon. The wood of this tree is perhaps tougher than that of most of its genus; but as the trunk is seldom either very straight or very high, it is not used so much as some other hickories, for the purposes of husbandry. Its average height may be estimated at about fifty feet, and its diameter at from eighteen inches to two feet.

The Blue Jay

Corvus cristatus, LINN.

(PLATE 21)

READER, look at the plate in which are represented three individuals of this beautiful species,—rogues though they be, and thieves, as I would call them, were it fit for me to pass judgment on their actions. See how each is enjoying the fruits of his knavery, sucking the egg which he has pilfered from the nest of some innocent dove or harmless partridge! Who could imagine that a form so graceful, arrayed by nature in a garb so resplendent, should harbour so much mischief;—that selfishness, duplicity, and malice should form the moral accompaniments of so much physical perfection! Yet so it is, and how like beings of a much higher order, are these gay deceivers! Aye, I could write you a whole chapter on this subject, were not my task of a different nature.

The Blue Jay is one of those birds that are found capable of subsisting in cold as well as in warm climates. It occurs as far north as the Canadas, where it makes occasional attacks upon the corn cribs of the farmers, and it is found in the most southern portions of the United States, where it abounds during the winter. Every where it manifests the same mischievous disposition. It imitates the cry of the Sparrow Hawk so perfectly, that the little birds in the neighbourhood hurry into the thick coverts, to avoid what they believe to be the attack of that marauder. It robs every nest it can find, sucks the eggs like the crow, or tears to pieces and devours the young birds. A friend once wounded a Grous (*Tetrao umbellus*), and marked the direction which it followed, but had not proceeded two hundred yards in pursuit, when he heard something fluttering in the bushes, and found his bird belaboured by two Blue Jays, who were picking out its eyes. The same person once put a Flying Squirrel into the cage of one of these birds, merely to preserve it for one night; but on looking into the cage about eleven o'clock next day, he found the animal partly eaten. A Blue Jay at Charleston destroyed all the birds of an aviary. One after another had been killed, and the rats were supposed to have been the culprits, but no crevice could be seen large enough to admit one. Then the mice were accused, and war was waged against them, but still the birds continued to be killed; first the smaller, then the larger, until at length the Keywest Pigeons; when it was discovered that a Jay which had been raised in the aviary was the depredator. He was taken out, and placed in a cage, with a quantity of corn, flour and several small birds which he had just killed. The birds he soon devoured, but the flour he would not condescend to eat, and refusing every other kind of food soon died. In the north, it is particularly fond of ripe chestnuts, and in visiting the trees is sure to select the choicest. When these fail, it attacks the beech nuts, acorns, pears, apples, and green corn.

While at Louisville, in Kentucky, in the winter of 1830, I purchased twenty-five of these birds, at the rate of 6¼ cents each, which I shipped to New Orleans, and afterwards to Liverpool, with the view of turning them out in the English woods. They were caught in common traps, baited with maize, and were brought to me one after another as soon as secured. In placing them in the large cage which I had ordered for the purpose of sending them abroad, I was surprised to see how cowardly each newly caught bird was when introduced to his brethren, who, on being in the cage a day or two, were as gay and frolicksome as if at liberty in the woods. The new comer, on the contrary, would run into a corner, place his head almost in a perpendicular position, and remain silent and sulky, with an appearance of stupidity quite foreign to his nature. He would suffer all the rest to walk over him and trample him down, without ever changing his position. If corn or fruit was presented to him, or even placed close to his bill, he would not so much as look at it. If touched with the hand, he would cower, lie down on his side, and remain motionless. The next day, however, things were altered: he was again a Jay, taking up corn, placing it between his feet, hammering it with his bill, splitting the grain, picking out the kernel, and dropping the divided husks. When the cage was filled, it was amusing to listen to their hammering; all mounted on their perch side by side, each pecking at a grain of maize, like so many blacksmiths paid by the piece. They drank a great deal, eat broken pacan nuts, grapes, dried fruits of all sorts, and especially fresh beef, of which they were extremely fond, roosted very peaceably close together, and were very pleasing pets. Now and then one would utter a cry of alarm, when instantly all would leap and fly about as if greatly concerned, making as much ado as if their most inveterate enemy had been in the midst of them. They bore the passage to Europe pretty well, and most of them reached Liverpool in good health; but a few days after their arrival, a disease occasioned by insects adhering to every part of their body, made such progress that some died every day. Many remedies were tried in vain, and only one individual reached London. The insects had so multiplied on it, that I immersed it in an infusion of tobacco, which, however, killed it in a few hours.

On advancing north, I observed that as soon as the Canada Jay made its appearance, the Blue Jay became more and more rare; not an individual did any of our party observe in Newfoundland or Labrador, during our stay there. On landing a few miles from Pictou, on the 22d of August 1833, after an absence of several months from the United States, the voice of a Blue Jay sounded melodious to me, and the sight of a Humming Bird quite filled my heart with delight.

These Jays are plentiful in all parts of the United States. In

Louisiana, they are so abundant as to prove a nuisance to the farmers, picking the newly planted corn, the pease, and the sweet potatoes, attacking every fruit tree, and even destroying the eggs of pigeons and domestic fowls. The planters are in the habit of occasionally soaking some corn in a solution of arsenic, and scattering the seeds over the ground, in consequence of which many Jays are found dead about the fields and gardens.

The Blue Jay is extremely expert in discovering a fox, a racoon, or any other quadruped hostile to birds, and will follow it, emitting a loud noise, as if desirous of bringing every Jay or Crow to its assistance. It acts in the same manner towards owls, and even on some occasions towards hawks.

This species breeds in all parts of the United States, from Louisiana to Maine, and from the Upper Missouri to the coast of the Atlantic. In South Carolina it seems to prefer for this purpose the live oak trees. In the lower parts of the Floridas it gives place in a great measure to the Florida Jay; nor did I meet with a single individual in the Keys of that peninsula. In Louisiana, it breeds near the planter's house, in the upper parts of the trees growing in the avenues, or even in the yards, and generally at a greater height than in the Middle States, where it is comparatively shy. It sometimes takes possession of the old or abandoned nest of a Crow or Cuckoo. In the Southern States, from Louisiana to Maryland, it breeds twice every year; but to the eastward of the latter State seldom more than once. Although it occurs in all places from the sea shore to the mountainous districts, it seems more abundant in the latter. The nest is composed of twigs and other coarse materials, lined with fibrous roots. The eggs are four or five, of a dull olive colour, spotted with brown.

The Blue Jay is truly omnivorous, feeding indiscriminately on all sorts of flesh, seeds, and insects. He is more tyrannical than brave, and, like most boasters, domineers over the feeble, dreads the strong, and flies even from his equals. In many cases in fact, he is a downright coward. The Cardinal Grosbeak will challenge him, and beat him off the ground. The Red Thrush, the Mocking Bird, and many others, although inferior in strength, never allow him to approach their nest with impunity; and the Jay, to be even with them, creeps silently to it in their absence, and devours their eggs and young whenever he finds an opportunity. I have seen one go its round from one nest to another every day, and suck the newly laid eggs of the different birds in the neighbourhood, with as much regularity and composure as a physician would call on his patients. I have also witnessed the sad disappointment it experienced, when, on returning to its own home, it found its mate in the jaws of a snake, the nest upset, and the eggs all gone. I have thought more than once on such occasions that, like all great culprits, when brought to a sense of their enormities, it evinced a strong feeling of remorse. While at Charleston, in November 1833, Dr WILSON of that city told me that on opening a division of his aviary, a Mocking Bird that he had kept for three years, flew at another and killed it, after which it destroyed several Blue Jays, which he had been keeping for me some months in an adjoining compartment.

The Blue Jay seeks for its food with great diligence at all times, but more especially during the period of its migration. At such a time, wherever there are chinquapins, wild chestnuts, acorns, or grapes, flocks will be seen to alight on the topmost branches of these trees, disperse, and engage with great vigour in detaching the fruit. Those that fall are picked up from the ground, and carried into a chink in the bark, the splinters of a fence rail, or firmly held under foot on a branch, and hammered with the bill until the kernel be procured.

As if for the purpose of gleaning the country in this manner, the Blue Jay migrates from one part to another during the day only. A person travelling or hunting by night, may now and then disturb the repose of a Jay, which in its terror sounds an alarm that is instantly responded to by all its surrounding travelling companions, and their multiplied cries make the woods resound far and near. While migrating, they seldom fly to any great distance at a time without alighting, for like true rangers they ransack and minutely inspect every portion of the woods, the fields, the orchards, and even the gardens of the farmers and planters. Always exceedingly garrulous, they may easily be followed to any distance, and the more they are chased the more noisy do they become, unless a hawk happen to pass suddenly near them, when they are instantly struck dumb, and, as if ever conscious of deserving punishment, either remain motionless for a while, or sneak off silently into the closest thickets, where they remain concealed as long as their dangerous enemy is near.

During the winter months they collect in large numbers about the plantations of the Southern States, approach the houses and barns, attend the feeding of the poultry, as well as of the cattle and horses in their separate pens, in company with the Cardinal Grosbeak, the Towhe Bunting, the Cow Bunting, the Starlings and Grakles, pick up every grain of loose corn they can find, search amid the droppings of horses along the roads, and enter the corn cribs, where many are caught by the cat and the sons of the farmer. Their movements on the wing are exceedingly graceful, and as they pass from one tree to another, their expanded wings and tail, exhibiting all the beauty of their graceful form and lovely tints, never fail to delight the observer.

The Black Vulture or Carrion Crow

Cathartes Jota, BONAP.

(PLATES 22, 24)

THE HABITS of this species are so intimately connected with those of the Turkey Buzzard (*Cathartes Aura*), that I cannot do better than devote this article to the description of both. And here, I beg leave to request of you, reader, that you allow me to present you with a copy of a paper which I published several years ago on the subject, and which was read, in my presence, to a numerous assemblage of the members of the Wernerian Natural History Society of Edinburgh, by my friend Mr NEILL, the Secretary of that Society. It is scarcely necessary for me to apologise for introducing here the observations which I then narrated, more especially as they referred principally to an interesting subject of discussion, which has been since resumed. They are as follows:—

"As soon as, like me, you shall have seen the Turkey Buzzard follow, with arduous closeness of investigation, the skirts of the forests, the meanders of creeks and rivers, sweeping over the whole of extensive plains, glancing his quick eye in all directions, with as much intentness as ever did the noblest of Falcons, to discover where below him lies the suitable prey; when, like me, you have repeatedly seen that bird pass over objects calculated to glut his voracious appetite, unnoticed, because unseen; and when you have also observed the greedy Vulture, propelled by hunger, if not famine, moving like the wind suddenly round his course, as the carrion attracts his eye; then will you abandon the deeply-rooted notion, that this bird possesses the faculty of discovering, by his sense of smell, his prey at an immense distance.

This power of smelling so acutely I adopted as a fact from my youth. I had read of this when a child; and many of the theorists, to whom I subsequently spoke of it, repeated the same with enthusiasm, the more particularly as they considered it an extraordinary gift of nature. But I had already observed, that nature, although wonderfully bountiful, had not granted more to any one individual than was necessary, and that no one was possessed of any two of the senses in a very high state of perfection; that if it had a good scent, it needed not so much acuteness of sight, and *vice versa*. When I visited the Southern States, and had lived, as it were, amongst these Vultures for several years, and discovered thousands of times that they did not smell me when I approached them, covered by a tree, until within a few feet; and that when so near, or at a greater distance, I shewed myself to them, they instantly flew away much frightened; the idea evaporated, and I assiduously engaged in a series of experiments, to prove to *myself*, at least, how far this acuteness of smell existed, or if it existed at all.

I sit down to communicate to you the results of those experiments, and leave for *you* to conclude how far and how long the world has been imposed on by the mere assertions of men who had never seen more than the skins of our Vultures, or heard the accounts from men caring little about observing nature closely.

My *First Experiment* was as follows:—I procured a skin of our common deer, entire to the hoofs, and stuffed it carefully with dried grass until filled rather above the natural size,—suffered the whole to become perfectly dry, and as hard as leather,—took it to the middle of a large open field,—laid it down on its back with the legs up and apart, as if the animal was dead and putrid. I then retired about a hundred yards, and in the lapse of some minutes, a Vulture, coursing round the field tolerably high, espied the skin, sailed directly towards it, and alighted within a few yards of it. I ran immediately, covered by a large tree, until within about forty yards, and from that place could spy the bird with ease. He approached the skin, looked at it with apparent suspicion, jumped on it, raised his tail, and voided freely (as you well know all birds of prey in a wild state generally do before feeding),—then approaching the eyes, that were here solid globes of hard, dried, and painted clay, attacked first one and then the other, with, however, no farther advantage than that of disarranging them. This part was abandoned; the bird walked to the other extremity of the pretended animal, and there, with much exertion, tore the stitches apart, until much fodder and hay was pulled out; but no flesh could the bird find or smell; he was intent on discovering some where none existed, and, after reiterated efforts, all useless, he took flight and coursed about the field, when, suddenly wheeling round and alighting, I saw him kill a small garter snake, and swallow it in an instant. The Vulture rose again, sailed about, and passed several times quite low over the stuffed deer-skin, as if loth to abandon so good looking a prey.

Judge of my feelings when I plainly saw that the Vulture, which could not discover, through its *extraordinary* sense of smell, that no flesh, either fresh or putrid, existed about that skin, could at a glance see a snake, scarcely as thick as a man's finger, alive, and destitute of odour, hundreds of yards distant. I concluded that, at all events, his ocular powers were much better than his sense of smell.

Second Experiment.—I had a large dead hog hauled some distance from the house, and put into a ravine, about twenty feet deeper than the surface of the earth around it, narrow and winding much, filled with briars and high cane. In this I made the negroes conceal the hog, by binding cane over it, until I thought it would puzzle either Buzzards, Carrion Crows, or any other birds to see it, and left it for two days. This was early in the month of July, when, in this latitude, a dead body becomes putrid and extremely fetid in a short time. I saw from time to time many Vultures, in search of food, sail over the field and ravine in all directions, but none discovered the carcass, although during this time several dogs had visited it, and fed plentifully on it. I tried to go near it, but the smell was so insufferable when within thirty yards, that I abandoned it, and the remnants were entirely destroyed at last through natural decay.

I then took a young pig, put a knife through its neck, and made it bleed on the earth and grass about the same place, and having covered it closely with leaves, also watched the result. The Vultures saw the fresh blood, alighted about it, followed it down into the ravine, discovered by the blood the pig, and devoured it, when yet quite fresh, within my sight.

Not contented with these experiments, which I already thought fully conclusive, having found two young Vultures, about the size of pullets, covered yet with down, and looking more like quadrupeds than birds, I had them brought home and put into a large coop in the yard, in the view of every body, and attended to their feeding myself. I gave them a great number of Red-headed Woodpeckers and Parokeets, birds then easy to procure, as they were feeding daily on the mulberry trees in the immediate neighbourhood of my orphans.

These the young Vultures could tear to pieces by putting both feet on the body, and applying the bill with great force. So accustomed to my going towards them were they in a few days, that when I approached the cage with hands filled with game for them, they immediately began hissing and gesticulating very much like young pigeons, and putting their bills to each other, as if expecting to be fed mutually, as their parent had done.

Two weeks elapsed, black feathers made their appearance, and the down diminished. I remarked an extraordinary increase of their legs and bill, and thinking them fit for trial, I closed three sides of the cage with plank, leaving the front only with bars for them to see through,—had the cage cleaned, washed, and sanded, to remove any filth attached to it from the putrid flesh that had been in it, and turned its front immediately from the course I usually took towards it with food for them.

I approached it often barefooted, and soon perceived that if I did not accidentally make a noise, the young birds remained in their silent upright attitudes, until I shewed myself to them by turning to the front of their prison. I frequently fastened a dead squirrel or rabbit, cut open, with all the entrails hanging loosely, to a long pole, and in this situation would put it to the back part of the cage; but no hissing, no movement, was made; when, on the contrary, I presented the end of the pole thus covered over the cage, no sooner would it appear beyond the edge, than my hungry birds would jump against the bars, hiss furiously, and attempt all in their power to reach the food. This was repeatedly done with fresh and putrid substances, all very congenial to their taste.

Satisfied within myself, I dropped these trials, but fed the birds until full grown, and then turned them out into the yard of the kitchen, for the purpose of picking up whatever substances might be thrown to them. Their voracity, however, soon caused their death: young pigs were not safe if within their reach; and young ducks, turkeys, or chickens, were such a constant temptation, that the cook, unable to watch them, killed them both, to put an end to their depredations.

Whilst I had these two young vultures in confinement, an extraordinary occurrence took place respecting an old bird of the same kind, which I cannot help relating to you. This bird, sailing over the yard, whilst I was experimenting with the pole and squirrels, saw the food, and alighted on the roof of one of the outhouses; then alighted on the ground, walked directly to the cage, and attempted to reach the food within. I approached it carefully, and it hopped off a short distance; as I retired, it returned, when always the appearances of the strongest congratulations would take place from the young towards this new comer. I directed several young negroes to drive it gently towards the stable, and to try to make it go in there. This would not do; but, after a short time, I helped to drive it into that part of the *gin-house* where the cotton seeds are deposited, and there caught it. I easily discovered that the bird was so emaciated, that to this state of poverty only I owed my success. I put it in with the young, who both at once jumped about him, making most extraordinary gestures of welcome, whilst the old bird, quite discomfited at his confinement, lashed both with great violence with his bill. Fearing the death of the young, I took them out, and fed plentifully the old bird; his appetite had become so great through fasting, that he ate too much, and died of suffocation.

I could enumerate many more instances, indicating that the power of smelling in these birds has been grossly exaggerated, and that, if they can smell objects at any distance, they can see the same objects much farther. I would ask any observer of the habits of birds, why if Vultures could smell at a great distance their prey, they should spend the greater portion of their lives hunting for it, when they are naturally so lazy, that, if fed in one place, they never leave it, and merely make such a change as is absolutely necessary to enable them to reach it. But I will now enter on their habits, and you will easily discover how this far famed power has originated.

Vultures are gregarious, and often associate in flocks of twenty, forty, or more;—hunting thus together, they fly in sight of each other, and thus cover an immense extent of country. A flock of twenty may easily survey an area of two miles, as they go turning in large circles, often intersecting each other in their lines, as if forming a vast chain of rounded links;—some are high, whilst others are low;—not a spot is passed unseen, and, consequently, the moment that a prey is discovered, the favoured bird rounds to, and, by the impetuosity of its movements, gives notice to its nearest companion, who immediately follows him, and is successively attended by all the rest. Thus the farthest from the discoverer being at a considerable distance, sails in a direct line towards the spot indicated to him by the flight of the others, who all have gone in a straight course before him, with the appearance of being impelled by this extraordinary power of smelling, so erroneously granted to them. If the object discovered is large, lately dead, and covered with a skin too tough to be eaten and torn asunder, and affords free scope to their appetites, they remain about it, and in the neighbourhood. Perched on high dead limbs, in such conspicuous positions, they are easily seen by other Vultures, who, through habit, know the meaning of such stoppages, and join the first flock, going also directly, and affording further evidence to those persons who are satisfied with appearance only. In this manner I have seen several hundreds of Vultures and Carrion Crows assembled near a dead ox at the dusk of evening, that had only two or three about it in the morning; when some of the later comers had probably travelled hundreds of miles searching diligently themselves for food, and probably would have had to go much farther, had they not espied this association.

Around the spot both species remain; some of them from time to time examining the dead body, giving it a tug in those parts most accessible, until putridity ensues. The accumulated number then fall to work, exhibiting a most disgusting picture of famished cannibals; the strongest driving the weakest, and the latter harassing the former with all the animosity that a disappointed hungry stomach can excite. They are seen jumping off the carcass, reattacking it, entering it, and wrestling for portions partly swallowed by two or more of them, hissing at a furious rate, and clearing every moment their nostrils from the filth that enters there, and stops their breathing. No doubt remains on my mind, that the great outward dimensions of these nostrils were allotted them for that especial and necessary purpose.

The animal is soon reduced to a mere skeleton, no portion of it being now too hard to be torn apart and swallowed, so that nothing is left but the bare bones. Soon all these bloody feeders are seen standing gorged, and scarcely able to take wing. At such times the observer may approach very near the group, whilst engaged in feeding, and see the Vultures in contact with the Dogs, who really by smelling have found the prey;—whenever this happens, it is with the greatest reluctance that the birds suffer themselves to be driven off, although frequently the sudden scowl or growl of the Dogs will cause nearly all the Vultures to rise a few yards in the air. I have several times seen the Buzzards feeding at one extremity of the carcass, whilst the Dogs were tearing the other; but if a single Wolf approached, or a pair of White-headed Eagles, driven by extreme hunger, then the place was abandoned to them until their wants were supplied.

The repast finished, each bird gradually rises to the highest branches of the nearest trees, and remains there until the full digestion of all the food they have swallowed is completed; from time to time opening their wings to the breeze, or to the sun, either to cool or to warm themselves. The traveller may then pass under them unnoticed; or, if regarded, a mere sham of flying off is made. The bird slowly recloses its wings, looks at the person as he passes, and remains there until hunger again urges him onwards. This takes often times more than a day, when gradually, and very often singly, each vulture is seen to depart.

They now rise to an immense height; cutting, with great elegance and ease, many circles through the air; now and then gently closing their wings, they launch themselves obliquely, with great swiftness, for several hundred yards, check and resume their portly movements, ascending until, like specks in the distance, they are seen altogether to leave that neighbourhood, to seek elsewhere the required means of subsistence.

Having heard it said, no doubt with the desire of proving that Buzzards smell their prey, that these birds usually fly against the breeze, I may state that, in my opinion, this action is simply used, because it is easier for birds to sustain themselves on the wing, encountering a moderate portion of wind, than when flying before it; but I have so often witnessed these birds bearing away under the influence of a strong breeze, as if enjoying it, that I consider either case as a mere incident connected with their pleasures or their wants.

Here, my dear Sir, let me relate one of those facts, curious in itself, and attributed to mere *instinct*, but which I cannot admit under that appellation, and which, in my opinion, so borders on *reason*, that, were I to call it by that name, I hope you will not look on my judgment as erroneous, without your further investigating the subject in a more general point of view.

During one of those heavy *gusts* that so often take place in Louisiana, in the early part of summer, I saw a flock of these birds, which had undoubtedly discovered that the current of air that was tearing all over them, was a mere sheet, raise themselves obliquely against it, with great force, slide through its impetuous current, and reassume *above* it, their elegant movements. The power given to them by nature of discerning the approaching death of a wounded animal, is truly remarkable. They will watch each individual thus assailed by misfortune, and follow it with keen perseverance, until the loss of life has rendered it their prey. A poor old emaciated horse or ox, a deer mired on the margin of the lake, where the timid animal has resorted to escape flies and musquitoes, so fatiguing in summer, is seen in distress with exultation by the Buzzard. He immediately alights; and, if the animal does not extricate itself, waits and gorges in peace on as much of the flesh as the nature of the spot will allow. They do more: they often watch the young kid, the lamb and the pig issuing from the mother's womb, and attack it with direful success; yet, notwithstanding this, they frequently pass over a healthy horse, hog, or other animal, lying as if dead, basking in the sunshine, without even altering their course in the least. Judge then, my dear Sir, how well they must see.

Opportunities of devouring young living animals are so very frequent around large plantations in this country, that to deny them would be ridiculous, although I have heard it attempted by European writers. During the terrifying inundations of the Mississippi, I have very frequently seen many of these birds alight on the dead floating bodies of animals, drowned by the waters in the lowlands, and washed by the current, gorging themselves at the expense of the squatter, who often loses the greater portion of his wandering flocks on such occasions. Dastardly withal, and such cowards are they, that our smaller hawks can drive them off any place: the little king-bird proves indeed a tyrant, whenever he espies the large marauder sailing about the spot where his dearest mate is all intent on incubation; and the eagle, if hungry, will chase him, force him to disgorge his food in a moment, and leave it at his disposal.

Many of those birds accustomed, by the privileges granted them by law, of remaining about cities and villages in our southern states, seldom leave them, and might almost be called a second set, differing widely in habits from those that reside constantly at a distance from these places. Accustomed to be fed, they are still more lazy; their appearance exhibits all the nonchalance belonging to the garrisoned half-paid soldier. To move is for them a hardship, and nothing but extreme hunger will make them fly down from the roof of the kitchen into the yard, or follow the vehicles employed in cleaning the streets of disagreeable substances, except where (at Natchez for instance), the number of these expecting parasites is so great that all the refuse of the town, within their reach, is insufficient: they then are seen following the scavengers' cart, hopping, flying, and alighting all about it, amidst grunting hogs and snarling dogs, until the contents, having reached a place of destination outside the suburbs, are deposited, and swallowed by them.

Whilst taking a view of this city from her lower ancient *fort*, I have for several days seen exhibitions of this kind.

I do not think that the vultures thus attached to cities are so much inclined to multiply as those more constantly resident in the forests, perceiving the diminution of number during the breeding season, and having remarked that many individuals known to me by particular marks made on them, and a *special cast of countenance*, were positively constant residents of town. The *Vultur Aura* is by no means so numerous as the *atratus*. I have seldom seen more than from twenty-five to thirty together; when, on the contrary, the latter are frequently associated to the number of an hundred.

The *Vultur Aura* is a more retired bird in habits, and more inclined to feed on dead game, snakes, lizards, frogs, and the dead fish that frequently are found about the sand-flats of rivers and borders of the sea-shore; is more cleanly in its appearance; and, as you will see by the difference in the drawings of both species, a neater and better formed bird. Its flight is also vastly superior in swiftness and elegance, requiring but a few flaps of its large wings to raise itself from the ground; after which it will sail for miles by merely turning either on one side or the other, and using its tail so slowly, to alter its course, that a person looking at it, whilst elevated and sailing, would be inclined to compare it to a machine fit to perform just a certain description of evolutions. The noise made by the vultures through the air, as they glide obliquely towards the earth, is often as great as that of our largest hawks, when falling on their prey; but they never reach the ground in this manner, always checking when about 100 yards high, and *going several rounds*, to *examine well the spot they are about to alight on*. The *Vultur Aura* cannot bear cold weather well; the few who, during the heat of summer, extend their excursions to the middle or northern states, generally return at the approach of winter; and I believe also, that very few of these birds breed east of the pine swamps of New Jersey. They are much attached to particular roosting-trees, and I know will come to them every night from a great distance. On alighting on these, each of them, anxious for a choice of place, creates always a general disturbance; and often, when quite dark, their hissing is heard in token of this inclination for supremacy. These roosting-trees of the Buzzards are generally in deep swamps, and mostly in high dead cypress trees; frequently, however, they roost with the carrion crows (*Vultur attratus*), and then it is on the largest dead timber of our fields, not unfrequently near the houses. Sometimes, also, this bird will roost close to the body of a thickly leaved tree: in such a position I have killed several when hunting wild turkeys by moonlight, mistaking them for these latter birds.

In Mississippi, Louisiana, Georgia, and Carolina, they prepare to breed early in the month of February, in common with most of the genus *Falco*. The most remarkable habit attached to their life is now to be seen: they assemble in parties of eight or ten, sometimes more, on large fallen logs, males and females, exhibiting the strongest desire to please mutually, and forming attachments in the choice of a mate, when each male, after many caresses, leads his partner off on the wing from the group, neither to mix nor associate with any more, until their offspring are well able to follow them in the air; after which, and until incubation takes place (about two weeks), they are seen sailing side by side the whole day.

These birds form no nest, yet are very choice respecting the place of deposite for their *two* eggs. Deep in the swamps, but always above the line of overflowing water-mark, a large hollow tree is sought, either standing or fallen, and the eggs are dropped on the mouldering particles inside, sometimes immediately near the entrance, at other times as much as twenty feet within. Both birds alternately incubate, and each feeds the other, by disgorging the contents of the stomach, or part of them, immediately before the bird that is sitting. Thirty-two days are required to bring forth the young from the shell; a thick down covers them completely; the parents, at that early period, and indeed for nearly two weeks, feed them by disgorging food considerably digested from their bills, in the manner of the common pigeons. The down acquires length, becomes thinner, and of a darker tint as the bird grows older. The young vultures, at three weeks, are large for their age, weighing then upwards of a pound, but extremely clumsy and inactive; unable to keep up their wings, then partly covered by large pin feathers, dragging them almost upon the ground, and bearing their whole weight on the full length of their legs and feet.

If approached at that time by a stranger or enemy, they hiss with a noise resembling that made by a strangling cat or fox, swell themselves, and hop sideways as fast as in their power. The parents, while sitting, and equally disturbed, act in the same manner; fly only a very short distance, waiting there the departure of the offender, to resume their duty. As the young grow larger, the parents simply throw their food before them; and, with all their exertions, seldom bring their offspring fat to the field. Their nests become so fetid, before the final departure of the young birds, that a person forced to remain there half an hour would be in danger of suffocation.

I have been frequently told, that the same pair will not abandon their first nest or place of deposit, unless broken up during incubation. This would attach to the vulture a constancy of affection that I cannot believe exists; as I do not think that pairing, in the manner described, is of any longer duration than the necessitous call of nature for the one season; and again, were they so inclined, they would never congregate in the manner they do, but would go in single pairs all their lives like eagles.

Vultures do not possess, in any degree, the power of bearing off their prey as falcons do, unless it be slender portions of entrails hanging by the bill. When chased by others from a carcass, it even renders them very awkward in their flight, and forces them to the earth again almost immediately.

Many persons in Europe believe that Buzzards prefer putrid flesh to any other. This is a mistake. Any flesh that they can at once tear with their very powerful bill in pieces, is swallowed, no matter how fresh. What I have said of their killing and devouring young animals, affords sufficient proofs of this; but it frequently happens that these birds are compelled to wait until the *hide* of their prey will yield to the bill. I have seen a large dead alligator, surrounded by vultures and carrion crows, of which nearly the whole of the flesh was so completely decomposed before these birds could perforate the tough skin of the monster, that, when at last it took place, their disappointment was apparent, and the matter, in an almost fluid state, abandoned by the vultures."

The above account of my experiments was read on the 16th day of December 1826, and was what I may call my "maiden speech." Well do I remember the uneasy feelings which I experienced: the audience was large, and composed of many of the most distinguished men of that enlightened country. My paper was a long one; and it contradicted all former opinions on the subject under discussion; yet the cheering appearance of kindness which every where met my eye, as I occasionally glanced around, gradually dispelled my uneasiness, and brought me to a state of confidence. The reading of the paper being at length accomplished, I was congratulated by the President, as well as by every member present. Many questions were put to me, all of which I answered as well as I could. My esteemed and learned friend, Professor JAMESON, requested permission to publish my paper in his valuable journal, which I most readily granted. Strolling homeward, I felt proud that I had at last broken the charm by which men had so long been held in ignorance respecting the history of our Vultures, assured that the breach which I had made upon a general and deeply rooted opinion, must gradually dissolve it, as well as many other absurdities which have for ages infested science, like the vile grub beneath the bark of the noblest forest tree, retarding its growth, until happily removed by the constant hammerings of the industrious Woodpecker!

I returned to America, urged by enthusiasm, to pursue the study of Nature in the majestic forests; and finding that doubts excited by persons prejudiced against me, existed in the minds of some individuals, I resolved to have my series of experiments repeated by some other person, in those districts where Vultures abound, and in the presence of a number of scientific men, with the view of satisfying the incredulous as much as in my power. My travels were continued, and I became acquainted with one of the best practical ornithologists our country affords, and moreover a man of general learning, my worthy and esteemed friend the Reverend JOHN BACHMAN of Charleston, South Carolina. To him I frequently wrote, requesting him to make experiments on the faculty of smelling in our vultures. In the winter of 1833–4, the following were made, and afterwards published in LOUDON's Magazine of Natural History (No. 38, March 1834, p. 164).

"On the 16th December 1833, I commenced a series of experiments on the habits of our Vultures, which continued till the end of the month, and these have been renewed at intervals till the 15th of January 1834. Written invitations were sent to all the Professors of the two Medical Colleges in this city, to the officers and some of the members of the Philosophical Society, and such other individuals as we believed might take an interest in the subject. Although Mr AUDUBON was present during most of this time, and was willing to render any assistance required of him, yet he desired that we might make the experiments ourselves—that we might adopt any mode that the ingenuity or experience of others could suggest, at arriving at the most correct conclusions. The manner in which these experiments were made, together with the results, I now proceed to detail.

There were two points in particular on which the veracity of AUDUBON had been assailed, *1st*, Whether the Vultures feed on fresh or putrid flesh, and, *2d*, Whether they are attracted to their food by the eye or scent.

On the first head it was unnecessary to make many experiments, it being a subject with which even the most casual observer amongst us is well acquainted. It is well known that the roof of our market-house is covered with these birds every morning, waiting for any little scrap of fresh meat that may be thrown to them by the butchers. At our slaughter-pens, the offal is quickly devoured by our vultures, whilst it is yet warm from the recent death of the slain animal. I have seen the *Vultur Aura* a hundred miles in the interior of the country, where he may be said to be altogether in a state of nature, regaling himself on the entrails of a deer which had been killed not an hour before. Two years ago, Mr Henry Ward, who is now in London, and who was in the employ of the

PLATE 1 Wild Turkey, *Meleagris gallopavo*

PLATE 2 Common Grackle, *Quiscalus quiscula*

PLATE 3   Bald Eagle, *Haliaeetus leucocephalus*

PLATE XXI.

Mocking Bird. TURDUS POLYGLOTTUS, Linn. Males & Females. 1.— *Florida Jessamine Gelsemium nitidum.*

PLATE 4 Northern Mockingbird, *Mimus polyglottos*

PLATE 5   Carolina Parakeet, *Conuropsis carolinensis*

PLATE XXVI

Carolina Parrot.

PSITTACUS CAROLINENSIS, Linn.
Male, Female, & Young.
Cockle bur, Xanthium strumarium.

PLATE 6 Carolina Parakeet, *Conuropsis carolinensis*

Carolina Parrot or Parrakeet

1. 2. Males . 3. Female . 4. Young.
Cockle bur

Drawn from Nature by J.J.Audubon.F.R.S.E.I.S.   Lith.ᵈ Printed & Col.ᵈ by J. T. Bowen, Phil.

PLATE 7 Carolina Parakeet, *Conuropsis carolinensis*

PLATE 8 Peregrine Falcon, *Falco peregrinus*

PLATE 9 Ruby-throated Hummingbird, *Archilochus colubris*

PLATE 10 Bald Eagle, *Haliaeetus leucocephalus*

PLATE 11 Bald Eagle, *Haliaeetus leucocephalus*

PLATE 12   Red-tailed Hawk, *Buteo jamaicensis*

PLATE 13 Osprey, *Pandion haliaetus*

PLATE 14   Passenger Pigeon, *Ectopistes migratorius*

PLATE 15   Passenger Pigeon, *Ectopistes migratorius*

PLATE 16   Ivory-billed Woodpecker, *Campephilus principalis*

PLATE LXVI

Ivory-billed Woodpecker IVORY PRINCIPALIS, Linn. *Male 1 Female 2, 3.*

PLATE 17 Ivory-billed Woodpecker, *Campephilus principalis*

PLATE 18 Wood Thrush, *Hylocichla mustelina*

PLATE 19 Wood Thrush, *Hylocichla mustelina*

PLATE 20.

Broad-winged Hawk.

FALCO PENNSYLVANICUS, Wils.

Male, 1 Female, 2

PLATE 20   Broad-winged Hawk, *Buteo platypterus*

Blue Jay.
CORVUS CRISTATUS,
Male. 1. Female. 2, 3.

PLATE 21 Blue Jay, *Cyanocitta cristata*

PLATE 22 Black Vulture, *Coragyps atratus*

PLATE 23 Mississippi Kite, *Ictinia mississippiensis*

PLATE 24 Black Vulture, *Coragyps atratus*

PLATE 25   Pileated Woodpecker, *Dryocopus pileatus*

PLATE 26 Eastern Phoebe, *Sayornis phoebe,* and Acadian Flycatcher,
Empidonax virescens

PLATE 27 Eastern Phoebe, *Sayornis phoebe*

PLATE 28 Snowy Owl, *Nyctea scandiaca*

PLATE 29 American Kestrel, *Falco sparverius*

PLATE 30 American Crow, *Corvus brachyrhynchos*

PLATE 31 Chimney Swift, *Chaetura pelagica*

PLATE 32 Golden Eagle, *Aquila chrysaetos*

Philosophical Society of this city, was in the habit of depositing at the foot of my garden, in the suburbs of Charleston, the fresh carcasses of the birds he had skinned, and in the course of half an hour, both species of Vulture, and particularly the Turkey Buzzard, came and devoured the whole. Nay, we discovered that Vultures fed on the bodies of those of their own species that had been thus exposed. A few days ago, a Vulture that had been killed by some boys in the neighbourhood, and that had fallen near the place where we were performing our experiments, attracted, on the following morning, the sight of a Turkey Buzzard, who commenced pulling off its feathers and feeding upon it. This brought down two of the Black Vultures, who joined him in the repast. In this instance, the former chased away the two latter to some distance,—an unusual occurrence, as the Black Vulture is the strongest bird, and generally keeps off the other species. We had the dead bird lightly covered with some rice chaff, where it still remains undiscovered by the Vultures.

2d, Whether is the Vulture attracted to its food by the sense of smell or sight? A number of experiments were tried to satisfy us on this head, and all led to the same result. A few of these I proceed to detail.

1st, A dead Hare (*Lepus timidus*), a Pheasant (*Phasianus colchicus*), a Kestrel (*Falco Tinnunculus*), a recent importation from Europe, together with a wheel-barrow full of offal from the slaughter-pens, were deposited on the ground, at the foot of my garden. A frame was raised above it at the distance of 12 inches from the earth; this was covered with brushwood, allowing the air to pass freely beneath it, so as to convey the effluvium far and wide; and although 25 days have now gone by, and the flesh has become offensive, not a single Vulture appears to have observed it, though hundreds have passed over it, and some very near it, in search of their daily food. Although the Vultures did not discover this dainty mess, the dogs in the vicinity, who appeared to have better olfactory nerves, frequently visited the place, and gave us much trouble in the prosecution of our experiments.

2d, I now suggested an experiment which would enable us to test the inquiry whether the Vulture would be attracted to an object by the sight alone. A coarse painting on canvass was made, representing a sheep skinned and cut open. This proved very amusing;—no sooner was this picture placed on the ground, than the Vultures observed it, alighted near, walked over it, and some of them commenced tugging at the painting. They seemed much disappointed and surprised, and after having satisfied their curiosity, flew away. This experiment was repeated more than fifty times, with the same result. The painting was then placed within fifteen feet of the place where the offal was deposited; they came as usual, walked around it, but in no instance evinced the slightest symptoms of their having scented the offal which was so near him.

3d, The most offensive portions of the offal were now placed on the earth; these were covered over by a thin canvass cloth; on this were strewed several pieces of fresh beef. The Vultures came, ate the flesh that was in sight, and although they were standing on a quantity beneath them, and although their bills were frequently within the eighth of an inch of this putrid matter, they did not discover it. We made a small rent in the canvass, and they at once discovered the flesh, and began to devour it. We drove them away, replaced the canvass with a piece that was entire; again they commenced eating the fresh pieces exhibited to their view, without discovering the hidden food they were trampling upon.

4th, The medical gentlemen who were present made a number of experiments to test the absurdity of a story, widely circulated in the United States, through the newspapers, that the eye of the Vulture, when perforated, and the sight extinguished, would in a few minutes be restored, in consequence of his placing his head under his wing, the down of which was said to renew his sight. The eyes were perforated; I need not add, that although they were refilled, and had the appearance of rotundity, yet the bird became blind, and that it was beyond the power of the healing art to restore his lost sight. His life was, however, preserved, by occasionally putting food in his mouth. In this situation they placed him in a small outhouse, hung the flesh of the hare (which had now become offensive) within his reach; nay, they frequently placed it within an inch of his nostrils, but the bird gave no evidence of any knowledge that his favourite food was so near him. This was repeated from time to time during an interval of twenty-four days (the period of his death), with the same results.

We were not aware that any other experiment could be made to enable us to arrive at more satisfactory conclusions; and as we feared, if prolonged, they might become offensive to the neighbours, we abandoned them."

As my humble name can scarcely be known to many of those into whose hands this communication may fall, I have thought proper to obtain the signature of some of the gentlemen who aided me in, or witnessed these experiments; and I must also add, that there was not an individual among the crowd of persons who came to judge for themselves, who did not coincide with those who have given their signatures to this certificate.

"We the subscribers, having witnessed the experiments made on the habits of the Vultures of Carolina (*Cathartes Aura and Cathartes Jota*), commonly called Turkey Buzzard and Carrion Crow, feel assured that they devour fresh as well as putrid food of any kind, and that they are guided to their food altogether through their sense of sight, and not that of smell.

ROBERT HENRY, A.M., President of the College of South Carolina.
JOHN WAGNER, M.D., Prof. of Surg. at the Med. Col. State So. Car.
HENRY R. FROST, M.D., Pro. Mat. Med. Col. State So. Car.
C. F. LEITNER, Lecturer on Bot. and Nat. His. So. Car.
B. B. STROBEL, M.D.
MARTIN STROBEL."

It now remains for me to present you with an account of those habits of the Black Vulture which have not been described above. This bird is a constant resident in all our Southern States, extends far up the Mississippi, and continues the whole year in Kentucky, Indiana, Illinois, and even in the State of Ohio as far as Cincinnati. Along the Atlantic coast, it is, I believe, rarely seen farther east than Maryland. It seems to give a preference to maritime districts, or the neighbourhood of water. Although shy in the woods, it is half domesticated in and about our cities and villages, where it finds food without the necessity of using much exertion. Charleston, Savannah, New Orleans, Natchez, and other cities, are amply provided with these birds, which may be seen flying or walking about the streets the whole day in groups. They also regularly attend the markets and shambles, to pick up the pieces of flesh thrown away by the butchers, and, when an opportunity occurs, leap from one bench to another, for the purpose of helping themselves. Hundreds of them are usually found, at all hours of the day, about the slaughter-houses, which are their favourite resort. They alight on the roofs and chimney-tops, wherever these are not guarded by spikes or pieces of glass, which, however, they frequently are, for the purpose of preventing the contamination by their ordure of the rain water, which the inhabitants of the Southern States collect in tanks, or cisterns, for domestic use. They follow the carts loaded with offal or dead animals, to the places in the suburbs where these are deposited, and wait the skinning of a cow or horse, when in a few hours they devour its flesh, in the company of the dogs, which are also accustomed to frequent such places. On these occasions, they fight with each other, leap about and tug in all the hurry and confusion imaginable, uttering a harsh sort of hiss or grunt, which may be heard at a distance of several hundred yards. Should eagles make their appearance at such a juncture, the Carrion Crows retire, and patiently wait until their betters are satisfied, but they pay little regard to the dogs. When satiated, they rise together, should the weather be fair, mount high in the air, and perform various evolutions, flying in large circles, and alternately plunging and rising, until they at length move off in a straight direction, or alight on the dead branches of trees, where they spread out their wings and tail to the sun or the breeze. In cold and wet weather they assemble round the chimney-tops, to receive the warmth imparted by the smoke. I never heard of their disgorging their food on such occasions, that being never done unless when they are feeding their young, or when suddenly alarmed or caught. In that case, they throw up the contents of their stomach with wonderful quickness and power.

No law exists for the protection of this or the other species, their usefulness alone affording them security in the Southern

States, although the people generally speak of a law with the view of preventing them from being molested. As to their propensity to attack live animals, at least those in a sickly state, although I could adduce numerous instances, it will suffice to produce the following attestations:—

"We the subscribers, natives of South Carolina, certify, that the Vultures of this State, commonly called the Turkey Buzzard and Carrion Crow, particularly the latter, will attack and destroy living animals, by feeding on them, such as young poultry, and the young of sheep and hogs; that they will also attack grown animals when in a helpless state, and destroy them in like manner.

PAUL S. H. LEE.   THOS. RIGGS.
STILES RIVERS.   THOS. W. BOONE.
L. WITSELL.   MALACHI FORD.
L. S. FISHBURNE.

SAINT BARTHOLOMEW PARISH, *Colleton District,*
32 miles from Charleston, 25th Jan. 1834."

"I hereby certify, that some years ago—I cannot specify the precise time, but have a perfect recollection of the fact—I saw a horse lying on the common, about half-a-mile from the city of Charleston, surrounded by a number of Buzzards, apparently feeding on him. My curiosity being excited by observing the horse move, I approached and drove off the Buzzards. They had already plucked out the eyes of the horse, and picked a wound in the anus, where I discovered a jet of blood from a small artery, which had been divided. I am well satisfied that the horse did not die for many hours afterwards. He struggled considerably whilst the Buzzards were operating on him, but was unable to rise from the ground.

B. B. STROBEL, M.D.

CHARLESTON, *5th Feb. 1834.*"

"I certify, that at my plantation, about four miles from the city of Charleston, one of my cattle, about two years old, in feeding in a ditch, got its horn so entangled in the root of a cane, as to be unable to get out. In this situation it was attacked by the Turkey Buzzard and Carrion Crow, who picked out one of its eyes, and would have killed it by feeding on it while alive, if it had not been discovered. It was extricated and driven home, but had been so much injured, that I had it knocked on the head to put it out of its misery.

GILBERT C. GEDDES.

CHARLESTON, *26th Feb. 1834.*"

The Carrion Crows of Charleston resort at night to a swampy wood across the Ashley river, about two miles from the city. I visited this roosting place in company with my friend JOHN BACHMAN, approaching it by a close thicket of undergrowth, tangled with vines and briars. When nearly under the trees on which the birds were roosted, we found the ground destitute of vegetation, and covered with ordure and feathers, mixed with the broken branches of the trees. The stench was horrible. The trees were completely covered with birds, from the trunk to the very tips of the branches. They were quite unconcerned; but, having determined to send them the contents of our guns, and firing at the same instant, we saw most of them fly off, hissing, grunting, disgorging, and looking down on their dead companions as if desirous of devouring them. We kept up a brisk fusilade for several minutes, when they all flew off to a great distance high in the air; but as we retired, we observed them gradually descending and settling on the same trees. The piece of ground was about two acres in extent, and the number of Vultures we estimated at several thousands. During very wet weather, they not unfrequently remain the whole day on the roost; but when it is fine, they reach the city every morning by the first glimpse of day.

The flight of this species, although laboured, is powerful and protracted. Before rising from the ground, they are obliged to take several leaps, which they do in an awkward sidelong manner. Their flight is continued by flappings, repeated eight or ten times, alternating with sailings of from thirty to fifty yards. The wings are disposed at right angles to the body, and the feet protrude beyond the tail, so as to be easily seen. In calm weather, they may be heard passing over you at the height of forty or fifty yards; so great is the force with which they beat the air. When about to alight, they allow their legs to dangle beneath, the better to enable them to alight.

They feed on all sorts of flesh, fresh or putrid, whether of quadrupeds or birds, as well as on fish. I saw a great number of them eating a dead shark near the wharf at St Augustine in East Florida; and I observed them many times devouring young cormorants and herons in the nest, on the keys bordering that peninsula.

The Carrion Crow and Turkey Buzzard possess great power of recollection, so as to recognise at a great distance a person who has shot at them, and even the horse on which he rides. On several occasions I have observed that they would fly off at my approach, after I had trapped several, when they took no notice of other individuals; and they avoided my horse in the pastures, after I had made use of him to approach and shoot them.

At the commencement of the love season, which is about the beginning of February, the gesticulation and parade of the males are extremely ludicrous. They first strut somewhat in the manner of the Turkey Cock, then open their wings, and, as they approach the female, lower their head, its wrinkled skin becoming loosened, so as entirely to cover the bill, and emit a puffing sound, which is by no means musical. When these actions have been repeated five or six times, and the conjugal compact sealed, the "happy pair" fly off, and remain together until their young come abroad. These birds form no nest, and consequently *never breed on trees*; the hollow of a prostrate log, or the excavation of a bank of earth, suffices for them. They *never lay more than two eggs*, which are deposited on the bare ground; they are about three inches in length, rather pointed at the smaller end, thick in the shell, with a pure white ground, marked towards the greater ends with large irregular dashes of black and dark brown. Twenty-one days are required for hatching them. The male and female sit by turns, and feed each other. The young are at first covered with a light cream-coloured down, and have an extremely uncouth appearance. They are fed by regurgitation, almost in the same manner as pigeons, and are abundantly supplied with food. When fledged, which is commonly about the beginning of June, they follow their parents through the woods. At this period, their head is covered with feathers to the very mandibles. The plumage of this part gradually disappears, and

the skin becomes wrinkled; but they are not in full plumage
till the second year. During the breeding season, they frequent the cities less, those remaining at that time being barren birds, of which there appear to be a good number. I
believe that the individuals which are no longer capable of
breeding, spend all their time in and about the cities, and
roost on the roofs and chimneys. They go out, in company
with the Turkey Buzzards, to the yards of the hospitals and
asylums, to feed on the remains of the provisions cooked
there, which are as regularly thrown out to them.

I have represented a pair of Carrion Crows or Black Vultures in full plumage, engaged with the head of our Common
Deer, the *Cervus virginianus.*

The Pileated Woodpecker

Picus pileatus, LINN.

(PLATE 25)

IT WOULD be difficult for me to say in what part of our extensive country I have not met with this hardy inhabitant of
the forest. Even now, when several species of our birds are becoming rare, destroyed as they are, either to gratify the palate
of the epicure, or to adorn the cabinet of the naturalist, the
Pileated Woodpecker is every where to be found in the wild
woods, although scarce and shy in the peopled districts.

Wherever it occurs it is a permanent resident, and, like its
relative the Ivory-billed Woodpecker, it remains pretty constantly in the place which it has chosen after leaving its parents. It is at all times a shy bird, so that one can seldom
approach it, unless under cover of a tree, or when he happens
accidentally to surprise it while engaged in its daily avocations. When seen in a large field newly brought into tillage,
and yet covered with girdled trees, it removes from one to another, cackling out its laughter-like notes, as if it found delight in leading you a wild-goose chase in pursuit of it. When
followed it always alights on the tallest branches or trunks of
trees, removes to the side farthest off, from which it every
moment peeps, as it watches your progress in silence; and so

well does it seem to know the distance at which a shot can reach it, that it seldom permits so near an approach. Often when you think the next step will take you near enough to fire with certainty, the wary bird flies off before you can reach it. Even in the wildest parts of Eastern Florida, where I have at times followed it, to assure myself that the birds I saw were of the same species as that found in our distant Atlantic States, its vigilance was not in the least abated. For miles have I chased it from one cabbage-tree to another, without ever getting within shooting distance, until at last I was forced to resort to stratagem, and seeming to abandon the chase, took a circuitous route, concealed myself in its course, and waited until it came up, when, it being now on the side of the trees next to me, I had no difficulty in bringing it down. I shall never forget, that, while in the Great Pine Forest of Pennsylvania, I spent several days in the woods endeavouring to procure one, for the same purpose of proving its identity with others elsewhere seen.

Their natural wildness never leaves them, even although they may have been reared from the nest. I will give you an instance of this, as related to me by my generous friend the Reverend JOHN BACHMAN of Charleston, who also speaks of the cruelty of the species. "A pair of Pileated Woodpeckers had a nest in an old elm tree, in a swamp which they occupied that year; the next spring early, two Blue Birds took possession of it, and there had young. Before these were half grown, the Woodpeckers returned to the place, and, despite of the cries and reiterated attacks of the Blue Birds, the others took the young, not very gently, as you may imagine, and carried them away to some distance. Next the nest itself was disposed of, the hole cleaned and enlarged, and there they raised a brood. The nest, it is true, was originally their own. The tree was large, but so situated, that, from the branches of another I could reach the nest. The hole was about 18 inches deep, and I could touch the bottom with my hand. The eggs, which were laid on fragments of chips, expressly left by the birds, were six, large, white and translucent. Before the Woodpeckers began to sit, I robbed them of their eggs, to see if they would lay a second time. They waited a few days as if undecided, when on a sudden I heard the female at work again in the tree; she once more deepened the hole, made it broader at bottom, and recommenced laying. This time she laid five eggs. I suffered her to bring out her young, both sexes alternately incubating, each visiting the other at intervals, peeping into the hole to see that all was right and well there, and flying off afterwards in search of food.

When the young were sufficiently grown to be taken out with safety, which I ascertained by seeing them occasionally peeping out of the hole, I carried them home, to judge of their habits in confinement, and attempted to raise them. I found it exceedingly difficult to entice them to open their bill in order to feed them. They were sullen and cross, nay, three died in a few days; but the others, having been fed on grasshoppers forcibly introduced into their mouths, were raised. In a short time they began picking up the grasshoppers thrown into their cage, and were fully fed with corn-meal, which they preferred eating dry. Their whole employment consisted in attempting to escape from their prison, regularly demolishing one every two days, although made of pine boards of tolerable thickness. I at last had one constructed with oak boards at the back and sides, and rails of the same in front. This was too much for them, and their only comfort was in passing and holding their bills through the hard bars. In the morning after receiving water, which they drank freely, they invariably upset the cup or saucer, and although this was large and flattish, they regularly turned it quite over. After this they attacked the trough which contained their food, and soon broke it to pieces, and when perchance I happened to approach them with my hand, they made passes at it with their powerful bills with great force. I kept them in this manner until winter. They were at all times uncleanly and unsociable birds. On opening the door of my study one morning, one of them dashed off by me, alighted on an apple-tree near the house, climbed some distance, and kept watching me from one side and then the other, as if to ask what my intentions were. I walked into my study:—the other was hammering at my books. They had broken one of the bars of the cage, and must have been at liberty for some hours, judging by the mischief they had done. Fatigued of my pets, I opened the door, and this last one hearing the voice of his brother, flew towards him and alighted on the same tree. They remained about half an hour, as if consulting each other, after which, taking to their wings together, they flew off in a southern direction, and with much more ease than could have been expected from birds so long kept in captivity. The ground was covered with snow, and I never more saw them. No birds of this species ever bred since in the hole spoken of in this instance, and I consider it as much wilder than the Ivory-billed Woodpecker."

While in the Great Pine Forest of Pennsylvania, of which I have repeatedly spoken, I was surprised to see how differently this bird worked on the bark of different trees, when searching for its food. On the hemlock and spruce, for example, of which the bark is difficult to be detached, it used the bill sideways, hitting the bark in an oblique direction, and proceeding in close parallel lines, so that when, after a while, a piece of the bark was loosened and broken off by a side stroke, the surface of the trunk appeared as if closely grooved by a carpenter using a gouge. In this manner the Pileated Woodpecker often, in that country, strips the entire trunks of the largest trees. On the contrary, when it attacked any other sort of timber, it pelted at the bark in a straightforward manner, detaching a large piece by a few strokes, and leaving the trunks smooth, no injury having been inflicted upon it by the bill.

This bird, when surprised, is subject to very singular and astonishing fits of terror. While in Louisiana, I have several times crept up to one occupied in searching for food, on the rotten parts of a low stump only a few inches from the ground, when, having got so near the tree as almost to touch it, I have taken my cap and suddenly struck the stump, as if with the intention of securing the bird; on which the latter instantly seemed to lose all power or presence of mind, and fell to the ground as if dead. On such occasions, if not immediately secured, it soon recovers, and flies off with more than its usual speed. When surprised when feeding on a tree, they now and then attempt to save themselves by turning round the trunk or branches, and do not fly away unless two persons be present, well knowing, it would seem, that flying is not always a sure means of escape. If wounded without falling, it mounts at once to the highest fork of the tree, where it squats and remains in silence. It is then very difficult to kill it, and sometimes, when shot dead, it clings so firmly to the bark that it may remain hanging for hours. When winged and brought to the ground, it cries loudly on the approach of its enemy, and essays to escape by every means in its power, often inflicting a severe wound if incautiously seized.

The Pileated Woodpecker is fond of Indian corn, chestnuts, acorns, fruits of every kind, particularly wild grapes, and insects of all descriptions. The maize it attacks while yet in its milky state, laying it bare, like the Redheads or Squirrels. For this reason, it often draws upon itself the vengeance of the farmer, who, however, is always disposed, without provocation, to kill the "Woodcock," or "Logcock" as it is commonly named by our country people.

The flight of this well known bird is powerful, and, on occasion, greatly protracted, resembling in all respects that of the Ivory-billed Woodpecker. Its notes are loud and clear, and the rolling sound produced by its hammerings, may be heard at the distance of a quarter of a mile. Its flesh is tough, of a bluish tint, and smells so strongly of the worms and insects on which it generally feeds, as to be extremely unpalatable. It almost always breeds in the interior of the forests, and frequently on trees placed in deep swamps over the water, appearing to give a preference to the southern side of the tree, on which I have generally found its hole, to which it retreats during winter or in rainy weather, and which is sometimes bored perpendicularly, although frequently not, as I have seen some excavated much in the form of that of the Ivory-billed Woodpecker. Its usual depth is from twelve to eighteen inches, its breadth from two and a half to three, and at the bottom sometimes five or six. It rears, I believe, only one brood in a season. The young follow their parents for a long time after coming abroad, receive food from them, and remain with them until the return of spring. The old birds, as well as the young, are fond of retiring at night to their holes, to which they return more especially in winter. My young friend, THOMAS LINCOLN, Esq. of the State of Maine, knew of one that seldom removed far from its retreat during the whole of the inclement season.

The observation of many years has convinced me, that Woodpeckers of all sorts have the bill longer when just fledged than at any future period of their life, and that through use it becomes not only shorter, but also much harder, stronger, and sharper. When the Woodpecker first leaves the nest, its bill may easily be bent; six months after, it resists the force of the fingers; and when the bird is twelve months old, the organ has acquired its permanent bony hardness. On measuring the bill of a young bird of this species not long able to fly, and that of an adult bird, I found the former seven-eighths of an inch longer than the latter. This difference I have represented in the plate. It is also curious to observe, that the young birds of this family, which have the bill tender, either search for larvæ in the most decayed or rotten stumps and trunks of trees, or hunt the deserted old fields, in search of blackberries and other fruits, as if sensible of their inaptitude for attacking the bark of sound trees or the wood itself.

The Mississippi Kite

Falco plumbeus, GMEL.

(PLATE 23)

WHEN, after many a severe conflict, the southern breezes, in alliance with the sun, have, as if through a generous effort, driven back for a season to their desolate abode the chill blasts of the north; when warmth and plenty are insured for a while to our happy lands; when clouds of anxious Swallows, returning from the far south, are guiding millions of Warblers to their summer residence; when numberless insects, cramped in their hanging shells, are impatiently waiting for the full expansion of their wings; when the vernal flowers, so welcome to all, swell out their bursting leaflets, and the rich-leaved Magnolia opens its pure blossoms to the Humming Bird;— then look up, and you will see the Mississippi Kite, as he comes sailing over the scene. He glances towards the earth with his fiery eye; sweeps along, now with the gentle breeze, now against it; seizes here and there the high-flying giddy bug, and allays his hunger without fatigue to wing or talon.

Suddenly he spies some creeping thing, that changes, like the chameleon, from vivid green to dull-brown, to escape his notice. It is the red-throated panting lizard that has made its way to the highest branch of a tree in quest of food. Casting upwards a sidelong look of fear, it remains motionless, so well does it know the prowess of the bird of prey: but its caution is vain; it has been perceived, its fate is sealed, and the next moment it is swept away.

The Mississippi Kite thus extends its migrations as high as the city of Memphis, on the noble stream whose name it bears, and along our eastern shores to the Carolinas, where it now and then breeds, feeding the while on lizards, small snakes, and beetles, and sometimes, as if for want of better employ, teaching the Carrion Crows and Buzzards to fly. At other times, congregating to the number of twenty or more, these birds are seen sweeping around some tree, catching the large locusts which abound in those countries at an early part of the season, and reminding one of the Chimney Swallows, which are so often seen performing similar evolutions, when endeavouring to snap off the little dried twigs of which their nests are composed.

Early in May, the thick-leaved Bay-Tree (*Magnolia grandiflora*), affords in its high tops a place of safety, in which the Hawk of the South may raise its young. These are out by the end of July, and are fed by the parent birds until well practised in the art of procuring subsistence. About the middle of August, they all wing their way southward.

The affection which the old birds display towards their young, and the methods which they occasionally employ to insure the safety of the latter, are so remarkable, that, before I proceed to describe their general habits, I shall relate a case in which I was concerned.

Early one morning, whilst I was admiring the beauties of nature, as the vegetable world lay embalmed in dew, I heard the cry of a bird that I mistook for that of a Pewee Flycatcher. It was prolonged, I thought, as if uttered in distress. After looking for the bird a long time in vain, an object which I had at first supposed to be something that had accidentally lodged in a branch, attracted my attention, as I thought I perceived it moving. It did move distinctly, and the cry that had ceased from the time when I reached the spot where I stood, was repeated, evidently coming from the object in view. I now took it for a young one of the Chuck-Will's-Widow, as it sat lengthwise on the branch. I shot at it, but perhaps did not hit it, as it only opened and closed its wings, as if surprised. At the report of the gun, the old bird came, holding food in her claws. She perceived me, but alighted, and fed her young with great kindness. I shot at both, and again missed, or at least did not succeed, which might have happened from my having only small shot in my gun. The mother flew in silence, sailed over head just long enough to afford me time to reload, returned, and to my great surprise gently lifted her young, and sailing with it to another tree, about thirty yards distant, deposited it there. My feelings at that moment I cannot express. I wished I had not discovered the poor bird; for who could have witnessed, without emotion, so striking an example of that affection which none but a mother can feel; so daring an act, performed in the midst of smoke, in the presence of a dreaded and dangerous enemy. I followed, however, and brought both to the ground at one shot, so keen is the desire of possession!

The young had the head of a fawn-colour, but I took little more notice of it, depositing the two birds under a log, whence I intended to remove them on my return, for the purpose of drawing and describing them. I then proceeded on my excursion to a lake a few miles distant. On coming back, what was my mortification, when I found that some quadruped had devoured both! My punishment was merited.

The Mississippi Kite arrives in Lower Louisiana about the middle of April in small parties of five or six, and confines itself to the borders of deep woods, or to those near plantations, not far from the shores of the rivers, lakes, or bayous. It never moves into the interior of the country, and in this respect resembles the *Falco furcatus*. Plantations lately cleared, and yet covered with tall dying girted trees, placed near a creek or bayou, seemed to suit it best.

Its flight is graceful, vigorous, protracted, and often extended to a great height, the Forked-tailed Hawk being the only species that can compete with it. At times it floats in the air, as if motionless, or sails in broad regular circles, when, suddenly closing its wings, it slides along to some distance, and renews its curves. Now it sweeps in deep and long undulations, with the swiftness of an arrow, passing almost within touching distance of a branch on which it has observed a small lizard, or an insect it longs for, but from which it again ascends disappointed. Now it is seen to move in hurried zigzags, as if pursued by a dangerous enemy, sometimes seeming to turn over and over like a Tumbling Pigeon. Again it is observed flying round the trunk of a tree to secure large insects, sweeping with astonishing velocity. While travelling, it moves in the desultory manner followed by Swallows; but at other times it is seen soaring at a great elevation among the large flocks of Carrion Crows and Turkey Buzzards, joined by the Forked-tailed Hawk, dashing at the former, and giving them chase, as if in play, until these cowardly scavengers sweep downwards, abandoning this to them disagreeable sport to the Hawks, who now continue to gambol undisturbed. When in pursuit of a large insect or a small reptile, it turns its body sidewise, throws out its legs, expands its talons, and generally seizes its prey in an instant. It feeds while on wing, apparently with as much ease and comfort, as when alighted on the branch of a tall tree. It never alights on the earth; at least I have never seen it do so, except when wounded, and then it appears extremely awkward. It never attacks birds or quadrupeds of any kind, with the view of destroying them for food, although it will chase a fox to a considerable distance, screaming loudly all the while, and soon forces a Crow to retreat to the woods.

The nest of this species is always placed in the upper branches of the tallest trees. I thought it gave the preference to those tall and splendid magnolias and white oaks, which adorn our Southern States. The nest resembles that of the dilapidated tenement of the Common American Crow, and is formed of sticks slightly put together, along with branches of Spanish moss (*Usnea*), pieces of vine bark, and dried leaves. The eggs are two or three, almost globular, of a light greenish tint, blotched thickly over with deep chocolate-brown and black. Only one brood is raised in the season, and I think the female sits more than half the time necessary for incubation. The young I also think obtain nearly the full plumage of the old bird before they depart from us, as I have examined these birds early in August, when the migration was already begun, without observing much difference in their general colour, except only in the want of firmness in the tint of the young ones.

Once, early in the month of May, I found a nest of this bird placed on a fine tall white oak near a creek, and observed that the female was sitting with unceasing assiduity. The male I saw bring her food frequently. Not being able to ascend the tree, I hired a Negro, who had been a sailor for some years, to climb it and bring down the eggs or young. This he did by first mounting another tree, the branches of which crossed the lower ones of the oak. No sooner had he reached the trunk of the tree on which the nest was placed, than the male was seen hovering about and over it in evident displeasure, screaming and sweeping towards the intruder the higher he advanced. When he attained the branch on which the nest was, the female left her charge, and the pair, infuriated at his daring, flew with such velocity, and passed so close to him, that I expected every moment to see him struck by them. The black tar, however, proceeded quietly, reached the nest, and took out the eggs, apprising me that there were three. I requested him to bring them down with care, and to throw off the nest, which he did. The poor birds, seeing their tenement cast down to the ground, continued sweeping around us so low and so long, that I could not resist the temptation thus offered of shooting them.

The Mississippi Kite is by no means a shy bird, and one may generally depend on getting near it when alighted; but to follow it while on wing were useless, its flight being usually so elevated, and its sweeps over a field or wood so rapid and varied, that you might spend many hours in vain in attempting to get up with it. Even when alighted, it perches so high, that I have sometimes shot at it, without producing any other effect than that of causing it to open its wings and close them again, as if utterly ignorant of the danger to which it had been exposed, while it seemed to look down upon me quite unconcerned. When wounded, it comes to the ground with great force, and seldom attempts to escape, choosing rather to defend itself, which it does to the last, by throwing itself on its back, erecting the feathers of its head, screaming loudly in the manner of the Pigeon Hawk, disgorging the contents of its stomach, stretching out its talons, and biting or clenching with great vigour. It is extremely muscular, the flesh tough and rigid.

These birds at times search for food so far from the spot where their nest has been placed, that I have on several occasions been obliged to follow their course over the woods, as if in search of a wild bee's hive, before I could discover it. There is scarcely any perceptible difference between the sexes as to size, and in colour they are precisely similar, only the female has less of the ferruginous colour on her primaries than the male. The stomach is thin, rugous, and of a deep orange colour.

The Pewee Flycatcher

Muscicapa fusca, BONAP.

(PLATES 26, 27)

CONNECTED with the biography of this bird are so many incidents relative to my own, that could I with propriety deviate from my proposed method, the present volume would contain less of the habits of birds than of those of the youthful days of an American woodsman. While young, I had a plantation that lay on the sloping declivities of a creek, the name of which I have already given, but as it will ever be dear to my recollection, you will, I hope, allow me to repeat it— the Perkioming. I was extremely fond of rambling along its rocky banks, for it would have been difficult to do so either without meeting with a sweet flower, spreading open its beauties to the sun, or observing the watchful King's-fisher perched on some projecting stone over the clear water of the stream. Nay, now and then, the Fish Hawk itself, followed by a White-headed Eagle, would make his appearance, and by his graceful aerial motions, raise my thoughts far above them into the heavens, silently leading me to the admiration of the sublime Creator of all. These impressive, and always delightful, reveries often accompanied my steps to the entrance of a small cave scooped out of the solid rock by the hand of nature. It was, I then thought, quite large enough for my study. My paper and pencils, with now and then a volume of EDGE-WORTH's natural and fascinating Tales or LAFONTAINE's Fables, afforded me ample pleasures. It was in that place, kind reader, that I first saw with advantage the force of parental affection in birds. There it was that I studied the habits of the Pewee; and there I was taught most forcibly that to destroy the nest of a bird, or to deprive it of its eggs or young, is an act of great cruelty.

I had observed the nest of this plain-coloured Flycatcher fastened, as it were, to the rock immediately over the arched entrance of this calm retreat. I had peeped into it: although empty, it was yet clean, as if the absent owner intended to re-visit it with the return of spring. The buds were already much swelled, and some of the trees were ornamented with blos-soms, yet the ground was still partially covered with snow, and the air retained the piercing chill of winter. I chanced one morning early to go to my retreat. The sun's glowing rays gave a rich colouring to every object around. As I entered the cave, a rustling sound over my head attracted my attention, and, on turning, I saw two birds fly off, and alight on a tree close by:—the Pewees had arrived! I felt delighted, and fear-ing that my sudden appearance might disturb the gentle pair, I walked off, not, however, without frequently looking at them. I concluded that they must have just come, for they seemed fatigued:—their plaintive note was not heard, their crests were not erected, and the vibration of the tail, so very conspicuous in this species, appeared to be wanting in power. Insects were yet few, and the return of the birds looked to me as prompted more by their affection to the place, than by any other motive. No sooner had I gone a few steps than the Pewees, with one accord glided down from their perches and entered the cave. I did not return to it any more that day, and as I saw none about it, or in the neighbourhood, I supposed that they must have spent the day within it. I concluded also that these birds must have reached this haven, either during the night, or at the very dawn of that morn. Hundreds of ob-servations have since proved to me that this species always mi-grates by night.

Filled with the thoughts of the little pilgrims, I went early next morning to their retreat, yet not early enough to surprise them in it. Long before I reached the spot, my ears were agreeably saluted by their well-known note, and I saw them darting about through the air, giving chase to some insects close over the water. They were full of gaiety, frequently flew into and out of the cave, and while alighted on a favourite tree near it, seemed engaged in the most interesting converse. The light fluttering or tremulous motions of their wings, the jetting of their tail, the erection of their crest, and the neatness of their attitudes, all indicated that they were no longer fatigued, but on the contrary refreshed and happy. On my going into the cave, the male flew violently towards the entrance, snapped his bill sharply and repeatedly, accompanying this action with a tremulous rolling note, the import of which I soon guessed. Presently he flew into the cave and out of it again, with a swiftness scarcely credible: it was like the passing of a shadow.

Several days in succession I went to the spot, and saw with pleasure that as my visits increased in frequency, the birds became more familiarized to me, and, before a week had elapsed, the Pewees and myself were quite on terms of intimacy. It was now the 10th of April; the spring was forward that season, no more snow was to be seen, Redwings and Grakles were to be found here and there. The Pewees, I observed, began working at their old nest. Desirous of judging for myself, and anxious to enjoy the company of this friendly pair, I determined to spend the greater part of each day in the cave. My presence no longer alarmed either of them. They brought a few fresh materials, lined the nest anew, and rendered it warm by adding a few large soft feathers of the common goose, which they found strewn along the edge of the water in the creek. There was a remarkable and curious twittering in their note while both sat on the edge of the nest at those meetings, and which is never heard on any other occasion. It was the soft, tender expression, I thought, of the pleasure they both appeared to anticipate of the future. Their mutual caresses, simple as they might have seemed to another, and the delicate manner used by the male to please his mate, rivetted my eyes on these birds, and excited sensations which I can never forget.

The female one day spent the greater part of the time in her nest; she frequently changed her position; her mate exhibited much uneasiness, he would alight by her sometimes, sit by her side for a moment, and suddenly flying out, would return with an insect, which she took from his bill with apparent gratification. About three o'clock in the afternoon, I saw the uneasiness of the female increase; the male showed an unusual appearance of despondence, when, of a sudden, the female rose on her feet, looked sidewise under her, and flying out, followed by her attentive consort, left the cave, rose high in the air, performing evolutions more curious to me than any I had seen before. They flew about over the water, the female leading her mate, as it were, through her own meanderings. Leaving the Pewees to their avocations, I peeped into their nest, and saw there their first egg, so white and so transparent—for I believe, reader, that eggs soon loose this peculiar transparency after being laid—that to me the sight was more pleasant than if I had met with a diamond of the same size. The knowledge that in an enclosure so frail, life already existed, and that ere many weeks would elapse, a weak, delicate, and helpless creature, but perfect in all its parts, would burst the shell, and immediately call for the most tender care and attention of its anxious parents, filled my mind with as much wonder as when, looking towards the heavens, I searched, alas! in vain, for the true import of all that I saw.

In six days, six eggs were deposited; but I observed that as they increased in number, the bird remained a shorter time in the nest. The last she deposited in a few minutes after alighting. Perhaps, thought I, this is a law of nature, intended for keeping the eggs fresh to the last. Kind reader, what are your thoughts on the subject? About an hour after laying the last egg, the female Pewee returned, settled in her nest, and, after arranging the eggs, as I thought, several times under her body, expanded her wings a little, and fairly commenced the arduous task of incubation.

Day after day passed by. I gave strict orders that no one should go near the cave, much less enter it, or indeed destroy any bird's nest on the plantation. Whenever I visited the Pewees, one or other of them was on the nest, while its mate was either searching for food, or perched in the vicinity, filling the air with its loudest notes. I not unfrequently reached out my hand near the sitting bird; and so gentle had they both become, or rather so well acquainted were we, that neither moved on such occasions, even when my hand was quite close to it. Now and then the female would shrink back into the nest, but the male frequently snapped at my fingers, and once left the nest as if in great anger, flew round the cave a few times, emitting his querulous whining notes, and alighted again to resume his labours.

At this very time, a Pewee's nest was attached to one of the rafters of my mill, and there was another under a shed in the cattle-yard. Each pair, any one would have felt assured, had laid out the limits of its own domain, and it was seldom that one trespassed on the grounds of its neighbour. The Pewee of the cave generally fed or spent its time so far above the mill on the creek, that he of the mill never came in contact with it. The Pewee of the cattle-yard confined himself to the orchard, and never disturbed the rest. Yet I sometimes could hear distinctly the notes of the three at the same moment. I had at that period an idea that the whole of these birds were descended from the same stock. If not correct in this supposition, I had ample proof afterwards that the brood of young Pewees, raised in the cave, returned the following spring, and established themselves farther up on the creek, and among the outhouses in the neighbourhood.

On some other occasion, I will give you such instances of the return of birds, accompanied by their progeny, to the place of their nativity, that perhaps you will become convinced, as I am at this moment, that to this propensity every country owes the augmentation of new species, whether of birds or of quadrupeds, attracted by the many benefits met with, as countries become more open and better cultivated: but now I will, with your leave, return to the Pewees of the cave.

On the thirteenth day, the little ones were hatched. One egg was unproductive, and the female, on the second day after the birth of her brood, very deliberately pushed it out of the nest. On examining this egg, I found it containing the embryo of a bird partly dried up, with its vertebræ quite fast to the shell, which had probably occasioned its death. Never have I since so closely witnessed the attention of birds to their young. Their entrance with insects was so frequently repeated, that I thought I saw the little ones grow as I gazed upon them. The old birds no longer looked upon me as an enemy, and would often come in close by me, as if I had been a post. I now took upon me to handle the young frequently; nay, several times I took the whole family out, and blew off the exuviæ of the feathers from the nest. I attached light threads to their legs: these they invariably removed, either with their bills, or with the assistance of their parents. I renewed them, however, until I found the little fellows habituated to them; and at last, when they were about to leave the nest, I fixed a light silver thread to the leg of each, loose enough not to hurt the part, but so fastened that no exertions of theirs could remove it.

Sixteen days had passed, when the brood took to wing; and the old birds, dividing the time with caution, began to arrange the nest anew. A second set of eggs were laid, and in the beginning of August a new brood made its appearance.

The young birds took much to the woods, as if feeling themselves more secure there than in the open fields; but before they departed, they all appeared strong, and minded not making long sorties into the open air, over the whole creek, and the fields around it. On the 8th of October, not a Pewee could I find on the plantation: my little companions had all set off on their travels. For weeks afterwards, however, I saw Pewees arriving from the north, and lingering a short time, as if to rest, when they also moved southward.

At the season when the Pewee returns to Pennsylvania, I had the satisfaction to observe those of the cave in and about it. There again, in the very same nest, two broods were raised. I found several Pewees nests at some distance up the creek, particularly under a bridge, and several others in the adjoining meadows, attached to the inner part of sheds erected for the protection of hay and grain. Having caught several of these birds on the nest, I had the pleasure of finding that two of them had the little ring on the leg.

I was now obliged to go to France, where I remained two years. On my return, which happened early in August, I had the satisfaction of finding three young Pewees in the nest of the cave; but it was not the nest which I had left in it. The old one had been torn off from the roof, and the one which I found there was placed above where it stood. I observed at once that one of the parent birds was as shy as possible, while the other allowed me to approach within a few yards. This was the male bird, and I felt confident that the old female had paid the debt of nature. Having inquired of the miller's son, I found that he had killed the old Pewee and four young ones, to make bait for the purpose of catching fish. Then the male Pewee had brought another female to the cave! As long as the plantation of Mill Grove belonged to me, there continued to be a Pewee's nest in my favourite retreat; but after I had sold it, the cave was destroyed, as were nearly all the beautiful rocks along the shores of the creek, to build a new dam across the Perkioming.

This species is so peculiarly fond of attaching its nest to rocky caves, that, were it called the Rock Flycatcher, it would be appropriately named. Indeed I seldom have passed near such a place, particularly during the breeding season, without seeing the Pewee, or hearing its notes. I recollect that, while travelling in Virginia with a friend, he desired that I would go somewhat out of our intended route, to visit the renowned Rock Bridge of that State. My companion, who had passed over this natural bridge before, proposed a wager that he could lead me across it before I should be aware of its existence. It was early in April; and, from the descriptions of this place which I had read, I felt confident that the Pewee Flycatcher must be about it. I accepted the proposal of my friend and trotted on, intent on proving to myself that, by constantly attending to one subject, a person must sooner or later become acquainted with it. I listened to the notes of the different birds, which at intervals came to my ear, and at last had the satisfaction to distinguish those of the Pewee. I stopped my horse, to judge of the distance at which the bird might be, and a moment after told my friend that the bridge was short of a hundred yards from us, although it was impossible for us to see the spot itself. The surprise of my companion was great. "How do you know this?" he asked, "for," continued he, "you are correct."—"Simply," answered I, "because I hear the notes of the Pewee, and know that a cave, or a deep rocky creek, is at hand." We moved on; the Pewees rose from under the bridge in numbers; I pointed to the spot and won the wager.

This rule of observation I have almost always found to work, as arithmeticians say, both ways. Thus the nature of the woods or place in which the observer may be, whether high or low, moist or dry, sloping north or south, with whatever kind of vegetation, tall trees of particular species, or low shrubs, will generally disclose the nature of their inhabitants.

The flight of the Pewee Flycatcher is performed by a fluttering light motion, frequently interrupted by sailings. It is slow when the bird is proceeding to some distance, rather rapid when in pursuit of prey. It often mounts perpendicularly from its perch after an insect, and returns to some dry twig, from which it can see around to a considerable distance. It then swallows the insect whole, unless it happen to be large. It will at times pursue an insect to a considerable distance, and seldom without success. It alights with great firmness, immediately erects itself in the manner of hawks, glances all around, shakes its wings with a tremulous motion, and vibrates its tail upwards as if by a spring. Its tufty crest is generally erected, and its whole appearance is neat, if not elegant. The Pewee has its particular stands, from which it seldom rambles far. The top of a fence stake near the road is often selected by it, from which it sweeps off in all directions, returning at intervals, and thus remaining the greater part of the morning and evening. The corner of the roof of the barn suits it equally well, and if the weather requires it, it may be seen perched on the highest dead twig of a tall tree. During the heat of the day it reposes in the shade of the woods. In the autumn it will choose the stalk of the mullein for its stand, and sometimes the projecting angle of a rock jutting over a stream. It now and then alights on the ground for an instant, but this happens principally during winter, or while engaged during spring in collecting the materials of which its nest is composed, in our Southern States, where many spend their time at this season.

I have found this species abundant in the Floridas in winter, in full song, and as lively as ever, also in Louisiana and the Carolinas, particularly in the cotton fields. None, however, to my knowledge, breed south of Charlestown in South Carolina, and very few in the lower parts of that State. They leave Louisiana in February, and return to it in October. Occasionally during winter they feed on berries of different kinds, and are quite expert at discovering the insects impaled on thorns by the Loggerhead Shrike, and which they devour with avidity. I met with a few of these birds on the Magdeleine Islands, on the coast of Labrador, and in Newfoundland.

The nest of this species bears some resemblance to that of the Barn Swallow, the outside consisting of mud, with which are firmly impacted grasses or mosses of various kinds deposited in regular strata. It is lined with delicate fibrous roots, or shreds of vine bark, wool, horse-hair, and sometimes a few feathers. The greatest diameter across the open mouth is from five to six inches, and the depth from four to five. Both birds work alternately, bringing pellets of mud or damp earth, mixed with moss, the latter of which is mostly disposed on the outer parts, and in some instances the whole exterior looks as if entirely formed of it. The fabric is firmly attached to a rock, or a wall, the rafter of a house, &c. In the barrens of Kentucky I have found the nests fixed to the side of those curious places called *sink-holes*, and as much as twenty feet below the surface of the ground. I have observed that when the Pewees return in spring, they strengthen their tenement by adding to the external parts attached to the rock, as if to prevent it from falling, which after all it sometimes does when several years old. Instances of their taking possession of the nest of the Republican Swallow (*Hirundo fulva*) have been observed in the State of Maine. The eggs are from four to six, rather elongated, pure white, generally with a few reddish spots near the larger end.

In Virginia, and probably as far as New York, they not unfrequently raise two broods, sometimes three, in a season. My learned friend, Professor NUTTALL, of Cambridge College, Massachusetts, thinks that the Pewee seldom raises more than one brood in the year in that State.

This species ejects the hard particles of the wings, legs,

abdomen, and other parts of insects, in small pellets, in the manner of owls, goatsuckers and swallows.

The Snowy Owl

Strix nyctea

(PLATE 28)

THIS beautiful bird is merely a winter visitor of the United States, where it is seldom seen before the month of November, and whence it retires as early as the beginning of February. It wanders at times along the sea coast, as far as Georgia. I have occasionally seen it in the lower parts of Kentucky, and in the State of Ohio. It is more frequently met with in Pennsylvania and the Jerseys; but in Massachusetts and Maine it is far more abundant than in any other parts of the Union.

The Snowy Owl hunts during the day, as well as in the dusk. Its flight is firm and protracted, although smooth and noiseless. It passes swiftly over its hunting ground, seizes its prey by instantaneously falling on it, and generally devours it on the spot. When the objects of its pursuit are on wing, such as ducks, grouse, or pigeons, it gains upon them by urging its speed, and strikes them somewhat in the manner of the Peregrine Falcon. It is fond of the neighbourhood of rivers and small streams, having in their course cataracts or shallow rapids, on the borders of which it seizes on fishes, in the manner of our wild cat. It also watches the traps set for musk-rats, and devours the animals caught in them. Its usual food, while it remains with us, consists of hares, squirrels, rats, and fishes, portions of all of which I have found in its stomach. In several fine specimens which I examined immediately after being killed, I found the stomach to be extremely thin, soft, and capable of great extension. In one of them I found the whole of a large house-rat, in pieces of considerable size, the head and the tail almost entire. This bird was very fat, and its intestines, which were thin, and so small as not to exceed a fourth of an inch in diameter, measured 4½ feet in length.

When skinned, the body of the Snowy Owl appears at first sight compact and very muscular, for the breast is large, as are the thighs and legs, these parts being covered with much flesh of a fine and delicate appearance, very much resembling that of a chicken, and not indelicate eating, but the thorax is very narrow for so large a bird. The keel of the breast-bone is fully an inch deep at its junction with the fourchette, which is wide. The heart and liver are large; the œsophagus is extremely wide, enabling the bird to swallow very large portions of its food at once. The skin may be drawn over the head without any difficulty, and from the body with ease. The male weighs 4 lb, the female 4¾ lb. avoirdupois.

The observations which I have made induce me to believe that the pure and rich light-yellowish whiteness of this species belongs to both sexes after a certain age. I have shot specimens which were, as I thought, so young as to be nearly of a uniform light-brown tint, and which puzzled me for several years, as I had at first conceived them to be of a different species. This, indeed, led me to think that, when young, these birds are brown. Others were more or less marked with broad transverse lines of deep brown or black; but I have seen specimens of both sexes perfectly free from spots, excepting on the occiput, where I have never missed them.

Some twenty years passed; and, during that time, scarcely was there a winter which did not bring several of these hardy natives of the north to the Falls of the Ohio at Louisville. At the break of day, one morning, when I lay hidden in a pile of floated logs, at the Falls of the Ohio, waiting for a shot at some wild geese, I had an opportunity of seeing this Owl secure fish in the following manner:—While watching for their prey on the borders of the "pots," they invariably lay flat on the rock, with the body placed lengthwise along the border of the hole, the head also laid down, but turned towards the water. One might have supposed the bird sound asleep, as it would remain in the same position until a good opportunity of securing a fish occurred, which I believe was never missed; for, as the latter unwittingly rose to the surface, near the edge, that instant the Owl thrust out the foot next the water, and, with the quickness of lightning, seized it, and drew it out. The Owl then removed to the distance of a few yards, devoured its prey, and returned to the same hole; or, if it had not perceived any more fish, flew only a few yards over the many pots there, marked a likely one, and alighted at a little distance from it. It then squatted, moved slowly towards the edge, and lay as before watching for an opportunity. Whenever a fish of any size was hooked, as I may say, the Owl struck the other foot also into it, and flew off with it to a considerable distance. In two instances of this kind, I saw the bird carry its prey across the Western or Indiana Shute, into the woods, as if to be quite out of harm's way. I never heard it utter a single note on such occasions, even when two birds joined in the repast, which was frequently the case, when the fish that had been caught was of a large size. At sun-rise, or shortly after, the Owls flew to the woods, and I did not see them until the next morning, when, after witnessing the same feats, I watched an opportunity, and killed both at one shot.

An old hunter, now residing in Maine, told me that one winter he lost so many musk-rats by the owls, that he resolved to destroy them. To effect this, without loss of ammunition, a great object to him, he placed musk-rats caught in the traps usually employed for the purpose, in a prominent spot, and in the centre of a larger trap. He said he seldom failed, and in this manner considerably "thinned the thieves," before the season was over. He found, however, more of the Great Grey Owl, *Strix cinerea*, than of the Snowy Owl. The latter he thought was much more cunning than the former.

In the course of a winter spent at Boston, I had some superb specimens of the Snowy Owl brought to me, one of which, a male, was alive, having only been touched in the wing. He stood upright, keeping his feathers close, but would not suffer me to approach him. His fine eyes watched every movement I made, and if I pretended to walk round him, the instant his head had turned as far as he could still see me, he would open his wings, and with large hops get to a corner of the room, when he would turn towards me, and again watch my approach. This bird had been procured on one of the sea-islands off Boston, by a gunner in my employ, who, after following it from one rock to another, with difficulty wounded it. In the course of the same winter, I saw one sailing high over the bay along with a number of gulls, which appeared to dislike his company, and chased it at a respectful distance, the owl seeming to pay no regard to them.

Several individuals have been procured near Charleston, in South Carolina, one on James' Island, another, now in the Charleston Museum, on Clarkson's plantation. A fine one was shot at Columbia, the seat of government for the State of that name, from the chimney of one of the largest houses in that town, and was beautifully preserved by Professor Gibbes of the Columbia College. I once met with one while walking with a friend near Louisville in Kentucky, in the middle of the day. It was perched on a broken stump of a tree in the centre of a large field; and, on seeing us, flew off, sailed round the field, and alighted again on the same spot. It evinced much impatience and apprehension, opening its wings several times as if intending to fly off; but, with some care, it was approached and shot. It proved to be a fine old female, the plumage of which was almost pure white. I have heard of individuals having been seen as far down the Mississippi as the town of Memphis. Some Indians assured me that they had shot one at the mouth of the Red River; and, while on the Arkansas River, I was frequently told of a large White Owl that had been seen there during winter.

So much has been said to me of its breeding in the northern parts of the State of Maine, that this may possibly be correct. In Nova Scotia they are abundant at the approach of winter; and Professor MacCulloch, of the University of Pictou, shewed me several beautiful specimens in his fine collection of North American Birds. Of its place and mode of breeding I know nothing; for, although every person to whom I spoke of this bird while in Labrador knew it, my party saw none there; and in Newfoundland we were equally unsuccessful in our search.

The American Sparrow-Hawk

Falco sparverius, LINN.

(PLATE 29)

WE HAVE few more beautiful hawks in the United States than this active little species, and I am sure, none half so abundant. It is found in every district from Louisiana to

Maine, as well as from the Atlantic shores to the western regions. Every one knows the Sparrow-Hawk, the very mention of its name never fails to bring to mind some anecdote connected with its habits, and, as it commits no depredations on poultry, few disturb it, so that the natural increase of the species experiences no check from man. During the winter months especially it may be seen in the Southern States about every old field, orchard, barn-yard, or kitchen-garden, but seldom indeed in the interior of the forest.

Beautifully erect, it stands on the highest fence-stake, the broken top of a tree, the summit of a grain stack, or the corner of the barn, patiently and silently waiting until it spy a mole, a field-mouse, a cricket, or a grasshopper, on which to pounce. If disappointed in its expectation, it leaves its stand and removes to another, flying low and swiftly until within a few yards of the spot on which it wishes to alight, when all of a sudden, and in the most graceful manner, it rises towards it and settles with incomparable firmness of manner, merely suffering its beautiful tail to vibrate gently for a while, its wings being closed with the swiftness of thought. Its keen eye perceives something beneath, when down it darts, secures the object in its talons, returns to its stand, and devours its prey piece by piece. This done, the little hunter rises in the air, describes a few circles, moves on directly, balances itself steadily by a tremulous motion of its wings, darts towards the earth, but, as if disappointed, checks it course, reascends and proceeds. Some unlucky finch crosses the field beneath it. The Hawk has marked it, and, anxious to secure its prize, sweeps after it; the chase is soon ended, for the poor affrighted and panting bird becomes the prey of the ruthless hunter, who, unconscious of wrong, carries it off to some elevated branch of a tall tree, plucks it neatly, tears the flesh asunder, and having eaten all that it can pick, allows the skeleton and wings to fall to the ground, where they may apprise the traveller that a murder has been committed.

Thus, reader, are the winter months spent by this little marauder. When spring returns to enliven the earth, each male bird seeks for its mate, whose coyness is not less innocent than that of the gentle dove. Pursued from place to place, the female at length yields to the importunity of her dear tormenter, when side by side they sail, screaming aloud their love notes, which if not musical, are doubtless at least delightful to the parties concerned. With tremulous wings they search for a place in which to deposit their eggs secure from danger, and now they have found it.

On that tall mouldering headless trunk, the hawks have alighted side by side. See how they caress each other! Mark! The female enters the deserted Woodpecker's hole, where she remains some time measuring its breadth and depth. Now she appears, exultingly calls her mate, and tells him there could not be a fitter place. Full of joy they gambol through the air, chase all intruders away, watch the Grakles and other birds to which the hole might be equally pleasing, and so pass the time, until the female has deposited her eggs, six, perhaps even seven in number, round, and beautifully spotted. The birds sit alternately, each feeding the other and watching with silent care. After a while the young appear, covered with white down. They grow apace, and now are ready to go abroad, when their parents entice them forth. Some launch into the air at once, others, not so strong, now and then fall to the ground; but all continue to be well provided with food, until they are able to shift for themselves. Together they search for grasshoppers, crickets, and such young birds as, less experienced than themselves, fall an easy prey. The family still resort to the same field, each bird making choice of a stand, the top of a tree, or that of the Great Mullein. At times they remove to the ground, then fly off in a body, separate, and again betake themselves to their stands. Their strength increases, their flight improves, and the field-mouse seldom gains her retreat before the little Falcon secures it for a meal.

The trees, of late so richly green, now disclose the fading tints of autumn; the cricket becomes mute, the grasshopper withers on the fences, the mouse retreats to her winter quarters, dismal clouds obscure the eastern horizon, the sun assumes a sickly dimness, hoarfrosts cover the ground, and the long night encroaches on the domains of light. No longer are heard the feathered choristers of the woods, who throng towards more congenial climes, and in their rear rushes the Sparrow-Hawk.

Its flight is rather irregular, nor can it be called protracted. It flies over a field, but seldom farther at a time; even in barren lands, a few hundred yards are all the extent it chooses to go before it alights. During the love season alone it may be seen sailing for half an hour, which is, I believe, the longest time I ever saw one on the wing. When chasing a bird, it passes along with considerable celerity, but never attains the speed of the Sharp-shinned Hawk or of other species. When teazing an Eagle or a Turkey Buzzard, its strength seems to fail in a few minutes, and if itself chased by a stronger hawk, it soon retires into some thicket for protection. Its migrations are pursued by day, and with much apparent nonchalance.

The cry of this bird so much resembles that of the European Kestrel, to which it seems allied, that, were it rather stronger in intonation, it might be mistaken for it. At times it emits its notes while perched, but principally when on the wing, and more continually before and after the birth of its young, the weaker cries of which it imitates when they have left the nest and follow their parents.

The Sparrow Hawk does not much regard the height of the place in which it deposits its eggs, provided it be otherwise suitable, but I never saw it construct a nest for itself. It prefers the hole of a Woodpecker, but now and then is satisfied with an abandoned crow's nest. So prolific is it, that I do not recollect having ever found fewer than five eggs or young in the nest, and, as I have already said, the number sometimes amounts to seven. The eggs are nearly globular, of a deep buff-colour, blotched all over with dark brown and black. This Hawk sometimes raises two broods in the season, in the Southern States, where in fact it may be said to be a constant resident; but in the Middle and Eastern States, seldom if ever more than one. Nay, I have thought that in the South the eggs of a laying are more numerous than in the North, although of this I am not quite certain.

So much attached are they to their stand, that they will return to it and sit there by preference for months in succession. My friend BACHMAN informed me that, through this circumstance, he has caught as many as seven in the same field, each from its favourite stump.

Although the greater number of these Hawks remove southward at the approach of winter, some remain even in the State of New York during the severest weather of that season.

These keep in the immediate neighbourhood of barns, where now and then they secure a rat or a mouse for their support. Sometimes this species is severely handled by the larger Hawks. One of them who had caught a Sparrow, and was flying off with it, was suddenly observed by a Red-tailed Hawk, which in a few minutes made it drop its prey: this contented the pursuer and enabled the pursued to escape.

THEODORE LINCOLN, Esq. of Dennisville, Maine, informed me that the Sparrow-Hawk is in the habit of attacking the Republican Swallow, while sitting on its eggs, deliberately tearing the bottle-neck-like entrance of its curious nest, and seizing the occupant for its prey. This is as fit a place as any to inform you, that the father of that gentleman, who has resided at Dennisville upwards of forty years, found the swallow just mentioned abundant there, on his arrival in that then wild portion of the country.

In the Floridas the Sparrow-Hawk pairs as early as February, in the Middle States about April, and in the northern parts of Maine seldom before June. Few are seen in Nova Scotia, and none in Newfoundland, or on the western coast of Labrador. Although abundant in the interior of East Florida, I did not observe one on any of the keys which border the coast of that singular peninsula. During one of my journeys down the Mississippi, I frequently observed some of these birds standing on low dead branches over the water, from which they would pick up the beetles that had accidentally fallen into the stream.

No bird can be more easily raised and kept than this beautiful Hawk. I once found a young male that had dropped from the nest before it was able to fly. Its cries for food attracted my notice, and I discovered it lying near a log. It was large, and covered with soft white down, through which the young feathers protruded. Its little blue bill and yet grey eyes made it look not unlike an owl. I took it home, named it Nero, and provided it with small birds, at which it would scramble fiercely, although yet unable to tear their flesh, in which I assisted it. In a few weeks it grew very beautiful, and became so voracious, requiring a great number of birds daily, that I turned it out, to see how it would shift for itself. This proved a gratification to both of us: it soon hunted for grasshoppers

and other insects, and on returning from my walks I now and
then threw a dead bird high in the air, which it never failed to
perceive from its stand, and towards which it launched with
such quickness as sometimes to catch it before it fell to the
ground. The little fellow attracted the notice of his brothers,
brought up hard by, who, accompanied by their parents, at
first gave it chase, and forced it to take refuge behind one of
the window-shutters where it usually passed the night, but
soon became gentler towards it, as if forgiving its desertion.
My bird was fastidious in the choice of food, would not touch
a Woodpecker, however fresh, and as he grew older, refused to
eat birds that were in the least tainted. To the last he continued kind to me, and never failed to return at night to his
favourite roost behind the window-shutter. His courageous
disposition often amused the family, as he would sail off from
his stand, and fall on the back of a tame duck, which, setting
up a loud quack, would waddle off in great alarm with the
Hawk sticking to her. But, as has often happened to adven-
turers of similar spirit, his audacity cost him his life. A hen and
her brood chanced to attract his notice, and he flew to secure
one of the chickens, but met one whose parental affection in-
spired her with a courage greater than his own. The conflict,
which was severe, ended the adventures of poor Nero.

I have often observed birds of this species in the Southern
States, and more especially in the Floridas, which were so
much smaller than those met with in the Middle and Northern Districts, that I felt almost inclined to consider them different; but after studying their habits and voice, I became
assured that they were the same. Another species allied to the
present, and alluded to by WILSON, has never made its appearance in our Southern States.

The American Crow

Corvus americanus

(PLATE 30)

THE Crow is an extremely shy bird, having found familiarity
with man no way to his advantage. He is also cunning—at

least he is so called, because he takes care of himself and his brood. The state of anxiety, I may say of terror, in which he is constantly kept, would be enough to spoil the temper of any creature. Almost every person has an antipathy to him, and scarcely one of his race would be left in the land, did he not employ all his ingenuity, and take advantage of all his experience, in counteracting the evil machinations of his enemies. I think I see him perched on the highest branch of a tree, watching every object around. He observes a man on horseback travelling towards him; he marks his movements in silence. No gun does the rider carry,—no, that is clear; but perhaps he has pistols in the holsters of his saddle!—of that the Crow is not quite sure, as he cannot either see them or "smell powder." He beats the points of his wings, jerks his tail once or twice, bows his head, and merrily sounds the joy which he feels at the moment. Another man he spies walking across the field towards his stand, but he has only a stick. Yonder comes a boy shouldering a musket loaded with large shot for the express purpose of killing crows! The bird immediately sounds an alarm; he repeats his cries, increasing their vehemence the nearer his enemy advances. All the crows within half a mile round are seen flying off, each repeating the well known notes of the trusty watchman, who, just as the young gunner is about to take aim, betakes himself to flight. But alas, he chances unwittingly to pass over a sportsman, whose dexterity is greater; the mischievous prowler aims his piece, fires;—down towards the earth broken-winged, falls the luckless bird in an instant. "It is nothing but a crow," quoth the sportsman, who proceeds in search of game, and leaves the poor creature to die in the most excruciating agonies.

Wherever within the Union the laws encourage the destruction of this species, it is shot in great numbers for the sake of the premium offered for each crow's head. You will perhaps be surprised, reader, when I tell you that in one single State, in the course of a season, 40,000 were shot, besides the multitudes of young birds killed in their nests. Must I add to this slaughter other thousands destroyed by the base artifice of laying poisoned grain along the fields to tempt these poor birds? Yes, I will tell you of all this too. The natural feelings of every one who admires the bounty of Nature in providing abundantly for the subsistence of all her creatures, prompt me to do so. Like yourself, I admire all her wonderful works, and respect her wise intentions, even when her laws are far beyond our limited comprehension.

The Crow devours myriads of grubs every day of the year, that might lay waste the farmer's fields; it destroys quadrupeds innumerable, every one of which is an enemy to his poultry and his flocks. Why then should the farmer be so ungrateful, when he sees such services rendered to him by a providential friend, as to persecute that friend even to the death? Unless he plead ignorance, surely he ought to be found guilty at the bar of common sense. Were the soil of the United States, like that of some other countries, nearly exhausted by long continued cultivation, human selfishness in such a matter might be excused, and our people might look on our Crows, as other people look on theirs; but every individual in the land is aware of the superabundance of food that exists among us, and of which a portion may well be spared for the feathered beings, that tend to enhance our pleasures by the sweetness of their song, the innocence of their lives, or their curious habits. Did not every American open his door and his heart to the wearied traveller, and afford him food, comfort and rest, I would at once give up the argument; but when I know by experience the generosity of the people, I cannot but wish that they would reflect a little, and become more indulgent toward our poor, humble, harmless, and even most serviceable bird, the Crow.

The American Crow is common in all parts of the United States. It becomes gregarious immediately after the breeding season, when it forms flocks sometimes containing hundreds, or even thousands. Towards autumn, the individuals bred in the Eastern Districts almost all remove to the Southern States, where they spend the winter in vast numbers.

The voice of our Crow is very different from that of the European species which comes nearest to it in appearance, so much so indeed, that this circumstance, together with others relating to its organization, has induced me to distinguish it, as you see, by a peculiar name, that of *Corvus Americanus.* I hope you will think me excusable in this, should my ideas prove to be erroneous, when I tell you that the Magpie of Europe is assuredly the very same bird as that met with in the western wilds of the United States, although some ornithologists have maintained the contrary, and that I am not disposed to make differences in name where none exist in nature. I consider our Crow as rather less than the European one, and the form of its tongue does not resemble that of the latter bird; besides the Carrion Crow of that country seldom associates in numbers, but remains in pairs, excepting immediately after it has brought its young abroad, when the family remains undispersed for some weeks.

Wherever our Crow is abundant, the Raven is rarely found, and *vice versa*. From Kentucky to New Orleans, Ravens are extremely rare, whereas in that course you find one or more Crows at every half mile. On the contrary, far up the Missouri, as well as on the coast of Labrador, few Crows are to be seen, while Ravens are common. I found the former birds equally scarce in Newfoundland.

Omnivorous like the Raven, our Crow feeds on fruits, seeds, and vegetables of almost every kind; it is equally fond of snakes, frogs, lizards, and other small reptiles; it looks upon various species of worms, grubs and insects as dainties; and if hard pressed by hunger, it will alight upon and devour even putrid carrion. It is as fond of the eggs of other birds as is the Cuckoo, and, like the Titmouse, it will, during a paroxysm of anger, break in the skull of a weak or wounded bird. It delights in annoying its twilight enemies the Owls, the Opossum, and the Racoon, and will even follow by day a fox, a wolf, a panther, or in fact any other carnivorous beast, as if anxious that man should destroy them for their mutual benefit. It plunders the fields of their superabundance, and is blamed for so doing, but it is seldom praised when it chases the thieving Hawk from the poultry-yard.

The American Crow selects with uncommon care its breeding place. You may find its nest in the interior of our most dismal swamps, or on the sides of elevated and precipitous rocks, but almost always as much concealed from the eye of man as possible. They breed in almost every portion of the Union, from the Southern Cape of the Floridas to the extremities of Maine, and probably as far westward as the Pacific

Ocean. The period of nestling varies from February to the beginning of June, according to the latitude of the place. Its scarcity on the coast of Labrador, furnishes one of the reasons that have induced me to believe it different from the Carrion Crow of Europe; for there I met with several species of birds common to both countries, which seldom enter the United States farther than the vicinity of our most eastern boundaries.

The nest, however, greatly resembles that of the European Crow, as much, in fact, as that of the American Magpie resembles the nest of the European. It is formed externally of dry sticks, interwoven with grasses, and is within thickly plastered with mud or clay, and lined with fibrous roots and feathers. The eggs are from four to six, of a pale greenish colour, spotted and clouded with purplish-grey and brownish-green. In the Southern States they raise two broods in the season, but to the eastward seldom more than one. Both sexes incubate, and their parental care and mutual attachment are not surpassed by those of any other bird. Although the nests of this species often may be found near each other, their proximity is never such as occurs in the case of the Fish-Crow, of which many nests may be seen on the same tree.

When the nest of this species happens to be discovered, the faithful pair raise such a hue and cry that every Crow in the neighbourhood immediately comes to their assistance, passing in circles high over the intruder until he has retired, or following him, if he has robbed it, as far as their regard for the safety of their own will permit them. As soon as the young leave the nest, the family associates with others, and in this manner they remain in flocks till spring. Many crows' nests may be found within a few acres of the same wood, and in this particular their habits accord more with those of the Rooks of Europe (*Corvus frugilegus*), which, as you very well know, breed and spend their time in communities. The young of our Crow, like that of the latter species, are tolerable food when taken a few days before the period of their leaving the nest.

The flight of the American Crow is swift, protracted, and at times performed at a great elevation. They are now and then seen to sail among the Turkey Buzzards or Carrion Crows, in company with their relatives the Fish-Crows, none of the other birds, however, shewing the least antipathy towards them, although the Vultures manifest dislike whenever a White-headed Eagle comes among them.

In the latter part of autumn and in winter, in the Southern States, this Crow is particularly fond of frequenting burnt grounds. Even while the fire is raging in one part of the fields, the woods, or the prairies, where tall grass abounds, the Crows are seen in great numbers in the other, picking up and devouring the remains of mice and other small quadrupeds, as well as lizards, snakes, and insects, which have been partly destroyed by the flames. At the same season they retire in immense numbers to roost by the margins of ponds, lakes, and rivers, covered with a luxuriant growth of rank weeds or cat-tails. They may be seen proceeding to such places more than an hour before sunset, in long straggling lines, and in silence, and are joined by the Grakles, Starlings, and Reed Birds, while the Fish-Crows retire from the very same parts to the interior of the woods many miles distant from any shores.

No sooner has the horizon brightened at the approach of day, than the Crows sound a reveillé, and then with mellowed notes, as it were, engage in a general thanksgiving for the peaceful repose they have enjoyed. After this they emit their usual barking notes, as if consulting each other respecting the course they ought to follow. Then parties in succession fly off to pursue their avocations, and relieve the reeds from the weight that bent them down.

The Crow is extremely courageous in encountering any of its winged enemies. Several individuals may frequently be seen pursuing a Hawk or an Eagle with remarkable vigour, although I never saw or heard of one pouncing on any bird for the purpose of preying on it. They now and then teaze the Vultures, when those foul birds are alighted on trees, with their wings spread out, but they soon desist, for the Vultures pay no attention to them.

The most remarkable feat of the Crow, is the nicety with which it, like the Jay, pierces an egg with its bill, in order to carry it off, and eat it with security. In this manner I have seen it steal, one after another, all the eggs of a wild Turkey's nest. You will perceive, reader, that I endeavour to speak of the Crow with all due impartiality, not wishing by any means to conceal its faults, nor withholding my testimony to its merits, which are such as I can well assure the farmer, that were it not for its race, thousands of corn stalks would every year fall prostrate, in consequence of being cut over close to the ground by the destructive grubs which are called "cutworms."

I never saw a pet Crow in the United States, and therefore cannot say with how much accuracy they may imitate the human voice, or, indeed, if they possess the power of imitating it at all, which I very much doubt, as in their natural state they never evince any talents for mimicry. I cannot say if it possess the thieving propensities attributed by authors to the European Crow.

Its gait, while on the ground, is elevated and graceful, its ordinary mode of progression being a sedate walk, although it occasionally hops when under excitement. It not unfrequently alights on the backs of cattle, to pick out the worms lurking in their skin, in the same manner as the Magpie, Fish-Crow, and Cow-bird. Its note or cry may be imitated by the syllables *cāw*, *cāw*, *cāw*, being different from the cry of the European Carrion Crow, and resembling the distant bark of a small dog.

At Pittsburgh in Pennsylvania I saw a pair of Crows perfectly white, in the possession of Mr LAMPDIN, the owner of the museum there, who assured me that five which were found in the nest were of the same colour.

I have placed the pensive oppressed Crow of our country on a beautiful branch of the Black Walnut tree, loaded with nuts, on the lower twig of which I have represented the delicate nest of our Common Humming Bird, to fulfil the promise which I made when writing the history of that species for my first volume.

In conclusion, I would again address our farmers, and tell them that if they persist in killing Crows, the best season for doing so is when their corn begins to ripen.

The Chimney Swallow, or American Swift

Cypselus pelasgius, TEMM.

(PLATE 31)

SINCE our country has furnished thousands of convenient places for this Swallow to breed in, free from storms, snakes, or quadrupeds, it has abandoned, with a judgment worthy of remark, its former abodes in the hollows of trees, and taken possession of the chimneys, which emit no smoke in the summer season. For this reason, no doubt, it has obtained the name by which it is generally known. I well remember the time when, in Lower Kentucky, Indiana, and Illinois, many resorted to excavated branches and trunks, for the purpose of breeding; nay, so strong is the influence of original habit, that not a few still betake themselves to such places, not only to roost, but also to breed, especially in those wild portions of our country that can scarcely be said to be inhabited. In such instances, they appear to be as nice in the choice of a tree, as they generally are in our cities in the choice of a chimney, wherein to roost, before they leave us. Sycamores of gigantic growth, and having a mere shell of bark and wood to support them, seem to suit them best, and wherever I have met with one of those patriarchs of the forest rendered habitable by decay, there I have found the Swallows breeding in spring and summer, and afterwards roosting until the time of their departure. I had a tree of this kind cut down, which contained about thirty of their nests in its trunk, and one in each of the hollow branches.

The nest, whether placed in a tree or chimney, consists of small dry twigs, which are procured by the birds in a singular manner. While on wing, the Chimney Swallows are seen in great numbers whirling round the tops of some decayed or dead tree, as if in pursuit of their insect prey. Their movements at this time are extremely rapid; they throw their body suddenly against the twig, grapple it with their feet, and by an instantaneous jerk, snap it off short, and proceed with it to the place intended for the nest. The Frigate Pelican sometimes employs the same method for a similar purpose, carrying away the stick in its bill, in place of holding it with its feet.

The Swallow fixes the first sticks on the wood, the rock, or the chimney wall, by means of its saliva, arranging them in a semicircular form, crossing and interweaving them, so as to extend the framework outwards. The whole is afterwards glued together with saliva, which is spread around it for an inch or more, to fasten it securely. When the nest is in a chimney, it is generally placed on the east side, and is from five to eight feet from the entrance; but in the hollow of a tree, where only they breed in communities, it is placed high or low according to convenience. The fabric, which is very frail, now and then gives way, either under the pressure of the parents and young, or during sudden bursts of heavy rain, when the whole is dashed to the ground. The eggs are from four to six, and of a pure white colour. Two broods are raised in the season.

The flight of this species is performed somewhat in the manner of the European Swift, but in a more hurried although continued style, and generally by repeated flappings, unless when courtship is going on, on which occasion it is frequently seen sailing with its wings fixed as it were, both sexes as they glide through the air issuing a shrill rattling twitter, and the female receiving the caresses of the male. At other times it is seen ranging far and wide at a considerable elevation over the forests and cities; again, in wet weather, it flies close over the ground; and anon it skims the water, to drink and bathe. When about to descend into a hollow tree or a chimney, its flight, always rapid, is suddenly interrupted as if by magic, for down it goes in an instant, whirling in a peculiar manner, and whirring with its wings, so as to produce a sound in the chimney like the rumbling of very distant thunder. They never alight on trees or on the ground. If one is caught and placed on the latter, it can only move in a very awkward fashion. I believe that the old birds sometimes fly at night, and have reason to think that the young are fed at such times, as I have heard the whirring sound of the former, and the acknowledging cries of the latter, during calm and clear nights.

When the young accidentally fall, which sometimes happens, although the nest should remain, they scramble up again, by means of their sharp claws, lifting one foot after another, in the manner of young Wood Ducks, and supporting themselves with their tail. Some days before the young are able to fly, they scramble up the walls to near the mouth of the chimney, where they are fed. Any observer may discover this, as he sees the parents passing close over them, without entering the funnel. The same occurrence takes place when they are bred in a tree.

In the cities, these birds make choice of a particular chimney for their roosting place, where, early in spring, before they have begun building, both sexes resort in multitudes, from an hour or more before sunset, until long after dark. Before entering the aperture, they fly round and over it many times, but finally go in one at a time, until hurried by the lateness of the hour, several drop in together. They cling to the wall with their claws, supporting themselves also by their sharp tail, until the dawn, when, with a roaring sound, the whole pass out almost at once. Whilst at St Francisville in Louisiana, I took the trouble of counting how many entered one chimney before dark. I sat at a window not far from the spot, and reckoned upwards of a thousand, having missed a considerable number. The place at that time contained about a hundred houses, and no doubt existed in my mind that the greater number of these birds were on their way southward, and had merely stopped there for the night.

Immediately after my arrival at Louisville, in the State of Kentucky, I became acquainted with the hospitable and amiable Major WILLIAM CROGHAN and his family. While talking one day about birds, he asked me if I had seen the trees in which the Swallows were supposed to spend the winter, but which they only entered, he said, for the purpose of roosting. Answering in the affirmative, I was informed that on my way back to town, there was a tree remarkable on account of the immense numbers that resorted to it, and the place in which it stood was described to me. I found it to be a sycamore, nearly destitute of branches, sixty or seventy feet high, between seven and eight feet in diameter at the base, and about five for the distance of forty feet up, where the stump of a broken hollowed branch, about two feet in diameter, made out from the main stem. This was the place at which the Swallows entered. On closely examining the tree, I found it hard, but hollow to near the roots. It was now about four o'clock after noon, in the month of July. Swallows were flying over Jeffersonville, Louisville, and the woods around, but there were none near the tree. I proceeded home, and shortly after returned on foot. The sun was going down behind the Silver Hills; the evening was beautiful; thousands of Swallows were flying closely above me, and three or four at a time were pitching into the hole, like bees hurrying into their hive. I remained, my head leaning on the tree, listening to the roaring noise made within by the birds as they settled and arranged themselves, until it was quite dark, when I left the place, although I was convinced that many more had to enter. I did not pretend to count them, for the number was too great, and the birds rushed to the entrance so thick as to baffle the attempt. I had scarcely returned to Louisville, when a violent thunderstorm passed suddenly over the town, and its appearance made me think that the hurry of the Swallows to enter the tree was caused by their anxiety to avoid it. I thought of the Swallows almost the whole night, so anxious had I become to ascertain their number, before the time of their departure should arrive.

Next morning I rose early enough to reach the place long before the least appearance of daylight, and placed my head against the tree. All was silent within. I remained in that posture probably twenty minutes, when suddenly I thought the great tree was giving way, and coming down upon me. Instinctively I sprung from it, but when I looked up to it again, what was my astonishment to see it standing as firm as ever. The Swallows were now pouring out in a black continued stream. I ran back to my post, and listened in amazement to the noise within, which I could compare to nothing else than the sound of a large wheel revolving under a powerful stream. It was yet dusky, so that I could hardly see the hour on my watch, but I estimated the time which they took in getting out at more than thirty minutes. After their departure, no noise was heard within, and they dispersed in every direction with the quickness of thought.

I immediately formed the project of examining the interior of the tree, which, as my kind friend, Major CROGHAN, had told me, proved the most remarkable I had ever met with. This I did, in company with a hunting associate. We went provided with a strong line and a rope, the first of which we, after several trials, succeeded in throwing across the broken branch. Fastening the rope to the line we drew it up, and pulled it over until it reached the ground again. Provided with the longest cane we could find, I mounted the tree by the rope, without accident, and at length seated myself at ease on the broken branch; but my labour was fruitless, for I could see nothing through the hole, and the cane, which was about fifteen feet long, touched nothing on the sides of the tree within that could give any information. I came down fatigued and disappointed.

The next day I hired a man, who cut a hole at the base of the tree. The shell was only eight or nine inches thick, and the axe soon brought the inside to view, disclosing a matted mass of exuviæ, with rotten feathers reduced to a kind of mould, in which, however, I could perceive fragments of insects and quills. I had a passage cleared, or rather bored through this mass, for nearly six feet. This operation took up a good deal of time, and knowing by experience that if the birds should notice the hole below, they would abandon the tree, I had it carefully closed. The Swallows came as usual that night, and I did not disturb them for several days. At last, provided with a dark lantern, I went with my companion about nine in the evening, determined to have a full view of the interior of the tree. The hole was opened with caution. I scrambled up the sides of the mass of exuviæ, and my friend followed. All was perfectly silent. Slowly and gradually I brought the light of the lantern to bear on the sides of the hole above us, when we saw the Swallows clinging side by side, covering the whole surface of the excavation. In no instance did I see one above another. Satisfied with the sight, I closed the lantern. We then caught and killed with as much care as possible more than a hundred, stowing them away in our pockets and bosoms, and slid down into the open air. We observed that, while on this visit, not a bird had dropped its dung upon us. Closing the entrance, we marched towards Louisville perfectly elated. On examining the birds which we had procured, a hundred and fifteen in number, we found only six females. Eighty-seven were adult males; of the remaining twenty-two the sex could not be ascertained, and I had no doubt that they were young of that year's first brood, the flesh and quill-feathers being tender and soft.

Let us now make a rough calculation of the number that clung to the tree. The space beginning at the pile of feathers and moulded exuviæ, and ending at the entrance of the hole above, might be fully 25 feet in height, with a breadth of 15 feet, supposing the tree to be 5 feet in diameter at an average. There would thus be 375 feet square of surface. Each square foot, allowing a bird to cover a space of 3 inches by 1½, which is more than enough, judging from the manner in which they were packed, would contain 32 birds. The number of Swallows, therefore, that roosted in this single tree was 9000.

I watched the motions of the Swallows, and when the young birds that had been reared in the chimneys of Louisville, Jeffersonville, and the houses of the neighbourhood, or the trees suited for the purpose, had left their native recesses, I visited the tree on the 2d day of August. I concluded that the numbers resorting to it had not increased; but I found many more females and young than males, among upwards of fifty, which were caught and opened. Day after day I watched the tree. On the 13th of August, not more than two or three hundred came there to roost. On the 18th of the same month, not one did I see near it, and only a few scattered individuals were passing, as if moving southward. In September I entered the tree at night, but not a bird was in it. Once more I went to it in February, when the weather was very cold; and perfectly satisfied that all these Swallows had left our country, I finally closed the entrance, and left off visiting it.

May arrived, bringing with its vernal warmth the wanderers of the air, and I saw their number daily augmenting, as they resorted to the tree to roost. About the beginning of June, I took it in my head to close the aperture above, with a bundle of straw, which with a string I could draw off whenever I might chuse. The result was curious enough; the birds as usual came to the tree towards night; they assembled, passed and repassed, with apparent discomfort, until I perceived many flying off to a great distance, on which I removed the straw, when many entered the hole, and continued to do so until I could no longer see them from the ground.

I left Louisville, having removed my residence to Henderson, and did not see the tree until five years after, when I still found the Swallows resorting to it. The pieces of wood with which I had closed the entrance had rotted, or had been carried off, and the hole was again completely filled with exuviæ and mould. During a severe storm, their ancient tenement at length gave way, and came to the ground.

General WILLIAM CLARK assured me that he saw this species on the whole of his route to the Pacific, and there can be no doubt that in those wilds it still breeds in trees or rocky caverns.

Its food consists entirely of insects, the pellets composed of the indigestible parts of which it disgorges. It is furnished with glands which supply the unctuous matter with which it fastens its nest.

This species does not appear to extend its migrations farther east than the British provinces of New Brunswick and Nova Scotia. It is unknown in Newfoundland and Labrador; nor was it until the 29th of May that I saw some at Eastport in Maine, where a few breed.

The Golden Eagle

Falco Chrysaëtos, LINN.

(PLATE 32)

IN THE early part of February 1833, while at Boston in Massachusetts, I chanced to call on Mr GREENWOOD, the proprietor of the Museum of that city, who informed me that he had purchased a very fine Eagle, the name of which he was desirous of knowing. The bird was produced, and as I directed my eye towards its own deep, bold and stern one, I recognised it at once as belonging to the species whose habits I have here to describe, and I determined to obtain possession of it. Mr GREENWOOD, who is a very kind as well as talented person, being asked if he would part with the noble bird, readily answered in the affirmative, and left to me to determine its value, which I accordingly did, and carried off my purchase. His report of the manner in which the royal prisoner had been secured, was as follows:—"The man from which I bought it had it in the same cage it is now in, on the top of his market-waggon and when I asked its price, said that the Eagle had been caught in a spring-trap set for foxes on the white mountains of New Hampshire. One morning the trap was missing, but on searching for it, it was at last discovered more than a mile from its original place, and held the bird by one of its toes only. The eagle flew about through the woods for several hundred yards, but was at last with difficulty secured. This took place a few days ago."

The Eagle was immediately conveyed to my place of residence, covered by a blanket, to save him, in his adversity, from the gaze of the people. I placed the cage so as to afford me a good view of the captive, and I must acknowledge that as I watched his eye, and observed his looks of proud disdain, I felt towards him not so generously as I ought to have done. At times I was half inclined to restore to him his freedom, that he might return to his native mountains; nay, I several times thought how pleasing it would be to see him spread out his broad wings and sail away towards the rocks of his wild haunts; but then, reader, some one seemed to whisper that I ought to take the portrait of the magnificent bird, and I abandoned the more generous design of setting him at liberty, for the express purpose of shewing you his semblance.

I occupied myself a whole day in watching his movements; on the next I came to a determination as to the position in which I might best represent him; and on the third thought of how I could take away his life with the least pain to him. I consulted several persons on the subject, and among others my most worthy and generous friend, GEORGE PARKMAN, Esq. M. D., who kindly visited my family every day. He spoke of suffocating him by means of burning charcoal, of killing him by electricity, &c. and we both concluded that the first method would probably be the easiest for ourselves, and the least painful to him. Accordingly the bird was removed in his prison into a very small room, and closely covered with blankets, into which was introduced a pan of lighted charcoal, when the windows and door were fastened, and the blankets tucked in beneath the cage. I waited, expecting every moment to hear him fall down from his perch; but after listening for *hours*, I opened the door, raised the blankets, and peeped under them amidst a mass of suffocating fumes. There stood the Eagle on his perch, with his bright unflinching eye turned towards me, and as lively and vigorous as ever! Instantly re-closing every aperture, I resumed my station at the door, and towards midnight, not having heard the least noise, I again took a peep at my victim. He was still uninjured, although the air of the closet was insupportable to my son and myself, and that of the adjoining apartment began to feel unpleasant. I persevered, however, for ten hours in all, when finding that the charcoal fumes would not produce the desired effect, I re-tired to rest wearied and disappointed.

Early next morning I tried the charcoal anew, adding to it a quantity of sulphur, but we were nearly driven from our home in a few hours by the stifling vapours, while the noble bird continued to stand erect, and to look defiance at us whenever we approached his post of martyrdom. His fierce demeanour precluded all internal application, and at last I was compelled to resort to a method always used as the last expe-dient, and a most effectual one. I thrust a long pointed piece of steel through his heart, when my proud prisoner instantly fell dead, without even ruffling a feather.

I sat up nearly the whole of another night to outline him, and worked so constantly at the drawing, that it nearly cost me my life. I was suddenly seized with a spasmodic affection, that much alarmed my family, and completely prostrated me for some days; but, thanks to my heavenly Preserver, and the immediate and unremitting attention of my most worthy friends Drs PARKMAN, SHATTUCK, and WARREN, I was soon restored to health, and enabled to pursue my labours. The drawing of this Eagle took me fourteen days, and I had never before laboured so incessantly excepting at that of the Wild Turkey.

The Golden Eagle, although a permanent resident in the United States, is of rare occurrence there, it being seldom that one sees more than a pair or two in the course of a year, unless he be an inhabitant of the mountains, or of the large plains spread out at their base. I have seen a few of them on the wing along the shores of the Hudson, others on the upper parts of the Mississippi, some among the Alleghanies, and a pair in the State of Maine. At Labrador we saw an individual sailing, at the height of a few yards, over the moss-covered surface of the dreary rocks.

Although possessed of a powerful flight, it has not the speed of many Hawks, nor even of the White-headed Eagle. It cannot, like the latter, pursue and seize on the wing the prey it longs for, but is obliged to glide down through the air for a certain height to insure the success of its enterprise. The keenness of its eye, however, makes up for this defect, and enables it to spy, at a great distance, the objects on which it preys; and it seldom misses its aim, as it falls with the swiftness of a meteor towards the spot on which they are concealed. When at a great height in the air, its gyrations are uncommonly beautiful, being slow and of wide circuit, and becoming the majesty of the king of birds. It often continues them for hours at a time, with apparently the greatest ease.

The nest of this noble species is always placed on an inaccessible shelf of some rugged precipice,—never, that I am aware of, on a tree. It is of great size, flat, and consists merely of a few dead sticks and brambles, so bare at times that the eggs might be said to be deposited on the naked rock. They are generally two, sometimes three, having a length of 3½ inches, and a diameter at the broadest part of 2½ . The shell is thick and smooth, dull white, brushed over, as it were, with undefined patches of brown, which are most numerous at the larger end. The period at which they are deposited, is the end of February or the beginning of March. I have never seen the young when newly hatched, but know that they do not leave the nest until nearly able to provide for themselves, when their parents drive them off from their home, and finally from their hunting grounds. A pair of these birds bred on the rocky shores of the Hudson for eight successive years, and in the same chasm of the rock.

Their notes are harsh and sharp, resembling at times the barking of a dog, especially about the breeding season, when they become extremely noisy and turbulent, flying more swiftly than at other times, alighting more frequently, and evincing a fretfulness which is not so observable after their eggs are laid.

They are capable of remaining without food for several days at a time, and eat voraciously whenever they find an opportunity. Young fawns, racoons, hares, wild turkeys, and other large birds, are their usual food, and they devour putrid flesh only when hard pressed by hunger, none alighting on carrion at any other time. They are nice in cleaning the skin or plucking the feathers of their prey, although they swallow their food in large pieces, often mixed with hair and bones, which they afterwards disgorge. They are muscular, strong, and hardy, capable of bearing extreme cold without injury, and of pursuing their avocations in the most tempestuous weather. A full grown female weighs about twelve pounds, the male about two pounds and a half less. This species seldom removes far from its place of residence, and the attachment of two individuals of different sexes appears to continue for years.

They do not obtain the full beauty of their plumage until the fourth year, the Ring-tailed Eagle of authors being the young in the dress of the second and third years. Our northwestern Indians are fond of ornamenting their persons and implements of war with the tail-feathers of this Eagle, which they kill or raise expressly for that purpose.

I conclude my account of this species with an anecdote relating to it given in one of Dr RUSH's lectures upon the effects of fear on man. During the revolutionary war, a company of soldiers were stationed near the highlands of the Hudson River. A Golden Eagle had placed her nest in a cleft of the rocks half way between the summit and the river. A soldier was let down by his companions suspended by a rope fastened around his body. When he reached the nest, he suddenly found himself attacked by the Eagle; in self defence he drew the only weapon about him, his knife, and made repeated passes at the bird, when accidentally he cut the rope almost off. It began unravelling; those above hastily drew him up, and relieved him from his perilous situation at the moment when he expected to be precipitated to the bottom. The Doctor stated that so powerful was the effect of the fear the soldier had experienced whilst in danger, that ere three days had elapsed his hair became quite grey.

The Canada Goose

Anser canadensis, VIEILL.

(PLATE 33)

ALTHOUGH the Canada Goose is considered as a northern species, the number of individuals that remain at all seasons in the milder latitudes, and in different portions of the United States, fully entitles this bird to be looked upon as a permanent resident there. It is found to breed sparingly at the present day, by many of the lakes, lagoons, and large streams of our Western Districts, on the Missouri, the Mississippi, the lower parts of the Ohio, on Lake Erie, the lakes farther north, and in several large pools situated in the interior of the eastern parts of the States of Massachusetts and Maine. As you advance farther toward the east and north, you find it breeding more abundantly. While on my way to Labrador, I found it in the Magdeleine Islands, early in June, sitting on its eggs. In the Island of Anticosti there is a considerable stream, near the borders of which great numbers are said to be annually reared; and in Labrador these birds breed in every suitable marshy plain. The greater number of those which visit us from still more northern regions, return in the vernal season, like many other species, to the dismal countries which gave them birth.

Few if any of these birds spend the winter in Nova Scotia, my friend Mr THOMAS M'CULLOCH having informed me that he never saw one about Pictou at that period. In spring, as they proceed northward, thousands are now and then seen passing high in the air; but in autumn, the flocks are considerably smaller, and fly much lower. During their spring movements, the principal places at which they stop to wait for milder days are Bay Chaleur, the Magdeleine Islands, Newfoundland, and Labrador, at all of which some remain to breed and spend the summer.

The general spring migration of the Canada Goose, may be stated to commence with the first melting of the snows in our Middle and Western Districts, or from the 20th of March to the end of April; but the precise time of its departure is always determined by the advance of the season, and the vast flocks that winter in the great savannahs or swampy prairies south-west of the Mississippi, such as exist in Opellousas, on the borders of the Arkansas River, or in the dismal "Ever Glades" of the Floridas, are often seen to take their flight, and steer their course northward, a month earlier than the first of the above mentioned periods. It is indeed probable that the individuals of a species most remote from the point at which the greater number ultimately assemble, commence their flight earlier than those which have passed the winter in stations nearer to it.

It is my opinion that all the birds of this species, which leave our States and territories each spring for the distant north, pair before they depart. This, no doubt, necessarily results from the nature of their place of summer residence, where the genial season is so short as scarcely to afford them sufficient time for bringing up their young and renewing their plumage, before the rigours of advancing winter force them to commence their flight towards milder countries. This opinion is founded on the following facts:—I have frequently observed large flocks of Geese, in ponds, on marshy grounds, or even on dry sand bars, the mated birds renewing their courtship as early as the month of January, while the other individuals would be contending or coquetting for hours every day, until all seemed satisfied with the choice they had made, after which, although they remained together, any person could easily perceive that they were careful to keep in pairs. I have observed also that the older the birds, the shorter were the preliminaries of their courtship, and that the barren individuals were altogether insensible to the manifestations of love and mutual affection that were displayed around them. The bachelors and old maids, whether in regret, or not caring to be disturbed by the bustle, quietly moved aside, and lay down on the grass or sand at some distance from the rest; and whenever the flocks rose on wing, or betook themselves to the water, these forlorn birds always kept behind. This mode of preparing for the breeding season has appeared to me the more remarkable, that, on reaching the place appointed for their summer residence, the birds of a flock separate in pairs, which form their nests and rear their young at a considerable distance from each other.

It is extremely amusing to witness the courtship of the Canada Goose in all its stages; and let me assure you, reader, that although a Gander does not strut before his beloved with the pomposity of a Turkey, or the grace of a Dove, his ways are quite as agreeable to the female of his choice. I can imagine before me one who has just accomplished the defeat of another male after a struggle of half an hour or more. He advances gallantly towards the object of contention, his head scarcely raised an inch from the ground, his bill open to its full stretch, his fleshy tongue elevated, his eyes darting fiery glances, and as he moves he hisses loudly, while the emotion which he experiences, causes his quills to shake, and his feathers to rustle. Now he is close to her who in his eyes is all loveliness; his neck bending gracefully in all directions, passes all round her, and occasionally touches her body; and as she congratulates him on his victory, and acknowledges his affection, they move their necks in a hundred curious ways. At this moment fierce jealousy urges the defeated gander to renew his efforts to obtain his love; he advances apace, his eye glowing with the fire of rage; he shakes his broad wings, ruffles up his whole plumage, and as he rushes on the foe, hisses with the intensity of anger. The whole flock seems to stand amazed, and opening up a space, the birds gather round to view the combat. The bold bird who has been caressing his mate, scarcely deigns to take notice of his foe, but seems to send a scornful glance towards him. He of the mortified feelings, however, raises his body, half opens his sinewy wings, and with a powerful blow, sends forth his defiance. The affront cannot be borne in the presence of so large a company, nor indeed is there much disposition to bear it in any circumstances; the blow is returned with vigour, the aggressor reels for a moment, but he soon recovers, and now the combat rages. Were the weapons more deadly, feats of chivalry would now be performed; as it is, thrust and blow succeed each other like the strokes of hammers driven by sturdy forgers. But now, the mated gander has caught hold of his antagonist's head with his bill; no bull-dog could cling faster to his victim; he squeezes him with all the energy of rage, lashes him with his powerful wings, and at length drives him away, spreads out his pinions, runs with joy to his mate, and fills the air with cries of exultation.

But now, see yonder, not a couple, but half a dozen of ganders are engaged in battle! Some desperado, it seems, has
fallen upon a mated bird, and several bystanders, as if sensible
of the impropriety of such conduct, rush to the assistance of
the wronged one. How they strive and tug, biting, and striking with their wings! and how their feathers fly about! Exhausted, abashed, and mortified, the presumptuous intruder
retreats in disgrace;—there he lies almost breathless on the
sand!

Such are the conflicts of these ardent lovers, and so full of
courage and of affection towards their females are they, that
the approach of a male invariably ruffles their tempers as well
as their feathers. No sooner has the goose laid her first egg,
than her bold mate stands almost erect by her side, watching
even the rustling sound of the breeze. The least noise brings
from him a sound of anger. Should he spy a racoon making
its way among the grass, he walks up to him undauntedly,
hurls a vigorous blow at him, and drives him instantly away.
Nay I doubt if man himself, if unarmed, would come off unscathed in such an encounter. The brave gander does more;
for, if imminent danger excite him, he urges his mate to fly
off, and resolutely remains near the nest until he is assured of
her safety, when he also betakes himself to flight, mocking as
it were by his notes his disappointed enemy.

Suppose all to be peace and quiet around the fond pair, and
the female to be sitting in security upon her eggs. The nest is
placed near the bank of a noble stream or lake; the clear sky
is spread over the scene, the bright beams glitter on the
waters, and a thousand odorous flowers give beauty to the
swamp which of late was so dismal. The gander passes to and
fro over the liquid element, moving as if lord of the waters;
now he inclines his head with a graceful curve, now sips to
quench his thirst; and, as noontide has arrived, he paddles his
way towards the shore, to relieve for a while his affectionate
and patient consort. The lisping sounds of their offspring are
heard through the shell; their little bills have formed a breach
in the inclosing walls; full of life, and bedecked with beauty,
they come forth, with tottering steps and downy covering.
Toward the water they now follow their careful parent, they
reach the border of the stream, their mother already floats on

the loved element, one after another launches forth, and now the flock glides gently along. What a beautiful sight! Close by the grassy margin, the mother slowly leads her innocent younglings; to one she shews the seed of the floating grass, to another points out the crawling slug. Her careful eye watches the cruel turtle, the garfish, and the pike, that are lurking for their prey, and, with head inclined, she glances upwards to the eagle or the gull that are hovering over the water in search of food. A ferocious bird dashes at her young ones; she instantly plunges beneath the surface, and, in the twinkling of an eye, her brood disappear after her; now they are among the thick rushes, with nothing above water but their little bills. The mother is marching towards the land, having lisped to her brood in accents so gentle that none but they and her mate can understand their import, and all are safely lodged under cover until the disappointed eagle or gull bears away.

More than six weeks have now elapsed. The down of the goslings, which was at first soft and tufty, has become coarse and hairlike. Their wings are edged with quills, and their bodies bristled with feathers. They have increased in size, and, living in the midst of abundance, they have become fat, so that on shore they make their way with difficulty, and as they are yet unable to fly, the greatest care is required to save them from their numerous enemies. They grow apace, and now the burning days of August are over. They are able to fly with ease from one shore to another, and as each successive night the hoarfrosts cover the country, and the streams are closed over by the ice, the family joins that in their neighbourhood, which is also joined by others. At length they spy the advance of a snow-storm, when the ganders with one accord sound the order for their departure.

After many wide circlings, the flock has risen high in the thin air, and an hour or more is spent in teaching the young the order in which they are to move. But now, the host has been marshalled, and off it starts, shewing, as it proceeds, at one time an extended front, at another a single lengthened file, and now arraying itself in an angular form. The old males advance in front, the females follow, the young come in succession according to their strength, the weakest forming the rear. Should one feel fatigued, his position is changed in the ranks, and he assumes a place in the wake of another, who cleaves the air before him; perhaps the parent bird flies for a while by his side to encourage him. Two, three, or more days elapse before they reach a secure resting place. The fat with which they were loaded at their departure has rapidly wasted; they are fatigued, and experience the keen gnawings of hunger; but now they spy a wide estuary, towards which they direct their course. Alighting on the water, they swim to the beach, stand, and gaze around them; the young full of joy, the old full of fear, for well are they aware that many foes have been waiting their arrival. Silent all night remains the flock, but not inactive; with care they betake themselves to the grassy shores, where they allay the cravings of appetite, and recruit their wasted strength. Soon as the early dawn lightens the surface of the deep they rise into the air, extend their lines, and proceed southward, until arriving in some place where they think they may be enabled to rest in security, they remain during the winter. At length, after many annoyances, they joyfully perceive the return of spring, and prepare to fly away from their greatest enemy man.

The Canada Goose often arrives in our Western and Middle Districts as early as the beginning of September, and does not by any means confine itself to the seashore. Indeed, my opinion is, that for every hundred seen during the winter along our large bays and estuaries, as many thousands may be found in the interior of the country, where they frequent the large ponds, rivers, and wet savannahs. During my residence in the State of Kentucky, I never spent a winter without observing immense flocks of these birds, especially in the neighbourhood of Henderson, where I have killed many hundreds of them, as well as on the Falls of the Ohio at Louisville, and in the neighbouring country, which abounds in ponds over-grown with grasses and various species of Nympheæ, on the seeds of which they greedily feed. Indeed all the lakes situated within a few miles of the Missouri and Mississippi, or their tributaries, are still amply supplied with them from the middle of autumn to the beginning of spring. In these places, too, I have found them breeding, although sparingly. It seems to me more than probable, that the species bred abundantly in the temperate parts of North America before the white population extended over them. This opinion is founded on the relations of many old and respectable citizens of our country, and in particular of General GEORGE CLARK, one of the first settlers on the banks of the Ohio, who, at a very advanced age, assured me that, fifty years before the period when our conversation took place (about seventy-five years from the present time), wild geese were so plentiful at all seasons of the year, that he was in the habit of having them shot to feed his soldiers, then garrisoned near Vincennes, in the present State of Indiana. My father, who travelled down the Ohio shortly after BRADOCK's defeat, related the same to me; and I, as well as many persons now residing at Louisville in Kentucky, well remember that, twenty-five or thirty years ago, it was quite easy to procure young Canada Geese in the ponds around. So late as 1819, I have met with the nests, eggs, and young of this species near Henderson. However, as I have already said, the greater number remove far north to breed. I have never heard of an instance of their breeding in the Southern States. Indeed, so uncongenial to their constitution seems the extreme heat of these parts to be, that the attempts made to rear them in a state of domestication very rarely succeed.

The Canada Goose, when it remains with us to breed, begins to form its nest in March, making choice of some retired place not far from the water, generally among the rankest grass, and not unfrequently under a bush. It is carefully formed of dry plants of various kinds, and is of a large size, flat, and raised to the height of several inches. Once only did I find a nest elevated above the ground. It was placed on the stump of a large tree, standing in the centre of a small pond, about twenty feet high, and contained five eggs. As the spot was very secluded, I did not disturb the birds, anxious as I was to see in what manner they should convey the young to the water. But in this I was disappointed, for, on going to the nest, near the time at which I expected the process of incubation to terminate, I had the mortification to find that a racoon, or some other animal, had destroyed the whole of the eggs, and that the birds had abandoned the place. The greatest number of eggs which I have found in the nest of this species was nine, which I think is more by three than these birds usually lay in a wild state. In the nests of those which I have had in a domesticated state, I have sometimes counted as many as eleven, several of them, however, usually proving unproductive. The eggs measure, on an average, 3½ inches by 2½, are thick shelled, rather smooth, and of a very dull yellowish-green colour. The period of incubation is twenty-eight days. They never have more than one brood in a season, unless their eggs are removed or broken at an early period.

The young follow their parents to the water a day or two after they have issued from the egg, but generally return to land to repose in the sunshine in the evening, and pass the night there under their mother, who employs all imaginable care to ensure their comfort and safety, as does her mate, who never leaves her during incubation for a longer time than is necessary for procuring food, and takes her place at intervals. Both remain with their brood until the following spring. It is during the breeding-season that the gander displays his courage and strength to the greatest advantage. I knew one that appeared larger than usual, and of which all the lower parts were of a rich cream colour. It returned three years in succession to a large pond a few miles from the mouth of Green River in Kentucky, and whenever I visited the nest, it seemed to look upon me with utter contempt. It would stand in a stately attitude, until I reached within a few yards of the nest, when suddenly lowering its head, and shaking it as if it were dislocated from the neck, it would open its wings, and launch into the air, flying directly at me. So daring was this fine fellow, that in two instances he struck me a blow with one of his wings on the right arm, which, for an instant, I thought, was broken. I observed that immediately after such an effort to defend his nest and mate, he would run swiftly towards them, pass his head and neck several times over and around the female, and again assume his attitude of defiance.

Always intent on making experiments, I thought of endeavouring to conciliate this bold son of the waters. For this purpose I always afterwards took with me several ears of corn, which I shelled, and threw towards him. It remained untouched for several days; but I succeeded at last, and before the end of a week both birds fed freely on the grain even in my sight! I felt much pleasure on this occasion, and repeating my visit daily, found, that before the eggs were hatched, they would allow me to approach within a few feet of them, although they never suffered me to touch them. Whenever I attempted this the male met my fingers with his bill, and bit me so severely that I gave it up. The great beauty and courage of the male rendered me desirous of obtaining possession of him. I had marked the time at which the young were likely to appear, and on the preceding day I baited with corn a large coop made of twine, and waited until he should enter. He walked in, I drew the string, and he was my prisoner. The next morning the female was about to lead her offspring to the river, which was distant nearly half a mile, when I caught the whole of the young birds, and with them the mother too, who came within reach in attempting to rescue one of her brood, and had them taken home. There I took a cruel method of preventing their escape, for with a knife I pinioned each of them on the same side, and turned them loose in my garden, where I had a small but convenient artificial pond. For more than a fortnight, both the old birds appeared completely cowed. Indeed, for some days I felt apprehensive that they would abandon the care of the young ones. However, with much attention, I succeeded in rearing the latter by feeding them abundantly with the larvæ of locusts, which they ate greedily, as well as with corn-meal moistened with water, and the whole flock, consisting of eleven individuals, went on prosperously. In December the weather became intensely cold, and I observed that now and then the gander would spread his wings, and sound a loud note, to which the female first, and then all the young ones in succession, would respond, when they would all run as far as the ground allowed them in a southerly direction, and attempt to fly off. I kept the whole flock three years. The old pair never bred while in my possession, but two pairs of the young ones did, one of them raising three, the other seven. They all bore a special enmity to dogs, and shewed dislike to cats; but they manifested a still greater animosity towards an old swan and a wild turkey-cock which I had. I found them useful in clearing the garden of slugs and snails; and although they now and then nipped the vegetables, I liked their company. When I left

Henderson, my flock of geese was given away, and I have not since heard how it has fared with them.

On one of my shooting excursions in the same neighbourhood, I chanced one day to kill a wild Canada Goose, which, on my return, was sent to the kitchen. The cook, while dressing it, found in it an egg ready for being laid, and brought it to me. It was placed under a common hen, and in due time hatched. Two years afterwards the bird thus raised, mated with a male of the same species, and produced a brood. This goose was so gentle that she would suffer any person to caress her, and would readily feed from the hand. She was smaller than usual, but in every other respect as perfect as any I have ever seen. At the period of migration she shewed by her movements less desire to fly off than any other I have known; but her mate, who had once been free, did not participate in this apathy.

I have not been able to discover why many of those birds which I have known to have been reared from the egg, or to have been found when very young and brought up in captivity, were so averse to reproduce, unless they were naturally sterile. I have seen several that had been kept for more than eight years, without ever mating during that period, while other individuals had young the second spring after their birth. I have also observed that an impatient male would sometimes abandon the females of his species, and pay his addresses to a common tame goose, by which a brood would in due time be brought up, and would thrive. That this tardiness is not the case in the wild state I feel pretty confident, for I have observed having broods of their own many individuals which, by their size, the dulness of their plumage, and such other marks as are known to the practical ornithologist, I judged to be not more than fifteen or sixteen months old. I have therefore thought that in this, as in many other species, a long series of years is necessary for counteracting the original wild and free nature which has been given them; and indeed it seems probable that our attempts to domesticate many species of wild fowls, which would prove useful to mankind, have often been abandoned in despair, when a few years more of constant care might have produced the desired effect.

The Canada Goose, although immediately after the full development of its young it becomes gregarious, does not seem to be fond of the company of any other species. Thus, whenever the White-fronted Goose, the Snow Goose, the Brent Goose, or others, alight in the same ponds, it forces them to keep at a respectful distance; and during its migrations I have never observed a single bird of any other kind in its ranks.

The flight of this species of Goose is firm, rather rapid, and capable of being protracted to a great extent. When once high in the air, they advance with extreme steadiness and regularity of motion. In rising from the water or from the ground, they usually run a few feet with outspread wings; but when suddenly surprised and in full plumage, a single spring on their broad webbed feet is sufficient to enable them to get on wing. While travelling to some considerable distance, they pass through the air at the height of about a mile, steadily following a direct course towards the point to which they are bound. Their notes are distinctly heard, and the various changes made in the disposition of their ranks are easily seen. But although on these occasions they move with the greatest regularity, yet when they are slowly advancing from south to north at an early period of the season, they fly much lower, alight more frequently, and are more likely to be bewildered by suddenly formed banks of fog, or by passing over cities or arms of the sea where much shipping may be in sight. On such occasions great consternation prevails among them, they crowd together in a confused manner, wheel irregularly, and utter a constant cackling resembling the sounds from a disconcerted mob. Sometimes the flock separates, some individuals leave the rest, proceed in a direction contrary to that in which they came, and after a while, as if quite confused, sail towards the ground, once alighted on which they appear to become almost stupified, so as to suffer themselves to be shot with ease, or even knocked down with sticks. This I have known to take place on many occasions, besides those of which I have myself been a witness. Heavy snow-storms also cause them great distress, and in the midst of them some have been known to fly against beacons and lighthouses, dashing their heads against the walls in the middle of the day. In the night they are attracted by the lights of these buildings, and now and then a whole flock is caught on such occasions. At other times their migrations northward are suddenly checked by a change of weather, the approach of which seems to be well known to them, for they will suddenly wheel and fly back in a southern direction several hundred miles. In this manner I have known flocks to return to the places which they had left a fortnight before. Nay even during the winter months, they are keenly sensible to changes of temperature, flying north or south in search of feeding-grounds, with so much knowledge of the future state of the weather, that one may be assured when he sees them proceeding southward in the evening, that the next morning will be cold, and *vice versa*.

The Canada Goose is less shy when met with far inland, than when on the sea-coast, and the smaller the ponds or lakes to which they resort, the more easy it is to approach them. They usually feed in the manner of Swans and fresh-water Ducks, that is, by plunging their heads towards the bottom of shallow ponds or the borders of lakes and rivers, immersing their fore parts, and frequently exhibiting their legs and feet with the posterior portion of their body elevated in the air. They never dive on such occasions. If feeding in the fields or meadows, they nip the blades of grass sidewise, in the manner of the Domestic Goose, and after rainy weather, they are frequently seen rapidly patting the earth with both feet, as if to force the earth-worms from their burrows. If they dabble at times with their bills in muddy water, in search of food, this action is by no means so common with them as it is with Ducks, the Mallard for example. They are extremely fond of alighting in corn-fields covered with tender blades, where they often remain through the night and commit great havoc. Wherever you find them, and however remote from the haunts of man the place may be, they are at all times so vigilant and suspicious, that it is extremely rare to surprise them. In keenness of sight and acuteness of hearing, they are perhaps surpassed by no bird whatever. They act as sentinels towards each other, and during the hours at which the flock reposes, one or more ganders stand on the watch. At the sight of cattle, horses, or animals of the deer kind, they are seldom alarmed, but a bear or a cougar is instantly announced, and if on such occasions the flock is on the ground near water, the birds immediately betake themselves in silence to the latter, swim to the middle of the pond or river, and there remain until danger is over. Should their enemies pursue them in the water, the males utter loud cries, and the birds arrange themselves in close ranks, rise simultaneously in a few seconds, and fly off in a compact body, seldom at such times forming lines or angles, it being in fact only when the distance they have to travel is great that they dispose themselves in those forms. So acute is their sense of hearing, that they are able to distinguish the different sounds or footsteps of their foes with astonishing accuracy. Thus the breaking of a dry stick by a deer is at once distinguished from the same accident occasioned by a man. If a dozen of large turtles drop into the water, making a great noise in their fall, or if the same effect is produced by an alligator, the Wild Goose pays no regard to it; but however faint and distant may be the sound of an Indian's paddle, that may by accident have struck the side of his canoe, it is at once marked, every individual raises its head and looks intently towards the place from which the noise has proceeded, and in silence all watch the movements of their enemy.

These birds are extremely cunning also, and should they conceive themselves unseen, they silently move into the tall grasses by the margin of the water, lower their heads, and lie perfectly quiet until the boat has passed by. I have seen them walk off from a large frozen pond into the woods, to elude the sight of the hunter, and return as soon as he had crossed the pond. But should there be snow on the ice or in the woods, they prefer watching the intruder, and take to wing long before he is within shooting distance, as if aware of the ease with which they could be followed by their tracks over the treacherous surface.

The Canada Geese are fond of returning regularly to the place which they have chosen for resting in, and this they continue to do until they find themselves greatly molested while there. In parts of the country where they are little disturbed, they seldom go farther than the nearest sandbank or the dry shore of the places in which they feed; but in other parts they retire many miles to spots of greater security, and of such extent as will enable them to discover danger long before it can reach them. When such a place is found, and proves secure, many flocks resort to it, but alight apart in separate groups. Thus, on some of the great sand-bars of the Ohio, the Mississippi, and other large streams, congregated flocks, often amounting to a thousand individuals, may be seen at the approach of night, which they spend there, lying on the sand within a few feet of each other, every flock having its own sentinel. In the dawn of next morning they rise on their feet, arrange and clean their feathers, perhaps walk to the water to drink, and then depart for their feeding grounds.

When I first went to the Falls of the Ohio, the rocky shelvings of which are often bare for fully half a mile, thousands of wild geese of this species rested there at night. The breadth of the various channels that separate the rocky islands from either shore, and the rapidity of the currents which sweep along them, render this place of resort more secure than most others. The wild geese still betake themselves to these islands during winter for the same purpose, but their number has become very small; and so shy are these birds at present in the neighbourhood of Louisville, that the moment they are disturbed at the ponds where they go to feed each morning, were it but by the report of a single gun, they immediately return to their rocky asylums. Even there, however, they are by no means secure, for it not unfrequently happens that a flock alights within half gunshot of a person concealed in a pile of drifted wood, whose aim generally proves too true for their peace. Nay, I knew a gentleman, who had a large mill opposite Rock Island, and who used to kill the poor geese at the distance of about a quarter of a mile, by means of a small cannon heavily charged with rifle bullets; and, if I recollect truly, Mr TARASCON in this manner not unfrequently obtained a dozen or more geese at a shot. This was done at dawn, when the birds were busily engaged in trimming their plumage with the view of flying off in a few minutes to their feeding grounds. This war of extermination could not last long: the geese deserted the fatal rock, and the great gun of the mighty miller was used only for a few weeks.

While on the water, the Canada Goose moves with considerable grace, and in its general deportment resembles the wild Swan, to which I think it is nearly allied. If wounded in the wing, they sometimes dive to a small depth, and make off with astonishing address, always in the direction of the shore, the moment they reach which, you see them sneaking through the grass or bushes, their necks extended an inch or so above the ground, and in this manner proceeding so silently, that, unless closely watched, they are pretty sure to escape. If shot at and wounded while on the ice, they immediately walk off in a dignified manner, as if anxious to make you believe that they have not been injured, emitting a loud note all the while; but the instant they reach the shore they become silent, and make off in the manner described. I was much surprised one day, while on the coast of Labrador, to see how cunningly one of these birds, which, in consequence of the moult, was quite unable to fly, managed for a while to elude our pursuit. It was first perceived at some distance from the shore, when the boat was swiftly rowed towards it, and it swam before us with great speed, making directly towards the land; but when we came within a few yards of it, it dived, and nothing could be seen of it for a long time. Every one of the party stood on tiptoe to mark the spot at which it should rise, but all in vain, when the man at the rudder accidentally looked down over the stern and there saw the goose, its body immersed, the point of its bill alone above water, and its feet busily engaged in propelling it so as to keep pace with the movements of the boat. The sailor attempted to catch it while within a foot or two of him, but with the swiftness of thought it shifted from side to side, fore and aft, until delighted at having witnessed so much sagacity in a *goose*, I begged the party to suffer the poor bird to escape.

The crossing of the Canada Goose with the common domestic species has proved as advantageous as that of the wild with the tame Turkey, the cross breed being much larger than the original one, more easily raised, and more speedily fattened. This process is at present carried on to a considerable extent in our Western and Eastern States, where the hybrids are regularly offered for sale during autumn and winter, and where they bring a higher price than either of the species from which they are derived.

The Canada Goose makes its first appearance in the western country, as well as along our Atlantic coast, from the middle of September to that of October, arriving in flocks composed

of a few families. The young birds procured at this early season soon get into good order, become tender and juicy, and
therefore afford excellent eating. If a sportsman is expert and
manages to shoot the old birds first, he is pretty sure to capture the less wily young ones afterwards, as they will be very
apt to return to the same feeding places to which their parents
had led them at their first arrival. To await their coming to a
pond where they are known to feed is generally effectual, but
to me this mode of proceeding never afforded much pleasure,
more especially because the appearance of any other bird
which I wished to obtain would at once induce me to go after it, and thus frighten the game, so that I rarely procured
any on such occasions. But yet, as I have witnessed the killing
of many a fine goose, I hope you will suffer me to relate one
or two anecdotes connected with the shooting of this kind of
game.

Reader, I am well acquainted with one of the best sportsmen now living in the whole of the western country, one possessed of strength, activity, courage, and patience,—qualities
of great importance in a gunner. I have frequently seen him
mount a capital horse of speed and bottom at midnight, when
the mercury in the thermometer was about the freezing
point, and the ground was covered with snow and ice, the latter of which so encased the trees that you might imagine
them converted into glass. Well, off he goes at a round gallop, his steed rough shod, but nobody knows whither, save
myself, who am always by his side. He has a wallet containing
our breakfast, and abundance of ammunition, together with
such implements as are necessary on occasions like the present. The night is pitch-dark, and dismal enough; but who
cares! *He* knows the woods as well as any Kentucky hunter,
and in this respect I am not much behind him. A long interval has passed, and now the first glimpse of day appears in the
east. We know quite well where we are, and that we have travelled just twenty miles. The Barred Owl alone interrupts the
melancholy silence of the hour. Our horses we secure, and on
foot we move cautiously towards a "long pond," the feeding-
place of several flocks of geese, none of which have yet arrived, although the whole surface of open water is covered
with Mallards, Widgeons, Pintail Ducks, Blue-winged and

Green-winged Teals. My friend's gun, like mine, is a long and trusty one, and the opportunity is too tempting. On all fours we cautiously creep to the very edge of the pond; we now raise ourselves on our knees, level our pieces, and let fly. The woods resound with repeated echoes, the air is filled with Ducks of all sorts, our dogs dash into the half frozen water, and in a few minutes a small heap of game lies at our feet. Now, we retire, separate, and betake ourselves to different sides of the pond. If I may judge of my companion's fingers by the state of my own, I may feel certain that it would be difficult for him to fasten a button. There we are shivering, with contracted feet and chattering teeth; but the geese are coming, and their well known cry, *hauk, hauk, awhawk, awhawk,* resounds through the air. They wheel and wheel for a while, but at length gracefully alight on the water, and now they play and wash themselves, and begin to look about for food. There must be at least twenty of them. Twenty more soon arrive, and in less than half an hour we have before us a flock of a hundred individuals. My experienced friend has put a snow-white shirt over his apparel, and although I am greatly intent on observing his motions, I see that it is impossible even for the keen eye of the sentinel goose to follow them. Bang, bang, quoth his long gun, and the birds in dismay instantly start, and fly towards the spot where I am. When they approach I spring up on my feet, the geese shuffle, and instantaneously rise upright; I touch my triggers singly, and broken-winged and dead two birds come heavily to the ground at my feet. Oh that we had more guns! But the business at this pond has been transacted. We collect our game, return to our horses, fasten the necks of the geese and ducks together, and throwing them across our saddles, proceed towards another pond. In this manner we continue to shoot until the number of geese obtained would seem to you so very large that I shall not specify it.

At another time my friend proceeds alone to the Falls of the Ohio, and, as usual, reaches the margins of the stream long before day. His well-trained steed plunges into the whirls of the rapid current, and, with some difficulty, carries his bold rider to an island, where he lands drenched and cold. The horse knows what he has to do as well as his master, and while the former ranges about and nips the frozen herbage, the latter carefully approaches a well-known pile of drifted wood, and conceals himself in it. His famous dog Nep is close at his heels. Now the dull grey dawn gives him a dim view of the geese; he fires, several fall on the spot, and one severely wounded rises and alights in the Indian Chute. Neptune dashes after it, but as the current is powerful, the gunner whistles to his horse, who, with pricked ears, gallops up. He instantly vaults into the saddle, and now see them plunge into the treacherous stream. The wounded game is overtaken, the dog is dragged along, and at length on the Indiana shore the horse and his rider have effected a landing. Any other man than he of whose exploits I am the faithful recorder, would have perished long ago. But it is not half so much for the sake of the plunder that he undergoes all this labour and danger, as for the gratification it affords his kind heart to distribute the game among his numerous friends in Louisville.

On our eastern shores matters are differently managed. The gunners there shoot geese with the prospect of pecuniary gain, and go to work in another way. Some attract them with wooden geese, others with actual birds; they lie in ambush for many hours at a time, and destroy an immense number of them, by using extremely long guns; but as there is little sport in this sort of shooting, I shall say no more about it. Here the Canada Goose feeds much on a species of long slender grass, the *Zostera marina*, along with marine insects, crustacea, and small shell-fish, all of which have a tendency to destroy the agreeable flavour which their flesh has when their food consists of fresh-water plants, corn, and grass. They spend much of their time at some distance from the shores, become more shy, diminish in bulk, and are much inferior as food to those which visit the interior of the country. None of these, however, are at all to be compared with the goslings bred in the inland districts, and procured in September, when, in my opinion, they far surpass the renowned Canvass-backed Duck.

A curious mode of shooting the Canada Goose I have practised with much success. I have sunk in the sand of the bars to which these birds resort at night, a tight hogshead, to within an inch of its upper edges, and placing myself within it at the approach of evening, have drawn over me a quantity of brushwood, placing my gun on the sand, and covering it in like manner with twigs and leaves. The birds would sometimes alight very near me, and in this concealment I have killed several at a shot; but the stratagem answers for only a few nights in the season. During severe winters these birds are able to keep certain portions of the deepest parts of a pond quite open and free from ice, by their continued movements in the water; at all events, such open spaces occasionally occur in ponds and lakes, and are resorted to by the geese, among which great havoc is made.

It is alleged in the State of Maine that a distinct species of Canada Goose resides there, which is said to be much smaller than the one now under your notice, and is described as resembling it in all other particulars. Like the true Canada Goose, it builds a large nest, which it lines with its own down. Sometimes it is placed on the sea-shore, at other times by the margin of a fresh-water lake or pond. That species is distinguished there by the name of *Flight Goose*, and is said to be entirely migratory, whereas the Canada Goose is resident. But, notwithstanding all my exertions, I did not succeed in procuring so much as a feather of this alleged species.

While we were at Newfoundland, on our return from Labrador, on the 15th August 1833, small flocks of the Canada Goose were already observed flying southward. In that country their appearance is hailed with delight, and great numbers of them are shot. They breed rather abundantly by the lakes of the interior of that interesting country. In the harbour of Great Macatina in Labrador, I saw a large pile of young Canada Geese, that had been procured a few days before, and were already salted for winter use. The pile consisted of several hundred individuals, all of which had been killed before they were able to fly. I was told there that this species fed much on the leaves of the dwarf firs, and, on examining their gizzards, found the statement to be correct.

The young dive very expertly, soon after their reaching the water, at the least appearance of danger. In the Southern and Western States, the enemies of the Canada Goose are, by water, the Alligator, the Garfish, and the Turtle; and on land, the Cougar, the Lynx, and the Racoon. While in the air, they are liable to be attacked by the White-headed Eagle. It is a very hardy bird, and individuals have been kept in a state of captivity or domestication for upwards of forty years. Every portion of it is useful to man, for besides the value of the flesh as an article of food, the feathers, the quills, and the fat, are held in request. The eggs also afford very good eating.

The Clapper Rail, or Salt-water Marsh-Hen
Rallus crepitans, GMEL.
(PLATE 34)

ALTHOUGH this species is a constant resident, and extremely abundant along the salt-marshes and reedy sea islands of South Carolina, Georgia, Florida, Alabama, and Louisiana, to the mouths of the Mississippi, and probably farther south, at all seasons of the year, it leaves these districts in considerable numbers in spring, and extends its movements along the Atlantic shores as far as the Middle States. They confine themselves entirely to the salt-marshes in the immediate vicinity of the Atlantic, the islands and the channels between them and the main shores, but are never seen inland or on fresh waters, unless when, during high tides, they remove to the margins of the main, where, indeed, during heavy gales and high seas, these poor birds are forced to take refuge, in order to escape the destructive fury of the tempest that, notwithstanding their utmost exertions, destroys great numbers of them. On all such occasions the birds appear greatly intimidated and stupified, and as if out of their proper element. Those individuals which leave the south for a season, reach the shores of New Jersey about the middle of April, and return to the southern States about the beginning of October, to spend the winter along with their young, after which period none are to be found in the Middle Districts. Few if any ever go beyond Long Island in the State of New York; at least I have never seen or heard of one farther east. Their migrations take place under night, and in perfect silence; but the moment they arrive at their destination, they announce their presence by a continuation of loud cacklings, meant no doubt as an expression of their joy. Having studied the habits of these interesting birds in the Jerseys, in South Carolina, and in the Floridas, on the maritime borders of all of which they breed, I shall here attempt to describe them.

In these countries, from about the beginning of March to that of April, the salt-marshes resound with the cries of the Clapper Rail, which resemble the syllables *cac, cac, cac, cac, cā, cāhā, cāhā*. The commencement of the cry, which is heard quite as frequently during day as by night, is extremely loud and rapid, its termination lower and protracted. At the report of a gun, when thousands of these birds instantaneously burst forth with their cries, you may imagine what an uproar they make. This bird seems to possess the power of ventriloquism, for, when several hundred yards off, its voice often seems to be issuing from the grass around you. At this period, the males are very pugnacious, and combats are rife until each has selected a female for the season. The males stand erect and cry aloud the least sound they hear, guard their mates, and continue faithfully to protect them until the young make their appearance. These come more under the care of the mother, who leads them about until they have attained a considerable size, and are able to shift for themselves. The nest is large, constructed of marsh plants, and fastened to the stems in the midst of the thickest tufts, above high-water mark. The materials of which it is formed are so well interlaced with the plants around them, as to prevent their being washed away by extraordinarily high tides, which, however, sometimes carry off and destroy the eggs, as well as many of the sitting birds, whose attachment to them is so great, that they are now and then drowned while endeavouring to keep them safe. The nest is very deep, so that the eggs seem placed in the bottom of a bowl or funnel. They are from eight to fifteen in number, measure an inch and a half in length by one and an eighth in breadth, and have a pale buff colour, sparingly sprinkled with light umber and purplish spots. The period of incubation is fourteen days. When undisturbed, this species lays only one set of eggs in the season; but as the eggs are in request as a delicious article of food, they are gathered in great numbers, and I myself have collected so many as seventy-two dozens in the course of a day. The nest is generally open at top, and then is very easily discovered, although sometimes the reeds are so arranged about them as to conceal them from the view. When the birds are sitting, they suffer you to approach within a few feet; but, as if aware of your intention, they glide away in silence to some distance, and remain crouched among the grass until you have retired. When, on returning, the poor bird finds that her treasure has been stolen, she immediately proclaims her grief aloud, and in this is joined by her faithful mate. In a few days, however, more eggs are deposited, although, I believe, never in the same nest. This species may be called gregarious, yet the nests are seldom nearer to each other than five or ten yards. They are placed in the thickest and most elevated tufts of grass, principally near the edges of the many lagoons that everywhere intersect the sea marshes, so that a man may go from one to another, finding them with ease as he proceeds along the muddy shores. In the Jerseys, it forms almost a regular occupation to collect the eggs of this bird, and there I have seen twenty or more persons gathering them by thousands during the season; in fact, it is not an uncommon occurrence for an egger to carry home a hundred dozens in a day; and when this havock is continued upwards of a month, you may imagine its extent. The abundance of the birds themselves is almost beyond belief; but if you suppose a series of salt marshes twenty miles in length, and a mile in breadth, while at every eight or ten steps one or two birds may be met with, you may calculate their probable number.

During ebb, the Clapper Rail advances towards the edge of the waters as they recede, and searches, either among the grasses, or along the deep furrows made by the ebb and flow of the tides, for its food, which consists principally of small crabs, a species of salt-water snail attached to the rushes, the fry of fishes, aquatic insects, and plants. When the tide flows, they gradually return, and at high-water they resort to the banks, where they remain concealed until the waters begin to retreat. This species is by no means exclusively nocturnal, for it moves about in search of food during the whole of the day, in this respect resembling the Gallinules. Their courage is now and then brought to the test by the sudden approach of some of their winged enemies, such as a Hawk or an Owl, especially the Marsh Hawk, which is often attacked by them while sailing low over the grass in which they are commonly concealed. On such occasions, the Rail rises a few yards in the air, strikes at the marauder with bill and claws, screaming aloud all the while, and dives again among the grass, to the astonishment of the bird of prey, which usually moves off at full speed. They are not so fortunate in their encounters with such hawks as pounce from on high on their prey, such as the Red-tailed and Red-shouldered Hawks, against which they have no chance of defending themselves. Minxes, racoons, and wild cats destroy a great number of them during night, and many are devoured by turtles and ravenous fishes; but their worst enemy is man. My friend BACHMAN has shot so many as sixty in the course of four hours, and others have killed double that number in double the time.

The Salt-water Marsh Hen swims with considerable ease, though not swiftly or gracefully. While in this act, it extends its neck forward, and strikes the water with its feet, as if unwilling to move far at a time, the motion of its neck resembling that of the Gallinules. It dives well, remains a considerable time under water, and in this manner dexterously eludes its pursuers, although it certainly does not possess the power of holding fast to the bottom, as some persons have alleged. When hard pressed, it often sinks just below the surface, keeping the bill above in order to breathe, and in this position, if not detected, remains for a considerable time. If perceived and approached, it instantly dives, and uses its wings to accelerate its progress, but rises as soon as it comes to a place of safety.

Their movements on the ground, or over the partially submersed or floating beds of weeds, are extremely rapid, and they run swiftly off before a dog, the utmost exertions of which are required to force them on wing. Such an attempt by man would prove utterly futile, unless he were to come upon them unawares. When not pursued, and feeling secure, they walk in a deliberate manner, the body considerably inclined, now and then jerking the tail upwards, although by no means so frequently as Gallinules are wont to do. On the least appearance of danger, they lower the head, stretch out the neck, and move off with incomparable speed, always in perfect silence. They have thousands of paths among the rank herbage, crossing each other so often that they can very easily escape pursuit; and besides, they have a power of compressing their body to such a degree, as frequently to force a passage between two stems so close, that one could hardly believe it possible for them to squeeze themselves through. When put up, they fly slowly and generally straight before you, with their legs dangling, so that they are very easily shot by a quick sportsman, as they rarely fly far at a time on such occasions, but prefer pitching down again into the first tuft of rank grass in their way. When on their migrations, however, they pass low and swiftly over the marshes, or the water, stretched to their full extent, and with a constant beat of the wings.

The young, which are at first covered with down of a black colour, obtain their full plumage before the winter arrives, and after this undergo little change of colour, although they increase in size for a year after. In the Eastern States, this species is not held in much estimation as an article of food, perhaps in a great measure on account of the quantity of Soras met with there during early autumn, and which are certainly more delicate; but in the Southern States, especially during winter, they are considered good for the table, and a great number are killed and offered for sale in the markets. Numbers are destroyed by torch light, which so dazzles their eyes, as to enable persons fond of the sport to knock them down with poles or paddles during high tides. It is by day, however, that they are usually shot, and as this kind of sport is exceedingly pleasant, I will attempt to describe it.

About Charleston, in South Carolina, the shooting of Marsh Hens takes place from September to February, a few days in each month during the spring-tides. A light skiff or canoe is procured, the latter being much preferable, and paddled by one or two experienced persons, the sportsman standing in the bow, and his friend, if he has one with him, taking his station in the stern. At an early hour they proceed to the marshes, amid many boats containing parties on the same errand. There is no lack of shooting-grounds, for every creek of salt-water swarms with Marsh Hens. The sportsman who leads has already discharged his barrels, and on either side of his canoe a bird has fallen. As the boat moves swiftly towards them, more are raised, and although he may not be ready, the safety of the bird is in imminent jeopardy, for now from another bark double reports are heard in succession. The tide is advancing apace, the boats merely float along, and the birds, driven from place to place, seek in vain for safety. Here, on a floating mass of tangled weeds, stand a small group side by side. The gunner has marked them, and presently nearly the whole covey is prostrated. Now, onward to that great bunch of tall grass all the boats are seen to steer; shot after shot flies in rapid succession; dead and dying lie all around on the water; the terrified survivors are trying to save their lives by hurried flight; but their efforts are unavailing,—one by one they fall, to rise no more. It is a sorrowful sight, after all: see that poor thing gasping hard in the agonies of death, its legs quivering with convulsive twitches, its bright eyes fading into glazed obscurity. In a few hours, hundreds have ceased to breathe the breath of life; hundreds that erst revelled in the joys of careless existence, but which can never behold their beloved marshes again. The cruel sportsman, covered with mud and mire, drenched to the skin by the splashing of the paddles, his face and hands besmeared with powder, stands amid the wreck which he has made, exultingly surveys his slaughtered heaps, and with joyous feelings returns home with a cargo of game more than enough for a family thrice as numerous as his own. How joyful must be the congratulations of those which have escaped, without injury to themselves or their relatives! With what pleasure, perhaps, have some of them observed the gun of one of their murderers, or the powder-flask of another, fall overboard! How delighted have they been to see a canoe overturned by an awkward movement, and their enemies struggling to reach the shore, or sticking fast in the mud! Nor have the minx and racoon come off well, for notwithstanding the expertness of the former at diving, and the cunning of the latter, many have been shot, and the boatmen intend to make caps of their fur.

In the Carolinas there are some most expert marksmen, of whom I know two who probably were never surpassed. One of them I have seen shoot fifty Marsh-Hens at fifty successive shots, and the other, I am assured, has killed a hundred without missing one. I have heard or read of a French king, who,

on starting a partridge, could take a pinch of snuff, then point
his gun, and shoot the bird; but whether this be true or not
I cannot say, although I have witnessed as remarkable a feat,
for I have seen a Carolinian, furnished with two guns, shoot
at and kill four Marsh-Hens as they flew off at once around
him! On speaking once to a friend of the cruelty of destroying so many of these birds, he answered me as follows:—"It
gives variety to life; it is good exercise, and in all cases affords
a capital dinner, besides the pleasure I feel when sending a
mess of Marsh-Hens to a friend such as you."

The Great Blue Heron

Ardea Herodias, LINN.

(PLATES 35, 47)

THE State of Louisiana has always been my favourite portion
of the Union, although Kentucky and some other States have
divided my affections; but as we are on the banks of the fair
Ohio, let us pause a while, good Reader, and watch the
Heron. In my estimation, few of our waders are more interesting than the birds of this family. Their contours and movements are always graceful, if not elegant. Look on the one
that stands near the margin of the pure stream:—see his reflection dipping as it were into the smooth water, the bottom
of which it might reach had it not to contend with the numerous boughs of those magnificent trees. How calm, how
silent, how grand is the scene! The tread of the tall bird himself no one hears, so carefully does he place his foot on the
moist ground, cautiously suspending it for a while at each
step of his progress. Now his golden eye glances over the surrounding objects, in surveying which he takes advantage of
the full stretch of his graceful neck. Satisfied that no danger is
near, he lays his head on his shoulders, allows the feathers of
his breast to droop, and patiently awaits the approach of his
finned prey. You might imagine what you see to be the statue
of a bird, so motionless is it. But now, he moves; he has taken
a silent step, and with great care he advances; slowly does he
raise his head from his shoulders, and now, what a sudden

start! his formidable bill has transfixed a perch, which he beats to death on the ground. See with what difficulty he gulps it down his capacious throat! and now his broad wings open, and away he slowly flies to another station, or perhaps to avoid his unwelcome observers.

The "Blue Crane" (by which name this species is generally known in the United States) is met with in every part of the Union. Although more abundant in the low lands of our Atlantic coast, it is not uncommon in the countries west of the Alleghany Mountains. I have found it in every State in which I have travelled, as well as in all our "Territories." It is well known from Louisiana to Maine, but seldom occurs farther east than Prince Edward's Island in the Gulf of St. Lawrence, and not a Heron of any kind did I see or hear of in Newfoundland or Labrador. Westward, I believe, it reaches to the very bases of the Rocky Mountains. It is a hardy bird, and bears the extremes of temperature surprisingly, being in its tribe what the Passenger Pigeon is in the family of Doves. During the coldest part of winter the Blue Heron is observed in the State of Massachusetts and in Maine, spending its time in search of prey about the warm springs and ponds which occur there in certain districts. They are not rare in the Middle States, but more plentiful to the west and south of Pennsylvania, which perhaps arises from the incessant war waged against them.

Extremely suspicious and shy, this bird is ever on the lookout. Its sight is as acute as that of any falcon, and it can hear at a considerable distance, so that it is enabled to mark with precision the different objects it sees, and to judge with accuracy of the sounds which it hears. Unless under very favourable circumstances, it is almost hopeless to attempt to approach it. You may now and then surprise one feeding under the bank of a deep creek or bayou, or obtain a shot as he passes unawares over you on wing; but to walk up towards one would be a fruitless adventure. I have seen many so wary, that, on seeing a man at any distance within half a mile, they would take to wing; and the report of a gun forces one off his grounds from a distance at which you would think he could not be alarmed. When in close woods, however, and perched on a tree, they can be approached with a good chance of success.

The Blue Heron feeds at all hours of the day, as well as in

the dark and dawn, and even under night, when the weather is clear, his appetite alone determining his actions in this respect; but I am certain that when disturbed during dark nights it feels bewildered, and alights as soon as possible. When passing from one part of the country to another at a distance, the case is different, and on such occasions they fly under night at a considerable height above the trees, continuing their movements in a regular manner.

The commencement of the breeding season varies, according to the latitude, from the beginning of March to the middle of June. In the Floridas it takes place about the first of these periods, in the Middle Districts about the 15th of May, and in Maine a month later. It is at the approach of this period only that these birds associate in pairs, they being generally quite solitary at all other times; nay, excepting during the breeding season, each individual seems to secure for itself a certain district as a feeding ground, giving chase to every intruder of its own species. At such times they also repose singly, for the most part roosting on trees, although sometimes taking their station on the ground, in the midst of a wide marsh, so that they may be secure from the approach of man. This unsocial temper probably arises from the desire of securing a certain abundance of food, of which each individual in fact requires a large quantity.

The manners of this Heron are exceedingly interesting at the approach of the breeding season, when the males begin to look for partners. About sunrise you see a number arrive and alight either on the margin of a broad sand-bar or on a savannah. They come from different quarters, one after another, for several hours; and when you see forty or fifty before you, it is difficult for you to imagine that half the number could have resided in the same district. Yet in the Floridas I have seen hundreds thus collected in the course of a morning. They are now in their full beauty, and no young birds seem to be among them. The males walk about with an air of great dignity, bidding defiance to their rivals, and the females croak to invite the males to pay their addresses to them. The females utter their coaxing notes all at once, and as each male evinces an equal desire to please the object of his affection, he has to encounter the enmity of many an adversary, who, with little attention to politeness, opens his powerful bill, throws out his wings, and rushes with fury on his foe. Each attack is carefully guarded against, blows are exchanged for blows; one would think that a single well-aimed thrust might suffice to inflict death, but the strokes are parried with as much art as an expert swordsman would employ; and, although I have watched these birds for half an hour at a time as they fought on the ground, I never saw one killed on such an occasion; but I have often seen one felled and trampled upon, even after incubation had commenced. These combats over, the males and females leave the place in pairs. They are now mated for the season, at least I am inclined to think so, as I never saw them assemble twice on the same ground, and they become comparatively peaceable after pairing.

It is by no means a constant practice with this species to breed in communities, whether large or small; for although I have seen many such associations, I have also found many pairs breeding apart. Nor do they at all times make choice of the trees placed in the interior of a swamp, for I have found heronries in the pine-barrens of the Floridas, more than ten miles from any marsh, pond, or river. I have also observed nests on the tops of the tallest trees, while others were only a few feet above the ground: some also I have seen on the ground itself, and many on cactuses. In the Carolinas, where Herons of all sorts are extremely abundant, perhaps as much so as in the lower parts of Louisiana or the Floridas, on account of the numerous reservoirs connected with the rice plantations, and the still more numerous ditches which intersect the rice-fields, all of which contain fish of various sorts, these birds find it easy to procure food in great abundance. There the Blue Herons breed in considerable numbers, and if the place they have chosen be over a swamp, few situations can be conceived more likely to ensure their safety, for one seldom ventures into those dismal retreats at the time when these birds breed, the effluvia being extremely injurious to health, besides the difficulties to be overcome in making one's way to them.

Imagine, if you can, an area of some hundred acres, overgrown with huge cypress trees, the trunks of which, rising to a height of perhaps fifty feet before they send off a branch,

spring from the midst of the dark muddy waters. Their broad
tops, placed close together with interlaced branches, seem intent on separating the heavens from the earth. Beneath their
dark canopy scarcely a single sunbeam ever makes its way; the
mire is covered with fallen logs, on which grow matted
grasses and lichens, and the deeper parts with nympheæ and
other aquatic plants. The Congo snake and water-moccasin
glide before you as they seek to elude your sight, hundreds of
turtles drop, as if shot, from the floating trunks of the fallen
trees, from which also the sullen alligator plunges into the
dismal pool. The air is pregnant with pestilence, but alive with
musquitoes and other insects. The croaking of the frogs,
joined with the hoarse cries of the Anhingas and the screams
of the Herons, forms fit music for such a scene. Standing
knee-deep in the mire, you discharge your gun at one of the
numerous birds that are breeding high over head, when immediately such a deafening noise arises, that, if you have a
companion with you, it were quite useless to speak to him.
The frightened birds cross each other confusedly in their
flight; the young attempting to secure themselves, some of
them lose their hold, and fall into the water with a splash; a
shower of leaflets whirls downwards from the tree-tops, and
you are glad to make your retreat from such a place. Should
you wish to shoot Herons, you may stand, fire, and pick up
your game as long as you please; you may obtain several
species, too, for not only does the Great Blue Heron breed
there, but the White, and sometimes the Night Heron, as well
as the Anhinga, and to such places they return year after year,
unless they have been cruelly disturbed.

The nest of the Blue Heron, in whatever situation it may be
placed, is large and flat, externally composed of dry sticks, and
matted with weeds and mosses to a considerable thickness.
When the trees are large and convenient, you may see several
nests on the same tree. The full complement of eggs which
these birds lay is three, and in no instance have I found more.
Indeed, this is constantly the case with all the large species
with which I am acquainted, from *Ardea cærulea* to *Ardea occidentalis*; but the smaller species lay more as they diminish in
size, the Louisiana Heron having frequently four, and the
Green Heron five, and even sometimes six. Those of the

Great Blue Heron are very small compared with the size of the bird, measuring only two and a half inches by one and seven-twelfths; they are of a dull bluish-white, without spots, rather rough, and of a regular oval form.

The male and the female sit alternately, receiving food from each other, their mutual affection being as great as it is towards their young, which they provide for so abundantly, that it is not uncommon to find the nest containing a quantity of fish and other food, some fresh, and some in various stages of putrefaction. As the young advance they are less frequently fed, although still as copiously supplied whenever opportunity offers; but now and then I have observed them, when the nests were low, standing on their haunches, with their legs spread widely before them, and calling for food in vain. The quantity which they require is now so great that all the exertions of the old birds appear at times to be insufficient to satisfy their voracious appetite; and they do not provide for themselves until fully able to fly, when their parents chase them off, and force them to shift as they can. They are generally in good condition when they leave the nest; but from want of experience they find it difficult to procure as much food as they have been accustomed to, and soon become poor. Young birds from the nest afford tolerable eating; but the flesh of the old birds is by no means to my taste, nor so good as some epicures would have us to believe, and I would at any time prefer that of a Crow or young Eagle.

The principal food of the Great Blue Heron is fish of all kinds; but it also devours frogs, lizards, snakes, and birds, as well as small quadrupeds, such as shrews, meadow-mice, and young rats, all of which I have found in its stomach. Aquatic insects are equally welcome to it, and it is an expert flycatcher, striking at moths, butterflies, and libellulæ, whether on the wing or when alighted. It destroys a great number of young Marsh-Hens, Rails, and other birds; but I never saw one catch a fiddler or a crab; and the only seeds that I have found in its stomach were those of the great water-lily of the Southern States. It always strikes its prey through the body, and as near the head as possible. When the animal is strong and active, it kills it by beating it against the ground or a rock, after which it swallows it entire. While on the St John's River in East

Florida, I shot one of these birds, and on opening it on board, found in its stomach a fine perch quite fresh, but of which the head had been cut off. The fish, when cooked, I found excellent, as did Lieutenant PIERCY and my assistant Mr WARD, but Mr LEEHMAN would not so much as taste it. When on a visit to my friend JOHN BULOW, I was informed by him, that although he had several times imported gold fishes from New York, with the view of breeding them in a pond, through which ran a fine streamlet, and which was surrounded by a wall, they all disappeared in a few days after they were let loose. Suspecting the Heron to be the depredator, I desired him to watch the place carefully with a gun; which was done, and the result was, that he shot a superb specimen of the present species, in which was found the last gold fish that remained.

In the wild state it never, I believe, eats dead fish of any sort, or indeed any other food than that killed by itself. Now and then it strikes at a fish so large and strong as to endanger its own life; and I once saw one on the Florida coast, that, after striking a fish, when standing in the water to the full length of its legs, was dragged along for several yards, now on the surface, and again beneath. When, after a severe struggle, the Heron disengaged itself, it appeared quite overcome, and stood still near the shore, his head turned from the sea, as if afraid to try another such experiment. The number of fishes, measuring five or six inches, which one of these birds devours in a day, is surprising: Some which I kept on board the Marion would swallow, in the space of half an hour, a bucketful of young mullets; and when fed on the flesh of green turtles, they would eat several pounds at a meal. I have no doubt that, in favourable circumstances, one of them could devour several hundreds of small fishes in a day. A Heron that was caught alive on one of the Florida keys, near Key West, looked so emaciated when it came on board, that I had it killed to discover the cause of its miserable condition. It was an adult female that had bred that spring; her belly was in a state of mortification, and on opening her, we found the head of a fish measuring several inches, which, in an undigested state, had lodged among the entrails of the poor bird. How long it had suffered could only be guessed, but this undoubtedly was the cause of the miserable state in which it was found.

I took a pair of young Herons of this species to Charleston. They were nearly able to fly when caught, and were standing erect a few yards from the nest, in which lay a putrid one that seemed to have been trampled to death by the rest. They offered little resistance, but grunted with a rough uncouth voice. I had them placed in a large coop, containing four individuals of the *Ardea occidentalis*, who immediately attacked the new-comers in the most violent manner, so that I was obliged to turn them loose on the deck. I had frequently observed the great antipathy evinced by the majestic white species towards the blue in the wild state, but was surprised to find it equally strong in young birds which had never seen one, and were at that period smaller than the others. All my endeavours to remove their dislike were unavailing, for when placed in a large yard, the White Herons attacked the Blue, and kept them completely under. The latter became much tamer, and were more attached to each other. Whenever a piece of turtle was thrown to them, it was dexterously caught in the air and gobbled up in an instant, and as they became more familiar, they ate bits of biscuit, cheese, and even rhinds of bacon.

When wounded, the Great Blue Heron immediately prepares for defence, and woe to the man or dog who incautiously comes within reach of its powerful bill, for that instant he is sure to receive a severe wound, and the risk is so much the greater that birds of this species commonly aim at the eye. If beaten with a pole or long stick, they throw themselves on their back, cry aloud, and strike with their bill and claws with great force. I have shot some on trees, which, although quite dead, clung by their claws for a considerable time before they fell. I have also seen the Blue Heron giving chase to a Fish Hawk, whilst the latter was pursuing its way through the air towards a place where it could feed on the fish which it bore in its talons. The Heron soon overtook the Hawk, and at the very first lounge made by it, the latter dropped its quarry, when the Heron sailed slowly towards the ground, where it no doubt found the fish. On one occasion of this kind, the

Hawk dropped the fish in the water, when the Heron, as if vexed that it was lost to him, continued to harass the Hawk, and forced it into the woods.

The flight of the Great Blue Heron is even, powerful, and capable of being protracted to a great distance. On rising from the ground or on leaving its perch, it goes off in silence with extended neck and dangling legs, for eight or ten yards, after which it draws back its neck, extends its feet in a straight line behind, and with easy and measured flappings continues its course, at times flying low over the marshes, and again, as if suspecting danger, at a considerable height over the land or the forest. It removes from one pond or creek, or even from one marsh to another, in a direct manner, deviating only on apprehending danger. When about to alight, it now and then sails in a circular direction, and when near the spot it extends its legs, and keeps its wings stretched out until it has effected a footing. The same method is employed when it alights on a tree, where, however, it does not appear to be as much as its ease as on the ground. When suddenly surprised by an enemy, it utters several loud discordant notes, and mutes the moment it flies off.

This species takes three years in attaining maturity, and even after that period it still increases in size and weight. When just hatched they have a very uncouth appearance, the legs and neck being very long, as well as the bill. By the end of a-week the head and neck are sparingly covered with long tufts of silky down, of a dark grey colour, and the body exhibits young feathers, the quills large with soft blue sheaths. The tibio-tarsal joints appear monstrous, and at this period the bones of the leg are so soft, that one may bend them to a considerable extent without breaking them. At the end of four weeks, the body and wings are well covered with feathers of a dark slate colour, broadly margined with ferruginous, the latter colour shewing plainly on the thighs and the flexure of the wing; the bill has grown wonderfully, the legs would not now easily break, and the birds are able to stand erect on the nest or on the objects near it. They are now seldom fed oftener than once a-day, as if their parents were intent on teaching them that abstinence without which it would often be difficult for them to subsist in their after life. At the age of six or seven weeks they fly off, and at once go in search of food, each by itself.

In the following spring, at which time they have grown much, the elongated feathers of the breast and shoulders are seen, the males shew the commencement of the pendent crest, and the top of the head has become white. None breed at this age, in so far as I have been able to observe. The second spring, they have a handsome appearance, the upper parts have become light, the black and white marks are much purer, and some have the crest three or four inches in length. Some breed at this age. The third spring, the Great Blue Heron is as represented in the plate.

The males are somewhat larger than the females, but there is very little difference between the sexes in external appearance. This species moults in the Southern States about the beginning of May, or as soon as the young are hatched, and one month after the pendent crest is dropped, and much of the beauty of the bird is gone for the season. The weight of a full grown Heron of this kind, when it is in good condition, is about eight pounds; but this varies very much according to circumstances, and I have found some having all the appearance of old birds that did not exceed six pounds. The stomach consists of a long bag, thinly covered by a muscular coat, and is capable of containing several fishes at a time. The intestine is not thicker than the quill of a swan, and measures from eight and a half to nine feet in length.

The Puffin

Mormon arcticus, ILLIGER

(PLATE 36)

THE Sea Parrot, as this bird is usually called on the eastern coasts of the United States, as well as by the fishermen of Newfoundland and Labrador, sometimes proceeds as far south as the entrance of the River Savannah in Georgia, where I saw a good number in the winter of 1831–32. It is by no means, however, common with this species to extend its southward migrations so far, and I suspect it does so only in very severe weather. It is never plentiful off Long Island, but becomes more abundant the farther you proceed eastward, until you reach the entrance to the Bay of Fundy, where it is quite common, and on the Islands of which many breed, although not one perhaps now for a hundred that bred there twenty years ago. Those which proceed farther north leave the United States about the middle of April, and move along the coast, none ever crossing over the land to any extent. On my voyage to Labrador I observed Puffins every day; but although we reached that country in the early part of June, none had then begun to breed. As we approached the shores of that inhospitable land, we every now and then saw them around the vessel, now floating on the swelling wave, now disappearing under the bow, diving with the swiftness of thought, and sometimes rising on wing and flying swiftly, but low, over the sea. The nearer we approached the coast the more abundant did we find the Puffins, and sometimes they were so numerous as actually to cover the water to the extent of half an acre or more. At first we paid little attention to them, but as soon as I became aware that they had begun to breed, I commenced an investigation, of which I now proceed to lay before you the result.

The first breeding place which I and my party visited was a small island, a few acres in extent, and pleasant to the eye, on account of the thick growth of green grass with which it was covered. The shores were exceedingly rugged, the sea ran high, and it required all the good management of our captain to effect a safe landing, which, however, was at length accomplished at a propitious moment, when, borne on the summit of a great wave, we reached the first rocks, leaped out in an instant, and held our boat, while the angry waters rolled back and left it on the land. After securing the boat, we reached with a few steps the green sward, and directly before us found abundance of Puffins. Some already alarmed flew past us with the speed of an arrow, others stood erect at the entrance of their burrows, while some more timid withdrew within their holes as we advanced towards them. In the course of half an hour we obtained a good number. The poor things seemed not at all aware of the effect of guns, for they would fly straight towards us as often as in any other direction; but after a while they became more knowing, and avoided us with more care. We procured some eggs, and as no young ones were yet to be found, we went off satisfied. The soil was so light, and so easily dug, that many of the burrows extended to the depth of five or six feet, although not more than a few inches below the surface, and some of the poor birds underwent a temporary imprisonment in consequence of the ground giving way under our weight. The whole island was perforated like a rabbit-warren, and every hole had its entrance placed due south, a circumstance which allowed the birds to emerge in our sight almost all at once, presenting a spectacle highly gratifying to us all. Our visit to this island took place on the 28th of June 1833.

On the 12th of August, the day after my son procured the two Jerfalcons mentioned in the second volume of this work, our Captain, my friends GEORGE SHATTUCK and WILLIAM INGALLS, with four sailors, and another boat in company, went on a visit to "Perroket Island," distant about two miles from the harbour of Bras d'Or. The place is known to all the cod-fishers, and is celebrated for the number of Puffins that annually breed there. As we rowed towards it, although we found the water literally covered with thousands of these birds, the number that flew over and around the green island seemed much greater, insomuch that one might have imagined half the Puffins in the world had assembled there. This far-famed isle is of considerable extent, its shores are guarded by numberless blocks of rock, and within a few yards of it the water is several fathoms in depth. The ground rises in the form of an amphitheatre to the height of about seventy feet, the greatest length being from north to south, and its southern extremity fronting the Streight of Belleisle. For every burrow in the island previously visited by us there seemed to be a hundred here, on every crag or stone stood a Puffin, at the entrance of each hole another, and yet the sea was covered and the air filled by them. I had two double-barrelled guns and two sailors to assist me; and I shot for one hour by my watch, always firing at a single bird on wing. How many Puffins I killed in that time I take the liberty of leaving you to guess.

The burrows were all inhabited by young birds, of different

ages and sizes, and clouds of Puffins flew over our heads, each
individual holding a "lint" by the head. This fish, which measures four or five inches in length, and is of a very slender
form, with a beautiful silvery hue, existed in vast shoals in the
deep water around the island. The speed with which the birds
flew made the fish incline by the side of their neck. While flying the Puffins emitted a loud croaking noise, but they never
dropped the fish, and many of them, when brought down by
a shot, still held their prey fast. I observed with concern the
extraordinary affection manifested by these birds towards
each other; for whenever one fell dead or wounded on the
water, its mate or a stranger immediately alighted by its side,
swam round it, pushed it with its bill as if to urge it to fly or
dive, and seldom would leave it until an oar was raised to
knock it on the head, when at last, aware of the danger, it
would plunge below in an instant. Those which fell wounded
immediately ran with speed to some hole, and dived into it,
on which no further effort was made to secure them. Those
which happened to be caught alive in the hand bit most severely, and scratched with their claws at such a rate that we
were glad to let them escape. The burrows here communicated in various ways with each other, so that the whole island
was perforated as if by a multitude of subterranean labyrinths,
over which one could not run without the risk of falling at almost every step. The voices of the young sounded beneath
our feet like voices from the grave, and the stench was extremely disagreeable, so that as soon as our boats were filled
with birds we were glad to get away.

During the whole of our visit, the birds never left the place,
but constantly attended to their avocations. Here one would
rise from beneath our feet, there, within a few yards of us, another would alight with a fish, and dive into its burrow, or
feed the young that stood waiting at the entrance. The young
birds were far from being friendly towards each other, and
those which we carried with us kept continually fighting so
long as we kept them alive. They used their yet extremely
small and slender bills with great courage and pertinacity, and
their cries resembled the wailings of young whelps. The
smaller individuals were fed by the parents by regurgitation,
or received little pieces of fish which were placed in their

mouths; the larger picked up the fish that were dropped before them; but almost all of them seemed to crawl to the entrance of the holes for the purpose of being fed. In all the burrows that communicated with others, a round place was scooped out on one side of the avenue, in the form of an oven; while in those which were single, this oven-like place was found at the end, and was larger than the corridor. All the passages were flattish above, and rounded beneath, as well as on the sides. In many instances we found two birds sitting each on its egg in the same hole.

The Puffin never lays more than one egg, unless the first may have been destroyed or taken away; nor does it raise more than a single young one in the season. The time of incubation is probably from twenty-five to twenty-eight days, although I have not been able to ascertain the precise period. Both birds work in digging the hole, using their bills and feet; they also sit alternately on their egg, although the female engages more industriously in this occupation, while the male labours harder at the burrow. The egg is pure white when first deposited, but soon becomes soiled by the earth, as no nest is formed for its reception. It generally measures two and a half inches by one and three-fourths, but varies in size according to the age of the bird, as well as in shape, some being considerably more rounded at the smaller end than others. When boiled, the white is of a livid-blue colour. The captain and myself were the only persons of our party who tried to eat some. The eggs are certainly very bad, and are never collected by "The Eggers." The flesh of the birds is very dark, tough, and so fishy, as to be eatable only in cases of great want. Two Italians who had come to Labrador to purchase cod-fish, and were short of provisions, fed upon Puffins daily, to the great amusement of our party. The fishermen at times, when bait is scarce along the coast, destroy a great number of these birds, which they skin like rabbits, and then cut the flesh into slices.

The flight of the Puffin is firm, generally direct, now and then pretty well sustained. It is able to rise at once from the water or land, although at times it runs on both before taking to wing. This depends much on necessity, for if pushed it flies at once from the ground, or plunges under the surface of the water. There they swim, with the wings partially opened, at a small depth, passing along in the manner of Divers; and by this means they catch their prey; but at other times they dive to the bottom, many fathoms deep, for shell-fish and other objects.

During the love season, the males chase each other in the air, on the water, or beneath its surface, with so much quick-ness, as to resemble the ricochets of a cannon-ball. Having kept several for about a week, I threw them overboard in the harbour where we were at anchor, and where the water was beautifully clear. On leaving my gloved hand, they plunged through the air, entered the water, and swam off, assisting themselves by their wings to the distance of from fifty to an hundred yards. On coming up, they washed their plumage for a long time, and then dived in search of food. While on board, they ran about from the dark towards the light, keep-ing themselves erect, and moving with great briskness, until at times close to my feet, when they would watch my motions like hawks, and if I happened to look towards them, would instantly make for some hiding-place. They fed freely and were agreeable pets, only that they emitted an unpleasant grunting noise, and ran about incessantly during the night, when each footstep could be counted. When on rocky shores, or islands with large stones, I observed that the Puffins often flew from one crag or stone to another, alighting with ease, and then standing erect.

The young, while yet covered with down, are black, with a white patch on the belly. Their bills do not acquire much of the form which they ultimately have for several weeks; nor do they assume their perfect shape for years. I have examined many hundred individuals, among which I have found great differences in the size and form of the bill. In fact, the exis-tence of this diversity has induced many persons to think that we have several species of Puffin on our coasts; but, after hav-ing examined many specimens in Europe, I am decidedly of opinion that this species is the same that occurs in both con-tinents, and that we have only one more at all common on our eastern coasts. The sexes differ in no perceptible degree, only that the males are somewhat larger. When two years old they may be considered of their full size, although the bill continues to grow and acquires furrows, until it becomes as you see it in the Plate.

The Razor-billed Auk

Alca Torda, LINN.

(PLATE 37)

A FEW BIRDS of this species occasionally go as far south as New York during winter; but beyond that parallel I never met with one. From Boston eastward many are seen, and some breed on the Seal Islands off the entrance of the Bay of Fundy. These Auks generally arrive on our Atlantic coast about the beginning of November, and return northward to breed about the middle of April. During their stay with us, they are generally seen singly, and at a greater distance from the shores than the Guillemots or Puffins; and I have no doubt that they are able to procure shell-fish at greater depths than these birds. I have observed them fishing on banks where the bottom was fifteen or eighteen fathoms from the surface, and, from the length of time that they remained under water, felt no doubt that they dived to it. On my voyage round Nova Scotia and across the Gulf of St Lawrence, we saw some of them constantly. Some had eggs on the Magdeleine Islands, where, as the inhabitants informed us, these birds arrive about the middle of April, when the Gulf is still covered with ice. As we proceeded towards Labrador, they passed us every now and then in long files, flying at the height of a few yards from the water, in a rather undulating manner, with a constant beat of the wings, often within musket-shot of our vessel, and sometimes moving round us and coming so close as to induce us to believe that they had a wish to alight. The thermometer indicated 44°. The sight of these files of birds passing swiftly by was extremely pleasing; each bird would alternately turn towards us the pure white of its lower parts, and again the jetty black of the upper. As I expected ere many days should pass to have the gratification of inspecting their breeding grounds, I experienced great delight in observing them as they sped their flight toward the north.

After we had landed, we every day procured Auks, notwith-standing their shyness, which exceeded that of almost all the other sea-birds. The fishermen having given me an account of their principal breeding places, the Ripley proceeded toward them apace. One fair afternoon we came in view of the renowned Harbour of Whapati Guan, and already saw its cu-rious beacon, which, being in form like a huge mounted can-non placed on the elevated crest of a great rock, produced a most striking effect. We knew that the harbour was within the stupendous wall of rock before us, but our pilot, either from fear or want of knowledge, refused to guide us to it, and our captain, leaving the vessel in charge of the mate, was obliged to go off in a boat, to see if he could find a passage. He was absent more than an hour. The Ripley stood off and on, the yards were manned on the look-out, the sea was smooth and its waters as clear as crystal, but the swell rose to a prodigious height as it passed sluggishly over the great rocks that seemed to line the shallows over which we floated. We were under no apprehension of personal danger, however, for we had several boats and a very efficient crew; and besides, the shores were within cannon shot; but the idea of losing our gallant bark and all our materials on so dismal a coast haunted my mind, and at times those of my companions. From the tops our sailors called out "Quite shallow here, Sir." Up went the helm, and round swung the Ripley like a duck taken by surprise. Then suddenly near another shoal we passed, and were careful to keep a sharp look-out until our commander came up.

Springing upon the deck, and turning his quid rapidly from side to side, he called out, "All hands square the yards," and whispered to me "All's safe, my good Sir." The schooner ad-vanced towards the huge barrier, merrily as a fair maiden to meet her beloved; now she doubles a sharp cape, forces her way through a narrow pass; and lo! before you opens the noble harbour of Whapati Guan. All around was calm and solemn; the waters were smooth as glass, the sails fell against the masts, but the impetus which the vessel had received urged her along. The lead was heaved at every yard, and in a few minutes the anchor was dropped.

Reader, I wish you had been there, that you might yourself describe the wild scene that presented itself to our admiring gaze. We were separated from the rolling swell of the Gulf of St Lawrence by an immense wall of rock. Far away toward the east and north, rugged mounds innumerable rose one above another. Multitudes of frightened Cormorants croaked loudly as they passed us in the air, and at a distance fled divers Guillemots and Auks. The mossy beds around us shone with a brilliant verdure, the lark piped its sweet notes on high, and thousands of young codfish leaped along the surface of the deep cove as if with joy. Such a harbour I had never seen before; such another, it is probable, I may never see again; the noblest fleet that ever ploughed the ocean might anchor in it in safety. To augment our pleasures, our captain some days after piloted the Gulnare into it. But, you will say, "Where are the Auks, we have lost sight of them entirely." Never fear, good reader, we are in a delightful harbour, and anon you shall hear of them.

Winding up the basin toward the north-east, Captain Emery, myself, and some sailors, all well armed, proceeded one day along the high and precipitous shores to the distance of about four miles, and at last reached the desired spot. We landed on a small rugged island. Our men were provided with long poles, having hooks at their extremities. These sticks were introduced into the deep and narrow fissures, from which we carefully drew the birds and eggs. One place, in particular, was full of birds; it was a horizontal fissure, about two feet in height, and thirty or forty yards in depth. We crawled slowly into it, and as the birds affrighted flew hurriedly past us by hundreds, many of their eggs were smashed. The farther we advanced, the more dismal did the cries of the birds sound in our ears. Many of them, despairing of effecting their escape, crept into the surrounding recesses. Having collected as many of them and their eggs as we could, we returned, and glad were we once more to breathe the fresh air. No sooner were we out than the cracks of the sailors' guns echoed among the rocks. Rare fun to the tars, in fact, was every such trip, and, when we joined them, they had a pile of Auks on the rocks near them. The birds flew directly towards the muzzles of the guns, as readily as in any other course, and therefore it needed little dexterity to shoot them.

When the Auks deposit their eggs along with the Guillemots, which they sometimes do, they drop them in spots from which the water can escape without injuring them; but when they breed in deep fissures, which is more frequently the case, many of them lie close together, and the eggs are deposited on small beds of pebbles or broken stones raised a couple of inches or more, to let the water pass beneath them. Call this instinct if you will:—I really do not much care; but you must permit me to admire the wonderful arrangements of that Nature from which they have received so much useful knowledge. When they lay their eggs in such a horizontal cavern as that which I have mentioned above, you find them scattered at the distance of a few inches from each other; and there, as well as in the fissures, they sit flat upon them like Ducks, for example, whereas on an exposed rock, each bird stands almost upright upon its egg. Another thing quite as curious, which I observed, is, that, while in exposed situations, the Auk seldom lays more than one egg, yet in places of greater security I have, in many instances, found two under a single bird. This may perhaps astonish you, but I really cannot help it.

The Razor-billed Auks begin to drop their eggs in the beginning of May. In July we found numerous young ones, although yet small. Their bill then scarcely exhibited the form which it ultimately assumes. They were covered with down, had a lisping note, but fed freely on shrimps and small bits of fish, the food with which their parents supply them. They were very friendly towards each other, differing greatly in this respect from the young Puffins, which were continually quarrelling. They stood almost upright. Whenever a finger was placed within their reach, they instantly seized it, and already evinced the desire to bite severely so cordially manifested by the old birds of this species, which in fact will hang to your hand until choked rather than let go their hold. The latter when wounded threw themselves on their back, in the manner of Hawks, and scratched fiercely with their claws. They walked and ran on the rocks with considerable ease and celerity, taking to wing, however, as soon as possible. When thus disturbed while breeding, they fly round the spot many times before they alight again. Sometimes a whole flock will alight on the water at some distance, to watch your departure, before they will venture to return.

This bird lays one or two eggs, according to the nature of the place. The eggs measure at an average three inches and one-eighth, by two and one-eighth, and are generally pure white, greatly blotched with dark reddish-brown or black, the spots generally forming a circle towards the larger end. They differ considerably from those of the Common and the Thick-billed Guillemots, being less blunted at the smaller end. The eggs afford excellent eating; the yolk is of a pale orange colour, the white pale blue. The eggers collect but few of the eggs of this bird, they being more difficult to be obtained than those of the Guillemot, of which they take vast numbers every season.

The food of the Razor-billed Auk consists of shrimps, various other marine animals, and small fishes, as well as roe. Their flesh is by the fishers considered good, and I found it tolerable, when well stewed, although it is dark and therefore not prepossessing. The birds are two years in acquiring the full size and form of their bill, and, when full grown, they weighed about a pound and a half. The stomach is an oblong sac, the lower part of which is rather muscular, and answers the purpose of a gizzard. In many I found scales, remnants of fish, and pieces of shells. The intestines were upwards of three feet in length.

Immediately after the breeding season, these birds drop their quills, and are quite unable to fly until the beginning of October, when they all leave their breeding grounds for the sea, and move southward. The young at this period scarcely shew the white streak between the bill and the eye; their cheeks, like those of the old birds at this time, and the fore part of the neck, are dingy white, and remain so until the following spring, when the only difference between the young and the old is, that the former have the bill smaller and less furrowed, and the head more brown. The back, tail, and lower parts do not seem to undergo any material change.

The Wood Ibis

Tantalus loculator, LINN.

(PLATE 38)

THIS very remarkable bird, and all others of the same genus that are known to occur in the United States, are constant residents in some part of our Southern Districts, although they perform short migrations. A few of them now and then stray as far as the Middle States, but instances of this are rare; and I am not aware that any have been seen farther to the eastward than the southern portions of Maryland, excepting a few individuals of the Glossy and the White Ibises, which have been procured in Pennsylvania, New Jersey, and New York. The Carolinas, Georgia, the Floridas, Alabama, Lower Louisiana, including Opellousas, and Mississippi, are the districts to which they resort by preference, and in which they spend the whole year. With the exception of the Glossy Ibis, which may be looked upon as a bird of the Mexican territories, and which usually appears in the Union singly or in pairs, they all live socially in immense flocks, especially during the breeding season. The country which they inhabit is doubtless the best suited to their habits; the vast and numerous swamps, lagoons, bayous, and submersed savannahs that occur in the lower parts of our Southern States, all abounding with fishes and reptiles; and the temperature of these countries being congenial to their constitutions.

In treating of the bird now under your notice, Mr WILLIAM BARTRAM says, "This solitary bird does not associate in flocks, but is generally seen alone." This was published by WILSON, and every individual who has since written on the subject, has copied the assertion without probably having any other reason than that he believed the authors of it to state a fact. But the habits of this species are entirely at variance with the above quotation, to which I direct your attention not without a feeling of pain, being assured that Mr BARTRAM could have made such a statement only because he had few opportunities of studying the bird in question in its proper haunts.

The Wood Ibis is rarely met with single, even after the breeding season, and it is more easy for a person to see an hundred together at any period of the year, than to meet with one by itself. Nay, I have seen flocks composed of several thousands, and that there is a natural necessity for their flocking together I shall explain to you. This species feeds entirely on fish and aquatic reptiles, of which it destroys an enormous quantity, in fact more than it eats; for if they have been killing fish for half an hour and have gorged themselves, they suffer the rest to lie on the water untouched, when it becomes food for alligators, crows, and vultures, whenever these animals can lay hold of it. To procure its food, the Wood Ibis walks through shallow muddy lakes or bayous in numbers. As soon as they have discovered a place abounding in fish, they dance as it were all through it, until the water becomes thick with the mud stirred from the bottom by their feet. The fishes, on rising to the surface, are instantly struck by the beaks of the Ibises, which, on being deprived of life, they turn over and so remain. In the course of ten or fifteen minutes, hundreds of fishes, frogs, young alligators, and water-snakes cover the surface, and the birds greedily swallow them until they are completely gorged, after which they walk to the nearest margins, place themselves in long rows, with their breasts all turned towards the sun, in the manner of Pelicans and Vultures, and thus remain for an hour or so. When digestion is partially accomplished, they all take to wing, rise in spiral circlings to an immense height, and sail about for an hour or more, performing the most beautiful evolutions that can well be conceived. Their long necks and legs are stretched out to their full extent, the pure white of their plumage contrasts beautifully with the jetty black of the tips of their wings. Now in large circles they seem to ascend toward the upper regions of the atmosphere; now, they pitch towards the earth; and again, gently rising, they renew their gyrations. Hunger once more induces them to go in search of food, and, with extended front, the band sails rapidly towards another lake or bayou.

Mark the place, reader, and follow their course through cane-brake, cypress-swamp, and tangled wood. Seldom do they return to the same feeding place on the same day. You have reached the spot, and are standing on the margin of a dark-watered bayou, the sinuosities of which lead your eye into a labyrinth ending in complete darkness. The tall canes bow to each other from the shores; the majestic trees above them, all hung with funereal lichen, gently wave in the suffocating atmosphere; the bullfrog, alarmed, shrinks back into the water; the alligator raises his head above its surface, probably to see if the birds have arrived, and the wily cougar is stealthily advancing toward one of the Ibises, which he expects to carry off into the thicket. Through the dim light your eye catches a glimpse of the white-plumaged birds, moving rapidly like spectres to and fro. The loud clacking of their mandibles apprises you of the havock they commit among the terrified inhabitants of the waters, while the knell-like sounds of their feet come with a feeling of dread. Move, gently or not, move at all, and you infallibly lose your opportunity of observing the actions of the birds. Some old male has long marked you; whether it has been with eye or with ear, no matter. The first stick your foot cracks, his hoarse voice sounds the alarm. Off they all go, battering down the bending canes with their powerful pinions, and breaking the smaller twigs of the trees, as they force a passage for themselves.

Talk to me of the stupidity of birds, of the dulness of the Wood Ibis! say it is fearless, easily approached, and easily shot. I listen, but it is merely through courtesy; for I have so repeatedly watched its movements, in all kinds of circumstances, that I am quite convinced we have not in the United States a more shy, wary, and vigilant bird than the Wood Ibis. In the course of two years spent, I may say, among them, for I saw some whenever I pleased during that period, I never succeeded in surprising one, not even under night, when they were roosting on trees at a height of nearly a hundred feet, and sometimes rendered farther secure by being over extensive swamps.

My Journal informs me, that, one autumn while residing near Bayou Sara, being intent on procuring eight or ten of these birds, to skin for my learned and kind friend the Prince of Musignano, I took with me two servants, who were first-rate woodsmen, and capital hands at the rifle, and that notwithstanding our meeting with many hundreds of Wood Ibises, it took us three days to shoot fifteen, which were for the most part killed on wing with rifle-balls, at a distance of about a hundred yards. On that occasion we discovered that a flock roosted regularly over a large corn field covered with huge girted trees, the tops of which were almost all decayed. We stationed ourselves apart in the field, concealed among the tall ripened corn, and in silence awaited the arrival of the birds. After the sun had disappeared, the broad front of a great flock of Ibises was observed advancing towards us. They soon alighted in great numbers on the large branches of the dead trees; but whenever one of the branches gave way under their weight, all at once rose in the air, flew about several times, and alighted again. One of my companions, having a good opportunity, fired, and brought two down with a single bullet; but here the sport was ended. In five minutes after, not an Ibis was within a mile of the place, nor did any return to roost there for more than a month. When on the margin of a lake, or even in the centre of it—for all the lakes they frequent are exceedingly shallow—the first glimpse they have of a man induces them to exert all their vigilance; and should he after this advance a few steps, the birds fly off.

The name of "Wood Ibis" given to this bird, is not more applicable to it than to any other species; for every one with which I am acquainted resorts quite as much to the woods at particular periods. All our species may be found on wet sa vannahs, on islands surrounded even by the waters of the sea, the Florida Keys for example, or in the most secluded parts of the darkest woods, provided they are swampy, or are furnished with ponds. I have found the Wood, the Red, the White, the Brown, and the Glossy Ibises, around ponds in the centre of immense forests; and in such places, even in the desolate pine-barrens of the Floridas; sometimes several hundred miles from the sea coast, on the Red River, in the State of Louisiana, and above Natchez, in that of Mississippi, as well as within a few miles of the ocean. Yet, beyond certain limits, I never saw one of these birds.

One of the most curious circumstances connected with this species is, that although the birds are, when feeding, almost constantly within the reach of large alligators, of which they devour the young, these reptiles never attack them; whereas if a Duck or a Heron comes within the reach of their tails, it is immediately killed and swallowed. The Wood Ibis will wade up to its belly in the water, round the edges of "alligators' holes," without ever being injured; but should one of these birds be shot, an alligator immediately makes towards it and pulls it under water. The gar-fish is not so courteous, but gives chase to the Ibises whenever an opportunity occurs. The Snapping Turtle is also a great enemy to the young birds of this species.

The flight of the Wood Ibis is heavy at its rising from the ground. Its neck at that moment is deeply curved downward, its wings flap heavily but with great power, and its long legs are not stretched out behind until it has proceeded many yards. But as soon as it has attained a height of eight or ten feet, it ascends with great celerity, generally in a spiral direction, in silence if not alarmed, or, if frightened, with a rough croaking guttural note. When fairly on wing, they proceed in a direct flight, with alternate flappings and sailings of thirty or forty yards, the sailings more prolonged than the flappings. They alight on trees with more ease than Herons generally do, and either stand erect or crouch on the branches, in the manner of the Wild Turkey, the Herons seldom using the latter attitude. When they are at rest, they place their bill against the breast, while the neck shrinks as it were between the shoulders. In this position you may see fifty on the same tree, or on the ground, reposing in perfect quiet for hours at a time, although some individual of the party will be constantly on the look-out, and ready to sound the alarm.

In the spring months, when these birds collect in large flocks, before they return to their breeding places, I have seen thousands together, passing over the woods in a line more than a mile in extent, and moving with surprising speed at the height of only a few yards above the trees. When a breeding place has once been chosen, it is resorted to for years in succession; nor is it easy to make them abandon it after they have deposited their eggs, although, if much annoyed, they never return to it after that season.

Besides the great quantity of fishes that these Ibises destroy, they also devour frogs, young alligators, wood-rats, young rails and grakles, fiddlers and other crabs, as well as snakes and small turtles. They never eat the eggs of the alligator, as has been alleged, although they probably would do so, could they demolish the matted nests of that animal, a task beyond the power of *any* bird known to me. I never saw one eat any thing which either it or some of its fellows had not killed. Nor will it eat an animal that has been dead for some time, even although it may have been killed by itself. When eating, the clacking of their mandibles may be heard at the distance of several hundred yards.

When wounded, it is dangerous to approach them, for they bite severely. They may be said to be very tenacious of life. Although usually fat, they are very tough and oily, and therefore are not fit for food. The Negroes, however, eat them, having, previous to cooking them, torn off the skin, as they do with Pelicans and Cormorants. My own attempts, I may add, were not crowned with success. Many of the Negroes of Louisiana destroy these birds when young, for the sake of the oil which their flesh contains, and which they use in greasing machines.

The French Creoles of that State name them "Grands Flamans," while the Spaniards of East Florida know them by the name of "Gannets." When in the latter country, at St Augustine, I was induced to make an excursion, to visit a large pond or lake, where I was assured there were Gannets in abundance, which I might shoot off the trees, provided I was careful enough. On asking the appearance of the Gannets, I was told that they were large white birds, with wings black at the end, a long neck, and a large sharp bill. The description so far agreeing with that of the Common Gannet or Solan Goose, I proposed no questions respecting the legs or tail, but went off. Twenty-three miles, Reader, I trudged through the woods, and at last came in view of the pond; when, lo! its borders and the trees around it were covered with Wood Ibises. Now, as the good people who gave the information spoke according to their knowledge, and agreeably to their custom of calling the Ibises Gannets, had I not gone to the pond, I might have written this day that Gannets are found in the interior of the woods in the Floridas, that they alight on trees, &c. which, if *once* published, would in all probability have gone down to future times through the medium of compilers, and all perhaps without acknowledgment.

The Wood Ibis takes four years in attaining full maturity, although birds of the second year are now and then found breeding. This is rare, however, for the young birds live in flocks by themselves, until they have attained the age of about three years. They are at first of a dingy brown, each feather edged with paler; the head is covered to the mandibles with short downy feathers, which gradually fall off as the bird advances in age. In the third year, the head is quite bare, as well as a portion of the upper part of the neck. In the fourth year, the bird is as you see it in the plate. The male is much larger and heavier than the female, but there is no difference in colour between the sexes.

Louisiana Heron

Ardea Ludoviciana, WILS.

(PLATE 40)

DELICATE in form, beautiful in plumage, and graceful in its movements, I never see this interesting Heron, without calling it the Lady of the Waters. Watch its motions, as it leisurely walks over the pure sand beaches of the coast of Florida, arrayed in the full beauty of its spring plumage. Its pendent crest exhibits its glossy tints, its train falls gracefully over a well defined tail, and the tempered hues of its back and wings contrast with those of its lower parts. Its measured steps are so light that they leave no impression on the sand, and with its keen eye it views every object around with the most perfect accuracy. See, it has spied a small fly lurking on a blade of grass, it silently runs a few steps, and with the sharp point of its bill it has already secured the prey. The minnow just escaped from the pursuit of some larger fish has almost rushed upon the beach for safety; but the quick eye of the Heron has observed its motions, and in an instant it is swallowed alive. Among the herbage yet dripping with dew the beautiful bird picks its steps. Not a snail can escape its keen search, and as it moves around the muddy pool, it secures each water lizard that occurs. Now the sun's rays have dried up the dews, the flowers begin to droop, the woodland choristers have ended their morning concert, and like them, the Heron, fatigued with its exertions, seeks a place of repose under the boughs of the nearest bush, where it may in safety await the coolness of the evening. Then for a short while it again searches for food. Little difficulty does it experience in this; and at length, with the last glimpse of day, it opens its wings, and flies off towards its well-known roosting place, where it spends the night contented and happy.

This species, which is a constant resident in the southern parts of the peninsula of the Floridas, seldom rambles far from its haunts during the winter season, being rarely seen at that period beyond Savannah in Georgia to the eastward. To the west it extends to the broad sedgy flats bordering the mouths of the Mississippi, along the whole Gulf of Mexico, and perhaps much farther south. In the beginning of spring, it is found abundantly in the Carolinas, and sometimes as far east as Maryland, or up the Mississippi as high as Natchez. You never find it far inland: perhaps forty miles would be a considerable distance at any time of the year. It is at all seasons a social bird, moving about in company with the Blue Heron or the White Egret. It also frequently associates with the larger species, and breeds in the same places, along with the White Heron, the Yellow-crowned Heron, and the Night Heron; but more generally it resorts to particular spots for this purpose, keeping by itself, and assembling in great numbers. Those which visit the Carolinas, or the country of the Mississippi, make their appearance there about the first of April, or when the Egrets and other species of Heron seek the same parts, returning to the Floridas or farther south about the middle of September, although I have known some to remain there during mild winters. When this is the case, all the other species may be met with in the same places, as the Louisiana Heron is the most delicate in constitution of all. Whilst at St Augustine in Florida, in the month of January, I found this species extremely abundant there; but after a hard frost of a few days, they all disappeared, leaving the other Herons, none of which seemed to be affected by the cold, and returned again as soon as the Fahrenheit thermometer rose to 80°. There they were in full livery by the end of February, and near Charleston by the 5th of April.

Although timid, they are less shy than most other species, and more easily procured. I have frequently seen one alight at the distance of a few yards, and gaze on me as if endeavouring to discover my intentions. This apparent insensibility to danger has given rise to the appellation of *Egrette folle*, which is given to them in Lower Louisiana.

The flight of this beautiful Heron is light, rather irregular, swifter than that of any other species, and capable of being considerably protracted. They usually move in long files, rather widely separated, and in an undulating manner, with constant flappings. When proceeding towards their roosts, or when on their migrations, they pass as high over the country as other species; on the former occasion, they pass and repass over the same tract, thus enabling the gunner easily to shoot them, which he may especially calculate on doing at the approach of night, when they are gorged with food, and fly lower than in the morning. They may, however, be still more surely obtained on their arriving at their roosting place, where they alight at once among the lowest branches. On being shot at, they seldom fly to a great distance, and their attachment to a particular place is such that you are sure to find them there during the whole period of their stay in the country, excepting the breeding time. At the cry of a wounded one, they assail you in the manner of some Gulls and Terns, and may be shot in great numbers by any person fond of such sport.

On the 29th of April, while wading around a beautiful key of the Floridas, in search of certain crustaceous animals called the sea Cray-fish, my party and I suddenly came upon one of the breeding places of the Louisiana Heron. The southern exposures of this lovely island were overgrown with low trees and bushes matted together by thousands of smilaxes and other creeping plants, supported by various species of cactus. Among the branches some hundred pairs of these lovely birds had placed their nests, which were so low and so close to each other, that without moving a step one could put his hand into several. The birds thus taken by surprise rose affrighted into the air, bitterly complaining of being disturbed in their secluded retreat. The nests were formed of small dried sticks crossing each other in various ways. They were flat, had little lining, and each contained three eggs, all the birds being then incubating. Observing that many eggs had been destroyed by the Crows and Buzzards, as the shells were scattered on the ground, I concluded that many of the Herons had laid more than once, to make up their full complement of eggs; for my opinion is, that all our species, excepting the Green Heron, never lay more nor less than three, unless an accident should happen. The eggs of the Louisiana Heron measure one inch and six and a half twelfths in length, an inch and a quarter in breadth; they are nearly elliptical, of a beautiful pale blue colour inclining to green, smooth, and with a very thin shell. The period of incubation is twenty-one days. Like all other species of the genus, this raises only one brood in the season. The little island of which I have spoken lies exposed to the sea, and has an extent of only a few acres. The trees or bushes with which it was covered seemed to have been stunted by the effect produced by their having been for years the receptacles of the Herons' nests.

On the 19th May, in the same year, I found another breeding place of this species not far from Key West. The young birds, which stood on all the branches of the trees and bushes on the southern side of the place, were about the size of our Little Partridge. Their notes, by which we had been attracted to the spot, were extremely plaintive, and resembled the syllables *wiee, wiee, wiee.* When we went up to them, the old birds all flew to another key, as if intent on drawing us there; but in vain, for we took with us a good number of their young. It was surprising to see the little fellows moving about among the branches, clinging to them in all sorts of curious positions, and persevering in forcing their way toward the water, when over which they at once dropped, and swam off from us with great vigour and speed. When seized with the hand, they defended themselves to the utmost. At this early period, they plainly shewed the sprouting feathers of the crest. Many Crow Blackbirds had nests on the same mangroves, and a Fish-Hawk also had formed its nest there at a height of not more than five feet from the water. On the 24th of May, these Herons were fully fledged, and able to fly to a short distance. In this state we, with some difficulty, procured one alive. Its legs and feet were green, the bill black, but its eyes, like those of an adult bird, were of a beautiful red hue. Many were caught afterwards and taken as passengers on board the Marion. They fed on any garbage thrown to them by the sailors; but whenever another species came near them, they leaped towards its bill, caught hold of it as if it had been a fish, and hung to it until shaken off by their stronger associates. On several occasions, however, the *Ardea occidentalis* shook them off violently, and after beating them on the deck, swallowed them before they could be rescued!

The place farthest up on the Mississippi where I have found this species breeding was on Buffalo Creek, about forty miles below Natchez, and ten miles in a direct line from the great river. To the eastward I have found them, breeding in company with the Green Heron and the Night Heron, within a few miles of Charleston.

During summer and autumn, after the old birds have left their young, both are frequently seen in the rice-fields, feeding along the ditches by which the water is led to those places. At this season they are uncommonly gentle and easily approached.

The Louisiana Heron acquires the full beauty of its plumage the second year after its birth, although it continues for some time to increase in size. The train and crest lengthen for several years until they become as represented in the plate. To procure specimens in such complete plumage, however, requires some care, for this state does not last many days after pairing has taken place, and by the time the young are hatched much of this fine plumage has dropped. When autumn has come, only a few of the long barbs remain, and in winter no appearance of them can be seen.

The flesh of the young birds affords tolerable eating. The food of this species consists of small fry, water insects, worms, slugs, and snails, as well as leeches, tadpoles, and aquatic lizards.

The Mallard

Anas Boschas, LINN.

(PLATE 41)

ALTHOUGH it is commonly believed that the Mallard is found abundantly everywhere in the United States, I have received sufficient proof to the contrary. If authors had acknowledged that they state so on report, or had said that in the tame state the bird is common, I should not have blamed them. According to my observation, and I may be allowed to say that I have had good opportunities, this valuable species is extremely rare in the wild state, in the neighbourhood of Boston in Massachusetts; and in this assertion, I am supported by my talented and amiable friend Mr NUTTALL, who has resided there for many years. Farther eastward, this bird is so rare that it is scarcely known, and not one was seen by myself or my party beyond Portland in Maine. On the western coast of Labrador none of the inhabitants that we conversed with had ever seen the Mallard, and in Newfoundland the people were equally unacquainted with it, the species being in those countries replaced by the Black Duck, *Anas fusca*. From New York southward, the Mallards become more plentiful, and numbers of them are seen in the markets of Philadelphia, Baltimore, Richmond in Virginia, and other towns. Although they are very abundant in the Carolinas and Floridas, as well as in Lower Louisiana, they are much more so in the Western Country. The reason of this is merely that the Mallard, unlike the sea ducks, is rarely seen on salt water, and that its course from the countries where it chiefly breeds is across the interior of the continent. From our great lakes, they spread along the streams, betake themselves to the ponds, wet meadows, submersed savannahs, and inland swamps, and are even found in the thick beech woods, in early autumn, and indeed long before the males have acquired the dark green colour of the head. Many of them proceed beyond the limits of the United States.

It would be curious to know when this species was first domesticated; but, Reader, the solution of such a question is a task on which I shall not venture. In the domestic state every body knows the Mallard. When young it affords excellent food, and when old lays eggs. A bed made of its feathers is far preferable to the damp earth of the camp of an American woodsman, or the plank on which the trained soldier lays his wearied limbs at night. You may find many other particulars if you consult in chronological order all the compilers from ALDROVANDUS to the present day.

Be not startled, good Reader, when I tell you that many of these ducks are bred in the lakes near the Mississippi, nay even in some of the small ponds in the low lands or bottoms of the States of Kentucky, Indiana and Illinois; for in many parts of those districts I have surprised the females on their eggs, have caught the young when their mother was cautiously and with anxiety leading them for greater safety to some stream, and have shot many a fat one before the poor thing could fly, and when it was so plump, tender, and juicy, that I doubt much whether, you, like myself, should not much prefer them to the famed Canvass-backed Duck.

Look at that Mallard as he floats on the lake; see his elevated head glittering with emerald-green, his amber eyes glancing in the light! Even at this distance, he has marked you, and suspects that you bear no good will towards him, for he sees that you have a gun, and he has many a time been frightened by its report, or that of some other. The wary bird draws his feet under his body, springs upon them, opens his wings, and with loud quacks bids you farewell.

Now another is before you, on the margin of that purling streamlet. How brisk are all his motions compared with those of his brethren that waddle across your poultry-yard! how much more graceful in form and neat in apparel! The duck at home is the descendant of a race of slaves, and has lost his native spirit: his wings have been so little used that they can hardly raise him from the ground. But the free-born, the untamed duck of the swamps,—see how he springs on wing, and hies away over the woods.

The Mallards generally arrive in Kentucky and other parts of the Western Country, from the middle of September to the first of October, or as soon as the acorns and beech-nuts are fully ripe. In a few days they are to be found in all the ponds that are covered with seed-bearing grasses. Some flocks, which appear to be guided by an experienced leader, come directly down on the water with a rustling sound of their wings that can be compared only to the noise produced by an Eagle in the act of stooping upon its prey, while other flocks, as if they felt uneasy respecting the safety of the place, sweep around and above it several times in perfect silence, before they alight. In either case, the birds immediately bathe themselves, beat their bodies with their wings, dive by short plunges, and cut so many capers that you might imagine them to be stark mad. The fact, however, seems to be, that all this alacrity and gaiety only shews the necessity they feel of clearing themselves of the insects about their plumage, as well as the pleasure they experience on finding themselves in a milder climate, with abundance of food around them, after a hard journey of perhaps a day and a night. They wash themselves and arrange their dress, before commencing their meal; and in this other travellers would do well to imitate them.

Now, towards the grassy margins they advance in straggling parties. See how they leap from the water to bend the loaded tops of the tall reeds. Woe be to the slug or snail that comes in their way. Some are probing the mud beneath, and waging war against the leech, frog, or lizard, that is within reach of their bills; while many of the older birds run into the woods, to fill their crops with beech-nuts and acorns, not disdaining to swallow also, should they come in their way, some of the wood-mice that, frightened by the approach of the foragers, hie towards their burrows. The cackling they keep up would almost deafen you, were you near them; but it is suddenly stopped by the approach of some unusual enemy, and at once all are silent. With heads erected on out-stretched necks, they anxiously look around. It is nothing, however, but a bear, who being, like themselves, fond of mast, is ploughing up the newly fallen leaves with his muzzle, or removing an old rotting log in search of worms. The ducks resume their employment. But another sound is now heard, one more alarming. The bear raises himself on his hind legs, snuffs the air, and with a loud snort gallops off towards the depths of his canebrake. The ducks retreat to the water, betake themselves to the centre of the pool, and uttering half-stifled notes await the sight of the object they dread. There the enemy cunningly advances first covered by one tree, then by another. He has lost his chance of the bear, but as he is pushed by hunger, a Mallard will do for the bullet of his rusty rifle. It is an Indian, as you perceive by his red skin and flowing black hair, which, however, has been cut close from the sides of his head. In the centre of his dearly purchased blanket, a hole has been cut, through which he has thrust his bare head, and the ragged garment, like a horse's netting, is engaged as it were in flapping off the last hungry musquitoes of the season that are fast sucking the blood from his limbs. Watch him, Mallard, Nay, wait no longer, for I see him taking aim; better for you all to fly! No—well, one of you will certainly furnish him with a repast. Amid the dark wood rises the curling smoke, the report comes on my ear, the ducks all rise save a pair, that, with back downwards and feet kicking against the air, have been hit by the prowler. The free son of the forest slowly approaches the pool, judges at a glance of the depth of the mire, and boldly advances, until with a cane he draws the game towards him. Returning to the wood, he now kindles a little fire, the feathers fill the air around; from each wing he takes a quill, to clean the touch-hole of his gun in damp weather; the entrails he saves to bait some trap. In a short time the ducks are ready, and the hunter enjoys his meal, although brief time does he take in swallowing the savoury morsels. Soon, the glimmering light of the moon will see him again on his feet, and lead him through the woods, as he goes in pursuit of other game.

The Mallards that remain with us during the whole year, and breed on the banks of the Mississippi or Lake Michigan, or in the beautiful meadows that here and there border the Schuylkil in Pennsylvania, begin to pair in the very heart of winter; and although ducks are quite destitute of song, their courtships are not devoid of interest. The males, like other gay deceivers, offer their regards to the first fair one that attracts their notice, promise unremitting fidelity and affection, and repeat their offers to the next they meet. See that drake, how he proudly shews, first the beauty of his silky head, then the brilliancy of his wing-spots, and, with honeyed jabberings, discloses the warmth of his affection. He plays around this one, then around another, until the passion of jealousy is aroused in the breasts of the admired and flattered. Bickerings arise; the younger duck disdains her elder sister, and a third, who conceives herself a coquette of the first order, interposes, as if to ensure the caresses of the feathered beau. Many tricks are played by ducks, good Reader, but ere long, the females retire in search of a safe place in which they may deposit their eggs and rear their young. They draw a quantity of weeds around them, and form an ill-arranged sort of nest, in which from seven to ten eggs are laid. From their bodies they pluck the softest down, and placing it beneath the eggs, begin the long process of incubation, which they intermit only for short periods, when it becomes absolutely necessary to procure a little sustenance.

At length, in about three weeks, the young began to cheep in the shell, from which, after a violent struggle, they make their escape. What beautiful creatures! See how, with their little bills, they dry their downy apparel! Now in a long line, one after another, they follow their glad mother to the water, on arriving at which they take to swimming and diving, as if elated with joy for having been introduced into existence. The male, wearied and emaciated, is far away on some other pond. The unnatural barbarian cares nothing about his progeny, nor has a thought arisen in his mind respecting the lonely condition of his mate, the greatness of her cares, or the sadness that she may experience under the idea that she has been utterly forsaken by him who once called her his only and truly beloved. No, Reader, not a thought of this kind has he wasted on her whom he has left alone in charge of a set of eggs, and now of a whole flock of innocent ducklings, to secure which from danger, and see them all grow up apace, she manifests the greatest care and anxiety. She leads them along the shallow edges of grassy ponds, and teaches them to seize the small insects that abound there, the flies, the musquitoes, the giddy beetles that skim along the surface in circles and serpentine lines. At the sight of danger they run as it were on the water, make directly for the shore, or dive and disappear. In about six weeks, those that have escaped from the ravenous fishes and turtles have attained a goodly size; the quills appear on their wings; their bodies are encased with feathers; but as yet none are able to fly. They now procure their food by partial immersions of the head and neck in the manner of the old bird. At this period they are already fit for the table, and delicate as well as savoury food they afford. By the time that the leaves are changing their hues, the young Mallards take freely to their wings, and the old males join the congregated flocks.

The Squatters of the Mississippi raise a considerable number of Mallards, which they catch when quite young, and which, after the first year, are as tame as they can wish. These birds raise broods which are superior even to those of the wild ones, for a year or two, after which they become similar to the ordinary ducks of the poultry-yard. The hybrids produced between the Mallard and the Muscovy Duck are of great size, and afford excellent eating. Some of these half-breeds now and then wander off, become quite wild, and have by some persons been considered as forming a distinct species. They also breed, when tame, with the Black Duck (*Anas fusca*) and the Gadwal, the latter connection giving rise to a very handsome hybrid, retaining the yellow feet and barred plumage of the one, and the green head of the other parent.

I have found the Mallard breeding on large prostrate and rotten logs, three feet above the ground, and in the centre of a cane-brake, nearly a mile distant from any water. Once I found a female leading her young through the woods, and no doubt conducting them towards the Ohio. When I first saw her, she had already observed me, and had squatted flat among the grass, with her brood around her. As I moved onwards, she ruffled her feathers, and hissed at me in the manner of a goose, while the little ones scampered off in all directions. I had an excellent dog, well instructed to catch young birds without injuring them, and I ordered him to seek for them. On this the mother took to wing, and flew through the woods as if about to fall down at every yard or so. She passed and repassed over the dog, as if watching the success of his search; and as one after another the ducklings were brought to me, and struggled in my bird-bag, the distressed parent came to the ground near me, rolled and tumbled about, and so affected me by her despair, that I ordered my dog to lie down, while, with a pleasure that can be felt only by those who are parents themselves, I restored to her the innocent brood, and walked off. As I turned round to observe her, I really thought I could perceive gratitude expressed in her eye; and a happier moment I never felt while rambling in search of knowledge through the woods.

In unfrequented parts, the Mallards feed both by day and by night; but in places where they are much disturbed by gunners, they feed mostly by night, or towards evening and about sunrise. In extremely cold weather, they betake themselves to the sources of streams, and even to small springs, where they may be found along with the American Snipe. At times, after heavy falls of rain, they are seen searching for ground-worms over the corn-fields, and during the latter part of autumn, the rice plantations of Georgia and the Carolinas afford them excellent pasture grounds. I have thought indeed that at this season these birds perform a second migration as it were, for they then pour into the rice-fields by thousands from the interior. In the Floridas, they are at times seen in such multitudes as to darken the air, and the noise they make in rising from off a large submersed savannah, is like the rumbling of thunder. So numerous were the Mallards while I was at General HERNANDEZ's in East Florida, that a single Negro whom that gentleman kept as a hunter, would shoot from fifty to a hundred and twenty in a day, thus supplying the plantation with excellent food.

The flight of the Mallard is swift, strong, and well sustained. It rises either from the ground or from the water at a single spring, and flies almost perpendicularly for ten or fifteen yards, or, if in a thick wood, until quite above the tops of the tallest trees, after which it moves horizontally. If alarmed, it never rises without uttering several *quacks*; but on other occasions it usually leaves its place in silence. While travelling to any distance, the whistling sound of their wings may be heard a great way off, more especially in the quiet of night. Their progress through the air I have thought might be estimated at a mile and a half in the minute; and I feel very confident that when at full speed and on a long journey, they can fly at the rate of a hundred and twenty miles in the hour.

The Mallard is truly omnivorous, its food consisting of every thing that can possibly satisfy the cravings of its extraordinary appetite. Nor is it at all cleanly in this respect, for it will swallow any kind of offals, and feed on all sorts of garbage, even putrid fish, as well as on snakes and small quadrupeds. Nuts and fruits of all kinds are dainties to it, and it soon fattens on rice, corn, or any other grain. My friend JOHN BACHMAN, who usually raises a great number of Mallards every year, has the young fed on chopped fish, on which they thrive uncommonly well. So very greedy are these birds, that I have often observed a couple of them tugging for a long time against each other for the skin of an eel, which was already half swallowed by the one, while the other was engaged at the opposite end. They are expert fly-catchers, and are in the habit of patting with their feet the damp earth, to force ground-worms out of their burrows.

Besides man, the enemies of the Mallard are the White-headed Eagle, the Snowy Owl, the Virginian Owl, the racoon, the lynx, and the snapping turtle. Mallards are easily caught by snares, steel-traps baited with corn, and figure-of-four traps. As we have no decoys in the United States, I shall not trouble you with a new edition of the many accounts you will find in ornithological books of that destructive method of procuring Wild Ducks.

The eggs of this species measure two inches and a quarter in length, one inch and five-eighths in breadth. The shell is smooth, and of a plain light dingy green. They are smaller than those of the tame duck, and rarely so numerous. As soon as incubation commences, the males associate together in flocks, until the young are able to migrate. This species raises only one brood in the season, and I never found its nest with eggs in autumn. The female covers her eggs before she leaves them to go in search of food, and thus keeps them sufficiently warm until her return.

The White Ibis

Ibis alba, VIEILL.

(PLATE 42)

SANDY ISLAND, of which I have already spoken in my second volume, is remarkable as a breeding-place for various species of water and land birds. It is about a mile in length, not more than a hundred yards broad, and in form resembles a horse-shoe, the inner curve of which looks toward Cape Sable in Florida, from which it is six miles distant. At low water, it is surrounded to a great distance by mud flats abounding in food for wading and swimming birds, while the plants, the fruits, and the insects of the island itself, supply many species that are peculiar to the land. Besides the White Ibis, we found breeding there the Brown Pelican, the Purple, the Louisiana, the White, and the Green Herons, two species of Gallinule, the Cardinal Grosbeak, Crows, and Pigeons. The vegetation consists of a few tall mangroves, thousands of wild plum trees, several species of cactus, some of them nearly as thick as a man's body, and more than twenty feet high, different sorts of smilax, grape-vines, cane, palmettoes, Spanish bayonets, and the rankest nettles I ever saw,—all so tangled together, that I leave you to guess how difficult it was for my companions and myself to force a passage through them in search of birds' nests, which, however, we effected, although the heat was excessive, and the stench produced by the dead birds, putrid eggs, and the natural effluvia of the Ibises, was scarcely sufferable. But then, the White Ibis was there, and in thousands; and, although I already knew the bird, I wished to study its manners once more, that I might be enabled to present you with an account of them, which I now proceed to do,—endeavouring all the while to forget the pain of the numerous scratches and lacerations of my legs caused by the cactuses of Sandy Island.

As we entered that well-known place, we saw nests on every bush, cactus, or tree. Whether the number was one thousand or ten I cannot say, but this I well know:—I counted forty-seven on a single plum-tree. These nests of the White Ibis measure about fifteen inches in their greatest diameter, and are formed of dry twigs intermixed with fibrous roots and green branches of the trees growing on the island, which this bird easily breaks with its bill; the interior, which is flat, being finished with leaves of the cane and some other plants. The bird breeds only once in the year, and the full number of its eggs is three. They measure two inches and a quarter in length, with a diameter of one inch and five-eighths, are rough to the touch, although not granulated, of a dull white colour, blotched with pale yellow, and irregularly spotted with deep reddish-brown. They afford excellent eating, although when boiled they do not look inviting, the white resembling a livid-coloured jelly, and the yolk being of a reddish-orange, the former wonderfully transparent, instead of being opaque like that of most other birds. The eggs are deposited from the 10th of April to the 1st of May, and incubation is general by the 10th of the latter month. The young birds, which are at first covered with thick down of a dark grey colour, are fed by regurgitation. They take about five weeks to be able to fly, although they leave the nest at the end of three weeks, and stand on the branches, or on the ground, waiting the arrival of their parents with food, which consists principally of small fiddler crabs and cray-fish. On some occasions, I have found them at this age miles away from the breeding-places, and in this state they are easily caught. As soon as the young are able to provide for themselves, the old birds leave them, and the different individuals are then seen searching for food apart. While nestling or in the act of incubating, these Ibises are extremely gentle and unwary, unless they may have been much disturbed, for they almost allow you to touch them on the nest. The females are silent all the while, but the males evince their displeasure by uttering sounds which greatly resemble those of the White-headed Pigeon, and which may be imitated by the syllables *crooh, croo, croo.* The report of a gun scarcely alarms them at first, although at all other periods these birds are shy and vigilant in the highest degree.

The change in the colouring of the bill, legs, and feet of this bird, that takes place in the breeding-season, is worthy of remark, the bill being then of a deep orange-red, and the legs and feet of a red nearly amounting to carmine. The males at this season have the gular pouch of a rich orange colour, and somewhat resembling in shape that of the Frigate Pelican, although proportionally less. During winter, these parts are of a dull flesh colour. The irides also lose much of their clear blue, and resume in some degree the umber colour of the young birds. I am thus particular in these matters, because it is doubtful if any one else has ever paid attention to them.

While breeding, the White Ibises go to a great distance in search of food for their young, flying in flocks of several hundreds. Their excursions take place at particular periods, determined by the decline of the tides, when all the birds that are not sitting go off, perhaps twenty or thirty miles, to the great mud flats, where they collect abundance of food, with which they return the moment the tide begins to flow. As the birds of this genus feed by night as well as by day, the White Ibis attends the tides at whatever hour they may be. Some of those which bred on Sandy Key would go to the keys next the Atlantic, more than forty miles distant, while others made for the Ever Glades; but they never went off singly. They rose with common accord from the breeding-ground, forming themselves into long lines, often a mile in extent, and soon disappeared from view. Soon after the turn of the tide we saw them approaching in the same order. Not a note could you have heard on those occasions; yet if you disturb them when far from their nests, they utter loud hoarse cries resembling the syllables *hunk, hunk, hunk*, either while on the ground or as they fly off.

The flight of the White Ibis is rapid and protracted. Like all other species of the genus, these birds pass through the air with alternate flappings and sailings; and I have thought that the use of either mode depended upon the leader of the flock, for, with the most perfect regularity, each individual follows the motion of that preceding it, so that a constant appearance of regular undulations is produced through the whole line. If one is shot at this time, the whole line is immediately broken up, and for a few minutes all is disorder; but as they continue their course, they soon resume their former arrangement. The wounded bird never attempts to bite or to defend itself in any manner, although, if only winged, it runs off with more speed than is pleasant to its pursuer.

At other times the White Ibis, like the Red and the Wood Ibises, rises to an immense height in the air, where it performs beautiful evolutions. After they have thus, as it were, amused themselves for some time, they glide down with astonishing speed, and alight either on trees or on the ground. Should the sun be shining, they appear in their full beauty, and the glossy black tips of their wings form a fine contrast with the yellowish-white of the rest of their plumage.

This species is as fond of resorting to the ponds, bayous, or lakes that are met with in the woods, as the Wood Ibis itself. I have found it breeding there at a distance of more than three hundred miles from the sea, and remaining in the midst of the thickest forests until driven off to warmer latitudes by the approach of winter. This is the case in the State of Mississippi, not far from Natchez, and in all the swampy forests around Bayou Sara and Pointe Coupée, as well as the interior of the Floridas. When disturbed in such places, these Ibises fly at once to the tops of the tallest trees, emitting their hoarse *hunk*, and watch your motions with so much care that it is extremely difficult to get within shot of them.

The manner in which this bird searches for its food is very curious. The Woodcock and the Snipe, it is true, are probers as well as it, but their task requires less ingenuity than is exercised by the White or the Red Ibis. It is also true that the White Ibis frequently seizes on small crabs, slugs and snails, and even at times on flying insects; but its usual mode of procuring food is a strong proof that cunning enters as a principal ingredient in its instinct. The Cray-fish often burrows to the depth of three or four feet in dry weather, for before it can be comfortable it must reach the water. This is generally the case during the prolonged heats of summer, at which time the White Ibis is most pushed for food. The bird, to procure the Cray-fish, walks with remarkable care towards the mounds of mud which the latter throws up while forming its hole, and breaks up the upper part of the fabric, dropping the fragments into the deep cavity that has been made by the animal. Then the Ibis retires a single step, and patiently waits the result. The Cray-fish, incommoded by the load of earth, instantly sets to work anew, and at last reaches the entrance of its burrow; but the moment it comes in sight, the Ibis seizes it with his bill.

Whilst at Indian Key, I observed an immense quantity of beautiful tree snails, of a pyramidal or shortly conical form, some pure white, others curiously marked with spiral lines of bright red, yellow and black. They were crawling vigorously on every branch of each bush where there was not a nest of the White Ibis; but wherever that bird had fixed its habitation, not a live snail was to be seen, although hundreds lay dead beneath. Was this caused by the corrosive quality of the bird's ordure?

There is a curious though not altogether general difference between the sexes of this species as to the plumage:—the male has five of its primaries tipped with glossy black for several inches, while the female, which is very little smaller than the male, has only four marked in this manner. On examining more than a hundred individuals of each sex, I found only four exceptions, which occurred in females that were very old birds, and which, as happens in some other species, might perhaps have been undergoing the curious change exhibited by ducks, pheasants, and some other birds, the females of which when old sometimes assume the livery of the males.

Much, as you are aware, good Reader, has been said respecting the "oil bags" of birds. I dislike controversy, simply because I never saw the least indications of it in the ways of the Almighty Creator. Should I err, forgive me, but my opinion is, that these organs were not made without an object. Why should they consist of matter so conveniently placed, and so disposed as to issue under the least pressure, through apertures in the form of well defined tubes? The White Ibis, as well as the Wood Ibis, and all the other species of this genus, when in full health, has these oil bags of great size, and, if my eyes have not deceived me, makes great use of their contents. Should you feel anxious to satisfy yourself on this subject, I request of you to keep some Ibises alive for several weeks, as I have done, and you will have an opportunity of judging. And again, tell me if the fat contained in these bags is not the very best *lip-salve* that can be procured.

When any species of Ibis with which I am acquainted falls into the water on being wounded, it swims tolerably well; but I have never observed any taking to the water and swimming either by choice or to escape pursuit. While in the company of Mr JOSEPH MASON, a young man who was for some time employed by me, and who has drawn plants to some of my birds, although not so successfully as my amiable friend Miss MARTIN, or GEORGE LEHMAN, who finish those they draw as beautifully as my learned and valued friend WILLIAM MACGILLIVRAY of Edinburgh does his faithful drawings of birds, I chanced one morning to be on the look-out for White Ibises, in a delightful swamp not many miles from Bayou Sara. It was in the end of summer, and all around was pure and calm as the clear sky, the bright azure of which was reflected by the lake before us. The trees had already exchanged the verdure of their foliage for more mellow tints of diversified hue; the mast dropped from the boughs; some of the Warblers had begun to think of removing farther south; the Night Hawk, in company with the Chimney Swallow, was passing swiftly towards the land of their winter residence, and the Ibises had all departed for the Florida coasts, excepting a few of the white species, one of which we at length espied. It was perched about fifty yards from us towards the centre of the pool, and as the report of one of our guns echoed among the tall cypresses, down to the water, broken-winged, it fell. The exertions which it made to reach the shore seemed to awaken the half-torpid alligators that lay in the deep mud at the bottom of the pool. One shewed his head above the water, then a second and a third. All gave chase to the poor wounded bird, which, on seeing its dreaded and deadly foes, made double speed towards the very spot where we stood. I was surprised to see how much faster the bird swam than the reptiles, who, with jaws widely opened, urged their heavy bodies through the water. The Ibis was now within a few yards of us. It was the alligator's last chance. Springing forward as it were, he raised his body almost out of the water; his jaws nearly touched the terrified bird; when pulling three triggers at once, we lodged the contents of our guns in the throat of the monster. Thrashing furiously with his tail, and rolling his body in agony, the alligator at last sunk to the mud; and the Ibis, as if in gratitude, walked to our very feet, and there lying down, surrendered itself to us. I kept this bird until the succeeding spring, and by care and good nursing, had the pleasure of seeing its broken wing perfectly mended, when, after its long captivity, I restored it to liberty, in the midst of its loved swamps and woods.

The young bird of this species which I kept alive for some time, fed freely, after a few days captivity, on soaked Indian corn meal, but evinced great pleasure when cray-fishes were offered to it. On seizing one, it beat it sideways on the ground, until the claws and legs were broken off, after which it swallowed the body whole. It was fond of lying on its side in the sun for an hour or so at a time, pluming its body and nursing the sore wing. It walked lightly and very gracefully, though not so much so as the Herons. It did not molest its companions, and became very gentle and tame, following those who fed it like a common fowl.

The Creoles of Louisiana call this species "*Bec croche*," and also "*Petit Flaman*," although it is also generally known by the name of "Spanish Curlew." The flesh, which, as well as the skin, is of a dull orange colour, is extremely fishy, although the birds are often sold in our southernmost markets, and are frequently eaten by the Indians.

The White Ibis has been shot eastward as far as New Jersey. Of this I have been made aware by my generous friend EDWARD HARRIS, Esq. I never saw one farther up the Mississippi than Memphis.

The Whooping Crane

Grus americana, TEMM.

(PLATE 39)

THE VARIEGATED foliage of the woods indicates that the latter days of October have arrived; gloomy clouds spread over the heavens; the fierce blasts of the north, as if glad to escape from the dreary regions of their nativity, sport in dreadful revelry among the forests and glades. Showers of sleet and snow descend at intervals, and the careful husbandman gathers his flocks, to drive them to a place of shelter. The traveller gladly accepts the welcome of the forester, and as he seats himself by the blazing fire, looks with pleasure on the spinning wheels of the industrious inmates. The lumberer prepares to set out on his long voyage, the trapper seeks the retreats of the industrious beaver, and the red Indian is making arrangements for his winter hunts. The Ducks and Geese have already reached the waters of the western ponds; here a Swan or two is seen following in their train, and as the observer of nature stands watching the appearances and events of this season of change, he hears from on high the notes of the swiftly travelling but unseen Whooping Crane. Suddenly the turbid atmosphere clears, and now he can perceive the passing birds. Gradually they descend, dress their extended lines, and prepare to alight on the earth. With necks outstretched, and long bony legs extended behind, they proceed supported by wings white as the snow but tipped with jet, until arriving over the great savannah they wheel their circling flight, and slowly approach the ground, on which with half-closed wings, and outstretched feet they alight, running along for a few steps to break the force of their descent.

Reader, see the majestic bird shake its feathers, and again arrange them in order. Proud of its beautiful form, and prouder still of its power of flight, it stalks over the withering grasses with all the majesty of a gallant chief. With long and measured steps he moves along, his head erect, his eye glistening with delight. His great journey is accomplished, and being well acquainted with a country which has often been visited by him, he at once commences his winter avocations.

The Whooping Crane reaches the Western Country about the middle of October, or the beginning of November, in flocks of twenty or thirty individuals, sometimes of twice or thrice that number, the young by themselves, but closely followed by their parents. They spread from Illinois over Kentucky, and all the intermediate States, until they reach the Carolinas on the southern coast, the Floridas, Louisiana, and the countries bordering on Mexico, in all of which they spend the winter, seldom returning northward until about the middle of April, or towards the beginning of May. They are seen on the edges of large ponds supplied with rank herbage, on fields or savannahs, now in swampy woods, and again on extensive marshes. The interior of the country, and the neighbourhood of the sea shores, suit them equally well, so long as the temperature is sufficiently high. In the Middle States, it is very seldom indeed that they are seen; and to the eastward of these countries they are unknown; for all their migrations are performed far inland, and thus they leave and return to the northern retreats where, it is said, they breed and spend the summer. While migrating they appear to travel both by night and by day, and I have frequently heard them at the former, and seen them at the latter time, as they were proceeding toward their destination. Whether the weather be calm or tempestuous, it makes no difference to them, their power of flight being such as to render them regardless of the winds. Nay I have observed them urging their way during very heavy gales, shifting from high to low in the air with remarkable dexterity. The members of a flock sometimes arrange themselves in the form of an acute-angled triangle; sometimes they move in a long line; again they mingle together without order, or form an extended front; but in whatever manner they advance, each bird sounds his loud note in succession, and on all occasions of alarm these birds manifest the same habit. While with us they are also always met with in flocks. But now, Reader, allow me to refer to my journals, whence I shall extract some circumstances relative to this majestic bird, which I hope you will find not uninteresting.

Louisville, State of Kentucky, March 1810.—I had the gratification of taking ALEXANDER WILSON to some ponds within a few miles of town, and of shewing him many birds of this species, of which he had not previously seen any other than stuffed specimens. I told him that the white birds were the adults, and that the grey ones were the young. WILSON, in his article on the Whooping Crane, has alluded to this, but, as on other occasions, has not informed his readers whence the information came.

Henderson, November 1810.—The Sand Hill Crane arrived at the Long Pond on the 28th of last month. I saw two flocks of young ones there, and one of adults on the Slim Pond. Both old and young immediately set to digging through the mud, the rains having scarcely begun to cover those places with water, for during summer they become almost dry. The birds work very assiduously with their bills, and succeed in uncovering the large roots of the great water-lily, which often run to a depth of two or three feet. Several cranes are seen in the same hole, tugging at roots and other substances, until they reach the object of their desire, which they greedily devour. While thus engaged, they are easily approached; for if their heads are bent down they cannot see you, and until they raise themselves again, to take notice of what may be going on around the place, you may advance so as to get within shot. While I watched them at this work, they were perfectly silent; and as I lay concealed behind a large cypress tree, within thirty paces of a flock, thus buried, as it were, in the great holes they had formed, so as to put me in mind of a parcel of hogs or bears at their wallowing spots, I could plainly see the colour of their eyes, which is brown in the young, and yellow in the adult. After observing them as long as I wished, I whistled, on which they all at once raised their heads to see what the matter might be. I had so fair an opportunity that I could

not resist the temptation, especially as several of the birds had
their necks so close together that I felt confident I must kill
more than one of them. Accordingly, just as their last croaking notes were heard, and I saw them preparing to set to
work again, I fired. Only two flew up, to my surprise. They
came down the pond towards me, and my next shot brought
them to the ground. On walking to the hole, I found that I
had disabled seven in all. Those which were in different holes
farther off, all flew away, uttering loud cries, and did not return that afternoon. In the course of a week these birds
turned up the earth, and dug holes all over the dry parts of
the ponds. As soon as heavy rains fill the pools, the Cranes
abandon them, and resort to other places.

Natchez, November 1821.—The Sand-hill Cranes now resort
to the fields, in which corn, pease, and sweet potatoes have
been planted, as well as to the cotton plantations. They feed
on the grains and pease, dig up the potatoes, which they devour with remarkable greediness; and in the wet fields seize
on water insects, toads and frogs, but never, I believe, on
fishes.

Bayou Sara, April 12, 1822.—The Sand-hill Cranes have left
all the fields, and removed to the swamps and inner lakes. I
saw some catching young bull-frogs, water-lizards, and water-
snakes, as well as very small alligators. One struck at a young
snapping turtle, which, however, escaped. The Wood Ibises
and these birds do not agree together; the latter chase the former up to their bellies in the water.

April 16.—I saw nine beautiful adult birds apparently in
perfect plumage. They were round a fallen log, about twenty
yards from the water, all very busily occupied in killing a band
of young alligators, which had probably endeavoured to save
themselves from the attacks of the Cranes by crawling beneath the sides of the log. I shot at them without much effect, for, although I believe I wounded two of them, they all
flew off. On going up to the log, I found several young alligators, measuring from seven to eight inches in length, apparently dead, with their heads sadly bruised as if by a
powerful blow. This led me to think that they kill a number
of animals before they feed upon them, as the Wood Ibis is
wont to do. This afternoon I saw four of these young Cranes

tearing up the ground in search of cray-fish. One caught a butterfly as it was fluttering near, and instantly swallowed it.

This species feeds only during the day. Besides the objects which I have already mentioned, it now and then swallows a mole or a meadow-mouse, and not unfrequently, I think, snakes of considerable length. I opened one that had a garter-snake, more than fifteen inches long, in its stomach.

The wariness of this species is so remarkable, that it takes all the cunning and care of an Indian hunter to approach it at times, especially in the case of an old bird. The acuteness of their sight and hearing is quite wonderful. If they perceive a man approaching, even at the distance of a quarter of a mile, they are sure to take to wing. Should you accidentally tread on a stick and break it, or suddenly cock your gun, all the birds in the flock raise their heads and emit a cry. Shut the gate of a field after you, and from that moment they all watch your motions. To attempt to crawl towards them, even among long grass, after such an intimation, would be useless; and unless you lie in wait for them, and be careful to maintain a perfect silence, or may have the cover of some large trees, heaps of brushwood, or fallen logs, you may as well stay at home. They generally see you long before you perceive them, and so long as they are aware that you have not observed them, they remain silent; but the moment that, by some inadvertency, you disclose to them your sense of their presence, some of them sound an alarm. For my part, Reader, I would as soon undertake to catch a deer by fair running, as to shoot a Sand-hill Crane that had observed me. Sometimes, indeed, towards the approach of spring, when they are ready to depart for their breeding grounds, the voice of one will startle and urge to flight all within a mile of the spot. When this happens, all the birds around join into a great flock, gradually rise in a spiral manner, ascend to a vast height, and sail off in a straight course.

When wounded, these birds cannot be approached without caution, as their powerful bill is capable of inflicting a severe wound. Knowing this as I do, I would counsel any sportsman not to leave his gun behind, while pursuing a wounded Crane. One afternoon in winter, as I was descending the Mississippi, on my way to Natchez, I saw several Cranes standing on a large sand-bar. The sight of these beautiful birds excited in me a desire to procure some of them. Accordingly, taking a rifle and some ammunition, I left the flat-bottomed boat in a canoe, and told the men to watch for me, as the current was rapid at that place, the river being there narrowed by the sand-bar. I soon paddled myself to the shore, and having observed, that, by good management, I might approach the Cranes under cover of a huge stranded tree, I landed opposite to it, drew up my canoe, and laying myself flat on the sand, crawled the best way I could, pushing my gun before me. On reaching the log, I cautiously raised my head opposite to a large branch, and saw the birds at a distance somewhat short of a hundred yards. I took, as I thought, an excellent aim, although my anxiety to shew the boatmen how good a marksman I was rendered it less sure than it might otherwise have been. I fired, when all the birds instantly flew off greatly alarmed, excepting one which leaped into the air, but immediately came down again, and walked leisurely away with a drooping pinion. As I rose on my feet, it saw me, I believe, for the first time, cried out lustily, and ran off with the speed of an ostrich. I left my rifle unloaded, and in great haste pursued the wounded bird, which doubtless would have escaped had it not made towards a pile of drift wood, where I overtook it. As I approached it, panting and almost exhausted, it immediately raised itself to the full stretch of its body, legs, and neck, ruffled its feathers, shook them, and advanced towards me with open bill, and eyes glancing with anger. I cannot tell you whether it was from feeling almost exhausted with the fatigue of the chase; but, however it was, I felt unwilling to encounter my antagonist, and keeping my eye on him, moved backwards. The farther I removed, the more he advanced, until at length I fairly turned my back to him, and took to my heels, retreating with fully more speed than I had pursued. He followed, and I was glad to reach the river, into which I plunged up to the neck, calling out to my boatmen, who came up as fast as they could. The Crane stood looking angrily on me all the while, immersed up to his belly in the water, and only a few yards distant, now and then making thrusts at me with his bill. There he stood until the people came up; and highly delighted they were with my situation.

However, the battle was soon over, for, on landing, some of them struck the winged warrior on the neck with an oar, and we carried him on board.

While in the Floridas, I saw only a few of these birds alive, but many which had been shot by the Spaniards and Indians, for the sake of their flesh and beautiful feathers, of which latter they make fans and fly-brushes. None of these birds remain there during summer; and WILLIAM BARTRAM, when speaking of this species, must have mistaken the Wood Ibis for it.

The young are considerably more numerous than the old white birds; and this circumstance has probably led to the belief among naturalists that the former constitute a distinct species, to which the name of Canada Crane, *Grus canadensis*, has been given. This, however, I hope, I shall be able to clear up to your satisfaction. In the mean time, I shall continue my remarks.

According to circumstances, this species roosts either on the ground or on high trees. In the latter case, they leave their feeding-ground about an hour before sun-set, and going off in silence, proceed towards the interior of high land forests, where they alight on the largest branches of lofty trees, six or seven settling on the same branch. For half an hour or so, they usually dress their plumage, standing erect: but afterwards they crouch in the manner of Wild Turkeys. In this situation they are sometimes shot by moonlight. Those which resort to plantations, situated in the vicinity of large marshes, covered with tall grasses, cat's tails, and other plants, spend the night on some hillock, standing on one leg, the other being drawn under the body, whilst the head is thrust beneath the broad feathers of the shoulder. In returning towards the feeding grounds, they all emit their usual note, but in a very low undertone, leaving their roost at an earlier or later hour, according to the state of the weather. When it is cold and clear, they start very early; but when warm and rainy, not until late in the morning. Their motions toward night are determined by the same circumstances. They rise easily from the ground after running a few steps, fly low for thirty or forty yards, then rise in circles, crossing each other in their windings, like Vultures, Ibises, and some other birds. If startled or shot at, they utter loud and piercing cries. These cries, which I cannot compare to the sounds of any instrument known to me, I have heard at the distance of three miles, at the approach of spring, when the males were paying their addresses to the females, or fighting among themselves. They may be in some degree represented by the syllables *kewrr, kewrr, kewrooh*; and strange and uncouth as they are, they have always sounded delightful in my ear.

In December 1833, I sent my son to Spring Island, on the coast of Georgia, to which these birds are in the habit of resorting every winter. Mr HAMMOND, the proprietor of this island, treated him with all the hospitality for which the southern planters are celebrated. The Cranes, which were plentiful, resorted to the sweet potato fields, digging up their produce as expertly as a troop of negroes. They walked carefully over the little heaps, probed them in various parts in the manner of Woodcocks or Snipes, and whenever they hit upon a potato, removed the soil, took out the root, and devoured it in rather small pieces. In this manner they would search over the whole field, which was two miles in length, and rather more than a quarter of a mile in breadth, gleaning all the potatoes that had escaped the gatherers. They were so shy, however, that notwithstanding all the endeavours of my son, who is a good hand at getting in upon game, as well as a good shot, he only killed a young one, which was evidently of that year's brood, it being yet almost reddish-brown, the long feathers of the rump just beginning to shew, and the head yet covered with hairlike feathers to the mandible, and merely shewing between them the wrinkled skin so conspicuous in the old birds. The specimen procured on Spring Island was carefully examined and described, and the skin is now in the British Museum in London. Its flesh was tender and juicy, of a colour resembling that of young venison, and afforded excellent eating. This I have always found to be the case with young birds of this species, so long as they are in their brown livery, and even when they have begun to be patched with white; but in old birds the flesh becomes very dark, tough and unfit for the table, although the Seminole Indians shoot them on all occasions for food.

In captivity the Whooping Crane becomes extremely gentle,

and feeds freely on grain and other vegetable substances. A Mr MAGWOOD, residing near Charleston, in South Carolina, kept one for some time feeding it on maize. It accidentally wounded one of its feet on the shell of an oyster, and, although the greatest care was taken of it, died after lingering some weeks. Having myself kept one alive, I will give you an account of its habits.

It was nearly full-grown when I obtained it, and its plumage was changing from greyish-brown to white. Its figure you will see in the plate to which this article refers. I received it as a present from Captain CLACK of the United States Navy, commander of the Erie sloop of war. It had been wounded in the wing, on the coast of Florida, but the fractured limb had been amputated and soon healed. During a voyage of three months, it became very gentle, and was a great favourite with the sailors. I placed it in a yard, in company with a beautiful Snow Goose. This was at Boston. It was so gentle as to suffer me to caress it with the hand, and was extremely fond of searching for worms and grubs about the wood pile, probing every hole it saw with as much care and dexterity as an Ivory-billed Woodpecker. It also watched with all the patience of a cat the motions of some mice which had burrows near the same spot, killed them with a single blow, and swallowed them entire, one after another, until they were extirpated. I fed it on corn and garbage from the kitchen, to which were added bits of bread and cheese, as well as some apples. It would pick up the straws intended to keep its feet from being soiled, and arrange them round its body, as if intent on forming a nest. For hours at a time, it would stand resting on one foot in a very graceful posture; but what appeared to me very curious was, that it had a favourite leg for this purpose; and in fact none of my family ever found it standing on the other, although it is probable that this happened in consequence of the mutilation of the wing, the leg employed being that of the injured side. The stump of its amputated wing appeared to be a constant source of trouble, particularly at the approach of the winter: it would dress the feathers about it, and cover it with so much care, that I really felt for the poor fellow. When the weather became intensely cold, it regularly retired at the approach of night under a covered passage, where it spent the hours of darkness; but it always repaired to this place with marked reluctance, and never until all was quiet and nearly dark, and it came out, even when the snow lay deep on the ground, at the first appearance of day. Now and then it would take a run, extend its only wing, and, uttering a loud cry, leap several times in the air, as if anxious to return to its haunts. At other times it would look upwards, cry aloud as if calling to some acquaintance passing high in the air, and again use its ordinary note whenever its companion the Snow Goose sent forth her own signals. It seldom swallowed its food without first carrying it to the water, and dipping it several times, and now and then it would walk many yards for that express purpose. Although the winter was severe, the thermometer some mornings standing as low as 10°, the bird fattened and looked extremely well. So strong was the natural suspicion of this bird, that I frequently saw it approach some cabbage leaves with measured steps, look at each sideways before it would touch one of them, and after all, if it by accident tossed the leaf into the air when attempting to break it to pieces, it would run off as if some dreaded enemy were at hand.

The trachea of this bird, of which you will find a notice at p. 213, confirms my opinion that the Canada Crane and the Whooping Crane are merely the same species in different states of plumage, or in other words, at different ages; and, in truth, the differences are not greater than those exhibited by many other birds, both aquatic and terrestrial. In illustration of this subject I might adduce Ibises, Herons, Divers, and Grebes; but this is quite unnecessary.

In reading the accounts given of the Canada Crane of authors, I find no description of its manner of breeding. In the Fauna Boreali-Americana of Mr SWAINSON and Dr RICHARDSON, the eggs of both are described, and in NUTTALL's Manual those of the Whooping Crane also; but in these works the account given of the birds and of their eggs is such, that one might even, from comparing the descriptions, suppose them to be of the same species. I have never had the satisfaction of finding any of the breeding-places of the Whooping Crane; but I well know that many birds breed long before they have attained their full plumage. The supposed new species of

Heron described under the name of *Ardea Pealii,* by my excellent friend Prince CHARLES BONAPARTE, breeds as the White-headed Eagle sometimes does, the immature bird in a snow-white dress, the adult in purple and greyish-blue plumage. The young of *Ardea cærulea* were for some time considered to form a distinct species, they being white also, then blue and white, and finally dark blue. But the most remarkable instance of change of plumage in the Traders is exhibited in the Scarlet Ibis. My humble opinion is, that unless in cases where birds are at first of one colour, and that colour remains ever after, little dependence can be placed on the tints of the plumage as a specific character.

On looking over my notes, I find that I have omitted to inform you that the extraordinary strength of the thighs, legs, and feet of the Whooping Crane, tends greatly to make it more terrestrial than the Herons; and that the great size of their nostrils, which so much resemble those of the Vultures, is well adapted to keep the inner parts of the organ from the damp earth and other matters with which they are so often in contact, while searching in the ground or mud for roots and other vegetable substances, on which the bird principally feeds. I am convinced also, that this species does not attain its full size or perfect plumage until it is four or five years old. The beauty of the plumage may be improved in brilliancy during the breeding-season by a greater brightness in the colour of the bill, as in the Booby Gannet and White Ibis, as well as in the redness of the fleshy parts of the head.

The measurements of the adult bird of my plate, drawn at New Orleans, in the month of April, were as follows:— Length from tip of bill to end of claws, 5 feet 5 inches; to end of tail, 4 feet 6 inches; the drooping feathers 1 foot beyond; alar extent 7 feet 8 inches; length of wing 22 inches; naked part of thigh 5 inches; tarsus 11¼ inches; length of middle toe 4¼, of its claw ¾.

The measurements of the specimen kept at Boston:— Length from tip of bill to end of tail, 3 feet 9 inches; to end of claws, 4 feet 6 inches; tarsus 8 inches; naked part of thigh 3½. The elongated inner secondaries equalled the tail. The weight was 9 lb. 14¾ oz.

Measurements of that killed on Spring Island:—Length 4

feet 4½ inches, the claws being 7 inches beyond the tail, so that the length from the tip of the bill to the end of the tail was 3 feet 9½ inches; alar extent 5 feet 8 inches. Weight 8¾ lb.

In the Museum of the University of Edinburgh, there is a specimen of still smaller size.

My friend JOHN BACHMAN, in a note addressed to me, says, "I saw a pair of tame birds of this species, which, as they advanced in age, changed their colours from grey to white."

The Long-billed Curlew

Numenius longirostris, WILS.

(PLATE 43)

THE Long-billed Curlew is a constant resident in the southern districts of the United States, whereas the other species are only autumnal and winter visitors. It is well known by the inhabitants of Charleston that it breeds on the islands on the coast of South Carolina; and my friend the Reverend JOHN BACHMAN has been at their breeding grounds. That some individuals go far north to breed, is possible enough, but we have no authentic account of such an occurrence, although many *suppositions* have been recorded. All that I have to say on this subject is, that the bird in question is quite unknown in the Magdeleine Islands, where, notwithstanding the assertions of the fishermen, they acknowledged that they had mistaken Godwits for Curlews. In Newfoundland, I met with a well-informed English gentleman, who had resided in that island upwards of twenty years, and described the Common Curlew of Europe with accuracy, but who assured me that he had observed only two species of Curlew there, one about the size of the Whimbrel—the *Numenius hudsonicus,* the other smaller—the *N. borealis,* and that only in August and the beginning of September, when they spend a few days in that country, feed on berries, and then retire southward. Mr JONES of Labrador, and his brother-in-law, who is a Scotch gentleman, a scholar, and a sportsman, gave me the same account. None of my party observed an individual of the species in the course of our three months' stay in the country, although we saw great numbers of the true Esquimaux Curlew, *N. borealis*. Yet I would not have you to suppose that I do not give credit to the reports of some travellers, who have said that the Long-billed Curlew is found in the fur countries during summer. This may be true enough; but none of the great northern travellers, such as RICHARDSON, ROSS, PARRY, or FRANKLIN, have asserted this as a fact. Therefore if the bird of which I speak has been seen far north, it was in all probability a few stragglers that had perhaps been enticed to follow some other species. I am well aware of the propensity it has to ramble, as I have shot some in Missouri, Indiana, Kentucky, Arkansas, and Mississippi; but the birds thus obtained were rare in those districts, where the species only appears at remote periods; and in every instance of the kind I have found the individuals much less shy than usual, and apparently more perplexed than frightened by the sight of man.

Until my learned friend, Prince CHARLES BONAPARTE, corrected the errors which had been made respecting the Curlews of North America, hardly one of these birds was known from another by any naturalist, American or European. To WILSON, however, is due the merit of having first published an account of the Long-billed Curlew as a species distinct from the Common Curlew of Europe.

This bird is the largest of the genus found in North America. The great length of its bill is of itself sufficient to distinguish it from every other. The bill, however, in all the species, differs greatly, according to the age of the individual, and in the present Curlew I have seen it in some birds nearly three inches shorter than in others, although all were full grown. In many of its habits, the Long-billed Curlew is closely allied to the smaller species of Ibis; its flight and manner of feeding are similar, and it has the same number of eggs. Unlike the Ibis, however, which always breeds on trees, and forms a large nest, the Curlew breeds on the ground, forming a scanty receptacle for its eggs; yet, according to my friend BACHMAN, the latter, like the former, places its nests "so close together, that it is almost impossible for a man to walk between them, without injuring the eggs."

The Long-billed Curlew spends the day in the sea-marshes, from which it returns at the approach of night, to the sandy beaches of the sea-shores, where it rests until dawn. As the sun sinks beneath the horizon, the Curlews rise from their feeding-grounds in small parties, seldom exceeding fifteen or twenty, and more usually composed of only five or six individuals. The flocks enlarge, however, as they proceed, and in the course of an hour or so the number of birds that collect in the place selected for their nightly retreat, sometimes amounts to several thousands. As it was my good fortune to witness their departures and arrivals, in the company of my friend BACHMAN, I will here describe them.

Accompanied by several friends, I left Charleston one beautiful morning, the 10th of November 1831, with a view to visit Cole's Island, about twenty miles distant. Our crew was good, and although our pilot knew but little of the cuttings in and out of the numerous inlets and channels in our way, we reached the island about noon. After shooting various birds, examining the island, and depositing our provisions in a small summer habitation then untenanted, we separated; some of the servants went off to fish, others to gather oysters, and the gunners placed themselves in readiness for the arrival of the Curlews. The sun at length sunk beneath the water-line that here formed the horizon; and we saw the birds making their first appearance. They were in small parties of two, three, or five, and by no means shy. These seemed to be the birds which we had observed near the salt-marshes, as we were on our way. As the twilight became darker the number of Curlews increased, and the flocks approached in quicker succession, until they appeared to form a continuous procession, moving not in lines, one after another, but in an extended mass, and with considerable regularity, at a height of not more than thirty yards, the individuals being a few feet apart. Not a single note or cry was heard as they advanced. They moved for ten or more yards with regular flappings, and then sailed for a few seconds, as is invariably the mode of flight of this species, their long bills and legs stretched out to their full extent. They flew directly towards their place of rest, called the "Bird Banks," and were seen to alight without performing any of the evolutions which they exhibit when at their feeding-places, for they had not been disturbed that season.

But when we followed them to the Bird Banks, which are sandy islands of small extent, the moment they saw us land the congregated flocks, probably amounting to several thousand individuals all standing close together, rose at once, performed a few evolutions in perfect silence, and re-alighted as if with one accord on the extreme margins of the sand-bank close to tremendous breakers. It was now dark, and we left the place, although some flocks were still arriving. The next morning we returned a little before day; but again as we landed, they all rose a few yards in the air, separated into numerous parties, and dispersing in various directions, flew off towards their feeding-grounds, keeping low over the waters, until they reached the shores, when they ascended to the height of about a hundred yards, and soon disappeared.

Now, Reader, allow me to say a few words respecting our lodgings. Fish, fowl, and oysters had been procured in abundance; and besides these delicacies, we had taken with us from Charleston some steaks of beef, and a sufficiency of good beverage. But we had no cook, save your humble servant. A blazing fire warmed and lighted our only apartment. The oysters and fish were thrown on the hot embers; the steaks we stuck on sticks in front of them; and ere long every one felt perfectly contented. It is true we had forgotten to bring salt with us; but I soon proved to my merry companions that hunters can find a good substitute in their powder-flasks. Our salt on this occasion was gunpowder, as it has been with me many a time; and to our keen appetites, the steaks thus salted were quite as savoury as any of us ever found the best cooked at home. Our fingers and mouths, no doubt, bore marks of the "villanous saltpetre," or rather of the charcoal with which it was mixed, for plates or forks we had none; but this only increased our mirth. Supper over, we spread out our blankets on the log floor, extended ourselves on them with our feet towards the fire, and our arms under our heads for pillows. I need not tell you how soundly we slept.

The Long-billed Curlews are in general easily shot, but take a good charge. So long as life remains in them, they skulk off among the thickest plants, remaining perfectly silent. Should they fall on the water, they swim towards the shore. The birds

that may have been in company with a wounded one fly
off uttering a few loud whistling notes. In this respect, the
species differs from all the others, which commonly remain
and fly about you. When on land, they are extremely wary;
and unless the plants are high, and you can conceal yourself
from them, it is very difficult to get near enough. Some one
of the flock, acting as sentinel, raises his wings, as if about to
fly, and sounds a note of alarm, on which they all raise their
wings, close them again, give over feeding, and watch all your
motions. At times a single step made by you beyond a certain
distance is quite enough to raise them, and the moment it
takes place, they all scream and fly off. You need not follow
the flock. The best mode of shooting them is to watch their
course for several evenings in succession; for after having chosen a resting place, they are sure to return to it by the same
route, until greatly annoyed.

The food of the Long-billed Curlews consists principally of
the small crabs called fiddlers, which they seize by running after them, or by pulling them out of their burrows. They
probe the wet sand to the full length of their bill, in quest of
sea-worms and other animals. They are also fond of small
salt-water shell-fish, insects, and worms of any kind; but I
have never seen them searching for berries on elevated lands,
as the Esquimaux Curlews are wont to do. Their flesh is by
no means so delicate as that of the species just mentioned,
for it has usually a fishy taste, and is rarely tender, although
many persons consider it good. They are sold at all seasons
in the markets of Charleston, at about twenty-five cents the
pair.

Rambling birds of this species are sometimes seen as far as
the neighbourhood of Boston; for my learned friend Thomas
Nuttall says in his Manual, that "they get so remarkably fat,
at times, as to burst the skin in falling to the ground, and are
then superior in flavour to almost any other game bird of the
season. In the market of Boston, they are seen as early as the
8th of August." I found them rather rare in East Florida in
winter and spring. They were there seen either on large savannahs, or along the sea shore, mixed with marbled Godwits, Tell-tales, and other species.

The Snowy Heron

Ardea candidissima, GMEL.

(PLATE 44)

THIS beautiful species is a constant resident in Florida and Louisiana, where thousands are seen during winter, and where many remain during the breeding season. It is perhaps of a still more delicate constitution than the Blue Heron, *Ardea cærulea*, as no individuals remain in the neighbourhood of Charleston when the winter happens to be rather colder than usual. In its migrations eastward it rarely proceeds farther than Long Island in the State of New York; few are seen in Massachusetts, and none farther to the east. My friend Professor MACCULLOCH never heard of it in Nova Scotia, and I cannot imagine on what authority WILSON stated that it inhabits the sea-coast of North America to the Gulf of St Lawrence. My friend NUTTALL also asserts, without mentioning on what evidence, that, by pursuing an inland course, it reaches its final destination in the wilds of Canada. It has not been observed in any part of the western country; nay, it rarely ascends the Mississippi as high as Memphis, or about two hundred miles from the mouth of the Ohio, and cannot be said to be at all abundant much farther up the great river than Natchez. In fact, the maritime districts furnish its favourite places of resort, and it rarely proceeds farther inland than fifty or sixty miles, even in the flat portions of the Carolinas, but even in the Middle States, where it prefers the islands along the Atlantic coast.

While I was at Charleston, in March 1831, few had arrived from the Floridas by the 18th of that month, but on the 25th thousands were seen in the marshes and rice fields, all in full plumage. They reach the shores of New Jersey about the first week of May, when they may be seen on all parts of the coast between that district and the Gulf of Mexico. On the Mississippi, they seldom reach the low grounds about Natchez, where they also breed, earlier than the period at which they appear in the Middle States.

While migrating, they fly both by night and by day, in loose flocks of from twenty to a hundred individuals, sometimes arranging themselves in a broad front, then forming lines, and again proceeding in a straggling manner. They keep perfectly silent, and move at a height seldom exceeding a hundred yards. Their flight is light, undetermined as it were, yet well sustained, and performed by regular flappings, as in other birds of the tribe. When they have arrived at their destination, they often go to considerable distances to feed during the day, regularly returning at the approach of night to their roosts on the low trees and bushes bordering the marshes, swamps, and ponds. They are very gentle at this season, and at all periods keep in flocks when not disturbed. At the approach of the breeding season, many spend a great part of the day at their roosting places, perched on the low trees principally growing in the water, when every now and then they utter a rough guttural sort of sigh, raising at the same moment their beautiful crest and loose recurved plumes, curving the neck, and rising on their legs to their full height, as if about to strut on the branches. They act in the same manner while on the ground mating. Then the male, with great ardour, and with the most graceful motions, passes and repasses for several minutes at a time before and around the female, whose actions are similar, although she displays less ardour. When disturbed on such occasions, they rise high in the air, sail about and over the spot in perfect silence, awaiting the departure of the intruder, then sweep along, exhibiting the most singular movements, now and then tumbling over and over like the Tumbler Pigeon, and at length alight on a tree. On the contrary, when you intrude upon them while breeding, they rise silently on wing, alight on the trees near, and remain there until you depart.

The Snowy Herons breed in large communities; and so very social are they, that they do not appear even to attempt to disturb such other birds as are wont to breed among them, the Night Herons, for instance, the Green Herons, or the Boat-tailed Grakles. I have visited some of their breeding grounds, where several hundred pairs were to be seen, and several nests were placed on the branches of the same bush, so low at times that I could easily see into them, although others were situated at a height of ten or fifteen feet. In places where these birds are often disturbed, they breed in taller trees, though rarely on very high ones. In the Floridas I found their nests on low mangroves; but wherever they are placed you find them fronting the water, over which, indeed, these Herons seem fond of placing them. The nest, which is formed of dry sticks, is rather small, and has a shallow cavity. The eggs are three, one inch and five-eighths and a half in length, one and a quarter across, of a broadly elliptical form, and having a plain pale bluish-green colour. In the Middle Districts, the usual time of laying is about the middle of May; in the Carolinas a month sooner; and in the Floridas still earlier, as there, on the 19th of May, I found the young in great numbers walking off their nests on the mangrove branches, and, like those of the Louisiana Heron, which also breeds in the same places, trying to escape by falling into the water below, and swimming in search of hiding-places among the roots and hanging branches. Both sexes incubate. Many of the eggs are destroyed by Crows and Turkey Buzzards, which also devour the young, and many are carried off by men.

The young acquire the full beauty of their plumage in the course of the first spring, when they can no longer be distinguished from the old birds. The legs and feet are at first of a darkish olive, as is the bill, except at the base, where it is lighter, and inclining to yellow. At the approach of autumn, the crest assumes a form, and the feathers of the lower parts of the neck in front become considerably lengthened, the feet acquire a yellow tint, and the legs are marked with black on a yellowish ground; but the flowing feathers of the back do not appear until the approach of spring, when they grow rapidly, become recurved, and remain until the young are hatched, when they fall off.

The Snowy Heron, while in the Carolinas, in the month of April, resorts to the borders of the salt-water marshes, and feeds principally on shrimps. Many individuals which I opened there contained nothing else in their stomach. On the Mississippi, at the time when the shrimps are ascending the stream, these birds are frequently seen standing on floating logs, busily engaged in picking them up; and on such occasions their pure white colour renders them conspicuous and highly pleasing to the eye. At a later period, they feed on small fry, fiddlers, snails, aquatic insects, occasionally small lizards and young frogs. Their motions are generally quick and elegant, and, while pursuing small fishes, they run swiftly through the shallows, throwing up their wings. Twenty or thirty seen at once along the margins of a marsh or a river, while engaged in procuring their food, form a most agreeable sight. In autumn and early spring, they are fond of resorting to the ditches of the rice fields, not unfrequently in company with the Blue Herons. When, on being wounded in the wing one falls into the water, it swims off towards the nearest shore, and runs to hide itself by the side of some log, or towards a tree which if possible it climbs, ascending to its very top. When seized, they peck at you with great spirit, and are capable of inflicting a severe wound.

There is no difference between the sexes as to plumage, but the male is somewhat larger. When in good condition, its flesh is excellent eating, especially in early autumn, when it is generally very fat. Some may be seen for sale in the markets of New Orleans and other southern cities. They return southward from the Middle Districts early in October, but in the Carolinas they remain until the first frosts, when they all depart for the Floridas, where I found them during the whole winter in considerable numbers, associating with the Blue Herons.

The Brown Pelican

Pelecanus fuscus, LINN.

(PLATES 45, 46)

THE Brown Pelican, which is one of the most interesting of our American birds, is a constant resident in the Floridas, where it resorts to the Keys and the salt-water inlets, but never enters fresh-water streams, as the White Pelican is wont to do. It is rarely seen farther eastward than Cape Hatteras, but is found to the south far beyond the limits of the United States. Within the recollection of persons still living, its numbers have been considerably reduced, so much indeed that in the inner Bay of Charleston, where twenty or thirty years ago it was quite abundant, very few individuals are now seen, and these chiefly during a continuance of tempestuous weather.

There is a naked bar, a few miles distant from the main land, between Charleston and the mouth of the Santee, on which my friend JOHN BACHMAN some years ago saw a great number of these birds, of which he procured several; but at the present day, few are known to breed farther east than the salt-water inlets running parallel to the coast of Florida, forty or fifty miles south of St Augustine, where I for the first time met with this Pelican in considerable numbers.

My friend JOHN BULLOW, Esq. took me in his barge to visit the Halifax, which is a large inlet, and on which we soon reached an island where the Brown Pelicans had bred for a number of years, but where, to my great disappointment, none were then to be seen. The next morning, being ten or twelve miles farther down the stream, we entered another inlet, where I saw several dozens of these birds perched on the mangroves, and apparently sound asleep. I shot at them from a very short distance, and with my first barrel brought two to the water, but although many of them still remained looking at us, I could not send the contents of my second barrel to them, as the shot had unluckily been introduced into it before the powder. They all flew off one after another, and still worse, as the servants approached those which had fallen upon the water, they also flew away.

On arriving at the Keys of Florida, on board the Marion Revenue Cutter, I found the Pelicans pretty numerous. They became more abundant the farther south we proceeded, and I procured specimens at different places, but nowhere so many as at Key West. There you would see them flying within pistol-shot of the wharfs, the boys frequently trying to knock them down with stones, although I believe they rarely succeed in their efforts. The Marion lay at anchor several days at a short distance from this island, and close to another. Scarcely an hour of daylight passed without our having Pelicans around us, all engaged at their ordinary occupations, some fishing, some slumbering as it were on the bosom of the ocean, or on the branches of the mangroves. This place and all around for about forty miles, seemed to be favourite resorts of these birds; and as I had excellent opportunities of observing their habits, I consider myself qualified to present you with some account of them.

The flight of the Brown Pelican, though to appearance heavy, is remarkably well sustained, that bird being able not only to remain many hours at a time on wing, but also to mount to a great height in the air to perform its beautiful evolutions. Their ordinary manner of proceeding, either when single or in flocks, is by easy flappings and sailings alternating at distances of from twenty to thirty yards, when they glide along with great speed. They move in an undulated line, passing at one time high, at another low, over the water or land, for they do not deviate from their course on coming upon a key or a point of land. When the waves run high, you may see them "troughing," as the sailors say, or directing their course along the hollows. While on wing they draw in their head between their shoulders, stretch out their broad webbed feet to their whole extent, and proceed in perfect silence.

When the weather is calm, and a flood of light and heat is poured down upon nature by the genial sun, they are often, especially during the love season, seen rising in broad circles, flock after flock, until they attain a height of perhaps a mile, when they gracefully glide on constantly expanded wings, and course round each other, for an hour or more at a time, after which, in curious zigzags, and with remarkable velocity, they descend towards their beloved element, and settle on the water, on large sand-bars or on mangroves. It is interesting beyond description to observe flocks of Brown Pelicans thus going through their aërial evolutions.

Now, Reader, look at those birds standing on their strong column-like legs, on that burning sand-bar. How dexterously do they wield that great bill of theirs, as they trim their plumage! Now along each broad quill it passes, drawing it out and displaying its elasticity; and now with necks stretched to their full length, and heads elevated, they direct its point in search of the insects that are concealed along their necks and breasts. Now they droop their wings for a while, or stretch them alternately to their full extent; some slowly lie down on the sand, others remain standing, quietly draw their head over their broad shoulders, raise one of their feet, and placing their bill on their back, compose themselves to rest. There let them repose in peace. Had they alighted on the waters, you might have seen them, like a fleet at anchor, riding on the ever-rolling billows as unconcernedly as if on shore. Had they perched on yon mangroves, they would have laid themselves flat on the branches, or spread their wings to the sun or the breeze, as Vultures are wont to do.

But see, the tide is advancing; the billows chase each other towards the shores; the mullets joyful and keen leap along the surface, as they fill the bays with their multitudes. The slumbers of the Pelicans are over; the drowsy birds shake their heads, stretch open their mandibles and pouch by way of yawning, expand their ample wings, and simultaneously soar away. Look at them as they fly over the bay; listen to the sound of the splash they make as they drive their open bills, like a pock-net, into the sea, to scoop up their prey; mark how they follow that shoal of porpoises, and snatch up the frightened fishes that strive to escape from them. Down they go, again and again. What voracious creatures they are!

The Brown Pelicans are as well aware of the time of each return of the tide, as the most watchful pilots. Though but a short time before they have been sound asleep, yet without bell or other warning, they suddenly open their eyelids, and all leave their roosts, the instant when the waters, which have themselves reposed for a while, resume their motion. The Pelicans possess a knowledge beyond this, and in a degree much surpassing that of man with reference to the same subject: they can judge with certainty of the changes of weather. Should you see them fishing all together, in retired bays, be assured, that a storm will burst forth that day; but if they pursue their finny prey far out at sea, the weather will be fine, and you also may launch your bark and go to the fishing. Indeed, most sea-birds possess the same kind of knowledge, as I have assured myself by repeated observation, in a degree corresponding to their necessities; and the best of all prognosticators of the weather, are the Wild Goose, the Gannet, the Lestris, and the Pelican.

This species procures its food on wing, and in a manner quite different from that of the White Pelican. A flock will leave their resting place, proceed over the waters in search of fish, and when a shoal is perceived, separate at once, when each, from an elevation of from fifteen to twenty-five feet, plunges in an oblique and somewhat winding direction, spreading to the full stretch its lower mandible and pouch, as it reaches the water, and suddenly scoops up the object of its pursuit, immersing the head and neck, and sometimes the body, for an instant. It immediately swallows its prey, rises on wing, dashes on another fish, seizes and devours it, and thus continues, sometimes plunging eight or ten times in a few minutes, and always with unerring aim. When gorged, it rests on the water for a while, but if it has a brood, or a mate sitting on her eggs, it flies off at once towards them, no matter how heavily laden it may be. The generally received idea that Pelicans keep fish or water in their pouch, to convey them to their young, is quite erroneous. The water which enters the pouch when it is immersed, is immediately forced out between the partially closed mandibles, and the fish, unless larger than those on which they usually feed, is instantly swallowed, to be afterwards disgorged for the benefit of the young, either partially macerated, or whole, according to the age and size of the latter. Of all this I have satisfied myself, when within less than twenty yards of the birds as they were fishing; and I never saw them fly without the pouch being closely contracted towards the lower mandible. Indeed, although I now much regret that I did not make the experiment when I had the means of doing so, I doubt very much if a Pelican could fly at all with its burden so much out of trim, as a sailor would say.

They at times follow the porpoise, when that animal is in pursuit of prey, and as the fishes rise from the deep water towards the surface, come in cunningly for their share, falling upon the frightened shoal, and seizing one or more, which they instantly gobble up. But one of the most curious traits of the Pelican is, that it acts unwittingly as a sort of purveyor to the Gulls just as the Porpoise acts towards itself. The Black-headed Gull of WILSON, which is abundant along the coast of the Floridas in spring and summer, watches the motions of the Pelicans. The latter having plunged after a shoal of small fishes, of which it has caught a number at a time, in letting off the water from amongst them, sometimes allows a few to escape; but the Gull at that instant alights on the bill of the Pelican, or on its head, and seizes the fry at the moment they were perhaps congratulating themselves on their escape. This every body on board the Marion observed as well as myself, while that vessel was at anchor in the beautiful harbour of Key West, so that it is not again necessary for me to lay before you a certificate with numerous signatures. To me such sights were always highly interesting, and I doubt if in the course of my endeavours to amuse you, I ever felt greater pleasure than I do at this moment, when, with my journal at my side, and the Gulls and Pelicans in my mind's eye as distinctly as I could wish, I ponder on the faculties which Nature has bestowed on animals which we merely consider as possessed of instinct. How little do we yet know of the operations of the Divine Power! On the occasions just mentioned, the Pelicans did not manifest the least anger towards the Gulls. It is said that the Frigate Pelican or Man-of-war Bird, forces the Brown Pelican to disgorge its food, but of this I never saw an instance; nor do I believe it to be the case, considering the great strength and powerful bill of the Pelican compared with those of the other bird. Indeed, if I had been told that when the Frigate Bird assails the Pelican, the latter opens its large pouch and swallows it entire, I might as soon have believed the one story as the other. But of this more anon, when we come to the habits of the bird in question.

On the ground this species is by no means so active, for it walks heavily, and when running, which it now and then does while in play, or during courtship, it looks extremely awkward, as it then stretches out its neck, partially extends its wings, and reels so that one might imagine it ready to fall at each step. If approached when wounded and on the water, it swims off with speed, and when overtaken, it suddenly turns about, opens its large bill, snaps it violently several times in succession, causing it to emit a smart noise in the manner of owls, strikes at you, and bites very severely. While I was at Mr BULLOW's, his Negro hunter waded after one whose wing had been broken. The Pelican could not be seized without danger, and I was surprised to see the hunter draw his butcher's knife, strike the long blade through the open pouch of the bird, hook it, as it were, by the lower mandible, and at one jerk swing it up into the air with extreme dexterity, after which he broke its neck and dragged it ashore.

The pouch measures from six to ten inches in depth,

according to the age of the bird after the first moult. The superb male whose portrait is before you, and which was selected from among a great number, had it about the last mentioned size, and capable of holding a gallon of water, were the mandibles kept horizontal. This membrane is dried and used for keeping snuff, gunpowder and shot. When fresh it may be extended so as to become quite thin and transparent, like a bladder.

This Pelican seldom seizes fish that are longer than its bill, and the size of those on which it ordinarily feeds is much smaller. Indeed, several which I examined, had in the stomach upwards of a hundred fishes, which were only from two to three inches in length. That organ is long, slender, and rather fleshy. In some I found a great number of live blue-coloured worms, measuring two and a half inches in length, and about the thickness of a crow-quill. The gut is about the size of a swan's quill, and from ten to twelve feet in length, according to the age of the individual.

At all periods the Brown Pelican keeps in flocks, seldom amounting to more than fifty or sixty individuals of both sexes, and of different ages. At the approach of the pairing time, or about the middle of April, the old males and females separate from the rest, and remove to the inner keys or to large estuaries, well furnished with mangroves of goodly size. The young birds, which are much more numerous, remain along the shores of the open sea, unless during heavy gales.

Now let us watch the full grown birds. Some skirmishes have taken place, and the stronger males, by dint of loud snappings of their bill, some hard tugs of the neck and head, and some heavy beats with their wings, have driven away the weaker, which content themselves with less prized belles. The females, although quiet and gentle on ordinary occasions, are more courageous than the males, who, however, are assiduous in their attentions, assist in forming the nest, feed their mates while sitting, and even share the labour of incubation with them. Now see the mated birds, like the citizens of a newly laid out town in some part of our western country, breaking the dry sticks from the trees, and conveying them in their bills to yon mangrove isle. You see they place all their mansions on the south-west side, as if to enjoy the benefit of all the heat of that sultry climate. Myriads of mosquitoes buzz around them, and alight on the naked parts of their body, but this seems to give them no concern. Stick after stick is laid, one crossing another, until a strong platform is constructed. Now roots and withered plants are brought, with which a basin is formed for the eggs. Not a nest, you observe, is placed very low; the birds prefer the tops of the mangroves, although they do not care how many nests are on one tree, or how near the trees are to each other. The eggs, of which there are never more than three, are rather elliptical, and average three inches and one-eighth in length, by two inches and one-eighth in their greatest breadth. The shell is thick and rather rough, of a pure white colour, with a few faint streaks of a rosy tint, and blotches of a very pale hue, from the centre towards the crown of the egg.

The young are at first covered with cream-coloured down, and have the bill and feet disproportionately large. They are fed with great care, and so abundantly, that the refuse of their food, putrid and disgusting, lies in great quantities round them; but neither young nor old regard this, however offensive it may be to you. As the former grow the latter bring larger fish to them. At first the food is dropped in a well macerated state into their extended throats; afterwards the fish is given to them entire; and finally the parent birds merely place it on the edge of the nest. The young increase in size at a surprising rate. When half fledged they seem a mere mass of fat, their partially indurated bill has acquired considerable length, their wings droop by their sides, and they would be utterly unable to walk. The Vultures at this period often fall upon them and devour them in the absence of their parents. The Indians also carry them off in considerable numbers; and farther eastward, on the Halifax river, for instance, the Negroes kill all they can find, to make gombo soup of them during winter. The crows, less powerful, but quite as cunning, suck the eggs; and many a young one which has accidentally fallen from the nest, is sure to be picked up by some quadruped, or devoured by the Shark or Balacuda. When extensive depredations have thus been made, the birds abandon their breeding places, and do not return to them. The Pelicans in fact are, year after year, retiring from the vicinity of man, and although they afford but very unsavoury food at any period of their lives, will yet be hunted beyond the range of civilization, just as our best of all game, the Wild Turkey, is now, until to meet with them the student of nature will have to sail round Terra del Fuego, while he may be obliged to travel to the Rocky Mountains before he find the other bird. Should you approach a settlement of the Pelicans and fire a few shots at them, they all abandon the place, and leave their eggs or young entirely at your disposal.

At all seasons, the Negroes of the plantations on the eastern coast of the Floridas lie in wait for the Pelicans. There, observe that fellow, who, with rusty musket, containing a tremendous charge of heavy shot, is concealed among the palmettoes, on the brink of a kind of embankment formed by the shelly sand. Now comes a flock of Pelicans, forcing their way against the breeze, unaware of the danger into which they rush, for there, a few yards apart, several Negroes crouch in readiness to fire; and let me tell you, good shots they are. Now a blast forces the birds along the shore; off goes the first gun, and down comes a Pelican; shot succeeds shot; and now the Negroes run up to gather the spoil. They skin the birds like so many racoons, cut off the head, wings and feet; and should you come this way next year, you may find these remains bleached in the sun. Towards night, the sable hunters carry off their booty, marching along in Indian file, and filling the air with their extemporaneous songs. At home they perhaps salt, or perhaps smoke them; but in whatever way the Pelicans are prepared, they are esteemed good food by the sons of Africa.

The Brown Pelican is a strong and tough bird, although not so weighty as the white species. Its flesh is, in my opinion, always impure. It seems never satisfied with food, and it mutes so profusely, that not a spot of verdure can be seen on the originally glossy and deep-coloured mangroves on which it nestles; and I must say that, much as I admire it in some respects, I should be sorry to keep it near me as a pet.

During winter, when the mullets, a favourite fish with the Brown Pelican, as it is with me, retires into deeper water, these birds advance farther to seaward, and may be seen over all parts of the Gulf of Mexico, and between the Florida Reefs

and the opposite isles, especially during fine weather. They are
very sensible to cold, and in this respect are tender birds.
Now and then, at this season, they are seen on Lake Borgne
and over Lake Pontchartrain, but never on the Mississippi beyond the rise of the tides, the space higher up being abandoned to the White Pelican. The keenness of their sight is
probably equal to that of any hawk, and their hearing is also
very acute. They are extremely silent birds, but when excited
they utter a loud and rough grunt, which is far from musical.
The young take two years to attain maturity. Several persons
in the Floridas assured me that the Brown Pelicans breed at
all seasons of the year; but as I observed nothing to countenance such an idea, I would give it as my opinion that they
raise only one brood in the season.

Their bodies are greatly inflated by large air-cells; their
bones, though strong, are very light; and they are tough to
kill.

The Great White Heron
Ardea occidentalis
(PLATE 47)

I AM now about to present you with an account of the habits
of the largest species of the Heron tribe hitherto found in the
United States, and which is indeed remarkable not only for its
great size, but also for the pure white of its plumage at every
period of its life. Writers who have subdivided the family, and
stated that none of the True Herons are white, will doubtless
be startled when they, for the first time, look at my plate of
this bird. I think, however, that our endeavours to discover
the natural arrangement of things cannot be uniformly
successful, and it is clear that he only who has studied *all*
can have much chance of disposing all according to their
relations.

On the 24th of April 1832, I landed on Indian Key in
Florida, and immediately after formed an acquaintance with
Mr EGAN, of whom I have already several times spoken. He it
was who first gave me notice of the species which forms the

subject of this article, and of which I cannot find any description. The next day after that of my arrival, when I was prevented from accompanying him by my anxiety to finish a drawing, he came in with two young birds alive, and another lying dead in a nest, which he had cut off from a mangrove. You may imagine how delighted I was, when at the very first glance I felt assured that they were different from any that I had previously seen. The two living birds were of a beautiful white, slightly tinged with cream-colour, remarkably fat and strong for their age, which the worthy Pilot said could not be more than three weeks. The dead bird was quite putrid and much smaller. It looked as if it had accidentally been trampled to death by the parent birds ten or twelve days before, the body being almost flat and covered with filth. The nest with the two live birds was placed in the yard. The young Herons seemed quite unconcerned when a person approached them, although on displaying one's hand to them, they at once endeavoured to strike it with their bill. My Newfoundland dog, a well-trained and most sagacious animal, was whistled for and came up; on which the birds rose partially on their legs, ruffled all their feathers, spread their wings, opened their bills, and clicked their mandibles in great anger, but without attempting to leave the nest. I ordered the dog to go near them, but not to hurt them. They waited until he went within striking distance, when the largest suddenly hit him with its bill, and hung to his nose. Plato, however, took it all in good part, and merely brought the bird towards me, when I seized it by the wings, which made it let go its hold. It walked off as proudly as any of its tribe, and I was delighted to find it possessed of so much courage. These birds were left under the charge of Mrs EGAN, until I returned from my various excursions to the different islands along the coast.

On the 26th of the same month, Mr THRUSTON took me and my companions in his beautiful barge to some keys on which the Florida Cormorants were breeding in great numbers. As we were on the way we observed two tall white Herons standing on their nests; but although I was anxious to procure them alive, an unfortunate shot from one of the party brought them to the water. They were, I was told, able to fly, but probably had never seen a man before. While searching that day for nests of the Zenaida Dove, we observed a young Heron of this species stalking among the mangroves that bordered the key on which we were, and immediately pursued it. Had you been looking on, good Reader, you might have enjoyed a hearty laugh, although few of us could have joined you. Seven or eight persons were engaged in the pursuit of this single bird, which, with extended neck, wings, and legs, made off among the tangled trees at such a rate, that, anxious as I was to obtain it alive, I several times thought of shooting it. At length, however, it was caught, its bill was securely tied, its legs were drawn up, and fastened by a strong cord, and the poor thing was thus conveyed to Indian Key, and placed along with its kinsfolk. On seeing it, the latter immediately ran towards it with open bills, and greeted it with a most friendly welcome, passing their heads over and under its own in the most curious and indeed ludicrous manner. A bucketful of fish was thrown to them, which they swallowed in a few minutes. After a few days, they also ate pieces of pork-rhind, cheese, and other substances.

While sailing along the numerous islands that occur between Indian Key and Key West, I saw many birds of this species, some in pairs, some single, and others in flocks; but on no occasion did I succeed in getting within shot of one. Mr EGAN consoled me by saying that he knew some places beyond Key West where I certainly should obtain several, were we to spend a day and a night there for the purpose. Dr BENJAMIN STROBEL afterwards gave me a similar assurance. In the course of a week after reaching Key West, I in fact procured more than a dozen birds of different ages, as well as nests and eggs, and their habits were carefully examined by several of my party.

At three o'clock one morning, you might have seen Mr EGAN and myself, about eight miles from our harbour, paddling as silently as possible over some narrow and tortuous inlets, formed by the tides through a large flat and partially submersed key. There we expected to find many White Herons; but our labour was for a long time almost hopeless, for, although other birds occurred, we had determined to shoot nothing but the Great White Heron, and none of that species came near us. At length, after six or seven hours of hard labour, a Heron flew right over our heads, and to make sure of it, we both fired at once. The bird came down dead. It proved to be a female, which had either been sitting on her eggs or had lately hatched her young, her belly being bare, and her plumage considerably worn. We now rested a while, and breakfasted on some biscuit soaked in molasses and water, reposing under the shade of the mangroves, where the mosquitoes had a good opportunity of breaking their fast also. We went about from one key to another, saw a great number of White Herons, and at length, towards night, reached the Marion, rather exhausted, and having a solitary bird. Mr EGAN and I had been most of the time devising schemes for procuring others with less trouble, a task which might easily have been accomplished a month before, when, as he said, the birds were "sitting hard." He asked if I would return that night at twelve o'clock to the last key which we had visited. I mentioned the proposal to our worthy Captain, who, ever willing to do all in his power to oblige me, when the service did not require constant attendance on board, said that if I would go, he would accompany us in the gig. Our guns were soon cleaned, provisions and ammunition placed in the boats, and after supping we talked and laughed until the appointed time.

"Eight Bells" made us bound on our feet, and off we pushed for the islands. The moon shone bright in the clear sky; but as the breeze had died away, we betook ourselves to our oars. The state of the tide was against us, and we had to drag our boats several miles over the soapy shallows; but at last we found ourselves in a deep channel beneath the hanging mangroves of a large key, where we had observed the Herons retiring to roost the previous evening. There we lay quietly until day-break. But the mosquitoes and sandflies! Reader, if you have not been in such a place, you cannot easily conceive the torments we endured for a whole hour, when it was absolutely necessary for us to remain perfectly motionless. At length day dawned, and the boats parted, to meet on the other side of the key. Slowly and silently each advanced. A Heron sprung from its perch almost directly over our heads. Three barrels were discharged,—in vain; the bird flew on unscathed; the pilot and I had probably been too anxious. As the bird sped away, it croaked loudly, and the noise, together with the report of our guns, roused some hundreds of these Herons, which flew from the mangroves, and in the grey light appeared to sail over and around us like so many spectres. I almost despaired of procuring any more. The tide was now rising, and when we met with the other boat we were told, that if we had waited until we could have shot at them while perched, we might have killed several; but that now we must remain until full tide, for the birds had gone to their feeding grounds.

The boats parted again, and it was now arranged that whenever a Heron was killed, another shot should be fired exactly one minute after, by which each party would be made aware of the success of the other. Mr EGAN, pointing to a nest on which stood two small young birds, desired to be landed near it. I proceeded into a narrow bayou, where we remained quiet for about half an hour, when a Heron flew over us and was shot. It was a very fine old male. Before firing my signal shot, I heard a report from afar, and a little after mine was discharged I heard another shot, so I felt assured that two birds had been killed. When I reached the Captain's boat I found that he had in fact obtained two; but Mr EGAN had waited two hours in vain near the nest, for none of the old birds came up. We took him from his hiding place, and brought the Herons along with us. It was now nearly high water. About a mile from us, more than a hundred Herons stood on a mud-bar up to their bellies. The pilot said that now was our best chance, as the tide would soon force them to fly, when they would come to rest on the trees. So we divided, each choosing his own place, and I went to the lowest end of the key, where it was separated from another by a channel. I soon had the pleasure of observing all the Herons take to wing, one after another, in quick succession. I then heard my companions' guns, but no signal of success. Obtaining a good chance as I thought, I fired at a remarkably large bird, and distinctly heard the shot strike it. The Heron merely croaked, and pursued its course. Not another bird came near enough to be shot at, although many had alighted on the neighbouring key, and stood perched like so many newly finished statues of the purest alabaster, forming a fine contrast to the deep blue sky. The boats joined us. Mr EGAN had one bird, the Captain another, and both looked at me with surprise. We now started for the next key, where we expected to see more. When we had advanced several hundred yards along its low banks, we found the bird at which I had shot lying with extended wings in the agonies of death. It was from this specimen that the drawing was made. I was satisfied with the fruits of this day's excursion. On other occasions I procured fifteen more birds, and judging that number sufficient, I left the Herons to their occupations.

This species is extremely shy. Sometimes they would rise when at the distance of half a mile from us, and fly quite out of sight. If pursued, they would return to the very keys or mud-flats from which they had risen, and it was almost impossible to approach one while perched or standing in the water. Indeed, I have no doubt that half a dozen specimens of *Ardea Herodias* could be procured for one of the present, in the same time and under similar circumstances.

The Great White Heron is a constant resident on the Florida Keys, where it is found more abundant during the breeding season than anywhere else. They rarely go as far eastward as Cape Florida, and are not seen on the Tortugas, probably because these islands are destitute of mangroves. They begin to pair early in March, but many do not lay their eggs until the middle of April. Their courtships were represented to me as similar to those of the Great Blue Heron. Their nests are at times met with at considerable distances from each other, and although many are found on the same keys, they are placed farther apart than those of the species just mentioned. They are seldom more than a few feet above high water-mark, which in the Floridas is so low, that they look as if only a yard or two above the roots of the trees. From twenty to thirty nests which I examined were thus placed. They were large, about three feet in diameter, formed of sticks of different sizes, but without any appearance of lining, and quite flat, being several inches thick. The eggs are always three, measure two inches and three quarters in length, one inch and eight-twelfths in breadth, and have a rather thick shell, of a uniform plain light bluish-green colour. Mr EGAN told me that incubation continues about thirty days,

that both birds sit, (the female, however, being most assiduous,) and with their legs stretched out before them, in the
same manner as the young when two or three weeks old. The
latter, of which I saw several from ten days to a month old,
were pure white, slightly tinged with cream colour, and had
no indications of a crest. Those which I carried to Charleston,
and which were kept for more than a year, exhibited nothing
of the kind. I am unable to say how long it is before they attain their full plumage as represented in the plate, when, as
you see, the head is broadly but loosely and shortly tufted,
the feathers of the breast pendent, but not remarkably long,
and there are none of the narrow feathers seen in other
species over the rump or wings.

These Herons are sedate, quiet, and perhaps even less animated than the *A. Herodias.* They walk majestically, with
firmness and great elegance. Unlike the species just named,
they *flock* at their feeding grounds, sometimes a hundred or
more being seen together; and what is still more remarkable
is, that they betake themselves to the mud-flats or sand-bars
at a distance from the Keys on which they roost and breed.
They seem, in so far as I could judge, to be diurnal, an opinion corroborated by the testimony of Mr EGAN, a person of
great judgment, sagacity and integrity. While on these banks,
they stand motionless, rarely moving towards their prey, but
waiting until it comes near, when they strike it and swallow it
alive, or when large beat it on the water, or shake it violently,
biting it severely all the while. They never leave their feeding
grounds until driven off by the tide, remaining until the water reaches their body. So wary are they, that although they
may return to roost on the same keys, they rarely alight on
trees to which they have resorted before, and if repeatedly
disturbed they do not return, for many weeks at least. When
roosting, they generally stand on one foot, the other being
drawn up, and, unlike the Ibises, are never seen lying flat on
trees, where, however, they draw in their long neck, and place
their head under their wing.

I was often surprised to see that while a flock was resting by
day in the position just described, one or more stood with
outstretched necks, keenly eyeing all around, now and then
suddenly starting at the sight of a Porpoise or Shark in chase

of some fish. The appearance of a man or a boat, seemed to distract them; and yet I was told that nobody ever goes in pursuit of them. If surprised, they leave their perch with a rough croaking sound, and fly directly to a great distance, but never inland.

The flight of the Great White Heron is firm, regular, and greatly protracted. They propel themselves by regular slow flaps, the head being drawn in after they have proceeded a few yards, and their legs extended behind, as is the case with all other Herons. They also now and then rise high in the air, where they sail in wide circles, and they never alight without performing this circling flight, unless when going to feeding grounds on which other individuals have already settled. It is truly surprising that a bird of so powerful a flight never visits Georgia or the Carolinas, nor goes to the Mainland. When you see them about the middle of the day on their feeding grounds they "loom" to about double their size, and present a singular appearance. It is difficult to kill them unless with buck-shot, which we found ourselves obliged to use.

When I left Key West, on our return towards Charleston, I took with me two young birds that had been consigned to the care of my friend Dr B. STROBEL, who assured me that they devoured more than their weight of food per day. I had also two young birds of the *Ardea Herodias* alive. After bringing them on board, I placed them all together in a very large coop; but was soon obliged to separate the two species, for the white birds would not be reconciled to the blue, which they would have killed. While the former had the privilege of the deck for a few minutes, they struck at the smaller species, such as the young of *Ardea rufescens* and *A. Ludoviciana*, some of which they instantly killed and swallowed entire, although they were abundantly fed on the flesh of green Turtles. None of the sailors succeeded in making friends with them.

On reaching Indian Key, I found those which had been left with Mrs EGAN, in excellent health and much increased in size, but to my surprise observed that their bills were much broken, which she assured me had been caused by the great force with which they struck at the fishes thrown to them on the rocks of their enclosure,—a statement which I found confirmed by my own observation in the course of the day. It was almost as difficult to catch them in the yard, as if they had never seen a man before, and we were obliged to tie their bills fast, to avoid being wounded by them while carrying them on board. They thrived well, and never manifested the least animosity towards each other. One of them which accidentally walked before the coop in which the Blue Herons were, thrust its bill between the bars, and transfixed the head of one of these birds, so that it was instantaneously killed.

When we arrived at Charleston, four of them were still alive. They were taken to my friend JOHN BACHMAN, who was glad to see them. He kept a pair, and offered the other to our mutual friend Dr SAMUEL WILSON, who accepted them, but soon afterwards gave them to Dr GIBBES of Columbia College, merely because they had killed a number of Ducks. My friend BACHMAN kept two of these birds for many months; but it was difficult for him to procure fish enough for them, as they swallowed a bucketful of mullets in a few minutes, each devouring about a gallon of these fishes. They betook themselves to roosting in a beautiful arbour in his garden; where at night they looked with their pure white plumage like beings of another world. It is a curious fact, that the points of their bills, of which an inch at least had been broken, grew again, and were as regularly shaped at the end of six months as if nothing had happened to them. In the evening or early in the morning, they would frequently set, like pointer dogs, at moths which hovered over the flowers, and with a well-directed stroke of their bill seize the fluttering insect and instantly swallow it. On many occasions, they also struck at chickens, grown fowls and ducks, which they would tear up and devour. Once a cat which was asleep in the sunshine, on the wooden steps of the viranda, was pinned through the body to the boards, and killed by one of them. At last they began to pursue the younger children of my worthy friend, who therefore ordered them to be killed. One of them was beautifully mounted by my assistant Mr HENRY WARD, and is now in the Museum of Charleston. Dr GIBBES was obliged to treat his in the same manner; and I afterwards saw one of them in his collection. Of the fifteen skins of this species which I carried to Philadelphia, one was presented to the Academy of Natural Sciences of that beautiful city, another was given in exchange for various skins, and two I believe are now in the possession of GEORGE COOPER, Esq. of New York. Two were sent along with other specimens to Mr SELBY of Twizel House, Northumberland. On my arrival in England, I presented a pair to His Royal Highness the Duke of Sussex, who gave them to the British Museum, where I have since seen them mounted. I also presented a specimen to the Zoological Society of London.

Mr EGAN kept for about a year one of these birds, which he raised from the nest, and which, when well grown, was allowed to ramble along the shores of Indian Key in quest of food. One of the wings had been cut, and the bird was known to all the resident inhabitants, but was at last shot by some Indian Hunter, who had gone there to dispose of a collection of sea shells.

Some of the Herons feed on the berries of certain trees during the latter part of autumn and the beginning of winter. Dr B. B. STROBEL observed the Night Heron eating those of the "Gobolimbo," late in September at Key West.

Among the varied and contradictory descriptions of Herons, you will find it alleged that these birds seize fish while on wing by plunging the head and neck into the water; but this seems to me extremely doubtful. Nor, I believe, do they watch for their prey while perched on trees. Another opinion is, that Herons are always thin, and unfit for food. This, however, is by no means generally the case in America, and I have thought these birds very good eating when not too old.

Blue Heron

Ardea cærulea, LINN.

(PLATE 48)

ALONG with a few other Herons, this is, comparatively speaking, confined within narrow limits along our southern coast in winter. It occurs, however, in most parts of the Floridas, where it is a constant resident, and whence, at the approach of summer, vast multitudes are seen proceeding northward, in search of suitable places in which they may rear their young in security. Many, however, go southward, beyond the limits of the United States, and proceed coastwise to Texas and Mexico to spend the winter, especially the younger birds, when still in that singular white plumage which differs so much from that of the young of every other known species of this genus, except that of the Reddish Egret (*A. rufescens*). At New Orleans, where it arrives at the same period, both from Mexico and the Floridas, its first appearance in spring is about the beginning of March; at which time also multitudes leave the Floridas on their way eastward, to settle in Georgia, the Carolinas, and other States farther east, as far as Long Island in that of New York. Beyond this, I believe, no birds of the species have been met with. They rarely, if ever, proceed far inland, or leave the shores of our large rivers and estuaries. On the Mississippi, the swamps and lakes on the borders of which are so well adapted to the habits of these birds, few individuals are ever seen above Natchez. About the beginning of September, by which time the young are able to shift for themselves, they return southward.

When in the Floridas, during winter, I observed that the Blue Herons associated with other species, particularly the White Heron, *Ardea alba*, and the Louisiana Heron, *Ardea Ludoviciana*, all of which were in the habit of roosting together in the thick evergreen low bushes that cover the central parts of the islands along the coast. Their passage to and from their feeding places, is as regular as the rising and setting of the sun, and, unless frequently disturbed, they betake themselves every night to the same locality, and almost to the same spot. In the morning, they rise with one accord from the roosts on which they have been standing all night on one leg, the other drawn up among the feathers of the abdomen, their neck retracted, and their head and bill buried beneath their scapulars. On emerging from their retreats, they at once proceed to some distant place in search of food, and spend the day principally on the head waters of the rivers, and the fresh-water lakes of the interior, giving a decided preference to the soft mud banks, where small crabs or fiddlers are abundant, on which they feed greedily, when the inland ponds have been dried up, and consequently no longer supply them with such fishes as they are wont to feed upon.

There, and at this season, Reader, you may see this graceful Heron, quietly and in silence walking along the margins of the water, with an elegance and grace which can never fail to please you. Each regularly-timed step is lightly measured, while the keen eye of the bird seeks for and watches the equally cautious movements of the objects towards which it advances with all imaginable care. When at a proper distance, it darts forth its bill with astonishing celerity, to pierce and secure its prey, and this it does with so much precision, that, while watching some at a distance with a glass, I rarely observed an instance of failure. If fish is plentiful, on the shallows near the shore, when it has caught one, it immediately swallows it, and runs briskly through the water, striking here and there, and thus capturing several in succession. Two or three dashes of this sort, afford sufficient nourishment for several hours, and when the bird has obtained enough it retires to some quiet place, and remains there in an attitude of repose until its hunger returns. During this period of rest, however, it is as watchful as ever, and on hearing the least noise, or perceiving the slightest appearance of danger, spreads its wings, and flies off to some other place, sometimes to a very distant one. About an hour before sunset, they are again seen anxiously searching for food. When at length satisfied, they rise simultaneously from all parts of the marsh, or shore, arrange themselves into loose bodies, and ascending to the height of fifty or sixty yards in the air, fly in a straight course towards their roosting place. I saw very few of these birds during the winter, on or near the river St John in Florida; but on several occasions met with some on small ponds in the pine barrens, at a considerable distance from any large stream, whither they had been attracted by the great number of frogs.

The flight of the Blue Heron is rather swifter than that of the Egret, *Ardea candidissima*, and considerably more so than that of the Great Blue Heron, *Ardea Herodias*, but very similar to that of the Louisiana Heron, *Ardea Ludoviciana*. When the bird is travelling, the motion is performed by flappings in quick succession, which rapidly propel it in a direct line, until it is about to alight, when it descends in circular sailings of considerable extent towards the spot selected. During strong adverse winds, they fly low, and in a continuous line, passing at the necessary distance from the shores to avoid danger, whether at an early or a late hour of the day. I recollect that once, on such an occasion, when, on the 15th of March, I was in company with my friend JOHN BACHMAN, I saw a large flock about sunset arising from across the river, and circling over a large pond, eight miles distant from Charleston. So cautious were they, that although the flock was composed of several hundred individuals, we could not manage to get so much as a chance of killing one. I have been surprised to see how soon the Blue Herons become shy after reaching the districts to which they remove for the purpose of breeding from their great rendezvous the Floridas, where I never experienced any difficulty in procuring as many as I wished. In Louisiana, on the other hand, I have found them equally vigilant on their first arrival. On several occasions, when I had placed myself under cover, to shoot at some, while on their way to their roosts or to their feeding grounds, I found it necessary to shift from one place to another, for if one of them had been fired at and had fallen in a particular place, all that were in its company took care not to pass again near it, but when coming up diverged several hundred yards, and increased their speed until past, when they would assume their more leisurely flappings. In South Carolina, where they are very shy on their arrival, I have seen them fly off on hearing the very distant report of a gun, and alight on the tops of the tallest trees, where they would congregate in hundreds, and whence they would again fly off on the least apprehension of danger. But when once these Herons have chosen a place to nestle in, or reached one in which they bred the preceding year, they become so tame as to allow you to shoot as many as you are disposed to have.

While on Cayo Island, in the Gulf of Mexico, on the 10th of April 1837, I observed large flocks of the Blue and Green Herons, *Ardea cœrulea* and *A. virescens*, arriving from the westward about the middle of the day. They flew at a considerable height, and came down like so many hawks, to alight on the low bushes growing around the sequestered ponds;

and this without any other noise than the rustling of their
wings as they glided through the air towards the spot on
which they at once alighted. There they remained until sunset, when they all flew off, so that none were seen there next
day. This shews that although these species migrate both by
day and night, they are quite diurnal during the period of
their residence in any section of the country which they may
have chosen for a season. It is more than probable that it has
been from want of personal knowledge of the habits of these
birds, that authors have asserted that all Herons are noctur-
nally inclined. This certainly is by no means the case, although they find it advantageous to travel by night during
their migrations, which is a remarkable circumstance as opposed to their ordinary habits. In the instance above mentioned, I found the birds remarkably gentle, which was
probably owing to fatigue.

The Blue Heron breeds earlier or later according to the
temperature of the district to which it resorts for that purpose, and therefore earlier in Florida, where, however, considerable numbers remain, during the whole year than in
other parts of the United States. Thus I have found them in
the southern parts of that country, sitting on their eggs, on
the 1st of March, fully a month earlier than in the vicinity of
Bayou Sara, on the Mississippi, where they are as much in advance of those which betake themselves, in very small numbers indeed, to our Middle Districts, in which they rarely
begin to breed before the fifteenth of May.

The situations which they choose for their nests are exceedingly varied. I have found them sitting on their eggs on
the Florida Keys, and on the islands in the Bay of Galveston,
in Texas, in nests placed amidst and upon the most tangled
cactuses, so abundant on those curious isles, on the latter of
which the climbing Rattlesnake often gorges itself with the
eggs of this and other species of Heron, as well as with their
unfledged young. In the Lower parts of Louisiana, it breeds
on low bushes of the water-willow, as it also does in South
Carolina; whereas, on the islands on the coast of New Jersey,
and even on the mainland of that State, it places its nest on
the branches of the cedar and other suitable trees. Wherever
you find its breeding place, you may expect to see other birds

in company with it, for like all other species, excepting perhaps the Louisiana Heron, it rarely objects to admit into its society the Night Heron, the Yellow-crowned Heron, or the White Egret.

The heronries of the southern portions of the United States are often of such extraordinary size as to astonish the passing traveller. I confess that I myself might have been as sceptical on this point as some who, having been accustomed to find in all places the Heron to be a solitary bird, cannot be prevailed on to believe the contrary, had I not seen with my own eyes the vast multitudes of individuals of different species breeding together in peace in certain favourable localities. Such persons may be excused from giving that credit to my account of the Passenger Pigeon which posterity will, I trust, accord to it.

The nest of the Blue Heron, wherever situated, is loosely formed of dry sticks, sometimes intermixed with green leaves of various trees, and with grass or moss, according as these materials happen to be plentiful in the neighbourhood. It is nearly flat, and can scarcely be said to have a regular lining. Sometimes you see a solitary nest fixed on a cactus, a bush, or a tree; but a little beyond this you may observe from six to ten, placed almost as closely together as you would have put them had you measured out the space necessary for containing them. Some are seen low over the water, while others are placed high; for, like the rest of its tribe, this species is rather fond of placing its tenement over or near the liquid element.

The eggs are usually three, rarely four; and I have never found a nest of this species containing five eggs, as is stated by WILSON, who, probably found a nest of the Green Heron containing that number among others of the present species. They measure an inch and three quarters in length, by an inch and a quarter in breadth, being about the size of those of *Ardea candidissima*, though rather more elongated, and precisely of the same colour.

The young bird is at first almost destitute of feathers, but scantily covered with yellowish-white down. When fully fledged, its bill and legs are greenish-black, and its plumage pure white, or slightly tinged with cream-colour, the tips of the three outer primaries light greyish-blue. Of this colour the bird remains until the breeding season, when, however, some individuals exhibit a few straggling pale blue feathers. When they have entered on their second year, these young birds become spotted with deeper blue on some parts of the body, or on the head and neck, thus appearing singularly patched with that colour and pure white, the former increasing with the age of the bird in so remarkable a manner, that you may see specimens of these birds with portions even of the pendant feathers of their head or shoulders so marked. And these are produced by *full moultings*, by which I mean the unexpected appearance, as it were, of feathers growing out of the skin of the bird coloured entirely blue, as is the case in many of our land birds. In all these stages of plumage, and from the first spring after birth, the young birds breed with others, as is equally the case with *Ardea rufescens*. You may see a pure white individual paired with one of a full blue colour, or with one patched with blue and white. The young, after leaving their parents, remain separate from the old birds until the next breeding season. At no period can the young of this species be confounded with, or mistaken for that of the *Ardea candidissima*, by a person really acquainted with these birds, for the Blue Heron is not only larger than the latter, but the very colour of its feet and legs is perfectly distinctive. Indeed, during the time when the young Blue Heron is quite white (excepting on the tips of the outer primaries), it would be easier to confound it with the young of the Reddish Egret, *Ardea rufescens*, than with that of any other, were the feathers of its hind head and neck of the same curious curled appearance as those of that species.

My friend JOHN BACHMAN informs me, that in South Carolina, this species not unfrequently breeds in the company of the Louisiana Heron, the nests and eggs of which, he adds, are very similar. He has specimens of these birds in all the different stages which I have described. At New Orleans, the Blue Herons, during the transition of their plumage from white to blue, are called "Egrettes folles," or foolish Egrets, on account of their unusual tameness. My friend BACHMAN and I, shot, on the 6th and 9th of April, several specimens spotted with blue feathers, and having their crests and trains similarly mixed, although of full length; but in most of the specimens obtained, the white was still prevalent.

I have shot some in Louisiana, in autumn, in the same curious dress.

This species, though larger than the Snowy Heron, *Ardea candidissima*, is considerably inferior to it in courage; and I was much amused as well as surprised, when at Galveston Bay, on the 24th of April 1837, to see one of that species alight near a Purple Heron, attack it, and pursue it as far as I could follow them with my eyes. When the Blue Herons are on the sea-coast they not unfrequently repose on the large mud or sand bars, at some distance from the adjacent marshes; but they generally prefer roosting on trees or bushes, when there are any in their neighbourhood. The Creoles of Louisiana not unfrequently eat the flesh of this species, and although they by no means consider it equal to that of the Night Heron, some of them have assured me that it is not bad food. Like other birds of this family, they become larger with age, and the male is usually somewhat superior in size to the female; but, with this exception, no difference can be perceived in the external appearance of the sexes.

Blue-winged Teal

Anas discors, LINN.

(PLATE 49)

Is it not strange, Reader, that birds which are known to be abundant on the Saskatchewan River during the breeding season, and which have been observed as far north as the 57th parallel, should also be found breeding at nearly the same period in Texas? Stranger still it is that species should proceed from certain points, or winter quarters, to both of the above-mentioned regions, without paying any regard to the intermediate districts, which yet seem to be as well adapted for breeding in, as they afford thousands of convenient and secluded localities for that purpose. Yet these facts, and many others connected with Nature's wonderful arrangements, we may look upon as intended to increase the innate desire which every true lover of Nature has to study her beautiful and marvellous works.

Having for some years observed such habits exhibited by the Blue-winged Teal and other birds, I have been induced to believe in the existence of what I would term *a double sense of migration* in many species, acted upon both in spring and in autumn, and giving to them at the latter period, the power as well as the desire of removing from the higher latitudes to opposite or meridional parts, thus to enter into the formation of the Fauna of different countries, from which again they are instigated to return to the place of their nativity, and thence diverge toward new sections of the globe equally adapted to their wants. If these observations should prove not unfounded, we need no longer be surprised to meet in different portions of the world with species which hitherto were supposed to be inhabitants only of far distant shores.

The mouths of the Mississippi, surrounded by extensive flat marshes, which are muddy, and in some degree periodically inundated by the overflowings of that great stream, or by the tides of the Mexican Gulf, and having in the winter months a mildness of temperature favourable to almost all our species of Waders and Swimmers, may be looked upon as the great rendezvous of the Blue-winged Teals, which are seen arriving there coastways, in autumn and the greater part of winter, to meet the multitudes that have travelled across the interior from the north and west. At New Orleans, and during spring, when this bird is in full plumage, it is called by the Creoles of Louisiana "Sarcelle Printanniere;" and in autumn, when scarcely an individual can be seen retaining the beauty of its spring plumage, it is known as the "Sarcelle Automniere;" in consequence of which double appellation, many persons imagine that there are two Blue-winged Teals.

They are the first ducks that arrive in that part of the country, frequently making their appearance in the beginning of September, in large flocks, when they are exceedingly fat. They depart, however, when the cold becomes so intense as to form ice; and in this respect they differ from the Green-winged Teals, which brave the coldest weather of that country. Toward the end of February, however, they are as abundant as ever, but they are then poor, although their plumage is perfected, and the males are very beautiful. During their stay, they are seen on bayous and ponds, along the banks of the Mississippi, and on the large and muddy sand-bars around, feeding on grasses and their seeds, particularly in autumn, when they are very fond of the wild pimento. Many remain as late as the 15th of May, in company with the Shoveller and Gadwall Ducks, with which they are usually fond of associating.

On my reaching the south-western pass of the Mississippi, on the 1st April 1837, I found these birds very abundant there, in full plumage, and in flocks of various sizes. On the 11th of the same month, when about an hundred miles to the west-ward, we saw large and dense flocks flying in the same direc-tion. On the 15th, at Derniere Isle, the Blue-wings were very plentiful and gentle. Two days after, they were quite as nu-merous round Rabbit Island, in the Bay called Cote Blanche; and on the 26th they were found on all the ponds and salt bayous or inlets of Galveston Island in Texas, as well as on the water-courses of the interior, where I was assured that they bred in great numbers. Though on account of the nature of the localities in which these Teals breed, and which cannot be explored otherwise than in extremely light canoes, or by risk-ing being engulphed in oozy morasses covered with tall grass, we were not so fortunate as to find any of their nests, we could easily judge by their manœuvres both while on wing and on the water, that we were not far from their well-con-cealed treasures and the females which we procured unequiv-ocally exhibited the state of exhaustion common in the course of incubation.

During the months of September and October, this species is plentiful on the Ohio, and in the whole of the Western Country, through which they pass again in April, but without tarrying. On the other hand, they seem to prolong their stay at this season in our Eastern Districts more than in autumn; and this is also the case in South Carolina, as I learn from the observations of my friend JOHN BACHMAN, who has seen them mated there as early as February. I have found them in the Boston markets on the 8th of September, but it is very rare to see any of them there in full spring dress. I saw or heard of none when I was in Labrador and Newfoundland; from which it may be inferred that those found in the Fur Countries reach them through the interior. They also occur

on the Columbia River. On the 21st of March 1821, I saw
many Blue-winged Teals copulating on the Mississippi, a little
below Natchez; yet none of these birds have been known to
breed in that section of the country. They were at the time
mentioned on a sand-bar in company with some American
Widgeons, which also were similarly employed.

The flight of the Blue-winged Teal is extremely rapid and
well sustained. Indeed, I have thought that, when travelling,
it passes through the air with a speed equal to that of the
Passenger Pigeon. When flying in flocks in clear sunny
weather, the blue of their wings glistens like polished steel, so
as to give them the most lively appearance; and while they are
wheeling over the places in which they intend to alight, their
wings being alternately thrown in the shade and exposed to
the bright light, the glowing and varied lustre thus produced,
at whatever distance they may be, draws your eyes involuntarily towards them. When advancing against a stiff breeze, they
alternately shew their upper and lower surfaces, and you are
struck by the vivid steel-blue of their mantle, which resembles
the dancing light of a piece of glass suddenly reflected on a
distant object. During their flight, they almost constantly emit
their soft lisping note, which they also utter when alighted
and under apprehension of danger. I have never observed
them travelling in company with other ducks, but have seen
them at times passing over the sea at a considerable distance
from land. Before alighting, and almost under any circumstances, and in any locality, these Teals pass and repass several
times over the place, as if to assure themselves of the absence
of danger, or, should there be cause of apprehension, to
watch until it is over. They swim buoyantly, and generally in a
close body, at times nearly touching each other. Indeed, during their first appearance in autumn, when you are apt to
meet with a flock entirely composed of young birds, you may,
by using a little care, kill a considerable number at one shot.
I was assured by a gunner residing at New Orleans, that as
many as one hundred and twenty had been killed by himself
at a single discharge; and I myself saw a friend of mine
kill eighty-four by pulling together the triggers of his double-
barrelled gun!

The Blue-winged Teal is easily kept in captivity, and soon

becomes very docile. In this state it feeds freely on coarse corn meal, and I have no doubt that it could readily be domesticated, in which case, so tender and savoury is its flesh that it would quickly put the merits of the widely celebrated Canvass-backed Duck in the shade.

In the course of my stay in East Florida, at General HERNANDEZ's and Mr BULOW's, I have observed this Teal in company with the Red-breasted Snipe, the Tell-tale Godwit, and the Yellow-shank Snipe. I observed the same circumstance in Texas.

During the time of their residence on the Delaware River, they feed principally on the seeds of the wild oats, which I also found them to do whilst at Green Bay. I have been assured by persons residing on the island of Cuba, that the Blue-winged Teal is abundant, and breeds there.

The old males lose the spring plumage of the head almost entirely during a great portion of the autumn and winter, but it is reassumed sometimes as early as the beginning of January. The young of both sexes in their first plumage resemble the females, but the males acquire their full beauty before they are a year old.

Anhinga or Snake-Bird

Plotus Anhinga, LINN.

(PLATES 50, 51)

READER, the pleasures which I have experienced in the course of this chequered life of mine have been many;—perhaps many more than would have fallen to my share, had I not, fortunately for me, become a devoted and enthusiastic lover of Nature's beauteous and wondrous works, which, in truth, I have been from the earliest period to which my recollection extends; and those who have known me best will not for a moment consider it extravagant in me to say, that among the greatest pleasures I have known, has been that derived from pursuing and faithfully describing such of our American birds as were previously unknown or but little observed. Many sultry summer days I have passed amidst the most dismal swamps of the secluded woods of Louisiana, watching with anxiety and in silence the curious habits of the Anhinga; the female bird now sitting closely on her eggs, in a nest constructed by herself and securely placed on the widely extended branch of the tallest cypress, that, as if by magic planted, stood in the midst of an ample lake, while with keen eyes she watched every motion of the wily Buzzard and cunning Crow, lest either of these cowardly marauders might deprive her of her treasures; the partner of her cares and joys meanwhile, with outspread wings and fan-like tail, soaring on high, and glancing first anxiously towards her he loves, then in anger towards one and all of their numerous enemies. In wider and bolder circles he moves, rising higher and still higher, until at length, becoming a mere dusky speck, he almost vanishes from my sight amidst the expanse of the blue sky; but now, suddenly closing his wings, and rushing downwards like a meteor, I see him instantly alight erect upon the edge of the nest, and complacently gaze upon his beloved.

After some time, about three weeks perhaps, I have found the egg-shells beneath the great cypress tree, cast out of the nest by the intelligent and attentive mother, and floating on the green slime of the stagnant pool. Climbing to the nest itself, I have seen the tender young clad in down far softer than our sea-island cottons, writhing their slender and tremulous necks, and with open mouths and extended pouches seeking, as all infants are wont to seek, the food suited to their delicate frame. Then, retiring to some concealed spot, I have seen the mother arrive with a supply of finely masticated nutriment, compounded of various fishes from the lake, and furnish each of her progeny by regurgitation with its due proportion. Thus, also, I have watched the growth of the younglings, marking their daily progress, which varied according to the changes of temperature and the state of the atmosphere. At length, after waiting many days in succession, I have seen them stand, in an almost erect posture, on a space scarcely large enough to contain them. The parents seemed aware of the condition of their brood, and, affectionate as they still appeared to be, I thought their manner towards them was altered, and I felt grieved. Indeed, sorely grieved I was when, next week, I saw them discharge, as it were, their children, and force them from the nest into the waters that were spread below. It is true that, previous to this, I had seen the young Anhingas trying the power of their wings as they stood upright on the nest, flapping them many minutes at a time; yet, although thus convinced that they were nearly in a state to provide for themselves, it was not without a feeling of despondency that I saw them hurled into the air, and alight on the water. But, Reader, Nature in all this had acted beneficially; and I afterwards found that in thus expelling their young so soon, the old birds had in view to rear another brood in the same spot, before the commencement of unfavourable weather.

Many writers have described what they have been pleased to call the habits of the Anhinga; nay, some have presumed to offer comments upon them, and to generalize and form theories thereon, or even to inform us gravely and oracularly what they ought to be, when the basis of all their fancies was merely a dried skin and feathers appended. Leaving these ornithologists for the present to amuse themselves in their snug closets, I proceed to detail the real habits of this curious bird, as I have observed and studied them in Nature.

The Snake-Bird is a constant resident in the Floridas, and the lower parts of Louisiana, Alabama, and Georgia. Few remain during winter in South Carolina, or in any district to the eastward of that State; but some proceed as far as North Carolina in spring, and breed along the coast. I have found it in Texas in the month of May, on the waters of Buffalo Bayou, and the St Jacinto River, where it breeds, and where, as I was told, it spends the winter. It rarely ascends the Mississippi beyond the neighbourhood of Natchez, from which most of the individuals return to the mouths of that great stream, and the numerous lakes, ponds, and bayous in its vicinity, where I have observed the species at all seasons, as well as in the Floridas.

Being a bird which, by its habits, rarely fails to attract the notice of the most indifferent observer, it has received various names. The Creoles of Louisiana, about New Orleans, and as far up the Mississippi as Pointe Coupé, call it "Bec à Lancette," on account of the form of its bill; whilst at the mouths of the river it bears the name of "Water Crow." In the southern parts of Florida, it is called the "Grecian Lady," and in South Carolina it is best known by the name of "Cormorant." Yet in all these parts, it bears also the name of "Snake-Bird;" but it is nowhere with us called the "Black-bellied Darter," which, by the way, could only be with strict propriety applied to the adult male.

Those which, on the one hand, ascend the Mississippi, and, on the other, visit the Carolinas, arrive at their several places of resort early in April, in some seasons even in March, and there remain until the beginning of November. Although this bird is occasionally seen in the immediate vicinity of the sea, and at times breeds not far from it, I never met with an individual fishing in salt water. It gives a decided preference to rivers, lakes, bayous, or lagoons in the interior, always however in the lowest and most level parts of the country. The more retired and secluded the spot, the more willingly does the Snake-Bird remain about it. Sometimes indeed I have suddenly come on some in such small ponds, which I discovered by mere accident, and in parts of woods so very secluded, that I was taken by surprise on seeing them. The Floridas therefore are peculiarly adapted for this species, as there the torpid waters of the streams, bayous, and lakes, are most abundantly supplied with various species of fish, reptiles, and insects, while the temperature is at all seasons congenial, and their exemption from annoyance almost unparalleled. Wherever similar situations occur in other parts of the Southern States, there the Anhingas are met with in numbers proportioned to the extent of the favourable localities. It is very seldom indeed that any are seen on rapid streams, and more especially on clear water, a single instance of such an occurrence being all that I have observed. Wherever you may chance to find this bird, you will perceive that it has not left itself without the means of escape; you will never find one in a pond or bayou completely enclosed by tall trees, so as to obstruct its passage; but will observe that it generally prefers ponds or lakes, surrounded by deep and almost impenetrable morasses, and having a few large trees growing out of the water near their centre, from the branches of which they can easily mark the approach of an enemy, and make their escape in good time. Unlike the Fish-hawk and Kings-fisher, the Anhinga however never plunges or dives from an eminence in procuring its prey, although from its habit of occasionally dropping in silence to the water from its perch, for the purpose of afterwards swimming about and diving in the manner of the Cormorant, some writers have been led to believe that it does so.

The Black-bellied Darter, all whose names I shall use, for the purpose of avoiding irksome repetitions, may be considered as indefinitely gregarious; by which I mean that you may see eight or more together at times, during winter especially, or only two, as in the breeding season. On a few occasions, whilst in the interior of the southernmost parts of Florida, I saw about thirty individuals on the same lake. While exploring the St John's River of that country in its whole length, I sometimes saw several hundreds together. I procured a great number on that stream, on the lakes in its neighbourhood, and also on those near the plantation of Mr BULOW, on the eastern side of the Peninsula. I observed that the young Darters, as well as those of the Cormorants, Herons, and many other birds, kept apart from the old individuals, which they however joined in spring, when they had attained their full beauty of plumage.

The Anhinga is altogether a diurnal bird, and, like the Cormorant, is fond of returning to the same roosting place every evening about dusk, unless prevented by molestation. At times I have seen from three to seven alight on the dead top branches of a tall tree, for the purpose of there spending the night; and this they repeated for several weeks, until on my having killed some of them and wounded others, the rest abandoned the spot, and after several furious contests with a party that roosted about two miles off, succeeding in establishing themselves among them. At such times they seldom sit very near each other, as Cormorants do, but keep at a distance of a few feet or yards, according to the nature of the branches. Whilst asleep, they stand with the body almost erect, but never bend the tarsus so as to apply it in its whole length, as the Cormorant does; they keep their head snugly covered among their scapulars, and at times emit a wheezing sound, which I supposed to be produced by their breathing. In rainy weather they often remain roosted the greater part of the day, and on such occasions they stand erect, with their neck and head stretched upwards, remaining perfectly motionless, as if to allow the water to glide off their plumage. Now and then, however, they suddenly ruffle their feathers, violently shake themselves, and again compressing their form, resume their singular position.

Their disposition to return to the same roosting places is so decided that, when chased from their places of resort, they seldom fail to betake themselves to them during the day; and in this manner they may easily be procured with some care. Whilst at Mr BULOW's, I was almost daily in the habit of visiting a long, tortuous, bayou, many miles in extent, which at that season (winter) was abundantly supplied with Anhingas. There the Otter, the Alligator, and many species of birds, found an ample supply of food; and as I was constantly watching them, I soon discovered a roosting place of the Snake-Birds, which was a large dead tree. I found it impossible to get near them either by cautiously advancing in the boat, or by creeping among the briars, canes, and tangled palmettoes which profusely covered the banks. I therefore paddled directly to the place, accompanied by my faithful and sagacious Newfoundland dog. At my approach the birds flew off towards the upper parts of the stream, and as I knew that they might remain for hours, I had a boat sent after them with orders to the Negroes to start all that they could see. Dragging up my little bark, I then hid myself among the tangled plants, and, with my eyes bent on the dead tree, and my gun in readiness, I remained until I saw the beautiful bird alight and gaze around to see if all was right. Alas! it was not aware of its danger, but, after a few moments, during which I noted its curious motions, it fell dead into the water, while the reverberations consequent on the discharge of my gun alarmed the birds around, and by looking either up or down the bayou I could see many Anhingas speeding away to other parts. My dog, as obedient as the most submissive of servants, never stirred until ordered, when he would walk cautiously into the water, swim up to the dead bird, and having brought it to me, lie down gently in his place. In this manner, in the course of one day I procured fourteen of these birds, and wounded several others. I may here at once tell you that all the roosting places of the Anhinga which I have seen were over the water, either on the shore or in the midst of some stagnant pool; and this situation they seem to select because there they can enjoy the first gladdening rays of the morning sun, or bask in the blaze of its noontide splendour, and also observe with greater ease the approach of their enemies, as they betake themselves to it after feeding, and remain there until hunger urges them to fly off. There, trusting to the extraordinary keenness of their beautiful bright eyes in spying the marauding sons of the forest, or the not less dangerous enthusiast, who, probably like yourself, would venture through mud and slime up to his very neck, to get within rifle shot of a bird so remarkable in form and manners, the Anhingas, or "Grecian Ladies," stand erect, with their wings and tail fully or partially spread out in the sunshine, whilst their long slender necks and heads are thrown as it were in every direction by the most curious and sudden jerks and bendings. Their bills are open, and you see that the intense heat of the atmosphere induces them to suffer their gular pouch to hang loosely. What delightful sights and scenes these have been to me, good Reader! With what anxiety have I waded toward these birds, to watch their movements, while at the same time I cooled my over-heated body, and left behind on the shores myriads of hungry sand flies, gnats, mosquitoes, and ticks, that had annoyed me for hours! And oh! how great has been my pleasure when, after several failures, I have at last picked up the spotted bird, examined it with care, and then returned to the gloomy shore, to note my observations! Great too is my pleasure in now relating to you the results of my long personal experience, together with that of my excellent friend Dr BACHMAN, who has transmitted his observations on this bird to me.

WILSON, I am inclined to think, never saw a live Anhinga; and the notes, furnished by Mr ABBOT of Georgia, which he has published, are very far from being correct. In the supplementary volumes of American Ornithology published in Philadelphia, the Editor, who visited the Floridas, added nothing of importance beyond giving more accurate measurements of a single specimen than WILSON had given from the stuffed skins from which he made his figures, and which were in the museum of that city.

The peculiar form, long wings, and large fan-like tail of the

Anhinga, would at once induce a person looking upon it to conclude that it was intended by nature rather for protracted and powerful flight, than for spending as it does more than half of its time by day in the water, where its progress, one might suppose, would be greatly impeded by the amplitude of these parts. Yet how different from such a supposition is the fact? The Anhinga in truth is the very first of all fresh-water divers. With the quickness of thought it disappears beneath the surface, and that so as scarcely to leave a ripple on the spot; and when your anxious eyes seek around for the bird, you are astonished to find it many hundred yards distant, the head perhaps merely above water for a moment; or you may chance to perceive the bill alone gently cutting the water, and producing a line of wake not observable beyond the distance of thirty yards from where you are standing. With habits like these it easily eludes all your efforts to procure it. When shot at while perched, however severely wounded they may be, they fall at once perpendicularly, the bill downward, the wings and tail closed, and then dive and make their way under water to such a distance that they are rarely obtained. Should you, however, see them again, and set out in pursuit, they dive along the shores, attach themselves to roots of trees or plants by the feet, and so remain until life is extinct. When shot dead on the trees, they sometimes cling so firmly to the branches that you must wait some minutes before they fall.

The generally received opinion or belief that the Anhinga always swims with its body sunk beneath the surface is quite incorrect; for it does so only when in sight of an enemy, and when under no apprehension of danger it is as buoyant as any other diving bird, such as a Cormorant, a Merganser, a Grebe, or a Diver. This erroneous opinion has, however, been adopted simply because few persons have watched the bird with sufficient care. When it first observes an enemy, it immediately sinks its body deeper, in the manner of the birds just mentioned, and the nearer the danger approaches, the more does it sink, until at last it swims off with the head and neck only above the surface, when these parts, from their form and peculiar sinuous motion, somewhat resemble the head and part of the body of a snake. It is in fact from this circumstance that the Anhinga has received the name of

Snake-Bird. At such a time, it is seen constantly turning its head from side to side, often opening its bill as if for the purpose of inhaling a larger quantity of air, to enable it the better to dive, and remain under water so long that when it next makes its appearance it is out of your reach. When fishing in a state of security it dives precisely like a Cormorant, returns to the surface as soon as it has procured a fish or other article of food, shakes it, if it is not too large often throws it up into the air, and receiving it conveniently in the bill, swallows it at once, and recommences its search. But I doubt much if it ever seizes on any thing that it cannot thus swallow whole. They have the curious habit of diving under any floating substances, such as parcels of dead weeds or leaves of trees which have accidentally been accumulated by the winds or currents, or even the green slimy substances produced by putrefaction. This habit is continued by the species when in a perfect state of domestication, for I have seen one kept by my friend JOHN BACHMAN thus diving when within a few feet of a quantity of floating rice-chaff, in one of the tide-ponds in the neighbourhood of Charleston. Like the Common Goose, it invariably depresses its head while swimming under a low bridge, or a branch or trunk of a tree hanging over the water. When it swims beneath the surface of the water, it spreads its wings partially, but does not employ them as a means of propulsion, and keeps its tail always considerably expanded, using the feet as paddles either simultaneously or alternately.

The quantity of fish consumed by this bird is astonishing; and what I am about to relate on this subject will appear equally so. One morning Dr BACHMAN and I gave to an Anhinga a Black Fish, measuring nine and a half inches, by two inches in diameter; and although the head of the fish was considerably larger than its body, and its strong and spinous fins appeared formidable, the bird, which was then about seven months old, swallowed it entire, head foremost. It was in appearance digested in an hour and a half, when the bird swallowed three others of somewhat smaller size. At another time, we placed before it a number of fishes about seven and a half inches long, of which it swallowed nine in succession. It would devour at a meal forty or more fishes about three inches and a half long. On several occasions it was fed on

Plaice, when it swallowed some that were four inches broad, extending its throat, and compressing them during their descent into the stomach. It did not appear to relish eels, as it eat all the other sorts first, and kept them to the last; and after having swallowed them, it had great difficulty in keeping them down, but, although for a while thwarted, it would renew its efforts, and at length master them. When taken to the tide-pond at the foot of my friend's garden, it would now and then after diving return to the surface of the water with a cray-fish in its mouth, which it pressed hard and dashed about in its bill, evidently for the purpose of maiming it, before it would attempt to swallow it, and it never caught a fish without bringing it up to subject it to the same operation.

While residing near Bayou Sara, in the State of Mississippi, I was in the habit of occasionally visiting some acquaintances residing at Pointe Coupé, nearly opposite the mouth of the bayou. One day, on entering the house of an humble settler close on the western bank of the Mississippi, I observed two young Anhingas that had been taken out of a nest containing four, which had been built on a high cypress in a lake on the eastern side of the river. They were perfectly tame and gentle, and much attached to their foster-parents, the man and woman of the house, whom they followed wherever they went. They fed with equal willingness on shrimps and fish, and when neither could be had, contented themselves with boiled Indian corn, of which they caught with great ease the grains as they were thrown one by one to them. I was afterwards informed, that when a year old, they were allowed to go to the river and fish for themselves, or to the ponds on either side, and that they regularly returned towards night for the purpose of roosting on the top of the house. Both birds were males, and in time they fought hard battles, but at last each met with a female, which it enticed to the roost on the house-top, where all the four slept at night for a while. Soon after, the females having probably laid their eggs in the woods, they all disappeared, and were never again seen by the persons who related this curious affair.

The Anhinga is shy and wary when residing in a densely peopled part of the country, which, however, is rarely the case, as I have already mentioned; but when in its favourite secluded and peaceful haunts, where it has seldom or never been molested, it is easily approached and without difficulty procured; nay, sometimes one will remain standing in the same spot and in the same posture, until you have fired several bullets from your rifle at it. Its mode of fishing is not to plunge from a tree or stump in pursuit of its prey, but to dive while swimming in the manner of Cormorants and many other birds. Indeed, it could very seldom see a fish from above the surface of the turbid waters which it prefers.

It moves along the branches of trees rather awkwardly; but still it walks there, with the aid of its wings, which it extends for that purpose, and not unfrequently also using its bill in the manner of a Parrot. On the land, it walks and even runs with considerable ease, certainly with more expertness than the Cormorant, though much in the same style. But it does not employ its tail to aid it, for, on the contrary, it carries that organ inclined upwards, and during its progress from one place to another, the movements of its head and neck are continued. These movements, which, as I have said, resemble sudden jerkings of the parts to their full extent, become extremely graceful during the love season, when they are reduced to gentle curvatures. I must not forget to say, that during all these movements, the gular pouch is distended, and the bird emits rough guttural sounds. If they are courting on wing, however, in the manner of Cormorants, Hawks, and many other birds, they emit a whistling note, somewhat resembling that of some of our rapacious birds, and which may be expressed by the syllables *eek, eek, eek*, the first loudest, and the rest diminishing in strength. When they are on the water, their call-notes so much resemble the rough grunting cries of the Florida Cormorant, that I have often mistaken them for the latter.

The flight of the Anhinga is swift, and at times well sustained; but like the Cormorants, it has the habit of spreading its wings and tail before it leaves its perch or the surface of the water, thus frequently affording the sportsman a good opportunity of shooting it. When once on wing, they can rise to a vast height, in beautiful gyrations, varied during the love-season by zigzag lines chiefly performed by the male, as he plays around his beloved. At times they quite disappear from the gaze, lost as it were, in the upper regions of the air; and at other times, when much lower, seem to remain suspended in the same spot for several seconds. All this while, and indeed as long as they are flying, their wings are directly extended, their neck stretched to its full length, their tail more or less spread according to the movements to be performed, being closed when they descend, expanded and declined to either side when they mount. During their migratory expeditions, they beat their wings at times in the manner of the Cormorant, and at other times sail like the Turkey Buzzard and some Hawks, the former mode being more frequently observed when they are passing over an extent of woodland, the latter when over a sheet of water. If disturbed or alarmed, they fly with continuous beats of the wings, and proceed with great velocity. As they find difficulty in leaving their perch without previously expanding their wings, they are also, when about to alight, obliged to use them in supporting their body, until their feet have taken a sufficient hold of the branch on which they desire to settle. In this respect, they exactly resemble the Florida Cormorant.

There are facts connected with the habits of birds which might afford a pretty good idea of the relative temperatures of different parts of the country during a given season; and those observed with regard to the Anhinga seem to me peculiarly illustrative of this circumstance. I have found the "Grecian Lady" breeding on St John's River in East Florida, near Lake George, as early as the 23d of February; having previously seen many of them caressing each other on the waters, and again carrying sticks, fresh twigs, and other matters, to form their nests, and having also shot females with the eggs largely developed. Now, at the same period, perhaps not a single Anhinga is to be seen in the neighbourhood of Natchez, only a few about New Orleans, in the eastern parts of Georgia, and the middle maritime portions of South Carolina. In Louisiana this bird breeds in April or May, and in South Carolina rarely before June, my friend BACHMAN having found eggs, and young just hatched, as late as the 28th of that month. In North Carolina, where only a few pairs breed, it is later by a fortnight.

I have already expressed my opinion that birds which thus

breed so much earlier in one section of the country than in another, especially when at great distances, may, after producing one or even two broods, in the same year, still have time enough to proceed toward higher latitudes for the purpose of again breeding. Actual observations have moreover satisfied me that individuals of the same species produced in warm latitudes have a stronger disposition toward reproduction than those of more northern climates. This being the case, and most birds endowed with the power of migrating, having a tendency to exercise it, may we not suppose that the pair of Anhingas which bred on the St John's in February, might be inclined to breed again either in South Carolina or in the neighbourhood of Natchez, several months after. But, as yet, I have not been able to adduce positive proof of the accuracy of this opinion.

The nest of the Snake-bird is variously placed in different localities; sometimes in low bushes, and even on the common smilax, not more than eight or ten feet above the water, if the place be secluded, or on the lower or top branches of the highest trees, but always over the water. In Louisiana and the State of Mississippi, where I have seen a goodly number of nests, they were generally placed on very large and tall cypresses, growing out of the central parts of lakes and ponds, or overhanging the borders of lagoons, bayous, or rivers, distant from inhabited places. They are frequently placed singly, but at times amidst hundreds or even thousands of nests of several species of Herons, especially *Ardea alba* and *A. Herodias*, the Great White and Great Blue Herons. As however in all cases the form, size, and component materials are nearly the same, I will here describe a nest procured for the purpose by my friend BACHMAN.

It measured fully two feet in diameter, and was of a flattened form, much resembling that of the Florida Cormorant. The first or bottom layer was made of dry sticks of different sizes, some nearly half an inch in diameter, laid crosswise, but in a circular manner. Green branches with leaves on them, of the common myrtle, *Myrica cerifera*, a quantity of Spanish moss, and some slender roots, formed the upper and inside layer, which was as solid and compact as that of any nest of the Heron tribe. This nest contained four eggs; another

examined on the same day had four young birds; a third only
three; and in no instance has a nest of the Anhinga been
found with either eight eggs, or "two eggs and six young
ones," as mentioned by Mr ABBOTT, of Georgia, in his notes
transmitted to WILSON. Mr ABBOTT is however correct in
saying that this species "will occupy the same tree for a series
of years," and I have myself known a pair to breed in the same
nest three seasons, augmenting and repairing it every succeeding spring, as Cormorants and Herons are wont to do.
The eggs average two inches and five-eighths in length, by
one and a quarter in diameter, and are of an elongated oval
form, of a dull uniform whitish colour externally, being covered with a chalky substance, beneath which the shell, on being carefully scraped, is of a light blue, precisely resembling in
this respect the eggs of the different species of American
Cormorants with which I am acquainted.

The young when about a fortnight old are clad with a uniform buff-coloured down; their bill is black, their feet yellowish-white, their head and neck nearly naked; and now they
resemble young Cormorants, though of a different colour.
The wing feathers make their appearance through the down,
and are dark brown. The birds in the same nest differ as much
in size as those of Cormorants, the largest being almost twice
the size of the smallest. At this age they are in the habit of
raising themselves by placing their bills on the upper part of
the nest, or over a branch if convenient, and drawing themselves up by their jaws, which on such occasions they open
very widely. This habit is continued by young birds whilst
in confinement, and was also observed in the Cormorant,
Phalacrocorax Carbo, the young of which assisted themselves
with their bills while crawling about on the deck of the Ripley.
The action is indeed performed by the Anhinga at all periods
of its life. At an early age the young utter a low wheezing call,
and at times some cries resembling those of the young of the
smaller species of Herons. From birth they are fed by regurgitation, which one might suppose an irksome task to the parent birds, as during the act they open their wings and raise
their tails. I have not been able to ascertain the period of incubation, but am sure that the male and the female sit alternately, the latter however remaining much longer on the nest.

Young Anhingas when approached while in the nest cling tenaciously to it, until seized, and if thrown down, they merely float on the water, and are easily captured. On the contrary, the young Florida Cormorants throw themselves into the water, and dive at once.

When they are three weeks old, the quills and tail-feathers grow rapidly, but continue of the same dark-brown colour, and so remain until they are able to fly, when they leave the nest, although they still present a singular motley appearance, the breast and back being buff-coloured, while the wings and tail are nearly black. After the feathers of the wings and tail are nearly fully developed, those of the sides of the body and breast become visible through the down, and the bird appears more curiously mottled than before. The young male now assumes the colour of the adult female, which it retains until the beginning of October, when the breast becomes streaked with dusky; white spots shew themselves on the back, the black of which becomes more intense, and the crimpings on the two middle feathers of the tail, which have been more or less apparent from the first, are now perfect. By the middle of February, the male is in full plumage, but the eyes have not yet acquired their full colour, being only of a dull reddish-orange. In this respect also two differences are observed between the Anhinga and the Cormorants. The first is the rapid progress of the Anhinga towards maturity of plumage, the other the retaining of its complete dress through the whole of its life, no change taking place in its colours at each successive moult. The Cormorants, on the contrary, take three or four years to attain their full dress of the love season, which lasts only during that period of excitement. The progress of the plumage in the female Anhinga is as rapid as in the male, and the tints also remain unaltered through each successive moult.

Like all other carnivorous and piscivorous birds, the Anhinga can remain days and nights without food, apparently without being much incommoded. When overtaken on being wounded, and especially if brought to the ground, it seems to regard its enemies without fear. On several occasions of this kind, I have seen it watch my approach, or that of my dog, standing as erect as it could under the pain of its wounds, with its head drawn back, its bill open, and its throat swelled with anger until, when at a sure distance, it would dart its head forward and give a severe wound. One which had thus struck at my dog's nose, hung to it until dragged to my feet over a space of thirty paces. When seized by the neck, they scratch severely with their sharp claws, and beat their wings about you with much more vigour than you would suppose they could possess. Having witnessed the singular means employed by this bird in making its escape on sudden emergencies, I will here relate an instance, which evinces a kind of reason. Whilst ascending the St John's river in East Florida, along with Captain PIERCY of the U. S. Navy, our boat was rowed into a circular basin of clear shallow water, having a sandy bottom; such places being found occasionally in that country, produced by the flowing of springs from the more elevated sandy parts into the muddy rivers and lakes. We entered the cove by passing between the branches of low trees, over-hung by others of great height. The first object that attracted my attention was a female Anhinga perched on the opposite side of the cove, and, as I did not wish that it should be shot, we merely advanced towards it, when it began to throw its head about, and watch our motions. The place was small, and the enclosing trees high. Though it might have flown upwards and escaped, it remained perched, but evidently perturbed and apprehensive of danger. When the boat was at a short distance, however, it suddenly threw itself backward, cutting a somerset as it were, and, covered by the branches, darted straight through the tangled forest, and was soon out of sight. Never before nor since have I seen or heard of Anhingas flying through the woods.

For the following description of the Snake-bird's breeding grounds, a few miles distant from Charleston in South Carolina, I am indebted to my friend JOHN BACHMAN:—"On the 28th of June 1837, accompanied by Dr WILSON, Dr DRAYTON, and WILLIAM RAMSAY, Esq., I went to Chisholm Pond, about seven miles from the city, for the purpose of seeing the Anhingas while breeding. The day was fine, and in about an hour our horses brought us to the margin of the swamp. We soon discovered a bird flying over us, and making for the upper part of the pond toward a retired place, rendered almost inaccessible in consequence of its being a morass overgrown with vines and rushes. As there was no other way of examining their locality but by water, we hauled ashore a small leaky canoe which we found in the pond, caulked it in the best manner we could, so as to render it not unsafe, although after all we could do to it, we found it still very leaky. It proved uncomfortable enough, and could hold only two persons. So it was agreed that I should proceed in it, accompanied by a servant, who understood well how to paddle it.

"The pond is artificial, and such as in this country is called a 'Reserve.' It is situated at the upper part of rice fields, and is intended to preserve water sufficient, when needed, to irrigate and overflow the rice. It is studded with small islands, covered by a thick growth of a small species of Laurel (*Laurus geniculata*) and the Black Willow (*Salix nigra*), all entangled by various species of Smilax and other plants. These were at the time covered with Herons' nests of several kinds. Farther on the Night Herons also had formed a city. As I proceeded onwards in my search I found the difficulties increasing. The water became shallow, the mire deeper and softer, and the boat required the best of management to be propelled along, for now it was retarded by rushes and vines. Enormous live oaks and cypress trees reared their majestic branches towards the pure sky above, covered as they were with dangling masses of Spanish moss, reaching to the very surface of the water, and turning day into night. Alligators of great size wallowed in the mire, or were heard to plunge into it, from the many logs which ever and anon intercepted my progress, while terrapins, snakes, and other reptiles swarmed around. My situation was thus not altogether so very pleasant, and the less so as it was necessary for me to destroy as many mosquitoes as possible, and guard against being upset in such a truly 'dismal swamp.' We moved extremely slowly, yet advanced, and at last, having reached an open space where the trees were of small size and height, I espied the nest of the Anhinga before me! The female was sitting on it, but on our coming nearer she raised herself by her bill to a branch about one foot above, and there stood with outstretched neck, like a statue. It was cruel thus to disturb her in her own peaceful solitude; but naturalists, alas! seldom consider this long, when the object of their pursuit is in their view and almost within their grasp. Being now within twenty yards of the innocent and interesting creature, I pointed my short rifle towards her, and immediately fired; but the unsteadiness of the canoe, and perhaps that of a hand not accustomed to this weapon, saved her life. She remained in her statue-like posture, the rifle was reloaded, and thrice fired, without touching her; but at last a bullet having cut through the branch on which she stood, she spread her dark pinions, and launching into the air, was soon beyond the reach of my eyes, and I trust of further danger."

The same kind friend having procured eggs and young of this interesting bird, I will present you with his observations respecting them. He writes thus:—"I brought home three young Snake-birds, two of which I immediately undertook to raise and domesticate, entrusting the third to the care of one of our mutual friends. I found no difficulty in rearing one of them. The other, by neglect of my servant, died a few weeks afterwards, during a short personal absence. Whilst these two birds were yet in the same cage, it was curious indeed to see the smaller one when hungry incessantly trying to force its bill into the mouth and throat of the other, which, after being thus teased for a short time, would open its mouth to suffer the little one to thrust its whole head down the throat of its brother, from which it would receive the fish that the latter had previously swallowed. In this singular manner did the larger bird, which after awhile proved to be a male, continue to act as if the foster-parent of his little sister, which indeed seemed to be thrown upon his protection. The one still in my possession is fed on fish, which it picks up, tosses a few times in the air, and swallows at the first convenient opportunity, that is when the fish falls towards its mouth head foremost. At the onset, when the fish was large, I had it cut into pieces, thinking that the apparent slenderness of the bird's neck could not expand enough to swallow it whole; but I soon ascertained that this was unnecessary. Fish three times the size of the neck were tossed in the expanded jaws and gobbled at once, and immediately after, the bird would come to my feet, clicking its bill in such an unequivocal manner that I never failed to give it more. My pet was tame from the beginning of its captivity, and followed me about the house, the yard, and garden, until I thought it quite troublesome in consequence of its peculiar attachment to me. The one given to our friend was fed on fish and raw beef; but although it grew to its full size, never seemed to thrive as well as the one I had, and finally died of an affection causing spasms. This was a female, and although less bright in colour than the adult of the same sex, the two middle feathers of her tail were partially crimped, and her markings were the same. While in the young state I frequently carried it to a pond, believing that it would relish the water, and would improve in health; but I invariably found it to scramble towards the shore as soon as possible, as if dreading the element in which it was by nature destined to live. When thrown into the pond, it usually dived at once, but the next instant arose to the surface, and swam with all the buoyancy of a common duck. It is a fearless bird, keeping at bay the hens and turkeys in the yard, and never sparing any dog that chances to pass by it, dealing blows right and left with its sharp bill, and occasionally placing itself at the trough where they are fed, to prevent them from taking a morsel of food till he has tantalized them sufficiently, when he leaves them to share whatever he does not himself relish.

"It was not until my bird was fully fledged that I found it willing or anxious to go to the water, and then, whenever it saw me go toward the pond, it accompanied me as far as the gate of the garden, seeming to say 'Pray let me go.' On my opening this gate, it at once followed me waddling along like a duck, and no sooner was it in sight of its favourite element than it immediately let itself in, not with a plunge or a dive, but by dropping from a plank into the stream, where for a while it would swim like a duck, then, dipping its long neck, it would dive for the purpose of procuring fish. The water was clear enough to enable me to see all its movements, and after many various windings it would emerge at the distance of forty or fifty yards. This bird sleeps in the open air during warm nights, perched on the highest bar of the fence, with its head under its wings, placed there from above its back, and in rainy weather it often sits in the same position for nearly the whole day. It appears to be very susceptible of cold, retreating to the kitchen and near the fire, battling with the dogs or the cooks for the most comfortable place on the hearth. Whenever the sun shines, it spreads its wings and tail, rustles its feathers, and seems delighted with our warmest sunny days. When walking and occasionally hopping, it does not support itself by the tail, as Cormorants sometimes do. When fishes are presented to it, it seizes and swallows them greedily; but when these cannot be procured, we are forced to feed it on meat, when it opens its mouth, and receives the food placed in it. Occasionally it has spent several days without any food; but in those cases the bird became very troublesome, harassing all around by its incessant croakings, and giving blows to the servants, as if to remind them of their neglect.

"Once it made its escape, and flew off about a quarter of a mile into the pond. Some boys happening to be there in a canoe, the bird approached them with open mouth, for it was hungry and wanted food. They seeing such a strange creature pursuing them with a head somewhat like that of a snake, took alarm and paddled for the shore; but my bird followed in their wake, and landed as soon as they did. They now fled to the house, where the Anhinga also arrived, and was recognised by some members of the family, who sent it back to me; and I, to prevent its farther escape or loss, clipped one of its wings."

I saw the bird above mentioned at my friend's house at Charleston in the winter of 1836, when on my way to the Gulf of Mexico, and had many opportunities of watching its habits. It was killed by a beautiful retriever presented to me by the EARL OF DERBY, and its death occasioned sorrow both to my friend and myself, as he had given it to me for the purpose of being sent to that nobleman.

Ever since I have been acquainted with the Anhinga, I have thought that in form and habits it is intimately connected with the Cormorants, and was induced to compare their manners. In some respects I found them similar, in others different; but when I discovered that all these birds possess a remarkable peculiarity in the structure of their feathers, I thought that their generic affinity could not be denied. The Anhinga has its body and neck covered with what I would call *fibrous* feathers, having a very slender shaft; while its quills and tail-feathers are *compact*, that is, perfect in structure, strong, and elastic. Now the shafts of all these latter feathers are *tubular from their bases to their very extremities*, which, in so far as I know, is not the case in any other bird, excepting the Cormorants. They are all very elastic, like those in the tails of our largest Woodpeckers, the shafts of which, however, are filled with a spongy pith, as in all other land-birds, and in all the aquatic species which I have examined, including Divers and Grebes, as well as *Plungers*, such as Gannets, Kingsfishers, and Fishing Hawks. The quills and tail-feathers of the Cormorants and Anhinga, in short, have the barrel as in other birds, but the shaft *hollow, even to the tip, its walls being transparent, and of the same nature as the barrel.*

WILSON, who, it is acknowledged, made his figures from stuffed specimens in the Philadelphia Museum, had no positive proof that the bird which he took for a female was one, for he had not seen the Anhinga alive or recently killed. Even his continuator, Mr ORD, procured only males during his visit to the Floridas. But the female which I have represented was proved to be of that sex by dissection, and was examined by myself nineteen years ago near Bayou Sara. Since that time I have had numerous opportunities of satisfying myself as to this point, by examining birds in various stages.

The substances which I have found in many individuals of this species were fishes of various kinds, aquatic insects, crays, leeches, shrimps, tadpoles, eggs of frogs, water-lizards, young alligators, water-snakes, and small terrapins. I never observed any sand or gravel in the stomach. On some occasions I found it distended to the utmost, and, as I have already stated, the bird has great powers of digestion. Its excrements are voided in a liquid state, and squirted to a considerable distance, as in Cormorants, Hawks, and all birds of prey.

The flesh of the Anhinga, after the bird is grown, is dark, firm, oily, and unfit for food, with the exception of the smaller pectoral muscles of the female, which are white and delicate. The crimpings of the two middle tail-feathers become more deeply marked during the breeding season, especially in the male. When young, the female shews them only in a slight degree, and never has them so decided as the male.

American Avoset

Recurvirostra Americana, GMEL.

(PLATE 56)

THE FACT of this curious bird's breeding in the interior of our country accidentally became known to me in June 1814. I was at the time travelling on horseback from Henderson to Vincennes in the State of Indiana. As I approached a large shallow pond in the neighbourhood of the latter town, I was struck by the sight of several Avosets hovering over the margins and islets of the pond, and although it was late, and I was both fatigued and hungry, I could not resist the temptation of endeavouring to find the cause of their being so far from the sea. Leaving my horse at liberty, I walked toward the pond, when, on being at once assailed by four of the birds, I felt confident that they had nests, and that their mates were either sitting or tending their young. The pond, which was about two hundred yards in length, and half as wide, was surrounded by tall bulrushes extending to some distance from the margin. Near its centre were several islets, eight or ten yards in length, and disposed in a line. Having made my way through the rushes, I found the water only a few inches deep; but the mud reached above my knees, as I carefully advanced towards the nearest island. The four birds kept up a constant noise, remained on wing, and at times dived through the air until close to me, evincing their displeasure at my intrusion. My desire to shoot them however was restrained by my anxiety to study their habits as closely as possible; and as soon as I had searched the different inlets, and found three nests with eggs, and a female with her brood, I returned to my horse, and proceeded to Vincennes, about two miles distant. Next morning at sunrise I was snugly concealed amongst the rushes, with a fair view of the whole pond. In about an hour the male birds ceased to fly over me, and betook themselves to their ordinary occupations, when I noted the following particulars.

On alighting, whether on the water or on the ground, the American Avoset keeps its wings raised until it has fairly settled. If in the water, it stands a few minutes balancing its head and neck, somewhat in the manner of the Tell-tale Godwit.

After this it stalks about searching for food, or runs after it, sometimes swimming for a yard or so while passing from one shallow to another, or wading up to its body, with the wings partially raised. Sometimes they would enter among the rushes, and disappear for several minutes. They kept apart, but crossed each other's path in hundreds of ways, all perfectly silent, and without shewing the least symptom of enmity towards each other, although whenever a Sandpiper came near, they would instantly give chase to it. On several occasions, when I purposely sent forth a loud shrill whistle without stirring, they would suddenly cease from their rambling, raise up their body and neck, emit each two or three notes, and remain several minutes on the alert, after which they would fly to their nests, and then return. They search for food precisely in the manner of the Roseate Spoonbill, moving their heads to and fro sideways, while their bill is passing through the soft mud; and in many instances, when the water was deeper, they would immerse their whole head and a portion of the neck, as the Spoonbill and Red-breasted Snipe are wont to do. When, on the contrary, they pursued aquatic insects, such as swim on the surface, they ran after them, and on getting up to them, suddenly seized them by thrusting the lower mandible beneath them, while the other was raised a good way above the surface, much in the manner of the Black Shear-water, which however performs this act on wing. They were also expert at catching flying insects, after which they ran with partially expanded wings.

I watched them as they were thus engaged about an hour, when they all flew to the islets where the females were, emitting louder notes than usual. The different pairs seemed to congratulate each other, using various curious gestures; and presently those which had been sitting left the task to their mates and betook themselves to the water, when they washed, shook their wings and tail, as if either heated or tormented by insects, and then proceeded to search for food in the manner above described. Now, Reader, wait a few moments until I eat my humble breakfast.

About eleven o'clock the heat had become intense, and the Avosets gave up their search, each retiring to a different part of the pond, where, after pluming themselves, they drew their heads close to their shoulders, and remained perfectly still, as if asleep, for about an hour, when they shook themselves simultaneously, took to wing, and rising to the height of thirty or forty yards, flew off towards the waters of the Wabash River.

I was now desirous of seeing one of the sitting birds on its nest, and leaving my hiding place, slowly, and as silently as possible, proceeded toward the nearest islet on which I knew a nest to be, having the evening before, to mark the precise spot, broken some of the weeds, which were now withered by the heat of the sun. You, good Reader, will not, I am sure, think me prolix; but as some less considerate persons may allege that I am tediously so, I must tell them here that no student of Nature ever was, or ever can be, too particular while thus marking the precise situation of a bird's nest. Indeed, I myself have lost many nests by being less attentive. After this short but valuable lecture, you and I will do our best to approach the sitting bird unseen by it. Although a person can advance but slowly when wading through mud and water knee-deep, it does not take much time to get over forty or fifty yards, and thus I was soon on the small island where the Avoset was comfortably seated on her nest. Softly and on all four I crawled toward the spot, panting with heat and anxiety. Now, Reader, I am actually within three feet of the unheeding creature, peeping at her through the tall grasses. Lovely bird! how innocent, how unsuspecting, and yet how near to thine enemy, albeit he be an admirer of thy race! There she sits on her eggs, her head almost mournfully sunk among the plumage, and her eyes, unanimated by the sight of her mate, half closed, as if she dreamed of future scenes. Her legs are bent beneath her in the usual manner. I have seen this, and I am content. Now she observes me, poor thing, and off she scrambles,—running, tumbling, and at last rising on wing, emitting her clicking notes of grief and anxiety, which none but an inconsiderate or callous-hearted person could hear without sympathizing with her.

The alarm is sounded, the disturbed bird is floundering hither and thither over the pool, now lying on the surface as if ready to die, now limping to induce me to pursue her and abandon her eggs. Alas, poor bird! Until that day I was not aware that gregarious birds, on emitting cries of alarm, after having been scared from their nest, could induce other incubating individuals to leave their eggs also, and join in attempting to save the colony. But so it was with the Avosets, and the other two sitters immediately rose on wing and flew directly at me, while the one with the four younglings betook herself to the water, and waded quickly off, followed by her brood, which paddled along swimming, to my astonishment, as well as ducklings of the same size.

How far such cries as those of the Avoset may be heard by birds of the same species I cannot tell; but this I know, that the individuals which had gone toward the Wabash reappeared in a few minutes after I had disturbed the first bird, and hovered over me. But now, having, as I thought, obtained all desirable knowledge of these birds, I shot down five of them, among which I unfortunately found three females.

The nests were placed among the tallest grasses, and were entirely composed of the same materials, but dried, and apparently of a former year's growth. There was not a twig of any kind about them. The inner nest was about five inches in diameter, and lined with fine prairie grass, different from that found on the islets of the pond, and about two inches in depth, over a bed having a thickness of an inch and a half. The islets did not seem to be liable to inundation, and none of the nests exhibited any appearance of having been increased in elevation since the commencement of incubation, as was the case with those described by WILSON. Like those of most waders, the eggs were four in number, and placed with the small ends together. They measured two inches in length, one inch and three-eighths in their greatest breadth, and were, exactly as WILSON tells us, "of a dull olive colour, marked with large irregular blotches of black, and with others of a fainter tint." To this I have to add, that they are pear-shaped and smooth. As to the time of hatching, I know nothing.

Having made my notes, and picked up the dead birds, I carefully waded through the rushes three times around the whole pond, but, being without my dog, failed in discovering the young brood or their mother. I visited the place twice the following day, again waded round the pond, and searched all the islets, but without success: not a single Avoset was to be seen; and I am persuaded that the mother of the four younglings had removed them elsewhere.

Since that time my opportunities of meeting with the American Avoset have been few. On the 7th of November 1819, while searching for rare birds a few miles from New Orleans, I shot one which I found by itself on the margin of Bayou St John. It was a young male, of which I merely took the measurements and description. It was very thin, and had probably been unable to proceed farther south. Its stomach contained only two small fresh-water snails and a bit of stone. In May 1829, I saw three of these birds at Great Egg Harbour, but found no nests, although those of the Long-legged Avoset of WILSON were not uncommon. My friend JOHN BACHMAN considers them as rare in South Carolina, where, however, he has occasionally seen some on the gravelly shores of the sea islands.

On the 16th of April 1837, my good friend Captain NAPOLEON COSTE, of the United States Revenue Cutter the Campbell, on board of which I then was, shot three individuals of this species on an immense sand-bar, intersected by pools, about twelve miles from Derniere Island on the Gulf of Mexico, and brought them to me in perfect order. They were larger, and perhaps handsomer, than any that I have seen; and had been killed out of a flock of five while feeding. He saw several large flocks on the same grounds, and assured me that the only note they emitted was a single whistle. He also observed their manner of feeding, which he represented as similar to that described above.

My friend THOMAS NUTTALL says in a note, that he "found this species breeding on the islands of shallow ponds throughout the Rocky Mountains about midsummer. They exhibited great fear and clamour at the approach of the party, but no nests were found, they being then under march." Dr RICHARDSON states, that it is abundant on the Saskatchewan Plains, where it frequents shallow lakes, and feeds on insects and small fresh water crustacea.

The flight of the American Avoset resembles that of the *Himantopus nigricollis.* Both these birds pass through the air as if bent on removing to a great distance, much in the manner of the Tell-tale Godwit, or with an easy, rather swift and continued flight, the legs and neck fully extended. When plunging towards an intruder, it at times comes downwards, and passes by you, with the speed of an arrow from a bow, but usually in moving off again, it suffers its legs to hang considerably. I have never seen one of them exhibit the bending and tremulous motions of the legs spoken of by writers, even when raised suddenly from the nest; and I think that I am equally safe in saying, that the bill has never been drawn from a fresh specimen, or before it has undergone a curvature, which it does not shew when the bird is alive. The notes of this bird resemble the syllable *click*, sometimes repeated in a very hurried manner, especially under alarm.

Great American Egret

Ardea Egretta, GMEL.

(PLATE 52)

IN the third volume of this work, I have already intimated that the truly elegant Heron which now comes to be described, is a constant resident in the Floridas, that it migrates eastward sometimes as far as the State of Massachusetts, and up the Mississippi to the city of Natchez, and, lastly, that it is never seen far inland, by which I mean that its rambles into the interior seldom extend to more than fifty miles from the sea-shore, unless along the course of our great rivers. I have now to add that on my way to the Texas, in the spring of 1837, I found these birds in several places along the coast of the Gulf of Mexico, and on several of the islands scattered around that named Galveston, where, as well as in the Floridas, I was told that they spend the winter.

The Great American Egret breeds along the shores of the Gulf of Mexico, and our Atlantic States, from Galveston Island in the Texas to the borders of the State of New York, beyond which, although stragglers have been seen, none, in so far as I can ascertain, have been known to breed. In all low districts that are marshy and covered with large trees, on the margins of ponds or lakes, the sides of bayous, or gloomy

swamps covered with water, are the places to which it generally resorts during the period of reproduction; although I
have in a few instances met with their nests on low trees, and
on sandy islands at a short distance from the main land. As
early as December I have observed vast numbers congregated,
as if for the purpose of making choice of partners, when the
addresses of the males were paid in a very curious and to me
interesting manner. Near the plantation of JOHN BULOW,
Esq. in East Florida, I had the pleasure of witnessing this sort
of tournament or dress-ball from a place of concealment not
more than a hundred yards distant. The males, in strutting
round the females, swelled their throats, as Cormorants do at
times, emitted gurgling sounds, and raising their long plumes
almost erect, paced majestically before the fair ones of their
choice. Although these snowy beaux were a good deal irri-
tated by jealousy, and conflicts now and then took place, the
whole time I remained, much less fighting was exhibited than
I had expected from what I had already seen in the case of the
Great Blue Heron, *Ardea Herodias.* These meetings took
place about ten o'clock in the morning, or after they had all
enjoyed a good breakfast, and continued until nearly three in
the afternoon, when, separating into flocks of eight or ten individuals, they flew off to search for food. These manœuvres
were continued nearly a week, and I could with ease, from a
considerable distance mark the spot, which was a clear sand-
bar, by the descent of the separate small flocks previous to
their alighting there.

The flight of this species is in strength intermediate between that of *Ardea Herodias* and *A. rufescens,* and is well sustained. On foot its movements are as graceful as those of the
Louisiana Heron, its steps measured, its long neck gracefully
retracted and curved, and its silky train reminded one of the
flowing robes of the noble ladies of Europe. The train of this
Egret, like that of other species, makes its appearance a few
weeks previous to the love season, continues to grow and increase in beauty, until incubation has commenced, after which
period it deteriorates, and at length disappears about the time
when the young birds leave the nest, when, were it not for
the difference in size, it would be difficult to distinguish them
from their parents. Should you however closely examine the

upper plumage of an old bird of either sex, for both possess the train, you will discover that its feathers still exist, although shortened and deprived of most of their filaments. Similar feathers are seen in all other Herons that have a largely developed train in the breeding season. Even the few plumes hanging from the hind part of the *Ardea Herodias, A. Nycticorax,* and *A. violacea,* are subject to the same rule; and it is curious to see these ornaments becoming more or less apparent, according to the latitude in which these birds breed, their growth being completed in the southern part of Florida two months sooner than in our Middle Districts.

The American Egrets leave the Floridas almost simultaneously about the 1st of March, and soon afterwards reach Georgia and South Carolina, but rarely the State of New Jersey, before the middle of May. In these parts the young are able to fly by the 1st of August. On the Mule Keys off the coast of Florida, I have found the young well grown by the 8th of May; but in South Carolina they are rarely hatched until toward the end of that month or the beginning of June. In these more southern parts two broods are often raised in a season, but in the Jerseys there is, I believe, never more than one. While travelling, early in spring, between Savannah in Georgia and Charleston in South Carolina, I saw many of these Egrets on the large rice plantations, and felt some surprise at finding them much wilder at that period of their migrations than after they have settled in some locality for the purpose of breeding. I have supposed this to be caused by the change of their *thoughts* on such occasions, and am of opinion that birds of all kinds become more careless of themselves. As the strength of their attachment toward their mates or progeny increases through the process of time, as is the case with the better part of our own species, lovers and parents performing acts of heroism, which individuals having no such attachment to each other would never dare to contemplate. In these birds the impulse of affection is so great, that when they have young they allow themselves to be approached, so as often to fall victims to the rapacity of man, who, boasting of reason and benevolence, ought at such a time to respect their devotion.

The American Egrets are much attached to their roosting

places, to which they remove from their feeding grounds regularly about an hour before the last glimpse of day; and I cannot help expressing my disbelief in the vulgar notion of birds of this family usually feeding by night, as I have never observed them so doing even in countries where they were most abundant. Before sunset the Egrets and other Herons (excepting perhaps the Bitterns and Night Herons) leave their feeding grounds in small flocks, often composed of only a single family, and proceed on wing in the most direct course, at a moderate height, to some secure retreat more or less distant, according to the danger they may have to guard against. Flock after flock may be seen repairing from all quarters to these places of repose, which one may readily discover by observing their course.

Approach and watch them. Some hundreds have reached the well-known rendezvous. After a few gratulations you see them lower their bodies on the stems of the trees or bushes on which they have alighted, fold their necks, place their heads beneath the scapular feathers, and adjust themselves for repose. Daylight returns, and they are all in motion. The arrangement of their attire is not more neglected by them than by the most fashionable fops, but they spend less time at the toilet. Their rough notes are uttered more loudly than in the evening, and after a very short lapse of time they spread their snowy pinions, and move in different directions, to search for fiddlers, fish, insects of all sorts, small quadrupeds or birds, snails, and reptiles, all of which form the food of this species.

The nest of the Great White Egret, whether placed in a cypress one hundred and thirty feet high, or on a mangrove not six feet above the water, whether in one of those dismal swamps swarming with loathsome reptiles, or by the margin of the clear blue waters that bathe the Keys of Florida, is large, flat, and composed of sticks, often so loosely put together as to make you wonder how it can hold, besides itself, the three young ones which this species and all the larger Herons have at a brood. In a few instances only have I found it compactly built, it being the first nest formed by its owners. It almost always overhangs the water, and is resorted to and repaired year after year by the same pair. The eggs, which are never more than three, measure two inches and a quarter in length, an inch and five-eighths in breadth, and when newly laid are smooth, and of a pale blue colour, but afterwards become roughish and faded. When the nest is placed on a tall tree, the young remain in it, or on its borders, until they are able to fly; but when on a low tree or bush, they leave it much sooner, being capable of moving along the branches without fear of being injured by falling, and knowing that should they slip into the water they can easily extricate themselves by striking with their legs until they reach either the shore or the nearest bush, by clinging to the stem, of which they soon ascend to the top.

This Egret is shy and vigilant at all times, seldom allowing a person to come near unless during the breeding season. If in a rice-field of some extent, and at some distance from its margins, where cover can be obtained, you need not attempt to approach it; but if you are intent on procuring it, make for some tree, and desire your friend to start the bird. If you are well concealed, you may almost depend on obtaining one in a few minutes, for the Egrets will perhaps alight within twenty yards or less of you. Once, when I was very desirous of making a new drawing of this bird, my friend JOHN BACHMAN followed this method, and between us we carried home several superb specimens.

The long plumes of this bird being in request for ornamental purposes, they are shot in great numbers while sitting on their eggs, or soon after the appearance of the young. I know a person who, on offering a double-barrelled gun to a gentlemen near Charleston, for one hundred White Herons fresh killed, received that number and more the next day.

The Great Egret breeds in company with the Anhinga, the Great Blue Heron, and other birds of this family. The Turkey Buzzards and the Crows commit dreadful havoc among its young, as well as those of the other species. My friend JOHN BACHMAN gives me the following account of his visit to one of its breeding places, at the "Round O," a plantation about forty miles from Charleston: "Our company was composed of BENJAMIN LOGAN, S. LEE, and Dr MARTIN. We were desirous of obtaining some of the Herons as specimens for stuffing, and the ladies were anxious to procure many of their primary feathers for the purpose of making fans. The trees were high, from a hundred to a hundred and thirty feet, and our shot was not of the right size; but we commenced firing at the birds, and soon discovered that we had a prospect of success. Each man took his tree, and loaded and fired as fast as he could. Many of the birds lodged on the highest branches of the cypresses, others fell into the nest, and, in most cases, when shot from a limb, where they had been sitting, they clung to it for some time before they would let go. One thing surprised me: it was the length of time it took for a bird to fall from the place where it was shot, and it fell with a loud noise into the water. Many wounded birds fell some distance off, and we could not conveniently follow them on account of the heavy wading through the place. We brought home with us forty-six of the large White Herons, and three of the great Blues. Many more might have been killed, but we became tired of shooting them."

Trumpeter Swan

Cygnus Buccinator, RICHARDSON

(PLATES 54, 55)

THE HISTORY of the American Swans has been but very slightly traced. Few records of the habits of these majestic, elegant, and useful birds exist, on which much reliance can be placed; their geographical range still remains an unsolved problem; one species has been mistaken for another, and this by ornithologists who are said to be of the first order. The *Cygnus Bewickii* of Great Britain has been given as a North American Swan in place of *Cygnus Americanus* (well described by Dr SHARPLESS of Philadelphia) in the Fauna Boreali-Americana; and the latter bird has been taken for the Whistling Swan, *C. musicus* of BECHSTEIN, by the Prince of MUSIGNANO, who says in his Synopsis, p. 379, No. 321, that it is "very numerous in winter in Chesapeake Bay." It is possible that we may have more than two species of Swan within the limits of North America, but I am at present acquainted with only that which forms the subject of this article, and the *Cygnus Americanus* of SHARPLESS.

In a note contained in the Journals of LEWIS and CLARK, written in the course of the expedition of these daring travellers across the Rocky Mountains, it is stated that "the Swans are of two kinds, the large and small. The large Swan is the same with the one common in the Atlantic States. The small differs from the large only in size and note; it is about one fourth less, and its note is entirely different. These birds were first found below the great narrows of the Columbia, near the Chilluckittequaw nation. They are very abundant in this neighbourhood, and remained with the party all winter, and in number they exceed those of the larger species in the proportion of five to one." These observations are partly correct and partly erroneous. In fact, the smaller species of the two, which is the *C. Americanus* of SHARPLESS, is the only one abundant in the middle districts of our Atlantic coast, while the larger Swan, the subject of this article, is rarely if ever seen to the eastward of the mouths of the Mississippi. A perfect specimen of the small Swan mentioned by LEWIS and CLARK has been transmitted to me from the Columbia River by Dr TOWNSEND, and I find it to correspond in every respect with the *C. Americanus* of SHARPLESS. Dr TOWNSEND corroborates the observations of the two eminent travellers by stating, that the latter species is much more numerous than the large *C. Buccinator*.

The Trumpeter Swans make their appearance on the lower portions of the waters of the Ohio about the end of October. They throw themselves at once into the larger ponds or lakes at no great distance from the river, giving a marked preference to those which are closely surrounded by dense and tall cane-brakes, and there remain until the water is closed by ice, when they are forced to proceed southward. During mild winters I have seen Swans of this species in the ponds about Henderson until the beginning of March, but only a few individuals, which may have staid there to recover from their wounds. When the cold became intense, most of those which visited the Ohio would remove to the Mississippi, and proceed down that stream as the severity of the weather increased, or return if it diminished; for it has appeared to me,

that neither very intense cold nor great heat suit them so well
as a medium temperature. I have traced the winter migrations
of this species as far southward as the Texas, where it is abundant at times, and where I saw a pair of young ones in captivity, and quite domesticated, that had been procured in the
winter of 1836. They were about two years old, and pure
white, although of much smaller size than even the younger
one represented in the plate before you, having perhaps been
stinted in food, or having suffered from their wounds, as both
had been shot. The sound of their well-known notes reminded me of the days of my youth, when I was half-yearly in
the company of birds of this species.

At New Orleans, where I made the drawing of the young
bird here given, the Trumpeters are frequently exposed for
sale in the markets, being procured on the ponds of the interior, and on the great lakes leading to the waters of the Gulf
of Mexico. This species is unknown to my friend, the Rev.
JOHN BACHMAN, who, during a residence of twenty years in
South Carolina, never saw or heard of one there; whereas in
hard winters the *Cygnus Americanus* is not uncommon, although it does not often proceed farther southward than that
State. The waters of the Arkansas and its tributaries are annually supplied with Trumpeter Swans, and the largest individual
which I have examined was shot on a lake near the junction
of that river with the Mississippi. It measured nearly ten feet
in alar extent, and weighed above thirty-eight pounds. The
quills, which I used in drawing the feet and claws of many
small birds, were so hard, and yet so elastic, that the best
steel-pen of the present day might have blushed, if it could, to
be compared with them.

Whilst encamped in the Tawapatee Bottom, when on a fur-
trading voyage, our keel-boat was hauled close under the
eastern shore of the Mississippi, and our valuables, for I then
had a partner in trade, were all disembarked. The party consisted of twelve or fourteen French Canadians, all of whom
were pretty good hunters; and as game was in those days extremely abundant, the supply of Deer, Bear, Racoons, and
Opossums, far exceeded our demands. Wild Turkeys, Grous,
and Pigeons, might have been seen hanging all around; and
the ice-bound lakes afforded an ample supply of excellent fish,

which was procured by striking a strong blow with an axe on the ice immediately above the confined animal, and afterwards extricating it by cutting a hole with the same instrument. The great stream was itself so firmly frozen that we were daily in the habit of crossing it from shore to shore. No sooner did the gloom of night become discernible through the grey twilight, than the loud-sounding notes of hundreds of Trumpeters would burst on the ear; and as I gazed over the ice-bound river, flocks after flocks would be seen coming from afar and in various directions, and alighting about the middle of the stream opposite to our encampment. After pluming themselves awhile they would quietly drop their bodies on the ice, and through the dim light I yet could observe the graceful curve of their necks, as they gently turned them backwards, to allow their heads to repose upon the softest and warmest of pillows. Just a dot of black as it were could be observed on the snowy mass, and that dot was about half an inch of the base of the upper mandible, thus exposed, as I think, to enable the bird to breathe with ease. Not a single individual could I ever observe among them to act as a sentinel, and I have since doubted whether their acute sense of hearing was not sufficient to enable them to detect the approach of their enemies. The day quite closed by darkness, no more could be seen until the next dawn; but as often as the howlings of the numerous wolves that prowled through the surrounding woods were heard, the clanging cries of the Swans would fill the air. If the morning proved fair, the whole flocks would rise on their feet, trim their plumage, and as they started with wings extended, as if, racing in rivalry, the pattering of their feet would come on the ear like the noise of great muffled drums, accompanied by the loud and clear sounds of their voice. On running fifty yards or so to windward, they would all be on wing. If the weather was thick, drizzly, and cold, or if there were indications of a fall of snow, they would remain on the ice, walking, standing, or lying down, until symptoms of better weather became apparent, when they would all start off. One morning of this latter kind, our men formed a plot against the Swans, and having separated into two parties, one above, the other below them on the ice, they walked slowly, on a signal being given from the camp, toward the unsuspecting birds. Until the boatmen had arrived within a hundred and fifty yards of them, the Swans remained as they were, having become, as it would appear, acquainted with us, in consequence of our frequently crossing the ice; but then they all rose on their feet, stretched their necks, shook their heads, and manifested strong symptoms of apprehension. The gunners meanwhile advanced, and one of the guns going off by accident, the Swans were thrown into confusion, and scampering off in various directions took to wing, some flying up, some down the stream, others making directly toward the shores. The muskets now blazed, and about a dozen were felled, some crippled, others quite dead. That evening they alighted about a mile above the camp, and we never went after them again. I have been at the killing of several of these Swans, and I can assure you that unless you have a good gun well loaded with large buck-shot, you may shoot at them without much effect, for they are strong and tough birds.

To form a perfect conception of the beauty and elegance of these Swans, you must observe them when they are not aware of your proximity, and as they glide over the waters of some secluded inland pond. On such occasions, the neck, which at other times is held stiffly upright, moves in graceful curves, now bent forward, now inclined backwards over the body. Now with an extended scooping movement the head becomes immersed for a moment, and with a sudden effort a flood of water is thrown over the back and wings, when it is seen rolling off in sparkling globules, like so many large pearls. The bird then shakes its wings, beats the water, and as if giddy with delight shoots away, gliding over and beneath the surface of the liquid element with surprising agility and grace. Imagine, Reader, that a flock of fifty Swans are thus sporting before you, as they have more than once been in my sight, and you will feel, as I have felt, more happy and void of care than I can describe.

When swimming unmolested the Swan shews the body buoyed up; but when apprehensive of danger, it sinks considerably lower. If resting and basking in the sunshine, it draws one foot expanded curiously towards the back, and in that posture remains often for half an hour at a time. When making off swiftly, the tarsal joint, or knee as it is called, is seen about an inch above the water, which now in wavelets passes over the lower part of the neck and along the sides of the body, as it undulates on the planks of a vessel gliding with a gentle breeze. Unless during the courting season, or while passing by its mate, I never saw a swan with the wings raised and expanded, as it is alleged they do, to profit by the breeze that may blow to assist their progress; and yet I have pursued some in canoes to a considerable distance, and that without overtaking them, or even obliging them to take to wing. You, Reader, as well as all the world, have seen Swans labouring away on foot, and therefore I will not trouble you with a description of their mode of walking, especially as it is not much to be admired.

The flight of the Trumpeter Swan is firm, at times greatly elevated and sustained. It passes through the air by regular beats, in the same manner as Geese, the neck stretched to its full length, as are the feet, which project beyond the tail. When passing low, I have frequently thought that I heard a rustling sound from the motion of the feathers of their wings. If bound to a distant place, they form themselves in angular lines, and probably the leader of the flock is one of the oldest of the males; but of this I am not at all sure, as I have seen at the head of a line a grey bird, which must have been a young one of that year.

This Swan feeds principally by partially immersing the body and extending the neck under water, in the manner of fresh-water Ducks and some species of Geese, when the feet are often seen working in the air, as if to aid in preserving the balance. Often however it resorts to the land, and then picks at the herbage, not sidewise, as Geese do, but more in the manner of Ducks and poultry. Its food consists of roots of different vegetables, leaves, seeds, various aquatic insects, land snails, small reptiles and quadrupeds. The flesh of a cygnet is pretty good eating, but that of an old bird is dry and tough.

I kept a male alive upwards of two years, while I was residing at Henderson in Kentucky. It had been slightly wounded in the tip of the wing, and was caught after a long pursuit in a pond from which it could not escape. Its size, weight, and strength rendered the task of carrying it nearly two miles by no means easy; but as I knew that it would please my wife and my then very young children, I persevered. Cutting off the tip of the wounded wing, I turned it loose in the garden. Although at first extremely shy, it gradually became accustomed to the servants, who fed it abundantly, and at length proved so gentle as to come to my wife's call, to receive bread from her hand. "Trumpeter," as we named our bird, in accordance with the general practice of those who were in the habit of shooting this species, now assumed a character which until then had been unexpected, and laying aside his timidity became so bold at times as to give chase to my favourite Wild Turkey Cock, my dogs, children, and servants. Whenever the gates of our yard happened to be opened, he would at once make for the Ohio, and it was not without difficulty that he was driven home again. On one occasion, he was absent a whole night, and I thought he had fairly left us; but intimation came of his having travelled to a pond not far distant. Accompanied by my miller and six or seven of my servants, I betook myself to the pond, and there saw our Swan swimming buoyantly about as if in defiance of us all. It was not without a great deal of trouble that we at length succeeded in driving it ashore. Pet birds, good Reader, no matter of what species they are, seldom pass their lives in accordance with the wishes of their possessors; in the course of a dark and rainy night, one of the servants having left the gate open, Trumpeter made his escape, and was never again heard of.

With the manners of this species during the breeding season, its mode of constructing its nest, the number of its eggs, and the appearance of its young, I am utterly unacquainted. The young bird represented in the plate was shot near New Orleans, on the 16th of December 1822. A figure of the adult male you will find in Plate 55; and should I ever have opportunities of studying the habits of this noble bird, believe me I shall have much pleasure in laying before you the results. Dr RICHARDSON informs us that it "is the most common Swan in the interior of the Fur Countries. It breeds as far south as lat. 61°, but principally within the arctic circle, and in its migrations generally precedes the Geese a few days."

As the adult bird will be subsequently described, I judge it unnecessary at present to enter into a full detail of the external form and characters of the species, and will therefore confine myself to the colours and proportions of the individual represented.

American Flamingo

Phœnicopterus ruber, LINN.

(PLATE 53)

ON THE 7th of May 1832, while sailing from Indian Key, one of the numerous islets that skirt the south-eastern coast of the Peninsula of Florida, I for the first time saw a flock of Flamingoes. It was on the afternoon of one of those sultry days which, in that portion of the country, exhibit towards evening the most glorious effulgence that can be conceived. The sun, now far advanced toward the horizon, still shone with full splendour, the ocean around glittered in its quiet beauty, and the light fleecy clouds that here and there spotted the heavens, seemed flakes of snow margined with gold. Our bark was propelled almost as if by magic, for scarcely was a ripple raised by her bows as we moved in silence. Far away to seaward we spied a flock of Flamingoes advancing in "Indian line," with well-spread wings, outstretched necks, and long legs directed backwards. Ah! Reader, could you but know the emotions that then agitated my breast! I thought I had now reached the height of all my expectations, for my voyage to the Floridas was undertaken in a great measure for the purpose of studying these lovely birds in their own beautiful islands. I followed them with my eyes, watching as it were every beat of their wings; and as they were rapidly advancing towards us, Captain DAY, who was aware of my anxiety to procure some, had every man stowed away out of sight and our gunners in readiness. The pilot, Mr EGAN, proposed to offer the first taste of his "groceries" to the leader of the band. As I have more than once told you, he was a first-rate shot, and had already killed many Flamingoes. The birds were now, as I thought, within a hundred and fifty yards; when suddenly, to our extreme disappointment, their chief veered away, and was of course followed by the rest. Mr

EGAN, however, assured us that they would fly round the Key, and alight not far from us, in less than ten minutes, which in fact they did, although to me these minutes seemed almost hours. "Now they come," said the pilot, "keep low." This we did; but, alas! the Flamingoes were all, as I suppose, very old and experienced birds, with the exception of one, for on turning round the lower end of the Key, they spied our boat again, sailed away without flapping their wings, and alighted about four hundred yards from us, and upwards of one hundred from the shore, on a "soap flat" of vast extent, where neither boat nor man could approach them. I however watched their motions until dusk, when we reluctantly left the spot and advanced toward Indian Key. Mr LOGAN then told me that these birds habitually returned to their feeding-grounds toward evening, that they fed during the greater part of the night, and were much more nocturnal in their habits than any of the Heron tribe.

When I reached Key West, my first inquiries, addressed to Dr BENJAMIN STROBEL, had reference to the Flamingoes, and I felt gratified by learning that he had killed a good number of them, and that he would assist us in procuring some. As on that Key they are fond of resorting to the shallow ponds formerly kept there as reservoirs of water, for the purpose of making salt, we visited them at different times, but always without success; and, although I saw a great number of them in the course of my stay in that country, I cannot even at this moment boast of having had the satisfaction of shooting a single individual.

A very few of these birds have been known to proceed eastward of the Floridas beyond Charleston in South Carolina, and some have been procured there within eight or ten years back. None have ever been observed about the mouths of the Mississippi; and to my great surprise I did not meet with any in the course of my voyage to the Texas, where, indeed, I was assured they had never been seen, at least as far as Galveston Island. The western coast of Florida, and some portions of that of Alabama, in the neighbourhood of Pensacola, are the parts to which they mostly resort; but they are said to be there always extremely shy, and can be procured only by way-laying them in the vicinity of their feeding-grounds toward evening, when, on one occasion, Dr STROBEL shot several in the course of a few hours. Dr LEITNER also procured some in the course of his botanical excursions along the western coast of the Floridas, where he was at last murdered by some party of Seminole Indians, at the time of our last disastrous war with those children of the desert.

Flamingoes, as I am informed, are abundant on the Island of Cuba, more especially on the southern side of some of its shores, and where many islets at some distance from the mainland afford them ample protection. In their flight they resemble Ibises, and they usually move in lines, with the neck and legs fully extended, alternately flapping their wings for twenty or thirty yards and sailing over a like space. Before alighting they generally sail round the place for several minutes, when their glowing tints become most conspicuous. They very rarely alight on the shore itself, unless, as I am told, during the breeding season, but usually in the water, and on shallow banks, whether of mud or of sand, from which however they often wade to the shores. Their walk is stately and slow, and their cautiousness extreme, so that it is very difficult to approach them, as their great height enables them to see and watch the movements of their various enemies at a distance. When travelling over the water, they rarely fly at a greater height than eight or ten feet; but when passing over the land, no matter how short the distance may be, they, as well as Ibises and Herons, advance at a considerable elevation. I well remember that on one occasion, when near Key West, I saw one of them flying directly towards a small hummock of mangroves, to which I was near, and towards which I made, in full expectation of having a fine shot. When the bird came within a hundred and twenty yards, it rose obliquely, and when directly over my head, was almost as far off. I fired, but with no other effect than that of altering its course, and inducing it to rise still higher. It continued to fly at this elevation until nearly half a mile off, when it sailed downwards, and resumed its wonted low flight.

Although my friends Dr JOHN BACHMAN, Dr WILSON, and WILLIAM KUNHARDT, Esq. of Charleston, have been at considerable trouble in endeavouring to procure accounts of the nidification of these birds and their habits during the breeding season, and although they, as well as myself, have made many inquiries by letter respecting them, of persons residing in Cuba, all that has been transmitted to me has proved of little interest. I am not however the less obliged by the kind intentions of these individuals, one of whom, A. MALLORY, Esq. thus writes to Captain CROFT.

"Capt. CROFT,   *Matanzas, April 20, 1837.*

DEAR SIR,—"I have made inquiry of several of the fishermen, and salt-rakers, who frequent the keys to the windward of this place, in regard to the habits of the Flamingo, and have obtained the following information, which will be found, I believe, pretty correct: *1st*, They build upon nearly all the Keys to the windward, the nearest of which is called Collocino Lignas. *2dly*, It builds upon the ground. *3dly*, The nest is an irregular mass of earth dug in the salt ponds, and entirely surrounded by water. It is scooped up from the immediate vicinity to the height of two or three feet, and is of course hollow at the top. There is no lining, nor any thing but the bare earth. *4thly*, The number of the eggs is almost always two. When there is one, there has probably been some accident. The time of incubation is not known. The egg is white, and near the size of the Goose's egg. On scraping the shell, it has a bluish tinge. *5thly*, The colour of the young is nearly white, and it does not attain the full scarlet colour until two years old. *6thly*, When the young first leave the nest, they take to the water, and do not walk for about a fortnight, as their feet are almost as tender as jelly. I do not think it easy to procure an entire nest; but I am promised some of the eggs, this being the time to procure them. Very truly your obedient servant,

A. MALLORY."

Another communication is as follows:—"The Flamingo is a kind of bird that lives in lagoons having a communication with the sea. This bird makes its nest on the shore of the same lagoon, with the mud which it heaps up to beyond the level of the water. Its eggs are about the size of those of a goose; it only lays two or three at a time, which are hatched about the end of May. The young when they break the shell have no feathers, only a kind of cottony down which covers them. They immediately betake themselves to the water to harden their feet. They take from two to three months before their feathers are long enough to enable them to fly. The first year they are rose-coloured, and in the second they obtain their natural colour, being all scarlet; half their bill is black, and the points of the wings are all black; the eyes entirely blue. Its flesh is savoury, and its tongue is pure fat. It is easily tamed, and feeds on rice, maize-meal, &c. Its body is about a yard high, and the neck about half as much. The breadth of the nest, with little difference, is that of the crown of a hat. The way in which the female covers the eggs is by standing in the water on one foot and supporting its body on the nest. This bird always rests in a lagoon, supporting itself on one leg alternately; and it is to be observed that it always stands with its front to the wind."

An egg, presented to me by Dr BACHMAN, and of which two were found in the nest, measures three inches and three-eighths in length, two inches and one-eighth in breadth, and is thus of an elongated form. The shell is thick, rather rough or granulated, and pure white externally, but of a bluish tint when the surface is scraped off.

The following description is taken from specimens sent to me by JEAN CHARTRAND, Esq. from Cuba, and preserved in spirits, together with several dried skins.

The Ohio

To RENDER more pleasant the task which you have imposed upon yourself, of following an author through the mazes of descriptive ornithology, permit me, kind reader, to relieve the tedium which may be apt now and then to come upon you, by presenting you with occasional descriptions of the scenery and manners of the land which has furnished the objects that engage your attention. The natural features of that land are not less remarkable than the moral character of her inhabitants; and I cannot find a better subject with which to begin, than one of those magnificent rivers that roll the collected waters of her extensive territories to the ocean.

When my wife, my eldest son (then an infant), and myself were returning from Pennsylvania to Kentucky, we found it expedient, the waters being unusually low, to provide ourselves with a *skiff*, to enable us to proceed to our abode at Henderson. I purchased a large, commodious, and light boat of that denomination. We procured a mattress, and our friends furnished us with ready prepared viands. We had two stout Negro rowers, and in this trim we left the village of Shippingport, in expectation of reaching the place of our destination in a very few days.

It was in the month of October. The autumnal tints already decorated the shores of that queen of rivers, the Ohio. Every tree was hung with long and flowing festoons of different species of vines, many loaded with clustered fruits of varied brilliancy, their rich bronzed carmine mingling beautifully with the yellow foliage, which now predominated over the yet green leaves, reflecting more lively tints from the clear stream than ever landscape painter portrayed or poet imagined.

The days were yet warm. The sun had assumed the rich and glowing hue which at that season produces the singular phenomenon called there the "Indian Summer." The moon had rather passed the meridian of her grandeur. We glided down the river, meeting no other ripple of the water than that formed by the propulsion of our boat. Leisurely we moved along, gazing all day on the grandeur and beauty of the wild scenery around us.

Now and then a large catfish rose to the surface of the water, in pursuit of a shoal of fry, which, starting simultaneously from the liquid element, like so many silvery arrows, produced a shower of light, while the pursuer with open jaws seized the stragglers, and, with a splash of his tail, disappeared from our view. Other fishes we heard uttering beneath our bark a rumbling noise, the strange sounds of which we discovered to proceed from the white perch, for on casting our net from the bow we caught several of that species, when the noise ceased for a time.

Nature, in her varied arrangements, seems to have felt a partiality towards this portion of our country. As the traveller ascends or descends the Ohio, he cannot help remarking that alternately, nearly the whole length of the river, the margin, on one side, is bounded by lofty hills and a rolling surface, while on the other, extensive plains of the richest alluvial land are seen as far as the eye can command the view. Islands of varied size and form rise here and there from the bosom of the water, and the winding course of the stream frequently brings you to places where the idea of being on a river of great length changes to that of floating on a lake of moderate extent. Some of these islands are of considerable size and value; while others, small and insignificant, seem as if intended for contrast, and as serving to enhance the general interest of the scenery. These little islands are frequently overflowed during great *freshets* or floods, and receive at their heads prodigious heaps of drifted timber. We foresaw with great concern the alterations that cultivation would soon produce along those delightful banks.

As night came, sinking in darkness the broader portions of the river, our minds became affected by strong emotions, and wandered far beyond the present moments. The tinkling of bells told us that the cattle which bore them were gently roving from valley to valley in search of food, or returning to their distant homes. The hooting of the Great Owl, or the muffled noise of its wings as it sailed smoothly over the stream,

were matters of interest to us; so was the sound of the boatman's horn, as it came winding more and more softly from
afar. When daylight returned, many songsters burst forth with
echoing notes, more and more mellow to the listening ear.
Here and there the lonely cabin of a squatter struck the eye,
giving note of commencing civilization. The crossing of the
stream by a deer foretold how soon the hills would be covered with snow.

Many sluggish flat-boats we overtook and passed: some
laden with produce from the different head-waters of the
small rivers that pour their tributary streams into the Ohio;
others, of less dimensions, crowded with emigrants from distant parts, in search of a new home. Purer pleasures I never
felt; nor have you, reader, I ween, unless indeed you have felt
the like, and in such company.

The margins of the shores and of the river were at this season amply supplied with game. A Wild Turkey, a Grouse, or a
Blue-winged Teal, could be procured in a few moments; and
we fared well, for, whenever we pleased, we landed, struck up
a fire, and provided as we were with the necessary utensils,
procured a good repast.

Several of these happy days passed, and we neared our
home, when, one evening, not far from Pigeon Creek (a small
stream which runs into the Ohio, from the State of Indiana),
a loud and strange noise was heard, so like the yells of Indian
warfare, that we pulled at our oars, and made for the opposite
side as fast and as quietly as possible. The sounds increased,
we imagined we heard cries of "murder;" and as we knew
that some depredations had lately been committed in the
country by dissatisfied parties of Aborigines, we felt for a
while extremely uncomfortable. Ere long, however, our
minds became more calmed, and we plainly discovered that
the singular uproar was produced by an enthusiastic set of
Methodists, who had wandered thus far out of the common
way, for the purpose of holding one of their annual camp
meetings, under the shade of a beech forest. Without meeting
with any other interruption, we reached Henderson, distant
from Shippingport by water about two hundred miles.

When I think of these times, and call back to my mind the
grandeur and beauty of those almost uninhabited shores;

when I picture to myself the dense and lofty summits of the forest, that everywhere spread along the hills, and overhung the margins of the stream, unmolested by the axe of the settler; when I know how dearly purchased the safe navigation of that river has been by the blood of many worthy Virginians; when I see that no longer any Aborigines are to be found there, and that the vast herds of elks, deer and buffaloes which once pastured on these hills and in these valleys, making for themselves great roads to the several salt-springs, have ceased to exist; when I reflect that all this grand portion of our Union, instead of being in a state of nature, is now more or less covered with villages, farms, and towns, where the din of hammers and machinery is constantly heard; that the woods are fast disappearing under the axe by day, and the fire by night; that hundreds of steam-boats are gliding to and fro, over the whole length of the majestic river, forcing commerce to take root and to prosper at every spot; when I see the surplus population of Europe coming to assist in the destruction of the forest, and transplanting civilization into its darkest recesses;—when I remember that these extraordinary changes have all taken place in the short period of twenty years, I pause, wonder, and, although I know all to be fact, can scarcely believe its reality.

Whether these changes are for the better or for the worse, I shall not pretend to say; but in whatever way my conclusions may incline, I feel with regret that there are on record no satisfactory accounts of the state of that portion of the country, from the time when our people first settled in it. This has not been because no one in America is able to accomplish such an undertaking. Our IRVINGS and our COOPERS have proved themselves fully competent for the task. It has more probably been because the changes have succeeded each other with such rapidity, as almost to rival the movements of their pen. However, it is not too late yet; and I sincerely hope that either or both of them will ere long furnish the generations to come with those delightful descriptions which they are so well qualified to give, of the original state of a country that has been so rapidly forced to change her form and attire under the influence of increasing population. Yes; I hope to read, ere I close my earthly career, accounts from those delightful writers of the progress of civilization in our western country. They will speak of the CLARKS, the CROGHANS, the BOONS, and many other men of great and daring enterprise. They will analyze, as it were, into each component part, the country as it once existed, and will render the picture, as it ought to be, immortal.

The Prairie

ON MY RETURN from the Upper Mississippi, I found myself obliged to cross one of the wide Prairies, which, in that portion of the United States, vary the appearance of the country. The weather was fine, all around me was as fresh and blooming as if it had just issued from the bosom of nature. My napsack, my gun, and my dog, were all I had for baggage and company. But, although well moccassined, I moved slowly along, attracted by the brilliancy of the flowers, and the gambols of the fawns around their dams, to all appearance as thoughtless of danger as I felt myself.

My march was of long duration; I saw the sun sinking beneath the horizon long before I could perceive any appearance of woodland, and nothing in the shape of man had I met with that day. The track which I followed was only an old Indian trace, and as darkness overshaded the prairie, I felt some desire to reach at least a copse, in which I might lie down to rest. The Night-hawks were skimming over and around me, attracted by the buzzing wings of the beetles which form their food, and the distant howling of wolves, gave me some hope that I should soon arrive at the skirts of some woodland.

I did so, and almost at the same instant a fire-light attracting my eye, I moved towards it, full of confidence that it proceeded from the camp of some wandering Indians. I was mistaken:—I discovered by its glare that it was from the hearth of a small log cabin, and that a tall figure passed and repassed between it and me, as if busily engaged in household arrangements.

I reached the spot, and presenting myself at the door, asked the tall figure, which proved to be a woman, if I might take shelter under her roof for the night. Her voice was gruff, and her attire negligently thrown about her. She answered in the affirmative. I walked in, took a wooden stool, and quietly seated myself by the fire. The next object that attracted my notice was a finely formed young Indian, resting his head between his hands, with his elbows on his knees. A long bow rested against the log wall near him, while a quantity of arrows and two or three raccoon skins lay at his feet. He moved not; he apparently breathed not. Accustomed to the habits of the Indians, and knowing that they pay little attention to the approach of civilized strangers (a circumstance which in some countries is considered as evincing the apathy of their character), I addressed him in French, a language not unfrequently partially known to the people in that neighbourhood. He raised his head, pointed to one of his eyes with his finger, and gave me a significant glance with the other. His face was covered with blood. The fact was, that an hour before this, as he was in the act of discharging an arrow at a raccoon in the top of a tree, the arrow had split upon the cord, and sprung back with such violence into his right eye as to destroy it for ever.

Feeling hungry, I inquired what sort of fare I might expect. Such a thing as a bed was not to be seen, but many large untanned bear and buffalo hides lay piled in a corner. I drew a fine time-piece from my breast, and told the woman that it was late, and that I was fatigued. She had espied my watch, the richness of which seemed to operate upon her feelings with electric quickness. She told me that there was plenty of venison and jerked buffalo meat, and that on removing the ashes I should find a cake. But my watch had struck her fancy, and her curiosity had to be gratified by an immediate sight of it. I took off the gold chain that secured it from around my neck, and presented it to her. She was all ecstacy, spoke of its beauty, asked me its value, and put the chain round her brawny neck, saying how happy the possession of such a watch should make her. Thoughtless, and, as I fancied myself, in so retired a spot, secure, I paid little attention to her talk or her movements. I helped my dog to a good supper of venison, and was not long in satisfying the demands of my own appetite.

The Indian rose from his seat, as if in extreme suffering. He passed and repassed me several times, and once pinched me on the side so violently, that the pain nearly brought forth an exclamation of anger. I looked at him. His eye met mine; but his look was so forbidding, that it struck a chill into the more nervous part of my system. He again seated himself, drew his butcher-knife from its greasy scabbard, examined its edge, as I would do that of a razor suspected dull, replaced it, and again taking his tomahawk from his back, filled the pipe of it with tobacco, and sent me expressive glances whenever our hostess chanced to have her back toward us.

Never until that moment had my senses been awakened to the danger which I now suspected to be about me. I returned glance for glance to my companion, and rested well assured that, whatever enemies I might have, he was not of their number.

I asked the woman for my watch, wound it up, and under pretence of wishing to see how the weather might probably be on the morrow, took up my gun, and walked out of the cabin. I slipped a ball into each barrel, scraped the edges of my flints, renewed the primings, and returning to the hut, gave a favourable account of my observations. I took a few bear-skins, made a pallet of them, and calling my faithful dog to my side, lay down, with my gun close to my body, and in a few minutes was, to all appearance, fast asleep.

A short time had elapsed, when some voices were heard, and from the corner of my eyes I saw two athletic youths making their entrance, bearing a dead stag on a pole. They disposed of their burden, and asking for whisky, helped themselves freely to it. Observing me and the wounded Indian, they asked who I was, and why the devil that rascal (meaning the Indian, who, they knew, understood not a word of English) was in the house. The mother—for so she proved to be, bade them speak less loudly, made mention of my watch, and took them to a corner, where a conversation took place, the purport of which it required little shrewdness in me to guess. I tapped my dog gently. He moved his tail, and with indescribable pleasure I saw his fine eyes alternately fixed on me and raised towards the trio in the corner. I felt that he perceived danger in my situation. The Indian exchanged a last glance with me.

The lads had eaten and drunk themselves into such condition, that I already looked upon them as *hors de combat*; and the frequent visits of the whisky bottle to the ugly mouth of their dam I hoped would soon reduce her to a like state. Judge of my astonishment, reader, when I saw this incarnate fiend take a large carving-knife, and go to the grindstone to whet its edge. I saw her pour the water on the turning machine, and watched her working away with the dangerous instrument, until the cold sweat covered every part of my body, in despite of my determination to defend myself to the last. Her task finished, she walked to her reeling sons, and said, "There, that'll soon settle him! Boys, kill you ——, and then for the watch."

I turned, cocked my gun-locks silently, touched my faithful companion, and lay ready to start up and shoot the first who might attempt my life. The moment was fast approaching, and that night might have been my last in this world, had not Providence made preparations for my rescue. All was ready. The infernal hag was advancing slowly, probably contemplating the best way of despatching me, whilst her sons should be engaged with the Indian. I was several times on the eve of rising, and shooting her on the spot:—but she was not to be punished thus. The door was suddenly opened, and there entered two stout travellers, each with a long rifle on his shoulder. I bounced up on my feet, and making them most heartily welcome, told them how well it was for me that they should have arrived at that moment. The tale was told in a minute. The drunken sons were secured, and the woman, in spite of her defence and vociferations, shared the same fate. The Indian fairly danced with joy, and gave us to understand that, as he could not sleep for pain, he would watch over us. You may suppose we slept much less than we talked. The two strangers gave me an account of their once having been themselves in a somewhat similar situation. Day came, fair and rosy, and with it the punishment of our captives.

They were now quite sobered. Their feet were unbound, but their arms were still securely tied. We marched them into the woods off the road, and having used them as Regulators were wont to use such delinquents, we set fire to the cabin, gave all the skins and implements to the young Indian warrior, and proceeded, well pleased, towards the settlements.

During upwards of twenty-five years, when my wanderings extended to all parts of our country, this was the only time at which my life was in danger from my fellow creatures. Indeed, so little risk do travellers run in the United States, that no one born there ever dreams of any to be encountered on the road; and I can only account for this occurrence by supposing that the inhabitants of the cabin were not Americans.

Will you believe, good-natured reader, that not many miles from the place where this adventure happened, and where fifteen years ago, no habitation belonging to civilized man was expected, and very few ever seen, large roads are now laid out, cultivation has converted the woods into fertile fields, taverns have been erected, and much of what we Americans call comfort is to be met with. So fast does improvement proceed in our abundant and free country.

The Original Painter

As I was lounging one fair and very warm morning on the *Levee* at New Orleans, I chanced to observe a gentleman, whose dress and other accompaniments greatly attracted my attention. I wheeled about, and followed him for a short space, when, judging by every thing about him that he was a true original, I accosted him.

But here, kind reader, let me give you some idea of his exterior. His head was covered by a straw hat, the brim of which might cope with those worn by the fair sex in 1830; his neck was exposed to the weather; the broad frill of a shirt, then fashionable, flapped about his breast, whilst an extraordinary collar, carefully arranged, fell over the top of his coat. The latter was of a light green colour, harmonizing well with a pair of flowing yellow nankeen trowsers, and a pink waistcoat, from the bosom of which, amidst a large bunch of the splendid flowers of the Magnolia, protruded part of a young alligator, which seemed more anxious to glide through the muddy waters of some retired swamp, than to spend its life swinging to and fro among folds of the finest lawn. The gentleman held in one hand a cage full of richly-plumed Nonpareils, whilst in the other he sported a silk umbrella, on which I could plainly read "*Stolen from I*," these words being painted in large white characters. He walked as if conscious of his own importance, that is, with a good deal of pomposity, singing "My love is but a lassie yet," and that with such thorough imitation of the Scotch emphasis, that had not his physiognomy brought to my mind a denial of his being from "within a mile of Edinburgh," I should have put him down in my journal for a true Scot. But no:—his tournure, nay, the very shape of his visage, pronounced him an American, from the farthest parts of our eastern Atlantic shores.

All this raised my curiosity to such a height, that I accosted him with "Pray, Sir, will you allow me to examine the birds you have in that cage?" The gentleman stopped, straightened his body, almost closed his left eye, then spread his legs apart, and, with a look altogether quizzical, answered, "Birds, Sir, did you say birds?" I nodded, and he continued, "What the devil do you know about birds, Sir?"

Reader, this answer brought a blush into my face. I felt as if caught in a trap, for I was struck by the force of the gentleman's question; which, by the way, was not much in discordance with a not unusual mode of granting an answer in the United States. Sure enough, thought I, little or perhaps nothing do I know of the nature of those beautiful denizens of the air; but the next moment vanity gave me a pinch, and urged me to conceive that I knew at least as much about birds as the august personage in my presence. "Sir," replied I, "I am a student of nature, and admire her works, from the noblest figure of man to the crawling reptile which you have in your bosom." "Ah!" replied he, "a-a-a naturalist, I presume!" "Just so, my good Sir," was my answer. The gentleman gave me the cage; and I observed from the corner of one of my eyes, that his were cunningly inspecting my face. I examined the pretty finches as long as I wished, returned the cage, made a low bow, and was about to proceed on my walk, when this odd sort of being asked me a question quite accordant with my desire of knowing more of him: "Will you come with me, Sir? If you will, you shall see some more curious birds, some of which are from different parts of the world. I keep quite a collection." I assured him I should feel gratified, and accompanied him to his lodgings.

We entered a long room, where, to my surprise, the first objects that attracted my attention were a large easel, with a full-length unfinished portrait upon it, a table with pallets and pencils, and a number of pictures of various sizes placed along the walls. Several cages containing birds were hung near the windows, and two young gentlemen were busily engaged in copying some finished portraits. I was delighted with all I saw. Each picture spoke for itself: the drawing, the colouring, the handling, the composition, and the keeping—all proved, that, whoever was the artist, he certainly was possessed of superior talents.

I did not know if my companion was the painter of the picture, but, as we say in America, I strongly guessed, and without waiting any longer, paid him the compliments which I thought he fairly deserved. "Aye," said he, "the world is pleased with my work, I wish I were so too, but time and industry are required as well as talents, to make a good artist. If you will examine the birds, I'll to my labour." So saying, the artist took up his pallet, and was searching for a rest-stick, but not finding the one with which he usually supported his hand, he drew the rod of a gun, and was about to sit, when he suddenly threw down his implements on the table, and, taking the gun, walked to me, and asked if "I had ever seen a percussion-lock." I had not, for that improvement was not yet in vogue. He not only explained the superiority of the lock in question, but undertook to prove that it was capable of acting effectually under water. The bell was rung, a flat basin of water was produced, the gun was charged with powder, and the lock fairly immersed. The report terrified the birds, causing them to beat against the gilded walls of their prisons. I remarked this to the artist. He replied, "The devil take the birds!—more of them in the market; why, Sir, I wish to shew you that I am a marksman as well as a painter." The easel was cleared of the large picture, rolled to the further end of the room, and placed against the wall. The gun was loaded in a trice, and the painter, counting ten steps from the easel, and taking aim at the supporting-pin on the left, fired. The bullet struck the head of the wooden pin fairly, and sent the splinters in all directions. "A bad shot, sir," said this extraordinary person, "the ball ought to have driven the pin farther into the hole, but it struck on one side; I'll try at the hole itself." After reloading his piece, the artist took aim again, and fired. The bullet this time had accomplished its object, for it had passed through the aperture, and hit the wall behind. "Mr ——, ring the bell and close the windows," said the painter, and turning to me, continued, "Sir, I will shew you the *ne plus ultra* of shooting." I was quite amazed, and yet so delighted, that I bowed my assent. A servant having appeared, a lighted candle was ordered. When it arrived, the artist placed it in a proper position, and retiring some yards, put out the light with a bullet, in the manner which I have elsewhere, in this volume, described. When light was restored, I observed the uneasiness of the poor little alligator, as it strove to effect its escape from the artist's waistcoat. I mentioned this to him. "True, true," he replied, "I had quite forgot the reptile, he shall have a dram;" and unbuttoning his vest, unclasped a small chain, and placed the alligator in the basin of water on the table.

Perfectly satisfied with the acquaintance which I had formed with this renowned artist, I wished to withdraw, fearing I might inconvenience him by my presence. But my time was not yet come. He bade me sit down, and paying no more attention to the young pupils in the room than if they had been a couple of cabbages, said, "If you have leisure and will stay awhile, I will shew you how I paint, and will relate to you an incident of my life, which will prove to you how sadly situated an artist is at times." In full expectation that more eccentricities were to be witnessed, or that the story would prove a valuable one, even to a naturalist, who is seldom a painter, I seated myself at his side, and observed with interest how adroitly he transferred the colours from his glistening pallet to the canvas before him. I was about to compliment him on his facility of touch, when he spoke as follows:

"This is, sir, or, I ought to say rather, this will be the portrait of one of our best navy officers, a man as brave as

Cæsar, and as good a sailor as ever walked the deck of a seventy-four. Do you paint, Sir?" I replied "Not yet." "Not yet! what do you mean?" "I mean what I say: I intend to paint as soon as I can draw better than I do at present." "Good," said he, "you are quite right, to draw is the first object; but, sir, if you should ever paint, and paint portraits, you will often meet with difficulties. For instance, the brave Commodore, of whom this is the portrait, although an excellent man at every thing else, is the worst sitter I ever saw; and the incident I promised to relate to you, as one curious enough, is connected with his bad mode of sitting. Sir, I forgot to ask if you would take any refreshment—a glass of wine, or ——." I assured him I needed nothing more than his agreeable company, and he proceeded. "Well, Sir, the first morning that the Commodore came to sit, he was in full uniform, and with his sword at his side. After a few moments of conversation, and when all was ready on my part, I bade him ascend this *throne*, place himself in the attitude which I contemplated, and assume an air becoming an officer of the navy. He mounted, placed himself as I had desired, but merely looked at me as if I had been a block of stone. I waited a few minutes, when, observing no change on his placid countenance, I ran the chalk over the canvas, to form a rough outline. This done, I looked up to his face again, and opened a conversation which I thought would warm his warlike nature; but in vain. I waited and waited, talked and talked, until my patience—Sir, you must know I am not overburdened with phlegm—being almost run out, I rose, threw my pallet and brushes on the floor, stamped, walking to and fro about the room, and vociferated such calumnies against our navy, that I startled the good Commodore. He still looked at me with a placid countenance, and, as he has told me since, thought I had lost my senses. But I observed him all the while, and, fully as determined to carry my point, as he would be to carry off an enemy's ship, I gave my oaths additional emphasis, addressed him as a representative of the navy, and, steering somewhat clear of personal insult, played off my batteries against the craft. The Commodore walked up to me, placed his hand on the hilt of his sword, and told me, in a resolute manner, that if I intended to insult the navy, he would instantly cut off my ears. His features exhibited all the spirit and animation of his noble nature, and as I had now succeeded in rousing the lion, I judged it time to retreat. So, changing my tone, I begged his pardon, and told him he now looked precisely as I wished to represent him. He laughed, and returning to his seat, assumed a bold countenance. And now, Sir, see the picture?"

At some future period, I may present you with other instances of the odd ways in which this admired artist gave animation to his sitters. For the present, kind reader, we shall leave him finishing the Commodore, while we return to our proper studies.

Louisville in Kentucky

LOUISVILLE in Kentucky has always been a favourite place of mine. The beauty of its situation, on the banks of *La Belle Rivière*, just at the commencement of the famed rapids, commonly called the Falls of the Ohio, had attracted my notice, and when I removed to it, immediately after my marriage, I found it more agreeable than ever. The prospect from the town is such that it would please even the eye of a Swiss. It extends along the river for seven or eight miles, and is bounded on the opposite side by a fine range of low mountains, known by the name of the Silver Hills. The rumbling sound of the waters, as they tumble over the rock-paved bed of the rapids, is at all times soothing to the ear. Fish and game are abundant. But, above all, the generous hospitality of the inhabitants, and the urbanity of their manners, had induced me to fix upon it as a place of residence; and I did so with the more pleasure when I found that my wife was as much gratified as myself, by the kind attentions which were shewn to us, utter strangers as we were, on our arrival.

No sooner had we landed, and made known our intention of remaining, than we were introduced to the principal inhabitants of the place and its vicinity, although we had not brought a single letter of introduction, and could not but see, from their unremitting kindness, that the Virginian spirit of hospitality displayed itself in all the words and actions of our newly-formed friends. I wish here to name those persons who so unexpectedly came forward to render our stay among them agreeable, but feel at a loss with whom to begin, so equally deserving are they of our gratitude. The CROGHANS, the CLARKS (our great traveller included), the BERTHOUDS, the GALTS, the MAUPINS, the TARASCONS, the BEALS, and the BOOTHS, form but a small portion of the long list which I could give. The matrons acted like mothers towards my wife, the daughters proved agreeable associates, and the husbands and sons were friends and companions to me. If I absented myself on business or otherwise, for any length of time, my wife was removed to the hospitable abode of some friend in the neighbourhood until my return, and then, kind reader, I was several times obliged to spend a week or more with these good people, before they could be prevailed upon to let us return to our own residence. We lived for two years at Louisville, where we enjoyed many of the best pleasures which this life can afford; and whenever we have since chanced to pass that way, we have found the kindness of our former friends unimpaired.

During my residence at Louisville, much of my time was employed in my ever favourite pursuits. I drew and noted the habits of every thing which I procured, and my collection was daily augmenting, as every individual who carried a gun, always sent me such birds or quadrupeds as he thought might prove useful to me. My portfolios already contained upwards of two hundred drawings. Dr W. C. GALT, being a botanist, was often consulted by me, as well as his friend Dr FERGUSON. M. GILLY drew beautifully, and was fond of my pursuits. So was my friend, and now relative, N. BERTHOUD. As I have already said, our time was spent in the most agreeable manner, through the hospitable friendship of our acquaintance.

One fair morning, I was surprised by the sudden entrance into our counting-room of Mr ALEXANDER WILSON, the celebrated author of the "American Ornithology," of whose existence I had never until that moment been apprised. This happened in March 1810. How well do I remember him, as he then walked up to me! His long, rather hooked nose, the keenness of his eyes, and his prominent cheek-bones, stamped his countenance with a peculiar character. His dress, too, was of a kind not usually seen in that part of the country; a short coat, trowsers, and a waistcoat of grey cloth. His stature was not above the middle size. He had two volumes under his arm, and as he approached the table at which I was working, I thought I discovered something like astonishment in his countenance. He, however, immediately proceeded to disclose the object of his visit, which was to procure subscriptions for his work. He opened his books, explained the nature of his occupations, and requested my patronage.

I felt surprised and gratified at the sight of his volumes, turned over a few of the plates, and had already taken a pen to write my name in his favour, when my partner rather abruptly said to me in French, "My dear AUDUBON, what induces you to subscribe to this work? Your drawings are certainly far better, and again you must know as much of the habits of American birds as this gentleman." Whether Mr WILSON understood French or not, or if the suddenness with which I paused, disappointed him, I cannot tell; but I clearly perceived that he was not pleased. Vanity and the encomiums of my friend prevented me from subscribing. Mr WILSON asked me if I had many drawings of birds. I rose, took down a large portfolio, laid it on the table, and shewed him, as I would shew you, kind reader, or any other person fond of such subjects, the whole of the contents, with the same patience with which he had shewn me his own engravings.

His surprise appeared great, as he told me he never had the most distant idea that any other individual than himself had been engaged in forming such a collection. He asked me if it was my intention to publish, and when I answered in the negative, his surprise seemed to increase. And, truly, such was not my intention; for, until long after, when I met the Prince of Musignano in Philadelphia, I had not the least idea of presenting the fruits of my labours to the world. Mr WILSON now examined my drawings with care, asked if I should have any objections to lending him a few during his stay, to which I replied that I had none: he then bade me good morning, not, however, until I had made an arrangement to explore the woods in the vicinity along with him, and had promised to procure for him some birds, of which I had drawings in my collection, but which he had never seen.

It happened that he lodged in the same house with us, but his retired habits, I thought, exhibited either a strong feeling of discontent, or a decided melancholy. The Scotch airs which he played sweetly on his flute made me melancholy too, and I felt for him. I presented him to my wife and friends, and seeing that he was all enthusiasm, exerted myself as much as was in my power, to procure for him the specimens which he wanted. We hunted together, and obtained birds which he had never before seen; but, reader, I did not subscribe to his work, for, even at that time, my collection was greater than his. Thinking that perhaps he might be pleased to publish the results of my researches, I offered them to him, merely on condition that what I had drawn, or might afterwards draw and send to him, should be mentioned in his work, as coming from my pencil. I at the same time offered to open a correspondence with him, which I thought might prove beneficial to us both. He made no reply to either proposal, and before many days had elapsed, left Louisville, on his way to New Orleans, little knowing how much his talents were appreciated in our little town, at least by myself and my friends.

Some time elapsed, during which I never heard of him, or of his work. At length, having occasion to go to Philadelphia, I, immediately after my arrival there, inquired for him, and paid him a visit. He was then drawing a White-headed Eagle. He received me with civility, and took me to the Exhibition Rooms of REMBRANDT PEALE, the artist, who had then portrayed NAPOLEON crossing the Alps. Mr WILSON spoke not of birds or drawings. Feeling, as I was forced to do, that my company was not agreeable, I parted from him; and after that I never saw him again. But judge of my astonishment some time after, when on reading the thirty-ninth page of the ninth volume of American Ornithology, I found in it the following paragraph:—

"*March 23d, 1810.*—I bade adieu to Louisville, to which place I had four letters of recommendation, and was taught to expect much of every thing there; but neither received one act of civility from those to whom I was recommended, one subscriber, nor one new bird; though I delivered my letters, ransacked the woods repeatedly, and visited all the characters likely to subscribe. Science or literature has not one friend in this place."

The Eccentric Naturalist

"WHAT an odd looking fellow!" said I to myself, as while walking by the river, I observed a man landing from a boat, with what I thought a bundle of dried clover on his back; "how the boatmen stare at him! sure he must be an original!" He ascended with a rapid step, and approaching me asked if I could point out the house in which Mr AUDUBON resided. "Why, I am the man," said I, "and will gladly lead you to my dwelling."

The traveller rubbed his hands together with delight, and drawing a letter from his pocket, handed it to me without any remark. I broke the seal and read as follows: "My dear AUDUBON, I send you an odd fish, which you may prove to be undescribed, and hope you will do so in your next letter. Believe me always your friend B." With all the simplicity of a woodsman I asked the bearer where the odd fish was, when M. de T. (for, kind reader, the individual in my presence was none else than that renowned naturalist) smiled, rubbed his hands, and with the greatest good humour said, "I am that odd fish I presume, Mr AUDUBON." I felt confounded and blushed, but contrived to stammer an apology.

We soon reached the house, when I presented my learned guest to my family, and was ordering a servant to go to the boat for M. de T.'s luggage, when he told me he had none but what he brought on his back. He then loosened the pack of weeds which had first drawn my attention. The ladies were a little surprised, but I checked their critical glances for the moment. The naturalist pulled off his shoes, and while engaged in drawing his stockings, not up, but down, in order to cover the holes about the heels, told us in the gayest mood imaginable that he had walked a great distance, and had only taken a passage on board the *ark*, to be put on this shore, and that he was sorry his apparel had suffered so much from his late journey. Clean clothes were offered, but he would not accept them, and it was with evident reluctance that he performed the lavations usual on such occasions before he sat down to dinner.

At table, however, his agreeable conversation made us all forget his singular appearance; and, indeed, it was only as we strolled together in the garden that his attire struck me as exceedingly remarkable. A long loose coat of yellow nankeen, much the worse of the many rubs it had got in its time, and stained all over with the juice of plants, hung loosely about him like a sac. A waistcoat of the same, with enormous pockets, and buttoned up to the chin, reached below over a pair of tight pantaloons, the lower parts of which were buttoned down to the ankles. His beard was as long as I have known my own to be during some of my peregrinations, and his lank black hair hung loosely over his shoulders. His forehead was so broad and prominent that any tyro in phrenology would instantly have pronounced it the residence of a mind of strong powers. His words impressed an assurance of rigid truth, and as he directed the conversation to the study of the natural sciences, I listened to him with as much delight as Telemachus could have listened to Mentor. He had come to visit me, he said, expressly for the purpose of seeing my drawings, having been told that my representations of birds were accompanied with those of shrubs and plants, and he was desirous of knowing whether I might chance to have in my collection any with which he was unacquainted. I observed some degree of impatience in his request to be allowed at once to see what I had. We returned to the house, when I opened my portfolios and laid them before him.

He chanced to turn over the drawing of a plant quite new to him. After inspecting it closely, he shook his head, and told me no such plant existed in nature;—for, kind reader, M. de T. although a highly scientific man, was suspicious to a fault, and believed such plants only to exist as he had himself seen, or such as, having been discovered of old, had, according to Father MALEBRANCHE's expression, acquired a "venerable beard." I told my guest that the plant was common in the immediate neighbourhood, and that I should shew it him on the morrow. "And why to morrow, Mr AUDUBON? let us go now." We did so, and on reaching the bank of the river, I pointed to the plant. M. de T. I thought had gone mad. He plucked the plants one after another, danced, hugged me in his arms, and exultingly told me that he had got not merely a new species, but a new genus. When we returned home, the naturalist opened the bundle which he had brought on his back, and took out a journal rendered water-proof by means of a leather case, together with a small parcel of linen, examined the new plant, and wrote its description. The examination of my drawings then went on. You would be pleased, kind reader, to hear his criticisms, which were of the greatest advantage to me, for, being well acquainted with books as well as with nature, he was well fitted to give me advice.

It was summer, and the heat was so great that the windows were all open. The light of the candles attracted many insects, among which was observed a large species of Scarabæus. I caught one, and, aware of his inclination to believe only what he should himself see, I shewed him the insect, and assured him it was so strong that it would crawl on the table with the candlestick on its back. "I should like to see the experiment made, Mr AUDUBON," he replied. It was accordingly made, and the insect moved about, dragging its burden so as to make the candlestick change its position as if by magic, until coming upon the edge of the table, it dropped on the floor, took to wing, and made its escape.

When it waxed late, I shewed him to the apartment intended for him during his stay, and endeavoured to render him comfortable, leaving him writing materials in abundance. I was indeed heartily glad to have a naturalist under my roof. We had all retired to rest. Every person I imagined was in deep slumber save myself, when of a sudden I heard a great uproar in the naturalist's room. I got up, reached the place in a few moments, and opened the door, when, to my astonishment, I saw my guest running about the room naked, holding the handle of my favourite violin, the body of which he had battered to pieces against the walls in attempting to kill the bats which had entered by the open window, probably attracted by the insects flying around his candle. I stood amazed, but he continued jumping and running round and round, until he was fairly exhausted, when he begged me to procure one of the animals for him, as he felt convinced they belonged to "a new species." Although I was convinced of the contrary, I took up the bow of my demolished Cremona, and administering a smart tap to each of the bats as it came up, soon got specimens enough. The war ended, I again bade him good night, but could not help observing the state of the room. It was strewed with plants, which it would seem he had arranged into groups, but which were now scattered about in confusion. "Never mind, Mr AUDUBON," quoth the eccentric naturalist, "never mind, I'll soon arrange them again. I have the bats, and that's enough."

Several days passed, during which we followed our several occupations. M. de T. searched the woods for plants, and I for birds. He also followed the margins of the Ohio, and picked up many shells, which he greatly extolled. With us, I told him, they were gathered into heaps to be converted into lime. "Lime! Mr AUDUBON; why, they are worth a guinea a piece in any part of Europe." One day, as I was returning from a hunt in a cane-brake, he observed that I was wet and spattered with mud, and desired me to shew him the interior of one of these places, which he said he had never visited.

The Cane, kind reader, formerly grew spontaneously over the greater portions of the State of Kentucky and other Western Districts of our Union, as well as in many farther south. Now, however, cultivation, the introduction of cattle and horses, and other circumstances connected with the progress of civilization, have greatly altered the face of the country, and reduced the cane within comparatively small limits. It attains a height of from twelve to thirty feet, and a diameter of from one to two, and grows in great patches resembling osier-holts, in which occur plants of all sizes. The plants frequently grow so close together, and in course of time become so tangled, as to present an almost impenetrable thicket. A portion of ground thus covered with canes is called a *Cane-brake*.

If you picture to yourself one of these cane-brakes growing beneath the gigantic trees that form our western forests, interspersed with vines of many species, and numberless plants of every description, you may conceive how difficult it is for one to make his way through it, especially after a heavy shower of rain or a fall of sleet, when the traveller, in forcing his way through, shakes down upon himself such quantities of water, as soon reduce him to a state of the utmost discomfort. The hunters often cut little paths through the thickets with their knives, but the usual mode of passing through them is by pushing one's self backward, and wedging a way between the stems. To follow a bear or a cougar pursued by dogs through these brakes, is a task, the accomplishment of which may be imagined, but of the difficulties and dangers accompanying which I cannot easily give an adequate representation.

The canes generally grow on the richest soil, and are particularly plentiful along the margins of the great western rivers. Many of our new settlers are fond of forming farms in their immediate vicinity, as the plant is much relished by all kinds of cattle and horses, which feed upon it at all seasons, and again because these brakes are plentifully stocked with game of various kinds. It sometimes happens that the farmer clears a portion of the brake. This is done by cutting the stems, which are fistular and knotted, like those of other grasses, with a large knife or cutlass. They are afterwards placed in heaps, and when partially dried set fire to. The moisture contained between the joints is converted into steam, which causes the cane to burst with a smart report, and when a whole mass is crackling, the sounds resemble discharges of musquetry. Indeed, I have been told that travellers floating down the rivers, and unacquainted with these circumstances, have been induced to pull their oars with redoubled rigour, apprehending the attack of a host of savages, ready to scalp every one of the party.

A day being fixed, we left home after an early breakfast, crossed the Ohio, and entered the woods. I had determined that my companion should view a cane-brake in all its perfection, and after leading him several miles in a direct course, came upon as fine a sample as existed in that part of the country. We entered, and for some time proceeded without much difficulty, as I led the way, and cut down the canes which were most likely to incommode him. The difficulties gradually increased, so that we were presently obliged to turn our backs to the foe, and push ourselves on the best way we could. My companion stopped here and there to pick up a plant and examine it. After a while, we chanced to come upon the top of a fallen tree, which so obstructed our passage that we were on the eve of going round, instead of thrusting ourselves through amongst the branches, when, from its bed in the centre of the tangled mass, forth rushed a bear, with such force, and snuffing the air in so frightful a manner, that M. de T. became suddenly terror-struck, and, in his haste to escape, made a desperate attempt to run, but fell amongst the canes in such a way, that he looked as if pinioned. Perceiving him jammed in between the stalks, and thoroughly frightened, I could not refrain from laughing at the ridiculous exhibition which he made. My gaiety, however, was not very pleasing to the savant, who called out for aid, which was at once administered. Gladly would he have retraced his steps, but I was desirous that he should be able to describe a cane-brake, and enticed him to follow me, by telling him that our worst difficulties were nearly over. We proceeded, for by this time the bear was out of hearing.

The way became more and more tangled. I saw with delight that a heavy cloud, portentous of a thunder gust, was approaching. In the mean time, I kept my companion in such constant difficulties, that he now panted, perspired, and seemed almost overcome by fatigue. The thunder began to rumble, and soon after a dash of heavy rain drenched us in a few minutes. The withered particles of leaves and bark attached to the canes stuck to our clothes. We received many scratches from briars, and now and then a twitch from a nettle. M. de T. seriously inquired if we should ever get alive out of the horrible situation in which we were. I spoke of courage and patience, and told him I hoped we should soon get to the margin of the brake, which, however, I knew to be two miles distant. I made him rest, and gave him a mouthful of brandy from my flask; after which, we proceeded on our slow and painful march. He threw away all his plants, emptied his pockets of the fungi, lichens, and mosses which he had thrust into them, and finding himself much lightened, went on for thirty or forty yards with a better grace. But, kind reader, enough— I led the naturalist first one way, then another, until I had nearly lost myself in the brake, although I was well acquainted with it, kept him tumbling and crawling on his hands and knees, until long after mid-day, when we at length reached the edge of the river. I blew my horn, and soon shewed my companion a boat coming to our rescue. We were ferried over, and, on reaching the house, found more agreeable occupation in replenishing our empty coffers.

M. de T. remained with us for three weeks, and collected multitudes of plants, shells, bats, and fishes, but never again expressed a desire of visiting a cane-brake. We were perfectly reconciled to his oddities, and, finding him a most agreeable and intelligent companion, hoped that his sojourn might be of long duration. But, one evening when tea was prepared, and we expected him to join the family, he was nowhere to be found. His grasses and other valuables were all removed from his room. The night was spent in searching for him in the neighbourhood. No eccentric naturalist could be discovered. Whether he had perished in a swamp, or had been devoured by a bear or a gar-fish, or had taken to his heels, were matters of conjecture; nor was it until some weeks after, that a letter from him, thanking us for our attention, assured me of his safety.

Pitting of Wolves

THERE seems to be a universal feeling of hostility among men against the Wolf, whose strength, agility, and cunning, which latter is scarcely inferior to that of his relative master Reynard, tend to render him an object of hatred, especially to the husbandman, on whose flocks he is ever apt to commit depredations. In America, where this animal was formerly abundant, and in many parts of which it still occurs in considerable numbers, it is not more mercifully dealt with than in other parts of the world. Traps and snares of all sorts are set for catching it, while dogs and horses are trained for hunting the Fox. The Wolf, however, unless in some way injured, being more powerful and perhaps better winded than the Fox, is rarely pursued with hounds or any other dogs in open chase; but as his depredations are at times extensive and highly injurious to the farmer, the greatest exertions have been used to exterminate his race. Few instances have occurred among us of any attack made by Wolves on man, and only one has come under my own notice.

Two young Negroes who resided near the banks of the Ohio, in the lower part of the State of Kentucky, about twenty-three years ago, had sweethearts living on a plantation ten miles distant. After the labours of the day were over, they frequently visited the fair ladies of their choice, the nearest way to whose dwelling lay directly across a great cane brake. As to the lover every moment is precious, they usually took this route, to save time. Winter had commenced, cold, dark, and forbidding, and after sunset scarcely a glimpse of light or glow of warmth, one might imagine, could be found in that dreary swamp, excepting in the eyes and bosoms of the ardent youths, or the hungry Wolves that prowled about. The snow covered the earth, and rendered them more easy to be scented from a distance by the famished beasts. Prudent in a certain degree, the young lovers carried their axes on their shoulders, and walked as briskly as the narrow path would allow. Some transient glimpses of light now and then met their eyes, but so faint were they that they believed them to be caused by their faces coming in contact with the slender reeds covered with snow. Suddenly, however, a long and frightful howl burst upon them, and they instantly knew that it proceeded from a troop of hungry, perhaps desperate Wolves. They stopped, and putting themselves in an attitude of defence, awaited the result. All around was dark, save a few feet of snow, and the silence of night was dismal. Nothing could be done to better their situation, and after standing a few minutes in expectation of an attack, they judged it best to resume their march; but no sooner had they replaced their axes on their shoulders, and begun to move, than the foremost found himself assailed by several foes. His legs were held fast as if pressed by a powerful screw, and the torture inflicted by the fangs of the ravenous animal was for a moment excruciating. Several Wolves in the mean time sprung upon the breast of the other Negro, and dragged him to the ground. Both struggled manfully against their foes; but in a short time one of them ceased to move, and the other, reduced in strength, and perhaps despairing of maintaining his ground, still more of aiding his unfortunate companion, sprung to the branch of a tree, and speedily gained a place of safety near the top. The next morning, the mangled remains of his comrade lay scattered around on the snow, which was stained with blood. Three dead Wolves lay around, but the rest of the pack had disappeared, and Scipio, sliding to the ground, took up the axes, and made the best of his way home, to relate the sad adventure.

About two years after this occurrence, as I was travelling between Henderson and Vincennes, I chanced to stop for the night at a farmer's house by the side of the road. After putting up my horse and refreshing myself, I entered into conversation with mine host, who asked if I should like to pay a visit to the wolf-pits, which were about half a mile distant. Glad of the opportunity I accompanied him across the fields to the neighbourhood of a deep wood, and soon saw the engines of destruction. He had three pits, within a few hundred yards of each other. They were about eight feet deep, and broader at bottom, so as to render it impossible for the most active animal to escape from them. The aperture was covered with a revolving platform of twigs, attached to a central axis. On either surface of the platform was fastened a large piece of putrid venison, with other matters by no means pleasant to my olfactory nerves, although no doubt attractive to the Wolves. My companion wished to visit them that evening, merely as he was in the habit of doing so daily, for the purpose of seeing that all was right. He said that Wolves were very abundant that autumn, and had killed nearly the whole of his sheep and one of his colts, but that he was now "paying them off in full;" and added that if I would tarry a few hours with him next morning, he would beyond a doubt shew me some sport rarely seen in those parts. We retired to rest in due time, and were up with the dawn.

"I think," said my host, "that all's right, for I see the dogs are anxious to get away to the pits, and although they are nothing but curs, their noses are none the worse for that." As he took up his gun, an axe and a large knife, the dogs began to howl and bark, and whisked around us, as if full of joy.

When we reached the first pit, we found the bait all gone, and the platform much injured; but the animal that had been entrapped had scraped a subterranean passage for himself and so escaped. On peeping into the next, he assured me that "three famous fellows were safe enough" in it. I also peeped in and saw the Wolves, two black, and the other brindled, all of goodly size, sure enough. They lay flat on the earth, their ears laid close over the head, their eyes indicating fear more than anger. "But how are we to get them out?"—"How Sir," said the farmer, "why by going down to be sure, and ham-stringing them." Being a novice in these matters, I begged to be merely a looker-on. "With all my heart," quoth the farmer, "stand here, and look at me through the brush." Whereupon he glided down, taking with him his axe and knife, and leaving his rifle to my care. I was not a little surprised to see the cowardice of the Wolves. He pulled out successively their hind legs, and with a side stroke of the knife cut the principal tendon above the joint, exhibiting as little fear as if he had been marking lambs.

"Lo!" exclaimed the farmer, when he had got out, "we have forgot the rope; I'll go after it." Off he went accordingly, with as much alacrity as any youngster could shew. In a short time he returned out of breath, and wiping his forehead with the back of his hand—"Now for it." I was desired to raise and hold the platform on its central balance, whilst he, with all the dexterity of an Indian, threw a noose over the neck of one of the Wolves. We hauled it up motionless with fright, as if dead, its disabled legs swinging to and fro, its jaws wide open, and the gurgle in its throat alone indicating that it was alive. Letting him drop on the ground, the farmer loosened the rope by means of a stick, and left him to the dogs, all of which set upon him with great fury and soon worried him to death. The second was dealt with in the same manner; but the third, which was probably the oldest, as it was the blackest, shewed some spirit, the moment it was left loose to the mercy of the curs. This Wolf, which we afterwards found to be a female, scuffled along on its fore legs at a surprising rate, giving a snap every now and then to the nearest dog, which went off howling dismally with a mouthful of skin torn from its side. And so well did the furious beast defend itself, that apprehensive of its escape, the farmer levelled his rifle at it, and shot it through the heart, on which the curs rushed upon it, and satiated their vengeance on the destroyer of their master's flock.

Breaking Up of the Ice

WHILE proceeding up the Mississippi above its junction with the Ohio, I found, to my great mortification, that its navigation was obstructed by ice. The chief conductor of my bark, who was a Canadian Frenchman, was therefore desired to take us to a place suitable for winter-quarters, which he accordingly did, bringing us into a great bend of the river called Tawapatee Bottom. The waters were unusually low, the thermometer indicated excessive cold, the earth all around was covered with snow, dark clouds were spread over the heavens, and as all appearances were unfavourable to the hope of a speedy prosecution of our voyage, we quietly set to work. Our bark, which was a large keel-boat, was moored close to the shore, the cargo was conveyed to the woods, large trees were felled over the water, and were so disposed as to keep off the pressure of the floating masses of ice. In less than two days, our stores, baggage, and ammunition, were deposited in a great heap under one of the magnificent trees of which the forest was here composed, our sails were spread over all, and a complete camp was formed in the wilderness. Every thing around us seemed dreary and dismal, and had we not been endowed with the faculty of deriving pleasure from the examination of nature, we should have made up our minds to pass the time in a state similar to that of bears during their hybernation. We soon found employment, however, for the woods were full of game; and deer, turkeys, racoons, and opossums might be seen even around our camp; while on the ice that now covered the broad stream rested flocks of swans, to surprise which the hungry wolves were at times seen to make energetic but unsuccessful efforts. It was curious to see the snow-white birds all lying flat on the ice, but keenly intent on

watching the motions of their insidious enemies, until the latter advanced within the distance of a few hundred yards,
when the swans, sounding their trumpet-notes of alarm,
would all rise, spread out their broad wings, and after running
some yards and battering the ice until the noise was echoed
like thunder through the woods, rose exultingly into the air,
leaving their pursuers to devise other schemes for gratifying
their craving appetites.

The nights being extremely cold, we constantly kept up a
large fire, formed of the best wood. Fine trees of ash and
hickory were felled, cut up into logs of convenient size, and
rolled into a pile, on the top of which, with the aid of twigs,
a fire was kindled. There were about fifteen of us, some
hunters, others trappers, and all more or less accustomed to
live in the woods. At night, when all had returned from their
hunting-grounds, some successful and others empty-handed,
they presented a picture in the strong glare of the huge fire
that illuminated the forest, which it might prove interesting
to you to see, were it copied by a bold hand on canvass. Over
a space of thirty yards or more, the snow was scraped away,
and piled up into a circular wall, which protected us from the
cold blast. Our cooking utensils formed no mean display, and
before a week had elapsed, venison, turkeys, and racoons
hung on the branches in profusion. Fish, too, and that of excellent quality, often graced our board, having been obtained
by breaking holes in the ice of the lakes. It was observed that
the opossums issued at night from holes in the banks of the
river, to which they returned about day-break; and having
thus discovered their retreat, we captured many of them by
means of snares.

At the end of a fortnight our bread failed, and two of the
party were directed to proceed across the bend, towards a village on the western bank of the Mississippi, in quest of that
commodity; for although we had a kind of substitute for it in
the dry white flesh of the breast of the wild turkey, bread is
bread after all, and more indispensable to civilized man than
any other article of food. The expedition left the camp early
one morning; one of the party boasted much of his knowledge of woods, while the other said nothing, but followed.
They walked on all day, and returned next morning to the

camp with empty wallets. The next attempt, however, succeeded, and they brought on a sledge a barrel of flour and some potatoes. After a while, we were joined by many Indians, the observation of whose manners afforded us much amusement.

Six weeks were spent in Tawapatee Bottom. The waters had kept continually sinking, and our boat lay on her side high and dry. On both sides of the stream, the ice had broken into heaps, forming huge walls. Our pilot visited the river daily, to see what prospect there might be of a change. One night, while, excepting himself, all were sound asleep, he suddenly roused us with loud cries of "the ice is breaking! get up, get up, down to the boat lads, bring out your axes, hurry on, or we may lose her, here let us have a torch!" Starting up, as if we had been attacked by a band of savages, we ran pell-mell to the bank. The ice was indeed breaking up; it split with reports like those of heavy artillery, and as the water had suddenly risen from an overflow of the Ohio, the two streams seemed to rush against each other with violence, in consequence of which the congealed mass was broken into large fragments, some of which rose nearly erect here and there, and again fell with thundering crash, as the wounded whale, when in the agonies of death, springs up with furious force, and again plunges into the foaming waters. To our surprise, the weather, which in the evening had been calm and frosty, had become wet and blowy. The water gushed from the fissures formed in the ice, and the prospect was extremely dismal. When day dawned, a spectacle strange and fearful presented itself: the whole mass of water was violently agitated, its covering was broken into small fragments, and although not a foot of space was without ice, not a step could the most daring have ventured to make upon it. Our boat was in imminent danger, for the trees which had been placed to guard it from the ice were cut or broken into pieces, and were thrust against her. It was impossible to move her; but our pilot ordered every man to bring down great bunches of cane, which were lashed along her sides; and before these were destroyed by the ice, she was afloat and riding above it. While we were gazing on the scene, a tremendous crash was heard, which seemed to have taken place about a mile below, when suddenly the great dam of ice gave way. The current of the Mississippi had forced its way against that of the Ohio; and in less than four hours, we witnessed the complete breaking up of the ice.

During that winter, the ice was so thick on the Mississippi, that opposite St Louis, horses and heavy waggons crossed the river. Many boats had been detained in the same manner as our own, so that provisions and other necessary articles had become very scarce, and sold at a high price. This happened about twenty-eight years ago.

MISSOURI RIVER JOURNALS

Missouri River Journals

I LEFT home at ten o'clock of the morning, on Saturday the 11th of March, 1843, accompanied by my son Victor. I left all well, and I trust in God for the privilege and happiness of rejoining them all some time next autumn, when I hope to return from the Yellowstone River, an expedition undertaken solely for the sake of our work on the Quadrupeds of North America. The day was cold, but the sun was shining, and after having visited a few friends in the city of New York, we departed for Philadelphia in the cars, and reached that place at eleven of the night. As I was about landing, I was touched on the shoulder by a tall, robust-looking man, whom I knew not to be a sheriff, but in fact my good friend Jediah Irish, of the Great Pine Swamp. I also met my friend Edward Harris, who, with old John G. Bell, Isaac Sprague, and young Lewis Squires, are to be my companions for this campaign. We all put up at Mr. Sanderson's. Sunday was spent in visits to Mr. Bowen, Dr. Morton, and others, and we had many calls made upon us at the hotel. On Monday morning we took the cars for Baltimore, and Victor returned home to Minniesland. The weather was rainy, blustery, cold, but we reached Baltimore in time to eat our dinner there, and we there spent the afternoon and the night. I saw Gideon B. Smith and a few other friends, and on the next morning we entered the cars for Cumberland, which we reached the same evening about six. Here we had all our effects weighed, and were charged thirty dollars additional weight—a first-rate piece of robbery. We went on now by coaches, entering the gap, and ascending the Alleghanies amid a storm of snow, which kept us company for about forty hours, when we reached Wheeling, which we left on the 16th of March, and went on board the steamer, that brought us to Cincinnati all safe.

We saw much game on our way, such as Geese, Ducks, etc., but no Turkeys as in times of yore. We left for Louisville in the U. S. mail steamer, and arrived there before daylight on the 19th inst. My companions went to the Scott House, and I to William G. Bakewell's, whose home I reached before the family were up. I remained there four days, and was, of course, most kindly treated; and, indeed, during my whole stay in this city of my youth I did enjoy myself famously well, with dancing, dinner-parties, etc. We left for St. Louis on board the ever-to-be-remembered steamer "Gallant," and after having been struck by a log which did not send us to the bottom, arrived on the 28th of March.

On the 4th of April, Harris went off to Edwardsville, with the rest of my companions, and I went to Nicholas Berthoud, who began housekeeping here that day, though Eliza was not yet arrived from Pittsburgh. My time at St. Louis would have been agreeable to any one fond of company, dinners, and parties; but of these matters I am not, though I did dine at three different houses, *bon gré, mal gré*. In fact, my time was spent procuring, arranging, and superintending the necessary objects for the comfort and utility of the party attached to my undertaking. The Chouteaux supplied us with most things, and, let it be said to their honor, at little or no profit. Captain Sire took me in a light wagon to see old Mr. Chouteau one afternoon, and I found the worthy old gentleman so kind and so full of information about the countries of the Indians that I returned to him a few days afterwards, not only for the sake of the pleasure I enjoyed in his conversation, but also with the view to procure, both dead and alive, a species of Pouched Rat (*Pseudostoma bursarius*) wonderfully abundant in this section of country. One day our friend Harris came back, and brought with him the prepared skins of birds and quadrupeds they had collected, and informed me that they had removed their quarters to B——'s. He left the next day, after we had made an arrangement for the party to return the Friday following, which they did. I drew four figures of Pouched Rats, and outlined two figures of *Sciurus capistratus*, which is here called "Fox Squirrel."

The 25th of April at last made its appearance, the rivers were now opened, the weather was growing warm, and every object in nature proved to us that at last the singularly lingering winter of 1842 and 1843 was over. Having conveyed the whole of our effects on board the steamer, and being supplied with excellent letters, we left St. Louis at 11.30 A. M., with Mr. Sarpy on board, and a hundred and one trappers of all descriptions and nearly a dozen different nationalities, though the greater number were French Canadians, or Creoles of this State. Some were drunk, and many in that stupid mood which follows a state of nervousness produced by drinking and over-excitement. Here is the scene that took place on board the "Omega" at our departure, and what followed when the roll was called.

First the general embarkation, when the men came in pushing and squeezing each other, so as to make the boards they walked upon fairly tremble. The Indians, poor souls, were more quiet, and had already seated or squatted themselves on the highest parts of the steamer, and were tranquil lookers-on. After about three quarters of an hour, the crew and all the trappers (these are called *engagés*) were on board, and we at once pushed off and up the stream, thick and muddy as it was. The whole of the effects and the baggage of the *engagés* was arranged in the main cabin, and presently was seen Mr. Sarpy, book in hand, with the list before him, wherefrom he gave the names of these *attachés*. The men whose names were called nearly filled the fore part of the cabin, where stood Mr. Sarpy, our captain, and one of the clerks. All awaited orders from Mr. Sarpy. As each man was called, and answered to his name, a blanket containing the apparel for the trip was handed to him, and he was ordered at once to retire and make room for the next. The outfit, by the way, was somewhat scanty, and of indifferent quality. Four men were missing, and some appeared rather reluctant; however, the roll was ended, and one hundred and one were found. In many instances their bundles were thrown to them, and they were ordered off as if slaves. I forgot to say that as the boat pushed off from the shore, where stood a crowd of loafers, the men on board had congregated upon the hurricane deck with their rifles and guns of various sorts, all loaded, and began to fire what I should call a very disorganized sort of a salute, which lasted for something like an hour, and which has been renewed at intervals, though in a more desultory manner, at every village we have passed. However, we now find them passably good, quiet, and regularly sobered men. We have of course a motley set, even to Italians. We passed the mouth of the Missouri, and moved very slowly against the current, for it was not less than twenty minutes after four the next morning, when we reached St. Charles, distant forty-two miles. Here we stopped till half-past five, when Mr. Sarpy, to whom I gave my letters home, left us in a wagon.

April 26. A rainy day, and the heat we had experienced yesterday was now all gone. We saw a Wild Goose running on the shore, and it was killed by Bell; but our captain did not stop to pick it up, and I was sorry to see the poor bird dead, uselessly. We now had found out that our berths were too thickly inhabited for us to sleep in; so I rolled myself in my blanket, lay down on deck, and slept very sound.

27th. A fine clear day, cool this morning. Cleaned our boilers last night, landing where the "Emily Christian" is sunk, for a few moments; saw a few Gray Squirrels, and an abundance of our common Partridges in flocks of fifteen to twenty, very gentle indeed. About four this afternoon we passed the mouth of the Gasconade River, a stream coming from the westward, valuable for its yellow-pine lumber. At a woodyard above us we saw a White Pelican that had been captured there, and which, had it been clean, I should have bought. I saw that its legs and feet were red, and not yellow, as they are during autumn and winter. Marmots are quite abundant, and here they perforate their holes in the loose, sandy soil of the river banks, as well as the same soil wherever it is somewhat elevated. We do not know yet if it is *Arctomys monax*, or a new species. The weather being fine, and the night clear, we ran all night and on the morning of the 28th, thermometer 69° to 78° at sunrise, we were in sight of the seat of government, Jefferson. The State House stands prominent, with a view from it up and down the stream of about ten miles; but, with the exception of the State House and the Penitentiary, Jefferson is a poor place, the land round being sterile and broken. This is *said* to be 160 or 170 miles above St. Louis. We saw many Gray Squirrels this morning. Yesterday we passed under long lines of elevated shore, surmounted by stupendous rocks of limestone, with many curious holes in them, where we saw Vultures and Eagles enter towards dusk. Harris saw a Peregrine Falcon; the whole of these rocky shores are ornamented with a species of white cedar quite satisfactorily known to us. We took wood at several places; at one I was told that Wild Turkeys were abundant and Squirrels also, but as the squatter observed, "Game is very scarce, especially Bears." Wolves begin to be troublesome to the settlers who have sheep; they are obliged to drive the latter home, and herd them each night.

This evening the weather became cloudy and looked like rain; the weather has been very warm, the thermometer being at 78° at three this afternoon. We saw a pair of Peregrine Falcons, one of them with a bird in its talons; also a few White-fronted Geese, some Blue-winged Teal, and some Cormorants, but none with the head, neck, and breast pure white, as the one I saw two days ago. The strength of the current seemed to increase; in some places our boat merely kept her own, and in one instance fell back nearly half a mile to where we had taken in wood. At about ten this evening we came into such strong water that nothing could be done against it; we laid up for the night at the lower end of a willow island, and then cleaned the boilers and took in 200 fence-rails, which the French Canadians call "perches." Now a *perche* in French means a pole; therefore this must be *patois*.

29th. We were off at five this rainy morning, and at 9 A. M. reached Booneville, distant from St. Louis about 204 miles. We bought at this place an axe, a saw, three files, and some wafers; also some chickens, at one dollar a dozen. We found here some of the Santa Fé traders with whom we had crossed the Alleghanies. They were awaiting the arrival of their goods, and then would immediately start. I saw a Rabbit sitting under the shelf of a rock, and also a Gray Squirrel. It appears to me that *Sciurus macrourus* of Say relishes the bottom lands in preference to the hilly or rocky portions which alternately present themselves along these shores. On looking along the banks of the river, one cannot help observing the half-drowned young willows, and cotton trees of the same age, trembling and shaking sideways against the current; and methought, as I gazed upon them, of the danger they were in of being immersed over their very tops and thus dying, not through the influence of fire, the natural enemy of wood, but from the force of the mighty stream on the margin of which they grew, and which appeared as if in its wrath it was determined to overwhelm, and undo all that the Creator in His bountifulness had granted us to enjoy. The banks themselves, along with perhaps millions of trees, are ever tumbling, falling, and washing away from the spots where they may have stood and grown for centuries past. If this be not an awful exemplification of the real course of Nature's intention, that all should and must live and die, then, indeed, the philosophy of our learned men cannot be much relied upon!

This afternoon the steamer "John Auld" came up near us, but stopped to put off passengers. She had troops on board and a good number of travellers. We passed the *city* of Glasgow without stopping there, and the blackguards on shore were so greatly disappointed that they actually fired at us with rifles; but whether with balls or not, they did us no harm, for the current proved so strong that we had to make over to the opposite side of the river. We did not run far; the weather was still bad, raining hard, and at ten o'clock, with wood nearly exhausted, we stopped on the west shore, and there remained all the night, cleaning boilers, etc.

Sunday 30th. This morning was cold, and it blew a gale from the north. We started, however, for a wooding-place, but the "John Auld" had the advantage of us, and took what there was; the wind increased so much that the waves were actually running pretty high down-stream, and we stopped until one o'clock. You may depend my party was not sorry for this; and as I had had no exercise since we left St. Louis, as soon as breakfast was over we started—Bell, Harris, Squires, and myself, with our guns—and had quite a frolic of it, for we killed a good deal of game, and lost some. Unfortunately we landed at a place where the water had overflowed the country between the shores and the hills, which are distant about one mile and a half. We started a couple of Deer, which Bell and I shot at, and a female Turkey flying fast; at my shot it extended its legs downwards as if badly wounded, but it sailed on, and must have fallen across the muddy waters. Bell, Harris, and myself shot running exactly twenty-eight Rabbits, *Lepus sylvaticus*, and two Bachmans, two *Sciurus macrourus* of Say, two *Arctomys monax*, and a pair of *Tetrao umbellus*. The woods were alive with the Rabbits, but they were very wild; the Ground-hogs, Marmots, or *Arctomys*, were in great numbers, judging from the innumerable burrows we saw, and had the weather been calm, I have no doubt we would have seen many more. Bell wounded a Turkey hen so badly that the poor thing could not fly; but Harris frightened it, and it was off, and was lost. Harris shot an *Arctomys* without pouches, that had been forced out of its burrow by the water entering it; it stood motionless until he was within ten paces of it; when, ascertaining what it was, he retired a few yards, and shot it with No. 10 shot, and it fell dead on the spot. We found the woods filled with birds—all known, however, to us: Golden-crowned Thrush, Cerulean Warblers, Woodpeckers of various kinds, etc.; but not a Duck in the bayou, to my surprise. At one the wind lulled somewhat, and as we had taken all the fence-rails and a quantity of dry stuff of all sorts, we were ready to attempt our ascent, and did so. It was curious to see sixty or seventy men carrying logs forty or fifty feet long, some well dried and some green, on their shoulders, all of which were wanted by our captain, for some purpose or other. In a great number of instances the squatters, farmers, or planters, as they may be called, are found to abandon their dwellings or make towards higher grounds, which fortunately are here no farther off than from one to three miles. After we left, we met with the strength of the current, but with our stakes, fence-rails, and our dry wood, we made good headway. At one place we passed a couple of houses, with women and children, perfectly surrounded by the flood; these houses stood apparently on the margin of a river coming in from the eastward. The whole farm was under water, and all around was the very perfection of disaster and misfortune. It appeared to us as if the men had gone to procure assistance, and I was grieved that we could not offer them any. We saw several trees falling in, and beautiful, though painful, was the sight. As they fell, the spray which rose along their whole length was exquisite; but alas! these magnificent trees had reached the day of oblivion.

A few miles above New Brunswick we stopped to take in wood, and landed three of our Indians, who, belonging to the Iowa tribe, had to travel up La Grande Rivière. The wind lulled away, and we ran all night, touching, for a few minutes, on a bar in the middle of the river.

May 1. This morning was a beautiful one; our run last

night was about thirty miles, but as we have just begun this fine day, I will copy here the habits of the Pouched Rats, from my notes on the spot at old Mr. Chouteau's, and again at St. Louis, where I kept several alive for four or five days:—

Plantation of Pierre Chouteau, Sen., four miles west of St. Louis, April 13, 1843. I came here last evening in the company of Mr. Sarpy, for the express purpose of procuring some Pouched Rats, and as I have been fortunate enough to secure several of these strange creatures, and also to have seen and heard much connected with their habits and habitats, I write on the spot, with the wish that no recollection of facts be passed over. The present species is uncommonly abundant throughout this neighborhood, and is even found in the gardens of the city of St. Louis, upon the outskirts. They are extremely pernicious animals to the planter and to the gardener, as they devour every root, grass, or vegetable within their reach, and burrow both day and night in every direction imaginable, wherever they know their insatiable appetites can be recompensed for their labor. They bring forth from five to seven young, about the 25th of March, and these are rather large at birth. The nest, or place of deposit, is usually rounded, and about eight inches in diameter, being globular, and well lined with the hair of the female. This nest is not placed at the end of a burrow, or in any particular one of their long galleries, but oftentimes in the road that may lead to hundreds of yards distant. From immediately around the nest, however, many galleries branch off in divers directions, all tending towards such spots as are well known to the parents to afford an abundance of food. I cannot ascertain how long the young remain under the care of the mother. Having observed several freshly thrown-up mounds in Mr. Chouteau's garden, this excellent gentleman called to some negroes to bring spades, and to dig for the animals with the hope I might procure one alive. All hands went to work with alacrity, in the presence of Dr. Trudeau of St. Louis, my friends the father and son Chouteau, and myself. We observed that the "Muloë" (the name given these animals by the creoles of this country) had worked in two or more opposite directions, and that the main gallery was about a foot beneath the surface of the ground, except where it had crossed the walks, when the burrow was sunk a few inches deeper. The work led the negroes across a large square and two of the walks, on one side of which we found large bunches of carnations, from which the roots had been cut off obliquely, close to the surface of the ground, thereby killing the plants. The roots measured ⅞ of an inch, and immediately next to them was a rosebush, where ended the burrow. The other side was now followed, and ended amidst the roots of a fine large peach-tree; these roots were more or less gashed and lacerated, but no animal was there, and on returning on our tracks, we found that several galleries, probably leading outside the garden, existed, and we gave up the chase.

This species throws up the earth in mounds rarely higher than twelve to fifteen inches, and these mounds are thrown up at extremely irregular distances, being at times near to each other, and elsewhere ten to twenty, or even thirty, paces apart, yet generally leading to particular spots, well covered with grapes or vegetables of different kinds. This species remains under ground during the whole winter, inactive, and probably dormant, as they never raise or work the earth at this time. The earth thrown up is as if pulverized, and as soon as the animal has finished his labors, which are for no other purpose than to convey him securely from one spot to another, he closes the aperture, which is sometimes on the top, though more usually on the side towards the sun, leaving a kind of ring nearly one inch in breadth, and about the diameter of the body of the animal. Possessed of an exquisite sense of hearing and of feeling the external pressure of objects travelling on the ground, they stop their labors instantaneously on the least alarm; but if you retire from fifteen to twenty paces to the windward of the hole, and wait for a quarter of an hour or so, you see the "Gopher" (the name given to it by the Missourians—*Americans*) raising the earth with its back and shoulders, and forcing it out forward, leaving the aperture open during the process, and from which it at times issues a few steps, cuts the grasses around, with which it fills its pouches, and then retires to its hole to feed upon its spoils; or it sometimes sits up on its haunches and enjoys the sun, and it may then be shot, provided you are quick. If missed you see it no more, as it will prefer altering the course of its burrow and continuing its labors in quite a different direction. They may be caught in common steel-traps, and two of them were thus procured to-day; but they then injure the foot, the hind one. They are also not uncommonly thrown up by the plough, and one was caught in this manner. They have been known to destroy the roots of hundreds of young fruit-trees in the course of a few days and nights, and will cut roots of grown trees of the most valued kinds, such as apple, pear, peach, plum, etc. They differ greatly in their size and also in their colors, according to age, but not in the sexes. The young are usually gray, the old of a dark chestnut, glossy and shining brown, very difficult to represent in a drawing. The opinion commonly received and entertained, that these Pouched Rats fill their pouches with the earth of their burrows, and empty them when at the entrance, is, I think, quite erroneous; about a dozen which were shot in the act of raising their mounds, and killed at the very mouth of their burrows, had no earth in any of these sacs; the fore feet, teeth, nose, and the anterior portion of the head were found covered with adhesive earth, and most of them had their pouches filled either with blades of grass or roots of different sizes; and I think their being hairy rather corroborates the fact that these pouches are only used for food. In a word, they appear to me to raise the earth precisely in the manner employed by the Mole.

When travelling the tail drags on the ground, and they hobble along with their long front claws drawn underneath; at other times, they move by slow leaping movements, and can travel backwards almost as fast as forwards. When turned over they have much difficulty in replacing themselves in their natural position, and you may see them kicking with their legs and claws for a minute or two before they are right. They bite severely, and do not hesitate to make towards their enemies or assailants with open mouth, squealing like a rat. When they fight among themselves they make great use of the nose in the manner of hogs. They cannot travel faster than the slow walk of a man. They feed frequently while seated on the rump, using their fore paws and long claws somewhat like a squirrel. When sleeping they place the head beneath the breast, and become round, and look like a ball of earth.

They clean their whiskers and body in the manner of Rats, Squirrels, etc.

The four which I kept alive never drank anything, though water was given to them. I fed them on potatoes, cabbages, carrots, etc. They tried constantly to make their escape by gnawing at the floor, but in vain. They slept wherever they found clothing, etc., and the rascals cut the lining of my hunting-coat all to bits, so that I was obliged to have it patched and mended. In one instance I had some clothes rolled up for the washerwoman, and, on opening the bundle to count the pieces, one of the fellows caught hold of my right thumb, with fortunately a single one of its upper incisors, and hung on till I shook it off, violently throwing it on the floor, where it lay as if dead; but it recovered, and was as well as ever in less than half an hour. They gnawed the leather straps of my trunks during the night, and although I rose frequently to stop their work, they would begin anew as soon as I was in bed again. I wrote and sent most of the above to John Bachman from St. Louis, after I had finished my drawing of four figures of these most strange and most interesting creatures.

And now to return to this day: When we reached Glasgow, we came in under the stern of the "John Auld." As I saw several officers of the United States army I bowed to them, and as they all knew that I was bound towards the mighty Rocky Mountains, they not only returned my salutations, but came on board, as well as Father de Smet. They all of them came to my room and saw specimens and skins. Among them was Captain Clark, who married the sister of Major Sandford, whom you all know. They had lost a soldier overboard, two had deserted, and a fourth was missing. We proceeded on until about ten o'clock, and it was not until the 2d of May that we actually reached Independence.

May 2. It stopped raining in the night while I was sound asleep, and at about one o'clock we did arrive at Independence, distant about 379 miles from St. Louis. Here again was the "John Auld," putting out freight for the Santa Fé traders, and we saw many of their wagons. Of course I exchanged a hand-shake with Father de Smet and many of the officers I had seen yesterday. Mr. Meeks, the agent of Colonel

Veras, had 148 pounds of tow in readiness for us, and I drew on the Chouteaux for $30.20, for we were charged no less than 12½ to 25 cts. per pound; but this tow might have passed for fine flax, and I was well contented. We left the "Auld," proceeded on our way, and stopped at Madame Chouteau's plantation, where we put out some freight for Sir William Stuart. The water had been two feet deep in her house, but the river has now suddenly fallen about six feet. At Madame Chouteau's I saw a brother of our friend Pierre Chouteau, Senr., now at New York, and he gave me some news respecting the murder of Mr. Jarvis. About twenty picked men of the neighborhood had left in pursuit of the remainder of the marauders, and had sent one of their number back, with the information that they had remained not two miles from the rascally thieves and murderers. I hope they will overtake them all, and shoot them on the spot. We saw a few Squirrels, and Bell killed two Parrakeets.

May 3. We ran all last night and reached Fort Leavenworth at six this morning. We had an early breakfast, as we had intended to walk across the Bend; but we found that the ground was overflowed, and that the bridges across two creeks had been carried away, and reluctantly we gave up our trip. I saw two officers who came on board, also a Mr. Ritchie. The situation of the fort is elevated and fine, and one has a view of the river up and down for some distance. Seeing a great number of Parrakeets, we went after them; Bell killed one. Unfortunately my gun snapped twice, or I should have killed several more. We saw several Turkeys on the ground and in the trees early this morning. On our reaching the landing, a sentinel dragoon came to watch that no one tried to escape.

After leaving this place we fairly entered the Indian country on the west side of the river, for the State of Missouri, by the purchase of the Platte River country, continues for about 250 miles further on the east side, where now we see the only settlements. We saw a good number of Indians in the woods and on the banks, gazing at us as we passed; these are, however, partly civilized, and are miserable enough. Major Mason, who commands here at present, is ill, and I could not see him. We saw several fine horses belonging to different officers. We soon passed Watson, which is considered the head of steam navigation.

In attempting to pass over a shallow, but a short, cut, we grounded on a bar at five o'clock; got off, tried again, and again grounded broadside; and now that it is past six o'clock all hands are busily engaged in trying to get the boat off, but with what success I cannot say. To me the situation is a bad one, as I conceive that as we remain here, the washings of the muddy sands as they float down a powerful current will augment the bar on the weather side (if I may so express myself) of the boat. We have seen another Turkey and many Parrakeets, as well as a great number of burrows formed by the "Siffleurs," as our French Canadians call all and every species of Marmots; Bell and I have concluded that there must be not less than twenty to thirty of these animals for one in any portion of the Atlantic States. We saw them even around the open grounds immediately about Fort Leavenworth.

About half-past seven we fortunately removed our boat into somewhat deeper water, by straightening her bows against the stream, and this was effected by fastening our very long cable to a snag above us, about 200 yards; and now, if we can go backwards and reach the deep waters along shore a few hundred yards below, we shall be able to make fast there for the night. Unfortunately it is now raining hard, the lightning is vivid, and the appearance of the night forbidding.

Thursday, May 4. We had constant rain, lightning and thunder last night. This morning, at the dawn of day, the captain and all hands were at work, and succeeded in removing the boat several hundred yards below where she had struck; but unfortunately we got fast again before we could reach deep water, and all the exertions to get off were renewed, and at this moment, almost nine, we have a line fastened to the shore and expect to be afloat in a short time. But I fear that we shall lose most of the day before we leave this shallow, intricate, and dangerous channel.

At ten o'clock we found ourselves in deep water, near the shore on the west side. We at once had the men at work cutting wood, which was principally that of ash-trees of moderate size, which wood was brought on board in great quantities and lengths. Thank Heaven, we are off in a few minutes, and I hope will have better luck. I saw on the shore many "Gopher" hills, in all probability the same as I have drawn. Bell shot a Gray Squirrel which I believe to be the same as our *Sciurus carolinensis.* Friend Harris shot two or three birds, which we have not yet fully established, and Bell shot one Lincoln's Finch—strange place for it, when it breeds so very far north as Labrador. Caught a Woodpecker, and killed a Catbird, Water-thrush, seventeen Parrakeets, a Yellow Chat, a new Finch, and very curious, two White-throated Finches, one White-crown, a Yellow-rump Warbler, a Gray Squirrel, a Loon, and two Rough-winged Swallows. We saw Cerulean Warblers, Hooded Flycatchers, Kentucky Warblers, Nashville ditto, Blue-winged ditto, Red-eyed and White-eyed Flycatchers, Great-crested and Common Pewees, Redstarts, Towhee Buntings, Ferruginous Thrushes, Wood Thrush, Golden-crowned Thrush, Blue-gray Flycatcher, Blue-eyed Warbler, Blue Yellow-back, Chestnut-sided, Black-and-White Creepers, Nuthatch, Kingbirds, Red Tanagers, Cardinal Grosbeaks, common House Wren, Blue-winged Teals, Swans, large Blue Herons, Crows, Turkey-buzzards, and a Peregrine Falcon, Red-tailed Hawks, Red-headed, Red-bellied, and Golden-winged Woodpeckers, and Partridges. Also, innumerable "Gopher" hills, one Ground-hog, one Rabbit, two Wild Turkeys, one Whippoorwill, one Maryland Yellow-throat, and Swifts. We left the shore with a strong gale of wind, and after having returned to our proper channel, and rounded the island below our troublesome situation of last night, we were forced to come to under the main shore. Here we killed and saw all that is enumerated above, as well as two nests of the White-headed Eagle. We are now for the night at a wooding-place, where we expect to purchase some fresh provisions, if any there are; and as it is nine o'clock I am off to bed.

Friday, May 5. The appearance of the weather this morning was rather bad; it was cloudy and lowering, but instead of rain we have had a strong southwesterly wind to contend with, and on this account our day's work does not amount to much. At this moment, not eight o'clock, we have stopped through its influence.

At half-past twelve we reached the Black Snake Hills settlement, and I was delighted to see this truly beautiful site for a town or city, as will be no doubt some fifty years hence. The hills themselves are about 200 feet above the river, and slope down gently into the beautiful prairie that extends over some thousands of acres, of the richest land imaginable. Five of our trappers did not come on board at the ringing of the bell, and had to walk several miles across a bend to join us and be taken on again. We have not seen much game this day, probably on account of the high wind. We saw, however, a large flock of Willets, two Gulls, one Grebe, many Blue-winged Teals, Wood Ducks, and Coots, and one pair of mated Wild Geese. This afternoon a Black Squirrel was seen. This morning I saw a Marmot; and Sprague, a *Sciurus macrourus* of Say. On examination of the Finch killed by Harris yesterday, I found it to be a new species, and I have taken its measurements across this sheet of paper. It was first seen on the ground, then on low bushes, then on large trees; no note was heard. Two others, that were females to all appearance, could not be procured on account of their extreme shyness. We saw the Indigo-bird, Barn Swallows, Purple Martin, and Greenbacks; also, a Rabbit at the Black Snake Hills. The general aspect of the river is materially altered for the worse; it has become much more crooked or tortuous, in some places very wide with sand-banks naked and dried, so that the wind blows the sand quite high. In one place we came to a narrow and swift chute, four miles above the Black Snake Hills, that in time of extreme high water must be very difficult of ascent. During these high winds it is very hard to steer the boat, and also to land her. The settlers on the Missouri side of the river appear to relish the sight of a steamer greatly, for they all come to look at this one as we pass the different settlements. The thermometer has fallen sixteen degrees since two o'clock, and it feels now very chilly.

Saturday, May 6. High wind all night and cold this morning, with the wind still blowing so hard that at half-past seven we stopped on the western shore, under a range of high hills, but on the weather side of them. We took our guns and went off, but the wind was so high we saw but little; I shot a Wild Pigeon and a Whippoorwill, female, that gave me great trouble, as I never saw one so remarkably wild before. Bell shot two Gray Squirrels and several Vireos, and Sprague, a

Kentucky Warbler. Traces of Turkeys and of Deer were seen.
We also saw three White Pelicans, but no birds to be added to
our previous lot, and I have no wish to keep a strict account
of the number of the same species we daily see. It is now half-
past twelve; the wind is still very high, but our captain is anxious to try to proceed. We have cut some green wood, and a
considerable quantity of hickory for axe-handles. In cutting
down a tree we caught two young Gray Squirrels. A Pewee
Flycatcher, of some species or other, was caught by the stew-
ard, who ran down the poor thing, which was starved on account of the cold and windy weather. Harris shot another of
the new Finches, a male also, and I saw what I believe is the
female, but it flew upwards of 200 yards without stopping.
Bell also shot a small Vireo, which is in all probability a new
species (to me at least). We saw a Goshawk, a Marsh Hawk,
and a great number of Blackbirds, but could not ascertain the
species. The wind was still high when we left our stopping
place, but we progressed, and this afternoon came alongside
of a beautiful prairie of some thousands of acres, reaching to
the hills. Here we stopped to put out our Iowa Indians, and
also to land the goods we had for Mr. Richardson, the Indian
agent. The goods were landed, but at the wrong place, as the
Agent's agent would not receive them there, on account of a
creek above, which cannot at present be crossed with wagons.
Our Sac Indian chief started at once across the prairie towards
the hills, on his way to his wigwam, and we saw Indians on
their way towards us, running on foot, and many on horseback, generally riding double on skins or on Spanish saddles.
Even the squaws rode, and rode well too! We counted about
eighty, amongst whom were a great number of youths of different ages. I was heartily glad that our own squad of them
left us here. I observed that though they had been absent
from their friends and relatives, they never shook hands, or
paid any attention to them. When the freight was taken in we
proceeded, and the whole of the Indians followed along the
shore at a good round run; those on horseback at times
struck into a gallop. I saw more of these poor beings when we
approached the landing, perched and seated on the promon-
tories about, and many followed the boat to the landing.
Here the goods were received, and Major Richardson came

on board, and paid freight. He told us we were now in the country of the Fox Indians as well as that of the Iowas, that the number about him is over 1200, and that his district extends about seventy miles up the river. He appears to be a pleasant man; told us that Hares were very abundant—by the way, Harris saw one to-day. We are now landed on the Missouri side of the river, and taking in wood. We saw a Pigeon Hawk, found Partridges paired, and some also in flocks. When we landed during the high wind we saw a fine sugar camp belonging to Indians. I was pleased to see that many of the troughs they make are formed of bark, and that both ends are puckered and tied so as to resemble a sort of basket or canoe. They had killed many Wild Turkeys, Geese, and Crows, all of which they eat. We also procured a White-eyed and a Warbling Vireo, and shot a male Wild Pigeon. Saw a Gopher throwing out the dirt with his fore feet and not from his pouches. I was within four or five feet of it. Shot a Humming-bird, saw a Mourning Warbler, and Cedar-birds.

May 7, Sunday. Fine weather, but cool. Saw several Gray Squirrels and one Black. I am told by one of our pilots, who has killed seven or eight, that they are much larger than *Sciurus macrourus*, that the hair is coarse, that they are clumsy in their motions, and that they are found from the Black Snake Hills to some distance above the Council Bluffs.

We landed to cut wood at eleven, and we went ashore. Harris killed another of the new Finches, a male also; the scarcity of the females goes on, proving how much earlier the males sally forth on their migrations towards the breeding grounds. We saw five Sand-hill Cranes, some Goldfinches, Yellowshanks, Tell-tale Godwits, Solitary Snipes, and the woods were filled with House Wrens singing their merry songs. The place, however, was a bad one, for it was a piece of bottom land that had overflowed, and was sadly muddy and sticky. At twelve the bell rang for Harris, Bell, and me to return, which we did at once, as dinner was preparing for the table. Talking of dinner makes me think of giving you the hours, usually, of our meals. Breakfast at half-past six, dinner at half-past twelve, tea or supper at seven or later as the case may be. We have not taken much wood here; it is ash, but quite green. We saw Orchard Orioles, Blue-gray Flycatchers, Great-crested and Common Pewees, Mallards, Pileated Woodpeckers, Blue Jays, and Blue-birds; heard a Marsh Wren, saw a Crow, a Wood Thrush, and Water Thrush. Indigo-birds and Parrakeets plentiful. This afternoon we went into the pocket of a sand bar, got aground, and had to back out for almost a mile. We saw an abundance of Ducks, some White Pelicans, and an animal that we guessed was a Skunk. We have run about fifty miles, and therefore have done a good day's journey. We have passed the mouths of several small rivers, and also some very fine prairie land, extending miles towards the hills. It is now nine o'clock, a beautiful night with the moon shining. We have seen several Ravens, and White-headed Eagles on their nests.

May 8, Monday.   A beautiful calm day; the country we saw was much the same as that we passed yesterday, and nothing of great importance took place except that at a wooding-place on the very verge of the State of Missouri (the northwest corner) Bell killed a Black Squirrel which friend Bachman has honored with the name of my son John, *Sciurus Audubonii.* We are told that this species is not uncommon here. It was a good-sized adult male, and Sprague drew an outline of it. Harris shot another specimen of the new Finch. We saw Parrakeets and many small birds, but nothing new or very rare. This evening I wrote a long letter to each house, John Bachman, Gideon B. Smith of Baltimore, and J. W. H. Page of New Bedford, with the hope of having them forwarded from the Council Bluffs.

May 9, Tuesday.   Another fine day. After running until eleven o'clock we stopped to cut wood, and two Rose-breasted Grosbeaks were shot, a common Blue-bird, and a common Northern Titmouse. We saw White Pelicans, Geese, Ducks, etc. One of our trappers cut one of his feet dreadfully with his axe, and Harris, who is now the doctor, attended to it as best he could. This afternoon we reached the famous establishment of Belle Vue where resides the brother of Mr. Sarpy of St. Louis, as well as the Indian Agent, or, as he might be more appropriately called, the Custom House officer. Neither were at home, both away on the Platte River, about 300 miles off. We had a famous pack of rascally Indians awaiting our landing—filthy and half-starved. We landed some cargo for the establishment, and I saw a trick of the trade which made me laugh. Eight cords of wood were paid for with five tin cups of sugar and three of coffee—value at St. Louis about twenty-five cents. We have seen a Fish Hawk, Savannah Finch, Green-backed Swallows, Rough-winged Swallows, Martins, Parrakeets, Black-headed Gulls, Blackbirds, and Cow-birds; I will repeat that the woods are fairly alive with House Wrens. Blue Herons, *Emberiza pallida*—Clay-colored Bunting of Swainson—Henslow's Bunting, Crow Blackbirds; and, more strange than all, two large cakes of ice were seen by our pilots and ourselves. I am very much fatigued and will finish the account of this day to-morrow. At Belle Vue we found the brother-in-law of old Provost, who acts as clerk in the absence of Mr. Sarpy. The store is no great affair, and yet I am told that they drive a good trade with Indians on the Platte River, and others, on this side of the Missouri. We unloaded some freight, and pushed off. We saw here the first ploughing of the ground we have observed since we left the lower settlements near St. Louis. We very soon reached the post of Fort Croghan, so called after my old friend of that name with whom I hunted Raccoons on his father's plantation in Kentucky some thirty-eight years ago, and whose father and my own were well acquainted, and fought together in conjunction with George Washington and Lafayette, during the Revolutionary War, against "Merrie England." Here we found only a few soldiers, dragoons; their camp and officers having been forced to move across the prairie to the Bluffs, five miles. After we had put out some freight for the sutler, we proceeded on until we stopped for the night a few miles above, on the same side of the river. The soldiers assured us that their parade ground, and so-called barracks, had been four feet under water, and we saw fair and sufficient evidence of this. At this place our pilot saw the first Yellow-headed Troupial we have met with. We landed for the night under trees covered by muddy deposits from the great overflow of this season. I slept soundly, and have this morning, May 10, written this.

May 10, Wednesday. The morning was fine, and we were under way at daylight; but a party of dragoons, headed by a

lieutenant, had left their camp four miles distant from our anchorage at the same time, and reached the shore before we
had proceeded far; they fired a couple of rifle shots ahead of
us, and we brought to at once. The young officer came on
board, and presented a letter from his commander, Captain
Burgwin, from which we found that we had to have our cargo
examined. Our captain was glad of it, and so were we all;
for, finding that it would take several hours, we at once ate
our breakfast, and made ready to go ashore. I showed my credentials and orders from the Government, Major Mitchell of
St. Louis, etc., and I was therefore immediately settled comfortably. I desired to go to see the commanding officer, and
the lieutenant very politely sent us there on horseback,
guided by an old dragoon of considerable respectability. I was
mounted on a young white horse, Spanish saddle with holsters, and we proceeded across the prairie towards the Bluffs
and the camp. My guide was anxious to take a short cut, and
took me across several bayous, one of which was really up to
the saddle; but we crossed that, and coming to another we
found it so miry, that his horse wheeled after two or three
steps, whilst I was looking at him before starting myself; for
you all well know that an old traveller is, and must be, prudent. We now had to retrace our steps till we reached the very
tracks that the squad sent after us in the morning had taken,
and at last we reached the foot of the Bluffs, when my guide
asked me if I "could ride at a gallop," to which not answering him, but starting at once at a round run, I neatly passed
him ere his horse was well at the pace; on we went, and in a
few minutes we entered a beautiful dell or valley, and were in
sight of the encampment. We reached this in a trice, and rode
between two lines of pitched tents to one at the end, where I
dismounted, and met Captain Burgwin, a young man,
brought up at West Point, with whom I was on excellent and
friendly terms in less time than it has taken me to write this
account of our meeting. I showed him my credentials, at
which he smiled, and politely assured me that I was too well
known throughout our country to need any letters. While
seated in front of his tent, I heard the note of a bird new to
me, and as it proceeded from a tree above our heads, I looked
up and saw the first Yellow-headed Troupial alive that ever

came across my own migrations. The captain thought me probably crazy, as I thought Rafinesque when he was at Henderson; for I suddenly started, shot at the bird, and killed it. Afterwards I shot three more at one shot, but only one female amid hundreds of these Yellow-headed Blackbirds. They are quite abundant here, feeding on the surplus grain that drops from the horses' troughs; they walked under, and around the horses, with as much confidence as if anywhere else. When they rose, they generally flew to the very tops of the tallest trees, and there, swelling their throats, partially spreading their wings and tail, they issue their croaking note, which is a compound, not to be mistaken, between that of the Crow Blackbird and that of the Red-winged Starling. After I had fired at them twice they became quite shy, and all of them flew off to the prairies. I saw then two Magpies in a cage, that had been caught in nooses, by the legs; and their actions, voice, and general looks, assured me as much as ever, that they are the very same species as that found in Europe. Prairie Wolves are extremely abundant hereabouts. They are so daring that they come into the camp both by day and by night; we found their burrows in the banks and in the prairie, and had I come here yesterday I should have had a superb specimen killed here, but which was devoured by the hogs belonging to the establishment. The captain and the doctor—Madison by name—returned with us to the boat, and we saw many more Yellow-headed Troupials. The high Bluffs back of the prairie are destitute of stones. On my way there I saw abundance of Gopher hills, two Geese paired, two Yellow-crowned Herons, Red-winged Starlings, Cowbirds, common Crow Blackbirds, a great number of Baltimore Orioles, a Swallow-tailed Hawk, Yellow Red-poll Warbler, Field Sparrow, and Chipping Sparrow. Sprague killed another of the beautiful Finch. Robins are very scarce, Parrakeets and Wild Turkeys plentiful. The officers came on board, and we treated them as hospitably as we could; they ate their lunch with us, and are themselves almost destitute of provisions. Last July the captain sent twenty dragoons and as many Indians on a hunt for Buffaloes. During the hunt they killed 51 Buffaloes, 104 Deer, and 10 Elks, within 80 miles of the camp. The Sioux Indians are great enemies to the Potowatamies, and

very frequently kill several of the latter in their predatory excursions against them. This kind of warfare has rendered the
Potowatamies very cowardly, which is quite a remarkable
change from their previous valor and daring. Bell collected six
different species of shells, and found a large lump of pumice
stone which does float on the water. We left our anchorage
(which means tied to the shore) at twelve o'clock, and about
sunset we did pass the real Council Bluff. Here, however, the
bed of the river is utterly changed, though you may yet see
that which is now called the Old Missouri. The Bluffs stand,
truly speaking, on a beautiful bank almost forty feet above the
water, and run off on a rich prairie, to the hills in the background in a gentle slope, that renders the whole place a fine
and very remarkable spot. We tied up for the night about
three miles above them, and all hands went ashore to cut
wood, which begins to be somewhat scarce, of a good quality. Our captain cut and left several cords of green wood for
his return trip, at this place; Harris and Bell went on shore,
and saw several Bats, and three Turkeys. This afternoon a
Deer was seen scampering across the prairies until quite out
of sight. Wild-gooseberry bushes are very abundant, and the
fruit is said to be very good.

May 11, Thursday. We had a night of rain, thunder, and
heavy wind from the northeast, and we did not start this
morning till seven o'clock, therefore had a late breakfast.
There was a bright blood-red streak on the horizon at four
o'clock that looked forbidding, but the weather changed as
we proceeded, with, however, showers of rain at various intervals during the day. We have now come to a portion of the
river more crooked than any we have passed; the shores on
both sides are evidently lower, the hills that curtain the distance are further from the shores, and the intervening space is
mostly prairie, more or less overflowed. We have seen one
Wolf on a sand-bar, seeking for food, perhaps dead fish. The
actions were precisely those of a cur dog with a long tail, and
the bellowing sound of the engine did not seem to disturb
him. He trotted on parallel to the boat for about one mile,
when we landed to cut drift-wood. Bell, Harris, and I went
on shore to try to have a shot at him. He was what is called a
brindle-colored Wolf, of the common size. One hundred

trappers, however, with their axes at work, in a few moments rather stopped his progress, and when he saw us coming, he turned back on his track, and trotted off, but Bell shot a very small load in the air to see the effect it would produce. The fellow took two or three leaps, stopped, looked at us for a moment, and then started on a gentle gallop. When I overtook his tracks they appeared small, and more rounded than usual. I saw several tracks at the same time, therefore more than one had travelled over this great sandy and muddy bar last night, if not this morning. I lost sight of him behind some large piles of drift-wood, and could see him no more. Turkey-buzzards were on the bar, and I thought that I should have found some dead carcass; but on reaching the spot, nothing was there. A fine large Raven passed at one hundred yards from us, but I did not shoot. Bell found a few small shells, and Harris shot a Yellow-rumped Warbler. We have seen several White Pelicans, Geese, Black-headed Gulls, and Green-backed Swallows, but nothing new. The night is cloudy and intimates more rain. We are fast to a willowed shore, and are preparing lines to try our luck at catching a Catfish or so. I was astonished to find how much stiffened I was this morning, from the exercise I took on horseback yesterday, and think that now it would take me a week, at least, to accustom my body to riding as I was wont to do twenty years ago. The timber is becoming more scarce as we proceed, and I greatly fear that our only opportunities of securing wood will be those afforded us by that drifted on the bars.

May 12, Friday. The morning was foggy, thick, and calm. We passed the river called the *Sioux Pictout*, a small stream formerly abounding with Beavers, Otters, Muskrats, etc., but now quite destitute of any of these creatures. On going along the banks bordering a long and wide prairie, thick with willows and other small brush-wood, we saw four Black-tailed Deer immediately on the bank; they trotted away without appearing to be much alarmed; after a few hundred yards, the two largest, probably males, raised themselves on their hind feet and pawed at each other, after the manner of stallions. They trotted off again, stopping often, but after a while disappeared; we saw them again some hundreds of yards farther on, when, becoming suddenly alarmed, they bounded off until out of sight. They did not trot or run irregularly as our Virginian Deer does, and their color was of a brownish cast, whilst our common Deer at this season is red. Could we have gone ashore, we might in all probability have killed one or two of them. We stopped to cut wood on the opposite side of the river, where we went on shore, and there saw many tracks of Deer, Elk, Wolves, and Turkeys. In attempting to cross a muddy place to shoot at some Yellow-headed Troupials that were abundant, I found myself almost mired, and returned with difficulty. We only shot a Blackburnian Warbler, a Yellow-winged ditto, and a few Finches. We have seen more Geese than usual as well as Mallards and Wood Ducks. This afternoon the weather cleared up, and a while before sunset we passed under Wood's Bluffs, so called because a man of that name fell overboard from his boat while drunk. We saw there many Bank Swallows, and afterwards we came in view of the Blackbird Hill, where the famous Indian chief of that name was buried, at his request, on his horse, whilst the animal was alive. We are now fast to the shore opposite this famed bluff. We cut good ash wood this day, and have made a tolerable run, say forty miles.

Saturday, May 13. This morning was extremely foggy, although I could plainly see the orb of day trying to force its way through the haze. While this lasted all hands were engaged in cutting wood, and we did not leave our fastening-place till seven, to the great grief of our commander. During the wood cutting, Bell walked to the top of the hills, and shot two Lark Buntings, males, and a Lincoln's Finch. After a while we passed under some beautiful bluffs surmounted by many cedars, and these bluffs were composed of fine white sandstone, of a soft texture, but very beautiful to the eye. In several places along this bluff we saw clusters of nests of Swallows, which we all looked upon as those of the Cliff Swallow, although I saw not one of the birds. We stopped again to cut wood, for our opportunities are not now very convenient. Went out, but only shot a fine large Turkey-hen, which I brought down on the wing at about forty yards. It ran very swiftly, however, and had not Harris's dog come to our assistance, we might have lost it. As it was, however, the dog pointed, and Harris shot it, with my small shot-gun, whilst I was squatted on the ground amid a parcel of low bushes. I was astonished to see how many of the large shot I had put into her body. This hen weighed 11¾ pounds. She had a nest, no doubt, but we could not find it. We saw a good number of Geese, though fewer than yesterday; Ducks also. We passed many fine prairies, and in one place I was surprised to see the richness of the bottom lands. We saw this morning eleven Indians of the Omaha tribe. They made signals for us to land, but our captain never heeded them, for he hates the red-skins as most men hate the devil. One of them fired a gun, the group had only one, and some ran along the shore for nearly two miles, particularly one old gentleman who per-severed until we came to such bluff shores as calmed down his spirits. In another place we saw one seated on a log, close by the frame of a canoe; but he looked surly, and never altered his position as we passed. The frame of this boat resembled an ordinary canoe. It is formed by both sticks giving a half circle; the upper edges are fastened together by a long stick, as well as the centre of the bottom. Outside of this stretches a Buffalo skin without the hair on; it is said to make a light and safe craft to cross even the turbid, rapid stream—the Missouri. By simply looking at them, one may suppose that they are suf-ficiently large to carry two or three persons. On a sand-bar af-terwards we saw three more Indians, also with a canoe frame, but we only interchanged the common yells usual on such oc-casions. They looked as destitute and as hungry as if they had not eaten for a week, and no doubt would have given much for a bottle of whiskey. At our last landing for wood-cutting, we also went on shore, but shot nothing, not even took aim at a bird; and there was an Indian with a flint-lock rifle, who came on board and stared about until we left, when he went off with a little tobacco. I pity these poor beings from my heart! This evening we came to the burial-ground bluff of Sergeant Floyd, one of the companions of the never-to-be-forgotten expedition of Lewis and Clark, over the Rocky Mountains, to the Pacific Ocean. A few minutes afterwards, before coming to Floyd's Creek, we started several Turkey-cocks from their roost, and had we been on shore could have accounted for more than one of them. The prairies are be-coming more common and more elevated; we have seen more evergreens this day than we have done for two weeks at least. This evening is dark and rainy, with lightning and some distant thunder, and we have entered the mouth of the Big Sioux River, where we are fastened for the night. This is a clear stream and abounds with fish, and on one of the branches of this river is found the famous red clay, of which the precious pipes, or calumets are manufactured. We will try to procure some on our return homeward. It is late; had the weather been clear, and the moon, which is full, shining, it was our intention to go ashore, to try to shoot Wild Turkeys; but as it is pouring down rain, and as dark as pitch, we have thrown our lines overboard and perhaps may catch a fish. We hope to reach Vermilion River day after to-morrow. We saw abundance of the birds which I have before enumerated.

May 14, Sunday. It rained hard and thundered during the night; we started at half-past three, when it had cleared, and the moon shone brightly. The river is crooked as ever, with large bars, and edged with prairies. Saw many Geese, and a Long-billed Curlew. One poor Goose had been wounded in the wing; when approached, it dived for a long distance and came up along the shore. Then we saw a Black Bear, swimming across the river, and it caused a commotion. Some ran for their rifles, and several shots were fired, some of which almost touched Bruin; but he kept on, and swam very fast. Bell shot at it with large shot and must have touched it. When it reached the shore, it tried several times to climb up, but each time fell back. It at last succeeded, almost immediately started off at a gallop, and was soon lost to sight. We stopped to cut wood at twelve o'clock, in one of the vilest places we have yet come to. The rushes were waist-high, and the whole underbrush tangled by grape vines. The Deer and the Elks had beaten paths which we followed for a while, but we saw only their tracks, and those of Turkeys. Harris found a heronry of the common Blue Heron, composed of about thirty nests, but the birds were shy and he did not shoot at any. Early this morning a dead Buffalo floated by us, and after a while the body of a common cow, which had probably belonged to the fort above this. Mr. Sire told us that at this point, two years ago, he overtook three of the deserters of the company, who had left a keel-boat in which they were going down to St.

Louis. They had a canoe when overtaken; he took their guns from them, destroyed the canoe, and left them there. On asking him what had become of them, he said they had walked back to the establishment at the mouth of Vermilion River, which by land is only ten miles distant; ten miles, through such woods as we tried in vain to hunt in, is a walk that I should not like at all. We stayed cutting wood for about two hours, when we started again; but a high wind arose, so that we could not make headway, and had to return and make fast again, only a few hundred yards from the previous spot. On such occasions our captain employs his wood-cutters in felling trees, and splitting and piling the wood until his return downwards, in about one month, perhaps, from now. In talking with our captain he tells us that the Black Bear is rarely seen swimming this river, and that one or two of them are about all he observes on going up each trip. I have seen them swimming in great numbers on the lower parts of the Ohio, and on the Mississippi. It is said that at times, when the common Wolves are extremely hard pressed for food, they will eat certain roots which they dig up for the purpose, and the places from which they take this food look as if they had been spaded. When they hunt a Buffalo, and have killed it, they drag it to some distance—about sixty yards or so—and dig a hole large enough to receive and conceal it; they then cover it with earth, and lie down over it until hungry again, when they uncover, and feed upon it. Along the banks of the rivers, when the Buffaloes fall, or cannot ascend, and then die, the Wolves are seen in considerable numbers feeding upon them. Although cunning beyond belief in hiding at the report of a gun, they almost instantly show themselves from different parts around, and if you wish to kill some, you have only to hide yourself, and you will see them coming to the game you have left, when you are not distant more than thirty or forty yards. It is said that though they very frequently hunt their game until the latter take to the river, they seldom, if ever, follow after it. The wind that drove us ashore augmented into a severe gale, and by its present appearance looks as if it would last the whole night. Our fire was comfortable, for, as you know, the thermometer has been very changeable since noon. We have had rain also, though not continuous, but

quite enough to wet our men, who, notwithstanding have cut
and piled about twelve cords of wood, besides the large quantity we have on board for to-morrow, when we hope the
weather will be good and calm.

May 15, Monday.   The wind continued an irregular gale the
whole of the night, and the frequent logs that struck our
weather side kept me awake until nearly daybreak, when I
slept about two hours; it unfortunately happened that we
were made fast upon the weather shore. This morning the
gale kept up, and as we had nothing better to do, it was proposed that we should walk across the bottom lands, and attempt to go to the prairies, distant about two and a half miles.
This was accordingly done; Bell, Harris, Mr. La Barge—the
first pilot—a mulatto hunter named Michaux, and I, started at
nine. We first crossed through tangled brush-wood, and high-
grown rushes for a few hundreds of yards, and soon perceived
that here, as well as all along the Missouri and Mississippi, the
land is highest nearest the shore, and falls off the farther one
goes inland. Thus we soon came to mud, and from mud to
muddy water, as *pure* as it runs in the Missouri itself; at every
step which we took we raised several pounds of mud on our
boots. Friend Harris very wisely returned, but the remainder
of us proceeded through thick and thin until we came in sight
of the prairies. But, alas! between us and them there existed a
regular line of willows—and who ever saw willows grow far
from water? Here we were of course stopped, and after attempting in many places to cross the water that divided us
from the dry land, we were forced back, and had to return as
best we could. We were mud up to the very middle, the perspiration ran down us, and at one time I was nearly exhausted; which proves to me pretty clearly that I am no
longer as young, or as active, as I was some thirty years ago.
When we reached the boat I was glad of it. We washed,
changed our clothes, dined, and felt much refreshed. During
our excursion out, Bell saw a Virginian Rail, and our sense of
smell brought us to a dead Elk, putrid, and largely consumed
by Wolves, whose tracks were very numerous about it. After
dinner we went to the heronry that Harris had seen yesterday
afternoon; for we had moved only one mile above the place
of our wooding before we were again forced on shore. Here

we killed four fine individuals, all on the wing, and some capital shots they were, besides a Raven. Unfortunately we had many followers, who destroyed our sport; therefore we returned on board, and at half-past four left our landing-place, having cut and piled up between forty and fifty cords of wood for the return of the "Omega." The wind has lulled down considerably, we have run seven or eight miles, and are again fast to the shore. It is reported that the water has risen two feet, but this is somewhat doubtful. We saw abundance of tracks of Elk, Deer, Wolf, and Bear, and had it been anything like tolerably dry ground, we should have had a good deal of sport. Saw this evening another dead Buffalo floating down the river.

May 16, Tuesday. At three o'clock this fair morning we were under way, but the water has actually risen a great deal, say three feet, since Sunday noon. The current therefore is very strong, and impedes our progress greatly. We found that the Herons we had killed yesterday had not yet laid the whole of their eggs, as we found one in full order, ripe, and well colored and conditioned. I feel assured that the Ravens destroy a great many of their eggs, as I saw one helping itself to two eggs, at two different times, on the same nest. We have seen a great number of Black-headed Gulls, and some Black Terns, some Indians on the east side of the river, and a Prairie Wolf, dead, hung across a prong of a tree. After a while we reached a spot where we saw ten or more Indians who had a large log cabin, and a field under fence. Then we came to the establishment called that of Vermilion River, and met Mr. Cerré, called usually Pascal, the agent of the Company at this post, a handsome French gentleman, of good manners. He dined with us. After this we landed, and walked to the fort, if the place may so be called, for we found it only a square, strongly picketed, without portholes. It stands on the immediate bank of the river, opposite a long and narrow island, and is backed by a vast prairie, all of which was inundated during the spring freshet. He told me that game was abundant, such as Elk, Deer, and Bear; but that Ducks, Geese, and Swans were extremely scarce this season. Hares are plenty—no Rabbits. We left as soon as possible, for our captain is a pushing man most truly. We passed some remarkable bluffs of blue and light limestone, towards the top of which we saw an abundance of Cliff-Swallows, and counted upwards of two hundred nests. But, alas! we have finally met with an accident. A plate of one of our boilers was found to be burned out, and we were obliged to stop on the west side of the river, about ten miles below the mouth of the Vermilion River. Here we were told that we might go ashore and hunt to our hearts' content; and so I have, but shot at nothing. Bell, Michaux, and I, walked to the hills full three miles off, saw an extraordinary quantity of Deer, Wolf, and Elk tracks, as well as some of Wild Cats. Bell started a Deer, and after a while I heard him shoot. Michaux took to the top of the hills, Bell about midway, and I followed near the bottom; all in vain, however. I started a Woodcock, and caught one of her young, and I am now sorry for this evil deed. A dead Buffalo cow and calf passed us a few moments ago. Squires has seen one other, during our absence. We took at Mr. Cerré's establishment two *engagés* and four Sioux Indians. We are obliged to keep bright eyes upon them, for they are singularly light-fingered. The woods are filled with wild-gooseberry bushes, and a kind of small locust not yet in bloom, and quite new to me. The honey bee was not found in this country twenty years ago, and now they are abundant. A keel-boat passed, going down, but on the opposite side of the river. Bell and Michaux have returned. Bell wounded a large Wolf, and also a young Deer, but brought none on board, though he saw several of the latter. Harris killed one of the large new Finches, and a Yellow-headed Troupial. Bell intends going hunting to-morrow at daylight, with Michaux; I will try my luck too, but do not intend going till after breakfast, for I find that walking eight or ten miles through the tangled and thorny underbrush, fatigues me considerably, though twenty years ago I should have thought nothing of it.

May 17, Wednesday. This was a most lovely morning. Bell went off with Michaux at four A. M. I breakfasted at five, and started with Mr. La Barge. When we reached the hunting-grounds, about six miles distant, we saw Bell making signs to us to go to him, and I knew from that that they had some fresh meat. When we reached them, we found a very large Deer that Michaux had killed. Squires shot a Woodcock, which I ate for my dinner, in company with the captain. Michaux had brought the Deer—Indian fashion—about two miles. I was anxious to examine some of the intestines, and we all three started on the tracks of Michaux, leaving Squires to keep the Wolves away from the dead Deer. We went at once towards a small stream meandering at the foot of the hills, and as we followed it, Bell shot at a Turkey-cock about eighty yards; his ball cut a streak of feathers from its back, but the gobbler went off. When we approached the spot where Michaux had opened the Deer, we did so cautiously, in the hope of then shooting a Wolf, but none had come; we therefore made our observations, and took up the tongue, which had been forgotten. Bell joined us, and as we were returning to Squires we saw flocks of the Chestnut-collared Lark or Ground-finch, whose exact measurement I have here given, and almost at the same time saw Harris. He and Bell went off after the Finches; we pursued our course to Squires, and waited for their return. Seeing no men to help carry the Deer, Michaux picked it up, Squires took his gun, etc., and we made for the river again. We had the good luck to meet the barge coming, and we reached our boat easily in a few minutes, with our game. I saw upwards of twelve of Harris' new Finch (?) a Marsh Hawk, Henslow's Bunting, *Emberiza pallida*, Robins, Wood Thrushes, Bluebirds, Ravens, the same abundance of House Wrens, and all the birds already enumerated. We have seen floating eight Buffaloes, one Antelope, and one Deer; how great the destruction of these animals must be during high freshets! The cause of their being drowned in such extraordinary numbers might not astonish one acquainted with the habits of these animals, but to one who is not, it may be well enough for me to describe it. Some few hundred miles above us, the river becomes confined between high bluffs or cliffs, many of which are nearly perpendicular, and therefore extremely difficult to ascend. When the Buffaloes have leaped or tumbled down from either side of the stream, they swim with ease across, but on reaching these walls, as it were, the poor animals try in vain to climb them, and becoming exhausted by falling back some dozens of times, give up the ghost, and float down the turbid stream; their bodies have been known to pass, swollen and putrid, the city of St. Louis. The most extraordinary part of the history of these drowned Buffaloes is, that the different tribes of Indians on the shores, are ever on the lookout for them, and no matter how putrid their flesh may be, provided the hump proves at all fat, they swim to them, drag them on shore, and cut them to pieces; after which they cook and eat this loathsome and abominable flesh, even to the marrow found in the bones. In some instances this has been done when the whole of the hair had fallen off, from the rottenness of the Buffalo. Ah! Mr. Catlin, I am now sorry to see and to read your accounts of the Indians *you* saw—how very different they must have been from any that I have seen! Whilst we were on the top of the high hills which we climbed this morning, and looked towards the valley beneath us, including the river, we were undetermined as to whether we saw as much land dry as land overflowed; the immense flat prairie on the east side of the river looked not unlike a lake of great expanse, and immediately beneath us the last freshet had left upwards of perhaps two or three hundred acres covered by water, with numbers of water fowl on it, but so difficult of access as to render our wishes to kill Ducks quite out of the question. From the tops of the hills we saw only a continual succession of other lakes, of the same form and nature; and although the soil was of a fair, or even good, quality, the grass grew in tufts, separated from each other, and as it grows green in one spot, it dies and turns brown in another. We saw here no "carpeted prairies," no "velvety distant landscape;" and if these things are to be seen, why, the sooner we reach them the better. This afternoon I took the old nest of a Vireo, fully three feet above my head, filled with dried mud; it was attached to two small prongs issuing from a branch fully the size of my arm; this proves how high the water must have risen. Again, we saw large trees of which the bark had been torn off by the rubbing or cutting of the ice, as high as my shoulder. This is accounted for as follows: during the first breaking up of the ice, it at times accumulates, so as to form a complete dam across the river; and when this suddenly gives way by the heat of the atmosphere, and the great pressure of the waters above the dam, the whole rushes on suddenly and overflows the country around, hurling the ice against any trees in its course.

Sprague has shot two *Emberiza pallida*, two Lincoln's Finches, and a Black and Yellow Warbler, *Sylvicola maculosa*. One of our trappers, who had gone to the hills, brought on board two Rattlesnakes of a kind which neither Harris nor myself had seen before. The four Indians we have on board are three Puncas and one Sioux; the Puncas were formerly attached to the Omahas; but, having had some difficulties among themselves, they retired further up the river, and assumed this new name. The Omahas reside altogether on the west side of the Missouri. Three of the Puncas have walked off to the establishment of Mr. Cerré to procure moccasins, but will return to-night. They appear to be very poor, and with much greater appetites than friend Catlin describes them to have. Our men are stupid, and very superstitious; they believe the rattles of snakes are a perfect cure for the headache; also, that they never die till after sunset, etc. We have discovered the female of Harris's Finch, which, as well as in the White-crowned Finch, resembles the male almost entirely; it is only a very little paler in its markings. I am truly proud to name it *Fringilla Harrisii*, in honor of one of the best friends I have in this world.

May 18, Thursday. Our good captain called us all up at a quarter before four this fair morning, to tell us that four barges had arrived from Fort Pierre, and that we might write a few letters, which Mr. Laidlow, one of the partners, would take to St. Louis for us. I was introduced to that gentleman and also to Major Dripps, the Indian agent. I wrote four short letters, which I put in an envelope addressed to the Messieurs Chouteau & Co., of St. Louis, who will post them, and we have hopes that some may reach their destination. The names of these four boats are "War Eagle," "White Cloud," "Crow-feather," and "Red-fish." We went on board one of them, and found it comfortable enough. They had ten thousand Buffalo robes on the four boats; the men live entirely on Buffalo meat and pemmican. They told us that about a hundred miles above us the Buffalo were by thousands, that the prairies were covered with dead calves, and the shores lined with dead of all sorts; that Antelopes were there also, and a great number of Wolves, etc.; therefore we shall see them after a while. Mr. Laidlow told me that he would be

back at Fort Pierre in two months, and would see us on our
return. He is a true Scot, and apparently a clean one. We gave
them six bottles of whiskey, for which they were very thankful; they gave us dried Buffalo meat, and three pairs of moccasins. They breakfasted with us, preferring salt meat to fresh
venison. They departed soon after six o'clock, and proceeded
rapidly down-stream in Indian file. These boats are strong and
broad; the tops, or roofs, are supported by bent branches of
trees, and these are covered by water-proof Buffalo hides;
each has four oarsmen and a steersman, who manages the
boat standing on a broad board; the helm is about ten feet
long, and the rudder itself is five or six feet long. They row
constantly for sixteen hours, and stop regularly at sundown;
they, unfortunately for us, spent the night about two miles
above us, for had we known of their immediate proximity we
should have had the whole of the night granted for writing
long, long letters. Our prospect of starting to-day is somewhat doubtful, as the hammering at the boilers still reaches
my ears. The day is bright and calm. Mr. Laidlow told us that
on the 5th of May the snow fell two feet on the level, and destroyed thousands of Buffalo calves. We felt the same storm
whilst we were fast on the bar above Fort Leavenworth. This
has been a day of almost pure idleness; our tramps of yesterday and the day previous had tired me, and with the exception of shooting at marks, and Sprague killing one of Bell's
Vireo, and a Least Pewee, as well as another female of
Harris's Finch, we have done nothing. Bell this evening went
off to look for Bats, but saw none.

May 19, Friday.   This has been a beautiful, but a very dull
day to us all. We started by moonlight at three this morning,
and although we have been running constantly, we took the
wrong channel twice, and thereby lost much of our precious
time; so I look upon this day's travel as a very poor one. The
river was in several places inexpressibly wide and shallow. We
saw a Deer of the common kind swimming across the stream;
but few birds were killed, although we stopped (unfortunately) three times for wood. I forgot to say yesterday two
things which I should have related, one of which is of a dismal and very disagreeable nature, being no less than the account given us of the clerks of the Company having killed one

of the chiefs of the Blackfeet tribe of Indians, at the upper settlement of the Company, at the foot of the great falls of the
Missouri, and therefore at the base of the Rocky Mountains,
and Mr. Laidlow assured us that it would be extremely dangerous for us to go that far towards these Indians. The other
thing is that Mr. Laidlow brought down a daughter of his, a
half-breed of course, whom he is taking to St. Louis to be ed-
ucated. We saw another Deer crossing the river, and have shot
only a few birds, of no consequence.

May 20, Saturday. We have not made much progress this
day, for the wind rose early, and rather ahead. We have passed
to-day Jacques River, or, as I should call it, La Rivière à
Jacques, named after a man who some twenty or more years
ago settled upon its banks, and made some money by collecting Beavers, etc., but who is dead and gone. Three White
Wolves were seen this morning, and after a while we saw a
fourth, of the brindled kind, which was trotting leisurely on,
about 150 yards distant from the bank, where he had probably
been feeding on some carrion or other. A shot from a rifle was
quite enough to make him turn off up the river again, but farther from us, at a full gallop; after a time he stopped again,
when the noise of our steam pipe started him, and we soon
lost sight of him in the bushes. We saw three Deer in the flat
of one of the prairies, and just before our dinner we saw,
rather indistinctly, a number of Buffaloes, making their way
across the hills about two miles distant; after which, however,
we saw their heavy tracks in a well and deep cut line across the
said hills. Therefore we are now in what is pronounced to be
the "Buffalo country," and may expect to see more of these
animals to-morrow. We have stopped for wood no less than
three times this day, and are fast for the night. Sprague killed
a *Pipilo arcticus*, and Bell three others of the same species. We
procured also another Bat, the *Vespertilio subulatus* of Say,
and this is all. The country around us has materially changed,
and we now see more naked, and to my eyes more completely
denuded, hills about us, and less of the rich bottoms of alluvial land, than we passed below our present situation. I will
not anticipate the future by all that we hear of the country
above, but will continue steadily to accumulate in this, my
poor journal, all that may take place from day to day. Three

of our Indian rascals left us at our last wooding-ground, and have gone towards their miserable village. We have now only one Sioux with us, who will, the captain says, go to Fort Pierre in our company. They are, all that we have had as yet, a thieving and dirty set, covered with vermin. We still see a great number of Black-headed Gulls, but I think fewer Geese and Ducks than below; this probably on account of the very swampy prairie we have seen, and which appears to become scarce as we are advancing in this strange wilderness.

May 21, Sunday. We have had a great deal that interested us all this day. In the first place we have passed no less than five of what are called rivers, and their names are as follows: Manuel, Basil, L'Eau qui Court, Ponca Creek, and Chouteau's River, all of which are indifferent streams of no magnitude, except the swift-flowing L'Eau qui Court, which in some places is fully as broad as the Missouri itself, fully as muddy, filled with quicksands, and so remarkably shallow that in the autumn its navigation is very difficult indeed. We have seen this day about fifty Buffaloes; two which we saw had taken to the river, with intent to swim across it, but on the approach of our thundering, noisy vessel, turned about and after struggling for a few minutes, did make out to reach the top of the bank, after which they travelled at a moderate gait for some hundreds of yards; then, perhaps smelling or seeing the steamboat, they went off at a good though not very fast gallop, on the prairie by our side, and were soon somewhat ahead of us; they stopped once or twice, again resumed their gallop, and after a few diversions in their course, made to the hill-tops and disappeared altogether. We stopped to wood at a very propitious place indeed, for it was no less than the fort put up some years ago by Monsieur Le Clerc. Finding no one at the spot, we went to work cutting the pickets off his fortifications till we were loaded with the very best of dry wood. After we left that spot, were found several *Pipilo arcticus* which were shot, as well as a Say's Flycatcher. The wind rose pretty high, and after trying our best to stem the current under very high cliffs, we were landed on Poncas Island, where all of us excepting Squires, who was asleep, went on shore to hunt, and to shoot whatever we might find. It happened that this island was well supplied with game; we saw many Deer, and Bell killed a young Doe, which proved good as fresh meat. Some twelve or fourteen of these animals were seen, and Bell saw three Elks which he followed across the island, also a Wolf in its hole, but did not kill it. Sprague saw a Forked-tailed Hawk, too far off to shoot at. We passed several dead Buffaloes near the shore, on which the Ravens were feeding gloriously. The *Pipilo arcticus* is now extremely abundant, and so is the House Wren, Yellow-breasted Chat, etc. We have seen this day Black-headed Gulls, Sandpipers, and Ducks, and now I am going to rest, for after my long walk through the deep mud to reach the ridge on the islands, I feel somewhat wearied and fatigued. Three Antelopes were seen this evening.

May 22, Monday. We started as early as usual, *i. e.*, at half-past three; the weather was fine. We breakfasted before six, and immediately after saw two Wild Cats of the common kind; we saw them running for some hundreds of yards. We also saw several large Wolves, noticing particularly one pure white, that stood and looked at us for some time. Their movements are precisely those of the common cur dog. We have seen five or six this day. We began seeing Buffaloes again in small gangs, but this afternoon and evening we have seen a goodly number, probably more than a hundred. We also saw fifteen or twenty Antelopes. I saw ten at once, and it was beautiful to see them running from the top of a high hill down to its base, after which they went round the same hill, and were lost to us. We have landed three times to cut wood, and are now busy at it on Cedar Island. At both the previous islands we saw an immense number of Buffalo tracks, more, indeed, than I had anticipated. The whole of the prairies as well as the hills have been so trampled by them that I should have considered it quite unsafe for a man to travel on horseback. The ground was literally covered with their tracks, and also with bunches of hair, while the bushes and the trunks of the trees, between which they had passed, were hanging with the latter substance. I collected some, and intend to carry a good deal home. We found here an abundance of what is called the White Apple, but which is anything else but an apple. The fruit grows under the ground about six inches; it is about the size of a hen's egg, covered with a woody, hard pellicle, a sixteenth of an inch thick, from which the fruit can be drawn without much difficulty; this is quite white; the exterior is a dirty, dark brown. The roots are woody. The flowers were not in bloom, but I perceived that the leaves are ovate, and attached in fives. This plant is collected in great quantities by the Indians at this season and during the whole summer, and put to dry, which renders it as hard as wood; it is then pounded fine, and makes an excellent kind of mush, upon which the Indians feed greedily. I will take some home. We found pieces of crystallized gypsum; we saw Meadow Larks whose songs and single notes are quite different from those of the Eastern States; we have not yet been able to kill one to decide if new or not. We have seen the Arkansas Flycatcher, Sparrow-hawks, Geese, etc. The country grows poorer as we ascend; the bluffs exhibit oxide of iron, sulphur, and also magnesia. We have made a good day's run, though the wind blew rather fresh from the northwest. Harris shot a Marsh Hawk, Sprague a Nighthawk, and some small birds, and I saw Martins breeding in Woodpeckers' holes in high and large cotton-trees. We passed the "Grand Town" very early this morning; I did not see it, however. Could we have remained on shore at several places that we passed, we should have made havoc with the Buffaloes, no doubt; but we shall have enough of that sport ere long. They all look extremely poor and shabby; we see them sporting among themselves, butting and tearing up the earth, and when at a gallop they throw up the dust behind them. We saw their tracks all along both shores; where they have landed and are unable to get up the steep cliffs, they follow along the margin till they reach a ravine, and then make their way to the hills, and again to the valleys; they also have roads to return to the river to drink. They appear at this season more on the west side of the Missouri. The Elks, on the contrary, are found on the islands and low bottoms, well covered with timber; the common Deer is found indifferently everywhere. All the Antelopes we have seen were on the west side. After we had left our first landing-place a few miles, we observed some seven or eight Indians looking at us, and again retiring to the woods, as if to cover themselves; when we came nearly opposite them, however, they all came to the shore, and made signs to induce us to land. The boat did not stop for their pleasure, and after we had fairly passed them they began firing at us, not with blank cartridges, but with well-directed rifle-balls, several of which struck the "Omega" in different places. I was standing at that moment by one of the chimneys, and saw a ball strike the water a few feet beyond our bows; and Michaux, the hunter, heard its passing within a few inches of his head. A Scotchman, who was asleep below, was awakened and greatly frightened by hearing a ball pass through the partition, cutting the lower part of his pantaloons, and deadening itself against a trunk. Fortunately no one was hurt. Those rascals were attached to a war party, and belong to the Santee tribes which range across the country from the Mississippi to the Missouri. I will make no comment upon their conduct, but I have two of the balls that struck our boat; it seems to be a wonder that not one person was injured, standing on deck as we were to the number of a hundred or more. We have not seen Parrakeets or Squirrels for several days; Partridges have also deserted us, as well as Rabbits; we have seen Barn Swallows, but no more Rough-winged. We have yet plenty of Red-headed Woodpeckers. Our captain has just sent out four hunters this evening, who are to hunt early to-morrow morning, and will meet the boat some distance above; Squires has gone with them. How I wish I were twenty-five years younger! I should like such a tramp greatly; but I do not think it prudent now for me to sleep on the ground when I can help it, while it is so damp.

May 23, Tuesday. The wind blew from the south this morning and rather stiffly. We rose early, and walked about this famous Cedar Island, where we stopped to cut large red cedars for one and a half hours; we started at half-past five, breakfasted rather before six, and were on the lookout for our hunters. *Hunters!* Only two of them had ever been on a Buffalo hunt before. One was lost almost in sight of the river. They only walked two or three miles, and camped. Poor Squires' first experience was a very rough one; for, although they made a good fire at first, it never was tended afterwards, and his pillow was formed of a buck's horn accidentally picked up near the place. Our Sioux Indian helped himself to another, and they all felt chilly and damp. They had forgotten to take any spirits with them, and their condition was miserable. As the orb of day rose as red as blood, the party started, each taking a different direction. But the wind was unfavorable; it blew up, not down the river, and the Buffaloes, Wolves, Antelopes, and indeed every animal possessed of the sense of smell, had scent of them in time to avoid them. There happened however to be attached to this party two good and true men, that may be called hunters. One was Michaux; the other a friend of his, whose name I do not know. It happened, by hook or by crook, that these two managed to kill four Buffaloes; but one of them was drowned, as it took to the river after being shot. Only a few pieces from a young bull, and its tongue, were brought on board, most of the men being too lazy, or too far off, to cut out even the tongues of the others; and thus it is that thousands multiplied by thousands of Buffaloes are murdered in senseless play, and their enormous carcasses are suffered to be the prey of the Wolf, the Raven and the Buzzard. However, the hunters all returned safely to the boat, and we took them in, some tired enough, among whom was friend Squires. He had worn out his moccasins, and his feet were sore, blistered, and swollen; he was thirsty enough too, for in taking a drink he had gone to a beautiful clear spring that unfortunately proved to be one of magnesia, which is common enough in this part of our country, and this much increased his thirst. He drank four tumblers of water first, then a glass of grog, ate somewhat of a breakfast, and went to bed, whence I called him a few minutes before dinner. However, he saw some Buffaloes, and had hopes of shooting one, also about twenty Antelopes. Michaux saw two very large White Wolves. At the place where we decided to take the fatigued party in, we stopped to cut down a few dead cedars, and Harris shot a common Rabbit and one Lark Finch. Bell and Sprague saw several Meadow-larks, which I trust will prove new, as these birds have quite different notes and songs from those of our eastern birds. They brought a curious cactus, some handsome well-scented dwarf peas, and several other plants unknown to me. On the island I found abundance of dwarf wild-cherry bushes in full blossom, and we have placed all these plants in press. We had the misfortune to get aground whilst at dinner, and are now fast till to-morrow morning; for all our efforts to get the boat off, and they have been many, have proved ineffectual. It is a bad spot, for we are nearly halfway from either shore. I continued my long letter for home, and wrote the greatest portion of another long one to John Bachman. I intend to write till a late hour this night, as perchance we may reach Fort Pierre early next week.

May 24, Wednesday. We remained on the sand bar till four this afternoon. The wind blew hard all day. A boat from Fort Pierre containing two men passed us, bound for Fort Vermilion; one of them was Mr. Charity, one of the Company's associate traders. The boat was somewhat of a curiosity, being built in the form of a scow; but instead of being made of wood, had only a frame, covered with Buffalo skins with the hair on. They had been nine days coming 150 miles, detained every day, more or less, by Indians. Mr. Charity gave me some leather prepared for moccasins—for a consideration, of course. We have seen Buffaloes, etc., but the most important animal to us was one of Townsend's Hare. We shot four Meadow-larks that have, as I said, other songs and notes than ours, but could not establish them as new. We procured a Red-shafted Woodpecker, two Sparrow-hawks, two Arkansas Flycatchers, a Blue Grosbeak, saw Say's Flycatcher, etc. I went on shore with Harris's small double-barrelled gun, and the first shot I had was pretty near killing me; the cone blew off, and passed so near my ear that I was stunned, and fell down as if shot, and afterwards I was obliged to lie down for several minutes. I returned on board, glad indeed that the accident was no greater. We passed this afternoon bluffs of sulphur, almost pure to look at, and a patch that has burnt for two years in succession. Alum was found strewn on the shores. A toad was brought, supposed to be new by Harris and Bell. We landed for the night on an island so thick with underbrush that it was no easy matter to walk through; perhaps a hundred Buffalo calves were dead in it, and the smell was not pleasant, as you may imagine. The boat of Mr. Charity went off when we reached the shore, after having escaped from the bar. We have seen more White Wolves this day, and few Antelopes. The whole country is trodden down by the heavy Buffaloes, and this renders the walking both fatiguing and somewhat dangerous. The garlic of this country has a red blossom, otherwise it looks much like ours; when Buffalo have fed for some time on this rank weed, their flesh cannot be eaten.

May 25, Thursday. The weather looked cloudy, and promised much rain when we rose this morning at five o'clock; our men kept busy cutting and bringing wood until six, when the "Omega" got under way. It began raining very soon afterwards and it has continued to this present moment. The dampness brought on a chilliness that made us have fires in each of the great cabins. Michaux brought me two specimens of *Neotoma floridana*, so young that their eyes were not open. The nest was found in the hollow of a tree cut down for firewood. Two or three miles above us, we saw three Mackinaw barges on the shore, just such as I have described before; all these belonged to the (so-called) Opposition Company of C. Bolton, Fox, Livingstone & Co., of New York, and therefore we passed them without stopping; but we had to follow their example a few hundred yards above them, for we had to stop also; and then some of the men came on board, to see and talk to their old acquaintances among our extraordinary and motley crew of trappers and *engagés*. On the roofs of the barges lay much Buffalo meat, and on the island we left this morning probably some hundreds of these poor animals, mostly young calves, were found dead at every few steps; and since then we have passed many dead as well as many groups of living. In one place we saw a large gang swimming across the river; they fortunately reached a bank through which they cut their way towards the hills, and marched slowly and steadily on, paying no attention to our boat, as this was far to the lee of them. At another place on the west bank, we saw eight or ten, or perhaps more, Antelopes or Deer of some kind or other, but could not decide whether they were the one or the other. These animals were all lying down, which would be contrary to the general habit of our common Deer, which never lie down during rain, that I am aware of. We have had an extremely dull day of it, as one could hardly venture out of the cabin for pleasure. We met with several difficulties among sand-bars. At three o'clock we passed the entrance into the stream known as White River; half an hour ago we were obliged to land, and send the yawl to try for the channel, but we are now again on our way, and have still the hope of reaching Great Cedar Island this evening, where we must stop to cut wood.—*Later.* Our attempt to reach the island I fear will prove abortive, as we are once more at a standstill for want of deeper water, and the yawl has again gone ahead to feel for a channel. Within the last mile or so, we must have passed upwards of a hundred drowned young Buffalo calves, and many large ones. I will await the moment when we must make fast somewhere, as it is now past eight o'clock. The rain has ceased, and the weather has the appearance of a better day to-morrow, overhead at least. Now it is after nine o'clock; we are fastened to the shore, and I will, for the first time since I left St. Louis, sleep in my cabin, and between sheets.

May 26, Friday. The weather was fine, but we moved extremely slowly, not having made more than ten miles by twelve o'clock. The captain arranged all his papers for Fort Pierre. Three of the best walkers, well acquainted with the road, were picked from among our singularly mixed crew of *engagés*, and were put ashore at Big Bend Creek, on the banks of a high cliff on the western side; they ascended through a ravine, and soon were out of sight. We had stopped previously to cut wood, where our men had to lug it fully a quarter of a mile. We ourselves landed of course, but found the prairie so completely trodden by Buffaloes that it was next to impossible to walk. Notwithstanding this, however, a few birds were procured. The boat continued on with much difficulty, being often stopped for the want of water. At one place we counted over a hundred dead Buffalo calves; we saw a great number, however, that did reach the top of the bank, and proceeded to feeding at once. We saw one animal, quite alone, wading and swimming alternately, till it had nearly crossed the river, when for reasons unknown to us, and when only about fifty yards from the land, it suddenly turned about, and swam and waded back to the western side, whence it had originally come; this fellow moved through the water as represented in this very imperfect sketch, which I have placed here, and with his tail forming nearly half a circle by its erection during the time he swam. It was mired on several occasions while passing from one shoal or sand-bar to another. It walked, trotted, or galloped, while on the solid beach, and ultimately, by swimming a few hundred yards, returned to the side from whence it had started, though fully half a mile below the exact spot. There now was heard on board some talk about the *Great Bend*, and the captain asked me whether I would like to go off and camp, and await his arrival on the other side tomorrow. I assured him that nothing would give us more pleasure, and he gave us three stout young men to go with us to carry our blankets, provisions, etc., and to act as guides and hunters. All was ready by about five of the afternoon, when Harris, Bell, Sprague, and I, as well as the three men, were put ashore; and off we went at a brisk walk across a beautiful, level prairie, whereon in sundry directions we could see small groups of Buffaloes, grazing at leisure. Proceeding along, we saw a great number of Cactus, some Bartram Sandpipers, and a Long-billed Curlew. Presently we observed a village of prairie Marmots, *Arctomys ludovicianus*, and two or three of our party diverged at once to pay them their respects. The mounds which I passed were very low indeed; the holes were opened, but I saw not one of the owners. Harris, Bell, and Michaux, I believe, shot at some of them, but killed none, and we proceeded on, being somewhat anxious to pitch our camp for the night before dark. Presently we reached the hills and were surprised at their composition; the surface looked as if closely covered with small broken particles of coal, whilst the soil was of such greasy or soapy nature, that it was both painful and fatiguing to ascend them. Our guides assured us that such places were never in any other condition, or as they expressed it, were "never dry." Whilst travelling about these remarkable hills, Sprague saw one of Townsend's Hare, and we started the first and only Prairie Hen we have seen since our departure from St. Louis. Gradually we rose on to the very uppermost crest of the hills we had to cross, and whilst reposing ourselves for some minutes we had the gratification of seeing around us one of the great panoramas this remarkable portion of our country affords. There was a vast extent of country beneath and around us. Westward rose the famous Medicine Hill, and in the opposite direction were the wanderings of the Missouri for many miles, and from the distance we were then from it, the river appeared as if a small, very circuitous streamlet. The Great Bend was all in full view, and its course almost resembled that of a chemist's retort, being formed somewhat like the scratch of my pen thus:—

The walk from our landing crossing the prairies was quite four miles, whilst the distance by water is computed to be twenty-six. From the pinnacle we stood on, we could see the movements of our boat quite well, and whilst the men were employed cutting wood for her engines, we could almost count every stroke of their axes, though fully two miles distant, as the crow flies. As we advanced we soon found ourselves on the ridges leading us across the Bend, and plainly saw that we were descending towards the Missouri once more. *Chemin faisant*, we saw four Black-tailed Deer, a shot at which Michaux or Bell, who were in advance, might perhaps have had, had not Harris and Sprague taken a route across the declivity before them, and being observed by these keen-sighted animals, the whole made off at once. I had no fair opportunity of witnessing their movements; but they looked swiftness itself, combined with grace. They were not followed, and we reached the river at a spot which evidently had been previously camped on by Indians; here we made our minds up to stop at once, and arrange for the night, which now promised to be none of the fairest. One man remained with us to prepare the camp, whilst Michaux and the others started in search of game, as if blood-hounds. Meantime we lighted a large and glowing fire, and began preparing some supper. In less than half an hour Michaux was seen to return with a load on his back, which proved to be a fine young buck of the Black-tailed Deer. This produced animation at once. I examined it carefully, and Harris and Sprague returned promptly from the point to which they had gone. The darkness of the night, contrasting with the vivid glare of our fire, which threw a bright light on the skinning of the Deer, and was reflected on the trunks and branches of the cottonwood trees, six of them in one clump, almost arising from the same root, gave such superb effect that I retired some few steps to enjoy the truly fine picture. Some were arranging their rough couches, whilst others were engaged in carrying wood to support our fire through the night; some brought water from the great, muddy stream, and others were busily at work sharpening long sticks for skewers, from which large pieces of venison were soon seen dropping their rich juices upon the brightest of embers. The very sight of this sharpened our appetites, and it must have been laughable to see how all of us fell to, and ate of this first-killed Black-tailed Deer. After a hearty meal we went to sleep, one and all, under the protection of God, and not much afraid of Indians, of whom we have not seen a specimen since we had the pleasure of being fired on by the Santees. We slept very well for a while, till it began to sprinkle rain; but it was only a very slight shower, and I did not even attempt to shelter myself from it. Our fires were mended several times by one or another of the party, and the short night passed on, refreshing us all as only men can be refreshed by sleep under the sky, breathing the purest of air, and happy as only a clear conscience can make one.

May 27, Saturday. At half-past three this morning my ears were saluted by the delightful song of the Red Thrush, who kept on with his strains until we were all up. Harris and Bell went off, and as soon as the two hunters had cleaned their rifles they followed. I remained in camp with Sprague for a while; the best portions of the Deer, *i. e.*, the liver, kidneys, and tongue, were cooked for breakfast, which all enjoyed. No Wolves had disturbed our slumbers, and we now started in search of quadrupeds, birds, and adventures. We found several plants, all new to me, and which are now in press. All the ravines which we inspected were well covered by cedars of the red variety, and whilst ascending several of the hills we found them in many parts partially gliding down as if by the sudden effects of very heavy rain. We saw two very beautiful Avocets feeding opposite our camp; we saw also a Hawk nearly resembling what is called Cooper's Hawk, but having a white rump. Bell joined the hunters and saw some thousands of Buffalo; and finding a very large bull within some thirty yards of them, they put in his body three large balls. The poor beast went off, however, and is now, in all probability, dead. Many fossil remains have been found on the hills about us, but we saw none. These hills are composed of limestone rocks, covered with much shale. Harris thinks this is a different formation from that of either St. Louis or Belle Vue—but, alas! we are not much of geologists. We shot only one of Say's Flycatcher, and the Finch we have called *Emberiza pallida*, but of which I am by no means certain, for want of more exact descriptions than those of a mere synopsis. Our boat made its appearance at two o'clock; we had observed from the hill-tops that it had been aground twice. At three our camp was broken up, our effects removed, our fire left burning, and our boat having landed for us, and for cutting cedar trees, we got on board, highly pleased with our camping out, especially as we found all well on board. We had not proceeded very far when the difficulties of navigation increased so much that we grounded several times, and presently saw a few Indians on the shore; our yawl was out sounding for a passage amid the many sand-bars in view; the Indians fired, not balls, but a salute, to call us ashore. We neared shore, and talked to them; for, they proving to be Sioux, and our captain being a good scholar in that tongue, there was no difficulty in so doing. He told them to follow us, and that he would come-to. They ran to their horses on the prairie, all of which stood still, and were good-looking, comparatively speaking, leaped on their backs without saddles or stirrups, and followed us with ease at a walk. They fired a second salute as we landed; there were only four of them, and they are all at this moment on board. They are fine-looking fellows; the captain introduced Harris and me to the chief, and we shook hands all round. They are a poor set of beggars after all. The captain gave them supper, sugar and coffee, and about one pound of gunpowder, and the chief coolly said: "What is the use of powder, without balls?" It is quite surprising that these Indians did not see us last night, for I have no doubt our fire could have been seen up and down the river for nearly twenty miles. But we are told their lodges are ten miles inland, and that may answer the question. I shall not be sorry now to go to bed. Our camp of the *Six Trees* is deserted and silent. The captain is

almost afraid he may be forced to leave half his cargo somewhere near this, and proceed to Fort Pierre, now distant fifty
miles, and return for the goods. The Indians saw nothing of
the three men who were sent yesterday to announce our approach to Fort Pierre.

Sunday, May 28. This morning was beautiful, though
cool. Our visiting Indians left us at twelve last night, and I
was glad enough to be rid of these beggars by trade. Both
shores were dotted by groups of Buffaloes as far as the eye
could reach, and although many were near the banks they
kept on feeding quietly till we nearly approached them; those
at the distance of half a mile never ceased their avocations. A
Gray Wolf was seen swimming across our bows, and some
dozens of shots were sent at the beast, which made it open its
mouth and raise its head, but it never stopped swimming
away from us, as fast as possible; after a while it reached a
sand-bar, and immediately afterwards first trotted, and then
galloped off. Three Buffaloes also crossed ahead of us, but at
some distance; they all reached the shore, and scrambled up
the bank. We have run better this morning than for three or
four days, and if fortunate enough may reach Fort Pierre
sometime to-morrow. The prairies appear better now, the
grass looks green, and probably the poor Buffaloes will soon
regain their flesh. We have seen more than 2,000 this morning up to this moment—twelve o'clock.

We reached Fort George at about three this afternoon. This
is what is called the "Station of the Opposition line;" some
Indians and a few lodges are on the edge of the prairie.
Sundry bales of Buffalo robes were brought on board, and
Major Hamilton, who is now acting Indian agent here until
the return of Major Crisp, came on board also. I knew his father thirty-five years ago. He pointed out to us the cabin on
the opposite shore, where a partner of the "Opposition line"
shot at and killed two white men and wounded two others, all
of whom were remarkable miscreants. We are about thirty
miles below Fort Pierre. Indians were seen on both sides the
river, ready to trade both here and at Fort Pierre, where I am
told there are five hundred lodges standing. The Indian dogs
which I saw here so very closely resemble wild Wolves, that I
feel assured that if I was to meet with one of them in the

woods, I should most assuredly kill it as such. A few minutes after leaving Fort George, we stopped to sound the channel, and could not discover more than three and a half feet of water; our captain told us we would proceed no farther this day, but would camp here. Bell, Harris, and Sprague went off with guns; Squires and I walked to Fort George, and soon met a young Englishman going towards our boat on a "Buffalo Horse" at a swift gallop; but on being hailed he reined up. His name was Illingsworth; he is the present manager of this establishment. He welcomed us, and as he was going to see Captain Sire, we proceeded on. Upon reaching the camp we found a strongly built log cabin, in one end of which we met Mr. Cutting, who told me he had known Victor in Cuba. This young gentleman had been thrown from his horse in a recent Buffalo chase, and had injured one foot so that he could not walk. A Buffalo cow had hooked the horse and thrown the rider about twenty feet, although the animal had not been wounded. We also met here a Mr. Taylor, who showed me the petrified head of a Beaver, which he supposed to be that of a Wolf; but I showed him the difference in the form at once. I saw two young Wolves about six weeks old, of the common kind, alive. They looked well, but their nature was already pretty apparently that of the parents. I saw an abundance of semi-wolf Dogs, and their howlings were distressing to my ear. We entered the lodge of a trader attached to our company, a German, who is a clever man, has considerable knowledge of botany, and draws well. There were about fifteen lodges, and we saw a greater number of squaws and half-breed children than I had expected. But as every clerk and agent belonging to the companies has "a wife," as it is *called*, a spurious population soon exhibits itself around the wigwams. I will not comment upon this here. We returned before dark to our boat, and I am off to bed.

Monday, May 29.   I was up early, and as soon as breakfast was over, Major Hamilton and myself walked to Fort George. We found the three gentlemen to whom I showed the plate of quadrupeds, and afterwards I went to their store to see skins of Wolves and of the Swift Fox. I found a tolerably good Fox skin which was at once given me; I saw what I was assured were two distinct varieties (for I cannot call them

species) of Wolves. Both, however, considering the difference
in size, were old and young of the same variety. They both
had the top of the back dark gray, and the sides, belly, legs,
and tail, nearly white. When I have these two sorts in the
flesh, I may derive further knowledge. I looked at the Indian
Dogs again with much attention, and was assured that there
is much cross breeding between these Dogs and Wolves, and
that all the varieties actually come from the same root.

Harris now joined us, and found he had met a brother of
Mr. Cutting in Europe. The gentlemen from the fort came
back to the boat with us; we gave them a luncheon, and later
a good substantial dinner, the like of which, so they told us,
they had not eaten for many a day. Mr. Illingsworth told us
much about Buffaloes; he says the hunting is usually more or
less dangerous. The Porcupine is found hereabouts and feeds
on the leaves and bark as elsewhere, but not unfrequently retires into the crevices of rocks, whenever no trees of large size
are to be found in its vicinity. Elks, at times, assemble in
groups of from fifty to two hundred, and their movements are
as regular as those of a flock of White Pelicans, so that if the
oldest Elk starts in any one direction, all the rest follow at
once in his tracks. Where he stops, they all stop, and at times
all will suddenly pause, range themselves as if a company of
dragoons, ready to charge upon the enemy; which, however,
they seldom if ever attempt. After dinner Mr. Illingsworth
told me he would go and shoot a Buffalo calf for me—we will
see. Bell, Harris, Squires, and myself went off to shoot some
Prairie-dogs, as the *Arctomys ludovicianus* is called. After
walking over the hills for about one mile, we came to the "village," and soon after heard their cries but not their barkings.
The sound they make is simply a "chip, chip, chip," long and
shrill enough, and at every cry the animal jerks its tail, without however erecting it upright, as I have seen them represented. Their holes are not perpendicular, but oblique, at an
angle of about forty degrees, after which they seem to deviate; but whether sideways or upwards, I cannot yet say. I shot
at two of them, which appeared to me to be standing, not
across their holes, but in front of them. The first one I never
saw after the shot; the second I found dying at the entrance
of the burrow, but at my appearance it worked backwards. I

drew my ramrod and put the end in its mouth; this it bit hard but kept working backwards, and notwithstanding my efforts, was soon out of sight and touch. Bell saw two enter the same hole, and Harris three. Bell saw some standing quite erect and leaping in the air to see and watch our movements. I found, by lying down within twenty or thirty steps of the hole, that they reappeared in fifteen or twenty minutes. This was the case with me when I shot at the two I have mentioned. Harris saw one that, after coming out of its hole, gave a long and somewhat whistling note, which he thinks was one of invitation to its neighbors, as several came out in a few moments. I have great doubts whether their cries are issued at the appearance of danger or not. I am of opinion that they are a mode of recognition as well as of amusement. I also think they feed more at night than in the day. On my return to the boat, I rounded a small hill and started a Prairie Wolf within a few steps of me. I was unfortunately loaded with No. 3 shot. I pulled one trigger and then the other, but the rascal went off as if unhurt for nearly a hundred yards, when he stopped, shook himself rather violently, and I saw I had hit him; but he ran off again at a very swift rate, his tail down, stopped again, and again shook himself as before, after which he ran out of my sight between the hills. Buffalo cows at this season associate together, with their calves, but if pursued, leave the latter to save themselves. The hides at present are not worth saving, and the Indians as well as the white hunters, when they shoot a Buffalo, tear off the hide, cut out the better portions of the flesh, as well as the tongue, and leave the carcass to the Wolves and Ravens. By the way, Bell saw a Magpie this day, and Harris killed two Black-headed Grosbeaks. Bell also saw several Evening Grosbeaks to-day; therefore there's not much need of crossing the Rocky Mountains for the few precious birds that the talented and truth-speaking Mr. —— brought or sent to the well-paying Academy of Natural Sciences of Philadelphia! The two men sent to Fort Pierre a few days ago have returned, one this evening, in a canoe, the other this afternoon, by land.

May 30, Tuesday. We had a fine morning, and indeed a very fair day. I was called up long before five to receive a Buffalo calf, and the head of another, which Mr. Illingsworth had the goodness to send me. Sprague has been busy ever since breakfast drawing one of the heads, the size of nature. The other entire calf has been skinned, and will be in strong pickle before I go to bed. Mr. Illingsworth killed two calves, one bull, and one cow. The calves, though not more than about two months old, as soon as the mother was wounded, rushed towards the horse or the man who had struck her. The one bull skinned was so nearly putrid, though so freshly killed, that its carcass was thrown overboard. This gentleman, as well as many others, assured us that the hunting of Buffaloes, for persons unaccustomed to it, was very risky indeed; and said no one should attempt it unless well initiated, even though he may be a first-rate rider. When calves are caught alive, by placing your hands over the eyes and blowing into the nostrils, in the course of a few minutes they will follow the man who performs this simple operation. Indeed if a cow perchance leaves her calf behind during a time of danger, or in the chase, the calf will often await the approach of man and follow him as soon as the operation mentioned is over. Mr. Illingsworth paid us a short visit, and told us that Mr. Cutting was writing to his post near Fort Union to expect us, and to afford us all possible assistance. We made a start at seven, and after laboring over the infernal sand-bars until nearly four this afternoon, we passed them, actually cutting our own channel with the assistance of the wheel. Whilst we were at this, we were suddenly boarded by the yawl of the "Trapper," containing Mr. Picotte, Mr. Chardon, and several others. They had left Fort Pierre this morning, and had come down in one hour and a half. We were all duly presented to the whole group, and I gave to each of these gentlemen the letters I had for them. I found them very kind and affable. They dined after us, being somewhat late, but ate heartily and drank the same. They brought a first-rate hunter with them, of whom I expect to have much to say hereafter. Mr. Picotte promised me the largest pair of Elk horns ever seen in this country, as well as several other curiosities, all of which I will write about when I have them. We have reached Antelope River, a very small creek on the west side. We saw two Wolves crossing the river, and Harris shot a Lark Finch. We have now no difficulties before us, and hope to reach Fort Pierre very early to-morrow morning.

Fort Pierre, May 31, Wednesday. After many difficulties we reached this place at four o'clock this afternoon, having spent the whole previous part of the day, say since half-past three this morning, in coming against the innumerable bars—only *nine miles!* I forgot to say last evening, that where we landed for the night our captain caught a fine specimen of *Neotoma floridana,* a female. We were forced to come-to about a quarter of a mile above Fort Pierre, after having passed the steamer "Trapper" of our Company. Bell, Squires, and myself walked to the Fort as soon as possible, and found Mr. Picotte and Mr. Chardon there. More kindness from strangers I have seldom received. I was presented with the largest pair of Elk horns I ever saw, and also a skin of the animal itself, most beautifully prepared, which I hope to give to my beloved wife. I was also presented with two pairs of moccasins, an Indian riding-whip, one collar of Grizzly Bear's claws, and two long strings of dried white apples, as well as two Indian dresses. I bought the skin of a fine young Grizzly Bear, two Wolf skins, and a parcel of fossil remains. I saw twelve young Buffalo calves, caught a few weeks ago, and yet as wild, apparently, as ever. Sprague will take outlines of them to-morrow morning, and I shall draw them. We have put ashore about one-half of our cargo and left fifty of our *engagés,* so that we shall be able to go much faster, in less water than we have hitherto drawn. We are all engaged in finishing our correspondence, the whole of the letters being about to be forwarded to St. Louis by the steamer "Trapper." I have a letter of seven pages to W. G. Bakewell, James Hall, J. W. H. Page, and Thomas M. Brewer, of Boston, besides those to my family. We are about one and a half miles above the Teton River, or, as it is now called, the Little Missouri, a swift and tortuous stream that finds its source about 250 miles from its union with this great river, in what are called the Bad Lands of Teton River, where it seems, from what we hear, that the country has been at one period greatly convulsed, and is filled with fossil remains. I saw the young Elk belonging to our captain, looking exceedingly shabby, but with the most beautiful eyes I ever beheld in any animal of the Deer kind. We have shot nothing to-day. I have heard all the notes of the Meadow Lark found here and they are utterly different from those of our common species. And now that I am pretty well fatigued with writing letters and this journal, I will go to rest, though I have matter enough in my poor head to write a book. We expect to proceed onwards some time to-morrow.

June 1, Thursday. I was up at half-past three, and by four Sprague and I walked to the Fort, for the purpose of taking sketches of young Buffalo calves. These young beasts grunt precisely like a hog, and I would defy any person not seeing the animals to tell one sound from the other. The calves were not out of the stable, and while waiting I measured the Elk horns given me by Mr. Picotte. They are as follows: length, 4 feet 6½ inches; breadth 27 to 27½ inches; circumference at the skull 16 inches, round the knob 12 inches; between the knobs 3 inches. This animal, one of the largest ever seen in this country, was killed in November last. From seventeen to twenty-one poles are necessary to put up a lodge, and the poles when the lodge is up are six or seven feet above the top. The holes at the bottom, all round, suffice to indicate the number of these wanted to tighten the lodge. In time Sprague made several outline sketches of calves, and I drew what I wished. We had breakfast very early, and I ate some good bread and fresh butter. Mr. Picotte presented me with two pipe-stems this morning, quite short, but handsome. At eleven we were on our way, and having crossed the river, came alongside of the "Trapper," of which Mr. John Durack takes the command to St. Louis. The name of our own captain is Joseph A. Sire. Mr. Picotte gave me a letter for Fort Union, as Mr. Culbertson will not be there when we arrive. One of Captain Sire's daughters and her husband are going up with us. She soled three pairs of moccasins for me, as skilfully as an Indian. Bell and Harris shot several rare birds. Mr. Bowie promised to save for me all the curiosities he could procure; he came on board and saw the plates of quadrupeds, and I gave him an almanac, which he much desired.

After we had all returned on board, I was somewhat surprised that Sprague asked me to let him return with the "Omega" to St. Louis. Of course I told him that he was at liberty to do so, though it will keep me grinding about double as much as I expected. Had he said the same at New York, I could have had any number of young and good artists, who would have leaped for joy at the very idea of accompanying such an expedition. Never mind, however.

We have run well this afternoon, for we left Fort Pierre at two o'clock, and we are now more than twenty-five miles above it. We had a rascally Indian on board, who hid himself for the purpose of murdering Mr. Chardon; the latter gave him a thrashing last year for thieving, and Indians never forget such things—he had sworn vengeance, and that was enough. Mr. Chardon discovered him below, armed with a knife; he talked to him pretty freely, and then came up to ask the captain to put the fellow ashore. This request was granted, and he and his bundle were dropped overboard, where the water was waist deep; the fellow scrambled out, and we heard, afterward, made out to return to Fort Pierre. I had a long talk with Sprague, who thought I was displeased with him—a thing that never came into my head—and in all probability he will remain with us. Harris shot a pair of Arkansas Flycatchers, and Squires procured several plants, new to us all. Harris wrote a few lines to Mr. Sarpy at St. Louis, and I have had the pleasure to send the Elk horns, and the great balls from the stomachs of Buffalo given me by our good captain. I am extremely fatigued, for we have been up since before daylight. *At 12 o'clock of the night.* I have got up to scribble this, which it is not strange that after all I saw this day, at this curious place, I should have forgotten. Mr. Picotte took me to the storehouse where the skins procured are kept, and showed me eight or ten packages of White Hare skins, which I feel assured are all of Townsend's Hare of friend Bachman, as no other species are to be met with in this neighborhood during the winter months, when these animals migrate southward, both in search of food and of a milder climate.

June 2, Friday. We made an extremely early start about three A. M. The morning was beautiful and calm. We passed Cheyenne River at half-past seven, and took wood a few miles above it. Saw two White Pelicans, shot a few birds. My hunter, Alexis Bombarde, whom I have engaged, could not go shooting last night on account of the crossing of this river, the Cheyenne, which is quite a large stream. Mr. Chardon gave me full control of Alexis, till we reach the Yellowstone. He is a first-rate hunter, and powerfully built; he wears his hair long about his head and shoulders, as I was wont to do; but being a half-breed, his does not curl as mine did. Whilst we are engaged cutting wood again, many of the men have gone after a Buffalo, shot from the boat. We have seen more Wolves this day than ever previously. We saw where carcasses of Buffaloes had been quite devoured by these animals, and the diversity of their colors and of their size is more wonderful than all that can be said of them. Alexis Bombarde, whom hereafter I shall simply call *Alexis*, says that with a small-bored rifle common size, good shot will kill any Wolf at sixty or eighty yards' distance, as well as bullets. We passed one Wolf that, crossing our bows, went under the wheel and yet escaped, though several shots were fired at it. I had a specimen of *Arvicola pennsylvanicus* brought to me, and I was glad to find this species so very far from New York. These animals in confinement eat each other up, the strongest one remaining, often maimed and covered with blood. This I have seen, and I was glad to have it corroborated by Bell. We are told the Buffalo cows are generally best to eat in the month of July; the young bulls are, however, tough at this season. Our men have just returned with the whole of the Buffalo except its head; it is a young bull, and may prove good. When they reached it, it was standing, and Alexis shot at it twice, to despatch it as soon as possible. It was skinned and cut up in a very few minutes, and the whole of the flesh was brought on board. I am now astonished at the poverty of the bluffs which we pass; no more of the beautiful limestone formations that we saw below. Instead of those, we now run along banks of poor and crumbling clay, dry and hard now, but after a rain soft and soapy. Most of the cedars in the ravines, formerly fine and thrifty, are now, generally speaking, dead and dried up. Whether this may be the effect of the transitions of the weather or not, I cannot pretend to assert. We have seen more Wolves to-day than on any previous occasions. We have made a good day's work of it also, for I dare say that when we stop for the night, we shall have travelled sixty miles. The water is rising somewhat, but not to hurt our progress. We have seen young Gadwall Ducks, and a pair of Geese that had young ones swimming out of our sight.

June 3, Saturday. Alexis went off last night at eleven o'clock, walked about fifteen miles, and returned at ten this morning; he brought three Prairie Dogs, or, as I call them, Prairie Marmots. The wind blew violently till we had run several miles; at one period we were near stopping. We have had many difficulties with the sand-bars, having six or seven times taken the wrong channel, and then having to drop back and try our luck again. The three Marmots had been killed with shot quite too large, and not one of them was fit for drawing, or even skinning. Sprague and I have taken measurements of all their parts, which I give at once. [*Here follow forty-two measurements, all external, of the male and female.*] I received no further intelligence about the habits of this species, except that they are quite numerous in every direction. We passed four rivers to-day; the Little Chayenne, the Moroe, the Grand, and the Rampart. The Moroe is a handsome stream and, I am told, has been formerly a good one for Beaver. It is navigable for barges for a considerable distance. Just before dinner we stopped to cut drift-wood on a sand-bar, and a Wolf was seen upon it. Bell, Harris, and some one else went after it. The wily rascal cut across the bar and, hiding itself under the bank, ran round the point, and again stopped. But Bell had returned towards the very spot, and the fellow was seen swimming off, when Bell pulled the trigger and shot it dead, in or near the head. The captain sent the yawl after it, and it was brought on board. It was tied round the neck and dipped in the river to wash it. It smelled very strong, but I was heartily glad to have it in my power to examine it closely, and to be enabled to take very many measurements of this the first Wolf we have actually procured. It was a male, but rather poor; its general color a grayish yellow; its measurements are as follows [*omitted*]. We saw one Goose with a gosling, several Coots, Grebes, Blue Herons, Doves, Magpies, Red-shafted Woodpeckers, etc. On a sand-bar Bell counted ten Wolves feeding on some carcass. We also saw three young whelps. This morning we saw a large number of Black-headed Gulls feeding on a dead Buffalo with some Ravens; the Gulls probably were feeding on the worms, or other insects about the carcass. We saw four Elks, and a large gang of Buffaloes. One Wolf was seen crossing the river towards our boat; being fired at, it wheeled round, but turned towards us again, again wheeled round, and returned to where it had started. We ran this evening till our wood was exhausted, and I do not know how we will manage to-morrow. Good-night. God bless you all.

June 4, Sunday. We have run pretty well, though the wind has been tolerably high; the country we have passed this day is somewhat better than what we saw yesterday, which, as I said, was the poorest we have seen. No occurrence of interest has taken place. We passed this morning the old Riccaree Village, where General Ashley was so completely beaten as to lose eighteen of his men, with the very weapons and ammunition that he had trafficked with the Indians of that village, against all the remonstrances of his friends and interpreters; yet he said that it proved fortunate for him, as he turned his steps towards some other spot, where he procured one hundred packs of Beaver skins for a mere song. We stopped to cut wood at an old house put up for winter quarters, and the wood being ash, and quite dry, was excellent. We are now fast for the night at an abandoned post, or fort, of the Company, where, luckily for us, a good deal of wood was found cut. We saw only one Wolf, and a few small gangs of Buffaloes. Bell shot a Bunting which resembles Henslow's, but we have no means of comparing it at present. We have collected a few plants during our landing. The steam is blowing off, and therefore our day's run is ended. When I went to bed last night it was raining smartly, and Alexis did not go off, as he did wish. By the way, I forgot to say that along with the three Prairie Marmots, he brought also four Spoon-billed Ducks, which we ate at dinner to-day, and found delicious. Bell saw many Lazuli Finches this morning. Notwithstanding the tremendous shaking of our boat, Sprague managed to draw four figures of the legs and feet of the Wolf shot by Bell yesterday, and my own pencil was not idle.

June 5, Monday. Alexis went off in the night sometime, and came on board about three o'clock this morning; he had seen nothing whatever, except the traces of Beavers and of Otters, on Beaver Creek, which, by the way, he had to cross on a raft. Speaking of rafts, I am told that one of these, made of two bundles of rushes, about the size of a man's body, and fastened together by a few sticks, is quite sufficient to take two men and two packs of Buffalo robes across this muddy river. In the course of the morning we passed Cannon Ball River, and the very remarkable bluffs about it, of which we cannot well speak until we have stopped there and examined their nature. We saw two Swans alighting on the prairie at a considerable distance. We stopped to take wood at Bowie's settlement, at which place his wife was killed by some of the Riccaree Indians, after some Gros Ventres had assured him that such would be the case if he suffered his wife to go out of the house. She went out, however, on the second day, and was shot with three rifle-balls. The Indians took parts of her hair and went off. She was duly buried; but the Gros Ventres returned some time afterwards, took up the body, and carried off the balance of her hair. They, however, reburied her; and it was not until several months had elapsed that the story came to the ears of Mr. Bowie. We have also passed Apple Creek, but the chief part is yet to be added. At one place where the bluffs were high, we saw five Buffaloes landing a few hundred yards above us on the western side; one of them cantered off immediately, and by some means did reach the top of the hills, and went out of our sight; the four others ran, waded, and swam at different places, always above us, trying to make their escape. At one spot they attempted to climb the bluff, having unconsciously passed the place where their leader had made good his way, and in their attempts to scramble up, tumbled down, and at last became so much affrighted that they took to the river for good, with the intention to swim to the shore they had left. Unfortunately for them, we had been gaining upon them; we had all been anxiously watching them, and the moment they began to swim we were all about the boat with guns and rifles, awaiting the instant when they would be close under our bows. The moment came; I was on the lower deck among several of the people with guns, and the firing was soon heavy; but not one of the Buffaloes was stopped, although every one must have been severely hit and wounded. Bell shot a load of buckshot at the head of one, which disappeared entirely under the water for perhaps a minute. I sent a ball through the neck of the last of the four, but all ineffectually, and off they went, swimming to the opposite shore; one lagged behind the rest, but, having found footing on a sand-bar, it rested awhile, and again swam off to rejoin its companions. They all reached the shore, but were quite as badly off on that side as they had been on the other, and their difficulties must have been great indeed; however, in a short time we had passed them. Mr. Charles Primeau, who is a good shot, and who killed the young Buffalo bull the other day, assured me that it was his opinion the whole of these would die before sundown, but that Buffaloes swimming were a hundred times more difficult to kill than those on shore. I have been told also, that a Buffalo shot by an Indian, in the presence of several whites, exhibited some marks on the inside of the skin that looked like old wounds, and that on close examination they found no less than six balls in its paunch. Sometimes they will run a mile after having been struck through the heart; whilst at other times they will fall dead without such desperate shot. Alexis told me that once he shot one through the thigh, and that it fell dead on the spot. We passed this afternoon a very curious conical mound of earth, about which Harris and I had some curiosity, by which I lost two pounds of snuff, as he was right, and I was wrong. We have seen Geese and Goslings, Ravens, Blue Herons, Bluebirds, Thrushes, Red-headed Woodpeckers and Red-shafted ditto, Martins, an immense number of Rough-winged Swallows about their holes, and Barn Swallows. We heard Killdeers last evening. Small Crested Flycatchers, Summer Yellow-birds, Maryland Yellow-throats, House Wrens are seen as we pass along our route; while the Spotted Sandpiper accompanies us all along the river. Sparrow Hawks, Turkey Buzzards, Arctic Towhee Buntings, Cat-birds, Mallards, Coots, Gadwalls, King-birds, Yellow-breasted Chats, Red Thrushes, all are noted as we pass. We have had a good day's run; it is now half-past ten. The wind has been cold, and this evening we have had a dash of rain. We have seen only one Wolf. We have heard some wonderful stories about Indians and white men, none of which I can well depend upon. We have stopped for the night a few miles above where the "Assiniboin" steamer was burnt with all her cargo uninsured, in the year 1835. I heard that after she had run ashore, the men started to build a scow to unload the cargo; but that through some accident the vessel was set on fire, and that a man and a woman who alone had been left on board, walked off to the island, where they remained some days unable to reach shore.

June 6, Tuesday. This morning was quite cold, and we had a thick white frost on our upper deck. It was also extremely cloudy, the wind from the east, and all about us looked dismal enough. The hands on board seemed to have been busy the whole of the night, for I scarcely slept for the noise they made. We soon came to a very difficult part of the river, and had to stop full three hours. Meanwhile the yawl went off to seek and sound for a channel, whilst the wood-cutters and the carriers—who, by the way, are called "charrettes"—followed their work, and we gathered a good quantity of drift-wood, which burns like straw. Our hopes of reaching the Mandan Village were abandoned, but we at last proceeded on our way and passed the bar; it was nearly dinner-time. Harris and Bell had their guns, and brought two Arctic Towhee Buntings and a Black-billed Cuckoo. They saw two large flocks of Geese making their way westward. The place where we landed showed many signs of Deer, Elk, and Buffaloes. I saw trees where the latter had rubbed their heavy bodies against the bark, till they had completely robbed the tree of its garment. We saw several Red-shafted Woodpeckers, and other birds named before. The Buffalo, when hunted on horseback, does *not* carry its tail erect, as has been represented in books, but close between the legs; but when you see a Buffalo bull work its tail sideways in a twisted rolling fashion, *then* take care of him, as it is a sure sign of his intention to rush against his pursuer's horse, which is very dangerous, both to hunter and steed. As we proceeded I saw two fine White-headed Eagles alighting on their nest, where perhaps they had young—and how remarkably late in the season this species does breed here! We also saw a young Sandhill Crane, and on an open prairie four Antelopes a few hundred yards off. Alexis tells me that at this season this is a rare occurrence, as the females are generally in the brushwood now; but in this instance the male and three females were on open prairie. We have passed what is called the Heart River, and the Square Hills, which, of course, are by no means square, but simply more level than the generality of those we have passed for upwards of three weeks. We now saw four barges belonging to our company, and came to, above them, as usual. A Mr. Kipp, one of the partners, came on board; and Harris, Squires, and myself had time to write each a short letter to our friends at home. Mr. Kipp had a peculiar looking crew who appeared not much better than a set of bandits among the Pyrenees or the Alps; yet they seem to be the very best sort of men for trappers and boatmen. We exchanged four of our men for four of his, as the latter are wanted at the Yellowstone. The country appears to Harris and to myself as if we had outrun the progress of vegetation, as from the boat we observed oaks scarcely in leaflets, whilst two hundred miles below, and indeed at a much less distance, we saw the same timber in nearly full leaf; flowers are also scarce. A single Wolf was seen by some one on deck. Nothing can be possibly keener than the senses of hearing and sight, as well as of smell, in the Antelope. Not one was ever known to jump up close to a hunter; and the very motion of the grasses, as these are wafted by the wind, will keep them awake and on the alert Immediately upon the breaking up of the ice about the Mandan Village, three Buffaloes were seen floating down on a large cake; they were seen by Mr. Primeau from his post, and again from Fort Pierre. How much further the poor beasts travelled, no one can tell. It happens not infrequently, when the river is entirely closed in with ice, that some hundreds of Buffaloes attempt to cross; their aggregate enormous weight forces the ice to break, and the whole of the gang are drowned, as it is impossible for these animals to climb over the surrounding sharp edges of the ice. We have seen not less than three nests of White-headed Eagles this day. We are fast ashore about sixteen miles below the Mandan Villages, and will, in all probability, reach there to-morrow morning at an early hour. It is raining yet, and the day has been a most unpleasant one.

June 7, Wednesday.   We had a vile night of rain, and wind from the northeast, which is still going on, and likely to continue the whole of this blessed day. Yesterday, when we had a white frost, ice was found in the kettles of Mr. Kipp's barges.

We reached Fort Clark and the Mandan Villages at half-past seven this morning. Great guns were fired from the fort and from the "Omega," as our captain took the guns from the "Trapper" at Fort Pierre. The site of this fort appears a good one, though it is placed considerably below the Mandan Village. We saw some small spots cultivated, where corn, pumpkins, and beans are grown. The fort and village are situated on the high bank, rising somewhat to the elevation of a hill. The Mandan mud huts are very far from looking poetical, although Mr. Catlin has tried to render them so by placing them in regular rows, and all of the same size and form, which is by no means the case. But different travellers have different eyes! We saw more Indians than at any previous time since leaving St. Louis; and it is possible that there are a hundred huts, made of mud, all looking like so many potato winter-houses in the Eastern States. As soon as we were near the shore, every article that could conveniently be carried off was placed under lock and key, and our division door was made fast, as well as those of our own rooms. Even the axes and poles were put by. Our captain told us that last year they stole his cap and his shot-pouch and horn, and that it was through the interference of the first chief that he recovered his cap and horn; but that a squaw had his leather belt, and would not give it up. The appearance of these poor, miserable devils, as we approached the shore, was wretched enough. There they stood in the pelting rain and keen wind, covered with Buffalo robes, red blankets, and the like, some partially and most curiously besmeared with mud; and as they came on board, and we shook hands with each of them, I felt a clamminess that rendered the ceremony most repulsive. Their legs and naked feet were covered with mud. They looked at me with apparent curiosity, perhaps on account of my beard, which produced the same effect at Fort Pierre. They all looked very poor; and our captain says they are the *ne plus ultra* of thieves. It is said there are nearly three thousand men, women, and children that, during winter, cram themselves into these miserable hovels. Harris and I walked to the fort about nine o'clock. The walking was rascally, passing through mud and water the whole way. The yard of the fort itself was as bad. We entered Mr. Chardon's own room, crawled up a crazy ladder, and in a low garret I had the great pleasure of seeing alive the Swift or Kit Fox which he has given to me. It ran swiftly from one corner to another, and, when approached, growled somewhat in the manner of a common Fox. Mr. Chardon told me that good care would be taken of it until our return, that it would be chained to render it more gentle, and that I would find it an easy matter to take it along. I sincerely hope so. Seeing a remarkably fine skin of a large Cross Fox which I wished to buy, it was handed over to me. After this, Mr. Chardon asked one of the Indians to take us into the village, and particularly to show us the "Medicine Lodge." We followed our guide through mud and mire, even into the Lodge. We found this to be, in general terms, like all the other lodges, only larger, measuring twenty-three yards in diameter, with a large squarish aperture in the centre of the roof, some six or seven feet long by about four wide. We had entered this curiosity shop by pushing aside a wet Elk skin stretched on four sticks. Looking around, I saw a number of calabashes, eight or ten Otter skulls, two very large Buffalo skulls with the horns on, evidently of great age, and some sticks and other magical implements with which none but a "Great Medicine Man" is acquainted. During my survey there sat, crouched down on his haunches, an Indian wrapped in a dirty blanket, with only his filthy head peeping out. Our guide spoke to him; but he stirred not. Again, at the foot of one of the posts that support the central portion of this great room, lay a parcel that I took for a bundle of Buffalo robes; but it moved presently, and from beneath it half arose the emaciated body of a poor blind Indian, whose skin was quite shrivelled; and our guide made us signs that he was about to die. We all shook both hands with him; and he pressed our hands closely and with evident satisfaction. He had his pipe and tobacco pouch by him, and soon lay down again. We left this abode of mysteries, as I was anxious to see the interior of one of the common huts around; and again our guide led us through mud and mire to his own lodge, which we entered in the same way as we had done the other. All these lodges have a sort of portico that leads to the door, and on the tops of most of them I observed Buffalo skulls. This lodge contained the whole family of our guide—several women and children, and another man, perhaps a son-in-law or a brother. All these, except the man, were on the outer edge of the lodge, crouching on the ground, some suckling children; and at nearly equal distances apart were placed berths, raised about two feet above the ground, made of leather, and with square apertures for the sleepers or occupants to enter. The man of whom I have spoken was lying down in one of these, which was all open in front. I walked up to him, and, after disturbing his happy slumbers, shook hands with him; he made signs for me to sit down; and after Harris and I had done so, he rose, squatted himself near us, and, getting out a large spoon made of boiled Buffalo horn, handed it to a young girl, who brought a great rounded wooden bowl filled with pemmican, mixed with corn and some other stuff. I ate a mouthful or so of it, and found it quite palatable; and Harris and the rest then ate of it also. Bell was absent; we had seen nothing of him since we left the boat. This lodge, as well as the other, was dirty with water and mud; but I am told that in dry weather they are kept cleaner, and much cleaning do they need, most truly. A round, shallow hole was dug in the centre for the fire; and from the roof descended over this a chain, by the aid of which they do their cooking, the utensil being attached to the chain when wanted. As we returned towards the fort, I gave our guide a piece of tobacco, and he appeared well pleased. He followed us on board, and as he peeped in my room, and saw the dried and stuffed specimens we have, he evinced a slight degree of curiosity. Our captain, Mr. Chardon, and our men have been busily engaged in putting ashore that portion of the cargo designed for this fort, which in general appearance might be called a poor miniature representation of Fort Pierre. The whole country around was overgrown with "Lamb's quarters" (*Chenopòdium album*), which I have no doubt, if boiled, would take the place of spinach in this wild and, to my eyes, miserable country, the poetry of which lies in the imagination of those writers who have described the "velvety prairies" and "enchanted castles" (of mud), so common where we now are. We observed a considerable difference in the color of these Indians, who, by the way, are almost all Riccarees; many appeared, and in fact are, redder than others; they are lank, rather tall, and very alert, but, as I have said before, all look poor and dirty. After dinner we went up the muddy bank again to look at the cornfields, as the small patches that are meanly cultivated are called. We found poor, sickly looking corn about two inches high, that had been represented to us this morning as full six inches high. We followed the prairie, a very extensive one, to the hills, and there found a deep ravine, sufficiently impregnated with saline matter to answer the purpose of salt water for the Indians to boil their corn and pemmican, clear and clean; but they, as well as the whites at the fort, resort to the muddy Missouri for their drinking water, the only fresh water at hand. Not a drop of spirituous liquor has been brought to this place for the last two years; and there can be no doubt that on this account the Indians have become more peaceable than heretofore, though now and then a white man is murdered, and many horses are stolen. As we walked over the plain, we saw heaps of earth thrown up to cover the poor Mandans who died of the small-pox. These mounds in many instances appear to contain the remains of several bodies and, perched on the top, lies, pretty generally, the rotting skull of a Buffalo. Indeed, the skulls of the Buffaloes seem as if a kind of relation to these most absurdly superstitious and ignorant beings. I could not hear a word of the young Grizzly Bear of which Mr. Chardon had spoken to me. He gave me his Buffalo head-dress and other trifles—as he was pleased to call them; all of which will prove more or less interesting and curious to you when they reach Minniesland. He presented Squires with a good hunting shirt and a few other things, and to all of us, presented moccasins. We collected a few round cacti; and I saw several birds that looked much the worse for the cold and wet weather we have had these last few days. Our boat has been thronged with Indians ever since we have tied to the shore; and it is with considerable difficulty and care that we can stop them from intruding into our rooms when we are there. We found many portions of skulls lying on the ground, which, perhaps, did at one period form the circles of them spoken of by Catlin. All around the village is filthy beyond description. Our captain tells us that no matter what weather we may have to-morrow, he will start at daylight, even if he can only go across the river, to get rid of these wolfish-looking vagabonds of Indians. I sincerely hope that we may have a fair day and a long run, so that the air around us may once more be pure and fresh from the hand of Nature. After the Riccarees had taken possession of this Mandan Village, the remains of that once powerful tribe removed about three miles up the river, and there have now fifteen or twenty huts, containing, of course, only that number of families. During the worst periods of the epidemic which swept over this village with such fury, many became maniacs, rushed to the Missouri, leaped into its turbid waters, and were seen no more. Mr. Primeau, wife, and children, as well as another half-breed, have gone to the fort, and are to remain there till further orders. The fort is in a poor condition, roofs leaking, etc. Whilst at the fort this afternoon, I was greatly surprised to see a tall, athletic Indian thrashing the dirty rascals about Mr. Chardon's door most severely; but I found on inquiry that he was called "the soldier," and that he had authority to do so whenever the Indians intruded or congregated in the manner this *canaille* had done. After a while the same tall fellow came on board with his long stick, and immediately began belaboring the fellows on the lower guards; the latter ran off over the planks, and scrambled up the muddy banks as if so many affrighted Buffaloes. Since then we have been comparatively quiet; but I hope they will all go off, as the captain is going to put the boat from the shore, to the full length of our spars. The wind has shifted to the northward, and the atmosphere has been so chilled that a House Swallow was caught, benumbed with cold, and brought to me by our captain. Harris, Bell, and I saw a Cliff Swallow take refuge on board; but this was not caught. We have seen Say's Flycatcher, the Ground Finch, Cow Buntings, and a few other birds. One of the agents arrived this afternoon from the Gros Ventre, or Minnetaree Village, about twelve miles above us. He is represented as a remarkably brave man, and he relates some strange adventures of his prowess. Several *great warriors* have condescended to shake me by the hand; their very touch is disgusting—it will indeed be a deliverance to get rid of all this "Indian poetry." We are, nevertheless, to take a few to the Yellowstone. Alexis has his wife, who is, in fact, a good-looking young woman; an old patroon, Provost, takes one of his daughters along; and we have, besides, several red-skinned single gentlemen. We were assured that the northern parts of the hills, that form a complete curtain to the vast prairie on which we have walked this afternoon, are still adorned with patches of snow that fell there during last winter. It is now nine o'clock, but before I go to rest I cannot resist giving you a description of the curious exhibition that we have had on board, from a numerous lot of Indians of the first class, say some forty or fifty. They ranged themselves along the sides of the large cabin, squatting on the floor. Coffee had been prepared for the whole party, and hard sea-biscuit likewise. The coffee was first given to each of them, and afterwards the biscuits, and I had the honor of handing the latter to the row on one side of the boat; a box of tobacco was opened and laid on the table. The man who came from the Gros Ventres this afternoon proved to be an excellent interpreter; and after the captain had delivered his speech to him, he spoke loudly to the group, and explained the purport of the captain's speech. They grunted their approbation frequently, and were, no doubt, pleased. Two individuals (Indians) made their appearance highly decorated, with epaulets on the shoulders, red clay on blue uniforms, three cocks' plumes in their head-dress, rich moccasins, leggings, etc. These are men who, though in the employ of the Opposition company, act truly as friends; but who, meantime, being called "Braves," never grunted, bowed, or shook hands with any of us. Supper over and the tobacco distributed, the whole body arose simultaneously, and each and every one of these dirty wretches we had all to shake by the hand. The two braves sat still until all the rest had gone ashore, and then retired as majestically as they had entered, not even shaking hands with our good-humored captain. I am told that this performance takes place once every year, on the passing of the Company's boats. I need not say that the coffee and the two biscuits apiece were gobbled down in less than no time. The tobacco, which averaged about two pounds to each man, was hid in their robes or blankets for future use. Two of the Indians, who must have been of the highest order, and who distributed the "rank weed," were nearly naked; one had on only a breech-clout and one legging, the other was in no better case. They are now all ashore except one or more who are going with us to the Yellowstone; and I will now go to my rest. Though I have said "Good-night," I have arisen almost immediately, and I must write on, for we have other scenes going on both among the trappers below and some of the people above. Many Indians, squaws as well as men, are bartering and trading, and keep up such a babble that Harris and I find sleep impossible; needless to say, the squaws who are on board are of the lowest grade of morality.

June 8, Thursday. This morning was fair and cold, as you see by the range of the thermometer, 37° to 56°. We started at a very early hour, and breakfasted before five, on account of the village of Gros Ventres, where our captain had to stop. We passed a few lodges belonging to the tribe of the poor Mandans, about all that remained. I only counted eight, but am told there are twelve. The village of the Gros Ventres (Minnetarees) has been cut off from the bank of the river by an enormous sand-bar, now overgrown with willows and brush, and we could only see the American flag flying in the cool breeze. Two miles above this, however, we saw an increasing body of Indians, for the prairie was sprinkled with small parties, on horse and on foot. The first who arrived fired a salute of small guns, and we responded with our big gun. They had an abundance of dogs harnessed to take wood back to the village, and their yells and fighting were severe upon our ears. Some forty or more of the distinguished blackguards came on board; and we had to close our doors as we did yesterday. After a short period they were feasted as last evening; and speeches, coffee, and tobacco, as well as some gunpowder, were given them, which they took away in packs, to be divided afterward. We took one more passenger, and lost our interpreter, who is a trader with the Minnetarees. The latter are by no means as fine-looking a set of men as those we have seen before, and I observed none of that whiteness of skin among them. There were numbers of men, women, and children. We saw a crippled and evidently tame Wolf, and two Indians, following us on the top of the hills. We saw two Swans on a bar, and a female Elk, with her young fawn, for a few minutes. I wished that we had been ashore, as I know full well that the mother would not leave her young; and the mother killed, the young one would have been easily caught alive. We are now stopping for the night, and our men are cutting wood. We have done this, I believe, four times to-day, and have run upward of sixty miles. At the last wood-cutting place, a young leveret was started by the men, and after a short race, the poor thing squatted, and was killed by the stroke of a stick. It proved to be the young of *Lepus townsendii*, large enough to have left the mother, and weighing rather more than a pound. It is a very beautiful specimen. The eyes are very large, and the iris pure amber color. Its hair is tightly, but beautifully curled. Its measurements are as follows [*omitted*]. Bell will make a fine skin of it to-morrow morning. We have had all sorts of stories related to us; but Mr. Kipp, who has been in the country for twenty-two years, is evidently a person of truth, and I expect a good deal of information from him. Our captain told us that on a previous voyage some Indians asked him if, "when the great Medicine" (meaning the steamer) "was tired, he gave it whiskey." Mr. Sire laughed, and told them he did. "How much?" was the query. "A barrelful, to be sure!" The poor wretches at first actually believed him, and went off contented, but were naturally angry at being undeceived on a later occasion. I have now some hope of finding a young of the Antelope alive at Fort Union, as Mr. Kipp left one there about ten days ago. I am now going to bed, though our axemen and "charettes" are still going; and I hope I may not be called up to-morrow morning, to be ready for breakfast at half-past four. Harris and Bell went off with Alexis. Bell fired at a bird, and a large Wolf immediately made its appearance. This is always the case in this country; when you shoot an animal and hide yourself, you may see, in less than half an hour, from ten to thirty of these hungry rascals around the carcass, and have fine fun shooting at them. We have had a windy day, but a good run on the whole. I hope to-morrow may prove propitious, and that we shall reach Fort Union in five more days.

June 9, Friday. Thermometer 42°, 75°, 66°. We had a heavy white frost last night, but we have had a fine, pleasant day on the whole, and to me a most interesting one. We passed the Little Missouri (the real one) about ten this morning.

It is a handsome stream, that runs all the way from the Black Hills, one of the main spurs of the mighty Rocky Mountains. We saw three Elks swimming across it, and the number of this fine species of Deer that are about us now is almost inconceivable. We have heard of burning springs, which we intend to examine on our way down. We started a Goose from the shore that had evidently young ones; she swam off, beating the water with wings half extended, until nearly one hundred yards off. A shot from a rifle was fired at her, and happily missed the poor thing; she afterwards lowered her neck, sank her body, and with the tip of the bill only above water, kept swimming away from us till out of sight. Afterwards one of the trappers shot at two Geese with two young ones. We landed at four o'clock, and Harris and Bell shot some Bay-winged Buntings and *Emberiza pallida*, whilst Sprague and I went up to the top of the hills, bounding the beautiful prairie, by which we had stopped to repair something about the engine. We gathered some handsome lupines, of two different species, and many other curious plants. From this elevated spot we could see the wilderness to an immense distance; the Missouri looked as if only a brook, and our steamer a very small one indeed. At this juncture we saw two men running along the shore upwards, and I supposed they had seen an Elk or something else, of which they were in pursuit. Meantime, gazing around, we saw a large lake, where we are told that Ducks, Geese, and Swans breed in great numbers; this we intend also to visit when we come down. At this moment I heard the report of a gun from the point where the men had been seen, and when we reached the steamboat, we were told that a Buffalo had been killed. From the deck I saw a man swimming round the animal; he got on its side, and floated down the stream with it. The captain sent a parcel of men with a rope; the swimmer fastened this round the neck of the Buffalo, and with his assistance, for he now swam all the way, the poor beast was brought alongside; and as the tackle had been previously fixed, it was hauled up on the fore deck. Sprague took its measurements with me, which are as follows: length from nose to root of tail, 8 feet; height of fore shoulder to hoof, 4 ft. 9½ in.; height at the rump to hoof, 4 ft. 2 in. The head was cut off, as well as one fore and one hind foot. The head is so full of symmetry, and so beautiful, that I shall have a drawing of it to-morrow, as well as careful ones of the feet. Whilst the butchers were at work, I was highly interested to see one of our Indians cutting out the milk-bag of the cow and eating it, quite fresh and raw, in pieces somewhat larger than a hen's egg. One of the stomachs was partially washed in a bucket of water, and an Indian swallowed a large portion of this. Mr. Chardon brought the remainder on the upper deck and ate it uncleaned. I had a piece well cleaned and tasted it; to my utter astonishment, it was very good, but the idea was repulsive to me; besides which, I am not a meat-eater, as you know, except when other provisions fail. The animal was in good condition; and the whole carcass was cut up and dispersed among the men below, reserving the nicer portions for the cabin. This was accomplished with great rapidity; the blood was washed away in a trice, and half an hour afterwards no one would have known that a Buffalo had been dressed on deck. We now met with a somewhat disagreeable accident; in starting and backing off the boat, our yawl was run beneath the boat; this strained it, and sprung one of the planks so much that, when we landed on the opposite side of the river, we had to haul it on shore, and turn it over for examination; it was afterwards taken to the forecastle to undergo repairs to-morrow, as it is often needed. Whilst cutting wood was going on, we went ashore. Bell shot at two Buffaloes out of eight, and killed both; he would also have shot a Wolf, had he had more bullets. Harris saw, and shot at, an Elk; but he knows little about still hunting, and thereby lost a good chance. A negro fire-tender went off with his rifle and shot two of Townsend's Hares. One was cut in two by his ball, and he left it on the ground; the other was shot near the rump, and I have it now hanging before me; and, let me tell you, that I never before saw so beautiful an animal of the same family. My drawing will be a good one; it is a fine specimen, an old male. I have been hearing much of the prevalence of scurvy, from living so constantly on dried flesh, also about the small-pox, which destroyed such numbers of the Indians. Among the Mandans, Riccarées, and Gros Ventres, hundreds died in 1837, only a few surviving; and the Assiniboins were nearly exterminated. Indeed it is said that in the various attacks of this scourge 52,000 Indians have perished. This last visitation of the dread disease has never before been related by a traveller, and I will write more of it when at Fort Union. It is now twenty minutes to midnight; and, with walking and excitement of one kind or another, I am ready for bed. Alexis and another hunter will be off in an hour on a hunt.

June 10, Saturday. I rose at half-past three this morning. It was clear and balmy; our men were cutting wood, and we went off shooting. We saw a female Elk that was loath to leave the neighborhood; and Bell shot a Sharp-tailed Grouse, which we ate at our supper and found pretty good, though sadly out of season. As we were returning to the boat, Alexis and his companion went off after Buffaloes that we saw grazing peaceably on the bank near the river. Whilst they were shooting at the Buffaloes, and almost simultaneously, the fawn of the female Elk was seen lying asleep under the bank. It rose as we approached, and Bell shot at it, but missed; and with its dam it went briskly off. It was quite small, looking almost red, and was beautifully spotted with light marks of the color of the Virginia Deer's fawn. I would have given five dollars for it, as I saw it skipping over the prairie. At this moment Alexis came running, and told the captain they had killed two Buffaloes; and almost all the men went off at once with ropes, to bring the poor animals on board, according to custom. One, however, had been already dressed. The other had its head cut off, and the men were tugging at the rope, hauling the beast along over the grass. Mr. Chardon was seated on it; until, when near the boat, the rope gave way, and the bull rolled over into a shallow ravine. It was soon on board, however, and quickly skinned and cut up. The two hunters had been absent three-quarters of an hour. At the report of the guns, two Wolves made their appearance, and no doubt fed at leisure on the offal left from the first Buffalo. Harris saw a gang of Elks, consisting of between thirty and forty. We have passed a good number of Wild Geese with goslings; the Geese were shot at, notwithstanding my remonstrances on account of the young, but fortunately all escaped. We passed some beautiful scenery when about the middle of the "Bend," and almost opposite had the pleasure of seeing five Mountain

Rams, or Bighorns, on the summit of a hill. I looked at them through the telescope; they stood perfectly still for some minutes, then went out of sight, and then again were in view. One of them had very large horns; the rest appeared somewhat smaller. Our captain told us that he had seen them at, or very near by, the same place last season, on his way up. We saw many very curious cliffs, but not one answering the drawings engraved for Catlin's work. We passed Knife River, *Rivière aux Couteaux*, and stopped for a short time to take in wood. Harris killed a Sparrow Hawk, and saw several Red-shafted Woodpeckers. Bell was then engaged in saving the head of the Buffalo cow, of which I made a drawing, and Sprague an outline, notwithstanding the horrible motion of our boat. We passed safely a dangerous chain of rocks extending across the river; we also passed White River; both the streams I have mentioned are insignificant. The weather was warm, and became cloudy, and it is now raining smartly. We have, however, a good quantity of excellent wood, and have made a good run, say sixty miles. We saw what we supposed to be three Grizzly Bears, but could not be sure. We saw on the prairie ahead of us some Indians, and as we neared them, found them to be Assiniboins. There were about ten altogether, men, squaws, and children. The boat was stopped, and a smart-looking, though small-statured man came on board. He had eight plugs of tobacco given him, and was asked to go off; but he talked a vast deal, and wanted powder and ball. He was finally got rid of. During his visit, our Gros Ventre chief and our Sioux were both in my own cabin. The first having killed three of that tribe and scalped them, and the Sioux having a similar record, they had no wish to meet. A few miles above this we stopped to cut wood. Bell and Harris went on shore; and we got a White Wolf, so old and so poor that we threw it overboard. Meantime a fawn Elk was observed crossing the river, coming toward our shore; it was shot at twice, but missed; it swam to the shore, but under such a steep bank that it could not get up. Alexis, who was told of this, ran down the river bank, reached it, and fastened his suspenders around its neck, but could not get it up the bank. Bell had returned, and went to his assistance, but all in vain; the little thing was very strong, and floundered and

PLATE CCI

Canada Goose
ANSER CANADENSIS.

PLATE 33 Canada Goose, *Branta canadensis*

PLATE 34   Clapper Rail, *Rallus longirostris*

PLATE 35 Great Blue Heron, *Ardea herodias*

PLATE 36 Atlantic Puffin, *Fratercula arctica*

PLATE 37 Razorbill, *Alca torda*

Wood Stork TANTALUS LOCULATOR

PLATE 38 Wood Stork, *Mycteria americana*

PLATE 39 Whooping Crane, *Grus americana*

PLATE 40 Tricolored Heron, *Egretta tricolor*

PLATE 41 Mallard, *Anas platyrhynchos*

PLATE 42 White Ibis, *Eudocimus albus*

PLATE CCXXXI

Long-billed Curlew. NUMENIUS LONGIROSTRIS. *1 Adt. 2 Young. 3 ..... of Animal.*

PLATE 43 Long-billed Curlew, *Numenius americanus*

PLATE 44 Snowy Egret, *Egretta thula*

PLATE 45   Brown Pelican, *Pelecanus occidentalis*

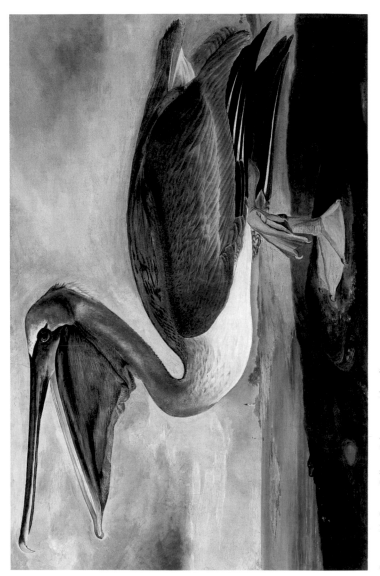

PLATE 46 Brown Pelican, *Pelecanus occidentalis*

PLATE 47 Great Blue Heron, *Ardea herodias*

PLATE 48 Little Blue Heron, *Egretta caerulea*

PLATE CCCXII

Blue-Winged Teal.
ANAS DISCORS. L.
Male 1. Female 2.

PLATE 49 Blue-winged Teal, *Anas discors*

PLATE 50 Anhinga, *Anhinga anhinga*

Black-billed Darter
PLOTUS ANHINGA. ♂

PLATE 51 Anhinga, *Anhinga anhinga*

PLATE 52 Great Egret, *Casmerodius albus*

PLATE 53 Greater Flamingo, *Phoenicopterus ruber*

PLATE 54 Trumpeter Swan, *Cygnus buccinator*

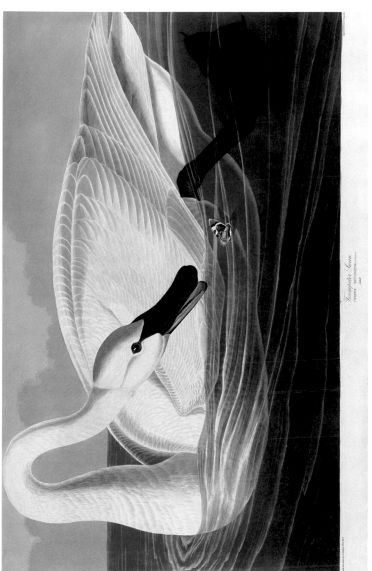

PLATE 55 Trumpeter Swan, *Cygnus buccinator*

PLATE 56 American Avocet, *Recurvirostra americana*

Plate XXXIX

No 8.

Drawn from Nature by J.J. Audubon, F.R.S. F.L.S

Drawn on Stone by R. Trembly

Leopard Spermophile

Lith. Printed & Col. by J.T. Bowen, Phil.

PLATE 57 Thirteen-lined Ground Squirrel, *Citellus tridecemlineatus*

Plate XLIV

Canada Pouched Rat.

Drawn from Nature by J.J. Audubon F.R.S. F.L.S.

Lith. Printed & Cold by J.T. Bowen, Philada.

PLATE 58 Plains Pocket Gopher, *Geomys bursarius*

Plate XXIX

Nº 6

Drawn from Nature by J.J. Audubon. FRS. FLS.

Drawn on Stone by R. Trembly

Rocky Mountain Neotoma

Printed by Nagel & Weingaertner N.Y.

PLATE 59 Bushy-tailed Woodrat, *Neotoma cinerea drummondi*

Drawn from Nature by J.J. Audubon, F.R.S.F.L.S.   Prairie Dog.   Prairie Marmot Squirrel.

On Stone by Wm E. Hitchcock.   Lith. Printed & Col. by J.T. Bowen, Phil.

PLATE 60 Black-tailed Prairie Dog, *Cynomys ludovicianus*

Plate XLVI

Drawn from Nature by J.J. Audubon, F.R.S.F.L.S

On Stone by W. E. Hitchcock

American Beaver.

Lith. Printed & Col.^d by J.T. Bowen, Philad.^a

PLATE 61 American Beaver, *Castor canadensis*

PLATE 62 American Badger, *Taxidea taxus*

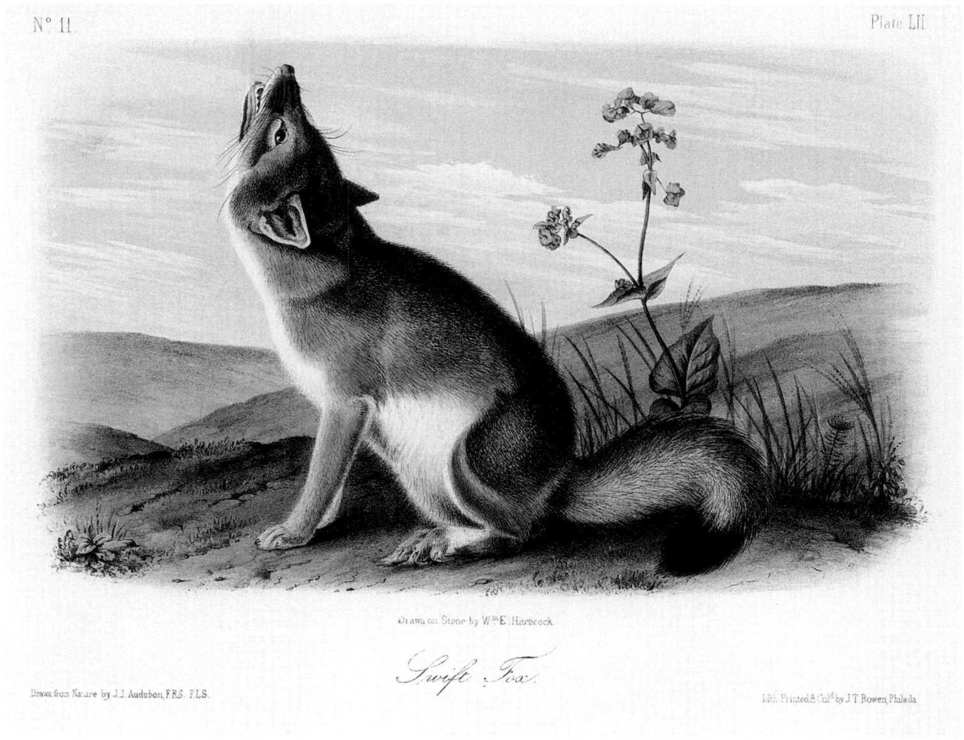
N° 11
Plate LII
Drawn on Stone by Wm E. Hitchcock
Swift Fox.
Drawn from Nature by J.J. Audubon, F.R.S. F.L.S.
Lith. Printed & Col.d by J.T. Bowen, Philada.

PLATE 63 Swift Fox, *Vulpes velox*

Plate LVII

American Bison or Buffalo

PLATE 64   American Bison, *Bison bison*

struggled till it broke the tie, and swam swiftly with the current down the river, and was lost. A slight rope would have secured it to us. This was almost the same spot where the captain caught one alive last season with the yawl; and we could have performed the same feat easily, had not the yawl been on deck undergoing repairs. We pushed off, and very soon saw more Indians on the shore, also Assiniboins. They had crossed the "Bend" below us, and had brought some trifles to trade with us; but our captain passed on, and the poor wretches sat and looked at the "Great Medicine" in astonishment. Shortly after this, we saw a Wolf attempting to climb a very steep bank of clay; he fell down thrice, but at last reached the top and disappeared at once. On the opposite shore another Wolf was lying down on a sand-bar, like a dog, and might readily have been taken for one. We have stopped for the night at nine o'clock; and I now have done my day's putting-up of memoranda and sketches, intending to enlarge upon much after I return home. I forgot to say that last evening we saw a large herd of Buffaloes, with many calves among them; they were grazing quietly on a fine bit of prairie, and we were actually opposite to them and within two hundred yards before they appeared to notice us. They stared, and then started at a handsome canter, suddenly wheeled round, stopped, closed up their ranks, and then passed over a slight knoll, producing a beautiful picturesque view. Another thing I forgot to speak of is a place not far below the Little Missouri, where Mr. Kipp assured us we should find the remains of a petrified forest, which we hope to see later.

June 11, Sunday. This day has been tolerably fine, though windy. We have seen an abundance of game, a great number of Elks, common Virginian Deer, Mountain Rams in two places, and a fine flock of Sharp-tailed Grouse, that, when they flew off from the ground near us, looked very much like large Meadow Larks. They were on a prairie bordering a large patch of Artemisia, which in the distance presents the appearance of acres of cabbages. We have seen many Wolves and some Buffaloes. One young bull stood on the brink of a bluff, looking at the boat steadfastly for full five minutes; and as we neared the spot, he waved his tail, and moved off briskly. On another occasion, a young bull that had just landed at the foot of a very steep bluff was slaughtered without difficulty; two shots were fired at it, and the poor thing was killed by a rifle bullet. I was sorry, for we did not stop for it, and its happy life was needlessly ended. I saw near that spot a large Hawk, and also a very small Tamias, or Ground Squirrel. Harris saw a Spermophile, of what species none of us could tell. We have seen many Elks swimming the river, and they look almost the size of a well-grown mule. They stared at us, were fired at, at an enormous distance, it is true, and yet stood still. These animals are abundant beyond belief hereabouts. We have seen much remarkably handsome scenery, but nothing at all comparing with Catlin's descriptions; his book must, after all, be altogether a humbug. Poor devil! I pity him from the bottom of my soul; had he studied, and kept up to the old French proverb that says, "Bon renommé vaut mieux que ceinture doré," he might have become an "honest man"—the quintessence of God's works. We did hope to have reached L'Eau Bourbeux (the Muddy River) this evening, but we are now fast ashore, about six miles below it, about the same distance that we have been told we were ever since shortly after dinner. We have had one event: our boat caught fire, and burned for a few moments near the stern, the effects of the large, hot cinders coming from the chimney; but it was almost immediately put out, thank God! Any inattention, with about 10,000 lbs. of powder on board, might have resulted in a sad accident. We have decided to write a short letter of thanks to our truly gentlemanly captain, and to present him with a handsome six-barrelled pistol, the only thing we have that may prove of service to him, although I hope he may never need it. Sprague drew four figures of the Buffalo's foot; and Bell and I have packed the whole of our skins. We ran to-day all round the compass, touching every point. The following is a copy of the letter to Captain Sire, signed by all of us.

FORT UNION, MOUTH OF YELLOWSTONE,
UPPER MISSOURI, *June 11th, 1843*

DEAR SIR,—We cannot part with you previous to your return to St. Louis, without offering to you our best wishes, and our thanks for your great courtesy, assuring you how highly we appreciate, and feel grateful for, your uniform kindness and gentlemanly deportment to each and all of us. We are most happy to add that our passage to the Yellowstone River has been devoid of any material accident, which we can only attribute to the great regularity and constant care with which you have discharged your arduous duties in the difficult navigation of the river.

We regret that it is not in our power, at this moment, to offer you a suitable token of our esteem, but hope you will confer on us the favor of accepting at our hands a six-barrelled, silver-mounted pistol, which we sincerely hope and trust you may never have occasion to use in defence of your person. We beg you to consider us,

Your well-wishers and friends, etc.,

Fort Union, June 12, Monday. We had a cloudy and showery day, and a high wind besides. We saw many Wild Geese and Ducks with their young. We took in wood at two places, but shot nothing. I saw a Wolf giving chase, or driving away four Ravens from a sand-bar; but the finest sight of all took place shortly before we came to the mouth of the Yellowstone, and that was no less than twenty-two Mountain Rams and Ewes mixed, and amid them one young one only. We came in sight of the fort at five o'clock, and reached it at seven. We passed the Opposition fort three miles below this; their flags were hoisted, and ours also. We were saluted from Fort Union, and we fired guns in return, six in number. The moment we had arrived, the gentlemen of the fort came down on horseback, and appeared quite a cavalcade. I was introduced to Mr. Culbertson and others, and, of course, the introduction went the rounds. We walked to the fort and drank some first-rate port wine, and returned to the boat at half-past nine o'clock. Our captain was pleased with the letter and the pistol. Our trip to the this place has been the quickest on record, though our boat is the slowest that ever undertook to reach the Yellowstone. Including all stoppages and detentions, we have made the trip in forty-eight days and seven hours from St. Louis. We left St. Louis April 25th, at noon; reaching Fort Union June 12th, at seven in the evening.

June 13, Tuesday. We had a remarkably busy day on board and on shore, but spent much of our time writing letters. I wrote home at great length to John Bachman, N. Berthoud, and Gideon B. Smith. We walked to the fort once and back again, and dined on board with our captain and the gentle-

men of the fort. We took a ride also in an old wagon, somewhat at the risk of our necks, for we travelled too fast for the
nature of what I was told was the road. We slept on board the
"Omega," probably for the last time.

We have been in a complete state of excitement unloading
the boat, reloading her with a new cargo, and we were all
packing and arranging our effects, as well as writing letters.
After dinner our belongings were taken to the landing of the
fort in a large keel-boat, with the last of the cargo. The room
which we are to occupy during our stay at this place is rather
small and low, with only one window, on the west side.
However, we shall manage well enough, I dare say, for the
few weeks we are to be here. This afternoon I had a good deal
of conversation with Mr. Culbertson, and found him well disposed to do all he can for us; and no one can ask for more politeness than is shown us. Our captain having invited us to
remain with him to-night, we have done so, and will breakfast
with him to-morrow morning. It is his intention to leave as
early as he can settle his business here. All the trappers are
gone to the fort, and in a few weeks will be dispersed over different and distant parts of the wilderness. The filth they had
left below has been scraped and washed off, as well indeed as
the whole boat, of which there was need enough. I have
copied this journal and send it to St. Louis by our good captain; also one box of skins, one pair Elk horns, and one bundle of Wolf and other skins.

June 14, Wednesday. At six this morning all hands rose
early; the residue of the cargo for St. Louis was placed on
board. Our captain told us time was up, and we all started for
the fort on foot, quite a short distance. Having deposited our
guns there, Bell, Squires, and I walked off to the wooding-
place, where our captain was to remain a good while, and it
was there we should bid him adieu. We found this walk one
of the worst, the very worst, upon which we ever trod; full of
wild rose-bushes, tangled and matted with vines, burs, and
thorns of all sorts, and encumbered by thousands of pieces of
driftwood, some decayed, some sunk in the earth, while others were entangled with the innumerable roots exposed by
floods and rains. We saw nothing but a few Ravens. When
nearly half way, we heard the trampling of galloping horses,

and loud hallooings, which we found to proceed from the wagon of which we have spoken, which, loaded with men, passed us at a speed one would have thought impossible over such ground. Soon after we had a heavy shower of rain, but reached the boat in good order. Harris and Sprague, who had followed us, came afterwards. I was pretty hot, and rather tired. The boat took on wood for half an hour after we arrived; then the captain shook us all by the hand most heartily, and we bade him God speed. I parted from him really with sorrow, for I have found him all I could wish during the whole passage; and his position is no sinecure, to say naught of the rabble under his control. All the wood-cutters who remained walked off by the road; and we went back in the wagon over a bad piece of ground—much easier, however, than returning on foot. As we reached the prairies, we travelled faster, and passed by the late garden of the fort, which had been abandoned on account of the thieving of the men attached to the Opposition Company, at Fort Mortimer. Harris caught a handsome snake, now in spirits. We saw Lazuli Finches and several other sorts of small birds. Upon reaching the fort, from which many great guns were fired as salutes to the steamer, which were loudly returned, I was amused at the terror the firing occasioned to the squaws and their children, who had arrived in great numbers the previous evening; they howled, fell down on the earth, or ran in every direction. All the dogs started off, equally frightened, and made for the distant hills. Dinner not being ready, three of us took a walk, and saw a good number of Tamias holes, many cacti of two sorts, and some plants hitherto uncollected by us. We saw a few Arctic Ground Finches and two Wolves. After dinner Mr. Culbertson told us that if a Wolf made its appearance on the prairie near the fort, he would give it chase on horseback, and bring it to us, alive or dead; and he was as good as his word. It was so handsomely executed, that I will relate the whole affair. When I saw the Wolf (a white one), it was about a quarter of a mile off, alternately standing and trotting; the horses were about one-half the distance off. A man was started to drive these in; and I thought the coursers never would reach the fort, much less become equipped so as to overhaul the Wolf. We were all standing on the platform of the fort, with our heads only above the palisades; and I was so fidgety that I ran down twice to tell the hunters that the Wolf was making off. Mr. Culbertson, however, told me he would see it did not make off; and in a few moments he rode out of the fort, gun in hand, dressed only in shirt and breeches. He threw his cap off within a few yards, and suddenly went off with the swiftness of a jockey bent on winning a race. The Wolf trotted on, and ever and anon stopped to gaze at the rider and the horse; till, finding out the meaning (too late, alas! for him), he galloped off with all his might; but the horse was too swift for the poor cur, as we saw the rider gaining ground rapidly. Mr. Culbertson fired his gun off as a signal, I was told, that the Wolf would be brought in; and the horse, one would think, must have been of the same opinion, for although the Wolf had now reached the hills, and turned into a small ravine, the moment it had entered it, the horse dashed after, the sound of the gun came on the ear, the Wolf was picked up by Mr. Culbertson without dismounting, hardly slackening his pace, and thrown across the saddle. The rider returned as swiftly as he had gone, wet through with a smart shower that had fallen meantime; and the poor Wolf was placed at my disposal. The time taken from the start to the return in the yard did not exceed twenty minutes, possibly something less. Two other men who had started at the same time rode very swiftly also, and skirted the hills to prevent the Wolf's escape; and one of them brought in Mr. C.'s gun, which he had thrown on the ground as he picked up the Wolf to place it on the saddle. The beast was not quite dead when it arrived, and its jaws told of its dying agonies; it scratched one of Mr. C.'s fingers sorely; but we are assured that such things so often occur that nothing is thought of it.

And now a kind of sham Buffalo hunt was proposed, accompanied by a bet of a suit of clothes, to be given to the rider who would load and fire the greatest number of shots in a given distance. The horses were mounted as another Wolf was seen trotting off towards the hills, and Mr. Culbertson again told us he would bring it in. This time, however, he was mistaken; the Wolf was too far off to be overtaken, and it reached the hill-tops, made its way through a deep ravine full of large rocks, and was then given up. Mr. Culbertson was seen coming down without his quarry. He joined the riders, started with his gun empty, loaded in a trice, and fired the first shot; then the three riders came on at full speed, loading and firing first on one side, then on the other of the horse, as if after Buffaloes. Mr. C. fired eleven times before he reached the fort, and within less than half a mile's run; the others fired once less, each. We were all delighted to see these feats. No one was thrown off, though the bridles hung loose, and the horses were under full gallop all the time. Mr. Culbertson's mare, which is of the full Blackfoot Indian breed, is about five years old, and could not be bought for four hundred dollars. I should like to see some of the best English hunting gentlemen hunt in the like manner. We are assured that after dusk, or as soon as the gates of the fort are shut, the Wolves come near enough to be killed from the platform, as these beasts oftentimes come to the trough where the hogs are fed daily. We have seen no less than eight this day from the fort, moving as leisurely as if a hundred miles off. A heavy shower put off running a race; but we are to have a regular Buffalo hunt, where I must act only as a spectator; for, alas! I am now too near seventy to run and load whilst going at full gallop. Two gentlemen arrived this evening from the Crow Indian Nation; they crossed to our side of the river, and were introduced at once. One is Mr. Chouteau, son of Auguste Chouteau, and the other a Scotchman, Mr. James Murray, at whose father's farm, on the Tweed, we all stopped on our return from the Highlands of Scotland. They told us that the snow and ice was yet three feet deep near the mountains, and an abundance over the whole of the mountains themselves. They say they have made a good collection of robes, but that Beavers are very scarce. This day has been spent altogether in talking, sight-seeing, and enjoyment. Our room was small, dark, and dirty, and crammed with our effects. Mr. Culbertson saw this, and told me that to-morrow he would remove us to a larger, quieter, and better one. I was glad to hear this, as it would have been very difficult to draw, write, or work in; and yet it is the very room where the Prince de Neuwied resided for two months, with his secretary and bird-preserver. The evening was cloudy and cold; we had had several showers of rain since our bath in the bushes this morning, and I felt somewhat fatigued. Harris and I made our beds up; Squires fixed some Buffalo robes, of which nine had been given us, on a long old bedstead, never knowing it had been the couch of a foreign prince; Bell and Sprague settled themselves opposite to us on more Buffalo skins, and night closed in. But although we had lain down, it was impossible for us to sleep; for above us was a drunken man affected with a *goître*, and not only was his voice rough and loud, but his words were continuous. His oaths, both in French and English, were better fitted for the Five Points in New York, or St. Giles of London, than anywhere among Christians. He roared, laughed like a maniac, and damned himself and the whole creation. I thought that time would quiet him, but, no! for now clarionets, fiddles, and a drum were heard in the dining-room, where indeed they had been playing at different times during the afternoon, and our friend above began swearing at this as if quite fresh. We had retired for the night; but an invitation was sent us to join the party in the dining-room. Squires was up in a moment, and returned to say that a ball was on foot, and that "all the beauty and fashion" would be skipping about in less than no time. There was no alternative; we all got up, and in a short time were amid the *beau monde* of these parts. Several squaws, attired in their best, were present, with all the guests, *engagés*, clerks, etc. Mr. Culbertson played the fiddle very fairly; Mr. Guèpe the clarionet, and Mr. Chouteau the drum, as if brought up in the army of the great Napoleon. Cotillions and reels were danced with much energy and apparent enjoyment, and the company dispersed about one o'clock. We retired for the second time, and now occurred a dispute between the drunkard and another man; but, notwithstanding this, I was so wearied that I fell asleep.

June 15, Thursday. We all rose late, as one might expect; the weather was quite cool for the season, and it was cloudy besides. We did nothing else than move our effects to an upstairs room. The Mackinaw boats arrived at the fort about noon, and were unloaded in a precious short time; and all hands being called forth, the empty boats themselves were dragged to a ravine, turned over, and prepared for calking previous to their next voyage up or down, as the case might be. The gentlemen from these boats gave me a fine pair of

Deer's horns; and to Mr. Culbertson a young Gray Wolf, and also a young Badger, which they had brought in. It snarled and snapped, and sometimes grunted not unlike a small pig, but did not bite. It moved somewhat slowly, and its body looked flattish all the time; the head has all the markings of an adult, though it is a young of the present spring. Bell and Harris hunted a good while, but procured only a Lazuli Finch and a few other birds. Bell skinned the Wolf, and we put its hide in the barrel with the head of the Buffalo cow, etc. I showed the plates of the quadrupeds to many persons, and I hope with success, as they were pleased and promised me much. To-morrow morning a man called Black Harris is to go off after Antelopes for me; and the hunters for the men of the fort and themselves; and perhaps some of the young men may go with one or both parties. I heard many stories about Wolves; particularly I was interested in one told by Mr. Kipp, who assured us he had caught upwards of one hundred with baited fish-hooks. Many other tales were told us; but I shall not forget them, so will not write them down here, but wait till hereafter. After shooting at a mark with a bow made of Elk horn, Mr. Kipp presented it to me. We saw several Wolves, but none close to the fort. Both the common Crow and Raven are found here; Bell killed one of the former.

June 16, Friday. The weather was cool this morning, with the wind due east. I drew the young Gray Wolf, and Sprague made an outline of it. Bell, Provost, Alexis, and Black Harris went over the river to try to procure Antelopes; Bell and Alexis returned to dinner without any game, although they had seen dozens of the animals wanted, and also some Common Deer. The two others, who travelled much farther, returned at dusk with empty stomachs and a young fawn of the Common Deer. Harris and I took a long walk after my drawing was well towards completion, and shot a few birds. The Buffalo, old and young, are fond of rolling on the ground in the manner of horses, and turn quite over; this is done not only to clean themselves, but also to rub off the loose old coat of hair and wool that hangs about their body like so many large, dirty rags. Those about the fort are gentle, but will not allow a person to touch their bodies, not even the young calves of the last spring. Our young Badger is quite fond of lying on his back, and then sleeps. His general appearance and gait remind me of certain species of Armadillo. There was a good deal of talking and jarring about the fort; some five or six men came from the Opposition Company, and would have been roughly handled had they not cleared off at the beginning of trouble. Arrangements were made for loading the Mackinaw barges, and it is intended that they shall depart for St. Louis, leaving on Sunday morning. We shall all be glad when these boats with their men are gone, as we are now full to the brim. Harris has a new batch of patients, and enjoys the work of physician.

June 17, Saturday.   Warm and fair, with the river rising fast. The young fawn was hung up, and I drew it. By dinner-time Sprague had well prepared the Gray Wolf, and I put him to work at the fawn. Bell went shooting, and brought five or six good birds. The song of the Lazuli Finch so much resembles that of the Indigo Bird that it would be difficult to distinguish them by the note alone. They keep indifferently among the low bushes and high trees. He also brought a few specimens of *Spermophilus hoodii* of Richardson, of which the measurements were taken. Wolves often retreat into holes made by the sinking of the earth near ravines, burrowing in different directions at the bottoms of these. I sent Provost early this morning to the Opposition fort, to inquire whether Mr. Cutting had written letters about us, and also to see a fine Kit Fox, brought in one of their boats from the Yellowstone. Much has been done in the way of loading the Mackinaw boats. Bell has skinned the young Wolf, and Sprague will perhaps finish preparing the fawn. The hunters who went out yesterday morning have returned, and brought back a quantity of fresh Buffalo meat. Squires brought many fragments of a petrified tree. No Antelopes were shot, and I feel uneasy on this score. Provost returned and told me Mr. Cutting's men with the letters had not arrived, but that they were expected hourly. The Kit Fox had been suffocated to death by some dozens of bundles of Buffalo robes falling on it, while attached to a ladder, and had been thrown out and eaten by the Wolves or the dogs. This evening, quite late, I shot a fine large Gray Wolf. I sincerely hope to see some Antelopes tomorrow, as well as other animals.

June 18, Sunday. This day has been a beautiful, as well as a prosperous one to us. At daylight Provost and Alexis went off hunting across the river. Immediately after an early breakfast, Mr. Murray and three Mackinaw boats started for St. Louis. After the boats were fairly out of sight, and the six-pounders had been twice fired, and the great flag floated in the stiff southwesterly breeze, four other hunters went off over the river, and Squires was one of them. I took a walk with Mr. Culbertson and Mr. Chardon, to look at some old, decaying, and simply constructed coffins, placed on trees about ten feet above ground, for the purpose of finding out in what manner, and when it would be best for us to take away the skulls, some six or seven in number, all Assiniboin Indians. It was decided that we would do so at dusk, or nearly at dark. My two companions assured me that they never had walked so far from the fort unarmed as on this occasion, and said that even a *single* Indian with a gun and a bow might have attacked us; but if several were together, they would pay no attention to us, as that might be construed to mean war. This is a good lesson, however, and one I shall not forget. About ten o'clock Alexis came to me and said that he had killed two male Antelopes, and Provost one Deer, and that he must have a cart to bring the whole in. This was arranged in a few minutes; and Harris and I went across the river on a ferry flat, taking with us a cart and a most excellent mule. Alexis' wife went across also to gather gooseberries. The cart being made ready, we mounted it, I sitting down, and Harris standing up. We took an old abandoned road, filled with fallen timber and bushes innumerable; but Alexis proved to be an excellent driver, and the mule the most active and the strongest I ever saw. We jogged on through thick and thin for about two miles, when we reached a prairie covered with large bushes of Artemisia (called here "Herbe Sainte"), and presently, cutting down a slope, came to where lay our Antelope, a young male, and the skin of the Deer, while its carcass hung on a tree. These were placed in the cart, and we proceeded across the prairie for the other Antelope, which had been tied by the horns to a large bush of Artemisia, being alive when Alexis left it; but it was now dead and stiff. I looked at its eyes at once. This was a fine old male with its coat half shed. I was sorry enough it was dead. We placed it by its relation in the cart, jumped in, and off we went at a good round trot, not returning to the road, but across the prairie and immediately under the clay hills where the Antelope go after they have fed in the prairie below from early dawn until about eight o'clock; there are of course exceptions to the contrary. Part of the way we travelled between ponds made by the melting of the snows, and having on them a few Ducks and a Black Tern, all of which no doubt breed here. After we had passed the last pond, we saw three Antelopes several hundred yards to the lee of us; the moment they perceived us Alexis said they would be off; and so they were, scampering towards the hills until out of sight. We now entered the woods, and almost immediately Harris saw the head of a Deer about fifty yards distant. Alexis, who had only a rifle, would have shot him from the cart, had the mule stood still; but as this was not the case, Alexis jumped down, took a long, deliberate aim, the gun went off, and the Deer fell dead in its tracks. It proved to be a doe with very large milk-bags, and doubtless her fawn or fawns were in the vicinity; but Alexis could not find them in the dense bush. He and Harris dragged her to the cart, where I stood holding the mule. We reached the ferry, where the boat had awaited our return, placed the cart on board without touching the game; and, on landing at the fort, the good mule pulled it up the steep bank into the yard. We now had two Antelopes and two Deer that had been killed before noon. Immediately after dinner, the head of the old male was cut off, and I went to work outlining it; first small, with the camera, and then by squares. Bell was engaged in skinning both the bodies; but I felt vexed that he had carelessly suffered the Gray Wolf to be thrown into the river. I spoke to him on the subject of never losing a specimen till we were quite sure it would not be needed; and I feel well assured he is so honest a man and so good a worker that what I said will last for all time. While looking at the Deer shot this day, Harris and I thought that their tails were very long, and that the animals themselves were very much larger than those we have to the eastward; and we all concluded to have more killed, and examine and measure closely, as this one may be an exception. It was unfortunate we did not speak of this an hour sooner, as two Deer had been killed on this side the river by a hunter belonging to the fort; but Mr. Culbertson assured me that we should have enough of them in a few days. I am told that the Rocky Mountain Rams lost most of their young during the hard frosts of the early spring; for, like those of the common sheep, the lambs are born as early as the 1st of March, and hence their comparative scarcity. Harris and Bell have shot a handsome White Wolf, a female, from the ramparts; having both fired together, it is not known which shot was the fatal one. Bell wounded another in the leg, as there were several marauders about; but the rascal made off.

June 19, Monday. It began raining early this morning; by "early," I mean fully two hours before daylight. The first news I heard was from Mr. Chardon, who told me he had left a Wolf feeding out of the pig's trough, which is immediately under the side of the fort. The next was from Mr. Larpenteur, who opens the gates when the bell rings at sunrise, who told us he saw seven Wolves within thirty yards, or less, of the fort. I have told him since, with Mr. Chardon's permission, to call upon us before he opens these mighty portals, whenever he espies Wolves from the gallery above, and I hope that to-morrow morning we may shoot one or more of these bold marauders. Sprague has been drawing all day, and I a good part of it; and it has been so chilly and cold that we have had fires in several parts of the fort. Bell and Harris have gone shooting this afternoon, and have not yet returned. Bell cleaned the Wolf shot last night, and the two Antelopes; old Provost boiled brine, and the whole of them are now in pickle. There are some notions that two kinds of Deer are found hereabouts, one quite small, the other quite large; but of this I have no proof at present. The weather was too bad for Alexis to go hunting. Young Mr. McKenzie and a companion went across the river, but returned soon afterwards, having seen nothing but one Grizzly Bear. The water is either at a stand, or falling a little.—*Later.* Harris and Bell have returned, and, to my delight and utter astonishment, have brought two new birds: one a Lark, small and beautiful; the other like our common Golden-winged Woodpecker, but with a red mark instead of a black one along the lower mandible running backward. I am quite amazed at the differences of opinion respecting the shedding —or not shedding—of the horns of the Antelope; and this must be looked to with the greatest severity, for if these animals *do* shed their horns, they are no longer *Antelopes*. We are about having quite a ball in honor of Mr. Chardon, who leaves shortly for the Blackfoot Fort.

June 20, Tuesday. It rained nearly all night; and though the ball was given, I saw nothing of it, and heard but little, for I went to bed and to sleep. Sprague finished the drawing of the old male Antelope, and I mine, taking besides the measurements, etc., which I give here. . . . Bell has skinned the head and put it in pickle. The weather was bad, yet old Provost, Alexis, and Mr. Bonaventure, a good hunter and a first-rate shot, went over the river to hunt. They returned, however, without anything, though they saw three or four Deer, and a Wolf almost black, with very long hair, which Provost followed for more than a mile, but uselessly, as the rascal outwitted him after all. Harris and Bell are gone too, and I hope they will bring some more specimens of Sprague's Lark and the new Golden-winged Woodpecker.

To fill the time on this dreary day, I asked Mr. Chardon to come up to our room and give us an account of the small-pox among the Indians, especially among the Mandans and Riccarees, and he related as follows: Early in the month of July, 1837, the steamer "Assiniboin" arrived at Fort Clark with many cases of small-pox on board. Mr. Chardon, having a young son on the boat, went thirty miles to meet her, and took his son away. The pestilence, however, had many victims on the steamboat, and seemed destined to find many more among the helpless tribes of the wilderness. An Indian stole the blanket of one of the steamboat's watchmen (who lay at the point of death, if not already dead), wrapped himself in it, and carried it off, unaware of the disease that was to cost him his life, and that of many of his tribe—thousands, indeed. Mr. Chardon offered a reward immediately for the return of the blanket, as well as a new one in its stead, and promised that no punishment should be inflicted. But the robber was a great chief; through shame, or some other motive, he never came forward, and, before many days, was a corpse. Most of the Riccarees and Mandans were some eighty miles in the prairies, hunting Buffaloes and saving meat for the winter. Mr.

Chardon despatched an express to acquaint them all of the awful calamity, enjoining them to keep far off, for that death would await them in their villages. They sent word in return, that their corn was suffering for want of work, that they were not afraid, and would return; the danger to them, poor things, seemed fabulous, and doubtless they thought other reasons existed, for which this was an excuse. Mr. Chardon sent the man back again, and told them their crop of corn was nothing compared to their lives; but Indians are Indians, and, in spite of all entreaties, they moved *en masse*, to confront the awful catastrophe that was about to follow. When they reached the villages, they thought the whites had saved the Riccarees, and put the plague on them alone (they were Mandans). Moreover, they thought, and said, that the whites had a preventive medicine, which the whites would not give them. Again and again it was explained to them that this was not the case, but all to no purpose; the small-pox had taken such a hold upon the poor Indians, and in such malignant form, that they died oftentimes within the rising and setting of a day's sun. They died by hundreds daily; their bodies were thrown down beneath the high bluff, and soon produced a stench beyond description. Men shot their wives and children, and afterwards, driving several balls in their guns, would place the muzzle in their mouths, and, touching the trigger with their feet, blow their brains out. About this time Mr. Chardon was informed that one of the young Mandan chiefs was bent on shooting him, believing he had brought the pestilence upon the Indians. One of Mr. Chardon's clerks heard of this plot, and begged him to remain in the store; at first Mr. Chardon did not place any faith in the tale, but later was compelled to do so, and followed his clerk's advice. The young chief, a short time afterwards, fell a victim to this fearful malady; but probably others would have taken his life had it not been for one of those strange incidents which come, we know not why, nor can we explain them. A number of the chiefs came that day to confer with Mr. Chardon, and while they were talking angrily with him, he sitting with his arms on a table between them, a Dove, being pursued by a Hawk, flew in through the open door, and sat panting and worn out on Mr. Chardon's arm for more than a minute, when it flew off.

The Indians, who were quite numerous, clustered about him, and asked him what the bird came to him for? After a moment's thought, he told them that the bird had been sent by the white men, his friends, to see if it was true that the Mandans had killed him, and that it must return with the answer as soon as possible; he added he had told the Dove to say that the Mandans were his friends, and would never kill him, but would do all they could for him. The superstitious redmen believed this story implicitly; thenceforth they looked on Mr. Chardon as one of the Great Spirit's sons, and believed he alone could help them. Little, however, could be done; the small-pox continued its fearful ravages, and the Indians grew fewer and fewer day by day. For a long time the Riccarees did not suffer; the Mandans became more and more astounded at this, and became exasperated against both whites and Indians. The disease was of the most virulent type, so that within a few hours after death the bodies were a mass of rottenness. Men killed themselves, to die a nobler death than that brought by the dreaded plague. One young warrior sent his wife to dig his grave; and she went, of course, for no Indian woman dares disobey her lord. The grave was dug, and the warrior, dressed in his most superb apparel, with lance and shield in hand, walked towards it singing his own death song, and, finding the grave finished, threw down all his garments and arms, and leaped into it, drawing his knife as he did so, and cutting his body almost asunder. This done, the earth was thrown over him, the grave filled up, and the woman returned to her lodge to live with her children, perhaps only another day. A great chief, who had been a constant friend to the whites, having caught the pest, and being almost at the last extremity, dressed himself in his fineries, mounted his war-steed, and, fevered and in agony, rode among the villages, speaking against the whites, urging the young warriors to charge upon them and destroy them all. The harangue over, he went home, and died not many hours afterward. The exposure and exertion brought on great pains, and one of the men from the fort went to him with something that gave him temporary relief; before he died, he acknowledged his error in trying to create trouble between the whites and Indians, and it was his wish to be buried in front of the gate of the fort, with all his trophies around and above his body; the promise was given him that this should be done, and he died in the belief that the white man, as he trod on his grave, would see that he was humbled before him, and would forgive him. Two young men, just sickening with the disease, began to talk of the dreadful death that awaited them, and resolved not to wait for the natural close of the malady, the effects of which they had seen among their friends and relatives. One said the knife was the surest and swiftest weapon to carry into effect their proposed self-destruction; the other contended that placing an arrow in the throat and forcing it into the lungs was preferable. After a long debate they calmly rose, and each adopted his own method; in an instant the knife was driven into the heart of one, the arrow into the throat of the other, and they fell dead almost at the same instant. Another story was of an extremely handsome and powerful Indian who lost an only son, a beautiful boy, upon whom all his hopes and affections were placed. The loss proved too much for him; he called his wife, and, after telling her what a faithful husband he had been, said to her, "Why should we live? all we cared for is taken from us, and why not at once join our child in the land of the Great Spirit?" She consented; in an instant he shot her dead on the spot, reloaded his gun, put the muzzle in his mouth, touched the trigger, and fell back dead. On the same day another curious incident occurred; a young man, covered with the eruption, and apparently on the eve of death, managed to get to a deep puddle of mire or mud, threw himself in it, and rolled over and over as a Buffalo is wont to do. The sun was scorching hot, and the poor fellow got out of the mire covered with a coating of clay fully half an inch thick and laid himself down; the sun's heat soon dried the clay, so as to render it like unburnt bricks, and as he walked or crawled along towards the village, the mud drying and falling from him, taking the skin with it, and leaving the flesh raw and bleeding, he was in agony, and besought those who passed to kill him; but, strange to say, after enduring tortures, the fever left him, he recovered, and is still living, though badly scarred. Many ran to the river, in the delirium of the burning fever, plunged in the stream, and rose no more. The whites in the fort, as well as the Riccarees, took the disease after all.

The Indians, with few exceptions, died, and three of the whites. The latter had no food in the way of bread, flour, sugar, or coffee, and they had to go stealthily by night to steal small pumpkins, about the size of a man's fist, to subsist upon—and this amid a large number of wild, raving, mad Indians, who swore revenge against them all the while. This is a mere sketch of the terrible scourge which virtually annihilated two powerful tribes of Indians, and of the trials of the traders attached to the Fur Companies on these wild prairies, and I can tell you of many more equally strange. The mortality, as taken down by Major Mitchell, was estimated by that gentleman at 150,000 Indians, including those from the tribes of the Riccarees, Mandans, Sioux, and Blackfeet. The small-pox was in the very fort from which I am now writing this account, and its ravages here were as awful as elsewhere. Mr. Chardon had the disease, and was left for dead; but one of his clerks saw signs of life, and forced him to drink a quantity of hot whiskey mixed with water and nutmeg; he fell into a sound sleep, and his recovery began from that hour. He says that with him the pains began in the small of the back, and on the back part of his head, and were intense. He concluded by assuring us all that the small-pox had never been known in the civilized world, as it had been among the poor Mandans and other Indians. Only *twenty-seven* Mandans were left to tell the tale; they have now augmented to ten or twelve lodges in the six years that have nearly elapsed since the pestilence.

Harris and Bell came back bringing several small birds among which three or four proved to be a Blackbird nearly allied to the Rusty Grakle, but with evidently a much shorter and straighter bill. Its measurements will be given, of course. The weather is still lowering and cold, and it rains at intervals. We are now out of specimens of quadrupeds to draw from. Our gentlemen seem to remember the ball of last night, and I doubt not will go early to bed, as I shall.

June 21, Wednesday. Cloudy and lowering weather; however, Provost went off over the river, before daylight, and shot a Deer, of what kind we do not know; he returned about noon, very hungry. The mud was dreadful in the bottoms. Bell and young McKenzie went off after breakfast, but brought nothing but a Sharp-tailed Grouse, though McKenzie shot two Wolves. The one Harris shot last night proved to be an old female not worth keeping; her companions had seamed her jaws, for in this part of the world Wolves feed upon Wolves, and no mistake. This evening I hauled the beast under the ramparts, cut her body open, and had a stake driven quite fast through it, to hold it as a bait. Harris and Bell are this moment on the lookout for the rascals. Wolves here not only eat their own kind, but are the most mischievous animals in the country; they eat the young Buffalo calves, the young Antelopes, and the young of the Bighorn on all occasions, besides Hares of different sorts, etc. Buffaloes never scrape the snow with their feet, but with their noses, notwithstanding all that has been said to the contrary, even by Mr. Catlin. Bell brought home the hind parts, the head, and one forefoot of a new species of small Hare.

We are told these Hares are very plentiful, and yet this is the first specimen we have seen, and sorry am I that it amounts to no specimen at all. Harris and I walked several miles, but killed nothing; we found the nest of a Sparrowhawk, and Harris, assisted by my shoulders, reached the nest, and drew out two eggs. Sprague went across the hills eastward, and was fortunate enough to shoot a superb specimen of the Arctic Bluebird. This evening, Mr. Culbertson having told me the Rabbits, such as Bell had brought, were plentiful on the road to the steamboat landing, Harris, Bell, and I walked there; but although we were very cautious, we saw none, and only procured a Black-headed Grosbeak, which was shot whilst singing delightfully. To-morrow morning Mr. Chardon leaves us in the keel-boat for the Blackfoot Fort, and Mr. Kipp will leave for the Crows early next week.

June 22, Thursday. We rose very late this morning, with the exception of Provost who went out shooting quite early; but he saw nothing fit for his rifle. All was bustle after breakfast, as Mr. Chardon's boat was loading, the rigging being put in order, the men moving their effects, etc., and a number of squaws, the wives of the men, were moving to and fro for hours before the ultimate departure of the boat, which is called the "Bee." The cargo being arranged, thirty men went on board, including the commander, friend Chardon, thirteen squaws, and a number of children, all more or less half-breeds. The flag of Fort Union was hoisted, the four-pounder run out of the front gate, and by eleven o'clock all was ready. The keel-boat had a brass swivel on her bows, and fired first, then off went the larger gun, and many an Antelope and Deer were doubtless frightened at the report that echoed through the hills far and near. We bid adieu to our good friend Chardon; and his numerous and willing crew, taking the cordelle to their shoulders, moved the boat against a strong current in good style. Harris and Bell had gone shooting and returned with several birds, among which was a female Red-patched Woodpecker, and a Lazuli Finch. Dinner over, I went off with young McKenzie after Hares; found none, but started a Grizzly Bear from her lair. Owen McKenzie followed the Bear and I continued after Hares; he saw no more of Bruin, and I not a Hare, and we both returned to the fort after a tramp of three hours. As I was walking over the prairie, I found an Indian's skull (an Assiniboin) and put it in my game pouch. Provost made a whistle to imitate the noise made by the fawns at this season, which is used to great advantage to decoy the female Deer; shortly afterward Mr. Bonaventure returned, and a cart was sent off at once to bring in a doe which he had killed below. This species of Deer is much larger than the one we have in Virginia, but perhaps no more so than those in Maine; and as yet we cannot tell whether it may, or may not, prove a distinct species. We took all its measurements, and Bell and Provost are now skinning it. Its gross weight is 140 lbs., which I think is heavier than any doe I have seen before. The animal is very poor and evidently has fawns in the woods. The little new Lark that I have named after Sprague has almost all the habits of the Skylark of Europe. Whilst looking anxiously after it, on the ground where we supposed it to be singing, we discovered it was high over our heads, and that sometimes it went too high for us to see it at all. We have not yet been able to discover its nest. Bell is of opinion that the Red-collared Ground Finch has its nest in the deserted holes of the Ground Squirrel, and we intend to investigate this. He also believes that Say's Flycatcher builds in rocky caverns or fissures, as he found the nest of a bird in some such place, after having wounded one of this species, which retired into the fissures of the rock, which he examined in pursuit of the wounded bird. The nest had no eggs; we are going to pay it a visit. Bell was busy most of the day skinning birds, and Sprague drew a beautiful plant. I found a number of wild roses in bloom, quite sweet-scented, though single, and of a very pale rose-color.

June 23, Friday. We have had a fine, warm day. The hunters of Buffaloes started before daylight, and Squires accompanied them; they are not expected back till sometime to-morrow. Provost went across the river with them, and with the assistance of his bleating whistle, brought several does round him, and a good many Wolves. He killed two does, drew them to a tree, and hung his coat near them while he returned for help to bring them to the fort. The hunters have a belief that a garment hung near game freshly killed will keep the Wolves at bay for a time; but there are exceptions to all rules, as when he returned with the cart, a dozen hungry rascals of Wolves had completely devoured one doe and all but one ham of the other; this he brought to the fort. The does at this season, on hearing the "bleat," run to the spot, supposing, no doubt, that the Wolves have attacked their fawns, and in rushing to the rescue, run towards the hunter, who despatches them without much trouble, unless the woods are thickly overgrown with bushes and brush, when more diffi culty is experienced in seeing them, although one may hear them close by; but it is a cruel, deceitful, and unsportsmanlike method, of which I can never avail myself, and which I try to discountenance. Bell was busy all day with skins, and Sprague with flowers, which he delineates finely. Mr. Kipp presented me with a complete dress of a Blackfoot warrior, ornamented with many tufts of Indian hair from scalps, and also with a saddle. After dinner, Harris, who felt poorly all morning, was better, and we went to pay a visit at the Opposition fort. We started in a wagon with an old horse called Peter, which stands fire like a stump. In going, we found we could approach the birds with comparative ease, and we had the good fortune to shoot three of the new Larks. I killed two, and Harris one. When this species starts from the ground, they fly in a succession of undulations, which renders aim at them quite difficult; after this, and in the same manner, they elevate themselves to some considerable height, as if about to sing, and presently pitch towards the ground, where they run prettily, and at times stand still and quite erect for a few minutes; we hope to discover their nests soon. Young Meadow Larks, Red-shafted Woodpeckers, and the Red-cheeked ditto, are abundant. We reached Fort Mortimer in due time; passed first between several sulky, half-starved looking Indians, and came to the gate, where we were received by the "bourgeois," a young man by the name of Collins, from Hopkinsville, Ky. We found the place in a most miserable condition, and about to be carried away by the falling in of the banks on account of the great rise of water in the Yellowstone, that has actually dammed the Missouri. The current ran directly across, and the banks gave way at such a rate that the men had been obliged already to tear up the front of the fort and remove it to the rear. To-morrow they are to remove the houses themselves, should they stand the coming night, which appeared to me somewhat dubious. We saw a large athletic man who has crossed the mountains twice to the Pacific; he is a Philadelphian, named Wallis, who had been a cook at Fort Union four years, but who had finally deserted, lived for a time with the Crows, and then joined the Opposition. These persons were very polite to us, and invited us to remain and take supper with them; but as I knew they were short of provisions, I would not impose myself upon them, and so, with thanks for their hospitality, we excused ourselves and returned to Fort Union. As we were in search of birds, we saw a small, whitish-colored Wolf trotting across the prairie, which hereabouts is very extensive and looks well, though the soil is poor. We put Peter to a trot and gained on the Wolf, which did not see us until we were about one hundred yards off; he stopped suddenly, and then went off at a canter. Harris gave the whip to Peter, and off we went, evidently gaining rapidly on the beast, when it saw an Indian in its road; taking fright, it dashed to one side, and was soon lost in a ravine. We congratulated ourselves, on reaching the fort, that we had such good fortune as to be able to sup and sleep here, instead of at Fort Mortimer. Bell had taken a walk and brought in a few birds. The prairie is covered with cacti, and Harris and I suffered by them; my feet were badly pricked by the thorns, which penetrated my boots at the junction of the soles with the upper leathers. I have to-day heard several strange stories about Grizzly Bears, all of which I must have corroborated before I fully accept them. The Otters and Musk-rats of this part of the country are smaller than in the States; the first is the worst enemy that the Beaver has.

June 24, Saturday. Bell killed a small Wolf last night, and Harris wounded another. This morning Provost started at daylight, and Bell followed him; but they returned without game. After breakfast Harris went off on horseback, and brought in a Sharp-tailed Grouse. He saw only one Deer, species not identified. Sprague and I went off last, but brought in nothing new. This afternoon I thought would be a fair opportunity to examine the manners of Sprague's Lark on the wing. Bell drove Peter for me, and I killed four Larks; we then watched the flight of several. The male rises by constant undulations to a great height, say one hundred yards or more; and whilst singing its sweet-sounding notes, beats its wings, poised in the air like a Hawk, without rising at this time; after which, and after each burst of singing, it sails in divers directions, forming three quarters of a circle or thereabouts, then rises again, and again sings; the intervals between the singing are longer than those which the song occupies, and at times the bird remains so long in the air as to render it quite fatiguing to follow it with the eye. Sprague thought one he watched yesterday remained in the air about one hour. Bell and Harris watched one for more than half an hour, and this afternoon I gazed upon one, whilst Bell timed it, for thirty-six minutes. We continued on to Fort Mortimer to see its condition, were received as kindly as yesterday, and saw the same persons. It was four o'clock, and the men were all at dinner, having been obliged to wait until this time because they had no meat in the fort, and their hunters had returned only one hour and a half before. We found that the river had fallen about fourteen inches since last evening, and the men would not remove for the present. On our way homeward Bell shot a fifth Lark, and when we reached the ravine I cut out of a tree-stump the nest of an Arctic Bluebird, with six eggs in it, of almost the same size and color as those of the common Bluebird. Sprague had brought a female of his Lark, and her nest containing five eggs; the measurements of these two species I will write out to-morrow. Our Buffalo hunters are not yet returned, and I think that Squires will feel pretty well fatigued when he reaches the fort. Mr. Culbertson presented me with a pair of stirrups, and a most splendid Blackfoot crupper for my saddle. The day has been warm and clear. We caught seven catfish at the river near the fort, and most excellent eating they are, though quite small when compared with the monsters of this species on the Missouri below.

June 25, Sunday. This day has been warm and the wind high, at first from the south, but this afternoon from the north. Little or nothing has been done in the way of procuring birds or game, except that Harris and Mr. Denig brought in several Arkansas Flycatchers. Not a word from the hunters, and therefore they must have gone far before they met Buffaloes. A few more catfish have been caught, and they are truly excellent.

June 26, Monday. The hunters returned this afternoon about three o'clock; *i. e.*, Squires and McKenzie; but the carts did not reach the fort till after I had gone to bed. They have killed three Antelopes, three bull Buffaloes, and one Townsend's Hare, but the last was lost through carelessness, and I am sorry for it. The men had eaten one of the Antelopes, and the two others are fine males; Bell skinned one, and saved the head and the fore-legs of the other. One of them had the tips of the horns as much crooked inwardly (backwards) as the horns of the European Chamois usually are. This afternoon early Provost brought in a Deer of the large kind, and this also was skinned. After this Harris and Bell went off and brought in several Lazuli Finches, and a black Prairie Lark Finch of the species brought from the Columbia by Townsend and Nuttall. We caught several catfish and a very curious sturgeon, of which Sprague took an outline with the camera, and I here give the measurements. . . . It had run on the shore, and was caught by one of the men. I made a bargain this morning with the hunter Bonaventure Le Brun to procure me ten Bighorns, at $10.00 apiece, or the same price for any number he may get. Mr. Culbertson lent him old Peter, the horse, and I wrote a *petit billet* to Mr. John Collins, to ask him to have them ferried across the river, as our boat was away on a wood-cutting expedition. As Le Brun did not return, of course he was taken across, and may, perhaps, come back this evening, or early to-morrow morning, with something worth having. At this moment Bell has shot a Wolf from the ramparts, and sadly crippled another, but it made off somehow.

June 27, Tuesday. This morning was quite cool, and the wind from the north. After breakfast Bell and Owen McKenzie went off on horseback on this side of the river, to see how far off the Buffaloes are, and they may probably bring home some game. Sprague and I have been drawing all day yesterday and most of to-day. Provost has been making whistles to call the Deer; later he, Harris, and I, walked to the hills to procure the black root plant which is said to be the best antidote for the bite of the rattlesnake. We found the root and dug one up, but the plant is not yet in bloom. The leaves are long and narrow, and the flowers are said to resemble the dwarf sunflower. Harris shot two of what he calls the Small Shore Lark, male and female; but beyond the size being a little smaller than those found at Labrador, I cannot discover any specific difference. From the top of the hills we saw a grand panorama of a most extensive wilderness, with Fort Union beneath us and far away, as well as the Yellowstone River, and the lake across the river. The hills across the Missouri appeared quite low, and we could see the high prairie beyond, forming the background. Bell and McKenzie returned, having shot a Wolf in a curious manner. On reaching the top of a hill they found themselves close to the Wolf. Bell's horse ran quite past it, but young McKenzie shot and broke one fore-leg, and it fell. Bell then gave his horse to McKenzie, jumped off, ran to the Wolf, and took hold of it by the tail, pulling it towards the horses; but it got up and ran rapidly. Bell fired two shots in its back with a pistol without stopping it, then he ran as fast as he could, shot it in the side, and it fell. Bell says its tail was longer than usual, but it was not measured, and the Wolf was left on the prairie, as they had no means of bringing it in. They saw an Antelope, some Magpies, and a Swift Fox, but no Buffaloes, though they were fifteen miles from the fort. They ran a Long-tailed Deer, and describe its movements precisely as do Lewis and Clark.

Between every three or four short leaps came the long leap of fully twenty-five feet, if not more. The Kit or Swift Fox which they saw stood by a bunch of wormwood, and whilst looking at the hunters, was seen to brush off the flies with his paws.

I am now going to take this book to Lewis Squires and ask him to write in it his account of the Buffalo hunt.

(The following is in Mr. Squires' handwriting:)

"By Mr. Audubon's desire I will relate the adventures that befell me in my first Buffalo hunt, and I am in hopes that among the rubbish a trifle, at least, may be obtained which may be of use or interest to him. On the morning of Friday, the 23d, before daylight, I was up, and in a short time young McKenzie made his appearance. A few minutes sufficed to saddle our horses, and be in readiness for our contemplated hunt. We were accompanied by Mr. Bonaventure the younger, one of the hunters of the fort, and two carts to bring in whatever kind of meat might be procured. We were ferried across the river in a flatboat, and thence took our departure for the Buffalo country. We passed through a wooded bottom for about one mile, and then over a level prairie for about one mile and a half, when we commenced the ascent of the bluffs that bound the western side of the Missouri valley; our course then lay over an undulating prairie, quite rough, and steep hills with small ravines between, and over dry beds of streams that are made by the spring and fall freshets. Occasionally we were favored with a level prairie never exceeding two miles in extent. When the carts overtook us, we exchanged our horses for them, and sat on Buffalo robes on the bottom, our horses following on behind us. As we neared the place where the Buffaloes had been killed on the previous hunt, Bonaventure rode alone to the top of a hill to discover, if possible, their whereabouts; but to our disappointment nothing living was to be seen. We continued on our way watching closely, ahead, right and left. Three o'clock came and as yet nothing had been killed; as none of us had eaten anything since the night before, our appetites admonished us that it was time to pay attention to them. McKenzie and Bonaventure began to look about for Antelopes; but before any were 'comeatable,' I fell asleep, and was awakened by the report of a gun. Before we, in the carts, arrived at the spot from whence this report proceeded, the hunters had killed, skinned, and nearly cleaned the game, which was a fine male Antelope. I regretted exceedingly I was not awake when it was killed, as I might have saved the skin for Mr. Audubon, as well as the head, but I was too late. It was now about five o'clock, and one may well imagine I was *somewhat* hungry. Owen McKenzie commenced eating the raw liver, and offered me a piece. What others can eat, I felt assured I could at least taste. I accordingly took it and ate quite a piece of it; to my utter astonishment, I found it not only palatable but very good; this experience goes far to convince me that our prejudices make things appear more disgusting than fact proves them to be. Our Antelope cut up and in the cart, we proceeded on our 'winding way,' and scarcely had we left the spot where the entrails of the animal remained, before the Wolves and Ravens commenced coming from all quarters, and from places where a minute before there was not a sign of one. We had not proceeded three hundred yards at the utmost, before eight Wolves were about the spot, and others approaching. On our way, both going and returning, we saw a cactus of a conical shape, having a light straw-colored, double flower, differing materially from the flower of the flat cactus, which is quite common; had I had any means of bringing one in, I would most gladly have done so, but I could not depend on the carts, and as they are rather unpleasant companions, I preferred awaiting another opportunity, which I hope may come in a few days. We shot a young of Townsend's Hare, about seven or eight steps from us, with about a dozen shot; I took good care of it until I left the cart on my return to the fort, but when the carts arrived it had carelessly been lost. This I regretted very much, as Mr. Audubon wanted it. It was nearly sunset when Bonaventure discovered a Buffalo bull, so we concluded to encamp for the night, and run the Buffaloes in the morning. We accordingly selected a spot near a pond of water, which in spring and fall is quite a large lake, and near which there was abundance of good pasture; our horses were soon unsaddled and hoppled, a good fire blazing, and some of the Antelope meat roasting on sticks before it. As soon as a bit was done, we commenced operations, and it was soon gone 'the way of all flesh.' I never before ate meat without salt or pepper, and until then never fully appreciated these two *luxuries*, as they now seemed, nor can any one, until deprived of them, and seated on a prairie as we were, or in some similar situation. On the opposite side of the lake we saw a Grizzly Bear, but he was unapproachable. After smoking our pipes we rolled ourselves in our robes, with our saddles for pillows, and were soon lost in a sound, sweet sleep. During the night I was awakened by a crunching sound; the fire had died down, and I sat up and looking about perceived a Wolf quietly feeding on the remains of our supper. One of the men awoke at the same time and fired at the Wolf, but without effect, and the fellow fled; we neither saw nor heard more of him during the night. By daylight we were all up, and as our horses had not wandered far, it was the work of a few minutes to catch and saddle them. We rode three or four miles before we discovered anything, but at last saw a group of three Buffaloes some miles from us. We pushed on, and soon neared them; before arriving at their feeding-ground, we saw, scattered about, immense quantities of pumice-stone, in detached pieces of all sizes; several of the hills appeared to be composed wholly of it. As we approached within two hundred yards of the Buffaloes they started, and away went the hunters after them. My first intention of being merely a looker-on continued up to this moment, but it was impossible to resist following; almost unconsciously I commenced urging my horse after them, and was soon rushing up hills and through ravines; but my horse gave out, and disappointment and anger followed, as McKenzie and Bonaventure succeeded in killing two, and wounding a third, which escaped. As soon as they had finished them, they commenced skinning and cutting up one, which was soon in the cart, the offal and useless meat being left on the ground. Again the Wolves made their appearance as we were leaving; they seemed shy, but Owen McKenzie succeeded in killing one, which was old and useless. The other Buffalo was soon skinned and in the cart. In the meantime McKenzie and I started on horseback for water. The man who had charge of the keg had let it all run out, and most fortunately none of us had wanted water until now. We rode to a pond, the water of which was very salt and warm, but we had to drink this or none; we did so, filled our flasks for the rest of the party, and a few minutes afterward rejoined them. We started again for more meat to complete our load. I observed, as we approached the Buffaloes, that they stood gazing at us with their heads erect, lashing their sides with their tails; as soon as they discovered what we were at, with the quickness of thought they wheeled, and with the most surprising speed, for an animal apparently so clumsy and awkward, flew before us. I could hardly imagine that these enormous animals could move so quickly, or realize that their speed was as great as it proved to be; and I doubt if in this country one horse in ten can be found that will keep up with them. We rode five or six miles before we discovered any more. At last we saw a single bull, and while approaching him we started two others; slowly we wended our way towards them until within a hundred yards, when away they went. I had now begun to enter into the spirit of the chase, and off I started, full speed, down a rough hill in swift pursuit; at the bottom of the hill was a ditch about eight feet wide; the horse cleared this safely. I continued, leading the others by some distance, and rapidly approaching the Buffaloes. At this prospect of success my feelings can better be imagined than described. I kept the lead of the others till within thirty or forty yards of the Buffaloes, when I began making preparations to fire as soon as I was sufficiently near; imagine, if possible, my disappointment when I discovered that now, when all my hopes of success were raised to the highest pitch, I was fated to meet a reverse as mortifying as success would have been gratifying. My horse failed, and slackened his pace, despite every effort of mine to urge him on; the other hunters rushed by me at full speed, and my horse stopped altogether. I saw the others fire; the animal swerved a little, but still kept on. After breathing my horse a while, I succeeded in starting him up again, followed after them, and came up in time to fire one shot ere the animal was brought down. I think that I never saw an eye so ferocious in expression as that of the wounded Buffalo; rolling wildly in its socket, inflamed as the eye was, it had the most frightful appearance that can be imagined; and in fact, the picture presented by the Buffalo as a whole is quite beyond my powers of description. The fierce eyes, blood streaming from his sides, mouth, and nostrils, he was the wildest, most unearthly-

looking thing it ever fell to my lot to gaze upon. His suffer-
ings were short; he was soon cut up and placed in the cart,
and we retraced our steps homeward. Whilst proceeding towards our camping-ground for the night, two Antelopes were
killed, and placed on our carts. Whenever we approached
these animals they were very curious to see what we were;
they would run, first to the right, and then to the left, then
suddenly run straight towards us until within gun-shot, or
nearly so. The horse attracted their attention more than the
rider, and if a slight elevation or bush was between us, they
were easily killed. As soon as their curiosity was gratified they
would turn and run, but it was not difficult to shoot before
this occurred. When they turned they would fly over the
prairie for about a mile, when they would again stop and look
at us. During the day we suffered very much for want of water, and drank anything that had the appearance of it, and
most of the water, in fact all of it, was either impregnated with
salt, sulphur, or magnesia—most disgusting stuff at any other
time, but drinkable now. The worst of all was some rain-water
that we were obliged to drink, first placing our handkerchiefs
over the cup to strain it, and keep the worms out of our
mouths. I drank it, and right glad was I to get even this. We
rode about five miles to where we encamped for the night,
near a little pond of water. In a few minutes we had a good
fire of Buffalo dung to drive away mosquitoes that were in
clouds about us. The water had taken away our appetites completely, and we went to bed without eating any supper. Our
horses and beds were arranged as on the previous evening.
McKenzie and I intended starting for the fort early in the
morning. We saw a great many Magpies, Curlews, Plovers,
Doves, and numbers of Antelopes. About daylight I awoke
and roused McKenzie; a man had gone for the horses, but after a search of two hours returned without finding them; all
the party now went off except one man and myself, and all returned without success except Bonaventure, who found an
old horse that had been lost since April last. He was
despatched on this to the fort to get other horses, as we had
concluded that ours were either lost or stolen. As soon as he
had gone, one of the men started again in search of the run-
aways, and in a short time returned with them. McKenzie and

I soon rode off. We saw two Grizzly Bears at the lake again. Our homeward road we made much shorter by cutting off several turns; we overtook Bonaventure about four miles from our encampment, and passed him. We rode forty miles to the fort in a trifle over six hours. We had travelled in all about one hundred and twenty miles. Bonaventure arrived two hours after we did, and the carts came in the evening."

Wednesday, June 28. This is an account of Squires' Buffalo hunt, his first one, which he has kindly written in my journal and which I hope some day to publish. This morning was very cloudy, and we had some rain, but from ten o'clock until this moment the weather has been beautiful. Harris shot a handsome though rather small Wolf; I have made a large drawing, and Sprague a fine diminished one, of the rascal. The first news we had this morning was that the ferry flat had been stolen last night, probably by the deserters from the fort who have had the wish to return to St. Louis. Some person outside of the fort threw a large stone at an Indian woman, and her husband fired in the dark, but no one could be found on searching. There is much trouble and discomfort to the managers of such an establishment as this. Provost went shooting, but saw nothing. Young McKenzie and another man were sent to find the scow, but in vain. On their return they said a hunter from Fort Mortimer had brought a Bighorn, and skinned it, and that he would let me have it if I wished. I sent Bell and Squires, and they brought the skin in. It proves to be that of an old female in the act of shedding her winter coat, and I found that she was covered with abundance of downy wool like the Antelopes under similar circumstances. Mr. Larpenteur caught five small catfish, which we ate at breakfast. After dinner Le Brun returned home, but brought only the skin of a young female of the White-tailed Deer, and I was surprised to see that it had the germ of a horn about one inch long; the skin was quite red, and it is saved. A young Elk was brought in good condition, as the hunters here know how to save skins properly; it was too young, however, to take measurements. The horns were in velvet about six inches long. When one sees the powerful bones and muscles of this young animal, one cannot fail to think of the great strength of the creature when mature, and its ability to bear with ease the enormous antlers with which its head is surmounted. The flesh of the Antelope is not comparable with that of the Deer, being dry and usually tough. It is very rarely indeed that a fat Antelope is killed. Bell has been very busy in skinning small birds and animals. We procured a young Red-shafted Woodpecker, killed by an Indian boy with a bow and arrow. Mr. Kipp's "Mackinaw" was launched this evening, and sent across the river with men to relieve the charcoal-burners; she returned immediately and we expect that Mr. Kipp's crew will go off to-morrow about twelve. I was told a curious anecdote connected with a Grizzly Bear, that I will write down; it is as follows: One of the *engagés* of the Company was forced to run away, having killed an Indian woman, and made his way to the Crow Fort, three hundred miles up the Yellowstone River. When he arrived there he was in sad plight, having his own squaw and one or two children along, who had all suffered greatly with hunger, thirst, and exposure. They were received at the fort, but in a short time, less than a week afterwards, he again ran off with his family, and on foot. The discovery was soon made, and two men were sent after him; but he eluded their vigilance by keeping close in ravines, etc. The men returned, and two others with an Indian were despatched on a second search, and after much travel saw the man and his family on an island, where he had taken refuge from his pursuers. The Buffalo-hide canoe in which he had attempted to cross the river was upset, and it was with difficulty that he saved his wife and children. They were now unable to escape, and when talking as to the best way to secure their return to the fort, the soldiers saw him walk to the body of a dead Buffalo lying on the shore of the island, with the evident intention of procuring some of it for food. As he stooped to cut off a portion, to his utter horror he saw a small Grizzly Bear crawl out from the carcass. It attacked him fiercely, and so suddenly that he was unable to defend himself; the Bear lacerated his face, arms, and the upper part of his body in a frightful manner, and would have killed him, had not the Indian raised his gun and fired at the Bear, wounding him severely, while a second shot killed him. The *engagé* was too much hurt to make further effort to escape, and one of the Company's boats passing soon after, he and his family were taken back to the fort, where he was kept to await his trial.

June 29, Thursday. It rained hard during the night, but at dawn Provost went shooting and returned to dinner, having shot a doe, which was skinned and the meat saved. He saw a Grouse within a few feet of him, but did not shoot, as he had only a rifle. Bell and I took a long walk, and shot several birds. We both were surprised to find a flock of Cliff Swallows endeavoring to build nests beneath the ledges of a clay bank. Watching the moment when several had alighted against the bank, I fired, and killed three. Previous to this, as I was walking along a ravine, a White Wolf ran past within fifteen or twenty paces of me, but I had only very small shot, and did not care to wound where I could not kill. The fellow went off at a limping gallop, and Bell after it, squatting whenever the Wolf stopped to look at him; but at last the rascal lost himself in a deep ravine, and a few minutes after we saw him emerge from the shrubs some distance off, and go across the prairie towards the river. Bell saw two others afterwards, and if ever there was a country where Wolves are surpassingly abundant, it is the one we now are in. Wolves are in the habit of often lying down on the prairies, where they form quite a bed, working at bones the while. We found a nest of the Prairie Lark, with four eggs. We saw Arctic Bluebirds, Say's Flycatcher and Lazuli Finches. Say's Flycatcher has a note almost like the common Pewee. They fly over the prairies like Hawks, looking for grasshoppers, upon which they pounce, and if they lose sight of them, they try again at another place. We returned home to dinner, and after this a discussion arose connected with the Red-shafted Woodpecker. We determined to go and procure one of the young, and finding that these have pale-yellow shafts, instead of deep orange-red, such as the old birds have, the matter was tested and settled according to my statement. Harris and I went off after the doe killed this morning, and killed another, but as I have now skins enough, the measurements only were taken, and the head cut off, which I intend drawing to-morrow. Harris shot also a Grouse, and a Woodpecker that will prove a *Canadensis*; he killed the male also, but could not find it, and we found seven young Red-shafted Woodpeckers in one nest. I killed a female

Meadow Lark, the first seen in this country by us. Provost told me (and he is a respectable man) that, during the breeding season of the Mountain Ram, the battering of the horns is often heard as far as a mile away, and that at such times they are approached with comparative ease; and there is no doubt that it is during such encounters that the horns are broken and twisted as I have seen them, and not by leaping from high places and falling on their horns, as poetical travellers have asserted. The fact is that when these animals leap from any height they alight firmly on all their four feet. At this season the young are always very difficult to catch, and I have not yet seen one of them. Harris, Bell, and young McKenzie are going Bighorn hunting to-morrow, and I hope they will be successful; I, alas! am no longer young and alert enough for the expedition. We find the mosquitoes very troublesome, and very numerous.

June 30, Friday.   The weather was dark, with the wind at the northwest, and looked so like rain that the hunters did not start as they had proposed. Sprague, Harris, and Bell went out, however, after small game. I began drawing at five this morning, and worked almost without cessation till after three, when, becoming fatigued for want of practice, I took a short walk, regretting I could no longer draw twelve or fourteen hours without a pause or thought of weariness. It is now raining quite hard. Mr. Larpenteur went after a large tree to make a ferry-boat, and the new skiff was begun this morning. I sent Provost to Fort Mortimer to see if any one had arrived from below; he found a man had done so last evening and brought letters to Mr. Collins, requesting him to do all he can for us. He also reported that a party of Sioux had had a battle with the Gros Ventres, and had killed three of the latter and a white man who lived with them as a blacksmith. The Gros Ventres, on the other hand, had killed eight of the Sioux and put them to flight. The blacksmith killed two Sioux, and the enemies cut off one leg and one arm, scalped him, and left the mangled body behind them. It is said there is now no person living who can recollect the manner in which the bitter enmity of these two nations originated. The Yellowstone River is again rising fast, and Mr. Kipp will have tough times before he reaches Fort Alexander, which was built by Mr.

Alexander Culbertson, our present host, and the Company had it honored by his name. When a herd of Buffaloes is chased, although the bulls themselves run very swiftly off, their speed is not to be compared to that of the cows and yearlings; for these latter are seen in a few minutes to leave the bulls behind them, and as cows and young Buffaloes are preferable to the old males, when the hunters are well mounted they pursue the cows and young ones invariably. Last winter Buffaloes were extremely abundant close to this fort, so much so that while the people were engaged in bringing hay in carts, the Buffaloes during the night came close in, and picked up every wisp that was dropped. An attempt to secure them alive was made by strewing hay in such a manner as to render the bait more and more plentiful near the old fort, which is distant about two hundred yards, and which was once the property of Mr. Sublette and Co.; but as the hogs and common cattle belonging to the fort are put up there regularly at sunset, the Buffaloes ate the hay to the very gates, but would not enter the enclosure, probably on account of the different smells issuing therefrom. At this period large herds slept in front of the fort, but just before dawn would remove across the hills about one mile distant, and return towards night. An attempt was made to shoot them with a cannon—a four-pounder; three were killed and several wounded. Still the Buffaloes came to their sleeping ground at evening, and many were killed during the season. I saw the head of one Mr. Culbertson shot, and the animal must have been of unusual size.

July 1, Saturday. It was still raining when I got up, but a few minutes later the sun was shining through one of our windows, and the wind being at northwest we anticipated a fine day. The ground was extremely wet and muddy, but Harris and Bell went off on horseback, and returned a few minutes after noon. They brought some birds and had killed a rascally Wolf. Bell found the nest of the Arkansas Flycatcher. The nest and eggs, as well as the manners, of this bird resemble in many ways those of our King-bird. The nest was in an elm, twenty or twenty-five feet above the ground, and he saw another in a similar situation. Mr. Culbertson and I walked to the Pilot Knob with a spy-glass, to look at the present condition of Fort Mortimer. This afternoon Squires, Provost, and I walked there, and were kindly received as usual. We found all the people encamped two hundred yards from the river, as they had been obliged to move from the tumbling fort during the rain of last night. Whilst we were there a trapper came in with a horse and told us the following: This man and four others left that fort on the 1st of April last on an expedition after Beavers. They were captured by a party of about four hundred Sioux, who took them prisoners and kept him one day and a half, after which he was released, but his companions were kept prisoners. He crossed the river and found a horse belonging to the Indians, stole it, and reached the fort at last. He looked miserable indeed, almost without a rag of clothing, long hair, filthy beyond description, and having only one very keen, bright eye, which looked as if he was both proud and brave. He had subsisted for the last eleven days on pomme blanche and the thick leaves of the cactus, which he roasted to get rid of the thorns or spines, and thus had fared most miserably; for, previous to the capture of himself and his companions, he had upset his bull canoe and lost his rifle, which to a trapper is, next to life, his dependence. When he was asked if he would have some dinner, he said that he had forgotten the word, but would try the taste of meat again. Mr. Collins was very polite to me, and promised me a hunter for the whole of next week, expressly to shoot Bighorns. I hope this promise may be better kept than that of Mr. Chardon, who told me that should he have one killed within forty miles he would send Alexis back with it at once. We heard some had been killed, but this may not be true; at any rate, men are men all over the world, and a broken promise is not unheard-of. This evening Mr. Culbertson presented me with a splendid dress, as well as one to Harris and one to Bell, and promised one to Sprague, which I have no doubt he will have. Harris and Sprague went off to procure Woodpeckers' nests, and brought the most curious set of five birds that I ever saw, and which I think will puzzle all the naturalists in the world. The first was found near the nest, of which Sprague shot the female, a light-colored Red-shafted Woodpecker. It proved to be of the same color, but had the rudiments of black stripes on the cheeks.

Next, Sprague shot an adult yellow-winged male, with the markings principally such as are found in the Eastern States. Harris then shot a young Red-shafted, just fledged, with a black stripe on the cheek. His next shot was a light-colored Red-shafted male, with black cheeks, and another still, a yellow Red-shafted with a red cheek. After all this Mr. Culbertson proposed to run a sham Buffalo hunt again. He, Harris, and Squires started on good horses, went about a mile, and returned full tilt, firing and cracking. Squires fired four times and missed once. Harris did not shoot at all; but Mr. Culbertson fired eleven times, starting at the onset with an empty gun, snapped three times, and reached the fort with his gun loaded. A more wonderful rider I never saw.

July 2, Sunday. The weather was cool and pleasant this morning, with no mosquitoes, which indeed—plentiful and troublesome as they are—Provost tells me are more scarce this season than he ever knew them thus far up the Missouri. Sprague finished his drawing of the doe's head about dinner-time, and it looks well. After dinner he went after the puzzling Woodpeckers, and brought three, all different from each other. Mr. Culbertson, his squaw wife, and I rode to Fort Mortimer, accompanied by young McKenzie, and found Mr. Collins quite ill. We saw the hunters of that fort, and they promised to supply me with Bighorns, at ten dollars apiece in the flesh, and also some Black-tailed Deer, and perhaps a Grizzly Bear. This evening they came to the fort for old Peter and a mule, to bring in their game; and may success attend them! When we returned, Harris started off with Mr. Culbertson and his wife to see the condition of Mr. Collins, to whom he administered some remedies. Harris had an accident that was near being of a serious nature; as he was getting into the wagon, thinking that a man had hold of the reins, which was not the case, his foot was caught between the axletree and the wagon, he was thrown down on his arm and side, and hurt to some extent; fortunately he escaped without serious injury, and does not complain much this evening, as he has gone on the ramparts to shoot a Wolf. Sprague saw a Wolf in a hole a few yards from the fort, but said not a word of it till after dinner, when Bell and Harris went there and shot it through the head. It was a poor, miserable, crippled old beast, that could not get out of the hole, which is not more than three or four feet deep. After breakfast we had a hunt after Hares or Rabbits, and Harris saw two of them, but was so near he did not care to shoot at them. Whilst Harris and Mr. Culbertson went off to see Mr. Collins, Mr. Denig and I walked off with a bag and instruments, to take off the head of a three-years-dead Indian chief, called the White Cow. Mr. Denig got upon my shoulders and into the branches near the coffin, which stood about ten feet above ground. The coffin was lowered, or rather tumbled, down, and the cover was soon hammered off; to my surprise, the feet were placed on the pillow, instead of the head, which lay at the foot of the coffin—if a long box may so be called. Worms innumerable were all about it; the feet were naked, shrunk, and dried up. The head had still the hair on, but was twisted off in a moment, under jaw and all. The body had been first wrapped up in a Buffalo skin without hair, and then in another robe with the hair on, as usual; after this the dead man had been enveloped in an American flag, and over this a superb scarlet blanket. We left all on the ground but the head. Squires, Mr. Denig and young Owen McKenzie went afterwards to try to replace the coffin and contents in the tree, but in vain; the whole affair fell to the ground, and there it lies; but I intend to-morrow to have it covered with earth. The history of this man is short, and I had it from Mr. Larpenteur, who was in the fort at the time of his decease, or self-committed death. He was a good friend to the whites, and knew how to procure many Buffalo robes for them; he was also a famous orator, and never failed to harangue his people on all occasions. He was, however, consumptive, and finding himself about to die, he sent his squaw for water, took an arrow from his quiver, and thursting it into his heart, expired, and was found dead when his squaw returned to the lodge. He was "buried" in the above-mentioned tree by the orders of Mr. McKenzie, who then commanded this fort. Mr. Culbertson drove me so fast, and Harris so much faster, over this rough ground, that I feel quite stiff. I must not forget to say that we had another sham Buffalo chase over the prairie in front of the fort, the riders being Squires, young McKenzie, and Mr. Culbertson; and I was glad and proud to see that

Squires, though so inexperienced a hunter, managed to shoot five shots within the mile, McKenzie eleven, and Mr. Culbertson eight. Harris killed an old Wolf, which he thought was larger and fatter than any killed previously. It was very large, but on examination it was found to be poor and without teeth in the upper jaw.

July 3, Monday. We have had a warm night and day; after breakfast we all six crossed the river in the newly built skiff, and went off in divers directions. Provost and I looked thoroughly through the brushwood, and walked fully six miles from the fort; we saw three Deer, but so far were they that it was useless to shoot. Deer-shooting on the prairies is all hazard; sometimes the animals come tripping along within ten yards of you, and at other times not nearer can you get than one hundred and fifty yards, which was the case this day. The others killed nothing of note, and crossed the river back to the fort two hours at least before us; and we shot and bawled out for nearly an hour, before the skiff was sent for us. I took a swim, found the water very pleasant, and was refreshed by my bath. The Bighorn hunters returned this afternoon with a Bighorn, a female, and also a female Black-tailed Deer. I paid them $15 for the two, and they are to start again to-morrow evening, or the next day.

July 4, Tuesday. Although we had some fireworks going on last evening, after I had laid myself down for the night, the anniversary of the Independence of the United States has been almost the quietest I have ever spent, as far as my recollection goes. I was drawing the whole day, and Sprague was engaged in the same manner, painting a likeness of Mr. Culbertson. Harris and Bell went off to try and procure a buck of the Long White-tailed Deer, and returned after dinner much fatigued and hungry enough. Bell had shot at a Deer and wounded it very severely; the poor thing ran on, but soon lay down, for the blood and froth were gushing out of its mouth. Bell saw the buck lying down, and not being an experienced hunter, thought it was dead, and instead of shooting it again, went back to call Harris; when they returned, the Deer was gone, and although they saw it again and again, the Deer outwitted them, and, as I have said, they returned weary, with no Deer. After dinner I spoke to Mr.

Culbertson on the subject, and he told me that the Deer could probably be found, but that most likely the Wolves would devour it. He prepared to send young McKenzie with both my friends; the horses were soon saddled, and the three were off at a gallop. The poor buck's carcass was found, but several Wolves and Turkey Buzzards had fared well upon it; the vertebræ only were left, with a few bits of skin and portions of the horns in velvet. These trophies were all that they brought home. It was a superb and very large animal, and I am very sorry for the loss of it, as I am anxious to draw the head of one of such a size as they represent this to have been. They ran after a Wolf, which gave them leg bail. Meanwhile Squires and Provost started with the skiff in a cart to go up the river two miles, cross, and camp on the opposite shore. The weather became very gloomy and chill. In talking with Mr. Culbertson he told me that no wise man would ever follow a Buffalo bull immediately in his track, even in a hunt, and that no one well initiated would ever run after Buffaloes between the herd and another hunter, as the latter bears on the former ever and anon, and places him in imminent danger. Buffalo cows rarely, if ever, turn on the assailant, but bulls oftentimes will, and are so dangerous that many a fine hunter has been gored and killed, as well as his horse.

July 5, Wednesday.   It rained the whole of last night and the weather has been bad all day. I am at the Bighorn's head, and Sprague at Mr. Culbertson. Provost and Squires returned drenched and hungry, before dinner. They had seen several Deer, and fresh tracks of a large Grizzly Bear. They had waded through mud and water enough for one day, and were well fatigued. Harris and Bell both shot at Wolves from the ramparts, and as these things are of such common occurrence I will say no more about them, unless we are in want of one of these beasts. Harris and I went over to see Mr. Collins, who is much better; his hunters had not returned. We found the men there mostly engaged in playing cards and backgammon. The large patches of rose bushes are now in full bloom, and they are so full of sweet fragrance that the air is perfumed by them. The weather looks clear towards the north, and I expect a fine to-morrow. Old Provost has been telling me much of interest about the Beavers, once so plentiful, but now very scarce. It takes about seventy Beaver skins to make a pack of a hundred pounds; in a good market this pack is worth five hundred dollars, and in fortunate seasons a trapper sometimes made the large sum of four thousand dollars. Formerly, when Beavers were abundant, companies were sent with as many as thirty and forty men, each with from eight to a dozen traps, and two horses. When at a propitious spot, they erected a camp, and every man sought his own game; the skins alone were brought to the camp, where a certain number of men always remained to stretch and dry them.

July 6, Thursday. The weather has been pleasant, with the wind at northwest, and the prairies will dry a good deal. After breakfast Harris, Bell, and McKenzie went off on horseback. They saw a Red Fox of the country, which is different from those of the States; they chased it, and though it ran slowly at first, the moment it saw the hunters at full gallop, it ran swiftly from them. McKenzie shot with a rifle and missed it. They saw fresh tracks of the small Hare, but not any of the animals themselves. After dinner I worked at Mr. Culbertson's head and dress, and by evening had the portrait nearly finished. At four o'clock Harris, Bell, and Sprague went across the river in the skiff; Sprague to take a view of the fort, the others to hunt. Harris and Bell shot twice at a buck, and killed it, though only one buckshot entered the thigh. Whilst we were sitting at the back gate of the fort, we saw a parcel of Indians coming towards the place, yelling and singing what Mr. Culbertson told me was the song of the scalp dance; we saw through the telescope that they were fourteen in number, with their faces painted black, and that it was a detachment of a war party. When within a hundred yards they all stopped, as if awaiting an invitation; we did not hurry as to this, and they seated themselves on the ground and looked at us, while Mr. Culbertson sent Mr. Denig to ask them to come in by the front gate of the fort, and put them in the Indian house, a sort of camp for the fellows. They all looked miserably poor, filthy beyond description, and their black faces and foully smelling Buffalo robes made them appear to me like so many devils. The leader, who was well known to be a famous rascal, and was painted red, was a tall, well-formed man. The party had only three poor guns, and a few had coarse, common lances; every man had a knife, and the leader was armed with a stick in which were inserted three blades of butcher's-knives; a blow from this weapon would doubtless kill a man. Some of the squaws of the fort, having found that they were Assiniboins, went to meet them; they took one of these, and painted her face black, as a sign of friendship. Most of these mighty warriors had a lump of fresh Buffalo meat slung on his back, which was all traded for by Mr. Larpenteur, who gave them in exchange some dried meat, not worth the notice of Harris's dog, and some tobacco. The report of their expedition is as follows: Their party at first consisted of nearly fifty; they travelled several hundred miles in search of Blackfeet, and having discovered a small troop of them, they hid till the next morning, when at daylight (this is always the time they prefer for an attack) they rushed upon the enemy, surprised them, killed one at the onset, and the rest took to flight, leaving guns, horses, shields, lances, etc., on the ground. The Assiniboins took several guns and seven horses, and the scalp of the dead Indian. It happened that the man they killed had some time ago killed the father of their chief, and he was full of joy. After eating and resting awhile, they followed the trail of the Blackfeet, hoping to again surprise them; but not seeing them, they separated into small parties, and it is one of these parties that is now with us. The chief, to show his pride and delight at killing his enemy, has borrowed a drum; and the company have nearly ever since been yelling, singing, and beating that beastly tambour. Boucherville came to me, and told me that if the swamp over the river was sufficiently dried by to-morrow morning, he would come early with a companion for two horses, and would go after Bighorns. He returned this afternoon from a Buffalo hunt and had killed six. These six animals, all bulls, will suffice for Fort Mortimer only three days. A rascally Indian had stolen his gun and Bighorn bow; the gun he said he could easily replace, but the loss of the bow he regretted exceedingly.

July 7, Friday. This morning the dirty Indians, who could have washed had they so minded, were beating the tambour and singing their miserable scalp song, until Mr. Culbertson ordered the drum taken away, and gave them more tobacco and some vermilion to bedaub their faces. They were permitted to remain about the fort the remainder of the day, and the night coming they will again be sheltered; but they must depart to-morrow morning. After breakfast Sprague worked on the view of the fort. I went on with the portrait of Mr. Culbertson, who is about as bad a sitter as his wife, whose portrait is very successful, notwithstanding her extreme restlessness. After dinner Harris, Bell, and I started on foot, and walked about four miles from the fort; the day was hot, and horseflies and mosquitoes pretty abundant, but we trudged on, though we saw nothing; we had gone after Rabbits, the tracks of which had been seen previously. We walked immediately near the foot of the clay hills which run from about a mile from and above the fort to the Lord knows where. We first passed one ravine where we saw some very curious sandstone formations, coming straight out horizontally from the clay banks between which we were passing; others lay loose and detached; they had fallen down, or had been washed out some time or other. All were compressed in such a manner that the usual form was an oval somewhat depressed in the centre; but, to give you some idea of these formations, I will send you a rough sketch. Those in the banks extended from five to seven feet, and the largest one on the ground measured a little less than ten feet. Bell thought they would make good sharpening-stones, but I considered them too soft. They were all smooth, and the grain was alike in all. We passed two much depressed and very broken ravines, and at last reached the Rabbit ground. Whilst looking at the wild scenery around, and the clay hills on the other side of the Missouri opposite the fort, I thought that if all these were granite, the formation and general appearance would resemble the country of Labrador, though the grandeur and sublimity of the latter far surpass anything that I have seen since I left them forever. I must not forget to say that on our way we passed through some grasses with bearded shafts, so sharp that they penetrated our moccasins and entered our feet and ankles, and in the shade of a stumpy ash-tree we took off our moccasins and drew the spines out. The Lazuli Finches and Arctic Bluebirds sang in our view; but though we beat all the clumps of low bushes where the Rabbits must go in, whether during night or day, we did not start one. We saw a Wolf which ran close by, reached the brow of the hill, and kept where he could watch our every motion; this they do on all possible occasions. We were all very warm, so we rested awhile, and ate some service-berries, which I found good; the gooseberries were small and green, and almost choked Harris with their sharp acidity. On our return, as we were descending the first deep ravine, a Raven flew off close by; it was so near Bell that he had no time to shoot. I followed it and although loaded with No. 6 shot, I drew my trigger and the bird fell dead; only one shot had touched it, but that had passed through the lungs. After we reached the prairie I shot a Meadow Lark, but lost it, as we had unfortunately not taken Bragg (Harris's dog). We saw a patch of wood called in these regions a "Point;" we walked towards it for the purpose of shooting Deer. I was sent to the lower end, Bell took one side, and Harris the other, and the hound we had with us was sent in; no Deer there, however, and we made for the fort, which we reached hot and thirsty enough after our long walk. As soon as I was cooled I took a good swim. I think the Indians hereabouts poor swimmers; they beat the water with their arms, attempting to "nage à la brasse;" but, alas! it is too bad to mention. I am told, however, that there are no good specimens to judge from at the fort, so this is not much of an opinion. It is strange how very scarce snakes of every description are, as well as insects, except mosquitoes and horseflies. Young McKenzie had been sent to seek for the lost ferry-boat, but returned without success; the new one is expected to be put in the water to-morrow evening. Squires and Provost had the skiff carried overland three miles, and they crossed the river in it with the intention to remain hunting until Sunday night.

July 8, Saturday. Mr. Culbertson told me this morning that last spring early, during a snow-storm, he and Mr. Larpenteur were out in an Indian lodge close by the fort, when they heard the mares which had young colts making much noise; and that on going out they saw a single Wolf that had thrown down one of the colts, and was about doing the same with another. They both made towards the spot with their pistols; and, fearing that the Wolf might kill both the colts, fired before reaching the spot, when too far off to take aim. Master Wolf ran off, but both colts bear evidence of his teeth to this day. When I came down this morning early, I was delighted to see the dirty and rascally Indians walking off to their lodge on the other side of the hills, and before many days they will be at their camp enjoying their merriment (rough and senseless as it seems to me), yelling out their scalp song, and dancing. Now this dance, to commemorate the death of an enemy, is a mere bending and slackening of the body, and patting of the ground with both feet at once, in very tolerable time with their music. Our squaws yesterday joined them in this exemplary ceremony; one was blackened, and all the others painted with vermilion. The art of painting in any color is to mix the color desired with grease of one sort or another; and when well done, it will stick on for a day or two, if not longer. Indians are not equal to the whites in the art of dyeing Porcupine quills; their ingredients are altogether too simple and natural to equal the knowledge of chemicals. Mr. Denig dyed a good quantity to-day for Mrs. Culbertson; he boiled water in a tin kettle with the quills put in when the water boiled, to remove the oil attached naturally to them; next they were thoroughly washed, and fresh water boiled, wherein he placed the color wanted, and boiled the whole for a few minutes, when he looked at them to judge of the color, and so continued until all were dyed. Red, yellow, green, and black quills were the result of his labors. A good deal of vegetable acid is necessary for this purpose, as minerals, so they say here, will not answer. I drew at Mr. Culbertson's portrait till he was tired enough; his wife—a pure Indian—is much interested in my work. Bell and Sprague, after some long talk with Harris about geological matters, of which valuable science he knows a good deal, went off to seek a Wolf's hole that Sprague had seen some days before, but of which, with his usual reticence, he had not spoken. Sprague returned with a specimen of rattle-snake root, which he has already drawn. Bell saw a Wolf munching a bone, approached it and shot at it. The Wolf had been wounded before and ran off slowly, and Bell after it. Mr. Culbertson and I saw the race; Bell gained on the Wolf until within thirty steps when he fired again; the Wolf ran some distance further, and then fell; but Bell was now exhausted by the heat, which was intense, and left the animal where it lay without attempting to skin it. Squires and Provost returned this afternoon about three o'clock, but the first alone had killed a doe. It was the first one he had ever shot, and he placed seven buckshot in her body. Owen went off one way, and Harris and Bell another, but brought in nothing. Provost went off to the Opposition camp, and when he returned told me that a Porcupine was there, and would be kept until I saw it; so Harris drove me over, at the usual breakneck pace, and I bought the animal. Mr. Collins is yet poorly, their hunters have not returned, and they are destitute of everything, not having even a medicine chest. We told him to send a man back with us, which he did, and we sent him some medicine, rice, and two bottles of claret. The weather has been much cooler and pleasanter than yesterday.

July 9, Sunday. I drew at a Wolf's head, and Sprague worked at a view of the fort for Mr. Culbertson. I also worked on Mr. Culbertson's portrait about an hour. I then worked at the Porcupine, which is an animal such as I never saw or Bell either. Its measurements are: from nose to anterior canthus of the eye, 1⅝ in., posterior ditto, 2⅛; conch of ear, 3½; distances from eyes posteriorly, 2¼; fore feet stretched beyond nose, 3½; length of head around, 4⅛; nose to root of tail, 18½; length of tail vertebræ, 6⅜; to end of hair, 7¾; hind claws when stretched equal to end of tail; greatest breadth of palm, 1¼; of sole, 1⅜; outward width of tail at base, 3⅝; depth of ditto, 3⅛; length of palm, 1½; ditto of sole, 1⅞; height at shoulder, 11; at rump, 10¼; longest hair on the back, 8⅞; breadth between ears, 2¼; from nostril to split of upper lip, ¾; upper incisors, ⅝; lower ditto, ¾; tongue quite smooth; weight 11 lbs. The habits of this animal are somewhat different from those of the Canadian Porcupine. The one of this country often goes in crevices or holes, and young McKenzie caught one in a Wolf's den, along with the old Wolf and seven young; they climb trees, however.

Provost tells me that Wolves are oftentimes destroyed by wild horses, which he has seen run at the Wolves head down, and when at a proper distance take them by the middle of the back with their teeth, and throw them several feet in the air, after which they stamp upon their bodies with the fore feet until quite dead. I have a bad blister on the heel of my right foot, and cannot walk without considerable pain.

July 10, Monday.   Squires, Owen McKenzie, and Provost, with a mule, a cart, and Peter the horse, went off at seven this morning for Antelopes. Bell did not feel well enough to go with them, and was unable to eat his usual meal, but I made him some good gruel, and he is better now. This afternoon Harris went off on horseback after Rabbits, and he will, I hope, have success. The day has been fine, and cool compared with others. I took a walk, and made a drawing of the beautiful sugar-loaf cactus; it does not open its blossoms until after the middle of the day, and closes immediately on being placed in the shade.

July 11, Tuesday.   Harris returned about ten o'clock last night, but saw no Hares; how we are to procure any is more than I can tell. Mr. Culbertson says that it was dangerous for Harris to go so far as he did alone up the country, and he must not try it again. The hunters returned this afternoon, but brought only one buck, which is, however, beautiful, and the horns in velvet so remarkable that I can hardly wait for daylight to begin drawing it. I have taken all the measurements of this perfect animal; it was shot by old Provost. Mr. Culbertson—whose portrait is nearly finished—his wife, and I took a ride to look at some grass for hay, and found it beautiful and plentiful. We saw two Wolves, a common one and a prairie one. Bell is better. Sprague has drawn another cactus; Provost and I have now skinned the buck, and it hangs in the ice-house; the head, however, is untouched.

July 12, Wednesday.   I rose before three, and began at once to draw the buck's head. Bell assisted me to place it in the position I wanted, and as he felt somewhat better, while I drew, he finished the skin of the Porcupine; so that is saved. Sprague continued his painting of the fort. Just after dinner a Wolf was seen leisurely walking within one hundred yards of the fort. Bell took the repeating rifle, went on the ramparts, fired, and missed it. Mr. Culbertson sent word to young Owen McKenzie to get a horse and give it chase. All was ready in a few minutes, and off went the young fellow after the beast. I left my drawing long enough to see the pursuit, and was surprised to see that the Wolf did not start off on a gallop till his pursuer was within one hundred yards or so of him, and who then gained rapidly. Suddenly the old sinner turned, and the horse went past him some little distance. As soon as he could be turned about McKenzie closed upon him, his gun flashed twice; but now he was almost *à bon touchant*, the gun went off—the Wolf was dead. I walked out to meet Owen with the beast; it was very poor, very old, and good for nothing as a specimen. Harris, who had shot at one last night in the late twilight, had killed it, but was not aware of it till I found the villain this morning. It had evidently been dragged at by its brothers, who, however, had not torn it. Provost went over to the other fort to find out where the Buffaloes are most abundant, and did not return till late, so did no hunting. A young dog of this country's breed ate up all the berries collected by Mrs. Culbertson, and her lord had it killed for our supper this evening. The poor thing was stuck with a knife in the throat, after which it was placed over a hot fire outside of the fort, singed, and the hair scraped off, as I myself have treated Raccoons and Opossums. Then the animal was boiled, and I intend to taste one mouthful of it, for I cannot say that just now I should relish an entire meal from such peculiar fare. There are men, however, who much prefer the flesh to Buffalo meat, or even venison. An ox was broken to work this day, and worked far better than I expected. I finished at last Mr. Culbertson's portrait, and it now hangs in a frame. He and his wife are much pleased with it, and I am heartily glad they are, for in conscience I am not; however, it is all I could do, especially with a man who is never in the same position for one whole minute; so no more can be expected. The dog was duly cooked and brought into Mr. Culbertson's room; he served it out to Squires, Mr. Denig, and myself, and I was astonished when I tasted it. With great care and some repugnance I put a very small piece in my mouth; but no sooner had the taste touched my palate than I changed my dislike to liking, and found this victim of the canine order most excellent, and made a good meal, finding it fully equal to any meat I ever tasted. Old Provost had told me he preferred it to any meat, and his subsequent actions proved the truth of his words. We are having some music this evening, and Harris alone is absent, being at his favorite evening occupation, namely, shooting at Wolves from the ramparts.

July 13, Thursday. This has been a cloudy and a sultry day. Sprague finished his drawing and I mine. After dinner Mr. Culbertson, Squires, and myself went off nine miles over the prairies to look at the "meadows," as they are called, where Mr. Culbertson has heretofore cut his winter crop of hay, but we found it indifferent compared with that above the fort. We saw Sharp-tailed Grouse, and what we thought a new species of Lark, which we shot at no less than ten times before it was killed by Mr. Culbertson, but not found. I caught one of its young, but it proved to be only the Shore Lark. Before we reached the meadows we saw a flock of fifteen or twenty Bob-o-link, *Emberiza orizivora*, and on our return shot one of them (a male) on the wing. It is the first seen since we left St. Louis. We reached the meadows at last, and tied our nag to a tree, with the privilege of feeding. Mr. Culbertson and Squires went in the "meadows," and I walked round the so-called patch. I shot seven Arkansas Flycatchers on the wing. After an hour's walking, my companions returned, but had seen nothing except the fresh tracks of a Grizzly Bear. I shot at one of the White-rumped Hawks, of which I have several times spoken, but although it dropped its quarry and flew very wildly afterwards, it went out of my sight. We found the beds of Elks and their fresh dung, but saw none of these animals. I have forgotten to say that immediately after breakfast this morning I drove with Squires to Fort Mortimer, and asked Mr. Collins to let me have his hunter, Boucherville, to go after Mountain Rams for me, which he promised to do. In the afternoon he sent a man over to ask for some flour, which Mr. Culbertson sent him. They are there in the utmost state of destitution, almost of starvation, awaiting the arrival of the hunters like so many famished Wolves. Harris and Bell went across the river and shot a Wolf under the river bank, and afterwards a Duck, but saw nothing else. But during their absence we have had a fine opportunity of witnessing the agility and extreme strength of a year-old Buffalo bull belonging to the fort. Our cook, who is an old Spaniard, threw his lasso over the Buffalo's horns, and all the men in the fort at the time, hauled and pulled the beast about, trying to get him close to a post. He kicked, pulled, leaped sideways, and up and down, snorting and pawing until he broke loose, and ran, as if quite wild, about the enclosure. He was tied again and again, without any success, and at last got out of the fort, but was soon retaken, the rope being thrown round his horns, and he was brought to the main post of the Buffalo-robe press. There he was brought to a standstill, at the risk of breaking his neck, and the last remnant of his winter coat was removed by main strength, which was the object for which the poor animal had undergone all this trouble. After Harris returned to the fort he saw six Sharp-tailed Grouse. At this season this species have no particular spot where you may rely upon finding them, and at times they fly through the woods, and for a great distance, too, where they alight on trees; when, unless you accidentally see them, you pass by without their moving. After we passed Fort Mortimer on our return we saw coming from the banks of the river no less than eighteen Wolves, which altogether did not cover a space of more than three or four yards, they were so crowded. Among them were two Prairie Wolves. Had we had a good running horse some could have been shot; but old Peter is long past his running days. The Wolves had evidently been feeding on some carcass along the banks, and all moved very slowly. Mr. Culbertson gave me a grand pair of leather breeches and a very handsome knife-case, all manufactured by the Blackfeet Indians.

July 14, Friday. Thermometer 70°–95°. Young McKenzie went off after Antelopes across the river alone, but saw only one, which he could not get near. After breakfast Harris, Squires, and I started after birds of all sorts, with the wagon, and proceeded about six miles on the road we had travelled yesterday. We met the hunter from Fort Mortimer going for Bighorns for me, and Mr. Culbertson lent him a horse and a mule. We caught two young of the Shore Lark, killed seven of Sprague's Lark, but by bad management lost two, either from the wagon, my hat, or Harris's pockets. The weather was exceedingly hot. We hunted for Grouse in the wormwood bushes, and after despairing of finding any, we started up three from the plain, and they flew not many yards to the river. We got out of the wagon and pushed for them; one rose, and Harris shot it, though it flew some yards before he picked it up. He started another, and just as he was about to fire, his gunlock caught on his coat, and off went Mr. Grouse, over and through the woods until out of sight, and we returned slowly home. We saw ten Wolves this morning. After dinner we had a curious sight. Squires put on my Indian dress. McKenzie put on one of Mr. Culbertson's, Mrs. Culbertson put on her own *superb* dress, and the cook's wife put on the one Mrs. Culbertson had given me. Squires and Owen were painted in an awful manner by Mrs. Culbertson, the *Ladies* had their hair loose, and flying in the breeze, and then all mounted on horses with Indian saddles and trappings. Mrs. Culbertson and her maid rode astride like men, and all rode a furious race, under whip the whole way, for more than one mile on the prairie; and how amazed would have been any European lady, or some of our modern belles who boast their equestrian skill, at seeing the magnificent riding of this Indian princess—for that is Mrs. Culbertson's rank—and her servant. Mr. Culbertson rode with them, the horses running as if wild, with these extraordinary Indian riders, Mrs. Culbertson's magnificent black hair floating like a banner behind her. As to the men (for two others had joined Squires and McKenzie), I cannot compare them to anything in the whole creation. They ran like wild creatures of unearthly compound. Hither and thither they dashed, and when the whole party had crossed the ravine below, they saw a fine Wolf and gave the whip to their horses, and though the Wolf cut to right and left Owen shot at him with an arrow and missed, but Mr. Culbertson gave it chase, overtook it, his gun flashed, and the Wolf lay dead. They then ascended the hills and away they went, with our princess and her faithful attendant in the van, and by and by the group returned to the camp, running full speed till they entered the fort, and all this in the intense heat of this July afternoon. Mrs. Culbertson, herself a wonderful rider, possessed of both strength and grace in a marked degree, assured me that Squires was equal to any man in the country as a rider, and I saw for myself that he managed his horse as well as any of the party, and I was pleased to see him in his dress, ornaments, etc., looking, however, I must confess, after Mrs. Culbertson's painting his face, like a being from the infernal regions. Mr. Culbertson presented Harris with a superb dress of the Blackfoot Indians, and also with a Buffalo bull's head, for which Harris had in turn presented him with a gun-barrel of the short kind, and well fitted to shoot Buffaloes. Harris shot a very young one of Townsend's Hare, Mr. Denig gave Bell a Mouse, which, although it resembles *Mus leucopus* greatly, is much larger, and has a short, thick, round tail, somewhat blunted.

July 15, Saturday.   We were all up pretty early, for we propose going up the Yellowstone with a wagon, and the skiff on a cart, should we wish to cross. After breakfast all of us except Sprague, who did not wish to go, were ready, and along with two extra men, the wagon, and the cart, we crossed the Missouri at the fort, and at nine were fairly under way— Harris, Bell, Mr. Culbertson, and myself in the wagon, Squires, Provost, and Owen on horseback. We travelled rather slowly, until we had crossed the point, and headed the ponds on the prairie that run at the foot of the hills opposite. We saw one Grouse, but it could not be started, though Harris searched for it. We ran the wagon into a rut, but got out unhurt; however, I decided to walk for a while, and did so for about two miles, to the turning point of the hills. The wheels of our vehicle were very shackling, and had to be somewhat repaired, and though I expected they would fall to pieces, in some manner or other we proceeded on. We saw several Antelopes, some on the prairie which we now travelled on, and many more on the tops of the hills, bounding westward. We stopped to water the horses at a saline spring, where I saw that Buffaloes, Antelopes, and other animals come to allay their thirst, and repose on the grassy margin. The water was too hot for us to drink, and we awaited the arrival of the cart, when we all took a good drink of the river water we had brought with us. After waiting for nearly an hour to allow the horses to bait and cool themselves, for it was very warm, we proceeded on, until we came to another watering-place, a river, in fact, which during spring overflows its banks, but now has only pools of water here and there. We soaked our wheels again, and again drank ourselves. Squires, Provost, and Owen had left sometime before us, but were not out of our sight, when we started, and as we had been, and were yet, travelling a good track, we soon caught up with them. We shot a common Red-winged Starling, and heard the notes of what was supposed to be a new bird by my companions, but which to my ears was nothing more than the Short-billed Marsh Wren of Nuttall. We reached our camping-place, say perhaps twenty miles' distance, by four o'clock, and all things were unloaded, the horses put to grass, and two or three of the party went in "the point" above, to shoot something for supper. I was hungry myself, and taking the Red-wing and the fishing-line, I went to the river close by, and had the good fortune to catch four fine catfish, when, my bait giving out, I was obliged to desist, as I found that these catfish will not take parts of their own kind as food. Provost had taken a bath, and rowed the skiff (which we had brought this whole distance on the cart, dragged by a mule) along with two men, across the river to seek for game on the point opposite our encampment. They returned, however, without having shot anything, and my four catfish were all the fresh provisions that we had, and ten of us partook of them with biscuit, coffee, and claret. Dusk coming on, the tent was pitched, and preparations to rest made. Some chose one spot and some another, and after a while we were settled. Mr. Culbertson and I lay together on the outside of the tent, and all the party were more or less drowsy. About this time we saw a large black cloud rising in the west; it was heavy and lowering, and about ten o'clock, when most of us were pretty nearly sound asleep, the distant thunder was heard, the wind rose to a gale, and the rain began falling in torrents. All were on foot in a few moments, and considerable confusion ensued. Our guns, all loaded with balls, were hurriedly placed under the tent, our beds also, and we all crawled in, in the space of a very few minutes. The wind blew so hard that Harris was obliged to hold the flappers of the tent with both hands, and sat in the water a considerable time to do this. Old Provost alone did not come in, he sat under the shelving bank of the river, and kept dry. After the gale was over, he calmly lay down in front of the tent on the saturated ground, and was soon asleep. During the gale, our fire, which we had built to keep off the myriads of mosquitoes, blew in every direction, and we had to watch the embers to keep them from burning the tent. After all was over, we snugged ourselves the best way we could in our small tent and under the wagon, and slept soundly till daylight. Mr. Culbertson had fixed himself pretty well, but on arising at daylight to smoke his pipe, Squires immediately crept into his comfortable corner, and snored there till the day was well begun. Mr. Culbertson had my knees for a pillow, and also my hat, I believe, for in the morning, although the first were not hurt, the latter was sadly out of shape in all parts. We had nothing for our breakfast except some vile coffee, and about three quarters of a sea-biscuit, which was soon settled among us. The men, poor fellows, had nothing at all. Provost had seen two Deer, but had had no shot, so of course we were in a quandary, but it is now—

July 16, Sunday. The weather pleasant with a fine breeze from the westward, and all eyes were bent upon the hills and prairie, which is here of great breadth, to spy if possible some object that might be killed and eaten. Presently a Wolf was seen, and Owen went after it, and it was not until he had disappeared below the first low range of hills, and Owen also, that the latter came within shot of the rascal, which dodged in all sorts of manners; but Owen would not give up, and after shooting more than once, he killed the beast. A man had followed him to help bring in the Wolf, and when near the river he saw a Buffalo, about two miles off, grazing peaceably, as he perhaps thought, safe in his own dominions; but, alas! white hunters had fixed their eyes upon him, and from that moment his doom was pronounced. Mr. Culbertson threw down his hat, bound his head with a handkerchief, his saddle was on his mare, he was mounted and off and away at a swift gallop, more quickly than I can describe, not towards the Buffalo, but towards the place where Owen had killed the Wolf. The man brought the Wolf on old Peter, and Owen, who was returning to the camp, heard the signal gun fired by Mr. Culbertson, and at once altered his course; his mare was evidently a little heated and blown by the Wolf chase, but both hunters went after the Buffalo, slowly at first, to rest Owen's steed, but soon, when getting within running distance, they gave whip, overhauled the Bison, and shot at it twice with balls; this halted the animal; the hunters had no more balls, and now loaded with pebbles, with which the poor beast was finally killed. The wagon had been sent from the camp. Harris, Bell, and Squires mounted on horseback, and travelled to the scene of action. They met Mr. Culbertson returning to camp, and he told Bell the Buffalo was a superb one, and had better be skinned. A man was sent to assist in the skinning who had been preparing the Wolf which was now cooking, as we had expected to dine upon its flesh; but when Mr. Culbertson returned, covered with blood and looking like a wild Indian, it was decided to throw it away; so I cut out the liver, and old Provost and I went fishing and caught eighteen catfish. I hooked two tortoises, but put them back in the river. I took a good swim, which refreshed me much, and I came to dinner with a fine appetite. This meal consisted wholly of fish, and we were all fairly satisfied. Before long the flesh of the Buffalo reached the camp, as well as the hide. The animal was very fat, and we have meat for some days. It was now decided that Squires, Provost, and Basil (one of the men) should proceed down the river to the Charbonneau, and there try their luck at Otters and Beavers, and the rest of us, with the cart, would make our way back to the fort. All was arranged, and at half-past three this afternoon we were travelling towards Fort Union. But hours previous to this, and before our scanty dinner, Owen had seen another bull, and Harris and Bell joined us in the hunt. The bull was shot at by McKenzie, who stopped its career, but as friend Harris pursued it with two of the hunters and finished it I was about to return, and thought sport over for the day. However, at this stage of the proceedings Owen discovered another bull making his way slowly over the prairie towards us. I was the only one who had balls, and would gladly have claimed the privilege of running him, but fearing I might make out badly on my slower steed, and so lose meat which we really needed, I handed my gun and balls to Owen McKenzie, and Bell and I went to an eminence to view the chase. Owen approached the bull, which continued to advance, and was now less than a quarter of a mile distant; either it did not see, or did not heed him, and they came directly towards each other, until they were about seventy or eighty yards apart, when the Buffalo started at a good run, and Owen's mare, which had already had two hard runs this

morning, had great difficulty in preserving her distance.
Owen, perceiving this, breathed her a minute, and then applying the whip was soon within shooting distance, and fired
a shot which visibly checked the progress of the bull, and enabled Owen to soon be alongside of him, when the contents
of the second barrel were discharged into the lungs, passing
through the shoulder blade. This brought him to a stand. Bell
and I now started at full speed, and as soon as we were within
speaking distance, called to Owen not to shoot again. The
bull did not appear to be much exhausted, but he was so stiffened by the shot on the shoulder that he could not turn
quickly, and taking advantage of this we approached him; as
we came near he worked himself slowly round to face us, and
then made a lunge at us; we then stopped on one side and
commenced discharging our pistols with little or no effect,
except to increase his fury with every shot. His appearance
was now one to inspire terror had we not felt satisfied of our
ability to avoid him. However, even so, I came very near being overtaken by him. Through my own imprudence, I placed
myself directly in front of him, and as he advanced I fired at
his head, and then ran *ahead* of him, instead of veering to one
side, not supposing that he was able to overtake me; but turning my head over my shoulder, I saw to my horror, Mr. Bull
within three feet of me, prepared to give me a taste of his
horns. The next instant I turned sharply off, and the Buffalo
being unable to turn quickly enough to follow me, Bell took
the gun from Owen and shot him directly behind the shoulder blade. He tottered for a moment, with an increased jet of
blood from the mouth and nostrils, fell forward on his horns,
then rolled over on his side, and was dead. He was a very old
animal, in poor case, and only part of him was worth taking
to the fort. Provost, Squires, and Basil were left at the camp
preparing for their departure after Otter and Beaver as decided. We left them eight or nine catfish and a quantity of
meat, of which they took care to secure the best, namely the
boss or hump. On our homeward way we saw several
Antelopes, some quite in the prairie, others far away on the
hills, but all of them on the alert. Owen tried unsuccessfully
to approach several of them at different times. At one place
where two were seen he dismounted, and went round a small

hill (for these animals when startled or suddenly alarmed always make to these places), and we hoped would have had a shot; but alas! no! One of the Antelopes ran off to the top of another hill, and the other stood looking at him, and us perhaps, till Owen (who had been re-mounted) galloped off towards us. My surprise was great when I saw the other Antelope following him at a good pace (but not by bounds or leaps, as I had been told by a former traveller they sometimes did), until it either smelt him, or found out he was no friend, and turning round galloped speedily off to join the one on the lookout. We saw seven or eight Grouse, and Bell killed one on the ground. We saw a Sand-hill Crane about two years old, looking quite majestic in a grassy bottom, but it flew away before we were near enough to get a shot. We passed a fine pond or small lake, but no bird was there. We saw several parcels of Ducks in sundry places, all of which no doubt had young near. When we turned the corner of the great prairie we found Owen's mare close by us. She had run away while he was after Antelopes. We tied her to a log to be ready for him when he should reach the spot. He had to walk about three miles before he did this. However, to one as young and alert as Owen, such things are nothing. Once they were not to me. We saw more Antelope at a distance, here called "Cabris," and after a while we reached the wood near the river, and finding abundance of service-berries, we all got out to break branches of these plants, Mr. Culbertson alone remaining in the wagon; he pushed on for the landing. We walked after him munching our berries, which we found very good, and reached the landing as the sun was going down behind the hills. Young McKenzie was already there, having cut across the point. We decided on crossing the river ourselves, and leaving all behind us except our guns. We took to the ferry-boat, cordelled it up the river for a while, then took to the nearest sand-bar, and leaping into the mud and water, hauled the heavy boat, Bell and Harris steering and poling the while. I had pulled off my shoes and socks, and when we reached the shore walked up to the fort barefooted, and made my feet quite sore again; but we have had a rest and a good supper, and I am writing in Mr. Culbertson's room, thinking over all God's blessings on this delightful day.

July 17, Monday. A beautiful day, with a west wind. Sprague, who is very industrious at all times, drew some flowers, and I have been busy both writing and drawing. In the afternoon Bell went after Rabbits, but saw one only, which he could not get, and Sprague walked to the hills about two miles off, but could not see any portion of the Yellowstone River, which Mr. Catlin has given in his view, as if he had been in a balloon some thousands of feet above the earth. Two men arrived last evening by land from Fort Pierre, and brought a letter, but no news of any importance; one is a cook as well as a hunter, the other named Wolff, a German, and a tinsmith by trade, though now a trapper.

July 18, Tuesday. When I went to bed last night the mosquitoes were so numerous downstairs that I took my bed under my arm and went to a room above, where I slept well. On going down this morning, I found two other persons from Fort Pierre, and Mr. Culbertson very busy reading and writing letters. Immediately after breakfast young McKenzie and another man were despatched on mules, with a letter for Mr. Kipp, and Owen expects to overtake the boat in three or four days. An Indian arrived with a stolen squaw, both Assiniboins; and I am told such things are of frequent occurrence among these sons of nature. Mr. Culbertson proposed that we should take a ride to see the mowers, and Harris and I joined him. We found the men at work, among them one called Bernard Adams, of Charleston, S. C., who knew the Bachmans quite well, and who had read the whole of the "Biographies of Birds." Leaving the men, we entered a ravine in search of plants, etc., and having started an Owl, which I took for the barred one, I left my horse and went in search of it, but could not see it, and hearing a new note soon saw a bird not to be mistaken, and killed it, when it proved, as I expected, to be the Rock Wren; then I shot another sitting by the mouth of a hole. The bird did not fly off; Mr. Culbertson watched it closely, but when the hole was demolished no bird was to be found. Harris saw a Shrike, but of what species he could not tell, and he also found some Rock Wrens in another ravine. We returned to the fort and promised to visit the place this afternoon, which we have done, and procured three more Wrens, and killed the Owl, which proves to be precisely the resemblance of the Northern specimen of the Great Horned Owl, which we published under another name. The Rock Wren, which might as well be called the Ground Wren, builds its nest in holes, and now the young are well able to fly, and we procured one in the act. In two instances we saw these birds enter a hole here, and an investigation showed a passage or communication, and on my pointing out a hole to Bell where one had entered, he pushed his arm in and touched the little fellow, but it escaped by running up his arm and away it flew. Black clouds now arose in the west, and we moved homewards. Harris and Bell went to the mowers to get a drink of water, and we reached home without getting wet, though it rained violently for some time, and the weather is much cooler. Not a word yet from Provost and Squires.

July 19, Wednesday. Squires and Provost returned early this morning, and again I give the former my journal that I may have the account of the hunt in his own words. "As Mr. Audubon has said, he left Provost, Basil, and myself making ready for our voyage down the Yellowstone. The party for the fort were far in the blue distance ere we bid adieu to our camping-ground. We had wished the return party a pleasant ride and safe arrival at the fort as they left us, looking forward to a good supper, and what I *now* call a comfortable bed. We seated ourselves around some boiled Buffalo hump, which, as has been before said, we took good care to appropriate to ourselves according to the established rule of this country, which is, 'When you can, take the best,' and we had done so in this case, more to our satisfaction than to that of the hunters. Our meal finished, we packed everything we had in the skiff, and were soon on our way down the Yellowstone, happy as could be; Provost acting pilot, Basil oarsman, and your humble servant seated on a Buffalo robe, quietly smoking, and looking on the things around. We found the general appearance of the Yellowstone much like the Missouri, but with a stronger current, and the water more muddy. After a voyage of two hours Charbonneau River made its appearance, issuing from a clump of willows; the mouth of this river we found to be about ten feet wide, and so shallow that we were obliged to push our boat over the slippery mud for about forty feet. This passed, we entered a pond formed by the contraction of the mouth and the collection of mud and sticks thereabouts, the pond so formed being six or eight feet deep, and about fifty feet wide, extending about a mile up the river, which is very crooked indeed. For about half a mile from the Yellowstone the shore is lined with willows, beyond which is a level prairie, and on the shores of the stream just beyond the willows are a few scattered trees. About a quarter of a mile from the mouth of the river, we discovered what we were in search of, the Beaver lodge. To measure it was impossible, as it was not perfect, in the first place, in the next it was so muddy that we could not get ashore, but as well as I can I will describe it. The lodge is what is called the summer lodge; it was comprised wholly of brush, willow chiefly, with a single hole for the entrance and exit of the Beaver. The pile resembled, as much as anything to which I can compare it, a brush heap about six feet high, and about ten or fifteen feet base, and standing seven or eight feet from the water. There were a few Beaver tracks about, which gave us some encouragement. We proceeded to our camping-ground on the edge of the prairie; here we landed all our baggage; while Basil made a fire, Provost and I started to set our traps—the two extremes of hunters, the skilful old one, and the ignorant pupil; but I was soon initiated in the art of setting Beaver traps, and to the uninitiated let me say, 'First, find your game, then catch it,' if you can. The first we did, the latter we tried to do. We proceeded to the place where the greatest number of tracks were seen, and commenced operations. At the place where the path enters the water, and about four inches beneath the surface, a level place is made in the mud, upon which the trap is placed, the chain is then fastened to a stake which is firmly driven in the ground under water. The end of a willow twig is then chewed and dipped in the 'Medicine Horn,' which contains the bait; this consists of castoreum mixed with spices; a quantity is collected on the chewed end of the twig, the stick is then placed or stuck in the mud on the edge of the water, leaving the part with the bait about two inches above the surface and in front of the trap; on each side the bait and about six inches from it, two dried twigs are placed in the ground; this done, all's done, and we are ready for the visit of Monsieur Castor. We set two traps, and returned to our camp, where we had supper, then pitched our tent and soon were sound asleep, but before we were asleep we heard a Beaver dive, and slap his tail, which sounded like the falling of a round stone in the water; here was encouragement again. In the morning (Monday) we examined our traps and found— nothing. We did not therefore disturb the traps, but examined farther up the river, where we discovered other tracks and resolved to set our traps there, as Provost concluded that there was but one Beaver, and that a male. We returned to camp and made a good breakfast on Buffalo meat and coffee, *sans* salt, *sans* pepper, *sans* sugar, *sans* anything else of any kind. After breakfast Provost shot a doe. In the afternoon we removed one trap, Basil and I gathered some wild-gooseberries which I stewed for supper, and made a sauce, which, though *rather acid*, was very good with our meat. The next morning, after again examining our traps and finding nothing, we decided to raise camp, which was accordingly done; everything was packed in the skiff, and we proceeded to the mouth of the river. The water had fallen so much since we had entered, as to oblige us to strip, jump in the mud, and haul the skiff over; rich and rare was the job; the mud was about half thigh deep, and a kind of greasy, sticky, black stuff, with a something about it so very peculiar as to be *rather* unpleasant; however, we did not mind much, and at last got into the Yellowstone, scraped and washed the mud off, and encamped on a prairie about one hundred yards below the Charbonneau. It was near sunset; Provost commenced fishing; we joined him, and in half an hour we caught sixteen catfish, quite large ones. During the day Provost started to the Mauvaises Terres to hunt Bighorns, but returned unsuccessful. He baited his traps for the last time. During his absence thunder clouds were observed rising all around us; we stretched our tent, removed everything inside it, ate our supper of meat and coffee, and then went to bed. It rained some part of the night, but not enough to wet through the tent. The next morning (Tuesday) at daylight, Provost started to examine his traps, while we at the camp put everything in the boat, and sat down to await his return, when we proceeded on our voyage down the Yellowstone to Fort Mortimer, and from thence by land to Fort Union. Nothing of any interest occurred except that we saw two does, one young and one buck of the Bighorns; I fired at the buck which was on a high cliff about a hundred and fifty yards from us; I fired above it to allow for the falling of the ball, but the gun shot so well as to carry where I aimed. The animal was a very large buck; Provost says one of the largest he had seen. As soon as I fired he started and ran along the side of the hill which looked almost perpendicular, and I was much astonished, not only at the feat, but at the surprising quickness with which he moved along, with no apparent foothold. We reached Fort Mortimer about seven o'clock; I left Basil and Provost with the skiff, and I started for Fort Union on foot to send a cart for them. On my way I met Mr. Audubon about to pay a visit to Fort Mortimer; I found all well, despatched the cart, changed my clothes, and feel none the worse for my five days' camping, and quite ready for a dance I hear we are to have to-night."

This morning as I walked to Fort Mortimer, meeting Squires as he has said, well and happy as a Lark, I was surprised to see a good number of horses saddled, and packed in different ways, and I hastened on to find what might be the matter. When I entered the miserable house in which Mr. Collins sleeps and spends his time when not occupied out of doors, he told me thirteen men and seven squaws were about to start for the lakes, thirty-five miles off, to kill Buffaloes and dry their meat, as the last his hunters brought in was already putrid. I saw the cavalcade depart in an E. N. E. direction, remained a while, and then walked back. Mr. Collins promised me half a dozen balls from young animals. Provost was discomfited and crestfallen at the failure of the Beaver hunt; he brought half a doe and about a dozen fine catfish. Mr. Culbertson and I are going to see the mowers, and to-morrow we start on a grand Buffalo hunt, and hope for Antelopes, Wolves, and Foxes.

July 20, Thursday. We were up early, and had our breakfast shortly after four o'clock, and before eight had left the landing of the fort, and were fairly under way for the prairies. Our equipment was much the same as before, except that we had two carts this time. Mr. C. drove Harris, Bell, and myself, and the others rode on the carts and led the hunting horses, or runners, as they are called here. I observed a Rabbit running across the road, and saw some flowers different from any I had ever seen. After we had crossed a bottom prairie, we ascended between the high and rough ravines until we were on the rolling grounds of the plains. The fort showed well from this point, and we also saw a good number of Antelopes, and some young ones. These small things run even faster than the old ones. As we neared the Fox River some one espied four Buffaloes, and Mr. C., taking the telescope, showed them to me, lying on the ground. Our heads and carts were soon turned towards them, and we travelled within half a mile of them, concealed by a ridge or hill which separated them from us. The wind was favorable, and we moved on slowly round the hill, the hunters being now mounted. Harris and Bell had their hats on, but Owen and Mr. Culbertson had their heads bound with handkerchiefs. With the rest of the party I crawled on the ridge, and saw the bulls running away, but in a direction favorable for us to see the chase. On the word of command the horses were let loose, and away went the hunters, who soon were seen to gain on the game; two bulls ran together and Mr. C. and Bell followed after them, and presently one after another of the hunters followed them. Mr. C. shot first, and his bull stopped at the fire, walked towards where I was, and halted about sixty yards from me. His nose was within a few inches of the ground; the blood poured from his mouth, nose, and side, his tail hung down, but his legs looked as firm as ever, but in less than two minutes the poor beast fell on his side, and lay quite dead. Bell and Mr. Culbertson went after the second. Harris took the third, and Squires the fourth. Bell's shot took effect in the buttock, and Mr. Culbertson shot, placing his ball a few inches above or below Bell's; after this Mr. Culbertson ran no more. At this moment Squires's horse threw him over his head, fully ten feet; he fell on his powder-horn and was severely bruised; he cried to Harris to catch his horse, and was on his legs at once, but felt sick for a few minutes. Harris, who was as cool as a cucumber, neared his bull, shot it through the lungs, and it fell dead on the spot. Bell was now seen in full pursuit of his game, and Harris joined Squires, and followed the fourth, which, however, was soon out of my sight. I saw Bell shooting two or three times, and I heard the firing of Squires and perhaps Harris, but the weather was hot, and being afraid of injuring their horses, they let the fourth bull make his escape. Bell's bull fell on his knees, got up again, and rushed on Bell, and was shot again. The animal stood a minute with his tail partially elevated, and then fell dead; through some mishap Bell had no knife with him, so did not bring the tongue, as is customary. Mr. Culbertson walked towards the first bull and I joined him. It was a fine animal about seven years old; Harris's and Bell's were younger. The first was fat, and was soon skinned and cut up for meat. Mr. Culbertson insisted on calling it my bull, so I cut off the brush of the tail and placed it in my hat-band. We then walked towards Harris, who was seated on his bull, and the same ceremony took place, and while they were cutting the animal up for meat, Bell, who said he thought his bull was about three quarters of a mile distant, went off with me to see it; we walked at least a mile and a half, and at last came to it. It was a poor one, and the tongue and tail were all we took away, and we rejoined the party, who had already started the cart with Mr. Pike, who was told to fall to the rear, and reach the fort before sundown; this he could do readily, as we were not more than six miles distant. Mr. Culbertson broke open the head of "my" bull, and ate part of the brains raw, and yet warm, and so did many of the others, even Squires. The very sight of this turned my stomach, but I am told that were I to hunt Buffalo one year, I should like it "even better than dog meat." Mr. Pike did not reach the fort till the next morning about ten, I will say *en passant*. We continued our route, passing over the same road on which we had come, and about midway between the Missouri and Yellowstone Rivers. We saw more Antelopes, but not one Wolf; these rascals are never abundant where game is scarce, but where game is, there too are the Wolves. When we had travelled about ten miles further we saw seven Buffaloes grazing on a hill, but as the sun was about one hour high, we drove to one side of the road where there was a pond of water, and there stopped for the night; while the hunters were soon mounted, and with Squires they went off, leaving the men to arrange the camp. I crossed the pond, and having ascended the opposite bank, saw the bulls grazing as leisurely as usual. The hunters near them, they started down the hill, and the chase immediately began. One broke from the rest and was followed by Mr. C. who shot it, and then abandoned the hunt, his horse being much fatigued. I now counted ten shots, but all was out of my sight, and I seated myself near a Fox hole, longing for him. The hunters returned in time; Bell and Harris had killed one, but Squires had no luck, owing to his being unable to continue the chase on account of the injury he had received from his fall. We had a good supper, having brought abundance of eatables and drinkables. The tent was pitched; I put up my mosquito-bar under the wagon, and there slept very soundly till sunrise. Harris and Bell wedged together under another bar, Mr. C. went into the tent, and Squires, who is tough and likes to rough it with the hunters, slept on a Buffalo hide somewhere with Moncrévier, one of the most skilful of the hunters. The horses were all hoppled and turned to grass; they, however, went off too far, and had to be sent after, but I heard nothing of all this. As there is no wood on the prairies proper, our fire was made of Buffalo dung, which is so abundant that one meets these deposits at every few feet and in all directions.

July 21, Friday. We were up at sunrise, and had our coffee, after which Lafleur a mulatto, Harris, and Bell went off after Antelopes, for we cared no more about bulls; where the cows are, we cannot tell. Cows run faster than bulls, yearlings faster than cows, and calves faster than any of these. Squires felt sore, and his side was very black, so we took our guns and went after Black-breasted Lark Buntings, of which we saw many, but could not near them. I found a nest of them, however, with five eggs. The nest is planted in the ground, deep enough to sink the edges of it. It is formed of dried fine grasses and roots, without any lining of hair or wool. By and by we saw Harris sitting on a high hill about one mile off, and joined him; he said the bulls they had killed last evening were close by, and I offered to go and see the bones, for I expected that the Wolves had devoured it during the night. We travelled on, and Squires returned to the camp. After about two miles of walking against a delightful strong breeze, we reached the animals; Ravens or Buzzards had worked at the eyes, but only one Wolf, apparently, had been there. They were bloated, and smelt quite unpleasant. We returned to the camp and saw a Wolf cross our path, and an Antelope looking at us. We determined to stop and try to bring him to us; I lay on my back and threw my legs up, kicking first one and then the other foot, and sure enough the Antelope walked towards us, slowly and carefully, however. In about twenty minutes he had come two or three hundred yards; he was a superb male, and I looked at him for some minutes; when about sixty yards off I could see his eyes, and being loaded with buck-shot pulled the trigger without rising from my awkward position. Off he went; Harris fired, but he only ran the faster for some hundred yards, when he turned, looked at us again, and was off. When we reached camp we found Bell there; he had shot three times at Antelopes without killing; Lafleur had also returned, and had broken the foreleg of one, but an Antelope can run fast enough with three legs, and he saw no more of it. We now broke camp, arranged the horses and turned our heads towards the Missouri, and in four and three-quarter hours reached the landing. On entering the wood we again broke branches of service-berries, and carried a great quantity over the river. I much enjoyed the trip; we had our supper, and soon to bed in our hot room, where Sprague says the thermometer has been at 99° most of the day. I noticed it was warm when walking. I must not forget to notice some things which happened on our return. First, as we came near Fox River, we thought of the horns of our bulls, and Mr. Culbertson, who knows the country like a book, drove us first to Bell's, who knocked the horns off, then to Harris's, which was served in the same manner; this bull had been eaten entirely except the head, and a good portion of mine had been devoured also; it lay immediately under "Audubon's Bluff" (the name Mr. Culbertson gave the ridge on which I stood to see the chase), and we could see it when nearly a mile distant. Bell's horns were the handsomest and largest, mine next best, and Harris's the smallest, but we are all contented. Mr. Culbertson tells me that Harris and Bell have done wonders, for persons who have never shot at Buffaloes from on horseback. Harris had a fall too, during his second chase, and was bruised in the manner of Squires, but not so badly. I have but little doubt that Squires killed his bull, as he says he shot it three times, and Mr. Culbertson's must have died also. What a terrible destruction of life, as it were for nothing, or next to it, as the tongues only were brought in, and the flesh of these fine animals was left to beasts and birds of prey, or to rot on the spots where they fell. The prairies are literally *covered* with the skulls of the victims, and the roads the Buffalo make in crossing the prairies have all the appearance of heavy wagon tracks. We saw young Golden Eagles, Ravens, and Buzzards. I found the Short-billed Marsh Wren quite abundant, and in such localities as it is found eastward. The Black-breasted Prairie-bunting flies much like a Lark, hovering while singing, and sweeping round and round, over and above its female while she sits on the eggs on the prairie below. I saw only one Gadwall Duck; these birds are found in abundance on the plains where water and rushes are to be found. Alas! alas! eighteen Assiniboins have reached the fort this evening in two groups; they are better-looking than those previously seen by us.

July 22, Saturday. Thermometer 99°–102°. This day has been the hottest of the season, and we all felt the influence of this densely oppressive atmosphere, not a breath of air stirring. Immediately after breakfast Provost and Lafleur went across the river in search of Antelopes, and we remained looking at the Indians, all Assiniboins, and very dirty. When and where Mr. Catlin saw these Indians as he has represented them, dressed in magnificent attire, with all sorts of extravagant accoutrements, is more than I can divine, or Mr. Culbertson tell me. The evening was so hot and sultry that Mr. C. and I went into the river, which is now very low, and remained in the water over an hour. A dozen catfish were caught in the main channel, and we have had a good supper from part of them. Finding the weather so warm I have had my bed brought out on the gallery below, and so has Squires. The Indians are, as usual, shut *out* of the fort, all the horses, young Buffaloes, etc., shut *in*; and much refreshed by my bath, I say God bless you, and good-night.

July 23, Sunday. Thermometer 84°. I had a very pleasant night, and no mosquitoes, as the breeze rose a little before I lay down; and I anticipated a heavy thunder storm, but we had only a few drops of rain. About one o'clock Harris was called to see one of the Indians, who was bleeding at the nose profusely, and I too went to see the poor devil. He had bled quite enough, and Harris stopped his nostrils with cotton, put cold water on his neck and head—God knows when they had felt it before—and the bleeding stopped. These dirty fellows had made a large fire between the walls of the fort, but outside the inner gates, and it was a wonder that the whole establishment was not destroyed by fire. Before sunrise they were pounding at the gate to be allowed to enter, but, of course, this was not permitted. When the sun had fairly risen, some one came and told me the hill-tops were covered with Indians, probably Blackfeet. I walked to the back gate, and the number had dwindled, or the account been greatly exaggerated, for there seemed only fifty or sixty, and when, later, they were counted, there were found to be exactly seventy. They remained a long time on the hill, and sent a youth to ask for whiskey. But whiskey there is none for them, and very little for any one. By and by they came down the hill leading four horses, and armed principally with bows and arrows, spears, tomahawks, and a few guns. They have proved to be a party of Crees from the British dominions on the Saskatchewan River, and have been fifteen days in travelling here. They had seen few Buffaloes, and were hungry and thirsty enough. They assured Mr. Culbertson that the Hudson's Bay Company supplied them all with abundance of spirituous liquors, and as the white traders on the Missouri had none for them, they would hereafter travel with the English. Now ought not this subject to be brought before the press in our country and forwarded to England? If our Congress will not allow our traders to sell whiskey or rum to the Indians, why should not the British follow the same rule? Surely the British, who are so anxious about the emancipation of the blacks, might as well take care of the souls and bodies of the redskins. After a long talk and smoking of pipes, tobacco, flints, powder, gun-screws and vermilion were placed before their great chief (who is tattooed and has a most rascally look), who examined everything minutely, counting over the packets of vermilion; more tobacco was added, a file, and a piece of white cotton with which to adorn his head; then he walked off, followed by his son, and the whole posse left the fort. They passed by the garden, pulled up a few squash vines and some turnips, and tore down a few of the pickets on their way elsewhere. We all turned to, and picked a quantity of peas, which with a fine roast pig, made us a capital dinner. After this, seeing the Assiniboins loitering about the fort, we had some tobacco put up as a target, and many arrows were sent to enter the prize, but I never saw Indians—usually so skilful with their bows—shoot worse in my life. Presently some one cried there were Buffaloes on the hill, and going to see we found that four bulls were on the highest ridge standing still. The horses being got in the yard, the guns were gathered, saddles placed, and the riders mounted, Mr. C., Harris, and Bell; Squires declined going, not having recovered from his fall, Mr. C. led his followers round the hills by the ravines, and approached the bulls quite near, when the affrighted cattle ran down the hills and over the broken grounds, out of our sight, followed by the hunters. When I see game chased by Mr. Culbertson, I feel confident of its being killed, and in less than one hour he had killed two bulls, Harris and Bell each one. Thus these poor animals which two hours before were tranquilly feeding are now dead; short work this. Harris and Bell remained on the hills to watch the Wolves, and carts being ordered, Mr. C. and I went off on horseback to the second one he had killed. We found it entire, and I began to operate upon it at once; after making what measurements and investigations I desired, I saved the head, the tail, and a large piece of the silky skin from the rump. The meat of three of the bulls was brought to the fort, the fourth was left to rot on the ground. Mr. C. cut his finger severely, but paid no attention to that; I, however, tore a strip off my shirt and bound it up for him. It is so hot I am going to sleep on the gallery again; the thermometer this evening is 89°.

July 24, Monday. I had a fine sleep last night, and this morning early a slight sprinkling of rain somewhat refreshed the earth. After breakfast we talked of going to see if Mr. Culbertson's bull had been injured by the Wolves. Mr. C., Harris, and I went off to the spot by a roundabout way, and when we reached the animal it was somewhat swollen, but untouched, but we made up our minds to have it weighed, *coute qui coute*. Harris proposed to remain and watch it, looking for Hares meantime, but saw none. The Wolves must be migratory at this season, or so starved out that they have gone elsewhere, as we now see but few. We returned first to the fort, and mustered three men and Bell, for Sprague would not go, being busy drawing a plant, and finding the heat almost insupportable. We carried all the necessary implements, and found Harris quite ready to drink some claret and water which we took for him. To cut up so large a bull, and one now with so dreadful an odor, was no joke; but with the will follows the success, and in about one hour the poor beast had been measured and weighed, and we were once more *en route* for the fort. This bull measured as follows: from end of nose to root of tail, 131 inches; height at shoulder, 67 inches; at rump, 57 inches; tail vertebræ, 15½ inches, hair in length beyond it 11 inches. We weighed the whole animal by cutting it in parts and then by addition found that this Buffalo, which was an old bull, weighed 1777 lbs. avoirdupois. The flesh was all tainted, and was therefore left for the beasts of prey. Our road was over high hills, and presented to our searching eyes a great extent of broken ground, and here and there groups of Buffaloes grazing. This afternoon we are going to bring in the skeleton of Mr. Culbertson's second bull. I lost the head of my first bull because I forgot to tell Mrs. Culbertson that I wished to save it, and the princess had its skull broken open to enjoy its brains. Handsome, and really courteous and refined in many ways, I cannot reconcile to myself the fact that she partakes of raw animal food with such evident relish. Before our departure, in came six half-breeds, belonging, or attached to Fort Mortimer; and understanding that they were first-rate hunters, I offered them ten dollars in goods for each Bighorn up to eight or ten in number. They have promised to go to-morrow, but, alas! the half-breeds are so uncertain I cannot tell whether they will move a step or not. Mrs. Culbertson, who has great pride in her pure Indian blood, told me with scorn that "all such no-color fellows are lazy." We were delayed in starting by a very heavy gale of wind and hard rain, which cooled the weather considerably; but we finally got off in the wagon, the cart with three mules following, to bring in the skeleton of the Buffalo which Mr. Culbertson had killed; but we were defeated, for some Wolves had been to it, dragged it about twenty-five feet, and gnawed the ends of the ribs and the backbone. The head of Harris's bull was brought in, but it was smaller; the horns alone were pretty good, and they were given to Sprague. On our return Mrs. Culbertson was good enough to give me six young Mallards, which she had caught by swimming after them in the Missouri; she is a most expert and graceful swimmer, besides being capable of remaining under water a long time; all the Blackfoot Indians excel in swimming and take great pride in the accomplishment. We found three of the Assiniboins had remained, one of whom wanted to carry off a squaw, and probably a couple of horses too. He strutted about the fort in such a manner that we watched him pretty closely. Mr. Culbertson took his gun, and a six-barrelled pistol in his pocket; I, my double-barrelled gun, and we stood at the back gate. The fellow had a spear made of a cut-and-thrust sword, planted in a good stick covered with red cloth, and this he never put down at any time; but no more, indeed, do any Indians, who carry all their goods and chattels forever about their persons. The three gentlemen, however, went off about dusk, and took the road to Fort Mortimer, where six half-breeds from the Northeast brought to Fort Mortimer eleven head of cattle, and came to pay a visit to their friends here. All these men know Provost, and have inquired for him. I feel somewhat uneasy about Provost and La Fleur, who have now been gone four full days. The prairie is wet and damp, so I must sleep indoors. The bull we cut up was not a fat one; I think in good condition it would have weighed 2000 lbs.

July 25, Tuesday. We were all rather lazy this morning, but about dinner-time Owen and his man arrived, and told us they had reached Mr. Kipp and his boat at the crossings within about half a mile of Fort Alexander; that his men were all broken down with drawing the cordelle through mud and water, and that they had lost a white horse, which, however, Owen saw on his way, and on the morning of his start from this fort. About the same time he shot a large Porcupine, and killed four bulls and one cow to feed upon, as well as three rattlesnakes. They saw a large number of Buffalo cows, and we are going after them to-morrow morning bright and early. About two hours later Provost and La Fleur, about whom I had felt some uneasiness, came to the landing, and brought the heads and skins attached to two female Antelopes. Both had been killed by one shot from La Fleur, and his ball broke the leg of a third. Provost was made quite sick by the salt water he had drunk; he killed one doe, on which they fed as well as on the flesh of the "Cabris." Whilst following the Mauvaises Terres (broken lands), they saw about twenty Bighorns, and had not the horse on which Provost rode been frightened at the sight of a monstrous buck of these animals, he would have shot it down within twenty yards. They saw from fifteen to twenty Buffalo cows, and we hope some of the hunters will come up with them to-morrow. I have been drawing the head of one of these beautiful female Antelopes; but their horns puzzle me, and all of us; they seem to me as if they were *new* horns, soft and short; time, however, will prove whether they shed them or not. Our preparations are already made for preserving the skins of the Antelopes, and Sprague is making an outline which I hope will be finished before the muscles of the head begin to soften. Not a word from the six hunters who promised to go after Bighorns on the Yellowstone.

July 26, Wednesday. We were all on foot before daybreak and had our breakfast by an early hour, and left on our trip for Buffalo cows. The wagon was sent across by hauling it through the east channel, which is now quite low, and across the sand-bars, which now reach seven-eighths of the distance across the river. We crossed in the skiff, and walked to the ferry-boat—I barefooted, as well as Mr. Culbertson; others wore boots or moccasins, but my feet have been tender of late, and this is the best cure. Whilst looking about for sticks to support our mosquito bars, I saw a Rabbit standing before me, within a few steps, but I was loaded with balls, and should have torn the poor thing so badly that it would have been useless as a specimen, so let it live. We left the ferry before six, and went on as usual. We saw two Antelopes on entering the bottom prairie, but they had the wind of us, and scampered off to the hills. We saw two Grouse, one of which Bell killed, and we found it very good this evening for our supper. Twelve bulls were seen, but we paid no attention to them. We saw a fine large Hawk, apparently the size of a Red-tailed Hawk, but with the whole head white. It had alighted on a clay hill or bank, but, on being approached, flew off to another, was pursued and again flew away, so that we could not procure it, but I have no doubt that it is a species not yet described. We now crossed Blackfoot River, and saw great numbers of Antelopes. Their play and tricks are curious; I watched many of the groups a long time, and will not soon forget them. At last, seeing we should have no meat for supper, and being a party of nine, it was determined that the first animal seen should be run down and killed. We soon saw a bull, and all agreed to give every chance possible to Squires. Mr. C., Owen, and Squires started, and Harris followed without a gun, to see the chase. The bull was wounded twice by Squires, but no blood came from the mouth, and now all three shot at it, but the bull was not apparently hurt seriously; he became more and more furious, and began charging upon them. Unfortunately, Squires ran between the bull and a ravine quite close to the animal, and it suddenly turned on him; his horse became frightened and jumped into the ravine, the bull followed, and now Squires lost his balance; however, he threw his gun down, and fortunately clung to the mane of his horse and recovered his seat. The horse got away and saved his life, for, from what Mr. C. told me, had he fallen, the bull would have killed him in a few minutes, and no assistance could be afforded him, as Mr. C. and Owen had, at that moment, empty guns. Squires told us all; he had never been so bewildered and terrified before. The bull kept on running, and was shot at perhaps twenty times, for when he fell he had *twelve balls* in his side, and had been shot twice in the head. Another bull was now seen close by us, and Owen killed it after four shots. Whilst we were cutting up this one, La Fleur and some one else went to the other, which was found to be very poor, and, at this season smelling very rank and disagreeable. A few of the best pieces were cut away, and, as usual, the hunters ate the liver and fat quite raw, like Wolves, and we were now on the move again. Presently we saw seven animals coming towards us, and with the glass discovered there were six bulls and one cow. The hunters mounted in quick time, and away after the cow, which Owen killed very soon. To my surprise the bulls did not leave her, but stood about one hundred yards from the hunters, who were cutting her in pieces; the best parts were taken for dried meat. Had we not been so many, the bulls would, in all probability, have charged upon the butchers, but after a time they went off at a slow canter. At this moment Harris and I were going towards the party thus engaged, when a Swift Fox started from a hole under the feet of Harris' horse. I was loaded with balls, and he also; he gave chase and gained upon the beautiful animal with remarkable quickness. Bell saw this, and joined Harris, whilst I walked towards the butchering party. The Fox was overtaken by Harris, who took aim at it several times, but could not get sight on him, and the little fellow doubled and cut about in such a manner that it escaped into a ravine, and was seen no more. Now who will tell me that no animal can compete with this Fox in speed, when Harris, mounted on an Indian horse, overtook it in a few minutes? We were now in sight of a large band of cows and bulls, but the sun was low, and we left them to make our way to the camping-place, which we reached just before the setting of the sun. We found plenty of water, and a delightful spot, where we were all soon at work unsaddling our horses and mules, bringing wood for fires, and picking serviceberries, which we found in great quantities and very good. We were thirty miles from Fort Union, close to the three Mamelles, but must have travelled near fifty, searching for and running down the game. All slept well, some outside and others inside the tent, after our good supper. We had a clear, bright day, with the wind from the westward.

July 27, Thursday. This morning was beautiful, the birds singing all around us, and after our early breakfast, Harris, with La Fleur and Mr. Culbertson, walked to the top of the highest of the three Mamelles; Bell went to skinning the birds shot yesterday, among which was a large Titmouse of the Eastern States, while I walked off a short distance, and made a sketch of the camp and the three Mamelles. I hope to see a fair picture from this, painted by Victor, this next winter, God willing. During the night the bulls were heard bellowing, and the Wolves howling, all around us. Bell had seen evidences of Grizzly Bears close by, but we saw none of the animals. An Antelope was heard snorting early this morning, and seen for a while, but La Fleur could not get it. The snorting of the

Antelope is more like a whistling, sneezing sound, than like the long, clear snorting of our common Deer, and it is also very frequently repeated, say every few minutes, when in sight of an object of which the animal does not yet know the nature; for the moment it is assured of danger, it bounds three or four times like a sheep, and then either trots off or gallops like a horse. On the return of the gentlemen from the eminence, from which they had seen nothing but a Hawk, and heard the notes of the Rock Wren, the horses were gathered, and preparations made to go in search of cows. I took my gun and walked off ahead, and on ascending the first hill saw an Antelope, which, at first sight, I thought was an Indian. It stood still, gazing at me about five hundred yards off; I never stirred, and presently it walked towards me; I lay down and lowered my rifle; the animal could not now see my body; I showed it my feet a few times, at intervals. Presently I saw it coming full trot towards me; I cocked my gun, loaded with buck-shot in one barrel and ball in the other. He came within thirty yards of me and stopped suddenly, then turned broadside towards me. I could see his very eyes, his beautiful form, and his fine horns, for it was a buck. I pulled one trigger—it snapped, the animal moved not; I pulled the other, snapped again, and away the Antelope bounded, and ran swiftly from me. I put on fresh caps, and saw it stop after going a few hundred yards, and presently it came towards me again, but not within one hundred and fifty yards, when seeing that it would not come nearer I pulled the trigger with the ball; off it went, and so did the Antelope, which this time went quite out of my sight. I returned to camp and found all ready for a move. Owen went up a hill to reconnoitre for Antelopes and cows; seeing one of the former he crept after it. Bell followed, and at this moment a Hare leaped from the path before us, and stopped within twenty paces. Harris was not loaded with shot, and I only with buck-shot; however, I fired and killed it; it proved to be a large female, and after measuring, we skinned it, and I put on a label "Townsend's Hare, killed a few miles from the three Mamelles, July 27, 1843." After travelling for a good while, Owen, who kept ahead of us, made signs from the top of a high hill that Buffaloes were in sight. This signal is made by walking the rider's horse backwards and forwards several times. We hurried on towards him, and when we reached the place, he pointed to the spot where he had seen them, and said they were travelling fast, being a band of both cows and bulls. The hunters were mounted at once, and on account of Squires' soreness I begged him not to run; so he drove me in the wagon as fast as possible over hills, through plains and ravines of all descriptions, at a pace beyond belief. From time to time we saw the hunters, and once or twice the Buffaloes, which were going towards the fort. At last we reached an eminence from which we saw both the game and the hunters approaching the cattle, preparatory to beginning the chase. It seems there is no etiquette among Buffalo hunters, and this proved a great disappointment to friend Harris, who was as anxious to kill a cow, as he had been to kill a bull. Off went the whole group, but the country was not as advantageous to the pursuers, as to the pursued. The cows separated from the bulls, the latter making their way towards us, and six of them passed within one hundred yards of where I stood; we let them pass, knowing well how savage they are at these times, and turned our eyes again to the hunters. I saw Mr. C. pursuing one cow, Owen another, and Bell a third. Owen shot one and mortally wounded it; it walked up on a hill and stood there for some minutes before falling. Owen killed a second close by the one Mr. C. had now killed, Bell's dropped dead in quite another direction, nearly one mile off. Two bulls we saw coming directly towards us, so La Fleur and I went under cover of the hill to await their approach, and they came within sixty yards of us. I gave La Fleur the choice of shooting first, as he had a rifle; he shot and missed; they turned and ran in an opposite direction, so that I, who had gone some little distance beyond La Fleur, had no chance, and I was sorry enough for my politeness. Owen had shot a third cow, which went part way up a hill, fell, and kicked violently; she, however, rose and again fell, and kept kicking with all her legs in the air. Squires now drove to her, and I walked, followed by Moncrévier, a hunter; seeing Mr. C. and Harris on the bottom below we made signs for them to come up, and they fortunately did, and by galloping to Squires probably saved that young man from more danger; for though I cried to him at the top of my voice, the wind prevented him from hearing me; he now stopped, however, not far from a badly broken piece of ground over which had he driven at his usual speed, which I doubt not he would have attempted, some accident must have befallen him. Harris and Mr. C. rode up to the cow, which expired at that moment. The cow Mr. C. had killed was much the largest, and we left a cart and two men to cut up this, and the first two Owen had killed, and went to the place where the first lay, to have it skinned for me. Bell joined us soon, bringing a tongue with him, and he immediately began operations on the cow, which proved a fine one, and I have the measurements as follows: "Buffalo Cow, killed by Mr. Alexander Culbertson, July 27, 1843. Nose to root of tail, 96 inches. Height at shoulder, 60; at rump, 55½. Length of tail vertebræ, 13; to end of hair, 25; from brisket to bottom of feet, 21½; nose to anterior canthus, 10½; between horns at root, 11⅜; between tops of ditto, 17⅛; between nostrils, 2¼; length of ditto, 2½; height of nose, 3⅛; nose to opening of ear, 20; ear from opening to tip, 5; longest hair on head, 14 inches; from angle of mouth to end of under lip, 3½." Whilst we were at this, Owen and Pike were hacking at their cow. After awhile all was ready for departure, and we made for the "coupe" at two o'clock, and expected to have found water to enable us to water our horses, for we had yet some gallons of the Missouri water for our own use. We found the road to the "coupe," which was seen for many, many miles. The same general appearance of country shows throughout the whole of these dreary prairies; up one hill and down on the other side, then across a plain with ravines of more or less depth. About two miles west of the "coupe," Owen and others went in search of water, but in vain; and we have had to cross the "coupe" and travel fully two miles east of it, when we came to a mere puddle, sufficient however, for the night, and we stopped. The carts with the meat, and our effects, arrived after a while; the meat was spread on the grass, the horses and mules hoppled and let go, to drink and feed. All hands collected Buffalo dung for fuel, for not a bush was in sight, and we soon had a large fire. In the winter season this prairie fuel is too wet to burn, and oftentimes the hunters have to eat their meat raw, or go without their supper. Ours was cooked however; I made mine chiefly from the liver, as

did Harris; others ate boiled or roasted meat as they preferred. The tent was pitched, and I made a bed for Mr. C. and
myself, and guns, etc., were all under cover; the evening was
cool, the wind fresh, and no mosquitoes. We had seen plenty
of Antelopes; I shot at one twenty yards from the wagon with
small shot. Harris killed a Wolf, but we have seen very few,
and now I will wish you all good-night; God bless you!

July 28, Friday.   This morning was cold enough for a frost,
but we all slept soundly until daylight, and about half-past
three we were called for breakfast. The horses had all gone
but four, and, as usual, Owen was despatched for them. The
horses were brought back, our coffee swallowed, and we were
off, Mr. C. and I, in the wagon. We saw few Antelopes, no
Buffalo, and reached the ferry opposite the fort at half-past
seven. We found all well, and about eleven Assiniboins, all
young men, headed by the son of a great chief called "Le
mangeur d'hommes" (the man-eater). The poor wretched
Indian whom Harris had worked over, died yesterday morning, and was buried at once. I had actually felt chilly riding in
the wagon, and much enjoyed a breakfast Mrs. Culbertson
had kindly provided for me. We had passed over some very
rough roads, and at breakneck speed, but I did not feel stiff
as I expected, though somewhat sore, and a good night's rest
is all I need. This afternoon the cow's skin and head, and the
Hare arrived, and have been preserved. A half-breed well
known to Provost has been here to make a bargain with me
about Bighorns, Grizzly Bear, etc., and will see what he and
his two sons can do; but I have little or no confidence in these
gentry. I was told this afternoon that at Mouse River, about
two hundred miles north of this, there are eight hundred
carts in one gang, and four hundred in another, with an adequate number of half-breeds and Indians, killing Buffalo and
drying their meat for winter provisions, and that the animals
are there in millions. When Buffalo bulls are shot from a distance of sixty or seventy yards, they rarely charge on the
hunter, and Mr. Culbertson has killed as many as nine bulls
from the same spot, when unseen by these terrible beasts.
Beavers, when shot swimming, and killed, sink at once to the
bottom, but their bodies rise again in from twenty to thirty
minutes. Hunters, who frequently shoot and kill them by

moonlight, return in the morning from their camping-places, and find them on the margins of the shores where they had shot. Otters do the same, but remain under water for an hour or more.

July 29, Saturday. Cool and pleasant. About one hour after daylight Harris, Bell, and two others, crossed the river, and went in search of Rabbits, but all returned without success. Harris, after breakfast, went off on this side, saw none, but killed a young Raven. During the course of the forenoon he and Bell went off again, and brought home an old and young of the Sharp-tailed Grouse. This afternoon they brought in a Loggerhead Shrike and two Rock Wrens. Bell skinned all these. Sprague made a handsome sketch of the five young Buffaloes belonging to the fort. This evening Moncrévier and Owen went on the other side of the river, but saw nothing. We collected berries of the dwarf cherries of this part, and I bottled some service-berries to carry home.

July 30, Sunday. Weather cool and pleasant. After breakfast we despatched La Fleur and Provost after Antelopes and Bighorns. We then went off and had a battue for Rabbits, and although we were nine in number, and all beat the rose bushes and willows for several hundred yards, not one did we see, although their traces were apparent in several places. We saw tracks of a young Grizzly Bear near the river shore. After a good dinner of Buffalo meat, green peas, and a pudding, Mr. C., Owen, Mr. Pike, and I went off to Fort Mortimer. We had an arrival of five squaws, half-breeds, and a gentleman of the same order, who came to see our fort and our ladies. The princess went out to meet them covered with a fine shawl, and the visitors followed her to her own room. These ladies spoke both the French and Cree languages. At Fort Mortimer we found the hunters from the north, who had returned last evening and told me they had seen nothing. I fear that all my former opinions of the half-breeds are likely to be realized, and that they are all more *au fait* at telling lies, than anything else; and I expect now that we shall have to make a regular turn-out ourselves, to kill both Grizzly Bears and Bighorns. As we were riding along not far from this fort, Mr. Culbertson fired off the gun given him by Harris, and it blew off the stock, lock, and breech, and it was a wonder it did not kill him, or me, as I was sitting by his side. After we had been at home about one hour, we were all called out of a sudden by the news that the *Horse Guards* were coming, full gallop, driving the whole of their charge before them. We saw the horses, and the cloud of dust that they raised on the prairies, and presently, when the Guards reached the gates, they told us that they had seen a party of Indians, which occasioned their hurried return. It is now more than one hour since I wrote this, and the Indians are now in sight, and we think they were frightened by three or four squaws who had left the fort in search of "pommes blanches." Sprague has collected a few seeds, but I intend to have some time devoted to this purpose before we leave on our passage downwards. This evening five Indians arrived, among whom is the brother of the man who died a few days ago; he brought a horse, and an Elk skin, which I bought, and he now considers himself a rich man. He reported Buffaloes very near, and to-morrow morning the hunters will be after them. When Buffaloes are about to lie down, they draw all their four feet together slowly, and balancing the body for a moment, bend their fore legs, and fall on their knees first, and the hind ones follow. In young animals, some of which we have here, the effect produced on their tender skin is directly seen, as callous round patches without hair are found; after the animal is about one year old, these are seen no more. I am told that Wolves have not been known to attack men and horses in these parts, but they do attack mules and colts, always making choice of the fattest. We scarcely see one now-a-days about the fort, and yet two miles from here, at Fort Mortimer, Mr. Collins tells me it is impossible to sleep, on account of their howlings at night. When Assiniboin Indians lose a relative by death, they go and cry under the box which contains the body, which is placed in a tree, cut their legs and different parts of the body, and moan miserably for hours at a time. This performance has been gone through with by the brother of the Indian who died here.

July 31, Monday. Weather rather warmer. Mr. Larpenteur went after Rabbits, saw none, but found a horse, which was brought home this afternoon. Mr. C., Harris, Bell, and Owen went after Buffaloes over the hills, saw none, so that all this day has been disappointment to us. Owen caught a *Spermophilus hoodii*. The brother of the dead Indian, who gashed his legs fearfully this morning, went off with his wife and children and six others, who had come here to beg. One of them had for *a letter of recommendation* one of the advertisements of the steamer "Trapper," which will be kept by his chief for time immemorial to serve as a pass for begging. He received from us ammunition and tobacco. Sprague collected seeds this morning, and this afternoon copied my sketch of the three Mamelles. Towards sunset I intend to go myself after Rabbits, along the margins of the bushes and the shore. We have returned from my search after Rabbits; Harris and I each shot one. We saw five Wild Geese. Harris lost his snuff-box, which he valued, and which I fear will never be found. Squires to-day proposed to me to let him remain here this winter to procure birds and quadrupeds, and I would have said "yes" at once, did he understand either or both these subjects, or could draw; but as he does not, it would be useless.

August 1, Tuesday. The weather fine, and warmer than yesterday. We sent off four Indians after Rabbits, but as we foolishly gave them powder and shot, they returned without any very soon, having, of course, hidden the ammunition. After breakfast Mr. C. had a horse put in the cart, and three squaws went off after "pommes blanches," and Sprague and I followed in the wagon, driven by Owen. These women carried sticks pointed at one end, and blunt at the other, and I was perfectly astonished at the dexterity and rapidity with which they worked. They place the pointed end within six inches of the plant, where the stem enters the earth, and bear down upon the other end with all their weight and move about to the right and left of the plant until the point of the stick is thrust in the ground to the depth of about seven inches, when acting upon it in the manner of a lever, the plant is fairly thrown out, and the root procured. Sprague and I, who had taken with us an instrument resembling a very narrow hoe, and a spade, having rather despised the simple instruments of the squaws, soon found out that these damsels could dig six or seven, and in some cases a dozen, to our *one*. We collected some seeds of these plants as well as those of some others, and walked fully six miles, which has rendered my feet quite tender again. Owen told me that he had seen, on his late journey up the Yellowstone, Grouse, both old and young, with a black breast and with a broad tail; they were usually near the margin of a wood. What they are I cannot tell, but he and Bell are going after them to-morrow morning. Just after dinner Provost and La Fleur returned with two male Antelopes, skinned, one of them a remarkably large buck, the other less in size, both skins in capital order. We have taken the measurements of the head of the larger. The timber for our boat has been hauling across the sand-bar ever since daylight, and of course the work will proceed pretty fast. The weather is delightful, and at night, indeed, quite cool enough. I spoke to Sprague last night about remaining here next winter, as he had mentioned his wish to do so to Bell some time ago, but he was very undecided. My regrets that I promised you all so faithfully that I would return this fall are beyond description. I am, as years go, an old man, but I do not feel old, and there is so much of interest here that I forget oftentimes that I am not as young as Owen.

August 2, Wednesday. Bell and Owen started on their tour up the Yellowstone after Cocks of the Plain. Provost and Moncrévier went in the timber below after Deer, but saw none. We had an arrival of six Chippeway Indians, and afterwards about a dozen Assiniboins. Both these parties were better dressed, and looked better off than any previous groups that we have seen at this fort. They brought some few robes to barter, and the traffic was carried on by Mr. Larpenteur in his little shop, through a wicket. On the arrival of the Assiniboins, who were headed by an old man, one of the Chippeways discovered a horse, which he at once not only claimed, but tied; he threw down his new blanket on the ground, and was leading off the horse, when the other Indian caught hold of it, and said that he had fairly bought it, etc. The Chippeway now gave him his gun, powder, and ball, as well as his *looking-glass*, the most prized of all his possessions, and the Assiniboin, now apparently satisfied, gave up the horse, which was led away by the new (or old) owner. We thought the matter was ended, but Mr. Culbertson told us that either the horse or the Chippeway would be caught and brought back. The latter had mounted a fine horse which he had brought with him, and was leading the other away, when presently a gun was heard out of the fort, and Mr. C. ran to tell us that the horse of the Chippeway had been shot, and that the rider was running as fast as he could to Fort Mortimer. Upon going out we found the horse standing still, and the man running; we went to the poor animal, and found that the ball had passed through the thigh, and entered the belly. The poor horse was trembling like an aspen; he at last moved, walked about, and went to the river, where he died. Now it is curious that it was not the same Assiniboin who had sold the horse that had shot, but another of their party; and we understand that it was on account of an old grudge against the Chippeway, who, by the way, was a surly-looking rascal. The Assiniboins brought eight or ten horses and colts, and a number of dogs. One of the colts had a necklace of "pommes blanches," at the end of which hung a handful of Buffalo calves' hoofs, not more than ¾ inch long, and taken from the calves before birth, when the mothers had been killed. Harris and I took a ride in the wagon over the Mauvaises Terres above the fort, in search of petrified wood, but though we found many specimens, they were of such indifferent quality that we brought home but one. On returning we followed a Wolf path, of which there are hundreds through the surrounding hills, all leading to the fort. It is curious to see how well they understand the best and shortest roads. From what had happened, we anticipated a row among the Indians, but all seemed quiet. Mr. C. gave us a good account of Fort McKenzie. I have been examining the fawn of the Long-tailed Deer of this country, belonging to old Baptiste; the man feeds it regularly, and the fawn follows him everywhere. It will race backwards and forwards over the prairie back of the fort, for a mile or more, running at the very top of its speed; suddenly it will make for the gate, rush through and overwhelm Baptiste with caresses, as if it had actually lost him for some time. If Baptiste lies on the ground pretending to sleep, the fawn pushes with its nose, and licks his face as a dog would, till he awakens.

August 3, Thursday. We observed yesterday that the atmosphere was thick, and indicated the first appearance of the close of summer, which here is brief. The nights and mornings have already become cool, and summer clothes will not be needed much longer, except occasionally. Harris and Sprague went to the hills so much encrusted with shells. We have had some talk about going to meet Bell and Owen, but the distance is too great, and Mr. C. told me he was not acquainted with the road beyond the first twenty-five or thirty miles. We have had a slight shower, and Mr. C. and I walked across the bar to see the progress of the boat. The horse that died near the river was hauled across to the sand-bar, and will make good catfish bate for our fishers. This morning we had another visitation of Indians, seven in number; they were very dirty, wrapped in disgusting Buffalo robes, and were not allowed inside the inner gate, on account of their filthy condition.

August 4, Friday. We were all under way this morning at half-past five, on a Buffalo hunt, that is to say, the residue of *us*, Harris and I, for Bell was away with Owen, and Squires with Provost after Bighorns, and Sprague at Fort Mortimer. Tobacco and matches had been forgotten, and that detained us for half an hour; but at last we started in good order, with only one cart following us, which carried Pike and Moncrévier. We saw, after we had travelled ten miles, some Buffalo bulls; some alone, others in groups of four or five, a few Antelopes, but more shy than ever before. I was surprised to see how careless the bulls were of us, as some actually gave us chances to approach them within a hundred yards, looking steadfastly, as if not caring a bit for us. At last we saw one lying down immediately in our road, and determined to give him a chance for his life. Mr. C. had a white horse, a runaway, in which he placed a good deal of confidence; he mounted it, and we looked after him. The bull did not start till Mr. C. was within a hundred yards, and then at a gentle and slow gallop. The horse galloped too, but only at the same rate. Mr. C. thrashed him until his hands were sore, for he had no whip, the bull went off without even a shot being fired, and the horse is now looked upon as forever disgraced. About two miles farther another bull was observed lying down in our way, and it was concluded to run him with the white horse, accompanied, however, by Harris. The chase took place, and the bull was killed by Harris, but the white horse is now scorned by every one. A few pieces of meat, the tongue, tail, and head, were all that was taken from this very large bull. We soon saw that the weather was becoming cloudy, and we were anxious to reach a camping-place; but we continued to cross ranges of hills, and hoped to see a large herd of Buffaloes. The weather was hot "out of mind," and we continued till, reaching a fine hill, we saw in a beautiful valley below us seventy to eighty head, feeding peacefully in groups and singly, as might happen. The bulls were mixed in with the cows, and we saw one or two calves. Many bulls were at various distances from the main group, but as we advanced towards them they galloped off and joined the others. When the chase began it was curious to see how much swifter the cows were than the bulls, and how soon they divided themselves into parties of seven or eight, exerting themselves to escape from their murderous pursuers. All in vain, however; off went the guns and down went the cows, or stood bleeding through the nose, mouth, or bullet holes. Mr. C. killed three, and Harris one in about half an hour. We had quite enough, and the slaughter was ended. We had driven up to the nearest fallen cow, and approached close to her, and found that she was not dead, but trying to rise to her feet. I cannot bear to see an animal suffer unnecessarily, so begged one of the men to take my knife and stab her to the heart, which was done. The animals were cut up and skinned, with considerable fatigue. To skin bulls and cows and cut up their bodies is no joke, even to such as are constantly in the habit of doing it. Whilst Mr. Culbertson and the rest had gone to cut up another at some distance, I remained on guard to save the meat from the Wolves, but none came before my companions returned. We found the last cow quite dead. As we were busy about her the rain fell in torrents, and I found my blanket *capote* of great service. It was now nearly sundown, and we made up our minds to camp close by, although there was no water for our horses, neither any wood. Harris and I began collecting Buffalo-dung from all around, whilst the others attended to various other affairs. The meat was all unloaded and spread on the ground, the horses made fast, the fire burned freely, pieces of liver were soon cooked and devoured, coffee drunk in abundance, and we went to rest.

August 5, Saturday.   It rained in the night; but this morning the weather was cool, wind at northwest, and cloudy, but not menacing rain. We made through the road we had come yesterday, and on our way Harris shot a young of the Swift Fox, which we could have caught alive had we not been afraid of running into some hole. We saw only a few bulls and Antelopes, and some Wolves. The white horse, which had gone out as a *hunter*, returned as a *pack-horse*, loaded with the entire flesh of a Buffalo cow; and our two mules drew three more and the heads of all four. This morning at daylight, when we were called to drink our coffee, there was a Buffalo feeding within twenty steps of our tent, and it moved slowly towards the hills as we busied ourselves making preparations for our departure. We reached the fort at noon; Squires, Provost, and La Fleur had returned; they had wounded a Bighorn, but had lost it. Owen and Bell returned this afternoon; they had seen no Cocks of the plains, but brought the skin of a female Elk, a Porcupine, and a young White-headed Eagle. Provost tells me that Buffaloes become so very poor during hard winters, when the snows cover the ground to the depth of two or three feet, that they lose their hair, become covered with scabs, on which the Magpies feed, and the poor beasts die by hundreds. One can hardly conceive how it happens, notwithstanding these many deaths and the immense numbers that are murdered almost daily on these boundless wastes called prairies, besides the hosts that are drowned in the freshets, and the hundreds of young calves who die in early spring, so many are yet to be found. Daily we see so many that we hardly notice them more than the cattle in our pastures about our homes. But this cannot last; even now there is a perceptible difference in the size of the herds, and before many years the Buffalo, like the Great Auk, will have disappeared; surely this should not be permitted. Bell has been relating his adventures, our boat is going on, and I wish I had a couple of Bighorns. God bless you all.

August 6, Sunday.   I very nearly lost the skin of the Swift Fox, for Harris supposed the animal rotten with the great heat, which caused it to have an odor almost insupportable, and threw it on the roof of the gallery. Bell was so tired he did not look at it, so I took it down, skinned it, and with the assistance of Squires put the coat into pickle, where I daresay it will keep well enough. The weather is thick, and looks like a thunderstorm. Bell, having awaked refreshed by his night's rest, has given me the measurements of the Elk and the Porcupine. Provost has put the skin of the former in pickle, and has gone to Fort Mortimer to see Boucherville and others, to try if they would go after Bighorn to-morrow morning. This afternoon we had an arrival of Indians, the same who were here about two weeks ago. They had been to Fort Clark, and report that a battle had taken place between the Crees and Gros Ventres, and that the latter had lost. Antelopes often die from the severity of the winter weather, and are found dead and shockingly poor, even in the immediate vicinity of the forts. These animals are caught in pens in the manner of Buffaloes, and are despatched with clubs, principally by the squaws. In 1840, during the winter, and when the snow was deep on the prairies and in the ravines by having drifted there, Mr. Laidlow, then at Fort Union, caught four Antelopes by following them on horseback and forcing them into these drifts, which were in places ten or twelve feet deep. They were brought home on a sleigh, and let loose about the rooms. They were so very gentle that they permitted the children to handle them, although being loose they could have kept from them. They were removed to the carpenter's shop, and there one broke its neck by leaping over a turning-lathe. The others were all killed in some such way, for they became very wild, and jumped, kicked, etc., till all were dead. Very young Buffaloes have been caught in the same way, by the same gentleman, assisted by Le Brun and four Indians, and thirteen of these he took down the river, when they became somewhat tamed. The Antelopes cannot be tamed except when caught young, and then they can rarely be raised. Mr. Wm. Sublette, of St. Louis, had one however, a female, which grew to maturity, and was so gentle that it would go all over his house, mounting and descending steps, and even going on the roof of the house. It was alive when I first reached St. Louis, but I was not aware of it, and before I left, it was killed by an Elk belonging to the same gentleman. Provost returned, and said that Boucherville would go with him and La Fleur to-morrow morning early, *but I doubt it.*

August 7, Monday. Provost, Bell, and La Fleur started after breakfast, having waited nearly four hours for Boucherville. They left at seven, and the Indians were curious to know where they were bound, and looked at them with more interest than we all liked. At about nine, we saw Boucherville, accompanied by five men, all mounted, and they were surprised that Provost had not waited for them, or rather that he had left so early. I gave them a bottle of whiskey, and they started under the whip, and must have overtaken the first party in about two hours. To-day has been warmer than any day we have had for two weeks. Sprague has been collecting seeds, and Harris and I searching for stones with impressions of leaves and fern; we found several. Mr. Denig says the Assiniboins killed a Black Bear on White Earth River, about sixty miles from the mouth; they are occasionally killed there, but it is a rare occurrence. Mr. Denig saw the skin of a Bear at their camp last winter, and a Raccoon was also killed on the Cheyenne River by the Sioux, who knew not what to make of it. Mr. Culbertson has given me the following account of a skirmish which took place at Fort McKenzie in the Blackfoot country, which I copy from his manuscript.

"*August 28, 1834.* At the break of day we were aroused from our beds by the report of an enemy being in sight. This unexpected news created naturally a confusion among us all; never was a set of unfortunate beings so surprised as we were. By the time that the alarm had spread through the fort, we were surrounded by the enemy, who proved to be Assiniboins, headed by the chief Gauché (the Antelope). The number, as near as we could judge, was about four hundred. Their first attack was upon a few lodges of Piegans, who were encamped at the fort. They also, being taken by surprise, could not escape. We exerted ourselves, however, to save as many as we could, by getting them into the fort. But the foolish squaws, when they started from their lodges, each took a load of old saddles and skins, which they threw in the door, and stopped it so completely that they could not get in, and here the enemy massacred several. In the mean time our men were firing with muskets and shot-guns. Unfortunately for us, we could not use our cannon, as there were a great many Piegans standing between us and the enemy; this prevented us from firing a telling shot on them at once. The engagement continued nearly an hour, when the enemy, finding their men drop very fast, retreated to the bluffs, half a mile distant; there they stood making signs for us to come on, and give them an equal chance on the prairie. Although our force was much weaker than theirs, we determined to give them a trial. At the same time we despatched an expert runner to an encampment of Piegans for a reinforcement. We mounted our horses, and proceeded to the field of battle, which was a perfect level, where there was no chance to get behind a tree, or anything else, to keep off a ball. We commenced our fire at two hundred yards, but soon lessened the distance to one hundred. Here we kept up a constant fire for two hours, when, our horses getting fatigued, we concluded to await the arrival of our reinforcements. As yet none of us were killed or badly wounded, and nothing lost but one horse, which was shot under one of our men named Bourbon. Of the enemy we cannot tell how many were killed, for as fast as they fell they were carried off the field. After the arrival of our reinforcements, which consisted of one hundred and fifty mounted Piegans, we charged and fought again for another two hours, and drove them across the Maria River, where they took another stand; and here Mr. Mitchell's horse was shot under him and he was wounded. In this engagement the enemy had a decided advantage over us, as they were concealed in the bushes, while we were in the open prairie. However, we succeeded in making them retreat from this place back on to a high prairie, but they suddenly rushed upon us and compelled us to retreat across the Maria. Then they had us in their power; but for some reason, either lack of courage or knowledge, they did not avail themselves of their opportunity. They could have killed a great many of us when we rushed into the water, which was almost deep enough to swim our horses; they were close upon us, but we succeeded in crossing before they fired. This foolish move came near being attended with fatal consequences, which we were aware of, but our efforts to stop it were unsuccessful. We, however, did not retreat far before we turned upon them again, with the determination of driving them to the mountains, in which we succeeded. By this time it was so dark that we could see no more, and we concluded to return. During the day we lost seven killed, and twenty wounded. Two of our dead the enemy had scalped. It is impossible to tell how many of the enemy were killed, but their loss must have been much greater than ours, as they had little ammunition, and at the last none. Our Indians took two bodies and burned them, after scalping them. The Indians who were with us in this skirmish deserve but little credit for their bravery, for in every close engagement the whites, who were comparatively few, always were in advance of them. This, however, had one good effect, for it removed the idea they had of our being cowards, and made them believe we were unusually brave. Had it not been for the assistance we gave the Piegans they would have been cut off, for I never saw Indians behave more bravely than the enemy this day; and had they been well supplied with powder and ball they would have done much more execution. But necessity compelled them to spare their ammunition, as they had come a long way, and they must save enough to enable them to return home. And on our side had we been positive they were enemies, even after they had surprised us in the manner they did, we could have killed many of them at first, but thinking that they were a band of Indians coming with this ceremony to trade (which is not uncommon) we did not fire upon them till the balls and arrows came whistling about our heads; then only was the word given, 'Fire!' Had they been bold enough at the onset to have rushed into the fort, we could have done nothing but suffer death under their tomahawks."

Mr. Denig gave me the following "Bear Story," as he heard it from the parties concerned: "In the year 1835 two men set out from a trading-post at the head of the Cheyenne, and in the neighborhood of the Black Hills, to trap Beaver; their names were Michel Carrière and Bernard Le Brun. Carrière was a man about seventy years old, and had passed most of his life in the Indian country, in this dangerous occupation of trapping. One evening as they were setting their traps along the banks of a stream tributary to the Cheyenne, somewhat wooded by bushes and cottonwood trees, their ears were suddenly saluted by a growl, and in a moment a large she Bear rushed upon them. Le Brun, being a young and active man, immediately picked up his gun, and shot the Bear through the bowels. Carrière also fired, but missed. The Bear then pursued them, but as they ran for their lives, their legs did them good service; they escaped through the bushes, and the Bear lost sight of them. They had concluded the Bear had given up the chase, and were again engaged in setting their traps, when Carrière, who was a short distance from Le Brun, went through a small thicket with a trap and came directly in front of the huge, wounded beast, which, with one spring, bounded upon him and tore him in an awful manner. With one stroke of the paw on his face and forehead he cut his nose in two, and one of the claws reached inward nearly to the brain at the root of the nose; the same stroke tore out his right eye and most of the flesh from that side of his face. His arm and side were *literally torn to pieces*, and the Bear, after handling him in this gentle manner for two or three minutes, threw him upwards about six feet, when he lodged, to all appearance dead, in the fork of a tree. Le Brun, hearing the noise, ran to his assistance, and again shot the Bear and killed it. He then brought what he at first thought was the dead body of his friend to the ground. Little appearance of a human being was left to the poor man, but Le Brun found life was not wholly extinct. He made a *travaille* and carried him by short stages to the nearest trading-post, where the wounded man slowly recovered, but was, of course, the most mutilated looking being imaginable. Carrière, in telling the story, says that he fully believes it to have been the Holy Virgin that lifted him up and placed him in the fork of the tree, and thus preserved his life. The Bear is stated to have been as large as a common ox, and must have weighed, therefore, not far from 1500 lbs." Mr. Denig adds that he saw the man about a year after the accident, and some of the wounds were, even then, not healed. Carrière fully recovered, however, lived a few years, and was killed by the Blackfeet near Fort Union.

When Bell was fixing his traps on his horse this morning, I was amused to see Provost and La Fleur laughing outright at him, as he first put on a Buffalo robe under his saddle, a blanket over it, and over that his mosquito bar and his rain protector. These old hunters could not understand why he needed all these things to be comfortable; then, besides, he took a sack of ship-biscuit. Provost took only an old blanket, a few pounds of dried meat, and his tin cup, and rode off in his shirt and dirty breeches. La Fleur was worse off still, for he took no blanket, and said he could borrow Provost's tin cup; but he, being a most temperate man, carried the bottle of whiskey to mix with the brackish water found in the Mauvaises Terres, among which they have to travel till their return. Harris and I contemplated going to a quarry from which the stones of the powder magazine were brought, but it became too late for us to start in time to see much, and the wrong horses were brought us, being both *runners*, we went, however, across the river after Rabbits. Harris killed a Red-cheeked Woodpecker and shot at a Rabbit, which he missed. We had a sort of show by Moncrévier which was funny, and well performed; he has much versatility, great powers of mimicry, and is a far better actor than many who have made names for themselves in that line. Jean Baptiste told me the following: "About twelve years ago when Mr. McKenzie was the superintendent of this fort, at the season when green peas were plenty and good, Baptiste was sent to the garden about half a mile off, to gather a quantity. He was occupied doing this, when, at the end of a row, to his astonishment, he saw a very large Bear gathering peas also. Baptiste dropped his tin bucket, ran back to the fort as fast as possible, and told Mr. McKenzie, who immediately summoned several other men with guns; they mounted their horses, rode off, and killed the Bear; but, alas! Mr. Bruin had emptied the bucket of peas."

August 8, Tuesday. Another sultry day. Immediately after breakfast Mr. Larpenteur drove Harris and myself in search of geological specimens, but we found none worth having. We killed a *Spermophilus hoodii*, which, although fatally wounded, entered its hole, and Harris had to draw it out by the hind legs. We saw a family of Rock Wrens, and killed four of them. I killed two at one shot; one of the others must have gone in a hole, for though we saw it fall we could not find it. Another, after being shot, found its way under a flat stone, and was there picked up, quite dead, Mr. Larpenteur accidentally turning the stone up. We saw signs of Antelopes and of Hares (Townsend), and rolled a large rock from the top of a high hill. The notes of the Rock Wren are a prolonged cree-è-è-è. On our return home we heard that Boucherville and his five hunters had returned with nothing for me, and they had not met Bell and his companions. We were told also that a few minutes after our departure the roarings and bellowings of Buffalo were heard across the river, and that Owen and two men had been despatched with a cart to kill three fat cows but *no more*; so my remonstrances about useless slaughter have not been wholly unheeded. Harris was sorry he had missed going, and so was I, as both of us could have done so. The milk of the Buffalo cow is truly good and finely tasted, but the bag is never large as in our common cattle, and this is probably a provision of nature to render the cows more capable to run off, and escape from their pursuers. Bell, Provost, and La Fleur returned just before dinner; they had seen no Bighorns, and only brought the flesh of two Deer killed by La Fleur, and a young Magpie. This afternoon Provost skinned a calf that was found by one of the cows that Owen killed; it was *very* young, only a few hours old, but large, and I have taken its measurements. It is looked upon as a phenomenon, as no Buffalo cow calves at this season. The calving time is from about the 1st of February to the last of May. Owen went six miles from the fort before he saw the cattle; there were more than three hundred in number, and Harris and I regretted the more we had not gone, but had been fruitlessly hunting for stones. It is curious that while Harris was searching for Rabbits early this morning, he heard the bellowing of the bulls, and thought first it was the growling of a Grizzly Bear, and then that it was the fort bulls, so he mentioned it to no one. To-morrow evening La Fleur and two men will go after Bighorns again, and they are not to return before they have killed one male, at least. This evening we went a-fishing across the river, and caught ten good catfish of the upper Missouri species, the sweetest and best fish of the sort that I have eaten in any part of the country. Our boat is going on well, and looks pretty to boot. Her name will be the "Union," in consequence of the united exertions of my companions to do all that could be done, on this costly expedition. The young Buffaloes now about the fort have begun shedding their red coats, the latter-colored hair dropping off in patches about the size of the palm of my hand, and the new hair is dark brownish black.

August 9, Wednesday. The weather is cool and we are looking for rain. Squires, Provost, and La Fleur went off this morning after an early breakfast, across the river for Bighorns with orders not to return without some of these wild animals, which reside in the most inaccessible portions of the broken and lofty clay hills and stones that exist in this region of the country; they never resort to the low lands except when moving from one spot to another; they swim rivers well, as do Antelopes. I have scarcely done anything but write this day, and my memorandum books are now crowded with sketches, measurements, and descriptions. We have nine Indians, all Assiniboins, among whom *five* are chiefs. These nine Indians fed for three days on the flesh of only a single Swan; they saw no Buffaloes, though they report large herds about their village, fully two hundred miles from here. This evening I caught about one dozen catfish, and shot a *Spermophilus hoodii*, an old female, which had her pouches distended and filled with the seeds of the wild sunflower of this region. I am going to follow one of their holes and describe the same.

August 10, Thursday. Bell and I took a walk after Rabbits, but saw none. The nine Indians, having received their presents, went off with apparent reluctance, for when you begin to give them, the more they seem to demand. The horse-guards brought in another *Spermophilus hoodii*; after dinner we are going to examine one of their burrows. We have been, and have returned; the three burrows which we dug were as follows: straight downward for three or four inches, and gradually becoming deeper in an oblique slant, to the depth of eight or nine inches, but not more, and none of these holes extended more than six or seven feet beyond this. I was disappointed at not finding nests, or rooms for stores. Although I have said much about Buffalo running, and butchering in general, I have not given the particular manner in which the latter is performed by the hunters of this country,—I mean the white hunters,—and I will now try to do so. The moment that the Buffalo is dead, three or four hunters, their faces and hands often covered with gunpowder, and with pipes lighted, place the animal on its belly, and by drawing out each fore and hind leg, fix the body so that it cannot fall down again; an incision is made near the root of the tail, immediately above the root in fact, and the skin cut to the neck, and taken off in the roughest manner imaginable, downwards and on both sides at the same time. The knives are going in all directions, and many wounds occur to the hands and fingers, but are rarely attended to at this time. The pipe of one man has perhaps given out, and with his bloody hands he takes the one of his nearest companion, who has his own hands equally bloody. Now one breaks in the skull of the bull, and with bloody fingers draws out the hot brains and swallows them with peculiar zest; another has now reached the liver, and is gobbling down enormous pieces of it; whilst, perhaps, a third, who has come to the paunch, is feeding luxuriously on some—to me—disgusting-looking offal. But the main business proceeds. The flesh is taken off from the sides of the boss, or hump bones, from where these bones begin to the very neck, and the hump itself is thus destroyed. The hunters give the name of "hump" to the mere bones when slightly covered by flesh; and it is cooked, and very good when fat, young, and well broiled. The pieces of flesh taken from the sides of these bones are called *filets*, and are the best portion of the animal when properly cooked. The fore-quarters, or shoulders, are taken off, as well as the hind ones, and the sides, covered by a thin portion of flesh called the *depouille*, are taken out. Then the ribs are broken off at the vertebræ, as well as the boss bones. The marrow-bones, which are those of the fore and hind legs only, are cut out last. The feet usually remain attached to these; the paunch is stripped of its covering of layers of fat, the head and the backbone are left to the Wolves, the pipes are all emptied, the hands, faces, and clothes all bloody, and now a glass of grog is often enjoyed, as the stripping off the skins and flesh of three or four animals is truly very hard work. In some cases when no water was near, our supper was cooked without our being washed, and it was not until we had travelled several miles the next morning that we had any opportunity of cleaning ourselves; and yet, despite everything, we are all hungry, eat heartily, and sleep soundly. When the wind is high and the Buffaloes run towards it, the hunter's guns very often snap, and it is during their exertions to replenish their pans, that the powder flies and sticks to the moisture every moment accumulating on their faces; but nothing stops these daring and usually powerful men, who the moment the chase is ended, leap from their horses, let them graze, and begin their butcher-like work.

August 11, Friday. The weather has been cold and windy, and the day has passed in comparative idleness with me. Squires returned this afternoon alone, having left Provost and La Fleur behind. They have seen only two Bighorns, a female and her young. It was concluded that, if our boat was finished by Tuesday next, we would leave on Wednesday morning, but I am by no means assured of this, and Harris was quite startled at the very idea. Our boat, though forty feet long, is, I fear, too small. *Nous verrons!* Some few preparations for packing have been made, but Owen, Harris, and Bell are going out early to-morrow morning to hunt Buffaloes, and when they return we will talk matters over. The activity of Buffaloes is almost beyond belief; they can climb the steep defiles of the Mauvaises Terres in hundreds of places where men cannot follow them, and it is a fine sight to see a large gang of them proceeding along these defiles four or five hundred feet above the level of the bottoms, and from which pathway if one of the number makes a mis-step or accidentally slips, he goes down rolling over and over, and breaks his neck ere the level ground is reached. Bell and Owen saw a bull about three years old that leaped a ravine filled with mud and water, at least twenty feet wide; it reached the middle at the first bound, and at the second was mounted on the opposite bank, from which it kept on bounding, till it gained the top of quite a high hill. Mr. Culbertson tells me that these animals can endure hunger in a most extraordinary manner. He says that a large bull was seen on a spot half way down a precipice, where it had slid, and from which it could not climb upwards, and either could not or would not descend; at any rate, it did not leave the position in which it found itself. The party who saw it returned to the fort, and, on their way back on the *twenty-fifth* day after, they passed the hill, and saw the bull standing there. The thing that troubles them most is crossing rivers on the ice; their hoofs slip from side to side, they become frightened, and stretch their four legs apart to support the body, and in such situations the Indians and white hunters easily approach, and stab them to the heart, or cut the hamstrings, when they become an easy prey. When in large gangs those in the centre are supported by those on the outposts, and if the stream is not large, reach the shore and readily escape. Indians of different tribes hunt the Buffalo in different ways; some hunt on horseback, and use arrows altogether; they are rarely expert in reloading the gun in the close race. Others hunt on foot, using guns, arrows, or both. Others follow with patient perseverance, and kill them also. But I will give you the manner pursued by the Mandans. Twenty to fifty men start, as the occasion suits, each provided with two horses, one of which is a pack-horse, the other fit for the chase. They have quivers with from twenty to fifty arrows, according to the wealth of the hunter. They ride the pack horse bareback, and travel on, till they see the game, when they leave the pack-horse, and leap on the hunter, and start at full speed and soon find themselves amid the Buffaloes, on the flanks of the herd, and on both sides. When within a few yards the arrow is sent, they shoot at a Buffalo somewhat ahead of them, and send the arrow in an oblique manner, so as to pass through the lights. If the blood rushes out of the nose and mouth the animal is fatally wounded, and they shoot at it no more; if not, a second, and perhaps a third arrow, is sent before this happens. The Buffaloes on starting carry the tail close in between the legs, but when wounded they switch it about, especially if they wish to fight, and then the hunter's horse shies off and lets the mad animal breathe awhile. If shot through the heart, they occasionally fall dead on the instant; sometimes, if not hit in the right place, a dozen arrows will not stop them. When wounded and mad they turn suddenly round upon the hunter, and rush upon him in such a quick and furious manner that if horse and rider are not both on the alert, the former is overtaken, hooked and overthrown, the hunter pitched off, trampled and gored to death. Although the Buffalo is such a large animal, and to all appearance a clumsy one, it can turn with the quickness of thought, and when once enraged, will rarely give up the chase until avenged for the wound it has received. If, however, the hunter is expert, and the horse fleet, they outrun the bull, and it returns to the herd. Usually the greater number of the gang is killed, but it very rarely happens that some of them do not escape. This however is not the case when the animal is pounded, especially by the Gros Ventres, Black Feet, and Assiniboins. These pounds are called "parks," and the Buffaloes are made to enter them in the following manner: The park is sometimes round and sometimes square, this depending much on the ground where it is put up; at the end of the park is what is called a *precipice* of some fifteen feet or less, as may be found. It is approached by a funnel-shaped passage, which like the park itself is strongly built of logs, brushwood, and pickets, and when all is ready a young man, very swift of foot, starts at daylight covered over with a Buffalo robe and wearing a Buffalo headdress. The moment he sees the herd to be taken, he bellows like a young calf, and makes his way slowly towards the contracted part of the funnel, imitating the cry of the calf, at frequent intervals. The Buffaloes advance after the decoy; about a dozen mounted hunters are yelling and galloping behind them, and along both flanks of the herd, forcing them by these means to enter the mouth of the funnel. Women and children are placed behind the fences of the funnel to frighten the cattle, and as soon as the young man who acts as decoy feels assured that the game is in a fair way to follow to the bank or "precipice," he runs or leaps down the bank, over the barricade, and either rests, or joins in the fray. The poor Buffaloes, usually headed by a large bull, proceed, leap down the bank in haste and confusion, the Indians all yelling and pursuing till every bull, cow, and calf is impounded. Although this is done at all seasons, it is more general in October or November, when the hides are good and salable. Now the warriors are all assembled by the pen, calumets are lighted, and the chief smokes to the Great Spirit, the four points of the compass, and lastly to the Buffaloes. The pipe is passed from mouth to mouth in succession, and as soon as this ceremony is ended, the destruction commences. Guns shoot, arrows fly in all directions, and the hunters being on the outside of the enclosure, destroy the whole gang, before they jump over to clean and skin the murdered herd. Even the children shoot small, short arrows to assist in the destruction. It happens sometimes however, that the leader of the herd will be restless at the sight of the precipices, and if the fence is weak will break through it, and all his fellows follow him, and escape. The same thing sometimes takes place in the pen, for so full does this become occasionally that the animals touch each other, and as they cannot move, the very weight against the fence of the pen is quite enough to break it through; the smallest aperture is sufficient, for in a few minutes it becomes wide, and all the beasts are seen scampering over the prairies, leaving the poor Indians starving and discomfited. Mr. Kipp told me that while travelling from Lake Travers to the Mandans, in the month of August, he rode in a heavily laden cart for six successive days through masses of Buffaloes, which divided for the cart, allowing it to pass without opposition. He has seen the immense prairie back of Fort Clark look black to the tops of the hills, though the ground was covered with snow, so crowded was it with these animals; and the masses probably extended much further. In fact it is *impossible to describe or even conceive* the vast multitudes of these animals that exist even now, and feed on these ocean-like prairies.

August 12, Saturday. Harris, Bell, and Owen went after Buffaloes; killed six cows and brought them home. Weather cloudy, and rainy at times. Provost returned with La Fleur this afternoon, had nothing, but had seen a Grizzly Bear. The "Union" was launched this evening and packing, etc., is going on. I gave a memorandum to Jean Baptiste Moncrévier of the animals I wish him to procure for me.

August 13, Sunday. A most beautiful day. About dinner time I had a young Badger brought to me dead; I bought it, and gave in payment two pounds of sugar. The body of these animals is broader than high, the neck is powerfully strong, as well as the fore-arms, and strongly clawed fore-feet. It weighed 8½ lbs. Its measurements were all taken. When the pursuer gets between a Badger and its hole, the animal's hair rises, and it at once shows fight. A half-breed hunter told Provost, who has just returned from Fort Mortimer, that he was anxious to go down the river with me, but I know the man and hardly care to have him. If I decide to take him Mr. Culbertson, to whom I spoke of the matter, told me my only plan was to pay him by the piece for what he killed and brought on board, and that in case he did not turn out well between this place and Fort Clark, to leave him there; so I have sent word to him to this effect by Provost this afternoon. Bell is skinning the Badger, Sprague finishing the map of the river made by Squires, and the latter is writing. The half-breed has been here, and the following is our agreement: "It is understood that François Détaillé will go with me, John J. Audubon, and to secure for me the following quadrupeds—if possible—for which he will receive the prices here mentioned, payable at Fort Union, Fort Clark, or Fort Pierre, as may best suit him.

For each Bighorn male	$10.00
For a large Grizzly Bear	20.00
For a large male Elk	6.00
For a Black-tailed Deer, male or female	6.00
For Red Foxes	3.00
For small Gray Foxes	3.00
For Badgers	2.00
For large Porcupine	2.00

Independent of which I agree to furnish him with his passage and food, he to work as a hand on board. Whatever he kills for food will be settled when he leaves us, or, as he says, when he meets the Opposition boat coming up to Fort Mortimer." He will also accompany us in our hunt after Bighorns, which I shall undertake, notwithstanding Mr. Culbertson and Squires, who have been to the Mauvaises Terres, both try to dissuade me from what they fear will prove over-fatiguing; but though my strength is not what it was twenty years ago, I am yet equal to much, and my eyesight far keener than that of many a younger man, though that too tells me I am no longer a youth. . . .

The only idea I can give in *writing* of what are called the "Mauvaises Terres" would be to place some thousands of loaves of sugar of different sizes, from quite small and low, to large and high, all irregularly truncated at top, and placed somewhat apart from each other. No one who has not seen these places can form any idea of these resorts of the Rocky Mountain Rams, or the difficulty of approaching them, putting aside their extreme wildness and their marvellous activity. They form paths around these broken-headed cones (that are from three to fifteen hundred feet high), and run round them at full speed on a track that, to the eye of the hunter, does not appear to be more than a few inches wide, but which is, in fact, from a foot to eighteen inches in width. In some places there are piles of earth from eight to ten feet high, or even more, the tops of which form platforms of a hard and shelly rocky substance, where the Bighorn is often seen looking on the hunter far below, and standing immovable, as if a statue. No one can imagine how they reach these places, and that too with their young, even when the latter are quite small. Hunters say that the young are usually born in such places, the mothers going there to save the helpless little one from the Wolves, which, after men, seem to be their greatest destroyers. The Mauvaises Terres are mostly formed of grayish white clay, very sparsely covered with small patches of thin grass, on which the Bighorns feed, but which, to all appearance, is a very scanty supply, and there, and there only, they feed, as not one has ever been seen on the bottom or prairie land further than the foot of these most extraordinary hills. In wet weather, no man can climb any of them, and at such times they are greasy, muddy, sliding grounds. Oftentimes when a Bighorn is seen on a hill-top, the hunter has to ramble about for three or four miles before he can approach within gunshot of the game, and if the Bighorn ever sees his enemy, pursuit is useless. The tops of some of these hills, and in some cases whole hills about thirty feet high, are composed of a conglomerated mass of stones, sand, and clay, with earth of various sorts, fused together, and having a brick-like appearance. In this mass pumice-stone of various shapes and sizes is to be found. The whole is evidently the effect of volcanic action. The bases of some of these hills cover an area of twenty acres or more, and the hills rise to the height of three or four hundred feet, sometimes even to eight hundred or a thousand; so high can the hunter ascend that the surrounding country is far, far beneath him. The strata are of different colored clays, coal, etc., and an earth impregnated with a salt which appears to have been formed by internal fire or heat, the earth or stones of which I have first spoken in this account, lava, sulphur, salts of various kinds, oxides and sulphates of iron; and in the sand at the tops of some of the highest hills I have found marine shells, but so soft and crumbling as to fall apart the instant they were exposed to the air. I spent some time over various lumps of sand, hoping to find some perfect ones that would be hard enough to carry back to St. Louis; but 't was "love's labor lost," and I regretted exceedingly that only a few fragments could be gathered. I found globular and oval shaped stones, very heavy, apparently composed mostly of iron, weighing from fifteen to twenty pounds; numbers of petrified stumps from one to three feet in diameter; the Mauvaises Terres abound with them; they are to be found in all parts from the valleys to the tops of the hills, and appear to be principally of cedar. On the sides of the hills, at various heights, are shelves of rock or stone projecting out from two to six, eight, or even ten feet, and generally square, or nearly so; these are the favorite resorts of the Bighorns during the heat of the day, and either here or on the tops of the highest hills they are to be found. Between the hills there is generally quite a growth of cedar, but mostly stunted and crowded close together, with very large stumps, and between the stumps quite a good display of grass; on the summits, in some *few* places, there are table-lands, varying from an area of one to ten or fifteen acres; these are covered with a short, dry, wiry grass, and immense quantities of flat leaved cactus, the spines of which often warn the hunter of their proximity, and the hostility existing between them and his feet. These plains are not more easily travelled than the hillsides, as every step may lead the hunter into a bed of these pests of the prairies. In the valleys between the hills are ravines, some of which are not more than ten or fifteen feet wide, while their depth is beyond the reach of the eye. Others vary in depth from ten to fifty feet, while some make one giddy to look in; they are also of various widths, the widest perhaps a hundred feet. The edges, at times, are lined with bushes, mostly wild cherry; occasionally Buffaloes make paths across them, but this is rare. The only safe way to pass is to follow the ravine to the head, which is usually at the foot of some hill, and go round. These ravines are mostly between every two hills, although like every general rule there are variations and occasionally places where three or more hills make only one ravine. These small ravines all connect with some larger one, the size of which is in proportion to its tributaries. The large one runs to the river, or the water is carried off by a subterranean channel. In these valleys, and sometimes on the tops of the hills, are holes, called "sink holes;" these are formed by the water running in a small hole and working away the earth beneath the surface, leaving a crust incapable of supporting the weight of a man; and if an unfortunate steps on this crust, he soon finds himself in rather an unpleasant predicament. This is one of the dangers that attend the hunter in these lands; these holes eventually form a ravine such as I have before spoken of. Through these hills it is almost impossible to travel with a horse, though it is sometimes done by careful management, and a correct knowledge of the country. The sides of the hills are very steep, covered with the earth and stones of which I have spoken, all of which are quite loose on the surface; occasionally a bunch of wormwood here and there seems to assist the daring hunter; for it is no light task to follow the Bighorns through these lands, and the pursuit is attended with much danger, as the least slip at times would send one headlong into the ravines below. On the sides of these high hills the water has washed away the earth, leaving caves of various sizes; and, in fact, in some places all manner of fantastic forms are made by the same process. Occasionally in the valleys are found isolated cones or domes, destitute of vegetation, naked and barren. Throughout the Mauvaises Terres there are springs of water impregnated with salt, sulphur, magnesia, and many other salts of all kinds. Such is the water the hunter is compelled to drink, and were it not that it is as cold as ice it would be almost impossible to swallow it. As it is, many of these waters operate as cathartics or emetics; this is one of the most disagreeable attendants of hunting in these lands. Moreover, venomous snakes of many kinds are also found here. I saw myself only one copperhead, and a common garter-snake. Notwithstanding the rough nature of the country, the Buffaloes have paths running in all directions, and leading from the prairies to the river. The hunter sometimes, after toiling for an hour or two up the side of one of these hills, trying to reach the top in hopes that when there he will have for a short distance at least, either a level place or good path to walk on, finds to his disappointment that he has secured a point that only affords a place scarcely large enough to stand on, and he has the trouble of descending, perhaps to renew his disappointment in the same way, again and again, such is the deceptive character of the country. I was thus deceived time and again, while in search of Bighorns. If the hill does not terminate in a point it is connected with another hill, by a ridge so narrow that nothing but a Bighorn can walk on it. This is the country that the Mountain Ram inhabits, and if, from this imperfect description, any information can be derived, I shall be more than repaid for the trouble I have had in these tiresome hills. Whether my theory be correct or incorrect, it is this: These hills were at first composed of the clays that I have mentioned, mingled with an immense quantity of combustible material, such as coal, sulphur, bitumen, etc.; these have been destroyed by fire, or (at least the greater part) by volcanic action, as to this day, on the Black Hills and in the hills near where I have been, fire still exists; and from the immense quantities of pumice-stone and melted ores found among the hills, even were there no fire now to be seen, no one could doubt that it had, at some date or other, been there; as soon as this process had ceased, the rains washed out the loose material, and carried it to the rivers, leaving the more solid parts as we now find them; the action of water to this day continues. As I have said, the Bighorns are very fond of resorting to the shelves, or ledges, on the sides of the hills, during the heat of the day, when these places are shaded; here they lie, but are aroused instantly upon the least appearance of danger, and, as soon as they have discovered the cause of alarm, away they go, over hill and ravine, occasionally stopping to look round, and when ascending the steepest hill, there is no apparent diminution of their speed. They will ascend and descend places, when thus alarmed, so inaccessible that it is almost impossible to conceive how, and where, they find a foothold. When observed before they see the hunter, or while they are looking about when first alarmed, are the only opportunities the hunter has to shoot them; for, as soon as they start there is no hope, as to follow and find them is a task not easily accomplished, for where or how far they go when thus on the alert, heaven only knows, as but few hunters have ever attempted a chase. At all times they have to be approached with the greatest caution, as the least thing renders them on the *qui vive*. When not found on these shelves, they are seen on the tops of the most inaccessible and highest hills, looking down on the hunters, apparently conscious of their security, or else lying down tranquilly in some sunny spot quite out of reach. As I have observed before, the only times that these animals can be shot are when on these ledges, or when moving from one point to another. Sometimes they move only a few hundred yards, but it will take the hunter several hours to approach near enough for a shot, so long are the *détours* he is compelled to make. I have been thus baffled two or three times. The less difficult hills are found cut up by paths made by these animals; these are generally about eighteen inches wide. These animals appear to be quite as agile as the European Chamois, leaping down precipices, across ravines, and running up and down almost perpendicular hills. The only places I could find that seemed to afford food for them, was between the cedars, as I have before mentioned; but the places where they are most frequently found are barren, and without the least vestige of vegetation. From the character of the lands where these animals are found, their own shyness, watchfulness, and agility, it is readily seen what the hunter must endure, and what difficulties he must undergo to near these "Wild Goats." It is one constant time of toil, anxiety, fatigue, and danger. Such the country! Such the animal! Such the hunting!

August 16. Started from Fort Union at 12 M. in the Mackinaw barge "Union." Shot five young Ducks. Camped at the foot of a high bluff. Good supper of Chickens and Ducks.

Thursday, 17th. Started early. Saw three Bighorns, some Antelopes, and many Deer, fully twenty; one Wolf, twenty-two Swans, many Ducks. Stopped a short time on a bar. Mr. Culbertson shot a female Elk, and I killed two bulls. Camped at Buffalo Bluff, where we found Bear tracks.

Friday, 18th. Fine. Bell shot a superb male Elk. The two bulls untouched since killed. Stopped to make an oar, when I caught four catfish. "Kayac" is the French Missourian's name for Buffalo Bluffs, original French for Moose; in Assiniboin

"Tah-Tah," in Blackfoot "Sick-e-chi-choo," in Sioux "Tah-Tah." Fifteen to twenty female Elks drinking, tried to approach them, but they broke and ran off to the willows and disappeared. We landed and pursued them. Bell shot at one, but did not find it, though it was badly wounded. These animals are at times unwary, but at others vigilant, suspicious, and well aware of the coming of their enemies.

Saturday, 19th. Wolves howling, and bulls roaring, just like the long continued roll of a hundred drums. Saw large gangs of Buffaloes walking along the river. Headed Knife River one and a half miles. Fresh signs of Indians, burning wood embers, etc. I knocked a cow down with two balls, and Mr. Culbertson killed her. Abundance of Bear tracks. Saw a great number of bushes bearing the berries of which Mrs. Culbertson has given me a necklace. Herds of Buffaloes on the prairies. Mr. Culbertson killed another cow, and in going to see it I had a severe fall over a partially sunken log. Bell killed a doe and wounded the fawn.

Sunday, 20th. *Tamias quadrivittatus* runs up trees; abundance of them in the ravine, and Harris killed one. Bell wounded an Antelope. Thousands upon thousands of Buffaloes; the roaring of these animals resembles the grunting of hogs, with a rolling sound from the throat. Mr. C. killed two cows, Sprague killed one bull, and I made two sketches of it after death. The men killed a cow, and the bull would not leave her although shot four times. Stopped by the high winds all this day. Suffered much from my fall.

Monday, 21st. Buffaloes all over the bars and prairies, and many swimming; the roaring can be heard for miles. The wind stopped us again at eight o'clock; breakfasted near the tracks of Bears surrounded by hundreds of Buffaloes. We left our safe anchorage and good hunting-grounds too soon; the wind blew high, and we were obliged to land again on the opposite shore, where the gale has proved very annoying. Bear tracks led us to search for those animals, but in vain. Collected seeds. Shot at a Rabbit, but have done nothing. Saw many young and old Ducks,—Black Mallards and Gadwalls. I shot a bull and broke his thigh, and then shot at him thirteen times before killing. Camped at the same place.

Tuesday, 22d. Left early and travelled about twelve miles.

Went hunting Elks. Mr. Culbertson killed a Deer, and he and Squires brought the meat in on their backs. I saw nothing, but heard shots which I thought were from Harris. I ran for upwards of a mile to look for him, hallooing the whole distance, but saw nothing of him. Sent three men who hallooed also, but came back without further intelligence. Bell shot a female Elk and brought in part of the meat. We walked to the Little Missouri and shot the fourth bull this trip. We saw many Ducks. In the afternoon we started again, and went below the Little Missouri, returned to the bull and took his horns, etc. Coming back to the boat Sprague saw a Bear; we went towards the spot; the fellow had turned under the high bank and was killed in a few seconds. Mr. Culbertson shot it first through the neck, Bell and I in the body.

Wednesday, 23d. Provost skinned the Bear. No Prairie-Dogs caught. The wind high and cold. Later two Prairie-Dogs were shot; their notes resemble precisely those of the Arkansas Flycatcher. Left this afternoon and travelled about ten miles. Saw another Bear and closely observed its movements. We saw several drowned Buffaloes, and were passed by Wolves and Passenger Pigeons. Camped in a bad place under a sky with every appearance of rain.

Thursday, 24th. A bad night of wind, very cloudy; left early, as the wind lulled and it became calm. Passed "L'Ours qui danse," travelled about twenty miles, when we were again stopped by the wind. Hunted, but found nothing. The fat of our Bear gave us seven bottles of oil. We heard what some thought to be guns, but I believed it to be the falling of the banks. Then the Wolves howled so curiously that it was supposed they were Indian dogs. We went to bed all prepared for action in case of an attack; pistols, knives, etc., but I slept very well, though rather cold.

Friday, 25th. Fair, but foggy, so we did not start early. I found some curious stones with impressions of shells. It was quite calm, and we passed the two Riccaree winter villages. Many Eagles and Peregrine Falcons. Shot another bull. Passed the Gros Ventre village at noon; no game about the place. "La Main Gauche," an Assiniboin chief of great renown, left seventy warriors killed and thirty wounded on the prairie opposite, the year following the small-pox. The Gros Ventres are a courageous tribe. Reached the Mandan village; hundreds of Indians swam to us with handkerchiefs tied on their heads like turbans. Our old friend "Four Bears" met us on the shore; I gave him eight pounds of tobacco. He came on board and went down with us to Fort Clark, which we reached at four o'clock. Mr. Culbertson and Squires rode out to the Gros Ventre village with "Four Bears" after dark, and returned about eleven; they met with another chief who curiously enough was called "The Iron Bear."

Saturday, 26th. Fine, but a cold, penetrating wind. Started early and landed to breakfast. A canoe passed us with two men from the Opposition. We were stopped by the wind for four hours, but started again at three; passed the Butte Quarré at a quarter past five, followed now by the canoe, as the two fellows are afraid of Indians, and want to come on board our boat; we have not room for them, but will let them travel with us. Landed for the night, and walked to the top of one of the buttes from which we had a fine and very extensive view. Saw a herd of Buffaloes, which we approached, but by accident did not kill a cow. Harris, whom we thought far off, shot too soon and Moncrévier and the rest of us lost our chances. We heard Elks whistling, and saw many Swans. The canoe men camped close to us.

Sunday, 27th. Started early in company with the canoe. Saw four Wolves and six bulls, the latter to our sorrow in a compact group and therefore difficult to attack. They are poor at this season, and the meat very rank, but yet are fresh meat. The wind continued high, but we landed in the weeds assisted by the canoe men, as we saw a gang of cows. We lost them almost immediately though we saw their *wet tracks* and followed them for over a mile, but then gave up the chase. On returning to the river we missed the boat, as she had been removed to a better landing below; so we had quite a search for her. Mrs. Culbertson worked at the *parflèche* with Golden Eagle feathers; she had killed the bird herself. Stopped by the wind at noon. Walked off and saw Buffaloes, but the wind was adverse. Bell and Harris, however, killed a cow, a single one, that had been wounded, whether by shot or by an arrow no one can tell. We saw a bull on a sandbar; the poor fool took to the water and swam so as to meet us. We shot at him about a dozen times, I shot him through one eye, Bell, Harris, and Sprague about the head, and yet the animal made for our boat and came so close that Mr. Culbertson touched him with a pole, when he turned off and swam across the river, but acted as if wild or crazy; he ran on a sand-bar, and at last swam again to the opposite shore, in my opinion to die, but Mr. Culbertson says he may live for a month. We landed in a good harbor on the east side about an hour before sundown. Moncrévier caught a catfish that weighed sixteen pounds, a fine fish, though the smaller ones are better eating.

Monday, 28th. A gale all night and this morning also. We are in a good place for hunting, and I hope to have more to say anon. The men returned and told us of many Bear tracks, and four of us started off. Such a walk I do not remember; it was awful—mire, willows, vines, holes, fallen logs; we returned much fatigued and having seen nothing. The wind blowing fiercely.

Tuesday, 29th. Heavy wind all night. Bad dreams about my own Lucy. Walked some distance along the shores and caught many catfish. Two Deer on the other shore. Cut a cotton-tree to fasten to the boat to break the force of the waves. The weather has become sultry. Beavers during the winter oftentimes come down amid the ice, but enter any small stream they meet with at once. Apple River, or Creek, was formerly a good place for them, as well as Cannon Ball River. Saw a Musk-rat this morning swimming by our barge. Slept on a muddy bar with abundance of mosquitoes.

Wednesday, 30th. Started at daylight. Mr. Culbertson and I went off to the prairies over the most infernal ground I ever saw, but we reached the high prairies by dint of industry, through swamps and mire. We saw two bulls, two calves, and one cow; we killed the cow and the larger calf, a beautiful young bull; returned to the boat through the most abominable swamp I ever travelled through, and reached the boat at one o'clock, thirsty and hungry enough. Bell and all the men went after the meat and the skin of the young bull. I shot the cow, but missed the calf by shooting above it. We started later and made about ten miles before sunset.

Thursday, 31st. Started early; fine and calm. Saw large

flocks of Ducks, Geese, and Swans; also four Wolves. Passed Mr. Primeau's winter trading-house; reached Cannon Ball River at half-past twelve. No game; water good-tasted, but warm. Dinner on shore. Saw a Rock Wren on the bluffs here. Saw the prairie on fire, and signs of Indians on both sides. Weather cloudy and hot. Reached Beaver Creek. Provost went after Beavers, but found none. Caught fourteen catfish. Saw a wonderful example of the power of the Buffalo in working through the heavy, miry bottom lands.

Friday, September 1. Hard rain most of the night, and uncomfortably hot. Left our encampment at eight o'clock. Saw Buffaloes and landed, but on approaching them found only bulls; so returned empty-handed to the boat, and started anew. We landed for the night on a large sand-bar connected with the mainland, and saw a large gang of Buffaloes, and Mr. Culbertson and a man went off; they shot at two cows and killed one, but lost her, as she fell in the river and floated down stream, and it was dusk. A heavy cloud arose in the west, thunder was heard, yet the moon and stars shone brightly. After midnight rain came on. The mosquitoes are far too abundant for comfort.

Saturday, September 2. Fine but windy. Went about ten miles and stopped, for the gale was so severe. No fresh meat on board. Saw eight Wolves, four white ones. Walked six miles on the prairies, but saw only three bulls. The wind has risen to a gale. Saw abundance of Black-breasted Prairie Larks, and a pond with Black Ducks. Returned to the pond after dinner and killed four Ducks.

Sunday, 3d. Beautiful, calm, and cold. Left early and at noon put ashore to kill a bull, having no fresh meat on board. He took the wind and ran off. Touched on a bar, and I went overboard to assist in pushing off and found the water very pleasant, for our cold morning had turned into a hot day. Harris shot a Prairie Wolf. At half-past four saw ten or twelve Buffaloes. Mr. Culbertson, Bell, a canoe man, and I, went after them; the cattle took to the river, and we went in pursuit; the other canoe man landed, and ran along the shore, but could not head them. He shot, however, and as the cattle reached the bank we gave them a volley, but uselessly, and are again under way. Bell and Mr. C. were well mired and greatly exhausted in consequence. No meat for another day. Stopped for the night at the mouth of the Moreau River. Wild Pigeons, Sandpipers, but no fish.

Monday, 4th. Cool night. Wind rose early, but a fine morning. Stopped by the wind at eleven. Mr. Culbertson, Bell, and Moncrévier gone shooting. Many signs of Elk, etc., and flocks of Wild Pigeons. A bad place for hunting, but good for safety. Found Beaver tracks, and small trees cut down by them. Provost followed the bank and found their lodge, which he says is an old one. It is at present a mass of sticks of different sizes matted together, and fresh tracks are all around it. To dig them out would have proved impossible, and we hope to catch them in traps to-night. Beavers often feed on berries when they can reach them, especially Buffalo berries. Mr. Culbertson killed a buck, and we have sent men to bring it entire. The Beavers in this lodge are not residents, but vagrant Beavers. The buck was brought in; it is of the same kind as at Fort Union, having a longer tail, we think, than the kind found East. Its horns were very small, but it is skinned and in brine. We removed our camp about a hundred yards lower down, but the place as regards wood is very bad. Provost and I went to set traps for Beaver; he first cut two dry sticks eight or nine feet long; we reached the river by passing through the tangled woods; he then pulled off his breeches and waded about with a pole to find the depth of the water, and having found a fit spot he dug away the mud in the shape of a half circle, placed a bit of willow branch at the bottom and put the trap on that. He had two small willow sticks in his mouth; he split an end of one, dipped it in his horn of castoreum, or "medicine," as he calls his stuff, and left on the end of it a good mass of it, which was placed in front of the jaws of the trap next the shore; he then made the chain of the trap secure, stuck in a few untrimmed branches on each side, and there the business ended. The second one was arranged in the same way, except that there was no bit of willow under it. Beavers when caught in shallow water are often attacked by the Otter, and in doing this the latter sometimes lose their own lives, as they are very frequently caught in the other trap placed close by. Mr. Culbertson and Bell returned without having shot, although we heard one report whilst setting the traps. Elks are very numerous here, but the bushes crack and make so much noise that they hear the hunters and fly before them. Bell shot five Pigeons at once. Harris and Squires are both poorly, having eaten too indulgently of Buffalo brains. We are going to move six or seven hundred yards lower down, to spend the night in a more sheltered place. I hope I may have a large Beaver to-morrow.

Tuesday, 5th. At daylight, after some discussion about Beaver lodges, Harris, Bell, Provost, and I, with two men, went to the traps—nothing caught. We now had the lodge demolished outwardly, namely, all the sticks removed, under which was found a hole about two and a half feet in diameter, through which Harris, Bell, and Moncrévier (who had followed us) entered, but found nothing within, as the Beaver had gone to the river. Harris saw it, and also the people at the boat. I secured some large specimens of the cuttings used to build the lodge, and a pocketful of the chips. Before Beavers fell the tree they long for, they cut down all the small twigs and saplings around. The chips are cut above and below, and then split off by the animal; the felled trees lay about us in every direction. We left our camp at half-past five; I again examined the lodge, which was not finished, though about six feet in diameter. We saw a Pigeon Hawk giving chase to a Spotted Sandpiper on the wing. When the Hawk was about to seize the little fellow it dove under water and escaped. This was repeated five or six times; to my great surprise and pleasure, the Hawk was obliged to relinquish the prey. As the wind blew high, we landed to take breakfast, on a fine beach, portions of which appeared as if paved by the hand of man. The canoe men killed a very poor cow, which had been wounded, and so left alone. The wind fell suddenly, and we proceeded on our route till noon, when it rose, and we stopped again. Mr. Culbertson went hunting, and returned having killed a young buck Elk. Dined, and walked after the meat and skin, and took the measurements. Returning, saw two Elks driven to the hills by Mr. Culbertson and Bell. Met Harris, and started a monstrous buck Elk from its couch in a bunch of willows; shot at it while running about eighty yards off, but it was not touched. Meantime Provost had heard us from our dinner camp; loading his rifle he came within ten paces, when his gun snapped. We yet hope to get this fine animal. Harris found a Dove's nest with one young one, and an egg just cracked by the bird inside; the nest was on the ground. Curious all this at this late late season, and in a woody part of the country. Saw a Bat.

Wednesday, 6th. Wind blowing harder. Ransacked the point and banks both below and above, but saw only two Wolves; one a dark gray, the largest I have yet seen. Harris shot a young of the Sharp-tailed Grouse; Bell, three Pigeons; Provost went off to the second point below, about four miles, after Elks; Sprague found another nest of Doves on the ground, with very small young. The common Bluebird was seen, also a Whip-poor-will and a Night-Hawk. Wind high and from the south.

Thursday, 7th. About eleven o'clock last night the wind shifted *suddenly* to northwest, and blew so violently that we all left the boat in a hurry. Mrs. Culbertson, with her child in her arms, made for the willows, and had a shelter for her babe in a few minutes. Our guns and ammunition were brought on shore, as we were afraid of our boat sinking. We returned on board after a while; but I could not sleep, the motion making me very sea-sick; I went back to the shore and lay down after mending our fire. It rained hard for about two hours; the sky then became clear, and the wind wholly subsided, so I went again to the boat and slept till eight o'clock. A second gale now arose; the sky grew dark; we removed our boat to a more secure position, but I fear we are here for another day. Bell shot a *Caprimulgus*, so small that I have no doubt it is the one found on the Rocky Mountains by Nuttall, after whom I have named it. These birds are now travelling south. Mr. Culbertson and I walked up the highest hills of the prairie, but saw nothing. The river has suddenly risen two feet, the water rises now at the rate of eight inches in two and a half hours, and the wind has somewhat moderated. The little Whip-poor-will proves an old male, but it is now in moult. Left our camp at five, and went down rapidly to an island four miles below. Mr. Culbertson, Bell, Harris, and Provost went off to look for Elks, but I fear fruitlessly, as I see no tracks, nor do I find any of their beds. About ten o'clock Harris called me to hear the notes of the new Whip-poor-will; we heard two at once, and the sound was thus: "Oh-will, oh-will," repeated often and quickly, as in our common species. The night was beautiful, but cold.

Friday, 8th. Cloudy and remarkably cold; the river has risen 6½ feet since yesterday, and the water is muddy and thick. Started early. The effect of sudden rises in this river is wonderful upon the sand-bars, which are no sooner covered by a foot or so of water than they at once break up, causing very high waves to run, through which no small boat could pass without imminent danger. The swells are felt for many feet as if small waves at sea. Appearances of rain. The current very strong; but we reached Fort Pierre at half-past five, and found all well.

Saturday, 9th. Rain all night. Breakfasted at the fort. Exchanged our boat for a larger one. Orders found here obliged Mr. Culbertson to leave us and go to the Platte River establishment, much to my regret.

Sunday, 10th. Very cloudy. Mr. Culbertson gave me a *parflèche* which had been presented to him by "L'Ours de Fer," the Sioux chief. It is very curiously painted, and is a record of a victory of the Sioux over their enemies, the Gros Ventres. Two rows of horses with Indians dressed in full war rig are rushing onwards; small black marks everywhere represent the horse tracks; round green marks are shields thrown away by the enemy in their flight, and red spots on the horses, like wafers, denote wounds.

Monday, 11th. Cloudy; the men at work fitting up our new boat. Rained nearly all day, and the wind shifted to every point of the compass. Nothing done.

Tuesday, 12th. Partially clear this morning early, but rained by ten o'clock. Nothing done.

Wednesday, 13th. Rainy again. Many birds were seen moving southwest. Our boat is getting into travelling shape. I did several drawings of objects in and about the fort.

Thursday, 14th. Cloudy and threatening. Mr. Laidlow making ready to leave for Fort Union, and ourselves for our trip down the river. Mr. Laidlow left at half-past eleven, and we started at two this afternoon; landed at the farm belonging to the fort, and procured a few potatoes, some corn, and a pig.

Friday, 15th. A foggy morning. Reached Fort George. Mr. Illingsworth left at half-past ten. Wind ahead, and we were obliged to stop on this account at two. Fresh signs of both Indians and Buffaloes, but nothing killed.

Saturday, 16th. Windy till near daylight. Started early; passed Ebbett's new island. Bell heard Parrakeets. The day was perfectly calm. Found *Arvicola pennsylvanica.* Landed at the Great Bend for Black-tailed Deer and wood. Have seen nothing worthy our attention. Squires put up a board at our old camp the "Six Trees," which I hope to see again. The Deer are lying down, and we shall not go out to hunt again till near sunset. The note of the Meadow Lark here is now unheard. I saw fully two hundred flying due south. Collected a good deal of the Yucca plant.

Sunday, 17th. We had a hard gale last night with rain for about an hour. This morning was beautiful; we started early, but only ran for two hours, when we were forced to stop by the wind, which blew a gale. Provost saw fresh signs of Indians, and we were told that there were a few lodges at the bottom of the Bend, about two miles below us. The wind is north and quite cold, and the contrast between to-day and yesterday is great. Went shooting, and killed three Sharp-tailed Grouse. Left our camp about three o'clock as the wind abated. Saw ten or twelve Antelopes on the prairie where the Grouse were. We camped about a mile from the spot where we landed in May last, at the end of the Great Bend. The evening calm and beautiful.

Monday, 18th. The weather cloudy and somewhat windy. Started early; saw a Fish Hawk, two Gulls, two White-headed Eagles and abundance of Golden Plovers. The Sharp-tailed Grouse feeds on rose-berries and the seeds of the wild sun-flower and grasshoppers. Stopped at twenty minutes past nine, the wind was so high, and warmed some coffee. Many dead Buffaloes are in the ravines and on the prairies. Harris, Bell, and Sprague went hunting, but had no show with such a wind. Sprague outlined a curious hill. The wind finally shifted, and then lulled down. Saw Say's Flycatcher, with a Grosbeak. Saw two of the common Titlark. Left again at two, with a better prospect. Landed at sunset on the west side. Signs of Indians. Wolves howling, and found one dead on the shore, but too far gone to be skinned; I was sorry, as it was a beautiful gray one. These animals feed on wild plums in great quantities. Tried to shoot some Doves for my Fox and Badger, but without success. Pea-vines very scarce.

Tuesday, 19th. Dark and drizzly. Did not start until six. Reached Cedar Island, and landed for wood to use on the boat. Bell went off hunting. Wind north. Found no fit trees and left. Passed the burning cliffs and got on a bar. The weather fine, and wind behind us. Wolves will even eat the frogs found along the shores of this river. Saw five, all gray. At three o'clock we were obliged to stop on account of the wind, under a poor point. No game.

Wednesday, 20th. Wind very high. Tracks of Wild Cats along the shore. The motion of the boat is so great it makes me sea-sick. Sprague saw a Sharp-tailed Grouse. We left at half-past twelve. Saw immense numbers of Pin-tailed Ducks, but could not get near them. Stopped on an island to procure pea-vines for my young Deer, and found plenty. Our camp of last night was only two miles and a half below White River. Ran on a bar and were delayed nearly half an hour. Shot two Blue-winged Teal. Camped opposite Bijou's Hill.

Thursday, 21st. Wind and rain most of the night. Started early. Weather cloudy and cold. Landed to examine Burnt Hills, and again on an island for pea-vines. Fresh signs of Indians. Saw many Antelopes and Mule Deer. At twelve saw a bull on one side of the river, and in a few moments after a herd of ten cattle on the other side. Landed, and Squires, Harris, Bell, and Provost have gone to try to procure fresh meat; these are the first Buffaloes seen since we left Fort Pierre. The hunters only killed one bull; no cows among eleven bulls, and this is strange at this season. Saw three more bulls in a ravine. Stopped to camp at the lower end of great Cedar Island at five o'clock. Fresh signs of Buffaloes and Deer. We cut some timber for oars. Rain set in early in the evening, and it rained hard all night.

Friday, 22d. Raining; left at a quarter past eight, with the wind ahead. Distant thunder. Everything wet and dirty after a very uncomfortable night. We went down the river about a mile, when we were forced to come to on the opposite side by the wind and the rain. Played cards for a couple of hours.

No chance to cook or get hot coffee, on account of the heavy storm. We dropped down a few miles and finally camped till next day in the mud, but managed to make a roaring fire. Wolves in numbers howling all about us, and Owls hooting also. Still raining heavily. We played cards till nine o'clock to kill time. Our boat a quagmire.

Saturday, 23d. A cloudy morning; we left at six o'clock. Five Wolves were on a sand-bar very near us. Saw Red-shafted Woodpeckers, and two House Swallows. Have made a good run of about sixty miles. At four this afternoon we took in three men of the steamer "New Haven" belonging to the Opposition, which was fast on the bar, eight miles below. We reached Ponca Island and landed for the night. At dusk the steamer came up, and landed above us, and we found Messrs. Cutting and Taylor, and I had the gratification of a letter from Victor and Johnny, of July 22d.

Sunday, 24th. Cloudy, windy, and cold. Both the steamer and ourselves left as soon as we could see. Saw a Wolf on a bar, and a large flock of White Pelicans, which we took at first for a keel-boat. Passed the Poncas, L'Eau qui Court, Manuel, and Basil rivers by ten o'clock. Landed just below Basil River, stopped by wind. Hunted and shot one Raven, one Turkey Buzzard, and four Wood-ducks. Ripe plums abound, and there are garfish in the creek. Found feathers of the Wild Turkey. Signs of Indians, Elks, and Deer. Provost and the men made four new oars. Went to bed early.

Monday, 25th. Blowing hard all night, and began raining before day. Cold, wet, and misty. Started at a quarter past ten, passed Bonhomme Island at four, and landed for the night at five, fifteen miles below.

Tuesday, 26th. Cold and cloudy; started early. Shot a Pelican. Passed Jack's River at eleven. Abundance of Wild Geese. Bell killed a young White Pelican. Weather fairer but coldish. Sprague killed a Goose, but it was lost. Camped a few miles above the Vermilion River. Harris saw Raccoon tracks on Basil River.

Wednesday, 27th. Cloudy but calm. Many Wood-ducks, and saw Raccoon tracks again this morning. Passed the Vermilion River at half-past seven. My Badger got out of his cage last night, and we had to light a candle to secure it. We reached the Fort of Vermilion at twelve, and met with a kind reception from Mr. Pascal. Previous to this we met a barge going up, owned and commanded by Mr. Tybell, and found our good hunter Michaux. He asked me to take him down, and I promised him $20 per month to St. Louis. We bought two barrels of superb potatoes, two of corn, and a good fat cow. For the corn and potatoes I paid no less than $16.00.

Thursday, 28th. A beautiful morning, and we left at eight. The young man who brought me the calf at Fort George has married a squaw, a handsome girl, and she is here with him. Antelopes are found about twenty-five miles from this fort, but not frequently. Landed fifteen miles below on Elk Point. Cut up and salted the cow. Provost and I went hunting, and saw three female Elks, but the order was to shoot only bucks; a large one started below us, jumped into the river, and swam across, carrying his horns flat down and spread on each side of his back; the neck looked to me about the size of a flour-barrel. Harris killed a hen Turkey, and Bell and the others saw plenty but did not shoot, as Elks were the order of the day. I cannot eat beef after being fed on Buffaloes. I am getting an old man, for this evening I missed my footing on getting into the boat, and bruised my knee and my elbow, but at seventy and over I cannot have the spring of seventeen.

Friday, 29th. Rained most of the night, and it is raining and blowing at present. Crossed the river and have encamped at the mouth of the Iowa River, the boundary line of the Sioux and Omahas. Harris shot a Wolf. My knee too sore to allow me to walk. Stormy all day.

Saturday, 30th. Hard rain all night, the water rose four inches. Found a new species of large bean in the Wild Turkey. Mosquitoes rather troublesome. The sun shining by eight o'clock, and we hope for a good dry day. Whip-poor-wills heard last night, and Night-hawks seen flying. Saw a Long-tailed Squirrel that ran on the shore at the cry of our Badger. Michaux had the boat landed to bring on a superb set of Elk-horns that he secured last week. Abundance of Geese and Ducks. Weather clouding over again, and at two we were struck by a heavy gale of wind, and were obliged to land on the weather shore; the wind continued heavy, and the motion of the boat was too much for me, so I slipped on shore and with Michaux made a good camp, where we rolled ourselves in our blankets and slept soundly.

Sunday, October 1. The wind changed, and lulled before morning, so we left at a quarter past six. The skies looked rather better, nevertheless we had several showers. Passed the Sioux River at twenty minutes past eleven. Heard a Pileated Woodpecker, and saw Fish Crows. Geese very abundant. Landed below the Sioux River to shoot Turkeys, having seen a large male on the bluffs. Bell killed a hen, and Harris two young birds; these will keep us going some days. Stopped again by the wind opposite Floyd's grave; started again and ran about four miles, when we were obliged to land in a rascally place at twelve o'clock. Had hail and rain at intervals. Camped at the mouth of the Omaha River, six miles from the village. The wild Geese are innumerable. The wind has ceased and stars are shining.

Monday, 2d. Beautiful but *cold*. The water has risen nine inches, and we travel well. Started early. Stopped at eight by the wind at a vile place, but plenty of Jerusalem artichokes, which we tried and found very good. Started again at three, and made a good run till sundown, when we found a fair camping-place and made our supper from excellent young Geese.

Tuesday, 3d. A beautiful, calm morning; we started early. Saw three Deer on the bank. A Prairie Wolf travelled on the shore beside us for a long time before he found a place to get up on the prairie. Plenty of Sandhill Cranes were seen as we passed the Little Sioux River. Saw three more Deer, another Wolf, two Swans, several Pelicans, and abundance of Geese and Ducks. Passed Soldier River at two o'clock. We were caught by a snag that scraped and tore us a little. Had we been two feet nearer, it would have ruined our barge. We passed through a very swift cut-off, most difficult of entrance. We have run eighty-two miles and encamped at the mouth of the cut-off, near the old bluffs. Killed two Mallards; the Geese and Ducks are abundant beyond description. Brag, Harris' dog, stole and hid all the meat that had been cooked for our supper.

Wednesday, 4th. Cloudy and coldish. Left early and can't find my pocket knife, which I fear I have lost. We were stopped by the wind at Cabané Bluffs, about twenty miles above Fort Croghan; we all hunted, with only fair results. Saw some hazel bushes, and some black walnuts. Wind-bound till night, and nothing done.

Thursday, 5th.   Blew hard all night, but a clear and beautiful sunrise. Started early, but stopped by the wind at eight. Bell, Harris, and Squires have started off for Fort Croghan. As there was every appearance of rain we left at three and reached the fort about half-past four. Found all well, and were most kindly received. We were presented with some green corn, and had a quantity of bread made, also bought thirteen eggs from an Indian for twenty-five cents. Honey bees are found here, and do well, but none are seen above this place. I had an unexpected slide on the bank, as it had rained this afternoon; and Squires had also one at twelve in the night, when he and Harris with Sprague came to the boat after having played whist up to that hour.

Friday, 6th.   Some rain and thunder last night. A tolerable day. Breakfast at the camp, and left at half-past eight. Our man Michaux was passed over to the officer's boat, to steer them down to Fort Leavenworth, where they are ordered, but we are to keep in company, and he is to cook for us at night. The whole station here is broken up, and Captain Burgwin leaves in a few hours by land with the dragoons, horses, etc. Stopped at Belle Vue at nine, and had a kind reception; bought 6 lbs. coffee, 13 eggs, 2 lbs. butter, and some black pepper. Abundance of Indians, of four different nations. Major Miller, the agent, is a good man for this place. Left again at eleven. A fine day. Passed the Platte and its hundreds of snags, at a quarter past one, and stopped for the men to dine. The stream quite full, and we saw some squaws on the bar, the village was in sight. Killed two Pelicans, but only got one. Encamped about thirty miles below Fort Croghan. Lieutenant Carleton supped with us, and we had a rubber of whist.

Saturday, 7th.   Fine night, and fine morning. Started too early, while yet dark, and got on a bar. Passed McPherson's, the first house in the State of Missouri, at eight o'clock. Bell skinned the young of *Fringilla harrisi*. Lieutenant Carleton came on board to breakfast with us—a fine companion and a perfect gentleman. Indian war-whoops were heard by him and his men whilst embarking this morning after we left. We encamped at the mouth of Nishnebottana, a fine, clear stream. Went to the house of Mr. Beaumont, who has a pretty wife. We made a fine run of sixty or seventy miles.

Sunday, 8th. Cloudy, started early, and had rain by eight o'clock. Stopped twice by the storm, and played cards to relieve the dulness. Started at noon, and ran till half-past four. The wind blowing hard we stopped at a good place for our encampment. Presented a plate of the quadrupeds to Lieut. James Henry Carleton, and he gave me a fine Black Bear skin, and has promised me a set of Elk horns. Stopped on the east side of the river in the evening. Saw a remarkably large flock of Geese passing southward.

Monday, 9th. Beautiful and calm; started early. Bell shot a Gray Squirrel, which was divided and given to my Fox and my Badger. Squires, Carleton, Harris, Bell, and Sprague walked across the Bend to the Black Snake Hills, and killed six Gray Squirrels, four Parrakeets, and two Partridges. Bought butter, eggs, and some whiskey for the men; exchanged knives with the lieutenant. Started and ran twelve miles to a good camp on the Indian side.

Tuesday, 10th. Beautiful morning, rather windy; started early. Great flocks of Geese and Pelicans; killed two of the latter. Reached Fort Leavenworth at four, and, as usual everywhere, received most kindly treatment and reception from Major Morton. Lieutenant Carleton gave me the Elk horns. Wrote to John Bachman, Gideon B. Smith, and a long letter home.

Wednesday, 11th. Received a most welcome present of melons, chickens, bread, and butter from the generous major. Lieutenant Carleton came to see me off, and we parted reluctantly. Left at half-past six; weather calm and beautiful. Game scarce, paw-paws plentiful. Stopped at Madame Chouteau's, where I bought three pumpkins. Stopped at Liberty Landing and delivered the letters of Laidlow to Black Harris. Reached Independence Landing at sundown; have run sixty miles. Found no letters. Steamer "Lebanon" passed upwards at half-past eight.

Thursday, 12th. Beautiful and calm; stopped and bought

eggs, etc., at a Mr. Shivers', from Kentucky. Ran well to Lexington, where we again stopped for provisions; ran sixty miles to-day.

Friday, 13th. Heavy white frost, and very foggy. Started early and ran well. Tried to buy butter at several places, but in vain. At Greenville bought coffee. Abundance of Geese and White Pelicans; many Sandhill Cranes. Harris killed a Wood-duck. Passed Grand River; stopped at New Brunswick, where we bought excellent beef at 2½ cents a pound, but very inferior to Buffalo. Camped at a deserted wood yard, after running between sixty and seventy miles.

Saturday, 14th. A windy night, and after eight days' good run, I fear we shall be delayed to-day. Stopped by a high wind at twelve o'clock. We ran ashore, and I undertook to push the boat afloat, and undressing for the purpose got so deep in the mud that I had to spend a much longer time than I desired in very cold water. Visited two farm houses, and bought chickens, eggs, and butter; very little of this last. At one place we procured corn bread. The squatter visited our boat, and we camped near him. He seemed a good man; was from North Carolina, and had a fine family. Michaux killed two Hutchins' Geese, the first I ever saw in the flesh. Ran about twenty miles; steamer "Lebanon" passed us going downwards, one hour before sunset. Turkeys and Long-tailed Squirrels very abundant.

Sunday, 15th. Cold, foggy, and cloudy; started early. Passed Chariton River and village, and Glasgow; bought bread, and oats for my Deer. Abundance of Geese and Ducks. Passed Arrow Rock at eleven. Passed Boonesville, the finest country on this river; Rocheport, with high, rocky cliffs; six miles below which we encamped, having run sixty miles.

Monday, 16th. Beautiful autumnal morning, a heavy white frost and no wind. Started early, before six. The current very strong. Passed Nashville, Marion, and steamer "Lexington" going up. Jefferson City at twelve. Passed the Osage River and saw twenty-four Deer opposite Smith Landing; camped at sundown, and found Giraud, the "strong man." Ran sixty-one miles. Met the steamer "Satan," badly steered. Abundance of Geese and Ducks everywhere.

Tuesday, 17th. Calm and very foggy. Started early and

floated a good deal with the strong current. Saw two Deer. The fog cleared off by nine o'clock. Passed the Gasconade River at half-past nine. Landed at Pinckney to buy bread, etc. Buffaloes have been seen mired, and unable to defend themselves, and the Wolves actually eating their noses while they struggled, but were eventually killed by the Wolves. Passed Washington and encamped below it at sundown; a good run.

Wednesday, 18th. Fine and calm; started very early. Passed Mount Pleasant. Landed at St. Charles to purchase bread, etc. Provost became extremely drunk, and went off by land to St. Louis. Passed the Charbonnière River, and encamped about one mile below. The steamer "Tobacco Plant" landed on the shore opposite. Bell and Harris killed a number of Gray Squirrels.

Thursday, 19th. A heavy white frost, foggy, but calm. We started early, the steamer after us. Forced by the fog to stop on a bar, but reached St. Louis at three in the afternoon. Unloaded and sent all the things to Nicholas Berthoud's warehouse. Wrote home.

Left St. Louis October 22, in steamer "Nautilus" for Cincinnati.

Reached home at 3 P. M., November 6th, 1843, and thank God, found all my family quite well.

OTHER WRITINGS

Account of the Method of Drawing Birds employed by J. J. Audubon, Esq. F. R. S. E.

In a Letter to a Friend

A T A very early period of my life I arrived in the United States of America, where, prompted by an innate desire to acquire a thorough knowledge of the birds of this happy country, I formed the resolution, immediately on my landing, to spend, if not all my time in that study, at least all that portion generally called leisure, and to draw each individual of its natural size and colouring.

Having studied drawing for a short while in my youth under good masters, I felt a great desire to make choice of a style more particularly adapted to the imitation of feathers than the drawings in water colours that I had been in the habit of seeing, and, moreover, to complete a collection not only valuable to the scientific class, but pleasing to every person, by adopting a different course of representation from the mere profile-like cut figures, given usually in works of that kind.

The first part of my undertaking proved for a long time truly irksome. I saw my attempt flat, and without that life that I have always thought absolutely necessary to render them distinguishable from all those priorly made; and had I not been impelled by the constant inviting sight of new and beautiful specimens which I longed to possess, I would probably have abandoned the task that I had set myself, very shortly after its commencement.

Discoveries, however, succeeded each other sufficiently rapidly to give me transient hopes, and *regularity of application* at length made me possessor of a style that I have continued to follow to this day.

Immediately after the establishment of this style, I *destroyed* and disposed of nearly all the drawings I had accumulated, (upwards of 200,) and with fresh vigour began again, having all my improvements about me.

The woods that I continually trod contained not only birds of richest feathering, but each tree, each shrub, each flower, attracted equally my curiosity and attention, and my anxiety to have all those in my portfolios introduced the thought of joining as much as possible *nature as it existed.*

I formed a plan of proceeding, with a view never to alter it very materially. I had remarked that few works contained the females or young of the different species; that in many cases, indeed, those latter had frequently been represented as different, and that such mistakes must prove extremely injurious to the advancement of science. My plan was then to form sketches in my *mind's eye,* each representing, if possible, each family as if employed in their most constant and natural avocations, and to complete those family pictures as chance might bring perfect specimens.

The knowledge I had already acquired of the habits of most of them enabled me to arrange my individuals in rough outlines, finishing probably at the time only one of the number intended to complete it, and putting the drawing thus begun aside, sometimes for *months,* and sometimes for *years.*

I knew well that closet naturalists would expect drawings exhibiting, in the old way, all those parts that are called by them *necessary characteristics;* and to content these gentlemen I have put in all my representations of groups always either parts or entire specimens, showing fully all that may be defined of those particulars.

My drawings have all been made after individuals fresh killed, mostly by myself, and put up before me by means of wires, &c. in the precise attitude represented, and copied with a closeness of *measurement* that I hope will always correspond with *nature* when brought into contact.

The many foreshortenings unavoidable in groups like these have been rendered attainable by means of squares of equal dimensions affixed both on my paper and immediately behind the subjects before me. I may thus date the *real* beginning of my *present collection,* and observations of the habits of some of these birds, as far back as 1805, not, however, continued always with the same advantages that attended me during the first ten years that I spent in America, for since then I have often been forced to put aside for a while even the thoughts of birds, or the pleasures I have felt in watching their movements, and likewise to their sweet melodies, to attend more closely to the peremptory calls of other necessary business.

The long journies that I have performed through different parts of the country have been attended with many difficulties and perplexing disappointments, some of which have several times made my mind waver whether I should or should not abandon them all for ever.

Being quite unknown amongst naturalists, I have had to depend on my own exertions alone, without either correspondents or friends. I have followed slowly to be sure, but constantly my object. I have often listened to the different observations of men who accidentally had made remarks on different species of birds, but seldom, except when with the rough hunters and squaters of the frontiers, have I discovered naked facts in such relations. This has dissuaded me from ever taking any account given me for granted, until corroborated either by my own ocular opportunities or accumulated repetitions. The astonishing tendency that men have to *improve nature in their way*, by embellishing each of their descriptions of habits without any farther object in view than that of entertaining the better their hearers, has frequently deterred me from listening at all to such accounts, and has brought my physical system to a solitary state of habits and manners so different from those that usually accompany men, that frequently I feel uneasy, as well as awkward, if more than one or two companions are about me. To the improvement of my observations I have found this no detriment. On the contrary, I am persuaded that alone in the woods, or at my work, I can make better use of the whole of myself than in any other situation, and that thereby I have lost nothing in exchanging the pleasure of studying *men* for that of admiring the feathered race.

Pursuers of natural curiosities are extremely abundant in our age. New, quite unknown subjects are those the most sought for. The dried skin of an exotic specimen, of which the *colour* has not been described minutely, draws all attention, whilst the *habits* of that same specimen are scarcely inquired after, and those of individuals more interesting, being nearer and more easily obtained, are abandoned, and the pleasure, as well as the profit that might be derived from a complete study of their manners, and faculties, and worth, are set aside. I must acknowledge to you that that kind of curiosity has not animated me half so much as the desire of first knowing well all those commonly about me,—a task that in it-self I discovered to be extremely difficult, but through which I found the means of at least drawing valuable deductions.

I have *never* drawn from a stuffed specimen. My reason for this has been, that I discovered when in museums, where large collections of that kind are to be met with, that the per-sons *generally* employed for the purpose of mounting them possessed no further talents than that of filling the skins, until *plumply formed*, and adorning them with eyes and legs generally from their own fancy. Those persons, on inquiry, knew nothing of the anatomy of the subject before them; sel-dom the true *length* of the whole, or the *junction* either of the wings and legs with the body; nothing of their *gaits* and *al-lurements*, and not once in a hundred times was the bird in a natural position.

I would not from this have you conclude that museums and collections of stuffed specimens are entirely useless. On the contrary, I think them extremely well fitted to enhance (in youths particularly) the desire of examining afterwards the same subjects at large in all their beauty, the only means of detecting errors. But in forming works entirely with a view to distinguish the true from the false, nature *must* be seen first alive, and well studied, before attempts are made at repre-senting it. Take such advantages away from the naturalist, who ought to be artist also, and he fails as completely as Raphael himself must have done, had he not fed his pencil with all belonging to a mind perfectly imbued with a knowl-edge of real forms, muscles, bones, movements, and, lastly, that spiritual expression of feelings that paintings like his ex-hibit so beautifully.

Among the naturalists of the time, several who are distin-guished have said that representations of subjects ought to be entirely devoid of shades in all their parts; that the colouring of the figure, that must be precisely profile, cannot be under-stood by the student if differently represented. Why then should the best artists of the same age give us pictures with powerful breadth of lights and shades? and why, still more strange, should every individual who looks on such paintings feel not only pleased, but elevated at the grand conception of the painter, and at the nobleness of the subjects being so much like through their effect? My opinion is, that he who cannot conceive and determine the *natural* colouring of a shaded part, need not study either natural history or any thing else connected with it.

If I have joined to many of my drawings plants, insects, reptiles, or views, it has been with the hope to render them all more attractive to the generality of observers; and as I can assure you that all these were copied with the same exactness with which all the birds are represented, you will no doubt view them with as much pleasure.

Do not be surprised at finding that I have trampled upon many deeply-rooted prejudices and opinions attached to the habits of several individuals by men who had only heard and not seen. My wish to impart truths has been my guide in every instance;—all the observations respecting them are my own.

All the authors who have formed works of natural history have attached to the representation of each species a minute description of all their parts. This was done probably because the subjects were never or very seldom offered to view of their natural size; or perhaps, indeed, because these very authors were well aware of the want of accuracy in those figures, seldom drawn by themselves. In my work I wish to curtail these extremely tiresome descriptions; more anxious that those who study ornithology should compare at once my figures with the living specimen, than with a description so easily made to correspond with the drawings by any person who merely knows the technical appellations of each part and feathers, with the name of the colours chosen by authors for that purpose.

I shall neither describe the eggs of the species that I have procured nor the number. A glance at the drawings will answer the more readily, as you will see classed under each the date of the season, and the average number deposited by each bird when ready for incubation. Not so with the nests. I would wish to see these so well described *en masse*, that the young naturalists, when in the woods, would be able to know the artist by his work. This is often a difficult task, the more with those species who will oftentimes form their nests *differently*, and of *different materials*, according to localities and climate, and those that oftentimes take possession of that of quite another species.

If the greater number of figures given in a work are received as perfectly correct in all their parts, by comparing them with good specimens, and through such an examination the author is greeted with public confidence, why should the reader be tormented with descriptions? Where is the amateur of paintings who could bear the reading of a description of the structure, muscles, and expression of the face of such a man as Rembrandt, after gazing at the portrait of that eminent artist by himself? The study of ornithology must be a journey of pleasure. Each step must present to the traveller's view objects that are eminently interesting, varied in their appearance, and attracting to such a degree, as to excite in each individual thus happily employed the desire of knowing all respecting all he sees.

I would have liked to raise an everlasting monument, commemorating with a grand effect the history and portraits of the birds of America, by adding to each drawing of a single species a vignette exhibiting corresponding parts of the country where the specimen is most plentifully found; but having no taste for landscape-painting, and unable to employ a competent assistant for such a purpose, I with deep regret have relinquished the idea. I mention this to you, my dear friend, with hopes that at some future period some one better seconded by pecuniary means or talents may still engage in the undertaking. Sorry, notwithstanding, that as time flies Nature loses its primitiveness, and that pictures drawn in ten, or twenty, or more years, will no longer illustrate our delightful America pure from the hands of its Creator!

My Style of Drawing Birds

W HEN I first began the attempt of representing Birds on paper, I was far from possessing any knowledge of their Nature, and like hundreds of others when the object was put aside under the Idea that it was compleated by the possessing of Some Sort of a head and Tail—Two sticks in lieu of Legs, and other four to support the general fabric, I never troubled myself with the thoughts that *abutments* to prevent their falling backward or forward were Still requisite to insure the appearance of proper gravitation.—and oh what bills and claws I did produce, whithout speaking Just now of a Straight line for a back and a Tail Stuck in beyond the natural rump like an unshipped Rudder.—

Those persons who besides My Father saw my miserable attempts never failed to praise them to the Skies, and no one was perhaps ever more likely to be compleatly wrecked than I by those false affections.—My Father however talked very differently to me.—he constantly assured me that nothing in the world possessing Life and animation was easy to imitate, and that as I grew older he hoped I would become more & more assured of this.—he was so kind to me in every thing unconnected with my Mental improvement, that to have denied to Listen to him with speaking seriously would have been highly ungrateful, and his maxims becoming Laws as it were, I listened less to others, more to him and slowly improved.—

The first Collection of Drawings I made of this Sort were from European Specimen, procured by my Father or myself, and I Still have them in my possession.—they were all represented *strickly ornithologically*, which means neither more or less than in Stiff unmeaning profiles, such as are found in all works published since the begaining of the present century.— My next set was began in America, and there without my honoured Mentor I betook myself to the drawing of Specimen hung to a String by one foot with the desire to shew their every portion as the wings lay loosely Spread as well as the Taile—in this Manner I made some pretty fair sign Boards for Poulterers!

One day whilt watching the habits of a paire of Pewees at Millgrove I looked so intently on their innocent attitudes, that a thought struck my Mind like a flash of light, that nothing after all could ever answer my Anthusiastic desires to represent nature, than to attempt to Copy her in her own Way, alive and Moving!—then, on I went with forming hundreds of Outlines of my favourites the Pewees.—how good or bad I cannot tell, but I fancied I had mounted astep on the high Mount before Me.—I continued for Months together in simply outlining birds as I observed them either alighted or on wing but could finish none of my Sketches.—I procured Many Individuals of different Species and laying them on my table or on the ground tried to place them in Such attitudes as I had Sketched, but alas they were dead to all intense and neither Wing, leg or tail could I place according to the intention of my Wishes.—a Second thought came to my assistance;—by means of threads I raised or Lowered A head Wing or a Tail and by fastening the threads securely I had something like life before me, yet Much was wanting—when I saw the living bird I felt the blood rise to my temples and almost in despair spent about a Month without Drawing, but in deep thought and daily in the company of the feathered inhabitants of Dear Mill Grove.—I had drawn from the "Mankin" whilt under David and have obtained tolerable figures of our Species through this means, and cogitated how far a mankin of a bird would answer for all of them?—I laboured in wood cork and Wires, and formed a grotesque figure which I cannot describe in any other terms than by telling you that when sat up it was a very tolerable looking "Dodo"! a Friend present laughed heartily and raised my blood by assuring me, that as far as might wish to represent a Tame Gander or bird of that Sort my Model would do.—I gave it a kick, demolished it to atoms walked off and thought again.—

Young as I was, my impatience to obtain my desire filled my brains with different places—nay I not unfrequently dreamt that I had made a New discovery, and long before day one morning I leaped out of bed fully persuaded that I had obtained my object.—I ordered a horse to be sadled and without answering to any of the various questions put to me, mounted and moved off at a hard Gallop toward the then little Village of Noristown distant about Five Miles.—on arriving there not a door was open—nay It was not yet day light —I therefore rode toward the River took a bath and in time returned to the Town and entered the first oppened Shop— Enquired for Wire of different sizes, bought some, Leaped on my Steed and was at Mill Grove again in a very Short time.— the wife of my Tenant I really believe thought that I was mad, as on offering me Breakfast, I told her I wanted my Gun and a curious scene ensued about this which is not worth your While to hear—off to the Creek and down with the first Kings Fisher I met! I picked the bird up and carried it home by the bill, I sent for the Miller and made him fetch me a piece of soft board,—when he returned he found me filing into Sharp points pieces of my Wire, and proud to Show him the substance of my discovery, for a discovery I had now in my brains, I pierced the body of the Fishing bird and fixed it on the board—another Wire passed above his upper Mandible was made to hold the head in a pretty fair attitude, Smaller Skewers fixed the feet according to my notions, and even common pins came to my assistance in the placing the legs and feet.—the last Wire proved a delightful elevator to the Bird's Tail and at Last there Stood before me the real Mankin of a Kings Fisher!

Think not reader that my want of a breakfast was at all in my Way, no indeed—I sat to, outlined the bird, aided by compasses and My eyes coloured it and finished it without ever a thought having crossed My Mind as regarded the aleviation of Hunger.—My honest Miller Stood by me the while and was delighted to see me pleased—Reader this was what I Shall ever call my first attempt at Drawing actually from Nature, for then Even the eye of the Kings fisher was as if full of Life before me whenever I pressed its Lids aside with a finger.—

In those Happy days of my Youth, I was extremely fond of reading what I Still call the delightful Mental fables of Lafontaine—I had frequently perused the one entitled "L'hirondelle et les Petits oiseaux" and thought much of the Meaning imparted in the first Line which if I now recollect rightly goes on to say that "quiconque à beaucoup vu, peut avoir beaucoup retenue" To me this meant that to study

Nature was to ramble through her domains, Late and early and at every hour, that any where there I might if capable obtain a serviceable Lesson the benefits of which again would at least be serviceable to me—not perhaps in the manner thrugh which I would aggrandize My fortune, but in one by which I would be sure to abstain from the daily vices of the world, whilt by generous exercise I would enlarge my phisical and perhaps also My Mental powers.—"Early to bed and early to rise" was another Addage which I thought possessed much value ('tis a pity that this adage has not passed into a general law) but reader I have followed it ever since a Child and am grateful for the hint to this very day.—

As I travelled, mostly bent on the Study of birds and with a wish to represent all those found in our Woods to best of my powers, I gradually became acquainted with their forms and Habits, the use of my Wires was improved by an acquirement in the delineation connected with the Naked Eye, and as I produced a better imitation, the former one was destroyed and after a while I laid down what I was pleased to call a Constitution in My Manner of Drawing Birds formed on *Natural principles* which I Must try to lay briefly before you.—

The Gradual Knowledge of the form and Habits of the Birds of our Country impressed me with the Idea that each part of a familly Must possess a certain degree of Affinity distinguishable at sight from any one of them.—the Pewees which I knew by experience were positively Flycatchers led me to the discovery that in every bird truly of that Genus, when Standing still, their attitudes was principally pensive, that they sat uprightly, now & then glanced their eyes upward or side ways to watch the approach of their insect prey, that if in pursuit of this on wing their Movements through the air were each as all others of the Tribe &^{c} &^{c} &^{c}. Gallinaceous Birds I saw were possessed of equally peculiar positions and movements—amongst the Water birds, each also exibited Characteristical Manners, I observed that the Herons walked with elegance and stateliness, that cormorants which setting obliquely upright had a well Marked swelling of the abdomen in consequence of their very position whilt in Such hattitudes and after having collected many of these Materials of the

Mind, I in greater earnest than ever, fairly began the Very Collection of the Birds of America Many of which are now before you.—

The more I understood my Subjects the better I became able to represent them in what I hoped was a Natural position, the Bird once fixed with Wires or Squeres, and its Nature (as far as habits Went) previously Known to Me, I Studied it whilt thus placed as a "lay figure" before me, according to its Specificality, this lead me to Judge as it were before hand of its general form, of those of its bill, nostrils head, eye, legs or claws, as well as the Structure of its Wings and Tail—nay the very tongue was at times of importance to Me, and I thought that the More I understood of all these particulars, the better representations I Made of the Originals, Successfull or not, I leave for yourself to decide.—

My Drawings at first were taken altogether in Water Colours, but they wanted softness and a great deal of them to finish them to my liking in this Tedious Style.—I sat for a long time very dispirited at this—particularly when trying in vain to immitate birds of soft and downy plumage, such as is that of Most owls, Pigeons, Hawks and Herons, how this could be remedied required a New sett of thoughts or some accident, and here the latter came to my aid.—

One day after having finished the Miniature portrait of the dearest Friend I have in this World A portion of the face was injured by a drop of Water which had dried on the Spot, and although I laboured a great deal to make amend for this, it was all in Vain—recollecting Just then that whilt a pupil of David I had drawn heads and figures in different coloured Chalks, I resorted to a piece that matched the tint intended for the part, applied the pigment, rubed the place with a cork Stump and at once produced the desired effect!—

My Drawing of owls, Pigeons or Herons were much improved by applications of Such Materials, indeed after a few Years of patience Some of My attempts began almost to please Me and I have continued the same Style ever since and that is Now for More than Thirty Years.—Whilt travelling both in Europe and America, many persons have evinced the desire to draw birds in My Manner, and I have always felt much pleasure in Shewing it to any one by whom I hoped

Ornithological delineations or portraiture would be improved—Some have done So, others have not, but at the exception of My Friend W^{am} Swainson not another has aknowledged the "*recepe*"   Nay some have grown so bold as to Copy and publish figures from my own Work on the Birds of America without giving so much as a hint that they had done So, and some to whom I have *presented* with original Drawings of my own execution have had them reduced and engraved under a fallacious name—but after all I have some hope that wherever you will see them, their similitude to My Originals will prove to you at Once that they are Nought but piracies of My Style of Drawing Birds.—

Myself

THE precise period of my birth is yet an enigma to me, and I can only say what I have often heard my father repeat to me on this subject, which is as follows: It seems that my father had large properties in Santo Domingo, and was in the habit of visiting frequently that portion of our Southern States called, and known by the name of, Louisiana, then owned by the French Government.

During one of these excursions he married a lady of Spanish extraction, whom I have been led to understand was as beautiful as she was wealthy, and otherwise attractive, and who bore my father three sons and a daughter,—I being the youngest of the sons and the only one who survived extreme youth. My mother, soon after my birth, accompanied my father to the estate of Aux Cayes, on the island of Santo Domingo, and she was one of the victims during the ever-to-be-lamented period of the negro insurrection of that island.

My father, through the intervention of some faithful servants, escaped from Aux Cayes with a good portion of his plate and money, and with me and these humble friends reached New Orleans in safety. From this place he took me to France, where, having married the only mother I have ever known, he left me under her charge and returned to the United States in the employ of the French Government, acting as an officer under Admiral Rochambeau. Shortly afterward, however, he landed in the United States and became attached to the army under La Fayette.

The first of my recollective powers placed me in the central portion of the city of Nantes, on the Loire River, in France, where I still recollect particularly that I was much cherished by my dear stepmother, who had no children of her own, and that I was constantly attended by one or two black servants, who had followed my father from Santo Domingo to New Orleans and afterward to Nantes.

One incident which is as perfect in my memory as if it had occurred this very day, I have thought of thousands of times since, and will now put on paper as one of the curious things which perhaps did lead me in after times to love birds, and to finally study them with pleasure infinite. My mother had several beautiful parrots and some monkeys; one of the latter was a full-grown male of a very large species. One morning, while the servants were engaged in arranging the room I was in, "Pretty Polly" asking for her breakfast as usual, "*Du pain au lait pour le perroquet Migonne*," the man of the woods probably thought the bird presuming upon his rights in the scale of nature; be this as it may, he certainly showed his supremacy in strength over the denizen of the air, for, walking deliberately and uprightly toward the poor bird, he at once killed it, with unnatural composure. The sensations of my infant heart at this cruel sight were agony to me. I prayed the servant to beat the monkey, but he, who for some reason preferred the monkey to the parrot, refused. I uttered long and piercing cries, my mother rushed into the room, I was tranquillized, the monkey was forever afterward chained, and Migonne buried with all the pomp of a cherished lost one.

This made, as I have said, a very deep impression on my youthful mind. But now, my dear children, I must tell you somewhat of *my* father, and of his parentage.

John Audubon, my grandfather, was born and lived at the small village of Sable d'Olhonne, and was by trade a very humble fisherman. He appears to have made up for the want of wealth by the number of his children, twenty-one of whom he actually raised to man and womanhood. All were sons, with one exception; my aunt, one uncle, and my father, who was the twentieth son, being the only members of that extraordinary numerous family who lived to old age. In subsequent years, when I visited Sable d'Olhonne, the old residents assured me that they had seen the whole family, including both parents, at church many times.

When my father had reached the age of twelve years, his father presented him with a shirt, a dress of coarse material, a stick, and his blessing, and urged him to go and seek means for his future support and sustenance.

Some *kind* whaler or cod-fisherman took him on board as a "Boy." Of his life during his early voyages it would be useless to trouble you; let it suffice for me to say that they were of the usual most uncomfortable nature. How many trips he made I cannot say, but he told me that by the time he was seventeen he had become an able seaman before the mast; when twenty-one he commanded a fishing-smack, and went to the great Newfoundland Banks; at twenty-five he owned several small crafts, all fishermen, and at twenty-eight sailed for Santo Domingo with his little flotilla heavily loaded with the produce of the deep. "Fortune," said he to me one day, "now began to smile upon me. I did well in this enterprise, and after a few more voyages of the same sort gave up the sea, and purchased a small estate on the Isle à Vaches; the prosperity of Santo Domingo was at its zenith, and in the course of ten years I had realized something very considerable. The then Governor gave me an appointment which called me to France, and having received some favors there, I became once more a seafaring man, the government having granted me the command of a small vessel of war."

How long my father remained in the service, it is impossible for me to say. The different changes occurring at the time of the American Revolution, and afterward during that in France, seem to have sent him from one place to another as if a foot-ball; his property in Santo Domingo augmenting, however, the while, and indeed till the liberation of the black slaves there.

During a visit he paid to Pennsylvania when suffering from the effects of a sunstroke, he purchased the beautiful farm of Mill Grove, on the Schuylkill and Perkiomen streams. At this place, and a few days only before the memorable battle of Valley Forge, General Washington presented him with his portrait, now in my possession; and highly do I value it as a memento of that noble man and the glories of those days. At the conclusion of the war between England and her child of the West, my father returned to France and continued in the employ of the naval department of that country, being at one time sent to Plymouth, England, in a seventy-five-gun ship to exchange prisoners. This was, I think, in the short peace that took place between England and France in 1801. He returned to Rochefort, where he lived for several years, still in the employ of government. He finally sent in his resignation and returned to Nantes and La Gerbétière. He had many severe trials and afflictions before his death, having lost my two older brothers early in the French Revolution; both were officers in the army. His only sister was killed by the Chouans of La Vendée, and the only brother he had was not on good terms with him. This brother resided at Bayonne, and, I believe, had a large family, none of whom I have ever seen or known.

In personal appearance my father and I were of the same height and stature, say about five feet ten inches, erect, and with muscles of steel; his manners were those of a most polished gentleman, for those and his natural understanding had been carefully improved both by observation and by self-education. In temper we much resembled each other also, being warm, irascible, and at times violent; but it was like the blast of a hurricane, dreadful for a time, when calm almost instantly returned. He greatly approved of the change in France during the time of Napoleon, whom he almost idolized. My father died in 1818, regretted most deservedly on account of his simplicity, truth, and perfect sense of honesty. Now I must return to myself.

My stepmother, who was devotedly attached to me, far too much so for my good, was desirous that I should be brought up to live and die "like a gentleman," thinking that fine clothes and filled pockets were the only requisites needful to attain this end. She therefore completely spoiled me, hid my faults, boasted to every one of my youthful merits, and, worse than all, said frequently in my presence that I was the handsomest boy in France. All my wishes and idle notions were at once gratified; she went so far as actually to grant me *carte blanche* at all the confectionery shops in the town, and also of the village of Couéron, where during the summer we lived, as it were, in the country.

My father was quite of another, and much more valuable description of mind as regarded my future welfare; he believed not in the power of gold coins as efficient means to render a man happy. He spoke of the stores of the mind, and having suffered much himself through the want of education, he ordered that I should be put to school, and have teachers at home. "Revolutions," he was wont to say, "too often take place in the lives of individuals, and they are apt to lose in one day the fortune they before possessed; but talents and knowledge, added to sound mental training, assisted by honest industry, can never fail, nor be taken from any one once the possessor of such valuable means." Therefore, notwithstanding all my mother's entreaties and her tears, off to a school I was sent. Excepting only, perhaps, military schools, none were good in France at this period; the thunders of the Revolution still roared over the land, the Revolutionists covered the earth with the blood of man, woman, and child. But let me forever drop the curtain over the frightful aspect of this dire picture. To think of these dreadful days is too terrible, and would be too horrible and painful for me to relate to you, my dear sons.

The school I went to was none of the best; my private teachers were the only means through which I acquired the least benefit. My father, who had been for so long a seaman, and who was then in the French navy, wished me to follow in his steps, or else to become an engineer. For this reason I studied drawing, geography, mathematics, fencing, etc., as well as music, for which I had considerable talent. I had a good fencing-master, and a first-rate teacher of the violin; mathematics was hard, dull work, I thought; geography pleased me more. For my other studies, as well as for dancing, I was quite enthusiastic; and I well recollect how anxious I was then to become the commander of a corps of dragoons.

My father being mostly absent on duty, my mother suffered me to do much as I pleased; it was therefore not to be wondered at that, instead of applying closely to my studies, I preferred associating with boys of my own age and disposition, who were more fond of going in search of birds' nests, fishing, or shooting, than of better studies. Thus almost every day, instead of going to school when I ought to have gone, I usually made for the fields, where I spent the day; my little basket went with me, filled with good eatables, and when I returned home, during either winter or summer, it was replenished with what I called curiosities, such as birds' nests, birds' eggs, curious lichens, flowers of all sorts, and even pebbles gathered along the shore of some rivulet.

The first time my father returned from sea after this my room exhibited quite a show, and on entering it he was so pleased to see my various collections that he complimented me on my taste for such things: but when he inquired what else I had done, and I, like a culprit, hung my head, he left me without saying another word. Dinner over he asked my sister for some music, and, on her playing for him, he was so pleased with her improvement that he presented her with a beautiful book. I was next asked to play on my violin, but alas! for nearly a month I had not touched it, it was stringless; not a word was said on that subject. "Had I any drawings to show?" Only a few, and those not good. My good father looked at his wife, kissed my sister, and humming a tune left the room. The next morning at dawn of day my father and I were under way in a private carriage; my trunk, etc., were fastened to it, my violin-case was under my feet, the postilion was ordered to proceed, my father took a book from his pocket, and while he silently read I was left entirely to my own thoughts.

After some days' travelling we entered the gates of Rochefort. My father had scarcely spoken to me, yet there was no anger exhibited in his countenance; nay, as we reached the house where we alighted, and approached the door, near which a sentinel stopped his walk and presented arms, I saw him smile as he raised his hat and said a few words to the man, but so low that not a syllable reached my ears.

The house was furnished with servants, and everything seemed to go on as if the owner had not left it. My father bade me sit by his side, and taking one of my hands calmly said to me: "My beloved boy, thou art now safe. I have brought thee here that I may be able to pay constant attention to thy studies; thou shalt have ample time for pleasures, but the remainder *must* be employed with industry and care. This day is entirely thine own, and as I must attend to my duties, if thou wishest to see the docks, the fine ships-of-war, and walk round the wall, thou may'st accompany me." I accepted, and off together we went; I was presented to every officer we met, and they noticing me more or less, I saw much that day, yet still I perceived that I was like a prisoner-of-war on parole in the city of Rochefort.

My best and most amiable companion was the son of Admiral, or Vice-Admiral (I do not precisely recollect his rank) Vivien, who lived nearly opposite to the house where my father and I then resided; his company I much enjoyed, and with him all my leisure hours were spent. About this time my father was sent to England in a corvette with a view to exchange prisoners, and he sailed on board the man-of-war "L'Institution" for Plymouth. Previous to his sailing he placed me under the charge of his secretary, Gabriel Loyen Dupuy Gaudeau, the son of a fallen nobleman. Now this gentleman was of no pleasing nature to me; he was, in fact, more than too strict and severe in all his prescriptions to me, and well do I recollect that one morning, after having been set to a very arduous task in mathematical problems, I gave him the slip, jumped from the window, and ran off through the gardens attached to the Marine Secrétariat. The unfledged bird may stand for a while on the border of its nest, and perhaps open its winglets and attempt to soar away, but his youthful imprudence may, and indeed often does, prove inimical to his prowess, as some more wary and older bird, that has kept an eye toward him, pounces relentlessly upon the young adventurer and secures him within the grasp of his more powerful talons. This was the case with me in this instance. I had leaped from the door of my cage and thought myself quite safe, while I rambled thoughtlessly beneath the shadow of the trees in the garden and grounds in which I found myself; but the secretary, with a side glance, had watched my escape, and, ere many minutes had elapsed, I saw coming toward me a corporal with whom, in fact, I was well acquainted. On nearing me, and I did not attempt to escape, our past familiarity was, I found, quite evaporated; he bid me, in a severe voice, to follow him, and on my being presented to my father's secretary I was at once ordered on board the pontoon in port. All remonstrances proved fruitless, and on board the pontoon I was conducted, and there left amid such a medley of culprits as I cannot describe, and of whom, indeed, I have but little recollection, save that I felt vile myself in their vile company. My father returned in due course, and released me from these floating and most disagreeable lodgings, but not without a rather severe reprimand.

Shortly after this we returned to Nantes, and later to La Gerbétière. My stay here was short, and I went to Nantes to study mathematics anew, and there spent about one year, the remembrance of which has flown from my memory, with the exception of one incident, of which, when I happen to pass my hand over the left side of my head, I am ever and anon reminded. 'T is this: one morning, while playing with boys of my own age, a quarrel arose among us, a battle ensued, in the course of which I was knocked down by a round stone, that brought the blood from that part of my skull, and for a time I lay on the ground unconscious, but soon rallying, experienced no lasting effects but the scar.

During all these years there existed within me a tendency to follow Nature in her walks. Perhaps not an hour of leisure was spent elsewhere than in woods and fields, and to examine either the eggs, nest, young, or parents of any species of birds constituted my delight. It was about this period that I commenced a series of drawings of the birds of France, which I continued until I had upward of two hundred drawings, all bad enough, my dear sons, yet they were representations of birds, and I felt pleased with them. Hundreds of anecdotes respecting my life at this time might prove interesting to you, but as they are not in my mind at this moment I will leave them, though you may find some of them in the course of the following pages.

I was within a few months of being seventeen years old, when my stepmother, who was an earnest Catholic, took into her head that I should be confirmed; my father agreed. I was surprised and indifferent, but yet as I loved her as if she had been my own mother,—and well did she merit my deepest affection,—I took to the catechism, studied it and other matters pertaining to the ceremony, and all was performed to her liking. Not long after this, my father, anxious as he was that I should be enrolled in Napoleon's army as a Frenchman, found it necessary to send me back to my own beloved country, the United States of America, and I came with intense and indescribable pleasure.

On landing at New York I caught the yellow fever by walking to the bank at Greenwich to get the money to which my father's letter of credit entitled me. The kind man who commanded the ship that brought me from France, whose name was a common one, John Smith, took particular charge of me, removed me to Morristown, N. J., and placed me under the care of two Quaker ladies who kept a boarding-house. To their skilful and untiring ministrations I may safely say I owe the prolongation of my life. Letters were forwarded by them to my father's agent, Miers Fisher of Philadelphia, of whom I have more to say hereafter. He came for me in his carriage and removed me to his villa, at a short distance from Philadelphia and on the road toward Trenton. There I would have found myself quite comfortable had not incidents taken place which are so connected with the change in my life as to call immediate attention to them.

Miers Fisher had been my father's trusted agent for about eighteen years, and the old gentlemen entertained great mutual friendship; indeed it would seem that Mr. Fisher was actually desirous that I should become a member of his family, and this was evinced within a few days by the manner in which the good Quaker presented me to a daughter of no mean appearance, but toward whom I happened to take an unconquerable dislike. Then he was opposed to music of all descriptions, as well as to dancing, could not bear me to carry a gun, or fishing-rod, and, indeed, condemned most of my amusements. All these things were difficulties toward accomplishing a plan which, for aught I know to the contrary, had been premeditated between him and my father, and rankled the heart of the kindly, if somewhat strict Quaker. They troubled me much also; at times I wished myself anywhere but under the roof of Mr. Fisher, and at last I reminded him that it was his duty to install me on the estate to which my father had sent me.

One morning, therefore, I was told that the carriage was ready to carry me there, and toward my future home he and I went. You are too well acquainted with the position of Mill Grove for me to allude to that now; suffice it to say that we reached the former abode of my father about sunset. I was presented to our tenant, William Thomas, who also was a Quaker, and took possession under certain restrictions, which amounted to my not receiving more than enough money per quarter than was considered sufficient for the expenditure of a young gentleman.

Miers Fisher left me the next morning, and after him went my blessings, for I thought his departure a true deliverance; yet this was only because our tastes and educations were so different, for he certainly was a good and learned man. Mill Grove was ever to me a blessed spot; in my daily walks I thought I perceived the traces left by my father as I looked on the even fences round the fields, or on the regular manner with which avenues of trees, as well as the orchards, had been planted by his hand. The mill was also a source of joy to me, and in the cave, which you too remember, where the Pewees were wont to build, I never failed to find quietude and delight.

Hunting, fishing, drawing, and music occupied my every moment; cares I knew not, and cared naught about them. I purchased excellent and beautiful horses, visited all such neighbors as I found congenial spirits, and was as happy as happy could be. A few months after my arrival at Mill Grove, I was informed one day that an English family had purchased the plantation next to mine, that the name of the owner was Bakewell, and moreover that he had several very handsome and interesting daughters, and beautiful pointer dogs. I listened, but cared not a jot about them at the time. The place was within sight of Mill Grove, and Fatland Ford, as it was called, was merely divided from my estate by a road leading to the Schuylkill River. Mr. William Bakewell, the father of the family, had called on me one day, but, finding I was rambling in the woods in search of birds, left a card and an invitation to go shooting with him. Now this gentleman was an Englishman, and I such a foolish boy that, entertaining the greatest prejudices against all of his nationality, I did not return his visit for many weeks, which was as absurd as it was ungentlemanly and impolite.

Mrs. Thomas, good soul, more than once spoke to me on the subject, as well as her worthy husband, but all to no import; English was English with me, my poor childish mind was settled on that, and as I wished to know none of the race the call remained unacknowledged.

Frosty weather, however, came, and anon was the ground covered with the deep snow. Grouse were abundant along the fir-covered ground near the creek, and as I was in pursuit of game one frosty morning I chanced to meet Mr. Bakewell in the woods. I was struck with the kind politeness of his manner, and found him an expert marksman. Entering into conversation, I admired the beauty of his well-trained dogs, and, apologizing for my discourtesy, finally promised to call upon him and his family.

Well do I recollect the morning, and may it please God that I may never forget it, when for the first time I entered Mr. Bakewell's dwelling. It happened that he was absent from home, and I was shown into a parlor where only one young lady was snugly seated at her work by the fire. She rose on my entrance, offered me a seat, and assured me of the gratification her father would feel on his return, which, she added, would be in a few moments, as she would despatch a servant for him. Other ruddy cheeks and bright eyes made their transient appearance, but, like spirits gay, soon vanished from my sight; and there I sat, my gaze riveted, as it were, on the young girl before me, who, half working, half talking, essayed to make the time pleasant to me. Oh! may god bless her! It was she, my dear sons, who afterward became my beloved wife, and your mother. Mr. Bakewell soon made his appearance, and received me with the manner and hospitality of a true English gentleman. The other members of the family were soon introduced to me, and "Lucy" was told to have luncheon produced. She now arose from her seat a second time, and her form, to which I had previously paid but partial attention, showed both grace and beauty; and my heart followed every one of her steps. The repast over, guns and dogs were made ready.

Lucy, I was pleased to believe, looked upon me with some favor, and I turned more especially to her on leaving. I felt that certain "*je ne sais quoi*" which intimated that, at least, she was not indifferent to me.

To speak of the many shooting parties that took place with Mr. Bakewell would be quite useless, and I shall merely say that he was a most excellent man, a great shot, and possessed of extraordinary learning—aye, far beyond my comprehension. A few days after this first interview with the family the Perkiomen chanced to be bound with ice, and many a one from the neighborhood was playing pranks on the glassy surface of that lovely stream. Being somewhat of a skater myself, I sent a note to the inhabitants of Fatland Ford, inviting them to come and partake of the simple hospitality of Mill Grove farm, and the invitation was kindly received and accepted. My own landlady bestirred herself to the utmost in the procuring of as many pheasants and partridges as her group of sons could entrap, and now under my own roof was seen the whole of the Bakewell family, seated round the table which has never ceased to be one of simplicity and hospitality.

After dinner we all repaired to the ice on the creek, and there in comfortable sledges, each fair one was propelled by an ardent skater. Tales of love may be extremely stupid to the majority, so that I will not expatiate on these days, but to me, my dear sons, and under such circumstances as then, and, thank God, now exist, every moment was to me one of delight.

But let me interrupt my tale to tell you somewhat of other companions whom I have heretofore neglected to mention. These are two Frenchmen, by name Da Costa and Colmesnil. A lead mine had been discovered by my tenant, William Thomas, to which, besides the raising of fowls, I paid considerable attention; but I knew nothing of mineralogy or mining, and my father, to whom I communicated the discovery of the mine, sent Mr. Da Costa as a partner and partial guardian from France. This fellow was intended to teach me mineralogy and mining engineering, but, in fact, knew nothing of either; besides which he was a covetous wretch, who did all he could to ruin my father, and indeed swindled both of us to a large amount. I had to go to France and expose him to my father to get rid of him, which I fortunately accomplished at first sight of my kind parent. A greater scoundrel than Da Costa never probably existed, but peace be with his soul.

The other, Colmesnil, was a very interesting young Frenchman with whom I became acquainted. He was very poor, and I invited him to come and reside under my roof. This he did, remaining for many months, much to my delight. His appearance was typical of what he was, a perfect gentleman; he was handsome in form, and possessed of talents far above my own. When introduced to your mother's family he was much thought of, and at one time he thought himself welcome to my Lucy; but it was only a dream, and when once undeceived by her whom I too loved, he told me he must part with me. This we did with mutual regret, and he returned to France, where, though I have lost sight of him, I believe he is still living.

During the winter connected with this event your uncle Thomas Bakewell, now residing in Cincinnati, was one morning skating with me on the Perkiomen, when he challenged me to shoot at his hat as he tossed it in the air, which challenge I accepted with great pleasure. I was to pass by at full speed, within about twenty-five feet of where he stood, and to shoot only when he gave the word. Off I went like lightning, up and down, as if anxious to boast of my own prowess while on the glittering surface beneath my feet; coming, however, within the agreed distance the signal was given, the trigger pulled, off went the load, and down on the ice came the hat of my future brother-in-law, as completely perforated as if a sieve. He repented, alas! too late, and was afterward severely reprimanded by Mr. Bakewell.

Another anecdote I must relate to you on paper, which I have probably too often repeated in words, concerning my skating in those early days of happiness; but, as the world knows nothing of it, I shall give it to you at some length. It was arranged one morning between your young uncle, myself, and several other friends of the same age, that we should proceed on a duck-shooting excursion up the creek, and, accordingly, off we went after an early breakfast. The ice was in capital order wherever no air-holes existed, but of these a great number interrupted our course, all of which were, however, avoided as we proceeded upward along the glittering, frozen bosom of the stream. The day was spent in much pleasure, and the game collected was not inconsiderable.

On our return, in the early dusk of the evening, I was bid to lead the way; I fastened a white handkerchief to a stick, held it up, and we all proceeded toward home as a flock of wild ducks to their roosting-grounds. Many a mile had already been passed, and, as gayly as ever, we were skating swiftly along when darkness came on, and now our speed was increased. Unconsciously I happened to draw so very near a large air-hole that to check my headway became quite impossible, and down it I went, and soon felt the power of a most chilling bath. My senses must, for aught I know, have left me for a while; be this as it may, I must have glided with the stream some thirty or forty yards, when, as God would have it, up I popped at another air-hole, and here I did, in some way or another, manage to crawl out. My companions, who in the gloom had seen my form so suddenly disappear, escaped the danger, and were around me when I emerged from the greatest peril I have ever encountered, not excepting my escape from being murdered on the prairie, or by the hands of that wretch S—— B——, of Henderson. I was helped to a shirt from one, a pair of dry breeches from another, and completely dressed anew in a few minutes, if in motley and ill-fitting garments; our line of march was continued, with, however, much more circumspection. Let the reader, whoever he may be, think as he may like on this singular and, in truth, most extraordinary escape from death; it is the truth, and as such I have written it down as a wonderful act of Providence.

Mr. Da Costa, my tutor, took it into his head that my affection for your mother was rash and inconsiderate. He spoke triflingly of her and of her parents, and one day said to me that for a man of my rank and expectations to marry Lucy Bakewell was out of the question. If I laughed at him or not I cannot tell you, but of this I am certain, that my answers to his talks on this subject so exasperated him that he immediately afterward curtailed my usual income, made some arrangements to send me to India, and wrote to my father accordingly. Understanding from many of my friends that his plans were fixed, and finally hearing from Philadelphia, whither Da Costa had gone, that he had taken my passage from Philadelphia to Canton, I walked to Philadelphia, entered his room quite unexpectedly, and asked him for such an amount of money as would enable me at once to sail for France and there see my father.

The cunning wretch, for I cannot call him by any other name, smiled, and said: "Certainly, my dear sir," and afterward gave me a letter of credit on a Mr. Kauman, a half-agent, half-banker, then residing at New York. I returned to Mill Grove, made all preparatory plans for my departure, bid a sad adieu to my Lucy and her family, and walked to New York. But never mind the journey; it was winter, the country lay under a covering of snow, but withal I reached New York on the third day, late in the evening.

Once there, I made for the house of a Mrs. Palmer, a lady of excellent qualities, who received me with the utmost kindness, and later on the same evening I went to the house of your grand-uncle, Benjamin Bakewell, then a rich merchant of New York, managing the concerns of the house of Guelt, bankers, of London. I was the bearer of a letter from Mr. Bakewell, of Fatland Ford, to this brother of his, and there I was again most kindly received and housed.

The next day I called on Mr. Kauman; he read Da Costa's letter, smiled, and after a while told me he had nothing to give me, and in plain terms said that instead of a letter of credit, Da Costa—that rascal!—had written and advised him to have me arrested and shipped to Canton. The blood rose to my temples, and well it was that I had no weapon about me, for I feel even now quite assured that his heart must have received the result of my wrath. I left him half bewildered, half mad, and went to Mrs. Palmer, and spoke to her of my purpose of returning at once to Philadelphia and there certainly murdering Da Costa. Women have great power over me at any time, and perhaps under all circumstances. Mrs. Palmer quieted me, spoke religiously of the cruel sin I thought of committing, and, at last, persuaded me to relinquish the direful plan. I returned to Mr. Bakewell's low-spirited and mournful, but said not a word about all that had passed. The next morning my sad visage showed something was wrong, and I at last gave vent to my outraged feelings.

Benjamin Bakewell was a *friend* of his brother (may you ever be so toward each other). He comforted me much, went with me to the docks to seek a vessel bound to France, and offered me any sum of money I might require to convey me to my father's house. My passage was taken on board the brig "Hope," of New Bedford, and I sailed in her, leaving Da Costa and Kauman in a most exasperated state of mind. The fact is, these rascals intended to cheat both me and my father. The brig was bound direct for Nantes. We left the Hook under a very fair breeze, and proceeded at a good rate till we reached the latitude of New Bedford, in Massachusetts, when my captain came to me as if in despair, and said he must run into port, as the vessel was so leaky as to force him to have her unloaded and repaired before he proceeded across the Atlantic. Now this was only a trick; my captain was newly married, and was merely anxious to land at New Bedford to spend a few days with his bride, and had actually caused several holes to be bored below water-mark, which leaked enough to keep the men at the pumps. We came to anchor close to the town of New Bedford; the captain went on shore, entered a protest, the vessel was unloaded, the apertures bunged up, and after a week, which I spent in being rowed about the beautiful harbor, we sailed for La Belle France. A few days after having lost sight of land we were overtaken by a violent gale, coming fairly on our quarter, and before it we scudded at an extraordinary rate, and during the dark night had the misfortune to lose a fine young sailor overboard. At one part of the sea we passed through an immensity of dead fish floating on the surface of the water, and, after nineteen days from New Bedford, we had entered the Loire, and anchored off Painbœuf, the lower harbor of Nantes.

On sending my name to the principal officer of the customs, he came on board, and afterward sent me to my father's villa, La Gerbétière, in his barge, and with his own men, and late that evening I was in the arms of my beloved parents. Although I had written to them previous to leaving America, the rapidity of my voyage had prevented them hearing of my intentions, and to them my appearance was sudden and unexpected. Most welcome, however, I was; I found my father hale and hearty, and *chère maman* as fair and good as ever. Adored *maman*, peace be with thee!

I cannot trouble you with minute accounts of my life in France for the following two years, but will merely tell you that my first object being that of having Da Costa disposed of, this was first effected; the next was my father's consent to my marriage, and this was acceded to as soon as my good father had received answers to letters written to your grandfather, William Bakewell. In the very lap of comfort my time was happily spent; I went out shooting and hunting, drew every bird I procured, as well as many other objects of natural history and zoölogy, though these were not the subjects I had studied under the instruction of the celebrated David.

It was during this visit that my sister Rosa was married to Gabriel Dupuy Gaudeau, and I now also became acquainted with Ferdinand Rozier, whom you well know. Between Rozier and myself my father formed a partnership to stand good for nine years in America.

France was at that time in a great state of convulsion; the republic had, as it were, dwindled into a half monarchical, half democratic era. Bonaparte was at the height of success, overflowing the country as the mountain torrent overflows the plains in its course. Levies, or conscriptions, were the order of the day, and my name being French my father felt uneasy lest I should be forced to take part in the political strife of those days.

I underwent a mockery of an examination, and was received as midshipman in the navy, went to Rochefort, was placed on board a man-of-war, and ran a short cruise. On my return, my father had, in some way, obtained passports for Rozier and me, and we sailed for New York. Never can I forget the day when, at St. Nazaire, an officer came on board to examine the papers of the many passengers. On looking at mine he said: "My dear Mr. Audubon, I wish you joy; would to God that I had such papers; how thankful I should be to leave unhappy France under the same passport."

About a fortnight after leaving France a vessel gave us chase. We were running before the wind under all sail, but the unknown gained on us at a great rate, and after a while stood to the windward of our ship, about half a mile off. She fired a gun, the ball passed within a few yards of our bows; our captain heeded not, but kept on his course, with the United States flag displayed and floating in the breeze. Another and another shot was fired at us; the enemy closed upon us; all the passengers expected to receive her broadside. Our commander hove to: a boat was almost instantaneously lowered and alongside our vessel; two officers leaped on board, with about a dozen mariners; the first asked for the captain's papers, while the latter with his men kept guard over the whole.

The vessel which had pursued us was the "Rattlesnake" and was what I believe is generally called a privateer, which means nothing but a pirate; every one of the papers proved to be in perfect accordance with the laws existing between England and America, therefore we were not touched nor molested, but the English officers who had come on board robbed the ship of almost everything that was nice in the way of provisions, took our pigs and sheep, coffee and wines, and carried off our two best sailors despite all the remonstrances made by one of our members of Congress, I think from Virginia, who was accompanied by a charming young daughter. The "Rattlesnake" kept us under her lee, and almost within pistol-shot, for a whole day and night, ransacking the ship for money, of which we had a good deal in the run beneath a ballast of stone. Although this was partially removed they did not find the treasure. I may here tell you that I placed the gold belonging to Rozier and myself, wrapped in some clothing, under a cable in the bow of the ship, and there it remained snug till the "Rattlesnake" had given us leave to depart, which you may be sure we did without thanks to her commander or crew; we were afterward told the former had his wife with him.

After this rencontre we sailed on till we came to within about thirty miles of the entrance to the bay of New York, when we passed a fishing-boat, from which we were hailed and told that two British frigates lay off the entrance of the Hook, had fired an American ship, shot a man, and impressed so many of our seamen that to attempt reaching New York might prove to be both unsafe and unsuccessful. Our captain, on hearing this, put about immediately, and sailed for the east end of Long Island Sound, which we entered uninterrupted by any other enemy than a dreadful gale, which drove us on a sand-bar in the Sound, but from which we made off unhurt during the height of the tide and finally reached New York.

I at once called on your uncle Benjamin Bakewell, stayed with him a day, and proceeded at as swift a rate as possible to Fatland Ford, accompanied by Ferdinand Rozier. Mr. Da Costa was at once dismissed from his charge. I saw my dear Lucy, and was again my own master.

Perhaps it would be well for me to give you some slight information respecting my mode of life in those days of my youth, and I shall do so without gloves. I was what in plain terms may be called extremely extravagant. I had no vices, it is true, neither had I any high aims. I was ever fond of shooting, fishing, and riding on horseback; the raising of fowls of every sort was one of my hobbies, and to reach the maximum of my desires in those different things filled every one of my thoughts. I was ridiculously fond of dress. To have seen me going shooting in black satin smallclothes, or breeches, with silk stockings, and the finest ruffled shirt Philadelphia could afford, was, as I now realize, an absurd spectacle, but it was one of my many foibles, and I shall not conceal it. I purchased the best horses in the country, and rode well, and felt proud of it; my guns and fishing-tackle were equally good, always expensive and richly ornamented, often with silver. Indeed, though in America, I cut as many foolish pranks as a young dandy in Bond Street or Piccadilly.

I was extremely fond of music, dancing, and drawing; in all I had been well instructed, and not an opportunity was lost to confirm my propensities in those accomplishments. I was, like most young men, filled with the love of amusement, and not a ball, a skating-match, a house or riding party took place without me. Withal, and fortunately for me, I was not addicted to gambling; cards I disliked, and I had no other evil practices. I was, besides, temperate to an *intemperate* degree. I lived, until the day of my union with your mother, on milk, fruits, and vegetables, with the addition of game and fish at times, but never had I swallowed a single glass of wine or spirits until the day of my wedding. The result has been my uncommon, indeed iron, constitution. This was my constant mode of life ever since my earliest recollection, and while in France it was extremely annoying to all those round me. Indeed, so much did it influence me that I never went to dinners, merely because when so situated my peculiarities in my choice of food occasioned comment, and also because often not a single dish was to my taste or fancy, and I could eat nothing from the sumptuous tables before me. Pies, puddings, eggs, milk, or cream was all I cared for in the way of food, and many a time have I robbed my tenant's wife, Mrs. Thomas, of the cream intended to make butter for the Philadelphia market. All this time I was as fair and as rosy as a girl, though as strong, indeed stronger than most young men, and as active as a buck. And why, have I thought a thousand times, should I not have kept to that delicious mode of living? and why should not mankind in general be more abstemious than mankind is?

Before I sailed for France I had begun a series of drawings of the birds of America, and had also begun a study of their habits. I at first drew my subjects dead, by which I mean to say that, after procuring a specimen, I hung it up either by the head, wing, or foot, and copied it as closely as I possibly could.

In my drawing of birds only did I interest Mr. Da Costa. He always commended my efforts, nay he even went farther, for one morning, while I was drawing a figure of the *Ardea herodias*, he assured me the time might come when I should be a great American naturalist. However curious it may seem to the scientific world that these sayings from the lips of such a man should affect me, I assure you they had great weight with me, and I felt a certain degree of pride in these words even then.

Too young and too useless to be married, your grandfather William Bakewell advised me to study the mercantile business; my father approved, and to insure this training under the best auspices I went to New York, where I entered as a clerk for your great-uncle Benjamin Bakewell, while Rozier went to a French house at Philadelphia.

The mercantile business did not suit me. The very first venture which I undertook was in indigo; it cost me several hundred pounds, the whole of which was lost. Rozier was no more fortunate than I, for he shipped a cargo of hams to the West Indies, and not more than one-fifth of the cost was returned. Yet I suppose we both obtained a smattering of business.

Time passed, and at last, on April 8th, 1808, your mother and I were married by the Rev. Dr. Latimer, of Philadelphia, and the next morning left Fatland Ford and Mill Grove for Louisville, Ky. For some two years previous to this, Rozier and I had visited the country from time to time as merchants, had thought well of it, and liked it exceedingly. Its fertility and abundance, the hospitality and kindness of the people were sufficiently winning things to entice any one to go there with a view to comfort and happiness.

We had marked Louisville as a spot designed by nature to become a place of great importance, and, had we been as wise as we now are, I might never have published the "Birds of America;" for a few hundred dollars laid out at that period, in lands or town lots near Louisville, would, if left to grow over with grass to a date ten years past (this being 1835), have become an immense fortune. But young heads are on young shoulders; it was not to be, and who cares?

On our way to Pittsburg, we met with a sad accident, that nearly cost the life of your mother. The coach upset on the mountains, and she was severely, but fortunately not fatally hurt. We floated down the Ohio in a flatboat, in company with several other young families; we had many goods, and opened a large store at Louisville, which went on prosperously when I attended to it; but birds were birds then as now, and my thoughts were ever and anon turning toward them as the objects of my greatest delight. I shot, I drew, I looked on nature only; my days were happy beyond human conception, and beyond this I really cared not.

Victor was born June 12, 1809, at Gwathway's Hotel of the Indian Queen. We had by this time formed the acquaintance of many persons in and about Louisville; the country was settled by planters and farmers of the most benevolent and hospitable nature; and my young wife, who possessed talents far above par, was regarded as a gem, and received by them all with the greatest pleasure. All the sportsmen and hunters were fond of me, and I became their companion; my fondness for fine horses was well kept up, and I had as good as the country—and the country was Kentucky—could afford. Our most intimate friends were the Tarascons and the Berthouds, at Louisville and Shippingport. The simplicity and wholeheartedness of those days I cannot describe; man was man, and each, one to another, a brother.

I seldom passed a day without drawing a bird, or noting something respecting its habits, Rozier meantime attending the counter. I could relate many curious anecdotes about him, but never mind them; he made out to grow rich, and what more could *he* wish for?

In 1810 Alexander Wilson the naturalist—not the *American* naturalist—called upon me. About 1812 your uncle Thomas

W. Bakewell sailed from New York or Philadelphia, as a partner of mine, and took with him all the disposable money
which I had at that time, and there opened a mercantile
house under the name of "Audubon & Bakewell."

Merchants crowded to Louisville from all our Eastern
cities. None of them were, as I was, intent on the study of
birds, but all were deeply impressed with the value of dollars.
Louisville did not give us up, but we gave up Louisville. I
could not bear to give the attention required by my business,
and which, indeed, every business calls for, and, therefore, my
business abandoned me. Indeed, I never thought of it beyond
the ever-engaging journeys which I was in the habit of taking
to Philadelphia or New York to purchase goods; these journeys I greatly enjoyed, as they afforded me ample means to
study birds and their habits as I travelled through the beautiful, the darling forests of Ohio, Kentucky, and Pennsylvania.

Were I here to tell you that once, when travelling, and
driving several horses before me laden with goods and dollars,
I lost sight of the pack-saddles, and the cash they bore, to
watch the motions of a warbler, I should only repeat occurrences that happened a hundred times and more in those
days. To an ordinary reader this may appear very odd, but it
is as true, my dear sons, as it is that I am now scratching this
poor book of mine with a miserable iron pen. Rozier and myself still had some business together, but we became discour-
aged at Louisville, and I longed to have a wilder range; this
made us remove to Henderson, one hundred and twenty-five
miles farther down the fair Ohio. We took there the remainder of our stock on hand, but found the country so very new,
and so thinly populated that the commonest goods only were
called for. I may say our guns and fishing-lines were the principal means of our support, as regards food.

John Pope, our clerk, who was a Kentuckian, was a good
shot and an excellent fisherman, and he and I attended to the
procuring of game and fish, while Rozier again stood behind
the counter.

Your beloved mother and I were as happy as possible, the
people round loved us, and we them in return; our profits
were enormous, but our sales small, and my partner, who
spoke English but badly, suggested that we remove to St.

Geneviève, on the Mississippi River. I acceded to his request to go there, but determined to leave your mother and Victor at Henderson, not being quite sure that our adventure would succeed as we hoped. I therefore placed her and the children under the care of Dr. Rankin and his wife, who had a fine farm about three miles from Henderson, and having arranged our goods on board a large flatboat, my partner and I left Henderson in the month of December, 1810, in a heavy snowstorm. This change in my plans prevented me from going, as I had intended, on a long expedition. In Louisville we had formed the acquaintance of Major Croghan (an old friend of my father's), and of General Jonathan Clark, the brother of General William Clark, the first white man who ever crossed the Rocky Mountains. I had engaged to go with him, but was, as I have said, unfortunately prevented. To return to our journey. When we reached Cash Creek we were bound by ice for a few weeks; we then attempted to ascend the Mississippi, but were again stopped in the great bend called Tawapatee Bottom, where we again planted our camp till a thaw broke the ice. In less than six weeks, however, we reached the village of St. Geneviève. I found at once it was not the place for me; its population was then composed of low French Canadians, uneducated and uncouth, and the ever-longing wish to be with my beloved wife and children drew my thoughts to Henderson, to which I decided to return almost immediately. Scarcely any communication existed between the two places, and I felt cut off from all dearest to me. Rozier, on the contrary, liked it; he found plenty of French with whom to converse. I proposed selling out to him, a bargain was made, he paid me a certain amount in cash, and gave me bills for the residue. This accomplished, I purchased a beauty of a horse, for which I paid dear enough, and bid Rozier farewell. On my return trip to Henderson I was obliged to stop at a humble cabin, where I so nearly ran the chance of losing my life, at the hands of a woman and her two desperate sons, that I have thought fit since to introduce this passage in a sketch called "The Prairie," which is to be found in the first volume of my "Ornithological Biography."

Winter was just bursting into spring when I left the land of lead mines. Nature leaped with joy, as it were, at her own new-born marvels, the prairies began to be dotted with beauteous flowers, abounded with deer, and my own heart was filled with happiness at the sights before me. I must not forget to tell you that I crossed those prairies on foot at another time, for the purpose of collecting the money due to me from Rozier, and that I walked one hundred and sixty-five miles in a little over three days, much of the time nearly ankle deep in mud and water, from which I suffered much afterward by swollen feet. I reached Henderson in early March, and a few weeks later the lower portions of Kentucky and the shores of the Mississippi suffered severely by earthquakes. I felt their effects between Louisville and Henderson, and also at Dr. Rankin's. I have omitted to say that my second son, John Woodhouse, was born under Dr. Rankin's roof on November 30, 1812; he was an extremely delicate boy till about a twelvemonth old, when he suddenly acquired strength and grew to be a lusty child.

Your uncle, Thomas W. Bakewell, had been all this time in New Orleans, and thither I had sent him almost all the money I could raise; but notwithstanding this, the firm could not stand, and one day, while I was making a drawing of an otter, he suddenly appeared. He remained at Dr. Rankin's a few days, talked much to me about our misfortunes in trade, and left us for Fatland Ford.

My pecuniary means were now much reduced. I continued to draw birds and quadrupeds, it is true, but only now and then thought of making any money. I bought a wild horse, and on its back travelled over Tennessee and a portion of Georgia, and so round till I finally reached Philadelphia, and then to your grandfather's at Fatland Ford. He had sold my plantation of Mill Grove to Samuel Wetherell, of Philadelphia, for a good round sum, and with this I returned through Kentucky and at last reached Henderson once more. Your mother was well, both of you were lovely darlings of our hearts, and the effects of poverty troubled us not. Your uncle T. W. Bakewell was again in New Orleans and doing rather better, but this was a mere transient clearing of that sky which had been obscured for many a long day.

Determined to do something for myself, I took to horse, rode to Louisville with a few hundred dollars in my pockets, and there purchased, half cash, half credit, a small stock, which I brought to Henderson. *Chemin faisant*, I came in contact with, and was accompanied by, General Toledo, then on his way as a revolutionist to South America. As our flatboats were floating one clear moonshiny night lashed together, this individual opened his views to me, promising me wonders of wealth should I decide to accompany him, and he went so far as to offer me a colonelcy on what he was pleased to call "his Safe Guard." I listened, it is true, but looked more at the heavens than on his face, and in the former found so much more of peace than of war that I concluded not to accompany him.

When our boats arrived at Henderson, he landed with me, purchased many horses, hired some men, and coaxed others, to accompany him, purchased a young negro from me, presented me with a splendid Spanish dagger and my wife with a ring, and went off overland toward Natchez, with a view of there gathering recruits.

I now purchased a ground lot of four acres, and a meadow of four more at the back of the first. On the latter stood several buildings, an excellent orchard, etc., lately the property of an English doctor, who had died on the premises, and left the whole to a servant woman as a gift, from whom it came to me as a freehold. The pleasures which I have felt at Henderson, and under the roof of that log cabin, can never be effaced from my heart until after death. The little stock of goods brought from Louisville answered perfectly, and in less than twelve months I had again risen in the world. I purchased adjoining land, and was doing extremely well when Thomas Bakewell came once more on the tapis, and joined me in commerce. We prospered at a round rate for a while, but unfortunately for me, he took it into his brain to persuade me to erect a steam-mill at Henderson, and to join to our partnership an Englishman of the name of Thomas Pears, now dead.

Well, up went the steam-mill at an enormous expense, in a country then as unfit for such a thing as it would be now for me to attempt to settle in the moon. Thomas Pears came to Henderson with his wife and family of children, the mill was raised, and worked very badly. Thomas Pears lost his money and we lost ours.

It was now our misfortune to add other partners and petty agents to our concern; suffice it for me to tell you, nay, to assure you, that I was gulled by all these men. The new-born Kentucky banks nearly all broke in quick succession; and again we started with a new set of partners; these were your present uncle N. Berthoud and Benjamin Page of Pittsburg. Matters, however, grew worse every day; the times were what men called "bad," but I am fully persuaded the great fault was ours, and the building of that accursed steam-mill was, of all the follies of man, one of the greatest, and to your uncle and me the worst of all our pecuniary misfortunes. How I labored at that infernal mill! from dawn to dark, nay, at times all night. But it is over now; I am old, and try to forget as fast as possible all the different trials of those sad days. We also took it into our heads to have a steamboat, in partnership with the engineer who had come from Philadelphia to fix the engine of that mill. This also proved an entire failure, and misfortune after misfortune came down upon us like so many avalanches, both fearful and destructive.

About this time I went to New Orleans, at the suggestion of your uncle, to arrest S—— B——, who had purchased a steamer from us, but whose bills were worthless, and who owed us for the whole amount. I travelled down to New Orleans in an open skiff, accompanied by two negroes of mine; I reached New Orleans one day too late; Mr. B—— had been compelled to surrender the steamer to a prior claimant. I returned to Henderson, travelling part way on the steamer "Paragon," walked from the mouth of the Ohio to Shawnee, and rode the rest of the distance. On my arrival old Mr. Berthoud told me that Mr. B—— had arrived before me, and had sworn to kill me. My affrighted Lucy forced me to wear a dagger. Mr. B—— walked about the streets and before my house as if watching for me, and the continued reports of our neighbors prepared me for an encounter with this man, whose violent and ungovernable temper was only too well known. As I was walking toward the steam-mill one morning, I heard myself hailed from behind; on turning, I observed Mr. B—— marching toward me with a heavy club in his hand. I stood still, and he soon reached me. He complained of my conduct to him at New Orleans, and suddenly raising his bludgeon laid it about me. Though white with wrath, I spoke nor moved not till he had given me twelve severe blows, then, drawing my dagger with my left hand (unfortunately my right was disabled and in a sling, having been caught and much injured in the wheels of the steam-engine), I stabbed him and he instantly fell. Old Mr. Berthoud and others, who were hastening to the spot, now came up, and carried him home on a plank. Thank God, his wound was not mortal, but his friends were all up in arms and as hot-headed as himself. Some walked through my premises armed with guns; my dagger was once more at my side, Mr. Berthoud had his gun, our servants were variously armed, and our carpenter took my gun "Long Tom." Thus protected, I walked into the Judiciary Court, that was then sitting, and was blamed, *only*,—for not having killed the scoundrel who attacked me.

The "bad establishment," as I called the steam-mill, worked worse and worse every day. Thomas Bakewell, who possessed more brains than I, sold his town lots and removed to Cincinnati, where he has made a large fortune, and glad I am of it.

From this date my pecuniary difficulties daily increased; I had heavy bills to pay which I could not meet or take up. The moment this became known to the world around me, that moment I was assailed with thousands of invectives; the once wealthy man was now nothing. I parted with every particle of property I held to my creditors, keeping only the clothes I wore on that day, my original drawings, and my gun.

Your mother held in her arms your baby sister Rosa, named thus on account of her extreme loveliness, and after my own sister Rosa. *She* felt the pangs of our misfortunes perhaps more heavily than I, but never for an hour lost her courage; her brave and cheerful spirit accepted all, and no reproaches from her beloved lips ever wounded my heart. With her was I not always rich?

Finally I paid every bill, and at last left Henderson, probably forever, without a dollar in my pocket, walked to Louisville alone, by no means comfortable in mind, there went to Mr. Berthoud's, where I was kindly received; they were indeed good friends.

My plantation in Pennsylvania had been sold, and, in a word, nothing was left to me but my humble talents. Were those talents to remain dormant under such exigencies? Was I to see my beloved Lucy and children suffer and want bread, in the abundant State of Kentucky? Was I to repine because I had acted like an honest man? Was I inclined to cut my throat in foolish despair? No!! I *had* talents, and to them I instantly resorted.

To be a good draughtsman in those days was to me a blessing; to any other man, be it a thousand years hence, it will be a blessing also. I at once undertook to take portraits of the human "head divine," in black chalk, and, thanks to my master, David, succeeded admirably. I commenced at exceedingly low prices, but raised these prices as I became more known in this capacity. Your mother and yourselves were sent up from Henderson to our friend Isham Talbot, then Senator for Kentucky; this was done without a cent of expense to me, and I can never be grateful enough for his kind generosity.

In the course of a few weeks I had as much work to do as I could possibly wish, so much that I was able to rent a house in a retired part of Louisville. I was sent for four miles in the country, to take likenesses of persons on their death-beds, and so high did my reputation suddenly rise, as the best delineator of heads in that vicinity, that a clergyman residing at Louisville (I would give much now to recall and write down his name) had his dead child disinterred, to procure a fac-simile of his face, which, by the way, I gave to the parents as if still alive, to their intense satisfaction.

My drawings of birds were not neglected meantime; in this particular there seemed to hover round me almost a mania, and I would even give up doing a head, the profits of which would have supplied our wants for a week or more, to represent a little citizen of the feathered tribe. Nay, my dear sons, I thought that I now drew birds far better than I had ever done before misfortune intensified, or at least developed, my abilities. I received an invitation to go to Cincinnati, a flourishing place, and which you now well know to be a thriving town in the State of Ohio. I was presented to the president of the Cincinnati College, Dr. Drake, and immediately formed an engagement to stuff birds for the museum there, in concert with Mr. Robert Best, an Englishman of great talent. My salary was large, and I at once sent for your mother to come to me, and bring you. Your dearly beloved sister Rosa died shortly afterward. I now established a large drawing-school at Cincinnati, to which I attended thrice per week, and at good prices.

The expedition of Major Long passed through the city soon after, and well do I recollect how he, Messrs. T. Peale, Thomas Say, and others stared at my drawings of birds at that time.

So industrious were Mr. Best and I that in about six months we had augmented, arranged, and finished all we could do for the museum. I returned to my portraits, and made a great number of them, without which we must have once more been on the starving list, as Mr. Best and I found, sadly too late, that the members of the College museum were splendid promisers and very bad paymasters.

In October of 1820 I left your mother and yourselves at Cincinnati, and went to New Orleans on board a flat-boat commanded and owned by a Mr. Haromack. From this date my journals are kept with fair regularity, and if you read them you will easily find all that followed afterward.

In glancing over these pages, I see that in my hurried and broken manner of laying before you this very imperfect (but perfectly correct) account of my early life I have omitted to tell you that, before the birth of your sister Rosa, a daughter was born at Henderson, who was called, of course, Lucy. Alas! the poor, dear little one was unkindly born, she was always ill and suffering; two years did your kind and unwearied mother nurse her with all imaginable care, but notwithstanding this loving devotion she died, in the arms which had held her so long, and so tenderly. This infant daughter we buried in our garden at Henderson, but after removed her to the Holly burying-ground in the same place.

Hundreds of anecdotes I could relate to you, my dear sons, about those times, and it may happen that the pages that I am now scribbling over may hereafter, through your own medium, or that of some one else be published. I shall try, should God Almighty grant me life, to return to these less important portions of my history, and delineate them all with

the same faithfulness with which I have written the ornithological biographies of the birds of my beloved country.

Only one event, however, which possesses in itself a lesson
to mankind, I will here relate. After our dismal removal from
Henderson to Louisville, one morning, while all of us were
sadly desponding, I took you both, Victor and John, from
Shippingport to Louisville. I had purchased a loaf of bread
and some apples; before we reached Louisville you were all
hungry, and by the river side we sat down and ate our scanty
meal. On that day the world was with me as a blank, and my
heart was sorely heavy, for scarcely had I enough to keep my
dear ones alive; and yet through these dark ways I was being
led to the development of the talents I loved, and which have
brought so much enjoyment to us *all*, for it is with deep
thankfulness that I record that you, my sons, have passed your
lives almost continuously with your dear mother and myself.
But I will here stop with one remark.

One of the most extraordinary things among all these adverse circumstances was that I never for a day gave up listening to the songs of our birds, or watching their peculiar
habits, or delineating them in the best way that I could; nay,
during my deepest troubles I frequently would wrench myself
from the persons around me, and retire to some secluded part
of our noble forests; and many a time, at the sound of the
wood-thrush's melodies have I fallen on my knees, and there
prayed earnestly to our God.

This never failed to bring me the most valuable of thoughts
and always comfort, and, strange as it may seem to you, it was
often necessary for me to exert my will, and compel myself to
return to my fellow-beings.

LETTERS

To Lucy Audubon

Edinburgh Scotland December 9th 1826

My Beloved Wife,

After postponing day after day for the last Two weeks, writing to thee, full of hopes that each new day would bring some tidings of thee or of some one *connected* with me in America—I am forced to sit and write filled with fears and sorrow—Many of the Vessels that I wrote by have returned from America with full Cargoes, but nothing from thee = it is the more surprising because a fortnight since Dewitt Clinton answered a letter of mine dated Manchester and Inclosed me one of recommendations for Gen[l] Lafayette.

My Situation in Edinburgh borders almost on the Miraculous. Without education and scarce one of those qualities necessary to render a man able to pass thro the throng of the Learned here, I am positively look[d] on by all the Professors and many of the Principal persons here as a very extraordinary man—I brought here from Liverpool thirteen letters of most valuable introduction—after I had delivered them and my Drawings had been seen by a few of those Persons I requested then to engage all my acquaintances to call on me and see them also = for that purpose I remained each day for a week at my lodgings from 10 untill 2 and my room was constantly filled by persons of the first rank in Society—after this the Comittee of the Royal Institution having met, an order was passed to offer me the exibition rooms Gratis for some weeks—my Drawings were put up in the splendid room, all the news Papers took notice of them in a very handsome manner, and having continued to do so constantly, the rooms have been well attended when ever the weather has in the least permitted it—Last Saturday I took in 15£ it will continue open to the last of Christmas week, when I will remove them to *Glasgow* 50 miles from here where I expect to do well with them—I have had the pleasure of being introduced to several of the 1st Noblemen here and have found them extremely kind indeed =

About a fortnight since Sir William Jardine came to spend

a few days here purposely to see me—he was almost constantly with me. he and Mr Selby are engaged in a General
Ornithological Work and as I find I am a usefull man that
way, it is most Likely that I Shall be connected with them
with a good Share of credit and a good deal of Cash—they
both will be in in a few days when the matter will be discussed
over at length and probably arranged—

It is now a month since my work has been begun by M^r
William H. Lizars of this City—it is to come out in numbers
of 5 prints the size of Life and all in the same size paper of my
Largest Drawings called Double Elephant paper. They will be
brought up and finished in such superb style as to Eclipse all
of the Kind in Existence, the price of each number is Two
Guineas—and all Individuals have the privileges to subscribe
for all or any portion of it—Two of the Plates were finished
last week some of the Engravings Colored are put up in my
Exhibition rooms and are truly beautifull I think that the
midle of January the first number will be compleat and under
way to each subscriber. I shall send thee the very first and I
think it will please thee—it consists of the Turkey Male—the
Cuckoos on the Papaws—and three Small drawings that I
doubt thou dost not remember but will when thou seest
them I am sure—The Little Drawings in the center of these
beautifull Large Sheets have a fine effect and an air of Richness & wealth that cannot but help ensure success in this
Country—I cannot yet say that I will ultimately succeed, but
at present all bears a better aspect than I ever expected to see.
I think that under the Eyes of the most discerning people in
the World, I mean in Edinburgh, if it takes here it cannot fail
any where. It is not the Naturalists that I wish to please altogether I assure thee; it is the wealthy part of the commu-
nity. the first can only speak well or Ill of me but the Latters
will fill my Pockets—The University of Edinburgh having
subscribed I look^d to the rest of them 11 in number to follow
—I have here Strong friends who interest themselves considerably in the success of the Work who will bear me a good
hand—but I cannot do wonders at Once—I must wait patiently untill the first Number is finished and Exibit *that* for
although my Drawings are much admired if the work itself

was Inferior nothing could be done and untill I have it I cannot expect many Subscribers =

as soon as it is finished I will travel with it over all England Ireland and Scotland and then over the European Continent—taking my Collection with me to exibit it in all principal Cities to raise the means of Supporting my self well and I would Like most dearly to Add thyself and my Son's also. but can I or can I not expect it? alas it is not in my power to say. it does not depend on me or it would soon be accomplished—The first Professor of this Place Mr Jameson the conductor of the *Philosophical Journal*, President of the Wernerian Society &^{c} &^{c} gives a beautifull announcement of my Work in his present number, along with an a/c of mine, of the habits of the Buzard—try to see—it = Doct^r Brewster also announces it with my Introductory Letter to my Work— and Professor of Natural Philosophy John Willson also in *Blackwoods Magazine* these Three Journals prints upwards of 30,000 Copies so that my Name will Spread quickly enough = I am to deliver lectures on Natural History at the Wernarian Society at each of its meetings whilst here and I will do the same in all the Cities where I will be received as an honorary member—Professor Jameson who also is professor of Natural History told me that I would soon be a member of all the Societies here and that it would give my Work a great Standing thro out Europe = in the event of ultimate success I must have either my sons or some other persons to travel for me to see about the collecting of payment for the Work and to procure new subscribers constantly—as I conceive My Victor a well fit Man for such business, and as it would at once afford him the means of receiving a Most compleat Education and a Knowledge of Europe surpassing that of probably any other man in case I say of Success I will write for him Imediately When I hope No more constraint or opposition will be made to My Will = I am now better aware of the advantages of a familly in Unisson than ever and I am *quite* satisfied that by acting conjointly and by my advise we can realize a handsome fortune for each of us—it needs but Industry and perseverance = Going to America is a mere song, and I now find that most valuable voyages could be made by Procuring such articles as are wanted here and most plentifull there =

It is now about time to know from thee what thy *future Intentions* are. I Wish thee to act according to thy Dictates but wish to know what those dictates are—think that we are far devided and that either sickness or need may throw one or the other into a most chocking situation—without either friend or help for as thou sayest thyself "The World is not indulgent"—cannot We move together and feel and enjoy the mutual need of each other? Lucy my Friend think of all this very seriously. not a portion of the Hearth exists but will support us amply and we may feel happiness any where if carefull—When you receive this, sit and consider well, consult N. Berthoud, thy Son Victor or such a Person as Judge Mathews, then consult *thyself* and in a long, plain explanatory letter give me thy own Kind heart entire = in this Country John can receive an Education that America does not yet afford—and his propensities are such that attached to me he would be Left at my death Possessor of a Talent that would be the means of Support for his Life = I earnestly begged of thee in all my letters since I discovered that I was advancing in the World to urge him by all means to set to and begain a Colection of Drawings of all he can—and not to destroy one Drawing no matter how Indiferent. but to take all from Nature—I find here that although I have drawn much I really have not drawn half anough—Tell him to employ my Method of putting up Birds before him &^{c}—to draw fishes, Turtles—eggs—Trees—Landscapes all, all, he can draw. it will be most valuable to him—if he was Industrious and Work well and Closely, by the time he comes of age he would be quite able to have a Collection that would be a Litle fortune for him to begain upon =

I was much surprised at hearing of Charles Bonaparte in Liverpool last Week he came in the very Ship that took thy Watch to New York. the *Canada* =

The diference of Manners here from those of America are astonishing the great round of company I am thrown in has become fatiguing to me in the extreme, and does not agree with my early habits—I go to dine out at 6. 7. or 8 o'clock in the Evening and it is one or 2 in the Morning when the Party brakes up—then painting all day—with my Corespondance that Increases daily my head is like a Hornet's Nest and my body wearyed beyond calculations—Yet it has to be done—I *must not* refuse a single Invitation—

The Reverend W^am^ Bakewell the Son of Robert B. of London called on me here, and said that he was glad to see me at Last—Robt Bakewell had Long since heard of me—they are not a little proud I find to be connected with Mr A. the American Naturalist. This Cousin of thine for he calls *thee cousin Audubon* is maried to a Young Wife and has Two beautifull children quite young—he is at the Unitarian church and does not do well here—he ask^d^ me how it would do for him to go to America—but I cannot advise on a subject that I do not understand—perhaps, thou might. I see him and familly frequently—they look upon it as a mark of Kindness—but they really themselves are quite kind to me—

Edinburgh must be the handsomest City in the World—thou Wouldst Like it of all things *I think* for a Place of residence—When I send thee the first Number of the *Birds of America* I will also send a Book given me containing 51 Views of this Place—In the Event of you all removing from America keep those things I beg = finding that I was not going to London for some time I forwarded the Letters I had for Mrs Midlemist from here and requested her to Let me know where Charles's Wife resided that I could have the money paid her through the secretary of Legation at London = I have and Am most surprised that Charles Middlemist Should not have answered my Letters to him when *I conceive* it of the very greatest Importance to his future welfare—how is he and what does he do now = I regret extremely my not having brought *Barrels of Reptiles of all sorts* with me, I could get fine prices I assure thee and also for rare Bird Skins—seeds of Plants &^c^. but I thought I had enough to attend to—

I have very frequently spoke to thee respecting the very great Kindness I have experienced from the familly Rathbone of Liverpool—This Kindness they continue to me so constantly and in such a manner that I feel most anxious to repay them thr our humble means—W^am^ Rathbone is one of the Principal Members of the Royal Institution of Liverpool and one of the Wealthiest Merchant there—I wrote to thee from his Mother's House dated Green Bank to forward him some seeds—Dried flowers Leaves &^{c} and some Segments of Large trees—I Hope that thou will attend to those things for in the event of thy coming to England thou wouldst Land and come to their Care—and they would be as Kind to thee as they have been to me—The Seal with which I now close all my Principal Letters was given me by Mrs Rathbone the Mother of that excellent familly and accompanied by a Letter that would Honor any Man living—Keep allways directing thy Letters to them and Write to Mrs Rathbone herself She will be a Most Valuable Friend to thee—

since here I have painted Two Pictures in Oil now in the Exibition—One contains 11 Wild Turkeys with a Handsome Landscape—The Other is my Otter in a Trap—my Success in Oil Painting is truly wonderfull—and I am called an astonishing artist &^{c}—what diferent times I see here courted as I am from those I spent at the Beech Woods were certain people Scarce thought fit to Look upon me = I have written to Mr Bourgeat—Dr Pope, Judge Mathews N. Berthoud. Victor. W^{am} Bakewell all to no purpose so far it Seems—

I must now close this and bid thee Adieu for a while—I have to Copy it as I do all I write This task is an arduous one but the consolation of Seeing what I say to thee from time to time compensates me very amply—I very frequently forward thee the News Papers each of them contains my Name—I dined at the Antiquarian Society and was toasted by Lord Elgin—thou wilt see it in the Papers I sent thee—I would have forwarded thee Books and other Objects but uncertain if thou Would not come to Europe as soon as My Plans are *Solidly fixed* I thought best not to do so—but I assure thee I cannot at present conceive a failure on my Part—and May God grant that it be true—If I can procure on the whole of Two Years 300 Subscribers We will be rich indeed—God for ever Bless You—remember me Kindly to all about thee—Kiss My Son and believe me for ever thine Husband & friend—

To Lucy Audubon

Liverpool England May 15th 1827

My Dearest Friend—

I arrived here yesterday afternoon and as I met My REAL Friend W^{am} Rathbone he handed me thy last letter received a few minutes before of the 15th March. I will now set to and reply to each of its sentences but before will give an a/c again of my Journey from Edinburgh to this place after an absence of 38 days from the former. in the first place I spent a week at Mr Selby in Northumberland, a particular *acquaintance* of mine and there amongst other pleasures had 3 Subscribers. from thence to New Castle upon Tyne where I also spent a week. Saw old Bewick, and obtained 8 Subscribers. then to York in Yorkshire, also one week and 10 Subscribers. the Minster of York is the grandest Edifice I have seen since in this Country—I then came to Leeds   one Week and 5 Subscribers. to Manchester where in a few days I procured 18 Subscribers and here I am!

My Stay here Will be of a Short duration, I leave this on Thursday Morning, the very day 12 Months since I *sailed* from My Far beloved Country for London—

Just pause for a moment, think coolly, and wonder how thy husband is proceeding in Such a work as his. 44 Subscribers in 38 days; whom most pay An amount of 7,040 Guineas by the time the whole is compleat. what *thou* may feel is unfortunatly quite unknown to me, but *My Friend* Rathbone and all my *acquaintances* are astounded = The method I have taken although extremely expensive will insure me success at last. My Expenses are all relieved by my Industry and are paid by the paintings I make in Oil and Sell as I go. I sold last week a Copy of the Doves for 20 Guineas. I have determined to travel compleatly through every Town in England, Scotland and Ireland. will not visit the Continent unless forced to do so, as I am particularly anxious to concentrate my Business entirely within the Bounds of this Kingdom.—

It is alas quite useless for me to say that I would be HAPPIER if thou were with me when travelling thus, but I almost abandon this hope as (according to thy expressions) *thy habits* and thy *Ideas* of things are so diferent from mine—

I have seen thy Sister Ann this morning, and She will write to thee Shortly, I know her advises will be better come than mine—I am married, every one knows it—and yet I have no Wife nor I am Likely to possess one = I have come to a highly Civilized Country where Talents are appreciated and where any one with Industry and Care can live as well as any where under the Sun. without my Wife and my Children, nay I am denied the privilege of every Father in the World, that of Judging what is best for them to do—and I have perhaps lost sight of them for ever—Such is the Situation of thy husband that after Years of Labours, in the midst of encouragement, the Strongest pangs of Sorrows fret my poor mind constantly = I will say no more. I have no wish to give thee pain, and I will now answer thy Letter.—

The first Item is thy Watch. *I am Sorry I sent it. I am Sorry I Bought one for thee.* I am vexed I did not in that let thee have thy own way and have had thee purchase One—all I know about it, is that it was sent to New York to Messrs *Walker & Son* through the care of a Gentleman (Mr Rathbone) on whom I can rely. he has wrote there, expects one of the partners here in a few days and will make the Strictest enquiries about it. notwithstanding, I am quite Sure, that either that article and all besides that I have sent would have reached thee had thy Brother in Law Mr Gordon acted towards me *then* as he does *now* that the cards are quite turned as to my Standing and prospects—he *now* offers to forward any thing I have, but *then* would have nothing to do with them—he pretends to be thy friend and is my Ennemy!—The Watch I bought I Shewed to thy Sister and to Mr Gordon, I Shewed it with pride to all the familly Rathbone. I paid for it upwards of 50 Guineas and yet if it is not arrived, say so, and I will the day I receive thy answer to this, purchase another and give it to Mr Gordon *who has better Luck than I.*

The pleasure expressed in thy Last at my suceeding well; believe me Lucy I am thankfull to thee for; was it not for thy Sake *not a Step* would I go further, I would return to America and Hide Myself from the World willingly—but I try to succeed, I hope to do so now, I think I will, merely TO PROVE to thee perhaps, that I have loved thee, that I love thee still, much more than thou hast seemed to think or express ever since, the extravagancies of the command of Money ceased to take place in our household.

It is Impossible for me to say if I will remain here for ever, or for any particular number of Years—for the Same reason it is quite Impossible for me to say if, or not, I will return to America Shortly—thou knowest well, how anxiously and often I have repeated to thee when in America that I wished to draw More, to finish my Collection entirely. &ᶜ when thou wert allways for my making a Trial in Europe before end and Judge = I have done so, and I say, *all now* bids fair towards ultimate success but that I may not be *obliged* to go again to the woods and draw to finish my work is indeed uncertain—

Mʳ Lizars my Engraver an Honest *Scotchman* a Man *who hopes* as well as me that I will suceed as it will be as well as to me a Fortune in such a Case is in good Spirits, has begun the second Number and says that 500 Subscribers will make me and him Independant for the rest of our Days—at this great distance letter writting is next to nothing. a word, or a sentence, may be misunderstood, that is enough to need a all Series of Letters to correct the false Impression received. I May think thee cold to me, and thou me unkind to thyself when neither of us mean to cross our ultimate Intentions to please each other and during all that time We are 5,000 Miles apart—

I have almost a mind to say now, My Beloved Lucy I will go for thee *Myself* but I have not Subscribers enough for that, I cannot bear to be without thee, it vexes me, frets me to death.—but when I have been in London I may have such a number as to prompt me to go to America and bring thee over. recollect that I wish thy Happiness and nothing else but recollect also that I am becoming a Judge what is best for *both of us.*

depend on it *I will have nothing to do at all with Charles Middlemist* or any of the Name. I am sorry that thou hast given him a letter to me because he will bore me to death if he finds me out, which I Hope he will not.—The Man is Crazy he will Starve here unless he works and he will not Work it seems—Nothing in the World would have been more vexatious to thee to have been travelling with him I am sure:

The Segments have not arrived Yet. I saw John's Letter to Mʳ Bentley. the good Gentleman is as much vexed as I am that nothing reaches thee—the first week I am in London I will purchase thee one or Two head Dresses and May they reach thee. allways Say by what Vessel any thing comes from thee, and I will do the same for thee from here—Enquire of thy Old, New Married Friend Briggs about what has already been sent by me, also at the Custom House at New Orleans, and of Vincent Nolte & C° perhaps it may put thee in the way of getting what I have sent = Anne told me that thou had wrote to her, and said thou wert not well, but She would not Shew me thy Letter   She is a queer Woman to me—

It gives me great pleasure that the Familly Johnson are as Kind as they ought to be to thee—present them my Kind Respects and Friend Bourgeat also—Mrs Percy ought not to have lent thee, the Horses but given them to thee, I am sure *thou* and *I* have paid her 3 Times their value =

I have now nearly 100 Subscribers. I will write to thee often, be Happy and May God *Join* us again. write to me about every thing. dost thou Know Who Charles Briggs has Married?—

No Letters from Victor or Berthoud—Strange, very Strange. Kiss John, God Bless him and thou for ever—a Vessel goes direct tomorow to New Orleans   May this reach thee quickly and find thee well and Happy. for ever thine. oh My Lucy Why Why are we not together—adieu again thine forever

I have asked Mr Sully to have each of my Letters to him copied and forwarded to thee—I was Elected since I left Edinburgh, Member of the Literary & Philosophical Society of New Castle and the Antiquarian So.^y—also and at Manchester Member of Natural History So.^y but London I am told is the place where I will receive great Honours—God Bless thee, oh how I would kiss thee were thou here by me—

To Lucy Audubon

London August 6th 1827.

My Dearest Lucy
    I am still here although London is (comparatively Speaking) deserted; it was my intention to have left about 3 weeks

ago to travel again to augment the number of my Subscribers, but I was prevented from so doing on account of the tardiness of Mr Lizars my Engraver at Edinburgh who nearly exausted my patience by not Supplying the Subscribers, for Several months after my expectations, of the 1st number. = he began engraving the 2^d number the 1st of May last and I have been anxious to See it out also before my departure but after much delays and perplexities, I was forced last week to write to him to forward me the *Coppers engraved* here to have the Impressions, printed and Colored here. I received the whole Yesterday in good Order and I am truly glad of it. for London affords all sorts of facilities imaginable or necessary for the Publication of Such Immense Work and hereafter my *Principal* business will be carried on here = I have made arrangements with a Mr Havell an excellent Engraver who has a good establishment containing Printers—Colorors and Engravers So that I can have all under my eye when I am in London and no longer will be Stopp^d by the want of Paper, or Coppers that Mr Lizars was obliged to order from here; sometimes with risks and at all events with a considerable expense *extra* Indeed the difcrence of Cost from the Number which Mr Havell is engraving (The 3^d) and those done by Mr Lizars I save about 25 pounds Sterling which is nearly one fourth of what Mr L. charged—and yet the work is quite equal, and the sets colored by him are far Surpassing in beauty those of Mr L. = My Business is now I think in Such a train as will enable me to Keep it going this Year as the work is now able to pay for itself by good manegem^t and Industry and to try to give thee a true Idea of it I will explain more at length—

The Price that I pay Mr Havell for Engraving one Number or a sett consisting of 5 Plates with the lettering and Coppers

	S.^{gs} p.^{cs}
Included is	£42.0.0—
The Price of Coloring 100 sets @ 8/6	42.10.0—
Paper for D^o 1 Ream	14.1.0—
Printing of the 100 sets	11.5.0—
100 Tin Cases to forward the sets to each person	5.0.0—
	£114:16:0

These 100 sets thus delivered bring 210 Pounds as I charge 2 Guineas per number so that my having been able to pay for the 1st Number and also the 2^{d} will enable me to Keep going and if betwen this and January 1828 I procure 100 More Subscribers than I have at present, I will consider myself quite able to have thy Sweet self and Johny here. because every Subscriber after even Now is clear profit. the plates are of course my property and 1500 Copies may be Struck off before they will need any repair = to Collect my money I take a round to the diferent Cities where my Subscribers are and It is my Intention to go that round Twice or three times a Year So that I have really great Hopes of Success and the Prospect of having thee and our Sons once more Independant =

The expenses of Living in London are very great and I assure thee that if I had not been extremely carefull and very industrious; I would have ran ashore long ere now—which would be dreadfull after all my Labours and Success thus far.—I do any thing for money now a days—I positively last week made 22. Pounds 10 Shillings by drawing Trifles in a Scotch Lady's Album. that enabled me to purchase 6 Gilt frames to forward 6 Pictures to the Liverpool exibition where I Hope I may sell the whole of them—I Painted them since I came to London in Oil—one of Ducks—one of Rabbits.— one of Common Fowls, One of Pigeons, one of Partridges, one of an Otter—all measuring 42. Inches by 28. = My Prices for them are from 20 to 30 Guineas each according to the diference of value Judged by Myself and Some friends of Mine—if I Sell them It will put me quite a float and at my ease—I will begain as soon as time will permit 2 very Large Pictures of Peacocks, and Turkeys, for the Spring London exibition so as to have my name Cracked up here as well as in Edinburgh—but Dearest Wife thou must Know that Edinburgh is a *Mere* Village compared with this Massy Capital— the Duke of bedford own several Streets himself that would cover Louisville entirely =

It is now my Intention to remain in England as Long as I will have Drawings to Keep my Work going on; say 5 Years exclusive of the present year; and if in January Next I feel myself *substantially settled*. I will Write for thee to come and when that does take place I will have every thing ready to receive my Sweet Wife in comfort = It is useless to dwel on the pleasure I anticipate at such an event after Years of Labours & perplexities under which we have grown these 8 Years past!—

I received a Letter from friend Bourgeat the other day, thanks to him for it. I will forward him some fine Dogs from Liverpool—I have made arrangements with a Friend who will give me Some of the best Stock in this Country—John also will have 2 sent to him. and Should you come over instead of me going there (a thing I do not anticipate Just now and that I hope will not take place as it can only be so true a compleat failure of my Prospects) he may easily give them away—Dear Boy but little hunting or fishing in this Country for him. when I think of America Lucy and her beautifull Natural Forests and Songsters my Eyes fill involuntarily with big tears as if I was never more to See or hear all these Sweet Friends & compagnions of Mine = Should I go, of course I will take thee an excellent Pianno and plenty of Music but I hope to do better for thee—Thy last letter is dated April 29th thou hadst received, The Sparrs, Books, &^{c} and liked all, I am truly glad of it for it is allways my wish to please my Dearly beloved Lucy—I will always here after send what I have for thee to the especial Care of Mr Edouard Hollander New Orleans—he is the former Partner of Mr Nolte, who is now here and who assured me that he would forward any thing from me to thee or from thee to me with pleasure—So that I wish thou would write to that Gentleman on the Subject. and I will also from here Mr Nolte goes to America in a fortnight, and will take Letters to Victor and Mr Berthoud. I have only one letter from Victor and none from Berthoud. I hope thy Watch has now reached thee and thou art pleased with it—I Wrote to Mr Gordon to tell him to pay over the 200 Dollars that thou says has been paid to his house at New Orleans for me, but I have no answer from him—I would not be *extremely* surprised if I never do = I am in daily expectation of a Letter from thee now Neither Segments, nor Drawings have reached us yet. it is a pity that thou never wrote by what vessel they were sent—, I only received the Watch Papers inclosed in thy Last made by John—

I am living with Mrs Midlemist, She received the Other day a letter from her Son John who speaks of the health of Poor

Charles Midlemist in an alarming manner. I was rather Surprised that he did not Mention thy name at all—do my Beloved Wife try to Collect as Many Natural Curiosities as Possible to bring over with thee.—if the lest Chance of an absence could possibly take place, I would go for thee with pleasure but I do not at present contemplate such an event = I have found here a Nephew of My Friend Sully an Aimiable Young Man that I Knew in Philadelphia who is quite an agreable companion.—I wish I could Spend my Sundays with thy Self and flock and Jump to London on Monday Mornings untill I am ready to Jump you over! This is Sunday and if Tomorow Monday I Should receive a Letter from my Good Friend W^{am} Rathbone telling me to go to the great Musical Festivals at Liverpool I will take this Letter there myself. now that I have all my Business maneageable in London I can go and procure more Subscribers.—

I Enclose this in one of my Prospectus because I am anxious thou Should see the Names of my Subscribers = now Sweet Dearest Friend I must once more bid thee well and Happy   remember me Kindly to all about thee. urge my Son to continue the Violin, Drawing, every thing. I saw the other day in the Streets, near the Regent's Park 2 Lads about 9 Years of age performing Miracles together on the Violin and flute for their Livelihood—but London is filled with such things and a Stranger would Suppose that talents of the 1st Class goes here begging but it is not quite So bad as all that: I saw the other night at the Equestrian Theatre a Man Managing 12 Horses full gallops, Jumping from one to another without any Sadles or Bridles. Cutting Summer Sols &^{c} &^{c} = Last night I heard Mrs Vestris sing. I have seen all the great Actors, singers &^{c} &^{c} but not *Mathews* yet. I could see more of all these things but I am generally better employed and I am always uneasy when walking the Streets at Night. such quantities of Robberies are comitted and the Streets are litteraly filled at these hours with no very respectable Ladies I assure thee—Again and Again God Bless thee for ever, Kiss our Dear Son for me, send a Copy of all this to Victor if it pleases thee to do so and believe me Thine Friend & Husband for ever

W^{am} Rathbone wrote to me of his having received a Letter from thee, I was glad of that they are such excellent Generous Friends—

To Lucy Audubon

London November 2^d 1828.—

My Dearest Friend—

I returned from Paris yesterday and hasten to write to inform thee of my Success as fully as I can in a Single letter.— on my Arrival at Paris I called on Baron Cuvier, the greatest naturalist of the age and although I was unknown to him he received me with great kindness and subsequently has treated me with all the friendly treatment that I could have wished.— he introduced me to the Royal Academy of Natural Sciences where I exibitcd the 9 numbers of my Work then published consisting of 45 plates,—he was appointed by the Society to render an account of the merits of the Work and at another meeting did so in the most honourable and agreeable Words to myself—this report was immediatly published in the Moniteur and other newspapers and my name & work was soon the talk of the principal Societies, through this mean I have obtained the following names of Subscribers.—1. the King of France Charles X. 2 the Duke of Orleans, 3. The Dutchess of Orleans, 4. Prince Massena, 5. Baron Cuvier, 6. The Royal French Institut, 7. The Minister of the Interieur. 6 copies for the Government; /. Monsieur Redouté. and Monsieur Pitois /.—in all 14 Copies.—during my absence from London I have had in England an accession of 4 More So that since I left this Place my list as been augmented 18 Subscribers making in all now 144.—I think that thou will be pleased at these famous personnages whom I all saw. I spent 1 and ½ hour with the Duke of Orleans and have sold him 2 large Pictures.—My time in Paris was agreably and usefully spent.—I saw the highest rank of Society and all that Art and nature combined have brought together in that beautifull City.— with the advise of the Minister of the Interieur and the Baron Cuvier I have taken an agent in Paris named Pitois who will procure subscriptions on the whole Continent and is responsable to me for the amounts, remitted me at London, for a discount granted him of 15 PC^t on my prices here—I look upon this as a good Job also, as M. Pitois is one of the first & Most respectable Booksellers on the Continent, his principal house is at Strasburgh.—

I received Yesterday a letter from our Victor dated 12th of Sepr I cannot conceive why thy letters are so much longer coming than his, do send them all by Way of New Orleans,— I wrote this day a very long letter to Victor which if he receives it will make him open his eyes respecting my Publication that *you all* seem not to know any thing correct about.—do my Lucy understand me well—My Work will not be finished for 14 Years to Come from this very present date—and if it is thy Intention not to Join me before that time, I think will be best off both of us to separate, thou to Marry in America and I to Spend my Life most Miserably alone for the remainder of my days.—in the course of another Year I think that it will be impossible for me to do without an assistant and as betwen thyself, thy Brother William & Co My Son is swept off I must look to an utter Stranger—thy Views are diferent from mine and no doubt must remain so for ever to the great disadvantage of both—I regret on thy account that the Piano, the Dresses and other objects sent to thee prove not to be good and always have some mishaps by the time they reach thee—this is no encouragement for me I assure thee and I will not send any thing else—from thy last Two letters which reach^d me in Paris and which I have really Studied as much as my Knowledge of the English language will enable me to do, I have now Most Positively concluded never to write to thee to Join me untill indeed I find myself so overflowing with cash as to be able to give thee these extraordinary comforts without which it appears my being thy Husband is of but little Consequence—in every letter of thine thy words are the same thou artt *Comfortable in the extreme*, I wish I could say half as much—I am sick of being alone and from thee and how much longer I will bear is a little doubt-full. I have not Jumped yet into a fortune in Europe—I am I THINK doing extremely well in a pecuniary point of View and could maintain comfortably a Wife desirous to render her husband happy as I know some in the World—My Income now annually is rather more than 600 pound sterling or 2664 Dollars—I live extremely simply except indeed when obliged and for my future advantage to do the contrary—I work I fear rather more *now* than my constitution will well bear and when I am absent from London I am in a constant state of fears, Least something wrong Should take place—Not a friend have I on *this Earth* to whom I can Speak openly   all my business is locked up in my own bosom, Scarcely now can I give a Single letter of business to Copy—this is my Lucy the Situation of a Man who is Maried to a woman clever herself, aimiable as much as I possibly could wish but unfortunatly found of a Style of Life that that husband of hers cannot at present at least meet for the want of thousands per annum—I write now most Candidly, I write as a Man who esteems his Wife as a valuable friend, who loves her tenderly and would render her happy to the utmost of his means with all his heart and Soul—thou sayest in thy last that to Come to Europe without thy Children would break thy heart, and at the same time seem not to care about my heart being broken, because *they* will not come to Europe—depend upon it Lucy, our affections are not of adamante substance—distance, long separation works strongly on the mind and the Phisic at our Age; who knows but some many Years more of Such Separation as thou seemest willing to undergo will not unroot the feelings of our early days and that when we meet again we may find each others Strangers to both in New habits, manners & feelings?—thy means of living at present do not I am sure exceed 5 or 6 hundred Dollars per annum, why not receive that same sum from thy husband and half as much again and be with him—comfort him in times of troubles and sorrows and assist him in his labours? My paper is filled I must close, do write to me often. I will write again in a few days but my business demands are now I have hundreds of letters to write, Pictures to finish and have but Myself to do all—May God for ever bless thee and render thee happy & believe me thy truest Friend at last—

To Lucy Audubon

New York May 10th 1829.—
Sunday morning.—

My Dearest Friend—

I have been landed here from on board the Packet Ship the Columbia, Four days after an agreable passage of 35 from Portsmouth—I have written thee since then 2 Short letters to announce thee my safe arrival and my good health and now sit to write at length a letter which I sincerely hope and wish thee to read with due attention and believe to be in its whole contents the true sentiment of thy affectionnate Friend and husband.—

1. I have come to America to remain as long as consistent with the *safety* of the continuation of my publication in London without my personnal presence and according to future circumstance either to return to England on the 1st October next or if possible not untill the 1st of April 1830.—in this I must be guided entirely by the advises of my Friends in England W^{am} Rathbone, G. J. Children of the British Museum and Mr Robt Havell Junr my Engraver.—

2. I wish to employ and devote every moment of my Sojourn in America at Drawing such Birds and Plants as I think necessary to enable me to give my publication *throughout* the degree of perfection that *I am told* exists in that Portion already published and now before the Public. This intention is Known to no one Individual and I wish it to be kept perfectly a Secret between our *Two* Selves.—to accomplish the whole of this or as much as I can of it between now and my return to Europe I intend to remain as *Stationary* as possible in Such parts of the Country as will afford me most of the Subjects, and these parts I Know well.

3. I have left my business going on quite well and with hopes that my return there will not be *forced* upon me by disapointments.—my Engraver has in his hands all the Drawings wanted to compleat this present Year and those necessary to form the 1st Number of the next Year and my cash arrangements to meet my engagements with him I think have been and are prudently managed and Sure.—

4. The exact situation of my Stock on hand left in Europe I give thee here bona fidœ copied from the receipt I have on hand and with me here.—

Amount of Debts due me 1ˢᵗ Janʸ. .	1829	. . . .	£466.16.4.
Values of my Engraved Coppers—	″	. . . . .	504.0.0.
Stock of the Work ready for Sale—	″	. . . . .	262.8.0.
Cash in Wᵃᵐ Rathbone's hands—	″	. . . . .	132.5.0.
Sundry Paintings Frames Books &ᶜ &ᶜ—″		. . . . .	200.0.0.
		Sterling:	£ 1565.9.4.

about 6,960 Dollars =

———

I have with me 150 pounds 2 copies of my Work 200 $ plenty of clothes My Watch 100£. Gun 20 Pounds &ᶜ—

The Above my Dear Lucy is the present Stock of thy husband, raised in the 2 first Years of my Publication, the Two most dificult Years to be encountered; with a Stock of *Fame* not likely I hope to decrease but to Support me and enable me to live decently but not in afluence but respectably— *Should I be absent* untill the 1ˢᵗ of Jan.ʸ. next without drawing for money on England and my work is published with regularity there will be 500 pounds to be added of money either due to me or received for my account—and an additional Stock of Coppers of 252 pounds = the more my Subscribers augment in numbers the greater my profits and on that Score I have great hopes!!—*and good reasons for thus hoping!*—To my Lucy I now offer myself with my Stock wares and chattels and all the devotedness of heart attached to such an Anthusiastic being as I am—to which I prefer to add my Industry and humble Talents as long as able through health and our God's will, to render her days as comfortable as Such means may best afford with caution and prudence——

in return for these present offers I wish to receive as *True* and as *Frank* an answer as *I Know my Lucy will give me*, saying whether or no, the facts and the prospects, will entice her to Join her husband and to go to Europe with him; to enliven his Spirits and assist him with her kind advises—the "no" or the "Yes" will Stamp my future Years—if a no comes; *I never will put the question again* and *we probably* never will meet again——if a "Yes," a kind "Yes" comes bounding from thy heart, my heart will bound also, and *it seems* to me that It will give me nerve for further exertions! = We have been married a good time; circumstances have caused our Voyages to be very motled with Incidents of very diferent natures, but our *happy days* are the only days *I now remember.* the Tears that now almost blind me are the vouchers for my hearts emotions at the recollection of those happy days! I have no wish to *entice thee to come by persuasions*; I wish thee to consult *thy onself* and that only, and to write to me accordingly thy determination—*the amount* of thy own pecuniary means— and how soon I might expect thee *in Philadelphia* from after the time this reaches thee.—*I cannot go to Louisiana* without running risks incalculable of not receiving *regular news* from London. either go to Louisville and even to Wheeling on the Ohio and I will meet thee at the latter place at the time appointed by thyself.—

5. I do not wish to take John with us *unless it be to follow my profession* and I have no wish whatever to enforce this upon him = settle him at Louisville with whomever thou may like best—Some future Years may bring us *all* together!—Victor being Settled I feel happy on his a/c and *that is all a Father must desire*—

6. Thy determination must be prompt either "yes" or "no". = if coming thou must settle as quietly as prudence will permit, sell all that is at all cumbersome, and *Ship* whatever is not absolutely necessary for thy Journy; through M[r] Charles Briggs to the care of Mess[rs] Rathbone Brothers & C[o] Liverpool.—ascend the Ohio or sail direct for here or Philadelphia as may suit thy wishes best.—sell for cash at reduce prices rather than leave debts behind thee.—If thou determines on coming I wish thee to be with me before the 1st day of October because Should I be recalled to England on account of accidents we must sail on *that day* in the same vessel that has brought me here.—I have pitched on Philadelphia for remaining untill I have *thy answer to this* because the Market is good for my purpose and the Woods very diversified in their Trees. = when with me we can go somewhere else if time will permit. = do not forget to bring my old Journals and whatever Drawings of mine (of Birds) that thou may have. = I have brought an excellent and beautifull Gold

watch for Victor—perhaps Mr Berthoud would permit him to take care of thee to Wheeling or to Philadelphia.—I will now pass to other subjects.—

I have been received here with great Kindness by the Scientific Men of New York, Col^l Trumbull, Major Long, Mr Cooper &^{c} &^{c} have paid me many compliments—the Collector of the Custom house gave me a permit to enter my Books Gun &^{c} *free of Duty* and all the Public Institutions and exibitions are open to me.—I found my good old Friend Doct^r Pascallis quite well, his aimiable Daughter maried and the Mother of three Sweet children. = Doc^r Mitchel is now lost to himself and to the World I have seen him once half dead with drunkeness. = My Immense Book has been laid on the Table of the Lyceum and look^d at praised and I may have one or Two Subscribers here, a few more at Boston, Phil^a &^{c} Should I procure 20 in the whole U. States I will be proud of myself I have seen Messrs Walker and Sons and given them a letter from Friend W^{am} Rathbone, they will attend to the forwarding of my letters from Europe &^{c}.—direct to their care untill I write to the contrary.—It was my Intention to proceed to Philad^a Tomorow monday the 11th May but the President of the Lyceum desired me to remain here a few days more and I will do so with hopes to have a Subscriber or So. = I have written to Mr Sully to procure me a Boarding house in a private familly &^{c} and I expect his answer tomorow. = I will write to thee frequently perhaps Twice per week untill I hear from thee. = I Should like exceedingly to Spend a week or Two at Mr Johnson's with thee but it cannot be and probably for ever my eyes will not rest on Magnolia Woods or See the mocking thrush gaily gamboling full of Melody amongst the Fig trees of the South.—a Vessel arrived yesterday in 12 days from New Orleans the news of which Shook my frame as if electrified, to know that in So Short a time I might again See my Lucy and press her to my heart is a blessing beyond any thing I have felt since three Years. = thy Sister Ann was quite well when I left—I had a letter from Mr Gordon a few days before my Sailing and a Week or 2 before he called on me in London to view my Paintings.—I have here a beautifull Dog of King Charles breed; I will try to send it to my old Friend Bourgeat if I can prevail on any Captain or Passenger to take Charge of it.—remember me most kindly to them all.—Just before my departure from London I received Two letters from thee but of Such old dates that thou did not even Know of my having Spent 2 Months in Paris. = on the 15th I will send a Copy of this by Packet Ship. May God grant thee health and Happiness; believe me thy Friend for Life

Philadelphia May 16th Saturday 1829—

Dearest Wife & Friend—I came here the day before yesterday from New York.—I called Immediatly on my old Friend Sully whom I found well familly & all as Kind as ever.—I dined with them en famille = last night I rode out to Good Friend Ruben Haines, he was absent his Wife tried to Keep me the night but having a Companion refused with an Apology—called this Morning was again disapointed—returned to Philad^a crossed to New Jersey to procure a House to live & Draw in = have been *So far* disapointed in that but will be settle in a few days and I hope at Work—I have this morning rec^d 2 Letters from London one from Mr Havell My Engraver who announces me a *New Subscriber*, and one from friend Bentley—all well and going on well on the 4th April, from the Arrangements I have made I will receive letters by every Packett from Liverpool—

Now My Dearest Wife, My Lucy, Write to me soon and let me Know thy *resolution*—Sully nor his familly nor that of Rubens Haines Knew me—Grew so fat and my hair being cut off makes such a diference with my appearance—

God Bless thee for ever

thy Friend & Husband

If thou Hast opportunity read the New York Papers of this Date and 10 Days Inclusive to come—

To Lucy Audubon

Charleston,—S.C. 23^d Octr 1831

My Dearest Friend—

I have just finished a drawing which I began this morning of a very rare Species of Heron and I am determined ere another day passes or another Drawing is began to write to thee and give thee an account of our proceedings Since Fayetteville from whence I wrote my last—

We left the later place on the day I wrote in a cramped Coach and passed over a flat level and drary Country Crossing at every half miles or So Swamps all of which might be termed truly dismal—no birds, no quadrupeds no prospect (Save that of being Jolted)—the waters were all high—it took us 3 hours to Cross the Pedee River in a Canoe &^{c} &^{c} but at last on Sunday last (a week this day) we arrived at Charleston—put up at a boarding house to the owner of which I paid 10½ Dollars for 3 Meals and 2 nights rest—

I delivered my letters to Mr Lowndes who received me as all Strangers are when they present a letter of that Kind and we parted.—I pushed almost out of Town to deliver another to the Revd Mr Gilman.—There I found a Man of learning of Sound heart and willing to bear "The American Woodsman" a hand—he walked with me and—had already contrived to procure us Cheaper Lodgings &^{c} when lo he presented me in the Street to the Revd Mr Backman!—Mr Backman!! why my Lucy Mr Backman would have us all to Stay at his house—he would have us to make free there as if we were at our encampment at the head waters of Some unknown Rivers—he would not Suffer us to proceed farther South for 3 weeks. he talked—he looked as if his heart had been purposely made of the most benevolent Materials granted to Man by the Creator to render all about him most happy—Could I have resented his kind invitation? no!—it would have pained him as much as if grossely insulted. We removed to his house in a crack—found a room already arranged for Henry to Skin our Birds—another for me & Lehman to Draw and a third for thy Husband to rest his bones in on an excellent bed!

An Amiable Wife and Sister in Law Two fine young

Daughters and 3 paires more of Cherubs all of whom I already look upon as if brought up among them =

Out Shooting every Day—Skining, Drawing, Talking Ornithology the whole evening, noon and morning—in a Word my Lucy had I thee and our Dear Boys along I certainly would be as happy a mortal as Mr Backman himself is at this present moment, when he has Just returned from his Congregation—congratulat^d me on my days work and now sets amid his family in a room above and enjoying the results of his days work. This My Dearest Friend is the Situation of thy husband at Charleston South Carolina—Some hopes of one or Two Subscribers are afloat and time will enable me to let thee Know the result—

Charleston is less in Size than Baltimore—it lays flat in front of the Bay—the Population is about 30,000—Politics run high with the Tariff Men I have become acquainted with Several amiable Characters and further I Know not—

I have 3 Drawings under way—about 80 Skins—Some insects &^{c} Lehman and Henry behave well—Our expenses since Richmond Virginia have been very great—I have heard news from no one and that is all I can Say at present.—

I hope thou didst reach home Safely and Victor also—that our Dear John is well and Brother William coining Dollars or Doubloons as fast as he may wish to do So—remember me to all   write to me at St Augustine Florida after this reaches thee as often as thou may please—write often to England and to Nicholas—to Doc Harlan also and believe me thine Friend and husband for ever

To Robert Havell

New York April 20th 1833—

My Dear Mr Havell—

I have Just returned from Philadelphia were I Spent merely Two days to visit a few of my Friends there.—I have found here your letter of the   and I take great pleasure in writing to you although my press of business and of course my time is as nearly taken up as can be.—

The Numbers which you have sent by My Son's Victor's directions are arrived, but not yet out of the Ship.—by the last Packet that Sailed for London I forwarded *all* the numbers which had been here for many months, all of which were perfectly useless in this Country.—You must work them into the Volumes which I have requested Victor to have Coloured & bound as soon as possible.—

You will see, and I know you will be pleased at it, that I have not been slow at procuring Names on this side the Atlantic.—My Subscribers in America now amount to 55.—I procured a new one this day—

The success of My Work depends much on your own exertions in the finishing of the Plates as accuratly as you are able to do, and in seing that the Colourists do their duty.—Knowing you as I do, I naturally expect all your attention—I might speak otherwise had I not Known you So well as I do—*Americans* are *excellent Judges* of Work particularly of Such as are drawn from their Country's Soil—they are proud of every thing that is connected with America, and feel Mortified when ever any thing is done that does not come up to their Sanguine expectations.—

I Hope you will be able to go through the present Second volume early next Spring—after this the *Water Birds* will be a New Area—Allow me to ask of You to see that *the Bills, legs & feet* are *carefully* copied from my Drawings—to Naturalists these points are of the greatest importance—try to Imitate *constantly* the plates of *The Whippoorwill, The Broad Winged Hawk* and the beautiful plate of your Young Eagle of last Year.—in the Small plate soften the tints as much as you can—there will be no End to my Publications of Birds, or (which is the same) of my Sons Publications. My Youngest Son *draws Well*—Can you tell what is his or mine's work in the last Drawings You saw?—I look forward to the time when we Shall meet as a grand Jubilee and of much enjoyment—Can we not work at the 3^d Volume So as to bring out 7 or 8 Numbers per Annum?

My Youngest Son and I are going a long & tedious Journey this Spring & Summer.—I intend to Visit the Whole coast of

Labrador into Hudson's Bay and reach quebec by returning over Land—No White Man has ever tramped the Country I am about to Visit, and I hope the result will prove profitable to all Concerned.—I am heartily glad that my Son and you agree and go on So well.—all I regret is the unquiet State of England with Ireland—it Seems that this, in a very great measure puts a Stop to our business in England at least.—

After I leave this which will be on the 1ˢᵗ of May I Shall have no opportunities at all to hear from England until my return—there are *no Post offices in the Wilderness before us*—I therefor ask of You to do your best and contact My Son who is my Right Arm and hand in every thing connected with my Publication—he will pay you punctually as I have done myself and I am sure the more you Know him the more you will like him and be pleased with him.—

Do not think for a moment that I am *lecturing* You.—I have no Such thoughts—but merely wish to enjoin you to Keep a Masters eye over the Work in each of its departments.—Who Knows but that your Name if not your fortune is now connected with Mine and with my Familly?—

My good Wife & Son here Join in best wishes to you & your Dear Wife & Children and I remain as ever Your Friend

To Victor G. Audubon

New York 15ᵗʰ Sepʳ 1833—
My Dear Victor.—We have no news from you since my arrival here. indeed not a packet has come.—Since my last to you, we have been very much engaged at finishing Several Drawings belonging to the Two Numbers and the 3 extra Drawings, which I will forward you by the Packet of the 20ᵗʰ Instant direct to London.

It is several Years since my desire to prepare a reduced sise Edition of the Birds of America has existed in my mind; and as I Still look upon Such an edition as on the greatest profits we are to desire from our Publications I wish you to think of this undertaking carefully and cautiously—

An Edition of the size of the present Small plates cut down
So as to leave merely a Suficient margin, *perhaps* would prove
the best Size for all the plates—and if all the present Small
plates would answer after being carefully retouched and better finished, it would certainly prove a great saving in the expense besides which, all the Small birds would Stil be given
the Size of Nature.—The Midle and Large plates only would
have to be reduced, and *perhaps* again it would not be requisite to give *all the figures* represented in these large and midle
size plates; although to have them reduced Entire from the
original Drawings, might prove more acceptable to pur-
chasers—no Colouring to enter in this Edition—the letter
press attached to the plates, as in Wilson, Bonaparte and others.—The price of our great Work is Such that besides Public
Institutions and Men of great Wealth, few copies only can we
expect to sell without waiting patiently for opportunities to
do so.—A reduced Edition would be within almost every persons compass, and I believe would meet with a great Sale
both in Europe and in our Country—this Second Edition not
to appear before the Public or indeed not even to be thought
of or mentioned by *any one besides ourselves* until the full
Completion of our great Work—*but to be ready* if possible
from that moment—*the Trade* would take it with advantage
to ourselves &c. Now Should your Ideas coincide with mine
on this undertaking, it would be well for you to seek out a
trusty Engraver who would undertake the whole of the
Engraving, and who would go on with it at once, one possessed of Such talents as would answer to our wishes in the
Style of the Workmanship—Yourself taking out of his hands
into your possession each plate as soon as approved by yourself and Kept in good Order and Insured (*by the Way do you
see to the full Insurance of the present plates—Havell has Insured them for me, but I never saw the Policy and you never
have mentioned this subject. do so when next you write to us.*) *If
we can Spare the funds* for Such an undertaking My opinion is,
that the money which we can Spare could not be better employed—the Plates might be either on Copper on Steel or on
Wood, and the size of the Edition either that of the present
Small plates, or that of Bewick's Birds or of that of "*the
Zooligical Gardens*"—this I would leave to your taste, pru-

dence or Wishes—perhaps indeed Bewicks Size would prove the best if the Wood Cuts were equally good as his, Cheaper than any other and consequently more profitable to us all. Our Friend G. J. Children you can fully consider in, and to speak to him respecting this might prove advantageous—try to have Estimates, Know what number of impressions Wood, Copper or Steel would give and above all which might prove, the cheapest, best and most salable as well as well come or accepted by the Public at Large—Would France or Germany or England prove the best Country to carry on this enterprise— in a word act on this with the same prudence, care and taste which you have So well Shewn, since you have been at the Wheel in England. at all events let us know your thoughts on the Subject—

Our Friend Ed^d Harriss desires that you will order a Gun for him, Such as you sent for W. Bakewell, but which is now Brother John, and is the best Gun *Conway* of Manchester ever made. = to be forwarded to New York as soon as possible.—the size, weight & *quality* of *the Whole* full as good as that of John's—a pair of Extra Main Springs, Cocks and Several paires of Nipples—attend to this at once—Send the bill &^{c} in one common Pine box well secured from the Water and Insured.—

I have examined N°s 32 and 33. and must say that I look on these 10 plates as the best I ever saw of birds and that they do *Havell* and YOURSELF my beloved Son great credit—every thing is better—the birds are fac Simile of my Drawings—Soft and beautiful the Colouring is Clear transparent and true to Nature—the plants are Seriously better—I am delighted— never was *a Crow* for Instance represented in print before now.—If Havell goes on in this present Styles and principle, I will be bound that neither I or you will have a word of Complaint about his Works.—tell him this.—The little black capt Titmouse is not dark enough on the back and in my Drawing there must be *a White Spot at the lower end of the black cap* next the shoulders—this white Spot distinguishes our bird from the European of the Same name, *which is* a diferent Species.—See to that at once.—

If you can possibly do without me in England for another Year acquaint me immediatly—do the same Should the case prove vice versa. let me Know at what time *Water Birds* will be wanted in London ready for Publication to enable one to send you Some from here to add to some which you have.—

I hope the 20 Volumes will soon arrive here and that I will find them coloured after the new plan—I think I can dispose of these in the course of my approaching Campaign after Subscribers.—it is our Intention to leave this the day after the Packet which will carry the Drawings for the Completion of the 2ᵈ Volume will sail. the 20ᵗʰ Instant.—I will finish the manuscript for the letter press of the 2ᵈ Volume this Winter at Charleston—John Bachman has Studied the Habits of our birds for many many Years, and I Shall be quiet and comfortable under his roof—John will finish the Drawings begun &ᶜ—Mamma will not Suffer from Cold—when at Washington City I will try to have the Charleston Cutter at my orders for a while in the course of next Spring it is commanded by the same Captain who took me to the Floridas (Capⁿ Day) in a New Ship Called the Mᶜ Lane &ᶜ and if I have time, I will proceed in her as far as Tampico and take a Turn by the Arkansaw River &ᶜ—

I Shall expect that Havell will Engrave the 3 Small extra plates at the usual price of those Plates, and Charge the Colouring of them in the usual proportion also.—God bless You My Dear Victor—we are all Well and all unite in the same good Wishes for your health and Happiness.—

Your affectionatly Father & Friend

To John Bachman

London, 25ᵗʰ August 1834—

My Dear Bachman.—

You really are a Lazy Fellow!—I have been in England—Four months, have written to you God knows how often, and yet the *only* letter I have received from you reached us 15 Minutes ago.—Now when I receive letters I write in Answer at once you see; and If I receive none, I keep hammering at My

Friends doors like a Woodpecker on the bark of Some Tough
Tree, the inside of which It longs to see—

Your letter is of July 22^d and was most welcome I assure
you—To See your dear hand Writing has quite raised our
Spirits, the more especially as you give us intelligence of All
being well & Happy under your Roof. I wish I was there also,
for betwen you & I and the post I Hate this infernal Smoaky
London as I do the Devil!!—

I hear nothing more of Watterton—Your paper certainly
"used him up" and I have no one to trouble me on the like
Scores—I am heartily glad that what the *honest* Gentleman
Said of me has *So well* insured *his purpose*—Tell my Sweet
heart, and *our* Dear Daughters that I am most happy to hear
of their perseverance Industry and augmentation of their acquirements.—Tomorow we forward them Some Dresses,
Prints, and a book of Instruction in the Art of Painting
Miniatures given us by Cruickshank. Also a Box Containing a
2^d Volume for Mr Rees, and the Numbers for Charleston &
Columbia.—All those deliver and receive the money for.—*as
Soon as you Can!* We are going on now bravely, the 4th and 5th
Numbers of Water Birds are engraved, and the 3 which you
will see with this will give you an Idea of how they look.—We
will publish 7 Numbers of Water Birds by Decr next.—and 10
Next Year and So on to the Completion of the Work.—

As it seems that you have received only 4 lines from me, I
must repeat a great deal, and here goes.—

I have written So constantly for Two Months, that I was
obliged to leave off after having finished 100 Articles of
Biography and 13. Episodes.—I became swelled as I was at
your house &^{c} and have been Idle these 10 days to assist my
recovery—Mc Gillivray is assisting me as before, he says this
Volume will be Much superior to the first, & Larger—the fact
is that My late transfer, and our *Visitation* to you was of the
greatest benefit immaginable to My Studies—Since here I
have read, Selby's and Temminck's Works, but they are I am
sorry to say *not from Nature.* not a word could I find in them
but what was compilation.—I could not even be told at what
time the Golden Eagle laid her Eggs in Europe! Sir W^{am}
Jardine is published an enormous quantity of Trash all
Compilation, and takes the undue liberty of giving *figures*

from My Work and those of all others who may best suit his views.—

Mr Gould is publishing the Birds of England, of Europe &^{c} &^{c} &^{c}—in all sorts of Ways—Swainson has 17 Volumes in his head and on paper half finished.—I have seen him Twice only.—Yarrel who is a first rate *Naturalist* and a most excellent Man, is now publishing a beautiful Work (Wood Cuts) on the Fishes of this Country—Two Brothers *Meyers* are also publishing the Birds of England—in fact You could not pass a Bookseller's Shop from the extreme "West end" to Wapping without seing New books on Zoology in every Window—and "at most reduced Prices"!—Swainson has he says upward of 50,000 Insects! and more Bird Skins than his house will hold.—

Henry Ward is on the Pavé, a poor Miserable object who can Scarcely Make out a living for his Wife & himself—he exchanged, Sold &^{c} all his Bird Skins—pulled off the whole of his Stolen White Herons feathers; Sold these to the Shops for Ladies head dresses, and the mutilated Skins to a Jew, who offered them to Havell at ½ a Dollar apiece.—I Sold 52 pounds Sterling of Skins to the British Museum about a Month ago —and again 25£ worth Two days ago—& Havell has Sold a good Number More.—So I Shall not be a looser in that way.—My own *Double* Collection I have in Drawers at home—

Charles Bonaparte has written very kindly to Me, and it appears that what W^{am} Cooper of New York told me was Fudge.—On the 8th of Next Month about 500 Philosophers on Zoology will Meet at Edinburgh from all parts of these Mighty British Isles—I have other fish to fry—I go to Manchester &^{c} &^{c} to see the *Whole* of my Patrons, Start next Saturday and will be absent about one month or so, after which to France I go for another Month and on my return begin the printing of the 2^d Vol^e of Biographies.—This Coming Winter, I will Spend at Writing My *own Biography* to be published as soon as possible and to be Continued as God May be pleased to grant me Life!

Our Dear Sons are Studying every day—My Old Friend mends our socks Makes our Shirts, Reads to us at times, but drank No brandy Now a days—She has cast off her purchased

Sham Curls, wears her own dear grey locks and looks all the
better—John Can make a pretty good Portrait in black Chalk
and Victor a pretty Landscape in Oil.—They are studying
Music & other Matters—on the Whole we are Happy and
Contented as much as can be whilt absent from our Dear &
beloved Friends of Charleston.—Tell my Sweet heart, that
Cruikshank has Improved my Miniature very Considerably—
he has worked over the Hair &ᶜ—this picture goes to *Turner*
to be Engraved in Mezzotinto and you all shall hear report.
hereafter.—

Your having Shot a Chaffinch is indeed Curious enough;
but not More So than my having Seen a Yellow billed Cuckoo
Shot within 40 Miles of London.—

The Town is now what is called "*Empty*" that is the
Grandies are off Shooting Partridges, Grous hares & Pheasants—Parliament is prorogued and there is in fact not more
than a Million and half of People in town, one good or
bad half of whom are Beggars, thiefs & Blagguards of all
sorts—We have an unacountably hot Summer—indeed Just
Such as I Might have expected at New York.—Fruit has been
aboundant and Peaches has lowered in price to 25ᶜᵗˢ! The The-
atres, and Shows of all sorts prodigiously Crammed—as are
Now the different Watering places of Britain.—Victor told us
on his return from Paris, the Population there appeared as if
constituted of English alone—A few Cases of Cholera have
appeared but London is now healthy.—The queen of these
Realms has returned in perfect Safety, she was hissed at her
departure and groaned at on her return—The Irish are fighting like Devils and I hope their rows will open the Eyes of
their Merciless Landlords—

Now my Dear Bachman nothing in this World will give
more pleasure than to go with you to the Floridas and if You
will prepare yourself for November *1835* God willing I will be
your Companion there, and as much further as you chuse.—
this Year it is Impossible for I have much to do ere I return
to our Dear Shores, and I look upon my labours as a duty I
owe to My Familly and to My Almighty Maker.

When ever you have a good Opportunity of preserving *excellent* Wild Turkey Cocks Skins pray do so—the only one I
had, I have Sold for 20£ or *100 Dollars*! a female I Sold for

25$.—and if I had 50 Males I could get the same prices for each of them—Fine Anhingas, Small blue Herons—and Clean White Egrets Sell well—Insects are now very high.—I paid 20 Dollars the other day for 5 which on a/c of their beauty have been thought Cheap by Swainson. Common birds from any portion of the World are mere Drug.—I have some promisses of fine Dogs after the Shooting Season is over—and I hope to send you Some Shortly as I will be at Lord Stanleys Manor in about 2 Weeks.—

The Old Zoological Gardens are Much poorer than when I left England.—The New ones Carry the Day—in fact Novelty is the Motto of every Englishman and Scarcely any thing can live here longer than a Month at Most.—one Week generally sufices to kill the Integrity of general Subjects in exhibitions of all Sorts.—

What are Ravenell and Lightner doing—Maria sent us word that the former had gone to the Floridas.—& that the latter was delivering lectures.—I Shall have no objection to the Ladies D[   ]etting & Seeying the Aimiable Mr Dawson.—how is your Mother—and our good Friends the Lees and Mrs Davis? how is our good Doc^r Beau Wilson and the estimable W^{am} Kunhardt at this distance from you and all these Worthy Friends, depend upon it, the pleasure of hearing from them is always great & welcome—Tell Young Strobel that his Watch although long in Coming will be a good one.—is your Sister's health quite recovered (I mean Mrs Strobel) Where is B. Strobell?—remember us to Doc^r Frost and others.—

I send you My own Copy of Bewicks Works.—and also a Pamphlet on Swans from Yarrel.—and Why did you not Send me the Eggs of the Chuck Will's Widow & "other Matters"—I Might no doubt have had Some further opportunities of Speaking of these in my 2^d Volume.—I left at Your House several Drawings which I Want—send them to the Messrs Rathbone Brothers & Co Merchants Cornhill Liverpool.—or to Robt Havell if you have an opp^y for London.—

Now here is My 4th or 5th Episode to You and I beg an answer—With sincerest good Wishes from All to All believe me

ever Your faithful Friend

To John Bachman

Edinburgh Decr 3^d 1834.—

My Dear Backman.—

Six more days will finish the printing of the 2^d Vol. of ornithological Biographies! think how pleased I shall be when, I fully find myself half way in my Carier.—the week following that I shall send you a Copy direct to Charleston and you may yet be the first to read it in our Country.—I am quite Surprised at the extreme rarity of your letters to me.—Do Write to me at least as often as I to you—and when you write send me *abundance!*

If you have a chance of determining the Habits of Strix Flammea do so, especially the time of incubation, and dates of their depositing their eggs.—try to procure Some alive and Watch their Habits then.—Can you through Doc^r Wilson find the nest of Falco Dispar, eggs, &^{c}—you Know Ward Shot them on the Santee River.—also the eggs and as much of the Habits of the Anhinga or Snake bird.—Nest & eggs of the *Long billed Curlew.*—Watch all Bank Swallows closely, we have I believe 2 *Species* in America.—Watch the Night Heron too, for there exists a great difference of opinions in this country respecting their bird & ours—try for the Habits of the fresh Water Marsh Hen all you Can, also those of the Water Hen.—all you Can for Macgillivray's finch.—Indeed When ever you have leisure, I wish you would Make Observations and *Write them down!* Study all our *Dear Herons* as much as you Can also.—

I regret very much that Doc^r Leitner did not give us in writing his curious experiments on the Buzzard it would have come So well in my article on this species. Could you not get this from him and take care of it for us hereafter, for I doubt if he will publish himself?—

In my last I mentioned to you that Sir W^{am} Jardine receives a great number of Birds from Charleston—nay I am told that his Collection of our Birds is superb—I do not *treat* with him any more since he took it upon himself to republish some of my plates without leave.—do try to seek *his Friend* at Charleston.—

We intend returning to London in the Course of a fort-night, and as soon as there, I am going to set to and *Write* my 3ᵈ Vol. of biographies.—*My Life*, and prepare to go to America where I hope to find you one and All in good health & Happy!—

Birds eggs! Bird Eggs I long for!!—and another thing too, which is Money of which I wish I had a glorious Mint Just Now!—

The Museum here is now much improved and is very fine, thousands of Specimen that would please you to see and to study I am sure.—

I see *another* life of Wilson by Peabody of Boston, and *Another* is now preparing here for the press, so that poor Wilson will have lives enough after all; besides that of his eternal glory!

The Reviewers here are all agog waiting for my Volume, and I understand on the watch for general defence or attack on Waterton, ord & others.—what Shocking disapointment! —not a Word is there in the whole book even in Allu-sion to these beetles of darkness!—Black Wood Magazine Will Shine again, and So will Jameson's Journal.—Now when *you* have read the book do try and give it an honest pull in your own Way.—I have now Some hopes of being reviewed by *Ornithologists*, you are One and I expect Much from you. You will find the Name of John Bachman at least once in my book and that of our Dear Sweetheart at least Twice.—The title of the 20 Episodes are regularly as follows.—

The Runaway. a Curious subject you will say.—
The Lost one.—Melancholic tale
Force of the Waters.—
Squatters of Mississipi
Squatters of Labrador
Death of a Pirate
a ball at Newfoundland
Live Oakers.—
excursion in the Floridas—
Sᵗ John's River there.—
Florida Keys.—
D.°—D.°—continued
The Turtlers—

Burning of the Forests—
Moose Hunt—
Journey in New brunswick & Maine—
Bay of Fundy—
Codfishing at Labrador.—
Merchant of Savannah
Kentucky Barbecue.—
all of these; food for the Idle!

And Now my Dear Bachman the Printer's devill is come and I must close with our sincerest best Wishes & thancks to you and all under your Dear Hospitable roof.—adieu—

Yours

A Joiner's bill for Jobbing a Chapel in Bohemia. "For Solidly repairing St Joseph 4^d for cleaning and ornamenting the Holy ghost 6^d; for repairing the Virgin Mary before and behind, and making her Child 5 Shillings for turning a nose for the devil, putting a Horn upon his head and glueing a piece to his tail 4/6.^{d} Total 10/4!—"

The above is a literal translation from the German for your own amusement—

To John Bachman

London April 20th 1835.—To J. Bachman—

My 4th and last Vol. will contain (as far as I now Know) 125 Species—and glad Shall I be when I see or if I See the last plate *coloured*?

Here there are at present three Works publishing on the Birds of Europe—one by Mr Gould and the others by No one Knows who—at least I do not Know—Works on the Birds of *all the World* are innumerable—Cheap as dirt and more dirty than dirt—Sir William Jardine will encumber the Whole of God's Creation with Stuff as little like the objects of the Creator's formations as the Moon is unto Cheese—but who cares? as long as these miscellanies bring forth 5 Shillings per Vol to the pocket bag of the one who produces them as a

Hen that Hatches *Duck Eggs*, and whom I have no doubt is as much Surprised to see his progeniture go to Market as the Hen is at seing her Webbed brood take to the Water—but after all, *Ornithological Times*, are fast going bye—by the time my Work will be done the World will have ceased to think that such beings as birds exist under Heaven's canopy—Bugs—fishes and reptiles are, and will then go for a time—then geology will Move heavily above, as well as through the Earth—Africa will cease to be an unknown land—for ought I know the North passage into the Pacific will become easier of performance to Steamers, than the passage of one of Such Vehicles is now to the bar of Charleston—people will dive into the Antipodes—Fishes will Swim on Earth—quadrupeds all will fly, and birds exchanging their present Natures will build *churches* and again become the rage of the times!—

It is late—I must to my bed, and will proceed with more nonsense and some sense Tomorow—Good night. all—

It is now after our dinner; we are setting all around our little table—Talking and thinking deeply of our Friends in America—Nay the glasses have been Knocked together and a Sound health wished to every one and all; *connectively* and individually.—and Now my Worthy Friend I will go on with my notions, facts, and parables!—

This afternoon I attended a public auction of Sundries.—My Friend Thomas McCulloch' of Pictou, Nova Scotia, had there for Sale about 400 well *Mounted* Birds, all of which were disposed of—for how much do you think?—Why not exceeding 50 Dollars. Havell bought the great number of them—thus you May Judge of the value of Birds at present in London—McCulloch whilt in Nova Scotia, refused 500 pounds for this collection!—when he came here with it, he thought that at least that amount would be realised—Now *I* purchased about 15 pounds worth—and a few others bought to nearly double that sum—he refused 20 Dollars six weeks ago, for a Snowy Owl, that this afternoon produced Just 25 *cents*!! and all this because the World is all egog—for what? for *Bugs* the Size of *Water Melons*!—There is in fact a Bug, now in Havell's Shop for which the owner aske^d—how Much?—once, Twice, thrice?—you give it up?—no Less than 50 pounds Sterling!—250 Dollars for a Beetle—as large as my

fist it is true, but nought but a beetle after all—30 Guineas
have offered and *refused*—I almost wish I could be turned
into a Beetle myself!—by the way My Friend Melly is here—
he has called Twice upon us, and assured me that more than
8 Months since he sent you many hundred *Insects*, wrote to
you &ᶜ—because I assured him that you would be delighted
to enter into a corespondance with him, on Entomology—
but not a word has he had from you—his Insects were
Shipped direct from Liverpool to Charleston—Look out My
Friend, or you will have Some *Water*(Ton)-*beetle* about your
ears—do write to my learned Friend, who is besides, a most
excellent Man, and who has a collection of 13,000 Species of
Insects *named* and *described*—

I have agreed to exchange a Copy of my Work with Mʳ
Gould, for his publications—and have by me, 13 Numbers of
his Birds of Europe—his Century of Hymealan Birds—and
his Monograph of Trogons—I have also purchased a monograph of Parrots from a Mʳ Lear—When you & I are Old
Men—how pleasing it will be to us to look at these together—to quiz them all, and pass our *Veto* upon them!

Gould is a Man of great industry—has the advantage of
the Zoological Society's Museums, Gardens &ᶜ—and is in
corespondance with Temminck, Jardine, Selby, James Wilson
and the rest of the Scientific Gentry—his *Wife* makes his
drawings on Stone—She is a plain fine Woman, and although
their Works are not quite up to Nature, both deserve great
credit.—

Charles Bonaparte has not written to me for Many
Months—his Work on american Birds I fear is entirely
Stopped—France denied him the privilege of going there—
Most Shameful our days—

I expect Harlan to be elected a Fellow of the Linnean Society on the 25ᵗʰ Instant—he was to have been elected also at the
Zoological Society, but a revolution has taken place there
—Parties run high—Vigors is about to be dismissed the Council—&ᶜ &ᶜ—I shall attend the anniversary Meeting on the 29ᵗʰ
when it is expected that warm debates will take place—thank
goodness I have Nought to do in all those broils—

Swainson has lost his Wife, and I fear much of the good
opinion of the Scientific World—the Reviewers have spoken

Severely against him of late, and he very foolishly has answered to them—and lo! they have returned Such cuts, as would wound a heart of adamant—

When my 2.^{d} Vol. of Biog.' came out, he had a Copy—Now, my Vol. was not very favourable to all he says of our birds—therefore, he did not answer my letter to him—I wrote again, and again had no answer—his Wife died—I wrote to him a letter of condolance—offered him my services and my person and at last had a good letter from him—this is now more than two Months—not a word more from him, and *he is* Now in London but never has come near us—he suffers his Temper to run away with his good Sense—how many Men there are in this World who *suffer* through this wonderful medium?—

My Intention is to go to America with John next April or May—this time Twelve months—No more subscribers are, or can be expected in this Country—I hope I may gather Some in our dear own Land?? and take a tremendous concluding Journey, the Lord Knows where—but I Shall certainly go through the "Ever Glades" of Florida, then to the Mouth of the Sabine River and up it into the broad Prairies—I love the Prairies! and then on to the Rocky Mountains and——— So much for an Old Man!—before I leave England—the *whole* of my Letter press will be ready for Publication—My Life Shall be written—and Should death Stare me in the face, I shall Laugh at her, as being quite too late to hurt *my feelings!!*—Now I think I have written long enough to you—I wish to write to our Dear Sweet heart also, and thank her as well as you—we all Join in Kindest remembrances to all (do not forget Maria) and believe us ever your truest and Most sincerely attached Friend

To John Bachman

London Jany 22^d 1836.—

My Worthy Friend.—

The First Number of the *last* Volume of "The Birds of America" is now under the graver, and my Friend Robt Havell

Tells me that unless *I* keep him back, the Enormous Work will be finished and Compleat in *22 Months*, from this date!! how delicious is the Idea, and how comfortable Should I feel at this moment were I able fully to say to Havell *you shall not be detained a Moment!* But there are drawbacks in all undertakings, and in mine especially numerous ones—Nay I have Stil to Cross the broad Atlantic Twice at least, and go, and ransack the Wildest portions of our Southern Country.—Now if by the assistance of some one or Two, or more, *Worthy Friends*, Time might be saved me in Some portions of our Country I would the better be enabled to ransack others the more and the More effectually.—To render my *present* publication a Standard Work, I feel extremely desirous to do all in my power, as well as in the power of those who love and esteem me and are able to assist Me, to derive all imaginable *assistance* from all and every one with whom I am now acquainted with, and on whom I think I might look upon with reliance.—You my Dear Bachman are foremost on the list! Then to you I Now address myself as if the Man in distress for the want of that relief which May at all times be desired from a Friendly Christian!—Then take to your Gun at all your *leisure hours*, go the Woods, and go to the Shores, or if you Cannot at all, send Some Worthy one on whom you can and I Also Can depend—Note down every INSIGNIFI-CANT Incident brought forth to your Eye, and to your Minds eye, for of Course any Incident of Consequence, will compt one and these I am sure you will not forget to WRITE DOWN! Measure, the depth, the diametrical width, of every Nest you Meet with this *Coming Spring*—Mark the Substance of their outward and Inner formation.—See to the period of the first Deposits of the Eggs, ennumerate them—Nay measure them as the Nest themselves, save the Shells if you Can, but at all events describe them in *Writing* and on *the Spot!* What ever Yunglings you Meet with do describe, or put them in plain Whisky or common Rum, the Cheapest will answer for that as if the very best.—And Now When ever you secure an Adult, down with it in Spirits also with a Memorandum of the Date of your procuring the Same.—*Look not to the expense* in any portion of this for God granting me life I Shall pay for all, except for your own trouble, and that Must ever remain an unsettled account, which *Science* may *perhaps* some days balance with you—

Now My Dear Friend, do pray think of this, and recollect that in Twenty Two Months after you have received this letter, all exertions will be useless and as it were quite dead and for ever gone by.—recollect that my Efforts, and your efforts in this precious instance are all meant, and intended for the Sake of *our own* Dear Children, nay for ourselves Too! Now what I ask of you, to Me appears quite a simple affair.—Carolinians are Carolinians Stil, and well I remember how Kindly I was and hope Still to be treated by them.—Write a Circular to each of our Friends, request of them to go "a Shooting" Twice or thrice, Nay if you please put a general advertisement in the News Papers of Charleston (and I know they are all Friends of Science through their Editors) and request *every Man*, to send you Specimen's In.—have Barrells, or Jarrs, or Gallipots prepared of all Sorts and sizes, and in these place the Specimen and then have them Covered to the Brim with Common Whiskey or Rum. In this Manner you will procure in a fortnight of exertions *All* that South Carolina can afford.—and Should I not reach You before the *Warm weather setts in*, then have what you May have on hand Shipped either to Liverpool or to London—to the first place Care of Messrs Rathbone, and to the Latter Care of Robt Havell:—Now when I tell you that I want every Bird, I do indeed Mean every one that Can be procured from a paire of Turkey Buzzards, and a paire of Carrion Crows to any other Species whatever! but *one paire* will do provided you are assured of the Sexes being settled or ascertained, and as confusion might take place in the numbers of Species placed in a Barrell, it would be well to Keep, or Send Me a regular list of each Barrel's Contents—If you can Keep my Intentions secret, so much the Better—they are as follows—I am extremely desirous to give such Anatomical descriptions of each Species, as May here after lead to the formmation of a *positively Natural System* Without a Word of humbug or *theory!* and depend upon it that it prove Sooner or later the only Way to ascertain *even Species!*—Now Once More and I then Shall close the Subject, procure Me if you possibly Can *every Species* to be found Within Twenty Miles of Charleston IN THE

FLESH and in Spirits, Take Bonaparte's Synopsis and let it be your Guide, besides Yours and Mine own Discoveries.—the Wild Turkey to the Anhinga.—all Sorts of Herons, Hawks, Eagles, Marsh Hens—Grus, down to the very Sparrows all are wanted.—Gulls—Cormorants, Ducks, Geese &c &c &c.—All! All!!!—*Should Two hundred Species Cost Four hundred Dollars* Never Mind that.—do it and that is simply what I ask of You to do.—It will save Me One Year of Shooting and of ransacking the Woods singly, and with your Friends Two or Three "Battues" would do Miracles in this Way.—

Then to the Custom House do you go, and beg and pray of the Collector, and I hope it is the Same Worthy one, to ask of the Commanders of the Revenue Cutters that ply along the Florida Coast or *elsewhere* to do the same thing on all occasions, and if fortunate enough, I Shall indeed be enabled to leave behind us a Memento that Audubon was not unworthy of his Country!—beyond which all is trash in this World! Now to other Subjects.—I have Shipped per Packet "the England" Three hundred Copies of the third Volume of my Text, in six Boxes each Containing Fifty Copies, and have directed Mr Berthoud of New York to send One Case of these Volumes to your Care, and I Now beg of you to have them *Sold Not Given away! Here* that Volume has been fondly reviewed and is spoken of as far better than the formers, and I am proud of this in as much as the *Habits* of our Water Birds was not understood by the Great Wilson!

The Fire at New York has destroyed the whole of our Library.—our Bedding, Sheets, Implements of Drawing &c &c &c and *our Guns*. So that I am obliged to have Guns at least Made a new.—The Riots at Baltimore were also much against Us and there we have lost many a Number unpaid and undelivered of the Birds of America—Here, we thank God go on well, and are prospering, although Just Now we pay 200£ rent for the House we are in—No 58 is finished and Will be forwarded to America Next Week—No 59 up to plate 295 is already engraved, So that in Two Months from this date, I shall have at least exceeded Wilson in Numeric Species.—You will read of the Reviews here, and therefor I Must remain Mum on that Subject.—

Tell our Sweetheart that *whatever* Drawings She May have

on hand and ready for me, the Sooner She Sends them the better. I will pay her in Kisses at least when I Meet you all.

John and his Brother are now engaged at Copying in Oil a Picture of mine which I Sold the other day for One Hundred Guineas.—*and you may yet See the Copy.*—

I am happy to hear that no War is to take place between us and the French, at all events so the full impression here, and in Paris.—John and Myself propose to be with you all Sometimes Next Summer When I expect *you* will be ready to go along with us to the Sabine River &^{c}—

My Friend MacGillivray has published a Work on Ornithology which he has dedicated to Me, and as I Know him to be in fact my Friend I am quite proud of Such a Compliment from one of so much talent and Intrinsic Worth.—

We are all Well, hope that you are all in the same like plight and that yourselves and ourselves will continue to be So, and with Love and sincerest good wishes from all to all I wish you to believe me ever Your

Sincerest and Most attached Friend

I wish you *to keep* all that you may collect in Spirits for me, until we Meet under your roof, as I may then *describe* the Inner Structure of each Species, and thereby save much freight and extra expense.—Keep them in a cool place and now once more adieu.

To John Bachman

Mobile Feby. 24th 1837—

My Dearest Friends—

We left Charleston on the 17th Instant (Ed^d Harris, John & I) and arrived here last night. Our Journey was performed, first by the Railroad to Augusta, a pretty Village in Georgia— the weather was extremely cold; nay the Ice in the morning of the 18th was one half Inch deep.—at Augusta we took the Mail, and luckily for us had no others than ourselves in the coach—the roads, in Consequence of several previous days & nights of rain were as bad as can be; but we proceeded apace and had no accidents—having crossed Georgia, we entered the State of Alabama after crossing a bridge at Columbus—here the Swamps were Shockingly bad, and we feared that our goods & Chattels would have been wetted, but thanks to our Yankee Drivers (*the very best in the World*) all was Kept dry as corks—The next morning we breakfasted at the Village of   where 100 Creek Warriors were confined in Irons, preparatory to leaving for ever the Land of their births!—Some Miles onward we overtook about Two thousands of These once free owners of the Forest, marching towards this place under an escort of Rangers, and militia mounted Men, destined for distant Lands, unknown to them, and where alas, their future and latter days Must be Spent in the deepest of Sorrows, affliction and perhaps even phisical want—This View produced on my Mind an aflicting series of reflections more powerfuly felt than easy of description—the Numerous groups of Warriors, of half clad females and of naked babes, trudging through the Mire under the residue of their ever Scanty Stock of Camp furniture, and household uttensiles—the evident regret expressed in the masked countenances of Some, and the tears of others—the howlings of their numerous Dogs; and the cool demeanour of the Chiefs—all formed Such a Picture as I hope I never will again witness in reality—had Victor being with us, ample indeed would have been his means to paint Indians in sorrow—

We reached Montgomery at Night—remained there until 10 of the next day, and on board of a Steamer, Made down the River alabama—a Stream which although Much Smaller than the Mississipi resembles it very much.—like it, it is muddy, winding, and lined on its Shores, by heavy cane brakes, and bluffs of various elevations & formations—

Our Intentions to Visit the Famillies of our Friends the Lees were abandoned, and I wrote to them in Stead—We heard from different persons that they were all well Doing and in good health.—We Saw Many Southern Birds, but felt no difference in the climate—Indeed even *here*, the weather is cool, and the Country exhibits no appearance of Spring—

Our first enquiry at this place was for Judge Hitchcock, but he is absent—a Mr Martineau answered in his Stead, and introduced us to the Collector of Mobile, who in turn presented us to Cap^n Foster, who Commands a Cutter; a Jolly old Gentleman, who gave us to understand that he Should like a Tour with us, *provided* I could obtain Commodore Dallas' permission to do so.—he gave us some pleasing information of desired birds &^c, and we have concluded to go to Pensacola Tomorow, by Steamer to pay our regards to the Commodore.—our Intention is to Spend but one day there; to return here, and await the receipt of answers to letters sent to Mr Grimshaw and Cap^n Coste, who we are told is on the New orleans Station, and now at that place—thus far you perceive we are unabled to form our plans; but expect to be able to do so very soon, when I Shall not fail to give you all desirable information—

Mobile is a Small, compact, thriving place, of goodly appearance—there are about 10 Steamers that Ply up the Mobile & alabama Rivers—Some to New Orleans *daily*—and also Some to Pensacola *daily*—the Country around is flat & Swampy, and the accounts of the healthiness of the place, So varied that no one can depend on what is said on the Subject; at the exception, that the population is about 13,000 people during winter, and that in July & August, it is reduced to about 5,000!—to me this, and what I have seen, is suficient— My Mind therefor is made up never to seek refuge (Much less health) in either the Lower parts of alabama or any of our *Southern States*—

Need I say to You all, how dearly glad we Would be, to be enabled suddenly to accompany you to Church on Sunday next? I believe not!—My Spirits are not above par I assure you and this day, I have suffered much from the [   ] of Drinking *alabama Water*—Tomorow I expect to be cured, by a dance over the Waters of the Mexican Gulph—and then all will be right again—

John Bachman my Friend, the Salamanders are Stil asleep— Hares we have seen none of—Parokeets, by the hundreds, and also Wild Pigeons, and *Hutchins'* Geese—at Augusta Doc^r Wray was very Kind to us—here We have seen Frank Lee, who looks well, and is Happy—I wish I was as fortunate! Mr Logan leaves out of Town and we have not had time to

Call upon him, but will do so on our return—our expenses to
this place have amounted to *nearly* 200$—My Sweet heart
will be So good as to Write to My Lucy, and give her the *interest* if any of this letter—I send my Love to you all, and
thousands of Kisses on the wing—and now God bless you all
and believe me ever yours truly attached & sincere & thankful Friend

To John Bachman

London Octr 4th 1837.—

My Dear Friend.—

We received your *first letter* of the 16th of August last, Two
days ago, and curious enough it was that *you* Should have
then felt dumpish and Lazy, whilst all of us here, were happy
and Industriously employed.—When with you, you must recollect, that we often spoke of the very long time required to
receive answers to letters written on different sides of the Atlantic, and if to this you write once in three of Four Months,
why, we may wait long enough.—

We are glad to hear that all are not quite so Lazy as you acknowledge yourself to be, under your Roof.—As to my "regular built Love letters" to our sweet heart, I cannot think
what you have to do with them—and I can assure you that I
will continue to Speak to her, to Kiss her, and to Love her as
far as She may permit me to do without ever troubling myself
as regards your thoughts on the subject.—

Just as I had finished the last line, we heard a crash in the
Dining room below, Lucy went to enquire, and we soon
heard that a *Cat* had thrown down the Cage which contained
Maria's Sweet Grosbeak!—Off John & I flew both armed
with Pokers, and you know what Pokers can do? Mr Puss had
gone below Stairs into the Kitchen, and there we also made
our Way—Doors all to in a crack.—Pussy like all other sinners
much disconfitured.—Under the tables,—up towards the
windows—Would not do.—the first Stroke of my Teazers
confounded Mr Puss; John touched (Slightly) a few more

times; and taking the Devil by the Tail it was launched on the Pavement.—And the Bird is now quite safe, for I have passed a resolution that no Cat Shall poach on our grounds.—but now I will return to your letter.—

I am delighted to hear you say that you have *One* egg of the Flamingo for me, but when shall I see it is another affair?—You say also that you have young ones under way to make experiments as regards their progressive changes of plumage, but would it not be much better to send me one of these young birds to figure (a thing quite new to the World of Science) and thereby enable ourselves to fulfil the whole of our enquiries respecting this very remarkable Bird?—I have noted what you have gathered of their habits—but to Me the most essential point remains in darkness—to Wit—whether they set on their nests with leggs dangling on the outsides??? a thing which I cannot believe, until I hear *you* affirm it!—I am delighted to hear that you have at last settled the hash with the Squirrels.—I wrote a few days ago to our Friend Doc^r Wilson, to do all in his power to forward me in Rum onc or More Flamingoes as soon as possible, and in case my letter Should Miss him I trust that you will give him this Commission with my best Wishes.—Can you not procure a *Wood Ibis* in Rum? & a pair of Fresh Water Marsh Hens?—My Friends here, all say the Introduction of the Anatomy of our birds in my last Volume will prove most valuable.—I have written both to Kentucky and New Orleans for divers species of Birds, and hope to receive them in good time.—This day I have received a large packet of letters from Thomas McCullough of Pictou, containing Much valuable information.—he has made a Shipment of Birds for me, but they are not yet I believe arrived at Liverpool.

By the next Packet I send you a Jar of Bird Lime, and will then forward you all the information you can desire, and I have no doubt you will have a good of pleasure whilt catching birds in that Way.—I also send you a very agreable book, the Sixth report of the annual Meetings of the Scientific Gentry of Europe, in which you & I are Spoken of at prety considerable length.—you will be pleased to see what Richardson says about the Geographical distribution of the North American quadrupeds, Birds &^c &^c.—

Charles Bonaparte came to London about 2 Weeks ago, and has spent about 2 hours with us.—he has gone off to his Father's in law' estate, but will return again in a few days.—he was in Town only Two days.—he says that he will go on with his continuation of Wilson's Work?? he is now publishing the Birds of Mexico.—he openned his eyes when he saw all *our* New species, and complimented me highly on my *Industry* and *perseverance*; Where he will procure Specimen, and *Matter* to go on with his Work on the birds of our Country, you will easily guess! He is a most aimiable good Man, and I Know that you would enjoy his society much.—He Kissed me as if a Brother, and I really believe that he is My Friend.—he is desirous to corespond with you, and I assured him that you would willingly meet him half way.—How he procures specimen of Birds, quadrupeds and Reptiles from *Charleston* and Georgia is yet a secret to both you and I.—

I am working like a Trojan; N° 78 containing up to plate 390 will be out in a few days—My last Volume will be made up of 83 Numbers or 115 plates without the Eggs, and will contain 159 Species, as good as ever flew or swam. and the whole will be finished in March Next!—

The Hawk I received from Natchez proves quite New, and it is a superb bird. I have received a letter from Doc^r Jenkins of Natchez in which he says that it is not a very rare bird, giving me the measurements, colour of the eyes &^c—I think you will find the New Woodpecker when next you search for it in the Interior of the State. It looks so much like the Downy and Hairy Woodpeckers that unless you look to the bill, and the Tail you would at first sight suppose it to be one or other of these. but It is a good New Species.—Bonaparte looked at many of my birds as you may well suppose.—he is satisfied about Henslow bunting of which he has several specimen from Charleston. but he appeared quite astonished when I Spoke to him of the *Young birds* which Wilson, him, and Myself have published as distinct species.—He is about to publish an ornithological System! Swainson has published about half a Dozen.—Vigors has given one to the World, and is about hatching another.—Dorbigny and Temminck will also astonish us very soon with their lugubrations of these Matters—and I feel so very sickened at all these puerile attempts, that I cannot reconcile myself to attempt any thing of the Kind.—The better *Judgements* in this Country laugh at all these Memorials but as I have said; they positively sicken me.—I have heard once from Ed^d Harris; and his Brother in Law, Doc^r Spencer, is now in London.—Harris perhaps May come over this Winter, but I doubt it?—My Old Friend has been better in health than usual for the past 3 Weeks.—We are thus all well.—Maria & John have gone to St James' Theatre this evening.—Lucy is Knitting across the round table—Victor is reading the last received Number of "*Pickwick*" and as you see I am driving a good old Iron pen. = We have seen President Van Buren's Message!—how do you like it??—Not a Word have I heard from the Revenue Cutter the Campbell, or of Cap^n Coste.—I am rather afraid that his CREW drank my Rum, and therefore shot no bird for me?—You will be Surprised to read that whilt searching over my Old Journals, I came to an a/c of my having Shot the *Smew* or White Nun Mergus Albellus near *New Orleans* in the winter of 19/20!—and perhaps Still more so, when I say that in the autumn of 1819. I saw *Plectrophanes Picta* of Swainson, which I have thank goodness Drawn!—I have renewed the figures of about 20 Species.—and have proved *Clark's Crow* to be a true Nutcracker—the third Species now Known to exist in the World.—but I have found that Old Catesby did publish the Rocky Mountain blue bird of Nuttall, and that the last Flycatcher the latter gave me, is the M. nigricans of Swainson.— So that after all poor Townsend did only obtain 8 Species that were as yet unknown. I have seen abundance of Specimen of the Yellow billed Magpie, but it has not been named except by Me.—Bonap says that our Raven is distinct from the European Raven. and I am of opinion that many others of our birds will equally prove distinct, especially all Such as do not Inhabit the Northern portions of our Country during Summer, Such as the Strix flammea of Authors—Falco cyaneus &^{c} &^{c} &^{c}—but of this I will you better accounts in the appendix to my 4th Vol. of Biographies—In that I will give all additional memorandums connected with corrections, extensions or deductions.—I have heard once from Brewer, and curious it is that the Eggs intended for him, were actually Shipped to Me, and have arrived in England, and now are at our house.—I am going to reship them by the packet of the 20th Instant; which will take over for you a regular English Plumb Pudding!—

Game is exceedingly abundant this season, as well as fruits of every description grown in this Country. figs are Just now full ripe.—So are Peaches and Nectarines, and Grapes and Melons of various Kinds—the Queen (God bless her) is quite well—but will be better Still when married to the Duke of Wellington! Or Indeed after She has partaken of the Sumptuous fare of the Lord Mayor on the 9th of November next *in the City*! I had a letter from Harlan the other day, but nothing worthy of your Notice.—Gould is publishing the Birds of *Australia* from Stuffed Skins! Next to that a Monograph of the Caprimulgae, and Next to that the Next things he can get. Was your Marsh Hare published before my figure of it? I think I am about to send you Two Diplomas from the Zoological and Linnæan Societies!—How you will laugh when you have read that Yesterday, I was offered the Presidency of an Botanical Society in London! I had actually to Walk nearly 6 Miles to day to refuse the Compliment, and after this what am I next to expect.—Your Story of the Vultures is pretty good but quite too late for Waterton, who I believe has thrown his pen aside—what a pity?—A very learned Member of the Scientific association whilt at Liverpool, and during the learned Sitting of that brilliant congregation discovered a new Plant growing on the very back of a Dead fly—the Plant is of course very curious being new, and as dead flies are pretty abundant in both hemispheres during Winter, I would advise you to Muster up a pair of Specks and Identify the European and American House fly plant. Now that it waxes late I will Stop for a while, and Should I find any thing more to say will resume before the sailing of the Packet when of Course I will send you a perfect account of the ways and Manners of catching birds with Bird Lime.—until then adieu and God bless you all.—Remember us Kindly to all Friends, and believe me ever yours Most truly & most sincerely attached

Oct[r] 8th   Since writing my last of the 4th No less than three Packets have arrived here and at Liverpool, and yet not a

letter have we received by them for any one of us.—Charles
Bonaparte returned to London a few days ago, and came to
see me after I had gone to bed; but there he Came, sat by my
side and talked about birds for upwards of an hour, the consequences of which were that I scarcely closed my eyes afterwards that Night. The next morning he called again, when
Victor and I went off with him in search of private Lodgings
as he does not wish to be known that he is in London except
by Naturalists, and because he dislikes the Humbug of the
Nobles that are ever and anon at his Father in law, Joseph
Bonaparte.—He therefore is now in an humble Street. he
came the third time to us for the purpose of Shaving dressing
&^{c} and lastly that day whilt we were all at Dinner.—he had
Shot a great Number of Pheasants, Hares & Partridges, of
which he brought us some. The next morning I went with
him to hire a Cabriolet and horse—he is almost constantly
with Gould, at the Zoological Museum and Indeed every
where, where there are bird Skins. Me thinks that he is over
anxious to *pump me*, but I am now no longer a green horn,
and will not Write such accounts for him as I did when I sent
him all the Habits of the wild Turkey from Bayou Sarah to
New York, and for which He has received all credit, and I
scarcely any.—I cannot well imagine why he Should continue
Wilson's Ornithology after my Work is finished, unless it is
Merely to Arrange our Fauna in Squares, Circles, and Tri-
angles, in the Manner of Swainson and all other crazed Naturalists of the Closet.—but we Shall see?—

I Received the other day a packet from Thomas Mac-
Culloch of Pictou, nova Scotia, containing a good deal of
Information respecting certain species, and I expect Shortly
to receive the Birds which he has collected for me in Rum,
but which I am sorry to say are few.

I calculate that Just about now you will have received the 5
last numbers Shipped to America, and that you will be pleased
with them.—I have 8 pounds of Bird lime for you in the
House, and it will go in a few days with other things.—

I wish you would ask Doctor Geddings for Money for
me—when I last Saw him at Charleston he fairly promessed
to pay you on my account for the Birds of America, of which
has three Volumes.—Havell seems to have made up his mind

to go to America to live, and I think that he will go pretty soon after our Work is finished, if he does not undertake the Engraving of Bonapt's continuation of Wilson.—

To John Bachman

London April 14th 1838.—

My Dear Bachman.—

The last intelligence or your being Still in the land of the living, reached us this morning, and Eliza's letter is dated the 13th of last Month.

We have heard of the loss of your Venerable Mother with sorrow commensurate, but were almost happy at the thought that at her extraordinary American Old Age She was removed in peaceful quietude to that World towards which we are all doomed or blessed sooner or later to remove!

That yourself and the remainder of your Dear Familly are quite well is quite a comfort to us all at this distance from Charleston, and blessed Indeed Would I feel as at this moment were I able to say as much of each member of my own beloved Familly.—My Dearest Friend is Still ackeing, John has had a Violent attack of an ulcerated throat, but is now again up, and I trust will soon be able to resume his daily avocations.—

Our child is quite Well and as round as any One in love of her would possibly wish, indeed My Dear Bachman, it may be possible that ere this reaches you, both of us will be Grand Fathers! Nay Mr Phillips thinks that the *Chance* may be *a double*, and if So how blessed I will feel to have a pair of New borned Audubon's.—

Doctor Wilson's valuable letter reached me Two days ago, Old date, but full of fun, and Just what was wanted to raise the Spirits of an Hypocondraical of 53 Years of Age, and thank God yet able to put his fore finger and thumb up to his nose holding withal a pinch of the "American Gentleman".—(Snuff! Snuff!!) Flamingoes are now very far below par; indeed it will prove a curiosity to the World of Science, when that world will Know that John Bachmann D D himself, assisted by Samuel Wilson M. D. and about one half of a hundred persons besides have not been able to send me even *a Stuffed* Specimen in time for my Publication—So it is however and I drop the subject.—*What have you done with the Bird-lime?* How preciously lazy you have become; and yet we here are told that you are gone with your beloved Moiety to Liberty Hall. Would that I was there at this moment, with my Dearest Friend, our Children, our Sweet heart and all that have a Jot to do with either or all of our Party.—

alexander Gordon has been with you and now tell me what do you think of that Gentleman—he is somewhat learned and keen, and May be a Friend besides.—

Charles Bonaparte has treated me most Shockingly—he has published the whole of *our* Secrets, which I foolishly communicated to him after his giving me his word of honour that he would not do so, and Now I have *Cut him*, and he never will have from me the remaining unpublished Numbers of my Work.—(Which by the bye he calls a poor thing) and the latter simply because I at last refused to give him my Knowledge of the Migratory or Geographical distribution of our Birds—So Much for *a Prince!*

Will you not be surprised when I tell you that my last Volume of Illustrations will contain One hundred and Ninety five Species of Birds?—cutting off all young bird and Spurious Species; and yet Bonap. exceeds my list by upwards of 20 *false* Species—So much for the Cabinet Man—

Our Packets appear to have had very long passages to America, and I am sorry that you all Should have abandoned writing by way of New York, which after all is the best way—

You will be surprised when you see the last Numbers of the Work at the Numbers of Woodpeckers and owls which we Now *Must* Know to be found in North America, and My Opinions are (betwen you and I) that the Contents of our Fauna will not be filled by Me by about one good & solid hundred Species—

> God bless you all—
> Your Friend J. J. Audubon
> 4 Winepole Street—
> Cavendish Square
> London

Maria will not be confined until the Middle or latter end of July next, if then?—

———

I have thought it proper to write to you crossways, on finding that I have some more to say to you. First did you receive the Bird Lime, have you caught any Birds with it, and have written to Earl Derby? Has Leitner published the New Plants he discovered in the Floridas? I ask this latter question because in the 83ʳᵈ Number of my Work, Plate 411 I have represented a New Nymphia, which unpublished by him, I Should like in my letter press to Name after Docʳ Leitner's name, "Nymphia Leitnernia"—Have you not met with any New Woodpeckers? among our Small tribes? Depend upon it, both you & I have not been as diligent on this head as we ought to have been, as since my latter investigation of the Subject, I found that Alexʳ Wilson commited the same error with the P. Villosus which he did with the R. Crepitans; to wit, he has positively figured Picus Canadensis of Buffon and other Authors (an Eastern Species) and described another Species, which however on account of the regard I have for that Wonderfull Man I Shall retain the name of according to his description.—I have made bold enough to name a New Woodpecker after you, it is another Species of Hairy Woodpecker from the Columbia River sent to me by Townsend, and I think you will be quite astonished to see that at this Moment no less than 19 Species of this interesting Tribe are in my published Plates—Townsend has sent Two New Oyster Catchers, Two New Cormorants, a New something which I intend to name in the way of a subjenus allied to Tringa, a New Burrowing Owl or one described by Temminck and a New Species of Bombicilla, the generic name of which is also pointed out by the latter author.—&ᶜ &ᶜ—Will you believe that since Bonap has left London I have drawn One hundred Birds; Indeed I feel quite fagged, and now think that I never laboured harder than I have done within the last Two Months.—

A long article on general ornithology has been published of late in the Encyclopedia Britannica, in which my Work is Spoken of in most luxuriant Words, and some good hints are given to Students of Zoology generally, though on the whole I look upon the Article as far beneath what it ought to have been in such publication—Mr Gould the author of the Birds of Europe is about leaving this country for New holland, or as it is now Called Australia.—he takes his Wife and Bairns with him, a Waggon the size of a Squatters Cabin and all such apparatus as will encumber him not a little—he has never travelled in the Woods, never Salted his rump Stakes with Gun Powder and how he will take to it, will be "a sin to Crockett"—before this reaches you I dare say that you will have received my Plates up to 405 wherein you will see some 'rara aves', but believe me when I tell you that in the 6th Concluding Numbers you will be quite surprised at what you will see when you look over these. Do you recollect how Mr Doughty abused me in the Philadelphia papers? well he is now here, dines with us about once a week, and thank God I have it in my power to treat him with as Much Kindness as he then treated me with all to the Contrary—that ever was my way and this I trust I shall hold untill I am called to Another World! and now Good Night to you, and again God bless you All.—*J. J. A.*

To Robert Havell

Edinburgh March 13th 1839.—

My Dear Mr Havell

I received yours of the 8th Instant in Course, and would in all probability have answered to it, ere this, had I not known from what you say that along with disposing of your premisses and the Selling off of your Stock you were "as busy as a Bee in a Tar Barrel".—

I am glad Mr Bakewell called for the Parcel, but exceedingly surprised that I Should not have heard from that Gentleman on the subject.—

I have written to Mr Baker but have had no answer from him and as he is very frequently absent from England, I would advise you to Call on Mr Gould "Secretary"! and try to find from him whether he is at home or Not.—

I expect a box of Bird Skins every day from Havre (France) Should it come forward it me by Steamer as soon as possible. —I Shall expect *another* in about a fortnight, and although you may have given up your House by that time, I *think* that it would be well for you to make some arrangement with the tenants thereof to receive every letter addressed to your Care as well as packages, until you are about to leave this *Country.* and do not I pray you send us *tremandous* parcels by Mail bag as letters, for our postages upon Such things are truly awful.—

Our Policies upon the Plates are as follows—

"Union assurance office, fire, life, and Annuities."

Cornhill and N° 70, Baker Street, London.—"N° 213986 dated 7ᵗʰ Jan.ʸ 1839 for 3000£.—Signed *W. B. Lewis.*"

The other is Phoenix fire Office Lombard Street and Charing cross N° 687941. dated 7ᵗʰ Jan.ʸ 1839. on 2000£ pounds.

Signed E. Goodhart.

I wish you to have the goodness to attend to this matter particularly, and to be sure to have from the parties concerned a Written, and fully Valid document as regards the remauvell of the Plates from Your present Dwelling to the London Docks, so that No Squable may take place here after, betwen these Two assurance Companies and Myself, in the Case of a loss by fire.—have you received any Numbers from Mʳˢ Robinson of Leeds?—She Says that she forwarded these Numbers to you by Waggon, but I think the Lady is a deep one, and trys her utmost to take us in.—

When next We Meet I will tell you how grossly, have been the Mistakes that have occured in the Packing of Prints of my Work and in the forwarding Numbers where they were not Wanted, such as will make you Stare; and all this through the carelessness of the Individuals whom you have had as attendents in your Shop, and towards the Salary of whom I foolishly contributed, though in an indirect Manner.—Only think that I have of late received *here* No less than Twelve Nᵒˢ in return, some of them containing, not the plates in regular order, but 3, and 5 Copies of the same plate instead of *A Number.* How Much *I* have lost in this manner, it is impossible for me to Tell, but the Idle rascals who did the like of this deserve the severest of punishment. In some parcels I find

Land and Water birds mixed in Numbers published when no Land and Water birds had yet been issued. The Canada Goose of the *Third* Volume, was found rolled up with the *Carrion Crow* of the *Second Volume* &ᶜ &ᶜ &ᶜ.—alas! alas! depend upon it, that a Clever young Man as a Clerk is worth a hundred of thick-heads.—How can you tell for Instance that Mʳ Baker has not paid his balance to you because he has not received the Numbers intended for *him* but some parcels as erroneously and foolishly arranged as those which I have Lately received and now have in my Possession?

Do you not remember the piece of *Beef* found by Lord Kinnoul among some of the plates that were sent to him, and on account of Which we no doubt lost his subscription—I write all this not to Vex you, but to put you on your guard, to have your eyes broad oppen, and to Watch what is going on round you even at this late period, I speak from the heart, as your Friend.

ever Yours

P. S. Do not forget to send me a Correct list of what you Ship to America on my account, and that list not made out by any other person than either *yourself* or Mʳˢ *Havell* to whom present my best regards.—

To John Bachman

New York Jan.ʸ. 2ᵈ 1840.

My Dear Bachman.—

May the God that has granted us Life and all the enjoyments connected with these, continue to bless us, ours, and our Friends for many, many years to Come! Give our love and all the best wishes of our hearts to all those who now surround you, and be assured that now as well as ever since We have Known you our regards and all our Sentiments continue just the Same:—unbounded and grateful!—

Yours of the 24ᵗʰ Ulᵒ came to hand this morning, and could I whisper a useful word in the ear of the Postmaster general of these *Realms*, I certainly would ask of that Gentleman to ameliorate the expedition of the transit of all friendly inter-course by letters, and dispose of all that is otherwise intended in any manner best suited to the times.—

I wrote to our Sweet Heart as soon as I returned from my eastern Journey, and I believe gave her a full account of my proceedings and the success I met with in the way of procur-ing Subscribers to our Little Work. I think I said to her that in less than three Weeks I received Ninety six names, and as many as 41 of them in the beautiful Village of New Bedford Massachusetts!—The Purgatory of which you Speak, and which indeed I have and must have much to do with Stil; be-comes easier the further I proceed, and as you observe, there is nothing equal to the habit of doing things.—

We have experienced however a rather bungling sort of Stopage in our present publication, by having had about 300 N^{os} & Spoiled by the Binders at Phil^a and all of which we have been obliged to *Stop* as dead letters.—this Mischief will be got over next Week, and then we will forward you the actual quantum.—

I truly thank you for your criticisms on the Synopsis, and I feel as you do, that it is not all that it ought to have been, but as perfection is Scarcely expected to be found in our present World, I must rest contended with the Idea that I have done for the best.—

as regards the publication of the Little Work, and that of the quadrupeds of our Country, I think it necessary to pre-sent you with Two Special Lectures, and Philosopher like, I will begain with the first.—It appears from what you say that you expected that I Should have given (in the letter press) the whole of my Knowledge in the Ornithology of our Country; When in fact, this never entered my head. no! I have further prospects in View, and for the present, I thought (and that af-ter rather considerable reflection) that to abridge the amount of my former letter press, to that of the size and general ap-pearance of the present publication, none or few of our Sub-scribers would complain (especially as very few of them are Naturalists) but on the contrary would be pleased, that in my So doing I saved them a considerable addition of expense, which Just at present is a matter of no little consideration to the Public at Large.—My Intentions are to give the best of figures of our birds, taken from my own Original Drawings, and to give figures of all and every Species which are *Now Known* or may *become Known*, between the present day and the last day of Said publication.—but as I have Ten thousand of other Matters connected with this which I do not like to put in a lettre, I will wait until I see you at your Home and express a few Words about our quadrupeds as if "en passant."

I have thought very deeply on this most interesting talk, and Know I believe, that Such a publication will be fraught with dificulties innumerable, but *I trust* not insurmountable. provided We Join our Names together, and you push your able and broad Shoulders to the Wheel, I promise to you that I will give the very best figures of all our quadrupeds that ever have been thought of or expected, and that you and I can relate the greatest amount of *Truths* that to this time has appeared connected with their dark and hitherto ununderstood Histories!—My Hairs are grey, and I am growing old, but what of this? My Spirits are as enthusiastical as ever, my legs fully able to carry my body for Some Ten Years to come, and in about Two of these, I expect to see *the Illustrations* OUT, and ere the following *Twelve Months* have elapsed, their Histories Studied, their descriptions carefully prepared and the Book printed!—Only think of the quadrupeds of America being presented to the World of Science, by Audubon and Bachman; the latter, one of the very best of D. D.'s and the former the only American living F. R. S. L.! how our good and most learned Friend George Ord of Phil^a Will laugh, and Will thank us? how many copies of that magnificent Work Will that most generous Friend of poor Alex^r Wilson will subscribe to? aye Friend Bachman answer that question I pray you by return of Mail!—

I will leave this as soon as the weather will allow, as it is now So *perfectly* cold, that I dare not proceed toward "*purgatory*" until the thermometer has risen a few degrees at least; but, as soon as that is the fact, I will enter the area again, and go forth and beg and beg and beg! We have now upward of 160 Subscribers, and 15 to the quadrupeds *unconditional^ly* for I really know not at what Price *that Work* can be presented to the Public? perhaps when we meet we may be able to

Judge of this—I now expect to be at Charleston in about 5 or 6 Weeks, and when there, you and I may ransack the Woods and call on all our Friends for assistance in the way of procuring quadrupeds, in the fleet, for my Pencil, and the Pencil of our dearly beloved Sweetheart, as the first Number must be out by the 1ˢᵗ day of May Next!

Since I began this letter, I have been interrupted about one hundred times by our sweet little dear Lucy, upon whom, we are all doting, as we will do upon Miss Harriet, as soon as She begins to run across rooms, and our Carpets, and Around our legs.—all the Younger ones are a loving, and the Old Folk endeavoring to render *the whole household* comfortable, for the harder and Colder the Times and the weather becomes, the more all this appears to be interesting.—Tell Friend Docʳ Wilson, that I have noted the useful lessons of his valuable letter, which I intend to answer in a few days and from Somewhere. Meantime God bless you all.—

Your friend

To John Bachman

Minnie's Land, Novʳ 12ᵗʰ 1843—

My Dear Bachman.—

I reached my happy home this day week last at 3 o'clock, and found all well.—The next day Victor handed me your letter of the 1ˢᵗ Inst, to which I will now answer as much as I can do, in the absence of my Cargo of Skins &ᶜ which I trust will be at home early next week.—Now Friend we were never out of sight of the Coffee Pot, feather beds or White faces, and never failed in our being hungry and thirsty! Nay not even while on the Prairies feeding on the Jucy ribbs or humps of the Bison. Harris Stood the Journey quite well but lost flesh and weight. I gained 22 pounds and am as fat as a Grisley Bear in good Season.—Harris would have been better had he given up taking phisic almost every day.—The rest of my party got on well enough, and when *we* meet I will then say more on this subject.—

I have no less than 14 New Species of Birds, perhaps a few more, and I hope that will in a great measure deffray my terribly heavy expenses.—The variety of quadrupeds is small in the Country we visited, and I fear that I have not more than 3 or 4 New ones.—I have brought home alive a Deer which we all think will prove new.—I have also a live Badger and a Swift Fox.—I have first rate Skins in pickle of the Buffalo Bull, Cow, and Calves.—Elks, Big horns Antilopes, Black tailed Deer, the Deer I have alive and Sundry Wolves.—I have Townsends Hare, *Tamias quadrivtatus, Prairie Marmots* (Prairie Dog So called) a fine Grisley Bear &^{c} but I have no list. I have written much and taken ample and minute measurements of *every thing.*—

I have a large collection of dried plants principally flowers, and an abundance of precious seeds—one or 2 fishes, but there are no Shells in the Streams of the Country we have visited.—

You wish me to go to you but this is impossible—As soon as my collections reach me I will draw first all the Birds that they may be added to my present publication, and then 30 or 40 Species of Quadrupeds—I have brought home good Sketches of Scenery, Drawings of flowers, and also of the heads of Antilopes, Bighorns, Wolves and Buffaloes.

I am most heartily glad to hear that you are all well, and that is the case with us also.—

I came home with a beard and mustachios of 7 Months growth, and Johny has painted my head as it was, for I am now Shaved and much as usual except in fatness which is almost desagreable to me.—

Now that I am in the lap of Comfort and without the hard and continued exercise So lately my lot, I feel Somewhat lazy and disinclined even to write a long letter.—I tried to Copy my last Journal yesterday but could not write more than one hour, and yet I must do that as soon as possible as no man on earth can do it for me.—In a few days my things will be on and I will send you a Catalogue of what I have.—By the way I think that I have a new Porcupine?—Nous verrons.—I have the best a/c of the *habits* of the Buffalo, Beaver, Antilopes, Big horns &^{c} that were ever written and a great deal of Information of divers nature. Now remember me most Kindly to every Member of your Dear familly. I Wrote to Maria from St Louis, She must have received my letter.—remember me to Doc^r Wilson and all other Friends and believe me my Dear Friend Always yours

Truly and sincerely attached

Chronology

1785   Born Jean Rabine on April 26 in Les Cayes, Saint-Domingue (later Haiti), son of Jeanne Rabine and Captain Jean Audubon, a merchant and naval officer. (Mother, a 27-year-old chambermaid from Les Touches, near Nantes, France, had met Jean Audubon at sea and soon after moved in with him and his already-established mistress, Catherine "Sanitte" Bouffard. Father, born in 1744, was descended from a family of fishermen in Les Sables-d'Olonne, on the Bay of Biscay southwest of Nantes; he traded slaves, sugar, coffee, and cotton to France for fabrics, wine, and other goods. He had married Anne Moynet in France in 1772, and fathered at least two children by Sanitte Bouffard, including a daughter, Marie-Madeleine, born 1776.) Mother dies from illness at father's sugar plantation on November 10. (Audubon later refers to the circumstances of his birth as a "cloud" hanging over his life, and will invent a variety of stories to explain his origins.)

1787   Half-sister Rose Bouffard born on April 29 to Jean Audubon and Sanitte Bouffard.

1788   Sent to Nantes in summer to live with father's family.

1789   Father sells plantation to an absentee owner after widespread slave unrest and leaves Saint-Domingue for France.

1791   Half-sister Rose arrives in Nantes. Spends a relatively carefree childhood in Nantes and on his father's country estate, La Gerbetière, nine miles down the Loire from Nantes, near the village of Couëron. Begins to collect natural curiosities, such as birds' nests and eggs, flowers, and pebbles on trips through the surrounding fields.

1792   Half-sister Marie-Madeleine dies during slave uprising at Les Cayes.

1794   Formally adopted by his father and legal stepmother, Anne Moynet, receives the name Jean-Jacques Fougère

Audubon. Father purchases Mill Grove, farm near Norristown, Pennsylvania.

1796-97   Begins naval training, but fails candidacy test for the School of Hydrography. Returns to Nantes, where he begins "a series of drawings of the birds of France."

1803   Leaves for the United States to avoid conscription into Napoleon's army and to take over the management of his father's estate at Mill Grove, on the grounds of which a lead mine had been discovered. Passport identifies him as a "native of Louisiana."

1804   Falls in love with Lucy Bakewell (1787–1874), the daughter of his neighbor William Bakewell, who had immigrated to the United States from England in 1801. Attaches silver threads to the legs of Eastern Phoebes he has observed in a nearby cave (the first banding experiment recorded in North America). Develops wire constructions that allow him to fix freshly killed birds in lifelike attitudes while painting them.

1805   Returns to Nantes for a year-long visit with his family; seeks father's consent to marry, but is told to find a means of supporting himself first. In December, half-sister Rose marries Gabriel Loyen Du Puigaudeau. Embarks on a series of portraits of the birds of the Loire Valley for Lucy; acquires experience in taxidermy working with the young physician and naturalist Charles-Marie D'Orbigny. Begins to draw birds roughly to scale.

1806   Enters into business partnership with Ferdinand Rozier (son of a merchant friend of Jean Audubon); they travel to the United States and settle briefly at Mill Grove, attempting unsuccessfully to operate mine. Audubon begins clerkship with Lucy's uncle Benjamin Bakewell, a wholesale importer, in New York City. In the evenings, stuffs birds for prominent naturalist Dr. Samuel Mitchell. His work includes accomplished drawing of the Wood Thrush, evidence of a new interest in decorative yet scientifically accurate backgrounds.

1807   With Rozier, sets up a general store in Louisville, Kentucky. In his spare time, continues to sketch birds, now with the idea of assembling a collection: "I drew and noted the habits of everything which I procured, and my collection was daily augmenting."

1808   Marries Lucy Bakewell on her father's farm on April 5, and departs with her for Louisville, where they take up residence at the Indian Queen Hotel.

1809   Son Victor Gifford Audubon born at the Indian Queen on June 12.

1810   In March, meets Scottish ornithologist Alexander Wilson (declines to subscribe to his *American Ornithology*: "even at the time my collection was greater than his"). Settles with wife and child in Henderson, Kentucky. Begins to experiment with graphite for details and textures in bird portraits. In December, leaves with Rozier for St. Geneviève, Missouri, possible location for a new general store.

1811   In April, terminates professional relationship with Rozier. Returns to Henderson, where he establishes the trading firm of Audubon & Bakewell with wife's brother, Thomas Bakewell, who heads the New Orleans branch. In November, takes Lucy and Victor to father-in-law's farm in Norristown. On his return trip to Kentucky meets New Orleans merchant Victor Nolte, who offers free passage in one of his flatboats from Pittsburgh to Limestone, Ohio, and then rides on with him to Lexington. (Nolte later remembers Audubon as "an odd fish," who introduced himself, in spite of his strong French accent, as an "Heenglishman.")

1812   Naturalized as an American citizen on July 3. New Orleans office of Audubon & Bakewell fails. Son John Woodhouse Audubon born on November 30.

1813   Family moves into new log house beside store in Henderson, with four acres of orchard and meadow for livestock, poultry, caged wild birds, and pet rodents.

1815   Daughter Lucy born in December.

1816   Invests in the construction of steam-powered grist mill in Henderson. Partners Thomas Pears and Thomas Bakewell withdraw from the project before the mill has even begun to operate.

1817   Daughter Lucy dies during winter.

1818   Father dies in Nantes on February 19, beginning a protracted legal struggle among family members. Is visited during the summer by naturalist Constantine Rafinesque. Convinces tenant George Keats to invest with him in a Mississippi steamboat; both lose their entire stakes. (George's brother, the poet John Keats, "cannot help thinking Mr. Audubon a dishonest man.")

1819   Follows former business competitor Samuel Adams Bowen to New Orleans in unsuccessful attempt to regain possession of a boat sold to him. After his return, is assaulted by Bowen on the streets of Henderson and stabs him in self-defense. (Wound is not fatal and judge rules in Audubon's favor.) Business in Henderson fails. Sells his possessions and goes to Louisville, leaving the pregnant Lucy and his two sons behind. Jailed for debt in Louisville but is released after filing for bankruptcy. In the fall, the family is reunited, and daughter Rose is born. Audubon develops skill in portraiture, and makes a name for himself as a painter of deathbed portraits in chalk: "so high did my reputation rise . . . that a clergyman residing at Louisville had his dead child disinterred."

1820   Daughter Rose dies. Leaves for Cincinnati, where he is hired by Dr. Daniel Drake as taxidermist for the Western Museum in Cincinnati. Establishes drawing school with 25 students and, for the first time, displays his bird paintings in public, prompting a critic to observe that "there have been no exhibitions west of the mountains which can compare with them." Now actively in pursuit of the project of his life, "to Compleat a collection of the *Birds* of our Country, from *Nature*, all of Natural Size." Departs with young assistant Joseph Mason on a flatboat down the Ohio and Mississippi Rivers for New Orleans.

1821   Arrives in New Orleans in January; supports himself through portrait-painting and drawing lessons. In March, obtains a recommendation from painter John Vanderlyn. From June to October, works as a drawing instructor at

James Pirrie's Oakley Plantation, 130 miles north of New Orleans, where he acquires further ornithological expertise. Dismissed by the mistress of plantation, returns to New Orleans. Develops a full range of techniques for representing birds, including watercolor, pencil, and gouache. In December, joined in New Orleans by his wife and sons.

1822   Travels to Natchez with Mason. Lucy begins work as teacher on Beech Woods Plantation in West Feliciana and supports herself and her two sons until 1830. Audubon receives instruction in oil painting from Pennsylvania artist John Steen, a teacher of Thomas Cole. In winter, paints signs and steamboat murals in Shippingport, Kentucky.

1824   Receives commission to draw birds for engraving on a New Jersey banknote, his first published work. Publishes paper on the Swallow in *Annals of the Lyceum of New York*. Unsuccessfully attempts to gain support for publishing a folio of engravings of American birds from distinguished naturalists affiliated with the Academy of Natural Sciences at Philadelphia; while project is supported by painter Thomas Sully, French naturalist and illustrator Charles-Alexander Lesueur, and ornithologist Charles-Lucien Bonaparte (a nephew of Napoleon), it is opposed by George Ord, the editor of Alexander Wilson's *American Ornithology*, and Wilson's engraver, Alexander Lawson. Meets farmer and naturalist Edward Harris from Moorestown, New Jersey. On his return journey to New Orleans, works as itinerant portrait painter and begins saving money for trip abroad.

1826   Leaves for England, where he hopes to find support for his publishing plans; family remains in Louisiana. Wearing a wolfskin coat and sporting long, curly hair, he is widely feted as the incarnation of the "American Woodsman." Exhibits 250 paintings in the Royal Institution at Liverpool, at Manchester, and at the Royal Institution in Edinburgh. Befriended by influential families (such as the Rathbones in Liverpool), meets Sir Walter Scott, and gains the endorsement of Robert Jameson, Professor of Natural History at the University of Edinburgh, and ornithologists William Jardine and Prideaux John Selby, who take lessons with him. Publishes papers on the

Carrion Crow and the "Habits of the Turkey-Buzzard" in Edinburgh scientific journals. Introduced to William Home Lizars, who agrees to undertake the engraving and reproduction of his paintings. Begins drafts of ornithological observations, but Lizars advises against issuing text with plates to circumvent British copyright restrictions.

1827   Elected to the Royal Society of Edinburgh. Issues first prospectus for *Birds of America*. Begins to tour the country to solicit subscriptions for his self-published work: subscribers are asked to pay a total of £183. Lizars abandons work on Double Elephant Folio etchings after completing ten plates. Audubon hires the London firm of Havell & Son and works 17-hour days, making new drawings of birds and redrawing old ones, supervising the engraving and coloring of his work, keeping track of his subscriptions. Publishes paper "Notes on the Rattlesnake" in *Edinburgh New Philosophical Journal*.

1828   Visits Paris in September with zoologist William Swainson and his wife. Attends meeting at the Académie des Sciences, where Cuvier lauds his work as "the greatest monument yet erected by Art to Nature."

1829   After three years absence, returns to the United States to paint more birds in Camden and Great Egg Harbor, New Jersey, and the Great Pine Forest, Pennsylvania. Tries to convince wife to join him in England. *American Journal of Science and Arts* calls the first 49 plates of *Birds of America* "the most magnificent work of its kind ever executed in any country."

1830   Invited to the White House to dine with President Andrew Jackson. Sails for England with Lucy on April 1. Enlists young ornithologist William MacGillivray as scientific editor for *Ornithological Biography*, written to accompany *Birds of America*.

1831   Publishes first volume of *Ornithological Biography* (subsequent volumes appear in 1834, 1835, 1838, and 1839). Elected to the American Philosophical Society. Leaves for New York and embarks on a collecting trip to the South with assistant George Lehmann and taxidermist Henry Ward. Meets minister and fellow naturalist John Bachman in Charleston, the beginning of a collaboration that will last until the end of Audubon's life. Spends November and December hunting, drawing, and writing in Florida.

1832   Travels up the St. John's River and then through the Florida Keys. Son Victor ("my Right Arm and hand in every thing connected with my Publication") prepares to go to England to supervise work on his father's plates. Naturalist Charles Waterton joins with George Ord in Philadelphia to claim Audubon is an "ornithological impostor" (Waterton will publish 19 attacks on his work over the next few years). Audubon and his family spend the winter in Boston, where he purchases and paints a Golden Eagle.

1833   Sails for Labrador from Eastport, Maine, on June 6 with five assistants, including his son John. Appalled by the "eggers" (egg poachers) of Labrador. Returns to New York in September; spends the winter in Charleston with John Bachman.

1834   Family leaves New York on April 1 for Liverpool, where they canvass for new subscribers. They settle again in Edinburgh, where work continues on *Ornithological Biography*. Second volume, published in December, receives praise from *Blackwood's Magazine* and the *Edinburgh New Philosophical Journal*.

1836   Fire in New York in January ruins equipment needed for future expeditions. Returns to America in August with son John. Visited by Washington Irving. Spends November and December in Charleston.

1837   Travels to Pensacola, Florida, in February with son John and Edward Harris and then on to New Orleans and Houston. John Woodhouse Audubon marries Maria Rebecca Bachman, daughter of John Bachman, on June 21; in July, with Audubon, they sail for Liverpool.

1838   Fourth and final volume of the Folio edition of *Birds of America* is completed.

1839   Publishes *A Synopsis of the Birds of America* in July with help from MacGillivray. In September, leaves England with wife to settle in New York. Begins to plan publication of *The Viviparous Quadrupeds of North America*, in collaboration with his sons John Woodhouse and Victor as well as John Bachman, who warns Audubon that "the birds are a mere trifle compared to this." Son Victor marries Bachman's daughter Mary Eliza Bachman on December 4.

1840   Begins work on a seven-volume octavo edition of *The Birds of America*, lithographed by J. T. Bowen of Philadelphia (published 1840–44). Maria Bachman Audubon dies in September of tuberculosis, leaving John Woodhouse with two children, Lucy (born 1838) and Harriet (born 1839).

1841   Purchases 30-acre estate (Minnie's Land) in upper Manhattan and builds home. Mary Eliza Audubon dies on May 25, also from tuberculosis. Son John Woodhouse marries Caroline Hall on October 2.

1842   Moves to Minnie's Land. In September, tours New England and Canada in search of subscribers for royal octavo edition of *Birds of America* and *Quadrupeds*, for which he publishes a prospectus on October 20.

1843   Joins Edward Harris, Isaac Sprague (a botanical artist), John G. Bell (a taxidermist), and Lewis Squires in traveling party to search for new specimens for *Quadrupeds*. In St. Louis, the party is offered free transportation up the Missouri River by Pierre Chouteau, head of the American Fur Company. Ventures into Indian territory, where he encounters bands of Mandan, Ricaree, Minnetaree, Cree, and Assiniboin. Revels in the "ocean-like" prairies still filled with bison but also deplores the state of the "half-starved" and smallpox-stricken Indian tribes and begins to feel sorry for some of the animals the party shoots. Acquires animal skins and sketches wolves, bison, wolves, and pronghorns. Arrives on June 12 at Fort Union, at the mouth of the Yellowstone. Returns to Minnie's Land on November 6, "fat as a Grisley Bear in Good Season."

1845   Publishes first Imperial Folio volume of *Viviparous Quadrupeds of North America*, prepared in collaboration with

John Bachman, who is mainly responsible for the text (subsequent volumes appear in 1846 and 1848).

1846   Failing eyesight forces Audubon to withdraw from the *Quadrupeds* project; son John Woodhouse assumes the task of completing the paintings.

1848   Suffers stroke. John Bachman travels to Minnie's Land and finds Audubon's "mind . . . all in ruins."

1849   Son John Woodhouse embarks on a California gold-rush expedition, hoping to remedy the family's financial problems.

1850   Matthew Brady takes Audubon's portrait for inclusion in his "Gallery of Illustrious Americans."

1851   Dies at Minnie's Land on January 27. Buried at Trinity Church Cemetery in upper Manhattan, where Lucy plants his "favorite shrubs and weepers. . . . All but the remembrance of him and his goodness to me is gone forever."

Note on the Texts

This volume contains the complete text of John James Audubon's journal of 1820–21 (the "Mississippi River Journal"), portions of his 1826 journal, a selection of 45 "bird biographies" and seven episodes from his *Ornithological Biography* (1831–39), the complete text of his 1843 "Missouri River Journals," three miscellaneous pieces ("Account of the Method of Drawing Birds," "My Style of Drawing Birds," "Myself"), and a selection of 18 letters. Of these works, only two—*Ornithological Biography* and "Account of the Method of Drawing Birds"—were published during Audubon's lifetime; the texts of both are taken from the first printings. The remaining works (except for three letters published here for the first time) were published posthumously, often in editions that significantly alter or misrepresent the texts of Audubon's manuscripts; the texts of these works, as printed here, have been prepared from Audubon's manuscripts, unless manuscript sources are no longer known to be extant.

Audubon made the first entry in his Mississippi River Journal, the earliest of the several journals he is known to have kept during his lifetime, on October 12, 1820, at the outset of a voyage from Kentucky to New Orleans; the last entry was written in New Orleans on December 31, 1821. The text of the journal printed in this volume has been prepared from the holograph manuscript held by the Ernst Mayr Library of the Museum of Comparative Zoology, Harvard University; an earlier transcription by Howard Corning was published as *Journal of John James Audubon Made during His Trip to New Orleans in 1820–1821* (Boston: Club of Odd Volumes, 1929). In presenting the text of this journal, as well as other texts newly transcribed from manuscript sources, this volume retains Audubon's often unconventional or inconsistent punctuation, capitalization, and spelling (such as "betwen" for "between," "found" for "fond," "begain" for "begin," "Awk" for "Hawk"). Where Audubon canceled a word or phrase or made a correction, only his final wording has been reproduced; alterations apparently made by others (such as the insertion of "re" before "Maried" at 30.5 in this volume) have been disregarded. Emendation has been limited to the correction of slips of the pen—inadvertently repeated or omitted words; transposed, elided, or otherwise accidentally miswritten letters—and all such changes are noted below in the list of errors corrected. Where Audubon's omission of terminal punctuation might confuse a modern reader, a one-em space has been inserted in the text; similarly, quotation marks have been added where an opening or closing quotation mark has been omitted. In some cases, readings of Audubon's handwriting are conjectural, and they are presented without comment. Two instructions written in the margins of the manuscript of the Mississippi River Journal—"Begin here" (beside 3.2 in this volume) and "turn Back to the Bottom of this Sheet" (beside 55.35)—have been followed but are not included as part of the text of the journal. Audubon's copy of an illustration from William Turton's 1806 English-language edition of Linnaeus's *Systema naturae* has been reproduced on page 2; other manuscript illustrations appear on pages 19, 121, and 156. Three items that precede the text of the regular journal in Audubon's manuscript—a line labeled "Length of My Lucy's Foot," a hand-ruled mileage table, and a recipe for small beer—and other marginal notations are described in the notes to this volume. (All manuscript drawings are reprinted by permission of the President and Fellows of Harvard College. Copyright © 1999, President and Fellows of Harvard College.)

Audubon's 1826 journal recounts his journey to England, Scotland, and France to arrange for the publication and sale of the Double Elephant Folio *Birds of America* (1827–38). The journal was first published, together with journals from 1827, 1828, and 1829, as part of the section titled "The European Journals" in *Audubon and His Journals* (Boston: Charles Scribner's Sons, 1897). In editing *Audubon and His Journals*, Audubon's granddaughter Maria Audubon freely altered his prose, changing punctuation, spelling, vocabulary, and sentence structure and sometimes omitting entire sentences or paragraphs. The text of the selections from the 1826 journal printed here has been prepared, following the guidelines described above, from a microfilm copy of Audubon's manuscript (the original of which is in private hands). In six instances, Audubon's entries for a given date have not been reproduced in this volume in their entirety; omitted material is indicated by a line of three asterisks. No manuscript version is known to be extant of the last journal selection included in this volume (at 192.1-27); it is reprinted here without alteration from *The 1826 Journal of John James Audubon*, edited by Alice Ford (Norman: University of Oklahoma Press, 1967).

Audubon's *Ornithological Biography*, first published in five volumes between 1831 and 1839 by Adam Black in Edinburgh, was written to accompany the Double Elephant Folio; it contains almost 500 individual accounts, often referred to as "bird biographies," of the habits and habitats of each of the species illustrated in the Double Elephant Folio. Interspersed among these accounts in the first three

volumes of *Ornithological Biography* are 60 "Delineations of American Scenery and Manners," referred to by Audubon in a letter of
December 3, 1834, (and by others in later publications) as
"episodes." This volume includes 45 of the bird biographies and
seven of the episodes in two separate sections; they are presented
within each section in the order of their original appearance.

The texts of the selections from *Ornithological Biography* printed
here have been taken from the Edinburgh first edition. In preparing
that edition, Audubon enlisted the aid of his wife, Lucy Bakewell
Audubon, who helped to edit his prose and acted as copyist; he also
hired William MacGillivray, professor of comparative anatomy at Edinburgh University, as scientific editor. MacGillivray reviewed and
revised Audubon's bird biographies soon after they were drafted and
added anatomical descriptions to each one, as well as some anatomical illustrations. (Two American printings of individual volumes of
Ornithological Biography appeared soon after the first publication in
Edinburgh; Audubon intended them to correspond exactly to the
Edinburgh edition.) *Ornithological Biography* was not republished as
a separate work during Audubon's lifetime, but much of the text was
incorporated into the Royal Octavo edition of *Birds of America*
(1840–44). The later text includes minor alterations, probably made
by Audubon himself, intended to update the work scientifically, and
in some instances entries were expanded; more frequently, however,
the text of the Edinburgh edition was shortened fit the Royal Octavo edition's less ample format. The present volume does not print
the taxonomic synonymies, anatomical descriptions, or anatomical illustrations that follow Audubon's bird biographies in the Edinburgh
Ornithological Biography; plate numbering in the Edinburgh edition
has been altered to refer to the plate numbering in this volume (for
Audubon's original plate numbering, see the Note on the Plates).

The Missouri River Journals record Audubon's travels between
March 11 and November 6, 1843, while he was sketching and gathering specimens for his *Viviparous Quadrupeds of North America*
(1845–48). Audubon sent a copy of the journals to his friend and col-
laborator John Bachman; neither the copy nor Audubon's original
manuscript is known to be extant. The text presented in this volume
is printed from *Audubon and His Journals* (1897), edited by Maria
Audubon. Her bracketed corrections and explanatory notes have
been deleted here, but where she omitted material, the present text
includes her bracketed comments to that effect.

"Account of the Method of Drawing Birds," originally written as
a letter "to a friend," is printed here from the *Edinburgh Journal of
Science*, 8 (1828): 48–54. No manuscript of this letter is known to be
extant.

The text of "My Style of Drawing Birds" presented in this volume has been prepared from a facsimile of Audubon's manuscript (the original of which is in private hands) published in *My Style of Drawing Birds* (Overland Press, 1979); it is printed by permission of the Haydn Foundation, Ardsley, New York. (The version of "My Style of Drawing Birds" published in *Audubon and His Journals* differs considerably from the manuscript version.)

"Myself," an autobiographical account written by Audubon for his sons, was first published in *Scribner's* in March 1893, with an introduction by Maria Audubon in which she wrote that although "in one or two instances paragraphs and names which bear on purely family matters have been omitted," the text otherwise "has been left untouched." When she reprinted "Myself" four years later in *Audubon and His Journals*, Maria Audubon corrected some dates and the spelling of some names and altered punctuation. No manuscript of "Myself" is known to be extant. The text printed here is from *Audubon and His Journals*.

The final section of this volume contains a selection of 18 letters written by Audubon between December 1826 and November 1843. Most of these letters have been previously published in *Letters of John James Audubon, 1826–1840*, edited by Howard Corning (Boston: Club of Odd Volumes, 1930), or in periodicals; three letters, marked with an asterisk in the list that follows, appear here for the first time. The texts of the letters included in this volume have been newly prepared from Audubon's manuscripts. In a few instances, words or parts of words have been lost as a result of damage to the manuscripts caused by tearing when they were opened; such instances of manuscript mutilation are indicated in this volume with square brackets. (In one instance, at 820.35 in this volume, a space in Audubon's manuscript is indicated by a two-em space.) Postscripts written by others have not been included.

In the following list, the three institutions from which the manuscripts of letters have been obtained are indicated by the abbreviations noted immediately below:

APS   American Philosophical Society, Philadelphia, Pennsylvania. Reprinted by permission.

Houghton   Houghton Library, Harvard University, Cambridge, Massachusetts (bMS Am 1482). Reprinted by permission.

Princeton   The John James Audubon Collection, Manuscripts Division, Department of Rare Books and Special Collections, Princeton University Library, Princeton, New Jersey. Reprinted by permission of the Princeton University Library.

To Lucy Audubon, December 9, 1826. *Princeton* B2 F5
*To Lucy Audubon, May 15, 1827. *Princeton* B2 F6
To Lucy Audubon, August 6, 1827. *APS*
*To Lucy Audubon, November 2, 1828. *Princeton* B2 F10
To Lucy Audubon, May 10, 1829. *APS*
To Lucy Audubon, October 23, 1831. *APS*
To Robert Havell, April 20, 1833. *Houghton* 54
To Victor G. Audubon, September 15, 1833. *APS*
To John Bachman, August 25, 1834. *Houghton* 61
To John Bachman, December 3, 1834. *Houghton* 66
To John Bachman, April 20, 1835. *Houghton* 70
To John Bachman, January 22, 1836. *Houghton* 90
To John Bachman, February 24, 1837. *Houghton* 107
To John Bachman, October 4, 1837. *Houghton* 120
To John Bachman, April 14, 1838. *Houghton* 126
To Robert Havell, March 13, 1839. *Houghton* 139
To John Bachman, January 2, 1840. *Houghton* 149
*To John Bachman, November 12, 1843. *Houghton* 160

This volume presents the texts of the original editions and manuscripts chosen for inclusion here. It does not attempt to reproduce features of their typographic design, such as the display capitalization of chapter openings, or holographic features, such as the long "s" or variation in the length of dashes. Spelling, punctuation, and capitalization are often expressive features and are not altered, even when inconsistent or irregular. The following is a list of slips of the pen and typographical errors corrected, cited by page and line number: 3.6, whith; 9.2, one the; 10.31, Thermoter; 11.33, Natured Natured; 16.5, a Golconda; 17.25, Falks; 18.10, quen; 18.12, fliyng; 18.25, Sid; 18.32, foather; 21.28, Thermoter; 21.38, althoug; 23.31, Groun; 25.29, Sungs; 27.4, Wing; 28.18, Surprised; 29.14–15, a S^r; 31.13, bade; 35.17, an; 37.12, in was; 39.17, fling; 47.11, and agreable; 48.30, the feed; 48.37, by; 54.4, say; 57.11, brougt; 58.6, Clouds Ducks; 60.29, seinig; 61.18, of; 62.32, surprisind; 66.33, a 25; 64.4, 31th; 64.27, of will; 66.25–26, considerab; 67.11, Pud; 68.21, that a; 70.20, 1820; 71.16, 1820; 72.34, beyong; 76.10, Waked; 77.13, though; 80.7–8, Merodanda; 84.14, are Most Likely are; 84.29, fliyng; 86.30, Parell; 88.10, also so; 89.3, had being; 92.2, Swifness; 92.28, Side the; 96.13, relatiable; 97.2, My My; 98.1, 24^d; 105.21, throaded; 105.33, kept^d; 108.28, Greasted; 110.6, plentituss; 111.23, Judment; 112.8, wind; 113.7, Genius; 113.20, its Move; 115.4, Kind; 117.10, an explore; 120.21, sammer; 125.14, assiociating; 125.21, Daugher; 126.15, Avarocations; 126.20, evering; 126.30, Ortinthology; 126.31, arraning; 132.25, Incusive;

132.35, premidited; 134.29, beyong; 135.9, bad; 135.29, begainging; 136.10, althoug; 140.20, Daugher; 141.24, 1820; 141.29, feather; 146.14, felling; 148.27, fullil; 150.24, & &; 159.23, feeling; 160.24, side; 161.15, urges; 161.21, bring; 161.24, both Side; 162.6–7, unwarly; 164.4, Enable; 165.19, from clock.; 167.2, efface; 167.35, american; 168.8, slaped; 171.7, kew; 173.13, finished; 174.31, hair; 176.22, *Man*; 176.39, lodge; 177.4, wer; 177.5, beg; 177.14, become; 186.17, Worst; 186.34, Streamletlet; 187.15, most; 187.19, perhap, 189.7, hun^d; 206.22, a strutting; 224.32, on on; 249.38, blue-Bird; 292.19, where-/ever; 300.3, themselves,; 468.32, disat ance; 493.12, "Reserve."; 493.34, "dismal swamp."; 495.28, "Pray . . . go."; 532.19, navy."; 548.26, wa; 593.8, said; 664.32, thursting; 673.3, Owen,; 686.9, of the; 753.20, äirksome; 790.21, T——; 798.31, weleathy; 806.5, wat has; 806.12, be to them; 809.17, thee and; 809.30, pleased with bit; 811.22,;s2 the; 820.21 Virnigia; 820.22, is I; 822.9, opportunies; 826.21, engraged; 829.23, Worty; 833.7, the go; 833.9, unknow; 834.36, anniversy; 838.33, althoug; 844.27, Dowy; 845.8, Jame's; 845.12, Buren'; 846.25, Setting; 848.3, Bonapt'; 850.8, 83th; 850.11, name, Nymphaea; 850.13, his head; 850.28, in a; 851.7, imcuber; 851.25, know; 856.9, are are; 856.26, we never

Note on the Plates

The plates in this volume have been published with support from
FURTHERMORE . . .
the publication program of The J.M. Kaplan Fund.

This volume reproduces 64 works of art by John James Audubon in two sections of 32 plates each. Thirty-four of these plates have been taken from engravings published during Audubon's lifetime: 25 from the Double Elephant Folio *Birds of America* (1827–38; abbreviated in the list below as "DEF"), one from the Royal Octavo edition of *Birds of America* (1840–44), and eight from the Royal Octavo edition of *The Viviparous Quadrupeds of North America* (1845–48; abbreviated as "*Quadrupeds*"). The remaining plates have been taken from Audubon's original drawings, 25 of which were later engraved for the Double Elephant Folio (five remained unpublished during Audubon's lifetime; one, plate 26, is published here for the first time.)

The list below gives the current common and scientific name of the species represented in each plate (for birds, nomenclature follows the American Ornithologists' Union *Check-list of North American Birds* [6th Edition, 1983, and Supplement, 1997], and for mammals, Ronald M. Nowak and John L. Paradiso, eds., *Walker's Mammals of the World*, 5th edition [Baltimore: Johns Hopkins UP, 1991]). Also listed are Audubon's original title or caption, date and place of composition (when known), or engraver and date of engraving, and the source from which the plate was obtained. For additional information about Audubon's art and references to other studies, see: Annette Blaugrund and Theodore E. Stebbins Jr., eds., *John James Audubon: The Watercolors for* Birds of America (New York: Villard, 1993); Alice Ford, *Audubon's Animals: The Quadrupeds of North America* (New York: Thomas Y. Crowell, 1951); Waldemar H. Fries, *The Double Elephant Folio: The Story of Audubon's* Birds of America (Chicago: American Library Association, 1973); Susanne M. Low, *An Index and Guide to Audubon's* Birds of America (New York: Abbeville Press, 1988).

Sources are indicated by the following abbreviations:

AMNH   American Museum of Natural History, New York. Courtesy Department of Library Services, American Museum of Natural History.

Houghton	Houghton Library, Harvard University. Reprinted by permission.
NHML	Natural History Museum, London. Reprinted by permission.
NYHS	New-York Historical Society. All images copyright © Collection of the New-York Historical Society. Reprinted by permission.
Hirschl & Adler	Department of American Prints, Hirschl & Adler Galleries, New York. Reprinted by permission.

PLATE 1   Wild Turkey, *Meleagris gallopavo*
"Great American Cock Male—Vulgo (Wild Turkey—)
—MALEAGRIS GALLOPAVO"
Engraved by William H. Lizars, 1826; without later additions by
Robert Havell Jr. (DEF I)
Hirschl & Adler

PLATE 2   Common Grackle, *Quiscalus quiscula*
"Purple Grackle QUISCALUS VERSICOLOR"
Engraved by William H. Lizars, 1827; printed and colored by R.
Havell Sr. (DEF VII)
NHML

PLATE 3   Bald Eagle, *Haliaeetus leucocephalus*
"The Bird of Washington or Great American Sea Eagle FALCO
WASHINGTONIENSIS"
Engraved by Robert Havell Jr., 1827 (DEF XI)
Hirschl & Adler

PLATE 4   Northern Mockingbird, *Mimus polyglottos*
"Mocking-Bird TURDUS POLYGLOTTUS. Linn."
Engraved by Robert Havell Jr., 1827 (DEF XXI)
Hirschl & Adler

PLATE 5   Carolina Parakeet, *Conuropsis carolinensis*
"Carolina Parrot"
June 9, 1811; Henderson, Kentucky
Houghton (pfMS Am 21, HCL # 88, box 4)

PLATE 6   Carolina Parakeet, *Conuropsis carolinensis*
"Carolina Parrot PSITACUS CAROLINENSIS, Linn."
Engraved by Robert Havell Jr., 1828 (DEF XXVI)
Hirschl & Adler

PLATE 7   Carolina Parakeet, *Conuropsis carolinensis.*
"Carolina Parrot or Parrakeet"
William Hitchcock after Audubon, engraved by J.T. Bowen,
1842 (Royal Octavo 278)
Houghton

PLATE 8   Peregrine Falcon, *Falco peregrinus*
"Great-footed Hawk FALCO PEREGRINUS. Gmel."
Engraved by Robert Havell Jr., 1827 (DEF XVI)
AMNH

PLATE 9   Ruby-throated Hummingbird, *Archilochus colubris*
               "Ruby-throated Humming Bird TROCHILUS COLUBRIS"
               Engraved by Robert Havell Jr., 1828 (DEF XLVII)
               NHML

PLATE 10   Bald Eagle, *Haliaeetus leucocephalus*
               "White headed Eagle FALCO LEUCOCEPHALUS. Linn."
               Engraved by Robert Havell Jr., 1828 (DEF XXXI)
               Hirsch & Adler

PLATE 11   Bald Eagle, *Haliaeetus leucocephalus*
               "White-headed Eagle, Falco leucocephalus"
               November 23, 1820. Little Prairie, Mississippi; later engraved as
                   DEF XXXI
               NYHS

PLATE 12   Red-tailed Hawk, *Buteo jamaicensis*
               "Red Shouldered Hawk"
               1821, later reworked; later engraved as DEF LI
               NYHS

PLATE 13   Osprey, *Pandion haliaetus*
               "Fish Hawk or Osprey FALCO HALIAETUS"
               Engraved Robert Havell Jr., 1830 (DEF LXXXI)
               Hirschl & Adler

PLATE 14   Passenger Pigeon, *Ectopistes migratorius*
               "Chute de l'Ohio"
               December 11, 1809
               Houghton (pfMS Am 21, HCL # 49, Box 8)

PLATE 15   Passenger Pigeon, *Ectopistes migratorius*
               "Passenger Pigeon, Columba migratoria"
               1824; later engraved as DEF LXII
               NYHS

PLATE 16   Ivory-billed Woodpecker, *Campephilus principalis*
               "Ivory Bill Woodpeckers"
               November 28, 1812
               Houghton (pfMS Am 21, HCL # 31, Box 10)

PLATE 17   Ivory-billed Woodpecker, *Campephilus principalis*
               "Ivory-billed Woodpecker PICUS PRINCIPALIS. Linn."
               Engraved by Robert Havell Jr., 1829 (DEF LXVI)
               AMNH

PLATE 18   Wood Thrush, *Hylocichla mustelina*
               "Wood Thrush"
               August 14, 1806
               Houghton (pfMS Am 21, HL # 89, Box 9)

PLATE 19   Wood Thrush, *Hylocichla mustelina*
               "Wood Thrush, Turdus mustelinus"
               April 21, 1822; dogwood painted by Joseph Mason; later
                   engraved as DEF LXXIII
               NYHS

PLATE 20   Broad-winged Hawk, *Buteo platypterus*
            "Broad-Winged Hawk FALCO PENNSYLVANICUS. *Wils.*"
            Engraved by Robert Havell Jr., 1830 (DEF XCI)
            Hirschl & Adler

PLATE 21   Blue Jay, *Cyanocitta cristata*
            "Blue Jay CORVUS CRISTATUS"
            Engraved by Robert Havell Jr., 1831 (DEF CII)
            AMNH

PLATE 22   Black Vulture, *Coragyps atratus*
            "Black Vulture"
            1820; later engraved as DEF CVI
            NYHS

PLATE 23   Mississippi Kite, *Ictinia mississippiensis*
            "Mississippi Kite Male—Falco Mississippiensis"
            June 28, 1821; James Pirrie's plantation, Louisiana; later modified
                and engraved as DEF CXVII
            NYHS

PLATE 24   Black Vulture, *Coragyps atratus*
            [untitled]
            1829
            NYHS

PLATE 25   Pileated Woodpecker, *Pyrocopus pileatus*
            "Pileated Woodpecker"
            1829; later engraved as DEF CXI
            NYHS

PLATE 26   Eastern Phoebe, *Sayornis phoebe*, and Acadian Flycatcher,
                Empidonax virescens
            "Small Green-Crested Flycatcher, Muscicapa querula, and Pewit
                Flycatcher A.W. Muscicapa Nunciola"
            May 22, 1811; Henderson, Kentucky
            Houghton (pfMS Am 21, HCL # 85 and 86, box 8)

PLATE 27   Eastern Phoebe, *Sayornis phoebe*
            "Pewit Flycatcher—Muscicapa Fusca"
            c. 1825; later engraved as DEF CXX
            NYHS

PLATE 28   Snowy Owl, *Nyctea scandiaca*
            "Snowy Owl STRYX NYCTEA. Linn."
            Engraved by Robert Havell Jr., 1831 (DEF CXXI)
            AMNH

PLATE 29   American Kestrel, *Falco sparverius*
            "American Sparrow Hawk—*Falco Sparverius*"
            Later engraved as DEF CXLII
            NYHS

PLATE 30   American Crow, *Corvus brachyrhynchos*
            "American Crow CORVUS AMERICANUS"
            Engraved by Robert Havell Jr., 1833 (DEF CLVI)
            NHML

PLATE 31   Chimney Swift, *Chaetura pelagica*
            [untitled]
            c.1824/1829; later engraved as DEF CLVIII
            NYHS

PLATE 32   Golden Eagle, *Aquila chrysaetos*
            "Aquila Chrysaetos Sen / Golden Eagle Female Adult"
            1833; later engraved as DEF CLXXXI
            NYHS

PLATE 33   Canada Goose, *Branta canadensis*
            "Canada Goose ANSER CANADIENSIS. Vieill."
            Engraved by Robert Havell Jr., 1834 (DEF CCI)
            AMNH

PLATE 34   Clapper Rail, *Rallus longirostris*
            "Salt Water Marsh Hen RALLUS CREPITANS. Gm."
            Later engraved as DEF CCIV
            NYHS

PLATE 35   Great Blue Heron, *Ardea herodias*
            "Great Blue Heron, ARDEA HERODIAS"
            Later engraved as DEF CCXI
            NYHS

PLATE 36   Atlantic Puffin, *Fratercula arctica*
            [untitled]
            1833, Labrador; later engraved as DEF CCXIII
            NYHS

PLATE 37   Razorbill, *Alca torda*
            "Razor-billed Auk—*Alca Torda*"
            1833, Labrador; later engraved as DEF CCXIV
            NYHS

PLATE 38   Wood Stork, *Mycteria americana*
            "Wood Ibiss TANTALUS LOCULATOR"
            Engraved by Robert Havell Jr., 1834 (DEF CCXVI)
            Hirschl & Adler

PLATE 39   Whooping Crane, *Grus americana*
            [untitled]
            1821, New Orleans, with later additions; later engraved as DEF
                CCXXVI
            NYHS

PLATE 40   Tricolored Heron, *Egretta tricolor*
            "Louisiana Heron ARDEA LUDOVICIANA. Wils."
            1832; later engraved as DEF CCXVII
            NYHS

PLATE 41   Mallard, *Anas platyrhynchos*
            [untitled]
            1821–25; later engraved as DEF CCXXI
            NYHS

PLATE 42   White Ibis, *Eudocimus albus*
            "White Ibis IBIS ALBA"
            Engraved by Robert Havell Jr., 1834 (DEF CCXXII)
            Hirschl & Adler

PLATE 43   Long-billed Curlew, *Numenius americanus*
            "Long-billed Curlew NUMENIUS LONGIROSTRIS"
            Engraved by Robert Havell Jr., 1834 (DEF CCXXXI)
            Hirschl & Adler

PLATE 44   Snowy Egret, *Egretta thula*
            [untitled]
            1832; later engraved as DEF CCXLII
            NYHS

PLATE 45   Brown Pelican, *Pelecanus occidentalis*
            "Brown Pelican PELICANUS FUSCUS"
            Engraved by Robert Havell Jr., 1835 (DEF CCLI)
            Hirschl & Adler

PLATE 46   Brown Pelican, *Pelecanus occidentalis*
            [untitled]
            1821, New Orleans; later engraved as DEF CCCCXXI
            NYHS

PLATE 47   Great Blue Heron, *Ardea herodias*
            "Great White Heron ARDEA OCCIDENTALIS"
            Engraved by Robert Havell Jr., 1835 (DEF CCLXXXI)
            Hirschl & Adler

PLATE 48   Little Blue Heron, *Egretta caerulea*
            "Blue Heron ARDEA CAERULEA"
            Engraved by Robert Havell Jr., 1836 (DEF CCCVII)
            AMNH

PLATE 49   Blue-winged Teal, *Anas discors*
            "Blue-winged Teal ANAS DISCORS"
            Engraved by Robert Havell Jr., 1836 (DEF CCCXIII)
            AMNH

PLATE 50   Anhinga, *Anhinga anhinga*
            "*Bec à Lanette*, Black-bellied Darter . . . Snake Bird"
            1822
            NYHS

PLATE 51   Anhinga, *Anhinga anhinga*
            "Black-Bellied Darter PLOTUS ANHINGA"
            Engraved by Robert Havell Jr., 1836 (DEF CCCXVI)
            NHML

PLATE 52   Great Egret, *Casmerodius albus*
            "White Heron or Great White Heron"
            1821; later engraved as DEF CCCLXXXVI
            NYHS

PLATE 53   Greater Flamingo, *Phoenicopterus ruber*
              "American Flamingo PHOENICOPTERUS RUBER, Linn."
              Engraved by Robert Havell Jr., 1838 (DEF CCCCXXXI)
              NHML

PLATE 54   Trumpeter Swan, *Cygnus buccinator*
              [untitled]
              December 1821, New Orleans; later engraved as DEF CCCLXXVI
              NYHS

PLATE 55   Trumpeter Swan, *Cygnus buccinator*
              "Trumpeter Swan CYGNUS BUCCINATOR. Richardson"
              Engraved by Robert Havell Jr., 1836 (DEF CCCVI)
              AMNH

PLATE 56   American Avocet, *Recurvirostra americana*
              [untitled]
              November 7, 1821; later engraved as DEF CCCXVIII
              NYHS

PLATE 57   Thirteen-lined Ground Squirrel, *Citellus tridecemlineatus*
              "Leopard Spermophile"
              R. Trembly after Audubon (*Quadrupeds* 39)
              Houghton

PLATE 58   Plains Pocket Gopher, *Geomys bursarius*
              "Canada Pouched Rat"
              Unknown artist after Audubon (*Quadrupeds* 44)
              Houghton

PLATE 59   Bushy-tailed Woodrat, *Neotoma cinerea drummondi*
              "Rocky Mountain Neotoma"
              R. Trembly after Audubon (*Quadrupeds* 29)
              Houghton

PLATE 60   Black-tailed Prairie Dog, *Cynomys ludovicianus*
              "Prairie-Dog— Prairie Marmot Squirrel"
              W. E. Hitchcock after Audubon (*Quadrupeds* 99)
              AMNH

PLATE 61   American Beaver, *Castor canadensis*
              "American Beaver"
              W.E. Hitchcock after Audubon (*Quadrupeds* 46)
              AMNH

PLATE 62   American Badger, *Taxidea taxus*
              "American Badger"
              Unknown artist after Audubon (*Quadrupeds* 47)
              Houghton

PLATE 63   Swift Fox, *Vulpes velox*
              "Swift Fox"
              W. E. Hitchcock after Audubon (*Quadrupeds* 52)
              AMNH

PLATE 64   American Bison, *Bison bison*
              "American Bison or Buffalo"
              W. E. Hitchcock after Audubon (*Quadrupeds* 57)
              AMNH

Notes

In the notes below, the reference numbers denote page and line of this volume (the line count includes chapter headings). No note is made for information included in standard desk reference works such as Webster's *Collegiate, Biographical,* and *Geographical* dictionaries. For further information and references to other studies, see Carolyn E. Delatte, *Lucy Audubon: A Biography* (Baton Rouge: Louisiana State University Press, 1982); Alice Ford, *John James Audubon: A Biography* (Norman: University of Oklahoma Press, 1964; revised ed., New York: Abbeville Press, 1988); Francis Hobart Herrick, *Audubon the Naturalist: A History of His Life and Times* (New York: Appleton, 1917; revised ed. 1938); Jay Shuler, *Had I the Wings: The Friendship of Bachman and Audubon* (Athens: University of Georgia Press, 1995).

MISSISSIPPI RIVER JOURNAL

3.1   *Mississippi River Journal*]   In Audubon's manuscript, the text of the journal is preceded by several miscellaneous items: a vertical line about 10 inches long labeled "Length of My Lucy's foot—" and the scribbled note "Call at J. C. Wilkins 26ᵗʰ Natchez—"; a labeled schematic drawing of a bird adapted from a plate in volume one of William Turton's 1806 English translation of Linnaeus's *Systema naturae* (page 2 in this volume); a mileage chart, with part of the paper excised; a recipe for "Small Beer": "to one Botle of Porter put 8 of Watter about 3 ozᶜ brown Sugar—Shake the Whole in a Jug.—Botled after Matured—."

3.8–9   Joseph Mason . . . of age]   Joseph Robert Mason (1808–42) provided watercolor backgrounds for many images in *The Birds of America*; he later worked as an artist at Bartram's garden in Philadelphia.

3.36   Wᵃᵐ Harrison's Plantation]   William Henry Harrison (1773–1841), later President of the United States, owned a farm near North Bend, Ohio.

5.14   Talbut]   Senator Isham Talbot, a frequent guest of Audubon's in Henderson, Kentucky.

5.15   Your Mother]   Audubon wrote his journal at least in part for his first son, Victor Gifford Audubon (1809–60).

5.16   Wᵃᵐ B]   William Gifford Bakewell (1789–1871), Lucy Audubon's youngest brother.

8.11   Not so Stupid . . . Linné]   In William Turton's 1806 translation of Linnaeus's *Systema naturae*, which Audubon carried with him to New Orleans, the Snow Goose is described as "a very stupid bird."

8.14   Mr Brigs] Charles Briggs, English-born merchant who had befriended Audubon in Henderson, Kentucky, and later moved to New
Orleans.

12.32–33   Shawaney Town] Shawneetown, Illinois.

13.25   famous *Rock in Cave*] "Cave-in-Rock," a limestone cave on the
Illinois shore of the Ohio just above present-day Cave-in-Rock, Illinois; it had
served in 1797 as headquarters of highwayman and pirate Samuel Mason.

18.4   *Fort Massacre*] Fort Massac, on the north bank of the Ohio, ten
miles below Paducah, Kentucky.

19.15   S. Eagles] "Sea Eagles" (the young of the Bald Eagle, *Haliaeetus
leucocephalus*) were considered by Audubon to be a separate species, which he
later named "The Bird of Washington."

22.10   Iron Banks] *Mine au Fer*, on the Kentucky side of the Mississippi, 20 miles below the mouth of the Ohio.

23.10   the Head of N° 8.] Audubon's references in his Mississippi River
Journal to numbered islands follow the system used in *The Navigator*, a pilot
book by Zadok Cramer and others, published under varying titles in 12 editions through 1824.

25.37–38   began my Drawing] See plate 10 in this volume.

28.22   the first Chicasaw Bluff] At present-day Fort Pillow State Park,
Lauderdale County, Tennessee.

29.19   Major Croghan] William Croghan, a hero of the Revolutionary
War, on whose estate in Louisville, Kentucky, Audubon was a frequent guest.

30.30–31   he tried . . . ever] In Audubon's manuscript, parts of this passage have been canceled, possibly in another hand, and are illegible: "he
[   ] tried his opportunity [   ] we parted for ever."

31.17–24   T. W. Bakewell . . . Third Partner] Thomas Woodhouse
Bakewell (1788–1874), brother of Lucy Audubon, was Audubon's partner in
the construction of a steam-powered mill in Henderson, Kentucky; Thomas
Pears later became the third partner.

32.4   likeness . . . Berthoud] A native of Neuchâtel, Switzerland, who
had settled in Shippingport, Kentucky, in 1803; Audubon's portrait, completed in 1819, is in the J. B. Speed Art Museum, Louisville, Kentucky.

35.20   *The Pride of China*] Chinaberry ("Pride of India" or "China-
tree"), *Melia azedarach*.

35.23–24   *Fort Pickering*] Site of present-day Memphis, Tennessee.

41.38   Arkansas Fort] The Arkansas Post, at the junction of the White,
Mississippi, and Arkansas rivers, north of Arkansas City.

42.12   Mrs Harrison]   Anna Symmes, wife of William Henry Harrison.

42.17   J. Miller]   James Miller, first governor (1819–24) of the Arkansas Territory.

43.13   Doc^r *Drake*]   Daniel Henry Drake (1785–1852), a Cincinnati physician, editor, chemist, and merchant, who in 1820 had hired Audubon to stuff specimens for the Western Museum in Cincinnati.

45.17   Cordel]   Cordelle, a towing line or rope.

46.24   Mr *Barbour*]   Henry Barbour, a trader with bases at Arkansas Post, New Orleans, and Three Forks on the Arkansas River.

46.29   The Cadron]   A settlement south of the mouth of Cadron Creek near present-day Conway, Arkansas.

47.19   *Point Rock*]   Little Rock, which became the capital of Arkansas Territory on November 20, 1821.

48.31   *Sturnus depradatorius*]   Red-winged Blackbird, *Agelaius phoeniceus* (*Sturnus prædatorius* in Alexander Wilson's *American Ornithology*).

53.13–14   *Pointe Chico*]   Point Chicot, opposite present-day Greenville, Mississippi.

53.14   *Spanish Beard*]   Spanish moss.

55.2   the Carrion Crow]   See plate 24 in this volume.

57.20   *Walnut Hills*]   The site of present-day Vicksburg, Mississippi.

57.23   Warington]   Warrenton, now part of Vicksburg, Mississippi.

59.21   Mr Livingston's]   Edward Livingston (1764–1836), a New Orleans lawyer, served as military secretary and legal adviser to Andrew Jackson.

62.13   *Cook*]   Probably George Cooke (1793–1849), portrait, historical, and landscape painter.

69.3   *George Croghan*]   Kentucky-born soldier (1791–1849) who distinguished himself at Fort Stephenson during the War of 1812; son of William Croghan (see note 29.19).

73.3–4   Mr Prentice]   David Prentice, a millwright, had advised Audubon in the operation of his Henderson grist mill.

74.32   Jarvis the P. Painter]   John Wesely Jarvis (1780–1840), portrait and miniature painter, engraver, and sculptor. (See "The Original Painter," pages 528–33 in this volume.)

75.17   Doctor Hunter]   George Hunter (1755–c.1823), Philadelphia apothecary and mineralogist who, along with William Dunbar from Natchez, was appointed by President Jefferson in 1804 to explore the Red River, one of the boundaries of the newly purchased Louisiana Territory.

76.26   Mʳ *Pamar*] Roman Pamar, owner of a New Orleans establishment selling glass, china, and earthenware.

77.38   Mʳ *Laville*] J. F. Laville, a meat inspector.

79.13   Mʳ Louallier] Louis Louailler, former member of the Louisiana legislature.

82.33   Mʳˢ *André*] In a letter from Audubon to his wife dated May 24, 1821 (now at the American Philosophical Society, Philadelphia, and marked "Not used + not for general reading as he decided" by his granddaughter Maria Audubon; printed here by permission of the American Philosophical Society *Audubon Papers* [B/Au25]), Audubon included an account of his relationship with this sitter that he said was taken from his diary:

I was accosted on the day of x 1821, at the corner of   Street & Street the former I take allmost daily not to be seen so much on Levée Street lugging my Port Folio, the astonishment of many—by a femelle of a fine form but whose face thickly covered by a Veil that I could not then distinguish it and who addressed Me quickly in about the following words in French—"Pray sir are you the one sent by the French Academy to draw the Birds of America" I answered that I drew them for my pleasure,   "You are he that draws Likenesses in Black Chalk so remarkably strong," I answered again that I took Likenesses in that Style. "then call in 30 Minutes at Nº   in   Street and walk upstairs I will wait for you"—I Bowed, "do not follow me now" I bowed again and as I went from her the course I had at first, took my pencil and put down the Street and Number; I soon reached a Book store where I waited some time having a feeling of astonishment undescribable, recollecting however how far I had to Walk, I Started and suppose the Stranger Employed a Carriadge—

I arrived, and as I walkᵈ upstairs I Saw her Apparently waiting "I am glad you have come, walk in quickly." my feeling became so agitated, that I trembled like a Leaf—this She perceived, Shut the door with a double lock and throwing her veil back Shewed me one of the most beautifull face, I ever saw "have You been or are you Married" yes madam "Long" 12 Years "is your Wife in this City" no Madam "Your name Audubon" yes madam "Set down and be easy" and with the smile of an Angel "I will not hurt you" I felt such a blush and such Deathness through me I could not answer. She raised and handed Me a Glass of cordial, so strange was all this to me that I drank it for I needed it, but awkwardly gave her the glass to take back—

She sat again immediately opposite me, and looking Me steadfastly askᵈ me if I thought I could draw her face—indeed I fear not answerᵈ I "I am sure You can if you will but before I say more what is Your price?" Generally 25$ she smiled again most sweetly "will you Keep my name if you discover it and My residence a secret?" If you require it "I do You must promess that to me, keep it for ever sacred although I care not about any thing else"

I promised to keep her name and her place of residence to Myself "have you ever Drawn a full figure" Yes *"Naked"* had I been shot with a 48 pounder through the Heart my articulating Powers could not have been more suddenly stopped. "well why do you not answer" I answered Yes; She raised walk^d the room a few times and sitting again Said, "I want you to draw my Likeness and the whole of my form naked but as I think you cannot work now, leave your Port Folio and return in one hour be silent."

She had Judged of my feelings precisely, I took my hat She open^d the door and I felt like a Bird that makes his escape from a strong Cage, filled with sweet Meats. had I met a Stranger on the stairs No doubt I would have been suspected for a Thief. I walk^d away fast looking behind me—

My thoughts rolled on her conduct, She look^d as if perfect Mistress of herself and yet look^d *I then thought* too young not supposing her more than Sixteen (a mistake however) and apparently not at all afraid to disclose to my eyes her sacred beauties—I tried to prepare myself for the occasion, the time passed and I arrived again at the foot of the Stairs.

She again was waiting for me and beckoned to me to move quick, She shut the door as the first time, then coming to me "Well how do you feel now, Still trembling a litle, what a Man you are—come, come, I am anxious to see the outline you will make, take time and be sure do not embellish any parts With your briliant Imagination, have your paper Suficiently large, I have some beautifull and good Chalks, the drawing will be compleated in this room and You will please do it on this" raising She gave me a Large Sheet of Elephant paper out of an *Armoire*.

The die was cast, I felt at once Easy, ready and pleased—

I told her I was waitting for her convenience, She repeated the urgency of Secrecy which I again promessed—

The *Couch* in the room was superbly decorated She drew the Curtains and I heard her undress. "I must be nearly in the Position you will see me unless your taste Should think proper to alter it by Speaking" very well was my answer Although I felt yet very Strange and never will forget the moment "please to draw the Curtains and arrange the light to Suit yourself." when drawing hirelings in company with 20 more I never cared but for a good outline, but Shut up with a beautifull young woman as much a Stranger to me as I was to her, I could not well reconcile all the feelings that were necessary to draw well, without mingling with them some of a very diferent nature—

Yet I drew the Curtain and saw this Beauty. "will I do so" I Eyed her but drop^d my black Lead pencil "I am glad you are so timid, but tell me will I do so" perceiving at once that the Position, the light and all had been carefully Studied, before I told her I fear^d She Look^d only too well for my talent—She Smiled and I begun—

I drew 55 Minutes by my watch, when She desired I should close the curtains—She dressed in an Instant and came imediatly to look at what was done—

"Is it like me? will it be like me? I hope it will be a likeness. I am a litle Chill, can you work any more without me today." I told her I could correct my Sketch "Well be contented and work as much as you can, I wish it was done, it is a folly but all our Sex is more or Less So." She remarked very approprietly an error and made me correct it—She pulled a Bell, a Woman came in with a Waiter covered with Cakes & Wine, left it and passed through a door I had not perceived before—She insisted on My resting a while, make me drank, asked me a thousand questions about my familly, residence, Birds, Way of travelling or living &c &c and certainly is a well informed femelle, using the best expressions and in all her actions possessing the manners necessary to Insure Respect & wonder—

I worked nearly Two hours more and Casted all the outlines of the Drawing, it pleased her apparently very much   I soon found She had received good Lessons, I begged to know her name   "not to day and if you are not Carefull and silent you never will see me again"   I assured her I would   "I have thought well of you from hear say and hope not to be mistaken."

I felt now very diferent thoughts from those I had while She was undressing in her curtains and ask^d when I must return again "every day at the same hour untill done but never again with your port folio   I will manage this once through your drawings of Birds." for Ten days at the exception of one Sunday, that She went out of the City, I had the pleasure of this beautifull woman's Company about one hour naked, and Two talking on diferent subjects,   She admired my work more every day   at least was pleased to say So, and on the 5th sitting she worked herself in a style much superior to mine—

The second day She desired to Know What I would ask her for my work, I told her I would be satisfied with whatever she would please give me   "I take you at your word   it will be *un Souvenir*   one who hunts so much needs a good Gun or Two, this afternoon see if there is one in the City & give this on a/c if you wish to please me to the last"   She handed me five Dollars   "I must see it and if I do not like it you are not to have it."   I thank^d her and told her it proprably would be a high price piece   "well that probably is Necessary to insure the good quality, do what I bid."   I took the note, when gone, felt very undetermined, Yet I hunted through the stores, found a good one & gave the Note on a/c with my name, telling the Shopmen that I did not well Knew when I would Call for it.—She was much gratified I had found One, when I told her I was asked One hundred and Twenty Dollars "No more well we will say nothing about it untill I see how I am pleased with your part." I worked from day to day. drawing besides a 25 Dollars Likeness every day, to be sure a litle at the expense of my Eyes at night, but how could I complain, how many artists would have been delighted of such lessons.

I finished my Drawing, or rather she did for when I returned every day I allways found the work much advanced, she touch^d it she said not because she was fatigued of my company daily but because She felt happy in mingling her talents with mine in a piece She had had in contemplation to have done, even before She left the country She came from. I suppose from Italy or France but never could assertain—

She often took my pencil to compose a devise to have engraved on the Gun Barrels, and ask^d me to have one of my own, but this I declined and left

to her taste and will. She at last decided on one which she said I must absolutly have done for her sake and ordered me to have it finished in a few days.

She had a beautifull frame the last morning I went, on which she ask^d my
opinion, this of Course I gave as I thought her desires inclined. She put her
Name at the foot of the Drawing as if *her own* and mine in a dark Shadded
part of Drapery; when I had Closed it and put it in a true light She gazed at
it for some moments and assured Me her wish was at last Gratified, and taking me by one hand gave me a delightfull Kiss—"had you acted otherwise
than you have, you would have received a very diferent recompense, go, take
this (125$) be happy think of me sometimes as you rest on your Gun, keep for
ever my name a secret" I begged to kiss her hand, She held it out freely—
We parted probably for ever—

it is well that I should say that She had had heard of me in a circle a few
days after I had taken the B.C. Likeness and of my collection of Birds that she
then understood, I was from France purposely sent by the Academy of Paris,
but soon was assured of the contrary by my way of living; and that she ask^d
me to try my veracity—that she employed a servant to watch my ways and
that for several nights this servant had remained very late to see if I absented
from the Boat and that in fact She knew every Step I had taken since the day
She had resolved on employing me. She ask^d Me if I had not seen a Mulatto
Man standing near the Gates of Madame A. x dry. two days Successively; this
I recollected but never supposed that any one watch^d my Steps—She praised
the few drawings of Birds I shewed her the first day and assured me that She
had no doubt I would be well recompensed for Such a Collection—

She never ask^d me to go see her when we parted, I have tried several times
in vain, the Servants allways saying Madame is absent. I have felt a great desire to see the Drawing since to Judge of it as I allways can do best after some
time.

here my Journal takes to another subject and I Leave to thee to conclude
what thou may of this extraordinary femelle—

Since, I have wished often I could have Shewn that Drawing to Mr Vanderlyn.—

The Lady was kind, the Gun is good and here is the Inscriptions on it—
Ne refuse pas ce don d'une amie qui t'est reconnaissante puisse t'il t'égaler
en bonté [Don't refuse this gift of a friend who is in your debt—may it equal
you in goodness]—and under the Raming Rod—Property of Laforest
Audubon February 22^d 1821.—her name *I* Engraved on it where I do not believe it will ever be found—

88.18   A. Liautaud] Augustin Liautaud, a merchant of the New Orleans
firm of Liautaud Brothers & Dolhonde.

89.11   Guesnon] Philip Guesnon, a collection clerk for the Bank of
Orleans.

89.36   Governor Robertson] Thomas Bolling Robertson (1779–1828),
governor of Louisiana, 1820–24.

89.37   Mr Hawkins] Joseph Hawkins, New Orleans attorney.

93.11–12   Mr *Vanderlyn*] John Vanderlyn (1775–1852), portrait, historical, and landscape painter, known for his panoramas.

93.28   how long Kempbell . . . Waitted] John Philip Kemble (1757–1853) was said to have stopped acting when one of his performances was interrupted by the loud talking of a young lady.

94.7   One of his figures of Women] *Ariadne Asleep on the Island of Naxos* (1812).

94.30   Judge Towles] Thomas Towles (1784–1850), born in Virginia, had moved to Henderson County, Kentucky, in 1805.

97.10–11   Mr *Earl . . . Jackson*] Ralph Eleaser Whiteside Earl (c. 1785–1838), itinerant artist and painter of more than two dozen portraits of Andrew Jackson. In 1821, Earl displayed one of these portraits (now at the Tennessee State Museum) in New Orleans and Natchez.

98.26   Vanderlyn's Likeness] Vanderlyn completed several portraits of Jackson, among them a head-and-shoulders likeness (c. 1819, City Hall Collection, Charleston, South Carolina) widely reproduced in contemporary engravings and a larger portrait (1820, Art Commission of the City of New York). In 1824, Audubon posed for another full-length portrait of Jackson in the artist's New York City studio.

98.27   *Sully's* Plate] Thomas Sully (1783–1872), English-born portrait and miniature painter; an 1820 engraving by James Barton Longacre of Sully's 1819 portrait of Jackson was widely circulated.

98.31–32   Mr *Bossier* portrait] *Jean Baptiste Bossier*, 1821, crayon and ink over graphite on paper, Nelson-Atkins Museum of Art, Kansas City, Missouri.

99.4   B. Morgan's] Benjamin Morgan (d. 1826), president of the New Orleans branch of the Bank of the United States beginning in 1816.

99.22   Berwicks] Thomas Berwick (1753–1828), engraver of *General History of Quadrupeds* (1790) and *History of British Birds* (1791–1804).

101.8   Miss Perry] Eliza Pirrie, daughter of Mr. and Mrs. James Pirrie of Oakley Plantation, Bayou Sara, Louisiana.

103.6–7   Mr Hollander] Edward Hollander, New Orleans merchant and Russian consul.

103.8   Vincent Nolte] Audubon had met Nolte (1779–1856), a New Orleans merchant, in 1817; Nolte later provided him with letters of recommendation to influential friends in Liverpool.

104.24   Lavaters directions] Johann Kaspar Lavater (1741–1801), the inventor of "physiognomy" or phrenology.

107.17   Egg represented by Willson]   In *American Ornithology*, vol. 2, pl. 10, fig. 1.

125.6   W^am Brand]   William Brand (c. 1778–1849), New Orleans building contractor and architect.

130.19   My Father *Don Antonio*]   Francis Antonio Ildefonso Moreno y Arze de Sedella (1748–1829), a Capuchin priest who served as curate of St. Louis Cathedral in New Orleans, a position from which he essentially controlled Catholic affairs in the city, from 1795 until his death; the present location of Audubon's portrait is not known.

131.29–30   "*a l'œuvre on connoit L'Artizan*"]   "The artist is known by his work"; from Jean de La Fontaine's "Les Frelons et les mouches à miel" ("The Hornets and the Honeybees," *Fables* i. 21).

133.8   M. Basterop]   Probably Basterot (first name unknown), a portrait painter and drawing teacher who came to New Orleans in 1821.

133.18   *Bruster* the Painter]   Edmund Brewster (b. 1784/94?), portrait and landscape painter.

133. 26–27   My Wife's Mother's in Law]   Rebecca Smith Bakewell, Lucy Audubon's stepmother.

136.24   Miss *Bornet's* academy]   Clotilde Bornct was principal of the Female Academy in New Orleans.

138.17   E. Fiske . . . City]   Eben Fiske, a merchant, had served as agent for the firm of Audubon & Bakewell (est. 1811).

141.7   the Maire's Lady Mrs Rofignac]   Joseph Roffignac was mayor of New Orleans from 1820 to 1828.

143.21–22   Mr Selle & Mr Jany Painters]   Jean-B. ("John B.") Sel worked as a portrait and miniature painter in New Orleans from 1821 until his death in 1832; Jean Baptiste Jeannin (c. 1792–1863), an art teacher, became president of Central College in New Orleans in 1838.

147.8–9   Bonaparte's Service]   A procession and funeral service in honor of Napoleon I took place in New Orleans on December 19, 1821.

148.11   Mr Colas]   Louis Antoine Collas, also known as Lewis Collers (1775–1856), portrait painter and miniaturist active prior to 1816 at the court of the czar in St. Petersburg and between 1822 and 1829 in New Orleans.

149.6   Latham]   John Latham (1740–1837), physician, naturalist, and author of *General Synopsis of Birds* (1781–85).

1826 JOURNAL

159.3   My leaving the U. S.]   Audubon had left New Orleans on May 17, 1826, on the *Delos*, bound for Liverpool.

162.1–2   the Daughter of Titian] Titian's *Girl with a Basket of Fruits* (1555–58), long thought to represent the artist's daughter Lavinia.

162.11–13   Thomson's the 4 seasons . . . Indolence] *The Seasons* (1730) and *The Castle of Indolence* (1748), by Scottish poet and dramatist James Thomson (1700–48).

163.11   Genus Anas] In Linnaeus's *Systema naturae*, *Anas* includes ducks, swans, and geese.

163.24–25   such a Loaf . . . Market] Benjamin Franklin, *Autobiography*, part I.

163.37   Mr Ord] George Ord (1781–1866), naturalist and philologist, edited and completed Alexander Wilson's *American Ornithology*; he was one of Audubon's principal American critics.

165.14   Mr Swift] John Swift, of St. Francisville, Louisiana, Audubon's cabin mate.

165.27–30   Mr Rathbone . . . Mother] Richard Rathbone and his brother William Rathbone (1787–1868) were prominent Liverpool cotton merchants, who along with their mother, Hannah Mary Reynolds Rathbone (1761–1839), and sister Hannah Mary Rathbone ("Miss Rathbone") entertained Audubon at Green Bank, their estate near Liverpool. William, who became mayor of Liverpool in 1837, was married to Elizabeth Greg (d. 1882).

166.1   Bourgeat] Augustin Bourgeat, one of Audubon's Louisiana hunting companions.

166.3–4   Philemon & Baucis] See Ovid, *Metamorphoses*, viii.611–724.

167.6   W. Goddard] William Stanley Goddard (1757–1845), former headmaster of Winchester College, had been prebendary of St. Paul's since 1814.

168.5   Thomas Kinder] New York businessman in whose firm Thomas Bakewell, Audubon's brother-in-law, had received his mercantile training.

168.11   Adam Hodgsons] Business partner and cousin of Richard and William Rathbone.

170.34   Bonaparte's Birds . . . Dr Trail] Charles Lucien Bonaparte's *American Ornithology; or the Natural History of Birds Inhabiting the United States, not Given by Wilson* (vol. 1, 1825); Thomas Stewart Traill (1781–1862), physician and naturalist, editor of the eighth edition of the *Encyclopedia Britannica*.

170.38   Harlan's Fauna] *Fauna Americana: Being a Description of the Mammiferous Animals Inhabiting North America* (1825), by Quaker physician Richard Harlan (1796–1843), was the first systematic treatment of American mammals, living and fossil.

171.1   W^{am} Roscoe] William Roscoe, English poet, historian, and amateur botanist, author of *The Life of Lorenzo de' Medici* (1796) and *Life and Pontificate of Leo the Tenth* (1805).

172.2–3   the ride taken . . . Englishman] In his *Wanderings in South America* (1825), naturalist and adventurer Charles Waterton claimed to have ridden on a caiman, a South American crocodilian similar to an alligator.

173.13   my Male Pheasant] Audubon painted several sporting scenes while in England; his *English Pheasants Surprised by a Spanish Dog* is now owned by the American Museum of Natural History.

173.35   Dʳ Holme] Edward Holme (1770–1847), founder of the Manchester Natural History Society.

175.6   Hafs] Handkerchiefs.

175.16–17   Reverend J. Clowes] John Clowes (1743–1831), a Swedenborgian, was rector of St. John's Church in Manchester.

175.32   Nº 37] Snuff.

175.36–37   Political Starvation . . . Corn Law] The corn laws restricted the importation of grain to Britain; they were repealed in 1846, partly as a consequence of the Irish famine of 1845.

179.38–180.1   according to Johnson] The first meaning for "uncommonly" given in Johnson's *Dictionary* is "not frequently."

180.13   My Doves] Later engraved as plate XVII of the Double Elephant Folio *Birds of America*.

180.18   Rattlesnake . . . Mocking Birds] See plate 4 in this volume.

180.20   Mʳ Selby] Prideaux John Selby (1788–1867), British naturalist, whose *Illustrations of British Ornithology* (1821–34) were etched by William H. Lizars in Edinburgh.

181.6–7   Mʳ Lizars] William Home Lizars (1788–1859) aquatinted the first ten plates of *The Birds of America*, subsequently completed by R. Havell & Son, London.

181.20   Lawson the *Philadelphia Brute*] Alexander Lawson (1773–1846), engraver of Alexander Wilson's *American Ornithology*, rejected Audubon's work in 1824 as lacking "truth in form" and "correctness in lines."

181.26–27   Mʳ W. Heath] William Heath, ex-soldier, engraver, caricaturist, and painter of battle scenes (1795–1840), provided illustrations for *Martial Achievements of Britain and Her Allies* (1815).

182.8–9   *Professor Jameson*] Robert Jameson (1774–1836), founder of the Wernerian and Plinian Societies and professor of natural history at the University of Edinburgh.

182.33   Dʳ Hibbert and Dʳ Henry and Dʳ Knox] Samuel Hibbert

(1782–1848), secretary of the Society of Antiquaries of Scotland from 1823 to 1827; Charles Henry, a young physician at the Royal Infirmary in Edinburgh; Robert Knox (1791–1862), a Lecturer on Anatomy at the University of Edinburgh.

183.26 View of Edin^g] W. H. Lizars had engraved drawings by John Wilson Ewbank for James Browne's *Picturesque Views of Edinburgh* (1825).

184.2 Beech Woods] Louisiana plantation owned by Jane Middlemist Percy, where Lucy Audubon taught school for seven years.

184.11 Earl of Elgin] Thomas Bruce, Lord Elgin, seventh Earl (1771–1841).

184.12 Mr Innes] Gilbert Innes (1751–1832), deputy governor of the Royal Bank of Scotland.

184.33 Mr Skin] James Skene (1775–1864), watercolorist and curator of the library and museum of the Royal Society of Edinburgh.

185.12 W^{am} Allan] William Allan (1777–1841), Scottish painter of history and Russian scenes.

185.30 Dr Brewster] David Brewster (1781–1868), pioneer of modern experimental optics and inventor of the kaleidoscope, served as the editor of the *Edinburgh Journal of Science*.

185.34–35 my Letter . . . Carrion Crow] "Account of the Carrion Crow, or Vultur attratus," *Edinburgh Journal of Science* 6 (1827).

188.13 My Painting . . . fighting] Sold by Audubon's Edinburgh landlady in 1832, this painting is not now known to be extant.

188.19 Dr Mease] James Mease, physician, agriculturalist, and historian (1771–1846), who had introduced Audubon to prominent Philadelphians.

188.24 George Combe] Edinburgh lawyer and amateur phrenologist (1788–1856).

188.36 W^{am} Jardine] William Jardine (1800–74), author (with Prideaux J. Selby) of *Illustrations of Ornithology* (1826–43) and general editor of *The Naturalist's Library* (1833–46).

191.36 Basil Hall] Basil Hall (1788–1844), captain in the English Navy, explorer, and travel writer.

ORNITHOLOGICAL BIOGRAPHY

211.35–36 MACGILLIVRAY . . . 1828] "On the Covering of Birds, Considered Chiefly with Reference to the Description and Distinction of Species, Genera and Orders," *Edinburgh New Philosophical Journal* 4 (1828). William MacGillivray (1796–1852), author of *A History of British Birds* (1837–52), served as scientific editor of Audubon's *Ornithological Biography*.

217.16   *The Bird of Washington*] See note 19.15.

220.5   RANKIN] Adam Rankin, a physician, lived on Meadow Brook Farm outside Henderson, Kentucky.

221.40   J. G. CHILDREN] John George Children (1777–1852), head of the Department of Zoology, had also served as a librarian in the Department of Antiquities and as secretary of the London Royal Society (1826–27, 1835–37).

222.18–19   *"Mangeurs de Poulets,"*] Chicken-eaters.

222.31   *"Mangeurs de Canards."*] Duck-eaters.

222.32–33   *dejeuné à la fourchette*] Lunch with forks.

245.33–34   a figure . . . Illustrations] See *The Birds of America*, Double Elephant Folio Edition, plate CXXVI.

247.22   one of his letters] To Sarah Bache, Franklin's daughter, January 26, 1784.

250.40   Althæa] Hollyhock.

254.6–7   A figure . . . elsewhere] See plate 31 in this volume.

260.25–26   I may hereafter . . . account] Audubon's account of the Eastern Cottontail, "Gray Rabbit (*Lepus Sylvaticus*)," appears in *Viviparous Quadrupeds of North America*.

263.5   YOUNG's inn] In West Port, Kentucky, about 25 miles south of Louisville.

278.26–29   Having given you a description . . . fond.] A flowering dogwood (*Cornus florida*) appears in plate VIII of the Double Elephant Folio *Birds of America*; the tree reproduced in plate 19 in this volume was originally painted by Audubon's assistant Joseph Mason.

286.3–5   The drawing . . . 1812] This drawing is not known to be extant.

287.37–39   The tree . . . represented it] Pignut Hickory, *Carya glabra*, painted by Audubon's assistant George Lehman.

292.12   WILSON] Samuel Wilson, Charleston physician and friend of John Bachman.

293.24–28   a copy of a paper . . . that Society] A version of Audubon's paper, "Account of the Habits of the Turkey Buzzard (Vultur aura), Particularly with the View of Exploding the Opinion Generally Entertained of Its Extraordinary Power of Smelling, in a Letter to Professor Jameson," *Edinburgh New Philosophical Journal* 2 (1826–27), was read by Patrick Neill, printer of the *Journal,* on December 16, 1826.

302.17–18   *Vultur Aura . . . atratus*] Turkey Vulture, *Cathartes aura*; Black Vulture, *Coragyps atratus*.

306.39   Henry Ward]   English taxidermist who accompanied Audubon on his 1831–32 excursion to Florida.

311.31   B. B. STROBEL]   Benjamin Strobel, of Key West, was editor of *the Key West Gazette.*

318.38   THOMAS LINCOLN]   Son of Judge Theodore Lincoln, of Dennysville, Maine, at whose home Audubon and his family spent several weeks in the late summer of 1832. Thomas Lincoln accompanied Audubon on his 1833 expedition to Labrador.

321.34   *Falco furcatus*]   American Swallow-tailed Kite, *Elanoides forficatus.*

322.8   Tumbling Pigeon]   Breed of domestic pigeon characterized by the habit of turning over backward in flight.

325.3–4   EDGEWORTH's . . . Tales]   *Moral Tales for Young People* (1801) and *Popular Tales* (1804), by Maria Edgeworth (1767–1849).

336.24   MacCULLOCH]   Thomas McCulloch Sr. (1776–1843), Presbyterian minister, educator, and naturalist, founded Pictou Academy in Nova Scotia, where he established a natural history museum. His son, Thomas McCulloch Jr., later professor of natural history at Dartmouth College, sent Audubon samples of Nova Scotia bird life.

340.8   THEODORE LINCOLN]   See note 318.38.

341.39–30   another species . . . WILSON]   In his *American Ornithology,* vol. 2, Wilson suggests that the male kestrel is "very different from the female."

355.30   GEORGE PARKMAN]   Boston physician and expert on insanity, murdered in 1849 by John W. Webster, professor of chemistry at Harvard.

356.29   SHATTUCK, and WARREN]   George Cheyne Shattuck (1783–1854), a general practitioner in Boston; John Collins Warren (1778–1856), professor of anatomy and surgery at the Harvard Medical School.

372.30   Mr TARASCON]   Louis Anastasius Tarascon, of Shippingport, Kentucky, a miller.

376.26   *Zostera marina*]   Eelgrass.

388.37–38   *Ardea cærulea . . . occidentalis*]   Little Blue Heron, *Egretta caerulea*; Great Blue Heron, *Ardea herodias.*

390.6   JOHN BULOW]   John J. Bulow (d. 1836) owned a sugar plantation ("Bulow Ville") 45 miles south of St. Augustine, Florida, later destroyed during the Seminole War.

395.16–17   SHATTUCK . . . INGALLS]   George Cheyne Shattuck Jr. (1813–93), later a physician and dean of Harvard Medical School; William Ingalls, son of Dr. William Ingalls (1769–1851).

397.28   "The Eggers"]   Labrador nest raiders described by Audubon in "The Eggers of Labrador," *Ornithological Biography*, vol. 3.

400.4   the Ripley]   The 106-ton schooner aboard which Audubon undertook his 1833 expedition to Labrador.

401.15   the Gulnare]   British surveying ship which trailed the *Ripley* in Labrador.

404.27–28   BARTRAM . . . alone."]   Bartram's observations on the "wood pelican" appear in his *Travels* (1791), part II, ch. v.

406.20–21   Talk to me . . . Ibis!]   In his *Natural History of Carolina, Florida, and the Bahama Islands* (1731–48), Mark Catesby refers to the Wood Ibis (now known as the Wood Stork, *Mycteria americana*) as "a stupid bird, and void of fear, easily to be shot."

409.17–18   "Grands Flamans,"]   Great flamingoes.

421.13   General HERNANDEZ's]   Joseph M. Hernandez (b. 1792), owner of a sugar plantation 30 miles south of St. Augustine, Florida, on the site of present-day Washington Oaks Garden State Park.

422.27–28   SANDY ISLAND . . . volume]   In the second episode titled "The Florida Keys," *Ornithological Biography*, vol. 2.

427.29   Miss MARTIN]   Maria Martin (1796–1863), John Bachman's sister-in-law and later his wife, supplied many paintings of plants that Audubon used as backgrounds.

428.39   "*Bec croche*,"]   Hooked bill.

428.40   "*Petit flaman*,"]   Little flamingo.

429.7   EDWARD HARRIS]   Farmer, horsebreeder, and naturalist (1799–1863) from Moorestown, New Jersey.

431.17   The Sand Hill Crane]   Audubon considered the Sandhill Crane (*Grus canadensis*) to be a juvenile form of the Whooping Crane, rather than a distinct species.

435.8–9   BARTRAM . . . species]   Bartram describes the "savanna crane" (Sandhill Crane, *Grus canadensis*) in his *Travels*, II.vii.

435.14   Canada Crane]   Sandhill Crane (see note 431.17).

438.23   p. 213]   *Ornithological Biography*, vol. 3 (not included in this volume).

440.32–33   Mr JONES]   Master of the sealing station at Bradore Bay in

1833, the subject of a biographical sketch in the episode "The Squatters of Labrador," *Ornithological Biography*, vol. 2.

441.17–19   BONAPARTE . . . North America] See the article on the "Esquimaux Curlew" in Bonaparte's *American Ornithology*, vol. 4.

441.21–23   WILSON . . . Europe] In Wilson's *American Ornithology*, vol. 8.

455.37   Balacuda] Great Barracuda, *Sphyaena barracuda*.

462.17   *Ardea Herodias*] Audubon's "Great White Heron" is now considered a subspecies of the Great Blue Heron, *Ardea herodias*.

464.30   *Ardea rufescens . . . A. Ludoviciana*] Reddish Egret, *Egretta rufescens*; Tricolored Heron, *Egretta tricolor* (see plate 40 in this volume).

468.36   *Ardea candidissima*] Snowy Egret, *Egretta thula* (see plate 44 in this volume).

471.28–29   a nest . . . WILSON] In *American Ornithology*, vol. 8.

474.26–28   "Sarcelle Printanniere" . . . "Sarcelle Automniere"] "Spring teal" and "fall teal."

479.38–39   "Bec à Lancette,"] Lancet bill.

483.39   museum of that city] The Philadelphia Museum, founded in 1786 by Charles Willson Peale (1741–1827).

502.34–35   Dr RICHARDSON states] In Richardson and Swainson, *Fauna Boreali-Americana*, vol. 2, no. 143.

502.39   *Himantopus nigricollis*] Black-necked Stilt, *Himantopus mexicanus*.

505.6–7   *A. Nycticorax . . . violacea*] Black-crowned Night Heron, *Nycticorax nycticorax*; Yellow-crowned Night Heron, *Nycticorax violaceus*.

509.3–14   a note . . . one."] See Meriwether Lewis and William Clark, *Journals*, March 9, 1806.

509.21–22   Dr TOWNSEND] John Kirk Townsend (1809–51), physician, ornithologist, and author of *Narrative of a Journey across the Rocky Mountains to the Columbia River* (1839).

510.31   Tawapatee Bottom] Tywappitty Bottom, Missouri.

514.35–38   RICHARDSON . . . days."] In *Fauna Boreali-Americana*, vol. 2, no. 223.

515.28   Captain DAY] Lieutenant Robert Day, acting commander of the *Marion*, a United States revenue cutter, had taken Audubon to the Florida Keys in April 1832.

517.2   Dr LEITNER]   Edward Leitner (d. 1838), Charleston physician and botanist.

520.25   the month of October]   The Audubons returned from Pennsylvania in July 1812.

528.1   Regulators]   Described by Audubon in "The Regulators," another episode in *Ornithological Biography* (vol. 1), as "honest citizens . . . vested with the power suited to the necessity of preserving order on the frontiers."

528.22   a gentleman]   See note 74.32.

531.17–18   elsewhere . . . described]   In the episode "Kentucky Sports" (*Ornithological Biography*, vol. 1).

537.20   M. de T.]   Constantine Samuel Rafinesque (1783–1840), self-described "Botanist, Naturalist, Geologist, Geographer, Historian, Poet, Philosopher, Philologist, Economist, Philanthropist," was author, among many other works, of *Ichthyologia Ohiensis* (1820).

538.23   Telemachus . . . to Mentor]   *Odyssey*, ii. 225.

MISSOURI RIVER JOURNALS

553.13   Jediah Irish]   A millwright and lumberjack who acted as Audubon's host during a visit to the "Great Pine Forest," 15 miles from present-day Jim Thorpe, Pennsylvania. Audubon described this visit in "The Great Pine Swamp," *Ornithological Biography*, vol. 1.

553.14   Edward Harris]   See note 429.7. Harris's diary was published in 1951 as *Up the Missouri with Audubon*.

553.15–16   John G. Bell . . . Squires]   John G. Bell (1812–79), taxidermist; Isaac Sprague (1811–95), artist and illustrator of a number of works including Asa Gray's *Manual of Botany* (1848); Lewis M. Squires, Audubon's secretary and aide-de-camp during the trip.

553.17   at Mr. Sanderson's]   J. M. Sanderson ran Franklin House, a Philadelphia hotel.

553.17–18   visits to Mr. Bowen . . . others]   J. T. Bowen, lithographer of the Royal Octavo edition of *Birds of America* and of Audubon and Bachman's *Viviparous Quadrupeds of North America*; Samuel George Morton (1799–1851), physician and author of *Crania Americana* (1838).

553.23   Gideon B. Smith]   Native of Baltimore and co-founder, in 1832, of the Horticultural Society.

554.14   *bon gré, mal gré*]   Willy-nilly.

554.17–19   The Chouteaux . . . Captain Sire]   Pierre Chouteau Jr. (1789–1865) headed Pierre Chouteau Jr. and Company, which had succeeded the American Fur Company in the Missouri River trade in 1842 (but continued to be referred to as "The American Fur Company" or "The Company). Chouteau Jr.'s father, "Old" Jean Pierre Chouteau, was 85 years old at the time of Audubon's visit to St. Louis. Joseph A. Sire (1799–1854) commanded the Company's supply boat during the 1840s, transferring supplies to the Company outpost at the confluence of the Missouri and Yellowstone rivers, and furs back to St. Louis.

554.24–25   Pouched Rat (*Pseudostoma bursarius*)] Plains Pocket Gopher, *Geomys bursarius* (see plate 58).

554.32   *Sciurus capistratus*] Fox Squirrel, *Sciurus niger.*

554.40   Mr. Sarpy] John B. Sarpy (1798–1857), partner in Pierre Chouteau Jr. and Company.

556.25–26   *Arctomys monax*] Woodchuck, *Marmota monax.*

558.36   *Lepus sylvaticus*] Eastern Cottontail, *Sylvilagus floridanus.*

558.37   *Tetrao umbellus*] Ruffed Grouse, *Bonasa umbellus.*

559.37   La Grande Rivière] Grand River, Missouri.

560.35   Dr. Trudeau] James De Berty Trudeau (1817–87), Louisiana physician.

560.37   "Muloë"] From French *mulot,* field mouse.

563.27   Father de Smet] Pierre-Jean de Smet (1801–73), Belgian Jesuit missionary and author of *Oregon Missions and Travels over the Rocky Mountains in 1846* (1847).

563.29   Major Sandford] John F. A. Sanford, son-in-law of Pierre Chouteau Jr., served as Indian agent to the Mandans and agent of Chouteau's Company.

564.5–6   Madame Chouteau's plantation] Trading post at Chouteaus Landing (later Kansas City), established by Pierre Chouteau Sr. and run by the widow of his son François.

564.6–7   Sir William Stuart] William Drummond Stewart (1795/96–1871), Scottish nobleman, soldier, and hunter, author of *Altowan, or Incidents of Life and Adventure in the Rocky Mountains* (1846).

564.11   the murder of Mr. Jarvis] Antonio Chávez ("Jarvis"), a merchant, was robbed and killed on the Santa Fé road about 250 miles from Independence, Missouri. Two of the robbers were hanged in St. Louis in 1844.

565.13   "Siffleurs,"] Whistlers.

566.4   *Sciurus carolinensis*] Grey Squirrel, *Sciurus carolinensis.*

566.9   a new Finch] Named Harris's Finch, *Fringilla harrisii,* by Audubon; now known as Harris's Sparrow, *Zonotrichia querula.* (Thomas Nuttall had described this species in 1834.)

568.14–15   a small Vireo . . . species] Bell's Vireo, *Vireo bellii* Audubon.

570.20   *Sciurus Audubonii*] Named after John Woodhouse Audubon, who had collected a specimen in 1839 in Louisiana; now recognized as a variety of the Fox Squirrel, *Sciurus niger.*

570.36   Belle Vue] Company post at Bellevue, in Sarpy County, Nebraska, directed by Peter L'Abadie Sarpy (1805–65).

571.9   *Emberiza pallida*] Clay-colored Sparrow, *Spizella pallida.*

571.14   the brother-in-law of old Provost] Étienne Provost (1785–1850), *voyageur* from Chambly, Quebec, entered the fur trade in St. Louis in 1814/15 and began his official association with the American Fur Company in 1828; Clement (Lambert) Salle dit Lajoie was his brother-in-law.

571.21–22   my old friend of that name] See note 29.19.

572.5–6   Captain Burgwin] John Henry K. Burgwin, a captain of the 1st Dragoons, died in 1847 of wounds received in the assault on Pueblo de Taos, New Mexico.

572.10   Major Mitchell] David Dawson Mitchell (1806–61) was appointed superintendent of Indian affairs at St. Louis in 1841, after years of service with the American Fur Company.

573.25   Madison by name] Thomas C. Madison (d. 1866) served as an assistant surgeon with the U.S. Army before the Civil War and later as a surgeon for the Confederacy.

574.40   brindle-colored Wolf] A variety of the Gray Wolf, *Canis lupis.*

575.29   *Sioux Pictout*] Little Sioux River in present-day Harrison County, Iowa.

575.33–34   Black-tailed Deer] A subspecies of the Mule Deer, *Odocoileus hemionus.*

576.14–18   Wood's Bluffs . . . buried] Omaha chief Black Bird (Washinga-Sabba) was buried in 1800 in the vicinity of what is now Decatur, Nebraska.

577.33–35   burial-ground . . . Clark] Floyd's Bluff was washed away in 1857; Sergeant Charles Floyd is now buried in Sioux City, Iowa. (See Lewis and Clark, *Journals*, August 19 and 20, 1804.)

581.28   Mr. Cerré] Gabriel Pascal Cerré (b. 1798), member of an influential family of St. Louis traders.

584.10–11   Mr. Catlin . . . accounts] In *Letters and Notes on the Manners, Customs, and Condition of the North American Indians* (1841).

585.25–27   Mr. Laidlow . . . Dripps] William Laidlaw (1798/99–1851), head of Company operations at Fort Pierre; Andrew Drips (b. 1789), Indian agent for the tribes of the Upper Missouri beginning in June 1842.

587.12–13   La Rivière à Jacques]   The James or Dakota River.

587.32   *Pipilo arcticus*]   Rufous-sided Towhee, *Pipilo erythrophthalmus.*

588.13–14   Manuel . . . Chouteau's River]   Emanuel Creek, Bazile Creek, Niobrara (or Rapid) River, Ponca River, and Choteau Creek, in Nebraska and South Dakota.

588.31   Monsieur Le Clerc]   Narcisse Leclerc, independent Missouri River trader.

589.38   White Apple]   Edible tuber of the bread root or "prairie potato," *Psoralea esculenta*; also known as *pomme blanche.*

590.10–12   Meadow Larks . . . States]   Western Meadowlark, *Sturnella neglecta* Audubon.

590.20   the "Grand Town"]   "The large prairie-dog village which once covered several acres on the right bank of the Missouri, in the vicinity of the butte known as the Dome, or Tower, between Yankton and Fort Randall." (Elliott Coues's note, *Audubon and His Journals*)

593.11   Mr. Charity]   Company trader François La Charité.

593.19   Townsend's Hare]   White-tailed Jack Rabbit, *Lepus townsendii.*

594.11   *Neotoma floridana*]   Eastern Woodrat, *Neotoma florida.*

594.15–17   Opposition Company . . . New York]   The Union Fur Company (operating in conjunction with New York City fur distributor Bolton, Fox, and Livingston), the principal competitor of the Chouteau Company.

596.4–5   *Great Bend*]   Also known as the Grand Detour, four miles across by land, 26 around by water.

596.17   prairie Marmots, *Arctomys ludovicianus*]   Black-tailed Prairie Dog, *Cynomys ludovicianus* (plate 60 in this volume).

597.13   *Chemin faisant*]   On the way.

600.26–31   Fort George . . . Crisp]   In present-day Presho County, South Dakota, newly built in 1842 by the Union Fur Company. The acting Indian agent was Joseph V. Hamilton, the son of Thomas Hamilton, U.S. Army, who had been appointed as sub-agent in May 1843 at the request of Andrew Drips (for which "Crisp" is a misspelling).

601.9   Illingsworth]   James Illingsworth, bookkeeper for the Opposition Company at Fort George in 1844.

601.18   Mr. Taylor]   Robert W. Taylor, from St. Louis, a fur trader.

603.33   the talented . . . Mr. ——] John Kirk Townsend (see note 509.21–22).

604.27   Mr. Picotte] Honoré Picotte (1775?–1860), American Fur Company trader at Fort Pierre.

605.30   James Hall] Brother of John Woodhouse Audubon's second wife, Caroline Hall.

605.36   Teton River] Now known as the Bad River.

606.31   Mr. Culbertson] Alexander Culbertson (1809–78), the superintendent of Fort Union; married to Na-ta-wis-ta-cha ("Medicine Snake-Woman") of the Blackfeet.

606.34–35   Mr. Bowie] Probably Anthony R. Bouis, American Fur Company trader.

608.18   *Arvicola pennsylvanicus*] Meadow vole, *Microtus pennsylvanicus*.

609.18–19   the Moroe] The Moreau River, South Dakota.

610.12–14   the old Riccaree Village . . . men] Settlement of the Arikara, on the western bank of the Missouri in north central South Dakota, just above the mouth of the Grand River. In 1822, William H. Ashley, general of the St. Louis militia and lieutenant governor of Missouri, in conjunction with trapper Andrew Henry, undertook a large-scale expedition to the upper Missouri in order to open up the territory for trade; in April 1823 the Arikara attacked two of Ashley's keelboats and 14 of his men were killed.

612.8–9   Charles Primeau] Primeau, born in St. Louis, had joined the American Fur Company as a clerk in 1831.

612.39–613.1   where the "Assiniboin" . . . 1835] The Company steamship had grounded at the head of Sibley Island, eight miles south of present-day Bismarck, and caught fire before the cargo could be discharged.

613.17–18   the Mandan Village] The two villages of the Mandan, located approximately 150 miles south of the Canadian border, were occupied at the time of Audubon's arrival by the Arikara; smallpox had forced the Mandan to abandon them.

614.5   Mr. Kipp] Canadian-born James Kipp (1788–1885), formerly of the Columbia Fur Company, built Fort Floyd (later Fort Union) in 1828 and Fort Clark in 1831.

615.1   Fort Clark] The Company's Mandan Post, 14 miles west of present-day Washburn, North Dakota.

618.17–18   the poor Mandans . . . small-pox] Introduced by the American Fur Company in 1837 by the steamboat *St. Peter*, which unloaded at Fort Clark on June 20 and at Fort Union on June 24), the smallpox virus had spread rapidly in the region, decimating the Mandan, the Hidatsa, the

Arikara, the Assiniboin, and the Cree. The Mandan population alone was reduced from between 1,600 and 2,000 to less than 200.

625.40–626.1   Mountain Rams] Bighorn Sheep, *Ovis canadensis.*

628.15–16   "Bon renommé . . . doré."] A good reputation is worth more than a golden ring.

628.35   FORT UNION] Twenty-four miles southwest of present-day Williston, North Dakota, on the north side of the Missouri River, built by the American Fur Company on the site of Fort Floyd in 1828.

633.25   James Murray] Trader who in 1842 became head of the Company's Crow post, Fort Alexander, on the north bank of the Yellowstone.

635.12   Black Harris] Moses Harris, a native of Kentucky who had joined General William Ashley's fur-trading expedition in 1823.

636.20   *Spermophilus hoodii*] Thirteen-lined Ground Squirrel, *Citellus tridecemlineatus.* Plate 57 in this volume shows a pair of these squirrels with the Missouri-Yellowstone confluence in the background.

639.16   Mr. Larpenteur] Charles Larpenteur (1807–72), French-born trader on the Missouri, originally worked for the competing firm of Sublette and Campbell and joined the Company in 1834. He built Fort Alexander on the Yellowstone in 1842 and in the following decades worked alternately as a farmer in Iowa and as a trader and interpreter in the fur business.

639.32   Young Mr. McKenzie] Owen McKenzie, son of "King of the Missouri," Kenneth McKenzie (1797–1861), born at Fort Union, killed by trader Malcolm Clark in 1863.

639.37   a Lark . . . beautiful] "Sprague's Missouri Lark," now known as Sprague's Pipit, *Anthus spragueii* Audubon.

640.5   the Blackfoot Fort] Fort McKenzie.

644.29   a Blackbird] Brewer's Blackbird, *Euphagus cyanocephalus.*

648.6   Fort Mortimer] Fort Mortimer, North Dakota, built in 1842 on the site of old Fort William, was abandoned in 1846.

650.13   Mr. Denig] Edwin Thompson Denig (1812–62?), clerk at Fort Union, author of *Indian Tribes of the Upper Missouri* (1930).

650.33–34   the camera] Camera obscura.

651.39   Long-tailed Deer] White-tailed Deer, *Odocoileus virginianus.*

661.14–16   old fort . . . Sublette] Fort Sublette, named after William Sublette (1799–1845), one of four brothers active in the fur trade, was erected in September 1833 and absorbed by the Company a year later.

670.21   "nage à la brasse;"] Swim the breaststroke.

678.7   *Mus leucopus*]   White-footed mouse, *Peromyscus lecopus.*

681.27–682.32   However, at this stage . . . fort.]   This passage is a slightly modified version of Edward Harris's journal entry for July 16, 1843.

690.19   Mr. Pike]   Probably Auguste Pike Vasquez (1813–69), a trader who worked for the Company from 1843 to 1845.

691.15   Moncrévier]   John B. Moncravie (1797–1885), a French refugee from Bordeaux and former sergeant in the U.S. Army, became a clerk at Fort Union in 1833.

694.28–29   Congress will not allow . . . Indians]   Congress had prohibited the sale of liquor in Indian territory in 1832.

695.40   *coute qui coute*]   Whatever it costs.

700.23–24   the three Mamelles]   The "three Buttes" are located in the vicinity of present-day Sydney, Montana.

705.20   battue]   Hunt.

705.35   *au fait*]   By the way, casual.

707.9–10   my sketch . . . Mamelles]   "Camp at the Three Mamelles" (1843), reproduced in *Audubon and His Journals* (1897).

711.32   *capote*]   Hooded garment worn by mountain men, made from a blanket and usually belted around the waist.

726.26   Mauvaises Terres]   Clay hills behind Fort Union.

732.19   *Tamias quadrivittatus*]   Colorado Chipmunk, *Eutamisa quadrivittatus.*

739.28–30   *Caprimulgus* . . . named it]   Nuttall's Whip-poor-will, *Caprimulgus nuttallii*, now known as the Common Poorwill, *Phalaenoptilus nuttallii.*

748.21–22   Hutchins' Geese]   Now considered a subspecies of the Canada Goose, *Branta canadensis.*

OTHER WRITINGS

760.24   whilt under David]   Audubon claimed on several occasions to have studied under David, but his name does not appear among the references to pupils in David's papers.

761.37–40   "L'hirondelle . . . retenue"]   The second and third lines of La Fontaine's "The Swallow and the Small Birds" (*Fables*, i.8): "whoever has observed a lot can remember a lot."

766.6–7   "*Du pain . . . Migonne,*"]   Milkbread for the parrot Mignonne.

778.9   S—— B——] Samuel Adams Bowen, Audubon's Henderson business competitor; see Chronology, 1819.

789.3   General Toledo] José Alvarez de Toledo y Dubois, a Spanish refugee, militia leader, and confidence man who acted as an agent for opposing Spanish colonial factions in Mexico.

793.1   Robert Best] Chief curator at Drake's Western Museum in Cincinnati during Audubon's tenure there.

793.7–9   expedition of Major Long . . . Say] Titian Ramsay Peale was the assistant naturalist on Stephen Harriman Long's exploration of the Louisiana Territory in 1821; Thomas Say (1787–1834) was in charge of the zoological collections.

793.20   Mr. Haromack] Jacob Aumack (see page 3.4 in this volume).

LETTERS

799.16   John Willson] Under the pseudonym Christopher North, John Wilson (1785–1854) had praised Audubon's paintings in *Blackwood's Edinburgh Magazine* (21 [1827]: 112).

801.5   Reverend W^{am} Bakewell . . . Robert B.] William Johnstone Bakewell (b. 1794) was a minister in Chester, Edinburgh, and later Pittsburgh; Robert Bakewell was a geologist.

801.23–27   Mrs Midlemist . . . Middlemist] On his departure for England, Audubon had been entrusted with a sum of money intended for the wife of painter Charles Middlemist.

802.13   11 Wild Turkeys] *Wild Turkey Cock and Hen and Nine Chicks*, (*Meleagris gallipavo*), 1826 (Ernest Mayr Library, Museum of Comparative Zoology, Harvard University).

802.14   Otter in a Trap] Subject of a number of Audubon paintings.

802.19   Dr Pope] Nathaniel Wells Pope, physician in West Feliciana, Louisiana.

805.40   Mr Bentley] William Horton Bentley, a Manchester taxidermist and dealer in skins.

806.11   the Familly Johnson] William Garrett Johnson, of Beech Grove, West Feliciana, Louisiana, had hired Lucy Audubon as governess in 1822.

806.13   Mrs Percy] See note 184.2.

810.17   my Prospectus] Audubon's first prospectus for his *Birds of America*, issued on March 17, 1827.

810.30   Mrs Vestris] Madame Vestris (1797–1856), originally Lucy Elizabetta Bartolozzi, actress and singer.

810.31   *Mathews*]   Charles Mathews (1776–1835), theater manager and co-median; his son, comedian Charles James Mathews (1803–78), married "Madame Vestris" in 1838.

811.25   Monsieur Redouté]   Pierre-Joseph Redouté (1759–1840), botanical artist.

814.19   G. J. Children]   See note 221.40.

817.5–6   Col¹ Trumbull, Major Long, Mʳ Cooper]   John Trumbull (1756–1843), a painter; Stephen Harriman Long (1784–1864), of the U.S. Corps of Topographical Engineers, who had led the first scientific exploration of the Louisiana Territory in 1819–20; William Cooper (1797–1864), a naturalist and founding member of the New York Lyceum.

817.9–10   Doctʳ Pascallis]   Felix Pascalis-Ouvrière (c. 1750–1833), expert on yellow fever and amateur botanist.

817.11   Docʳ Mitchel]   Samuel Latham Mitchill (1764–1831), author of *The Fishes of New York* (1815); professor of natural history, chemistry, and agriculture at Columbia College, New York (1792–1801); U.S. congressman (1801–4; 1810–13) and senator (1804–9); founder in 1817 of the New York Lyceum of History.

818.12   Ruben Haines]   Reuben Haines (d. 1831), a Quaker farmer, corresponding secretary of the Academy of Natural Sciences.

819.21   Mʳ Gilman]   Samuel Gilman (1791–1858), Unitarian minister and author of the song "Fair Harvard."

819.35   Henry]   See note 306.39.

820.16   Politics . . . the Tariff Men]   The 1828 "tariff of abominations" had reinvigorated southern demands for nullification.

823.39   Bewick's Birds]   Thomas Bewick (see note 99.22) pioneered the technique of fine-line engraving on the end-grain of boxwood blocks, which unlike metal-plate engravings could be set with type, lowering production costs.

823.39–40   "*the Zooligical Gardens*"]   Probably William Swainson's *Zoological Illustrations* (1820–23).

824.24   Nᵒˢ 32 and 33]   Plates XLVI–XLXV in the Double Elephant Folio *Birds of America*.

826.17   Cruickshank]   The original miniature by Frederick Cruikshank became widely known through C. Turner's engraving, which Robert Havell published, along with Audubon's autograph, on January 12, 1835.

826.18   Mʳ Rees]   William J. Rees, of Statesbury, South Carolina, a new subscriber to *Birds of America*.

826.35 Temminck's Works] Dutch ornithologist Coenraad Jacob Temminck (1778–1858), whose *Manuel d'ornithologie ou tableau systematique des oiseaux qui se trouve en Europe* was published between 1820 and 1840.

827.6 Yarrel] William Yarrell (1784–1856), *A History of British Fishes* (1836).

827.8 Two Brothers *Meyers*] Henry Leonard Meyer, *Illustrations of British Birds* (1835–41), with plates drawn by various members of the Meyer family.

827.15 on the Pavé] On the streets.

827.27–28 W^am Cooper . . . Fudge] Audubon had named what he thought to be a new species of hawk in honor of Lord Stanley; Charles Bonaparte, in his supplement to Wilson's *American Ornithology*, had already named the same bird for William Cooper in 1828. Audubon's claim to "Cooper's Hawk" became the cause of much bitterness among himself, Cooper, and Bonaparte.

829.10–11 The Old Zoological . . . Day] The zoological gardens in the northeast corner of Regent's Park had opened in 1828; their popularity soon eclipsed that of older collections, such as the Exeter Change Menagerie in downtown London.

829.16 Ravenell and Lightner] Dr. Edmund Ravenel (1797–1871), Charleston physician, planter, and conchologist; Edward Leitner, see note 517.2.

829.20–21 the Lees and Mrs Davis] Paul Hutson Lee, Harriet Bachman's brother-in-law, owned a plantation at Round O, 30 miles southwest of Charleston; Mrs. Mary E. Davis was a family friend of the Bachmans in Charleston.

829.27 Doc^r Frost] Henry Frost, Professor of Materia Medica, Medical College of the State of South Carolina.

830.12–13 Strix Flammea] Barn Owl, *Tyto alba*.

830.16 Falco Dispar] White-tailed Kite ("Black-shouldered Kite"), *Elanus leucurus*.

831.12 *another* life of Wilson] William Bourn Oliver Peabody (1788–1847), *Life of Alexander Wilson* (1834).

832.27 one by Mr Gould] *Birds of Europe* (1832–37), by John Gould (1804–81), superintendent of stuffed birds at the London Zoological Society.

834.3 My Friend Melly] André Melly, Swiss-born entomologist.

834.14–15 Mr Gould . . . publications] John Gould and Nicholas Aylward Vigors, *A Century of Birds from the Himalaya Mountains* (1831–32) and the first part of Gould's *Monograph of the Trogonidae, or Family of Trogons*

(1835–38). Nicholas Aylward Vigors (1787–1840) was the secretary of the Zoological Society of London.

834.17–18   monograph . . . Mr Lear]   Edward Lear (1812–88) had illustrated the parrots in William Jardine's *Naturalist's Library* (1833–46).

834.23   James Wilson]   James Wilson (1795–1856), brother of John Wilson ("Christopher North"), published *Illustrations of Zoology* (1831).

834.28–30   Bonaparte . . . Stopped]   The final volume of Bonaparte's supplement to Wilson's *American Ornithology* had appeared in 1833.

838.1   Bonaparte's Synopsis]   "The Genera of North American Birds, and a Synopsis of the Species Found Within the Territory of the United States," *Annals of the Lyceum of New-York* (1826–28).

838.27   The Fire at New York]   In January 1836, a fire destroyed buildings in New York from Battery Park to Wall Street, including the warehouse in which Audubon's belongings had been stored.

838.30   Riots at Baltimore]   A week of rioting followed the announcement on March 24, 1834, that the Bank of Maryland would no longer be able to conduct its business; Audubon was later compensated for drawings ruined in an attack on the house of Reverdy Johnson, the Bank of Maryland's counsel.

838.34–35   N° 58 , . . N° 59 up to plate 295]   The Double Elephant Folio *Birds of America* was issued in numbers. No. 58 included plates CCLXXXVI to CXC; No. 59, CXCI to CCXCV.

838.40   our Sweetheart]   Maria Martin (see note 427.29).

839.11–12   a Work on Ornithology]   MacGillivray's *Descriptions of the Rapacious Birds of Great Britain* (1836).

840.9   100 Creek Warriors]   Audubon witnessed the roundup by the U.S. Army and the Alabama state militia of the last remnants of those Muskogee (Creek) Indians who had not been forcibly removed during the campaign of 1836. By March 8, 1837, nearly 4,000 Muskogee were concentrated near Montgomery, waiting to be transferred to a camp at Mobile Point.

840.40   Judge Hitchcock]   Henry Hitchcock, Mobile lawyer, judge, and contractor, a subscriber to *Birds of America*.

844.26   the New Woodpecker]   Audubon's Woodpecker, now considered a subspecies of the Hairy Woodpecker, *Picoides villosus*.

845.5   Doc^r Spencer]   John Spencer, of Moorestown, New Jersey, brother-in-law of Edward Harris.

845.10   the last . . . "*Pickwick*"]   Charles Dickens' novel *The Posthumous Papers of the Pickwick Club* was first issued in monthly parts from April 1836 to November 1837.

845.12   Van Buren's Message]   On September 5, 1837, President Martin Van Buren sent an address to the Congress on the financial panic that had swept through the United States.

845.17   a/c of my having Shot the *Smew*]   See page 138.9–10 in this volume.

845.20   *Plectrophanes Picta* of Swainson]   Painted Bunting, *Passerina ciris*.

845.24–25   Old Catesby . . . Nuttall]   See Catesby's discussion of the Eastern Bluebird, *Natural History*, vol. 1.

845.26   M. nigricans]   Black Phoebe, *Sayornis nigricans*.

845.34   Falco cyaneus]   Northern Harrier ("Marsh Hawk"), *Circus cyaneus*.

845.38   Brewer]   Thomas Mayo Brewer (1814–80), physician and author of *North American Oölogy* (1852).

846.9–10   Sumptuous fare . . . November]   On the occasion of Victoria's first state visit to the City of London, the Queen dined with the Lord Mayor of London, Sir John Cowan, and the City's aldermen in the Guildhall.

846.12–14   Birds of *Australia* . . . Caprimulgae]   John Gould's *The Birds of Australia, and the Adjacent Islands* (1837–38) was abandoned as incomplete on Gould's departure for Australia in 1838 and superseded by his 8-volume *The Birds of Australia* (1840–69); he published a *Monograph of the Ramphastidae; or Family of Toucans* (1834), and *A Monograph of the Trochilidae; or Humming-Birds* (1849–61), but no monograph on the nightjars (Caprimulgidae).

847.25–26   Fauna in Squares . . . in the Manner of Swainson]   Swainson espoused quinarianism, an idiosyncratic system of classification originally proposed in William MacLeay's *Hora Entomologicae* (1819).

847.37   Doctor Geddings]   Eli Geddings, Charleston physician.

848.25   Mr Phillips]   Benjamin Phillips, the Audubon family physician.

849.7   Liberty Hall]   Plantation northwest of Charleston, owned by Bachman's friend Dr. Charles Desel.

849.13–14   Charles Bonaparte . . . published]   In *Geographical and Comparative List of the Birds of Europe and North America* (1837).

850.11   "Nymphia Leitnernia"]   Yellow Water-lily, *Nymphea mexicana*.

850.15–16   P. Villosus . . . R. Crepitans]   Hairy Woodpecker, *Picoides villosus*; Clapper Rail, *Rallus longirostris*.

850.36   long article . . . ornithology]   The article, by James Wilson, appeared in the seventh edition.

851.14   Mr Doughty] Lithographer and landscape painter Thomas Doughty (1793–1856), who edited and published, along with his brother John, *The Cabinet of Natural History and American Rural Sports* (1830–33).

851.32   Mr Baker] Thomas Barwick Lloyd Baker (1807–86) of Christ Church, Oxford, a subscriber to *Birds of America*.

853.11–12   Lord Kinnoul] Thomas Robert, eleventh Earl of Kinnoul (1785–1866).

854.21   Synopsis] Audubon's *Synopsis of the Birds of North America* (1839), an index to the Double Elephant Folio and *Ornithological Biography*.

General Index

Abbot, John, 483, 490
Académie Royale des Sciences, 811
Adam, Lewis, 129, 139
Adams, Bernard, 684
Adams-Onís Treaty, 89
Adelaide, Queen of England, 828
Africa, 833
Alabama, 195, 270, 378, 404, 479, 516, 839–41
Alabama (steamboat), 65
Alabama River (Alabama), 840–41
Aldrovandi, Ulisse, 415
Allan, William, 185, 188
Allegheny Mountains, 195, 233, 286, 356, 385, 553, 557
Alligators, 55–56, 65, 77, 117, 120, 171, 271, 305, 371, 377, 388, 405–8, 428, 432, 482, 493, 497, 529, 531
Althæa, 250
Alves, Walter, 10
America, Illinois, 20
American Fur Company, 554, 586–87, 593, 605, 610, 620, 644, 658, 661
American Ornithology (Bonaparte), 170, 211, 834, 844, 847–48
American Ornithology (Wilson), 61–63, 71, 79–80, 83, 126, 149–54, 483, 534–37, 847
André (Andry), Madame, 82
Antelope River (South Dakota), 604
Anticosti Island, Québec, 359
Antiquarian Society (Society of Antiquaries, Edinburgh), 184–85, 186, 187, 802
Ants, 114, 202
Apple Creek, North Dakota, 611, 735
Apple trees, 105, 234, 289, 316, 562
Ariadne Asleep on the Island of Naxos (Vanderlyn), 140
Arkansas, 195, 441
Arkansas Post, 41–42, 44–52
Arkansas River, 45–51, 336, 360, 510, 825
Arkansas Territory, 32–55
Armadillos, 636
Arnaud, Felix, 73
Arrow Rock, Missouri, 748

Artemisia, 627, 637
Ash trees, 272, 548, 565, 570, 576, 610, 669
Ashley, Gen. William H., 610
Ashley River (South Carolina), 312
Asley, James, 23
Assiniboin (steamboat), 612–13, 640
Audubon, Anne Moynet (stepmother), 30–31, 75, 178, 765–66, 768–70, 772, 780
Audubon, Harriet (granddaughter), 856
Audubon, Jean (father), 28–30, 64, 139, 178, 365, 759, 765–74, 776, 778–81, 784, 787
Audubon, John Woodhouse (son), 3, 20–21, 23, 28, 31–32, 58, 72, 77, 92, 99, 104, 137–38, 143, 146–48, 159, 177, 192, 356, 395, 436, 570, 743, 749, 769, 788, 793–94, 800, 805–6, 808–10, 816, 820–21, 824–25, 827–28, 835, 839, 842, 845, 848–49, 857
Audubon, Lucy (daughter), 31, 793
Audubon, Lucy (granddaughter), 856
Audubon, Lucy Bakewell (wife), 3, 5, 8, 11, 13, 21, 23–24, 28, 30–32, 37, 44, 49, 58–59, 64, 72–75, 77–79, 81, 85–86, 92, 94, 96–102, 104, 112, 124, 129–31, 136–38, 140–43, 146–48, 159–92, 286, 520, 533–34, 536, 605, 735, 749, 763, 774–76, 778, 782–94, 825, 827–28, 842, 845, 848–49; letters to, 797–802, 803–6, 806–11, 811–13, 814–18, 818, 819–20
Audubon, Maria Rebecca Bachman (Mrs. John), 819–20, 826, 842, 845, 848–50
Audubon, Mary Eliza Bachman (Mrs. Victor), 819–20, 826, 848–49
Audubon, Pierre ("John") (grandfather), 766
Audubon, Rose (daughter), 32, 791, 793
Audubon, Rose Bonnitte (half-sister), 30–31, 178, 770, 781, 791
Audubon, Victor Gifford (son), 3, 20–21, 23, 28, 31–32, 58, 72, 77, 85, 92,

Ornithological Index

Nomenclature in this index follows the American Ornithologists' Union *Check-list of North American Birds* (6th Edition, 1983, and Supplement, 1997). Generic and specific names used by Audubon and his contemporaries are cross-referenced to current usage and also appear in parentheses following current names. Where Audubon uses a name for which a current designation cannot reliably be given, his original terminology appears in quotation marks. Page numbers in italics refer to chapters of Audubon's *Ornithological Biography* in this volume.

Guillemot
Black, 399, 401–3
Common. *See* Murre, Common
Thick-billed. *See* Murre, Thick-billed
Gull
Black-headed. *See* Gull, Franklin's;
Gull, Laughing
Common. *See* Gull, Ring-billed
Franklin's (Black-headed Gull), 571,
575, 581, 588–89, 609
Herring, 9, 19
Laughing (Black-headed Gull), 154,
452–53
Ring-billed (Common Gull), 79–81,
95, 137, 160
gulls, 14–15, 23, 28, 33–35, 37, 49, 66, 73,
335, 363, 412, 452, 567, 741, 838
Gyrfalcon (Jerfalcon), 395

Harrier, Northern (Marsh Hawk;
Prairie Hawk), 49–50, 52–53, 72, 81,
380, 568, 583, 590, 845
Hawk
Ash-colored. *See* Hawk, Sharp-
shinned
Black. *See* Hawk, Rough-legged
Broad-winged, *285–88*, 821; plate 20
Cooper's (Intrepid Hawk; Stanley
Hawk), 44, 48, 231–32, 598
Crested. *See* Caracara, Crested
Duck. *See* Falcon, Peregrine
Fish. *See* Osprey
Fork-tailed. *See* Kite, Swallow-tailed
Great-footed. *See* Falcon, Peregrine
Hen. *See* Hawk, Red-tailed
Intrepid. *See* Hawk, Cooper's
Marsh. *See* Harrier, Northern
Night. *See* Nighthawk, Common
Pigeon. *See* Merlin
Prairie. *See* Harrier, Northern
Red-shouldered (Winter Falcon;
Winter Hawk), 11, 35, 53, 72, 117,
381; plate 12
Red-tailed (American Buzzard; Hen
Hawk), 6, 23, 56, 68, *254–60*, 340,
381, 566, 698; plate 12
Rough-legged (Black Hawk), 15, 20,
24–25, 36, 55–56
Sharp-shinned (Ash-colored Hawk;
Slate-colored Hawk), 35, 112,
339

Slate-colored. *See* Hawk, Sharp-
shinned
Sparrow. *See* Kestrel, American
Stanley. *See* Hawk, Cooper's
Swallow-tailed. *See* Kite, Swallow-
tailed
"White-headed," 698–99
"White-rumped," 675
Winter. *See* Hawk, Red-shouldered
hawks, 10, 14, 47–48, 68, 77, 115, 190,
201, 223, 225, 229, 231, 244, 260, 263,
267, 279–81, 284–85, 287, 291–92,
301–2, 322, 331, 336, 339–40, 344, 346,
357, 380–81, 398, 402, 457, 469,
487–88, 497, 569, 628, 641, 649,
659, 701, 763, 837, 844. *See also*
falcons
Heron
Blue. *See* Heron, Great Blue; Heron,
Little Blue
Great Blue (Blue Crane; Blue
Heron; Great White Heron;
White Heron), 10, 33, 38, 40, 48,
75, 92, 114, 123, 152, *384–93*, 411, 414,
423, *457–66*, 467–68, 471, 489,
504–5, 507–8, 566, 571, 578, 580–81,
609, 612, 784, 827; plates 35, 47
Great White. *See* Heron, Great Blue
Green, 115, 388, 413–14, 423, 446,
469, 471
Little Blue (Blue Crane; Blue
Heron), 89, 115, 150, 388, 411, 439,
445, 448, *466–73*, 829; plate 48
Louisiana. *See* Heron, Tricolored
Purple. *See* Egret, Reddish
Snowy. *See* Egret, Snowy
Tricolored (Louisiana Heron), 151,
388, *410–14*, 423, 447, 464, 467–68,
471–72, 504; plate 40
White. *See* Egret, Great; Egret,
Snowy; Heron, Great Blue
Yellow-crowned. *See* Night-Heron,
Yellow-crowned
herons, 75, 313, 384–85, 387, 407–8, 411,
428, 438–39, 446, 457–58, 463–64,
466–67, 470–71, 481, 489–90, 493,
505–6, 516–17, 762–63, 819, 830, 837.
See also egrets
Hummingbird, Ruby-throated, 62,
107, *248–54*, 290, 319, 347, 569;
plate 9

Library of Congress Cataloging-in-Publication Data

Audubon, John James, 1785–1851.
  [Selections. 1999]
  Writings and drawings / John James Audubon.
    p. cm. — (The Library of America ; 113)
  Contents: Mississippi River journal — From 1826 journal —
From Ornithological biography — Missouri River journals —
Letters — Other writings.
  ISBN 1-883011-68-X (alk. paper)
  ISBN 1-883011-81-7 (gift edition)
  1. Audubon, John James, 1785–1851—Diaries. 2. Birds—
North America. 3. Natural history—North America.
I. Audubon, John James, 1785–1851. Mississippi River journal.
1999. II. Audubon, John James, 1785–1851. Journal.
Selections. 1999. III. Audubon, John James, 1785–1851.
Ornithological biography. Selections. 1999. IV. Audubon,
John James, 1785–1851. Missouri River journals. 1999.
V. Audubon, John James, 1785–1851. Correspondence.
Selections. 1999. VI. Mississippi River journal. VII. 1826
journal. VIII. Ornithological biography. IX. Mississippi
River journals. X. Title. XI. Series.
QL31.A9A3 1999
598′.092—dc21   CIP
[B]   99–18337

THE LIBRARY OF AMERICA SERIES

The Library of America fosters appreciation and pride in America's literary heritage by publishing, and keeping permanently in print, authoritative editions of its best and most significant writing. An independent nonprofit organization, it was founded in 1979 with seed money from the National Endowment for the Humanities and the Ford Foundation.

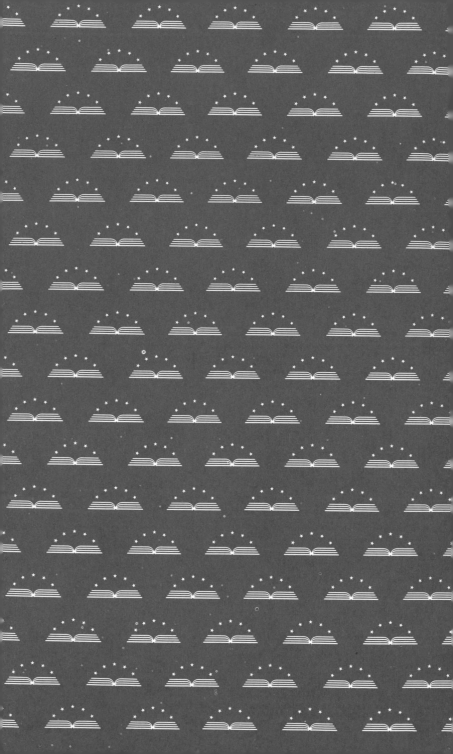